# THE HANDBOOK OF FIXED INCOME SECURITIES

# THE HANDBOOK OF FIXED INCOME SECURITIES

### Sixth Edition

**FRANK J. FABOZZI**

*Editor*

**McGraw-Hill**

New York   San Francisco   Washington, D.C.   Auckland   Bogotá
Caracas   Lisbon   London   Madrid   Mexico City   Milan
Montreal   New Delhi   San Juan   Singapore
Sydney   Tokyo   Toronto

**Library of Congress Cataloging-in-Publication Data**

The handbook of fixed income securities / Frank J. Fabozzi, Editor.—6th ed.
   p. cm.
   ISBN 0-07-135805-6 (hardcover)
   ISBN 0-07-137682-8 (paperback)
   1. Bonds—Handbooks, manuals, etc.  2. Preferred stocks—Handbooks, manuals, etc.  3.
Money market funds—Handbooks, manuals, etc.  4. Mutual funds—Handbooks, manuals,
etc.  5. Fixed-income securities—Handbooks, manuals, etc.  I. Fabozzi, Frank J.

HG4651.H265  2000
332.63′2046—dc2100                             00-035484

# McGraw-Hill

*A Division of The McGraw·Hill Companies*

*This book was set in Times Roman by Pro-Image Corporation.*

*Printed and bound by R. R. Donnelley & Sons Company.*

*This publication is designed to provide accurate and authoritative information in regard to the
subject matter covered. It is sold with the understanding that neither the author nor the publisher
is engaged in rendering legal, accounting, or other professional service. If legal advice or other
expert assistance is required, the services of a competent professional person should be sought.*
           *—From a declaration of Principles jointly adopted by a Committee
             of the American Bar Association and a Committee of Publishers.*

This book is printed on acid-free paper.

# C O N T E N T S

## Chapter 7

### Bond Market Indexes    155
*Frank K. Reilly and David J. Wright*

## PART 2

## GOVERNMENT AND PRIVATE DEBT OBLIGATIONS

## Chapter 8

### U.S. Treasury and Agency Securities    175
*Frank J. Fabozzi and Michael J. Fleming*

## Chapter 9

### Municipal Bonds    197
*Sylvan G. Feldstein, Frank J. Fabozzi, and Patrick M. Kennedy*

## Chapter 10

### Private Money Market Instruments    231
*Frank J. Fabozzi and Steven V. Mann*

## Chapter 11

## Corporate Bonds    253
*Frank J. Fabozzi, Richard S. Wilson, and Richard Todd*

## Chapter 12

## Medium-Term Notes    283
*Leland E. Crabbe*

## Chapter 13

## Inflation-Indexed Bonds (TIPS)    301
*John B. Brynjolfsson*

## Chapter 18

## PART 3

## CREDIT ANALYSIS

## Chapter 19

## Chapter 20

## Chapter 21

## Chapter 22

### Guidelines in the Credit Analysis of General Obligation and Revenue Municipal Bonds    491

*Sylvan G. Feldstein*

## Chapter 23

### High-Yield Analysis of Emerging Markets Debt    519

*Allen A. Vine*

## PART 4

## MORTGAGE-BACKED AND ASSET-BACKED SECURITIES

## Chapter 24

### Mortgages and Overview of Mortgage-Backed Securities    549

*Frank J. Fabozzi and Chuck Ramsey*

## Chapter 25

## Mortgage Pass-Throughs    573

*Lakhbir S. Hayre, Cyrus Mohebbi, Thomas A. Zimmerman*

## Chapter 26

## Collateralized Mortgage Obligations    619

*Lehman Brothers Inc.*

## Chapter 27

## Nonagency CMOS    649

*Frank J. Fabozzi, Anthony B. Sanders, David Yuen, and Chuck Ramsey*

## Chapter 28

## Chapter 29

## Chapter 30

## Chapter 31

## Chapter 32

# Securities Backed by Credit Card Receivables    739
*John N. McElravey*

## PART 5

# FIXED INCOME ANALYTICS AND MODELING


## Chapter 33

# Characteristics of and Strategies with Callable Securities    759
*Douglas Johnston*

## Chapter 34

# Valuation of Bonds with Embedded Options    773
*Frank J. Fabozzi, Andrew J. Kalotay, and George O. Williams*

# PART 6

# PORTFOLIO MANAGEMENT

## Chapter 43

# Management of a High-Yield Bond Portfolio    945

*J. Thomas Madden and Joseph Balestrino*

## Chapter 44

# Bond Immunization: An Asset/Liability Optimization Strategy    957

*Frank J. Fabozzi and Peter F. Christensen*

## Chapter 45

# Dedicated Bond Portfolios    969

*Frank J. Fabozzi and Peter F. Christensen*

## Chapter 46

# Managing Market Risk Proactively at Long-Term Investment Funds    985

*Lang Gibson*

## Chapter 47

## Improving Insurance Company Portfolio Returns    1011
*Kevin Edward Grant*

## Chapter 48

## International Bond Investing and Portfolio Management    1027
*Christopher B. Steward and Adam M. Greshin*

# PREFACE

This book is designed to provide extensive coverage of not only the wide range of fixed income products but also fixed income portfolio management strategies. Each chapter is written by an authority on the subject. Many of these authorities have written books, monographs, and/or articles on their topic.

The sixth edition of the *Handbook* is divided into eight parts. Part 1 provides general information about the investment features of fixed income securities and the associated risks. Coverage of yield measures, spot rates, forward rates, total return, price volatility measures (duration and convexity), and bond market indexes is included in this part.

Parts 2 covers bonds (domestic and foreign) and money market instruments. Credit analysis of these instruments is explained in Part 3. Part 4 describes mortgage-backed securities (passthroughs, collateralized mortgage obligations, and stripped mortgage-backed securities) and asset-backed securities.

Part 5 builds on the analytical framework in Part 1. In this part, two methodologies for valuing fixed income securities are discussed: the binomial method and the Monte Carlo method. A byproduct of these methods is the option-adjusted spread.

The more popular fixed income portfolio management strategies are covered in Part 6. In addition to active strategies and structured portfolio strategies (indexing, immunization, and dedication), coverage includes the importance of selecting a performance bogey.

Part 7 has two chapters on equity-linked securities. The securities not only are described, but the state-of-the valuation models and portfolio strategies are explained.

Part 8 covers derivative instruments and their portfolio management applications. Derivative instruments include futures/forward contracts, options, interest rate swaps, and interest rate agreements (caps and floors). The basic feature of each instrument is described as well as how it is valued and used to control the risk of a fixed income portfolio.

The following 14 chapters are new to the sixth edition:

Price Volatility Characteristics of Fixed Income Securities

Treasury and Agency Securities

Inflation-Indexed Bonds

Floating-Rate Securities

Commercial Mortgage-Backed Securities

Securities Backed by Automobile Loans

Securities Backed by Closed-End Home Equity Loans

Securities Backed by Manufacturing Housing Loans

Securities Backed by Credit Card Receivables

Characteristics of and Strategies with Callable Securities

Managing Indexed and Enhanced Indexed Bond Portfolios

Management of a High-Yield Bond Portfolio

Managing Market Risk Proactively at Long-Term Investment Funds

Convertible Securities and Their Valuation

The following 10 chapters have been significantly revised:

Municipal Bonds

International Bond Markets and Instruments

Brady Bonds

Mortgage Pass-Throughs

Nonagency CMOs

The Active Decisions in the Selection of Passive Management and Bogeys

Global Corporate Bond Portfolio Management

International Bond Investing and Portfolio Management

Convertibles Securities and Their Investment Characteristics

Controlling Interest Rate Risk with Futures and Options

*Frank J. Fabozzi, CFA*
*Editor*

# ACKNOWLEDGMENTS

I would like to extend my deep personal appreciation to the contributing authors and the following individuals who provided various forms of assistance in this project:

Scott Amero (BlackRock Financial Management)
Keith Anderson (BlackRock Financial Management)
Clifford Asness (AQR Capital Management)
Max Bublitz (Conesco)
Dwight Churchill (Fidelity Management and Research)
Claire Cohen (Fitch)
Peter DeRoot (Lehman Brothers)
Susan Dushock (Lehman Brothers)
Lev Dynkin (Lehman Brothers)
Wendell Fuller (Guardian Life Insurance Company)
Joe Geraci (Salomon Smith Barney)
Robert Gerber (Lord Abbett)
David Germany (Miller Anderson & Sherrerd)
Laurie Goodman (PaineWebber)
Alex Grant (Guardian Life Insurance Company)
Hy Grossman (Standard & Poor's)
Brad Gewehr (PaineWebber)
Frank Jones (Guardian Life Insurance Company)
George P. Kegler (Cassian Market Consultants)
Martin Leibowitz (TIAA-CREF)
Michael Marz (First Southwest)
Ed Murphy (Merchants Mutual Insurance Company)
Scott Pinkus (Goldman Sachs)
Robert Reitano (John Hancock Mutual Life Insurance Company)

Scott Richard (Miller Anderson & Sherrerd)
Ehud Ronn (University of Texas at Austin)
Peter Rubinstein (Prudential Securities)
Ron Ryan (Ryan Labs)
Dexter Senft (Lehman Brothers)
James E. Spiotto (Chapman and Cutler)
Vlad Stadnyk (Standard & Poor's)
Francis Trainer (Sanford C. Bernstein & Co.)
Doug Watson (Moody's Investors Service)

*Frank J. Fabozzi*

# CONTRIBUTORS

James S. Anderson
  Managing Director
  First Union Securities, Inc.

David Audley
  Chief Operating Officer
  Research Technology
  Merrill Lynch

Joseph Balestrino, CFA
  Senior Vice President
  Federated Investors

Anand K. Bhattacharya, Ph.D.
  Executive Vice President
  Countrywide Capital Markets Inc.

Mihir Bhattacharya
  Managing Director
  Deutsche Banc Alex. Brown

Jane S. Brauer, Ph.D.
  First Vice President
  Merrill Lynch

John B. Brynjolfsson, CFA
  Executive Vice President and Manager
  PIMCO Real Return Bond Fund
  Pacific Investment Management Company

Gerald W. Buetow, Jr., Ph.D., CFA
  President
  BFRC Services

Douglas Chen
  Assistant Vice President
  Merrill Lynch

Richard Chin
  Fixed-Income Research
  Goldman Sachs & Co.

Peter F. Christensen
  Managing Director
  ComTech, Incorporated

Kristina L. Clark
  Analyst
  First Union Securities, Inc.

Leland F. Crabbe, Ph.D.
  Director
  Credit Suisse Asset Management

Ravi F. Dattatreya, Ph.D.
  CEO
  Jasmine Networks, Inc.

Chris P. Dialynas
  Managing Director
  Pacific Investment Management Company

Sandra Durn
  Senior Vice President / Portfolio Manager
  Pacific Investment Management Company

Sylvan G. Feldstein, Ph.D.
  Assistant Vice President
  Investment Department
  Guardian Life Insurance Company

Michael G. Ferri, Ph.D.
  Foundation Professor of Finance
  George Mason University

Michael J. Fleming, Ph.D.
  Senior Economist
  Federal Reserve Bank of New York

H. Gifford Fong
  President
  Gifford Fong Associates

William J. Gartland, CFA
  Vice President
  Bloomberg Financial Market

Lang Gibson
  Vice President
  Fixed Income Strategies Research
  First Union Securities, Inc.

Kevin Edward Grant, CFA
  Portfolio Manager
  Fidelity Management and Research

Adam M. Greshin, CFA
  Principal
  Scudder Kemper Investments

**Lakhbir S. Hayre, D. Phil.**
Managing Director
Salomon Smith Barney, Inc.

**David S. Horowitz, CFA**
Portfolio Manager
Miller, Anderson & Sherrerd

**Jane Tripp Howe, CFA**
Director of Credit Research
Freedom Capital Management

**R. Russell Hurst**
Director
First Union Securities, Inc.

**Robert R. Johnson, Ph.D., CFA**
Senior Vice President
Association for Investment Management and
Research

**Douglas Johnston**
Senior Vice President
Fixed Income Research
Lehman Brothers Inc.

**Ronald N. Kahn, Ph.D.**
Managing Director
Barclays Global Investors

**Andrew J. Kalotay, Ph.D.**
President
Andrew J. Kalotay Associates

**Patrick M. Kennedy**
Vice President
Fixed Income Portfolio Manager
Pitcairn Trust Company

**David T. Kim**
Tokai Bank

**Nicholas C. Letica**
Managing Director
Bear Stearns & Co.

**J. Thomas Madden, CFA**
Executive Vice President
Federated Investors

**Jack Malvey, CFA**
Managing Director
Lehman Brothers

**Steven V. Mann, Ph.D.**
Associate Professor of Finance
The Darla Moore School of Business
University of South Carolina

**John M. Mawe**
Director
Prudential Securities, Inc.

**John N. McElravey**
Director, Asset-Backed Research
Banc One Capital Markets, Inc.

**Cyrus Mohebbi, Ph.D.**
Managing Director
Prudential Securities, Inc.

**Mortgage Research Group**
Lehman Brothers Inc.

**Mark Pitts, Ph.D.**
Principal
White Oak Capital Management Corp.

**Shrikant Ramamurthy**
Senior Vice President
Fixed-Income Research
Prudential Securities, Inc.

**Chuck Ramsey**
CEO
Mortgage Risk Assessment Corp.

**Frank K. Reilly, Ph.D., CFA**
Bernard J. Hank Professor of Finance
University of Notre Dame

**Scott F. Richard, DBA**
Portfolio Manager
Miller, Anderson & Sherrerd

**John C. Ritchie, Jr., Ph.D.**
Professor of Finance
Temple University

**Michael R. Rosenberg, Ph.D.**
Managing Director
Global Head of FX Research
Deutsche Bank

**W. Alexander Roever, CFA**
Managing Director, Head of Asset Backed
Research
Banc One Capital Markets, Inc.

**Anthony B. Sanders, Ph.D.**
Professor of Finance and Galbreath Distinguished
Scholar
The Ohio State University

**Glenn M. Schultz, CFA**
Director
Banc One Capital Markets, Inc.

**Christopher B. Steward, CFA**
Vice President
Wellington Management Company, LLP

**Anthony V. Thompson**
Director of ABS Research
Goldman, Sachs & Co.

**Richard Todd**
Vice President
Bear Stearns & Co.

**Allen A. Vine**
International Emerging Markets Specialist
Global High Yield Securities Research
Merrill Lynch

**Kenneth E. Volpert, CFA**
    Principal and Senior Portfolio Manager
    The Vanguard Group, Inc.

**Kenneth L. Walker**
    President
    T. Rowe Price Stable Asset Management, Inc.

**George O. Williams, Ph.D.**
    Vice President
    Fixed Income Research
    Lehman Brothers Inc.

**Richard S. Wilson**
    Consultant

**David J. Wright, Ph.D.**
    Professor of Finance
    University of Wisconsin—Parkside

**David Yuen, CFA**
    Susquehanna Advisors Group

# THE HANDBOOK OF FIXED INCOME SECURITIES

PART 1

# BACKGROUND

## CHAPTER 1

# OVERVIEW OF THE TYPES AND FEATURES OF FIXED INCOME SECURITIES

**Frank J. Fabozzi, Ph.D., CFA, CPA**
Adjunct Professor of Finance
School of Management
Yale University

**Michael G. Ferri, Ph.D.**
Foundation Professor of Finance
George Mason University

**Steven V. Mann, Ph.D.**
Associate Professor of Finance
The Darla Moore School of Business
University of South Carolina

This chapter will explore some of the most important features of bonds, preferred stock, and mortgage-backed securities, and provide the reader with a taxonomy of terms and concepts that will be useful in the reading of the specialized chapters to follow.

## BONDS

### Type of Issuer

One important characteristic of a bond is the nature of its issuer. Although foreign governments and firms raise capital in U.S. financial markets, the three largest issuers of debt are domestic corporations, municipal governments, and the federal government and its agencies. Each class of issuer, however, features additional and significant differences.

Domestic corporations, for example, include regulated utilities as well as unregulated manufacturers. Furthermore, each firm may sell different kinds of bonds: Some debt may be publicly placed, whereas other bonds may be sold directly to one or only a few buyers (referred to as a *private placement*); some debt is collateralized by specific assets of the company, whereas other debt may be unsecured. Municipal debt is also varied: "General obligation" bonds (GOs) are backed by the full faith, credit, and taxing power of the governmental unit issuing them; "revenue bonds," on the other hand, have a safety, or creditworthiness, that depends upon the vitality and success of the particular entity (such as toll roads, hospitals, or water systems) within the municipal government issuing the bond.

The U.S. Treasury has the most voracious appetite for debt, but the bond market often receives calls from its agencies. Federal government agencies include federally related institutions and government-sponsored enterprises.

It is important for the investor to realize that, by law or practice or both, these different borrowers have developed different ways of raising debt capital over the years. As a result, the distinctions among the various types of issuers correspond closely to differences among bonds in yield, denomination, safety of principal, maturity, tax status, and such important provisions as the call privilege, put features, and sinking fund. As we discuss the key features of fixed income securities, we will point out how the characteristics of the bonds vary with the obligor or issuing authority. A more extensive discussion is provided in later chapters in this book that explain the various instruments.

## Maturity

A key feature of any bond is its *term-to-maturity,* the number of years during which the borrower has promised to meet the conditions of the debt (which are contained in the bond's indenture). A bond's term-to-maturity is the date on which the debt will cease and the borrower will redeem the issue by paying the face value, or principal. One indication of the importance of the maturity is that the code word or name for every bond contains its maturity (and coupon). Thus, the title of the Anheuser Busch Company bond due, or maturing, in 2016 is given as "Anheuser Busch 8⅝s of 2016." In practice, the words *maturity, term,* and *term-to-maturity* are used interchangeably to refer to the number of years remaining in the life of a bond. Technically, however, *maturity* denotes the date the bond will be redeemed, and either *term* or *term-to-maturity* denotes the number of years until that date.

A bond's maturity is crucial for several reasons. First, maturity indicates the expected life of the instrument, or the number of periods during which the holder of the bond can expect to receive the coupon interest and the number of years before the principal will be paid. Second, the yield on a bond depends substantially on its maturity. More specifically, at any given point in time, the yield offered on a long-term bond may be greater than, less than, or equal to the yield offered on a short-term bond. As will be explained in Chapter 6, the effect of maturity on the yield depends on the *shape of the yield curve.* Third, the volatility of a bond's price is closely associated with maturity: Changes in the market level of rates will wrest much larger changes in price from bonds of long maturity than from otherwise similar debt of shorter life.[1] Finally, as explained in the next chapter, there are other risks associated with the maturity of a bond.

When considering a bond's maturity, the investor should be aware of any provisions that modify, or permit the issuer to modify, the maturity of a bond. Although corporate bonds (referred to as "corporates") are typically *term bonds* (issues that have a single maturity), they often contain arrangements by which the issuing firm either can or must retire the debt early, in full or in part. Many corporates, for example, give the issuer a *call privilege,* which permits the issuing firm to redeem the bond before the scheduled maturity under certain conditions (these conditions are discussed below). Many municipal bonds have the same provision. Although the U.S. government no longer issues bonds that have a call privilege, there are outstanding issues with this provision. Many industrials and some utilities have *sinking-fund provisions,* which mandate that the firm retire a substantial portion of the debt, in a prearranged schedule, during its life and before the stated maturity. Typically, municipal bonds are *serial bonds* or, in essence, bundles of bonds with differing maturities. (Some corporates are of this type, too.)

Usually, the maturity of a corporate bond is between 1 and 30 years. This is not to say that there are not outliers. In fact, financially sound firms have begun to issue longer-term debt in order to lock in long-term attractive financing. Some examples are Tennessee Valley Authority (TVA), $8\frac{1}{4}$ maturing on 4/15/42 (callable on 4/15/12); and Conrail, $7\frac{7}{8}$ maturing on 5/15/43 (noncallable). Recently, Walt Disney Corporation issued a 100-year bond.

Although classifying bonds as "short-term," "intermediate-term," and "long-term" is not universally accepted, the following classification is typically used. Bonds with a maturity of 1 to 5 years are generally considered short-term; bonds with a maturity between 5 and 12 years are viewed as intermediate-term (and are often called *notes*). Long-term bonds are those with a maturity greater than 12 years.

## Coupon and Principal

A bond's *coupon* is the periodic interest payment made to owners during the life of the bond. The coupon is always cited, along with maturity, in any quotation of a bond's price. Thus one might hear about the "ATT $5\frac{1}{8}$ due in 2001" or the "Ingersoll Rand 7.2 due in 2025" in discussions of current bond trading. In these examples, the coupon cited is in fact the *coupon rate,* that is, the rate of interest that, when multiplied by the *principal, par value, or face value* of the bond, provides the dollar value of the coupon payment. Typically, but not universally, for bonds issued in the United States the coupon payment is made

---

1. Chapter 5 discusses this point in detail.

in semiannual installments. An important exception is mortgage-backed and as-set-backed securities that usually deliver monthly cash flows. In contrast, for bonds issued in some European bond markets and all bonds issued in the *Euro-bond market,* the coupon payment is made once per year. Bonds may be *bearer bonds* or *registered bonds.* With bearer bonds, investors clip coupons and send them to the obligor for payment. In the case of registered issues, bond owners receive the payment automatically at the appropriate time. All new bond issues must be registered.

There are a few corporate bonds (mostly railroad issues), called *income bonds,* that contain a provision permitting the firm to omit or delay the payment of interest if the firm's earnings are too low. They have been issued as part of bankruptcy reorganizations or to replace a preferred-stock offering of the issuer. A variant of this bond type, *deferrable bonds* (also called *trust preferred* and *debt/equity hybrids*) witnessed explosive growth in the 1990s. Deferrable bonds are deeply subordinated debt instruments that give the issuer the option to defer coupon payment up to five years in the event of financial distress.

*Zero-coupon bonds* have been issued by corporations and municipalities since the early 1980s. For example, Coca-Cola Enterprises has a zero-coupon bond outstanding due June 20, 2020 that was issued on May 9, 1995. Although the U.S. Treasury does not issue zero-coupon debt with a maturity greater than one year, such securities have been created by government securities dealers. Merrill Lynch was the first to do this with its creation of Treasury Investment Growth Receipts (TIGRs) in August 1982. The most popular zero-coupon Trea-sury securities today are those created by government dealer firms under the Treasury's Separate Trading of Registered Interest and Principal Securities (STRIPS) program. Just how these securities—commonly referred to as *Trea-sury strips*—are created will be explained in Chapter 8. The investor in a zero-coupon security typically receives interest by buying the security at a price below its principal, or maturity value, and holding it to the maturity date. The reason for the issuance of zero-coupon securities is explained in Chapter 8. However, some zeros are issued at par and accrue interest during the bond's life, with the accrued interest and principal payable at maturity.

Governments and corporations also issue *inflation-indexed bonds* whose coupon payments are tied to an inflation index. These securities are designed to protect bondholders from the erosion of purchasing power of fixed nominal coupon payments due to inflation. For example, in January 1997, the U.S. Trea-sury auctioned a 10-year Treasury note whose semiannual coupon interest de-pends on the rate of inflation as measured by the Consumer Price Index for All Urban Consumers (i.e., CPI-U). The coupon payments are adjusted annually. These issues are referred to as Treasury Inflation-Protection Securities (TIPS). As of this writing, the Treasury issues TIPS with 10 and 30-year maturities. The first such 10-year issue matures in January 15, 2007 and carries a coupon rate of 3.375%. At issuance, the value of the CPI-U was 158.43548. On January 1, 1998, the CPI-U was 161.55484. Accordingly, the new semiannual coupon pay-ment (per $100 of par value) was computed as follows:

$$\$1.72027 = (0.03375/2) \times (161.55484/158.43548) \times \$100$$

For a conventional 10-year U.S. Treasury note with a fixed coupon rate, the semiannual coupon payment would have been $1.68875 (per $100 of par value). Some corporations followed the Treasury and issued inflation-indexed bonds of their own.[2]

There are securities that have a coupon rate that increases over time. These securities are called *step-up notes* because the coupon rate "steps up" over time. For example, a six-year step-up note might have a coupon rate that is 5% for the first two years, 5.8% for the next two years, and 6% for the last two years. Alternatively, there are securities that have a coupon rate that can decrease over time but never increase. For example, in June 1998, the Tennessee Valley Authority issued a 30-year 6.75% putable automatic-reset securities (PARRS), also known as *ratchet bonds*. Beginning five years after issuance and annually thereafter, the bond's coupon rate is automatically reset to either the current 30-year constant maturity Treasury yield plus 94 basis points, or to 6.75%, whichever is lower. The coupon rate may decline if Treasury yields decline, but it will never increase. This bond also contains a contingent put option such that if the coupon rate is lowered, the bond is putable at par. Ratchet bonds were designed as substitutes for callable bonds.

In contrast to a coupon rate that is fixed for the bond's entire life, the term *floating-rate security* or *floater* encompasses several different types of securities with one common feature: the coupon rate will vary over the instrument's life. The coupon rate is reset at designated dates based on the value of some reference rate adjusted for a spread. For example, a floater issued by Enron Corp. (due in March 2000) has a coupon formula equal to three-month LIBOR plus 45 basis points and delivers cash flows quarterly.

Typically, floaters have coupon rates that reset more than once a year (e.g., semiannually, quarterly, or monthly). Conversely, the term *adjustable-rate* or *variable-rate* security refers to those issues whose coupon rates reset not more frequently than annually.

There are several features about floaters that deserve mention. First, a floater may have a restriction on the maximum (minimum) coupon rate that will be paid at any reset date called a *cap* (*floor*). Second, while the reference rate for most floaters is an interest rate or an interest rate index, a wide variety of reference rates appear in the coupon formulas. A floater's coupon could be indexed to movements in foreign exchange rates, the price of a commodity (e.g., crude oil), movements in an equity index (e.g., the S&P 500), or movements in a bond index (e.g., the Merrill Lynch Corporate Bond Index). Third, while a floater's coupon rate normally moves the same direction as the reference rate

2. For examples of these issues see, Andrew Rossen, Michael Schumacher, and John Cassaudoumecq, "Corporate and Agency Inflation-Linked Securities," Chapter 18 in John Brynjolfsson and Frank J. Fabozzi (eds.), *Handbook of Inflation Indexed Bonds* (New Hope, PA: Frank J. Fabozzi Associates, 1999).

moves, there are floaters whose coupon rate moves in the opposite direction
from the reference rate. These securities are called *inverse floaters* or *reverse
floaters*. As an example, consider an inverse floater, issued by the Federal Home
Loan Bank in April 1999. This issue matures in April 2002 and delivers quarterly coupon payments according to the following formula:

$$18\% - 2.5 \times (\text{three-month LIBOR})$$

This inverse floater has a floor of 3% and a cap of 15.5%. Finally, *range notes*
are floaters whose coupon rate is equal to the reference rate (adjusted for a
spread) as long as the reference rate is within a certain range at the reset date.
If the reference rate is outside the range, the coupon rate is zero for that period.
Consider a range note issued by Sallie Mae in August 1996 that matures in
August 2003. This issue makes coupon payments quarterly. The investor earns
three-month LIBOR + 155 basis points for every day during this quarter that
three-month LIBOR is between 3% and 9%. Interest will accrue at 0% for each
day that three-month LIBOR is outside this range. As a result, this range note
has a floor of 0%.

Structures in the *high-yield* (*junk bond*) sector of the corporate bond market have introduced variations in the way coupon payments are made. For example, in a leveraged buyout or recapitalization financed with high-yield bonds,
the heavy interest payment burden the corporation must bear places severe cash-
flow constraints on the firm. To reduce this burden, firms involved in leveraged
buy-outs (LBOs) and recapitalizations have issued deferred-coupon structures
that permit the issuer to defer making cash interest payments for a period of
three to seven years. There are three types of deferred-coupon structures: (1)
deferred-interest bonds, (2) step-up bonds, and (3) payment-in-kind bonds.
These structures are described in Chapter 11.

Another high-yield bond structure allows the issuer to reset the coupon
rate so that the bond will trade at a predetermined price. The coupon rate may
reset annually or reset only once over the life of the bond. Generally, the coupon
rate will be the average of rates suggested by two investment banking firms.
The new rate will then reflect the level of interest rates at the reset date and the
credit spread the market wants on the issue at the reset date. This structure is
called an *extendible reset bond.* Notice the difference between this bond structure
and the floating-rate issue described earlier. With a floating-rate issue, the coupon rate resets based on a fixed spread to some benchmark, where the spread
is specified in the indenture and the amount of the spread reflects market conditions at the time the issue is first offered. In contrast, the coupon rate on an
extendible reset bond is reset based on market conditions suggested by several investment banking firms at the time of the reset date. Moreover, the new
coupon rate reflects the new level of interest rates and the new spread that investors seek.

One reason that debt financing is popular with corporations is that the
interest payments are tax-deductible expenses. As a result, the true after-tax cost
of debt to a profitable firm is usually much less than the stated coupon interest

rate. The level of the coupon on any bond is typically close to the level of yields for issues of its class at the time the bond is first sold to the public. Some bonds are initially issued at a price substantially below par value (called *original-issue discount bonds,* or *OIDs*), and their coupon rate is deliberately set below the current market rate. However, firms usually try to set the coupon at a level that will make the market price close to par value. This goal can be accomplished by placing the coupon rate near the prevailing market rate.

To many investors, the coupon is simply the amount of interest they will receive each year. However, the coupon has another major impact on an investor's experience with a bond. The coupon's size influences the volatility of the bond's price: The larger the coupon, the less the price will change in response to a change in market interest rates. Thus, the coupon and the maturity have opposite effects on the price volatility of a bond. This will be illustrated in Chapter 5.

The principal, par value, or face value of a bond is the amount to be repaid to the investor either at maturity or at those times when the bond is called or retired according to sinking-fund provisions. But the principal plays another role, too: It is the basis on which the coupon or periodic interest rests; the coupon is the product of the principal and the coupon rate. For most corporate issues, the face value is $1,000; many government bonds have larger principals starting with $10,000; and most municipal bonds come in denominations of $5,000.

Participants in the bond market use several measures to describe the potential return from investing in a bond: current yield, yield-to-maturity, yield-to-call for a callable bond, and yield-to-put for a putable bond. A *yield-to-worst* is often quoted for bonds. This is the lowest yield of the following: yield-to-maturity, yields to all possible call dates, and yields to all put dates. The calculation and limitations of these yield measures are explained and illustrated in Chapter 4.

The prices of most bonds are quoted as percentages of par or face value. To convert the price quote into a dollar figure, one simply divides the price by 100 (converting it to decimal) and then multiplies by the par value. The following table illustrates this.

| Par Value | Price Quote | Price as a Percentage of Par | Price in Dollars |
|---|---|---|---|
| $   1,000 | 91¾ | 91.75 | $    917.50 |
| 5,000 | 102½ | 102.5 | 5,125.00 |
| 10,000 | 87¼ | 87.25 | 8,725.00 |
| 25,000 | 100¾ | 100.875 | 25,218.75 |
| 100,000 | 71⁹⁄₃₂ | 71.28125 | 71,281.25 |

Treasury bonds and notes are quoted in 32nds of a percentage point, whereas corporate and municipal bonds are quoted in eighths of a percentage point. Care must be taken in translating quotes into dollar prices because the convention for Treasury bonds and notes is to quote, on dealer screens, the number of 32nds after the decimal. Specifically, for a Treasury note and bond, a quote of 91.24 means $91^{24}\!/_{32}$, or $91\frac{3}{4}$. A quote of 102.4 means $102^{4}\!/_{32}$, or $102\frac{1}{8}$. A plus sign ("+") following the number of 32nds indicates that a 64th ($\frac{1}{2}$ of a 32nd) is added to the price. For example, a quote of 98.18+ means $98^{37}\!/_{64}$.

## Call and Refunding Provisions

If a bond's indenture contains a *call feature* or *call provision,* the issuer retains the right to retire the debt, fully or partially, before the scheduled maturity date. The chief benefit of such a feature is that it permits the borrower, should market rates fall, to replace the bond issue with a lower-interest-cost issue. The call feature has added value for corporations and municipalities. It may in the future help them to escape the restrictions that frequently characterize their bonds (about the disposition of assets or collateral). The call feature provides an additional benefit to corporations, which might want to use unexpectedly high levels of cash to retire outstanding bonds or might wish to restructure their balance sheets.

The call provision is detrimental to investors, who run the risk of losing a high-coupon bond when rates begin to decline. When the borrower calls the issue, the investor must find other outlets, which presumably would have lower yields than the bond just withdrawn through the call privilege. Another problem for the investor is that the prospect of a call limits the appreciation in a bond's price that could be expected when interest rates decline.

Because the call feature benefits the issuer and places the investor at a disadvantage, callable bonds carry higher yields than bonds that cannot be retired before maturity. This difference in yields is likely to grow when investors believe that market rates are about to fall and that the borrower may be tempted to replace a high-coupon debt with a new, low-coupon bond. (Such a transaction is called *refunding.*) However, the higher yield alone is often not sufficient compensation to the investor for granting the call privilege to the issuer. Thus, the price at which the bond may be called, termed the *call price,* is normally higher than the principal or face value of the issue. The difference between call price and principal is the *call premium,* whose value may be as much as one year's interest in the first few years of a bond's life and may decline systematically thereafter.

An important limitation on the borrower's right to call is the *period of call protection,* or *deferment period,* which is a specified number of years in the early life of the bond during which the issuer may not call the debt. Such protection is another concession to the investor, and it comes in two forms. Some bonds are *noncallable* (often abbreviated NC) for any reason during the deferment period; other bonds are *nonrefundable* (NF) for that time. The distinction lies in the fact that nonrefundable debt may be called if the funds used to retire the bond issue are obtained from internally generated funds, such as the cash flow from operations or the sale of property or equipment, or from nondebt funding such as the sale of common stock. Thus, although the terminology is unfortunately confusing, a nonrefundable issue may be refunded under the circumstances just described and, as a result, offers less call protection than a noncallable bond, which cannot be called for any reason except to satisfy sinking-fund requirements, explained later. Beginning in early 1986, a number of corporations issued long-term debt with extended call protection, not refunding protection. A number are non-callable for the issue's life, such as Dow Chemical Company's 8⅝s due in 2006. The issuer is expressly prohibited from redeeming the issue prior to maturity. These *noncallable-for-life issues* are referred to as *bullet bonds*. If a bond does not have any protection against an early call, then it is said to be *currently callable*.

Since the mid-1990s, an increasing number of public debt issues include a so-called "make-whole" call provision. Make-whole call provisions have appeared routinely in privately-placed issues since the late 1980s. In contrast to the standard call feature that contains a call price fixed by a schedule, a make-whole call price varies inversely with the level of interest rates. A make-whole call price (i.e., redemption amount) is typically the sum of the present values of the remaining coupon payments and principal discounted at a yield on a Treasury security that matches the bond's remaining maturity plus a spread. For example on January 22, 1998 Aluminum Company of America (Alcoa) issued $300 million in bonds with a make-whole call provision that mature on January 15, 2028. These bonds are redeemable at any time in whole or in part at the issuer's option. The redemption price is the greater of (1) 100% of the principal amount plus accrued interest or (2) the make-whole redemption amount plus accrued interest. In this case, the make-whole redemption amount is equal to the sum of the present value of the remaining coupon and principal payments discounted as the Adjusted Treasury Rate plus 15 basis points.[3] The Adjusted Treasury Rate is the bond-equivalent yield on a U.S. Treasury security having a maturity comparable to the remaining maturity of the bonds to be redeemed. Each holder of the bonds will be notified at least 30 days but not more than 60 days prior to the redemption date. This issue is currently callable as are most issues with make-whole call provisions. Note that the make-whole call price increases as interest rates decrease so if the issuer refunds when interest rates have decreased, the bondholder receives a higher call price. Make-whole call provisions thus provides investors with some protection against reinvestment rate risk.

A key question is, When will the firm find it profitable to refund an issue? It is important for investors to understand the process by which a firm decides

---

3. A 30/360 day count convention is employed in this present value calculation.

whether to retire an old bond and issue a new one. A simple and brief example will illustrate that process and introduce the reader to the kinds of calculations a bondholder will make when trying to predict whether a bond will be refunded.

Suppose a firm's outstanding debt consists of $30 million par value of a bond with a coupon of 10%, a maturity of 15 years, and a lapsed deferment period. The firm can now issue a bond with a similar maturity for an interest rate of 7.8%. Assume that the issuing expenses and legal fees amount to $200,000. The call price on the existing bond issue is $105 per $100 par value. The firm must pay, adjusted for taxes, the sum of call premium and expenses. To simplify the calculations, assume a 30% tax rate. This sum is then $1,190,000.[4] Such a transaction would save the firm a yearly sum of $462,000 in interest (which equals the interest of $3 million on the existing bond less the $2.34 million on the new, adjusted for taxes) for the next 15 years.[5] The rate of return on a payment of $1,190,000 now in exchange for a savings of $462,000 per year for 15 years is about 38%. This rate far exceeds the firm's after-tax cost of debt (now at 7.8% times .7, or 5.46%) and makes the refunding a profitable economic transaction.

In municipal securities, refunding often refers to something different, although the concept is the same. Municipal bonds can be *prerefunded* prior to maturity (usually on a call date). Here, instead of issuing new bonds to retire the debt, the municipality will issue bonds and use the proceeds to purchase enough risk-free securities to fund all the cash flows on the existing bond issue. It places these in an irrevocable trust. Thus, the municipality still has two issues outstanding, but the old bonds receive a new label—they are prerefunded. If Treasury securities are used to prerefund the debt, the cash flows on the bond are guaranteed by Treasury obligations in the trust. Thus, they become AAA rated and trade at higher prices than previously. Municipalities often find this an effective means of lowering their cost of debt.

## Sinking-Fund Provision

The *sinking-fund provision,* which is typical for publicly and privately issued industrial bonds and not uncommon among certain classes of utility debt, requires the obligor to retire a certain amount of the outstanding debt each year. Generally, the retirement occurs in one of two ways. The firm may purchase the amount of bonds to be retired in the open market if their price is below par, or the company may make payments to the trustee who is empowered to monitor

---

4. Both expenses are tax deductible for the firm. The total expense is the call premium of $1.5 million plus the issuing expenses and legal fees of $200,000. The after-tax cost is equal to the before-tax cost times $(1 - \text{tax rate})$. Hence, the after-tax cost is $1.7 million times $(1 - .3)$, or $1,190,000.
5. The new interest expense would be $30 million times .078. The after-tax cost of the interest saving is $660,000 times $(1 - .3)$.

the indenture and who will call a certain number of bonds chosen by lottery. In the latter case, the investor would receive the prearranged call price, which is usually par value. The schedule of retirements varies considerably from issue to issue. Some issuers, particularly in the private-placement market, retire most if not all of their debt before maturity. In the public market, some companies may retire as little as 20 to 30% of the outstanding par value before maturity. Further, the indenture of many issues includes a deferment period that permits the issuer to wait five years or more before beginning the process of sinking-fund retirements. U.S. Treasury debt is generally free of this provision.

There are three advantages of a sinking-fund provision from the investor's perspective. The sinking-fund requirement ensures an orderly retirement of the debt so that the final payment, at maturity, will not be too large. Second, the provision enhances the liquidity of some debt, especially for smaller issues with thin secondary markets. Third, the prices of bonds with this requirement are presumably more stable because the issuer may become an active participant on the buy side when prices fall. For these reasons, the yields on bonds with sinking-fund provisions tend to be less than those on bonds without them.

The sinking fund, however, can work to the disadvantage of an investor. Suppose an investor is holding one of the early bonds to be called for a sinking fund. All of the time and effort put into analyzing the bond has now been wasted, and the investor will have to choose new instruments for purchase. Also, an investor holding a bond with a high coupon at the time rates begin to fall is still forced to relinquish the issue. For this reason, in times of high interest rates, one might find investors demanding higher yields from bonds with sinking funds than from other debt.

The sinking-fund provision may also harm the investor's position through the optional acceleration feature, a part of many corporate bond indentures. With this option, the corporation is free to retire more than the amount of debt the sinking fund requires (and often a multiple thereof) and to do it at the call price set for sinking-fund payments. Of course, the firm will exercise this option only if the price of the bond exceeds the sinking-fund price (usually near par), and this happens when rates are relatively low. If, as is typically the case, the sinking-fund provision becomes operative before the lapse of the call-deferment period, the firm can retire much of its debt with the optional acceleration feature and can do so at a price far below that of the call price it would have to pay in the event of refunding. The impact of such activity on the investor's position is obvious: The firm can redeem at or near par many of the bonds that appear to be protected from call and that have a market value above the face value of the debt.

## Put Provisions

A *putable bond* grants the investor the right to sell the issue back to the issuer at par value on designated dates. The advantage to the investor is that if interest rates rise after the issue date, thereby reducing the value of the bond, the investor can force the issuer to redeem the bond at par. Some issues with put provisions may restrict the amount that the bondholder may put back to the issuer on any one put date. Put options have been included in corporate bonds to deter unfriendly takeovers. Such put provisions are referred to as "poison puts."

Put options can be classified as *hard puts* and *soft puts.* A hard put is one in which the security must be redeemed by the issuer only for cash. In the case of a soft put, the issuer has the option to redeem the security for cash, common stock, another debt instrument, or a combination of the three. Soft puts are found in convertible debt, which we describe next.

## Convertible or Exchangeable Debt

A *convertible bond* is one that can be exchanged for specified amounts of common stock in the issuing firm: The conversion cannot be reversed, and the terms of the conversion are set by the company in the bond's indenture. The most important terms are *conversion ratio* and *conversion price.* The conversion ratio indicates the number of shares of common stock to which the holder of the convertible has a claim. For example, Amazon.com issued $1.25 billion in convertibles in January 1999 that mature in 2009. These convertibles carry a 4.75% coupon with a conversion ratio of 6.408 shares for each bond. This translates to a conversion price of $156.055 per share ($1,000 par value divided by the conversion ratio 6.408) at the time of issuance. The conversion price at issuance is also referred to as the *stated conversion price.*

The conversion privilege may be permitted for all or only some portion of the bond's life. The conversion ratio may decline over time. It is always adjusted proportionately for stock splits and stock dividends. Convertible bonds are typically callable by the issuer. This permits the issuer to force conversion of the issue. (Effectively, the issuer calls the bond, and the investor is forced to convert the bond or allow it to be called.) There are some convertible issues that have call protection. This protection can be in one of two forms: Either the issuer is not allowed to redeem the issue before a specified date, or the issuer is not permitted to call the issue until the stock price has increased by a predetermined percentage price above the conversion price at issuance.

An *exchangeable bond* is an issue that can be exchanged for the common stock of a corporation other than the issuer of the bond. For example, Bell Atlantic Corp. issued 5.75% coupon exchangeable bonds in February 1998 which can be exchanged for shares in Telecom Corp. of New Zealand. There are a handful of issues that are exchangeable into more than one security.

One significant innovation in the convertible bond market is the "Liquid Yield Option Note" (LYON) developed by Merrill Lynch Capital Markets in 1985. A LYON is a zero-coupon, convertible, callable, and putable bond.

Techniques for analyzing convertible and exchangeable bonds are described in Chapters 50 and 51.

## Medium-Term Notes

*Medium-term notes* are highly flexible debt instruments that can be easily structured in response to changing market conditions and investor tastes. "Medium-term" is a misnomer since these securities have ranged in maturity from nine months to 30 years and longer. Since the latter part of the 1980s, medium-term notes have become an increasingly important financing vehicle for corporations, federal agencies, and governments. Typically, medium-term notes are noncallable, unsecured, senior debt securities with fixed-coupon rates that carry an investment-grade credit rating. They generally differ from other bond offerings in their primary distribution process as will be discussed in Chapter 12. *Structured medium-term notes,* or simply *structured notes,* are debt instruments linked to a derivative position. For example, structured notes are usually created with an underlying swap transaction. This "hedging swap" allows the issuer to create securities with interesting risk/return features.

## Warrants

A *warrant* is an option a firm issues that permits the owner to buy from the firm a certain number of shares of common stock at a specified price. It is not uncommon for publicly held corporations to issue warrants with new bonds.

A valuable aspect of a warrant is its rather long life: Most warrants are in effect for at least two years from issuance, and some are perpetual.[6] Another key feature of the warrant is the *exercise price,* the price at which the warrant holder can buy stock from the corporation. This price is normally set at about 15% above the market price of common stock at the time the bond, and thus the warrant, is issued. Frequently, the exercise price will rise through time, according to the schedule in the bond's indenture. Another important characteristic of the warrant is its detachability. *Detachable warrants* are often actively traded on the American Stock Exchange. Other warrants can be exercised only by the bondholder, and these are called *nondetachable warrants.* The chief benefit to the investor is the financial leverage the warrant provides.

## PREFERRED STOCK

*Preferred stock* is a class of stock, not a debt instrument, but it shares characteristics of both common stock and debt. Like the holder of common stock, the preferred stockholder is entitled to dividends. Unlike those on common stock, however, preferred stock dividends are a specified percentage of par or face

---

6. This long life contrasts sharply with the short life during which many exchange-traded call options on common stock, similar to warrants, are exercisable.

value.[7] The percentage is called the *dividend rate;* it need not be fixed, but may float over the life of the issue.

Failure to make preferred stock dividend payments cannot force the issuer into bankruptcy. Should the issuer not make the preferred stock dividend payment, usually paid quarterly, one of two things can happen, depending on the terms of the issue. First, the dividend payment can accrue until it is fully paid. Preferred stock with this feature is called *cumulative preferred stock.* Second, if a dividend payment is missed and the security holder must forgo the payment, the preferred stock is said to be *noncumulative preferred stock.* Failure to make dividend payments may result in imposition of certain restrictions on management. For example, if dividend payments are in arrears, preferred stockholders might be granted voting rights.

Unlike debt, payments made to preferred stockholders are treated as a distribution of earnings. This means that they are not tax deductible to the corporation under the current tax code. (Interest payments, on the other hand, are tax deductible.) Although the after-tax cost of funds is higher if a corporation issues preferred stock rather than borrowing, there is a factor that reduces the cost differential: A provision in the tax code exempts 70% of qualified dividends from federal income taxation if the recipient is a qualified corporation. For example, if Corporation A owns the preferred stock of Corporation B, for each $100 of dividends received by A, only $30 will be taxed at A's marginal tax rate. The purpose of this provision is to mitigate the effect of double taxation of corporate earnings. There are two implications of this tax treatment of preferred stock dividends. First, the major buyers of preferred stock are corporations seeking tax-advantaged investments. Second, the cost of preferred stock issuance is lower than it would be in the absence of the tax provision because the tax benefits are passed through to the issuer by the willingness of buyers to accept a lower dividend rate.

Preferred stock has some important similarities with debt, particularly in the case of cumulative preferred stock: (1) The payments to preferred stockholders promised by the issuer are fixed, and (2) preferred stockholders have priority over common stockholders with respect to dividend payments and distribution of assets in the case of bankruptcy. (The position of noncumulative preferred stock is considerably weaker than cumulative preferred stock.) It is because of this second feature that preferred stock is called a *senior security.* It is senior to common stock. On a balance sheet, preferred stock is classified as equity.

Preferred stock may be issued without a maturity date. This is called *perpetual preferred stock.* Almost all preferred stock has a sinking-fund provision,

---

7. Almost all preferred stock limits the security holder to the specified amount. Historically, there have been issues entitling the preferred stockholder to participate in earnings distribution beyond the specified amount (based on some formula). Preferred stock with this feature is referred to as *participating preferred stock.*

and some preferred stock is convertible into common stock. A trademark product of Morgan Stanley is the Preferred Equity Redemption Cumulative Stock (PERCS). This is a preferred stock with a mandatory conversion at maturity.

Historically, utilities have been the major issuers of preferred stock, making up more than half of each year's issuance. Since 1985, major issuers have been in the financial industry—finance companies, banks, thrifts, and insurance companies.

There are three types of preferred stock: (1) fixed-rate preferred stock, (2) adjustable-rate preferred stock, and (3) auction and remarketed preferred stock. The dividend rate on an adjustable-rate preferred stock (ARPS) is reset quarterly and based on a predetermined spread from the highest of three points on the Treasury yield curve. Most ARPS are perpetual, with a floor and ceiling imposed on the dividend rate of most issues. For auction preferred stock (APS) the dividend rate is reset periodically, as with ARPS, but the dividend rate is established through an auction process. In the case of remarketed preferred stock (RP), the dividend rate is determined periodically by a remarketing agent who resets the dividend rate so that any preferred stock can be tendered at par and be resold (re-marketed) at the original offering price. An investor has the choice of dividend resets every 7 days or every 49 days.

## MORTGAGE-BACKED SECURITIES

A *mortgage-backed security* (MBS) is an instrument whose cash flow depends on the cash flows of an underlying pool of mortgages. There are three types of mortgage-backed securities: (1) mortgage pass-through securities, (2) collateralized mortgage obligations, and (3) stripped mortgage-backed securities. This chapter provides an overview of these securities. A detailed discussion of the structure and analysis of these securities is presented in Part 4 of this book.

### Mortgage Cash Flows

Because the cash flow for these securities depends on the cash flow from the underlying pool of mortgages, the first thing to define is a *mortgage*. A mortgage is a pledge of real estate to secure the loan originated for the purchase of that real property. The mortgage gives the lender (*mortgagee*) the right to foreclose on the loan and seize the property in order to ensure that the loan is paid off if the borrower (*mortgagor*) fails to make the contracted payments. The types of real estate properties that can be mortgaged are divided into two broad categories: residential and nonresidential (i.e., commercial and farm properties). The mortgage loan specifies the interest rate of the loan, the frequency of payment, and the number of years to maturity. Each monthly mortgage payment consists of the monthly interest, a scheduled amount in excess of the monthly interest that is applied to reduce the outstanding loan balance (this is called the *scheduled repayment of principal*), and any payments in excess of the mortgage payment. The latter payments are called *prepayments.*

In effect, the lender has granted the homeowner the right to prepay (or "call") all or part of the mortgage balance at any time. Homeowners prepay their mortgages for one of several reasons. First, they prepay the entire mortgage when they sell their home. Homes are sold for many reasons, among them a change of employment that requires moving or the purchase of a more expensive home. Second, if mortgage rates drop substantially after the mortgage loan was obtained, it may be beneficial for the homeowner to refinance the loan (even after paying all refinancing costs) at the lower interest rate. Third, if homeowners cannot meet their mortgage obligations, their property is repossessed and sold. The proceeds from the sale are used to pay off the mortgage loan. Finally, if the property is destroyed by fire or another insured catastrophe occurs, the insurance proceeds are used to pay off the mortgage.

## Mortgage Pass-Through Securities

A *mortgage pass-through security* (or simply *pass-through*) is created when one or more holders of mortgages form a collection (pool) of mortgages and sell shares or participation certificates in the pool. A pool may consist of several thousand mortgages or only a few mortgages. The cash flow of a pass-through depends on the cash flow of the underlying mortgages, which, as just explained, consists of monthly mortgage payments representing interest, the scheduled repayment of principal, and any prepayments. Payments are made to security holders each month.

There are three major types of pass-through securities, guaranteed by the following organizations: Government National Mortgage Association ("Ginnie Mae"), Federal Home Loan Mortgage Corporation ("Freddie Mac"), and Federal National Mortgage Association ("Fannie Mae"). The last two are government-sponsored entities. The Government National Mortgage Association is a wholly owned U.S. government corporation within the Department of Housing and Urban Development. The securities associated with these three entities are known as *agency pass-through securities.* There are also *nonagency pass-through securities,* issued by thrifts, commercial banks, and private conduits that are not backed by any agency.

While the preponderance of mortgage pass-through securities is backed by one- to four-family residential mortgages, there has been increased issuance of pass-throughs backed by other types of mortgages. These securities are called *commercial mortgage-backed securities.* The five major property types backing such securities are office space, retail property, industrial facilities, multifamily housing, and hotels.

## Collateralized Mortgage Obligations

The *collateralized mortgage obligation (CMO)* structure was developed to broaden the appeal of mortgage-backed products to traditional fixed income investors. A CMO is a security backed by a pool of pass-throughs or a pool of mortgage loans. CMOs are structured so that there are several classes of bond-holders with varying maturities. The different bond classes are called *tranches.* The rules for the distribution of the principal payments and the interest from the underlying collateral among the tranches are specified in the prospectus. By redirecting the cash flow (i.e., principal payments and interest) from the under-lying collateral, issuers have created classes of bonds that have different degrees of prepayment risk and are thereby more attractive to institutional investors to satisfy asset/liability objectives than a pass-through.

Numerous innovations in structuring CMOs have created classes of bonds with one or more of the following characteristics: (1) greater stability of cash flows over a wide range of prepayment speeds, (2) better matching of floating-rate liabilities, (3) substantial upside potential in a declining interest-rate envi-ronment but less downside risk in a rising interest-rate environment, or (4) prop-erties that allow them to be used for hedging mortgage-related products.

The various types of bonds include sequential-pay bonds, planned amor-tization class (PAC) bonds, accrual (or Z) bonds, floating-rate bonds, inverse floating-rate bonds, targeted amortization class (TAC) bonds, support bonds, and very accurately determined maturity (VADM) bonds.

The most prevalent type of commercial mortgage-backed security is a CMO.

## Stripped Mortgage-Backed Securities

A pass-through divides the cash flow from the underlying collateral on a pro rata basis to the security holders. *Stripped mortgage-backed securities,* intro-duced by Fannie Mae in 1986, are created by altering the distribution of principal and interest from a pro rata distribution to an *unequal* distribution.

Why are stripped mortgage-backed securities created? It is sufficient to say at this juncture that the risk/return characteristics of these instruments make them attractive for the purpose of hedging a portfolio of pass-throughs and mortgage loans.

There are two types of stripped MBSs: synthetic-coupon pass-throughs and interest-only/principal-only securities. The first generation of stripped mort-gage-backed securities were the synthetic-coupon pass-throughs because the un-equal distribution of coupon and principal resulted in a synthetic coupon rate that was different from the underlying collateral. In early 1987, stripped MBSs began to be issued in which all of the interest is allocated to one class (the interest-only, or IO, class) and all of the principal to the other class (the principal-only, or PO, class). The IO class receives no principal payments, and the PO class receives no interest.

## ASSET-BACKED SECURITIES

*Asset-backed securities* are securities collateralized by assets that are not mort-gage loans. In structuring an asset-backed security, issuers have drawn from the structures used in the mortgage-backed securities market. Asset-backed securities have been structured as pass-throughs and as structures with multiple bond classes called *pay-throughs,* which are similar to CMOs. Credit enhancement is provided by letters of credit, recourse to the issuer, overcollateralization, or senior/subordination.

Four common types of asset-backed securities are those backed by credit card receivables, home-equity loans, manufactured homes, and automobile loans. There are chapters in Part 4 dedicated to each of these securities. There are also asset-backed securities supported by a pool of Small Business Administration (SBA) loans, student loans, boat loans, equipment leases, recreational vehicle loans, and senior bank loans, and, possibly, the future royalties of your favorite entertainer.

## SUMMARY

This chapter has provided an overview of the types of fixed income securities and has explored the key features of these securities. It is our hope that this chapter will equip the reader with a general knowledge of the instruments and provide a conceptual and terminological background for the chapters that will investigate in more detail the features of these securities and the associated risks and returns.

## CHAPTER 2

# RISKS ASSOCIATED WITH INVESTING IN FIXED INCOME SECURITIES

**Ravi F. Dattatreya, Ph.D.**
CEO
Jasmine Networks, Inc.

**Frank J. Fabozzi, Ph.D., CFA, CPA**
Adjunct Professor of Finance
School of Management
Yale University

The return obtained from a fixed income security from the day it is purchased to the day it is sold can be divided into two parts: (1) the market value of the security when it is eventually sold and (2) the cash flows received from the security over the time period that it is held, plus any additional income from reinvestment of the cash flow. Several environmental factors affect one or both of these two parts. We can define the risk in any security as a measure of the impact of these market factors on the return characteristics of the security.

The different types of risk that an investor in fixed income securities is exposed to are as follows:

- Market, or interest-rate, risk
- Reinvestment risk
- Timing, or call, risk
- Credit, or default, risk
- Yield-curve, or maturity, risk
- Inflation, or purchasing power, risk
- Liquidity, risk
- Exchange rate, or currency, risk
- Volatility risk
- Political or legal risk

- Event risk

- Sector risk

Each risk is described in this chapter. They will become more clear as the securities are described in more detail in other chapters of this book.

## MARKET OR INTEREST-RATE RISK

The price of a typical fixed income security moves in the opposite direction of the change in interest rates: As interest rates rise (fall), the price of a fixed income security will fall (rise).[1] This property is illustrated in Chapter 4. For an investor who plans to hold a fixed income security to maturity, the change in its price before maturity is not of concern; however, for an investor who may have to sell the fixed income security before the maturity date, an increase in interest rates will mean the realization of a capital loss. This risk is referred to as *market risk,* or *interest-rate risk,* which is by far the biggest risk faced by an investor in the fixed income market.

It is customary to represent the market by the yield levels on Treasury securities. Most other yields are compared to the Treasury levels and are quoted as spreads off appropriate Treasury yields. To the extent that the yields of all fixed income securities are interrelated, their prices respond to changes in Treasury rates. As discussed in Chapter 5, the actual magnitude of the price response for any security depends on various characteristics of the security such as coupon, maturity, and the options embedded in the security (e.g., call and put provisions).

To control interest rate-risk, it is necessary to quantify it. The most commonly used measure of interest rate risk is *duration.* Duration is the approximate percentage change in the price of a bond or bond portfolio due to a 100 basis point change in yields. This measure and how it is computed is explained in Chapter 5.

## REINVESTMENT RISK

As explained in Chapter 4, the cash flows received from a security are usually (or are assumed to be) reinvested. The additional income from such reinvestment, sometimes called interest-on-interest, depends on the prevailing interest rate levels at the time of reinvestment as well as on the reinvestment strategy. The variability in the returns from reinvestment from a given strategy due to changes in market rates is called *reinvestment risk.* The risk here is that the interest rate at which interim cash flows can be reinvested will fall. Reinvestment

---

1. There are certain fixed income instruments whose price changes in the same direction as interest rates. Examples are put options and interest-only mortgage-backed securities.

risk is greater for longer holding periods. It is also greater for securities with large, early cash flows such as high-coupon bonds. This risk is analyzed in more detail in Chapter 4.

It should be noted that interest-rate risk and reinvestment risk oppose each other. For example, interest-rate risk is the risk that interest rates will rise, thereby reducing the price of a fixed income security. In contrast, reinvestment risk is the risk that interest rates will fall. A strategy based on these two offsetting risks is called "immunization" and is the topic of Chapter 44.

## TIMING OR CALL RISK

As explained in the previous chapter, many bonds contain a provision that allows the issuer to retire, or "call," all or part of the issue before the maturity date. The issuer usually retains this right to refinance the bond in the future if market interest rates decline below the coupon rate.

From the investor's perspective, there are three disadvantages of the call provision. First, the cash flow pattern of a callable bond is not known with certainty. Second, because the issuer may call the bonds when interest rates have dropped, the investor is exposed to reinvestment rate risk. That is, the investor will have to reinvest the proceeds received when the bond is called at lower interest rates. Finally, the capital appreciation potential of a bond will be reduced because the price of a callable bond may not rise much above the price at which the issuer may call the bond.

Many agency, corporate, and municipal bonds, and all mortgage-backed securities, have embedded in them the option on the part of the borrower to call, or terminate, the issue before the stated maturity date. Even though the investor is usually compensated for taking the risk of call by means of a lower price or a higher yield, it is not easy to determine if this compensation is sufficient. In any case, the returns from a bond with call risk can be dramatically different from those obtained from a noncallable bond. The magnitude of this risk depends upon the various parameters of the call as well as on market conditions. Timing risk is so pervasive in fixed income portfolio management that many market participants consider it second only to interest-rate risk in importance. A framework for analyzing callable bonds and mortgage-backed securities is presented in Chapters 34 and 35, respectively.

In the case of mortgage-backed securities, the cash flow depends on prepayments of principal made by the homeowners in the pool of mortgages that serves as collateral for the security. The timing risk in this case is called *prepayment risk*. It includes *contraction risk—the* risk that homeowners will prepay all or part of their mortgage when mortgage interest rates decline. If interest rates rise, however, investors would benefit from prepayments. The risk that prepayments will slow down when mortgage interest rates rise is called *extension risk*. Thus, timing risk in the case of mortgage-backed securities is called prepayment risk, which includes contraction risk and extension risk.

# CREDIT RISK OR DEFAULT RISK

*Credit risk,* or *default risk,* refers to the risk that the issuer of a fixed income security may default (i.e., the issuer will be unable to make timely principal and interest payments on the security). Credit risk is gauged by quality ratings assigned by commercial rating companies such as Moody's Investor Service, Standard & Poor's Corporation, and Fitch.

Because of this risk, most bonds are sold at a lower price than, or at a yield spread to, comparable U.S. Treasury securities, which are considered free of credit risk. However, except for the lowest credit securities (known as "speculative grade" or "high-yield" or "junk bonds"), the investor is normally concerned more with the changes in the perceived credit risk and/or the cost associated with a given level of credit risk than with the actual event of default. This is so because even though the actual default of an issuing corporation may be highly unlikely, the impact of a change in perceived credit risk or the spread demanded by the market for any given level of risk can have an immediate impact on the value of a security.

# YIELD-CURVE OR MATURITY RISK

In many situations, a bond of a given maturity is used as an alternative to another bond of a different maturity. An adjustment is made to account for the differential interest-rate risks in the two bonds. However, this adjustment makes an assumption about how the interest rates (i.e., yields) at different maturities will move.[2] To the extent that the yield movements deviate from this assumption, there is *yield-curve* or *maturity risk.*

In general, yield-curve risk is more important in hedging situations than in pure investment decisions. For example, if a trader is hedging a position or if a pension fund or an insurance company is acquiring assets so as to enable it to meet a given liability, then yield-curve risk should be carefully examined. However, if a pension fund has decided to invest in the intermediate-term sector, then the fine distinctions in maturity are less important.

Another situation where yield-curve risk should be considered is in the analysis of bond swap transactions where the potential incremental returns are dependent entirely on the parallel shift (or other equally arbitrary) assumption for the yield curve.

# INFLATION OR PURCHASING POWER RISK

*Inflation risk,* or *purchasing power risk,* arises because of the variation in the value of cash flows from a security due to inflation, as measured in terms of

---

2. Usually, a parallel shift assumption is made. That is, we assume that the yields at different maturities move by equal amounts.

purchasing power. For example, if an investor purchases a five-year bond in which he or she can realize a coupon rate of 7%, but the rate of inflation is 8%, then the purchasing power of the cash flow has declined. For all but inflation-adjusted securities, adjustable- or floating-rate bonds, an investor is exposed to inflation risk because the interest rate the issuer promises to make is fixed for the life of the security. To the extent that interest rates reflect the expected inflation rate, floating-rate bonds have a lower level of inflation risk.

## LIQUIDITY RISK

*Liquidity risk* is the risk that the investor will have to sell a bond below its true value where the true value is indicated by a recent transaction. The primary measure of liquidity is the size of the spread between the bid price and the ask price quoted by a dealer. The wider the bid-ask spread, the greater the liquidity risk. Exhibit 2–1 shows indicators of market liquidity by market sector as measured by bid-ask spreads where the spread is as a percent of the price.

A liquid market can generally be defined by "small bid-ask spreads which do not materially increase for large transactions."[3] How to define the bid-ask spread in a multiple dealer market is subject to interpretation. For example,

**E X H I B I T   2–1**

Indicators of Market Liquidity

| Sector | Bid-ask spreads (% of price) | |
|---|---|---|
| | Typical | Distressed |
| Treasuries | | |
| Bills | 0.002 | 0.005 |
| On-the-run notes and bonds | 0.003 | 0.006 |
| Off-the-run issues and bonds | 0.006 | 0.009 |
| Corporates (intermediates) | | |
| A rated Finance | 0.120 | 0.500 |
| B rated Industrials | 0.500 | 5.000 |
| Mortgage-backed securities | | |
| Fixed-rate generic | 0.060 | 0.250 |
| Municipals (long) | | |
| Aa/Aaa | 0.250 | 0.750 |

Adapted from Exhibit 1 in Robert I. Gerber, "A User's Guide to Buy-Side Bond Trading," Chapter 16 in Frank J. Fabozzi (ed.), *Managing Fixed Income Portfolios* (New Hope, PA: Frank J. Fabozzi, 1997), p. 279.

---

3. Robert I. Gerber, "A User's Guide to Buy-Side Bond Trading," Chapter 16 in Frank J. Fabozzi (ed.), *Managing Fixed Income Portfolios* (New Hope, PA: Frank J. Fabozzi, 1997), p. 278.

consider the bid-ask spread for four dealers. Each quote is for 92 plus the number of 32nds shown:

|  | Dealer | | | |
| --- | --- | --- | --- | --- |
|  | 1 | 2 | 3 | 4 |
| Bid price | 1 | 1 | 2 | 2 |
| Ask price | 4 | 3 | 4 | 5 |

The bid-ask spread for each dealer (in 32nds) is:

|  | Dealer | | | |
| --- | --- | --- | --- | --- |
|  | 1 | 2 | 3 | 4 |
| Bid-ask spread | 3 | 2 | 2 | 3 |

The bid-ask spread as computed above is measured relative to a dealer. The best bid-ask spread is 2 32nds for Dealers 2 and 3.

From the perspective of the *market overall,* the bid-ask spread can be computed by looking at the best bid price (high price at which one of the dealers is willing to buy the security) and the lowest ask price (lowest offer price at which one of the dealers is willing to sell the security). This liquidity measure is called the *market bid-ask spread.* For the four dealers, the highest bid price is 92 plus 2 32nds and the lowest ask price is 92 plus 3 32nds. Thus, the market bid-ask spread is 1 32nd.

For investors who plan to hold a bond until maturity and need not mark a position to market, liquidity risk is not a major concern. An institutional investor who plans to hold an issue to maturity but is periodically marked to market is concerned with liquidity risk. By marking a position to market, it is meant the security is revalued in the portfolio based on its current market price. For example, mutual funds are required to mark to market at the end of each day the holdings in their portfolio in order to compute the net asset value (NAV). While other institutional investors may not mark to market as frequently as mutual funds, they are marked to market when reports are periodically sent to clients or the board of directors or trustees.

Where are the prices obtained to mark a position to market? Typically, a portfolio manager will solicit indicative bids from several dealers and then use some process to determine the bid price used to mark the position. The less liquid the issue, the greater the variation there will be in the bid prices obtained by dealers. With an issue that has little liquidity, the price may have to be determined by a pricing service rather than by dealers. Moreover, lack of dealer indicative bids and concern with models used by pricing services may lead the manager to occasional override a bid (subject to internal approval beyond the control of the manager).

Bid-ask spreads, and therefore liquidity risk, change over time. Exhibit 2–1 shows estimates of the bid-ask spread by sector in distressed periods. Changing market liquidity is a concern to portfolio managers who are contemplating investing in new complex bond structures.

## EXCHANGE RATE OR CURRENCY RISK

A nondollar-denominated bond (i.e., a bond whose payments occur in a foreign currency) has unknown U.S. dollar cash flows. The dollar cash flows are dependent on the foreign-exchange rate at the time the payments are received. For example, suppose an investor purchases a bond whose payments are in Japanese yen. If the yen depreciates relative to the U.S. dollar, then fewer dollars will be received. The risk of this occurring is referred to as *exchange rate risk,* or *currency risk.* Of course, should the yen appreciate relative to the U.S. dollar, the investor will benefit by receiving more dollars.

In addition to the change in the exchange rate, an investor is exposed to the interest-rate, or market, risk in the local market. For example, if a U.S. investor purchases German government bonds denominated in euros, the proceeds received from the sale of that bond prior to maturity will depend on the level of interest rates in the German bond market, in addition to the exchange rate.

## VOLATILITY RISK

As will be explained in later chapters, the price of a bond with an embedded option depends on the level of interest rates and factors that influence the value of the embedded option. One of the factors is the expected volatility of interest rates. Specifically, the value of an option rises when expected interest-rate volatility increases. In the case of a callable bond or mortgage-backed security, because the investor has granted an option to the borrower, the price of the security falls because the investor has given away a more valuable option. The risks that a change in volatility will adversely affect the price of a security is called *volatility risk.*

## POLITICAL OR LEGAL RISK

Sometimes the government can declare withholding or other additional taxes on a bond or declare a tax-exempt bond taxable. In addition, a regulatory authority can conclude that a given security is unsuitable for investment entities that it regulates. These actions can adversely affect the value of the security. Similarly, it is also possible that a legal or regulatory action affects the value of a security positively. The possibility of any political or legal actions adversely affecting the value of a security is known as *political* or *legal risk.*

To illustrate political or legal risk, consider investors who purchase tax-exempt municipal securities. They are exposed to two types of political risk that can be more appropriately called *tax risk*. The first type of tax risk is that the federal income tax rate will be reduced. The higher the marginal tax rate, the greater the value of the tax-exempt nature of a municipal security. As the marginal tax rates decline, the price of a tax-exempt municipal security will decline. For example, proposals for a flat tax with a low tax rate significantly reduced the potential tax advantage of owning municipal bonds. As a result, tax-exempt municipal bonds began trading at lower prices. The second type of tax risk is that a municipal bond issued as tax-exempt will eventually be declared taxable by the Internal Revenue Service. This may occur because many municipal (revenue) bonds have elaborate security structures that could be subject to future adverse congressional actions and IRS interpretations. As a result of the loss of the tax exemption, the municipal bond will decline in value in order to provide a yield comparable to similar taxable bonds. For example, in June of 1980, the Battery Park City Authority sold $97.315 million in construction loan notes. At the time of issuance, the legal counsel thought that the interest on the note would be exempt from federal income taxation. In November of 1980, however, the IRS held that interest on these notes was not exempt, resulting in a lower price for the notes. The issue was not resolved until September 1981 when the Authority and the IRS signed a formal agreement resolving the matter so as to make the interest on the notes tax-exempt.

## EVENT RISK

Occasionally, the ability of an issuer to make interest and principal payments is seriously and unexpectedly changed by (1) a natural or industrial accident or (2) a takeover or corporate restructuring. These risks are referred to as *event risk*. The cancellation of plans to build a nuclear power plant illustrates the first type of event in relation to the utility industry.

An example of the second type of event risk is the takeover in 1988 of RJR Nabisco for $25 billion via a financing technique known as a *leveraged buyout* (LBO). In such a transaction, the new company incurred a substantial amount of debt to finance the acquisition of the firm. Because the corporation was required to service a substantially larger amount of debt, its quality rating was reduced to noninvestment grade quality. As a result, the change in yield spread to a benchmark Treasury, demanded by investors because of the LBO announcement, increased from about 100 basis points to 350 basis points.

There are also spillover effects of event risk on other firms. For example, if there is a nuclear accident, this will affect all utilities producing nuclear power.

## SECTOR RISK

Bonds in different sectors of the market respond differently to environmental changes because of a combination of some or all of the above risks, as well as others. Examples include discount versus premium coupon bonds, industrial versus utility bonds, and corporate versus mortgage-backed bonds. The possibility of adverse differential movement of specific sectors of the market is called *sector risk.*

## OTHER RISKS

The various risks of investing in the fixed income markets reviewed in this chapter do not represent the entire range of risks. In the marketplace, it is customary to combine almost all risks other than market risk (interest-rate risk) and refer to it as *basis risk.*

## SUMMARY

In this chapter, we have described 12 risks associated with investing in fixed income securities. Not all securities or investment strategies expose the investor to all of the risks we have discussed. As the instruments and portfolio management strategies are described in more detail throughout this book, these risks will be explained further.

## CHAPTER 3

# A REVIEW OF THE TIME VALUE OF MONEY

Frank J. Fabozzi, Ph.D., CFA, CPA
Adjunct Professor of Finance
School of Management
Yale University

The notion that money has a time value is one of the basic concepts in the analysis of any financial instrument. Money has a time value because of the opportunities for investing money at some interest rate. In this chapter, we review the three fundamental concepts involved in understanding the time value of money: future value, present value, and yield. These concepts are applied in the next chapter, where we discuss bond pricing and yield measures.

## FUTURE VALUE

Suppose an investor places $1,000 in a bank account and the bank agrees to pay interest of 7% a year. At the end of one year, the account will contain $1,070, or $1,000, the original principal, plus $70 interest. Suppose that the investor decides to let the $1,070 remain in the bank account for another year and that the bank agrees to continue paying interest of 7% a year. The amount in the bank account at the end of the second year will equal $1,144.90, determined as follows:

| | |
|---|---|
| Principal at beginning of year 2 | $1,070.00 |
| Interest for year 2 ($1,070 × .07) | 74.90 |
| Total in bank account | $1,144.90 |

In terms of our original $1,000 investment, the $1,144.90 represents the following:

| | |
|---|---|
| Original investment at beginning of year 1 | $1,000.00 |
| Interest for year 1 ($1,000 × .07) | 70.00 |
| Interest for year 2 based on original investment | 70.00 |
| Interest for year 2 earned on interest for year 1 ($70 × .07) | 4.90 |
| Total | $1,144.90 |

The additional interest of $4.90 in year 2 above the $70 interest earned on the original principal of $1,000 is the interest on the interest earned in year 1.

After eight years, $1,000 will grow to $1,718.19 if allowed to accumulate tax-free at an annual interest rate of 7%. We refer to the amount at the end of eight years as the *future value*.

Notice that the total interest at the end of eight years is $718.19. The total interest represents $560 of interest earned on the original principal ($70 × 8) plus $158.19 ($718.19 − $560) earned by the reinvestment of the interest.

## Computing the Future Value of an Investment

To compute the amount to which $1,000 will grow by the end of eight years if interest is earned at an annual interest rate of 7%, the following formula is used:

$$\$1,000 \ (1.07)^8 = \$1,718.19$$

To generalize the formula, suppose $1,000 is invested for $N$ periods at an annual interest rate of $i$ (expressed as a decimal). Then, the future value $N$ periods from now can be expressed as follows:

$$\$1,000 \ (1 + i)^N$$

For example, if $1,000 is invested for four years at an annual interest rate of 10% ($i = .10$), then it will grow to $1,464.10:

$$\$1,000 \ (1.10)^4 = \$1,000 \ (1.4641) = \$1,464.10$$

The expression $(1 + i)^N$ is the amount to which $1 will grow at the end of $N$ years if an annual interest rate of $i$ is earned. This expression is called the *future value of $1*. By multiplying the future value of $1 by the original principal, we can determine the future value of the original principal.

For example, we just demonstrated that the future value of $1,000 invested for four years at an annual interest rate of 10% is $1,464.10. The future value of $1 is $1.4641. Therefore, if instead of $1,000, $50,000 is invested, the future value is

$$\$50,000 \ (1.4641) = \$73,205.00$$

We can generalize the formula for the future value as follows:

$$FV = P(1 + i)^N$$

where

$FV$ = Future value ($)
$\ P$ = Original principal ($)
$\ \ i$ = Interest rate (in decimal form)
$\ N$ = Number of years

Most calculators have an option that computes this value. Alternatively, there are tables available that provide the value of $(1 + i)^N$. Exhibit 3–1 is an abridged future value table that provides the value of $(1 + i)^N$. Notice that at the intersection of the 10-percent column and four-period row, the value is 1.4641. This is the same value computed for $(1.10)^4$ in the above illustration.

The following three illustrations show how to apply the future value formula.

**Illustration 1.**    A pension fund manager invests $10 million in a financial instrument that promises to pay 8.7% per year for five years. The future value of the $10 million investment is $15,175,665, as shown below:

$$P = \$10,000,000$$
$$i = .087$$
$$N = 5$$
$$FV = \$10,000,000\ (1.087)^5$$
$$= \$10,000,000\ (1.5175665)$$
$$= \$15,175,665$$

**Illustration 2.**    Suppose that a life insurance company has guaranteed a payment of $14 million to a pension fund four years from now. If the life insurance company receives a premium of $11 million and can invest the entire premium for four years at an annual interest rate of 6.5%, will it have sufficient funds from this investment to meet the $14 million obligation?

The future value of the $11 million investment at the end of four years is $14,151,130, as shown below:

$$P = \$11,000,000$$
$$i = .065$$
$$N = 4$$
$$FV = \$11,000,000\ (1.065)^4$$
$$= \$11,000,000\ (1.2864664)$$
$$= \$14,151,130$$

Because the future value is expected to be $14,151,130, the life insurance company will have sufficient funds from this investment to satisfy the $14 million obligation to the pension fund.

**Illustration 3.**    The portfolio manager of a tax-exempt fund is considering investing $400,000 in an instrument that pays an annual interest rate of 5.7% for four years. At the end of four years, the portfolio manager plans to reinvest the proceeds for three more years and expects that, for the three-year period, an

EXHIBIT 3-1

Future Value of $1 at the End of N Periods

**Interest Rate**

| Period | 1% | 2% | 3% | 4% | 5% | 6% | 7% | 8% | 9% | 10% | 11% | 12% | 13% | 14% | 15% |
|---|---|---|---|---|---|---|---|---|---|---|---|---|---|---|---|
| 1 | 1.0100 | 1.0200 | 1.0300 | 1.0400 | 1.0500 | 1.0600 | 1.0700 | 1.0800 | 1.0900 | 1.100 | 1.1100 | 1.1200 | 1.1300 | 1.1400 | 1.1500 |
| 2 | 1.0201 | 1.0404 | 1.0609 | 1.0816 | 1.1025 | 1.1236 | 1.1449 | 1.1664 | 1.1881 | 1.2100 | 1.2321 | 1.2544 | 1.2769 | 1.2996 | 1.3225 |
| 3 | 1.0303 | 1.0612 | 1.0927 | 1.1249 | 1.1576 | 1.1910 | 1.2250 | 1.2597 | 1.2950 | 1.3310 | 1.3676 | 1.4049 | 1.4429 | 1.4815 | 1.5209 |
| 4 | 1.0406 | 1.0824 | 1.1255 | 1.1699 | 1.2155 | 1.2625 | 1.3108 | 1.3605 | 1.4116 | 1.4641 | 1.5181 | 1.5735 | 1.6305 | 1.6890 | 1.7490 |
| 5 | 1.0510 | 1.1041 | 1.1593 | 1.2167 | 1.2763 | 1.3382 | 1.4026 | 1.4693 | 1.5386 | 1.6105 | 1.6851 | 1.7623 | 1.8424 | 1.9254 | 2.0114 |
| 6 | 1.0615 | 1.1262 | 1.1941 | 1.2653 | 1.3401 | 1.4185 | 1.5007 | 1.5869 | 1.6771 | 1.7716 | 1.8704 | 1.9738 | 2.0820 | 2.1950 | 2.3131 |
| 7 | 1.0721 | 1.1487 | 1.2299 | 1.3159 | 1.4071 | 1.5036 | 1.6058 | 1.7138 | 1.8280 | 1.9487 | 2.0762 | 2.2107 | 2.3526 | 2.5023 | 2.6600 |
| 8 | 1.0829 | 1.1717 | 1.2668 | 1.3686 | 1.4775 | 1.5938 | 1.7182 | 1.8509 | 1.9926 | 2.1436 | 2.3045 | 2.4760 | 2.6554 | 2.8526 | 3.0590 |
| 9 | 1.0937 | 1.1951 | 1.3048 | 1.4233 | 1.5513 | 1.6895 | 1.8385 | 1.9990 | 2.1719 | 2.3579 | 2.5580 | 2.7731 | 3.0040 | 3.2519 | 3.5179 |
| 10 | 1.1046 | 1.2190 | 1.3439 | 1.4802 | 1.6289 | 1.7908 | 1.9672 | 2.1589 | 2.3674 | 2.5937 | 2.8394 | 3.1058 | 3.3946 | 3.7072 | 4.0456 |
| 11 | 1.1157 | 1.2434 | 1.3842 | 1.5395 | 1.7103 | 1.8983 | 2.1049 | 2.3316 | 2.5804 | 2.8531 | 3.1518 | 3.4785 | 3.8359 | 4.2262 | 4.6524 |
| 12 | 1.1268 | 1.2682 | 1.4258 | 1.6010 | 1.7595 | 2.0122 | 2.2522 | 2.5182 | 2.8127 | 3.1384 | 3.4984 | 3.8960 | 4.3345 | 4.8179 | 5.3502 |
| 13 | 1.1381 | 1.2936 | 1.4685 | 1.6651 | 1.8856 | 2.1329 | 2.4098 | 2.7196 | 3.0658 | 3.4523 | 3.8833 | 4.3635 | 4.8980 | 5.4924 | 6.1528 |
| 14 | 1.1495 | 1.3195 | 1.5126 | 1.7317 | 1.9799 | 2.2609 | 2.5785 | 2.9372 | 3.3417 | 3.7975 | 4.3104 | 4.8871 | 5.5347 | 6.2613 | 7.0757 |
| 15 | 1.1610 | 1.3459 | 1.5580 | 1.8009 | 2.0789 | 2.3966 | 2.7590 | 3.1722 | 3.6425 | 4.1772 | 4.7846 | 5.4736 | 6.2543 | 7.1379 | 8.1371 |
| 16 | 1.1726 | 1.3728 | 1.6047 | 1.8730 | 2.1829 | 2.5404 | 2.9522 | 3.4259 | 3.9703 | 4.5950 | 5.3109 | 6.1304 | 7.0673 | 8.1372 | 9.3576 |
| 17 | 1.1843 | 1.4002 | 1.6528 | 1.9479 | 2.2920 | 2.6928 | 3.1588 | 3.7000 | 4.3276 | 5.0545 | 5.8951 | 6.8660 | 7.9861 | 9.2765 | 10.761 |
| 18 | 1.1961 | 1.4282 | 1.7024 | 2.0258 | 2.4066 | 2.8543 | 3.3799 | 3.9960 | 4.7171 | 5.5599 | 6.5435 | 7.6900 | 9.0243 | 10.575 | 12.375 |
| 19 | 1.2081 | 1.4568 | 1.7535 | 2.1068 | 2.5270 | 3.0256 | 3.6165 | 4.3157 | 5.1417 | 6.1159 | 7.2633 | 8.6128 | 10.197 | 12.055 | 14.231 |
| 20 | 1.2202 | 1.4859 | 1.8061 | 2.1911 | 2.6533 | 3.2071 | 3.8697 | 4.6610 | 5.6044 | 6.7275 | 8.0623 | 9.6463 | 11.523 | 13.743 | 46.366 |
| 21 | 1.2324 | 1.5157 | 1.8603 | 2.2788 | 2.7860 | 3.3966 | 4.1406 | 5.0388 | 6.1088 | 7.4002 | 8.9491 | 10.803 | 13.021 | 15.667 | 18.821 |
| 22 | 1.2447 | 1.5460 | 1.9161 | 2.3699 | 2.9253 | 3.6035 | 4.4304 | 5.4365 | 6.6586 | 8.1403 | 9.9335 | 12.100 | 14.714 | 17.861 | 21.644 |
| 23 | 1.2572 | 1.5769 | 1.9736 | 2.4647 | 3.0715 | 3.8197 | 4.7405 | 5.8715 | 7.2579 | 8.9543 | 11.026 | 13.552 | 16.627 | 20.361 | 24.891 |
| 24 | 1.2697 | 1.6084 | 2.0328 | 2.5633 | 3.2251 | 4.0489 | 5.0724 | 6.3412 | 7.9111 | 9.8497 | 12.239 | 15.178 | 18.788 | 23.212 | 28.625 |
| 25 | 1.2824 | 1.6406 | 2.0938 | 2.6658 | 3.3864 | 4.2919 | 5.4274 | 6.8485 | 8.6231 | 10.834 | 13.585 | 17.000 | 21.230 | 26.461 | 32.918 |
| 26 | 1.2953 | 1.6734 | 2.1566 | 2.7725 | 3.5557 | 4.5494 | 5.8074 | 7.3964 | 9.3992 | 11.918 | 15.080 | 19.040 | 23.990 | 30.166 | 37.856 |
| 27 | 1.3082 | 1.7069 | 2.2213 | 2.8834 | 3.7335 | 4.8223 | 6.2139 | 7.9881 | 10.245 | 13.110 | 16.739 | 21.324 | 27.109 | 34.389 | 43.535 |
| 28 | 1.3213 | 1.7410 | 2.2879 | 2.9987 | 3.9201 | 5.1117 | 6.6488 | 8.6271 | 11.167 | 14.421 | 18.580 | 23.883 | 30.633 | 39.204 | 50.065 |
| 29 | 1.3345 | 1.7758 | 2.3566 | 3.1187 | 4.1161 | 5.4184 | 7.1143 | 9.3173 | 12.172 | 15.863 | 20.624 | 26.749 | 34.616 | 44.693 | 57.575 |
| 30 | 1.3478 | 1.8114 | 2.4273 | 3.2434 | 4.3219 | 5.7435 | 7.6123 | 10.062 | 13.267 | 17.449 | 22.892 | 29.959 | 39.116 | 50.950 | 66.211 |

annual interest rate of 7.2% can be earned. The future value of this investment is $615,098.

The future value of the $400,000 investment for four years at 5.7% is as follows:

$$P = \$400,000$$
$$i = .057$$
$$N = 4$$
$$FV = \$400,000 \ (1.057)^4$$
$$= \$400,000 \ (1.248245)$$
$$= \$499,298$$

The future value of $499,298 reinvested for three years at 7.2% is computed below:

$$i = .072$$
$$N = 3$$
$$FV = \$499,298 \ (1.072)^3$$
$$= \$499,298 \ (1.231925)$$
$$= \$615,098$$

### Fractional Periods

In our illustrations, we have computed the future value for whole years. The future value formula, however, is the same if an investment is made for part of a year. Most pocket calculators can accommodate fractional exponents.

For example, suppose that $100,000 is invested for seven years and three months. Because three months is 0.25 of one year, $N$ in the future value formula is 7.25. Assuming an annual interest rate of 5%, the future value of $100,000 invested for seven years and three months is $142,437, as shown below:

$$P = \$100,000$$
$$i = .05$$
$$N = 7.25$$
$$FV = \$100,000 \ (1.05)^{7.25}$$
$$= \$100,000 \ (1.424369)$$
$$= \$142,437$$

## Compounding More than One Time per Year

An investment may pay interest more than one time per year. For example, interest may be paid semiannually, quarterly, monthly, weekly, or daily. Our future value formula can handle interest payments that are made more than once per year. This is done by adjusting the annual interest rate and the exponent. The annual interest rate is divided by the number of times that interest is paid per year. The exponent, which represents the number of years, is multiplied by the number of times interest is paid per year.

Mathematically, we can express the future value when interest is paid $m$ times per year as follows:

$$FV = P(1 + i)^n$$

where

$i$ = Annual interest rate divided by $m$
$n$ = Number of interest payments ($= N \times m$)

***Illustration 4.*** Suppose that a portfolio manager invests \$1 million in an investment that promises to pay an annual interest rate of 6.4% for six years. Interest on this investment is paid semiannually. The future value is \$1,459,340, as shown below:

$$P = \$1,000,000$$
$$m = 2$$
$$i = .032 \ (=.064/2)$$
$$N = 6$$
$$n = 12 \ (= 6 \times 2)$$
$$FV = \$1,000,000 \ (1.032)^{12}$$
$$= \$1,000,000 \ (1.459340)$$
$$= \$1,459,340$$

If interest is paid only once per year, this future value would be \$1,450,941 instead of \$1,459,340. The higher future value when interest is paid semiannually reflects the more frequent opportunity for reinvesting the interest paid.

## Future Value of an Ordinary Annuity

Suppose that an investor expects to receive \$10,000 a year from some investment for each of the next five years starting one year from now. Each time the investor receives the \$10,000, he plans to invest it. Let's assume that the investor can earn an annual interest rate of 6% each time \$10,000 is invested. How much money will the investor have at the end of five years?

Our future value formula makes it simple to determine to what amount each \$10,000 investment will grow. This calculation is illustrated graphically in Exhibit 3–2. The total future value of \$56,371.30 shown in Exhibit 3–2 is composed of the five payments of \$10,000, or \$50,000, plus \$6,371.30 of interest earned by investing the \$10,000 annual payments.

**E X H I B I T   3–2**

Future Value of an Ordinary Annuity of $10,000 per Year for 5 Years

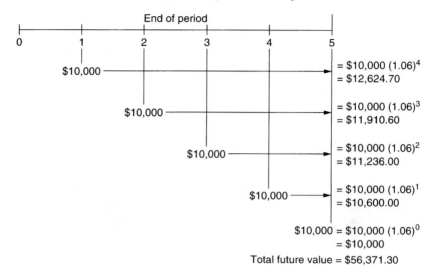

When the same amount of money is received (or paid) periodically, it is referred to as an *annuity.* When the first receipt occurs one period from now, it is referred to as an *ordinary annuity.*

The following formula can be used to calculate the future value of an ordinary annuity:

$$FV = A \left[ \frac{(1 + i)^N - 1}{i} \right]$$

where

$A$ = Amount of the annuity ($)
$i$ = Annual interest rate (in decimals)

The term in the square brackets is the *future value of an ordinary annuity of $1 per year.* Multiplying the future value of an ordinary annuity of $1 by the amount of the annuity produces the future value of an ordinary annuity of any amount.

For example, if $10,000 is invested at 6% each year for the next five years, starting one year from now, we have

$A$ = $10,000
$i$ = .06
$N$ = 5

therefore,

$$FV = \$10,000 \left[ \frac{(1.06)^5 - 1}{.06} \right]$$

$$= \$10,000 \left[ \frac{1.3382256 - 1}{.06} \right]$$

$$= \$10,000 \ (5.63710)$$

$$= \$56,371$$

This value agrees with our earlier calculation.

Tables are available that provide the future value of an ordinary annuity of $1 per period. Exhibit 3–3 is an abridged version. The value from the table should be multiplied by the annuity payment to obtain the future value of the annuity. For example, from Exhibit 3–3 the future value of an ordinary annuity of $1 per period for 5 periods assuming a 6% interest rate per period is 5.6371. Hence, the future value of an ordinary annuity of $10,000 is $10,000 times 5.6371, or $56,371.

## PRESENT VALUE

We illustrated how to compute the future value of an investment. Now we will illustrate how to work the process in reverse; that is, given the future value of an investment, we will illustrate how to determine the amount of money that must be invested today in order to realize the future value. The amount of money that must be invested today is called the *present value.*

### Present Value of an Amount to Be Received in the Future

What we are interested in is how to determine the amount of money that must be invested today, earning an interest rate of $i$ for $N$ years, in order to produce a specific future value. This can be done by solving the future value formula given earlier for $P$, the original principal:

$$P = FV \left[ \frac{1}{(1 + i)^N} \right]$$

Instead of using $P$ in the above formula, we shall denote the present value as PV. Therefore, the present value formula can be rewritten as

$$PV = FV \left[ \frac{1}{(1 + i)^N} \right]$$

The term in the square brackets is equal to the present value of $1; that is, it indicates how much must be set aside today, earning an interest rate of $i$, in order to have $1 $N$ years from now. Present value tables are available. Exhibit 3–4 shows the present value of $1, which is found by dividing 1 by $(1 + i)^N$.

# EXHIBIT 3-3

Future Value of an Ordinary Annuity of $1 per Period for N Periods

**Interest Rate**

| Number of Periods | 1% | 2% | 3% | 4% | 5% | 6% | 7% | 8% | 9% | 10% | 11% | 12% | 13% | 14% | 15% |
|---|---|---|---|---|---|---|---|---|---|---|---|---|---|---|---|
| 1 | 1.0000 | 1.0000 | 1.0000 | 1.0000 | 1.0000 | 1.0000 | 1.0000 | 1.0000 | 1.0000 | 1.0000 | 1.0000 | 1.0000 | 1.0000 | 1.0000 | 1.0000 |
| 2 | 2.0100 | 2.0200 | 2.0300 | 2.0400 | 2.0500 | 2.0600 | 2.0700 | 2.0800 | 2.0900 | 2.1000 | 2.1100 | 2.1200 | 2.1300 | 2.1400 | 2.1500 |
| 3 | 3.0301 | 3.0604 | 3.0909 | 3.1216 | 3.1525 | 3.1836 | 3.2149 | 3.2463 | 3.2781 | 3.3100 | 3.3421 | 3.3744 | 3.4069 | 3.4396 | 3.4725 |
| 4 | 4.0604 | 4.1216 | 4.1836 | 4.2465 | 4.3101 | 4.3746 | 4.4399 | 4.5061 | 4.5731 | 4.6410 | 4.7097 | 4.7793 | 4.8498 | 4.9211 | 4.9934 |
| 5 | 5.1010 | 5.2040 | 5.3091 | 5.4163 | 5.5256 | 5.6371 | 5.7507 | 5.8666 | 5.9847 | 6.1051 | 6.2278 | 6.3528 | 6.4803 | 6.6101 | 6.7424 |
| 6 | 6.1520 | 6.3081 | 6.4684 | 6.6630 | 6.8019 | 6.9753 | 7.1533 | 7.3359 | 7.5233 | 7.7156 | 7.9129 | 8.1152 | 8.3227 | 8.5355 | 8.7537 |
| 7 | 7.2135 | 7.4343 | 7.6625 | 7.8893 | 8.1420 | 8.3938 | 8.6540 | 8.9228 | 9.2004 | 39.4872 | 9.7833 | 10.809 | 10.405 | 10.730 | 11.066 |
| 8 | 8.2857 | 8.5830 | 8.8923 | 9.2142 | 9.5491 | 9.8975 | 10.259 | 10.636 | 11.028 | 11.435 | 11.859 | 12.299 | 12.757 | 13.232 | 13.726 |
| 9 | 9.3685 | 9.7546 | 10.159 | 10.582 | 11.026 | 11.491 | 11.978 | 12.487 | 13.021 | 13.579 | 14.164 | 14.775 | 15.416 | 16.085 | 16.785 |
| 10 | 10.462 | 10.949 | 11.463 | 12.006 | 12.577 | 13.180 | 13.816 | 14.486 | 15.192 | 15.937 | 16.722 | 17.548 | 18.420 | 19.337 | 20.603 |
| 11 | 11.566 | 12.168 | 12.807 | 13.486 | 14.206 | 14.971 | 15.783 | 16.645 | 17.560 | 18.531 | 19.561 | 20.654 | 21.814 | 23.044 | 24.649 |
| 12 | 12.682 | 13.412 | 14.192 | 15.025 | 15.917 | 16.869 | 17.888 | 18.977 | 20.140 | 21.384 | 22.713 | 24.133 | 25.650 | 27.270 | 29.001 |
| 13 | 13.809 | 14.680 | 15.617 | 16.626 | 17.713 | 18.882 | 20.140 | 21.495 | 22.953 | 24.522 | 26.212 | 28.029 | 29.985 | 32.088 | 34.851 |
| 14 | 14.947 | 15.973 | 17.086 | 18.291 | 19.598 | 21.015 | 22.550 | 24.214 | 26.019 | 27.975 | 30.095 | 32.392 | 34.883 | 37.581 | 40.504 |
| 15 | 16.096 | 17.293 | 18.598 | 20.023 | 21.578 | 23.276 | 25.129 | 27.152 | 29.360 | 31.772 | 34.405 | 37.729 | 40.418 | 43.842 | 47.580 |
| 16 | 17.257 | 18.639 | 20.156 | 21.824 | 23.657 | 25.672 | 27.888 | 30.324 | 33.003 | 35.949 | 39.190 | 42.753 | 46.672 | 50.980 | 55.717 |
| 17 | 18.430 | 20.012 | 21.761 | 23.697 | 25.840 | 28.212 | 30.840 | 33.750 | 36.973 | 40.544 | 44.501 | 48.883 | 53.739 | 59.117 | 65.075 |
| 18 | 19.614 | 21.412 | 23.414 | 25.645 | 28.132 | 30.905 | 33.999 | 37.450 | 41.301 | 45.599 | 50.396 | 55.749 | 61.725 | 68.394 | 75.836 |
| 19 | 20.810 | 22.840 | 25.116 | 27.671 | 30.539 | 33.760 | 37.379 | 41.446 | 46.018 | 51.159 | 56.940 | 63.439 | 70.749 | 78.969 | 88.211 |
| 20 | 22.019 | 24.297 | 26.870 | 29.778 | 33.066 | 36.785 | 40.995 | 45.762 | 51.160 | 57.275 | 64.203 | 72.052 | 80.947 | 91.024 | 102.44 |
| 21 | 23.239 | 25.783 | 28.676 | 31.969 | 35.719 | 39.992 | 44.865 | 50.422 | 56.764 | 64.002 | 72.265 | 81.698 | 92.470 | 104.76 | 118.81 |
| 22 | 24.471 | 27.299 | 30.536 | 34.248 | 38.505 | 43.392 | 49.005 | 55.456 | 62.873 | 71.402 | 81.214 | 92.502 | 105.49 | 120.43 | 137.63 |
| 23 | 25.716 | 28.845 | 32.452 | 36.617 | 41.430 | 46.995 | 53.436 | 60.893 | 69.531 | 79.543 | 91.148 | 104.60 | 120.20 | 138.29 | 159.27 |
| 24 | 26.973 | 30.421 | 34.426 | 39.082 | 44.502 | 50.815 | 58.176 | 66.764 | 76.789 | 88.497 | 102.17 | 118.15 | 136.83 | 158.65 | 184.16 |
| 25 | 28.243 | 32.030 | 36.459 | 41.645 | 47.727 | 54.864 | 63.249 | 73.105 | 84.700 | 98.347 | 114.41 | 133.33 | 155.62 | 181.87 | 212.79 |
| 26 | 29.525 | 33.670 | 38.553 | 44.311 | 51.113 | 59.156 | 68.676 | 79.954 | 93.323 | 109.18 | 128.00 | 150.33 | 176.85 | 208.33 | 245.71 |
| 27 | 30.820 | 35.344 | 40.709 | 47.084 | 54.669 | 63.705 | 74.483 | 87.350 | 102.72 | 121.09 | 143.08 | 169.37 | 200.84 | 238.49 | 283.56 |
| 28 | 32.129 | 37.051 | 42.930 | 49.967 | 58.402 | 68.528 | 80.697 | 95.338 | 112.96 | 134.20 | 159.82 | 190.69 | 227.95 | 272.88 | 327.10 |
| 29 | 33.450 | 38.792 | 45.218 | 52.966 | 62.232 | 73.639 | 87.346 | 103.96 | 124.13 | 148.63 | 178.40 | 214.58 | 258.58 | 312.09 | 377.16 |
| 30 | 34.784 | 40.568 | 47.575 | 56.084 | 66.438 | 79.058 | 94.460 | 113.28 | 136.30 | 164.49 | 199.02 | 241.33 | 293.20 | 356.78 | 434.74 |

# EXHIBIT 3-4

Present Value of $1

| Period | 1% | 2% | 3% | 4% | 5% | 6% | 7% | 8% | 9% | 10% | 11% | 12% | 13% | 14% | 15% | 16% | 18% | 20% |
|--------|------|------|------|------|------|------|------|------|------|------|------|------|------|------|------|------|------|------|
| 1 | .9901 | .9804 | .9709 | .9615 | .9524 | .9434 | .9346 | .9259 | .9174 | .9091 | .9009 | .8929 | .8850 | .8772 | .8696 | .8621 | .8475 | .8333 |
| 2 | .9803 | .9612 | .9426 | .9246 | .9070 | .8900 | .8734 | .8573 | .8417 | .8264 | .8116 | .7972 | .7831 | .7695 | .7561 | .7432 | .7182 | .6944 |
| 3 | .9706 | .9423 | .9151 | .8890 | .8638 | .8396 | .8163 | .7938 | .7722 | .7513 | .7312 | .7118 | .6931 | .6750 | .6675 | .6407 | .6086 | .5787 |
| 4 | .9610 | .9238 | .8885 | .8548 | .8227 | .7921 | .7629 | .7350 | .7084 | .6830 | .6587 | .6355 | .6133 | .5921 | .5718 | .5523 | .5158 | .4823 |
| 5 | .9515 | .9057 | .8626 | .8219 | .7835 | .7473 | .7130 | .6806 | .6499 | .6209 | .5935 | .5674 | .5428 | .5194 | .4972 | .4761 | .4371 | .4019 |
| 6 | .9420 | .8880 | .8375 | .7903 | .7462 | .7050 | .6663 | .6302 | .5963 | .5645 | .5346 | .5066 | .4803 | .4556 | .4323 | .4104 | .3704 | .3349 |
| 7 | .9327 | .8706 | .8131 | .7599 | .7107 | .6651 | .6227 | .5835 | .5470 | .5132 | .4817 | .4523 | .4251 | .3996 | .3759 | .3538 | .3139 | .2791 |
| 8 | .9235 | .8535 | .7894 | .7307 | .6768 | .6274 | .5820 | .5403 | .5019 | .4665 | .4339 | .4039 | .3762 | .3506 | .3269 | .3050 | .2660 | .2326 |
| 9 | .9143 | .8368 | .7664 | .7026 | .6446 | .5919 | .5439 | .5002 | .4604 | .4241 | .3909 | .3606 | .3329 | .3075 | .2843 | .2630 | .2255 | .1938 |
| 10 | .9053 | .8203 | .7441 | .6756 | .6139 | .5584 | .5083 | .4632 | .4224 | .3855 | .3522 | .3220 | .2946 | .2697 | .2472 | .2267 | .1911 | .1615 |
| 11 | .8963 | .8043 | .7224 | .6496 | .5847 | .5268 | .4751 | .4289 | .3875 | .3505 | .3173 | .2875 | .2607 | .2366 | .2149 | .1954 | .1619 | .1346 |
| 12 | .8874 | .7885 | .7014 | .6246 | .5568 | .4970 | .4440 | .3971 | .3555 | .3186 | .2858 | .2567 | .2307 | .2076 | .1869 | .1685 | .1372 | .1122 |
| 13 | .8787 | .7730 | .6810 | .6006 | .5303 | .4688 | .4150 | .3677 | .3262 | .2897 | .2575 | .2292 | .2042 | .1821 | .1625 | .1452 | .1163 | .0935 |
| 14 | .8700 | .7579 | .6611 | .5775 | .5051 | .4423 | .3878 | .3405 | .2992 | .2633 | .2320 | .2046 | .1807 | .1597 | .1413 | .1252 | .0985 | .0779 |
| 15 | .8613 | .7430 | .6419 | .5553 | .4810 | .4173 | .3624 | .3152 | .2745 | .2394 | .2090 | .1827 | .1599 | .1401 | .1229 | .1079 | .0835 | .0649 |
| 16 | .8528 | .7284 | .6232 | .5339 | .4581 | .3936 | .3387 | .2919 | .2519 | .2176 | .1883 | .1631 | .1415 | .1229 | .1069 | .0930 | .0708 | .0541 |
| 17 | .8444 | .7142 | .6050 | .5434 | .4363 | .3714 | .3166 | .2703 | .2311 | .1978 | .1696 | .1456 | .1252 | .1078 | .0929 | .0802 | .0600 | .0451 |
| 18 | .8360 | .7002 | .5874 | .4936 | .4155 | .3503 | .2959 | .2502 | .2120 | .1799 | .1528 | .1300 | .1108 | .0946 | .0808 | .0691 | .0508 | .0376 |
| 19 | .8277 | .6864 | .5703 | .4746 | .3957 | .3305 | .2765 | .2317 | .1945 | .1635 | .1377 | .1161 | .0981 | .0829 | .0703 | .0596 | .0431 | .0313 |
| 20 | .8195 | .6730 | .5537 | .4564 | .3769 | .3118 | .2584 | .2145 | .1784 | .1486 | .1240 | .1037 | .0868 | .0728 | .0611 | .0514 | .0365 | .0261 |
| 21 | .8114 | .6598 | .5375 | .4388 | .3589 | .2942 | .2415 | .1987 | .1637 | .1351 | .1117 | .0926 | .0768 | .0638 | .0531 | .0443 | .0309 | .0217 |
| 22 | .8034 | .6468 | .5219 | .4220 | .3418 | .2775 | .2257 | .1839 | .1502 | .1228 | .1007 | .0826 | .0680 | .0560 | .0462 | .0382 | .0262 | .0181 |
| 23 | .7954 | .6342 | .5067 | .4057 | .3526 | .2618 | .2109 | .1703 | .1378 | .1117 | .0907 | .0738 | .0601 | .0491 | .0402 | .0329 | .0222 | .0151 |
| 24 | .7876 | .6217 | .4919 | .3901 | .3101 | .2470 | .1971 | .1577 | .1264 | .1015 | .0817 | .0659 | .0532 | .0431 | .0349 | .0284 | .0188 | .0126 |
| 25 | .7798 | .6095 | .4776 | .3751 | .2953 | .2330 | .1842 | .1460 | .1160 | .0923 | .0736 | .0588 | .0471 | .0378 | .0304 | .0245 | .0160 | .0105 |
| 26 | .7720 | .5976 | .4637 | .3607 | .2812 | .2198 | .1722 | .1352 | .1064 | .0839 | .0663 | .0525 | .0417 | .0331 | .0264 | .0211 | .0135 | .0087 |
| 27 | .7644 | .5859 | .4502 | .3468 | .2678 | .2074 | .1609 | .1252 | .0976 | .0763 | .0597 | .0469 | .0369 | .0291 | .0230 | .0182 | .0115 | .0073 |
| 28 | .7568 | .5744 | .4371 | .3335 | .2551 | .1956 | .1504 | .1159 | .0895 | .0693 | .0538 | .0419 | .0326 | .0255 | .0200 | .0157 | .0097 | .0061 |
| 29 | .7493 | .5631 | .4243 | .3207 | .2429 | .1846 | .1406 | .1073 | .0822 | .0630 | .0485 | .0374 | .0289 | .0224 | .0174 | .0135 | .0082 | .0051 |
| 30 | .7419 | .5521 | .4120 | .3083 | .2314 | .1741 | .1314 | .0994 | .0754 | .0573 | .0437 | .0334 | .0256 | .0196 | .0151 | .0116 | .0070 | .0042 |

**Interest (Discount) Rate**

The columns show the interest rate. The rows show the number of periods. The present value of $1 obtained from Exhibit 3–4 is then multiplied by the future value to determine the present value. For example, the present value of $1,000 seven years from now, assuming 12% interest compounded annually, is

$$PV = \$1,000 \ (\text{PV of \$1 from Exhibit 3–4})$$
$$= \$1,000 \ (.4523)$$
$$= \$452.30$$

The process of computing the present value is also referred to as *discounting*. Therefore, the present value is sometimes referred to as the *discounted value*, and the interest rate is referred to as the *discount rate*.

There are two facts you should note about present value. Look again at Exhibit 3–4. Select any interest rate and look down the column. Notice that the present value decreases. That is, the greater the number of periods over which interest could be earned, the less must be set aside today for a given dollar amount to be received in the future. Next, select any period and look across the row. As you look across, the interest rate increases and the present value decreases. The higher the interest rate that can be earned on any amount invested today, the less must be set aside to obtain a specified future value.

The following two illustrations demonstrate how to compute the present value.

**Illustration 5.**    A pension fund manager knows that he must satisfy a liability of $9 million six years from now. Assuming that an annual interest rate of 7.5% can be earned on any sum invested today, the pension fund manager must invest $5,831,654 today in order to have $9 million six years from now, as shown below:

$$FV = \$9,000,000$$
$$i = .075$$
$$N = 6$$
$$PV = \$9,000,000 \left[ \frac{1}{(1.075)^6} \right]$$
$$= \$9,000,000 \left[ \frac{1}{1.543302} \right]$$
$$= \$9,000,000 \ (.647961)$$
$$= \$5,831,654$$

**Illustration 6.**    Suppose a money manager has the opportunity to purchase a financial instrument that promises to pay $800,000 four years from now. The price of the financial instrument is $572,000. Should the money manager invest in this financial instrument if she wants a 7.8% annual interest rate?

To answer this, the money manager must determine the present value of the $800,000 to be received four years from now. The present value is $592,400, as shown below:

$$FV = \$800,000$$

$$i = .078$$

$$N = 4$$

$$PV = \$800,000 \left[ \frac{1}{(1.078)^4} \right]$$

$$= \$800,000 \left[ \frac{1}{1.350439} \right]$$

$$= \$800,000 \ (.740500)$$

$$= \$592,400$$

Because the price of the financial instrument is only $572,000, the money manager will realize more than a 7.8% annual interest rate if the financial instrument is purchased and the issuer pays $800,000 four years from now.

### Fractional Periods

If a future value is to be received or paid over a fractional part of a year, the number of years is adjusted accordingly. For example, if $1,000 is to be received nine years and three months from now and the interest rate is 7%, the present value is determined as follows:

$$F = \$1,000$$

$$i = .07$$

$$N = 9.25 \text{ years (3 months is .25 years)}$$

$$PV = \$1,000 \left[ \frac{1}{(1.07)^{9.25}} \right]$$

$$= \$1,000 \left[ \frac{1}{1.86982} \right]$$

$$= \$1,000 \ (.53481)$$

$$= \$534.81$$

## Present Value of a Series of Future Values

In most applications in investment management and asset/liability management, a financial instrument will offer a series of future values. To determine the present value of a series of future values, the present value of each future value must first be computed. Then the present values are added together to obtain the present value of the series of future values. This procedure is demonstrated in the following illustration.

**Illustration 7.**    An investor is considering the purchase of a financial instrument that promises to make the following payments:

| Years from Now | Promised Payment by Issuer |
|:---:|:---:|
| 1 | $ 100 |
| 2 | 100 |
| 3 | 100 |
| 4 | 100 |
| 5 | 1,100 |

This financial instrument is selling for $1,243.83. Assume that the investor wants a 6.25% annual interest rate on this investment. Should he purchase this investment?

To answer this question, the investor first must compute the present value of the future amounts that will be received, as follows:

| Years from Now | Future Value of Payment | Present Value of $1 at 6.25% | Present Value of Payment |
|:---:|:---:|:---:|:---:|
| 1 | $ 100 | 0.9412 | $   94.12 |
| 2 | 100 | 0.8858 | 88.58 |
| 3 | 100 | 0.8337 | 83.37 |
| 4 | 100 | 0.7847 | 78.47 |
| 5 | 1,100 | 0.7385 | 812.35 |

Total present value = $1,156.89

Because the present value of the series of future values promised by the issuer of this financial instrument is less than the price of $1,243.83, the investor would earn an annual interest rate of less than 6.25%. Thus, this financial instrument is unattractive.

## Present Value of an Ordinary Annuity

One way to compute the present value of an ordinary annuity is to compute the present value of each future value and then total the present values. There is a formula that can be employed to compute—in one step—the present value of an ordinary annuity:

$$PV = A \left[ \frac{1 - \dfrac{1}{(1 + i)^N}}{i} \right]$$

where

$A$ = Amount of the annuity ($)

The term in the brackets is the *present value of an ordinary annuity of $1 for N years*. Exhibit 3–5 provides the present value of an ordinary annuity of $1 for $N$ periods for selected interest rates. The present value of an ordinary annuity is computed by multiplying the value from Exhibit 3–5 by the annuity payment. The following illustration shows how to apply the formula.

**Illustration 8.**   An investor has the opportunity to purchase a financial instrument that promises to pay $500 a year for the next 20 years, beginning one year from now. The financial instrument is being offered for a price of $5,300. The investor seeks an annual interest rate of 5.5% on this investment. Should she purchase this financial instrument?

Because the first payment is to be received one year from now, the financial instrument is offering a 20-year annuity of $500 per year. The present value of this ordinary annuity is calculated as follows:

$$A = \$500$$
$$i = .055$$
$$N = 20$$

$$PV = \$500 \left[ \frac{1 - \dfrac{1}{(1.055)^{20}}}{.055} \right]$$

$$= \$500 \left[ \frac{1 - \dfrac{1}{2.917757}}{.055} \right]$$

$$= \$500 \left[ \frac{1 - .342729}{.055} \right]$$

$$= \$500 \,(11.950382)$$

$$= \$5,975.19$$

Because the present value of an ordinary annuity of $500 per year when discounted at 5.5% exceeds the price of the financial instrument ($5,300), this financial instrument offers an annual interest rate greater than 5.5%. Therefore, it is an attractive investment for this investor.

# EXHIBIT 3-5

Present Value of an Ordinary Annuity of $1 per Period for N Periods

**Interest (Discount) Rate**

| Number of Periods | 1% | 2% | 3% | 4% | 5% | 6% | 7% | 8% | 9% | 10% | 11% | 12% | 13% | 14% | 15% |
|---|---|---|---|---|---|---|---|---|---|---|---|---|---|---|---|
| 1 | 0.9901 | 0.9804 | 0.9709 | 0.9615 | 0.9524 | 0.9434 | 0.9346 | 0.9259 | 0.9174 | 0.9091 | 0.9009 | 0.8929 | 0.8850 | 0.8772 | 0.8696 |
| 2 | 1.9704 | 1.9416 | 1.9135 | 1.8861 | 1.8594 | 1.8334 | 1.8080 | 1.7833 | 1.7591 | 1.7355 | 1.7125 | 1.6901 | 1.6681 | 1.6467 | 1.6257 |
| 3 | 2.9410 | 2.8839 | 2.8286 | 2.7751 | 2.7232 | 2.6730 | 2.6243 | 2.5771 | 2.5313 | 2.4869 | 2.4437 | 2.4018 | 2.3612 | 2.3216 | 2.2832 |
| 4 | 3.9020 | 3.8077 | 3.7171 | 3.6299 | 3.5460 | 3.4651 | 3.3872 | 3.3121 | 3.2397 | 3.1699 | 3.1024 | 3.0373 | 2.9745 | 2.9137 | 2.8550 |
| 5 | 4.8534 | 4.7135 | 4.5797 | 4.4518 | 4.3295 | 4.2124 | 4.1002 | 3.9927 | 3.8897 | 3.7908 | 3.6959 | 3.6048 | 3.5172 | 3.4331 | 3.3522 |
| 6 | 5.7955 | 5.6014 | 5.4172 | 5.2421 | 5.0757 | 4.9173 | 4.7665 | 4.6229 | 4.4859 | 4.3553 | 4.2305 | 4.1114 | 3.9976 | 3.8887 | 3.7845 |
| 7 | 6.7282 | 6.4720 | 6.2303 | 6.0021 | 5.7864 | 5.5824 | 5.3893 | 5.2064 | 5.0330 | 4.8684 | 4.7122 | 4.5638 | 4.4226 | 4.2883 | 4.1604 |
| 8 | 7.6517 | 7.3255 | 7.0197 | 6.7327 | 6.4632 | 6.2098 | 5.9713 | 5.7466 | 5.5348 | 5.3349 | 5.1461 | 4.9676 | 4.7988 | 4.6389 | 4.4873 |
| 9 | 8.5660 | 8.1622 | 7.7861 | 7.4353 | 7.1078 | 6.8017 | 6.5152 | 6.2469 | 5.9952 | 5.7590 | 5.5371 | 5.3282 | 5.1317 | 4.9464 | 4.7716 |
| 10 | 9.4713 | 8.9826 | 8.5302 | 8.1109 | 7.7217 | 7.3601 | 7.0236 | 6.7101 | 6.4177 | 6.1446 | 5.8892 | 5.6502 | 5.4263 | 5.2161 | 5.0188 |
| 11 | 10.3676 | 9.7876 | 9.2526 | 8.7605 | 8.3064 | 7.8869 | 7.4987 | 7.1390 | 6.8052 | 6.4951 | 6.2065 | 5.9377 | 5.6870 | 5.4527 | 5.2337 |
| 12 | 11.2551 | 10.5753 | 9.9540 | 9.3851 | 8.8633 | 8.3838 | 7.9427 | 7.5361 | 7.1607 | 6.8137 | 6.4924 | 6.1944 | 5.9177 | 5.6603 | 5.4206 |
| 13 | 12.1337 | 11.3484 | 10.6350 | 9.9856 | 9.3936 | 8.8527 | 8.3577 | 7.9038 | 7.4869 | 7.1034 | 6.7499 | 6.4235 | 6.1218 | 5.8424 | 5.5831 |
| 14 | 13.0037 | 12.1062 | 11.2961 | 10.5631 | 9.8986 | 9.2950 | 8.7455 | 8.2442 | 7.7862 | 7.3667 | 6.9819 | 6.6282 | 6.3025 | 6.0021 | 5.7245 |
| 15 | 13.8651 | 12.8493 | 11.9379 | 11.1184 | 10.3797 | 9.7122 | 9.1079 | 8.5595 | 8.0607 | 7.6061 | 7.1909 | 6.8109 | 6.4624 | 6.1422 | 5.8474 |
| 16 | 14.7179 | 13.5777 | 12.5611 | 11.6523 | 10.8378 | 10.1059 | 9.4466 | 8.8514 | 8.3126 | 7.8237 | 7.3792 | 6.9740 | 6.6039 | 6.2651 | 5.9542 |
| 17 | 15.5623 | 14.2919 | 13.1661 | 12.1657 | 11.2741 | 10.4773 | 9.7623 | 9.1216 | 8.5436 | 8.0216 | 7.5488 | 7.1196 | 6.7291 | 6.3729 | 6.0472 |
| 18 | 16.3983 | 14.9920 | 13.7535 | 12.6593 | 11.6896 | 10.8276 | 10.0591 | 9.3719 | 8.7556 | 8.2014 | 7.7016 | 7.2497 | 6.8399 | 6.4674 | 6.1280 |
| 19 | 17.2260 | 15.6785 | 14.3238 | 13.1339 | 12.0853 | 11.1581 | 10.3356 | 9.6036 | 8.9501 | 8.3649 | 7.8393 | 7.3658 | 6.9380 | 6.5504 | 6.1982 |
| 20 | 18.0456 | 16.3514 | 14.8775 | 13.5903 | 12.4622 | 11.4699 | 10.5940 | 9.8181 | 9.1285 | 8.5136 | 7.9633 | 7.4694 | 7.0248 | 6.6231 | 6.2593 |
| 21 | 18.8570 | 17.0122 | 15.4150 | 14.0292 | 12.8212 | 11.7641 | 10.8355 | 10.0168 | 9.2922 | 8.6487 | 8.0751 | 7.5620 | 7.1016 | 6.6870 | 6.3125 |
| 22 | 19.6604 | 17.6580 | 15.9369 | 14.4511 | 13.1630 | 12.0416 | 11.0612 | 10.2007 | 9.4424 | 8.7715 | 8.1757 | 7.6446 | 7.1695 | 6.7429 | 6.3587 |
| 23 | 20.4558 | 18.2922 | 16.4436 | 14.8568 | 13.4886 | 12.3034 | 11.2722 | 10.3711 | 9.5802 | 8.8832 | 8.2664 | 7.7184 | 7.2297 | 6.7921 | 6.3988 |
| 24 | 21.2434 | 18.9139 | 16.9355 | 15.2470 | 13.7986 | 12.5504 | 11.4693 | 10.5288 | 9.7066 | 8.9847 | 8.3481 | 7.7843 | 7.2829 | 6.8351 | 6.4338 |
| 25 | 22.0232 | 19.5235 | 17.4131 | 15.6221 | 14.0939 | 12.7834 | 11.6536 | 10.6748 | 9.8226 | 9.0770 | 8.4218 | 7.8431 | 7.3300 | 6.8729 | 6.4642 |
| 26 | 22.7952 | 20.1210 | 17.8768 | 15.9828 | 14.3752 | 13.0032 | 11.8258 | 10.8100 | 9.9290 | 9.1609 | 8.4881 | 7.8957 | 7.3717 | 6.9061 | 6.4906 |
| 27 | 23.5596 | 20.7069 | 18.3270 | 16.3296 | 14.6430 | 13.2105 | 11.9867 | 10.9352 | 10.0266 | 9.2372 | 8.5478 | 7.9426 | 7.4086 | 6.9352 | 6.5135 |
| 28 | 24.3164 | 21.2813 | 18.7641 | 16.6631 | 14.8981 | 13.4062 | 12.1371 | 11.0511 | 10.1161 | 9.3066 | 8.6016 | 7.9844 | 7.4412 | 6.9607 | 6.5335 |
| 29 | 25.0658 | 21.8444 | 19.1885 | 16.9837 | 15.1411 | 13.5907 | 12.2777 | 11.1584 | 10.1983 | 9.3696 | 8.6501 | 8.0218 | 7.4701 | 6.9830 | 6.5509 |
| 30 | 25.8077 | 22.3965 | 19.6004 | 17.2920 | 15.3725 | 13.7648 | 12.4090 | 11.2578 | 10.2737 | 9.4269 | 8.6938 | 8.0552 | 7.4957 | 7.0027 | 6.5660 |

## YIELD (INTERNAL RATE OF RETURN)

The yield on any investment is computed by determining the interest rate that will make the present value of the cash flow from the investment equal to the price of the investment. Mathematically, the yield on any investment, $y$, is the interest rate that will make the following relationship hold:

$$p = \frac{C_1}{(1 + y)^1} + \frac{C_2}{(1 + y)^2} + \frac{C_3}{(1 + y)^3} + \cdots + \frac{C_N}{(1 + y)^N}$$

where

$C_t$ = Cash flow in year $t$
$p$ = Price
$N$ = Number of years

The individual terms that are being summed on the right-hand side of the above relationship are the present values of the cash flow. The yield calculated from the above relationship is also called the *internal rate of return.*

Solving for the yield ($y$) requires a trial-and-error procedure. The objective is to find the interest rate that will make the present value of the cash flows equal to the price. The following two illustrations demonstrate how it is carried out.

***Illustration 9.*** A financial instrument offers the following annual payments:

| Years from Now | Promised Annual Payments (Cash Flow to Investor) |
|:---:|:---:|
| 1 | $2,000 |
| 2 | 2,000 |
| 3 | 2,500 |
| 4 | 4,000 |

Suppose that the price of this financial instrument is $7,704. What is the yield, or internal rate of return, offered by this financial instrument?

To compute the yield, we must try different interest rates until we find one that makes the present value of the cash flows equal to $7,704 (the price of the financial instrument). Trying an annual interest rate of 10% gives the following present value:

| Years from Now | Promised Annual Payments (Cash Flow to Investor) | Present Value of Cash Flow at 10% |
|:---:|:---:|:---:|
| 1 | $2,000 | $1,818 |
| 2 | 2,000 | 1,652 |
| 3 | 2,500 | 1,878 |
| 4 | 4,000 | 2,732 |
| | | Total present value = $8,080 |

Because the present value computed using a 10% interest rate exceeds the price of $7,704, a higher interest rate must be tried. If a 14% interest rate is assumed, the present value is $7,348, as shown below:

| Years from Now | Promised Annual Payments (Cash Flow to Investor) | Present Value of Cash Flow at 14% |
|:---:|:---:|:---:|
| 1 | $2,000 | $1,754 |
| 2 | 2,000 | 1,538 |
| 3 | 2,500 | 1,688 |
| 4 | 4,000 | 2,368 |
| | Total present value = | $7,348 |

At 14%, the present value of the cash flows is less than the price of the financial instrument. Therefore, a lower interest rate must be tried. A 12% interest rate gives the following results:

| Years from Now | Promised Annual Payments (Cash Flow to Investor) | Present Value of Cash Flow at 12% |
|:---:|:---:|:---:|
| 1 | $2,000 | $1,786 |
| 2 | 2,000 | 1,594 |
| 3 | 2,500 | 1,780 |
| 4 | 4,000 | 2,544 |
| | Total present value = | $7,704 |

The present value of the cash flow is equal to the price of the financial instrument when a 12% interest rate is used. Therefore, the yield is 12%.

Although the formula for the yield is based on annual cash flows, the formula can be generalized to any number of periodic payments in a year. The generalized formula for determining the yield is

$$p = \frac{C_1}{(1 + y)^1} + \frac{C_2}{(1 + y)^2} + \frac{C_3}{(1 + y)^3} + \cdots + \frac{C_n}{(1 + y)^n}$$

where

$C_t$ = Cash flow in period $t$
$n$ = Number of periods

Keep in mind that the yield computed is now the yield for the period. That is, if the cash flows are semiannual, the yield is a semiannual yield. If the cash flows are monthly, the yield is a monthly yield. The annual interest rate is computed by multiplying the yield for the period by the appropriate factor (the frequency of payments per year). We reconsider this procedure for annualizing yields later.

**Illustration 10.**    An investor is considering the purchase of a financial instrument that promises the following *semiannual* cash flows:

10 payments of $50 every six months.

$1,000 10 six-month periods (five years) from now.

Suppose that the price of this financial instrument is $1,243.88. What yield is this financial instrument offering?

The yield can be computed by a trial-and-error procedure, as summarized in the table below:

| Annual Interest Rate | Semi-annual Interest Rate | Present Value of 10 Six-Month Payments of $50[a] | Present Value of $1,000 10 Six-Month Periods from Now[b] | Total Present Value |
|---|---|---|---|---|
| 6.000% | 3.000% | $426.51 | $744.09 | $1,160.60 |
| 5.500 | 2.750 | 432.00 | 762.40 | 1,194.40 |
| 5.000 | 2.500 | 437.50 | 781.20 | 1,218.80 |
| 4.500 | 2.250 | 443.31 | 800.51 | 1,243.83 |

[a] $50 × present value of an ordinary annuity of $1 for 10 periods.
[b] $1,000 × present value of $1 10 periods from now.

As can be seen from the calculation, when a semiannual interest rate of 2.250% is used to find the present value of the cash flows, the present value is equal to the price of $1,243.83. Hence, 2.250% is the six-month yield. Doubling this yield would give an annual interest rate of 4.5%.

## Yield Calculation When There Is Only One Cash Flow

There is a special case when it is not necessary to go through the time-consuming trial-and-error procedure to determine the yield. This is the case where only one cash flow is provided by the investment. The formula to determine the yield is

$$y = (\text{Future value per dollar invested})^{1/n} - 1$$

where

$n$ = Number of periods until the cash flow will be received

$$\text{Future value per dollar invested} = \frac{\text{Cash flow from investment}}{\text{Amount invested (or price)}}$$

**Illustration 11.** An investment offers a payment 20 years from now of $84,957. The price of the investment is $20,000. The yield for this investment is 7.50%, as shown below:

$$\text{Future value per dollar invested} = \frac{\$84,957}{\$20,000} = 4.24785$$

$$y = (4.24785)^{1/20} - 1$$

$$= 1.07499 - 1$$

$$= 0.74999, \text{ or } 7.5\%$$

## Annualizing Yields

We might want to annualize interest rates by simply multiplying by the frequency of payments per year. The resulting rate is called the *annual interest rate*. For example, if we computed a semiannual yield, we can annualize it by multiplying by 2. Alternatively, if we had an annual interest rate and wanted to determine a semiannual interest rate, we can divide by 2.

This procedure for computing the annual interest rate, given a periodic (weekly, monthly, quarterly, semiannual, etc.) interest rate is not correct. To see why, suppose that $100 is invested for one year at an annual interest rate of 8%. At the end of one year, the interest is $8. Suppose, instead, that $100 is invested for one year at an annual interest rate of 8%, but interest is paid semiannually at 4% (one-half the annual interest rate). The future value at the end of one year is $108.16. Interest is therefore $8.16 on a $100 investment. The interest rate, or yield, on the $100 investment is therefore 8.16% ($8.16/$100). The 8.16% is called the *effective annual yield.*

To obtain the effective annual yield associated with a periodic interest rate, the following formula can be used:

$$\text{Effective annual yield} = (1 + \text{Periodic interest rate})^m - 1$$

where

$m$ = Frequency of payments per year

For instance, in the previous example, the periodic yield is 4% and the frequency of payments is twice per year. Therefore,

$$\text{Effective annual yield} = (1.04)^2 - 1$$

$$= 1.0816 - 1$$

$$= .0816, \text{ or } 8.16\%$$

If interest is paid quarterly, then the periodic interest rate is 2% (8%/4), and the effective annual yield is 8.24%, as shown below:

$$\text{Effective annual yield} = (1.02)^4 - 1$$

$$= 1.0824 - 1$$

$$= .0824, \text{ or } 8.24\%$$

We can also determine the periodic interest rate that will produce a given annual interest rate. For example, suppose we wanted to know what quarterly interest rate would produce an effective annual yield of 12%. The following formula can be used:

$$\text{Periodic interest rate} = (1 + \text{Effective annual yield})^{1/m} - 1$$

Applying this formula to determine the quarterly interest rate to produce an effective annual yield of 12%, we find that

$$\text{Periodic interest rate} = (1.12)^{1/4} - 1$$
$$= 1.0287 - 1$$
$$= .0287, \text{ or } 2.87\%.$$

## SUMMARY

In this chapter, several basic mathematical concepts are presented—future value, present value, and yield (or internal rate of return). In the next chapter, we will see how these concepts can be applied to price fixed income securities and calculate various yield measures.

## CHAPTER 4

# BOND PRICING AND RETURN MEASURES

Frank J. Fabozzi, Ph.D., CFA, CPA
Adjunct Professor of Finance
School of Management
Yale University

In this chapter, the pricing of fixed income securities and the various measures of computing return (or yield) from holding a fixed income security will be explained and illustrated. The chapter is organized as follows. In the first section, we extend the present value analysis reviewed in the previous chapter to explain how a bond's price is determined. Then we turn to yield measures, first focusing on conventional yield measures for a fixed-rate coupon bond (yield-to-maturity and yield-to-call in the case of a callable bond) and a floating-rate coupon bond. After highlighting the deficiencies of the conventional yield measures, a better measure of return—total return—is then presented.

## BOND PRICING

The price of any financial instrument is equal to the present value of the expected cash flow. The interest rate or discount rate used to compute the present value depends on the yield offered on comparable securities in the market. In this chapter, we shall explain how to compute the price of a noncallable bond. The pricing of callable bonds is explained in Part 5.

### Determining the Cash Flow

The first step in determining the price of a bond is to determine its cash flow. The cash flow of an option-free bond (i.e., noncallable/nonputable bond) consists of (1) periodic coupon interest payments to the maturity date and (2) the par (or maturity) value at maturity. Although the periodic coupon payments can be made over any time interval (weekly, monthly, quarterly, semiannually, or annually), most bonds issued in the United States pay coupon interest semiannually. In our illustrations, we shall assume that the coupon interest is paid semiannually. Also, to simplify the analysis, we shall assume that the next coupon payment for the bond will be made exactly six months from now. Later in this section, we explain how to price a bond when the next coupon payment is less than six months from now.

In practice, determining the cash flow of a bond is not simple, even if we ignore the possibility of default. The only case in which the cash flow is known with certainty is for fixed-rate coupon, option-free bonds. For callable bonds, the cash flow depends on whether the issuer elects to call the issue. In the case of a putable bond, it depends on whether the bondholder elects to put the issue. In either case, the date that the option will be exercised is not known. Thus, the cash flow is uncertain. For mortgage-backed and asset-backed securities, the cash flow depends on prepayments. The amount and timing of future prepayments are not known, and therefore the cash flow is uncertain. When the coupon rate is floating rather than fixed, the cash flow depends on the future value of the reference rate. The techniques discussed in Part 5 have been developed to cope with the uncertainty of cash flows. In this chapter, the basic elements of bond pricing, where the cash flow is assumed to be known, are presented.

The cash flow for an option-free bond consists of an annuity (that is, the fixed coupon interest paid every 6 months) and the par or maturity value. For example, a 20-year bond with a 9% (4.5% per 6 months) coupon rate and a par or maturity value of $1,000 has the following cash flows:

$$\text{Semiannual coupon interest} = \$1,000 \times .045$$
$$= \$45$$
$$\text{Maturity value} = \$1,000$$

Therefore, there are 40 semiannual cash flows of $45, and a $1,000 cash flow 40 six-month periods from now.

Notice the treatment of the par value. It is *not* treated as if it will be received 20 years from now. Instead, it is treated on a consistent basis with the coupon payments, which are semiannual.

## Determining the Required Yield

The interest rate or discount rate that an investor wants from investing in a bond is called the *required yield.* The required yield is determined by investigating the yields offered on comparable bonds in the market. By comparable, we mean option-free bonds of the same credit quality and the same maturity.[1]

The required yield is typically specified as an annual interest rate. When the cash flows are semiannual, the convention is to use one-half the annual interest rate as the periodic interest rate with which to discount the cash flows.

---

1. In Chapter 5, we introduce a measure of interest rate risk known as *duration.* Instead of talking in terms of a bond with the same maturity as being comparable, we can recast the analysis in terms of the same duration.

As explained at the end of the previous chapter, a periodic interest rate that is one-half the annual yield will produce an effective annual yield that is greater than the annual interest rate.

Although one yield is used to calculate the present value of all cash flows, there are theoretical arguments for using a different yield to discount the cash flow for each period. Essentially, the theoretical argument is that each cash flow can be viewed as a zero-coupon bond, and therefore the cash flow of a bond can be viewed as a package of zero-coupon bonds. The appropriate yield for each cash flow would then be based on the theoretical rate on a zero-coupon bond with a maturity equal to the time that the cash flow will be received. For purposes of this chapter, however, we shall use only one yield to discount all cash flows. In Chapters 6 and 34, this issue is reexamined.

## Determining the Price

Given the cash flows of a bond and the required yield, we have all the necessary data to price the bond. The price of a bond is equal to the present value of the cash flows, and it can be determined by adding (1) the present value of the semiannual coupon payments and (2) the present value of the par or maturity value.

Because the semiannual coupon payments are equivalent to an ordinary annuity, the present value of the coupon payments and maturity value can be calculated from the following formula:[2]

$$ c\left[\frac{1 - \left[\frac{1}{(1 + i)^n}\right]}{i}\right] + \frac{M}{(1 + i)^n} $$

where

$C$ = Semiannual coupon payment ($)
$n$ = Number of periods (number of years times 2)
$i$ = Periodic interest rate (required yield divided by 2) (in decimal)
$M$ = Maturity value

**Illustration 1.**   Compute the price of a 9% coupon bond with 20 years to maturity and a par value of $1,000 if the required yield is 12%.

The cash flows for this bond are as follows: (1) 40 semiannual coupon payments of $45 and (2) $1,000 40 six-month periods from now. The semiannual or periodic interest rate is 6%.

---

2. The formula is the same as the formula for the present value of an ordinary annuity for $n$ periods given in the previous chapter. Instead of using $A$ to represent the annuity, we have used $c$, the semiannual coupon payment.

The present value of the 40 semiannual coupon payments of $45 discounted at 6% is $677.08, as shown below:

$$c = \$45$$

$$n = 40$$

$$i = .06$$

$$\$45 \left[ \frac{1 - \left[ \dfrac{1}{(1.06)^{40}} \right]}{.06} \right]$$

$$= \$45 \left[ \frac{1 - \left[ \dfrac{1}{10.28572} \right]}{.06} \right]$$

$$= \$45 \left[ \frac{1 - .097222}{.06} \right]$$

$$= \$45 \,(15.04630)$$

$$= \$677.08$$

The present value of the par or maturity value 40 *six-month periods* from now discounted at 6% is $97.22, as shown below:

$$M = \$1,000$$

$$n = 40$$

$$i = .06$$

$$\$1,000 \left[ \frac{1}{(1.06)^{40}} \right]$$

$$= \$1,000 \left[ \frac{1}{10.28572} \right]$$

$$= \$1,000 \,(.097222)$$

$$= \$97.22$$

The price of the bond is then equal to the sum of the two present values:

| | |
|---|---:|
| Present value of coupon payments | $677.08 |
| Present value of par (maturity) value | 97.22 |
| Price | $774.30 |

**Illustration 2.**   Compute the price of the bond in Illustration 1, assuming that the required yield is 7%.

The cash flows are unchanged, but the periodic interest rate is now 3.5% (7%/2).

The present value of the 40 semiannual coupon payments of $45 discounted at 3.5% is $960.98, as shown below:

$$c = \$45$$

$$n = 40$$

$$i = .035$$

$$\$45\left[\frac{1 - \left[\frac{1}{(1.035)^{40}}\right]}{.035}\right]$$

$$= \$45\left[\frac{1 - \left[\frac{1}{3.95926}\right]}{.035}\right]$$

$$= \$45\left[\frac{1 - .252572}{.035}\right]$$

$$= \$45\ (21.35509)$$

$$= \$960.98$$

The present value of the par or maturity value of $1,000 *40 six-month periods from now* discounted at 3.5% is $252.57, as shown below:

$$M = \$1,000$$

$$n = 40$$

$$= .035$$

$$\$1,000\left[\frac{1}{(1.035)^{40}}\right]$$

$$= \$1,000\left[\frac{1}{3.95926}\right]$$

$$= \$1,000\ (.252572)$$

$$= \$252.57$$

The price of the bond is then equal to the sum of the two present values:

| | |
|---|---|
| Present value of coupon payments | $  960.98 |
| Present value of par (maturity) value | 252.57 |
| Price | $1,213.55 |

## Relationship between Required Yield and Price at a Given Time

The price of an option-free bond changes in the direction opposite to the change in the required yield. The reason is that the price of the bond is the present value of the cash flows. As the required yield increases, the present value of the cash flows decreases; hence, the price decreases. The opposite is true when the required yield decreases: The present value of the cash flows increases and, therefore, the price of the bond increases.

We can see this by comparing the price of the 20-year, 9% coupon bond that we priced in Illustrations 1 and 2. When the required yield is 12%, the price of the bond is $774.30. If, instead, the required yield is 7%, the price of the bond is $1,213.55. Exhibit 4–1 shows the price of the 20-year, 9% coupon bond for required yields from 5% to 14%.

If we graphed the price/yield relationship for any option-free bond, we would find that it has the "bowed" shape shown in Exhibit 4–2. This shape is referred to as *convex*. The convexity of the price/yield relationship has important implications for the investment properties of a bond. We've devoted Chapter 5 to examine this relationship more closely.

## The Relationship between Coupon Rate, Required Yield, and Price

For a bond issue at a given point in time, the coupon rate and the term-to-maturity are fixed. Consequently, as yields in the marketplace change, the only variable that an investor can change to compensate for the new yield required in the market is the price of the bond. As we saw in the previous section, as the required yield increases (decreases), the price of the bond decreases (increases).

**EXHIBIT  4–1**

Price/Yield Relationship for a 20-Year, 9 Percent Coupon Bond

| Required Yield | Price of Bond |
|---|---|
| 5% | $1,502.05 |
| 6 | 1,346.72 |
| 7 | 1,213.55 |
| 8 | 1,098.96 |
| 9 | 1,000.00 |
| 10 | 914.21 |
| 11 | 839.54 |
| 12 | 774.30 |
| 13 | 717.09 |
| 14 | 666.71 |

**E X H I B I T   4–2**

Price/Yield Relationship

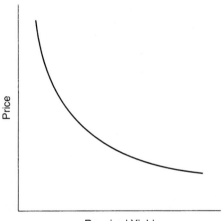

Generally, when a bond is issued, the coupon rate is set at approximately the prevailing yield in the market.[3] The price of the bond will then be approximately equal to its par value. For example, in Exhibit 4–1, we see that when the required yield is equal to the coupon rate, the price of the bond is its par value. Consequently, we have the following properties:

*When the coupon rate equals the required yield, the price equals the par value.*

*When the price equals the par value, the coupon rate equals the required yield.*

When yields in the marketplace rise above the coupon rate at *a given time,* the price of the bond has to adjust so that the investor can realize some additional interest. This adjustment is accomplished by having the bond's price fall below the par value. The difference between the par value and the price is a capital gain and represents a form of interest to the investor to compensate for the coupon rate being lower than the required yield. When a bond sells below its par value, it is said to be selling at a *discount* We can see this in Exhibit 4–1. When the required yield is greater than the coupon rate of 9%, the price of the bond is always less than the par value. Consequently, we have the following properties:

*When the coupon rate is less than the required yield, the price is less than the par value.*

---

3. The exception is an original-issue discount bond such as a zero-coupon bond.

*When the price is less than the par value, the coupon rate is less than the required yield.*

Finally, when the required yield in the market is below the coupon rate, the price of the bond must be above its par value. This occurs because investors who could purchase the bond at par would be getting a coupon rate in excess of what the market requires. As a result, investors would bid up the price of the bond because its yield is attractive. It will be bid up to a price that offers the required yield in the market. A bond whose price is above its par value is said to be selling at a *premium*. Exhibit 4–1 shows that for a required yield less than the coupon rate of 9%, the price of the bond is greater than its par value. Consequently, we have the following properties:

*When the coupon rate is greater than the required yield, the price is greater than the par value.*

*When the price is greater than the par value, the coupon rate is greater than the required yield.*

## Time Path of a Bond

If the required yield is unchanged between the time the bond is purchased and the maturity date, what will happen to the price of the bond? For a bond selling at par value, the coupon rate is equal to the required yield. As the bond moves closer to maturity, the bond will continue to sell at par value. Thus, for a bond selling at par, its price will remain at par as the bond moves toward the maturity date.

The price of a bond will *not* remain constant for a bond selling at a premium or a discount. For all discount bonds the following is true: As the bond moves toward maturity, its price will increase if *the required yield* does not change. This can be seen in Exhibit 4–3, which shows the price of the 20-year, 9% coupon bond as it moves toward maturity, assuming that the required yield remains at 12%. For a bond selling at a premium, the price of the bond declines as it moves toward maturity. This can also be seen in Exhibit 4–3, which shows the time path of the 20-year, 9% coupon bond selling to yield 7%.

## Reasons for the Change in the Price of a Bond

The price of a bond will change because of one or more of the following reasons:

• *A change in the level of interest rates in the economy.* For example, if interest rates in the economy increase (fall) because of Fed policy, the price of a bond will decrease (increase).

• *A change in the price of the bond selling at a price other than par as it moves toward maturity without any change in the required yield.* As we

**EXHIBIT 4-3**

Time Paths of 20-Year, 9 Percent Coupon Discount and Premium Bonds

| Years Remaining to Maturity | Price of Discount Bond[a] | Price of Premium Bond[b] |
|:---:|:---:|:---:|
| 20 | $774.30 | $1,213.55 |
| 18 | 780.68 | 1,202.90 |
| 16 | 788.74 | 1,190.69 |
| 14 | 798.91 | 1,176.67 |
| 12 | 811.75 | 1,160.59 |
| 10 | 827.95 | 1,142.13 |
| 8 | 848.42 | 1,120.95 |
| 6 | 874.24 | 1,096.63 |
| 4 | 906.85 | 1,068.74 |
| 2 | 948.02 | 1,036.73 |
| 1 | 972.50 | 1,019.00 |
| 0 | 1,000.00 | 1,000.00 |

[a] Selling to yield 12%.
[b] Selling to yield 7%.

demonstrated, over time a discount bond's price increases if yields do not change; a premium bond's price declines over time if yields do not change.

- *For non-Treasury bonds, a change in the required yield due to changes in the spread to Treasuries.* If the Treasury rate does not change but the spread to Treasuries changes (narrows or widens), non-Treasury bond prices will change.

- *A change in the perceived credit quality of the issuer.* Assuming that interest rates in the economy and yield spreads between non-Treasuries and Treasuries do not change, the price of a non-Treasury bond will increase (decrease) if its perceived credit quality has improved (deteriorated).

- *For bonds with embedded options (e.g., callable bonds, putable bonds, and convertible bonds), the price of the bond will change as the factors that affect the value of the embedded options change.*

## Pricing a Zero-Coupon Bond

So far, we have determined the price of coupon-bearing bonds. Some bonds do not make any periodic coupon payments. Instead, the investor realizes interest by the difference between the maturity value and the purchase price.

The pricing of a zero-coupon bond is no different from the pricing of a coupon bond: Its price is the present value of the expected cash flows. In the case of a zero-coupon bond, the only cash flow is the maturity value. Therefore, the price of a zero-coupon bond is simply the present value of the maturity value. The number of periods used to discount the maturity value is double the number of years to maturity. This treatment is consistent with the manner in which the maturity value of a coupon bond is handled.

**Illustration 3.**    The price of a zero-coupon bond that matures in 10 years and has a maturity value of $1,000 if the required yield is 8.6%, is equal to the present value of $1,000 20 periods from now discounted at 4.3%. That is,

$$\$1,000\left[\frac{1}{(1.043)^{20}}\right] = \$430.83$$

# Determining the Price When the Settlement Date Falls between Coupon Periods

In our illustrations, we assumed that the next coupon payment is six months away. This means that settlement occurs on the day after a coupon date. Typically, an investor will purchase a bond between coupon dates, so that the next coupon payment is less than six months away. To compute the price, we have to answer the following three questions:

• How many days are there until the next coupon payment?

• How should we determine the present value of cash flows received over fractional periods?

• How much must the buyer compensate the seller for the coupon interest earned by the seller for the fraction of the period that the bond was held?

The first question is the day count question. The second is the compounding question. The last question asks how accrued interest is determined. Below we address these questions.

### Day Count

Market conventions for each type of bond dictate the answer to the first question: the number of days until the next coupon payment.

For Treasury coupon securities, a nonleap year is assumed to have 365 days. The number of days between settlement and the next coupon payment is therefore the actual number of days between the two dates. The day count convention for a coupon-bearing Treasury security is said to be "actual/actual," which means the actual number of days in a month and the actual number of days in the coupon period. For example, consider a Treasury bond whose last coupon payment was on March 1; the next coupon would be six months later on September 1. Suppose this bond is purchased with a settlement date of July 17. The actual number of days between July 17 (the settlement date) and September 1 (the date of the next coupon payment) is 46 days (the actual number of days in the coupon period is 184), as shown below:

| | |
|---|---|
| July 17 to July 31 | 14 days |
| August | 31 days |
| September 1 | 1 day |
| | 46 days |

In contrast to the actual/actual day count convention for coupon-bearing Treasury securities, for corporate and municipal bonds and agency securities, the day count convention is "30/360." That is, each month is assumed to have 30 days and each year 360 days. For example, suppose that the security in our previous example is not a coupon-bearing Treasury security but instead either a coupon-bearing corporate bond, municipal bond, or agency security. The number of days between July 17 and September 1 is shown below:

| | |
|---|---|
| Remainder of July | 13 days |
| August | 30 days |
| September 1 | 1 day |
| | 44 days |

## Compounding

Once the number of days between the settlement date and the next coupon date is determined, the present value formula must be modified because the cash flows will not be received six months (one full period) from now. The Street convention is to compute the price is as follows:

1. Determine the number of days in the coupon period.

2. Compute the following ratio:

$$w = \frac{\text{Number of days between settlement and next coupon payment}}{\text{Number of days in the coupon period}}$$

   For a corporate bond, a municipal bond, and an agency security, the number of days in the coupon period will be 180 because a year is assumed to have 360 days. For a coupon-bearing Treasury security, the number of days is the actual number of days. The number of days in the coupon period is called the *basis*.

3. For a bond with $n$ coupon payments remaining to maturity, the price is

$$p = \frac{c}{(1 + i)^w} + \frac{c}{(1 + i)^{1+w}} + \frac{c}{(1 + i)^{2+w}} + \cdots + \frac{c}{(1 + i)^{n-1+w}}$$
$$+ \frac{M}{(1 + i)^{n-1+w}}$$

where

$p$ = Price ($)
$c$ = Semiannual coupon payment ($)
$M$ = Maturity value
$n$ = Number of coupon payments remaining
$i$ = Periodic interest rate (required yield divided by 2) (in decimal)

The period (exponent) in the formula for determining the present value can be expressed generally as $t - 1 + w$. For example, for the first cash flow, the period is $1 - 1 + w$, or simply $w$. For the second cash flow, it is $2 - 1 + w$, or simply $1 + w$. If the bond has 20 coupon payments remaining, the last period is $20 - 1 + w$, or simply $19 + w$.

**Illustration 4.**   Suppose that a corporate bond with a coupon rate of 10% maturing March 1, 2006 is purchased with a settlement date of July 17, 2000. What would the price of this bond be if it is priced to yield 6.5%?

The next coupon payment will be made on September 1, 2000. Because the bond is a corporate bond, based on a 30/360 day count convention, there are 44 days between the settlement date and the next coupon date. The number of days in the coupon period is 180. Therefore,

$$w = \frac{44}{180} = 0.24444$$

The number of coupon payments remaining, $n$, is 12. The semiannual interest rate is 3.25% (6.5%/2).

The calculation based on the formula for the price is given in Exhibit 4–4. The price of this corporate bond would be $120.0281 per $100 par value. The price calculated in this way is called the *full price* or *dirty price* because it reflects the portion of the coupon interest that the buyer will receive but that the seller has earned.

**Accrued Interest and the Clean Price**
The buyer must compensate the seller for the portion of the next coupon interest payment the seller has earned but will not receive from the issuer because the issuer will send the next coupon payment to the buyer. This amount is called *accrued interest* and depends on the number of days from the last coupon payment to the settlement date.[4] The accrued interest is computed as follows:

---

4. Accrued interest is not computed for all bonds. No accrued interest is computed for bonds in default or income bonds. A bond that trades without accrued interest is said to be traded "flat."

**EXHIBIT 4–4**

Price Calculation When a Bond Is Purchased between Coupon Payments

| Period | Cash Flow per $100 of Par | Present Value of $1 at 3.25% | Present Value of Cash Flow |
|---|---|---|---|
| 0.24444 | $  5.000 | $0.992212 | $  4.961060 |
| 1.24444 | 5.000 | 0.960980 | 4.804902 |
| 2.24444 | 5.000 | 0.930731 | 4.653658 |
| 3.24444 | 5.000 | 0.901435 | 4.507175 |
| 4.24444 | 5.000 | 0.873060 | 4.365303 |
| 5.24444 | 5.000 | 0.845579 | 4.227896 |
| 6.24444 | 5.000 | 0.818963 | 4.094815 |
| 7.24444 | 5.000 | 0.793184 | 3.965922 |
| 8.24444 | 5.000 | 0.768217 | 3.841087 |
| 9.24444 | 5.000 | 0.744036 | 3.720181 |
| 10.24444 | 5.000 | 0.720616 | 3.603081 |
| 11.24444 | 105.000 | 0.697933 | 73.283000 |
|  |  | Total | $120.028100 |

$$AI = c \left[ \frac{\text{Number of days from last coupon payment to settlement date}}{\text{Number of days in coupon period}} \right]$$

where

$AI$ = Accrued interest ($)

$c$ = Semiannual coupon payment ($)

**Illustration 5.**  Let's continue with the hypothetical corporate bond in Illustration 4. Because the number of days between settlement (July 17, 2000) and the next coupon payment (September 1, 2000) is 44 days and the number of days in the coupon period is 180, the number of days from the last coupon payment date (March 1, 2000) to the settlement date is 136 (180 − 44). The accrued interest per $100 of par value is

$$AI = \$5\left(\frac{136}{180}\right) = \$3.777778$$

The full or dirty price includes the accrued interest that the seller is entitled to receive. For example, in the calculation of the full price in Exhibit 4–4, the next coupon payment of $5 is included as part of the cash flow. The *clean price* or *flat price* is the full price of the bond minus the accrued interest.

The price that the buyer pays the seller is the full price. It is important to note that in calculation of the full price, the next coupon payment is a discounted value, but in calculation of accrued interest it is an undiscounted value. Because of this market practice, if a bond is selling at par and the settlement date is not a coupon date, the yield will be slightly less than the coupon rate. Only when the settlement date and coupon date coincide is the yield equal to the coupon rate for a bond selling at par.

In the U.S. market, the convention is to quote a bond's clean or flat price. The buyer, however, pays the seller the full price. In some non-U.S. markets, the full price is quoted.

## CONVENTIONAL YIELD MEASURES

In the previous section, we explained how to compute the price of a bond given the required yield. In this section, we'll show how various yield measures for a bond are calculated given its price. First let's look at the sources of potential return from holding a bond.

An investor who purchases a bond can expect to receive a *dollar* return from one or more of the following sources:

• The coupon interest payments made by the issuer

• Any capital gain (or capital loss—negative dollar return) when the bond matures, is called, or is sold

• Income from reinvestment of the coupon interest payments

This last source of dollar return is referred to as *interest-on-interest.*

Three yield measures are commonly cited by market participants to measure the potential return from investing in a bond—current yield, yield-to-maturity, and yield-to-call. These yield measures are expressed as a *percent* return rather than a dollar return. However, any yield measure should consider each of the three potential sources of return cited above. Below we discuss these three yield measures and assess whether they consider the three sources of potential return.

## Current Yield

The current yield relates the *annual* coupon interest to the market price. The formula for the current yield is

$$\text{Current yield} = \frac{\text{Annual dollar coupon interest}}{\text{Price}}$$

***Illustration 6.***  The current yield for an 18-year, 6% coupon bond selling for $700.89 per $1,000 par value is 8.56%, as shown below:

$$\text{Annual dollar coupon interest} = \$1,000 \times .06$$

$$= \$60$$

$$\text{Current yield} = \frac{\$60}{\$700.89} = .0856, \text{ or } 8.56\%$$

The current yield considers only the coupon interest and no other source of return that will affect an investor's return. For example, in Illustration 6, no consideration is given to the capital gain that the investor will realize when the bond matures. No recognition is given to a capital loss that the investor will realize when a bond selling at a premium matures. In addition, interest-on-interest from reinvesting coupon payments is ignored.

## Yield-to-Maturity

In the previous chapter, we explained how to compute the yield or internal rate of return on any investment. The yield is the interest rate that will make the present value of the cash flows equal to the price (or initial investment). The yield-to-maturity is computed in the same way as the yield; the cash flows are those that the investor would realize by holding the bond to maturity. For a semiannual-pay bond, doubling the interest rate or discount rate gives the yield-to-maturity.

Recall from the previous chapter that the calculation of a yield involves a trial-and-error procedure. Practitioners usually use calculators or software to obtain a bond's yield-to-maturity. The following illustration shows how to compute the yield-to-maturity for a bond.

***Illustration 7.***  In Illustration 6, we computed the current yield for an 18-year, 6% coupon bond selling for $700.89. The maturity value for this bond is $1,000. The yield-to-maturity for this bond is 9.5%, as shown in Exhibit 4–5. Cash flows for the bond are

• 36 coupon payments of $30 every six months

• $1,000 36 six-month periods from now

Different interest rates must be tried until one is found that makes the present value of the cash flows equal to the price of $700.89. Because the coupon rate on the bond is 6% and the bond is selling at a discount, the yield must be greater than 6%. Exhibit 4–5 shows the present value of the cash flows of the bond for semiannual interest rates from 3.25% to 4.75% (corresponding to annual interest rates from 6.5% to 9.50%). As can be seen, when a 4.75% interest

**E X H I B I T   4–5**

Computation of Yield-to-Maturity for an 18-Year, 6 Percent Coupon Bond
Selling at $700.89

---

Objective: Find, by trial and error, the semiannual interest rate that will make the
present value of the following cash flows equal to $700.89:

  36 coupon payments of $30 every six months
  $1,000 36 6-month periods from now

| Annual Interest Rate | Semi-annual Rate | Present Value of 36 Payments of $30[a] | Present Value of $1,000 10 Periods from Now[b] | Present Value of Cash Flows |
|---|---|---|---|---|
| 6.50% | 3.25% | $631.20 | $316.20 | $947.40 |
| 7.00 | 3.50 | 608.71 | 289.83 | 898.54 |
| 7.50 | 3.75 | 587.42 | 265.72 | 853.14 |
| 8.00 | 4.00 | 567.25 | 243.67 | 810.92 |
| 8.50 | 4.25 | 548.12 | 223.49 | 771.61 |
| 9.00 | 4.50 | 529.98 | 205.03 | 735.01 |
| 9.50 | 4.75 | 512.76 | 188.13 | 700.89 |

---

$$^a 30\left[\dfrac{1 - \left[\dfrac{1}{(1 + \text{Semiannual interest rate})^{36}}\right]}{\text{Semiannual interest rate}}\right]$$

$$^b \$1,000\left[\dfrac{1}{(1 + \text{Semiannual interest rate})^{36}}\right]$$

rate is used, the present value of the cash flows is $700.89. Therefore, the yield-to-maturity is 9.50% (4.75% × 2).

The yield-to-maturity considers the coupon income and any capital gain or loss that the investor will realize by *holding the bond to maturity.* The yield-to-maturity also considers the timing of the cash flows. It does consider interest-on-interest; *however, it assumes that the coupon payments can be reinvested at an interest rate equal to the yield-to-maturity.* So, if the yield-to-maturity for a bond is 9.5%, to earn that yield, the coupon payments must be reinvested at an interest rate equal to 9.5%. The following example clearly demonstrates this.

Suppose an investor has $700.89 and places the funds in a certificate of deposit that pays 4.75% every six months for 18 years or 9.5% per year. At the end of 18 years, the $700.89 investment will grow to $3,726. Instead, suppose the investor buys a 6%, 18-year bond selling for $700.89. This is the same as the price of our bond in Illustration 7. The yield-to-maturity for this bond is 9.5%. The investor would expect that at the end of 18 years, the total dollars from the investment will be $3,726.

Let's look at what he will receive. There will be 36 semiannual interest payments of $30, which will total $1,080. When the bond matures, the investor will receive $1,000. Thus, the total dollars that he will receive is $2,080 if he holds the bond to maturity, but this is $1,646 less than the $3,726 necessary to produce a yield of 9.5% (4.75% semiannually). How is this deficiency supposed to be made up? If the investor reinvests the coupon payments at a semiannual interest rate of 4.75% (or a 9.5% annual rate), it is a simple exercise to demonstrate that the interest earned on the coupon payments will be $1,646. Consequently, of the $3,025 total dollar return ($3,726 − $700.89) necessary to produce a yield of 9.5%, about 54% ($1,646 divided by $3,025) must be generated by reinvesting the coupon payments.

Clearly, the investor will realize the yield-to-maturity stated at the time of purchase only if (1) the coupon payments can be reinvested at the yield-to-maturity and (2) if the bond is held to maturity. With respect to the first assumption, the risk that an investor faces is that future reinvestment rates will be less than the yield-to-maturity at the time the bond is purchased. This risk is referred to as *reinvestment risk*. If the bond is not held to maturity, the price at which the bond may have to be sold is less than its purchase price, resulting in a return that is less than the yield-to-maturity. The risk that a bond will have to be sold at a loss because interest rates rise is referred to as *interest rate risk.*

## Reinvestment Risk

There are two characteristics of a bond that determine the degree of reinvestment risk. First, for a given yield-to-maturity and a given coupon rate, the longer the maturity, the more the bond's total dollar return is dependent on the interest-on-interest to realize the yield-to-maturity at the time of purchase. That is, the greater the reinvestment risk. The implication is that the yield-to-maturity measure for long-term coupon bonds tells little about the potential yield that an investor may realize if the bond is held to maturity. In high-interest-rate environments, the interest-on-interest component for long-term bonds may be as high as 80% of the bond's potential total dollar return.

The second characteristic that determines the degree of reinvestment risk is the coupon rate. For a given maturity and a given yield-to-maturity, the higher the coupon rate, the more dependent the bond's total dollar return will be on the reinvestment of the coupon payments in order to produce the yield-to-maturity at the time of purchase. This means that if maturity and yield-to-maturity are hold constant, premium bonds will be more dependent on interest-on-interest than bonds selling at par. For zero-coupon bonds, none of the bond's total dollar return is dependent on interest-on-interest; a zero-coupon bond carries no reinvestment risk if held to maturity.

## Interest Rate Risk

As we explained in the previous section, a bond's price moves in the direction opposite to the change in interest rates. As interest rates rise (fall), the price of a bond will fall (rise). For an investor who plans to hold a bond to maturity, the change in the bond's price before maturity is of no concern; however, for an investor who may have to sell the bond prior to the maturity date, an increase in interest rates after the bond is purchased will mean the realization of a capital loss. Not all bonds have the same degree of interest-rate risk. In the next chapter, the characteristics of a bond that determine its interest-rate risk will be discussed.

Given the assumptions underlying yield-to-maturity, we can now demonstrate that yield-to-maturity has limited value in assessing the potential return of bonds. Suppose that an investor who has a five-year investment horizon is considering the following four option-free bonds:

| Bond | Coupon Rate | Maturity | Yield-to-Maturity |
|------|-------------|----------|-------------------|
| W | 5% | 3 years | 9.0% |
| X | 6 | 20 | 8.6 |
| Y | 11 | 15 | 9.2 |
| Z | 8 | 5 | 8.0 |

Assuming that all four bonds are of the same credit quality, which one is the most attractive to this investor? An investor who selects Bond Y because it offers the highest yield-to-maturity is failing to recognize that the bond must be sold after five years, and the selling price of the bond will depend on the yield required in the market for 10-year, 11% coupon bonds at that time. Hence, there could be a capital gain or capital loss that will make the return higher or lower than the yield-to-maturity promised now. Moreover, the higher coupon rate on Bond Y relative to the other three bonds means that more of this bond's return will be dependent on the reinvestment of coupon interest payments.

Bond W offers the second highest yield-to-maturity. On the surface, it seems to be particularly attractive because it eliminates the problem faced by purchasing Bond Y of realizing a possible capital loss when the bond must be sold before the maturity date. In addition, the reinvestment risk seems to be less than for the other three bonds because the coupon rate is the lowest. However, the investor would not be eliminating the reinvestment risk because after three years, she must reinvest the proceeds received at maturity for two more years. The return that the investor will realize will depend on interest rates three years from now, when the investor must roll over the proceeds received from the maturing bond.

Which is the best bond? The yield-to-maturity doesn't seem to help us identify the best bond. The answer depends on the expectations of the investor. Specifically, it depends on the interest rate at which the coupon interest payments can be reinvested until the end of the investor's investment horizon. Also, for bonds with a maturity longer than the investment horizon, it depends on the investor's expectations about interest rates at the end of the investment horizon.

Consequently, any of these bonds can be the best investment vehicle based on some reinvestment rate and some future interest rate at the end of the investment horizon. In the next section, we shall present an alternative return measure for assessing the potential performance of a bond.

### Yield-to-Maturity for a Zero-Coupon Bond

In the previous chapter, we explained that when there is only one cash flow, it is much easier to compute the yield on an investment. A zero-coupon bond is characterized by a single cash flow resulting from an investment. Consequently, the following formula, presented in the previous chapter, can be applied to compute the yield-to-maturity for a zero-coupon bond:

$$y = \text{(Future value per dollar invested)}^{1/n} - 1$$

where

$$y = \text{One-half the yield-to-maturity}$$

$$\text{Future value per dollar invested} = \frac{\text{Maturity value}}{\text{Price}}$$

Once again, doubling $y$ gives the yield-to-maturity. *Remember that the number of periods used in the formula is double the number of years.*

***Illustration 8.*** The yield-to-maturity for a zero-coupon bond selling for $274.78 with a maturity value of $1,000, maturing in 15 years, is 8.8%, as computed below:

$$n = 15 \times 2 = 30$$

$$\text{Future value per dollar invested} = \frac{\$1,000.00}{\$274.78} = 3.639275$$

$$y = (3.639275)^{1/30} - 1$$
$$= (3.639275)^{.033333} - 1$$
$$= 1.044 - 1$$
$$= .044, \text{ or } 4.4\%$$

Doubling 4.4% gives the yield-to-maturity of 8.8%.

### Relationship between Coupon Rate, Current Yield, and Yield-to-Maturity

The following relationship should be recognized between the coupon rate, current yield, and yield-to-maturity:

| Bond Selling at: | Relationship |
|---|---|
| Par | Coupon rate = Current yield = Yield-to-maturity |
| Discount | Coupon rate < Current yield <Yield-to-maturity |
| Premium | Coupon rate > Current yield >Yield-to-maturity |

## Problem with the Annualizing Procedure

As we pointed out at the end of the previous chapter, multiplying a semiannual interest rate by 2 will give an underestimate of the effective annual yield. The proper way to annualize the semiannual yield is by applying the following formula:

$$\text{Effective annual yield} = (1 + \text{Periodic interest rate})^k - 1$$

where

$$k = \text{Number of payments per year}$$

For a semiannual-pay bond, the formula can be modified as follows:

$$\text{Effective annual yield} = (1 + \text{Semiannual interest rate})^2 - 1$$

or

$$\text{Effective annual yield} = (1 + y)^2 - 1$$

For example, in Illustration 7, the semiannual interest rate is 4.75%, and the effective annual yield is 9.73%, as shown below:

$$\text{Effective annual yield} = (1.0475)^2 - 1$$
$$= 1.0973 - 1$$
$$= .0973, \text{ or } 9.73\%$$

Although the proper way for annualizing a semiannual interest rate is given in the formula above, the convention adopted in the bond market is to double the semiannual interest rate. The yield-to-maturity computed in this manner—doubling the semiannual yield—is called a *bond-equivalent yield*. In fact, this convention is carried over to yield calculations for other types of fixed income securities.

# Yield-to-Call

For a callable bond, investors also compute another yield (or internal rate of return) measure, the *yield-to-call*. The cash flows for computing the yield-to-call are those that would result if the issue were called on some assumed call date. Two commonly used call dates are the *first call date* and the *first par call date*. The yield-to-call is the interest rate that will make the present value of the cash flows if the bond is held to the assumed call date equal to the price of the bond (i.e., the full price).

**Illustration 9.**  In Illustrations 6 and 7, we computed the current yield and yield-to-maturity for an 18-year, 6% coupon bond selling for $700.89. Suppose that this bond is first callable in five years at $1,030. The cash flows for this bond if it is called in five years are

- 10 coupon payments of $30 every six months
- $1,030 in 10 six-month periods from now

The interest rate we seek is one that will make the present value of the cash flows equal to $700.89. From Exhibit 4–6, it can be seen that when the interest rate is 7.6%, the present value of the cash flows is $700.11, which is close enough to $700.89 for our purposes. Therefore, the yield-to-call on a bond-equivalent basis is 15.2% (double the periodic interest rate of 7.6%).

According to the conventional approach, conservative investors will compute the yield-to-call and yield-to-maturity for a callable bond selling at a pre-

---

**EXHIBIT  4–6**

Computation of Yield-to-Call for an 18-Year, 6 Percent Coupon Bond Callable in 5 Years at $1,030, Selling at $700.89

Objective: Find, by trial and error, the semiannual interest rate that will make the present value of the following cash flows equal to $700.89:

> 10 coupon payments of $30 every six months
> $1,030 10 6-month periods from now

| Annual Interest Rate | Semi-annual Rate | Present Value of 10 Payments of $30[a] | Present Value of $1,030 10 Periods from Now[b] | Present Value of Cash Flows |
|---|---|---|---|---|
| 11.20% | 5.60% | $225.05 | $597.31 | $822.36 |
| 11.70 | 5.85 | 222.38 | 585.35 | 805.73 |
| 12.20 | 6.10 | 219.76 | 569.75 | 789.51 |
| 12.70 | 6.35 | 217.19 | 556.50 | 773.69 |
| 13.20 | 6.60 | 214.66 | 543.58 | 758.24 |
| 13.70 | 6.85 | 212.18 | 531.00 | 743.18 |
| 14.20 | 7.10 | 209.74 | 518.73 | 728.47 |
| 14.70 | 7.35 | 207.34 | 506.78 | 714.12 |
| 15.20 | 7.60 | 204.99 | 495.12 | 700.11 |

[a] $\$30 \left[ \dfrac{1 - \left[ \dfrac{1}{(1 + \text{Semiannual interest rate})^{10}} \right]}{\text{Semiannual interest rate}} \right]$

[b] $\$1,030 \left[ \dfrac{1}{(1 + \text{Semiannual interest rate})^{10}} \right]$

mium, selecting the lower of the two as a measure of potential return. It is the smaller of the two yield measures that investors would use to evaluate the yield for a bond. Some investors calculate not just the yield to the first call date and yield to first par call date, but the yield to all possible call dates. Because most bonds can be called at any time after the first call date, the approach has been to compute the yield to every coupon anniversary date following the first call date. Then, all calculated yields-to-call and the yield-to-maturity are compared. The lowest of these yields is called the *yield-to-worst*. The conventional approach would have us believe that this yield is the appropriate one a conservative investor should use.

Let's take a closer look at the yield-to-call as a measure of the potential return of a callable bond. The yield-to-call does consider all three sources of potential return from owning a bond. However, as in the case of the yield-to-maturity, it assumes that all cash flows can be reinvested at the computed yield—in this case, the yield-to-call—until the assumed call date. As we noted earlier in this chapter, this assumption may be inappropriate. Moreover, the yield-to-call assumes that (1) the investor will hold the bond to the assumed call date and (2) the issuer will call the bond on that date.

The assumptions underlying the yield-to-call are often unrealistic. They do not take into account how an investor will reinvest the proceeds if the issue is called. For example, consider two bonds, M and N. Suppose that the yield-to-maturity for bond M, a five-year noncallable bond, is 10%, whereas for bond N the yield-to-call, assuming that the bond will be called in three years, is 10.5%. Which bond is better for an investor with a five-year investment horizon? It's not possible to tell from the yields cited. If the investor intends to hold the bond for five years and the issuer calls the bond after three years, the total dollars that will be available at the end of five years will depend on the interest rate that can be earned from reinvesting funds from the call date to the end of the investment horizon.

More will be said about the analysis of callable bonds in Part 5.

## Yield (Internal Rate of Return) for a Portfolio

The yield for a portfolio of bonds is not simply the average or weighted average of the yield-to-maturity of the individual bond issues. It is computed by determining the cash flows for the portfolio and then finding the interest rate that will make the present value of the cash flows equal to the market value of the portfolio.[5] As with any yield measure, it suffers from the same assumptions.

---

5. In the next chapter, the concept of duration will be discussed. A good approximation to the yield for a portfolio can be obtained by using duration to weight the yield-to-maturity of the individual bonds in the portfolio.

***Illustration 10.***  Consider the following three-bond portfolio:[6]

| Bond | Coupon Rate | Maturity | Par Value | Price Value | Yield-to-Maturity |
|------|-------------|----------|-----------|-------------|-------------------|
| A | 7.0% | 5 years | $ 10,000,000 | $ 9,209,000 | 9.0% |
| B | 10.5 | 7 | 20,000,000 | 20,000,000 | 10.5% |
| C | 6.0 | 3 | 30,000,000 | 28,050,000 | 8.5 |

The portfolio's total market value is $57,259,000. The cash flow for each bond in the portfolio and for the whole portfolio is given below:

| Period Cash Flow Received | Bond A | Bond B | Bond C | Portfolio |
|---------------------------|--------|--------|--------|-----------|
| 1 | $    350,000 | $ 1,050,000 | $    900,000 | $ 2,300,000 |
| 2 | 350,000 | 1,050,000 | 900,000 | 2,300,000 |
| 3 | 350,000 | 1,050,000 | 900,000 | 2,300,000 |
| 4 | 350,000 | 1,050,000 | 900,000 | 2,300,000 |
| 5 | 350,000 | 1,050,000 | 900,000 | 2,300,000 |
| 6 | 350,000 | 1,050,000 | 30,900,000 | 32,300,000 |
| 7 | 350,000 | 1,050,000 | — | 1,400,000 |
| 8 | 350,000 | 1,050,000 | — | 1,400,000 |
| 9 | 350,000 | 1,050,000 | — | 1,400,000 |
| 10 | 10,350,000 | 1,050,000 | — | 11,400,000 |
| 11 | — | 1,050,000 | — | 1,050,000 |
| 12 | — | 1,050,000 | — | 1,050,000 |
| 13 | — | 1,050,000 | — | 1,050,000 |
| 14 | — | 21,050,000 | — | 21,050,000 |

To determine the yield (internal rate of return) for this three-bond portfolio, the interest rate that makes the present value of the cash flows shown in the last column of the table above equal to $57,259,000 (the total market value of the portfolio) must be found. If an interest rate of 4.77% is used, the present value of the cash flows will equal $57,259,000. Doubling 4.77% gives 9.54%, which is the yield on the portfolio on a bond-equivalent basis.

## Yield Measure for Floating-Rate Securities

The coupon rate for a floating-rate security changes periodically based on some reference rate (such as LIBOR).[7] Because the value for the reference rate in the

---

6. To simplify the illustration, it is assumed that the coupon payment date is the same for each bond.

7. Floating-rate securities are discussed in Chapter 14.

future is not known, it is not possible to determine the cash flows. This means that a yield-to-maturity cannot be calculated.

A conventional measure used to estimate the potential return for a floating-rate security is the security's *discounted margin*. This measure estimates the average spread or margin over the reference rate that the investor can expect to earn over the life of the security. The procedure for calculating the discounted margin is as follows:

1. Determine the cash flows assuming that the reference rate does not change over the life of the security.

2. Select a margin (spread).

3. Discount the cash flows found in step (1) by the current value of the reference rate plus the margin selected in step (2).

4. Compare the present value of the cash flows as calculated in step (3) to the price. If the present value is equal to the security's price, the discounted margin is the margin assumed in step (2). If the present value is not equal to the security's price, go back to step (2) and try a different margin.

For a security selling at par, the discounted margin is simply the spread over the reference rate.

***Illustration 11.***    To illustrate the calculation, suppose that a six-year floating-rate security selling for 99.3098 pays a rate based on some reference rate index plus 80 basis points. The coupon rate is reset every six months. Assume that the current value for the reference rate is 10%. Exhibit 4–7 shows the calculation of the discounted margin for this security. The second column shows the current discounted value for the reference rate (10%). The third column sets forth the cash flows for the security. The cash flow for the first 11 periods is equal to one-half the current value for the reference rate (5%) plus the semiannual spread of 40 basis points multiplied by 100. In the 12th six-month period, the cash flow is 5.4 plus the maturity value of 100. The top row of the last five columns shows the assumed margin. The rows below the assumed margin show the present value of each cash flow. The last row gives the total present value of the cash flows. For the five assumed yield spreads, the present value is equal to the price of the floating-rate security (99.3098) when the assumed margin is 96 basis points. Therefore, the discounted margin on a semiannual basis is 48 basis points and 96 basis points on an annual basis. (Notice that the discounted margin is 80 basis points, the same as the spread over the reference rate, when the security is selling at par.)

There are two drawbacks of the discounted margin as a measure of the potential return from investing in a floating-rate security. First, this measure assumes that the reference rate will not change over the life of the security. Second, if the floating-rate security has a cap or floor, this is not taken into

**EXHIBIT 4–7**

Calculation of the Discounted Margin for a Floating-Rate Security

| Floating-rate security: | Maturity = 6 years |
| | Coupon rate = Reference rate + 80 basis points |
| | Reset every six months |

| | | | Present Value of Cash Flow: Assumed Annual Yield Spread (in bp) | | | | |
|---|---|---|---|---|---|---|---|
| Period | Reference Rate | Cash Flow[a] | 80 | 84 | 88 | 96 | 100 |
| 1 | 10% | 5.4 | 5.1233 | 5.1224 | 5.1214 | 5.1195 | 5.1185 |
| 2 | 10 | 5.4 | 4.8609 | 4.8590 | 4.8572 | 4.8535 | 4.8516 |
| 3 | 10 | 5.4 | 4.6118 | 4.6092 | 4.6066 | 4.6013 | 4.5987 |
| 4 | 10 | 5.4 | 4.3755 | 4.3722 | 4.3689 | 4.3623 | 4.3590 |
| 5 | 10 | 5.4 | 4.1514 | 4.1474 | 4.1435 | 4.1356 | 4.1317 |
| 6 | 10 | 5.4 | 3.9387 | 3.9342 | 3.9297 | 3.9208 | 3.9163 |
| 7 | 10 | 5.4 | 3.7369 | 3.7319 | 3.7270 | 3.7171 | 3.7122 |
| 8 | 10 | 5.4 | 3.5454 | 3.5401 | 3.5347 | 3.5240 | 3.5186 |
| 9 | 10 | 5.4 | 3.3638 | 3.3580 | 3.3523 | 3.3409 | 3.3352 |
| 10 | 10 | 5.4 | 3.1914 | 3.1854 | 3.1794 | 3.1673 | 3.1613 |
| 11 | 10 | 5.4 | 3.0279 | 3.0216 | 3.0153 | 3.0028 | 2.9965 |
| 12 | 10 | 105.4 | 56.0729 | 55.9454 | 55.8182 | 55.5647 | 55.4385 |
| Present value | | | 100.0000 | 99.8269 | 99.6541 | 99.3098 | 99.1381 |

[a] For periods 1–11: Cash flow = 100 (Reference rate + Assumed margin) (0.5)
For period 12: Cash flow = 100 (Reference rate + Assumed margin) (0.5) + 100

consideration. Techniques described in Chapter 34 can allow interest rate volatility to be considered and can handle caps or floors.

## TOTAL RETURN ANALYSIS

If conventional yield measures such as the yield-to-maturity and yield-to-call offer little insight into the potential return of a bond, what measure of return can be used? The proper measure is one that considers all three sources of potential dollar return over the investment horizon. This requires that an investor first project the total future dollars over an investment horizon. The return is then the interest rate that will make the bond's price (full price) grow to the projected total future dollars at the end of the investment horizon. The yield computed in this way is known as the *total return,* also referred to as the *horizon return.* In this section, we explain this measure and demonstrate how it can be applied in assessing the potential return from investing in a bond.

# Calculating the Total Return

The total return requires that the investor specify

- An investment horizon
- A reinvestment rate
- A selling price for the bond at the end of the investment horizon (which depends on the assumed yield at which the bond will sell at the end of the investment horizon)

More formally, the steps for computing a total return over some investment horizon are as follows.

**Step 1:** Compute the total coupon payments plus the interest-on-interest based on an assumed reinvestment rate. The reinvestment rate is one-half the annual interest rate that the investor believes can be earned on the reinvestment of coupon interest payments.

The total coupon payments plus interest-on-interest can be calculated using the formula for the future value of an annuity (given in the previous chapter) as shown:

$$\text{Coupon plus interest-on-interest} = \text{Semiannual coupon} \left[ \frac{[(1 + r)^h - 1)]}{r} \right]$$

where

$h$ = Length of the investment horizon (in semiannual periods)
$r$ = Assumed semiannual reinvestment rate

**Step 2:** Determine the projected sale price at the end of the investment horizon. The projected sale price will depend on the projected yield on comparable bonds at the end of the investment horizon.

**Step 3:** Add the values computed in steps 1 and 2. The sum is the *total future dollars* that will be received from the investment given the assumed reinvestment rate and projected required yield at the end of the investment horizon.

**Step 4:** To obtain the semiannual total return, use the following formula:[8]

$$\left( \frac{\text{Total future dollars}}{\text{Purchase price of bond}} \right)^{1/h} - 1$$

**Step 5:** Because coupon interest is assumed to be paid semiannually, double the interest rate found in step 4. The resulting interest rate is the total return expressed on a bond-equivalent basis. Alternatively, the total return can be expressed on an effective annual interest rate basis by using the following formula:

---

8. This formula is the same formula as given in the previous chapter for calculating the yield on an investment when there is only one cash flow and, as expected, for calculating the yield on a zero-coupon bond given earlier in this chapter.

$$(1 + \text{Semiannual total return})^2 - 1$$

***Illustration 12.***    Suppose that an investor with a three-year investment horizon is considering purchasing a 20-year, 8% coupon bond for $828.40. The yield-to-maturity for this bond is 10%. The investor expects that he can reinvest the coupon interest payments at an annual interest rate of 6% and that at the end of the investment horizon the 17-year bond will be selling to offer a yield-to-maturity of 7%. The total return for this bond is computed in Exhibit 4–8.

Objections to the total-return analysis cited by some portfolio managers are that it requires them to make assumptions about reinvestment rates and future yields and forces a portfolio manager to think in terms of an investment horizon. Unfortunately, some portfolio managers find comfort in meaningless measures such as the yield-to-maturity because it is not necessary to incorporate any expectations. As explained below, the total-return framework enables the portfolio manager to analyze the performance of a bond based on different interest rate-scenarios for reinvestment rates and future market yields. By investigating multiple scenarios, the portfolio manager can see how sensitive the bond's performance is to each scenario. There is no need to assume that the reinvestment rate will be constant for the entire investment horizon.

For portfolio managers who want to use the market's expectations of short-term reinvestment rates and the yield on the bond at the end of the investment horizon, implied forward rates can be calculated from the yield curve. Implied forward rates are explained in Chapter 6, and are calculated based on arbitrage arguments. A total return computed using implied forward rates is called an *arbitrage free total return*.

## Scenario Analysis

Because the total return depends on the reinvestment rate and the yield at the end of the investment horizon, portfolio managers assess performance over a wide range of scenarios for these two variables. This approach is referred to as *scenario analysis*.

***Illustration 13.***    Suppose a portfolio manager is considering the purchase of bond A, a 20-year, 9% noncallable bond selling at $109.896 per $100 of par value. The yield-to-maturity for this bond is 8%. Assume also that the portfolio manager's investment horizon is three years and that the portfolio manager believes the reinvestment rate can vary from 3% to 6.5% and the yield at the end of the investment horizon from 5% to 12%.

The top panel of Exhibit 4–9 shows the total future dollars at the end of three years under various scenarios. The bottom panel shows the total return (based on the effective annualizing of the six-month total return). The portfolio manager knows that the maximum and minimum total return for the scenarios

**E X H I B I T   4–8**

Illustration of Total Return Calculation

**Assumptions:**
  Bond = 8% 20-year bond selling for $828.40 (yield-to-maturity is 10%)
  Annual reinvestment rate = 6%
  Investment horizon = 3 years
  Yield for 17-year bonds at end of investment horizon = 7%

**Step 1:**  Compute the total coupon payments plus the interest-on-interest assuming an annual reinvestment rate of 6%, or 3% every six months. The coupon payments are $40 every six months for three years or six periods (the investment horizon). The total coupon interest plus interest-on-interest is

$$\text{Coupon plus interest-on-interest} =$$

$$\$40\left[\frac{(1.03)^6 - 1}{.03}\right] = \$258.74$$

**Step 2:**  The projected sale price at the end of 3 years, assuming that the required yield-to-maturity for 17-year bonds is 7%, is found by determining the present value of 34 coupon payments of $40 plus the present value of the maturity value of $1,000, discounted at 3.5%. The price can be shown to be $1,098.51.

**Step 3:**  Adding the amount in steps 1 and 2 gives total future dollars of $1,357.25.

**Step 4:**  Compute the following:

$$= \left(\frac{\$1,357.25}{828.40}\right)^{1/6} - 1$$

$$= (1.63840)^{.16667} - 1$$

$$1.0858 - 1$$

$$= .0858, \text{ or } 8.58\%$$

**Step 5:**  Doubling 8.58% gives a total return of 17.16% on a bond-equivalent basis. On an effective annual interest-rate basis, the total return is

$$(1.0858)^2 - 1$$

$$= 1.1790 - 1$$

$$= .1790$$

$$= 17.90\%$$

analyzed will be 16.72% and −1.05%, respectively, and the scenarios under which each will be realized. If the portfolio manager faces three-year liabilities guaranteeing, say, 6%, the major consideration is scenarios that will produce a three-year total return of less than 6%. These scenarios can be determined from Exhibit 4–9.

**E X H I B I T   4–9**

Scenario Analysis for Bond A

| Bond A: | 9% coupon, 20-year noncallable bond |
| Price: | $109.896 |
| Yield to maturity: | 8.00% |
| Investment Horizon: | 3 years |

| | **Yield at end of horizon** | | | | | | | |
|---|---|---|---|---|---|---|---|---|
| | 5.00% | 6.00% | 7.00% | 8.00% | 9.00% | 10.00% | 11.00% | 12.00% |
| | **Horizon price** | | | | | | | |
| | 145.448 | 131.698 | 119.701 | 109.206 | 100.000 | 91.9035 | 84.763 | 78.4478 |

| | **Total future dollars** | | | | | | | |
|---|---|---|---|---|---|---|---|---|
| Reinvestment rate | 5.00% | 6.00% | 7.00% | 8.00% | 9.00% | 10.00% | 11.00% | 12.00% |
| 3.0% | 173.481 | 159.731 | 147.734 | 137.239 | 128.033 | 119.937 | 112.796 | 106.481 |
| 3.5 | 173.657 | 159.907 | 147.910 | 137.415 | 128.209 | 120.113 | 112.972 | 106.657 |
| 4.0 | 173.834 | 160.084 | 148.087 | 137.592 | 128.387 | 120.290 | 113.150 | 106.834 |
| 4.5 | 174.013 | 160.263 | 148.266 | 137.771 | 128.565 | 120.469 | 113.328 | 107.013 |
| 5.0 | 174.192 | 160.443 | 148.445 | 137.950 | 128.745 | 120.648 | 113.508 | 107.193 |
| 5.5 | 174.373 | 160.623 | 148.626 | 138.131 | 128.926 | 120.829 | 113.689 | 107.374 |
| 6.0 | 174.555 | 160.806 | 148.809 | 138.313 | 129.108 | 121.011 | 113.871 | 107.556 |
| 6.5 | 174.739 | 160.989 | 148.992 | 138.497 | 129.291 | 121.195 | 114.054 | 107.739 |

| | **Total return (effective rate)** | | | | | | | |
|---|---|---|---|---|---|---|---|---|
| Reinvestment rate | 5.00% | 6.00% | 7.00% | 8.00% | 9.00% | 10.00% | 11.00% | 12.00% |
| 3.0% | 16.44 | 13.28 | 10.37 | 7.69 | 5.22 | 2.96 | 0.87 | −1.05 |
| 3.5 | 16.48 | 13.32 | 10.41 | 7.73 | 5.27 | 3.01 | 0.92 | −0.99 |
| 4.0 | 16.52 | 13.36 | 10.45 | 7.78 | 5.32 | 3.06 | 0.98 | −0.94 |
| 4.5 | 15.56 | 13.40 | 10.50 | 7.83 | 5.37 | 3.11 | 1.03 | −0.88 |
| 5.0 | 16.60 | 13.44 | 10.54 | 7.87 | 5.42 | 3.16 | 1.08 | −0.83 |
| 5.5 | 16.64 | 13.49 | 10.59 | 7.92 | 5.47 | 3.21 | 1.14 | −0.77 |
| 6.0 | 16.68 | 13.53 | 10.63 | 7.97 | 5.52 | 3.26 | 1.19 | −0.72 |
| 6.5 | 16.72 | 13.57 | 10.68 | 8.02 | 5.57 | 3.32 | 1.25 | −0.66 |

***Illustration 14.***    Suppose that the same portfolio manager owns bond B, a 14-year noncallable bond with a coupon rate of 7.25% and a current price of $94.553 per $100 par value. The yield-to-maturity is 7.9%. Exhibit 4–10 reports the total future dollars and total return over a three-year investment horizon under the same scenarios as Exhibit 4–9. A portfolio manager considering swapping from bond B to bond A would compare the relative performance of the two bonds as reported in Exhibits 4–9 and 4–10. Exhibit 4–11 shows the difference between the performance of the two bonds in basis points. This com-

**E X H I B I T   4–10**

Scenario Analysis for Bond B

| Bond B: | 7.25% coupon, 14-year noncallable bond |
|---|---|
| Price: | $94.553 |
| Yield to maturity: | 7.90% |
| Investment horizon: | 3 years |

|  | *Yield at end of horizon* | | | | | | | |
|---|---|---|---|---|---|---|---|---|
|  | **5.00%** | **6.00%** | **7.00%** | **8.00%** | **9.00%** | **10.00%** | **11.00%** | **12.00%** |
|  | *Horizon price* | | | | | | | |
|  | 118.861 | 109.961 | 101.896 | 94.5808 | 87.9386 | 81.9009 | 76.4066 | 71.4012 |

|  | *Total future dollars* | | | | | | | |
|---|---|---|---|---|---|---|---|---|
| **Reinvestment rate** | **5.00%** | **6.00%** | **7.00%** | **8.00%** | **9.00%** | **10.00%** | **11.00%** | **12.00%** |
| 3.0% | 141.443 | 132.543 | 124.478 | 117.163 | 110.521 | 104.483 | 98.989 | 93.983 |
| 3.5 | 141.585 | 132.685 | 124.620 | 117.448 | 110.663 | 104.625 | 99.131 | 94.125 |
| 4.0 | 141.728 | 132.828 | 124.763 | 117.448 | 110.806 | 104.768 | 99.273 | 94.268 |
| 4.5 | 141.872 | 132.971 | 124.907 | 117.592 | 110.949 | 104.912 | 99.417 | 94.412 |
| 5.0 | 142.017 | 133.116 | 125.051 | 117.736 | 111.094 | 105.056 | 99.562 | 94.557 |
| 5.5 | 142.162 | 133.262 | 125.197 | 117.882 | 111.240 | 105.202 | 99.708 | 94.703 |
| 6.0 | 142.309 | 133.409 | 125.344 | 118.029 | 111.387 | 105.349 | 99.855 | 94.849 |
| 6.5 | 142.457 | 133.556 | 125.492 | 118.176 | 111.534 | 105.497 | 100.002 | 94.997 |

|  | *Total return (effective rate)* | | | | | | | |
|---|---|---|---|---|---|---|---|---|
| **Reinvestment rate** | **5.00%** | **6.00%** | **7.00%** | **8.00%** | **9.00%** | **10.00%** | **11.00%** | **12.00%** |
| 3.0% | 14.37 | 11.92 | 9.60 | 7.41 | 5.34 | 3.38 | 1.54 | −0.20 |
| 3.5 | 14.41 | 11.96 | 9.64 | 7.45 | 5.38 | 3.43 | 1.59 | −0.15 |
| 4.0 | 14.44 | 12.00 | 9.68 | 7.50 | 5.43 | 3.48 | 1.64 | −0.10 |
| 4.5 | 14.48 | 12.04 | 9.72 | 7.54 | 5.48 | 3.53 | 1.69 | −0.05 |
| 5.0 | 14.52 | 12.08 | 9.77 | 7.58 | 5.52 | 3.57 | 1.74 | 0.00 |
| 5.5 | 14.56 | 12.12 | 9.81 | 7.63 | 5.57 | 3.62 | 1.79 | 0.05 |
| 6.0 | 14.60 | 12.16 | 9.85 | 7.67 | 5.61 | 3.67 | 1.84 | 0.10 |
| 6.5 | 14.64 | 12.20 | 9.90 | 7.72 | 5.66 | 3.72 | 1.89 | 0.16 |

parative analysis assumes that the two bonds are of the same investment quality and ignores the financial accounting and tax consequences associated with the disposal of bond B to acquire bond A.

# Evaluating Potential Bond Swaps

Portfolio managers commonly swap an existing bond in a portfolio for another bond. Bond swaps can be categorized as pure yield pickup swaps, substitution

## EXHIBIT 4–11

Scenario Analysis Showing the Relative Performance of Bonds A and B

| Total Return for Bond A minus Total Return for Bond B (in basis points) | | | | | | | | |
|---|---|---|---|---|---|---|---|---|
| Reinvestment rate | 5.00% | 6.00% | 7.00% | 8.00% | 9.00% | 10.00% | 11.00% | 12.00% |
| 3.0% | 207 | 136 | 77 | 28 | −12 | −43 | −67 | −85 |
| 3.5 | 207 | 136 | 77 | 28 | −11 | −42 | −66 | −84 |
| 4.0 | 207 | 136 | 77 | 28 | −11 | −42 | −66 | −84 |
| 4.5 | 207 | 136 | 77 | 29 | −11 | −42 | −66 | −83 |
| 5.0 | 207 | 137 | 78 | 29 | −10 | −41 | −65 | −83 |
| 5.5 | 208 | 137 | 78 | 29 | −10 | −41 | −65 | −82 |
| 6.0 | 208 | 137 | 78 | 30 | −10 | −41 | −64 | −82 |
| 6.5 | 208 | 137 | 78 | 30 | −9 | −40 | −64 | −81 |

swaps, intermarket spread swaps, or rate anticipation swaps. Total return analysis can be used to assess the potential return from a swap.

- *Pure yield pickup swap:* Switching from one bond to another that has a higher yield is called a pure yield pickup swap. The swap may be undertaken to achieve either higher current coupon income or higher yield-to-maturity, or both. No expectation is made about changes in interest rates, yield spreads, or credit quality.

- *Rate anticipation swap:* A portfolio manager who has expectations about the future direction of interest rates will use bond swaps to position the portfolio to take advantage of the anticipated interest-rate move. These are known as rate anticipation swaps. If rates are expected to fall, for example, bonds with a greater price volatility will be swapped for existing bonds in the portfolio with lower price volatility (to take advantage of the larger change in price that will result if interest rates do in fact decline). The opposite will be done if rates are expected to rise.

- *Intermarket spread swap:* These swaps are undertaken when the portfolio manager believes that the current yield spread between two bonds in the market is out of line with its historical yield spread and that the yield spread will realign by the end of the investment horizon. Yields spreads between bonds exist for the following reasons: (1) there is a difference in the credit quality of bonds (for example, between Treasury bonds and double-A-rated public utility bonds of the same maturity), or (2) there are differences in the features of corporate bonds that make them more or less attractive to investors (for example, callable and noncallable bonds, and putable and non-putable bonds).

• *Substitution swap:* In a substitution swap, a portfolio manager swaps one bond for another bond that is thought to be identical in terms of coupon, maturity, price sensitivity to interest-rate changes, and credit quality but that offers a higher yield. This swap depends on a capital market imperfection. Such situations sometimes exist in the bond market because of temporary market imbalances. The risk that the portfolio manager faces is that the bond purchased may not be identical to the bond for which it is exchanged. For example, if credit quality is not the same, the bond purchased may be offering a higher yield because of higher credit risk rather than because of a market imbalance.

## Comparing Municipal and Corporate Bonds

The conventional methodology for comparing the relative performance of a tax-exempt municipal bond and a taxable corporate bond is to compute the *taxable equivalent yield*. The taxable equivalent yield is the yield that must be earned on a taxable bond in order to produce the same yield as a tax-exempt municipal bond. The formula is

$$\text{Taxable equivalent yield} = \frac{\text{Tax-exempt yield}}{1 - \text{Marginal tax rate}}$$

For example, suppose an investor in the 39.6% marginal tax bracket is considering a 10-year municipal bond with a yield-to-maturity of 4.5%. The taxable equivalent yield is

$$\frac{4.5\%}{1 - .396} = 7.45\%$$

If the yield-to-maturity offered on a comparable quality corporate bond with 10 years to maturity is more than 7.45%, those who use this approach would recommend that the corporate bond be purchased. If, instead, a yield-to-maturity of less than 7.45% on a comparable corporate bond is offered, the investor should invest in the municipal bond.

What's wrong with this approach? The tax-exempt yield of the municipal bond and the taxable equivalent yield suffer from the same limitations we discussed with respect to yield-to-maturity. Consider the difference in reinvestment opportunities for a corporate and a municipal bond. For the former, coupon payments will be taxed; therefore, the amount to be reinvested is not the entire coupon payment but an amount net of taxes. In contrast, because the coupon payments are free from taxes for a municipal bond, the entire coupon can be reinvested.

The total return framework can accommodate this situation by allowing us to explicitly incorporate the reinvestment opportunities. There is another advantage to the total return framework as compared to the conventional taxable equivalent yield approach. Changes in tax rates (because the investor expects either his or her tax rate to change or the tax structure to change) can be incorporated into the total return framework.

## SUMMARY

In this chapter, the pricing of bonds and the calculation of various yield measures have been described. The price of a bond is equal to the present value of the expected cash flow. For bonds with embedded options, the cash flow is difficult to estimate. The required yield used to discount the cash flow is determined by the yield offered on comparable securities.

The two most popular yield measures cited in the bond market are the yield-to-maturity and yield-to-call. Both yield measures consider the coupon interest and any capital gain (or loss) at the maturity date or call date in the case of the yield-to-call. The coupon interest and capital gain (or loss), however, are only two of the three components of potential dollar return from owning a bond until it matures or is called. The other component is the reinvestment of coupon income, commonly referred to as the interest-on-interest component. This component can be as large as 80% of a bond's total dollar return. The yield-to-maturity assumes that the coupon payments can be reinvested at the calculated yield-to-maturity. The yield-to-call assumes that the coupon payments can be reinvested at the calculated yield-to-call.

A better measure of the potential return from holding a bond over a predetermined investment horizon is the total return measure. This measure considers all three sources of potential dollar return and can be used to analyze bond swaps.

## CHAPTER 5

# MEASURING INTEREST RATE RISK

**Frank J. Fabozzi, Ph.D., CFA**
Adjunct Professor of Finance
School of Management
Yale University

**Gerald W. Buetow, Jr., Ph.D., CFA**
President
BFRC Services

**Robert R. Johnson, Ph.D., CFA**
Senior Vice President
Association for Investment Management and Research

The value of a bond changes in the opposite direction of the change in interest rates. A long bond position's value will decline if interest rates rise, resulting in a loss. For a short bond position, a loss will be realized if interest rates fall. However, an investor wants to know more than simply when a position will realize a loss. To control interest rate risk, an investor must be able to quantify what will result.

The key to measuring interest rate risk is the accuracy of the estimate is of the value of the position after an adverse rate change. A valuation model is used to determine the value of a position after an adverse rate move. Consequently, if a reliable valuation model is not used, there is no way to properly measure interest rate risk exposure.

There are two approaches to measuring interest rate risk—the *full valuation approach* and the *duration/convexity approach*. We begin with a discussion of the full valuation approach. The balance of the chapter is devoted to the duration/convexity approach. As a background to the duration/convexity ap-

---

Parts of this chapter are adapted from several chapters in Frank J. Fabozzi, *Duration, Convexity, and Other Bond Risk Measures* (New Hope, PA: Frank J. Fabozzi Associates, 1999) and from Gerald W. Buetow and Robert R. Johnson, "A Primer on Effective Duration and Convexity," in Frank J. Fabozzi (ed.), *Professional Perspectives on Fixed Income Portfolio Management: Volume 1* (New Hope, PA: Frank J. Fabozzi Associates, 2000).

proach, we discuss the price volatility characteristics of option-free bonds and bonds with embedded options. We then look at how duration can be used to estimate interest rate risk and distinguish between various duration measures (effective, modified, and Macaulay). Next we show how a measure referred to as "convexity" can be used to improve the duration estimate of the price volatility of a bond to rate changes. In the next to the last section we show the relationship between duration and another measure of price volatility used by investors, the price value of a basis point (or dollar value of an 01). In the last section we discuss the importance of incorporating yield volatility in estimates of exposure to interest rate risk.

# THE FULL VALUATION APPROACH

The most obvious way to measure the interest rate risk exposure of a bond position or a portfolio is to re-value it when interest rates change. The analysis is performed for a given scenario with respect to interest rate changes. For example, an investor may want to measure the interest rate exposure to a 50 basis point, 100 basis point, and 200 basis point instantaneous change in interest rates. This approach requires the re-valuation of a bond or bond portfolio for a given interest rate change scenario and is referred to as the *full valuation approach*. It is sometimes referred to scenario analysis because it involves assessing the exposure to interest rate change scenarios.

To illustrate this approach, suppose that an investor has a $10 million par value position in a 9% coupon 20-year bond. The bond is option-free. The current price is 134.6722 for a yield (i.e., yield to maturity) of 6%. The market value of the position is $13,467,220 (134.6722% × $10 million). Since the investor owns the bond, she is concerned with a rise in yield since this will decrease the market value of the position. To assess the exposure to a rise in market yields, the investor decides to look at how the value of the bond will change if yields change instantaneously for the following three scenarios: (1) 50 basis point increase, (2) 100 basis point increase, and (3) 200 basis point increase. This means that the investor wants to assess what will happen to the bond position if the yield on the bond increases from 6% to (1) 6.5%, (2) 7%, and (3) 8%. Because this is an option-free bond, valuation is straightforward. We will assume that one yield is used to discount each of the cash flows. That is, we will assume a flat yield curve. The price of this bond per $100 par value and the market value of the $10 million par position is shown in Exhibit 5–1. Also shown is the change in the market value and the percentage change.

In the case of a portfolio, each bond is valued for a given scenario and then the total value of the portfolio is computed for the scenario. For example, suppose that a manager has a portfolio with the following two option-free bonds: (1) 6% coupon five-year bond and (2) 9% coupon 20-year bond. For the shorter term bond, $5 million of par value is owned and the price is 104.3760 for a

**EXHIBIT 5-1**

Illustration of Full Valuation Approach to Assess the Interest Rate Risk of a Bond Position for Three Scenarios

Current bond position: 9% coupon 20-year bond (option-free)
Price: 134.6722
Yield to maturity: 6%
Par value owned: $10 million
Market value of position: $13,467,220.00

| Scenario | Yield Change (bp) | New Yield | New Price | New Market Value ($) | Percentage Change in Market Value (%) |
|----------|-------------------|-----------|-----------|----------------------|---------------------------------------|
| 1 | 50 | 6.5% | 127.7606 | 12,776,060 | −5.13% |
| 2 | 100 | 7.0% | 121.3551 | 12,135,510 | −9.89% |
| 3 | 200 | 8.0% | 109.8964 | 10,989,640 | −18.40% |

yield of 5%. For the longer term bond, $10 million of par value is owned and the price is 134.6722 for a yield of 6%. Suppose that the manager wants to assess the interest rate risk of this portfolio for a 50, 100, and 200 basis point increase in interest rates assuming both the five-year yield and 20-year yield change by the same number of basis points. Exhibit 5–2 shows the exposure. Panel a of the exhibit shows the market value of the five-year bond for the three scenarios. Panel b does the same for the 20-year bond. Panel c shows the total market value of the portfolio and the percentage change in the market value for the three scenarios.

In Exhibit 5–2, it is assumed that both the five-year and the 20-year yields changed by the same number of basis points. The full valuation approach can also handle scenarios where the yield curve does not change in a parallel fashion. Exhibit 5–3 illustrates this for our portfolio that includes the five-year and 20-year bonds. The scenario analyzed is a yield curve shift scenario combined with scenarios for shifts in the level of yields. In the illustration in Exhibit 5–3, the following yield changes for the five-year and 20-year yields are assumed:

| Scenario | Change in 5-year Rate (bp) | Change in 20-year Rate (bp) |
|----------|----------------------------|------------------------------|
| 1 | 50 | 10 |
| 2 | 100 | 50 |
| 3 | 200 | 100 |

The last panel in Exhibit 5–3 shows how the market value of the portfolio changes for each scenario.

**E X H I B I T    5–2**

Illustration of Full Valuation Approach to Assess the Interest Rate Risk
of a Bond Portfolio for Three Scenarios Assuming a Parallel Shift
in the Yield Curve

Two bond portfolio (both bonds are option-free bonds)

*Panel a*

| Bond 1: | 6% coupon 5-year bond | Par value: | $5,000,000 |
|---|---|---|---|
| Initial price: | 104.3760 | Market value: | $5,218,800 |
| Yield: | 5% | | |

| Scenario | Yield Change (bp) | New Yield | New Price | New Market Value ($) |
|---|---|---|---|---|
| 1 | 50 | 5.5% | 102.1600 | 5,108,000 |
| 2 | 100 | 6.0% | 100.0000 | 5,000,000 |
| 3 | 200 | 7.0% | 95.8417 | 4,792,085 |

*Panel b*

| Bond 2: | 9% coupon 20-year bond | Par value: | $10,000,000 |
|---|---|---|---|
| Initial price: | 134.6722 | Market value: | $13,467,220 |
| Yield: | 6% | | |

| Scenario | Yield Change (bp) | New Yield | New Price | New Market Value ($) |
|---|---|---|---|---|
| 1 | 50 | 6.5% | 127.7602 | 12,776,020 |
| 2 | 100 | 7.0% | 121.3551 | 12,135,510 |
| 3 | 200 | 8.0% | 109.8964 | 10,989,640 |

*Panel c*

Portfolio Market value: $18,686,020.00

| Scenario | Yield Change (bp) | Market Value of Bond 1 ($) | Bond 2 ($) | Portfolio ($) | Percentage Change in Market Value (%) |
|---|---|---|---|---|---|
| 1 | 50 | 5,108,000 | 12,776,020 | 17,884,020 | −4.29% |
| 2 | 100 | 5,000,000 | 12,135,510 | 17,135,510 | −8.30% |
| 3 | 200 | 4,792,085 | 10,989,640 | 15,781,725 | −15.54% |

The full valuation approach seems straightforward. If one has a good valuation model, assessing how the value of a portfolio or individual bond will
change for different scenarios for parallel and nonparallel yield curve shifts
measures the interest rate risk of a portfolio.

A common question that often arises when using the full valuation approach is what scenarios should be evaluated to assess interest rate risk exposure.

**E X H I B I T   5–3**

Illustration of Full Valuation Approach to Assess the Interest Rate Risk of a Bond Portfolio for Three Scenarios Assuming a Nonparallel Shift in the Yield Curve

**Two bond portfolio (both bonds are option-free bonds)**

*Panel a*

Bond 1:              6% coupon 5-year bond    Par value:          $5,000,000
Initial price:        104,3760                Market value:       $5,218,800
Yield:               5%

| Scenario | Yield Change (bp) | New Yield | New Price | New Market Value ($) |
|----------|-------------------|-----------|-----------|----------------------|
| 1 | 50 | 5.5% | 102.1600 | 5,108,000 |
| 2 | 100 | 6.0% | 100.000 | 5,000,000 |
| 3 | 200 | 7.0% | 95,8417 | 4,792,085 |

*Panel b*

Bond 2:                                        Par value:          $10,000,000
Initial price:        134.6722                 Market value:       $13,467,220

| Scenario | Yield Change (bp) | New Yield | New Price | New Market Value ($) |
|----------|-------------------|-----------|-----------|----------------------|
| 1 | 10 | 6.1% | 133.2472 | 13,324,720 |
| 2 | 50 | 6.5% | 127.7605 | 12,776,050 |
| 3 | 100 | 7.0% | 121.3551 | 12,135,510 |

*Panel c*

Portfolio Market value: $18,686,020.00

| Scenario | Market Value of Bond 1 ($) | Market Value of Bond 2 ($) | Market Value of Portfolio ($) | Percentage Change in Market Value (%) |
|----------|------------|------------|-----------|-----------|
| 1 | 5,108,000 | 13,324,720 | 18,432,720 | −1.36% |
| 2 | 5,000,000 | 12,776,050 | 17,776,050 | −4.87% |
| 3 | 4,792,085 | 12,135,510 | 16,927,595 | −9.41% |

For some regulated entities, there are specified scenarios established by regulators. For example, it is common for regulators of depository institutions to require entities to determine the impact on the value of their bond portfolio for a 100, 200, and 300 basis point instantaneous change in interest rates (up and down). (Regulators tend to refer to this as "simulating" interest rate scenarios rather than scenario analysis.) Risk managers and highly leveraged investors such as hedge funds tend to look at extreme scenarios to assess exposure to interest rate changes. This practice is referred to as *stress testing*.

Of course, in assessing how changes in the yield curve can affect the exposure of a portfolio, there are an infinite number of scenarios that can be evaluated. The state-of-the-art technology involves using a complex statistical procedure to determine a likely set of yield curve shift scenarios from historical data.

We can use the full valuation approach to assess the exposure of a bond or portfolio to interest rate change to evaluate any scenario, assuming—and this must be repeated continuously—*that the investor has a good valuation model to estimate what the price of the bonds will be in each interest rate scenario.* While the full valuation approach is the recommended approach for assessing the position of a single bond or a portfolio of a few bonds, for a portfolio with a large number of bonds and with even a minority of those bonds being complex (i.e., having embedded options), the full valuation process is time consuming. Investors want one measure they can use to get an idea of how a portfolio or a even a single bond will change if rates change in a parallel fashion rather than having to revalue a portfolio to obtain that answer. Such a measure is duration. We will discuss this measure as well as a supplementary measure (convexity). To build a foundation to understand the limitations of these measures, we describe next the basic price volatility characteristics of bonds. The fact that there are limitations of using one or two measures to describe the interest rate exposure of a position or portfolio should not be surprising. What is important to understand is that these measures provide a starting point for assessing interest rate risk.

## PRICE VOLATILITY CHARACTERISTICS OF BONDS

The characteristics of a bond that affect its price volatility are: (1) maturity, (2) coupon rate, and (3) presence of embedded options. We will also see how the level of yields affects price volatility.

### Price Volatility Characteristics of Option-Free Bonds

We begin by focusing on option-free bonds (i.e., bonds that do not have embedded options). A fundamental characteristic of an option-free bond is that the price of the bond changes in the opposite direction from a change in the bond's required yield. Exhibit 5–4 illustrates this property for four hypothetical bonds assuming a par value of $100.

When the price/yield relationship for any option-free bond is graphed, it exhibits the shape shown in Exhibit 5–5. Notice that as the required yield increases, the price of an option-free bond declines. However, this relationship is not linear (i.e., not a straight line relationship). The shape of the price/yield

**E X H I B I T   5–4**

Price/Yield Relationship for Four Hypothetical Option-Free Bonds

| | Price ($) | | | |
|---|---|---|---|---|
| **Yield (%)** | **6%/5 Year** | **6%/20 Year** | **9%/5 Year** | **9%/20 Year** |
| 4.00 | 108.9826 | 127.3555 | 122.4565 | 168.3887 |
| 5.00 | 104.3760 | 112.5514 | 117.5041 | 150.2056 |
| 5.50 | 102.1600 | 106.0195 | 115.1201 | 142.1367 |
| 5.90 | 100.4276 | 101.1651 | 113.2556 | 136.1193 |
| 5.99 | 100.0427 | 100.1157 | 112.8412 | 134.8159 |
| 6.00 | 100.0000 | 100.0000 | 112.7953 | 134.6722 |
| 6.01 | 99.9574 | 99.8845 | 112.7494 | 134.5287 |
| 6.10 | 99.5746 | 98.8535 | 112.3373 | 133.2472 |
| 6.50 | 97.8944 | 94.4479 | 110.5280 | 127.7605 |
| 7.00 | 95.8417 | 89.3225 | 108.3166 | 121.3551 |
| 8.00 | 91.8891 | 80.2072 | 104.0554 | 109.8964 |

**E X H I B I T   5–5**

Price/Yield Relationship for a Hypothetical Option-Free Bond

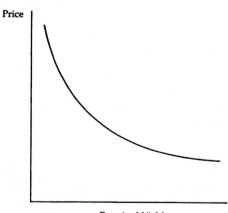

relationship for any option-free bond is referred to as *convex*. This price/yield relationship is for an instantaneous change in the required yield.

The price sensitivity of a bond to changes in the required yield can be measured in terms of the dollar price change or the percentage price change. Exhibit 5–6 uses the four hypothetical bonds in Exhibit 5–4 to show the percentage change in each bond's price for various changes in yield, assuming that the initial yield for all four bonds is 6%. An examination of Exhibit 5–6 reveals the following properties concerning the price volatility of an option-free bond:

*Property 1:* Although the price moves in the opposite direction from the change in required yield, the percentage price change is not the same for all bonds.

*Property 2:* For small changes in the required yield, the percentage price change for a given bond is roughly the same, whether the required yield increases or decreases.

*Property 3:* For large changes in required yield, the percentage price change is not the same for an increase in required yield as it is for a decrease in required yield.

*Property 4:* For a given large change in basis points in the required yield, the percentage price increase is greater than the percentage price decrease.

While the properties are expressed in terms of percentage price change, they also hold for dollar price changes.

**E X H I B I T   5–6**

Instantaneous Percentage Price Change for Four Hypothetical Bonds (Initial yield for all four bonds is 6%)

| | *Percentage Price Change* | | | |
|---|---|---|---|---|
| **New Yield** | **6%/5 Year** | **6%/20 Year** | **9%/5 Year** | **9%/20 Year** |
| 4.00 | 8.98 | 27.36 | 8.57 | 25.04 |
| 5.00 | 4.38 | 12.55 | 4.17 | 11.53 |
| 5.50 | 2.16 | 6.02 | 2.06 | 5.54 |
| 5.90 | 0.43 | 1.17 | 0.41 | 1.07 |
| 5.99 | 0.04 | 0.12 | 0.04 | 0.11 |
| 6.01 | −0.04 | −0.12 | −0.04 | −0.11 |
| 6.10 | −0.43 | −1.15 | −0.41 | −1.06 |
| 6.50 | −2.11 | −5.55 | −2.01 | −5.13 |
| 7.00 | −4.16 | −10.68 | −3.97 | −9.89 |
| 8.00 | −8.11 | −19.79 | −7.75 | −18.40 |

The implication of Property 4 is that if an investor is long a bond, the price appreciation that will be realized if the required yield decreases is greater than the capital loss that will be realized if the required yield increases by the same number of basis points. For an investor who is short a bond, the reverse is true: the potential capital loss is greater than the potential capital gain if the yield changes by a given number of basis points.

## Bond Features that Affect Interest Rate Risk

The degree of sensitivity of a bond's price to changes in market interest rates (i.e., a bond's interest rate risk) depends on various features of the issue, such as maturity, coupon rate, and embedded options.

### The Impact of Maturity

All other factors constant, *the longer the bond's maturity, the greater the bond's price sensitivity to changes in interest rates.* For example, for a 6% 20-year bond selling to yield 6%, a rise in the yield required by investors to 6.5% will cause the bond's price to decline from 100 to 94.4479, a 5.55% price decline. For a 6% five-year bond selling to yield 6%, the price is 100. A rise in the yield required by investors from 6% to 6.5% would decrease the price to 97.8944. The decline in the bond's price is only 2.11%.

### The Impact of Coupon Rate

A property of a bond is that all other factors constant, *the lower the coupon rate, the greater the bond's price sensitivity to changes in interest rates.* For example, consider a 9% 20-year bond selling to yield 6%. The price of this bond would be 134.6722. If the yield required by investors increases by 50 basis points to 6.5%, the price of this bond would fall by 5.13% to 127.7605. This decline is less than the 5.55% decline for the 6% 20-year bond selling to yield 6%.

An implication is that zero-coupon bonds have greater price sensitivity to interest rate changes than same-maturity bonds bearing a coupon rate and trading at the same yield.

### The Impact of Embedded Options

In Chapter 1 we discussed the various embedded options that may be included in a bond issue. The value of a bond with embedded options will change depending on how the value of the embedded options change when interest rates change. For example, as interest rates decline, the price of a callable bond may not increase as much as an otherwise option-free bond (that is, a bond with no embedded options).

To understand why, we decompose the price of a callable bond into two parts, as shown below:

price of callable bond

= price of option-free bond − price of embedded call option

The reason for subtracting the price of the embedded call option from the price of the option-free bond is that the call option is a benefit to the issuer and a disadvantage to the bondholder. This reduces the price of a callable bond relative to an option-free bond.

Now, when interest rates decline, the price of an option-free bond increases. However, the price of the embedded call option increases when interest rates decline because the call option becomes more valuable to the issuer. So, when interest rates decline both components increase, *but* the change in the price of the callable bond depends on the relative price change of the two components. Typically, a decline in interest rates will result in an increase in the price of the callable bond but not by as much as the price change of an otherwise comparable option-free bond.

Similarly, when interest rates rise, the price of a callable bond will not fall by as much as an otherwise option-free bond. The reason is that the price of the embedded call option declines. When interest rates rise, the price of the option-free bond declines but is partially offset by the decrease in the price of the embedded call option.

## Price Volatility Characteristics of Bonds with Embedded Options

In this section we examine the price/yield relationship for bonds with both types of options (calls and puts) and implications for price volatility.

### Bonds with Call and Prepay Options

In the discussion below, we will refer to a bond that may be called or is prepayable as a callable bond. Exhibit 5–7 shows the price/yield relationship for an option-free bond and a callable bond. The convex curve given by *a-a'* is the price/yield relationship for an option-free bond. The unusual shaped curve denoted by *a-b* in the exhibit is the price/yield relationship for the callable bond.

The reason for the price/yield relationship for a callable bond is as follows. When the prevailing market yield for comparable bonds is higher than the coupon rate on the callable bond, it is unlikely that the issuer will call the issue. For example, if the coupon rate on a bond is 7% and the prevailing market yield on comparable bonds is 12%, it is highly unlikely that the issuer will call a 7% coupon bond so that it can issue a 12% coupon bond. Since the bond is unlikely to be called, the callable bond will have a similar price/yield relationship as an otherwise comparable option-free bond. Consequently, the callable bond is going to be valued as if it is an option-free bond. However, since there is still some value to the call option, the bond won't trade exactly like an option-free bond.

As yields in the market decline, the concern is that the issuer will call the bond. The issuer won't necessarily exercise the call option as soon as the market

**EXHIBIT  5–7**

Price/Yield Relationship for a Callable Bond and an Option-Free Bond

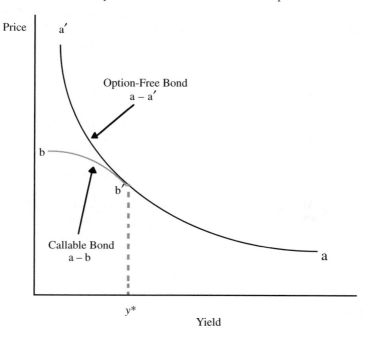

yield drops below the coupon rate. Yet, the value of the embedded call option increases as yields approach the coupon rate from higher yield levels. For example, if the coupon rate on a bond is 7% and the market yield declines to 7.5%, the issuer will most likely not call the issue. However, market yields are at a level at which the investor is concerned that the issue may eventually be called if market yields decline further. Cast in terms of the value of the embedded call option, that option becomes more valuable to the issuer and therefore it reduces the price relative to an otherwise comparable option-free bond.[1] In Exhibit 5–7, the value of the embedded call option at a given yield can be measured by the difference between the price of an option-free bond (the price shown on the curve *a-a′*) and the price on the curve *a-b*. Notice that at low yield levels (below *y\** on the horizontal axis), the value of the embedded call option is high.

Let's look at the difference in the price volatility properties relative to an option-free bond given the price/yield relationship for a callable bond shown in

---

1. For readers who are already familiar with option theory, this characteristic can be restated as follows: When the coupon rate for the issue is below the market yield, the embedded call option is said to be "out-of-the-money." When the coupon rate for the issue is above the market yield, the embedded call option is said to be "in-the-money."

Exhibit 5–7. Exhibit 5–8 blows up the portion of the price/yield relationship for the callable bond where the two curves in Exhibit 5–7 depart (segment b-b' in Exhibit 5–7). We know from our discussion of the price/yield relationship that for a large change in yield of a given number of basis points, the price of an option-free bond increases by more than it decreases (Property 4 above). Is that what happens for a callable bond in the region of the price/yield relationship shown in Exhibit 5–8? No, it is not. In fact, as can be seen in the exhibit, the opposite is true! That is, for a given large change in yield, the price appreciation is less than the price decline.

The price volatility characteristic of a callable bond is important to understand. The characteristic of a callable bond that its price appreciation is less than its price decline when rates change by a large number of basis points is referred to as *negative convexity*.[2] But notice from Exhibit 5–7 that callable bonds don't exhibit this characteristic at every yield level. When yields are high (relative to the issue's coupon rate), the bond exhibits the same price/yield relationship as an option-free bond and therefore at high yield levels also has the characteristic that the gain is greater than the loss. Because market participants have referred to the shape of the price/yield relationship shown in Exhibit 5–8 as negative convexity, market participants refer to the relationship for an

**E X H I B I T   5–8**

Negative Convexity Region of the Price/Yield Relationship for a
Callable Bond

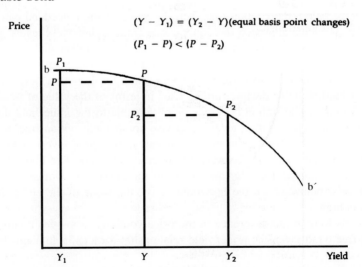

---

2. Mathematicians refer to this shape as being "concave."

option-free bond as *positive convexity.* Consequently, a callable bond exhibits negative convexity at low yield levels and positive convexity at high yield levels.

As can be seen from the exhibits, when a bond exhibits negative convexity, as rates decline the bond compresses in price. That is, at a certain yield level there is very little price appreciation when rates decline. When a bond enters this region, the bond is said to exhibit "price compression."

### Bonds with Embedded Put Options

Putable bonds may be redeemed by the bondholder on the dates and at the put price specified in the indenture. Typically, the put price is par value. The advantage to the investor is that if yields rise such that the bond's value falls below the put price, the investor will exercise the put option. If the put price is par value, this means that if market yields rise above the coupon rate, the bond's value will fall below par and the investor will then exercise the put option.

The value of a putable bond is equal to the value of an option-free bond plus the value of the put option. Thus, the difference between the value of a putable bond and the value of an otherwise comparable option-free bond is the value of the embedded put option. This can be seen in Exhibit 5–9 which shows the price/yield relationship for a putable bond (the curve $a'$-$b$) and an option-free bond (the curve $a$-$a'$).

At low yield levels (low relative to the issue's coupon rate), the price of the putable bond is basically the same as the price of the option-free bond

### EXHIBIT 5-9

Price/Yield Relationship for a Putable Bond and an Option-Free Bond

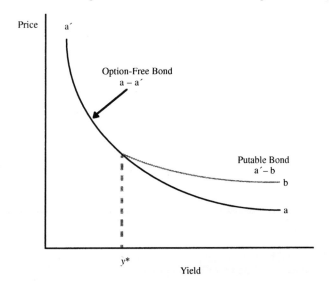

because the value of the put option is small. As rates rise, the price of the putable bond declines, but the price decline is less than that for an option-free bond. The divergence in the price of the putable bond and an otherwise comparable option-free bond at a given yield level is the value of the put option. When yields rise to a level where the bond's price would fall below the put price, the price at these levels is the put price.

## Interest Rate Risk for Floating-Rate Securities

The change in the price of a fixed-rate coupon bond when market interest rates change is due to the fact that the bond's coupon rate differs from the prevailing market interest rate. For a floating-rate security, the coupon rate is reset periodically based on the prevailing value for the reference rate plus the quoted margin. The quoted margin is set for the life of the security. The price of a floating-rate security will fluctuate depending on three factors.

First, the longer the time to the next coupon reset date, the greater the potential price fluctuation.[3] For example, consider a floating-rate security whose coupon resets every six months and the coupon formula is the six-month Treasury rate plus 20 basis points. Suppose that on the coupon reset date the six-month Treasury rate is 5.8%. If on the day after the coupon is reset, the six-month Treasury rate rises to 6.1%, this means that this security is offering a six-month coupon rate that is less than the prevailing six-month rate for the remaining six months. The price of the security must decline to reflect this. Suppose instead that the coupon resets every month at the one-month Treasury rate and that this rate rises immediately after the coupon rate is reset. In this case, while the investor would be realizing a sub-market one-month coupon rate, it is for only a month. The price decline will be less than for the security that resets every six months.

The second reason why a floating-rate security's price will fluctuate is that the required margin that investors demand in the market changes. For example, consider once again the security whose coupon formula is the six-month Treasury rate plus 20 basis points. If market conditions change such that investors want a margin of 30 basis points rather than 20 basis points, this security would be offering a coupon rate that is 10 basis points below the market rate. As a result, the security's price will decline.

Finally, a floating-rate security will typically have a cap. Once the coupon rate as specified by the coupon formula rises above the cap rate, the coupon will be set at the cap rate and the security will then offer a below market coupon rate and its price will decline. In fact, once the cap is reached, the security's price will react much the same way to changes in market interest rates as that

---

3. As explained in Chapter 1, the coupon reset formula is set at the reset date at the beginning of the period but is not paid until the end of the period.

of a fixed-rate coupon security. This risk for a floating-rate security is called *cap risk*.

## The Impact of the Yield Level

Because of credit risk, different bonds trade at different yields, even if they have the same coupon rate, maturity, and embedded options. How, then, holding other factors constant, does the level of interest rates affect a bond's price sensitivity to changes in interest rates? As it turns out, the higher the level of interest rates that a bond trades, the lower the price sensitivity.

To see this, we can compare a 6% 20-year bond initially selling at a yield of 6%, and a 6% 20-year bond initially selling at a yield of 10%. The former is initially at a price of 100, and the latter 65.68. Now, if the yield on both bonds increases by 100 basis points, the first bond trades down by 10.68 points (10.68%) to a price of 89.32. After the assumed increase in yield, the second bond will trade at a price of 59.88, for a price decline of only 5.80 points (or 8.83%). Thus, we see that the bond that trades at a lower yield is more volatile in both percentage price change and absolute price change, as long as the other bond characteristics are the same. An implication is that, for a given change in interest rates, price sensitivity is lower when the level of interest rates in the market is high, and price sensitivity is higher when the level of interest rates is low.

## DURATION

With the background about the price volatility characteristics of a bond, we can now turn to an alternate approach to full valuation: the duration/convexity approach. *Duration is a measure of the approximate sensitivity of a bond's value to rate changes.* More specifically, *it is the approximate percentage change in value for a 100 basis point change in rates.* We'll see in this section that duration is the first approximation of the percentage price change. To improve the estimate provided by duration a measure called "convexity" can be used. Hence, using duration combined with "convexity" to estimate the percentage price change of a bond to changes in interest rates is called the duration/convexity approach.

## Calculating Duration

The duration of a bond is estimated as follows:

$$\frac{\text{price if yields decline} - \text{price if yields rise}}{2(\text{initial price})(\text{change in yield in decimal})}$$

If we let

$\Delta y$ = change in yield in decimal

$V_0$ = initial price

$V_-$ = price if yields decline by $\Delta y$

$V_+$ = price if yields increase by $\Delta y$

then duration can be expressed as

$$\text{duration} = \frac{V_- - V_+}{2(V_0)(\Delta y)} \tag{5-1}$$

For example, consider a 9% coupon 20-year option-free bond selling at 134.6722 to yield 6% (see Exhibit 5–4). Let's change (i.e., shock) the yield down and up by 20 basis points and determine what the new prices will be for the numerator. If the yield is decreased by 20 basis points from 6.0% to 5.8%, the price would increase to 137.5888. If the yield increases by 20 basis points, the price would decrease to 131.8439. Thus,

$\Delta y$ = 0.002

$V_0$ = 134.6722

$V_-$ = 137.5888

$V_+$ = 131.8439

Then,

$$\text{duration} = \frac{137.5888 - 131.8439}{2 \times (134.6722) \times (0.002)} = 10.66$$

Duration is interpreted as the approximate percentage change in price for a 100 basis point change in rates. Consequently, a duration of 10.66 means that the approximate change in price for this bond is 10.66% for a 100 basis point change in rates.

A common question asked about this interpretation of duration is the consistency between the yield change that is used to compute duration using Eq. (5–1) and the interpretation of duration. For example, recall that in computing the duration of the 9% coupon 20-year bond, we used a 20 basis point yield change to obtain the two prices to use in the numerator of Eq. (5–1). Yet, we interpret the duration computed as the approximate percentage price change for a 100 basis point change in yield. The reason is that regardless of the yield change used to estimate duration in Eq. (5–1), the interpretation is the same. If we used a 25 basis point change in yield to compute the prices used in the numerator of Eq. (5–1), the resulting duration is interpreted as the approximate percentage price change for a 100 basis point change in yield. Later we will use different changes in yield to illustrate the sensitivity of the computed duration.

## Approximating the Percentage Price Change Using Duration

The following formula is used to approximate the percentage price change for a given change in yield and a given duration:

$$\text{approximate percentage price change} = -\text{duration} \times \Delta y \times 100 \quad (5\text{–}2)$$

The reason for the negative sign on the right-hand side of Eq. (5–2) is due to the inverse relationship between price change and yield change.

For example, consider the 9% 20-year bond trading at 134.6722 whose duration we just showed is 10.66. The approximate percentage price change for a 10 basis point increase in yield (i.e., $\Delta y = +0.001$) is:

$$\text{approximate percentage price change} = -10.66 \times (+0.001) \times 100 = -1.066\%$$

How good is this approximation? The actual percentage price change is $-1.06\%$ (as shown in Exhibit 5–6 when yield increases to 6.10%). Duration, in this case, did an excellent job in estimating the percentage price change. We would come to the same conclusion if we used duration to estimate the percentage price change if the yield declined by 10 basis points (i.e., $\Delta y = -0.001$). In this case, the approximate percentage price change would be $+1.066\%$ (i.e., the direction of the estimated price change is the reverse but the magnitude of the change is the same). Exhibit 5–6 shows that the actual percentage price change is $+1.07\%$.

In terms of estimating the new price, let's see how duration performed. The initial price is 134.6722. For a 10 basis point increase in yield, duration estimates that the price will decline by 1.066%. Thus, the price will decline to 133.2366 (found by multiplying 134.6722 by one minus 0.1066). The actual price from Exhibit 5–4 if the yield increases by 10 basis points is 133.2472. Thus, the price estimated using duration is close to the actual price. For a 10 basis point decrease in yield, the actual price from Exhibit 5–4 is 136.1193 and the estimated price using duration is 136.1078 (a price increase of 1.066%). Consequently, the new price estimated by duration is close to the actual price for a 10 basis point change in yield.

Let's look at how well duration does in estimating the percentage price change if the yield increases by 200 basis points instead of 10 basis points. In this case, $\Delta y$ is equal to $+0.02$. Substituting into Eq. (5–2) we have

$$\text{approximate percentage price change} = -10.66 \times (+0.02) \times 100 = -21.32\%$$

How good is this estimate? From Exhibit 5–6 we see that the actual percentage price change when the yield increases by 200 basis points to 8% is $-18.40\%$. Thus, the estimate is not as accurate as when we used duration to approximate the percentage price change for a change in yield of only 10 basis points. If we use duration to approximate the percentage price change when the yield decreases by 200 basis points, the approximate percentage price change in this scenario is $+21.32\%$. The actual percentage price change as shown in Exhibit 5–6 is $+25.04\%$.

Again, let's look at the use of duration in terms of estimating the new price. Since the initial price is 134.6722 and a 200 basis point increase in yield will decrease the price by 21.32%, the estimated new price using duration is 105.9601 (found by multiplying 134.6722 by one minus 0.2132). From Exhibit 5–4 the actual price if the yield is 8% is 109.8964. Consequently, the estimate is not as accurate as the estimate for a 10 basis point change in yield. The estimated new price using duration for a 200 basis point decrease in yield is 163.3843 compared to the actual price (from Exhibit 5–4) of 168.3887. Once again, the estimation of the price using duration is not as accurate as for a 10 basis point change. *Notice that whether the yield is increased or decreased by 200 basis points, duration underestimates what the new price will be.* We will see why shortly.

Let's summarize what we found in our application of duration to approximate the percentage price change:

| Yield Change (bp) | Initial Price | New Price | | Percent Price Change | | Comment |
|---|---|---|---|---|---|---|
| | | Based on Duration | Actual | Based on Duration | Actual | |
| +10 | 134.6722 | 133.2366 | 133.2472 | −1.066 | −1.06 | estimated price close to new price |
| −10 | 134.6722 | 136.1078 | 136.1193 | +1.066 | +1.07 | estimated price close to new price |
| +200 | 134.6722 | 105.9601 | 109.8964 | −21.320 | −18.40 | underestimates new price |
| −200 | 134.6722 | 163.3843 | 168.3887 | +21.320 | +25.40 | underestimates new price |

Look again at Eq. (5–2). Notice that whether the change in yield is an increase or a decrease, the approximate percentage price change will be the same except that the sign is reversed. This violates Property 3 and Property 4 with respect to the price volatility of option-free bonds when yields change. Recall that Property 3 states that the percentage price change will not be the same for a large increase and decrease in yield by the same number of basis points. This is one reason why we see that the estimate is inaccurate for a 200 basis point yield change. Why did the duration estimate of the price change do a good job for a small change in yield of 10 basis points? Recall from Property 2 that the percentage price change will be approximately the same whether there is an increase or decrease in yield by a small number of basis points. We can also explain these results in terms of the graph of the price/yield relationship. We will do this next.

## Graphical Depiction of Using Duration to Estimate Price Changes

The shape of the price/yield relationship for an option-free bond is convex. Exhibit 5–10 shows this relationship. In the exhibit a tangent line is drawn to

## E X H I B I T  5–10

Price/Yield Relationship for an Option-Free Bond with a Tangent Line

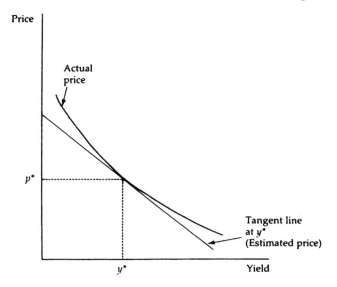

the price/yield relationship at yield $y^*$. (For those unfamiliar with the concept of a tangent line, it is a straight line that just touches a curve at one point within a relevant (local) range. In Exhibit 5–10, the tangent line touches the curve at the point where the yield is equal to $y^*$ and the price is equal to $p^*$. The tangent line can be used to estimate the new price if the yield changes. If we draw a vertical line from any yield (on the horizontal axis), as in Exhibit 5–10, the distance between the horizontal axis and the tangent line represents the price approximated by using duration starting with the initial yield $y^*$.

Now how is the tangent line, used to approximate what the new price will be if yields change, related to duration? Duration tells us the approximate percentage price change. Given the initial price and the approximate percentage price change provided by duration (i.e., as given by Eq. (5–2)), the approximate new price can be estimated. Mathematically, it can be demonstrated that the estimated price that is provided by duration is on the tangent line.

This helps us understand why duration did an effective job of estimating the percentage price change, or equivalently the new price, when the yield changes by a small number of basis points. Look at Exhibit 5–11. Notice that for a small change in yield, the tangent line does not depart much from the price/yield relationship. Hence, when the yield changes up or down by 10 basis points, the tangent line does a good job of estimating the new price, as we found in our earlier numerical illustration.

Exhibit 5–11 also shows what happens to the estimate using the tangent line when the yield changes by a large number of basis points. Notice that the

**EXHIBIT 5-11**

Estimating the New Price Using a Tangent Line

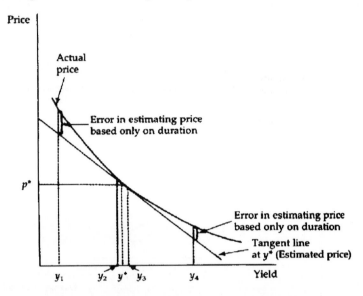

error in the estimate gets larger the further one moves from the initial yield. The estimate is less accurate the more convex the bond. This is illustrated in Exhibit 5–12.

Also note that regardless of the magnitude of the yield change, the tangent line always underestimates what the new price will be for an option-free bond because the tangent line is below the price/yield relationship. This explains why we found in our illustration that when using duration we underestimated what the actual price will be.

## Rate Shocks and Duration Estimate

In calculating duration using Eq. (5–1), it is necessary to shock interest rates (yields) up and down by the same number of basis points to obtain the values for $V_-$ and $V_+$. In our illustration, 20 basis points was arbitrarily selected. But how large should the shock be? That is, how many basis points should be used to shock the rate?

In Exhibit 5–13, the duration estimate for our four hypothetical bonds using Eq. (5–1) for rate shocks of 1 basis point to 200 basis points is reported. The duration estimates for the two five-year bonds are not affected by the size of the shock. The two five-year bonds are less convex than the two 20-year bonds. But even for the two 20-year bonds, for the size of the shocks reported

**E X H I B I T   5–12**

Estimating the New Price for a Large Yield Change for Bonds with Different Convexities

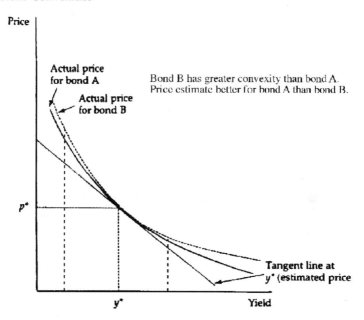

**E X H I B I T   5–13**

Duration Estimates for Different Rate Shocks

| Bond | 1 bp | 10 bps | 20 bps | 50 bps | 100 bps | 150 bps | 200 bps |
|------|------|--------|--------|--------|---------|---------|---------|
| 6% 5 year | 4.27 | 4.27 | 4.27 | 4.27 | 4.27 | 4.27 | 4.27 |
| 6% 20 year | 11.56 | 11.56 | 11.56 | 11.57 | 11.61 | 11.69 | 11.79 |
| 9% 5 year | 4.07 | 4.07 | 4.07 | 4.07 | 4.07 | 4.08 | 4.08 |
| 9% 20 year | 10.66 | 10.66 | 10.66 | 10.67 | 10.71 | 10.77 | 10.86 |

Initial yield: 6%

in Exhibit 5–13, the duration estimates are not materially affected by the greater convexity.

   Thus, it would seem that the size of the shock is unimportant. However, the results reported in Exhibit 5–13 are for option-free bonds. When we deal with more complicated securities, small rate shocks that do not reflect the types of rate changes that may occur in the market do not permit the determination

of how prices can change because expected cash flows may change when dealing
with bonds with embedded options. In comparison, if large rate shocks are used,
we encounter the asymmetry caused by convexity. Moreover, large rate shocks
may cause dramatic changes in the expected cash flows for bonds with embedded options that may be far different from how the expected cash flows will
change for smaller rate shocks.

There is another potential problem with using small rate shocks for complicated securities. The prices that are inserted into the duration formula as given
by Eq. (5–1) are derived from a valuation model. In Chapters 34 and 35 we
will discuss various valuation models and their underlying assumptions. The
duration measure depends crucially on a valuation model. If the rate shock is
small and the valuation model used to obtain the prices for Eq. (5–1) is poor,
dividing poor price estimates by a small shock in rates in the denominator will
have a significant affect on the duration estimate.

What is done in practice by dealers and vendors of analytical systems?
Each system developer uses rate shocks they believe to be realistic based on
historical rate changes.

## Modified Duration versus Effective Duration

One form of duration that is cited by practitioners is *modified duration*. Modified
duration is the approximate percentage change in a bond's price for a 100 basis
point change in yield *assuming that the bond's expected cash flows do not
change when the yield changes*. What this means is that in calculating the values
of $V_-$ and $V_+$ in Eq. (5–1), the same cash flows used to calculate $V_0$ are used.
Therefore, the change in the bond's price when the yield is changed is due
solely to discounting cash flows at the new yield level.

The assumption that the cash flows will not change when the yield is
changed makes sense for option-free bonds such as noncallable Treasury securities. This is because the payments made by the U.S. Department of the Treasury to holders of its obligations do not change when interest rates change.
However, the same cannot be said for bonds with embedded options (i.e., callable and putable bonds and mortgage-backed securities). For these securities, a
change in yield may significantly alter the expected cash flows.

Earlier we showed the price/yield relationship for callable and prepayable
bonds. Failure to recognize how changes in yield can alter the expected cash
flows will produce two values used in the numerator of Eq. (5–1) that are not
good estimates of how the price will actually change. The duration is then not
a good number to use to estimate how the price will change.

In later chapters where valuation models for bonds with embedded options
will be discussed, it will be explained how these models take into account how
changes in yield will affect the expected cash flows. Thus, when $V_-$ and $V_+$ are
the values produced from these valuation models, the resulting duration takes

into account both the discounting at different interest rates and how the expected cash flows may change. When duration is calculated in this manner, it is referred to as *effective duration* or *option-adjusted duration.* Exhibit 5–14 summarizes the distinction between modified duration and effective duration.

The difference between modified duration and effective duration for bonds with embedded options can be quite dramatic. For example, a callable bond could have a modified duration of 5 but an effective duration of only 3. For certain collateralized mortgage obligations, the modified duration could be 7 and the effective duration 20! Thus, using modified duration as a measure of the price sensitivity of a security with embedded options to changes in yield would be misleading. The more appropriate measure for any bond with an embedded option is effective duration.

## Macaulay Duration and Modified Duration

It is worth comparing the relationship between modified duration and Macaulay duration. Modified duration can also be written as:[4]

$$\frac{1}{(1 + yield/k)} \left[ \frac{1 \times \mathrm{PVCF}_1 + 2 \times \mathrm{PVCF}_2 + \cdots + n \times \mathrm{PVCF}_n}{k \times \mathrm{Price}} \right] \quad (5\text{–}3)$$

where

$k$ = number of periods, or payments, per year (e.g., $k = 2$ for semi-annual-pay bonds and $k = 12$ for monthly-pay bonds)

$n$ = number of periods until maturity (i.e., number of years to maturity times $k$)

yield = yield to maturity of the bond

**E X H I B I T   5–14**

Modified Duration versus Effective Duration

| *Duration* |
| --- |
| Interpretation: Generic description of the sensitivity of a bond's price (as a percentage of initial price) to a change in yield |

| *Modified Duration* | *Effective Duration* |
| --- | --- |
| Duration measure in which it is assumed that yield changes do not change the expected cash flows | Duration measure in which recognition is given to the fact that yield changes may change the expected cash flows |

---

4. More specifically, this is the formula for the modified duration of a bond on a coupon anniversary date.

PVCF$_t$ = present value of the cash flow in period $t$ discounted at the yield to maturity

The expression in the brackets of the modified duration formula given by Eq. (5–3) is a measure formulated in 1938 by Frederick Macaulay.[5] This measure is popularly referred to as *Macaulay duration*. Thus, modified duration is commonly expressed as:

$$\text{Modified duration} = \frac{\text{Macaulay duration}}{(1 + \text{yield}/k)}$$

The general formulation for duration as given by Eq. (5–1) provides a short-cut procedure for determining a bond's modified duration. Because it is easier to calculate the modified duration using the short-cut procedure, most vendors of analytical software will use Eq. (5–1) rather than Eq. (5–3) to reduce computation time.

However, it must be clearly understood that modified duration is a flawed measure of a bond's price sensitivity to interest rate changes for a bond with an embedded option and therefore so is Macaulay duration. The use of the formula for duration given by Eq. (5–3) *misleads* the user because it masks the fact that changes in the expected cash flows must be recognized for bonds with embedded options. Although Eq. (5–3) will give the same estimate of percent price change for an option-free bond as Eq. (5–1), Eq. (5–1) is still better because it acknowledges that cash flows and thus value can change due to yield changes.

## Interpretations of Duration

At the outset of this section we defined duration as the approximate percentage change in price for a 100 basis point change in rates. If you understand this definition, you need never use the equation for the approximate percentage price change given by Eq. (5–2) and you can easily calculate the change in a bond's value.

For example, suppose we want to know the approximate percentage change in price for a 50 basis point change in yield for our hypothetical 9% coupon 20-year bond selling for 134.6722. Since the duration is 10.66, a 100 basis point change in yield would change the price by about 10.66%. For a 50 basis point change in yield the price will change by approximately 5.33% (= 10.66%/2). So, if the yield changes by 50 basis points, the price will change by 5.33% from 134.6722 to 127.4942.

Now let's look at some other definitions or interpretations of duration that have been used.

---

5. Frederick Macaulay, *Some Theoretical Problems Suggested by the Movement of Interest Rates, Bond Yields, and Stock Prices in the U.S. Since 1856* (New York: National Bureau of Economics Research, 1938).

## Duration is the "First Derivative"

Sometimes a market participant will refer to duration as the "first derivative of the price/yield function" or simply the "first derivative." First, "derivative" here has nothing to do with "derivative instruments" (i.e., futures, swaps, options, etc.). A derivative as used in this context is obtained by differentiating a mathematical function. There are first derivatives, second derivatives, and so on. When market participants say that duration is the first derivative, here is what they mean. If it were possible to write a mathematical equation for a bond in closed form, the first derivative would be the result of differentiating that equation the first time. While it is a correct interpretation of duration, it is an interpretation that in no way helps us understand what the interest rate risk is of a bond. That is, it is an operationally meaningless interpretation.

Why is it an operationally meaningless interpretation? Go back to the $10 million bond position with a duration of 6. Suppose a client is concerned with the exposure of the bond to changes in interest rates. Now, tell that client the duration is 6 and that it is the first derivative of the price function for that bond. What have you told the client? Not much. In contrast, tell that client that the duration is 6 and that duration is the approximate price sensitivity of a bond to a 100 basis point change in rates and you've told them a great deal with respect to the bond's interest rate risk.

## Duration is Some Measure of Time

When the concept of duration was originally introduced by Macaulay in 1938, he used it as a gauge of the time that the bond was outstanding. More specifically, Macaulay defined duration as the weighted average of the time to each coupon and principal payment of a bond. Subsequently, duration has too often been thought of in temporal terms, i.e., years. This is most unfortunate for two reasons.

First, in terms of dimensions, there is nothing wrong with expressing duration in terms of years because that is the proper dimension of this value. But the proper interpretation is that duration is the price volatility of a zero-coupon bond with that number of years to maturity. So, when a manager says a bond has a duration of 4 years, it is not useful to think of this measure in terms of time, but that the bond has the price sensitivity to rate changes of a four-year zero-coupon bond.

Second, thinking of duration in terms of years makes it difficult for managers and their clients to understand the duration of some complex securities. Here are a few examples. For a mortgage-backed security that is an interest-only security, the duration is negative. What does a negative number of, say, −4 mean? In terms of our interpretation as a percentage price change, it means that when rates change by 100 basis points, the price of the bond changes by about 4% but the change is in the same direction as the change in rates.

As a second example, consider the duration of an option that expires in one year. Suppose that it is reported that its duration is 60. What does that mean? To someone who interprets duration in terms of time, does that mean 60 years, 60 days, 60 seconds? It doesn't mean any of these. It simply means that the option tends to have the price sensitivity to rate changes of a 60-year zero-coupon bond.

### Forget First Derivatives and Temporal Definitions

The bottom line is that one should not care if it is technically correct to think of duration in terms of years (volatility of a zero-coupon bond) or in terms of first derivatives. There are even some who interpret duration in terms of the "half life" of a security. Subject to the limitations that we will describe later, duration is used as a measure of the sensitivity of a security's price to changes in yield. We will fine tune this definition as we move along.

Users of this interest rate risk measure are interested in what it tells them about the price sensitivity of a bond (or a portfolio) to changes in rates. Duration provides the investor with a feel for the dollar price exposure or the percentage price exposure to potential rate changes.

## Portfolio Duration

A portfolio's duration can be obtained by calculating the weighted average of the duration of the bonds in the portfolio. The weight is the proportion of the portfolio that a security comprises. Mathematically, a portfolio's duration can be calculated as follows:

$$w_1 D_1 + w_2 D_2 + w_3 D_3 + \cdots + w_K D_K$$

where

$w_i$ = market value of bond i/market value of the portfolio
$D_i$ = duration of bond $i$
$K$ = number of bonds in the portfolio

To illustrate this calculation, consider the following three-bond portfolio in which all three bonds are option free:

| Bond | Price ($) | Yield (%) | Par Amount Owned | Market Value | Duration |
|------|-----------|-----------|------------------|--------------|----------|
| 10% 5-year | 100.0000 | 10 | $4 million | $4,000,000 | 3.861 |
| 8% 15-year | 84.6275 | 10 | 5 million | 4,231,375 | 8.047 |
| 14% 30-year | 137.8590 | 10 | 1 million | 1,378,586 | 9.168 |

In this illustration, it is assumed that the next coupon payment for each bond is exactly six months from now (i.e., there is no accrued interest). The market value for the portfolio is $9,609,961. Since each bond is option free, the modified duration can be used. The market price per $100 par value of each bond, its yield, and its duration are given below:

In this illustration, $K$ is equal to 3 and:

$$w_1 = \$4,000,000/\$9,609,961 = 0.416 \quad D_1 = 3.861$$

$$w_2 = \$4,231,375/\$9,609,961 = 0.440 \quad D_2 = 8.047$$

$$w_3 = \$1,378,586/\$9,609,961 = 0.144 \quad D_3 = 9.168$$

The portfolio's duration is:

$$0.416 \ (3.861) + 0.440 \ (8.047) + 0.144 \ (9.168) = 6.47$$

A portfolio duration of 6.47 means that for a 100 basis point change in the yield of all three bonds, the market value of the portfolio will change by approximately 6.47%. But keep in mind, the yield on all three bonds must change by 100 basis points for the duration measure to be useful. This is a *critical assumption* and its importance cannot be overemphasized.[6]

An alternative procedure for calculating the duration of a portfolio is to calculate the dollar price change for a given number of basis points for each security in the portfolio and then add up all the price changes. Dividing the total of the price changes by the initial market value of the portfolio produces a percentage price change that can be adjusted to obtain the portfolio's duration.

For example, consider the three-bond portfolio shown above. Suppose that we calculate the dollar price change for each bond in the portfolio based on its respective duration for a 50 basis point change in yield. We would then have:

| Bond | Market Value | Duration | Change in Value for 50 bp Yield Change |
|------|-------------|----------|----------------------------------------|
| 10% 5-year | $4,000,000 | 3.861 | $77,220 |
| 8% 15-year | 4,231,375 | 8.047 | 170,249 |
| 14% 30-year | 1,378,586 | 9.168 | 63,194 |
| | | Total | $310,663 |

Thus, a 50 basis point change in all rates changes the market value of the three-bond portfolio by $310,663. Since the market value of the portfolio is $9,609,961, a 50 basis point change produced a change in value of 3.23% ($310,663 divided by $9,609,961). Since duration is the approximate percentage change for a 100 basis point change in rates, this means that the portfolio duration is 6.46 (found by doubling 3.23). This is the same value for the portfolio's duration as found earlier.

---

6. This is equivalent to saying that the correlation between the yield change for every maturity is equal to 1.

# CONVEXITY

The duration measure indicates that regardless of whether interest rates increase or decrease, the approximate percentage price change is the same. However, as we noted earlier, this is not consistent with Property 3 of a bond's price volatility. Specifically, while for small changes in yield the percentage price change will be the same for an increase or decrease in yield, for large changes in yield this is not true. This suggests that duration is only a good approximation of the percentage price change for small changes in yield.

We demonstrated this property earlier using a 9% 20-year bond selling to yield 6% with a duration of 10.66. For a 10 basis point change in yield, the estimate was accurate for both an increase or decrease in yield. However, for a 200 basis point change in yield the approximate percentage price change was off considerably.

The reason for this result is that duration is in fact a first (linear) approximation for a small change in yield.[7] The approximation can be improved by using a second approximation. This approximation is referred to as "convexity." *The use of this term in the industry is unfortunate since the term convexity is also used to describe the shape or curvature of the price/yield relationship.* The *convexity measure* of a security can be used to approximate the change in price that is not explained by duration.

## Convexity Measure

The convexity measure of a bond is approximated using the following formula:

$$\text{convexity measure} = \frac{V_+ + V_- - 2V_0}{2V_0(\Delta y)^2} \tag{5-4}$$

where the notation is the same as used earlier for duration as given by Eq. (5–1).

For our hypothetical 9% 20-year bond selling to yield 6%, we know that for a 20 basis point change in yield ($\Delta y = 0.002$):

$$V_0 = 134.6722, \quad V_- = 137.5888, \quad \text{and} \quad V_+ = 131.8439$$

Substituting these values into the convexity measure given by Eq. (5–4):

$$\text{Convexity measure} = \frac{131.8439 + 137.5888 - 2(134.6722)}{2(134.6722)(0.002)^2} = 81.96$$

We'll see how to use this convexity measure shortly. Before doing so,

---

7. The reason it is a linear approximation can be seen in Exhibit 5–11 where the tangent line is used to estimate the new price. That is, a straight line is being used to approximate a non-linear (i.e., convex) relationship.

there are three points that should be noted. First, there is no simple interpretation of the convexity measure. Second, in contrast to duration, it is more common for market participants to refer to the value computed in Eq. (5–4) as the "convexity of a bond" rather than the "convexity measure of a bond." Finally, the convexity measure reported by dealers and vendors will differ for an option-free bond. The reason is that the value obtained from Eq. (5–4) is often scaled for the reason explained after we demonstrate how to use the convexity measure.

## Convexity Adjustment to Percentage Price Change

Given the convexity measure, the approximate percentage price change adjustment due to the bond's convexity (i.e., the percentage price change not explained by duration) is:

$$\text{Convexity adjustment} = \text{Convexity measure} \times (\Delta y)^2 \times 100$$

For example, for the 9% coupon bond maturing in 20 years, the convexity adjustment to the percentage price change based on duration if the yield increases from 6% to 8% is

$$81.96 \times (0.02)^2 \times 100 = 3.28\%$$

If the yield decreases from 6% to 4%, the convexity adjustment to the approximate percentage price change based on duration would also be 3.28%.

The approximate percentage price change based on duration and the convexity adjustment is found by adding the two estimates. So, for example, if yields change from 6% to 8%, the estimated percentage price change would be:

$$\text{Estimated change using duration} = -21.32\%$$
$$\underline{\text{Convexity adjustment} = \phantom{0}+3.28\%}$$
$$\text{Total estimated percentage price change} = -18.04\%$$

The actual percentage price change is −18.40%.

For a decrease of 200 basis points, from 6% to 4%, the approximate percentage price change would be as follows:

$$\text{Estimated change using duration} = +21.32\%$$
$$\underline{\text{Convexity adjustment} = \phantom{0}+3.28\%}$$
$$\text{Total estimated percentage price change} = +24.60\%$$

The actual percentage price change is +25.04%. Thus, duration combined with the convexity adjustment does a better job of estimating the sensitivity of a bond's price change to large changes in yield.

Notice that when the convexity measure is positive, we have the situation described earlier that the gain is greater than the loss for a given large change in rates. That is, the bond exhibits positive convexity. We can see this in the example above. However, if the convexity measure is negative, we have the situation where the loss will be greater than the gain. For example, suppose that a callable bond has an effective duration of 4 and a convexity measure of $-30$. This means that the approximate percentage price change for a 200 basis point change is 8%. The convexity adjustment for a 200 basis point change in rates is then

$$-30 \times (0.02)^2 \times 100 = -1.2$$

The convexity adjustment is $-1.2\%$ and therefore the bond exhibits the negative convexity property illustrated in Exhibit 5–7. The approximate percentage price change after adjusting for convexity is:

$$
\begin{aligned}
\text{Estimated change using duration} &= -8.0\% \\
\text{Convexity adjustment} &= \underline{-1.2\%} \\
\text{Total estimated percentage price change} &= -9.2\%
\end{aligned}
$$

For a decrease of 200 basis points, the approximate percentage price change would be as follows:

$$
\begin{aligned}
\text{Estimated change using duration} &= +8.0\% \\
\text{Convexity adjustment} &= \underline{-1.2\%} \\
\text{Total estimated percentage price change} &= +6.8\%
\end{aligned}
$$

Notice that the loss is greater than the gain—a property called negative convexity that we discussed earlier and illustrated in Exhibit 5–7.

## Scaling the Convexity Measure

The convexity measure as given by Eq. (5–4) means nothing in isolation. It is the substitution of the computed convexity measure into Eq. (5–5) that provides the estimated adjustment for convexity. Therefore, it is possible to scale the convexity measure in any way and obtain the same convexity adjustment.

For example, in some books the convexity measure is defined as follows:

$$\text{Convexity measure} = \frac{V_+ + V_- - 2V_0}{V_0(\Delta y)^2} \qquad (5\text{–}6)$$

Equation (5–6) differs from Eq. (5–4) since it does not include 2 in the denominator. Thus, the convexity measure computed using Eq. (5–6) will be double the convexity measure using Eq. (5–4). So, for our earlier illustration, since the convexity measure using Eq. (5–4) is 81.96, the convexity measure using Eq. (5–6) would be 163.92.

Which is correct, 81.96 or 163.92? The answer is both. The reason is that the corresponding equation for computing the convexity adjustment would not be given by Eq. (5–5) if the convexity measure is obtained from Eq. (5–6). Instead, the corresponding convexity adjustment formula would be:

Convexity adjustment = (Convexity measure/2) $\times$ $(\Delta y)^2$ $\times$ 100    (5–7)

Equation (5–7) differs from Eq. (5–5) in that the convexity measure is divided by 2. Thus, the convexity adjustment will be the same whether one uses Eq. (5–4) to get the convexity measure and Eq. (5–5) to get the convexity adjustment or one uses Eq. (5–6) to compute the convexity measure and Eq. (5–7) to determine the convexity adjustment.

Some dealers and vendors scale the convexity measure in a different way. One can also compute the convexity measure as follows:

$$\text{Convexity measure} = \frac{V_+ + V_- - 2V_0}{2V_0(\Delta y)^2(100)} \qquad (5\text{–}8)$$

Equation (5–8) differs from Eq. (5–4) by the inclusion of 100 in the denominator. In our illustration, the convexity measure would be 0.8196 rather than 81.96 using Eq. (5–4). The convexity adjustment formula corresponding to the convexity measure given by Eq. (5–8) is then

Convexity adjustment = Convexity measure $\times$ $(\Delta y)^2$ $\times$ 10,000    (5–9)

Similarly, one can express the convexity measure as shown in Eq. (5–10):

$$\text{Convexity measure} = \frac{V_+ + V_- - 2V_0}{V_0(\Delta y)^2(100)} \qquad (5\text{–}10)$$

For the bond we have been using in our illustrations, the convexity measure is 1.6392. The corresponding convexity adjustment is:

Convexity adjustment = (Convexity measure/2) $\times$ $(\Delta y)^2$ $\times$ 10,000    (5–11)

Consequently, the convexity measure (or just simply "convexity" as it is referred to by some market participants) that could be reported for this option-free bond are 81.96, 163.92, 0.8196, or 1.6392. All of these values are correct, but they mean nothing in isolation. To use them to obtain the convexity adjustment to the price change estimated by duration requires knowing how they are computed so that the correct convexity adjustment formula is used. *It is the convexity adjustment that is important—not the convexity measure in isolation.*

It is also important to understand this when comparing the convexity measures reported by dealers and vendors. For example, if one dealer shows a portfolio manager Bond A with a duration of 4 and a convexity measure of 50, and a second dealer shows the manager Bond B with a duration of 4 and a convexity measure of 80, which bond has the greater percentage price change response to changes in interest rates? Since the duration of the two bonds is identical, the bond with the larger convexity measure will change more when rates decline. However, not knowing how the two dealers computed the convexity measure means that the manager does not know which bond will have the greater convexity adjustment. If the first dealer used Eq. (5–4) while the second dealer used

Eq. (5–6), then the convexity measures must be adjusted in terms of either equation. For example, using Eq. (5–4), the convexity measure of 80 computed using Eq. (5–6) is equal to a convexity measure of 40 based on Eq. (5–4).

## Modified Convexity and Effective Convexity

The prices used in Eq. (5–4) to calculate convexity can be obtained by either assuming that when the yield changes the expected cash flows do not change or they do change. In the former case, the resulting convexity is referred to as *modified convexity*. (Actually, in the industry, convexity is not qualified by the adjective "modified.") In contrast, *effective convexity* assumes that the cash flows do change when yields change. This is the same distinction made for duration.

As with duration, there is little difference between modified convexity and effective convexity for option-free bonds. However, for bonds with embedded options there can be quite a difference between the calculated modified convexity and effective convexity measures. In fact, for all option-free bonds, either convexity measure will have a positive value. For bonds with embedded options, the calculated effective convexity can be negative when the calculated modified convexity measures is positive.

## Illustrations of Effective Duration and Convexity

As noted earlier, modified duration and effective duration are two ways to measure the price sensitivity of a fixed income security. Modified duration ignores any effect on cash flows that might take place as a result of changes in interest rates. Effective duration does not ignore the potential for such changes in cash flows. For example, bonds with embedded options will have very different cash flow properties as interest rates (or yields) change. Modified duration ignores these effects completely. In order to apply effective duration, an available interest rate model and corresponding valuation model are needed. The example in this section shows how to compute the effective duration of securities with cash flows that are dependent upon interest rates.

There is no difference between modified and effective duration for option-free or straight bonds. In fact, it can be shown that they are mathematically identical when the change in rates (or yields) becomes very small. As shown in the example, even for bonds with embedded options, the differences between the two measures are minimal over certain ranges of yields. For example, when the embedded option is far out-of-the-money, the cash flows of the bond are not affected by small changes in yields, resulting in almost no difference in cash flows between the two measures.

Convexity (sometimes referred to as standard convexity) suffers the same limitations as modified duration and is therefore not generally useful for securities with embedded options. However, similar to the duration measures, in ranges of rates (or yields) where the cash flows are not materially affected by small changes in yields, the two convexity measures are almost identical.

The following example illustrates how to calculate and interpret effective duration and effective convexity for option-free bonds and bonds with embedded options.

Suppose we need to measure the interest rate sensitivity of the following three securities:

1. A five-year, 6.70% coupon option-free semiannual coupon bond, with a current price of 102.75% of par

2. A five-year, 6.25% coupon bond, callable at par in years 2 through 5 on the semiannual coupon dates, with a current price of 99.80% of par

3. A five-year, 5.75% coupon bond, putable at par in years 2 through 5 on the semiannual coupon dates, with a current price of 100.11% of par

The cash flows of these securities are very different as interest rates change. Consequently, the sensitivities to changes in interest rates are also very different.

Using an interest rate model that is based on the existing term structure,[8] the term structure of interest rates is shifted up and down by 10 basis points (bps) and the resulting price changes are recorded. Using the notation for duration and convexity earlier in this chapter, $V_-$ corresponds to the price after a downward shift in interest rates, $V_+$ corresponds to the price after an upward shift in interest rates, $V_0$ is the current price, and $\Delta y$ is the assumed shift in the term structure.[9] Exhibit 5–15 shows these prices for each bond using Eq. (5–1) for duration and Eq. (5–6) for the convexity measure.

It is very important to realize the importance of the valuation model in this exercise. The model must account for the change in cash flows of the securities as interest rates change. The callable and putable bonds have very different cash flow characteristics that depend on the level of interest rates. The valuation model used must account for this property. (Note that when calculating the measures, users are cautioned not to round values. Since the denominators of both the duration and convexity terms are very small, any rounding will have a significant impact on results.)

---

8. The Black-Derman-Toy no arbitrage binomial model was used to perform this analysis. Fischer Black, Emanuel Derman, and William Toy, "A One-Factor Model of Interest Rates and Its Application to Treasury Bond Options," *Financial Analysts Journal* (January–February 1990), pp. 24–32.

9. Note that shifting the term structure in a parallel manner will result in a change in yields equal to the shift for option-free bonds.

## E X H I B I T   5–15

Original Prices and Resulting Prices from a Downward and Upward 10 Basis Point Interest Rate Shift and the Corresponding Effective Duration and Effective Convexity for Three Bonds based on the Black-Derman-Toy Model

| | Price Changes Following 10 bp Shift | | |
|---|---|---|---|
| **Variable** | **Original Price** $V_0$ | **Upward Shift of** 10 bp $V_+$ | **Downward Shift of** 10 bp $V_-$ |
| Option-Free Bond Price | 102.7509029 | 102.3191235 | 103.1848805 |
| Callable Bond Price | 99.80297176 | 99.49321718 | 100.1085624 |
| Putable Bond Price | 100.1089131 | 99.84237604 | 100.3819059 |

| *Effective Duration and Effective Convexity Measures Calculated from Using the Price Changes Resulting from the 10 bp Shifts in the Term Structure* | | |
|---|---|---|
| | **Effective Duration** | **Effective Convexity** |
| Option-Free Bond | 4.21 | 21.39 |
| Callable Bond | 3.08 | −41.72 |
| Putable Bond | 2.70 | 64.49 |

## Option-Free Bond

The effective duration for the straight bond is found by recording the price changes from shifting the term structure up $(V_+)$ and down $(V_-)$ by 10 bps and then substituting these values into Eq. (5–1). The prices are shown in Exhibit 5–15. Consequently, the computation is:

$$\text{Effective duration} = \frac{103.1848805 - 102.3191235}{2(102.7509029)(0.001)} = 4.21$$

Similarly, the calculation for effective convexity is found by substituting the corresponding prices into Eq. (5–6):

$$\text{Effective convexity} = \frac{103.1848805 + 102.3191235 - 2(102.7509029)}{102.7509029(0.001)^2}$$
$$= 21.39$$

For the option-free bond, the modified duration is 4.21 and the convexity is 21.40. These are very close to the effective measures shown in Exhibit 5–15. This demonstrates that, for option-free bonds, the two measures are almost the same for small changes in yields.

Exhibit 5–16 shows the effects of the term structure shifts on the effective duration and effective convexity of the straight bond. The effective duration

**EXHIBIT 5–16**

Effective Duration and Effective Convexity for Various Shifts in the Term Structure for Three Bonds

| Term Structure Shift (bps) | Option-Free Bond | | Callable Bond | | Putable Bond | |
|---|---|---|---|---|---|---|
| | Effective Duration | Effective Convexity | Effective Duration | Effective Convexity | Effective Duration | Effective Convexity |
| −500 | 4.40 | 23.00 | 1.91 | 4.67 | 4.46 | 23.46 |
| −250 | 4.30 | 22.19 | 1.88 | 4.55 | 4.37 | 22.66 |
| 0 | 4.21 | 21.39 | 3.08 | −41.72 | 2.70 | 64.49 |
| 250 | 4.12 | 20.62 | 4.15 | 20.85 | 1.87 | 7.07 |
| 500 | 4.03 | 19.87 | 4.07 | 20.10 | 1.81 | 4.23 |
| 1000 | 3.85 | 18.42 | 3.89 | 18.66 | 1.77 | 4.03 |

increases as yields decrease because as yields decrease the slope of the price/yield relationship for option-free bonds becomes steeper and effective duration (and modified duration) is directly proportional to the slope of this relationship. For example, the effective duration at very low yields (−500 bps shift) is 4.40 and decreases to 3.85 at very high rates (+1000 bps). Exhibit 5–17 illustrates this phenomenon; as yields increase notice how the slope of the price/yield relationship decreases (becomes more horizontal or flatter).

**EXHIBIT 5–17**

Price/Yield Relationship of the Option-Free Bond

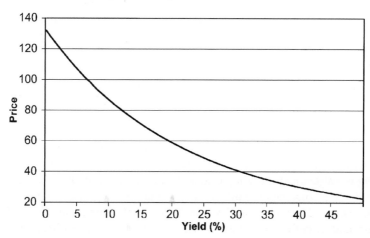

As the term structure shifts up (i.e., as rates rise), the yield to maturity on a straight bond increases by approximately the same amount. As the yield increases, the bond's convexity decreases. Exhibit 5–17 illustrates this property. As yields increase, the curvature (or the rate of change of the slope) decreases. The results in Exhibit 5–16 for the straight bond also bear this out. The effective convexity values become smaller as yields increase. For example, the effective convexity at very low yields (−500 bp shift) is 23.00 and decreases to 18.43 at very high rates (+1000 bp shift).

These are both well-documented properties of option-free bonds. The modified duration and convexity numbers for the straight bond are almost identical to the effective measures for the straight bond shown in Exhibit 5–16.

### Callable Bond

The effective duration for the callable bond is found by recording the price changes from shifting the term structure up ($V_+$) and down ($V_-$) by 10 bps and then substituting these values into Eq. (5–1). The prices are shown in Exhibit 5–15. Note that these prices take into account the changing cash flows resulting from the embedded call option. Consequently, the computation is:

$$\text{Effective duration} = \frac{100.1085624 - 99.4932178}{2(99.800297)(0.001)} = 3.08$$

Similarly, the calculation for effective convexity is found by substituting the corresponding prices into Eq. (5–6):

$$\text{Effective convexity} = \frac{100.1085624 + 99.49321718 - 2(99.80297176)}{99.80297176(0.001)^2}$$
$$= -41.72$$

The relationship between the shift in rates and effective duration is shown in Exhibit 5–16 and in Exhibit 5–18. As rates increase, the effective duration of the callable bond becomes larger. For example, the effective duration at very low yields (−500 bp shift) is 1.91 and increases to 3.89 at very high rates (+1000 bps). This reflects the fact that as rates increase the likelihood of the bond being called decreases and, as a result, the bond behaves more like an option-free bond; hence its effective duration increases. Conversely, as rates drop, this likelihood increases and the bond and its effective duration behave more like a bond with a two-year maturity because of the call option becoming effective in two years. As rates decrease significantly, the likelihood of the issuer calling the bond in two years increases. Consequently, at very low and intermediate rates the difference between the effective duration measure and modified duration is large and at very high rates the difference is small.

Effective convexity measures the curvature of the price/yield relationship of bonds. Low values for effective convexity simply mean that the relationship

**EXHIBIT 5–18**

Price/Yield Relationship of the Callable Bond

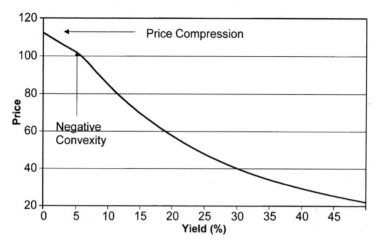

is becoming linear (an effective convexity of zero represents a linear relationship). As shown in Exhibit 5–16, the effective convexity values of the callable bond at extremely low interest rates (i.e., for the −250 bp and −500 bp shifts in the term structure) are very small positive numbers (4.55 and 4.67, respectively). This means that the relationship is almost linear but exhibits slight convexity. This is due to the call option being delayed by two years. At these extremely low interest rates, the callable bond exhibits slight positive convexity because the price compression at the call price is not complete for another two years.[10] If this bond were immediately callable, the price/yield relationship would exhibit positive convexity at high yields and negative convexity at low yields. At the current level of interest rates, the effective convexity is negative as expected. At these rate levels, the embedded call option causes enough price compression to cause the curvature of the price/yield relationship to be negatively convex (i.e., concave). Exhibit 5–18 illustrates these properties. It is at these levels that the embedded option has a significant effect on the cash flows of the callable bond.

Exhibit 5–16 shows that for large positive yield curve shifts (i.e., for the +250 bp, +500 bp, and +1000 bp shifts in the term structure), the effective

---

10. As noted earlier in this chapter, price compression for a callable bond refers to the property that a callable bond's price appreciation potential is severely limited as yields decline. As shown in Exhibit 5–18, as yields fall below a certain level (i.e., where the yield corresponds to the call price), the price appreciation of the callable bond is being compressed.

convexity of the callable bond becomes positive and very close to the effective convexity values of the straight bond. For example, the effective convexity at the +250 bp shift is 20.85 for the callable bond and 20.62 for the straight bond. The only reason they are not the same is because the coupon rates of the bonds are not equal. Consequently, at very low and intermediate rates the difference between effective convexity and the standard convexity is large and at very high rates the difference is small. The intuition behind these findings is straightforward. At low rates, the cash flows of the callable bond are severely affected by the likelihood of the embedded call option being exercised by the issuer. At high rates, the embedded call option is so far out-of-the-money that it has almost no affect on the cash flows of the callable bond and so the callable bond behaves like a straight bond.

**Putable Bond**

The effective duration for the putable bond is found by recording the price changes from shifting the term structure up $(V_+)$ and down $(V_-)$ by 10 bps and then substituting these values into Eq. (5–1). The prices are shown in Exhibit 5–15. Note that these prices take into account the changing cash flows resulting from the embedded put option. Consequently, the computation is:

$$\text{Effective duration} = \frac{100.3819059 - 99.84237604}{2(100.1089131)(0.001)} = 2.70$$

Similarly, the calculation for effective convexity is found by substituting the corresponding prices into Eq. (5–6):

$$\text{Effective convexity} = \frac{100.3819059 + 99.84237604 - 2(100.1089131)}{100.1089131(0.001)^2}$$
$$= 64.49$$

Because the putable bond behaves so differently from the other two bonds, the effective duration and effective convexity values are very different. As rates increase, the bond behaves more like a two-year bond because the owner will, in all likelihood, exercise his right to put the bond back at the put price as soon as possible. As a result, the effective duration of the putable bond is expected to decrease as rates increase. This is due to the embedded put option severely affecting the cash flows of the putable bond. Conversely, as rates fall, the putable bond behaves more like a five-year straight bond since the embedded put option is so far out-of-the-money and has little effect on the cash flows of the putable bond. Effective duration should reflect these properties. Exhibit 5–16 shows that this is indeed the case. For example, the effective duration at very low yields (−500 bp shift) is 4.46 and decreases to 1.77 at very high rates (+1000 bps). Consequently, at very high rates and intermediate rates the difference between the effective duration and modified duration measures is large and at low rates the difference is small.

Exhibit 5–16 shows that the effective convexity of the putable bond is positive for all rate shifts as would be expected, but it becomes smaller as rates increase (i.e., for the +250 bp, +500 bp, and +1000 bp shifts in the term structure). As rates increase, the putable bond price/yield relationship will become linear because of the bond's price truncation at the put price.[11] This is the reason for the small effective convexity values for the putable bond for the three positive shifts in the term structure (7.07, 4.23, and 4.03, respectively). It is at these levels that the embedded put option has a significant effect on the cash flows of the putable bond. Consequently, at very high rates and intermediate rates the difference between the effective convexity and standard convexity is very large. Exhibit 5–19 illustrates these properties.

At very low rates (i.e., for the 250 bp and 500 bp downward shifts in the term structure), the putable bond behaves like a five-year straight bond because the put option is so far out-of-the-money. Therefore, as the term structure is shifted downward, the putable bond's effective convexity values approach those of a comparable five-year option-free bond. Comparing the effective convexity measures for the putable bond and the option-free bond illustrates this characteristic. For example, the effective convexity at the −250 bp shift is 22.66 for the putable bond and 22.19 for the straight bond. The two convexity measures are almost identical. In fact, they would be identical if their coupon rates were equal.

**E X H I B I T   5–19**

Price/Yield Relationship of the Putable Bond

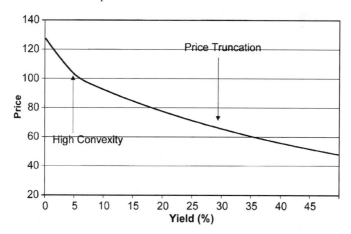

11. Price truncation for a putable bond refers to the property that the putable bond's price depreciation potential is severely limited as yields increase. As shown in Exhibit 5–19, as yields rise above a certain level (i.e., where the yield corresponds to the put price), the price depreciation of the putable bond is truncated.

Exhibit 5–19 illustrates these properties. Also notice how the transition from low yields to high yields forces the price/yield relationship to have a very high convexity at intermediate levels of yields. For example, the current effective convexity of the putable bond is 64.49 compared to 21.39 for the straight bond and −41.72 for the callable bond. This is because as yields increase, the embedded put option moves from out-of-the-money to in- and the behavior of the bond goes from that of a five-year bond to a two-year bond as a result. This corresponding price truncation causes the price/yield relationship to have to transition very quickly from the five year (high effective duration) to the two year (low effective duration) resulting in very high effective convexity.

### Putting it All Together

Notice in Exhibit 5–16 how effective duration changes much more across yields for the callable and putable bonds than it does for the option-free bond. This is to be expected because the embedded options have such a significant influence over cash flows as yields change over a wide spectrum. Interestingly, at high (low) yields the callable (putable) bond's effective duration is very close to the straight bond. This is where the embedded call (put) option is so far out-of-the-money that the two securities behave similarly. The same intuition holds for the effective convexity measures.

As explained and illustrated earlier, the common use of effective duration and effective convexity is to estimate the percentage price changes in fixed income securities for assumed changes in yield. In fact, it is not uncommon for effective duration and effective convexity to be presented in terms of estimated percentage price change for a given change in yield (typically 100 bp). Exhibits 5–20 and 5–21 show this alternative presentation for a ±100 bp changes in yield using Eqs. (5–2) and (5–7).

## PRICE VALUE OF A BASIS POINT

Some managers use another measure of the price volatility of a bond to quantify interest rate risk—*the price value of a basis point* (PVBP). This measure, also called the *dollar value of an 01* (DV01), is the absolute value of the change in the price of a bond for a 1 basis point change in yield. That is,

PVBP = | initial price − price if yield is changed by 1 basis point |

Does it make a difference if the yield is increased or decreased by 1 basis point? It does not because of Property 2—the change will be about the same for a small change in basis points.

To illustrate the computation, we use the values in Exhibit 5–4. If the initial yield is 6%, we can compute the PVBP by using the prices for either the yield at 5.99% or 6.01%. The PVPB for both for each bond is shown below:

EXHIBIT 5-20

Percentage Price Changes Assuming an Increase in Yield of 100 bps and Effective Duration and Effective Convexity for Various Shifts in the Term Structure

| Term Structure Shift (bp) | Option-Free Bond | | | Callable Bond | | | Putable Bond | | |
|---|---|---|---|---|---|---|---|---|---|
| | % Price Change Using Effective Duration | % Price Change Using Effective Convexity | Total % Price Change | % Price Change Using Effective Duration | % Price Change Using Effective Convexity | Total % Price Change | % Price Change Using Effective Duration | % Price Change Using Effective Convexity | Total % Price Change |
| −500 | −4.40 | 0.11500 | −4.28500 | −1.91 | 0.02335 | −1.88665 | −4.46 | 0.11730 | −4.34270 |
| −250 | −4.30 | 0.11095 | −4.18905 | −1.88 | 0.02275 | −1.85725 | −4.37 | 0.11330 | −4.25670 |
| 0 | −4.21 | 0.10695 | −4.10305 | −3.08 | −0.20860 | −3.28860 | −2.70 | 0.32245 | −2.37755 |
| 250 | −4.12 | 0.10310 | −4.01690 | −4.15 | 0.10425 | −4.04575 | −1.87 | 0.03535 | −1.83465 |
| 500 | −4.03 | 0.09935 | −3.93065 | −4.07 | 0.10050 | −3.96950 | −1.81 | 0.02115 | −1.78885 |
| 1000 | −3.85 | 0.09210 | −3.75790 | −3.89 | 0.09330 | −3.79670 | −1.77 | 0.02015 | −1.74985 |

# EXHIBIT 5-21

Percentage Price Changes Assuming a Decrease in Yield of 100 bps and Effective Duration and Effective Convexity for Various Shifts in the Term Structure

| Term Structure Shift (bp) | Option-Free Bond | | | Callable Bond | | | Putable Bond | | |
|---|---|---|---|---|---|---|---|---|---|
| | % Price Change Using Effective Duration | % Price Change Using Effective Convexity | Total % Price Change | % Price Change Using Effective Duration | % Price Change Using Effective Convexity | Total % Price Change | % Price Change Using Effective Duration | % Price Change Using Effective Convexity | Total % Price Change |
| −500 | 4.40 | 0.1150 | 4.5150 | 1.91 | 0.0234 | 1.9334 | 4.46 | 0.1173 | 4.5773 |
| −250 | 4.30 | 0.1110 | 4.4110 | 1.88 | 0.0228 | 1.9028 | 4.37 | 0.1133 | 4.4833 |
| 0 | 4.21 | 0.1070 | 4.3170 | 3.08 | −0.2086 | 2.8714 | 2.70 | 0.3225 | 3.0225 |
| 250 | 4.12 | 0.1031 | 4.2231 | 4.15 | 0.1043 | 4.2543 | 1.87 | 0.0354 | 1.9054 |
| 500 | 4.03 | 0.0994 | 4.1294 | 4.07 | 0.1005 | 4.1705 | 1.81 | 0.0212 | 1.8312 |
| 1000 | 3.85 | 0.0921 | 3.9421 | 3.89 | 0.0933 | 3.9833 | 1.77 | 0.0202 | 1.7902 |

| Coupon | 6.0% | 6.0% | 9.0% | 9.0% |
|---|---|---|---|---|
| Maturity | 5 | 20 | 5 | 20 |
| Initial price | $100.0000 | $100.0000 | $112.7953 | $134.6722 |
| Price at 5.99% | 100.0427 | 100.1157 | 112.8412 | 134.8159 |
| PVBP at 5.99% | $0.0427 | $0.1157 | $0.0459 | $0.1437 |
| Price at 6.01% | 99.9574 | 99.8845 | 112.7494 | 134.5287 |
| PVPB at 6.01% | $0.0426 | $0.1155 | $0.0459 | $0.1435 |

The PVBP is related to duration. In fact, PVBP is simply a special case of dollar duration. We know that the duration of a bond is the approximate percentage price change for a 100 basis point change in interest rates. We also know how to compute the approximate percentage price change for any number of basis points given a bond's duration using Eq. (5–2). Given the initial price and the approximate percentage price change for 1 basis point, we can compute the change in price for a 1 basis point change in rates.

For example, consider the 9% 20-year bond. The duration for this bond is 10.66. Using Eq. (5–2), the approximate percentage price change for a 1 basis point increase in interest rates (i.e., $\Delta y = 0.0001$) ignoring the negative sign in Eq. (5–2) is:

$$10.66 \times (0.0001) \times 100 = 0.1066\%$$

Given the initial price of 134.6722, the dollar price change estimated using duration is

$$0.1066\% \times 134.6722 = \$0.1435$$

This is the same price change as shown above for a PVPB for this bond. Below is (1) the PVPB based on a 1 basis point increase for each bond and (2) the estimated price change using duration for a 1 basis point increase for each bond:

| Coupon | 6.0% | 6.0% | 9.0% | 9.0% |
|---|---|---|---|---|
| Maturity | 5 | 20 | 5 | 20 |
| Maturity | 5 | 20 | 5 | 20 |
| PVBP for 1 bp increase | $0.0426 | $0.1155 | $0.0459 | $0.1435 |
| Duration of bond | 4.2700 | 11.5600 | 4.0700 | 10.6600 |
| Duration estimate | $0.0427 | $0.1156 | $0.0459 | $0.1436 |

## THE IMPORTANCE OF YIELD VOLATILITY

What we have not considered thus far is the volatility of interest rates. All other factors equal, the higher the coupon rate, the lower the price volatility of a bond to changes in interest rates. In addition, the higher the level of yields, the lower the price volatility of a bond to changes in interest rates. This is illustrated in Exhibit 5–22 which shows the price/yield relationship for an option-free bond. When the yield level is high ($Y_H$ in the exhibit) a change in interest rates does not produce a large change in the initial price ($P_H$ in the exhibit). However, when the yield level is low ($Y_L$ in the exhibit) a change in interest rates of the same number of basis points as shown when the yield is high does produce a large change in the initial price ($P_L$ in the exhibit).

This can also be cast in terms of duration properties: the higher the coupon, the lower the duration and the higher the yield level the lower the duration. Given these two properties, a 10-year non-investment grade bond has a lower duration than a current coupon 10-year Treasury note since the former has a higher coupon rate and trades at a higher yield level. Does this mean that a 10-year non-investment grade bond has less interest rate risk than a current coupon 10-year Treasury note? Consider also that a 10-year Swiss government bond has a lower coupon rate than a current coupon 10-year U.S. Treasury note and trades at a lower yield level. Therefore, a 10-year Swiss government bond will have a higher duration than a current coupon 10-year Treasury note. Does this mean that a 10-year Swiss government bond has greater interest rate risk than a current coupon 10-year U.S. Treasury note? The missing link is the relative volatility of rates which we shall refer to as *yield volatility or interest rate volatility*.

The greater the expected yield volatility, the greater the interest rate risk for a given duration and current value of a position. In the case of non-

**EXHIBIT   5–22**

The Effect of Yield Level on Price Volatility

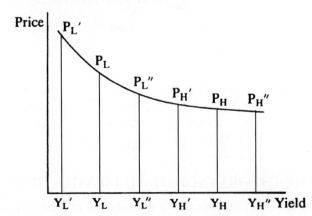

$$(Y_H' - Y_H) = (Y_H - Y_H'') = (Y_L' - Y_L) = (Y_L - Y_L'')$$
$$(P_H - P_H') < (P_L - P_L') \text{ and}$$
$$(P_H - P_H'') < (P_L - P_L'')$$

investment grade bonds, while their durations are less than current coupon Treasuries of the same maturity, the yield volatility of non-investment grade bonds
is greater than that of current coupon Treasuries. For the 10-year Swiss government bond, while the duration is greater than for a current coupon 10-year U.S.
Treasury note, the yield volatility of 10-year Swiss bonds is considerably less
than that of 10-year U.S. Treasury notes.

A framework that ties together the price sensitivity of a bond position to
rate changes and yield volatility is the value-at-risk (VaR) framework. Risk in
this framework is defined as the maximum estimated loss in market value of a
given position that is expected to happen with a specified probability.

CHAPTER **6**

# THE STRUCTURE OF INTEREST RATES

Frank J. Fabozzi, Ph.D., CFA, CPA
Adjunct Professor of Finance
School of Management
Yale University

There is no single interest rate for any economy; rather, there is an interdependent structure of interest rates. The interest rate that a borrower has to pay depends on a myriad of factors. In this chapter, we describe these factors. We begin with a discussion of the *base interest rate:* The interest rate on U.S. government securities. Next we explain the factors that affect the yield spread or risk premium for non-Treasury securities. Finally, we focus on one particular factor that affects the interest rate demanded in an economy for a particular security: maturity. The relationship between yield and maturity (or term) is called the *term structure of interest rates,* and this relationship is critical in the valuation of securities. Determinants of the *general* level of interest rates in the economy will not be discussed.

## THE BASE INTEREST RATE

The securities issued by the U.S. Department of the Treasury are backed by the full faith and credit of the U.S. government. Consequently, market participants throughout the world view them as having no credit risk. Therefore interest rates on Treasury securities are the benchmark interest rates throughout the U.S. economy, as well as in international capital markets. The large sizes of Treasury issues have contributed to making the Treasury market the most active and hence the most liquid market in the world.

The minimum interest rate or *base interest rate* that investors will demand for investing in a non-Treasury security is the yield offered on a comparable maturity for an on-the-run Treasury security. For example, if an investor wanted to purchase a 10-year U.S. bond on January 14, 2000, the minimum yield he would seek is 6.68%, the on-the-run U.S. Treasury yield reported in Exhibit 6–1. The base interest rate is also referred to as the *benchmark interest rate.*

**E X H I B I T   6–1**

Various Yield and Yield Spreads in the United States

---

**a. Yields for On-The-Run Treasuries on January 14, 2000***

| Maturity | Yield |
|----------|-------|
| 3 months | 5.41% |
| 6 months | 5.68 |
| 1-year | 6.11 |
| 2 years | 6.43 |
| 5 years | 6.58 |
| 10 years | 6.68 |
| 30 years | 6.69 |

**b. Average 90-Day Yield Spreads on Investment Grade Industrial Corporate Bonds by Rating and Maturity as of January 14, 2000 (In Basis Points)****

| Maturity | AAA | AA | A | BBB |
|----------|-----|-----|-----|-----|
| 2 years | 51 | 61 | 68 | 103 |
| 3 years | 58 | 66 | 80 | 107 |
| 5 years | 63 | 74 | 88 | 116 |
| 10 years | 85 | 93 | 121 | 148 |
| 30 years | 98 | 107 | 137 | 172 |

*Source: Lehman Brothers, *Relative Value Report*, January 18, 2000, T-4.

**Source: Lehman Brothers, *Relative Value Report*, January 18, 2000, T-9.

## RISK PREMIUM

Market participants describe interest rates on non-Treasury securities as trading at a spread to a particular on-the-run Treasury security. For example, if the yield on a 10-year non-Treasury security is 7.68% and the yield on a 10-year Treasury security is 6.68%, the spread is 100 basis points. This spread reflects the additional risks the investor faces by acquiring a security that is not issued by the U.S. government, and therefore can be called a *risk premium*. Thus, we can express the interest rate offered on a non-Treasury security as

Base interest rate + Spread

or equivalently,

Base interest rate + Risk premium

The factors that affect the spread include: (1) the type of issuer, (2) the issuer's perceived creditworthiness, (3) the term or maturity of the instrument, (4) provisions that grant either the issuer or the investor the option to do something, (5) the taxability of the interest received by investors, and (6) the expected liquidity of the issue.

## Types of Issuers

A key feature of a debt obligation is the nature of the issuer. In addition to the U.S. government, there are agencies of the U.S. government, municipal governments, corporations (domestic and foreign), and foreign governments that issue bonds.

The bond market is classified by the type of issuer. These are referred to as *market sectors*. The spread between the interest rate offered in two sectors of the bond market with the same maturity is referred to as an *intermarket-sector spread*.

Excluding the Treasury market sector, other market sectors have a wide range of issuers, each with different abilities to satisfy bond obligations. For example, within the corporate market sector, issuers are classified as utilities, transportations, industrials, and banks and finance companies. The spread between two issues within a market sector is called an *intramarket-sector spread*.

## Perceived Creditworthiness of Issuer

Default risk or credit risk refers to the risk that the issuer of a bond may be unable to make timely payment of principal or interest payments. Most market participants rely primarily on commercial rating companies to assess the default risk of an issuer. We discuss these rating companies in Chapter 11.

The spread between Treasury securities and non-Treasury securities that are identical in all respects except for quality is referred to as a *credit spread* or *quality spread*. Panel b of Exhibit 6–2 shows the average 90-day credit spread between U.S. Treasury securities and industrial corporate bond issues by maturity for the week of January 14, 2000.

## Term-to-Maturity

As we explained in Chapter 5, the price of a bond will fluctuate over its life as yields in the market change. As demonstrated in that chapter, the volatility of a bond's price is dependent on its maturity. With all other factors constant, the longer the maturity of a bond, the greater the price volatility resulting from a change in market yields.

The spread between any two maturity sectors of the market is called a *yield curve spread* or *maturity spread*. The relationship between the yields on comparable securities with different maturities, as mentioned earlier, is called the term structure of interest rates.

The term-to-maturity topic is very important, and we have devoted more time to this topic later in this chapter.

## Inclusion of Options

It is not uncommon for a bond issue to include a provision that gives the bond-holder or the issuer an option to take some action against the other party. An option that is included in a bond issue is referred to as an *embedded option.* We discussed the various types of embedded options in Chapter 1. The most common type of option in a bond issue is the call provision, which grants the issuer the right to retire the debt, fully or partially, before the scheduled maturity date. The inclusion of a call feature benefits issuers by allowing them to replace an old bond issue with a lower-interest-cost issue when interest rates in the market decline. In effect, a call provision allows the issuer to alter the maturity of a bond. The exercise of a call provision is disadvantageous to the bondholder because the bondholder must reinvest the proceeds received at a lower interest rate.

The presence of an embedded option affects both the spread of an issue relative to a Treasury security and the spread relative to otherwise comparable issues that do not have an embedded option. In general, market participants will require a larger spread to a comparable Treasury security for an issue with an embedded option that is favorable to the issuer (such as a call option) than for an issue without such an option. In contrast, market participants will require a smaller spread to a comparable Treasury security for an issue with an embedded option that is favorable to the investor (such as a put option or a conversion option). In fact, the interest rate on a bond with an option that is favorable to an investor may be less than that on a comparable Treasury security.

## Taxability of Interest

Unless exempted under the federal income tax code, interest income is taxable at the federal level. In addition to federal income taxes, there may be state and local taxes on interest income.

The federal tax code specifically exempts the interest income from qualified municipal bond issues. Because of this tax exemption, the yield on municipal bonds is less than on Treasuries with the same maturity. The difference in yield between tax-exempt securities and Treasury securities is typically measured not in basis points but in percentage terms. More specifically, it is measured as the percentage of the yield on a tax-exempt security relative to a comparable Treasury security.

The yield on a taxable bond issue after federal income taxes are paid is equal to

$$\text{After-tax yield} = \text{Pretax yield} \times (1 - \text{Marginal tax rate})$$

For example, suppose a taxable bond issue offers a yield of 9% and is acquired by an investor facing a marginal tax rate of 39.6%. The after-tax yield would then be

$$\text{After-tax yield} = .09 \times (1 - 0.396) = 0.0544 = 5.44\%$$

Alternatively, we can determine the yield that must be offered on a taxable bond issue to give the same after-tax yield as a tax-exempt issue. This yield is called the *equivalent taxable yield* and is determined as follows:

$$\text{Equivalent taxable yield} = \frac{\text{Tax-exempt yield}}{(1 - \text{Marginal tax rate})}$$

For example, consider an investor facing a 39.6% marginal tax rate who purchases a tax-exempt issue with a yield of 5.44%. The equivalent taxable yield is then

$$\text{Equivalent taxable yield} = \frac{0.0544}{(1 - 0.396)} = .09 = 9\%$$

Notice that the lower the marginal tax rate, the lower the equivalent taxable yield. For example, in our previous example, if the marginal tax rate is 25% rather than 39.6%, the equivalent taxable yield would be 7.25% rather than 9%, as shown below:

$$\text{Equivalent taxable yield} = \frac{0.0544}{(1 - 0.25)} = .0725 = 7.25\%$$

State and local governments may tax interest income on bond issues that are exempt from federal income taxes. Some municipalities exempt interest income from all municipal issues from taxation, others do not. Some states exempt interest income from bonds issued by municipalities within the state but tax the interest income from bonds issued by municipalities outside of the state. The implication is that two municipal securities of the same quality rating and the same maturity may trade at some spread because of the relative demand for bonds of municipalities in different states. For example, in a high-income-tax state such as New York, the demand for bonds of municipalities will drive down their yield relative to municipalities in a low-income-tax state such as Florida, holding all credit issues aside.

Municipalities are not permitted to tax the interest income from securities issued by the U.S. Treasury. Thus, part of the spread between Treasury securities and taxable non-Treasury securities of the same maturity reflects the value of the exemption from state and local taxes.

## Expected Liquidity of an Issue

Bonds trade with different degrees of liquidity. The greater the expected liquidity at which an issue will trade, the lower the yield that investors require. As noted earlier, Treasury securities are the most liquid securities in the world. The lower yield offered on Treasury securities relative to non-Treasury securities reflects the difference in liquidity as well as perceived credit risk. Even within the Treasury market, on-the-run issues have greater liquidity than off-the-run issues.

## THE TERM STRUCTURE OF INTEREST RATES

In future chapters, we will see the key role that the term structure of interest rates plays in the valuation of bonds. For this reason, we devote a good deal of space to this important topic.

## The Yield Curve

The graphical depiction of the relationship between the yield on the bonds of the same credit quality but different maturities is known as the *yield curve*. In the past, most market participants have constructed yield curves from the observations of prices and yields in the Treasury market. Two reasons account for this tendency. First, Treasury securities are free of default risk, and differences in creditworthiness do not affect yield estimates. Second, as the most active bond market, the Treasury market offers the fewest problems of illiquidity or infrequent trading. Exhibit 6–2 shows the shape of three hypothetical Treasury yield curves that have been observed in the United States, as well as other countries.

Exhibit 6–3 shows the bellwether yield curves for government bond issues for four countries (U.S., Germany, U.K., and Japan) for four different maturities on January 13, 2000. Notice that as of January 17, 2000, all of the yield curves except that of the United Kingdom were upward sloping. The German and Japanese yield curves were steep relative to the U.S. yield curve. The U.K. yield curve was inverted.

From a practical viewpoint, as we explained earlier in this chapter, the key function of the Treasury yield curve is to serve as a benchmark for pricing bonds and setting yields in other sectors of the debt market, such as bank loans, mortgages, corporate debt, and international bonds. However, market participants are coming to realize that the traditionally constructed Treasury yield curve is an unsatisfactory measure of the relation between required yield and maturity. The key reason is that securities with the same maturity may actually carry different yields. As we will explain, this phenomenon reflects the impact of differences in the bonds' coupon rates. Hence, it is necessary to develop more accurate and reliable estimates of the Treasury yield curve. We will show the problems posed by traditional approaches to the Treasury yield curve and we will explain the

**EXHIBIT  6–2**

Four Hypothetical Yield Curves

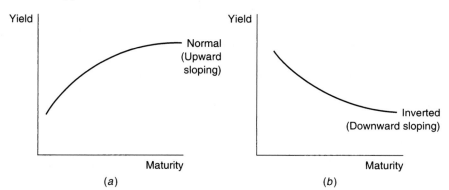

(a)                                                  (b)

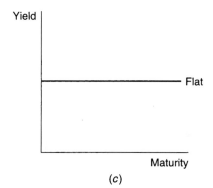

(c)

**EXHIBIT  6–3**

Bellwether Government Yield Curves for the United States, Germany, United Kingdom, and Japan on January 17, 2000

| Maturity | United States | Germany | United Kingdom | Japan |
|----------|---------------|---------|----------------|-------|
| 2 years  | 6.39%         | 4.27%   | 6.48%          | 0.35% |
| 5 years  | 6.52          | 4.93    | 6.28           | 1.00  |
| 10 years | 6.62          | 5.50    | 5.66           | 1.78  |
| 30 years | 6.65          | 6.10    | 4.59           | 2.27  |

Source: Lehman Brothers, *Relative Value Report,* January 18, 2000, Figure 1, REL-4.

proper approach to building a yield curve. The approach consists of identifying yields that apply to zero-coupon bonds and, therefore, eliminates the problem of nonuniqueness in the yield-maturity relationship.

## Using the Yield Curve to Price a Bond

The price of a bond is the present value of its cash flows. However, in our discussion of the pricing of a bond in Chapter 4, we assumed that one interest rate should be used to discount all the bond's cash flows. The appropriate interest rate is the yield on a Treasury security with the same maturity as the bond, plus an appropriate risk premium or spread.

However, there is a problem with using the Treasury yield curve to determine the appropriate yield at which to discount the cash flow of a bond. To illustrate this problem, consider two hypothetical five-year Treasury bonds, A and B. The difference between these two Treasury bonds is the coupon rate, which is 12% for A and 3% for B. The cash flow for these two bonds per $100 of par value for the 10 six-month periods to maturity would be as follows:

| Period | Cash Flow for A | Cash Flow for B |
|--------|-----------------|-----------------|
| 1–9    | $  6.00         | $  1.50         |
| 10     | 106.00          | 101.50          |

Because of the different cash flow patterns, it is not appropriate to use the same interest rate to discount all cash flows. Instead, each cash flow should be discounted at a unique interest rate that is appropriate for the time period in which the cash flow will be received. But what should be the interest rate for each period?

The correct way to think about bonds A and B is not as bonds but as packages of cash flows. More specifically, they are packages of zero-coupon instruments. Thus, the interest earned is the difference between the maturity value and the price paid. For example, bond A can be viewed as 10 zero-coupon instruments: One with a maturity value of $6 maturing six months from now, a second with a maturity value of $6 maturing one year from now, a third with a maturity value of $6 maturing 1.5 years from now, and so on. The final zero-coupon instrument matures 10 six-month periods from now, and has a maturity value of $106. Likewise, bond B can be viewed as 10 zero-coupon instruments: One with a maturity value of $1.50 maturing six months from now, one with a maturity value of $1.50 maturing one year from now, one with a maturity value of $1.50 maturing 1.5 years from now, and so on. The final zero-coupon instrument matures 10 six-month periods from now and has a maturity value of $101.50. Obviously, in the case of each coupon bond, the value or price of the bond is equal to the total value of its component zero-coupon instruments.

In general, any bond can be viewed as a package of zero-coupon instruments. That is, each zero-coupon instrument in the package has a maturity equal to its coupon payment date or, in the case of the principal, the maturity date. The value of the bond should equal the value of all the component zero-coupon instruments. If this does not hold, a market participant may generate riskless profits by stripping the security and creating stripped securities.

To determine the value of each zero-coupon instrument, it is necessary to know the yield on a zero-coupon Treasury with that same maturity. This yield is called the *spot rate,* and the graphical depiction of the relationship between the spot rate and its maturity is called the *spot-rate curve.* Because there are no zero-coupon Treasury debt issues with a maturity greater than one year, it is not possible to construct such a curve solely from observations of Treasury yields. Rather, it is necessary to derive this curve from theoretical considerations as applied to the yields of actual Treasury securities. Such a curve is called a *theoretical spot-rate curve.*

## Constructing the Theoretical Spot-Rate Curve

The theoretical spot-rate curve is constructed from the yield curve based on the observed yields of Treasury bills and Treasury coupon securities. The process of creating a theoretical spot-rate curve in this way is called *bootstrapping.*[1] To explain this process, we use the data for the hypothetical price, annualized yield (yield-to-maturity), and maturity of the 20 Treasury securities shown in Exhibit 6–4.

Throughout the analysis and illustrations to come, it is important to remember that the basic principle of bootstrapping is that the value of a Treasury coupon security should be equal to the value of the package of zero-coupon Treasury securities that duplicates the coupon bond's cash flow.

Consider the six-month Treasury bill in Exhibit 6–4. As explained in Chapter 10, a Treasury bill is a zero-coupon instrument. Therefore, its annualized yield of 8% is equal to the spot rate. Similarly, for the one-year Treasury bill, the cited yield of 8.3% is the one-year spot rate. Given these two spot rates, we can compute the spot rate for a theoretical 1.5-year zero-coupon Treasury. The price of a theoretical 1.5-year Treasury should equal the present value of three cash flows from an actual 1.5-year coupon Treasury, where the yield used

---

1. In practice, the securities used to construct the theoretical spot-rate curve are the most recently auctioned Treasury securities of a given maturity. Such issues are referred to as the *on-the-run Treasury issues.* As we explain in Chapter 8, there are actual zero-coupon Treasury securities with a maturity greater than one year that are outstanding in the market. These securities are not issued by the U.S. Treasury but are created by market participants from actual coupon Treasury securities. It would seem logical that the observed yield on zero-coupon Treasury securities can be used to construct an actual spot-rate curve. However, there are problems with this approach. First, the liquidity of these securities is not as great as that of the coupon Treasury market. Second, there are maturity sectors of the zero-coupon Treasury market that attract specific investors who may be willing to trade yield in exchange for an attractive feature associated with that particular maturity sector, thereby distorting the term structure relationship.

**E X H I B I T    6–4**

Maturity and Yield-to-Maturity for 20 Hypothetical Treasury Securities

| Maturity | Coupon Rate | Yield-to-Maturity | Price |
|---|---|---|---|
| 0.50 years | 0.0000 | 0.0800 | $ 96.15 |
| 1.00 | 0.0000 | 0.0830 | 92.19 |
| 1.50 | 0.0850 | 0.0890 | 99.45 |
| 2.00 | 0.0900 | 0.0920 | 99.64 |
| 2.50 | 0.1100 | 0.0940 | 103.49 |
| 3.00 | 0.0950 | 0.0970 | 99.49 |
| 3.50 | 0.1000 | 0.1000 | 100.00 |
| 4.00 | 0.1000 | 0.1040 | 98.72 |
| 4.50 | 0.1150 | 0.1060 | 103.16 |
| 5.00 | 0.0875 | 0.1080 | 92.24 |
| 5.50 | 0.1050 | 0.1090 | 98.38 |
| 6.00 | 0.1100 | 0.1120 | 99.14 |
| 6.50 | 0.0850 | 0.1140 | 86.94 |
| 7.00 | 0.0825 | 0.1160 | 84.24 |
| 7.50 | 0.1100 | 0.1180 | 96.09 |
| 8.00 | 0.0650 | 0.1190 | 72.62 |
| 8.50 | 0.0875 | 0.1200 | 82.97 |
| 9.00 | 0.1300 | 0.1220 | 104.30 |
| 9.50 | 0.1150 | 0.1240 | 95.06 |
| 10.00 | 0.1250 | 0.1250 | 100.00 |

for discounting is the spot rate corresponding to the cash flow. Using $100 as par, the cash flow for the 1.5-year coupon Treasury is as follows:

$$0.5 \text{ years} \quad .085 \times \$100 \times .5 \quad\quad\quad = \$ \ \ 4.25$$

$$1.0 \text{ years} \quad .085 \times \$100 \times .5 \quad\quad\quad = \$ \ \ 4.25$$

$$1.5 \text{ years} \quad .085 \times \$100 \times .5 + 100 \quad = \$104.25$$

The present value of the cash flow is then

$$\frac{4.25}{(1 + z_1)^1} + \frac{4.25}{(1 + z_2)^2} + \frac{104.25}{(1 + z_3)^3}$$

where

$z_1$ = One-half the annualized six-month theoretical spot rate
$z_2$ = One-half the one-year theoretical spot rate
$z_3$ = One-half the 1.5-year theoretical spot rate

Because the six-month spot rate and one-year spot rate are 8.0% and 8.3%, respectively, we know that

$$z_1 = .04 \quad \text{and} \quad z_2 = .0415.$$

We can compute the present value of the 1.5-year coupon Treasury security as

$$\frac{4.25}{(1.0400)^1} + \frac{4.25}{(1.0415)^2} + \frac{104.25}{(1 + z_3)^3}$$

Because the price of the 1.5-year coupon Treasury security (from Exhibit 6–4) is $99.45, the following relationship must hold:

$$99.45 = \frac{4.25}{(1.0400)^1} + \frac{4.25}{(1.0415)^2} + \frac{104.25}{(1 + z_3)^3}$$

We can solve for the theoretical 1.5-year spot rate as follows:

$$99.45 = 4.08654 + 3.91805 + \frac{104.25}{(1 + z_3)^3}$$

$$91.44541 = \frac{104.25}{(1 + z_3)^3}$$

$$(1 + z_3)^3 = 1.140024$$

$$z_3 = .04465$$

Doubling this yield, we obtain the bond-equivalent yield of .0893 or 8.93%, which is the theoretical 1.5-year spot rate. That rate is the rate that the market would apply to a 1.5-year zero-coupon Treasury security, if such a security existed.

Given the theoretical 1.5-year spot rate, we can obtain the theoretical two-year spot rate. The cash flow for the two-year coupon Treasury in Exhibit 6–4 is

| | | |
|---|---|---|
| 0.5 years | $.090 \times \$100 \times .5$ | $= \$ \ 4.50$ |
| 1.0 years | $.090 \times \$100 \times .5$ | $= \$ \ 4.50$ |
| 1.5 years | $.090 \times \$100 \times .5$ | $= \$ \ 4.50$ |
| 2.0 years | $.090 \times \$100 \times .5 + 100$ | $= \$104.50$ |

The present value of the cash flow is then

$$\frac{4.50}{(1 + z_1)^1} + \frac{4.50}{(1 + z_2)^2} + \frac{4.50}{(1 + z_3)^3} + \frac{104.50}{(1 + z_4)^4}$$

where

$z_4$ = One-half the two-year theoretical spot rate

Because the six-month spot rate, one-year spot rate, and 1.5-year spot rate are 8.0%, 8.3%, and 8.93%, respectively, then

$$z_1 = .04 \quad z_2 = .0415 \quad \text{and} \quad z_3 = .04465$$

Therefore, the present value of the two-year coupon Treasury security is

$$\frac{4.50}{(1.0400)^1} + \frac{4.50}{(1.0415)^2} + \frac{4.50}{(1.04465)^3} + \frac{104.50}{(1 + z_4)^4}$$

Because the price of the two-year coupon Treasury security is \$99.64, the following relationship must hold:

$$99.64 = \frac{4.50}{(1.0400)^1} + \frac{4.50}{(1.0415)^2} + \frac{4.50}{(1.04465)^3} + \frac{104.50}{(1 + z_4)^4}$$

We can solve for the theoretical two-year spot rate as follows:

$$99.64 = 4.32692 + 4.14853 + 3.94730 + \frac{104.50}{(1 + z_4)^4}$$

$$87.21725 = \frac{104.50}{(1 + z_4)^4}$$

$$(1 + z_4)^4 = 1.198158$$

$$z_4 = .046235$$

Doubling this yield, we obtain the theoretical two-year spot rate bond-equivalent yield of 9.247%.

One can follow this approach sequentially to derive the theoretical 2.5-year spot rate from the calculated values of $z_1$, $z_2$, $z_3$, and $z_4$ (the six-month, one-year, 1.5-year, and two-year rates), and the price and coupon of the bond with a maturity of 2.5 years. Further, one could derive theoretical spot rates for the remaining 15 half-yearly rates. The spot rates thus obtained are shown in Exhibit 6–5. They represent the term structure of interest rates for maturities up to ten years, at the particular time to which the bond price quotations refer.

## Why Treasuries Must Be Priced Based on Spot Rates

Financial theory tells us that the theoretical price of a Treasury security should be equal to the present value of the cash flows where each cash flow is discounted at the appropriate theoretical spot rate. What we did not do, however, is demonstrate the economic force that ensures that the actual market price of a Treasury security does not depart significantly from its theoretical price.

To demonstrate this, we will use the 20 hypothetical Treasury securities introduced in Exhibit 6–4. The longest maturity bond given in that exhibit is

**EXHIBIT  6–5**

Theoretical Spot Rates

| Maturity | Yield-to-Maturity | Theoretical Spot Rate |
|---|---|---|
| 0.50 years | 0.0800 | 0.08000 |
| 1.00 | 0.0830 | 0.08300 |
| 1.50 | 0.0890 | 0.08930 |
| 2.00 | 0.0920 | 0.09247 |
| 2.50 | 0.0940 | 0.09468 |
| 3.00 | 0.0970 | 0.09787 |
| 3.50 | 0.1000 | 0.10129 |
| 4.00 | 0.1040 | 0.10592 |
| 4.50 | 0.1060 | 0.10850 |
| 5.00 | 0.1080 | 0.11021 |
| 5.50 | 0.1090 | 0.11175 |
| 6.00 | 0.1120 | 0.11584 |
| 6.50 | 0.1140 | 0.11744 |
| 7.00 | 0.1160 | 0.11991 |
| 7.50 | 0.1180 | 0.12405 |
| 8.00 | 0.1190 | 0.12278 |
| 8.50 | 0.1200 | 0.12546 |
| 9.00 | 0.1220 | 0.13152 |
| 9.50 | 0.1240 | 0.13377 |
| 10.00 | 0.1250 | 0.13623 |

the 10-year, 12.5% coupon bond selling at par with a yield-to-maturity of 12.5%. Suppose that a government dealer buys the issue at par and strips it, expecting to sell the zero-coupon Treasury securities at the yields-to-maturity indicated in Exhibit 6–5 for the corresponding maturity. (We will discuss stripping coupon Treasury securities in Chapter 8.)

Exhibit 6–6 shows the price that would be received for each zero-coupon Treasury security created. The price for each is the present value of the cash flow from the stripped Treasury discounted at the yield-to-maturity corresponding to the maturity of the security (from Exhibit 6–4). The total proceeds received from selling the zero-coupon Treasury securities created would be $104.1880 per $100 of par value of the original Treasury issue. This would result in an arbitrage profit of $4.1880 per $100 of the 10-year, 12.5% coupon Treasury security purchased.

To understand why the government dealer has the opportunity to realize this profit, look at the third column of Exhibit 6–6, which shows how much the government dealer paid for each cash flow by buying the entire package of cash flows (i.e., by buying the bond). For example, consider the $6.25 coupon pay-

**E X H I B I T   6–6**

Illustration of Arbitrage Profit from Coupon Stripping

| Maturity | Cash Flow | Present Value at 12.5% | Yield-to-Maturity | Present Value at Yield-to-Maturity |
|---|---|---|---|---|
| 0.50 years | $6.25 | 5.8824 | 0.0800 | $6.0096 |
| 1.00 | 6.25 | 5.5363 | 0.0830 | 5.7618 |
| 1.50 | 6.25 | 5.2107 | 0.0890 | 5.4847 |
| 2.00 | 6.25 | 4.9042 | 0.0920 | 5.2210 |
| 2.50 | 6.25 | 4.6157 | 0.0940 | 4.9676 |
| 3.00 | 6.25 | 4.3442 | 0.0970 | 4.7040 |
| 3.50 | 6.25 | 4.0886 | 0.1000 | 4.4418 |
| 4.00 | 6.25 | 3.8481 | 0.1040 | 4.1663 |
| 4.50 | 6.25 | 3.6218 | 0.1060 | 3.9267 |
| 5.00 | 6.25 | 3.4087 | 0.1080 | 3.6938 |
| 5.50 | 6.25 | 3.2082 | 0.1090 | 3.4863 |
| 6.00 | 6.25 | 3.0195 | 0.1120 | 3.2502 |
| 6.50 | 6.25 | 2.8419 | 0.1140 | 3.0402 |
| 7.00 | 6.25 | 2.6747 | 0.1160 | 2.8384 |
| 7.50 | 6.25 | 2.5174 | 0.1180 | 2.6451 |
| 8.00 | 6.25 | 2.3693 | 0.1190 | 2.4789 |
| 8.50 | 6.25 | 2.2299 | 0.1200 | 2.3210 |
| 9.00 | 6.25 | 2.0987 | 0.1220 | 2.1528 |
| 9.50 | 6.25 | 1.9753 | 0.1240 | 1.9930 |
| 10.00 | 106.25 | 31.6046 | 0.1250 | 31.6046 |
| Total | | 100.0000 | | $104.1880 |

ment in four years. By buying the 10-year Treasury bond priced to yield 12.5%, the dealer effectively pays a price based on 12.5% (6.25% semiannually) for that coupon payment, or, equivalently, $3.8481. Under the assumptions of this illustration, however, investors were willing to accept a lower yield-to-maturity, 10.4% (5.2% semiannually), to purchase a zero-coupon Treasury security with four years to maturity. Thus, investors were willing to pay $4.1663. On this one coupon payment, the government dealer realizes a profit equal to the difference between $4.1663 and $3.8481 (or $0.3182). From all the cash flows, the total profit is $4.1880. In this instance, coupon stripping shows that the sum of the parts is greater than the whole.

Suppose that, instead of the observed yield-to-maturity from Exhibit 6-4, the yields investors want are the same as the theoretical spot rates shown in

Exhibit 6-5. If we use these spot rates to discount the cash flows, the total proceeds from the sale of the zero-coupon Treasury securities would be equal to $100, making coupon stripping uneconomic.

In our illustration of coupon stripping, the price of the Treasury security is less than its theoretical price. Suppose instead that the price of the Treasury security is greater than its theoretical price. In such cases, investors can purchase a package of zero-coupon Treasury securities such that the cash flow of the package of securities replicates the cash flow of the mispriced coupon Treasury security. By doing so, the investor will realize a yield higher than the yield on the coupon Treasury security. For example, suppose that the market price of the 10-year Treasury security we used in our illustration (Exhibit 6–6) is $106. By buying the 20 zero-coupon bonds shown in Exhibit 6–6 with a maturity value identical to the cash flow shown in the second column, the investor is effectively purchasing a 10-year Treasury coupon security at a cost of $104.1880 instead of $106.

The process of coupon stripping and reconstituting prevents the actual spot-rate curve observed on zero-coupon Treasuries from departing significantly from the theoretical spot-rate curve. As more stripping and reconstituting occurs, forces of demand and supply will cause rates to return to their theoretical spot-rate levels. This is what has happened in the Treasury market.

## Forward Rates

Consider an investor who has a one-year investment horizon and is faced with the following two alternatives:

*Alternative 1:* Buy a one-year Treasury bill.

*Alternative 2:* Buy a six-month Treasury bill and when it matures in six months, buy another six-month Treasury bill.

The investor will be indifferent between the two alternatives if they produce the same return over the one-year investment horizon. The investor knows the spot rate on the six-month Treasury bill and the one-year Treasury bill. However, she does not know what yield will be available on a six-month Treasury bill that will be purchased six months from now. The yield on a six-month Treasury bill six months from now is called a *forward rate*. Given the spot rate for the six-month Treasury bill and the one-year bill, we wish to determine the forward rate on a six-month Treasury bill that will make the investor indifferent between the two alternatives. That rate can be readily determined.

At this point, however, we need to digress briefly and recall several present value and investment relationships. First, if you invested in a one-year Treasury bill, you would receive $100 at the end of one year. The price of the one-year Treasury bill would be

$$\frac{100}{(1 + z_2)^2}$$

where

$z_2$ is one-half the bond-equivalent yield of the theoretical one-year spot rate.

Second, suppose you purchased a six-month Treasury bill for $X$. At the end of six months, the value of this investment would be

$$X(1 + z_1)$$

where

$z_1$ is one-half the bond-equivalent yield of the theoretical six-month spot rate.

Let $f$ represent one-half the forward rate (expressed as a bond-equivalent yield) on a six-month Treasury bill available six months from now. If the investor were to renew her investment by purchasing that bill at that time, then the future dollars available at the end of one year from the $X$ investment would be

$$X(1 + z_1)(1 + f)$$

Third, it is easy to use that formula to find out how many $X$ the investor must invest in order to get $100 one year from now. This can be found as follows:

$$X(1 + z_1)(1 + f) = 100$$

which gives us

$$X = \frac{100}{(1 + z_1)(1 + f)}$$

We are now prepared to return to the investor's choices and analyze what that situation says about forward rates. The investor will be indifferent between the two alternatives confronting her if she makes the same dollar investment and receives $100 from both alternatives at the end of one year. That is, the investor will be indifferent if

$$\frac{100}{(1 + z_2)^2} = \frac{100}{(1 + z_1)(1 + f)}$$

Solving for $f$, we get

$$f = \frac{(1 + z_2)^2}{(1 + z_1)^1} - 1$$

Doubling $f$ gives the bond-equivalent yield for the six-month forward rate six months from now.

We can illustrate the use of this formula with the theoretical spot rates shown in Exhibit 6–5. From that exhibit, we know that

Six-month bill spot rate = .080   so   $z_1$ = .0400

One-year bill spot rate = .083   so   $z_2$ = .0415

Substituting into the formula, we have

$$f = \frac{(1.0415)^2}{1.0400} - 1$$

$$= .043$$

Therefore, the forward rate on a six-month Treasury security, quoted on a bond-equivalent basis, is 8.6% (.043 × 2). Let's confirm our results. The price of a one-year Treasury bill with a $100 maturity value is

$$\frac{100}{(1.0415)^2} = 92.19$$

If $92.19 is invested for six months at the six-month spot rate of 8%, the amount at the end of six months would be

$$92.19 \ (1.0400) = 95.8776$$

If $95.8776 is reinvested for another six months in a six-month Treasury offering 4.3% for six months (8.6% annually), the amount at the end of one year would be

$$95.8776(1.043) = 100$$

Both alternatives will have the same $100 payoff if the six-month Treasury bill yield six months from now is 4.3% (8.6% on a bond-equivalent basis). This means that, if an investor is guaranteed a 4.3% yield (8.6% bond-equivalent basis) on a six-month Treasury bill six months from now, she will be indifferent between the two alternatives.

We used the theoretical spot rates to compute the forward rate. The resulting forward rate is also called the *implied forward rate.*

We can take this sort of analysis much further. It is not necessary to limit ourselves to implied forward rates six months from now. The yield curve can be used to calculate the implied forward rate for any time in the future for any investment horizon. For example, the following can be calculated:

• The two-year implied forward rate five years from now

• The six-year implied forward rate two years from now

• The seven-year implied forward rate three years from now

# Relationship between Spot Rates and Short-Term Forward Rates

Suppose an investor purchases a five-year zero-coupon Treasury security for $58.42 with a maturity value of $100. He could instead buy a six-month Treasury bill and reinvest the proceeds every six months for five years. The number of dollars that will be realized depends on the six-month forward rates. Suppose that the investor can actually reinvest the proceeds maturing every six months at the implied six-month forward rates. Let's see how many dollars would accumulate at the end of five years. The implied six-month forward rates were calculated for the yield curve given in Exhibit 6–5. Letting $f_t$ denote the six-month forward rate beginning $t$ six-month periods from now, the semiannual implied forward rates using the spot rates shown in that exhibit are as follows:

$$f_1 = .043000 \quad f_2 = .050980 \quad f_3 = .051005 \quad f_4 = .051770$$

$$f_5 = .056945 \quad f_6 = .060965 \quad f_7 = .069310 \quad f_8 = .064625$$

$$f_9 = .062830$$

If he invests the $58.48 at the six-month spot rate of 4% (8% on a bond-equivalent basis) and reinvests at the above forward rates, the number of dollars accumulated at the end of five years would be

$$\$58.48(1.04)(1.043)(1.05098)(1.051005)(1.05177)(1.056945) \times$$
$$(1.060965)(1.069310)(1.064625)(1.06283) = \$100$$

Therefore, we see that if the implied forward rates are realized, the $58.48 investment will produce the same number of dollars as an investment in a five-year zero-coupon Treasury security at the five-year spot rate. From this illustration, we can see that the five-year spot rate is related to the current six-month spot rate and the implied six-month forward rates.

In general, the relationship between a $t$-period spot rate, the current six-month spot rate, and the implied six-month forward rates is as follows:

$$z_t = [(1 + z_1)(1 + f_1)(1 + f_2)(1 + f_3) \ldots (1 + f_{t-1})]^{1/t} - 1$$

Why should an investor care about forward rates? There are actually very good reasons for doing so. Knowledge of the forward rates implied in the current long-term rate is relevant in formulating an investment policy. In addition, forward rates are key inputs into the valuation of bonds with embedded options.

For example, suppose an investor wants to invest for one year (two six-month periods); the current six-month or short rate $(z_1)$ is 7%, and the one-year (two-period) rate $(z_2)$ is 6%. Using the formulas we have developed, the investor finds that by buying a two-period security, she is effectively making a forward contract to lend money six months from now at the rate of 5% for six months. If the investor believes that the second-period rate will turn out to be higher than 5%, it will be to her advantage to lend initially on a one-period contract, then at the end of the first period to reinvest interest and principal in the one-period contract available for the second period.

## Determinants of the Shape of the Term Structure

If we plot the term structure—the yield-to-maturity, or the spot rate, at successive maturities against maturity—what will it look like? Exhibit 6–2 shows three shapes that have appeared with some frequency over time. Panel (a) shows an upward-sloping yield curve; that is, yield rises steadily as maturity increases. This shape is commonly referred to as a *normal* or *upward-sloping yield curve.* Panel (*b*) shows a *downward-sloping* or *inverted yield curve,* where yields decline as maturity increases. Finally, panel (*c*) shows a *flat yield curve.*

Two major theories have evolved to account for these shapes: the *expectations theory* and the *market segmentation theory.*

There are three forms of the expectations theory: the *pure expectations theory,* the *liquidity theory,* and the *preferred habitat theory.* All share a hypothesis about the behavior of short-term forward rates and also assume that the forward rates in current long-term bonds are closely related to the market's expectations about future short-term rates. These three theories differ, however, on whether other factors also affect forward rates, and how. The pure expectations theory postulates that no systematic factors other than expected future short-term rates affect forward rates; the liquidity theory and the preferred habitat theory assert that there are other factors. Accordingly, the last two forms of the expectations theory are sometimes referred to as *biased expectations theories.*

### The Pure Expectations Theory

According to the pure expectations theory, the forward rates exclusively represent expected future rates. Thus, the entire term structure at a given time reflects the market's current expectations of future short-term rates. Under this view, a rising term structure, as shown in panel (*a*) of Exhibit 6–2, must indicate that the market expects short-term rates to rise throughout the relevant future. Similarly, a flat term structure reflects an expectation that future short-term rates will be mostly constant, and a falling term structure must reflect an expectation that future short-term rates will decline steadily.

We can illustrate this theory by considering how an expectation of a rising short-term future rate would affect the behavior of various market participants to result in a rising yield curve. Assume an initially flat term structure, and suppose that economic news leads market participants to expect interest rates to rise.

• Market participants interested in a long-term investment would not want to buy long-term bonds because they would expect the yield structure to rise sooner or later, resulting in a price decline for the bonds and a capital loss on the long-term bonds purchased. Instead, they would want to invest in short-term debt obligations until the rise in yield had occurred, permitting them to reinvest their funds at the higher yield.

• Speculators expecting rising rates would anticipate a decline in the price of long-term bonds and therefore would want to sell any long-term bonds they own and possibly to "short-sell" some they do not now own. (Should interest rates rise as expected, the price of longer-term bonds will fall. Because the speculator sold these bonds short and can then purchase them at a lower price to cover the short sale, a profit will be earned.) The proceeds received from the selling of long-term debt issues or the shorting of longer-term bonds will be invested in short-term debt obligations.

• Borrowers wishing to acquire long-term funds would be pulled toward borrowing now, in the long end of the market, by the expectation that borrowing at a later time would be more expensive.

All these responses would tend either to lower the net demand for, or to increase the supply of, long-maturity bonds, and two responses would increase demand for short-term debt obligations. This would require a rise in long-term yields in relation to short-term yields; that is, these actions by investors, speculators, and borrowers would tilt the term structure upward until it is consistent with expectations of higher future interest rates. By analogous reasoning, an unexpected event leading to the expectation of lower future rates will result in a downward-sloping yield curve.

Unfortunately, the pure expectations theory suffers from one serious shortcoming. It does not account for the risks inherent in investing in bonds and like instruments. If forward rates were perfect predictors of future interest rates, then the future prices of bonds would be known with certainty. The return over any investment period would be certain and independent of the maturity of the instrument initially acquired and of the time at which the investor needed to liquidate the instrument. However, with uncertainty about future interest rates and hence about future prices of bonds, these instruments become risky investments in the sense that the return over some investment horizon is unknown.

There are two risks that cause uncertainty about the return over some investment horizon. The first is the uncertainty about the price of the bond at the end of the investment horizon. For example, an investor who plans to invest for five years might consider the following three investment alternatives: (1) invest in a five-year bond and hold it for five years, (2) invest in a 12-year bond and sell it at the end of five years, and (3) invest in a 30-year bond and sell it at the end of five years. The return that will be realized for the second and third alternatives is not known because the price of each long-term bond at the end of five years is not known. In the case of the 12-year bond, the price will depend on the yield on seven-year debt securities five years from now; and the price of the 30-year bond will depend on the yield on 25-year bonds five years from now. Because forward rates implied in the current term structure for a future seven-year bond and a future 25-year bond are not perfect predictors of the actual future rates, there is uncertainty about the price for both bonds five years from now. Thus, there is price risk: The risk that the price of the bond will be lower than currently expected at the end of the investment horizon. As explained in the previous chapter, an important feature of price risk is that it increases as the maturity of the bond increases.

The second risk involves the uncertainty about the rate at which the proceeds from a bond that matures during the investment horizon can be reinvested, and is known as reinvestment risk. For example, an investor who plans to invest for five years might consider the following three alternative investments: (1) invest in a five-year bond and hold it for five years, (2) invest in a six-month instrument and, when it matures, reinvest the proceeds in six-month instruments over the entire five-year investment horizon, and (3) invest in a two-year bond and, when it matures, reinvest the proceeds in a three-year bond. The risk in the second and third alternatives is that the return over the five-year investment horizon is unknown because rates at which the proceeds can be reinvested are unknown.

Several interpretations of the pure expectations theory have been put forth by economists. These interpretations are not exact equivalents, nor are they consistent with each other, in large part because they offer different treatments of price risk and reinvestment risk.[2]

The broadest interpretation of the pure expectations theory suggests that investors expect the return for any investment horizon to be the same, regardless of the maturity strategy selected.[3] For example, consider an investor who has a five-year investment horizon. According to this theory, it makes no difference if a five-year, 12-year, or 30-year bond is purchased and held for five years because the investor expects the return from all three bonds to be the same over five years. A major criticism of this very broad interpretation of the theory is that, because of price risk associated with investing in bonds with a maturity greater than the investment horizon, the expected returns from these three very different bond investments should differ in significant ways.[4]

A second interpretation, referred to as the *local expectations* form of the pure expectations theory, suggests that the return will be the same over a short-term investment horizon starting today. For example, if an investor has a six-month investment horizon, buying a five-year, 10-year or 20-year bond will produce the same six-month return. It has been demonstrated that the local

2. These formulations are summarized by John Cox, Jonathan Ingersoll, Jr., and Stephen Ross, "A Re-Examination of Traditional Hypotheses about the Term Structure of Interest Rates," *Journal of Finance,* September 1981, pp. 769–799.

3. F Lutz, "The Structure of Interest Rates," *Quarterly Journal of Economics,* 1940–41, pp. 36–63.

4. Cox, Ingersoll, and Ross, pp. 774–775.

expectations formulation, which is narrow in scope, is the only interpretation of the pure expectations theory that can be sustained in equilibrium.[5]

The third interpretation of the pure expectations theory suggests that the return an investor will realize by rolling over short-term bonds to some investment horizon will be the same as holding a zero-coupon bond with a maturity that is the same as that investment horizon. (A zero-coupon bond has no reinvestment risk, so that future interest rates over the investment horizon do not affect the return.) This variant is called the *return-to-maturity expectations* interpretation. For example, let's once again assume that an investor has a five-year investment horizon. If he buys a five-year zero-coupon bond and holds it to maturity, his return is the difference between the maturity value and the price of the bond, all divided by the price of the bond. According to the return-to-maturity expectations, the same return will be realized by buying a six-month instrument and rolling it over for five years. At this time, the validity of this interpretation is subject to considerable doubt.

## The Liquidity Theory

We have explained that the drawback of the pure expectations theory is that it does not account for the risks associated with investing in bonds. Nonetheless, we have just shown that there is indeed risk in holding a long-term bond for one period, and that risk increases with the bond's maturity because maturity and price volatility are directly related.

Given this uncertainty, and the reasonable consideration that investors typically do not like uncertainty, some economists and financial analysts have suggested a different theory. This theory states that investors will hold longer-term maturities if they are offered a long-term rate higher than the average of expected future rates by a risk premium that is positively related to the term to maturity.[6] Put differently, the forward rates should reflect both interest rate expectations and a liquidity premium (which is really a risk premium), and the premium should be higher for longer maturities.

According to this theory, which is called the *liquidity theory of the term structure,* the implied forward rates will not be an unbiased estimate of the market's expectations of future interest rates because they include a liquidity premium. Thus, an upward-sloping yield curve may reflect expectations that future interest rates either will rise or will be flat (or even fall), but with a liquidity premium increasing fast enough with maturity so as to produce an upward-sloping yield curve.

## The Preferred Habitat Theory

Another theory, known as the preferred habitat theory, also adopts the view that the term structure reflects the expectation of the future path of interest rates as

---

5. Cox, Ingersoll, and Ross, p. 788.
6. John R. Hicks, *Value and Capital,* second ed. (London: Oxford University Press, 1946), pp. 141–145.

well as a risk premium. However, the preferred habitat theory rejects the assertion that the risk premium must rise uniformly with maturity.[7] Proponents of the preferred habitat theory say that the latter conclusion could be accepted if all investors intend to liquidate their investment at the shortest possible date and all borrowers are anxious to borrow long. This assumption can be rejected because institutions have holding periods dictated by the nature of their liabilities.

The preferred habitat theory asserts that, to the extent that the demand and supply of funds in a given maturity range do not match, some lenders and borrowers will be induced to shift to maturities showing the opposite imbalances. However, they will need to be compensated by an appropriate risk premium that reflects the extent of aversion to either price or reinvestment risk.

Thus, this theory proposes that the shape of the yield curve is determined by both expectations of future interest rates and a risk premium, positive or negative, to induce market participants to shift out of their preferred habitat. Clearly, according to this theory, yield curves sloping up, down, flat, or humped are all possible.

### Market Segmentation Theory

The market segmentation theory recognizes that investors have preferred habitats dictated by the nature of their liabilities. This theory also proposes that the major reason for the shape of the yield curve lies in asset/liability management constraints (either regulatory or self-imposed) and creditors (borrowers) restricting their lending (financing) to specific maturity sectors.[8] However, the market segmentation theory differs from the preferred habitat theory in that it assumes that neither investors nor borrowers are willing to shift from one maturity sector to another to take advantage of opportunities arising from differences between expectations and forward rates. Thus, for the segmentation theory, the shape of the yield curve is determined by supply of and demand for securities within each maturity sector.

## SUMMARY

In all economies, there is not just one interest rate but a structure of interest rates. The difference between the yields on any two bonds is called the yield spread. The base interest rate is the yield on a Treasury security. The yield spread between a non-Treasury security and a comparable on-the-run Treasury security is called a risk premium. The factors that affect the spread include (1) the type of issuer (e.g., agency, corporate, municipality), (2) the issuer's perceived creditworthiness as measured by the rating system of commercial rating companies,

---

7. Franco Modigliani and Richard Sutch, "Innovations in Interest Rate Policy," *American Economic Review,* May 1966, pp. 178–197.
8. This theory was suggested in J. M. Culbertson, "The Term Structure of Interest Rates," *Quarterly Journal of Economics,* November 1957, pp. 489–504.

(3) the term or maturity of the instrument, (4) the embedded options in a bond issue (e.g., call, put, or conversion provisions), (5) the taxability of interest income at the federal and municipal levels, and (6) the expected liquidity of the issue.

The relationship between yield and maturity is referred to as the term structure of interest rates. The graphical depiction of the relationship between the yield on bonds of the same credit quality but different maturities is known as the yield curve. Because the yield on Treasury securities is the base rate from which a non-government bond's yield often is benchmarked, the most commonly constructed yield curve is the Treasury yield curve.

There is a problem with using the Treasury yield curve to determine the one yield at which to discount all the cash payments of any bond. Each cash flow should be discounted at a unique interest rate that is applicable to the time period in which the cash flow is to be received. Because any bond can be viewed as a package of zero-coupon instruments, its value should equal the value of all the component zero-coupon instruments. The rate on a zero-coupon bond is called the spot rate. The theoretical spot-rate curve for Treasury securities can be estimated from the Treasury yield curve using a method known as bootstrapping.

Under certain assumptions, the market's expectation of future interest rates can be extrapolated from the theoretical Treasury spot-rate curve. The resulting forward rate is called the implied forward rate. Spot rates include the current six-month spot rate and the implied six-month forward rates.

Several theories have been proposed about the determinants of the term structure: the pure expectations theory, the biased expectations theories (the liquidity theory and the preferred habitat theory), and the market segmentation theory. All the expectation theories hypothesize that the one-period forward rates represent the market's expectations of future actual rates. The pure expectations theory asserts that these rates constitute the only factor. The biased expectations theories assert that there are other factors that determine the term structure.

## CHAPTER 7

# BOND MARKET INDEXES

**Frank K. Reilly, Ph.D., CFA**
Bernard J. Hank Professor of Finance
University of Notre Dame

**David J. Wright, Ph.D.**
Professor of Finance
University of Wisconsin–Parkside

The value of nonmunicipal bonds outstanding in the United States at over $7 trillion exceeds the combined value of equity in the United States, and a similar comparison holds for world capital markets where the value of fixed income securities exceeds the total value of equity. The only instance where this capital comparison does not hold is in some emerging market countries where the bond markets have not yet developed. Given the economic dominance of fixed income markets, it is difficult to understand why there has not been greater concern and analysis of bond market indexes. Part of the reason for a lack of analysis of bond market indexes is the relatively short history of these indexes. Specifically, in contrast to stock market indexes that have been in existence for over 100 years, total rate-of-return bond indexes were not developed until the 1970s, and those created were limited to U.S. investment-grade bonds. For example, indexes for U.S. high-yield bonds, where the market has grown to over $350 billion, were not established until the mid-1980s, which is also when international government bond indexes were initially created.

There are four parts to this chapter. The first considers the major uses for bond market indexes. The second is concerned with the difficulty of building and maintaining a bond market index compared to the requirements for a stock market index. The third section contains a description of the indexes available in three major categories. Finally, we present the risk/return characteristics of the alternative bond market sectors and examine the correlations among the alternative indexes.

## USES OF BOND INDEXES

An analysis of bond market indexes is important and timely for several reasons. First, the bond portfolios of both pension funds and individuals have grown substantially in recent years; sales of fixed income mutual funds have exceeded equity mutual fund sales in a number of years. With the increase in the number and size of bond portfolios, investors and portfolio managers have increasingly come to rely on bond indexes *as benchmarks for measuring performance* and, in the case of those managing on a performance-fee basis, determining compensation. There are numerous indexes of differing construction that purport to measure the aggregate bond market and the major sectors of the market (government, corporate, and mortgages). An obvious concern is the choice of an appropriate index that will provide an accurate benchmark of bond market behavior.

Second, benchmarks for *bond index funds* have become increasingly popular because those who monitor the performance of bond portfolios have discovered that, similar to equity managers, most bond portfolio managers have not been able to outperform the aggregate bond market. The amount of money invested in bond index funds grew from $3 billion in 1984 to over $200 billion in 1999. Given the total size and growth of the bond market, it is estimated that bond index funds could grow to $300 billion by the early 2000s.

The behavior of a particular index is critical to fixed income managers who attempt to replicate its performance in an index fund. Clearly, if all indexes move together, one would be indifferent to the choice of a particular index. We examine the return correlations between the various indexes and their risk/return characteristics. The analysis of long-term risk/return and correlations is important because index numbers may differ markedly over short periods of time, yet still exhibit similar long-run movements.

Portfolio managers of a bond index fund need to rebalance their assets to replicate the composition, maturity, and duration of the bond market. As shown in Reilly, Kao, and Wright, the composition of the bond market changed dramatically during the 1980s and there have been further changes during the 1990s.[1] It is possible to use the indexes to document the intertemporal changes in the makeup, maturity, and duration of the bond market that have influenced its risk and return characteristics.

Third, because of the size and importance of the bond market, there has been and will continue to be substantial fixed income research; the bond market indexes can provide accurate and timely measurement of the risk/return of these assets and the characteristics of the market, as noted above. For example, the time-series properties of equity index returns have been extensively examined, but these same tests were not applied to bond market returns. Our investigation indicated significant autocorrelation in bond market index returns, which were

---

1. Frank K. Reilly, Wenchi Kao, and David J. Wright, "Alternative Bond Market Indexes," *Financial Analysts Journal* 48, no. 3 (May/June 1992), pp. 44–58.

explained by examining the intertemporal behavior of U.S. Treasury securities with different maturities.[2]

## BUILDING AND MAINTAINING A BOND INDEX

To construct a *stock* market index, you have to select a sample of stocks, decide how to weight each component, and select a computational method. Once you have done this, adjustment for stock splits is typically automatic, and the pricing of the securities is fairly easy because most of the sample stocks are listed on a major stock exchange or actively traded in the OTC market. Mergers or significant changes in the performance of the firms in an index may necessitate a change in the index components. Other than such events, a stock could continue in an index for decades. (On average, the DJIA has about one change per year.)

In contrast, the creation, computation, and maintenance of a bond market index is more difficult for several reasons. First, *the universe of bonds is broader and more diverse than that of stocks.* It includes U.S. Treasury issues, agency series, municipal bonds, and a wide variety of corporate bonds spanning several segments (industrials, utilities, financials) and ranging from high-quality, AAA-rated bonds to bonds in default. Furthermore, within each group, issues differ by coupon and maturity as well as sinking funds and call features. As a result of this diversity, an aggregate bond market series can be subdivided into numerous subindexes; the Merrill Lynch aggregate series, for example, contains over 150 subindexes.

Second, *the universe of bonds changes constantly.* A firm will typically have one common stock issue outstanding, which may vary in size over time as the result of additional share sales or repurchases. In contrast, a major corporation will have several bond issues outstanding at any point in time, and these issues will change constantly because of maturities, sinking funds, and call features. This change in the universe of bonds outstanding also makes it more difficult to determine the market value of bonds outstanding, which is necessary when computing market-value-weighted rates of return.

Third, *the volatility of bond prices varies across issues and over time.* As indicated in Chapter 5 bond price volatility is influenced by the *duration* and *convexity* of the bond. These factors change constantly with the maturity, coupon, market yield, and call features of the bond. As maturity changes constantly and market yields become more volatile, which in turn affects embedded call options, it becomes more difficult to estimate the duration, convexity, and implied volatility of an individual bond issue or an aggregate bond series.

Finally, *there can be significant problems in the pricing of individual bond issues.* Individual bond issues are generally not as liquid as stocks. While most

---

2. Ibid.

stock issues are listed on exchanges or traded in an active OTC market with an electronic quotation system (NASDAQ), most bonds are traded on a fragmented OTC market without a consolidated quotation system. This problem is especially acute for corporate bonds. Several studies have examined this problem and noted the significant effects of using alternative sources for bond prices.[3]

## DESCRIPTION OF ALTERNATIVE BOND INDEXES

This section contains three subsections to reflect three major sectors of the global bond market: (1) U.S. investment grade bonds (including Treasury bonds), (2) U.S. high-yield bonds, and (3) international government bonds. In each case, we examine the overall constraints and computational procedures employed for the indexes in the three sectors.

Several characteristics are critical in judging or comparing bond indexes. First is the *sample of securities,* including the number of bonds as well as specific requirements for including the bonds in the sample, such as maturity and size of issue. It is also important to know what issues have been excluded from the index. Second is the *weighting of returns* for individual issues. Specifically, are the returns market-value weighted or equally weighted? Third, users of indexes need to consider the *quality of the price data* used in the computation. Are the bond prices used to compute rates of return based upon actual market transactions as they almost always are for stock indexes? Alternatively, are the prices provided by bond traders based upon recent actual transactions or are they the traders' current "best estimate"? Finally, are they based on "matrix pricing" that involves a computer model that estimates a price using current and historical relationships? Fourth, what *reinvestment assumption* does the rate of return calculation use for interim cash flows?

## U.S. Investment-Grade Bond Indexes

Four firms publish ongoing rate-of-return investment-grade bond market indexes. Three of them publish a comprehensive set of indexes that span the universe of U.S. bonds: Lehman Brothers (LB), Merrill Lynch (ML), and Salomon Smith Barney (SSB). The fourth firm, Ryan Labs (RL), concentrates on a long series for the government bond sector.

Exhibit 7–1 summarizes the major characteristics of the indexes created and maintained by these firms. Three of the four firms (LB, ML, and SSB)

---

3. In this regard, see Kenneth P. Nunn, Jr., Joanne Hill, and Thomas Schneeweis, "Corporate Bond Price Data Sources and Return/Risk Measurement," *Journal of Financial and Quantitative Analysis* 21, no. 2 (June 1986), pp. 197–208; and Oded Sarig and Arthur Warga, "Bond Price Data and Bond Market Liquidity," *Journal of Financial and Quantitative Analysis* 24, no. 3 (September 1989), pp. 367–378.

**EXHIBIT 7-1**

Summary of Bond-Market Indexes

| Name of Index | Number of Issues | Maturity | Size of Issues | Weighting | Pricing | Reinvestment Assumption | Subindexes Available |
|---|---|---|---|---|---|---|---|
| **U.S. Investment-Grade Bond Indexes** | | | | | | | |
| Lehman Brothers Aggregate | 5,000+ | Over 1 year | Over $100 million | Market value | Trader priced and model priced | No | Government, gov./corp., corporate, mortgage-backed, asset-backed |
| Merrill Lynch Composite | 5,000+ | Over 1 year | Over $50 million | Market value | Trader priced and model priced | In specific bonds | Government, gov./corp., corporate, mortgage |
| Ryan Treasury Composite | 118 | Over 1 year | All Treasury | Market value and equal | Market priced | In specific bonds | Treasury |
| Salomon Smith Barney Composite | 5,000+ | Over 1 year | Over $50 million | Market value | Trader priced | In one-month T-bill | Broad inv. grade, Treas.-agency, corporate, mortgage |
| **U.S. High-Yield Bond Indexes** | | | | | | | |
| First Boston | 423 | All maturities | Over $75 million | Market value | Trader priced | Yes | Composite and by rating |
| Lehman Brothers | 624 | Over 1 year | Over $100 million | Market value | Trader priced | No | Composite and by rating |
| Merrill Lynch | 735 | Over 1 year | Over $25 million | Market value | Trader priced | Yes | Composite and by rating |
| Salomon Smith Barney | 299 | Over 7 years | Over $50 million | Market value | Trader priced | Yes | Composite and by rating |
| **Global Government Bond Index (Initial Date of Index)** | | | | | | | |
| Lehman Brothers (January 1987) | 800 | Over 1 year | Over $200 million | Market value | Trader priced | Yes | Composite and 13 countries, local and U.S. dollars |
| Merrill Lynch (December 1985) | 9,736 | Over 1 year | Over $100 million | Market value | Trader priced | Yes | Composite and 9 countries, local and U.S. dollars |
| J. P. Morgan (12/31/85) | 445 | Over 1 year | Over $200 million | Market value | Trader priced | Yes in Index | Composite and 11 countries, local and U.S. dollars |
| Salomon Smith Barney (12/31/84) | 525 | Over 1 year | Over $250 million | Market value | Trader priced | Yes at local short-term rate | Composite and 14 countries, local and U.S. dollars |

Source: Frank K. Reilly, Wenchi Kao, and David J. Wright, "Alternative Bond Market Indexes," *Financial Analysts Journal* 48, no. 3 (May–June, 1992); Frank K. Reilly and David J. Wright, "An Analysis of High Yield Bond Benchmarks," *Journal of Fixed Income* 3, no. 4 (March 1994); Frank K. Reilly and David J. Wright, "Global Bond Markets: An Analysis of Performance and Benchmarks," mimeo (March 1994).

include numerous bonds (over 5,000), and there is substantial diversity in a sample that includes Treasuries, corporates, and mortgage securities. In contrast, the Ryan series is limited to Treasury bonds and has a sample size that has varied over time, based upon the Treasury issues outstanding (i.e., from 26 to 118 issues). All of the indexes require bonds to have maturities of at least one year. The required minimum size of an issue varies from $25 million (ML and LB) to $50 million (SSB); while the Treasury issues used by Ryan are substantially larger. All the series include only investment-grade bonds (rated BBB or better) and exclude convertible bonds and floating-rate bonds. The three broad-based indexes by LB, ML, and SSB also exclude government flower bonds, while Ryan has included these bonds in its index because flower bonds were a significant factor in the government bond market during the 1950s.

The two major alternatives for weighting are *relative market value* of the issues outstanding and *equal weighting* (also referred to as *unweighted*). The justification for market-value weighting is that it reflects the relative economic importance of the issue and is a logical weighting for an investor with no preferences regarding asset allocation. Although this theoretical argument is reasonable, it is important to recognize that in the real world it is difficult to keep track of the outstanding bonds, given the possibility of calls, sinking funds, and redemptions. Alternatively, equal weighting is reasonable for an investor who has no prior assumptions regarding the relative importance of individual issues. Also, equal weighting is consistent if one is assuming the random selection of issues. Finally, an equally weighted index is easier to compute and the results are unambiguous because it is not necessary to worry about outstanding market value due to calls and so on. The three large-sample indexes are value-weighted while Ryan Labs has created both a value-weighted and an equal-weighted series.

As noted, one of the major problems with computing returns for a bond index is that continuous transaction prices are not available for most bonds. Ryan can get recent transaction prices for its Treasury issues, while SSB gets all prices from its traders. As noted, these trader prices may be based on a recent actual transaction, the trader's current bid price, or what the trader would bid if he or she made a market in the bond. Both LB and ML use a combination of trader pricing and matrix prices based on a computer model. It is contended that most of the individual issues are priced by traders, so most of the value of each index is based on trader prices.

The indexes also treat interim cash flows differently. Both ML and Ryan assume that cash flows are immediately reinvested in the bonds that generated the cash flows. SSB assumes that flows are reinvested at the one-month T-bill rate, while LB does not assume any reinvestment of the funds. Obviously, immediate reinvestment in the same bond is the most aggressive assumption, while no reinvestment is the most conservative.

# U.S. High-Yield Bond Indexes

There are two notable points about high-yield (HY) bond indexes. First, they have a shorter history than the investment-grade bond indexes. This is not surprising because, as shown in several studies, this market only became a recognizable factor in 1977 and its major growth began in about 1982.[4] Therefore, the fact that HY bond indexes began in about 1984 is reasonable.

Second, earlier we noted the general difficulty of creating and maintaining bond indexes because of the constant changes in the size and characteristics of the sample and the significant pricing problems. The fact is, these difficulties are magnified when dealing with the HY bond market because it experiences larger sample changes due to defaults and more frequent redemptions. In addition, the illiquidity and bond pricing problems in the HY bond market are a quantum leap above those faced in the government and investment-grade corporate bond market.

As shown in Exhibit 7–1, four investment firms have created HY bond indexes (First Boston [FB], Lehman Brothers [LB], Merrill Lynch [ML], and Salomon Smith Barney [SSB]).[5] The investment firms have also created indexes for rating categories within the HY bond universe: BB, B, and CCC bonds.

The summary of characteristics in Exhibit 7–1 indicates that there are substantial differences among the HY bond indexes. This contrasts with relatively small differences in the characteristics of investment-grade bond indexes. The number of issues in the alternative HY bond indexes varies from 299 HY bonds in the Salomon Smith Barney (SSB) series to 735 bonds in the Merrill Lynch High Yield Master (ML) series. Some of the differences in sample size can be traced to the maturity-size constraints of the particular index. The large number of bonds in the ML series can be partially explained by its maturity guideline, which includes all HY bonds with a maturity over one year compared to a seven-year maturity requirement for the SSB series.

The minimum issue size is also important because ML has a minimum issue size requirement of $25 million compared to $50 million (SSB), $75 million (FB), and $100 million (LB). The only surprise is the large sample of bonds in the LB index (624) compared to the other HY bond indexes, which have much smaller size constraints than LB's $100 million.

---

4. Edward I. Altman, "Revisiting the High Yield Bond Market," *Financial Management* 21, no. 2 (Summer 1992), pp. 78–92; Rayner Cheung, Joseph C. Bencivenga, and Frank J. Fabozzi, "Original-Issue High Yield Bonds: Historical Return and Default Experiences 1977–1989," *Journal of Fixed Income* 2, no. 2 (September 1992), pp. 58–76; Martin S. Fridson, "The State of the High Yield Bond Market: Overshooting or Return to Normalcy?" *Journal of Applied Corporate Finance* 7, no. 1 (Spring 1994), pp. 85–97.

5. Drexel Burnham also created an index before its demise in 1989. Blume and Keim created an index but subsequently substituted an SSB series. There is also an index of high-yield bond mutual funds created by Lipper Analytical.

Notably, there are significant differences in how the alternative indexes handle defaulted issues. The treatment varies, from dropping issues the day they default (ML) to retaining them for an unlimited period subject to size and other constraints (FB, LB). In contrast, there is no difference in return weighting i.e., all use market-value weighting.

All the bonds in the HY bond indexes are trader priced except for ML, which uses matrix pricing for a few of its illiquid issues. The difficulty with trader pricing is that when bond issues do not trade, the price provided is a trader's best estimate of what the price "should be." Matrix pricing is likewise a problem because each issue has unique characteristics that may not be considered by the computer program. Obviously, this means that it is possible to get significantly different prices from alternative traders or matrix pricing programs.

All the indexes except LB assume the reinvestment of interim cash flows, but at different rates—that is, the individual bond rate, the average portfolio rate, or a T-bill rate. Finally, the average maturity and the duration for the indexes are consistent with the constraints on the index: FB, LB, and ML have one-year minimums and lower durations; while SSB, with a seven-year minimum is at the high end.

In summary, there are significant differences in the characteristics of the alternative HY bond indexes in terms of the samples and pricing. One would expect these differences to have a significant impact on the risk/return performance and the correlations among indexes.[6]

## Global Government Bond Market Indexes

Similar to the HY bond indexes, these global-based indexes are relatively new (beginning in 1985) because there was limited interest in these markets prior to the 1980s. The summary description in Exhibit 7–1 indicates numerous similarities among the indexes by the four investment firms (J. P. Morgan [JP], Lehman Brothers [LB], Merrill Lynch [ML], and Salomon Smith Barney [SSB]) with the exception of minimum size that varied from $100 million (ML) to $250 million (SSB). In turn, this issue size constraint had an impact on the sample sizes that ranged from JP at 445 to ML with over 9,000 bonds. Beyond this issue size and sample size difference, the indexes are the same regarding market-value weighting and trader pricing. All of them assume the reinvestment of cash flows with small differences in the reinvested security.

---

6. For a detailed analysis of the alternative HY bond indexes, see Frank K. Reilly and David J. Wright, "An Analysis of High-Yield Bond Benchmarks," *Journal of Fixed Income* 3, no. 4 (March 1994), pp. 6–25.

## RISK/RETURN CHARACTERISTICS

The presentation of the risk/return results is divided into two subsections. The first subsection presents and discusses the results for the U.S. indexes, including government and investment-grade bonds as well as HY bonds. The second subsection provides a similar presentation for global bond indexes, including both domestic and U.S. dollar returns.

## U.S. Investment-Grade and HY Bonds

The arithmetic and geometric average annual rates of return and risk measures are contained in Exhibit 7–2 for the period beginning in 1986, when the data are available for almost all the series except the Altman defaulted bond series, which began in 1987. We show the Lehman Brothers index for U.S. investment-grade bonds because it has been shown that all of the investment-grade bond series are very highly correlated.[7] The SB broad investment-grade (BIG) index is provided because of its popularity.

When viewing the results in Exhibit 7–2 and Exhibit 7–3, one is struck by two factors. The first is the generally high level of mean returns over this 13-year period wherein the investment-grade bonds experienced average annual returns of approximately 10% and the HY bonds attained returns of almost 12%.

The second observation is that the relationship between return and risk (measured as the annualized standard deviation of returns) was generally consistent with expectations. The investment-grade bond indexes typically had lower returns and risk, while the HY bond indexes had higher returns and risk measures. The major deviations were the very high-risk segments (CCC rated bonds and defaulted bonds), which experienced returns about in line with HY debt, but risk substantially above all other assets.[8] The BB rated bonds experienced abnormally positive results because they experienced returns similar to other HY bonds but experienced risk similar to investment-grade debt.

## Global Government Bonds

These results will be considered in two parts, involving results in local currency and in U.S. dollars. The results in Exhibits 7–4 show significant consistency between the risk and returns in local currency for the alternative countries. Germany experienced the lowest return and risk, while the U.K. had a much higher rate of return (12% versus about 7.5%) but also experienced higher risk (almost

---

7. Reilly, Kao, and Wright, *Op cit.*
8. For a detailed analysis of defaulted debt securities, see Frank K. Reilly, David J. Wright and Edward I. Altman, "Including Defaulted Debt in the Capital Markets Asset Spectrum," *Journal of Fixed Income* 8, no. 3 (December 1998): 33–48.

## EXHIBIT 7-2

Rates of Return, Risk, and Annual Ranges for U.S. and Global Bond Index (1986–1998)

| | Geometric Mean Annual Return | Arithmetic Mean Annual Return | Annualized Standard Deviation of Monthly Returns | Coefficient of Variation* | Minimum Annual Return | Maximum Annual Return |
|---|---|---|---|---|---|---|
| **U.S. Bond Index** | | | | | | |
| Lehman Bros. Govt/Corp | 9.11 | 9.28 | 4.77 | 0.51 | -3.51 | 19.24 |
| Lehman Bros. Government | 8.91 | 9.07 | 4.75 | 0.52 | -3.37 | 18.34 |
| Lehman Bros. Corporate | 9.73 | 9.94 | 5.05 | 0.51 | -3.93 | 22.25 |
| Lehman Bros. Mortgage | 9.04 | 9.16 | 3.91 | 0.43 | -1.61 | 16.80 |
| Lehman Bros. Aggregate | 9.08 | 9.23 | 4.46 | 0.48 | -2.92 | 18.47 |
| Salomon Smith Barney Broad Invest. Grade | 9.10 | 9.25 | 4.51 | 0.49 | -2.85 | 18.55 |
| Merrill Lynch High Yield Master (Composite) | 11.15 | 11.58 | 5.37 | 0.46 | -4.34 | 34.58 |
| Lehman Bros. High Yield BB Grade | 11.49 | 11.77 | 4.93 | 0.42 | -0.39 | 25.03 |
| Lehman Bros. High Yield B Grade | 10.69 | 11.32 | 7.04 | 0.62 | -8.62 | 43.28 |
| Lehman Bros. High Yield CCC Grade | 8.67 | 11.16 | 12.05 | 1.08 | -22.64 | 83.16 |
| Altman Default Index ('87–'98) | 6.87 | 9.21 | 14.07 | 1.53 | -26.91 | 43.10 |
| **Merrill Lynch Global Bond Indexes in $U.S.** | | | | | | |
| ML Global with U.S. | 10.37 | 10.58 | 6.71 | 0.63 | 1.69 | 22.96 |
| ML Global without U.S. | 11.92 | 12.54 | 10.91 | 0.87 | -4.12 | 35.93 |
| Canada | 10.14 | 10.53 | 8.80 | 0.84 | -9.77 | 23.68 |
| France | 13.25 | 13.83 | 11.19 | 0.81 | -6.83 | 33.83 |
| Germany | 10.86 | 11.66 | 12.08 | 1.04 | -9.04 | 37.52 |
| Japan | 11.23 | 12.33 | 14.80 | 1.20 | -14.21 | 40.05 |
| U.K. | 13.44 | 14.23 | 13.64 | 0.96 | -3.76 | 46.31 |
| U.S. | 8.91 | 9.08 | 4.87 | 0.54 | -3.35 | 18.45 |
| **Merrill Lynch Global Bond Indexes in Local Currency** | | | | | | |
| Canada | 10.94 | 11.13 | 6.14 | 0.55 | -4.33 | 21.28 |
| France | 10.70 | 10.88 | 4.29 | 0.39 | -4.37 | 20.21 |
| Germany | 7.65 | 7.76 | 3.06 | 0.39 | -1.26 | 16.03 |
| Japan | 6.39 | 6.52 | 4.86 | 0.75 | 2.92 | 13.45 |
| U.K. | 12.22 | 12.45 | 6.88 | 0.55 | -5.65 | 21.20 |

**EXHIBIT 7–3**

Geometric Mean Return versus the Standard Deviation of U.S. Bond Index Returns (1986–1998)

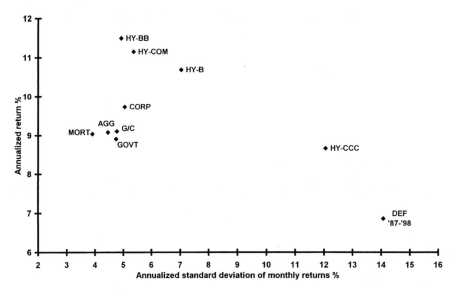

**EXHIBIT 7–4**

Geometric Mean Return versus the Standard Deviation of Country Bond Index Returns in Local Currency (1986–1998)

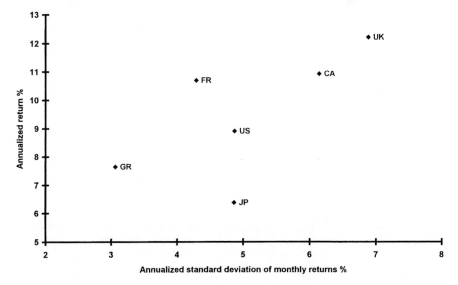

7% for the U.K. versus 3% for Germany). The only country that deviated from
the main security market line was Japan, which experienced mid-range risk but
a very low return (less than 5%).

The return/risk results in U.S. dollars are contained in Exhibit 7–5. The
graph in Exhibit 7–5 makes it clear that the results change substantially with
the conversion to U.S. dollars. Specifically, the U.S. is clearly the low risk/
return market, followed by Canada, while the other four countries (France, Germany, Japan, and the U.K.) all experienced much higher returns (9 to 10% for
the U.S. and Canada versus 11 to 13% for the four countries) and larger risk (5
to 9% for U.S. and Canada versus 11 to 15% for the others). France had the
best risk-adjusted returns during this time period.

In addition to the individual countries, there is a global index with and
without the U.S. Notably, both of these indexes are equal to or above the average
line, which is probably because of the reduced risk due to global diversification.

## CORRELATION RELATIONSHIPS

The correlations will likewise be presented in two parts: U.S. bond market results
and global bond market results.

## E X H I B I T   7–5

Geometric Mean Return versus the Standard Deviation of Country Bond
Index Returns in U.S. Dollars (1986–1998)

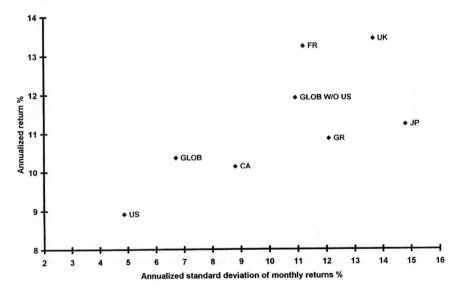

## U.S. Investment-Grade and HY Bonds

The correlation results in Exhibit 7–6 confirm some expectations about relationships among sectors of the bond market but also provide some unique results. The expected relationships are those among the five investment-grade bond indexes. Because all of these are investment grade, which implies that there is a small probability of default, the major factor influencing returns is interest-rate changes based upon the Treasury yield curve. Therefore, since they have a common determinant, they are very highly correlated. Specifically the correlations among the Lehman Bros. indexes range from about 0.90 to 0.99, with the results for the mortgage bond sector at the low end because of the impact of embedded call options on mortgage bonds. The correlations with the SSB BIG index is somewhat lower because of the higher average maturity of the bonds in this index.

The HY bond results show two distinct patterns. First, the correlations among the HY indexes are quite high, ranging from 0.84 to 0.96. Second, the correlations among investment-grade bonds and HY bonds have a greater range and are significantly lower, generally ranging from about 0.10 to 0.66. Not surprising, the highest correlations are between BB rated bonds and investment-grade bonds, while the lowest correlations (several insignificant) are between investment-grade bonds and CCC rated bonds.

The correlations with defaulted debt were unique. The correlations between defaulted debt and investment-grade debt are generally negative but not significant. In contrast, the correlations among defaulted debt and various HY bonds are substantially higher and generally exceed the correlations between B and CCC-rated debt and investment-grade debt.

## Global Government Bond Correlations

Again, the discussion is in two parts to consider the local currency and U.S. dollar results. Exhibit 7–7 contains correlations among returns in local currencies. The correlations of Canada with all non-U.S. countries indicate a similar relationship (about .40), while the U.S.-Canada correlation was about 0.70. In turn, France had fairly similar correlations with all the countries except a much higher correlation with Germany—its major trading partner in Europe. Japan had correlations with the European countries between 0.30 and 0.43 and only a mid-range correlations with the United States—about 0.38. This is even though Japan and the United States conduct significant trade.

Exhibit 7–8 contains correlations among returns in U.S. dollars. The results differ from local currency results as well as from normal expectations. Typically, correlations decline when one goes from local currency to U.S. currency because of the effect of random exchange-rate changes, which reduce the relationships. This is generally what happened for correlations among these

EXHIBIT 7-6

Correlation Coefficients of the U.S. Bond Index Monthly Returns (1986–1998)

| | LB Govt./Corp. | LB Govt. | LB Corp. | LB Mort. | SSB BIG. | ML HY Master | LB HY BB | LB HY B | LB HY CCC | Altman Default |
|---|---|---|---|---|---|---|---|---|---|---|
| LB Govt./Corp. | 1.000 | | | | | | | | | |
| LB Govt. | 0.996* | 1.000 | | | | | | | | |
| LB Corp. | 0.970* | 0.943* | 1.000 | | | | | | | |
| LB Mort. | 0.907* | 0.895* | 0.905* | 1.000 | | | | | | |
| SSB B.I.G. | 0.870* | 0.873* | 0.826* | 0.845* | 1.000 | | | | | |
| ML HY Master | 0.390* | 0.333* | 0.520* | 0.404* | 0.344* | 1.000 | | | | |
| LB HY BB | 0.543* | 0.491* | 0.656* | 0.530* | 0.455* | 0.882* | 1.000 | | | |
| LB HY B | 0.303* | 0.251* | 0.425* | 0.337* | 0.284* | 0.955* | 0.852* | 1.000 | | |
| LB HY CCC | 0.147 | 0.099 | 0.265* | 0.191* | 0.140 | 0.843* | 0.687* | 0.867* | 1.000 | |
| Altman Default ('87–'98) | −0.124 | −0.171* | −0.009 | −0.056 | −0.134 | 0.551* | 0.395* | 0.553* | 0.587* | 1.000 |

* Significant at the 5% level.

**EXHIBIT** 7-7

Correlation Coefficients Among Monthly Global Bond Index Returns in Local Currency (1986–1998)

| | Ryan U.S. | ML Canada | ML France | ML Germany | ML Japan | ML U.K. | ML Global w/o U.S. | ML Global with U.S. |
|---|---|---|---|---|---|---|---|---|
| Ryan U.S. | 1.000 | | | | | | | |
| ML Canada | 0.708 | 1.000 | | | | | | |
| ML France | 0.483 | 0.396 | 1.000 | | | | | |
| ML Germany | 0.485 | 0.423 | 0.745 | 1.000 | | | | |
| ML Japan | 0.379 | 0.327 | 0.294 | 0.434 | 1.000 | | | |
| ML U.K. | 0.488 | 0.503 | 0.557 | 0.621 | 0.377 | 1.000 | | |
| ML Global w/o U.S. | 0.301 | 0.249 | 0.182 | 0.350 | 0.491 | 0.328 | 1.000 | |
| ML Global with U.S. | 0.596 | 0.449 | 0.308 | 0.451 | 0.539 | 0.432 | 0.943 | 1.000 |

All of the correlation coefficients are significant at the 5% level.
The ML Global returns are expressed in U.S. dollars.

# EXHIBIT 7-8

Correlation Coefficients Among Monthly Global Bond Index Returns in U.S. Dollars (1986–1998)

| | Ryan U.S. | ML Canada | ML France | ML Germany | ML Japan | ML U.K. | ML Global w/o U.S. | ML Global with U.S. |
|---|---|---|---|---|---|---|---|---|
| Ryan U.S. | 1.000 | | | | | | | |
| ML Canada | 0.533* | 1.000 | | | | | | |
| ML France | 0.327* | 0.140 | 1.000 | | | | | |
| ML Germany | 0.277* | 0.123 | 0.949* | 1.000 | | | | |
| ML Japan | 0.186* | 0.102 | 0.616* | 0.640* | 1.000 | | | |
| ML U.K. | 0.341* | 0.291* | 0.633* | 0.625* | 0.515* | 1.000 | | |
| ML Global w/o U.S. | 0.301* | 0.216* | 0.816* | 0.834* | 0.928* | 0.732* | 1.000 | |
| ML Global with U.S. | 0.598* | 0.360* | 0.793* | 0.792* | 0.851* | 0.718* | 0.943* | 1.000 |

* Significant at the 5% level.

countries and the United States: there were big differences in the correlations with Canada, Germany and Japan but smaller changes with France and the U.K. In contrast, the correlations among the European countries and with Japan consistently experienced large *increases* when returns were in U.S. dollars—typically by over 0.20. For example, the correlations between France and Germany went from about 0.75 to about 0.95. This implies that during this period the exchange-rate correlations were quite high and became a cause for stronger return correlations. Notably, toward the end of the period, the EU currency was introduced.

## CONCLUSION

Bond market indexes are a relatively new but important factor to those who analyze bonds or manage bond portfolios. They have several significant uses, including acting as performance benchmarks, as benchmarks for investors who want to invest through bond index funds, and as a means to determine fixed-income asset risk/return characteristics and correlations as inputs into the asset-allocation decision. Clearly, although bond indexes are very difficult to create and maintain, they are worth the effort.

A brief analysis of the risk/return characteristics of alternative bond series indicated that most of the series had results in line with expectations. The outliers were the very risky securities (CCC bonds and defaulted bonds) and low-risk HY bonds (BB rated). The global bond results were heavily impacted by the currency effect. Local currency results were consistent except for Japan, which was below the market line. The U.S. dollar results were quite consistent in terms of risk and return, with almost all countries showing benefits from the weak dollar, especially France. The global index results were slightly above the aggregate line, apparently due to the benefits of global diversification.

The analysis of correlations for U.S. bond indexes confirmed prior studies that there is very high correlation among bond series within either the investment-grade or the HY bond sector (typically between 0.90 and 0.99). In contrast, there is significantly lower correlation between investment-grade and HY bonds. (The correlations were typically between 0.20 and 0.40.) Defaulted debt had no correlation with investment-grade debt but had fairly significant correlation with HY debt.

The correlations among the global indexes in local currencies typically showed fairly low relationships with other countries (about 0.40), except United States-Canada and France-Germany (about 0.70). The correlations changed when we considered returns in U.S. dollars. Specifically, all the correlations with the United States declined by about 0.20, while many of the correlations among non-U.S. countries increased by about 0.20 due to the weak U.S. dollar during this period, which affected these countries simultaneously.

Two final points. First, it is important to remember that the significance of many of the empirical results of risk/return and correlations are reduced because of the relatively short 13-year time period. Second, even though these results are not as powerful as one would want, the important point is that it is currently possible to do such analysis related to the bond market because there are a number of very well-constructed and diverse bond indexes available, as described herein. Such an analysis of the bond market and its components is critical for investors and portfolio managers making asset allocation and portfolio performance decisions.

## PART 2

# GOVERNMENT AND PRIVATE DEBT OBLIGATIONS

## CHAPTER 8

# U.S. TREASURY AND AGENCY SECURITIES

**Frank J. Fabozzi, Ph.D., CFA, CPA**
Adjunct Professor of Finance
School of Management
Yale University

**Michael J. Fleming, Ph.D.***
Senior Economist
Federal Reserve Bank of New York

U.S. Treasury securities are direct obligations of the U.S. government issued by the Department of the Treasury. They are backed by the full faith and credit of the U.S. government and are therefore considered to be free of credit risk. Treasuries are used extensively by market participants for pricing other securities, hedging positions, and assessing the market's views of future developments. Agency securities, in contrast, are obligations of specific entities that are either part of or sponsored by the U.S. government. Agency securities do not typically have an explicit government backing, but are nevertheless viewed as having low credit risk. In this chapter, we discuss U.S. Treasury and agency securities.

## TREASURY SECURITIES

U.S. Treasury securities play a prominent role in financial markets for several reasons. As noted, Treasuries are issued by the federal government and are considered to be free of credit risk. Issuance to pay off maturing debt and raise needed cash has created a stock of marketable Treasuries that totaled $3.2 trillion on June 30, 1999.[1] The creditworthiness and supply of Treasuries has resulted

---

* The views expressed in this chapter are not necessarily reflective of views at the Federal Reserve Bank of New York or the Federal Reserve System.
1. The stock of nonmarketable Treasury securities on the same date totaled $2.4 trillion. Of this, $2.0 trillion was non-public debt (held in government accounts), $0.2 trillion was held by private investors in the form of U.S. savings bonds, and $0.2 trillion was held in a special series by state and local governments (Monthly Statement of the Public Debt, www.publicdebt.ustreas.gov/opd/opddload.htm). This section focuses on marketable Treasury securities.

in a highly liquid round-the-clock secondary market with high levels of trading activity and narrow bid-ask spreads. These features have made Treasuries benchmark securities—for pricing other fixed-income securities, for hedging positions, and for assessing the market's views of future economic and policy developments.

An additional inducement to holding Treasury securities is that their interest income is free of state and local taxes. Many of the largest holders of Treasuries do not benefit from this feature, however, as they do not pay state or local taxes. In particular, foreign and international investors held 34% of the publicly held debt as of December 31, 1998, state and local treasuries held 13%, and Federal Reserve Banks held 12%.[2] The remaining 41% of the public debt was held by banks and insurance companies (11%), other financial institutions (14%), other companies (7%), and individuals (9%).

## Types of Securities

Treasuries are issued as either *discount* or *coupon securities*. Discount securities pay a fixed amount at maturity, called face value or par value, with no intervening interest payments. Discount securities are so called because they are issued at a price below face value with the return to the investor being the difference between the face value and the issue price. Coupon securities are issued with a stated rate of interest, pay interest every six months, and are redeemed at par value (or principal value) at maturity. Coupon securities are issued at a price close to par value with the return to the investor being primarily the coupon payments received over the security's life.

The Treasury issues securities with original maturities of one year or less as discount securities. These securities are called *Treasury bills*. The Treasury currently issues bills with original maturities of 13 weeks (3 months), 26 weeks (6 months), and 52 weeks (1 year), as well as cash-management bills with various maturities. On June 30, 1999, Treasury bills accounted for $648 billion (20.0%) of the $3.2 trillion in outstanding marketable Treasury securities, as shown in Exhibit 8–1.

Securities with original maturities of more than one year are issued as coupon securities. Coupon securities with original maturities of more than 1 year, but not more than 10 years, are called *Treasury notes*. Coupon securities with original maturities of more than 10 years are called *Treasury bonds*. The Treasury currently issues notes with maturities of 2 years, 5 years, and 10 years, and bonds with maturities of 30 years. While a few issues of the outstanding bonds are callable, the Treasury has not issued new callable Treasury securities since 1984. On June 30, 1999 Treasury notes accounted for $1.9 trillion (57.8%)

---

2. The publicly held debt includes marketable and nonmarketable securities held in non-government accounts. Figures are calculated from Table 1.41 of the *Federal Reserve Bulletin.*

**EXHIBIT 8–1**

Marketable U.S. Treasury Securities

| Issue Type | Security Type | Issues | Amount Outstanding (June 30, 1999) |
|---|---|---|---|
| Treasury bills | discount | cash-management, 13-week, 26-week, 52-week | $648 billion |
| Treasury notes | coupon | 2-year, 5-year, 10-year | $1,869 billion |
| Treasury bonds | coupon | 30-year | $633 billion |
| Treasury inflation-indexed securities | coupon | 10-year, 30-year | $85 billion |

Source: Department of the Treasury, Monthly Statement of the Public Debt for amounts outstanding (www.publicdebt.ustreas.gov / opd / opddload.htm).

of the outstanding marketable Treasury securities, and Treasury bonds accounted for $633 billion (19.6%).

In January 1997, the Treasury began selling inflation-indexed securities. The principal of these securities is adjusted for inflation using the consumer price index for urban consumers. Semi-annual interest payments are a fixed percentage of the inflation-adjusted principal and the inflation-adjusted principal is paid at maturity. On June 30, 1999, Treasury inflation-indexed notes and bonds accounted for $85 billion (2.6%) of the outstanding marketable Treasury securities. As these securities are discussed in detail in Chapter 13, the remainder of this section focuses on nominal (or fixed-rate) Treasuries.

## The Primary Market

Marketable Treasuries are sold in the primary market through sealed-bid, *single-price* (or *uniform price*) *auctions*. Each auction is announced several days in advance by means of a Treasury Department press release or press conference. The announcement provides details of the offering, including the offering amount and the term and type of security being offered, and describes some of the auction rules and procedures.

Treasury auctions are open to all entities. Bids must be made in multiples of $1,000 (with a $1,000 minimum) and submitted to a Federal Reserve Bank (or branch) or to the Treasury's Bureau of the Public Debt. Competitive bids must be made in terms of yield and must typically be submitted by 1:00 p.m. eastern time on auction day. Noncompetitive bids must typically be submitted by noon on auction day. While most tenders (or formal offers to buy) are submitted electronically, both competitive and noncompetitive tenders can be made on paper.[3]

All noncompetitive bids from the public up to $1 million for bills and $5 million for coupon securities are accepted. The lowest yield (i.e., highest price) competitive bids are then accepted up to the yield required to cover the amount offered (less the amount of noncompetitive bids). The highest yield accepted is called the *stop-out yield.* All accepted tenders (competitive and noncompetitive) are awarded at the stop-out yield. There is no maximum acceptable yield, and the Treasury does not add to or reduce the size of the offering according to the strength of the bids.

Historically, the Treasury auctioned securities through *multiple-price* (or *discriminatory*) *auctions.* With multiple-price auctions, the Treasury still accepted the lowest-yielding bids up to the yield requird to sell the amount offered (less the amount of noncompetitive bids), but accepted bids were awarded at the particular yields bid, rather than at the stop-out yield. Noncompetitive bids were awarded at the weighted-average yield of the accepted competitive bids rather than at the stop-out yield. In September 1992, the Treasury started conducting single-price auctions for the two- and five-year notes. In November 1998, the Treasury adopted the single-price method for all auctions.

Within an hour following the 1:00 p.m. auction deadline, the Treasury announces the auction results. Announced results include the stop-out yield, the associated price, and the proportion of securities awarded to those investors who bid exactly the stop-out yield. Also announced is the quantity of noncompetitive tenders, the median-yield bid, and the ratio of the total amount bid for by the public to the amount awarded to the public (called the *bid-to-cover ratio*). For notes and bonds, the announcement includes the coupon rate of the new security. The coupon rate is set to be that rate (in increments of $\frac{1}{8}$ one percent) that produces the price closest to, but not above, par when evaluated at the yield awarded to successful bidders.

Accepted bidders make payment on issue date through a Federal Reserve account or account at their financial institution, or they provide payment in full with their tender. Marketable Treasury securities are issued in book-entry form and held in the commercial book-entry system operated by the Federal Reserve Banks or in the Bureau of the Public Debt's Treasury Direct book-entry system.

## Primary Dealers
While the primary market is open to all investors, the *primary government securities dealers* play a special role. Primary dealers are firms with which the

---

3. Commercial bidders, such as broker/dealers and depository institutions, are encouraged to submit tenders electronically by computer, although paper tenders are accepted. Non-commercial bidders are encouraged to submit tenders electronically by phone or Internet, although mailed-in paper tenders are accepted. Bidding procedures are described in detail on the Bureau of the Public Debt's website at www.publicdebt.ustreas.gov.

Federal Reserve Bank of New York interacts directly in the course of its open market operations. They include large diversified securities firms, money center banks, and specialized securities firms, and are foreign-as well as U.S.-owned. Among their responsibilities, primary dealers are expected to participate meaningfully in Treasury auctions, make reasonably good markets to the Federal Reserve Bank of New York's trading desk, and supply market information and commentary to the Fed. The dealers must also maintain certain designated capital standards. The 30 primary dealers as of September 1, 1999 are listed in Exhibit 8–2.

Historically, Treasury auction rules tended to facilitate bidding by the primary dealers. In August 1991, however, Salomon Brothers Inc. admitted deliberate and repeated violations of auction rules. While the rules preclude any bidder from being awarded more than 35% of any issue, Salomon amassed significantly larger positions by making unauthorized bids on behalf of their customers. For the five-year note auctioned February 21, 1991, for example, Salomon bid for 105% of the issue (including two unauthorized customer bids) and was awarded 57% of the issue. Rule changes enacted later that year allowed any government securities broker or dealer to submit bids on behalf of customers and facilitated competitive bidding by non-primary dealers.[4]

**Auction Schedule**

To minimize uncertainty surrounding auctions, and thereby reduce borrowing costs, the Treasury offers securities on a regular, predictable schedule as shown in Exhibit 8–3. Thirteen-week and 26-week Treasury bills are offered every week. They are announced for auction on Thursday, auctioned on the following Monday, and issued on the following Thursday (one week after they are announced for auction). Fifty-two week bills are offered every four weeks. They are announced for auction on a Thursday, auctioned on the following Tuesday, and issued on the following Thursday. Cash-management bills are issued when required by the Treasury's short-term cash-flow needs, and are therefore not offered on a regular schedule.

Two-year notes are offered every month. They are announced for auction on a Wednesday, auctioned on the following Wednesday, and issued on the last day of the month (or the first day of the following month).

The remaining coupon securities are issued as a part of the Treasury's Quarterly Refunding in February, May, August, and November. The Treasury holds a press conference on the first Wednesday of the refunding months (or on the last Wednesday of the preceding months) at which it announces details of the upcoming auctions. The auctions then take place on the following Tuesday (five-year), Wednesday (10-year), and Thursday (30-year), with issuance on the

---

4. For further information on the auction violations and subsequent rule changes, see the *Joint Report on the Government Securities Market,* published by the Department of the Treasury, the Securities and Exchange Commission, and the Board of Governors of the Federal Reserve System in January 1992.

**EXHIBIT  8–2**

Primary Government Securities Dealers as of September 1, 1999

| | |
|---|---|
| ABN AMRO Incorporated | Greenwich Capital Markets, Inc. |
| Aubrey G. Lanston & Co., Inc. | HSBC Securities (USA) Inc. |
| Banc of America Securities LLC | J. P. Morgan Securities, Inc. |
| Banc One Capital Markets, Inc. | Lehman Brothers Inc. |
| Barclays Capital Inc. | Merrill Lynch Government Securities |
| Bear, Stearns & Co., Inc. | Inc. |
| Chase Securities Inc. | Morgan Stanley & Co. Incorporated |
| CIBC Oppenheimer Corp. | Nesbitt Burns Securities Inc. |
| Credit Suisse First Boston Corporation | Nomura Securities International, Inc. |
| Daiwa Securities America Inc. | Paine Webber Incorporated |
| Deutsche Bank Securities Inc. | Paribas Corporation |
| Donaldson, Lufkin & Jenrette Securities | Prudential Securities Incorporated |
| Corp. | SG Cowen Securities Corporation |
| Dresdner Kleinwort Benson North | Salomon Smith Barney Inc. |
| America LLC. | Warburg Dillon Read LLC. |
| Fuji Securities Inc. | Zions First National Bank |
| Goldman, Sachs & Co. | |

Source: Federal Reserve Bank of New York (www.ny.frb.org / pihome / news / announce /).

**EXHIBIT  8–3**

Auction Schedule for U.S. Treasury Securities

Issue frequency and typical issue sizes as of August 1999 are reported
for the seven regularly issued Treasury securities. Public issue sizes exclude amounts issued to refund maturities of Federal Reserve Banks as
well as certain amounts issued to foreign and international monetary authorities with accounts at Federal Reserve Banks.

| Issue | Issue Frequency | Public Issue Size |
|---|---|---|
| 13-week bill | weekly | $7.5–8.0 billion |
| 26-week bill | weekly | $7.5–8.0 billion |
| 52-week bill | every 4 weeks | $10.0 billion |
| 2-year note | monthly | $15.0 billion |
| 5-year note | quarterly | $15.0 billion |
| 10-year note | quarterly | $12.0 billion |
| 30-year bond | semi-annually | $10.0 billion |

Source: Bloomberg for issue sizes.

15th of the refunding month. Five- and 10-year notes are offered at every re-funding whereas 30-year bonds are only offered at the February and August refundings.

While the Treasury seeks to maintain a regular issuance cycle, its borrow-ing needs change over time. Most recently, the improved fiscal situation has reduced the Treasury's borrowing needs resulting in decreased issuance and a declining stock of outstanding Treasury securities.[5] To maintain large, liquid issues, the Treasury eliminated regular issuance of the three-year note in 1998 and reduced issuance of the five-year note from monthly to quarterly. At the August 1999 Quarterly Refunding press conference, the Treasury announced that 30-year issuance would be cut to twice a year from three times, and that it was considering reducing the frequency of 52-week bill and two-year note issuance.

In addition to maintaining a regular issuance cycle, the Treasury tries to maintain a constant issue size for securities of a given maturity. As shown in Exhibit 8–3, typical public issue sizes as of August 1999 were $7.5–$8.0 billion for 13- and 26-week bills, $10.0 billion for the 52-week bill, $15.0 billion for two- and five-year notes, $12.0 billion for the 10-year note, and $10.0 billion for the 30-year bond.[6] Issue sizes have fallen in recent years, particularly for Treasury bills, as illustrated by the decline in 13-week issue sizes from the $11–14 billion range in 1996 and early 1997, to the $7.5–$8.0 billion range in 1999.

### Reopenings

While the Treasury typically offers new securities at auction, it sometimes offers additional amounts of existing securities. Such additional offerings are called reopenings. Current Treasury practice is to issue every 13-week bill as a re-opening of a previously issued 26-week bill, and every fourth 26-week bill as a reopening of a previously issued 52-week bill. Coupon securities, in contrast, are reopened on an *ad hoc* basis only, to expand the size of an issue and improve its liquidity. In 1998, there were two reopenings of fixed-rate coupon securities: the 30-year bond issued in November 1997 was reopened at the February auc-tion, and the 10-year note issued in May was reopened at the August auction.

## The Secondary Market

Secondary trading in Treasury securities occurs in a multiple-dealer over-the-counter market rather than through an organized exchange. Trading takes place

---

5. Gross Treasury issuance fell from $2.2 trillion in 1997 to $2.0 trillion in 1998 (Bond Market Association, www.bondmarkets.com/research/tsyiss.shtml) and the stock of marketable Treasuries fell $121 billion to $3.2 trillion over the 12 months ending June 30, 1999 (Monthly Statement of the Public Debt, www.publicdebt.ustreas.gov/opd/opddload.htm).

6. Public issue sizes exclude amounts issued to Federal Reserve Banks to refund maturing securities. Coupon security issue sizes also exclude amounts issued to foreign and international mon-etary authorities with accounts at Federal Reserve Banks; bill security issue sizes typically include these amounts to the extent that they are a refunding of maturing securities.

around the clock during the week, from the three main trading centers of Tokyo, London, and New York. As shown in Exhibit 8–4, the vast majority of trading takes place during New York trading hours, roughly 7:30 a.m. to 5:00 p.m. eastern time. The primary dealers are the principal market makers, buying and selling securities from customers for their own accounts at their quoted bid and ask prices. For the first half of 1999, primary dealers reported daily trading activity in the secondary market that averaged $198 billion per day.[7]

### Interdealer Brokers

In addition to trading with their customers, the dealers trade among themselves through *interdealer brokers*. The brokers provide the dealers with proprietary electronic screens that post the best bid and offer prices called in by the dealers,

---

**EXHIBIT 8–4**

### Trading Volume of U.S. Treasury Securities by Half Hour
Mean half-hourly trading volume as a percentage of mean daily trading volume is plotted for the April 4 to August 19 1994, period. The times on the horizontal axis indicate the beginning of intervals.

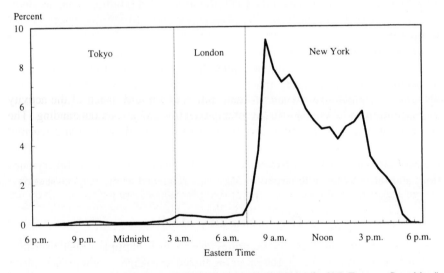

Source: Chart 2 in Michael J. Fleming, "The Round-the-Clock Market for U.S. Treasury Securities," Federal Reserve Bank of New York *Economic Policy Review* (July 1997).

---

7. Federal Reserve Bank of New York (www.ny.frb.org/pihome/statistics/). As the data are collected from all of the primary dealers but no other entities, trades between primary dealers are counted twice, and trades between non-primary dealers are not counted at all. The figure excludes financing transactions, such as repurchase agreements and reverse repurchase agreements.

along with the associated quantities bid or offered (minimums are $5 million for bills and $1 million for notes and bonds). The dealers execute trades by calling the brokers, who post the resulting trade price and size on their screens. The dealer who initiates a trade by "hitting" a bid or "taking" an offer pays the broker a small fee.

Interdealer brokers thus facilitate information flows in the market while providing anonymity to the trading dealers. For the most part, the brokers act only as agents and serve only the primary dealers and a number of non-primary dealers. The brokers include Cantor Fitzgerald Securities, Garban LLC, Hilliard Farber & Co., Inc., Intercapital Government Securities, Inc., Liberty Brokerage Inc., and Tullett & Tokyo Securities, Inc.

**Federal Reserve**
The Federal Reserve is another important participant in the secondary market for Treasury securities by virtue of its Treasury holdings, open market operations, and surveillance activities. The Federal Reserve Banks held $465 billion in Treasuries as of March 31, 1999, or 12% of the publicly held stock. The Federal Reserve Bank of New York buys and sells Treasuries through open market operations as one of the tools used to implement the monetary policy directives of the Federal Open Market Committee (FOMC). Finally, the New York Fed follows and analyzes the Treasury market and communicates market developments to other government agencies, including the Federal Reserve Board and the U.S. Treasury.

**Trading Activity**
While the Treasury market is extremely active and liquid, much of the activity is concentrated in a small number of the roughly 235 issues outstanding. The most recently issued securities of a given maturity, called *on-the-run* or *current securities,* are particularly active. Analysis of data from GovPX, Inc., a firm that tracks interdealer trading volume, shows that on-the-run issues accounted for 71% of trading activity in 1998. Older issues of a given maturity are called *off-the-run securities.* While nearly all Treasury securities are off-the-run, they accounted for only 23% of interdealer trading in 1998.

The remaining 6% of interdealer trading in 1998 occurred in *when-issued securities.* When-issued securities are securities that have been announced for auction, but not yet issued. When-issued trading facilitates price discovery for new issues and can serve to reduce uncertainty about bidding levels surrounding auctions. The when-issued market also enables dealers to sell securities to their customers in advance of the auctions, and thereby bid competitively with relatively little risk. While most Treasury market trades settle the following day, trades in the when-issued market settle on the issue date of the new security.

There are also notable differences in trading activity by issue type, as shown in Exhibit 8–5. According to 1998 data from GovPX, the on-the-run Treasury notes are the most actively traded securities, with average daily trading

**E X H I B I T   8-5**

Daily Trading Volume of U.S. Treasury Securities

Mean daily interdealer trading volume is reported by issue for when-
issued, on-the-run, and off-the-run Treasury securities. The when-issued
figures are estimated only over days on which the securities traded
when-issued. The off-the-run figures are per-security averages, estimated
over all off-the-run securities of a given issue. Figures are in millions of
dollars.

| Issue | When-issued | On-the-run | Off-the-run |
|---|---|---|---|
| 13-week bill | 627 | 1,265 | 160 |
| 26-week bill | 441 | 919 | 79 |
| 52-week bill | 1,841 | 2,123 | 96 |
| 2-year note | 2,093 | 7,320 | 97 |
| 5-year note | 1,095 | 6,629 | 18 |
| 10-year note | 584 | 4,538 | 7 |
| 30-year bond | 270 | 818 | 6 |

Source: Authors' calculations, based on 1998 data from GovPX, Inc.

of $7.3 billion for the two-year, $6.6 billion for the five-year, and $4.5 billion
for the 10-year.[8] Trading activity in when-issued securities is similarly concentrated, with the most active securities being the two-year note ($2.1 billion), the
52-week bill ($1.8 billion), and the five-year note ($1.1 billion). In contrast, off-
the-run trading is concentrated in the more frequently issued shorter-term issues,
with the most active being the three-month bill ($160 million per issue), the
two-year note ($97 million per issue), and the 52-week bill ($96 million per
issue). Trading in longer-term off-the-run securities is extremely thin, with mean
daily per-issue trading of just $18 million for the five-year note and $7 million
for the 10-year note.

## Quoting Conventions for Treasury Bills
The convention in the Treasury market is to quote bills on a discount basis. The
yield on a discount basis is computed as:

$$Y_d = \frac{(F - P)}{F} \times \frac{360}{t}$$

where

---

8. GovPX tracks trading activity among five of the six major interdealer brokers and thus covers
   most, but not all, of the interdealer market.

$Y_d$ = the yield on a discount basis
$F$ = the face value
$P$ = the price
$t$ = the number of days to maturity

For example, the 26-week bill auctioned July 26, 1999 sold at a price ($P$) of $97.715 per $100 face value ($F$). At issue, the bill had 182 days to maturity ($t$). The yield on a discount basis is then calculated as:

$$Y_d = \frac{(\$100 - \$97.715)}{\$100} \times \frac{360}{182} = 0.0452 \text{ or } 4.52\%$$

Conversely, given the yield on a discount basis, the price can be computed as:

$$P = F - \left( F \times Yd \times \frac{t}{360} \right)$$

For our example,

$$P = \$100 - \left( \$100 \times 4.52\% \times \frac{182}{360} \right) = \$97.715$$

The discount rate differs from more standard return measures for two reasons: First, the measure compares the dollar return to the face value rather than to the price. Second, the return is annualized based on a 360-day year rather than a 365-day year. Nevertheless, the discount rate can be converted to a bond-equivalent yield (as discussed in Chapter 4), and such yields are often reported alongside the discount rate.

Treasury bill discount rates are typically quoted to two decimal places in the secondary market, so that a quoted discount rate might be 4.87%. For more active issues, the last digit is often split into halves and quarters, so that a quoted rate might be 4.875% or 4.8725%.

Typical bid-ask spreads in the interdealer market for the on-the-run bill issues are 0.5 basis points, as shown in Exhibit 8–6. A basis point equals one one-hundredth of a percentage point, so that quotes for a half basis point spread might be 4.875%/4.87%. Exhibit 8–6 also shows that spreads vary with market conditions, ranging from 0 to 2 basis points most of the time. A zero spread is called a "locked market" and can persist in the interdealer market because of the transaction fee paid to the broker who mediates a trade. Bid-ask spreads are typically wider outside of the interdealer market, and for less active issues.

## Quoting Conventions for Treasury Coupon Securities

In contrast to Treasury bills, Treasury notes and bonds are quoted in the secondary market on a price basis in points where one point equals one percent of

**E X H I B I T   8-6**

Bid-Ask Spreads for U.S. Treasury Securities

Statistics for the spread between the best bid and the best offer in the
interdealer market are reported for the on-the-run securities of each issue.
Bill spreads are reported in yield terms in basis points and coupon spreads
are reported in price terms in points.

| Issue | Median Spread | 95% Range |
|-------|---------------|-----------|
| 13-week bill | 0.5 basis points | 0–2.0 basis points |
| 26-week bill | 0.5 basis points | 0–2.0 basis points |
| 52-week bill | 0.5 basis points | 0–2.0 basis points |
| 2-year note | 1/128 point | 0–1/64 point |
| 5-year note | 1/64 point | 0–5/128 point |
| 10-year note | 1/64 point | 0-2/32 point |
| 30-year bond | 2/32 point | 0–6/32 point |

Source: Authors' calculations, based on 1995 data from GovPX, Inc.

par.[9] The points are split into units of 32nds, so that a price of 96-14, for example, refers to a price of 96 and $14/32$ or 96.4375. The 32nds are themselves
split by the addition of a plus sign or a number, with a plus sign indicating that
half a 32nd (or $1/64$) is added to the price and a number indicating how many
eighths of 32nds (or 256ths) are added to the price. A price of 96-14+ therefore
refers to a price of 96 and $14\frac{1}{2}/32$ or 96.453125, while a price of 96-142 refers
to a price of 96 and $14\frac{2}{8}/32$ or 96.4453125. The yield to maturity, discussed
in Chapter 4, is typically reported alongside the price.

Typical bid-ask spreads in the interdealer market for the on-the-run coupon
issues range from $1/128$ point for the 2-year note to $2/32$ point for the 30-year
bond, as shown in Exhibit 8–6. A 2-year note might therefore be quoted as 99-
082/99-08+ whereas a 30-year bond might be quoted as 95-23/95-25. As with
bills, the spreads vary with market conditions, and are usually wider outside of
the interdealer market and for less active issues.

## Zero-Coupon Treasury Securities

The Treasury does not issue zero-coupon notes or bonds. These securities are
created from existing Treasury notes and bonds through coupon stripping. Coupon stripping is the process of separating the coupon payments of a security

9. Notes and bonds are quoted in yield terms in when-issued trading because coupon rates are not
   set until after these securities are auctioned.

from the principal and from one another. After stripping, each piece of the original security can trade by itself, entitling its holder to a particular payment on a particular date. A newly issued 30-year Treasury bond, for example, can be split into its 60 semi-annual coupon payments (called the *coupon strips*) and its principal payment (called the *principal strip*) resulting in 61 individual securities. As the components of stripped Treasuries consist of single payments (with no intermediate coupon payments), they are referred to as zero coupons or zeros.

The Treasury introduced its *Separate Trading of Registered Interest and Principal Securities* (STRIPS) program in February 1985 to improve the liquidity of the zero-coupon market. The program allows the individual components of eligible Treasury securities to be held separately in the Federal Reserve's book entry system. Institutions with book-entry accounts can request that a security be stripped into its separate components by sending instructions to a Federal Reserve Bank. Each stripped component receives its own CUSIP (or identification) number and can then be traded and registered separately. The components of stripped Treasuries remain direct obligations of the U.S. government. The STRIPS program was originally limited to new coupon security issues with maturities of 10 years or longer, but was expanded to include all new coupon issues in September 1997.

Since May 1987, the Treasury has also allowed the components of a stripped Treasury security to be reassembled into their fully constituted form. An institution with a book-entry account assembles the principal component and all remaining interest components of a given security and then sends instructions to a Federal Reserve Bank requesting the reconstitution.

As of July 31, 1999, $223 billion of Treasury notes and bonds were held in stripped form, representing 13% of the $1.7 trillion in eligible fixed-rate coupon securities.[10] There is wide variation across issue types and across issues of a particular type in the rate of stripping. As of July 31, 32% of eligible bonds were stripped but only 5% of eligible notes were stripped. Among the notes, one issue was 54% stripped on July 31, while 31 eligible note issues were not stripped at all. On a flow basis, securities were stripped at a rate of $12.3 billion per month in the first seven months of 1999, and reconstituted at a rate of $11.5 billion per month.

## AGENCY SECURITIES

Agency securities are direct obligations of federal government agencies or government-sponsored enterprises. *Federal agencies* are entities of the U.S. government, such as the Tennessee Valley Authority. *Government-sponsored enter-*

---

10. Figures are from Table V of the Treasury's Monthly Statement of the Public Debt (www.publicdebt.ustreas.gov/opd/opddload.htm)

*prises* are publicly chartered but privately owned and operated entities, such as the Federal National Mortgage Association (Fannie Mae), the Federal Home Loan Mortgage Corporation (Freddie Mac), the Federal Home Loan Banks, the Farm Credit Banks, and the Student Loan Marketing Association (Sallie Mae). The agencies issue debt securities to finance activities supported by public policy, including home ownership, farming, and education.[11]

Agency securities are not typically backed by the full faith and credit of the U.S. government, as is the case with Treasury securities. Agency securities are therefore not considered to be risk-free instruments, but rather trade with some credit risk. Nevertheless, agency securities are considered to be of very high credit quality because of the strong fundamentals of their underlying businesses and because of the agencies' government affiliation. Several of the agencies have authority to borrow directly from the U.S. Treasury. Additionally, there is a perception among market participants that the government implicitly backs the agency issues and would be reluctant to let an agency default on its obligations. Agency issues are also attractive to investors because their interest income is exempt from state and local taxation for many of the issuers (it is not exempt for Fannie Mae or Freddie Mac issues).

## Types of Securities

Agency securities are issued in a variety of types and maturities. Discount notes are short-term obligations issued at a discount from par with maturities ranging from one day to 360 days. Medium-term notes are fixed- or floating-rate coupon securities and are offered with a range of maturities. More generally, the agencies offer a wide variety of securities-with various attributes, including callable and non-callable securities, fixed-rate, floating-rate, indexed, and zero-coupon securities, and securities denominated in U.S. dollars or in another currency.

An important recent development in the agency securities market is the introduction of agency benchmark programs, including *Fannie Mae's Benchmark Notes program* and *Freddie Mac's Reference Notes program*. The programs provide for the regular issuance of coupon securities in large sizes for a range of maturities. The programs are intended to produce a yield curve for liquid agency securities and thereby appeal to investors who might typically buy Treasury securities. The initial benchmark programs were limited to non-callable securities, but callable programs have since been introduced.

## The Primary Market

The agencies use a variety of methods to distribute their securities including allocation to dealers, competitive dealer bidding, direct sales to investors, and

---

11. Several of the agencies also guarantee and/or issue asset-backed securities. Agency mortgage-backed securities are discussed in Chapter 24.

sales to investors through dealers. The most common distribution mechanism for agency securities is to allocate them among members of a selling group of dealers. The selling group provides market and trading information to the issuing agency before and during the allocation, and may support secondary trading in the issue after allocation. In compensation for their services, the selling group members retain a percentage of the proceeds from the sold securities.

The quantity of agency securities sold in the primary market has increased rapidly in recent years, as shown in Exhibit 8–7. In 1990, the agencies issued $637 billion in debt securities, $582 billion in short-term debt (securities with a maturity of one year or less) and $55 billion in long-term debt. In 1998, the agencies issued $6.4 trillion in debt securities, $5.8 trillion in short-term debt and $0.6 trillion in long-term debt.

Rising issuance has resulted in a growing stock of agency debt outstanding, as shown in Exhibit 8–8. The outstanding debt of the agencies stood at $1.3 trillion on December 31, 1998, up from $412 billion on December 31, 1989.[12] The growth in agency debt is attributable to three issuers, Fannie Mae,

**EXHIBIT   8–7**

Agency Debt Issuance, 1990–1998

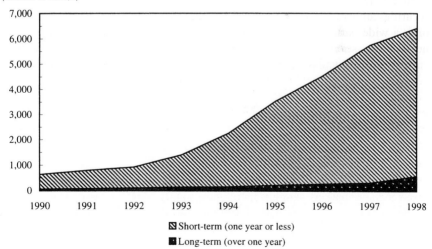

Debt Issuance
(billions of dollars)

☒ Short-term (one year or less)
■ Long-term (over one year)

Source: Bond Market Association (www.bondmarkets.com/research/faiss.shtml).

---

12. Note that agency debt issuance in 1998 ($6.4 trillion) significantly exceeded the stock of debt outstanding on December 31, 1998 ($1.3 trillion). This is because most agency debt is of such a short-term that it turns over numerous times within a year.

**EXHIBIT 8-8**

Agency Debt Outstanding, 1989–1998

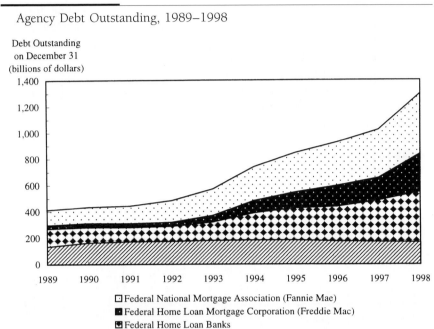

Debt Outstanding
on December 31
(billions of dollars)

☐ Federal National Mortgage Association (Fannie Mae)
■ Federal Home Loan Mortgage Corporation (Freddie Mac)
◨ Federal Home Loan Banks
▨ All Other Agencies

Source: Table 1.44, *Federal Reserve Bulletin.*

Freddie Mac, and the Federal Home Loan Banks, which together accounted for 87% of the outstanding debt at the end of 1998.

## The Secondary Market

Like Treasury securities, agency securities trade in a multiple dealer over-the-counter secondary market. Also like Treasuries, trading among dealers is screen-based, through interdealer brokers. Trading volume is significantly lower than that in the Treasury market, but it is still reasonably high relative to that in other fixed income markets, and has increased strongly in recent years. Daily primary dealer trading in the first half of 1999 averaged $53 billion per day, with $41 billion in discount notes and $12 billion in coupon securities. In contrast, dealer trading in 1991 averaged $5.6 billion per day.[13]

---

13. Figures for 1999 are from the Federal Reserve Bank of New York (www.ny.frb.org/pihome/ statistics/) and figures for 1991 are from Table 1.42 of the *Federal Reserve Bulletin.*

# EXHIBIT 8-9

Agencies

| Agency | Purpose | Debt Outstanding (December 31, 1998) |
|---|---|---|
| Federal National Mortgage Association (Fannie Mae) | Promote liquid secondary market for residential mortgages | $460.2 billion |
| Federal Home Loan Mortgage Corporation (Freddie Mac) | Promote liquid secondary market for residential mortgages | $287.4 billion |
| Federal Home Loan Banks | Supply credit for residential mortgages | $382.1 billion |
| Farm Credit Banks | Supply credit to agricultural sector | $63.5 billion |
| Farm Credit System Financial Assistance Corporation | Finance recapitalization of Farm Credit System institutions | $1.3 billion |
| Federal Agricultural Mortgage Corporation (Farmer Mac) | Promote liquid secondary market for agricultural and rural housing loans | $1.8 billion |
| Student Loan Marketing Association (Sallie Mae) | Increase availability of student loans | $35.4 billion |
| Financing Corporation | Finance recapitalization of Federal Savings and Loan Insurance Corporation | $8.2 billion |
| Resolution Funding Corporation | Finance recapitalization of savings and loan industry | $30.0 billion |
| Tennessee Valley Authority | Promote development of Tennessee River and adjacent areas | $26.5 billion |

Source: Table 1.44, *Federal Reserve Bulletin* and Federal Agricultural Mortgage Corporation for debt outstanding.

# Issuing Agencies

As previously mentioned, agency securities are direct obligations of federal agencies or government-sponsored enterprises. Federal agencies are entities of the federal government. They include the Commodity Credit Corporation, the Export-Import Bank of the United States, the Federal Housing Administration, the Farmers Home Administration, the Government National Mortgage Association (Ginnie Mae), the Tennessee Valley Authority (TVA), the Rural Electrification Administration, and the Small Business Administration. Historically, a number of federal agencies issued their own debt securities. In 1974, the Federal Financing Bank was set up to consolidate agency borrowing and thereby reduce borrowing costs. The TVA still issues its own debt securities, however, and accounts for nearly all of the outstanding debt issued directly by federal agencies.

Government-sponsored enterprises (GSEs) are privately owned and operated entities chartered by Congress to decrease the cost of funding for certain sectors of the economy. The GSEs are granted certain privileges to help them achieve their public purposes, and in turn are limited to certain activities. As mentioned, the agencies' securities are seen to have an implicit government guarantee and agency security interest income is exempt from state and local taxation for many of the issuers. The agencies themselves are exempt from state and local income taxes, and are exempt from SEC registration fees.

The largest GSEs were chartered to provide credit to the housing sector. They include the Federal National Mortgage Association (Fannie Mae), the Federal Home Loan Mortgage Corporation (Freddie Mac), and the Federal Home Loan Banks. Another set of GSEs was established to provide credit to the agricultural sector. It includes the Farm Credit Banks, the Farm Credit System Financial Assistance Corporation, and the Federal Agricultural Mortgage Corporation (Farmer Mac). One GSE, the Student Loan Marketing Association (Sallie Mae), was established to provide funds to support higher education. Two other GSEs, the Financing Corporation and the Resolution Funding Corporation, were established to recapitalize the savings and loan industry.

The remainder of this section provides a brief overview of each of the agencies with debt securities outstanding. The information is summarized in Exhibit 8–9.

## Federal National Mortgage Association (Fannie Mae)

The Federal National Mortgage Association (Fannie Mae) is a stockholder-owned corporation chartered in 1938 to develop a secondary market for residential mortgages. Fannie Mae buys home loans from banks and other mortgage lenders in the primary market, and holds the mortgages until they mature, or issues securities backed by pools of the mortgages. In addition to promoting a liquid secondary market for mortgages, Fannie Mae is charged with providing access to mortgage finance for low-income families and underserved areas. Fannie Mae's housing mission is overseen by the U.S. Department of Housing and Urban Development (HUD), and its safety and soundness is overseen by the Office of Federal Housing Enterprise Oversight (OFHEO).

Fannie Mae issues a variety of securities including discount notes and medium-term notes. In January 1998, Fannie Mae initiated a new debt issuance program called Benchmark Notes. The program is an aggregation of Fannie Mae's intermediate-term debt issuance into large, regularly scheduled non-callable issues. Each month, Fannie Mae issues a new benchmark security, re-opens an old one, or passes for that month. New issues range in size from $2 billion to $5 billion. Fannie Mae established its program to provide greater liquidity and efficiency to the market, and promotes its securities as higher-yielding alternatives to off-the-run Treasury securities. The benchmark program was extended to callable securities in April 1999, and to longer-term issues (a 30-year non-callable) in May 1999. Total Fannie Mae debt issuance in 1998 was $843 billion, with $696 billion in short-term debt and $147 billion in long-term debt.[14] On December 31, 1998, Fannie Mae had debt securities outstanding of $460 billion.

### Federal Home Loan Mortgage Corporation (Freddie Mac)

The Federal Home Loan Mortgage Corporation (Freddie Mac) is a stockholder-owned corporation chartered in 1970 to improve the liquidity of the secondary mortgage market. Freddie Mac purchases mortgage loans from individual lenders, and sells securities backed by the mortgages to investors, or holds the mortgages until they mature. Like Fannie Mae, Freddie Mac is charged with providing access to mortgage finance for low-income families and underserved areas. Also like Fannie Mae, Freddie Mac is regulated by HUD for its housing mission and by OFHEO for safety and soundness.

Freddie Mac issues a variety of debt securities including discount notes and medium-term notes. In April 1998, Freddie Mac established its own benchmark securities program called Reference Notes. Each month, Freddie Mac issues a new benchmark security in the two to ten year sector, or reopens an old one. Each new issue is between $3 billion and $5 billion, with reopening offerings of at least $1 billion. Like Fannie Mae, Freddie Mac promotes its benchmark securities as an alternative to the declining supply of Treasury notes and bonds. Also like Fannie Mae, Freddie Mac extended its benchmark program to callable securities in April 1999. Total Freddie Mac debt issuance in 1998 was $2.2 trillion, $2.1 trillion in short-term securities and $126 billion in long-term securities. On December 31, 1998, Freddie Mac had $287 billion in outstanding debt.

---

14. Debt issuance in 1998 for each of the agencies is from the Bond Market Association (www.bondmarkets.com/research/faiss.shtml) while debt outstanding on December 31, 1998 is from Table 1.44 of the *Federal Reserve Bulletin.*

## Federal Home Loan Bank System

The Federal Home Loan Bank System (FHLBank System) is a GSE established in 1932 to increase credit to the housing sector. It consists of 12 federally chartered privately owned Federal Home Loan Banks that are charged with supporting residential mortgage lending by over 6,500 member-stockholder institutions. It does this by making loans to the member institutions, which in turn provide mortgages to homebuyers. The Federal Housing Finance Board regulates the FHLBank System for mission as well as safety and soundness issues.

FHLBank debt issuance is conducted through the system's fiscal agent, the Office of Finance. The FHLBanks sells a variety of debt securities including discount notes and medium-term notes. In July 1999, the FHLBanks initiated their own benchmark securities program called the Tap Issue Program. The program reopens coupon securities of four common maturities up to twice a day for three months through a competitive auction. Like the other benchmark programs, the Tap Issue Program is intended to increase issuance size, trading volume, and liquidity, and thereby increase demand for the agency's securities. In 1998, the FHLBanks issued $2.5 trillion in debt securities, $2.3 trillion in short-term debt and $277 billion in long-term debt. The FHLBanks had $382 billion in outstanding debt as of December 31, 1998.

## Farm Credit System

The Farm Credit System (FCS) is a GSE established in 1916 to provide credit to the agricultural sector. The FCS lends money to farmers through a network of borrower-owned financial institutions and related service organizations. Six Farm Credit Banks and one Agricultural Credit Bank make direct long-term real estate loans to farmers through 32 Federal Land Bank Associations. The banks also provide loan funds to various credit associations, which in turn make short-, intermediate-, and long-term loans to farmers. The FCS is regulated by the Farm Credit Administration.

The Federal Farm Credit Banks Funding Corporation is the system's fiscal entity, providing funds to system institutions through the issuance of debt securities. The FCS issues discount notes, medium-term notes, and other debt securities. In 1998, the FCS issued $301 billion in debt securities, $274 billion in short-term debt and $27 billion in long-term debt. On December 31, 1998 the FCS had $63.5 billion in outstanding debt.

## Farm Credit System Financial Assistance Corporation

The Farm Credit Financial Assistance Corporation was chartered in 1988 to finance the recapitalization of FCS institutions. Between 1988 and 1990, the corporation raised $1.3 billion through the issuance of debt securities, which it provided to system institutions in return for preferred stock. Unlike most GSEs, debt securities of this corporation are fully guaranteed by the U.S. Treasury. On December 31, 1998, the full $1.3 billion in issued debt securities was outstanding.

## Federal Agricultural Mortgage Corporation (Farmer Mac)

The Federal Agricultural Mortgage Corporation (Farmer Mac) is a stockholder-owned corporation chartered in 1988 to promote a liquid secondary market for agricultural real estate and rural housing loans. It does this by buying qualified loans from lenders and grouping the loans into pools against which it issues securities. Farmer Mac thus performs a role for the agricultural mortgage market similar to that performed by Fannie Mae and Freddie Mac for the residential mortgage market. Farmer Mac issues discount notes and medium-term notes, and had debt securities outstanding of $1.8 billion on December 31, 1998.

## Student Loan Marketing Association (Sallie Mae)

The Student Loan Marketing Association (Sallie Mae) is a stockholder-owned corporation established in 1972 to increase the availability of student loans. Sallie Mae purchases insured student loans from lenders and makes loans to lenders secured by student loans. Sallie Mae was reorganized in 1997 in a step towards privatization, and is scheduled to be dissolved as a GSE by September 30, 2008.

Sallie Mae issues discount notes, medium-term notes, and other debt securities. It issued $475 billion in debt securities in 1998, $469 billion in short-term debt and $6 billion in long-term debt. As of December 31, 1998, Sallie Mae had debt securities outstanding of $35.4 billion.

## Financing Corporation

The Financing Corporation (FICO) was established in 1987 to finance the recapitalization of the Federal Savings and Loan Insurance Corporation (FSLIC). Between 1987 and 1989, FICO issued debt obligations with an aggregate principal of $8.2 billion. The Federal Home Loan Bank System provided capital to purchase zero-coupon Treasury securities to repay the principal. Interest payments were to be funded by an assessment on FSLIC-insured institutions, although assessments were eventually expanded to include banks as well as savings and loans. The full $8.2 billion in issued debt securities was outstanding as of December 31, 1998.

## Resolution Funding Corporation

The Resolution Funding Corporation (REFCorp) was established in 1989 as the funding arm of the Resolution Trust Corporation to finance the recapitalization of the savings and loan industry. REFCorp issued $30.0 billion in debt securities between 1989 and 1991. Interest payments on REFCorp bonds are guaranteed by the U.S. government, and the principal is protected by the purchase of zero-coupon bonds with a face value equal to those of REFCorp bonds. The full $30.0 billion in issued debt securities was outstanding on December 31, 1998.

## Tennessee Valley Authority

The Tennessee Valley Authority (TVA) is a government-owned corporation established in 1933 to promote development of the Tennessee River and adjacent areas. The TVA manages the river system for flood control, navigation, power generation, and other purposes, and is the nation's largest producer of electricity.

The TVA issues discount notes as well as longer-term coupon securities called Power Bonds. Interest and principal on Power Bonds are paid from the proceeds of TVA's power program. The TVA issued $31 billion in debt securities in 1998, $25 billion in short-term debt and $7 billion in long-term debt. The TVA had debt securities outstanding of $26.5 billion on December 31, 1998.

## SUMMARY

U.S. Treasury securities are obligations of the U.S. government issued by the Department of the Treasury. They trade in a highly liquid secondary, and are used by market participants as benchmark securities. Treasury issuance and debt outstanding have recently declined with the improved federal fiscal situation and are expected to continue declining in future years. The Treasury has taken a number of steps to maintain the liquidity of the market, including reducing the issuance frequency of some security issues and eliminating other issues altogether.

Agency securities are obligations of entities that are either part of or sponsored by the U.S. government. Agency securities are viewed as having very low credit risk although they are not risk-free. Agency security issuance and amount outstanding have grown strongly in recent years due to the growth of the housing GSEs: Fannie Mae, Freddie Mac, and the Federal Home Loan Bank System. The agencies have recently introduced benchmark security programs designed to appeal to investors who might typically buy Treasury securities.

# CHAPTER 9

# MUNICIPAL BONDS

**Sylvan G. Feldstein, Ph.D.**
Assistant Vice President
Investment Department
Guardian Life Insurance Company

**Frank J. Fabozzi, Ph.D., CFA, CPA**
Adjunct Professor of Finance
School of Management
Yale University

**Patrick M. Kennedy**
Vice President
Fixed Income Portfolio Manager
Pitcairn Trust Company

The U.S. bond market can be divided into two major sectors: the taxable bond market and the tax-exempt bond market. The former sector includes bonds issued by the U.S. government, U.S. government agencies and sponsored enterprises, and corporations. The tax-exempt bond market is one in which the interest from bonds that are issued and sold is exempt from federal income taxation. Interest may or may not be taxable at the state and local level. The interest on U.S. Treasury securities is exempt from state and local taxes, but the distinction in classifying a bond as tax-exempt is the tax treatment at the federal income tax level.

The Federal Reserve Board estimates that the size of the tax-exempt bond market as of June 1999 totals $1.5 trillion. This makes the municipal bond market about 11% of the domestic bond market, which makes municipal debt the fourth largest sector. United States Treasuries and agencies account for a dominant 38% of the domestic bond market. The mortgage-backed security sector (MBS) has the second largest representation while U.S. corporate debt ranks third. The municipal sector is certainly one of the larger components of the domestic bond market, but it is clearly different from the 89% of the bond market that is taxable.

The majority of tax-exempt securities are issued by state and local governments and by their creations, such as "authorities" and special districts. Consequently, the terms *municipal market and tax-exempt market* are often used interchangeably. Although not all municipal bonds are tax-exempt securities, most are.

The major motivation for investing in municipal bonds is their tax advantage. With the increase in the marginal tax rates resulting from the 1993 Tax Act, more investors are purchasing municipal securities. The primary owners of municipal bonds are individual investors; the remainder of the investors consist of mutual funds, commercial banks, and property and casualty insurance companies. Although certain institutional investors such as pension funds have no need for tax-advantaged investments, there have been instances where such institutional investors have crossed into the municipal bond market to take advantage of higher yields. These investors have also purchased municipal bonds when municipal bonds were expected to outperform taxable bonds. Institutional investors that are natural purchasers of taxable bonds, but at times purchase municipal debt, are known as "crossover buyers."

Traditionally the household sector has owned the largest portion of the municipal bond market. Another substantial owner has been the mutual fund industry. However, examination of Federal Reserve Board data indicates that there have been three major changes among holders. First, the percentage holdings of commercial banks has dropped significantly since 1986. In general, The Tax Reform Act of 1986 reduced the benefits commercial banks received by owning municipal bonds. Commercial banks responded to this change by reducing their municipal bond holdings and investing in assets that provided greater benefits.

Households account for the next substantial ownership change. In 1990, household ownership of municipal bonds reached a peak of 49% for the 20-year period. However, by 1997, household ownership declined to 31%. If commercial banks and households both decreased their holdings, then other groups had to increase their ownership. Federal Reserve Board data indicate that mutual funds dramatically increased their holdings. In 1979, mutual funds held 1% of the municipal market; by the second quarter of 1999, mutual funds increased their share to 34%. During 1997, mutual funds became the largest holder of municipal bonds.

Insurance companies and personal bank trust accounts have had relatively stable ownership of municipal bonds. Insurance companies typically adjust their holdings of municipal bonds according to profitability and the relative value municipal bonds offer compared to taxable bonds. Trust accounts are relatively stable purchasers of municipal bonds. A typical trust account will purchase bonds near par, collect the tax-exempt income and hold the bonds to maturity.

In the past, investing in municipal bonds has been considered second in safety only to that of U.S. Treasury securities; however, there have now developed among investors ongoing concerns about the credit risks of municipal bonds. This is true regardless of whether or not the bonds are given investment-grade credit ratings by the commercial rating companies. There are several reasons for this: (1) the financial crisis of several major municipal issuers beginning with the City of New York billion-dollar financial crisis in 1975, and more recently with the default of Orange County, California; (2) the federal bankruptcy law (which became effective October 1979) that makes it easier for municipal bond issuers to seek protection from bondholders by filing for bankruptcy; (3) the proliferation of innovative financing techniques and legally untested security structures, highlighted by the default of the Washington Public Power Supply System (WPPSS) in the early 1980s; (4) the cutbacks in federal grant and aid programs that will affect the ability of certain municipal issuers to meet their obligations; and (5) fundamental changes in the American economy that may cause economic hardship for municipal issuers in some regions of the country and thus difficulty in meeting their obligations.

One reason for concern is that an issuer's credit quality can vary. Granted, nearly half of all newly issued bonds are insured, earning them the coveted triple-A credit rating.[1] However, only about 36% of outstanding bonds are insured. This dramatically increases the number of potential changes in credit quality. In 1998 Standard and Poor's had 647 upgrades and 126 downgrades. The dollar volume of debt upgrades was $92.2 billion compared to $6.8 billion of downgrades. The five-year average for upgrades is 4.2% of the 13,800 Public Finance issues rated by Standard and Poor's and the five-year average for downgrades is 1.7%. While these statistics are impressively favorable, one must remember that these statistics are indicative of the extremely favorable economic environment during this period. Under less favorable environment conditions, downgrades could exceed upgrades. This fact is evident by viewing Exhibit 9–1, which shows downgrades exceeding upgrades during the early 1990s. Additionally, there are variations among sectors. In 1998, the tax-backed sector accounted for most of the rating upgrades while the housing sector had more downgrades than upgrades. As can be seen, the credit quality of the issuers is not static. Even though the risk of monetary default in the municipal market is considered to be less than one percent, the risk of a decline in credit quality for an individual issuer is larger. Investors are concerned about declines in credit quality because the marketplace requires higher yields from lower rated bonds. If a bond's credit quality declines, the bond's yield will rise and its price will fall.

## FEATURES OF MUNICIPAL SECURITIES

In Chapter 1 the various features of fixed income securities were described. These include call and refunding provisions, sinking-fund provisions, and put

---

1. Credit quality ratings are denoted by assigning a letter rating to an issue. Triple-A denotes the highest credit quality while D is the lowest. Investment grade ratings range from triple-A to triple-B. Junk bonds/high yield ratings range from double-B to D. Nationally Recognized Statistical Rating Organizations (Moody's, S&P, and Fitch) rate the issuers' ability to make timely payments of principal and interest. The rating is the agency's opinion of the general creditworthiness of an obligor, or the creditworthiness of an obligor with respect to a particular debt security or other financial obligation based on relevant risk factors.

**EXHIBIT   9–1**

Standard & Poor's Rating Actions

|        | Upgrades | | Downgrades | |
|--------|----------|--------------------------|----------|--------------------------|
|        | **Number** | **Dollar Volume (Billions)** | **Number** | **Dollar Volume (Billions)** |
| 1998   | 647      | 92.20                    | 126      | 6.80                     |
| 1997   | 746      | 98.60                    | 113      | 15.70                    |
| 1996   | 672      | 53.70                    | 190      | 29.30                    |
| 1995   | 324      | 20.00                    | 289      | 66.40                    |
| 1994   | 293      | 19.30                    | 324      | 36.50                    |
| 1993*  | 248      | 25.00                    | 239      | 10.00                    |
| 1992*  | 410      | 31.00                    | 489      | 49.00                    |
| 1991*  | 145      | 9.00                     | 607      | 51.00                    |

* Approximate dollar volume.

provisions. Such provisions can also be included in municipal securities. In one type of municipal structure discussed below, a revenue bond, there is a special call feature wherein the issuer must call the entire issue if the facility is destroyed.

## Coupon Features

The coupon rate on a municipal issue can be fixed throughout the life of the issue or it can be reset periodically. When the coupon rate is reset periodically, the issue is referred to as a *floating-rate* or *variable-rate* issue. In general form, the coupon reset formula for a floating-rate issue is

% of reference rate ± Spread

Typically, when the reference rate is a municipal index, the coupon reset formula is

Reference rate ± Spread

Reference rates that have been used for municipal issues include the J. J. Kenny Municipal Index, LIBOR, Bond Market Association "BMA" rate, and Treasury bills. The coupon rate on a floating-rate issue need not change in the same direction as the reference rate. There are derivative municipal bonds whose coupon rate changes in the opposite direction to the change in the reference rate. That is, if the reference rate increases from the previous coupon reset date, the coupon rate on the issue declines. Such issues are referred to as *inverse floating-rate issues.* Some municipal issues have a fixed coupon rate and are issued at a discount from their maturity value. Issues whose original-issue price is less than its maturity value are referred to as *original-issue discount bonds* (OIDs). The difference between the par value and the original-issue price represents tax-exempt interest that the investor realizes by holding the issue to maturity.

Two types of municipal issues do not distribute periodic interest to the investor. The first type is called a *zero-coupon bond.* The coupon rate is zero and the original issue price is below the maturity value. Zero-coupon bonds are therefore OIDs. The other type of issue that does not distribute periodic interest is one in which a coupon rate is stated but the coupon is not distributed to the investor. Instead, the interest is accrued and all interest is paid to the investor at the maturity date along with the maturity value. Later in this chapter we will discuss the important aspects an investor should be aware of when considering the purchase of OIDs in the secondary market.

## Maturity Date

The maturity date is the date on which the issuer is obligated to pay the par value. Corporate issuers of debt generally schedule their bonds to mature in one or two different years in the future. Municipal issuers, on the other hand, frequently schedule their bonds to mature serially over many years. Such bonds are called *serial bonds.* It is common for a municipal issue to have 10 or more different maturities.

After the last of the serial maturities, some municipal issues lump together large sums of debt into one or two years—much the way corporate bonds are issued. These bonds, called *term bonds,* have become increasingly popular in the municipal market because active secondary markets for them can develop if the term issue is of sufficient size.

## The Legal Opinion

Municipal bonds have legal opinions. The relationship of the legal opinion to the safety of municipal bonds for both general obligation and revenue bonds is threefold. First, bond counsel should check to determine if the issuer is indeed legally able to issue the bonds. Second, bond counsel is to see that the issuer has properly prepared for the bond sale by having enacted the various required ordinances, resolutions, and trust indentures and without violating any other laws and regulations. This preparation is particularly important in the highly technical areas of determining if the bond issue is qualified for tax exemption under federal law and if the issue has not been structured in such a way as to violate federal arbitrage regulations. Third, bond counsel is to certify that the security safeguards and remedies provided for the bondholders and pledged either by the bond issuer or by third parties, such as banks with letter-of-credit agreements, are actually supported by federal, state, and local government laws and regulations.

The popular notion is that much of the legal work done in a bond issue is boilerplate in nature, but from the bondholder's point of view the legal opinions and document reviews should be the ultimate security provisions. The reason is that if all else fails, the bondholder may have to go to court to enforce his or her security rights. Therefore, the integrity and competence of the lawyers who review the documents and write the legal opinions that are usually summarized and stated in the official statements are very important.

## TYPES OF MUNICIPAL OBLIGATIONS

The number of municipal bond issuers is remarkable. One broker/dealer's estimate places the total at 60,055. Also, Bloomberg Financial Markets' (Bloomberg)[2] database contains 55,000 active issuers. Even more noteworthy is the number of different issues. Interactive Data (formerly Muller Data Corporation)[3] claims that it provides daily prices for over 1.2 million individual issues in its database. Bloomberg's database contains over 2.7 million cusips (including matured bonds). Bloomberg's database contains 1.7 million issues with complete description pages. The number of different issues to choose from is staggering. Considering all the different types of issuers in the market—states, state agencies, cities, airports, colleges and universities, hospitals, school districts, toll roads and bridges, public power facilities, seaport facilities, water and sewer authorities, solid waste facilities, and other special purpose districts—your investment choices for investors are overwhelming. Some of the issuers are extremely large and issue billions of dollars of debt. Some are extremely small and may only have $1 to $2 million in outstanding debt. Obviously, the characteristics of these issuers and their debt are very different, and both require independent and careful analysis. However, municipal bonds can be categorized into two broad security structures. In terms of municipal bond security structures, there are basically two different types. The first type is the general obligation bond, and the second is the revenue bond.

---

2. Bloomberg Financial Markets is a multimedia distributor of information services that combines news, data, and analysis for global financial markets and business. The "BLOOMBERG," the company's core business, is a computer network that delivers real-time financial information and links the world's financial markets and financial professionals.

3. Interactive Data is a securities information provider that specializes in data collection and internally authored evaluations. Data are delivered electronically to financial institutions and authorized redistribution vendors. Fixed income coverage encompasses the municipal and taxable bond markets. Interactive Data is a financial information company of Pearson, PLC.

# General Obligation Bonds

General obligation bonds are debt instruments issued by states, counties, special districts, cities, towns, and school districts. They are secured by the issuer's general taxing powers. Usually, a general obligation bond is secured by the issuer's unlimited taxing power. For smaller governmental jurisdictions such as school districts and towns, the only available unlimited taxing power is on property. For larger general obligation bond issuers such as states and big cities, the tax revenues are more diverse and may include corporate and individual income taxes, sales taxes, and property taxes. The security pledges for these larger issuers such as states are sometimes referred to as being *full faith and credit obligations.*

Additionally, certain general obligation bonds are secured not only by the issuer's general taxing powers to create monies accumulated in the general fund but also from certain identified fees, grants, and special charges, which provide additional revenues from outside the general fund. Such bonds are known as being *double barreled* in security because of the dual nature of the revenue sources. Also, not all general obligation bonds are secured by unlimited taxing powers. Some have pledged taxes that are limited as to revenue sources and maximum property-tax millage amounts. Such bonds are known as *limited-tax general obligation bonds.*

# Revenue Bonds

The second basic type of security structure is found in a revenue bond. Such bonds are issued for either project or enterprise financings in which the bond issuers pledge to the bondholders the revenues generated by the operating projects financed. Below are examples of the specific types of revenue bonds that have been issued over the years.

### Airport Revenue Bonds
The revenues securing airport revenue bonds usually come from either traffic-generated sources—such as landing fees, concession fees, and airline apron-use and fueling fees—or lease revenues from one or more airlines for the use of a specific facility such as a terminal or hangar.

### College and University Revenue Bonds
The revenues securing college and university revenue bonds usually include dormitory room rental fees, tuition payments, and sometimes the general assets of the college or university as well.

### Hospital Revenue Bonds
The security for hospital revenue bonds is usually dependent on federal and state reimbursement programs (such as Medicaid and Medicare), third-party com-

mercial payers (such as Blue Cross and private insurance), health maintenance organizations (HMOs), and individual patient payments.

### Single-Family Mortgage Revenue Bonds

Single-family mortgage revenue bonds are usually secured by the mortgages and mortgage loan repayments on single-family homes. Security features vary but can include Federal Housing Administration (FHA), Federal Veterans Administration (VA), or private mortgage insurance.

### Multifamily Revenue Bonds

These revenue bonds are usually issued for multifamily housing projects for senior citizens and low-income families. Some housing revenue bonds are usually secured by mortgages that are federally insured; others receive federal government operating subsidies, such as under section 8, or interest-cost subsidies, such as under section 236; and still others receive only local property-tax reductions as subsidies.

### Industrial Development and Pollution Control Revenue Bonds

Bonds have been issued for a variety of industrial and commercial activities that range from manufacturing plants to shopping centers. They are usually secured by payments to be made by the corporations or businesses that use the facilities.

### Public Power Revenue Bonds

Public power revenue bonds are secured by revenues to be produced from electrical operating plants and distribution systems. Some bonds are for a single issuer, who constructs and operates power plants and then sells the electricity. Other public power revenue bonds are issued by groups of public and private investor-owned utilities for the joint financing of the construction of one or more power plants. This last arrangement is known as a *joint power* financing structure. During the past several years, this sector has started to undergo the most dramatic changes since electricity was invented. In many states the electric utility industry is transforming to a deregulated industry. In a deregulated environment, customers will have the ability to choose an electric provider; therefore electric providers will face competition. This means this sector will experience new and different challenges and investors will need to analyze this sector differently.

### Resource Recovery Revenue Bonds

A resource recovery facility converts refuse (solid waste) into commercially salable energy, recoverable products, and a residue to be landfilled. The major revenues for a resource recovery revenue bond usually are (1) the "tipping fees" per ton paid by those who deliver the garbage to the facility for disposal; (2) revenues from steam, electricity, or refuse-derived fuel sold to either an electric power company or another energy user; and (3) revenues from the sale of recoverable materials such as aluminum and steel scrap.

### Seaport Revenue Bonds

The security for seaport revenue bonds can include specific lease agreements with the benefiting companies or pledged marine terminal and cargo tonnage fees.

### Sewer Revenue Bonds

Revenues for sewer revenue bonds come from hookup fees and user charges. For many older sewer bond issuers, substantial portions of their construction budgets have been financed with federal grants.

### Sports Complex and Convention Center Revenue Bonds

Sports complex and convention center revenue bonds usually receive revenues from sporting or convention events held at the facilities and, in some instances, from earmarked outside revenues such as local motel and hotel room taxes.

### Toll Road and Gas Tax Revenue Bonds

There are generally two types of highway revenue bonds. The bond proceeds of the first type are used to build such specific revenue-producing facilities as toll roads, bridges, and tunnels. For these pure enterprise-type revenue bonds, the pledged revenues usually are the monies collected through the tolls. The second type of highway bond is one in which the bondholders are paid by earmarked revenues outside of toll collections, such as gasoline taxes, automobile registration payments, and driver's license fees.

### Water Revenue Bonds

Water revenue bonds are issued to finance the construction of water treatment plants, pumping stations, collection facilities, and distribution systems. Revenues usually come from connection fees and charges paid by the users of the water systems.

## Hybrid and Special Bond Securities

Though having certain characteristics of general obligation and revenue bonds, the following types of municipal bonds have more unique security structures as well.

### Refunded Bonds

Although originally issued as either revenue or general obligation bonds, municipals are sometimes *refunded*. A refunding usually occurs when the original bonds are escrowed or collateralized either by direct obligations guaranteed by the U.S. government, or by other types of securities. The maturity schedules of the securities in the escrow fund are such so as to pay when due the bond's maturity value, coupon, and premium payments (if any) on the refunded bonds.

Once this cash flow match is in place, the refunded bonds are no longer secured as either general obligation or revenue bonds. The bonds are now supported by the ties held in the escrow fund. Such bonds, if escrowed with securities guaranteed by the U.S. government, have little if any credit risk. They are the safest municipal bond investments available.

Usually, an escrow fund is an irrevocable trust established by the original bond issuer with a commercial bank or state treasurer's office. Government securities are deposited in an escrow fund that will be used to pay debt service on the refunded bonds. A pure escrow fund is one in which the deposited securities are solely direct or guaranteed obligations of the U.S. government, whereas a *mixed* escrow fund is one in which the permitted securities, as defined by the trust indenture, are not exclusively limited to direct or guaranteed U.S. government securities. Other securities that could be placed in mixed escrow funds include federal agency bonds, certificates of deposit from banks, other municipal bonds, and even annuity policies from commercial insurance companies. The escrow agreement should indicate what is in the escrow fund and if substitutions of lower credit-quality investments are permitted.

Still another type of refunded bond is a *crossover refunded bond.* Typically, proceeds from crossover refunding bonds are used to purchase securities that are placed in an escrow account. Usually, the crossover refunding bonds are secured by maturing principal and interest from the escrowed securities *only until the crossover date* and the bonds to be refunded continue to be secured by the issuer's own revenues until the crossover date, which is usually the first call date of the bonds to be refunded. On that date, the crossover occurs and the bonds to be refunded are redeemed from maturing securities in the escrow fund, which could include U.S. government securities or other investments, such as certificates of deposit. In turn, the security for the refunding bonds reverts back to the issuer's own revenues.

Here we focus primarily on the pure escrow-backed bonds, not the mixed escrow or crossover bonds. The escrow fund for a refunded municipal bond can be structured so that the refunded bonds are to be called at the first possible date or a subsequent call date established in the original bond indenture. The call price usually includes a premium of from 1 to 3% above par. This type of structure usually is used for those refundings that either reduce the issuer's interest payment expenses or change the debt maturity schedule. Such bonds are known in the industry as *prerefunded* municipal bonds. Prerefunded municipal bonds usually are to be retired at their first or subsequent respective callable dates, but some escrow funds for refunding bonds have been structured differently. In such refundings, the maturity schedules of the securities in the escrow funds match the regular debt-service requirements on the bonds as originally stated in the bond indentures. Such bonds are known as *escrowed-to-maturity,* or ETM, bonds. It should be noted that under the Tax Reform Law of 1986 such ETM refundings still can be done. In the secondary market there are ETM refunded municipal bonds outstanding. However, we note that the investor or trader should determine whether all earlier calls have been legally defeased before purchasing an ETM bond.

## "Dedicated Tax-Backed" and "Structured/Asset-Backed" Bonds

More recently, states and local governments have issued increasing amounts of bonds where the debt service is to be paid from so-called "dedicated" revenues such as sales taxes, tobacco settlement payments, fees, and penalty payments. Many are structured to mimic the asset-backed bonds that are common in the taxable market. The "assets" providing the security for the municipal bonds are the "dedicated" revenues instead of credit-card receivables, home equity loans, and auto loan repayments that are commonly used to secure the taxable asset-backed bonds.

## Insured Bonds

Insured bonds, in addition to being secured by the issuer's revenues, are also backed by insurance policies written by commercial insurance companies. The insurance, usually structured as an insurance contract, is supposed to provide prompt payment to the bondholders if a default should occur. These bonds are discussed in more detail later in this chapter.

## Lease-Backed Bonds

Lease-backed bonds are usually structured as revenue-type bonds with annual payments. In some instances the payments may come only from earmarked tax revenues, student tuition payments, or patient fees. In other instances the underlying lessee governmental unit makes annual appropriations from its general fund.

## Letter of Credit-Backed Bonds

Some municipal bonds, in addition to being secured by the issuer's cash flow revenues, also are backed by commercial bank letters of credit. In some instances, the letters of credit are irrevocable and, if necessary, can be used to pay the bondholders. In other instances the issuers are required to maintain investment-quality worthiness before the letters of credit can be drawn upon.

## Life Care Revenue Bonds

Life care, or Continuing Care Retirement Community (CCRC), bonds are issued to construct long-term residential facilities for older citizens. Revenues are usually derived from initial lump-sum payments made by the residents and operating revenues.

## Moral Obligation Bonds

A moral obligation bond is a security structure for state-issued bonds that indicates that if revenues are needed for paying bondholders, the state legislature involved is legally authorized, though not required, to make an appropriation out of general state-tax revenues.

## Municipal Utility District Revenue Bonds

Municipal utility district revenue bonds are usually issued to finance the construction of water and sewer systems as well as roadways in undeveloped areas. The security is usually dependent on the commercial success of the specific development project involved, which can range from the sale of new homes to the renting of space in shopping centers and office buildings.

## New Housing Authority Bonds

New housing authority bonds are secured by a contractual pledge of annual contributions from HUD. Monies from Washington are paid directly to the paying agent for the bonds, and the bondholders are given specific legal rights to enforce the pledge. These bonds can no longer be issued.

## Tax Allocation Bonds

These bonds are usually issued to finance the construction of office buildings and other new buildings in formerly blighted areas. They are secured by property taxes collected on the improved real estate.

## "Territorial" Bonds

These are bonds issued by United States territorial possessions such as Puerto Rico, the Virgin Islands, and Guam. The bonds are tax-exempt throughout most of the country. Also, the economies of these issuers are influenced by positive special features of the United States corporate tax codes that are not available to the states.

## "Troubled City" Bailout Bonds

There are certain bonds that are structured to appear as pure revenue bonds but in essence are not. Revenues come from general purpose taxes and revenues that otherwise would have gone to a state's or city's general fund. Their bond structures were created to bail out underlying general obligation bond issuers from severe budget deficits. Examples are the New York State *Municipal Assistance Corporation for the City of New York Bonds* (MAC) and the state of Illinois *Chicago School Finance Authority Bonds*.

# Money Market Products

Tax-exempt money products include notes, commercial paper, variable-rate demand obligations, and a hybrid of the last two products.

**Notes**

Municipal notes include tax anticipation notes (TANs), revenue anticipation notes (RANs), grant anticipation notes (GANs), and bond anticipation notes (BANs). These are temporary borrowings by states, local governments, and special jurisdictions. Usually, notes are issued for a period of 12 months, though it is not uncommon for notes to be issued for periods of as short as 3 months and for as long as 3 years. TANs and RANs (also known as TRANS) are issued in anticipation of the collection of taxes or other expected revenues. These are borrowings to even out the cash flows caused by the irregular flows of income into the treasuries of the states and local units of government. BANs are issued in anticipation of the sale of long-term bonds.

Tax-exempt money market products generally have some type of credit support. This may come in the form of an irrevocable letter of credit, a line of credit, a municipal bond insurance policy, an escrow agreement, a bond purchase agreement, or a guaranteed investment contract. With a bond purchase agreement, a bank obligates itself to purchase the debt if the remarketing agent cannot resell the instrument or make a timely payment. In the case of a guaranteed investment contract, either an insurance company or a bank invests sufficient proceeds so that the cash flow generated from a portfolio of supporting assets can meet the obligation of the issue.

**Commercial Paper**

As with commercial paper issued by corporations, tax-exempt commercial paper is used by municipalities to raise funds on a short-term basis ranging from 1 day to 270 days. The dealer sets interest rates for various maturity dates and the investor then selects the desired date. Thus the investor has considerable choice in selecting a maturity to satisfy investment objectives. Provisions in the 1986 Tax Act, however, have restricted the issuance of tax-exempt commercial paper. Specifically, this act limits the new issuance of municipal obligations that is tax exempt, and as a result, every maturity of a tax-exempt commercial issuance is considered a new debt issuance. Consequently, very limited issuance of tax-exempt commercial paper exists. Instead, issuers use one of the next two products to raise short-term funds.

**Variable-Rate Demand Obligations (VRDOS)**

Variable-rate demand obligations are floating-rate obligations that have a nominal long-term maturity but have a coupon rate that is reset either daily or every 7 days. The investor has an option to put the issue back to the trustee at any time with 7 days' notice. The put price is par plus accrued interest.

**Commercial Paper/VRDO Hybrid**

The commercial paper/VRDO hybrid is customized to meet the cash flow needs of an investor. As with tax-exempt commercial paper, there is flexibility in structuring the maturity, because the remarketing agent establishes interest rates for a range of maturities. Although the instrument may have a long nominal maturity, there is a put provision as with a VRDO. Put periods can range from 1 day to over 360 days. On the put date, the investor can put back the bonds, receiving principal and interest, or the investor can elect to extend the maturity at the new interest rate and put date posted by the remarketing agent at that time. Thus the investor has two choices when initially purchasing this instrument: The interest rate and the put date. Interest is generally paid on the put date if the date is within 180 days. If the put date is more than 180 days forward, interest is paid semiannually. Some commercial paper dealers market these products under a proprietary name. Lehman markets these simply as money market municipals. Goldman Sachs refers to these securities as flexible rate notes, and Salomon Smith Barney markets them as ROCs (Reset Option Certificates).

## Municipal Derivative Securities

In recent years, a number of municipal products have been created from the basic fixed-rate municipal bond. This has been done by splitting up cash flows of newly issued bonds as well as bonds existing in the secondary markets. These products have been created by dividing the coupon interest payments and principal payments into two or more bonds classes, or *tranches*. The resulting bond classes may have far different yield and price volatility characteristics than the underlying fixed-rate municipal bond from which they were created. By expanding the risk/return profile available in the municipal marketplace, institutional investors have more flexibility in structuring municipal bond portfolios either to satisfy a specific asset/liability objective or to make an interest rate or yield curve bet more efficiently.

The name *derivative securities* has been attributed to these bond classes because they derive their value from the underlying fixed-rate municipal bond. Much of the development in this market has paralleled that of the taxable, and specifically the mortgage-backed securities, market. The ability of investment bankers to create these securities has been enhanced by the development of the municipal swap market.

A common type of derivative security is one in which two classes of securities, a *floating-rate security* and an *inverse floating-rate bond,* are created from a fixed-rate bond. Two types of inverse-floaters dominate the market: auction rate securities and the later-developed TOB (Tender Option Bond) product. TOB programs, in various forms, have existed since the beginning-to-mid 1980s. Widespread use did not occur until the 1990s.

Initially, inverse-floaters took the form of auction rate securities. Salomon Smith Barney's proprietary auction rate product is called ARS (Auction Rate Securities) and IRS (Inverse Rate Securities). Lehman's proprietary product is called RIBS (Residual Interest Bonds) and SAVRS (Select Auction Variable Rate

Securities), and Goldman's proprietary product is called PARS (Periodic Auction Rate Securities) and INFLOS, which are inverse floaters.

With these auction rate securities the coupon rate on the floating-rate security is reset based on the results of a Dutch auction. The auction can take place anywhere between 7 days and 6 months (but the frequency is for a given security). The coupon rate on the floating-rate security changes in the same direction as market rates. The inverse floating-rate bond receives the residual interest; that is, the coupon interest paid on this bond is the difference between the fixed-rate on the underlying bond and the floating-rate security. Thus the coupon rate on the inverse floating-rate bond changes in the opposite direction of interest rates.

The sum of interest paid on the auction-rate floater and inverse floater (plus fees associated with the auction) must always equal the sum of the fixed-rate bond from which they were created. A floor (a minimum interest rate) is established on the inverse floater. Typically the floor is zero. As a result, a cap (maximum interest rate) will be imposed on the floater such that the combined floor of zero on the inverse floater and the cap on the floater is equal to the total interest rate on the fixed-rate bond from which they were created.

New issuance of auction-rate derivatives, however, has been largely supplanted by TOB programs as the primary vehicle to create inverse floaters. Functionally, TOBs are similar to the auction rate product. Both derivatives are inverse floaters. Auction-rate floaters, however, are primarily sold to corporations, whereas TOB floaters are sold to money market funds. Auction floaters are ineligible to be sold to money market funds. When corporations have less use for tax-exempt income, the demand and liquidity in auction-rate securities can substantially decrease. Tax-exempt money market funds, unlike corporations, have a continuous need for tax-exempt interest. This demand provides a more stable buying base for the TOB floaters. To take advantage of this money-market demand, TOBs feature a liquidity facility, which makes these floating-rate derivatives putable and therefore money-market eligible. These liquidity facilities typically last 364 days and are provided by highly rated banks or broker-dealers.

TOBs are created through trusts. Given this structure, certain provisions must exist for the unwinding of a TOB. For example, if the remarketing agent fails to sell out the floating-rate class or the underlying bond falls below a minimum collateral value a mandatory tender event is triggered. When a mandatory tender event occurs, the liquidity provider pays the floater holder par plus accrued interest. The trustee simultaneously terminates the trust and liquidates the bonds. The proceeds from this sale are used to first pay par plus accrued interest to the liquidity provider, then any accrued fees. Finally, the inverse floating-rate investor receives the residual value.

Several proprietary programs have been developed to market and sell plain-vanilla TOBs, which are used by mutual bond funds and insurance companies. Additionally, TOBs are used in more exotic combination trades by a few

Wall Street structured products areas. Salomon Smith Barney's proprietary program is called "ROCs & ROLs." The short-term certificates are called ROCs or (Residual Option Certificates). The inverse-floaters are called the "ROLs" or (Residual Option Longs), Lehman's is called RIBS and Trust Receipts, and Morgan Stanley's proprietary program is called municipal trust certificates.

## THE COMMERCIAL CREDIT RATING OF MUNICIPAL BONDS

Of the municipal bonds that were rated by a commercial rating company in 1929 and plunged into default in 1932, 78% had been rated double-A or better, and 48% had been rated triple-A. Since then the ability of rating agencies to assess the creditworthiness of municipal obligations has evolved to a level of general industry acceptance and respectability. In most instances, they adequately describe the financial conditions of the issuers and identify the credit-risk factors. However, a small but significant number of recent instances have caused market participants to reexamine their reliance on the opinions of the rating agencies.

As examples, the troubled bonds of the Washington Public Power Supply System (WPPSS) and Orange County, California should be mentioned. Two major commercial rating companies, Moody's and Standard & Poor's, gave their highest ratings to the WPPSS bonds in the early 1980s. Moody's gave the WPPSS Projects 1, 2, and 3 bonds its very highest credit rating of Aaa and the Projects 4 and 5 bonds its rating of A1. This latter investment-grade rating is defined as having the strongest investment attributes within the upper medium grade of creditworthiness. Standard & Poor's also had given the WPPSS Projects 1, 2, and 3 bonds its highest rating of AAA and Projects 4 and 5 bonds its rating of A+ . While these high-quality ratings were in effect WPPSS sold over $8 billion in long-term bonds. By 1990, over $2 billion of these bonds were in default.

Orange County, California also had very strong credit ratings before its filing for bankruptcy protection on December 6, 1994. This would be the largest municipal bankruptcy filing in U.S. history. The Orange County debacle was unique. The county's problem were not caused by local economic problems, like Philadelphia's crisis in the early 1990s nor were they caused by budget problems like New York City's situation in 1975. Orange County's problems were created by the county Treasurer-Tax Collector's investment strategy for the Orange County Investment Pool. The investment pool was highly leveraged and contained a large percentage of inverse floaters. As interest rates rose in 1994, the value of the investments decreased and the institutions that provided the financial leverage decided to terminate those financial agreements. The problem was that if the investment pool were liquidated, the amount of assets would be insufficient to cover all of the loans. Since the pool did not have sufficient assets to cover its debt, the county chose to seek the safety of bankruptcy protection.

The county's voluntary bankruptcy filing was unprecedented. It was a signal to investors that the county did not necessarily intend to repay all of its obligations. In most other cases of severe financial hardship, the municipalities tried to meet all of their obligations and did not even suggest that they might wish not to fulfill their obligations. What troubled most investors was that Orange County was a vibrant and economically strong area and in all likelihood could fulfill its obligations. This created a different situation for investors and brought the question of an issuer's ability to pay versus its willingness to pay. This was something that municipal investors rarely, if ever, questioned before Orange County.

Another area investors rarely questioned prior to Orange County was the investment strategies that were being used to manage operating fund investments and other state and local investment funds or pools. It was a common perception that state and local government finance officials invested conservatively and followed policies that emphasized safety of principal and maintenance of liquidity. Immediately following the onset of the Orange County debacle, large investors started to question state and local officials on their investment policies, and their use of financial leverage and derivative securities. Because Orange County received high-quality credit ratings prior to its problems, investors started to question the reliability of the commercial credit rating agencies.

The Washington Public Power Supply System and Orange County, California are the more notable issuers that had high-quality ratings prior to their problems, but they are not isolated instances. In fact, since 1975 all of the major municipal defaults in the industry initially had been given investment-grade ratings by Moody's and Standard & Poor's. Of course, it should be noted that in the majority of instances, ratings of the commercial rating companies adequately reflect the condition of the credit. However, unlike 30 years ago when the commercial rating companies would not rate many kinds of revenue bond issues, today they seem to view themselves as assisting in the capital formation process.

Today, many large institutional investors, underwriters, and traders use the ratings of the commercial rating agencies as starting points and rely on their own in-house municipal credit analysts for determining the creditworthiness of municipal bonds. However, other investors do not perform their own credit-risk analysis, but instead rely entirely upon credit-risk ratings by Moody's and Standard & Poor's. In this section, we discuss the rating categories of these two commercial rating companies.

We note that there is also a third, and smaller, commercial rating company, Fitch. It has enhanced its market presence and is particularly known in the industry for its health care and Continuing Care Retirement Community ratings, among others.

## Moody's Investors Service

The municipal bond rating system used by Moody's grades the investment quality of municipal bonds in a nine-symbol system that ranges from the highest investment quality, which is Aaa, to the lowest credit rating, which is C. The respective nine alphabetical ratings and their definitions are found in Exhibit 9–2.

Municipal bonds in the top four categories (Aaa, Aa, A, and Baa) are considered to be of investment-grade quality. Additionally, bonds in the Aa through Caa categories are refined by numeric modifiers 1, 2 and 3 with "1" indicating the top third of the rating category, "2" the middle third and "3" the bottom third. Moody's also may use the prefix *Con.* before a credit rating to indicate that the bond security is dependent on (1) the completion of a construction project; (2) earnings of a project with little operating experience; (3) rentals be paid once the facility is constructed; or (4) some other limiting condition.

The municipal note rating system used by Moody's is designated by investment-grade categories of Moody's Investment Grade (MIG), as shown in Exhibit 9–3.

Moody's also provides credit ratings for tax-exempt commercial paper. These are promissory obligations not having an original maturity in excess of nine months. Moody's uses three designations all considered to be of investment grade, for indicating the relative repayment capacity of the rated issuers, as shown in Exhibit 9–4.

## Standard & Poor's

The municipal bond rating system used by Standard & Poor's grades the investment quality of municipal bonds in a 10-symbol system that ranges from

**E X H I B I T   9–2**

Moody's Municipal Bond Ratings

| Rating | Definition |
|--------|------------|
| Aaa | Best quality; carry the smallest degree of credit risk |
| Aa | High quality; margins of protection not quite as large as the Aaa bonds |
| A | Upper medium grade; security adequate but could be susceptible to impairment |
| Baa | Medium grade; neither highly protected nor poorly secured—lack outstanding investment characteristics and sensitive to changes in economic circumstances |
| Ba | Speculative; protection is very moderate |
| B | Highly speculative; sensitive to day-to-day economic circumstances |
| Caa | Poor standing; may be in default but with recovery prospects |
| Ca | Likely to be in default with poor recovery prospects |
| C | In default with no recovery expected |

**EXHIBIT   9–3**

Moody's Municipal Note Ratings*

| Rating | Definition |
|--------|------------|
| MIG 1 | Best quality |
| MIG 2 | High quality |
| MIG 3 | Adequate quality |

*A short issue having a demand feature (i.e., payment relying on external liquidity and usually payable upon demand rather than fixed maturity dates) is differentiated by Moody's with the use of the symbols VMIG1 through VMIG3.

**EXHIBIT   9–4**

Moody's Tax-Exempt Commercial Paper Ratings

| Rating | Definition |
|--------|------------|
| Prime 1 (P-1) | Superior capacity for repayment |
| Prime 2 (P-2) | Strong capacity for repayment |
| Prime 3 (P-3) | Acceptable capacity for repayment |

the highest investment quality, which is AAA, to the lowest credit rating, which is D. Bonds within the top four categories (AAA, AA, A, and BBB) are considered by Standard & Poor's as being of investment-grade quality. The respective 10 alphabetical ratings and definitions are shown in Exhibit 9–5.

Standard & Poor's also uses a plus (+) or minus (−) sign to show relative standing within the rating categories ranging from AA to CCC. Additionally, Standard & Poor's uses the letter p to indicate a provisional rating that is intended to be removed upon the successful and timely completion of the construction project. The (r) denotes issues that Standard & Poor's believes may experience high volatility in expected return due to noncredit risks. Such issues could be derivatives or hybrid securities.

The municipal note rating system used by Standard & Poor's grades the investment quality of municipal notes in a four-symbol system that ranges from highest investment quality, SP-1+, to the lowest credit rating, SP-3. Notes within the top three categories (i.e., SP-1+, SP-1, and SP-2) are considered by Standard & Poor's as being of investment-grade quality. The respective ratings and summarized definitions are shown in Exhibit 9–6.

Standard & Poor's also rates tax-exempt commercial paper in the same four categories as taxable commercial paper. The four tax-exempt commercial paper rating categories are shown in Exhibit 9–7.

**EXHIBIT 9–5**

Standard & Poor's Municipal Bond Ratings

| Rating | Definition |
|--------|------------|
| AAA | Highest rating; extremely strong security |
| AA | Very strong security; differs from AAA in only a small degree |
| A | Strong capacity but more susceptible to adverse economic effects than two above categories |
| BBB | Adequate capacity but adverse economic conditions more likely to weaken capacity |
| BB | Lowest degree of speculation; risk exposure |
| B | Speculative; risk exposure |
| CCC | Speculative; major risk exposure |
| CC | Highly vulnerable to nonpayment |
| C | Bankruptcy petition may be filed |
| D | Bonds in default with interest and/or repayment of principal in arrears |

**EXHIBIT 9–6**

Standard & Poor's Municipal Note Ratings

| Rating | Definition |
|--------|------------|
| SP-1 | Strong capacity to pay principal and interest. Those issues determined to possess overwhelming safety characteristic will be given a plus (+) designation. |
| SP-2 | Satisfactory capacity to pay principal and interest. |
| SP-3 | Speculative capacity to pay principal and interest. |

## Fitch

A third, and smaller, rating company is Fitch. The alphabetical ratings and definitions used by Fitch are given in Exhibit 9–8. Plus (+) and minus (−) signs are used with a rating to indicate the relative position of a credit within the rating category. Plus and minus signs are not used for the AAA category.

## MUNICIPAL BOND INSURANCE

Using municipal bond insurance is one way to help reduce credit risk within a portfolio. Insurance on a municipal bond is an agreement by an insurance company to pay debt service that is not paid by the bond issuer. Municipal bond

**EXHIBIT  9–7**

Standard & Poor's Tax-Exempt Commercial Paper Ratings

| Rating | Definition |
|--------|------------|
| A-1+ | Extremely strong degree of safety |
| A-1 | Strong degree of safety |
| A-2 | Satisfactory degree of safety |
| A-3 | Adequate degree of safety |
| B | Speculative capacity for timely payment |
| C | Doubtful payment for capacity |
| D | Used when principal or interest payments are not made on the due date |

**EXHIBIT  9–8**

Fitch Municipal Bond Ratings

| Rating | Definition |
|--------|------------|
| AAA | Highest credit quality |
| AA | Very high credit quality |
| A | High credit quality |
| BBB | Good |
| BB | Speculative |
| B | Highly speculative |
| CCC | High default risk |
| CC | High default risk |
| C | High default risk |
| DDD, DD, D | In default |

insurance contracts insure the payment of debt service on a municipal bond to the bondholder. That is, the insurance company promises to pay the issuer's obligation to the bondholder if the issuer does not do so.

The insurance usually is for the life of the issue. If the trustee or investor has not had his bond paid by the issuer on its due date, he notifies the insurer and presents the defaulted bond and coupon. Under the terms of the insurance contract, the insurer is generally obligated to pay sufficient monies to cover the value of the defaulted insured principal and coupon interest when they come due.

Because municipal bond insurance reduces the credit risk for the investor, the marketability of certain municipal bonds can be greatly expanded. Municipal bonds that benefit most from the insurance would include lower-quality bonds,

bonds issued by smaller governmental units not widely known in the financial community, bonds that have a sound though complex and difficult-to-understand security structure, and bonds issued by infrequent local-government borrowers who do not have a general market following among investors.

Of course, a major factor for an issuer to obtain bond insurance is that its creditworthiness without the insurance is substantially lower than what it would be with the insurance. That is, the interest cost savings are only of sufficient magnitude to offset the cost of the insurance premium when the underlying creditworthiness of the issuer is lower. There are two major groups of municipal bond insurers. The first includes the "monoline" companies that are primarily in the business of insuring municipal bonds. Almost all of the companies that are now insuring municipal bonds can be characterized as monoline in structure. The second group of municipal bond insurers includes the "multiline" property and casualty companies that usually have a wide base of business, including insurance for fires, collisions, hurricanes, and health problems. Most new issues in the municipal bond market today are insured by the insurers described below. By the year 2000, over 50% of all new issues came with bond insurance.

The monoline companies are primarily in the business of insuring municipal bonds, and their respective assets, as determined in various state statutes and administrative rulings, are dedicated to paying bond principal and interest claims. The active insurers are: AMBAC Indemnity Corporation (AMBAC); Financial Guaranty Insurance Company (FGIC); Financial Security Assurance, Inc. (FSA); and Municipal Bond Investors Assurance Corporation (MBIA Corp.).

It is commonly understood that when referring to insured bonds, you are also referring to bonds that receive a triple-A rating due to presence of the insurance coverage. However, in the future, the market place might need to refine this notion. In 1997, ACA Financial Guaranty Corp. was started and became the first "A" rated bond insurer. ACA mostly focuses on the domestic finance and asset-backed sectors. This event has the potential to change the market in terms of broadening the quality range of issuers that can utilize insurance as a credit enhancement. Sub-investment grade, particularly double-B rated issuers and non-rated issuers now have access to insurance and greater access to the capital markets. Asset Guaranty Insurance Company (double-A) has also provided underwriting capacity to non-investment grade and non-rated issuers. Asset Guaranty Insurance Co. operates under the umbrella of Enhance Financial Services Group.

## VALUATION METHODS

The traditional method for evaluating municipal bonds is relatively straightforward. First an investor determines the maturity of the bond, considers the offered price (discount, par, or premium), evaluates any call features or sinking funds, and then considers credit quality. If it is a premium bond and callable, then the investor places more emphasis on the call dates. If the bond is callable and sells at a discount, then the calls are not much of a factor and the bond is valued using its maturity date. Basically, the investor is determining the relative attractiveness of the bond based on a yield-to-worst calculation. The credit quality is quantified and the appropriate yield premium for the specific credit quality is added to the base yield-to-worst calculation. Since investors do not perform an option adjusted-spread analysis (OAS), the yield premium that is applied is a nominal yield premium. The benchmark yields that are used to value the bonds come from a variety of sources, such as, yield levels from the primary market, trading levels of similar bonds in the secondary market, and benchmark (triple-A GO, generic sector, state specific) interest rate curves.

An investor interested in purchasing a municipal bond must be able to compare the promised yield on a municipal bond with that of a comparable taxable bond. Using the yield computed using the traditional approaches, the following general formula is used to determine the *equivalent taxable yield* for a tax-exempt bond:

$$\text{Equivalent taxable yield} = \frac{\text{Tax-exempt yield}}{(1 - \text{Marginal tax rate})}$$

For example, suppose an investor in the 40% marginal tax bracket is considering the acquisition of a tax-exempt bond that offers a tax-exempt yield of 6%. The equivalent taxable yield is 10%, as shown below.

$$\text{Equivalent taxable yield} = \frac{.06}{(1 - .40)} = .10 = 10\%$$

When computing the equivalent taxable yield, the traditionally computed yield-to-maturity is not the tax-exempt yield if the issue is selling below par (i.e., selling at a discount) because only the coupon interest is exempt from federal income taxes. Instead, the yield-to-maturity after an assumed capital gains tax is computed and used in the numerator of the formula.

The yield-to-maturity after an assumed capital gains tax is calculated in the same manner as the traditional yield-to-maturity. However, instead of using the redemption value in the calculation, the net proceeds after an assumed tax on any capital gain are used.

There is a major drawback in employing the equivalent taxable yield formula to compare the relative investment merits of a taxable and tax-exempt bond. Recall from the discussion in Chapter 4 that the yield-to-maturity measure assumes that the entire coupon interest can be reinvested at the computed yield. Consequently, taxable bonds with the same yield-to-maturity cannot be compared because the total dollar returns may differ from the computed yield. The same problem arises when attempting to compare taxable and tax-exempt bonds, especially because only a portion of the coupon interest on taxable bonds can be reinvested, although the entire coupon payment is available for reinvestment in the case of municipal bonds. The total return framework that should be employed compare taxable and tax-exempt bonds is discussed in Chapter 4.

The traditional method of evaluating a municipal bond leaves much to be desired. The basic problem is that the call risk is not analyzed properly. The yield-to-worst calculation ignores the fact that interest rates can change in the future and the actual timing of the cash flows may not be the same as what was projected. If an investor evaluates a bond to its maturity date, then this investor will be surprised if the bonds are called several years earlier. Conversely, if the investor evaluates a bond to a specific call date and the bond isn't called, then this investor will realize a stream of cash flows which is different from what was anticipated. The result of the traditional methodology is that most callable municipal bonds are priced too richly and the cost of non-callable bonds with extra convexity is cheap. This is especially true for longer dated bonds. More information about OAS analysis can be found in the section, "Fixed Income Analytics and Modeling" of this book.

## TAX PROVISIONS AFFECTING MUNICIPALS

Federal tax rate levels affect municipal bond values and strategies employed by investors. There are three provisions in the Internal Revenue Code that investors in municipal securities should recognize. These provisions deal with the tax treatment of OIDs, alternative minimum tax, and the deductibility of interest expense incurred to acquire municipal securities. Moreover, there are state and local taxes that an investor must be aware of.

### Tax Treatment of OIDs

When purchasing OIDs in the secondary market investors should analyze the bond carefully due to the complex tax treatment of OIDs. Few investors think about tax implications when investing in municipal debt. After all, the interest earned on most municipal bonds is exempt from federal taxes and in many cases state and local taxes. If investors do think about taxes they probably think about selling bonds at a higher price than the original tax cost. Most investors believe this would create a capital gain and absent this situation there should be no tax impact. Sounds straightforward, but the municipal world isn't simplistic. Several years ago the marketplace was introduced to the Revenue Reconciliation Act of 1993 and since then investing in municipals has become more complex. Currently, profit from bonds purchased in the secondary market after April 30, 1993 could be free from any tax implications, taxed at the capital gains rate, ordinary income rate or a combination of the two rates. To understand this situation, it is essential to understand the rule of *de minimis*.

In basic terms the rule of *de minimis* states that a bond is to be discounted up to 0.25% from the face value for each remaining year of a bond's life before it is affected by ordinary income taxes. This price is commonly referred to as the market discount cutoff price. If the bond is purchased at a market discount, but the price is higher than the market discount cutoff price then any profits will be taxed at the capital gains rate. If the purchase price is lower than the market discount cutoff price, then any profits may be taxed as ordinary income or a combination of the ordinary income rate and the capital gains rate. The exact tax burden depends on several factors.

The rule of *de minimis* is especially complicated for OID bonds. For these bonds, a revised issue price must be calculated as well as the market discount cutoff price. The revised issue price does change over time since the OID must be accreted over the life of the bond. The rule of *de minimis* doesn't apply to the OID segment, but it does apply to the market discount segment. The market discount segment is equal to the purchase price (secondary market price) minus the revised issue price. If an OID bond is purchased in the secondary market at a price greater than the revised issue price the bond is considered to have an acquisition premium and the rule of *de minimis* doesn't apply. If the OID bond is purchased at a price below the revised issue price and above the market discount cutoff price then the OID bond is purchased at a market discount and any profits will be taxed at the capital gains rate. Finally, if the purchase price of the OID bond is lower than the market discount cutoff price then any profits may be taxed as ordinary income or a combination of the ordinary income rate and the capital gains rate. The exact tax burden depends on several factors. The OID topic is complicated. More specific details can be found in the IRS Publications 550 and 1212.[4]

## Alternative Minimum Tax

*Alternative minimum taxable income* (AMTI) is a taxpayer's taxable income with certain adjustments for specified tax preferences designed to cause AMTI to approximate economic income. For both individuals and corporations, a taxpayer's liability is the greater of (1) the tax computed at regular tax rates on taxable income, and (2) the tax computed at a lower rate on AMTI. This parallel tax system, the alternative minimum tax (AMT), is designed to prevent taxpayers from avoiding significant tax liability as a result of taking advantage of exclusions from gross income, deductions, and tax credits otherwise allowed under the Internal Revenue Code.

There are different rules for determining AMTI for individuals and corporations. The latter are required to calculate their minimum tax liability using two methods. Moreover, there are special rules for property and casualty companies.

---

4. Also several articles on the topic, such as Bloomberg's, "Taxing Tax-Exempt Bonds," May 1995, are available.

One of the tax preference items that must be included is certain tax-exempt municipal interest. As a result of the AMT, the value of the tax-exempt feature is reduced. However, the interest of some municipal issues is not subject to the AMT. Under the current tax code, tax-exempt interest earned on all private activity bonds issued after August 7, 1986, must be included in AMTI. There are two exceptions. First, interest from bonds that are issued by 501(c)(3) organizations (i.e., not-for-profit organizations) is not subject to AMTI. The second exception is interest from bonds issued for the purpose of refunding if the original bonds were issued before August 7, 1986. The AMT does not apply to interest on governmental or nonprivate activity municipal bonds. An implication is that those issues that are subject to the AMT will trade at a higher yield than those exempt from AMT.

## Deductibility of Interest Expense Incurred to Acquire Municipals

Some investment strategies involve the borrowing of funds to purchase or carry securities. Ordinarily, interest expense on borrowed funds to purchase or carry investment securities is tax deductible. There is one exception that is relevant to investors in municipal bonds. The Internal Revenue Service specifies that interest paid or accrued on "indebtedness incurred or continued to purchase or carry obligations, the interest on which is wholly exempt from taxes," is not tax deductible. It does not make any difference if any tax-exempt interest is actually received by the taxpayer in the taxable year. In other words, interest is not deductible on funds borrowed to purchase or carry tax-exempt securities.

Special rules apply to commercial banks. At one time, banks were permitted to deduct all the interest expense incurred to purchase or carry municipal securities. Tax legislation subsequently limited the deduction first to 85% of the interest expense and then to 80%. The 1986 tax law eliminated the deductibility of the interest expense for bonds acquired after August 6, 1986. The exception to this nondeductibility of interest expense rule is for *bank-qualified issues*. These are tax-exempt obligations sold by small issuers after August 6, 1986, and purchased by the bank for its investment portfolio.

An issue is bank qualified if: (1) it is a tax-exempt issue other than private activity bonds, but including any bonds issued by 501(c)(3) organizations, and (2) it is designated by the issuer as bank qualified and the issuer or its subordinate entities reasonably do not intend to issue more than $10 million of such bonds. A nationally recognized and experienced bond attorney should include in the opinion letter for the specific bond issue that the bonds are bank qualified.

## State and Local Taxes

The tax treatment of municipal bonds varies by state. There are three types of taxes that can be imposed: (1) an income tax on coupon income; (2) a tax on realized capital gains; and (3) a personal property tax.

Many states levy an individual income tax. Coupon interest from obligations by in-state issuers is exempt from state individual income taxes in most states. A few states levy individual income taxes on coupon interest whether the issuer is in state or out of state.

State taxation of realized capital gains is often ignored by investors when making investment decisions. In many states, a tax is levied on a base that includes income from capital transactions (i.e., capital gains or losses). In many states where coupon interest is exempt if the issuer is in state, the same exemption will not apply to capital gains involving municipal bonds.

Some states levy a personal property tax on municipal bonds. The tax resembles more of an income tax than a personal property tax. Before 1995, some state and local governments levied this tax on residents who owned municipal bonds where the issuer of the bond was located outside of the investor's home state. While residents owning municipal bonds where the issuer was located within the investor's home state's boundaries were exempt from such tax, this tax was declared unconstitutional by the U.S. Supreme Court because it violated the federal Commerce Clause by favoring in-state businesses over out-of-state business. The determining case was *Fulton Corporation* v. *Janice H. Faulkner, Secretary of Revenue of North Carolina,* No. 94-1239 (U.S. S.C. Feb. 21, 1996). After the court ruled on this case, many state and local governments, which levied a similar tax, repealed the tax or chose not to collect it.

In determining the effective tax rate imposed by a particular state, an investor must consider the impact of the deductibility of state taxes on federal income taxes. Moreover, in some states, *federal* taxes are deductible in determining state income taxes.

## YIELD RELATIONSHIPS WITHIN THE MUNICIPAL BOND MARKET

### Differences within an Assigned Credit Rating

Bond buyers primarily use the credit ratings assigned by the commercial rating companies, Standard & Poor's and Moody's, as a starting point for pricing an issue. The final market-derived bond price is determined by the assigned credit rating and adjustments by investors to reflect their own analysis of creditworthiness and perception of marketability. For example, insured municipal bonds tend to have yields that are substantially higher than noninsured superior-investment quality municipal bonds even though most insured bonds are given triple-A ratings by the commercial rating companies. Additionally, many investors have geographical preferences among bonds, in spite of identical credit quality and otherwise comparable investment characteristics.

### Differences between Credit Ratings

With all other factors constant, the greater the credit risk perceived by investors, the higher the return expected by investors. The spread between municipal bonds of different credit quality is not constant over time. Reasons for the change in spreads are: (1) the outlook for the economy and its anticipated impact on issuers; (2) federal budget financing needs; and (3) municipal market supply-and-demand factors. During periods of relatively low interest rates, investors sometimes increase their holdings of issues of lower credit quality in order to obtain additional yield. This narrows the spread between high-grade and lower-grade credit issues. During periods in which investors anticipate a poor economic climate, there is often a "flight to quality" as investors pursue a more conservative, credit-risk exposure. This widens the spread between high-grade and lower-grade credit issues.

Another factor that causes shifts in the spread between issues of different, quality is the temporary oversupply of issues within a market sector. For example, a substantial new-issue volume of high-grade state general obligation bonds may tend to decrease the spread between high-grade and lower-grade revenue bonds. In a weak market environment, it is easier for high-grade municipal bonds to come to market than for weaker credits. Therefore, it is not uncommon for high grades to flood weak markets at the same time there is a relative scarcity of medium- and low-grade municipal bond issues.

## Differences between in-State and General Market

Bonds of municipal issuers located in certain states (for example, New York, California, Arizona, Maryland, and Pennsylvania) usually yield considerably less than issues of identical credit quality that come from other states that trade in the "general market." There are three reasons for the existence of such spreads. First, states often exempt interest from in-state issues from state and local personal income taxes. Interest from out-of-state issues is generally not exempt. Consequently, in states with high income taxes (e.g., New York and California), strong investor demand for in-state issues will reduce their yields relative to bonds of issues located in states where state and local income taxes are not important considerations (e.g., Illinois and Wisconsin). Second, in some states, public funds deposited in banks must be collateralized by the bank accepting the deposit. This requirement is referred to as pledging. Acceptable collateral for pledging will typically include issues of certain in-state issuers. For those qualifying issues, pledging tends to increase demand (particularly for the shorter maturities) and reduce yields relative to nonqualifying comparable issues. The third reason is that investors in some states exhibit extreme reluctance to purchase issues from issuers outside of their state or region. In-state parochialism tends to decrease relative yields of issues from states in which investors exhibit this behavior.

## Differences between Maturities

One determinant of the yield on a bond is the number of years remaining to maturity. As explained in Chapter 6, the yield curve depicts the relationship at a given point in time between yields and maturity for bonds that are identical in every way except maturity. When yields increase with maturity, the yield curve is said to be normal or have a *positive slope*. Therefore, as investors lengthen their maturity, they require a greater yield. It is also possible for the yield curve to be "inverted," meaning that long-term yields are less than short-term yields. If short-, intermediate-, and long-term yields are roughly the same, the yield curve is said to be *flat*.

In the taxable bond market, it is not unusual to find all three shapes for the yield curve at different points in the business cycle. However, in the municipal bond market, the yield curve is typically normal or upward sloping. Consequently, in the municipal bond market, long-term bonds generally offer higher yields than short- and intermediate-term bonds.

## Insured Municipal Bonds

In general, although insured municipal bonds sell at yields lower than they would without the insurance, they tend to have yields higher than other Aaa/AAA-rated bonds such as deep-discount refunded bonds. Of course, supply-and-demand forces and in-state taxation factors can distort market trading patterns from time to time. Insured bonds as a generic group may not be viewed as having the same superior degree of safety as either refunded bonds secured with escrowed U.S. Treasuries or those general obligation bonds of states that have robust and growing economies, fiscally conservative budgetary operations and very low debt burdens.

## PRIMARY AND SECONDARY MARKETS

The municipal market can be divided into the primary market and the secondary market. The primary market is where all new issues of municipal bonds are sold for the first time. The secondary market is the market where previously issued municipal securities are traded.

## Primary Market

A substantial number of municipal obligations are brought to market each week. A state or local government can market its new issue by offering bonds publicly to the investing community or by placing them privately with a small group of investors. When a public offering is selected, the issue usually is underwritten by investment bankers or municipal bond departments of commercial banks. Public offerings may be marketed by either competitive bidding or direct negotiations with underwriters. When an issue is marketed via competitive bidding, the issue is awarded to the bidder submitting the best bid.

Most states mandate that general obligation issues be marketed through competitive bidding, but generally this is not required for revenue bonds. Usually state and local governments require a competitive sale to be announced in a recognized financial publication, such as *The Bond Buyer,* which is the trade publication for the municipal bond industry. *The Bond Buyer* also provides information on upcoming competitive sales and most negotiated sales, as well as the results of previous weeks.

# Secondary Market

Municipal bonds are traded in the over-the-counter market supported by municipal bond dealers across the country. Markets are maintained on smaller issuers (referred to as *local credits)* by regional brokerage firms, local banks, and some of the larger Wall Street firms. Larger issuers (referred to as *general market names)* are supported by the larger brokerage firms and banks, many of whom have investment banking relationships with these issuers. There are brokers who serve as intermediaries in the sale of large blocks of municipal bonds among dealers and large institutional investors. Additionally, beginning in 2000, bonds in the secondary market as well as some new issue competitive and negotiated bond issues began to be auctioned and sold over the Internet by large and small broker-dealers to institutional and individual investors.

In the municipal bond markets, an odd lot of bonds is $25,000 or less in par value for retail investors. For institutions, anything below $100,000 in par value is considered an odd lot. Dealer spreads depend on several factors. For the retail investor, the spread can range from as low as one-quarter of one point ($12.50 per $5,000 of par value) on large blocks of actively traded bonds to four points ($200 per $5,000 of par value) for odd-lot sales of an inactive issue. For retail investors, the typical commission should be between 1½ and 2½ points. For institutional investors, the dealer spread rarely exceeds one-half of one point ($25 per $5,000 of par value).

The convention for both corporate and Treasury bonds is to quote prices as a percentage of par value with 100 equal to par. Municipal bonds, however, generally are traded and quoted in terms of yield (yield-to-maturity or yield-to-call). The price of the bond in this case is called a *basis price.* Certain long-maturity revenue bonds are exceptions. A bond traded and quoted in dollar prices (actually, as a percentage of par value) is called a *dollar bond.*

It should be noted that many institutional investors, for trading and bond purchasing purposes, price bonds off the "MMD" scale. This is a daily index of generic "AAA's" prices covering the full yield curve, provided by Thomson Financial and available to subscribers over the Internet. Also, the Municipal Securities Rulemaking Board (MSRB) in Washington, D.C. reports on a daily basis for no charge actual trades and prices of specific bonds. The Internet address is: "www.investinginbonds.com," which is the home page of the Bond Market Association (BMA), the trade association for the sell side.

# BOND INDEXES

The major provider of total return based indices to institutional investors is Lehman Brothers. Investors use the Lehman Brothers Municipal Index to measure relative total return performance and to enhance a fund manager's ability to outperform the market. Lehman began publishing municipal indices in January of 1980 and by mid-2000 compiles returns and statistics on over 2,500 benchmarks. They are broad-based performance measures for the tax-exempt bond market. Similar to all bond indices provided by Lehman Brothers, the municipal indices are rules based and market value weighted. As of May 2000, the Lehman Municipal index contained 39,149 bonds with a market value of $694 billion. To be included in the index, bonds must have a minimum credit rating of Baa/BBB. They must have an outstanding par value of at least $5 million and be part of a transaction of $50 million or greater. The bonds must have been issued after December 31, 1990, and have a remaining maturity of at least one year.

In addition to investment grade indices, Lehman Brothers offers total return benchmarks for the noninvestment grade tax-exempt market. To insure statistically significant, representative benchmarks for the lower capitalized states, Lehman provides state specific municipal benchmarks with reduced liquidity requirements.

Many investors utilize Lehman indices as performance measures for a given market or market segment. The benchmarks are also employed to identify and quantify portfolio bets versus the general market and/or a given peer group. Indices are also used to identify relative value opportunities as well as a proxy for the outstanding market. Given the consistent methodologies, The Lehman indices are often used when comparing tax-exempt and taxable fixed income markets.

# OFFICIAL STATEMENT

An official statement describing the issue and the issuer is prepared for new offerings. Often a preliminary official statement is issued prior to the final official statement. These statements are known as the OS and POS. These statements provide potential investors with a wealth of information. The statements contain basic information about the amount of bonds to be issued, maturity dates, coupons, the use of the bond proceeds, the credit ratings, a general statement about the issuer and discloses the name of the underwriter and members of the selling group. Much of this information can be found on the cover page or in the first few pages of the official statement. It also contains detailed information about the security and sources of payments for the bonds, sources and uses of funds, debt service requirements, relevant risk factors, issuer's financial statements, a summary of the bond indenture, relevant agreements, notice of any known existing or pending litigation, the bond insurance policy specimen (if insured) and the form of opinion of bond counsel. The official statement contains most of the information an investor will need in order to make an informed and educated investment decision.


## REGULATION OF THE MUNICIPAL SECURITIES MARKET

As an outgrowth of abusive stock market practices, Congress passed the Securities Act of 1933 and the Securities Exchange Act of 1934. The 1934 Act created the Securities and Exchange Commission (SEC), granting it regulatory authority over the issuance and trading of *corporate* securities. Congress specifically exempted municipal securities from both the registration requirements of the 1933 Act and the periodic-reporting requirements of the 1934 Act. However, antifraud provisions did apply to offerings of or dealings in municipal securities.

The exemption afforded municipal securities appears to have been due to: (1) the desire for governmental comity; (2) the absence of recurrent abuses in transactions involving municipal securities; (3) the greater level of sophistication of investors in this segment of the securities markets (i.e., institutional investors dominated the market); and (4) the fact that there were few defaults by municipal issuers. Consequently, from the enactment of the two federal securities Acts in the early 1930s to the early 1970s, the municipal securities market can be characterized as relatively free from federal regulation.

In the early 1970s, however, circumstances changed. As incomes rose, individuals participated in the municipal securities market to a much greater extent. As a result, public outcries over selling practices occurred with greater frequency. For example, in the early 1970s, the SEC obtained seven injunctions against 72 defendants for fraudulent municipal trading practices. According to the SEC, the abusive practices involved both disregard by the defendants as to whether the particular municipal bonds offered to individuals were in fact appropriate investment vehicles for the individuals to whom they were offered, and misrepresentation failure to disclose information necessary for individuals to assess the credit rise, of the municipal issuer, especially in the case of revenue bonds. Moreover, the financial problems of some municipal issuers, notably New York City, made market participants aware that municipal issuers have the potential to experience severe and bankruptcy-type financial difficulties.

Congress passed the Securities Act Amendment of 1975 to broaden regulation in the municipals market. The legislation brought brokers and dealers in the municipal securities market, including banks that underwrite and trade municipal securities, within the regulatory scheme of the Securities Exchange Act of 1934. In addition, the legislation mandated that the SEC establish a 15-member Municipal Securities Rule Making Board (MSRB) as an independent, self-regulatory agency, whose primary responsibility is to develop rules governing the activities of banks, brokers, and dealers in municipal securities. Rules adopted by the MSRB must be approved by the SEC. The MSRB has no enforcement or inspection authority. This authority is vested with the SEC, the National Association of Securities Dealers, and certain regulatory banking agencies such as the Federal Reserve Bank. The Securities Act Amendment of 1975 does *not* require that municipal issuers comply with the registration requirement of the 1933 Act or the periodic-reporting requirement of the 1934 Act. There have been, however, several legislative proposals to mandate financial disclosure. Although none has been passed, there is clearly pressure to improve disclosure. Even in the absence of federal legislation dealing with the regulation of financial disclosure, underwriters began insisting upon greater disclosure as it became apparent that the SEC was exercising stricter application of the antifraud provisions. Moreover writers recognized the need for improved disclosure to sell municipal securities to an investing public that has become much more concerned about credit risk by municipal issuers. On June 28, 1989, the Securities and Exchange Commission formally approved the first bond disclosure rule, effective January 1, 1990. The following paragraphs summarize its contents. The rule applies to all new issue municipal securities offerings of $1 million or more. Exemptions have been added for securities offered in denominations of $100,000 or more, if such securities

- Are sold to no more than 35 "sophisticated investors"
- Have a maturity of 9 months or less
- Are variable-rate demand instruments

Before bidding or purchasing an offering, underwriters must obtain and review official statements that are deemed final by the issuer, with the omission of no more than the following information:

- Offering price
- Interest rate
- Selling compensation
- Aggregate principal amount
- Principal amount per maturity
- Delivery dates
- Other terms or provisions required by an issuer of such a security to be specified in a competitive bid, ratings, other terms of the securities depending on such matters, and the identity of the underwriters

The underwriters shall contract with an issuer or its designated agent to receive copies of a final official statement within seven business days after any final agreement to purchase, offer, or sell any offering and in sufficient time to accompany any confirmation that requests payment from any customer.

Except for competitively bid offerings, the underwriters shall send, no later than the next business day, to any potential customer, on request, a single copy of the most recent preliminary official statement, if any.

Underwriters are required to distribute the final official statement to any potential customer, on request, within 90 days, or 25 days if the final official statement is available from a repository.

## Material Event Disclosure under SEC Rule 15c2-12

The first phase of the implementation of amendments to Rule 15c2-12, that took effect on July 3, 1995, required dealers to determine that issuers before issuing new municipal bonds made arrangements to disclose in the future financial information *at least* annually as well as notices of the occurrence of any of 11 material events as specified in the Rule. This resulted in the creation of state information depositories ("SIDs") and municipal securities information repositories ("NRMSIRs") to which issuers are to deliver annual information and notices. The SIDs and NRMSIRs make this information available to the public. The second phase went into effect on January 1, 1996 and required dealers to have in-house procedures in place to provide reasonable assurance that they will receive prompt notice of the any material that is required to be disclosed by the issuers.

## CHAPTER 10

# PRIVATE MONEY MARKET INSTRUMENTS

**Frank J. Fabozzi, Ph.D., CFA, CPA**
Adjunct Professor of Finance
School of Management
Yale University

**Steven V. Mann, Ph.D.**
Associate Professor of Finance
The Darla Moore School of Business
University of South Carolina

Historically, the money market has been defined as the market for assets maturing in one year or less. The assets traded in this market include Treasury bills, commercial paper, some medium-term notes, bankers acceptances, federal agency discount paper, short-term municipal obligations, certificates of deposit, repurchase agreements, floating-rate instruments, and federal funds. Although several of these assets have maturities greater than one year, they are still classified as part of the money market.

In Chapter 8, Treasury bills are discussed. In this chapter, we will cover private money market instruments: commercial paper, bankers acceptances, certificates of deposit, repurchase agreements, and federal funds. Medium-term notes have maturities ranging from nine months to 30 years. These securities are discussed in Chapter 12.

## COMMERCIAL PAPER

A corporation that needs long-term funds can raise those funds in either the equity or bond market. If, instead, a corporation needs short-term funds, it may attempt to acquire those funds via bank borrowing. An alternative to bank borrowing for large corporations with strong credit ratings is commercial paper. Commercial paper is short-term unsecured promissory notes issued in the open market as an obligation of the issuing entity.

The commercial paper market once was limited to entities with strong credit ratings, but in recent years some lower-credit-rated corporations have issued commercial paper by obtaining credit enhancements or other collateral to allow them to enter the market as issuers. Issuers of commercial paper are not restricted to U.S. corporations. Foreign corporations and sovereign issuers also issue commercial paper.

Although the original purpose of commercial paper was to provide short-term funds for seasonal and working capital needs, it has been issued for other purposes in recent years, frequently for "bridge financing." For example, suppose that a corporation needs long-term funds to build a plant or acquire equipment. Rather than raising long-term funds immediately, the issuer may elect to postpone the offering until more favorable capital market conditions prevail. The funds raised by issuing commercial paper are used until longer-term securities are sold. Commercial paper has been used as bridge financing to finance corporate takeovers.[1]

The maturity of commercial paper is typically less than 270 days; the most common maturity range is 30 to 50 days or less.[2] There are reasons for this. First, the Securities Act of 1933 requires that securities be registered with the SEC. Special provisions in the 1933 act exempt commercial paper from registration so long as the maturity does not exceed 270 days. To avoid the costs associated with registering issues with the SEC, issuers rarely issue commercial paper with a maturity exceeding 270 days. To pay off holders of maturing paper, issuers generally issue new commercial paper. Another consideration in determining the maturity is whether the paper would be eligible collateral by a bank if it wanted to borrow from the Federal Reserve Bank's discount window. In order to be eligible, the maturity of the paper may not exceed 90 days. Because eligible paper trades at a lower cost than paper that is not eligible, issuers prefer to issue paper whose maturity does not exceed 90 days.

The risk that the investor faces is that the borrower will be unable to issue new paper at maturity. As a safeguard against "rollover risk," commercial paper issuers secure backup lines of credit sometimes called "liquidity enhancements." Most commercial issuers maintain 100% backing because the credit rating agencies that rate commercial paper (Duff and Phelps, Fitch, Moody's, and Standard & Poor's) usually require a bank line of credit as a precondition for a rating.

Investors in commercial paper are institutional investors. Money market mutual funds purchase roughly one-third of all the commercial paper issued. Pension funds, commercial bank trust departments, state and local governments, and nonfinancial corporations seeking short-term investments purchase the balance. The minimum round-lot transaction is $100,000. Some issuers will sell commercial paper in denominations of $25,000.

---

1. Commercial paper has also been used as an integral part of an interest rate swap transaction. We discuss interest-rate swaps in Chapter 57.

2. *Money Market Instruments* (New York: Merrill Lynch Money Markets, Inc., 1989), p. 16.

## Issuers of Commercial Paper

Corporate issuers of commercial paper can be divided into financial companies and nonfinancial companies. The majority of commercial paper outstanding was issued by financial companies. As of June 1997, financial firms issued 78% of all commercial paper outstanding.[3]

There are three types of financial companies: captive finance companies, bank-related finance companies, and independent finance companies. Captive finance companies are subsidiaries of equipment-manufacturing companies. Their primary purpose is to secure financing for the customers of the parent company. The three major U.S. automobile manufacturers, for example, have captive finance companies: General Motors Acceptance Corporation (GMAC), Ford Credit, and Chrysler Financial. GMAC is by the far the largest issuer of commercial paper in the United States. Another captive finance company, General Electric Capital Corporation, is a major issuer of commercial paper. Bank holding companies may have a finance company subsidiary that provides loans to individuals and businesses to acquire a wide range of products. Independent finance companies are those that are not subsidiaries of equipment-manufacturing firms or bank holding companies.

Although the typical issuers of commercial paper are those with high credit ratings, smaller and less well-known companies with lower credit ratings have been able to issue paper in recent years. They have been able to do so by means of credit support from a firm with a high credit rating (such paper is called *credit-supported commercial paper*) or by collateralizing the issue with high-quality assets (such paper is called *asset-backed commercial paper*). An example of credit-supported commercial paper is an issue supported by a letter of credit. The terms of such a letter of credit specify that the bank issuing it guarantees that the bank will pay off the paper when it comes due, if the issuer fails to. Banks charge a fee for letters of credit. From the issuer's perspective, the fee enables it to enter the commercial paper market and obtain funding at a lower cost than bank borrowing. Paper issued with this credit enhancement is referred to as *LOC paper.* The credit enhancement may also take the form of a surety bond from an insurance company.[4] Asset-backed commercial paper is issued by large corporations through special purpose vehicles that pool the assets and issue the securities. The assets underlying these securities consist of credit card receivables, auto and equipment leases, health care receivables, and even small business loans.

---

3. See Dusan Stojanovic and Mark D. Vaughan, "Who's Minding the Shop?" *The Regional Economist,* St. Louis Federal Reserve, April 1998, pp. 1–8.
4. A surety bond is a policy written by an insurance company to protect another party against loss or violation of a contract.

## Directly Placed versus Dealer-Placed Paper

Commercial paper is classified as either direct paper or dealer paper. *Direct paper* is sold by the issuing firm directly to investors without using a securities dealer as an intermediary. A large majority of the issuers of direct paper are financial companies. Because they require a continuous source of funds in order to provide loans to customers, they find it cost-effective to establish a sales force to sell their commercial paper directly to investors.

In the case of dealer-placed commercial paper, the issuer uses the services of a securities firm to sell its paper. Commercial paper sold in this way is referred to as *dealer paper*. Competitive pressures have forced dramatic reductions in the underwriting fees charged by dealer firms.

Historically, the dealer market has been dominated by large investment banking firms because commercial banks were prohibited from underwriting commercial paper by the Glass-Steagall Act. In June 1987, however, the Fed granted subsidiaries of bank holding companies permission to underwrite commercial paper. Although investment banking firms still dominate the dealer market, commercial banks are making inroads.

## The Secondary Market

Commercial paper is the largest segment (just under $1 trillion) of the money market exceeding even U.S. Treasury bills as of 1997.[5] Despite this fact, secondary trading activity is much smaller. The typical investor in commercial paper is an entity that plans to hold it until maturity, given that an investor can purchase commercial paper with the specific maturity desired. Should an investor's economic circumstances change such that there is a need to sell the paper, it can be sold back to the dealer, or, in the case of directly placed paper, the issuer will repurchase it.

## Yields on Commercial Paper

Like Treasury bills, commercial paper is a discount instrument. That is, it is sold at a price less than its maturity value. The difference between the maturity value and the price paid is the interest earned by the investor, although some commercial paper is issued as an interest-bearing instrument. For commercial paper, a year is treated as having 360 days.

The yield offered on commercial paper tracks that of other money market instruments. Exhibit 10–1 is a time series plot of weekly observations of three-month commercial paper yields and three-month U.S. Treasury bills for the

---

5. See footnote 3.

**E X H I B I T   10-1**

3-month CP vs. 3-month T-bills

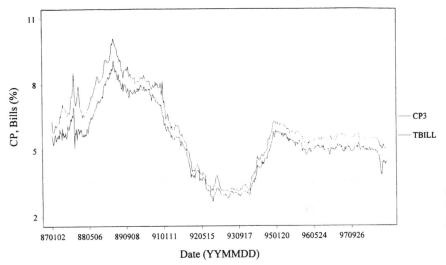

Date (YYMMDD)

Source: Federal Reserve Statistical Release H.15

period of January 1, 1987 to December 31, 1998.[6] The average spread between the two yields over this period was 55.43 basis points with a minimum of 12 basis points and a maximum of 221 basis points. The commercial paper rate is higher than that on Treasury bills for three reasons. First, the investor in commercial paper is exposed to credit risk. Second, interest earned from investing in Treasury bills is exempt from state and local income taxes. As a result, commercial paper has to offer a higher yield to offset this tax advantage. Finally, commercial paper is less liquid than Treasury bills. The liquidity premium demanded is probably small, however, because investors typically follow a buy-and-hold strategy with commercial paper and so are less concerned with liquidity. The rate on commercial paper is higher by a few basis points than the rate on certificates of deposit, which we discuss later in this chapter. The higher yield available on commercial paper is attributable to the poorer liquidity relative to certificates of deposit.

## BANKERS ACCEPTANCES

Simply put, a bankers acceptance is a vehicle created to facilitate commercial trade transactions. The instrument is called a bankers acceptance because a bank

---

6. Source: Federal Reserve Statistical Release H.15.

accepts the ultimate responsibility to repay a loan to its holder. The use of bankers acceptances to finance a commercial transaction is referred to as *acceptance financing*.

The transactions in which bankers acceptances are created include (1) the importing of goods into the United States, (2) the exporting of goods from the United States to foreign entities, (3) the storing and shipping of goods between two foreign countries where neither the importer nor the exporter is a U.S. firm,[7] and (4) the storing and shipping of goods between two entities in the United States.

Bankers acceptances are sold on a discounted basis just as Treasury bills and commercial paper. The major investors in bankers acceptances are money market mutual funds and municipal entities.

## Illustration of the Creation of a Bankers Acceptance

The best way to explain the creation of a bankers acceptance is by an illustration. Several entities are involved in our transaction:

- Car Imports Corporation of America ("Car Imports"), a firm in New Jersey that sells automobiles
- Germany Autos Inc. ("GAI"), a manufacturer of automobiles in Germany
- Hoboken Bank of New Jersey ("Hoboken Bank"), a commercial bank in Hoboken, New Jersey
- Berlin National Bank ("Berlin Bank"), a bank in Germany
- High-Caliber Money Market Fund, a mutual fund in the United States that invests in money market instruments

Car Imports and GAI are considering a commercial transaction. Car Imports wants to import 15 cars manufactured by GAI. GAI is concerned with the ability of Car Imports to make payment on the 15 cars when they are received.

Acceptance financing is suggested as a means for facilitating the transaction. Car Imports offers $300,000 for the 15 cars. The terms of the sale stipulate payment to be made to GAI 60 days after it ships the 15 cars to Car Imports. GAI determines whether it is willing to accept the $300,000. In considering the offering price, GAI must calculate the present value of the $300,000 because it will not be receiving the payment until 60 days after shipment. Suppose that GAI agrees to these terms.

Car Imports arranges with its bank, Hoboken Bank, to issue a letter of credit. The letter of credit indicates that Hoboken Bank will make good on the payment of $300,000 that Car Imports must make to GAI 60 days after shipment. The letter of credit, or time draft, will be sent by Hoboken Bank to GAL's bank, Berlin Bank. Upon receipt of the letter of credit, Berlin Bank will notify

---

7. Bankers acceptances created from these transactions are called *third-country acceptances*.

GAI, who will then ship the 15 cars. After the cars are shipped, GAI presents the shipping documents to Berlin Bank and receives the present value of $300,000. GAI is now out of the picture.

Berlin Bank presents the time draft and the shipping documents to Hoboken Bank. The latter will then stamp "accepted" on the time draft. By doing so, the Hoboken Bank has created a bankers acceptance. This means that Hoboken Bank agrees to pay the holder of the bankers acceptance $300,000 at the maturity date. Car Imports will receive the shipping documents so that it can procure the 15 cars it signs a note or some other type of financing arrangement with Hoboken Bank.

At this point, the holder of the bankers acceptance is the Berlin Bank. It has two choices. It can retain the bankers acceptance as an investment in its loan portfolio, or it can request that the Hoboken Bank make a payment of the present value of $300,000. Let's assume that Berlin Bank requests payment of the present value of $300,000.

Now the holder of the bankers acceptance is Hoboken Bank. It has two choices: retain the bankers acceptance as an investment as part of its loan portfolio or sell it to an investor. Suppose that Hoboken Bank chooses the latter, and that High-Caliber Money Market Fund is seeking a high-quality investment with the same maturity as that of the bankers acceptance. The Hoboken Bank sells the bankers acceptance to the money market fund at the present value of $300,000. Rather than sell the instrument directly to an investor, Hoboken Bank could sell it to a dealer who would then resell it to an investor such as a money market fund. In either case, at the maturity date, the money market fund presents the bankers acceptance to Hoboken Bank, receiving $300,000, which the bank in turn recovers from Car Imports.

### Credit Risk

Investing in bankers acceptances exposes the investor to credit risk. This is the risk that neither the borrower nor the accepting bank will be able to pay the principal due at the maturity date. Accordingly, bankers acceptances will offer a higher yield then Treasury bills of the same maturity. Exhibit 10–2 presents a time series plot of weekly observations of the spread (in basis points) between three-month bankers acceptances and three-month U.S. Treasury bills for the period January 1, 1987 to December 31, 1998.[8] The average spread over this period was 45.82 basis points with a minimum of 2 basis points and a maximum of 214 basis points.

### Eligible Bankers Acceptance

An accepting bank that has decided to retain a bankers acceptance in its portfolio may be able to use it as collateral for a loan at the discount window of the Federal Reserve. The reason we say it "may" is that bankers acceptances must

8. Source: Federal Reserve Statistical Release H.15.

**E X H I B I T    10–2**

Spread Between BAs and T-bills

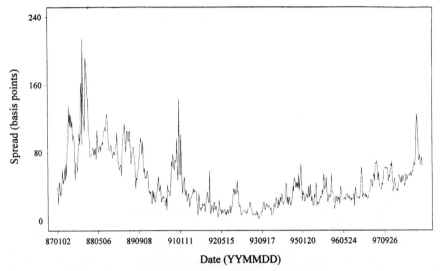

Date (YYMMDD)

Source: Federal Reserve Statistical Release H.15

meet certain eligibility requirements established by the Federal Reserve. One requirement for eligibility is maturity, which with few exceptions cannot exceed six months. The other requirements for eligibility are too detailed to review here, but the basic principle is simple: The bankers acceptance should be financing a self-liquidating commercial transaction. Conversely, *finance bills* are acceptances that are not related to specific transactions and are generally ineligible.

Eligibility is also important because the Federal Reserve imposes a reserve requirement on funds raised via bankers acceptances that are ineligible. Bankers acceptances sold by an accepting bank are potential liabilities of the bank, but no reserve requirements are imposed for eligible bankers acceptances. Consequently, most bankers acceptances satisfy the various eligibility criteria. Finally, the Federal Reserve also imposes a limit on the amount of eligible bankers acceptances that may be issued by a bank.

**Rates Banks Charge on Bankers Acceptances**

To calculate the rate to be charged the customer for issuing a bankers acceptance, the bank determines the rate for which it can sell its bankers acceptance in the open market. To this rate it adds a commission. In the case of ineligible bankers acceptances, a bank will add an amount to offset the cost of the reserve requirements imposed.

# LARGE-DENOMINATION NEGOTIABLE CDS

A *certificate of deposit* (CD) is a certificate issued by a bank or thrift that indicates a specified sum of money has been deposited at the issuing depository institution. CDs are issued by banks and thrifts to raise funds for financing their business activities. A CD bears a maturity date and a specified interest rate, and it can be issued in any denomination. CDs issued by banks are insured by the Federal Deposit Insurance Corporation but only for amounts up to $100,000. As for maturity, there is no limit on the maximum, but by Federal Reserve regulations CDs cannot have a maturity of less than seven days.

A CD may be nonnegotiable or negotiable. In the former case, the initial depositor must wait until the maturity date of the CD to obtain the funds. If the depositor chooses to withdraw funds prior to the maturity date, an early withdrawal penalty is imposed. In contrast, a negotiable CD allows the initial depositor (or any subsequent owner of the CD) to sell the CD in the open market prior to the maturity date.

Negotiable CDs were introduced in the early sixties. At that time, the interest rate that banks could pay on various types of deposits was subject to ceilings administered by the Federal Reserve (except for demand deposits, defined as deposits of less than one month that by law could pay no interest). For complex historical reasons, these ceiling rates started very low, rose with maturity, and remained below market rates up to some fairly long maturity. Before introduction of the negotiable CD, those with money to invest for, say, one month had no incentive to deposit it with a bank because they would get a below-market rate, unless they were prepared to tie up their capital for a much longer period of time. When negotiable CDs came along, those investors could buy a three-month or longer negotiable CD yielding a market interest rate and recoup all or more than the investment (depending on market conditions) by selling it in the market.

This innovation was critical in helping banks to increase the amount of funds raised in the money market, a position that had languished in the earlier postwar period. It also motivated competition among banks, ushering in a new era. There are now two types of negotiable CDs. The first is the large-denomination CD, usually issued in denominations of $1 million or more. These are the negotiable CDs whose history we described above.

In 1982, Merrill Lynch entered the retail CD business by opening up a primary and secondary market in small-denomination (less than $100,000) CDs. While it made the CDs of its numerous banking and savings institution clients available to retail customers, Merrill Lynch also began to give these customers the negotiability enjoyed by institutional investors by standing ready to buy back CDs prior to maturity. Today, several retail-oriented brokerage firms offer CDs that are salable in a secondary market. These are the second type of negotiable CD. Our focus in this chapter, though, is on the large-denomination negotiable CD, and we refer to them simply as CDs throughout the chapter.

The largest group of CD investors comprises investment companies, and money market funds make up the bulk of them. Far behind are banks and bank trust departments, followed by municipal entities and corporations.

## CD Issuers

CDs can be classified into four types, based on the issuing bank. First are CDs issued by domestic banks. Second are CDs that are denominated in U.S. dollars but are issued outside of the United States. These CDs are called *Eurodollar CDs* or *Euro CDs*. Euro CDs are U.S. dollar-denominated CDs, issued primarily in London by U.S., Canadian, European, and Japanese banks. Branches of large U.S. banks once were the major issuers of Euro CDs. A third type of CD is the *Yankee CD*, which is a CD denominated in U.S. dollars and issued by a foreign bank with a branch in the United States. Finally, *thrift CDs* are those issued by savings and loan associations and savings banks.

## Yields on CDs

Unlike Treasury bills, commercial paper, and bankers acceptances, yields on domestic CDs are quoted on an interest-bearing basis. CDs with a maturity of one year or less pay interest at maturity. For purposes of calculating interest, a year is treated as having 360 days. Term CDs issued in the United States normally pay interest semiannually, again with a year taken to have 360 days.

The yields posted on CDs vary depending on three factors: (1) the credit rating of the issuing bank, (2) the maturity of the CD, and (3) the supply and demand for CDs. With respect to the third factor, banks and thrifts issue CDs as part of their liability management strategy, so the supply of CDs will be driven by the demand for bank loans and the cost of alternative sources of capital to fund these loans. Moreover, bank loan demand will depend on the cost of alternative funding sources such as commercial paper. When loan demand is weak, CD rates decline. When demand is strong, the rates rise. The effect of maturity depends on the shape of the yield curve.

Credit risk has become more of an issue. At one time, domestic CDs issued by money center banks traded on a no-name basis. Recent financial crises in the banking industry, however, have caused investors to take a closer look at issuing banks. Prime CDs (those issued by high-rated domestic banks) trade at a lower yield than nonprime CDs (those issued by lower-rated domestic banks). Because of the unfamiliarity investors have with foreign banks, generally Yankee CDs trade at a higher yield than domestic CDs.

Euro CDs offer a higher yield than domestic CDs. There are three reasons for this. First, there are reserve requirements imposed by the Federal Reserve on CDs issued by U.S. banks in the United States that do not apply to issuers of Euro CDs. The reserve requirement effectively raises the cost of funds to the issuing bank because it cannot invest all the proceeds it receives from the issuance of a CD, and the amount that must be kept as reserves will not earn a return for the bank. Because it will earn less on funds raised by selling domestic CDs, the domestic issuing bank will pay less on its domestic CD than a Euro CD. Second, the bank issuing the CD must pay an insurance premium to the FDIC, which again raises the cost of funds. Finally, Euro CDs are dollar obligations that are payable by an entity operating under a foreign jurisdiction, exposing the holders to a risk (referred to as *sovereign risk*) that their claim may not be enforced by the foreign jurisdiction. As a result, a portion of the spread between the yield offered on Euro CDs and domestic CDs reflects what can be termed a *sovereign risk premium.* This premium varies with the degree of confidence in the international banking system.

During the 1990s, the liquidity of the Eurodollar CDs has increased dramatically and the perception of higher risk has diminished considerably. Exhibit 10–3 presents the spread (in basis points) between three-month LIBOR and three-month CDs for the period January 1, 1987 to December 31, 1998.[9] The patterns evident from the graph are consistent with Eurodollar CDs and domestic CDs being viewed as substitutes as of the late 1990s. Specifically, the spread's

**E X H I B I T   10–3**

Spread Between Euro CDs and Domestic CDs

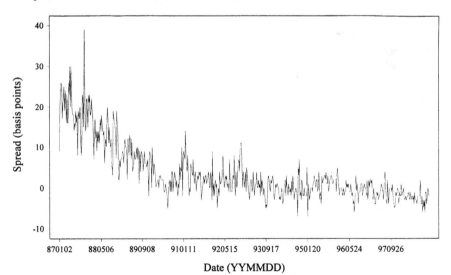

Source: Federal Reserve Statistical Release H.15

---

9. Source: Federal Reserve Statistical Release H.15. The CD rates are an average of dealer offering rates on nationally traded CDs.

long-term trend is toward zero and there is a marked reduction in the spread's volatility. Over this period, the mean spread fell from 19.52 basis points in 1987 to negative 2.23 basis points in 1998. These results suggest that Eurodollar CDs have risk/liquidity characteristics equivalent to or even slightly better than domestic CDs.

CD yields are higher than yields on Treasury securities of the same maturity. Exhibit 10–4 presents a time series of the weekly observations of the spread between yield on domestic CDs and the yield on three-month U.S. Treasury bills for the period January 1, 1987 to December 31, 1998. The average spread over this period was 57.19 basis points with a minimum of 7 basis points and a maximum of 230 basis points.[10] The spread is due mainly to the credit risk that a CD investor is exposed to and the fact that CDs offer less liquidity. The spread due to credit risk will vary with economic conditions and confidence in the banking system, increasing when there is a flight to quality or when there is a crisis in the banking system. For example, three prominent spikes in the spread during this time period are the stock market crash in October 1987, the Persian Gulf War in January 1991, and the financial crisis that ensued after the Russian debt default and ruble devaluation in August 1998.

**E X H I B I T   10–4**

Spread Between CDs and T-bills

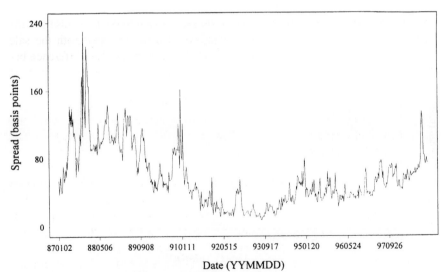

Date (YYMMDD)

Source: Federal Reserve Statistical Release H.15

---

10. Source: Federal Reserve Statistical Release H.15.

At one time, there were more than 30 dealers who made markets in CDs. The presence of that many dealers provided good liquidity to the market. Today, fewer dealers are interested in making markets in CDs, and the market can be characterized as an illiquid one.

## REPURCHASE AGREEMENTS

A *repurchase agreement* is the sale of a security with a commitment by the seller to buy the security back from the purchaser at a specified price at a designated future date. Basically, a repurchase agreement is a collateralized loan, where the collateral is a security. The agreement is best explained with an illustration.

Suppose a government securities dealer has purchased $10 million of a particular Treasury security. Where does the dealer obtain the funds to finance that position? Of course, the dealer can finance the position with its own funds or by borrowing from a bank. Typically, however, the dealer uses the repurchase agreement or "repo" market to obtain financing. In the repo market, the dealer can use the $10 million of the Treasury security as collateral for a loan. The term of the loan and the interest rate that the dealer agrees to pay (called the "repo rate") are specified. When the term of the loan is one day, it is called an *overnight repo;* a loan for more than one day is called a *term repo.* Alternatively, *open maturity* repos give both counterparties the option to terminate the repo each day. This structure reduces the settlement costs if counterparties choose to continuously roll over overnight repos.

The transaction is referred to as a repurchase agreement because it calls for the sale of the security and its repurchase at a future date. Both the sale price and the purchase price are specified in the agreement. The difference between the purchase (repurchase) price and the sale price is the dollar interest cost of the loan.

Let us return to the dealer who needs to finance $10 million of a Treasury security that it purchased and plans to hold overnight. Suppose that a customer of the dealer has excess funds of $10 million. (The customer might be a municipality with tax receipts that it has just collected, and no immediate need to disburse the funds.) The dealer would agree to deliver ("sell") $10 million of the Treasury security to the customer for an amount determined by the repo rate and buy ("repurchase") the same Treasury security from the customer for $10 million the next day. Suppose that the overnight repo rate is 6.5 percent. Then, as will be explained below, the dealer would agree to deliver the Treasury securities for $9,998,195 and repurchase the same securities for $10 million the next day. The $1,805 difference between the "sale" price of $9,998,195 and the repurchase price of $10 million is the dollar interest on the financing. From the customer's perspective, the agreement is called a *reverse* repo.

The formula following is used to calculate the dollar interest on a repo transaction:

$$\text{Dollar interest} = (\text{Dollar principal}) \times (\text{Repo rate}) \times \left(\frac{\text{Repo term}}{360}\right)$$

Notice that the interest is computed on a 360-day basis. In our example, at a repo rate of 6.5% and a repo term of one day (overnight), the dollar interest is $1,805, as we show below:

$$= \$9,998,195 \times 0.065 \times \frac{1}{360}$$

$$= \$1,805$$

The advantage to the dealer of using the repo market for borrowing on a short-term basis is that the rate is less than the cost of bank financing. We will explain why later in this section. From the customer's perspective, the repo market offers an attractive yield on a short-term secured transaction that is highly liquid.

The example illustrates financing a dealer's long position in the repo market, but dealers can also use the market to cover a short position. For example, suppose a government dealer sold $10 million of Treasury securities two weeks ago and must now cover the position—that is, deliver the securities. The dealer can do a reverse repo (agree to buy the securities and sell them back). Of course, the dealer eventually would have to buy the Treasury security in the market in order to cover its short position.

There is a good deal of Wall Street jargon describing repo transactions. To understand it, remember that one party is lending money and accepting security as collateral for the loan; the other party is borrowing money and giving collateral to borrow money. When someone lends securities in order to receive cash (i.e., borrow money), that party is said to be *reversing out* securities. A party that lends money with the security as collateral is said to be *reversing in* securities. The expressions *to repo securities* and *to do repo* are also used. The former means that someone is going to finance securities using the security as collateral; the latter means that the party is going to invest in a repo. Finally, the expressions *selling collateral* and *buying collateral* are used to describe a party financing a security with a repo on the one hand, and lending on the basis of collateral on the other.

The collateral in a repo is not limited to government securities. Money market instruments, federal agency securities, and mortgage-backed securities are also used. Moreover, repos can include *substitution clauses* that permit the counterparty to substitute alternative securities as collateral over the repo's life.

## Credit Risks

Despite the fact that there may be high-quality collateral underlying a repo transaction, both parties to the transaction are exposed to credit risk. The failure of a few small government securities dealer firms involving repo transactions in the 1980s has made market participants more cautious about the creditworthiness of the counterparty to a repo.[11]

Why does credit risk occur in a repo transaction? Consider our initial example, in which the dealer used $10 million of government securities as collateral to borrow. If the dealer cannot repurchase the government securities, the customer may keep the collateral; if interest rates on government securities have increased subsequent to the repo transaction, however, the market value of the government securities will decline, and the customer will own securities with a market value less than the amount it loaned to the dealer. If the market value of the security rises instead, the dealer firm will be concerned with the return of the collateral, which then has a market value higher than the loan.

Repos are now more carefully structured to reduce credit risk exposure. The amount loaned is less than the market value of the security used as collateral, which provides the lender with some cushion should the market value of the security decline. The amount by which the market value of the security used as collateral exceeds the value of the loan is called *margin*.[12] The amount of margin is generally between 1% and 3%. For borrowers of lower creditworthiness or when less liquid securities are used as collateral, the margin can be 10% or more.

Another practice to limit credit risk is to mark the collateral to market on a regular basis. When market value changes by a certain percentage, the repo position is adjusted accordingly. Suppose that a dealer firm has borrowed $20 million using collateral with a market value of $20.4 million. The margin is 2%. Suppose further that the market value of the collateral drops to $20.1 million. A repo agreement can specify either (1) a margin call or (2) repricing of the repo. In the case of a margin call, the dealer firm is required to put up additional collateral with a market value of $300,000 in order to bring the margin up to $400,000. If repricing is agreed upon, the principal amount of the repo will be changed from $20 million to $19.7 million (the market value of $20.1 million divided by 1.02). The dealer would then send the customer $300,000.

One concern in structuring a repo is delivery of the collateral to the lender. The most obvious procedure is for the borrower to deliver the collateral to the lender. At the end of the repo term, the lender returns the collateral to the borrower in exchange for the principal and interest payment. This procedure may be too costly, though, particularly for short-term repos, because of the costs associated with delivering the collateral. The cost of delivery would be factored into the transaction by a lower repo rate offered by the borrower. The risk of the lender not taking possession of the collateral is that the borrower may sell the security or use the same security as collateral for a repo with another party.

---

11. Failed firms include Drysdale Government Securities, Lion Capital, RTD Securities, Inc., Belvill Bressler & Schulman, Inc., and ESM Government Securities, Inc.
12. Margin is also referred to as the "haircut."

As an alternative to delivering the collateral, the lender may agree to allow the borrower to hold the security in a segregated customer account. Of course, the lender still faces the risk that the borrower uses the collateral fraudulently by offering it as collateral for another repo transaction.

Another method is for the borrower to deliver the collateral to the lender's custodial account at the borrower's clearing bank. The custodian then has possession of the collateral that it holds on behalf of the lender. This practice reduces the cost of delivery because it is merely a transfer within the borrower's clearing bank. If, for example, a dealer enters into an overnight repo with Customer A, the next day the collateral is transferred back to the dealer. The dealer can then enter into a repo with Customer B for, say, five days without having to redeliver the collateral. The clearing bank simply establishes a custodian account for Customer B and holds the collateral in that account.

There have been a number of well-publicized losses by nondealer institutional investors—most notably Orange County, California—that have resulted from the use of repurchase agreements. Such losses did not occur as a result of credit risk. Rather, it was the use of repos to make a leverage bet on the movement of interest rates. That is, the repo was not used as a money market instrument but as a leveraging vehicle. This can be accomplished by mismatching the maturity of repos and reverse repos. For example, if one has a view that rates will rise, one could borrow money via a term repo (say three months) and lend money overnight. Conversely, if rates are expected to fall, one could reverse the maturity mismatch. Leverage can be increased many times if market participants are able to borrow and lend a single piece of collateral multiple times.

## Participants in the Market

Because it is used by dealer firms (investment banking firms and money center banks acting as dealers) to finance positions and cover short positions, the repo market has evolved into one of the largest sectors of the money market. Financial and nonfinancial firms participate in the markets as both sellers and buyers, depending on the circumstances they face. Thrifts and commercial banks are typically *net sellers* of collateral (i.e., net borrowers of funds); money market funds, bank trust departments, municipalities, and corporations are typically *net buyers* of collateral (i.e., providers of funds).

Although a dealer firm uses the repo market as the primary means for financing its inventory and covering short positions, it will also use the repo market to run a matched book where it takes on repos and reverse repos with the same maturity. The firm will do so to capture the spread at which it enters into the repo and reverse repo agreement. For example, suppose that a dealer firm enters into a term repo of 10 days with a money market fund and a reverse repo rate with a thrift for 10 days in which the collateral is identical. This means that the dealer firm is borrowing funds from the money market fund and lending money to the thrift. If the rate on the repo is 7.5% and the rate on the reverse repo is 7.55%, the dealer firm is borrowing at 7.5% and lending at 7.55%, locking in a spread of 0.05% (five basis points).

Another participant is the repo broker. To understand the role of the repo broker, suppose that a dealer firm has shorted $50 million of a security. It will then survey its regular customers to determine if it can borrow via a reverse repo the security it shorted. Suppose that it cannot find a customer willing to do a repo transaction (repo from the customer's point of view, reverse repo from the dealer's). At that point, the dealer firm will use the services of a repo broker. When the collateral is difficult to acquire, it is said to be a *hot* or *special* issue.

### The Fed and the Repo Market

The Federal Reserve influences short-term interest rates through its open market operations—that is, by the outright purchase or sale of government securities. This is not the common practice followed by the Fed, however. It uses the repo market instead to implement monetary policy by purchasing or selling collateral. By buying collateral (i.e., lending funds), the Fed injects money into the financial markets, thereby exerting downward pressure on short-term interest rates. When the Fed buys collateral for its own account, this is called a *system repo*. The Fed also buys collateral on behalf of foreign central banks in repo transactions that are referred to as *customer repos*. It is primarily through system repos that the Fed attempts to influence short-term rates. By selling securities for its own account, the Fed drains money from the financial markets, thereby exerting upward pressure on short-term interest rates. This transaction is called a *matched sale*.

Note the language that is used to describe the transactions of the Fed in the repo market. When the Fed lends funds based on collateral, we call it a *system* or *customer repo*, not a reverse repo. Borrowing funds using collateral is called a *matched sale*, not a repo. The jargon is confusing, which is why we used the terms of *buying collateral* and *selling collateral* to describe what parties in the market are doing.

In September 1999, the Federal Reserve made a number of policy changes involving its repo operations. These changes were designed to quell liquidity concerns resulting from Y2K. First, as a permanent change, the Fed increased their maximum term for a term repo from 60 days to 90 days. Second, around the calendar turn, the Fed broadened the acceptable collateral for Fed repos to include agency mortgage-backed securities, Treasury STRIPS, and agency zeros. Third, the Fed announced it will sell options on repos for specific December 1999 and January 2000 dates with a repo rate equal to the fed funds rate plus 150 basis points. The latter two changes are in effect only for the Y2k period.

## Determinants of the Repo Rate

There is no one repo rate; rates vary from transaction to transaction, depending on several factors:

**Quality.** The higher the credit quality and liquidity of the collateral, the lower the repo rate.

**Term of the repo.** The effect of the term of the repo on the rate depends on the shape of the yield curve.

**Delivery requirement.** As noted earlier, if delivery of the collateral to the lender is required, the repo rate will be lower. If the collateral can be deposited with the bank of the borrower, a higher repo rate is paid.

**Availability of collateral.** The more difficult it is to obtain the collateral, the lower the repo rate. To understand why this is so, remember that the borrower (or equivalently, the seller of the collateral) has a security that is a hot or special issue. The party that needs the collateral will be willing to lend funds at a lower repo rate in order to obtain the collateral.

The factors above determine the repo rate on a particular transaction; the federal funds rate discussed below determines the general level of repo rates. The repo rate will be a rate below the federal funds rate. The reason is that a repo involves collateralized borrowing, whereas a federal funds transaction is unsecured borrowing.

## FEDERAL FUNDS

The rate determined in the federal funds market is the major factor that influences the rate paid on all the other money market instruments described in this chapter. When the Federal Reserve formulates and executes monetary policy, it sets a target level for the federal funds rate. Announcements of changes in monetary policy specify the changes in the Fed's target for this rate. The Federal Reserve influences the level of the federal funds rate through open market operations. Exhibit 10–5 presents a time series plot of weekly observations (sampled on Wednesdays) of the daily effective federal funds rate for the period January 1, 1987 to December 31, 1998.[13]

Depository institutions (commercial banks and thrifts) are required to maintain reserves. The reserves are deposits at their district Federal Reserve Bank, which are called federal funds. The level of the reserves that a bank must maintain is based on its average daily deposits over the previous 14 days. Of all depository institutions, commercial banks are by far the largest holders of federal funds.

No interest is earned on federal funds. Consequently, a depository institution that maintains federal funds in excess of the amount required incurs an opportunity cost—the loss of interest income that could be earned on the excess

---

13. Source: Federal Reserve Statistical release H.15. The weekly observations are averages of the seven calendar days ending on Wednesday of the current week.

**E X H I B I T   10–5**

Daily Effective Federal Funds Rate

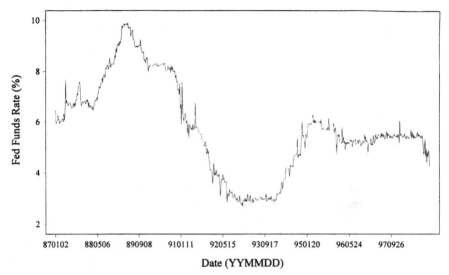

**Date (YYMMDD)**

Source: Federal Reserve Statistical Release H.15

reserves. At the same time, there are depository institutions whose federal funds are less than the amount required. Typically, smaller banks have excess reserves, whereas money center banks find themselves short of reserves and must make up the shortfall. Banks maintain federal funds desks whose managers are responsible for the bank's federal funds position.

One way that banks with less than the required reserves can bring reserves to the required level is to enter into a repo with a nonbank customer. An alternative is for the bank to borrow federal funds from a bank that has excess reserves. The market in which federal funds are bought (borrowed) by banks that need these funds and sold (lent) by banks that have excess federal funds is called the *federal funds market* The equilibrium interest rate, which is determined by the supply and demand for federal funds, is the federal funds rate.

The federal funds rate and the repo rate are tied together because both are a means for a bank to borrow. The federal funds rate is higher because the lending of federal funds is done on an unsecured basis; this differs from the repo, in which the lender has a security as collateral. The spread between the two rates varies depending on market conditions; typically the spread is around 25 basis points.

The term of most federal funds transactions is overnight, but there are longer-term transactions that range from one week to six months. Trading typically takes place directly between the buyer and seller-usually between a large bank and one of its correspondent banks. Some federal funds transactions require the use of a broker.

## SUMMARY

Money market instruments are debt obligations that at issuance have a maturity of one year or less. Commercial paper is a short-term unsecured promissory note issued in the open market that represents the obligation of the issuing entity. It is sold on a discount basis. To avoid SEC registration, the maturity of commercial paper is less than 270 days. Generally, commercial paper maturity is less than 90 days so that it will qualify as eligible collateral for the bank to borrow from the Federal Reserve Bank's discount window. Financial and nonfinancial corporations issue commercial paper, with the majority issued by the former. Direct paper is sold by the issuing firm directly to investors without using a securities dealer as an intermediary; with dealer-placed commercial paper, the issuer uses the services of a securities firm to sell its paper. There is little liquidity in the commercial paper market.

A bankers acceptance is a vehicle created to facilitate commercial trade transactions, particularly international transactions. They are called bankers acceptances because a bank accepts the responsibility to repay a loan to the holder of the vehicle created in a commercial transaction in case the debtor fails to perform. Bankers acceptances are sold on a discounted basis, as are Treasury bills and commercial paper.

Certificates of deposit (CDs) are issued by banks and thrifts to raise funds for financing their business activities. Unlike Treasury bills, commercial paper, and bankers acceptances, yields on domestic CDs are quoted on an interest-bearing basis. A floating-rate CD is one whose coupon interest rate changes periodically in accordance with a predetermined formula.

A repurchase agreement is a lending transaction in which the borrower uses a security as collateral for the borrowing. The transaction is referred to as a repurchase agreement because it specifies the sale of a security and its subsequent repurchase at a future date. The difference between the purchase (repurchase) price and the sale price is the dollar interest cost of the loan. An overnight repo is for one day; a loan for more than one day is called a term repo. The collateral in a repo may be a Treasury security, money market instrument, federal agency security, or mortgage-backed security. The parties to a repo are exposed to credit risk, limited by margin and mark-to-market practices included in a repo agreement. Dealers use the repo market to finance positions and cover short positions, and to run a matched book so that they can earn spread income. The Fed uses the repo market to implement monetary policy. Factors that determine the repo rate are the federal funds rate, the quality of the collateral, the term of the repo, the delivery requirement, and the availability of the collateral.

The federal funds market is the market where depository institutions borrow (buy) and sell (lend) federal funds. The federal funds rate, which is the rate at which all money market interest rates are anchored, is determined in this market. The federal funds rate is higher than the repo rate because borrowing done in the federal funds market is unsecured borrowing.

## CHAPTER 11

# CORPORATE BONDS

**Frank J. Fabozzi, Ph.D., CFA, CPA**
Adjunct Professor of Finance
School of Management
Yale University

**Richard S. Wilson**
Consultant

**Richard Todd**
Vice President
Bear Stearns & Co.

A corporate bond is a debt instrument setting forth the obligation of the issuer to satisfy the terms of the agreement. Essentially an IOU, it can be quite a complex instrument, although the essential features may be relatively simple. The maker, or issuer, agrees to pay a certain amount or a percentage of the face, or principal, value (also known as par value) to the owner of the bond, either periodically over the life of the issue or in a lump sum upon the bond's retirement or maturity. Failure to pay the principal and/or interest when due (and to meet other of the debt's provisions) in accordance with the terms of the instrument constitutes legal default and court proceedings can be instituted to enforce the contract. Bondholders, as creditors, have a prior legal claim over common and preferred stockholders as to both income and assets of the corporation for the principal and interest due them and may have a prior claim over other creditors if liens or mortgages are involved. It is important to recognize, however, that a superior legal status will not prevent bondholders from suffering financial loss when the ability of a corporation to generate cash flow adequate to pay its obligations is seriously eroded.

Bond prices can and do undergo sizeable changes as the general level of interest rates changes, reflecting changing supply-and-demand conditions for loanable funds. Bonds can be acquired for income, emphasizing the relative sureness and attractiveness of periodic interest receipts and tending to ignore price fluctuations. On the other hand, fixed income securities can be among the

---

Previous versions of this chapter were coauthored with Harry Sauvain and John Ritchie, Jr.

most speculative investment vehicles available when bought on margin or when a low-quality issue is purchased.

Corporate bonds are usually issued in denominations of $1,000 and multiples thereof. In common usage, a corporate bond is assumed to have a par value of $1,000 unless otherwise explicitly specified. A security dealer who says he or she has five bonds to sell means five bonds each of $1,000 principal amount. If the promised rate of interest (coupon rate) is 6%, the annual amount of interest on each bond is $60 and the semiannual interest is $30.

Although there are technical differences between bonds, notes, and debentures, we will use Wall Street convention and call fixed income debt by the general term—*bonds*.

## THE CORPORATE TRUSTEE

The promises of corporate bond issuers and the rights of investors who buy them are set forth in great detail in contracts generally called *indentures*. If bondholders were handed the complete indenture, some may have trouble understanding the legalese and have even greater difficulty in determining from time to time if the corporate issuer is keeping all the promises made. These problems are solved for the most part by bringing in a *corporate trustee* as a third party to the contract. The indenture is made out to the corporate trustee as a representative of the interests of bondholders; that is, the trustee acts in a fiduciary capacity for investors who own the bond issue.

A corporate trustee is a bank or trust company with a corporate trust department and officers who are experts in performing the functions of a trustee. This is no small task. The corporate trustee must, at the time of issue, authenticate the bonds issued—that is, keep track of all the bonds sold and make sure that they do not exceed the principal amount authorized by the indenture. It must then be a watchdog for the bondholders by seeing to it that the issuer complies with all the covenants of the indenture. These covenants are many and technical, and they must be watched during the entire period that a bond issue is outstanding. We will describe some of these covenants in subsequent pages.

It is very important that corporate trustees be competent and financially responsible. To this end, there is a federal statute known as the Trust Indenture Act, which requires that for all corporate bond offerings in the amount of more than $5 million sold in interstate commerce there must be a corporate trustee. The indenture must include adequate requirements for performance of the trustee's duties on behalf of bondholders; there must be no conflict between the trustee's interest as a trustee and any other interest it may have, especially if it is also a creditor of the issuer; and there must be provision for reports by the trustee to bondholders. If a corporate issuer fails to pay interest or principal, the trustee may declare a default and take such action as may be necessary to protect the rights of bondholders. If the corporate issuer has promised in the indenture to always maintain an amount of current assets equal to two times the amount of current liabilities, the trustee must watch the corporation's balance sheet and see that the promise is kept. If the issuer fails to maintain the prescribed amounts, the trustee must take action on behalf of the bondholders. However, it must be emphasized that the trustee is paid by the debt issuer and can only do what the indenture provides. The indenture may contain a clause stating that the trustee undertakes to perform such duties and only such duties as are specifically set forth in the indenture, and no implied covenants or obligations shall be read into the indenture against the trustee. Also, the trustee is usually under no obligation to exercise the rights or powers under the indenture at the request of bondholders unless it has been offered reasonable security or indemnity. The trustee is not bound to make investigations into the facts surrounding documents delivered to it, but it may do so if it sees fit.

The terms of bond issues set forth in bond indentures are always a compromise between the interests of the bond issuer and those of investors who buy bonds. The issuer always wants to pay the lowest possible rate of interest and to be tied up as little as possible with legal covenants. Bondholders want the highest possible interest rate, the best security, and a variety of covenants to restrict the issuer in one way or another. As we discuss the provisions of bond indentures, keep this opposition of interests in mind and see how compromises are worked out in practice.

## SOME BOND FUNDAMENTALS

Bonds can be classified by a number of characteristics, which we will use for ease of organizing this section.

## Bonds Classified by Issuer Type

The five broad categories of corporate bonds sold in the United States based on the type of issuer are public utilities, transportations, industrials, banks and finance companies, and international or Yankee issues. Finer breakdowns are often made by market participants to create homogeneous groupings. For example, public utilities are subdivided into telephone or communications, electric companies, gas distribution and transmission companies, and water companies. The transportation industry can be subdivided into airlines, railroads, and trucking companies. Like public utilities, transportation companies often have various degrees of regulation or control by state and/or federal government agencies. Industrials are a catchall class, but even here, finer degrees of distinction may be needed by analysts. The industrial grouping includes manufacturing and mining concerns, retailers, and service-related companies. Even the Yankee or international borrower sector can be more finely tuned. For example, one might classify the issuers into categories such as supranational borrowers (International

Bank for Reconstruction and Development and the European Investment Bank), sovereign issuers (Canada, Australia, United Kingdom), and foreign municipalities and agencies.

## Corporate Debt Maturity

A bond's maturity is the date on which the issuer's obligation to satisfy the terms of the indenture is fulfilled. On that date the principal is repaid with any premium and accrued interest that may be due. However, as we shall see later when discussing debt redemption, the final maturity date as stated in the issue's title may or may not be the date when the contract terminates. Many issues can be retired prior to maturity.

Thus, although we often talk about long-term and short-term bonds, our long-term holdings may turn out to be relatively short. Also, investors' perceptions of what constitutes short- and long-term maturity for bonds has undergone considerable change over time. A half-century ago some experts viewed bonds with maturities of 5 to 15 years as short-term issues and those with maturities from 15 to 40 years as intermediate-term paper. Such is not the case today. Issues maturing within a year are usually viewed as the equivalent of cash items. Debt maturing more than one year from the reference date to five years later is generally thought of as short-term. Intermediate-term debt matures in 5 to 12 years, whereas long-term debt obviously matures in more than 12 years. These are not hard-and-fast classifications. Some think short-term bonds mature within 2 to 3 years and intermediate-term issues not longer than 8 to 10 years.

Before the Great Depression, there were a number of long-term bond issues with maturities of 100 or more years. Many were issued by railroads and others came out of corporate reorganizations. In a few cases, maturities were as long as 999 years from the date of issue. Today, only a few such issues are around. Investors prefer bonds to mature within their lifetime, not during the lifetime of some progeny centuries away.

Since the early 1970s, the average maturity of domestically issued new corporate debt shortened distinctly. Investor preference for shorter maturities is attributed to the increased volatility of bond prices caused by higher interest rates. All other things being the same, shorter maturity means reduced price risk. However, the shorter maturity structure of corporate debt increases pressures on corporate financial managers. It becomes more difficult to match long-lived assets with long-term liabilities. Years ago, a matching of assets and liabilities was deemed the proper course for corporations to follow. Now that isn't necessarily so. The more frequent refinancings necessary to replace a heavier volume of maturing debt also add to the burden of the corporate financial officer and to the pressures on the corporate bond market. More of a company's cash flow might have to be directed to paying off these obligations as they become due.

# Interest Payment Characteristics

The three main interest payment classifications of domestically issued corporate bonds are straight-coupon bonds, zero-coupon bonds, and floating-rate, or variable-rate, bonds. Floating-rate issues are discussed in Chapter 14 and the other two types are examined below.

However, before we get into interest-rate characteristics, let us briefly discuss bond types. We refer to the interest rate on a bond as the *coupon*. This is technically wrong, as bonds issued today do not have coupons attached. Instead, bonds are represented by a certificate, similar to a stock certificate, with a brief description of the terms printed on both sides. These are called *registered bonds*. The principal amount of the bond is noted on the certificate, and the interest-paying agent or trustee has the responsibility of making payment by check to the registered holder on the due date. Years ago, bonds were issued in *bearer* or coupon, form with coupons attached for each interest payment. However, the registered form is considered safer and entails less paperwork. As a matter of fact, the registered bond certificate is on its way out as more and more issues are sold in *book-entry* form. This means that only one master or global certificate is issued. It is held by a central securities depository that issues receipts denoting interests in this global certificate.

Straight-coupon bonds have an interest rate set for the life of the issue, however long or short that may be; they are also called *fixed-rate* bonds. Most fixed-rate bonds in the United States pay interest semiannually and at maturity. For example, a bond with an interest rate of 9% maturing on June 15, 2010, will pay $45 per $1,000 par amount each June 15 and December 15, including June 15, 2010. Of course, at maturity the par amount is also paid. Bonds with interest payable once a year are uncommon among domestic issues but are the norm for issues sold in continental Europe. From time to time, investors may encounter bonds with other payment patterns such as quarterly or even monthly.

Interest payments due on Sundays or holidays are normally paid on the next business day without additional interest for the extra day or two the company has use of the monies. Interest on corporate bonds is based on a year of 360 days made up of twelve 30-day months. It does not matter whether the month is February, April, or May; all months for this purpose are of the same length. The 9% bond pays interest of $90 per year per $1,000 face value. Interest accrues at the rate of $7.50 a month or $0.25 per day. The corporate calendar day count convention is referred to as *30/360*.

Most fixed-rate corporate bonds pay interest in a standard fashion. However, there are some variations of which you should be aware. Most domestic bonds pay interest in U.S. dollars. However, starting in the early 1980s, issues were marketed with principal and interest payable in other currencies such as the Australian, New Zealand, or Canadian dollar or the British pound. Generally, interest and principal payments are converted from the foreign currency to U.S. dollars by the paying agent unless it is otherwise notified. The bondholders bear any costs associated with the dollar conversion. Foreign currency issues provide investors with another way of diversifying a portfolio, but not without risk. The holder bears the currency, or exchange rate, risk in addition to all of the other risks associated with debt instruments.

There are a few issues of bonds that can participate in the fortunes of the issuer over and above the stated coupon rate. These are called *participating bonds,* as they share in the profits of the issuer or the rise in certain assets over and above certain minimum levels. Another type of bond rarely encountered today is the *income bond.* These bonds promise to pay a stipulated interest rate, but the payment is contingent on sufficient earnings and is in accordance with the definition of available income for interest payments contained in the indenture. Repayment of principal is not contingent. Interest may be cumulative or noncumulative. If payments are cumulative, unpaid interest payments must be made up at some future date. If noncumulative, once the interest payment is past, it does not have to be repaid. Failure to pay interest on income bonds is not an act of default and is not a cause for bankruptcy. Income bonds have been issued by some financially troubled corporations emerging from reorganization proceedings.

Zero-coupon bonds are, just as the name implies, bonds without coupons or an interest rate. Essentially, zero-coupon bonds pay only the principal portion at some future date. These bonds are issued at discounts to par; the difference constitutes the return to the bondholder. The difference between the face amount and the offering price when first issued is called the *original-issue discount* (OID). The rate of return depends on the amount of the discount and the period over which it accretes. For example, a five-year zero-coupon bond yielding 9% on a semiannual basis must be priced at 64.39% of par. If due in 7 years, the price would be 59%; in 10 years, 41.46%; and in 15 years, only 26.70%.

Zeros were first publicly issued in the corporate market in the spring of 1981 and were an immediate hit with investors. The rapture only lasted a couple of years because of changes in the income tax laws that made ownership more costly on an after-tax basis. Also, these changes reduced the tax advantages to issuers. However, tax-deferred investors, such as pension funds, could still take advantage of zero-coupon issues. One important risk is eliminated in a zero-coupon investment—the reinvestment risk. Because there is no coupon to reinvest, there isn't any reinvestment risk. Of course, although this is beneficial in declining interest-rate markets, the reverse is true when interest rates are rising. The investor will not be able to reinvest an income stream at rising reinvestment rates. Investors tend to find zeros less attractive in lower interest-rate markets because compounding is not as meaningful as when rates are higher. Also, the lower the rates are, the more likely that they will rise again, making a zero-coupon investment worth less in the eyes of potential holders.

In bankruptcy, a zero-coupon bond creditor can claim the original offering price plus accrued and unpaid interest to the date of the bankruptcy filing, but not the principal amount of $1,000. Zero-coupon bonds have been sold at deep discounts and the liability of the issuer at maturity may be substantial. The accretion of the discount on the corporation's books is not put away in a special fund for debt retirement purposes. There are no sinking funds on most of these issues. One hopes that corporate managers properly invest the proceeds and run the corporation for the benefit of all investors so that there will not be a cash crisis at maturity. The potentially large balloon repayment creates a cause for concern among investors. Thus, it is most important to invest in higher-quality issues so as to reduce the risk of a potential problem. If one wants to speculate in lower-rated bonds, then that investment should throw off some cash return.

Finally, a variation of the zero-coupon bond is the deferred-interest bond (DIB), also known as a zero/coupon bond. These bonds have generally been subordinated issues of speculative-grade issuers, also known as *junk* issuers. Most of the issues are structured so that they do not pay cash interest for the first five years. At the end of the deferred-interest period, cash interest accrues, and is paid semiannually until maturity, unless the bonds are redeemed earlier. The deferred-interest feature allows newly restructured, highly leveraged companies and others with less-than-satisfactory cash flows to defer the payment of cash interest over the early life of the bond. Hopefully, when cash interest payments start, the company will be able to service the debt. If it has made excellent progress in restoring its financial health, the company may be able to redeem or refinance the debt rather than have high interest outlays.

An offshoot of the deferred-interest bond is the pay-in-kind (PIK) debenture. With PIKs, cash interest payments are deferred at the issuer's option until some future date. Instead of just accreting the original-issue discount as with DIBs or zeros, the issuer pays out the interest in additional pieces of the same security. The option to pay cash or in-kind interest payments rests with the issuer, but in many cases the issuer has little choice because provisions of other debt instruments often prohibit cash interest payments until certain indenture or loan tests are satisfied. The holder just gets more pieces of paper, but these at least can be sold in the market without giving up one's original investment; PIKs, DIBs, and zeros do not have provisions for the resale of the interest portion of the instrument. An investment in this type of bond, because it is issued by speculative-grade companies, requires careful analysis of the issuer's cash flow prospects and ability to survive.

## SECURITY FOR BONDS

Shylock demanded a pound of flesh as his security. Investors who buy corporate bonds don't go quite that far, but they do like some kind of security. Either real property (using a mortgage) or personal property may be pledged to offer security beyond that of the general credit standing of the issue. In fact, the kind of security or the absence of a specific pledge of security is usually indicated by the title of a bond issue. However, the best security is a strong general credit that can repay the debt from earnings.

# Mortgage Bond

Readers of *The Wall Street Journal* may have seen an advertisement for "$50,000,000 issue of Metropolitan Edison, First Mortgage Bonds, 9% Series, due December 1, 2008." That title says several things about this bond issue.

It says that the issuer has granted the bondholders a first-mortgage lien on substantially all of its properties. That is good from the viewpoint of bondholders. But in return the issuer got a lower rate of interest on the bonds than if the issue were unsecured. A debenture issue (i.e., unsecured debt) of the same company at that time might have carried an interest rate of 9.25% to 9.375%. A *lien* is a legal right to sell mortgaged property to satisfy unpaid obligations to bondholders. In practice, foreclosure of a mortgage and sale of mortgaged property is unusual. If a default occurs, there is usually a financial reorganization on the part of the issuer, in which provision is made for settlement of the debt to bondholders. The mortgage lien is important, though, because it gives the mortgage bondholders a very strong bargaining position relative to other creditors in determining the terms of a reorganization.

Often first-mortgage bonds are issued in series with bonds of each series secured equally by the same first mortgage. The title of the bond issue mentioned above includes "9% Series," which says that the issue is one of a series. Many companies, particularly public utilities, have a policy of financing part of their capital requirements continuously by long-term debt. They want some part of their total capitalization in the form of bonds because the cost of such capital is ordinarily less than that of capital raised by sale of stock. So, as a principal amount of debt is paid off, they issue another series of bonds under the same mortgage. As they expand and need a greater amount of debt capital, they can add new series of bonds. It is a lot easier and more advantageous to issue a series of bonds under one mortgage and one indenture than it is to create entirely new bond issues with different arrangements for security. This arrangement is called a *blanket mortgage.* When property is sold or released from the lien of the mortgage, additional property or cash may be substituted or bonds may be retired in order to provide adequate security for the debtholders.

When a bond indenture authorizes the issue of additional series of bonds with the same mortgage lien as those already issued, the indenture imposes certain conditions that must be met before an additional series may be issued. Bondholders do not want their security impaired; these conditions are for their benefit. It is common for a first-mortgage bond indenture to specify that property acquired by the issuer subsequent to the granting of the first-mortgage lien shall be subject to the first-mortgage lien. This is termed the *after-acquired clause.* Then the indenture usually permits the issue of additional bonds up to some specified percentage of the value of the after-acquired property, such as 60%. The other 40%, or whatever the percentage may be, must be financed in some other way. This is intended to ensure that there will be additional assets with a value significantly greater than the amount of additional bonds secured by the mortgage. Another customary kind of restriction on the issue of additional series is a requirement that earnings in an immediately preceding period must be equal to some number of times the amount of annual interest on all outstanding mortgage bonds including the new or proposed series (1.5, 2, or some other number). For this purpose, *earnings* are usually defined as earnings before income tax. Still another common provision is that additional bonds may be issued to the extent that earlier series of bonds have been paid off.

You seldom see a bond issue with the term *second mortgage* in its title. The reason is that this term has a connotation of weakness. Sometimes companies get around that difficulty by using such words as *first and consolidated, first and refunding,* or *general and refunding mortgage bonds.* Usually this language means that a bond issue is secured by a first mortgage on some part of the issuer's property but by a second or even third lien on other parts of its assets. A general and refunding mortgage bond is generally secured by a lien on all of the company's property *subject* to the prior lien of first mortgage bonds, if any are still outstanding.

## Collateral Trust Bonds

Some companies do not own fixed assets or other real property and so have nothing on which they can give a mortgage lien to secure bondholders. Instead, they own securities of other companies; they are *holding companies,* and the other companies are *subsidiaries.* To satisfy the desire of bondholders for security, they pledge stocks, notes, bonds, or whatever other kind of obligations they own. These assets are termed *collateral* (or personal property), and bonds secured by such assets are *collateral trust bonds.* Some companies own both real property and securities. They may use real property to secure mortgage bonds and use securities for collateral trust bonds.

The legal arrangement for collateral trust bonds is much the same as that for mortgage bonds. The issuer delivers to a corporate trustee under a bond indenture the securities pledged, and the trustee holds them for the benefit of the bondholders. When voting common stocks are included in the collateral, the indenture permits the issuer to vote the stocks so long as there is no default on its bonds. This is important to issuers of such bonds because usually the stocks are those of subsidiaries, and the issuer depends on the exercise of voting rights to control the subsidiaries.

Indentures usually provide that, in event of default, the rights to vote stocks included in the collateral are transferred to the trustee. Loss of the voting right would be a serious disadvantage to the issuer because it would mean loss of control of subsidiaries. The trustee may also sell the securities pledged for whatever prices they will bring in the market and apply the proceeds to payment of the claims of collateral trust bondholders. These rather drastic actions, however, are not usually taken immediately on an event of default. The corporate trustee's primary responsibility is to act in the best interests of bondholders, and their interests may be served for a time at least by giving the defaulting issuer a proxy to vote stocks held as collateral and thus preserve the holding company structure. It may also defer the sale of collateral when it seems likely that bondholders would fare better in a financial reorganization than they would by sale of collateral.

Collateral trust indentures contain a number of provisions designed to protect bondholders. Generally, the market or appraised value of the collateral must be maintained at some percentage of the amount of bonds outstanding. The percentage is greater than 100 so that there will be a margin of safety. If collateral value declines below the minimum percentage, additional collateral must be provided by the issuer. There is almost always provision for withdrawal of some collateral provided other acceptable collateral is substituted.

Collateral trust bonds may be issued in series in much the same way that mortgage bonds are issued in series. The rules governing additional series of bonds require that adequate collateral must be pledged, and there may be restrictions on the use to which the proceeds of an additional series may be put. All series of bonds are issued under the same indenture and have the same claim on collateral.

## Equipment Trust Certificates

The desire of borrowers to pay the lowest possible rate of interest on their obligations generally leads them to offer their best security and to grant lenders the strongest claim on it. Many years ago, the railway companies developed a way of financing purchase of cars and locomotives, called *rolling stock,* that enabled them to borrow at just about the lowest rates in the corporate bond market.

Railway rolling stock has for a long time been regarded by investors as excellent security for debt. This equipment is sufficiently standardized that it can be used by one railway as well as another. And it can be readily moved from the tracks of one railroad to those of another. There is generally a good market for lease or sale of cars and locomotives. The railroads have capitalized on these characteristics of rolling stock by developing a legal arrangement for giving investors a legal claim on it that is different from, and generally better than, a mortgage lien.

The legal arrangement is one that vests legal title to railway equipment in a trustee, which is better from the standpoint of investors than a first-mortgage lien on property. A railway company orders some cars and locomotives from a manufacturer. When the job is finished, the manufacturer transfers the legal title to the equipment to a trustee. The trustee leases it to the railroad that ordered it and at the same time sells *equipment trust certificates* (ETCs) in an amount equal to a large percentage of the purchase price, normally 80%. Money from sale of certificates is paid to the manufacturer. The railway company makes an initial payment of rent equal to the balance of the purchase price, and the trustee gives that money to the manufacturer. Thus the manufacturer is paid off. The trustee collects lease rental money periodically from the railroad and uses it to pay interest and principal on the certificates. These interest payments are known as dividends. The amounts of lease rental payments are worked out carefully so that they are enough to pay the equipment trust certificates. At the end of some period of time, such as 15 years, the certificates are paid off, the trustee sells the equipment to the railroad for some nominal price, and the lease is terminated.

Railroad ETCs are usually structured in serial form; that is, a certain amount becomes payable at specified dates until the final installment. For example, a $60 million ETC might mature $4 million on each June 15 from 2000 through 2014. Each of the 15 maturities may be priced separately to reflect the shape of the yield curve, investor preference for specific maturities, and supply-and-demand considerations. The advantage of a serial issue from the investor's point of view is that the repayment schedule matches the decline in the value of the equipment used as collateral. Hence, principal repayment risk is reduced. From the issuer's side, serial maturities allow for the repayment of the debt periodically over the life of the issue, making less likely a crisis at maturity due to a large repayment coming due at one time.

The beauty of this arrangement from the viewpoint of investors is that the railroad does not legally own the rolling stock until all the certificates are paid. In case the railroad does not make the lease rental payments, there is no big legal hassle about foreclosing a lien. The trustee owns the property and can take it back because failure to pay the rent breaks the lease. The trustee can lease the equipment to another railroad and continue to make payments on the certificates from new lease rentals.

This description emphasizes the legal nature of the arrangement for securing the certificates. In practice, these certificates are regarded as obligations of the railway company that leased the equipment and are shown as liabilities in its balance sheet. In fact, the name of the railway appears in the title of the certificates. In the ordinary course of events, the trustee is just an intermediary who performs the function of holding title, acting as lessor, and collecting the money to pay the certificates. It is significant that even in the worst years of a depression, railways have paid their equipment trust certificates, though they did not pay bonds secured by mortgages. Although railroads have issued the largest amount of equipment trust certificates, airlines have also utilized this form of financing.

## Debenture Bonds

After all the emphasis upon security, you might think that usury-minded investors would not buy bonds without something to secure them. But not so! Investors often buy large issues of unsecured bonds just as they buy first-mortgage bonds. These unsecured bonds are termed *debentures*. As a matter of fact, with the exception of the utility industry and specifically structured special purpose financings, nearly all other corporate debt sold is unsecured.

Debentures are not secured by a specific pledge of designated property, but that does not mean that they have no claim on property of issuers or on their earnings. Debenture bondholders have the claim of general creditors on all assets of the issuer not pledged specifically to secure other debt. And they even have a claim on pledged assets to the extent that these assets have value greater than necessary to satisfy secured creditors. In fact, if there are no pledged assets and no secured creditors, debenture bondholders have first claim on all assets along with other general creditors.

These unsecured bonds are sometimes issued by companies that are so strong financially and have such a high credit rating that to offer security would be gilding the lily. Such companies can simply turn a deaf ear to investors who want security and still sell their debentures at relatively low interest rates. But debentures are sometimes issued by companies that have already sold mortgage bonds and given liens on most of their property. These debentures rank below the mortgage bonds or collateral trust bonds in their claim on assets, and investors may regard them as relatively weak. This is the kind that bears the higher rates of interest.

Even though there is no pledge of security, the indentures for debenture bonds may contain a variety of provisions designed to afford some protection to investors. Frequently the amount of a debenture bond issue is limited to the amount of the initial issue. This limit is to keep issuers from weakening the position of debenture holders by running up additional unsecured debt. Sometimes additional debentures may be issued a specified number of times in a recent accounting period, provided that the issuer has earned its bond interest on all existing debt plus the additional issue.

If a company has no secured debt, it is customary to provide that debentures will be secured equally with any secured bonds that may be issued in the future. This is known as the *negative pledge clause*. Some provisions of debenture bond issues are intended to give the corporate trustee early warning of deterioration in the issuer's financial condition. The issuer may be required to always maintain a specified minimum amount of net working capital—the excess of current assets over current liabilities—equal to not less than the amount of debentures outstanding. The corporate trustee must watch the issuer's balance sheet and, on failure to maintain the required amount of net working capital, take whatever action is appropriate in the interest of debenture holders. Another common restriction is one limiting the payment of cash dividends by the issuer. Another restriction limits the proportion of current earnings that may be used to pay dividends. However, the trend in recent years, at least with investment-grade companies, is away from indenture restrictions.

## Subordinated and Convertible Debentures

You might think that debenture bonds have about the weakest possible claim on the assets and earnings of a corporate issuer, but that is not so. Many companies have issued *subordinated debenture bonds.* The term *subordinated* means that such an issue ranks after secured debt, after debenture bonds, and often after some general creditors in its claim on assets and earnings. Owners of this kind of bond stand last in line among creditors when an issuer fails financially.

Because subordinated debentures are weaker in their claim on assets, issuers would have to offer a higher rate of interest unless they also offer some special inducement to buy the bonds. The inducement can be an option to convert bonds into stock of the issuer at the discretion of bondholders. If the issuer prospers and the market price of its stock rises substantially in the market, the bondholders can convert bonds to stock worth a great deal more than what they paid for the bonds. This conversion privilege may also be included in the provisions of debentures that are not subordinated. Convertible securities are discussed in Part 7.

The bonds may be convertible into the common stock of a corporation other than that of the issuer. Such issues are called *exchangeable bonds.* There are also issues indexed to a commodity's price or its cash equivalent at the time of maturity or redemption.

## Guaranteed Bonds

Sometimes a corporation may guarantee the bonds of another corporation. Such bonds are referred to as *guaranteed bonds.* The guarantee, however, does not mean that these obligations are free of default risk. The safety of a guaranteed bond depends upon the financial capability of the guarantor to satisfy the terms of the guarantee, as well as the financial capability of the issuer. The terms of the guarantee may call for the guarantor to guarantee the payment of interest and/or repayment of the principal. A guaranteed bond may have more than one corporate guarantor. Each guarantor may be responsible for not only its pro rata share but also the entire amount guaranteed by the other guarantors.

## PROVISIONS FOR PAYING OFF BONDS

What would you pay for a bond that promises to pay interest in the amount of $50 or $60 a year from now to eternity but never promises to repay the principal? The right to receive interest in perpetuity may very well be worth $1,000, depending upon the current level of interest rates in the market, but investors generally dislike the absence of a promise to pay a fixed amount of principal on some specified date in the future; therefore, there is no such thing as a perpetual bond in the U.S. financial markets.

## Call and Refund Provisions

One important question in the negotiation of terms of a new bond issue is whether the issuer shall have the right to redeem the bonds before maturity, either as a whole or in part. Issuers generally want to have this right, and investors do not want them to have it. Both sides think that at some time in the future the general level of interest rates in the market may decline to a level well below that prevailing at the time bonds are issued. If so, issuers want to redeem all of the bonds outstanding and replace them with new bond issues at lower interest rates. But this is exactly what investors do not want. If bonds are redeemed when interest rates are low, investors have to take their money back and reinvest it at a low rate.

A common practice is a provision that denies the issuer a right to redeem bonds during the first 5 or 10 years following the date of issue if the proceeds from the redemption are from lower-cost funds obtained with issues ranking equally with or superior to the debt to be redeemed. This type of redemption is called *refunding*. However, when long-term issues have these refunding bars, or prohibitions, they are usually immediately callable, in whole or in part, if the source of funds is not lower-interest-cost money. Such sources may include retained earnings, the proceeds from a common stock sale, or funds from the disposition of property. Although the redemption price is often at a premium, there are many cases where the call price is 100% of par.

Many short- to intermediate-term bonds and notes are not callable for the first three to seven years (in some cases, not callable for the life of the issue). Thereafter, they may be called for any reason. Bond market participants often confuse refunding protection with call protection. Call protection is much more absolute in that bonds cannot be redeemed for any reason. Refunding restrictions only provide protection against one type of redemption, as mentioned above. Failure to recognize this difference has resulted in unnecessary losses for some investors.

In the 1990s, there was a significant reduction in callable issues. (This is discussed further in Chapter 42.) At one time, long-term industrial issues generally had 10 years of refunding protection but were immediately callable. Electric utilities most often had 5 years of refunding protection, although during times of high interest rates, issues with 10 years of refunding protection were sold.

As a rule, corporate bonds are callable at a premium above par. Generally, the amount of the premium declines as the bond approaches maturity. The initial amount of the premium may be as much as one year's interest or as little as interest for half a year. When less than the entire issue is called, the specific bonds to be called are selected randomly or on a pro rata basis. If the bonds selected on a random basis are bearer bonds, the serial numbers of the certificates are published in *The Wall Street Journal* and major metropolitan dailies.

## Outright Redemptions

For lack of a better term, we will use *outright redemptions* to describe the call of debt at general redemption prices. In the spring of 1973, Bristol-Myers Company called for redemption at 107.538 one-third, or $25 million, of its 8⅝% debentures due 1995. Trading as high as 111 in 1972 and about 108–109 when the call was announced, there were obviously some losses involved. Some market participants were confused by the call as they did not know the difference between nonrefundable and currently callable.

In 1977, NCR Corporation redeemed $75 million of its 9¾% debentures due 2000 at 107.88. The bonds were trading at 111–111½. The company was in a strong cash position and projected cash flow was substantially in excess of expected capital spending plans. Thus, NCR took action to improve its balance sheet and to reduce leverage through the call of this debt.

In 1983, a good example of an industrial redemption involved Archer Daniels Midland Company 16% sinking-fund debentures due May 15, 2011. The bonds were sold May 12, 1981, at 99½ and had the standard redemption/ refunding provisions (i.e., currently callable but nonrefundable prior to May 15, 1991). On June 1, 1983, the company announced the call of the bonds for August 1 at 113.95 plus accrued interest. On May 31, the bonds traded at 120. The source of the funds, according to the company, was from the two common stock offerings in January and June. Bondholders brought legal action, but the court allowed the redemption to proceed. On August 6, 1984, Archer Daniels Midland sold $100 million of 13% sinking-fund debentures due 8/1/2014 at 97.241, for a yield of 13.375%. The financial press reported that the investor reception was lukewarm. Would you like to guess one of the reasons for this?

## Sinking-Fund Provision

Term bonds may be paid off by operation of a *sinking fund.* Those last two words are often misunderstood to mean that the issuer accumulates a fund in cash, or in assets readily sold for cash, that is used to pay bonds at maturity. It had that meaning many years ago, but too often the money supposed to be in a sinking fund was not all there when it was needed. In modern practice, there is no fund, and *sinking* means that money is applied periodically to redemption of bonds before maturity. Corporate bond indentures require the issuer to retire a specified portion of an issue each year. This kind of provision for repayment of corporate debt may be designed to liquidate all of a bond issue by the maturity date, or it may be arranged to pay only a part of the total by the end of the term. If only a part is paid, the remainder is called a *balloon maturity.*

The issuer may satisfy the sinking-fund requirement in one of two ways. A cash payment of the face amount of the bonds to be retired may be made by the corporate debtor to the trustee. The latter then calls the bonds by lot for redemption. Bonds have serial numbers, and numbers may be randomly selected for redemption. Owners of bonds called in this manner turn them in for redemption; *interest payments stop at the redemption date.* Alternatively, the issuer can deliver to the trustee bonds with a total face value equal to the amount that must be retired. The bonds are purchased by the *issuer* in the open market. This option is elected by the issuer when the bonds are selling below par. A few corporate bond indentures, however, prohibit the open market purchase of the bonds by the issuer.

Many electric utility bond issues can satisfy the sinking-fund requirement by a third method. Instead of actually retiring bonds, the company may certify to the trustee that it has utilized unfunded property credits in lieu of the sinking fund. That is, it has made property and plant investments that have not been utilized for issuing bonded debt. For example, if the sinking-fund requirement is $1 million, it may give the trustee $1 million in cash to call bonds; it may deliver to the trustee $1 million of bonds it purchased in the open market; or it may certify that it made additions to its property and plant in the required amount, normally $1,667 of plant for each $1,000 sinking-fund requirement. In this case, it could satisfy the sinking fund with certified property additions of $1,667,000.

The issuer is granted a special call price to satisfy any sinking-fund requirement. Usually, the sinking-fund call price is the par value if the bonds were originally sold at par. When issued at a price in excess of par, the sinking-fund call price generally starts at the issuance price and scales down to par as the issue approaches maturity.

There are two advantages of a sinking-fund requirement from the bondholder's perspective. First, default risk is reduced because of the orderly retirement of the issue before maturity. Second, if bond prices decline as a result of an increase in interest rates, price support may be provided by the issuer or its fiscal agent, because it must enter the market on the buy side in order to satisfy the sinking-fund requirement. However, the disadvantage is that the bonds may be called at the special sinking-fund call price at a time when interest rates are lower than rates prevailing at the time of issuance. In that case, the bonds will be selling above par but may be retired by the issuer at the special call price that may be equal to par value.

Usually, the periodic payments required for sinking-fund purposes will be the same for each period. Gas company issues often have increasing sinking-fund requirements. However, a few indentures might permit variable periodic payments, where the periodic payments vary based upon prescribed conditions set forth in the indenture. The most common condition is the level of earnings of the issuer. In such cases, the periodic payments vary directly with earnings. An issuer prefers such flexibility; however, an investor may prefer fixed periodic payments because of the greater default risk protection provided under this arrangement.

Many corporate bond indentures include a provision that grants the issuer the option to retire more than the amount stipulated for sinking-fund retirement.

This option, referred to as an *accelerated sinking-fund provision,* effectively reduces the bondholder's call protection because, when interest rates decline, the issuer may find it economically advantageous to exercise this option at the special sinking-fund call price to retire a substantial portion of an outstanding issue.

With the exception of finance companies, industrial issues almost always include sinking-fund provisions. Finance companies, on the other hand, almost always do not. The inclusion or absence of a sinking-fund provision in public utility debt obligations depends upon the type of public utility. Pipeline issues almost always include sinking-fund provisions, whereas telephone issues do not. Electric utility companies have varying sinking-fund provisions. There can be a mandatory sinking fund where bonds have to be retired or, as mentioned above, a nonmandatory sinking fund in which it may utilize certain property credits for the sinking-fund requirement. If the sinking fund applies to a particular issue, it is called a *specific* sinking fund. There are also *nonspecific* sinking funds (also known as *funnel, tunnel, blanket,* or *aggregate sinking funds*) where the requirement is based upon the total bonded debt outstanding of an issuer. Generally, it might require a sinking-fund payment of 1% of all bonds outstanding as of year-end. The issuer can apply the requirement to one particular issue or to any other issue or issues. Again, the blanket sinking fund may be mandatory (where bonds have to be retired) or nonmandatory (whereby it can utilize unfunded property additions). Companies with blanket sinking funds include Alabama Power Company, Georgia Power Company, Consumers Power Company, and Pacific Gas and Electric Company, among others. In some years, they might actually retire bonds, whereas in other years they may certify unfunded property additions. The blanket sinking fund of Baltimore Gas and Electric Company is mandatory.

## Maintenance and Replacement Funds

Calls under *maintenance and replacement fund* (M&R) *provisions* first occurred in 1977–78. They shocked bondholders, as calls were thought to be unlikely under these provisions, which were little known and used. However, due to the steep decline in interest rates in 1985 and early 1986, some electric utility companies decided to make use of the M&R calls again. Now investors recognize this type of redemption, but because the calls were around the par level and the bonds with above-market-level coupons were trading at higher prices, the results still hurt.

Florida Power & Light Company retired $63.7 million out of $125 million of its 10⅛% bonds due March 1, 2005, at 100.65 on September 2, 1977, through the M&R provisions. The regular redemption price at the time was 110.98 and the issue was well within the refunding period, which expired on February 28, 1980 (call price starting March 1, 1980, was 109.76).

In 1977 and 1978, Carolina Power & Light deposited nearly $79 million with its trustee under the M&R fund provisions. The company, on June 2, 1978, called $46 million of its privately held 11⅛% bonds due 1994 and $32.7 million of the public 11% bonds of 1984 at the special redemption price of par. The company's announcement stated the following:

> The funds deposited were derived at the time from cash flow; however, if it is assumed that the eventual result is the replacement of the interest cost of the bonds to be redeemed with bonds at a probable interest cost of about 9% for 30 years, it is apparent that there will be a significant reduction of interest costs with an attendant improvement in fixed-charge coverages. The security of the total body of bondholders is improved and the maturities lengthened. These debt management actions are a positive demonstration to customers, stockholders and regulators that the management of the company continues to exercise appropriate cost control measures.

Of course, some bondholders objected to the retirements, claiming that, as the calls were within the refunding protected periods, the companies were barred from these special debt redemptions. They also claimed that the prospectuses and offering statements were unclear. However, a *careful* reading of the prospectuses revealed that the debt could be redeemed at the special redemption prices for the replacement fund or from certain other deposited cash. The general redemption prices applied to other redemptions, provided that none of the bonds could be redeemed *at the general redemption price* before the end of the refunding protected period if such redemption was for the purpose or in anticipation of refunding the bonds through the use of borrowed funds at a lower interest cost. The M&R provisions were allowed exceptions, and the courts have upheld companies' rights to redeem bonds in accordance with their terms.

Not all electric utility companies provide maintenance and replacement fund requirements for all of their mortgage debt. Some of the more recent issues lack the M&R provisions, although, as long as some of the older issues are still outstanding with these clauses, the M&R provisions apply. A number of issues subject to M&R clauses may be retired at the higher general redemption price and not the lower special call price. Others are protected from M&R redemption through the end of the refunding protected period, and in some cases certain property credits *must* be used before cash could be deposited with the trustee.

## Redemption through the Sale of Assets and Other Means

Because mortgage bonds are secured by property, bondholders want the integrity of the collateral to be maintained. Bondholders would not want a company to sell a plant (which has been pledged as collateral) and then to use the proceeds for a distribution to shareholders. Therefore, release-of-property and substitution-of-property clauses are found in most bond indentures.

Wisconsin Michigan Power retired $9.9 million of its 9¼% bonds due 2000 on February 28, 1977, through the release-of-property clause at a redemption price of 100.97. On June 30, 1976, the company sold its gas business for

$16,920,000 to an affiliate, Wisconsin Natural Gas. Of the proceeds, $16,520,000 was deposited with the trustee under the mortgage per the release and substitution-of-property clause, and a portion of these funds was released to the company against certified property additions. The balance was used to redeem the 9¼'s as interest rates dropped to a level where the company thought it was to its advantage to retire high-coupon debt.

On December 7, 1983, Virginia Electric and Power Company said it would redeem its $100 million 15¾% bonds due April 1, 1989 (the highest public coupon), with the proceeds (so-called release moneys) from the sale of ownership interests in some nuclear facilities. Property sales are not unusual for electric utility companies and a number have been negotiated in recent years.

Many utility bond issues contain provisions regarding the confiscation of assets by a governmental body through the right of eminent domain or the disposition of assets by order of or to any governmental authority. In a number of cases, bonds *must* be redeemed if the company receives more than a certain amount in cash. Washington Water Power Company must apply the proceeds of $15 million or more to the retirement of debt in the case of government takeover of its property. The redemption price may be either the special or regular, depending on the issue. In 1984, Pacific Power & Light Company sold an electric distribution system to the Emerald People's Utility District for $25 million. It applied these proceeds to the redemption of half of the outstanding 14¾% mortgage bonds due 2010 at the special redemption price of 100. This issue was not the highest-coupon bond outstanding in the company's capitalization. There were some 18s of 1991, but these were exempt from the special provisions for the retirement of bonds with the proceeds from property sold to governmental authorities. In April 1988, Utah Power & Light company retired some 13% bonds due 2012 with funds obtained from the condemnation of some of its property in Kaneb, Utah, and the sale of electric assets to a couple of other cities.

On December 13, 1983, InterNorth, Inc., announced the call on February 1, 1984, of $90.5 million out of $200 million of its 17½% debentures due August 1, 1991, at the regular redemption price of 112.32. The refunding protected period expired September 30, 1988. However, the proceeds were obtained from the sale of its Northern Propane Gas Co. unit. Because these are unsecured debentures and not mortgage bonds, there was no release and substitution of property clause and no special call price. On October 1, 1984, it redeemed another $23,875,000 of these 17½% debentures at 109.86 with funds obtained from the December 1983 sale of two tanker ships.

## CORPORATE BOND RATINGS

At any one time, the yields that investors obtain by purchasing bonds in the market may vary according to how investors estimate the uncertainty of future payment of dollar amounts of interest and principal exactly as set forth in bond indentures. This uncertainty is often called *financial risk* because it depends upon the financial ability of issuers to make those payments. If an issuer can pay, it will. Failure by a company to pay usually means intervention of a court of law on behalf of bondholders and court supervision of the conduct of business. In any event, a default is a disaster for an issuer.

Professional bond investors have ways of analyzing information about companies and bond issues to estimate the uncertainty of future ability to pay. These techniques are explained in Part 3 of this book. However, most individual bond investors and some institutional bond investors make no such elaborate studies. In fact, they rely largely upon bond ratings published by several organizations that do the job of bond analysis and express their conclusions by a system of ratings. The three major nationally recognized statistical rating organizations (NRSROs) in the United States are Moody's Investors Service, Inc. (Moody's); Standard & Poor's Corporation (S&P); and Fitch (the entity resulting from the April 2000 merger of Fitch IBCA and Duff & Phelps Credit Rating Co.). These ratings are used by market participants as a factor in the valuation of securities on account of their independent and unbiased nature.

Rating definitions are released by these firms in their various publications. Investors are urged to read these definitions. It should be remembered that they are not "buy," "hold," or "sell" indicators. They do not state whether an issue is "cheap" or "dear" among the multitude of bond issues. They do not point to the direction of the market. Although only a guide to the issuer's ability and willingness to meet the terms of the issue, they are a very important factor in the bond investment decision.

The rating systems use similar symbols, as shown in Exhibit 11–1. The bonds in the four highest rating categories are known as *high grade,* or *investment grade,* meaning that financial risk is relatively low and the probability of future payment relatively high. Lower-rated bonds have speculative elements, and the repayment of principal and interest in accordance with the terms of the issue is not ensured.

## EVENT RISK

In recent years, one of the more talked-about topics among corporate bond investors is *event risk.* Over the last couple of decades, corporate bond indentures have become less restrictive, and corporate managements have been given a free rein to do as they please without regard to bondholders. Management's main concern or duty is to enhance shareholder wealth. As for the bondholder, all a company is required to do is to meet the terms of the bond indenture including the payment of principal and interest. With few restrictions and the optimization of shareholder wealth of paramount importance for corporate managers, it is no wonder that bondholders became concerned when merger mania and other

## EXHIBIT 11-1

Summary of Rating Symbols and Definitions

| Moody's | S&P | Fitch* | D&P* | Brief Definition |
|---------|-----|--------|------|------------------|
| *Investment Grade—High Creditworthiness* | | | | |
| Aaa | AAA | AAA | AAA | Gilt edge, prime, maximum safety |
| Aa1 | AA+ | AA+ | AA+ | |
| Aa2 | AA | AA | AA | Very high grade, high quality |
| Aa3 | AA− | AA− | AA− | |
| A1 | A+ | A+ | A+ | |
| A2 | A | A | A | Upper medium grade |
| A3 | A− | A− | A− | |
| Baa1 | BBB+ | BBB+ | BBB+ | |
| Baa2 | BBB | BBB | BBB | Lower medium grade |
| Baa3 | BBB− | BBB− | BBB− | |
| *Distinctly Speculative—Low Creditworthiness* | | | | |
| Ba1 | BB+ | BB+ | BB+ | |
| Ba2 | BB | BB | BB | Low grade, speculative |
| Ba3 | BB− | BB− | BB− | |
| B1 | B+ | B+ | | |
| B2 | B | B | B | Highly speculative |
| B3 | B− | B− | | |
| *Predominantly Speculative—Substantial Risk or in Default* | | | | |
| | CCC+ | | | |
| Caa | CCC | CCC | CCC | Substantial risk, in poor standing |
| | CCC− | | | |
| Ca | CC | CC | | May be in default, extremely speculative |
| C | C | C | | Even more speculative than those above |
| | CI | | | CI = Income bonds— no interest is being paid |
| | | DDD | | Default |
| | | DD | DD | |
| | D | D | | |

*As of this writing, the merged entity of Fitch IBCA and D&P has not announced its rating symbols.

Source: Richard S. Wilson and Frank J. Fabozzi, *Corporate Bonds: Structures and Analysis* (New Hope, PA: Frank J. Fabozzi Associates, 1996).

events swept the nation's boardrooms. Events such as decapitalizations, restructurings, recapitalizations, mergers, acquisitions, leveraged buyouts, and share repurchases, among other things, often caused substantial changes in a corporation's capital structure, namely, greatly increased leverage and decreased equity. Bondholders' protection was sharply reduced and debt quality ratings lowered, in many cases to speculative-grade categories. Along with greater risk came lower bond valuations. Shareholders were being enriched at the expense of bondholders.

In reaction to the increased activity of corporate raiders and mergers and acquisitions, some companies incorporated "poison puts" in their indentures. These are designed to thwart unfriendly takeovers by making the target company unpalatable to the acquirer. The poison put provides that the bondholder can require the company to repurchase the debt under certain circumstances arising out of specific designated events such as a change in control. Poison puts may not deter a proposed acquisition but could make it more expensive. In some cases if the board of directors approves the change in control—a "friendly" transaction (and all takeovers are friendly if the price is right)—the poison put provisions will not become effective. The designated event of change in control generally means either that continuing directors no longer constitute a majority of the board of directors or that a person, including affiliates, becomes the beneficial owner, directly or indirectly, of stock with at least 20% of the voting rights. Many times, in addition to a designated event, a rating change to below investment grade must occur within a certain period for the put to be activated. Some issues provide for a higher interest rate instead of a put as a designated event remedy.

Event risk has caused some companies to include other special debt retirement features in their indentures. An example is the *maintenance of net worth clause* included in the indentures of some lower-rated bond issues. In this case, an issuer covenants to maintain its net worth above a stipulated level, and if it fails to do so, it must begin to retire its debt at par. Usually the redemptions affect only part of the issue and continue periodically until the net worth recovers to an amount above the stated figure or the debt is retired. In other cases, the company is required only to *offer to redeem* a required amount. An offer to redeem is not mandatory on the bondholders' part; only those holders who want their bonds redeemed need do so. In a number of instances in which the issuer is required to call bonds, the bondholders may elect not to have bonds redeemed. This is not much different from an offer to redeem. It may protect bondholders from the redemption of the high-coupon debt at lower interest rates. However, if a company's net worth declines to a level low enough to activate such a call, it would probably be prudent to have one's bonds redeemed.

Protecting the value of debt investments against the added risk caused by corporate management activity is not an easy job. Investors should carefully analyze the issuer's fundamentals to determine if the company may be a candidate for restructuring. Attention to news and equity investment reports can make the task easier. Also, the indenture should be reviewed to see if there are any protective features. However, even these can often be circumvented by sharp legal minds. Toward this end, some of the debt rating services issue commentary on indenture features of corporate bonds, noting the degree of protection against event risk. Of course, large portfolios can reduce risk with broad diversification among industry lines, but price declines do not always affect only the issue at risk; they also can spread across the board and take the innocent down with them. This happened in the fall of 1988 with the leveraged buyout of RJR Nabisco, Inc. The whole industrial bond market suffered as buyers and traders withdrew from the market, new issues were postponed, and secondary market activity came to a standstill. The impact of the initial leveraged buyout bid announcement on yield spreads for RJR Nabisco's debt to a benchmark Treasury increased from about 100 basis points to 350 basis points. The RJR transaction showed that size was not an obstacle. Therefore, other large firms that investors previously thought were unlikely candidates for a leveraged buyout were fair game. The spillover effect caused yield spreads to widen for other major corporations.

## SPECULATIVE-GRADE BONDS

Speculative-grade bonds are those rated below investment grade by the rating agencies, i.e., BB+ and lower by Standard & Poor's Corporation, and Ba1 and less by Moody's Investors Service, Inc. They may also be unrated, but not all unrated debt is speculative. Also known as "junk bonds," promoters have given these securities other euphemisms, such as "high-yield interest bonds," "high-yield opportunity debt," and "high-yield securities." While some of these terms may be misleading to the uninitiated, they are used throughout the investment world with "junk" and "high yield" being the most popular. We will also use "junk" and "high yield" in our discussion below. Speculative-grade bonds may not be high-yielders at all as they may not be paying any interest, and there may be little hope for the resumption of interest payments; even the return expected from a reorganization or liquidation may be low. Some high-yield instruments may not be speculative-grade at all as they may carry investment grade ratings. The higher yields may be due to fears of premature redemption of high-coupon bonds in a lower interest rate environment. The higher yields may be caused by a sharp decline in the securities markets which has driven down the prices of all issues including those with investment merit. By using the term "high-yield securities" some may be attempting to whitewash the risks associated with these securities. But surely, an above average yield should denote extra risk to investors since there is "no free lunch" in the investment markets.

While the term "junk" tarnishes the entire less-than-investment-grade spectrum, it is applicable to some specific situations. Junk bonds are not useless stuff, trash or rubbish as the term is defined. At times, investors overpay for their speculative-grade securities so they feel that they may have purchased junk or worthless garbage. But isn't this also the case when they have overpaid for high-grade securities? There are other times when profits may be made from buying junk bonds; certainly then, these bonds are not junk but something that may be quite attractive. Also, not all securities in this low grade sector of the market are on the verge of default or bankruptcy. Many issues might be on the fringe of the investment grade sector. Market participants should be discriminating in the choice of their terminology.

## Types of Issuers

Several types of issuers fall into the less-than-investment-grade high yield category. These categories are discussed below.

### Original Issuers

Original issuers include young, growing concerns lacking the stronger balance sheet and income statement profile of many established corporations, but often with lots of promise. Also called "venture capital situations" or "growth or emerging market companies," the debt is often sold with a story projecting future financial strength. From this we get the term "story bond." There are also the established operating firms with financials neither measuring up to the strengths of investment-grade corporations nor possessing the weaknesses of companies on the verge of bankruptcy. Subordinated debt of investment grade issuers may be included here. A bond rated at the bottom rung of the investment grade category (Baa and BBB) or at the top end of the speculative grade category (Ba and BB) is known as a "businessman's risk."

### Fallen Angels

"Fallen angels" are companies with investment-grade rated debt that have come upon hard times with deteriorating balance sheet and income statement financial parameters are included in this category. They may be in default or near bankruptcy. In these cases, investors are interested in the workout value of the debt in a reorganization or liquidation, whether within or without the bankruptcy courts. Some refer to these issues as "special situations." Over the years they have fallen on hard times; some have recovered and others have not.

### Restructurings and Leveraged Buyouts

These are companies which have deliberately increased their debt burden with a view towards maximizing shareholder value. The shareholders may be the existing public group to which the company pays a special extraordinary dividend with the funds coming from borrowings and the sale of assets. Cash is paid out, net worth decreased and leverage increased, and ratings drop on existing debt. Newly issued debt gets junk bond status because of the company's weakened financial condition. In 1988, The Kroger Co. declared a dividend of about $3.2 billion in cash and junior subordinated discount notes. Funds were obtained through bank borrowings with repayment to be made from asset sales and retained future cash flow. The proceeds did not go towards building the company, but towards its weakening and dismantling, at least over the intermediate term. Prior to the special dividend the senior debt was rated A2 by Moody's. It fell to B1 in 1988 and recovered to Ba1 where it stood at the end of 1994.

In a leveraged buyout (LBO), a new and private shareholder group owns and manages the company. The debt issue's purpose may be to retire other debt from commercial and investment banks and institutional investors incurred to finance the LBO. The debt to be retired is called bridge financing as it provides a bridge between the initial LBO activity and the more permanent financing. One example is Ann Taylor, Inc.'s 1989 debt financing for bridge loan repayment. The proceeds of BCI Holding Corporation's 1986 public debt financing and bank borrowings were used to make the required payments to the common shareholders of Beatrice Companies, pay issuance expenses, retire certain Beatrice debt, and for working capital.

## Unique Features of Some Issues

Often actions taken by management that result in the assignment of a non-investment-grade bond rating result in a heavy interest payment burden. This places severe cash flow constraints on the firm. To reduce this burden, firms involved with heavy debt burdens have issued bonds with *deferred coupon structures* that permit the issuer to avoid using cash to make interest payments for a period of three to seven years. There are three types of deferred coupon structures: (1) deferred-interest bonds, (2) step-up bonds, and (3) payment-in-kind bonds.

*Deferred interest bonds* are the most common type of deferred coupon structure. These bonds sell at a deep discount and do not pay interest for an initial period, typically from three to seven years. (Because no interest is paid for the initial period, these bonds are sometimes referred to as zero-coupon bonds.) *Step-up bonds* do pay coupon interest, but the coupon rate is low for an initial period and then increases ("step up") to a higher coupon rate. Finally, *payment-in-kind (PIK) bonds* give the issuers an option to pay cash at a coupon payment date or give the bondholder a similar bond (i.e., a bond with the same coupon rate and a par value equal to the amount of the coupon payment that would have been paid). The period during which the issuer can make this choice varies from five to ten years.

In late 1987, an issue came to market with a structure allowing the issuer to reset the coupon rate so that the bond will trade at a predetermined price.[1]

---

1. Most of the bonds have a coupon reset formula that requires the issuer to reset the coupon so that the bond will trade at a price of $101.

The coupon rate may reset annually or even more frequently, or reset only one time over the life of the bond. Generally, the coupon rate at the reset date will be the average of rates suggested by two investment banking firms. The new rate will then reflect: (1) the level of interest rates at the reset date and (2) the credit spread the market wants on the issue at the reset date. This structure is called an *extendible reset bond.*

Notice the difference between an extendible reset bond and a typical floating-rate issue. In a floating-rate issue, the coupon rate resets according to a fixed spread over the reference rate, with the index spread specified in the indenture. The amount of the index spread reflects market conditions at the time the issue is offered. The coupon rate on an extendible reset bond, in contrast, is reset based on market conditions (as suggested by several investment banking firms) at the time of the reset date. Moreover, the new coupon rate reflects the new level of interest rates and the new spread that investors seek.

The advantage to investors of extendible reset bonds is that the coupon rate will reset to the market rate—both the level of interest rates and the credit spread—in principle keeping the issue at par value. In fact, experience with extendible reset bonds has not been favorable during periods of difficulties in the high-yield bond market. The sudden substantial increase in default risk has meant that the rise in the rate needed to keep the issue at par value was so large that it would have insured the bankruptcy of the issuer. As a result, the rise in the coupon rate has been insufficient to keep the issue at the stipulated price.

Some speculative-grade bond issues started to appear in 1992 granting the issuer a limited right to redeem a portion of the bonds during the noncall period if the proceeds are from an initial public stock offering. In a few cases, proceeds from a secondary stock offering are also a permissible source of funds. Called "clawback" provisions, they merit careful attention by inquiring bond investors. According to Merrill Lynch's High Yield Securities Research Department, an increasing number of high yield issues have clawbacks. In the nearly three-year period ending June 30, 1994, of the almost 700 high-yield issues in its sample, close to 25%, came with clawbacks. The percentage of the issue that can be retired with stock proceeds ranges from 20% to 100% with the clawback period usually limited to the first three years after issuance. The redemption prices are around 110% of par, give or take a coupon of points. Investors should be fore-warned of clawbacks since they can lose bonds at the point in time just when the issuer's finances have been strengthened through access to the equity market. Also, the redemption may reduce the amount of the outstanding bonds to a level at which their liquidity in the aftermarket may suffer.

## DEFAULT RATES AND RECOVERY RATES

We now turn our attention to the various aspects of the historical performance of corporate issuers with respect to fulfilling their obligations to bondholders. Specifically, we will look at two aspects of this performance. First, we will look at the default rate of corporate borrowers. From an investment perspective, default rates by themselves are not of paramount significance: it is perfectly possible for a portfolio of bonds to suffer defaults and to outperform Treasuries at the same time, provided the yield spread of the portfolio is sufficiently high to offset the losses from default. Furthermore, because holders of defaulted bonds typically recover some percentage of the face amount of their investment, the *default loss rate* is substantially lower than the default rate. Therefore, it is important to look at default loss rates or, equivalently, *recovery rates.*

## Default Rates

A default rate can be measured in different ways. A simple way to define a default rate is to use the issuer as the unit of study. A default rate is then measured as the number of issuers that default divided by the total number of issuers at the beginning of the year. This measure gives no recognition to the amount defaulted nor the total amount of issuance. Moody's, for example, uses this default rate statistic in its study of default rates.[2] The rationale for ignoring dollar amounts is that the credit decision of an investor does not increase with the size of the issuer. The second measure is to define the default rate as the par value of all bonds that defaulted in a given calendar year, divided by the total par value of all bonds outstanding during the year. Edward Altman who has performed extensive analysis of default rates for speculative-grade bonds measures default rates in this way. We will distinguish between the default rate statistic below by referring to the first as the *issuer default rate* and the second as the *dollar default rate.*

With either default rate statistic, one can measure the default for a given year or an average annual default rate over a certain number of years. Researchers who have defined dollar default rates in terms of an average annual default rate over a certain number of years have measured it as:

$$\frac{\text{Cumulative \$ value of all defaulted bonds}}{\text{Cumulative \$ value of all issuance} \times \text{Weighted avg. no. of years outstanding}}$$

Alternatively, some researchers report a cumulative annual default rate. This is done by not normalizing by the number of years. For example, a cumulative annual dollar default rate is calculated as:

$$\frac{\text{Cumulative \$ value of all defaulted bonds}}{\text{Cumulative \$ value of all issuance}}$$

There have been several excellent studies of corporate bond default rates. We will not review each of these studies since the findings are similar. Here we

2. Moody's Investors Service, *Corporate Bond Defaults and Default Rates: 1970–1994,* Moody's Special Report, January 1995, p. 13. Different issuers within an affiliated group of companies are counted separately.

will look at a study by Moody's that covers the period 1970 to 1994.[3] Over this 25-year period, 640 of the 4,800 issuers in the study defaulted on more than $96 billion of publicly offered long-term debt. A default in the Moody's study is defined as "any missed or delayed disbursement of interest and/or principal." Issuer default rates are calculated. The Moody's study found that the lower the credit rating, the greater the probability of a corporate issuer defaulting.

There have been extensive studies focusing on default rates for speculative-grade issuers. In their 1987 study, Altman and Nammacher[4] found that the annual default rate for speculative-grade corporate debt was 2.15%, a figure that Altman[5] later updated to 2.40%. Drexel Burnham Lambert's (DBL), the now defunct investment banking firm that at one time was the major underwriter of speculative-grade bonds, estimates have also shown default rates of about 2.40% per year.[6] Asquith, Mullins, and Wolff,[7] however, found that nearly one out of every three speculative-grade bonds defaults. The large discrepancy arises because researchers use three different definitions of "default rate"; even if applied to the same universe of bonds (which they are not), all three results could be valid simultaneously.[8]

Altman and Nammacher define the default rate as the par value of all speculative-grade bonds that defaulted in a given calendar year, divided by the total par value outstanding during the year. That is the dollar default rate is calculated. Their estimates (2.15% and 2.40%) are simple averages of the annual dollar default rates over a number of years. DBL took the cumulative dollar value of all defaulted speculative-grade bonds, divided by the cumulative dollar value of all speculative-grade bond issuance, and further divided by the weighted average number of years outstanding to obtain an average annual dollar default rate. Asquith, Mullins, and Wolff use a cumulative dollar default rate statistic. For all bonds issued in a given year, the default rate is the total par value of defaulted issues as of the date of their study, divided by the total part amount originally issued to obtain a cumulative default rate. Their result (that about one in three speculative-grade bonds defaults) is not normalized by the number of years outstanding.

---

3. Moody's Investors Service, *Corporate Bond Defaults and Default Rates: 1970–1994.*
4. Edward I. Altman and Scott A. Nammacher, *Investing in Junk Bonds* (New York: John Wiley, 1987).
5. Edward I. Altman, "Research Update: Mortality Rates and Losses, Bond Rating Drift," unpublished study prepared for a workshop sponsored by Merrill Lynch Merchant Banking Group, High Yield Sales and Trading, 1989.
6. As reported in various annual issues of *High Yield Market Report: Financing America's Future* (New York and Beverly Hills: Drexel Burnham Lambert Incorporated).
7. Paul Asquith, David W. Mullins, Jr., and Eric D. Wolff, "Original Issue High Yield Bonds: Aging Analysis of Defaults, Exchanges, and Calls," *Journal of Finance* (September 1989), pp. 923–952.
8. As a parallel, we know that the mortality rate in the United States is currently less than 1% per year, but we also know that 100% of all humans (eventually) die.

While all three measures are useful indicators of bond default propensity, they are not direct comparable. Even when restated on an annualized basis, they do not all measure the same quantity. The default statistics from all studies, however, are surprisingly similar once cumulative rates have been annualized. A majority of studies place the annual dollar default rates for all original issue high-yield bonds between 3% and 4%.

## Recovery Rates

There have been several studies that have focused on recovery rates or default loss rates for corporate debt. Measuring the amount recovered is not a simply task. The final distribution to claimants when a default occurs may consist of cash and securities. Often it is difficult to track what was received and then determine the present value of any non-cash payments received.

Here we review recovery information as reported in the Moody's study that we cited earlier. Moody's uses the trading price at the time of default as a proxy for the amount recovered. The recovery rate is the trading price at that time divided by the par value. Moody's found that the recovery rate was 38% for all bonds.

While default rates are the same regardless of the level of seniority, recovery rates differ. The study found that the higher the level of seniority, the greater the recovery rate.

## CHAPTER 12

# MEDIUM-TERM NOTES*

Leland F. Crabbe, Ph.D.
Director
Credit Suisse Asset Management

Over the past two decades, medium-term notes (MTNs) have emerged as a major source of funding for U.S. and foreign corporations, federal agencies, supranational institutions, and sovereign countries. U.S. corporations have issued MTNs since the early 1970s. At that time, the market was established as an alternative to short-term financing in the commercial paper market and long-term borrowing in the bond market; hence the name *medium term*. Through the 1970s, however, only a few corporations issued MTNs, and by 1981 outstandings amounted to only about $800 million. In the 1980s, the U.S. MTN market evolved from a relatively obscure niche market dominated by the auto finance companies into a major source of debt financing for several hundred large corporations. In the 1990s, the U.S. market has continued to attract a diversity of new borrowers, and outside the United States, the Euro-MTN market has grown at a phenomenal rate.

Most MTNs are noncallable, unsecured, senior debt securities with fixed coupon rates and investment-grade credit ratings. In these features, MTNs are similar to investment-grade corporate bonds. However, they have generally differed from bonds in their primary distribution process. MTNs have traditionally been sold on a best-efforts basis by investment banks and other broker-dealers acting as agents. In contrast to an underwriter in the conventional bond market, an agent in the MTN market has no obligation to underwrite MTNs for the issuer, and the issuer is not guaranteed funds. Also, unlike corporate bonds, which are typically sold in large, discrete offerings, MTNs are usually sold in relatively small amounts either on a continuous or on an intermittent basis.

Borrowers with MTN programs have great flexibility in the types of securities they may issue. As the market for MTNs has evolved, issuers have taken advantage of this flexibility by issuing MTNs with less conventional features.

---

* This chapter is adapted from Leland E. Crabbe, "Anatomy of the Medium-Term Note Market," *Federal Reserve Bulletin,* August 1993, pp.751–768.

Many MTNs are now issued with floating interest rates or with rates that are computed according to unusual formulas tied to equity or commodity prices. Also, many include calls, puts, and other options. Furthermore, maturities are not necessarily "medium term"—they have ranged from nine months to 30 years and longer. Moreover, like corporate bonds, MTNs are now often sold on an underwritten basis, and offering amounts are occasionally as large as those of bonds. Indeed, rather than denoting a narrow security with an intermediate maturity, an MTN is more accurately defined as a highly flexible debt instrument that can easily be designed to respond to market opportunities and investor preferences.

The emergence of the MTN market has transformed the way that corporations raise capital and that institutions invest. In recent years, this transformation has accelerated because of the development of derivatives markets, such as swaps, options, and futures, that allow investors and borrowers to transfer risk to others in the financial system who have different risk preferences. A growing number of transactions in the MTN market now involve simultaneous transactions in a derivatives market.

This chapter discusses the history and economics of the MTN market, analyzes statistics on MTNs collected by the Federal Reserve, and reviews developments in the U.S. and Euro-MTN markets.[1]

## BACKGROUND OF THE MTN MARKET[2]

General Motors Acceptance Corporation (GMAC) created the MTN market in the early 1970s as an extension of the commercial paper market. To improve their asset/liability management, GMAC and the other auto finance companies needed to issue debt with a maturity that matched that of their auto loans to dealers and consumers. However, underwriting costs made bond offerings with short maturities impractical, and maturities on commercial paper cannot exceed 270 days. The auto finance companies therefore began to sell MTNs directly to investors. In the 1970s, the growth of the market was hindered by illiquidity in the secondary market and by securities regulations requiring approval by the Securities and Exchange Commission (SEC) of any amendment to a registered

---

1. The Federal Reserve Board conducts a survey of borrowing by U.S. corporations in the public MTN market, the largest sector of the worldwide market. The Federal Reserve collects these data to improve its estimates of new securities issues of U.S. corporations, as published in the *Federal Reserve Bulletin,* and to improve estimates of corporate securities outstanding, as shown in the flow of funds accounts.

2. Material in this and the next two sections was originally presented in Leland Crabbe, "Corporate Medium-Term Notes," *The Continental Bank Journal of Applied Corporate Finance,* Winter 1992, pp.90–102.

public offering. The latter, in particular, increased the costs of issuance significantly because borrowers had to obtain the approval of the SEC each time they changed the posted coupon rates on their MTN offering schedule. To avoid this regulatory hurdle, some corporations sold MTNs in the private placement market.

In the early 1980s, two institutional changes set the stage for rapid growth of the MTN market. First, in 1981 major investment banks acting as agents committed resources to assist in primary issuance and to provide secondary market liquidity. By 1984, the captive finance companies of the three large automakers had at least two agents for their MTN programs. The ongoing financing requirements of these companies and the competition among agents established a basis for the market to develop. Because investment banks stood ready to buy back MTNs in the secondary market, investors became more receptive to adding MTNs to their portfolio holdings. In turn, the improved liquidity and consequent reduction in the cost of issuance attracted new borrowers to the market.

Second, the adoption by the SEC of Rule 415 in March 1982 served as another important institutional change. Rule 415 permits delayed or continuous issuance of so-called shelf-registered corporate securities. Under shelf registrations, issuers register securities that may be sold for two years after the effective date of the registration without the requirement of another registration statement each time new offerings are made. Thus shelf registration enables issuers to take advantage of brief periods of low interest rates by selling previously registered securities on a moment's notice. In contrast, debt offerings that are not made from shelf registrations are subject to a delay of at least 48 hours between the filing with the SEC and the subsequent offering to the public.

The ability of borrowers to sell a variety of debt instruments with a broad range of coupons and maturities under a single prospectus supplement is another advantage of a shelf-registered MTN program. Indeed, a wide array of financing options have been included in MTN filings.[3] For example, MTN programs commonly give the borrower the choice of issuing fixed- or floating-rate debt.[4] Furthermore, several "global" programs allow for placements in the U.S. market or in the Euromarket. Other innovations that reflect the specific funding needs of issuers include MTNs collateralized by mortgages issued by thrift institutions,

---

3. For example, MTNs have been callable, putable, and extendible; they have had zero coupons, step-down or step-up coupons, or inverse floating rates; and they have been foreign-currency denominated or indexed, and commodity indexed.

4. The most common indexes for floating-rate MTNs are the following: the London interbank offered rate (LIBOR), commercial paper, Treasury bills, federal funds, and the prime rate. MTN programs typically give the issuer the option of making floating-rate interest payments monthly, quarterly, or semiannually.

equipment trust certificates issued by railways, amortizing notes issued by leasing companies, and subordinated notes issued by bank holding companies. Another significant innovation has been the development of asset-backed MTNs, a form of asset securitization used predominantly to finance trade receivables and corporate loans. This flexibility in types of instruments that may be sold as MTNs, coupled with the market timing benefits of shelf registration, enables issuers to respond readily to changing market opportunities.

In the early and mid-1980s, when finance companies dominated the market, most issues of MTNs were fixed rate, noncallable, and unsecured, with maturities of five years or less. In recent years, as new issuers with more diverse financing needs have established programs, the characteristics of new issues have become less generic. For example, maturities have lengthened as industrial and utility companies with longer financing needs have entered the market. Indeed, in July 1993, Walt Disney Company issued a note with a 100-year maturity off its medium-term note shelf registration. A growing volume of placements of notes with long maturities have made the designation *medium term* something of a misnomer.

## MECHANICS OF THE MARKET

The process of raising funds in the public MTN market usually begins when a corporation files a shelf registration with the SEC.[5] Once the SEC declares the registration statement effective, the borrower files a prospectus supplement that describes the MTN program. The amount of debt under the program generally ranges from $100 million to $1 billion. After establishing an MTN program, a borrower may enter the MTN market continuously or intermittently with large or relatively small offerings. Although underwritten corporate bonds may also be issued from shelf registrations, MTNs provide issuers with more flexibility than traditional underwritings in which the entire debt issue is made at one time, typically with a single coupon and a single maturity.

The registration filing usually includes a list of the investment banks with which the corporation has arranged to act as agents to distribute the notes to investors. Most MTN programs have two to four agents. Having multiple agents encourages competition among investment banks and thus lowers financing costs. The large New York-based investment banks dominate the distribution of MTNs.

Through its agents, an issuer of MTNs posts offering rates over a range of maturities: for example, 9 months to a year, a year to 18 months, 18 months

---

5. SEC-registered MTNs have the broadest market because they have no resale or transfer restrictions and generally fit within an investor's investment guidelines.

to 2 years, and annually thereafter (see Exhibit 12–1). Many issuers post rates as a yield spread over a Treasury security of comparable maturity. The relatively attractive yield spreads posted at the maturities of three, four, and five years shown in Exhibit 12–1 indicate that the issuer desires to raise funds at these maturities. The investment banks disseminate this offering rate information to their investor clients.

When an investor expresses interest in an MTN offering, the agent contacts the issuer to obtain a confirmation of the terms of the transaction. Within a maturity range, the investor has the option of choosing the final maturity of the note sale, subject to agreement by the issuing company. The issuer will lower its posted rates once it raises the desired amount of funds at a given maturity. In the example in Exhibit 12–1, the issuer might lower its posted rate for MTNs with a five-year maturity to 40 basis points over comparable Treasury securities after it sells the desired amount of debt at this maturity. Of course, issuers also change their offering rate scales in response to changing market conditions. Issuers may withdraw from the market by suspending sales or, alternatively, by posting narrow offering spreads at all maturity ranges. The proceeds from primary trades in the MTN market typically range from $1 million to $25 million,

**E X H I B I T   12–1**

An Offering Rate Schedule for a Medium-Term Note Program

| Medium-Term Notes | | Yield Spread of MTN over Treasury Securities (basis points) | Treasury Securities | |
|---|---|---|---|---|
| Maturity Range | Yield (percent) | | Maturity | Yield (percent) |
| 9 months to 12 months | (a) | (a) | 9 months | 3.35 |
| 12 months to 18 months | (a) | (a) | 12 months | 3.50 |
| 18 months to 2 years | (a) | (a) | 18 months | 3.80 |
| 2 years to 3 years | 4.35 | 35 | 2 years | 4.00 |
| 3 years to 4 years | 5.05 | 55 | 3 years | 4.50 |
| 4 years to 5 years | 5.60 | 60 | 4 years | 5.00 |
| 5 years to 6 years | 6.05 | 60 | 5 years | 5.45 |
| 6 years to 7 years | 6.10 | 40 | 6 years | 5.70 |
| 7 years to 8 years | 6.30 | 40 | 7 years | 5.90 |
| 8 years to 9 years | 6.45 | 40 | 8 years | 6.05 |
| 9 years to 10 years | 6.60 | 40 | 9 years | 6.20 |
| 10 years | 6.70 | 40 | 10 years | 6.30 |

[a] No rate posted.

but the size of transactions varies considerably.[6] After the amount of registered debt is sold, the issuer may "reload" its MTN program by filing a new registration with the SEC.

Although MTNs are generally offered on an agency basis, most programs permit other means of distribution. For example, MTN programs usually allow the agents to acquire notes for their own account and for resale at par or at prevailing market prices. MTNs may also be sold on an underwritten basis. In addition, many MTN programs permit the borrower to bypass financial intermediaries by selling debt directly to investors.

## THE ECONOMICS OF MTNS AND CORPORATE BONDS

In deciding whether to finance with MTNs or with bonds, a corporate borrower weighs the interest cost, flexibility, and other advantages of each security.[7] The growth of the MTN market indicates that MTNs offer advantages that bonds do not. However, most companies that raise funds in the MTN market have also

---

6. Financing strategies vary among the borrowers. Some corporate treasurers prefer to "go in for size" on one day with financings in the $50 million to $100 million range, reasoning that smaller offerings are more time-consuming. Furthermore, a firm may be able to maintain a "scarcity value" for its debt by financing intermittently with large offerings, rather than continuously with small offerings. Other treasurers prefer to raise $50 million to $100 million over the course of several days with $2 million to $10 million drawdowns. These corporate treasurers argue that a daily drawdown of $50 million is an indication that they should have posted a lower offering rate. In regard to the posting of offering rates, some treasurers post an absolute yield, whereas others post a spread over Treasuries, usually with a cap on the absolute yield. A few active borrowers typically post rates daily in several maturity sectors; less active borrowers post only in the maturity sector in which they seek financing and suspend postings when they do not require funds.

7. Apart from the distribution process, MTNs have several less significant features that distinguish them from underwritten corporate bonds. First, MTNs are typically sold at par, whereas traditional underwritings are frequently sold at slight discounts or premiums to par. Second, the settlement for MTNs is in same-day funds, whereas corporate bonds generally settle in next-day funds. Although MTNs with long maturities typically settle five business days after the trade date (as is the convention in the corporate bond market), MTNs with short maturities sometimes have a shorter settlement period.

Finally, semiannual interest payments to noteholders are typically made on a fixed cycle without regard to the offering date or the maturity date of the MTN; in contrast, corporate bonds typically pay interest on the first or fifteenth day of the month at six-month and annual intervals from the date of the offering. The interest payment convention in the MTN market usually results in a short or a long first coupon and in a short final coupon. Consider, for example, an MTN program that pays interest on March 1 and September 1 and at maturity of the notes. A $100,000 MTN sold on May 1 with a 9% coupon and a 15-month maturity from such a program would distribute a "short" first coupon of $3,000 on September 1, a full coupon of $4,500 on March 1, and a "short" final coupon of $3,750 plus the original principal on August 1 of the following year. Like corporate bonds, interest on fixed-rate MTNs is calculated on the basis of a 360-day year of 12 30-day months.

continued to issue corporate bonds, suggesting that each form of debt has advantages under particular circumstances.

## Offering Size, Liquidity, and Price Discrimination

The amount of the offering is the most important determinant of the cost differential between the MTN and corporate bond markets. For large, standard financings (such as $300 million of straight debt with a 10-year maturity) the all-in interest cost to an issuer of underwritten corporate bonds may be lower than the all-in cost of issuing MTNs. This cost advantage arises from economies of scale in underwriting and, most important, from the greater liquidity of large issues. As a result, corporations that have large financing needs for a specific term usually choose to borrow with bonds. From an empirical point of view, the liquidity premium, if any, on small offerings has yet to be quantified. Nevertheless, the sheer volume of financing in the MTN market suggests that any liquidity premium that may exist for small offerings is not a significant deterrent to financing. According to market participants, the interest cost differential between the markets has narrowed in recent years as liquidity in the MTN market has improved. Many borrowers estimate that the premium is now only about 5 to 10 basis points.[8]

Furthermore, many borrowers believe that financing costs are slightly lower in the MTN market because its distribution process allows borrowers to price discriminate. Consider an example of a company that needs to raise $100 million. With a bond offering, the company may have to raise the offering yield significantly, for example, from 6% to 6.25%, to place the final $10 million with the marginal buyer. In contrast, with MTNs the company could raise $90 million by posting a yield of 6%; to raise the additional $10 million, the company could increase its MTN offering rates or issue at a different maturity. Consequently, because all of the debt does not have to be priced to the marginal buyer, financing costs can be lower with MTNs.

## The Flexibility of MTNs

Even if conventional bonds enjoy an interest cost advantage, this advantage may be offset by the flexibility that MTNs afford. Offerings of investment-grade straight bonds are clustered at standard maturities of 2, 3, 5, 7, 10, and 30 years. Also, because the fixed costs of underwritings make small offerings impractical, corporate bond offerings rarely amount to less than $100 million. These insti-

---

8. Commissions to MTN agents typically range from 0.125% to 0.75% of the principal amount of the note sale, depending on the stated maturity and the credit rating assigned at the time of issuance. Fees to underwriters of bond offerings are somewhat higher.

tutional conventions tend to keep corporations from implementing a financing policy of matching the maturities of assets with those of liabilities. By contrast, drawdowns from MTN programs over the course of a month typically amount to $30 million, and these drawdowns frequently have different maturities and special features that are tailored to meet the needs of the borrower. This flexibility of the MTN market allows companies to match more closely the maturities of assets and liabilities.

The flexibility of continuous offerings also plays a role in a corporation's decision to finance with MTNs. With MTNs, a corporation can "average out" its cost of funds by issuing continuously rather than coming to market on a single day. Therefore, even if bond offerings have lower average yields, a risk-averse borrower might still elect to raise funds in the MTN market with several offerings in a range of $5 million to $10 million over several weeks, rather than with a single $100 million bond offering.

The flexibility of the MTN market also allows borrowers to take advantage of funding opportunities. By having an MTN program, an issuer can raise a sizable amount of debt in a short time; often, the process takes less than half an hour. Bonds may also be sold from a shelf registration, but the completion of the transaction may be delayed by the arrangement of a syndicate, the negotiation of an underwriting agreement, and the "preselling" of the issue to investors. Furthermore, some corporations require that underwritten offerings receive prior approval by the president of the company or the board of directors. In contrast, a corporate treasurer may finance with MTNs without delay and at his or her discretion.[9]

## Discreet Funding with MTNs

The MTN market also provides corporations with the ability to raise funds discreetly because the issuer, the investor, and the agent are the only market participants that have to know about a primary transaction. In contrast, the investment community obtains information about underwritten bond offerings from a variety of sources.

Corporations often avoid the bond market in periods of heightened uncertainty about interest rates and the course of the economy, such as the period after the 1987 stock market crash. Underwritings at such times could send a signal of financial distress to the market. Similarly, corporations in distressed industries, such as commercial banking in the second half of 1990, can use the MTN market to raise funds quietly rather than risk negative publicity in the

---

9. The administrative costs may be lower with MTNs than with bonds. After the borrower and the investor have agreed to the terms of a transaction in the MTN market, the borrower files a one-page pricing supplement with the SEC, stating the sale date, the rate of interest, and the maturity date of the MTN. In contrast, issuers of corporate bonds sold from shelf registrations are required to file a prospectus supplement.

high-profile bond market. Thus, during periods of financial turmoil, the discreet nature of the MTN market makes it an attractive alternative to the bond market.

## Reverse Inquiry in the MTN Market

Another advantage of MTNs is that investors often play an active role in the issuance process through the phenomenon known as *reverse inquiry.* For example, suppose an investor desires to purchase $15 million of A-rated finance company debt with a maturity of six years and nine months. Such a security may not be available in the corporate bond market, but the investor may be able to obtain it in the MTN market through reverse inquiry. In this process, the investor relays the inquiry to an issuer of MTNs through the issuer's agent. If the issuer finds the terms of the reverse inquiry sufficiently attractive, it may agree to the transaction even if it was not posting rates at the maturity that the investor desires.

According to market participants, trades that stem from reverse inquiries account for a significant share of MTN transactions. Reverse inquiry not only benefits the issuer by reducing borrowing costs but also allows investors to use the flexibility of MTNs to their advantage. In response to investor preferences, MTNs issued under reverse inquiry often include embedded options and frequently pay interest according to unusual formulas. This responsiveness of the MTN market to the needs of investors is one of the most important factors driving the growth and acceptance of the market.

## THE FEDERAL RESERVE BOARD'S SURVEY OF U.S. CORPORATE MTNS

Since 1997, the Federal Reserve Board has been obtaining the data on the issuance of MTNs from the Depository Trust Company (DTC), a national clearinghouse for the settlement of securities trades and a custodian for securities. The DTC performs these functions for almost all activity in the domestic market. Before 1997, the data were based on surveys of U.S. corporations that borrow in the MTN market. The participation rate in that survey was 100%.

Because nearly all corporate MTNs are cleared through the DTC, their records provide an accurate measure of the volume of MTN financing by U.S. corporations in the U.S. public market. However, although the U.S. corporate sector is the largest segment of the MTN market, MTNs have been issued in other markets and by non-U.S. corporations. For example, several U.S. corporations have issued MTNs in the Euromarket. Also, the survey does not include MTNs issued in the U.S. public market by government-sponsored agencies such as the Federal National Mortgage Association, by supranational institutions, and by non-U.S. corporations. Furthermore, although the database includes MTNs issued by bank holding companies, it does not include deposit notes and bank notes offered by banks because these securities are exempt from SEC registration. Perhaps most important, the database does not include privately placed MTNs. The private-placement market is particularly attractive to issuers who wish to gain access to U.S. investors without having to obtain SEC approval for a public offering. According to MTN agents, non-U.S. corporations are the largest borrowers in the market for privately placed MTNs. Because the financing costs are usually lower in the public market than in the less-liquid private market, most U.S. corporations choose to issue public, SEC-registered MTNs.

## Issuance Volume and Industry of the Issuers

From 1983 through 1998, the volume of MTN issuance in the public market increased in each year, rising from $5.5 billion in 1983 to $149.2 billion in 1998, and totaled $960 billion over the 16-year period. Similarly, the number of borrowers increased from 12 in 1983 to a peak of 224 in 1991.[10]

Borrowers in the MTN market span a wide array of industry groups. In the financial sector, major borrowers include auto finance companies, bank holding companies, business and consumer credit institutions, and securities brokers. In the nonfinancial sector, participants in the MTN market include utilities, telephone companies, manufacturers, service firms, and wholesalers and retailers. Within industry groups, the auto finance companies have been the heaviest borrowers, raising $162 billion over the period. In relative terms, however, issuance by auto finance companies declined from an 87% share of the MTN market in 1983 to 13% in 1998.

In the early to mid-1980s, financial companies dominated the MTN market. Indeed, in 1983, only two nonfinancial companies issued MTNs, and they accounted for less than 1% of the issuance volume. In recent years, however, nonfinancial companies have increased their share of the market, and in the 1990s, they have accounted for about 20% of MTN issuance.

The increase in the volume of MTN issuance reflects a dramatic increase in the number of new borrowers in the market. In each year from 1984 through 1992, at least 20 companies issued MTNs for the first time, and most of the new entrants have been nonfinancial companies. In 1991, for example, 66 new borrowers entered the market, of which 55 were nonfinancial companies.

## The Volume of Corporate MTNs Outstanding and the Components of Net Borrowing

Outstanding MTNs and issuer use of MTN programs have increased sharply since 1989. In the aggregate, outstanding MTNs increased from $76 billion in

---

10. Data on the volume of issuance can be found in the Fed's website, Tables 1-A and 1-B at *http://federalreserve.gov/releases/medterm/medterm.pdf.*

1989 to $380 billion in 1998. Over this period, outstandings of nonfinancial firms increased from $18.5 billion to $81.2 billion, while outstandings of financial corporations increased from $57.5 billion to $298 billion. For individual firms, outstandings of MTNs averaged $889 million in 1998, compared with $350 million in 1989.

The data on net borrowing, that is, the year-over-year change in outstandings, can be dissected to determine the sources of growth in the market. For the market as a whole, new entrants accounted for about one-third of net borrowing in 1990, one-fourth of net borrowing in 1991, and less than one-fifth in 1992. Thus, firms that had already issued MTNs accounted for most of the recent growth in the market. In the financial sector, in particular, new entrants accounted for only a small proportion of the growth, simply because a large share of the financial firms that could enter the MTN market did so in the 1980s. Among nonfinancial firms, in contrast, new entrants have continued to fuel a significant share of the growth in the market.

## Credit Ratings

The corporations issuing MTNs have had high credit ratings. Since 1983, 99% of MTNs have been rated investment grade (Baa or higher) at the time of issuance. In 1998, $86 billion of the $149 billion in MTN offerings were rated single A, and only one firm issuing $159 million, had a rating of Ba or lower. Outstanding MTNs also tend to have high credit ratings, but not as high as the ratings on new offerings because of the preponderance of rating downgrades in recent years. Nevertheless, 99% of outstanding MTNs were rated investment grade at year-end 1998.

## Maturities and Yield Spreads

Maturities on MTNs reflect the financing needs of the borrowers. Financial firms tend to issue MTNs with maturities matched to the maturity of loans made to their customers. Consequently, in the financial sector, maturities are concentrated in a range of 1 to 5 years, and only a small proportion are longer than 10 years. Nonfinancial firms, in contrast, often use MTNs to finance long-lived assets, such as plant and equipment. As a result, maturities on MTNs issued by nonfinancial corporations cover a wider range, and in 1992, 25% to 30% were longer than 10 years.

Yields on fixed-rate MTNs, commonly quoted as a yield spread over a Treasury security of comparable maturity, reflect the credit risk of the borrower. Other factors held constant, Baa-rated MTNs have higher yield spreads than A-rated MTNs, which in turn have higher yield spreads than Aa-rated MTNs. Yield spreads also vary over time, particularly over the course of the business cycle.

**EXHIBIT   12–2**

Yield Spreads between Two-Year Medium-Term Notes of Financial
Companies and Two-Year Treasury Notes, Selected Ratings. October
1987–December 1992

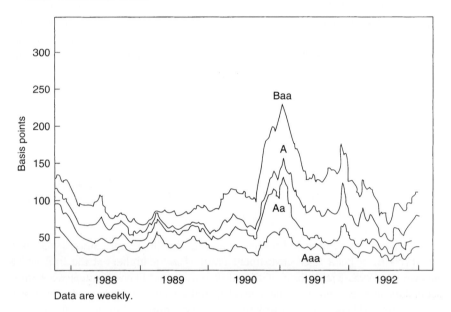

Data are weekly.

## DEVELOPMENTS IN THE MTN MARKET

Several changes have occurred in the MTN market as a result of innovations in
other capital markets. Among the most important changes in the MTN market
are the increasing use of "structured" MTNs, the increasing participation by
banking organizations in the market, and the development of a system for book-
entry clearing and settlement of MTN transactions. Also, foreign corporations
have begun to use the MTN market more frequently since the adoption of SEC
Rule 144A in April 1990. The first two changes are discussed below.[11]

### Structured MTNs

In recent years, an increasing share of MTNs have been issued as part of structured transactions. In a structured MTN, a corporation issues an MTN and si-

---

11. For a discussion of the development of the book-entry clearing and settlement of MTN trans-
    actions and Rule 144A, see Leland E. Crabbe, "Anatomy of the Medium-Term Note Market,"
    *Federal Reserve Bulletin,* August 1993, pp. 751–768.

multaneously enters into one or several swap agreements to transform the cash flows that it is obligated to make. The simplest type of structured MTN involves a "plain vanilla" interest rate swap.[12] In such a financing, a corporation might issue a three-year, floating-rate MTN that pays LIBOR plus a premium semiannually. At the same time, the corporation negotiates a swap transaction in which it agrees to pay a fixed rate of interest semiannually for three years in exchange for receiving LIBOR from a swap counterparty. As a result of the swap, the borrower has synthetically created a fixed-rate note because the floating-rate payments are offsetting.

At first glance, structured transactions seem needlessly complicated. A corporation could simply issue a fixed-rate MTN. However, as a result of the swap transaction, the corporation may be able to borrow at a lower rate than it would pay on a fixed-rate note. Indeed, most MTN issuers decline to participate in structured financings unless they reduce borrowing costs at least 10 or 15 basis points. Issuers demand this compensation because, compared with conventional financings, structured financings involve additional expenses, such as legal and accounting costs and the cost of evaluating and monitoring the credit risk of the swap counterparty. For complicated structured transactions, most issuers require greater compensation.

Many structured transactions originate with investors through a reverse inquiry. This process begins when an investor has a demand for a security with specific risk characteristics. The desired security may not be available in the secondary market, and regulatory restrictions or bylaws prohibit some investors from using swaps, options, or futures to create synthetic securities. Through a reverse inquiry, an investor will use MTN agents to communicate its desires to MTN issuers. If an issuer agrees to the inquiry, the investor will obtain a security that is custom-tailored to its needs. The specific features of these transactions vary in response to changes in market conditions and investor preferences. For example, in 1991 many investors desired securities with interest rates that varied inversely with short-term market interest rates. In response to investor inquiries, several corporations issued "inverse floating-rate" MTNs that paid an interest rate of, for example, 12% minus LIBOR. At the time of the transaction, the issuers of inverse floating-rate MTNs usually entered into swap transactions to eliminate their exposure to falling interest rates.

Although structured transactions in the MTN market often originate with investors, investment banks also put together such transactions. Most investment banks have specialists in derivative products who design securities to take advantage of temporary market opportunities. When an investment bank identifies an opportunity, it will inform investors and propose that they purchase a specialized security. If an investor tentatively agrees to the transaction, the MTN

---

12. Interest rate swaps are described in Chapter 57.

agents in the investment bank will contact an MTN issuer with the proposed structured transaction.

Most investors require that issuers of structured MTNs have triple-A or double-A credit ratings. By dealing with highly rated issuers, the investor reduces the possibility that the value of the structured MTN will vary with the credit quality of the issuer. In limiting credit risk, the riskiness of the structured MTN mainly reflects the specific risk characteristics that the investor prefers.[13] Consequently, federal agencies and supranational institutions, which have triple-A ratings, issue a large share of structured MTNs. The credit quality profile of issuers of structured MTNs has changed slightly in recent years, however, as some investors have become more willing to purchase structured MTNs from single-A corporations. In structured transactions with lower-rated borrowers, the investor receives a higher promised yield as compensation for taking on greater credit risk.

Market participants estimate that structured MTNs accounted for 20% to 30% of MTN volume in the 1990s, compared with less than 5% in the late 1980s. The growth of structured MTNs highlights the important role of derivative products in linking various domestic and international capital markets. Frequently, the issuers of structured MTNs are located in a different country from that of the investors.

The increasing volume of structured transactions is testimony to the flexibility of MTNs. When establishing MTN programs, issuers build flexibility into the documentation that will allow for a broad range of structured transactions. Once the documentation is in place, an issuer is able to reduce borrowing costs by responding quickly to temporary opportunities in the derivatives market.

The flexibility of MTNs is also evident in the wide variety of structured MTNs that pay interest or repay principal according to unusual formulas. Some of the common structures include the following: (1) floating-rate MTNs tied to the federal funds rate, LIBOR, commercial paper rates, or the prime rate, many of which have included caps or floors on rate movements; (2) step-up MTNs, the interest rate on which increases after a set period; (3) LIBOR differential notes, which pay interest tied to the spread between, say, deutsche mark LIBOR and French franc LIBOR; (4) dual-currency MTNs, which pay interest in one currency and principal in another; (5) equity-linked MTNs, which pay interest according to a formula based on an equity index, such as the Standard & Poor's 500 or the Nikkei; and (6) commodity-linked MTNs, which have interest tied to a price index or to the price of specific commodities such as oil or gold. The terms and features of structured MTNs continue to evolve in response to changes in the preferences of investors and developments in financial markets.

---

13. An additional reason for the high credit quality of structured MTNs is that some investors, such as money market funds, face regulatory restrictions on the credit ratings of their investments. See Leland Crabbe and Mitchell A. Post, "The Effect of SEC Amendments to Rule 2a-7 on the Commercial Paper Market," *Finance and Economics Discussion Series* 199 (Board of Governors of the Federal Reserve System, May 1992).

## Bank Notes

Banking organizations are major participants in the MTN market. Like other corporations, bank holding companies must file registration documents with the SEC when issuing public securities. Consequently, the Federal Reserve survey captures MTNs issued by bank holding companies. From 1983 to 1995, 45 bank holding companies raised funds in the MTN market, and from 1989 to 1995, outstanding MTNs of bank holding companies increased from $9.3 billion to $28 billion. Although most of these MTNs have senior status in relation to other debt outstanding, a few bank holding companies have issued subordinated MTNs. Subordinated MTNs of bank holding companies typically have long maturities of about 10 years. Under regulatory capital requirements, subordinated debt with a maturity of 5 years or longer qualifies as tier 2 capital.

In contrast to public offerings by bank holding companies, securities issued by banks are exempt from registration under section 3(a)2 of the Securities Act of 1933. In recent years, a growing number of banks have issued exempt securities, called *bank notes,* that have characteristics in common with certificates of deposit (CDs), MTNs, and short-term bonds.

Like CDs, most bank notes are senior, unsecured debt obligations issued by the bank. However, in the event of the insolvency of the issuing institution, insured and uninsured deposits have priority over bank notes. As with institutional CDs, nearly all bank notes are sold to institutional investors in minimum denominations of $250,000 to $1 million. Bank notes are not covered by FDIC insurance, nor are they subject to FDIC insurance assessments. CDs, in contrast, are insured for $100,000 per depositor. Furthermore, in the event of a bank failure, the FDIC could choose to protect the financial interests of some or all depositors or other creditors without treating bank notes in the same manner.

Like MTNs, bank notes may be offered continuously or intermittently in relatively small amounts that typically range from $5 million to $25 million. In addition, as with MTNs, most medium-term bank notes have maturities that range from one to five years.[14] However, ratings on senior bank notes are typically one notch higher than the ratings on senior MTNs, which are issued at the holding company level. Reflecting these differences in ratings and priority in the firms' capital structures, the yields on banks notes usually are significantly lower than the yields on MTNs of comparable maturity.

Some bank notes, which are similar to corporate bonds, are sold in large, underwritten, discrete offerings that range from $50 million to $1 billion. However, they differ from corporate bonds in that they are not registered with the SEC.

---

14. Banks also issue bank notes with shorter maturities that range from seven days to one year. These short-term bank notes are sold to money market investors with interest calculated on a CD basis or discount basis. As with medium-term bank notes, short-term bank notes are issued at the bank level, and they are not insured. Short-term bank notes differ from commercial paper in that commercial paper is an obligation of the bank holding company.

# EURO-MTNS

MTNs have become a major source of financing in international financial markets, particularly in the Euromarket. Like Eurobonds, Euro-MTNs are not subject to national regulations, such as registration requirements.[15] Although Euro-MTNs and Eurobonds can be sold throughout the world, the major underwriters and dealers are located in London, where most offerings are distributed.

Although the first Euro-MTN program was established in 1986, the market represented a minor source of financing throughout the 1980s. In the 1990s, the Euro-MTN market has grown at a phenomenal rate, with outstandings increasing from less than $10 billion in early 1990 to $470 billion year-end 1995. New borrowers account for most of this growth, as a majority of the 560 entities that have established Euro-MTN programs did so in the 1990s. As in the U.S. market, flexibility is the driving force behind the rapid growth of the Euro-MTN market. Under a single documentation framework, an issuer with a Euro-MTN program has great flexibility in the size, currency denomination, and structure of offerings. Furthermore, reverse inquiry gives issuers of Euro-MTNs the opportunity to reduce funding costs by responding to investor preferences.

The characteristics of Euro-MTNs are similar, but not identical, to MTNs issued in the U.S. market. In both markets, most MTNs are issued with investment-grade credit ratings, but the ratings on Euro-MTNs tend to be higher. In 1992, for example, 68% of Euro-MTNs had Aaa or Aa ratings, compared with 13% of U.S. corporate MTNs. In both markets, most offerings have maturities of one to five years. However, offerings with maturities longer than 10 years account for a smaller percentage of the Euromarket than of the U.S. market. In both markets, dealers have committed to provide liquidity in the secondary market, but by most accounts the Euromarket is less liquid.

In many ways, the Euro-MTN market is more diverse than the U.S. market. For example, the range of currency denominations of Euro-MTNs is broader, as would be expected. The Euromarket also accommodates a broader cross-section of borrowers, both in terms of the country of origin and the type of borrower, which includes sovereign countries, supranational institutions, finan-

---

15. Bonds and MTNs may be classified as either domestic or international. By definition, a domestic offering is issued in the home market of the issuer. For example, MTNs sold in the United States by U.S. companies are domestic MTNs in the U.S. market. Similarly, MTNs sold in France by French companies are domestic MTNs in the French market. Bonds and MTNs sold in the international market can be further classified as foreign or Euro. Foreign offerings are sold by foreign entities in a domestic market of another country. For example, bonds sold by foreign companies and sovereigns in the U.S. market are foreign bonds, known as "Yankee bonds." Eurobonds and Euro-MTNs are international securities offerings that are not sold in a domestic market. As a practical matter, statisticians, tax authorities, and market participants often disagree about whether particular securities should be classified as domestic, foreign, or Euro.

cial institutions, and industrial companies. Similarly, Euro-MTNs have a more diverse investor base, but the market is not as deep as the U.S. market.

In several respects, the evolution of the Euro-MTN market has paralleled that of the U.S. market. Two of the more important developments have been the growth of structured Euro-MTNs and the emergence of large, discrete offerings. Structured transactions represent 50% to 60% of Euro-MTN issues, compared with 20% to 30% in the U.S. market. In the Euro-MTN market, many of the structured transactions involve a currency swap in which the borrower issues an MTN that pays interest and principal in one currency and simultaneously agrees to a swap contract that transforms required cash flow into another currency. Most structured Euro-MTNs arise from investor demands for debt instruments that are otherwise unavailable in the public markets. To be able to respond to investor-driven structured transactions, issuers typically build flexibility into their Euro-MTN programs. Most programs allow for issuance of MTNs with unusual interest payments in a broad spectrum of currencies with a variety of options.

Large, discrete offerings of Euro-MTNs first appeared in 1991, and about 40 of these offerings occurred in 1992. They are similar to Eurobonds in that they are underwritten and are often syndicated using the fixed-price reoffering method. As a result of this development, the distinction between Eurobonds and EuroMTNs has blurred, just as the distinction between corporate bonds and MTNs has blurred in the U.S. market.

The easing of regulatory restrictions by foreign central banks has played an important role in the growth of the Euro-MTN market. For example, in recent years MTNs denominated in deutsche marks have emerged as a major sector in the Euromarket as a result of regulatory changes made by the Bundesbank in August 1992. Under the previous rules, foreign borrowers could only issue debt denominated in deutsche marks through German subsidiaries or other German financial firms, and maturities could not be shorter than two years.. Debt denominated in deutsche marks also had to be listed on a German exchange, and these offerings were subject to German law, clearing, and payment procedures. These rules effectively precluded issuers from establishing multicurrency Euro-MTN programs with a deutsche mark option.

In the August 1992 deregulation, the Bundesbank removed the minimum maturity requirement on debt denominated in deutsche marks issued by foreign non-banks, and it eliminated or simplified issuance procedures for all issuers. Although the new rules require that a "German bank" act as an arranger or dealer, the definition is broad enough to include German branches and subsidiaries of foreign banks. The arranger is required to notify the Bundesbank monthly of the volume and frequency of issues denominated in deutsche marks. As a result of the Bundesbank's deregulation, from 1991 to 1993, the share of Euro-MTN offerings denominated in deutsche marks increased from 1.4% to 13.5%, while the volume of issuance in deutsche marks rose from $268 million to $10.66 billion. Other central banks have instituted similar liberalizations that may result in rapid growth of MTNs denominated in other currencies, such as the Swiss franc and the French franc.

## OUTLOOK FOR THE MTN MARKET

Few innovations in finance have been as successful as the medium-term note. Its success derives from its remarkable adaptability to the needs of both borrowers and investors. The success can be measured by the number of borrowers, the diversity of note structures, and the amount of outstanding MTNs, all of which have increased dramatically over the past decade.

The adoption of SEC Rule 415 in 1982 was the key event that removed the regulatory impediments to continuous offerings of corporate notes. Other regulatory changes, such as SEC Rule 144A and liberalizations by European central banks, have been instrumental in the development of new sectors in the MTN market. As a result of these regulatory changes, financial markets have become more efficient.

## CHAPTER 13

# INFLATION-INDEXED BONDS (TIPS)

John B. Brynjolfsson, CFA
Executive Vice President and Manager
PIMCO Real Return Bond Fund
Pacific Investment Management Company

Inflation is the key driver of investment performance. It determines how much each dollar of return is worth, and it dictates asset returns themselves. Consider the 17-year period from 1983 to 2000, a period marked by falling inflation. Falling raw material prices allowed corporate margins to expand. Simultaneously, falling interest rates positively impacted the price to earnings multipliers being applied to those expanded corporate earnings. The result was doubly explosive equity returns. For different reasons, the inflation-adjusted returns of bonds and cash were similarly favorably impacted by falling inflation during this period. The opposite happens during bouts of rising inflation. The 17-year inflationary period from 1966 to 1983 represented one of the worst investment climates in modern history, for equities, bonds, and cash.

Recently, investors have found a weapon that effectively offsets this threat to stable and predictable investment returns—and that weapon is the subject matter of this chapter.

TIPS (Treasury Inflation Protection Securities)[1] are bonds that promise to protect and grow investors' purchasing power. The U.S. Treasury delivers on this promise by adjusting the principal of TIPS based upon changes in the consumer price index (CPI).[2] It repays the bondholders principal in an amount that

---

I wish to thank my colleagues at PIMCO and Anthony Faillace for their contributions and support.

1. United States Secretary of the Treasury Robert Rubin coined the term "TIPS" in 1996, before the official launch of "Treasury Inflation-Indexed Securities" (TIIS) in January, 1997. Market participants have gravitated to a generic use of the acronym "TIPS" to refer to all forms of inflation-indexed bonds, singular and plural. For clarity, this chapter will do the same. Other terms sometimes used to describe this class of bonds include "Inflation Indexed Bonds," "IPBS," "TIIS," "Inflation-Linked Bonds," "Linkers" and "Real Return Bonds."

2. The Bureau of Labor Statistics, an independent economics-oriented agency of the U.S. Department of Labor, is responsible for gathering and reporting price changes at the consumer level. The CPI series used to calculate TIPS is the non-seasonally adjusted Consumer Price Index for all Urban Consumers (CPI-U). See the discussion about the CPI later in this chapter.

exactly maintains the purchasing power of their original investment, as defined by the CPI. In addition, the U.S. Treasury pays interest in an amount that also maintains the purchasing power of the stream of semiannual interest payments by calculating coupon payments based upon the CPI-indexed principal amounts. (See Exhibit 13–1.)

The U.S. Treasury launched the TIPS program in 1997, and through the middle of 2000 issued over $100 billion of the securities. According to Federal Reserve Bank statistics, on a typical day more than $500 million of the securities are traded. Since the 1940s at least 15 governments and numerous corporations have issued similarly structured securities. In the U.K., inflation-indexed securities account for more than 20% of government bonds outstanding. For clarity, we will focus our discussion on the U.S. Treasury TIPS and introduce substantive differences of other TIPS where appropriate.

TIPS are best known as a defensive hedge against the fear of inflation, but they offer tactical and strategic advantages as well. Tactically, investors are attracted to the opportunity TIPS afford to speculate on changes in inflation and real interest rates. Strategically, individual and institutional investors with long-term objectives are attracted to TIPS high real yield, low correlation to traditional financial assets and muted volatility. They sense TIPS will help them achieve their long-term investment goals, and reduce risk in the process.

The unique characteristics of TIPS qualify them as a fundamental asset class, as are equities, traditional bonds, and cash. TIPS have relatively high correlation with one-another, and unusually low correlation with other asset classes. As a whole they form a large, investable, and easily benchmarked universe.

In addition to TIPS correlative appeal, their novelty and scope attest to their importance as an investment instrument. This chapter has two goals; the first and most important is to introduce market participants to this important new investment instrument. The second is to provide portfolio managers with a comprehensive examination of the investment qualities that make TIPS unique.

**EXHIBIT 13–1**

Schematic Cash Flow of TIPS

| | Purchase | First Annual Coupon | Interim Annual Coupon | Last Annual Coupon | Principal | Return (per annum) |
|---|---|---|---|---|---|---|
| Date | 1/15/00 | 1/15/01 | 1/15/05 | 1/15/10 | 1/15/10 | 1/15/10 |
| Real $ Cash Flow | (1,000) | 40.00 | 40.00 | 40.00 | 1,000 | 4.00 |
| CPI (Base = 200) | 200.0 | 206.0 | 231.8 | 268.7 | 268.7 | 3.00 |
| Indexed Principal | 1,000 | 1,030 | 1,159 | 1,343 | 1,343 | (na) |
| Nominal $ Cash Flow | (1,000) | 41.20 | 46.37 | 53.76 | 1343.92 | 7.12 |

Source: *Pacific Investment Management Company*

We begin with the mechanics of TIPS cash flows. We explore real yield and real duration, two measures that are analogous to a nominal bond's yield to maturity and effective duration. The marketplace section narrates a brief history of TIPS, including their trading characteristics. The valuation and performance section presents a framework, and evaluates the TIPS market of the first quarter of 2000 in the context of that framework. The investors section discusses how professional managers and institutions are using TIPS within portfolios and in asset-liability management. The Issuers section introduces the suppliers of TIPS and explains why they utilize the prevailing structures. We then address common investor concerns, specifically on taxes and deflation.

# MECHANICS AND MEASUREMENT
## How TIPS Work

The merit of TIPS is that while the principal and interest repaid to investors fluctuates based on the level of the CPI, the purchasing power of each payment is fixed. As a consequence, the *real yield* of TIPS (the growth in purchasing power that a hold-to-maturity investor will earn) is fixed. The assumptions corresponding to Exhibit 13–1 are described below:

- Issuance date of 1/15/00
- Issuance price of $100.00
- 10-year maturity
- 4% real coupon paid annually, and
- 3% annualized inflation rate.

If the CPI for the TIPS issuance date is 200.0 and the CPI for a coupon date one year later is 206.0, year-over-year inflation would be reported as 3.00%. The TIPS' adjusted principal would be 1.03 times its original value, or $1,030 per $1,000 of "original face."

This indexed principal is used to calculate the coupon paid. In other words, the Treasury calculates the amount of each coupon payment, *after the principal has been adjusted for inflation*. This exhibit shows that the compounding effect of a 4% real coupon with a 3% inflation rate results in a *nominal* cash flow annualized return of 7.12%.

The calculations of actual Treasury TIPS cash flows and returns are only somewhat more complicated. TIPS pay interest semiannually at one-half their stated annual coupon rate. The inflation-indexed principal is accrued daily, based on an interpolation between the two most recent monthly CPI figures reported prior to the settlement month. And lastly, Treasury uses a rather arcane rounding procedure for interim and final calculations (included in Bloomberg analytics). (See Exhibit 13–2.)

**E X H I B I T   13–2**

Bloomberg Screen Illustrating Actual Settlement Calculations

P066 Govt   YA

**INFLATION-INDEXED YIELD ANALYSIS**

| PRICE 95 ⅝ | | CUSIP 9128272M | REAL COUPON 3 ⅜ |
|---|---|---|---|
| SETTLEMENT DATE 12/31/1999 | | REAL CPN ACCRUED INT | 1.549932 |

| YIELD CALCULATIONS | MATURITY 1/15/2007 | ECONOMIC FACTORS | |
|---|---|---|---|
| STREET REAL YIELD | 4.096 | BASE CPI VALUE 1/15/1997 | 158.43548 |
| TREASURY YIELD EQUIVALENT | 4.096 | | |
| | | REFERENCE CPI 12/31/1999 | 168.19032 |
| | | CPURNSA <INDEX> 10/99 | 168.20000 |
| | | CPURNSA <INDEX> 9/99 | 167.90000 |
| INFLATION ASSUMPTION 2.6041% | | CPI @ LAST CPN DATE | 166.20000 |
| YIELD W/INFLATION ASSUMPTION | 6.736 | FLAT INDEX RATIO | 1.04901 |
| YIELD WITHOUT INFLATION | 4.096 | ACCRUED RATIO GROWTH | 0.01256 |
| | | INDEX RATIO | 1.06157 |

Personal default Yield Betas now available. Type COVR<GO>.

| SENSITIVITY ANALYSIS | | | PAYMENT INVOICE | |
|---|---|---|---|---|
| FOR VARIOUS REAL vs NOMINAL | | | FACE 1000M | |
| YIELD-BETA ASSUMPTIONS ( SEE <HELP> ) | | | FLAT | 1003115.81 |
| YIELD-BETA ASSUMPTION | 0.000 0.500 1.000 | | INFLATION ACCRUAL | 12010.50 |
| EFFECTIVE DURATION | 0.000 3.001 6.003 | | GROSS AMOUNT | 1015126.31 |
| RISK | 0.000 3.096 6.193 | | CPN ACCR. 169 DAYS | 16453.61 |
| CONVEXITY | 0.000 0.105 0.422 | | NET AMOUNT | 1031579.93 |

Inflation Compensation    61570.00

*Source:* Bloomberg Financial Markets

**The Consumer Price Index (CPI)**
The specific CPI series used for TIPS indexation is the "Non-Seasonally Adjusted, All-Urban Consumer Price Index" (NSA CPI-U), and is reported monthly. Unlike the seasonally adjusted series, the NSA CPI-U is not subject to revision. One consequence of utilizing the NSA CPI-U is that the series includes predictable seasonal fluctuations in inflation. For example, each December when inflation is typically muted by year-end price-cutting and inventory liquidations, the Non-Seasonally Adjusted CPI-U index tends to fall slightly below its trend growth rate, while in certain other months it tends to rise slightly above the underlying trend.

The CPI report that measures the price level in a given month, for example May, is typically reported on or near the 15th of the following month, in this case June. The two weeks between June 15th and July 1st when the TIPS accruals begin, allow for potential delays in the official release of the CPI and eliminate the need to calculate day-counts across month-end. The last daily accrual occurs on July 31st, about seven weeks after the CPI is reported. So, the May CPI is fully incorporated into the August 1st TIPS principal.

This relatively quick 15-day turnaround of CPI reports into TIPS indexation is described as a three-month lag because the May (month 5) CPI is fully incorporated into the TIPS by August 1st (month 8). To calculate the TIPS principal for any settlement date other than the first of a month, for example July 10th, calculate as follows:

1. Find the TIPS principal that applies to July 1st: this is based on the April NSA CPI-U report (month 7 − 3 = month 4).

2. Find the TIPS principal that applies to August 1st: this is based on the May NSA CPI-U report (month 8 − 3 = month 5).

3. Divide 9, the number of days accrual (the 10th day of the month − the 1st day of the month) by 31 (the number of days in that month).

4. Linearly interpolate by adding 9/31st of the difference between the July 1st and August 1st TIPS' principal values to the July 1st value.

## Real Frame of Reference, Real Yield, Nominal Yield, and Break-Even Inflation Rate

### Real Frame of Reference

A nominal frame of reference looks at investments in terms of dollars, without regard to any change in purchasing power of those dollars. In contrast, a real frame of reference takes into account the loss of purchasing power due to inflation. Put another way, it calculates how many bushels of wheat, baskets of apples, or more generally the standard of living to which a given dollar amount corresponds. If it costs 100 "real dollars" to purchase a basket of consumer goods in the year 2000, in the year 2020, 100 "real dollars" will still purchase that same basket.

Any investment can be described from either a *real* or *nominal* frame of reference. To directly compare the expected returns of any two investments one must choose either a real or a nominal frame of reference. For example, in *Stocks For the Long Run, 1998*, Jeremy Siegel describes equities from 1926 through 1997 as having generated *either* a 7.2% real return *or* a 10.6% nominal return.

Ideally, the frame of reference would be dictated by one's goals, but in practice the choice is heavily influenced by the characteristics of the investment instrument. For instance, conventional bonds are easily described in a *nominal* frame of reference because they have fixed *nominal* coupons and principal. TIPS, on the other hand, are more easily described within a *real* frame of reference because they have fixed *real* coupons and principal. Not surprisingly, TIPS' *real* yield, *real* duration, and other real characteristics are relatively intuitive and as easy to calculate as a nominal bond's yield to maturity, effective duration, and other nominal characteristics.

### Real Yield

The real yield of a TIPS bond represents the annualized growth rate of purchasing power earned by holding the security to maturity. Real yield can easily be calculated on a standard bond calculator by entering the TIPS quoted market price, coupon rate and maturity date. The calculator does not know the bond is a TIPS, or that the price and coupon rate are *real*. It is the user's responsibility to interpret the result as the "real yield."[3]

The *real* yield of a *nominal* bond is more difficult to calculate, as it can only be precisely determined with the benefit of hindsight. In practice, when analysts speak of a nominal bond's real yield they may be: (1) referring to its "current" real yield (approximated by subtracting the current year-over-year inflation from the bond's nominal yield), (2) guesstimating the nominal bond's "expected" real yield based on expectations of future inflation, or (3) speaking of historical realized real yields on bonds that have matured.

## Nominal Yield
The opposite situation occurs with nominal yields. While the nominal yield of a conventional bond is easily determined, the nominal yield of TIPS is more difficult to pin-down. The nominal yield realized by holding TIPS to maturity depends upon the average level and trajectory of inflation over the bond's life-time. Ignoring the trajectory of the inflation rate, and focusing only on the average level of inflation, the realized nominal yield can be approximated as:

TIPS realized nominal yield $= (1 + \text{real yield}) \times (1 + \text{inflation}) - 1$

## Break-Even Inflation Rate
The break-even inflation rate is the rate that results in the holder of a TIPS "breaking-even" with the holder of a nominal bond. Using the above equation, the nominal yield of the TIPS can be set to equal the nominal yield of the conventional bond. Solving the equation for the break-even inflation rate:

Break-even inflation rate

$= (1 + \text{conventional nominal yield})/(1 + \text{TIPS real yield}) - 1$

If the conventional bond's nominal yield is 7% and the TIPS real yield is 4% (both expressed in simple annualized terms), the break-even inflation rate is 2.88%. For most purposes approximating the above equation as the simple difference between the two bonds' yields is appropriate—and general industry practice.

Exhibit 13–3 plots nominal yields, real yields, and their differences over a period including the fall of 1998. This period was notably marked by a sig-nificant deflationary scare. An astute investor might have construed the dramatic decline of the break-even inflation rate to below 1% as an opportunity.

Although the "break-even" inflation rate may be useful to assess market inflation expectations or to gauge break-even requirements for narrowly con-

---

3. Two phenomena that could cause a minor difference in TIPS quoted real yield from the "TIPS realized real yield" are: (1) real reinvestment rate of coupon cash flows; and (2) the time-lag between the "applicable" date for the CPI and the applicable date for TIPS indexing.

**EXHIBIT   13–3**

Bloomberg Screen Showing Break-even Inflation Rates

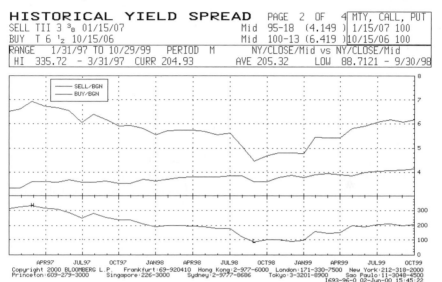

for explanation.                                          P066 **Govt    HS**

HISTORICAL YIELD SPREAD  PAGE  2  OF  4  MTY, CALL, PUT
SELL TII 3 ³⁄₈ 01/15/07                  Mid  95-18  (4.149 )  1/15/07 100
BUY  T 6 ¹⁄₂ 10/15/06                    Mid 100-13 (6.419 ) 10/15/06 100
RANGE   1/31/97 TO 10/29/99   PERIOD  M      NY/CLOSE/Mid vs NY/CLOSE/Mid
HI  335.72  - 3/31/97  CURR 204.93       AVE 205.32    LOW  88.7121 - 9/30/98

*Source:* Bloomberg Financial Markets

strained fixed-income investors, it generally overstates the risk-adjusted "break-even" inflation rate applicable to long-term strategies. In particular, the riskier nominal bonds embody inflation risk premiums. Researchers have estimated the embedded inflation risk premium in nominal bonds to be between 0.50% and 1.0%.[4]

Because TIPS pay in real dollars, exhibit low volatility, and have a low correlation to other assets, at least part of such inflation risk premiums should not be embodied in TIPS yields. Therefore, the risk-adjusted break-even inflation rate for TIPS equals the calculated break-even inflation rate minus an inflation risk premium. This means an investor can advantageously use TIPS even when

---

4. Citing the tremendous supply of TIPS, the illiquidity of TIPS, and the substantial exposure that TIPS have to changes in real interest rates, Lucas and Quek suggest that a part of (or the entire) "inflation-risk premium" may be offset. (See Gerald Lucas and Timothy Quek, "Valuing and Trading TIPS," Chapter 9 in John Brynjolfsson and Frank J. Fabozzi (eds.), *Handbook of Inflation Indexed Bonds* (New Hope, PA: Frank J. Fabozzi Associates, 1999).) For a more detailed discussion of implied break-evens and risk-premiums, see the seminal work on expectations and markets by M. Harrison and D. Kreps, "Martingales and Multiperiod Securities Markets," *Journal of Economic Theory* (1979), pp. 381–408.

his expected inflation rate equals the calculated break-even inflation rate. Such an investor will gain by lowering overall portfolio risk, or from "reallocating" the risk capacity created into other sectors.

## Real and Effective Duration

### Real Duration

Duration is the measure of a bond's market value sensitivity to changes in yields—real *or* nominal. The above section, describing real and nominal frames of reference, and real and nominal yields is pivotal to any discussion of duration. By definition, the *real* duration of TIPS is the percentage change in its market value associated with a 1.0% change in its *real* yield. For example, if the market value (MV) of TIPS is $1,000 and the market values associated with a 0.50% decrease and a 0.50% increase in the TIPS real yield are $1,051 and $951 respectively, the TIPS real duration is 10. In order to center the calculation at current yield levels, the 1.0% change in the definition is applied equally, as a 0.50% decrease and a 0.50% increase in yield.

Algebraically, the formula for TIPS real duration is:

$$100 \times [\text{MV(real yield} + 0.50\%) - \text{MV(real yield} - 0.50\%)]/\text{MV(real yield)}$$

Not surprisingly, the TIPS duration formula is identical to that of a nominal bond (excepting the frame of reference). It follows that TIPS duration can be calculated using a standard bond calculator. As with the calculation for real yield, it is the user's responsibility to remember that the result is the TIPS' *real* duration. (Using real duration within a dedicated TIPS portfolio is discussed in a later section.)

As relevant as real duration is to TIPS portfolio managers, it is critical to understand that TIPS real duration does not quantify the exposure of TIPS to changes in nominal yields. First, the correlation of real yields to nominal yields tends to be quite low—real duration measures sensitivity to phenomena that may impact nominal bonds in an opposite way, or not at all. Second, real yields tend to be significantly less volatile than nominal yields—so any given "real duration" tends to correspond to significantly less portfolio volatility than the same "nominal duration."

## Effective Duration

To compare TIPS' risk to that of nominal bonds so they may be included within a conventional bond portfolio, a manager needs a measure of TIPS sensitivity to changes in *nominal* interest rates. The method for determining market value change of TIPS as a function of nominal yield change is the "effective duration" calculation. The limitation is that since this calculation must infer a change in real yield from the given change in nominal yield, the measure is statistical rather than deterministic.

Initially this dilemma caused more than a few managers to conclude that the risk exposure of TIPS could not be managed within the context of a conventional fixed-income portfolio. But it was soon realized that in the 1980s, mortgage-backed securities overcame similar concerns. The calculation of effective duration for mortgages calls for an inference that a change in nominal Treasury yield will result in a change in the underlying yield of mortgage cash flows.

Similar to TIPS, yields underlying mortgage pricing are not perfectly correlated with Treasury yields. In fact, during the deflationary scare in the summer of 1998 mortgage prices dramatically underperformed what naïve calculations of mortgage effective durations would have predicted. For a brief period, as Treasury yields fell mortgage yields actually rose. Nonetheless, effective duration is broadly used to determine a mortgage's value change as a function of nominal yield change. It is incumbent upon fixed-income managers to manage the remaining mortgage basis risk.

Although crude, the best metric we have found for converting TIPS real yield into "effective duration" is to apply a 35% multiplicative factor to TIPS real durations. This approach is often described as a "35% yield beta"—a reference to the second coefficient (beta) of a linear regression of change in real yield against a change in nominal yield. Like mortgages, TIPS effective duration should only be used as a loose metric for nominal interest rate exposure because substantial risk (basis risk) remains.

Occasionally, nominal yields fall and TIPS real yields rise, meaning that TIPS experience negative effective durations. Conversely, occasionally nominal yields rise, and real yields rise even more, meaning TIPS experience capital losses more than three times what their *ex ante* effective durations predict. It is incumbent that managers, who use TIPS, manage the basis risk that TIPS embody beyond their modest effective duration.

Exhibit 13–4 plots the monthly change in TIPS '07 real yield on the vertical axis as a scatter chart, with the corresponding monthly change in nominal yield on the horizontal axis. The slope of the "best-fit" regression line shows that historically the "yield beta" over that period, at 17.56%, has been somewhat lower than the 35% that we use. The regression result will vary (as a function of the time period chosen to calculate the individual change), the time period included in the study, the securities chosen, and perhaps most importantly, the economic environment.

TIPS real duration measures risk as it relates to change in real yield and TIPS effective duration measures risk as it relates to changes in nominal yield. Two broader measures of TIPS risk are volatility and relative volatility. Volatility is simply the standard deviation of TIPS prices (or returns). It varies over time and across maturities as a function of the calculation period and measurement interval. Exhibit 13–5 graphs the historical price volatility of the first Treasury 10-year TIPS issued.

Relative volatility is a measure of TIPS volatility as a fraction of the volatility of another instrument such as a nominal bond having a comparable

**EXHIBIT  13–4**

Bloomberg Screen—Historical Regression Analysis—Monthly Yield Changes
of '07 TIPS vs. Monthly Yield Changes of '06 Treasury

```
<HELP> for explanation.                                    P064 Govt   MRA
<PAGE> for historical data,  <MENU> to Update Matrix.
HISTORICAL                    Name:TIPS V TENS              Page 1 of 4
REGRESSION  ANALYSIS  Set # 5
RANGE  2/28/97 TO 10/29/99  Correlation    R2    Standard Error   Observations
PERIOD M (D-W-M-Q-Y)         0.51857   0.26891    0.07665             33
Y = TII 3 3⁄8 01/15/07      Slope    Intercept   t-Test   Coefficient Error
X = T 6 1⁄2 10/15/06        0.17576   0.02558   3.37677       0.05205
          *Identifies latest observation
    .40
         ┌──────────────────────┐
         │ Y =  0.17  X +  0.03  │
   Y     └──────────────────────┘
    .20

    .00

   -.20

   -.40
     -1.00        -.50        .00        .50        1.00
                                X
Copyright 2000 BLOOMBERG L.P.   Frankfurt:69-920410  Hong Kong:2-977-6000  London:171-330-7500  New York:212-318-2000
Princeton:609-279-3000   Singapore:226-3000   Sydney:2-9777-8686  Tokyo:3-3201-8900   Sao Paulo:11-3048-4500
                                                                    I731-267-1 02-Jun-00 14:04:00
```

*Source:* Bloomberg Financial Markets

maturity. Exhibit 13–6 plots the price volatility of a comparable maturity Treasury. A comparison of Exhibits 13–5 and 13–6 from the beginning of 1998
through late 1999 illustrates the TIPS bond exhibited about one-third of the
price volatility as the comparable maturity nominal Treasury bond.

## MARKETPLACE

### A Brief History of TIPS

Conceptually, TIPS are such a fundamental economic instrument that it is possible they pre-date nominal bonds, and even coins. In essence, the buyer of these
bonds is simply "storing" (and earning a return on) a current basket of goods
he will consume in the future.

In ancient Mesopotamia, warehouse receipts referencing quantities of
grains and other goods were traded in a secondary market and were in some
ways preferred to the currency of the day.[5] These receipts "were" TIPS. They

---

5. Glyn Davies, *A History of Money* (Cardiff: University of Wales Press, 1994).

## EXHIBIT 13–5

Bloomberg Graph of TIPS Bond's 26-Week Rolling Price Volatility

*Source:* Bloomberg Financial Markets

could be traded and upon maturity their value would be redeemed in the form of a "real basket" of consumer goods.

In the United States, TIPS date back to the birth of the nation. In 1780, the state of Massachusetts created debt colorfully inscribed as follows:

> *Both Principal and Interest to be paid in the then current Money of said State, in a greater or less Sum, according as Five Bushels of CORN, Sixty-eight Pounds and four–seventh Parts of a Pound of BEEF, Ten Pounds of SHEEP'S WOOL, and Sixteen Pounds of SOLE LEATHER shall then cost, more or less than One Hundred Thirty Pounds current money, at the then current Prices of Said Articles.[6]*

Since World War II more than 15 countries have issued TIPS. A partial list is provided in Exhibit 13–7. As the exhibit suggests, TIPS are not just issued by countries experiencing run-away inflation. Countries often issue TIPS as they are embarking on successful disinflationary initiatives. For example, in Iceland from 1949 to 1954, inflation averaged over 15% per year. In 1955, the year

---

6. Willard Fisher, "The Tabular Standard in Massachusetts History," *Quarterly Journal of Economics* (May 1913), p. 454.

**EXHIBIT 13–6**

Bloomberg Graph of Conventional Treasury's 26-Week Rolling Price Volatility

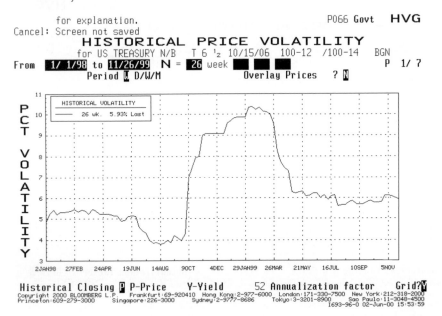

*Source:* Bloomberg Financial Markets

following the introduction of their TIPS, Iceland's recorded inflation rate fell to zero.[7]

## Quotation and Settlement

In the U.S. TIPS are quoted on a "Real-Clean" basis—as distinguished from a "Nominal-Dirty" basis. Fractions of a dollar are quoted as units of 1/32.

In this instance, "Real" implies U.S. TIPS prices are quoted on the basis of 100 *inflation-adjusted* units of principal. The quoted price 95-20 can be interpreted as 95 and 20/32 real dollars, meaning the investor is paying 95.625% of the *indexed* principal amount. While this may seem intuitive, it is not the only way to quote TIPS prices. If prices were quoted on a *nominal* basis, as they are in the U.K. Linker market, this same purchase would be quoted as 101.512 (95.625 × 1.06157 = the real price times the index ratio). Similarly,

---

7. *Statistical Abstract of Iceland,* Table 12.5, page 150.

**E X H I B I T 13-7**

Post War Introductions of Indexed Bonds and Inflation Rates

| Date | Country | Inflation Index | Inflation Rate |
|------|---------|-----------------|----------------|
| 1945 | Finland | WPI | 6.4 |
| 1952 | Sweden | CPI | 2.0 |
| 1955 | Iceland | CPI | 15.7 |
| 1966 | Chile | CPI | 22.2 |
| 1972 | Argentina | WPI | 19.7 |
| 1981 | United Kingdom | CPI | 14.0 |
| 1989 | Mexico | CPI | 114.8 |
| 1994 | Sweden | CPI | 4.4 |
| 1997 | United States | CPI | 3.0 |
| 1999 | France | CPI | 1.3 |

WPI: wholesale price index; Inflation: in year prior to introduction except Iceland, for which the prior 5-year average inflation is reported. Source: John Y. Campbell and Robert J. Shiller, "A Scorecard for Indexed Government Debt," NBER Working Paper #5587, May 1996. © 1996 John Y. Campbell and Robert J. Shiller and PIMCO.

to calculate the clean settlement price, which necessarily is paid in "nominal dollars," multiply the real price by the index ratio.

Clean means the quoted TIPS price does not include the accrued-interest amount that the buyer of a TIPS bond owes the seller. Just as with nominal bonds, the TIPS buyer must compensate the seller for coupon income that has been earned since the last coupon payment. Parties therefore can calculate the settlement proceeds by multiplying real accrued interest by the index ratio and adding the result to the clean settlement price. In practice, a computer algorithm as shown in Exhibit 13-2 can be used to incorporate prescribed rounding procedures.

Canadian and French TIPS are quoted similarly to U.S. TIPS, except of course local inflation indexes are referenced.

The U.K. Linker market is quoted on a "Nominal Clean Price" basis, and therefore some U.K. linkers trade at prices above $200 per $100 original face. This is because the country's Retail Price Index (RPI) has more than doubled since the Bank of England began issuing these bonds in the early 1980s.

In Australia and New Zealand Inflation-Indexed Bonds (IIBs) typically are quoted and traded on a "Real Yield" basis.

## Size, Growth, and Liquidity

By February 2000, the U.S. TIPS market had over $97 billion in market value outstanding, and was expected to grow $16 billion annually. The U.S. Treasury does not, however, explicitly announce the quantity or structure of its future debt issuance. But the U.S. Treasury does have a policy of avoiding surprises and it generally maintains a structure for its calendar of issuance.

In 1999, Treasury issued TIPS exclusively in the 10-year and 30-year sectors. The pattern for the 10-year sector has been to issue a new 10-year TIPS each January 15th and to reopen it as a 9.5-year on July 15th. The pattern for issuance in the 30-year sector had been similar; but in February of 2000 changed to a once a year issuance on October 15th.

If this pace continues through 2028, the TIPS market steady-state size would be an enormous \$320 billion. This steady state figure represents almost 20% of marketable long-term Treasury debt currently outstanding.

## Liquidity

The common metrics of liquidity are turnover, bid-ask spread and transactional size. TIPS are less liquid than conventional coupon Treasuries, but as measured by the bid-ask spread associated with transacting \$50 million, they are more liquid than most corporate bonds, non-agency mortgage pass-through bonds, and even some agency debentures. TIPS are significantly more liquid than other inflation-hedges such as real estate, commodity futures, precious metal contracts, natural gas partnerships, timberland deeds, and collectable possessions.

## VALUATION AND PERFORMANCE DYNAMICS

As with any bond, the holding period return of a TIPS bond is the sum of its yield and capital gains. For TIPS, changes in real yield determine capital gains. So perhaps the most important question for investors evaluating TIPS is: "What direction are real yields heading?"

Over the long-term we believe real yields in the U.S. should gravitate to levels below 3.5%. Historically and comparatively, even a 3.50% real return for a riskless instrument is high. Over the past 70 years, long-term Treasury bonds have realized real yields of just above 2% and short-term Treasury bills just below 1%, with both averages concealing significant volatility in real return. During 1999 real yields on long-term nominal Treasuries averaged about 3.5% and Treasury bills 2.5%. Internationally, the 30-year Canadian inflation-linked bonds and French bonds with real yields of 3.7% provided real yields above 3.6%. Australian, Swedish, and British bonds all had lower real yields.

### Determinants of Inflation and the Taylor Rule for Real Yields

Professor John Taylor of Stanford University presents a compelling thesis that there is an immutable link between the sustainable real economic growth rate and the sustainable real Fed-funds rate. "The Taylor Rule" argues that over the long-term, the real Fed-funds rate should average the long-term real economic growth rate of the economy, which he estimated to be about 2%.[8] If the monetary authority maintains the real Fed-funds rate above this for an extended period of time, the inflation rate will diverge towards deflation. If the authority maintains the real Fed-funds rate below this, the result will ultimately be hyperinflation. The implication is that TIPS real yields above 3.5% are overly generous.[9]

But in 1998 a different risk faced policy makers—the possibility of deflation. Paraphrasing Fed Chairman Alan Greenspan, we have to be mindful that the risks and costs of deflation may be as great as the risk and costs of inflation.

The implication is clear. Monetary policy should be balanced during the next decade. The Fed will likely manage a funds rate that averages at most 3.5% above inflation and substantially less than the 4% above inflation experienced during the 1980s and 1990s.

## INVESTORS

## Tactical Use (Within Fixed-Income Portfolios)

There are times when economic fundamentals, financial market dynamics or simply structure will result in TIPS performing exceptionally well, or as in 1999 less badly relative to other investments. All investors can benefit from understanding how to evaluate and purchase TIPS for tactical gain.

In electing to own TIPS for tactical purposes within a fixed-income portfolio an investor may make a relative valuation assessment by comparing them to debt instruments with similar credit, effective duration, and liquidity. After the investment decision is made, the investor must diligently manage the tracking risk, that is non-fixed income risk, associated with introducing tactical allocation to TIPS.

### International Relative Value Opportunities

The international market for inflation-indexed bonds is currently larger than the U.S. TIPS market. We believe that all global TIPS belong to the same asset class. Tactical opportunities exist in all these markets because no region is immune from ebbs and flows in the global supply and demand for capital. To some extent TIPS from different countries are interchangeable.

However, there are nuances that differentiate TIPS from one another. International TIPS provide investors with avenues to exploit a variety of currencies, monetary policies, and other local phenomena. These tactical opportunities can be reduced to perspectives regarding absolute global real yield levels, inflation rates, and inter-country differences from these global averages. Exhibit

---

8. More recently, particularly among proponents of "New Paradigm Economics," there is talk that 2.5% to 3.5% real economic growth may be sustainable.

9. Taylor's equations suggest that in periods of high inflation, high real rates may be temporarily called for.

13–8 illustrates relative value relationships along with ancillary data for seven of the larger government issuers of TIPS.

The second and third columns entitled "Hedged Carry" and "Real Yield" should be of particular interest as they report respectively a short-term measure and a long-term measure of relative value. Hedged carry is obtained by subtracting two-year government conventional yields from the TIPS nominal yield. Real yield incorporates the return of real principal and the interim real income that a TIPS holder will earn. The other columns provide the raw data needed to calculate hedge carry and more.

There are potential international risks not included in Exhibit 13–8 that can impact real yields. The first is the credit profile of the particular issuing country. To the extent that government issuers rarely default on debt instruments denominated in their own currencies, credit risk is low. A second factor is issuance. If a country issues more inflation-indexed supply than domestic and global strategic TIPS investors need, yields are likely to rise until sufficient tactical investors are attracted.

TIPS can be tactically used within equity and cash portfolios as well. Conceptually the motivation is similar. In the U.K. investors often allocate out of equities into TIPS as a defensive tactic—much as U.S. equity managers reallocate defensively into utility stocks to protect against violent market declines.

## E X H I B I T   13–8

Global TIPS Tactical Relative Value Summary (5/30/2000)

| Country | Hedged Carry | Real Yield | Inflation Outlook | Implied Yield | 2-Year Govt | Outstanding (all Maturities: billion US$) |
|---|---|---|---|---|---|---|
| Australia (Index Linked) | 0.81 | 3.40 | 3.50 | 6.90 | 6.09 | 4.47 |
| Canada (Real Return Bonds) | (0.26) | 3.80 | 2.20 | 6.00 | 6.26 | 8.50 |
| France (OATi) | (0.07) | 3.80 | 1.10 | 4.90 | 4.97 | 9.75 |
| Sweden (Index Linked Bonds) | 0.72 | 3.80 | 1.90 | 5.70 | 4.98 | 12.73 |
| UK (Index Linked Gilts) | (1.53) | 2.20 | 2.50 | 4.70 | 6.23 | 112.33 |
| US (Inflation-Indexed Securities) | (0.08) | 4.20 | 2.60 | 6.80 | 6.72 | 97.62 |

Source: PIMCO & Barclays Capital

# Strategic Use

Strategic allocations are more deliberate than tactical ones, and ultimately speak to the inherent investment qualities of TIPS. TIPS can play a significant role within such top-down strategic allocations. Enduring investor goals, such as matching liabilities, diversifying risks, controlling downside exposures, and achieving real return objectives typically drive these strategic allocations. In contrast, bottom-up valuation, market timing, and other opportunistic considerations are rarely important aspects of the strategic decision making process.

Investors typically make strategic asset allocations among the fundamental asset classes: equities, bonds, cash, and inflation hedges. Unadvisedly, some investors opt for finer gradations utilizing more unwieldy sets of narrowly defined asset classes such as large-capitalization, mid-cap, small cap equities, and government bonds at the top-level of their asset allocation framework.

Typically, the thread that holds the elements of an asset class together is that each element's returns are primarily driven by common, fundamental phenomena. Simply, correlations between members of the same asset class will be high, while correlations between assets that are members of different asset classes will be low.

For TIPS, inflation and real global interest rate are the identifying fundamental phenomena that drive returns. So, it is reasonable that all TIPS (Treasury, international, agency, and corporate) comprise a distinct asset class, separate from equities, (nominal) bonds, and cash. Real estate, commodities and certain other "inflation hedges" also fall into this TIPS asset class.

There are three general situations that warrant a strategic reallocation into TIPS. First, portfolio managers looking for higher returns without increased risk may investigate moving out of low risk assets such as cash. Second, those motivated toward preserving past gains might consider a defensive allocation out of higher risk assets such as equities or real estate. Importantly, a defensive allocation will tend to dramatically decrease or eliminate shortfall probability. (Shortfall probability is the likelihood that a portfolio will fall below a minimum acceptable threshold.) And, third, TIPS can be strategically utilized in an asset-liability management context.

## Asset-Liability Management (ALM)

Asset-liability management is closely related to asset allocation. Traditionally, asset allocation studies do not explicitly incorporate liabilities. They tend to focus on increasing absolute levels of return through allocations to higher returning assets or through diversification of assets, thereby reducing risk calculated without regard to liabilities.

ALM studies focus on reducing the mismatch between assets and liabilities. Traditionally, researchers have studied ALM in a conventional nominal frame of reference where the exposure of assets and liabilities to conventional yield changes are compared and to some extent matched. Liabilities are assumed to be nominal liabilities even when they are in fact inflation sensitive.

The large-scale introduction of TIPS by the U.S. Treasury has given asset-liability managers the ability to measure and manage both assets and liabilities that are predominantly real. This is a reprieve for the many investors discussed later.

Investors are no longer limited to choosing between asset allocation or asset-liability management. The two can be combined into a framework generally termed "surplus management"—optimizing the return and risk of surplus (assets net of liabilities).

### Risk/Return Optimization

The novelty of TIPS as an asset class in the U.S. poses challenges for strategic users of the securities. In particular, to include TIPS in a standard nominal Markowitz mean-variance optimization, the analyst must input appropriate expected return, variance, and correlation data for TIPS as well as other assets (or liabilities) included in the optimization.

Although conceptually inputs for such optimizations are forward looking, practitioners usually rely heavily on historical data. Since U.S. TIPS have existed since 1997, correlation matrices are built using asset class returns from 1997 forward, or from pro-forma estimates of TIPS returns prior to 1997. Although most optimization models function in a nominal frame of reference, some practitioners appropriately implement them in a real frame of reference.

### Managing Dedicated TIPS Portfolios Using Real Duration

After a TIPS allocation has been determined, an implementation strategy must be executed. For this, an investor chooses between active or passive management. In either case, real duration is a useful metric of exposure as it measures the allocation's relative sensitivity to changes (parallel shifts) in the real yield curve.

To construct a TIPS portfolio the practitioner needs first to choose a target "real duration" for the portfolio, then to devise a variety of candidate portfolio structures. The candidate portfolios might include a bulleted portfolio having all its TIPS close to the target duration, and a barbell portfolio with a combination of longer and shorter TIPS weighted to achieve the target duration.

To select the most advantageous portfolio structure from those with the same real duration, the practitioner need only concern herself with the exposure to changes in the general real yield curve slope of the various candidate portfolios. This is because the candidate portfolios have the same real yield duration, so their response to parallel shifts will be very similar.

### Investor Types: Pension Plans, Endowments, Foundations, and Individuals

Defined-benefit pension plans have both retired-lives and active-lives liabilities. Although TIPS as assets may match the active life portion of these plans extremely well, plan sponsors typically do not rely exclusively on TIPS to back their active-lives liabilities. Instead, they reach for higher expected returns by utilizing other asset classes with higher risk and return qualities. Given that TIPS and the active-lives liabilities are both linked to inflation,[10] sponsors realize that to reach for higher returns, they take on some risk of under-performance in inflationary environments. In addition to generic asset allocations, pension plans may use TIPS to protect a surplus, to offset substantial equity risk exposure, or to reduce the variability of annual funding requirements. Defined-contribution pension plans and their participants may also benefit from the inclusion of TIPS as described separately below.

Endowments, foundations, and other eleemosynary organizations also may have return objectives that are formulated in *real* terms. Typically their goal is to generate a 5% or higher real-return on their investment portfolio. (The IRS generally requires that 5% of charitable foundation's assets be spent on the delivery of charitable services each year—so a 5% real-return, net of expenses and contributions, is required to maintain the foundation's inflation-adjusted size.)

Establishing a real return target for investment performance makes sense for these organizations. Educational or charitable programs, whether they involve physical infrastructure or services, are often budgeted for utilizing inflation-adjusted dollars. Implicitly, such goals, objectives and plans represent real liabilities.

This suggests that eleemosynaries employ TIPS as a core pillar in their investment strategy. TIPS will not generally achieve 5% returns in isolation, but they go a long way toward engineering out much of the downside risk of return distributions. With the downside risk truncated, more aggressive use of a higher returning (riskier) asset can be used. As of this writing, eleemosynaries generally have used TIPS only at the margin.

*Individuals* save primarily to provide for retirement needs, and secondarily for children's education, bequeathment, and other goals. Younger individuals may be relatively immune to the damage that inflation can cause in the context of such liabilities. They hold a large proportion of their "wealth" in the intangible real asset known as human capital (future earning power). As individuals age the proportion of their real assets typically decrease as their financial assets increase—leaving those in their late 40's and older relatively vulnerable to the inflationary erosion of retirement living standards.

## ISSUERS

Although corporations and agencies can and do issue TIPS, governments are by far the largest issuers. By issuing TIPS, government officials make clearer their

---

10. More specifically, active-lives' liabilities are tied to increases in wages of employees. The pension plans may prescribe that an employee's retirement benefit is a fixed annuity, with each monthly payment being a fraction of employees' highest annual income. This income level is in turn not explicitly, but is generally, highly correlated with the CPI.

commitment to maintaining a low level of inflation. A government's willingness to assume the financial risk of inflation is a powerful signal to the market place regarding future policy. Donald T. Brash, Governor, Reserve Bank of New Zealand, characterized this attitude in a speech following New Zealand's introduction of these securities:

> *The only "cost" to Government is that, by issuing inflation-adjusted bonds, it foregoes the opportunity of reducing, through inflation, the real cost of borrowing... Since [the New Zealand] Government has no intention of stealing the money invested by bondholders, foregoing the right to steal through inflation hardly seems a significant penalty.*[11]

How can an investment instrument that makes so much sense for investors, as described in previous sections, also be advantageous to the issuer? Brash's quote provides one example of how investors gain, while the issuer forfeits something it considered worthless to begin with. Below we discuss the U.S. Treasury rationale for issuing TIPS.

## U.S. Treasury's Rationale

The Clinton administration has delivered on its promise to reduce the future interest burden of the Treasury's debt. Balancing the budget was the main target of this policy, but a secondary objective took aim at "Bond Market Vigilantes." The administration recognized that because of the "maturity premium" inherent in longer term debt, rolling over a three-year bond ten times would likely incur less interest cost than issuing a single 30-year bond. One of the most important programs Treasury embarked upon during this administration was a deliberate effort to reduce the average maturity of outstanding debt.

### TIPS Program

The TIPS program was instituted in this spirit. Like floating-rate debt, TIPS have long *stated* but short *effective* maturities, reducing the "roll-over risk" inherent in short-term debt. Additionally, TIPS explicitly provide market-based inflation forecasts for use by the Fed. TIPS reduce the expected cost of financing a government's debt because they are conceptually free of the inflation risk premium built into nominal long-term bond yields. Normally one might conclude that by relieving bond investors of this risk, the Treasury implicitly absorbs a burden or risk equal in magnitude. This is not the case here however.

By reducing nominal debt and increasing inflation-indexed (real) debt, the Treasury has in effect changed the structure of its liabilities to better match its only asset—its authority to tax. Put another way, the Treasury is the ideal issuer of inflation-indexed debt.

---

11. Donald T. Brash, "Monetary Policy and Inflation-Adjusted Bonds," An Address to the New Zealand Society of Actuaries (April 12, 1995).

The issuance of TIPS improves taxpayer welfare by eliminating the 0.5% to 1.0% inflation risk premium that researchers believe is embedded in nominal bond yields. At the margin investors are indifferent to accepting lower yields versus living with the higher risk of nominal debt—so conceptually they are no better or worse off. The elimination of this inflation risk premium is, therefore, a true welfare gain. In practice the welfare gains of issuing TIPS have been split between issuers and the investors.

## Moral Hazard

The government is both the issuer of TIPS (Department of Treasury) and publisher of the CPI (BLS, Department of Labor). The inherent ambiguity in measuring the CPI creates a moral hazard because the government can directly control the economic value of its liability. Fortunately, several factors mitigate the risk of the government publishing statistics which are not scientifically based.

First, professional integrity, a strong institutional infrastructure, and influential political constituencies combine to preclude the government from manipulating the CPI. Second, any confiscation of value through index distortions would be perceived by the financial community as an erosion of credibility or, if blatant, tantamount to default. Since the issuance process is a repeated-game of substantial proportion, such an erosion of credibility would have long-term repercussions on future debt issuance and other government promises that would greatly outweigh any apparent short-term economic or political benefits.

## International Issuers

The TIPS market in the U.K. is large and well developed, comprising about 20% of outstanding debt. Additionally, Canada, Australia, France, and Sweden have issued TIPS in large enough quantities to ensure reasonable market liquidity as well.

While each of these countries shares the basic inflation protection concept with their U.S. cousins, differences include market size, trading liquidity, time lag associated with the inflation indexation, taxation, day-count conventions, and quotation conventions. These differences substantially influence both observed quoted real yields and "true" real yields available to investors.

All of the TIPS issued by these five governments, together with those issued by the U.S. Treasury, make up a performance benchmark of liquid global inflation bonds known as the Barclays Capital Global Inflation-Linked Bond Index.

## Corporate Issuers and CPI-Floaters

In addition to the U.S. Treasury and foreign government issuers, U.S. corporations, agencies and municipalities have issued inflation-indexed bonds. Two of the earliest corporate issuers were the Tennessee Valley Authority and Salomon Brothers. Their inflation-indexed bonds were virtually identical in structure to U.S. Treasury TIPS. Other issuers, including Nationsbank, Toyota Motor Credit, the Student Loan Marketing Association (SLMA) and the Federal Home Loan Bank (FHLB), have chosen to structure their bonds as CPI-floaters.

A CPI floater is a hybrid between TIPS and a conventional floating-rate note (FRN). Like a TIPS its return is closely linked to CPI inflation. Like a conventional floating-rate note, its principal is fixed in size. The coupon rate of a CPI floater fluctuates and is typically defined as the CPI inflation rate plus a fixed percentage margin.

# OTHER ISSUES

## Taxation

U.S. TIPS are taxed similarly to zero-coupon bonds. They incur a tax liability on phantom income (income earned but not paid.) This does not mean that investors in TIPS pay more taxes or that they pay taxes sooner than holders of nominal bonds. In fact, if inflation, nominal yields, and tax rates are constant, the cash flow profile of taxes paid and payments received on TIPS is comparable to that of nominal bonds (assuming reinvestment of the excess coupon). In practice, many taxpayers hold TIPS in tax-exempt accounts (401K's etc) or within mutual funds (which are generally required to distribute taxable income.)

## Deflation Protection

Questions naturally arise regarding how TIPS would behave in a deflationary environment (one where prices are literally falling). Applying CPI-indexation, the current adjusted-principal value would be less than the prior adjusted principal value. This would impact semiannual interest payments accordingly.

Extending this premise, it is certainly possible for the adjusted principal value to fall below the original principal value—and therefore for coupon payments to be calculated on a shrinking base. Note, they would still be positive and almost equal to their original size. For example, even after 10 years of 1% deflation, and a resulting price level that was 10% lower than when it started, the semiannual coupon payments on a $1,000 TIPS would still be about $18 (rather than $20 originally). The final principal repayment would be treated even more favorably.

In particular, *the Treasury has guaranteed that for the maturity payment of principal (and only the maturity payment) the investor will not receive less than the original principal amount.*

In such deflationary circumstances, in order to maintain acceptable nominal returns, the Treasury would in effect be paying a higher real return than initially promised. The Treasury decided that the regulatory, institutional, and psychological benefits of providing this guarantee would facilitate distribution of the bonds to an extent that more than justifies the theoretical contingent cost to the government.

This government guarantee of 100% principal return distinguishes TIPS from all other inflation hedges.

## CONCLUSION

During the last two decades of the 20th Century, the financial markets enjoyed an unprecedented period of falling inflation and high real returns. But investors will inevitably relearn the history lesson taught thousands of years ago in Mesopotamia: The risk of secular inflation can never be completely eliminated.

Fortunately for investors, the decision by the U.S. Treasury to issue TIPS provides an attractive vehicle to hedge against the risk of inflation. The creation of this new asset class is sure to have broad-reaching implications for both institutional and retail investors. In time it is likely TIPS allocations will become an integral part of almost all portfolios. Negatively correlated to inflation sensitive financial asset classes, TIPS increase the efficiency of investment portfolios. The result is a dramatically superior risk/return trade-off, independent of inflation forecasts.

## CHAPTER 14

# FLOATING-RATE SECURITIES*

**Steven V. Mann, Ph.D.**
Associate Professor of Finance
The Darla Moore School of Business
University of South Carolina

**Frank J. Fabozzi, Ph.D., CFA**
Adjunct Professor of Finance
School of Management
Yale University

Under the rubric of floating-rate securities or simply *floaters,* there are several different types of securities with an essential feature in common: coupon interest will vary over the instrument's life. Floaters, which were first introduced into the European debt market and issued in the United States in the early 1970s, are now issued in every sector of the bond market—government, agency, corporate, municipal, mortgage and asset-backed—in the United States and in markets throughout the world. Although a floater's coupon formula may depend on a wide variety of economic variables (e.g., foreign exchange rates or commodity prices), a floater's coupon payments usually depends on the level of a money market interest rate (e.g., the London Interbank Offer Rate or LIBOR, Treasury bills). A floater's coupon rate can be reset semiannually, quarterly, monthly or weekly. The term "adjustable-rate" or "variable-rate" typically refers to those securities with coupon rates reset not more than annually or based on a longer-term interest rate. However, this is a distinction without a difference and we will refer to both floating-rate securities and adjustable-rate securities as floaters.

In this chapter, we will discuss the general features of floaters and present some illustrations of the major product types. Most market participants use "spread" or margin measures (e.g., adjusted simple margin, or discount margin) to assess the relative value of a floater. We will briefly describe these measures and note their limitations. Finally, we discuss several popular portfolio strategies which employ floaters.

---

* Parts of this chapter are adapted from Frank J. Fabozzi and Steven V. Mann, *Floating-Rate Securities* (New Hope, PA: Frank J. Fabozzi Associates, 2000).

# GENERAL FEATURES OF FLOATERS AND MAJOR PRODUCT TYPES

A floater is a debt security whose coupon rate is reset at designated dates based on the value of some designated reference rate. The coupon formula for a pure floater (i.e., a floater with no embedded options) can be expressed as follows:

$$\text{coupon rate} = \text{reference rate} \pm \text{quoted margin}$$

The quoted margin is the adjustment (in basis points) that the issuer agrees to make to the reference rate. For example, consider a floating-rate note issued by Enron Corp. that matured March 30, 2000. This floater delivered cash flows quarterly and had a coupon formula equal to three-month LIBOR plus 45 basis points.

As noted, the reference rate is the interest rate or index that appears in a floater's coupon formula and it is used to determine the coupon payment on each reset date within the boundaries designated by embedded caps and/or floors. The four most common reference rates are LIBOR, Treasury bills yields, Prime rates, and domestic CD rates and they appear in the coupon formulas of a wide variety of floating-rate products. There are other reference rates utilized in more specialized markets such as the markets for mortgage-backed securities and the municipal market. For example, the most common reference rates for adjustable-rate mortgages (ARMs) or collateralized mortgage obligation (CMO) floaters include: (1) the one-year Constant Maturity Treasury Rate (i.e., one-year CMT); (2) the 11th District Cost of Funds (COFI); (3) six-month LIBOR; and (4) the National Monthly Median Cost of Funds Index. In the municipal market the reference rate for floaters is often a Treasury rate or the prime rate. Alternatively, the reference rate could be a municipal index. Three popular municipal indexes are J. J. Kenney Index, Bond Buyer 40 Bond Index, and Merrill Lynch Municipal Securities Index.[1]

A floater often imposes limits on how much the coupon rate can float. Specifically, a floater may have a restriction on the maximum coupon rate that will be paid on any reset date. This is called a *cap*. Consider a hypothetical floater whose coupon formula is three-month LIBOR plus 50 basis points with a cap of 7.5%. If three-month LIBOR at a coupon reset date is 8%, then the coupon formula would suggest the new coupon rate is 8.5%. However, the cap restricts the maximum coupon rate to 7.5%. Needless to say, a cap is an unattractive feature from the investor's perspective.

In contrast, a floater may also specify a minimum coupon rate called a *floor*. For example, First Chicago (now 1st Chicago NBD Corp.) issued a floored floating-rate note in July 1993 that matures in July 2003. This issue delivers quarterly coupon payments with a coupon formula of three-month LIBOR plus

---

1. For a detailed description of each of these reference rates, see Frank J. Fabozzi and Steven V. Mann, *Floating Rate Securities* (New Hope, PA: Frank J. Fabozzi Associates, 2000).

12.5 basis points with a floor of 4.25%. So if three-month LIBOR ever fell below 4.125%, the coupon rate would remain at 4.25%. A floor is an attractive feature from the investor's perspective.

When a floater possesses both a cap and a floor, this feature is referred to as a *collar*. Thus, a collared floater's coupon rate has a maximum and a minimum value. For example, the Economic Development Corporation issued a collared floater in February 1993 that makes semiannual coupon payments and matures in 2003. The coupon formula is six-month LIBOR flat with a floor of 5% and a cap of 8%.[2]

While a floater's coupon rate typically moves in the same direction as the reference rate, there are floaters whose coupon rate moves in the opposite direction from the reference rate called *inverse floaters* or *reverse floaters*. A general formula for an inverse floater is:

$$K - L \times (\text{Reference rate})$$

From the formula, it is easy to see that as the reference rate goes up (down), the coupon rate goes down (up). As an example, consider an inverse floater issued by the Federal Home Loan Bank in April 1999 due in April 2002. This issue delivers quarterly coupon payments according to the formula:

$$18\% - 2.5 \times (\text{three-month LIBOR})$$

In addition, this inverse floater has a floor of 3% and a cap of 15.5%. Note that for this inverse floater, the value for L (called the *coupon leverage*) in the coupon reset formula is 2.5. Assuming neither the cap rate nor the floor rate are binding, this means that for every one basis point change in three-month LIBOR, the coupon rate changes by 2.5 basis points in the opposite direction.[3]

There is a wide variety of floaters that have special features that may appeal to certain types of investors. For example, some issues provide for a change in the quoted margin (i.e., the spread added to or subtracted from the reference in the coupon reset formula) at certain intervals over a floater's life. These issues are called *stepped spread floaters* because the quoted margin can either step to a higher or lower level over time. Consider Standard Chartered Bank's floater due in December 2006. From its issuance in December 1996 until December 2001, the coupon formula is three-month LIBOR plus 40 basis points. However, from December 2001 until maturity, the quoted margin "steps up" to 90 basis points.

A *range note* is a floater where the coupon payment depends upon the number of days that the specified reference rate stays within a preestablished collar. For instance, Sallie Mae issued a range note in August 1996 (due in August 2003) that makes coupon payments quarterly. For every day during the

---

2. Here, the term flat means without a quoted margin or a quoted margin of zero.
3. When L is greater than 1, the security is referred to as a *leveraged inverse floater.*

quarter that three-month LIBOR is between 3% and 9%, the investor earns three-month LIBOR plus 155 basis points. Interest will accrue at 0% for each day that three-month LIBOR is outside this collar.

There are also floaters whose coupon formula contains more than one reference rate. A *dual-indexed* floater is one such example. The coupon rate formula is typically a fixed percentage plus the difference between two reference rates. For example, the Federal Home Loan Bank System issued a floater in July 1993 (due in July 1996) whose coupon rate was the difference between the 10-year Constant Maturity Treasury Rate and three-month LIBOR plus 160 basis points.

Although the reference rate for most floaters is an interest rate or an interest rate index, numerous kinds of reference rates appear in coupon formulas. This is especially true for structured notes. Potential reference rates include movements in foreign exchange rates, the price of a commodity (e.g., gold), movements in an equity index (e.g., the Standard & Poor's 500 Index), or an inflation index (e.g., CPI). Financial engineers are capable of structuring floaters with almost any reference rate. For example, in April 1983, Merrill Lynch issued Stock Market Reset Term Notes which mature in December 1999. These notes deliver semiannual coupon payments using a formula of 0.65 multiplied by the annual return of the Standard & Poor's MidCap 400 during the calendar year. These notes have a cap rate of 10% and a floor rate of 3%.

## CALL AND PUT PROVISIONS

Just like fixed-rate issues, a floater may be *callable*. The call option gives the issuer the right to buy back the issue prior to the stated maturity date. The call option may have value to the issuer some time in the future for two basic reasons. First, market interest rates may fall so that the issuer can exercise the option to retire the floater and replace it with a fixed-rate issue. Second, the required margin decreases so that the issuer can call the issue and replace it with a floater with a lower quoted margin.[4] The issuer's call option is a disadvantage to the investor since the proceeds received must be reinvested either at a lower interest rate or a lower margin. Consequently, an issuer who wants to include a call feature when issuing a floater must compensate investors by offering a higher quoted margin.

For amortizing securities (e.g., mortgage-backed and some asset-backed securities) that are backed by loans that have a schedule of principal repayments, individual borrowers typically have the option to pay off all or part of their loan prior to the scheduled date. Any additional principal repayment above the sched-

---

4. The required margin is the spread (either positive or negative) the market requires as compensation for the risks embedded in the issue. If the required margin equals the quoted margin, a floater's price will be at par on coupon reset dates.

uled amount is called a *prepayment*. The right of borrowers to prepay is called the *prepayment option*. Basically, the prepayment option is analogous to a call option. However, unlike a call option, there is not a call price that depends on when the borrower pays off the issue. Typically, the price at which a loan is prepaid is its par value.

Floaters may also include a *put provision* which gives the security holder the option to sell the security back to the issuer at a specified price on designated dates. The specified price is called the *put price*. The put's structure can vary across issues. Some issues permit the holder to require the issuer to redeem the issue on any coupon payment date. Others allow the put to be exercised only when the coupon is adjusted. The time required for prior notification to the issuer or its agent varies from as little as four days to as long as a couple of months. The advantage of the put provision to the holder of the floater is that if after the issue date the margin required by the market for a floater to trade at par rises above the issue's quoted margin, the investor can force the issuer to redeem the floater at the put price and then reinvest the proceeds in a floater with the higher quoted margin.

## SPREAD MEASURES

There are several yield spread measures or margins that are routinely used to evaluate floaters. The four margins commonly used are spread for life, adjusted simple margin, adjusted total margin and discount margin. All of these spread measures are available on Bloomberg's Yield Analysis (YA) screen.

## Spread for Life

When a floater is selling at a premium/discount to par, a potential buyer of a floater will consider the premium or discount as an additional source of dollar return. *Spread for life* (also called *simple margin*) is a measure of potential return that accounts for the accretion (amortization) of the discount (premium) as well as the constant index spread over the security's remaining life.

## Adjusted Simple Margin

The *adjusted simple margin* (also called *effective margin*) is an adjustment to spread for life. This adjustment accounts for a one-time cost of carry effect when a floater is purchased with borrowed funds. Suppose a security dealer has purchased $10 million of a particular floater. Naturally, the dealer has a number of alternative ways to finance the position—borrowing from a bank, repurchase agreement, etc. Regardless of the method selected, the dealer must make a one-time adjustment to the floater's price to account for the cost of carry from the settlement date to next coupon reset date.

## Adjusted Total Margin

The *adjusted total margin* (also called *total adjusted margin*) adds one additional refinement to the adjusted simple margin. Specifically, the adjusted total margin is the adjusted simple margin plus the interest earned by investing the difference between the floater's par value and the carry-adjusted price.[5]

## Discount Margin

One common method of measuring potential return that employs discounted cash flows is *discount margin*. This measure indicates the average spread or margin over the reference rate the investor can expect to earn over the security's life given a particular assumed path that the reference rate will take to maturity. The assumption that the future levels of the reference rate are equal to today's level is the current market convention. The procedure for calculating the discount margin is as follows:

1. Determine the cash flows assuming that the reference rate does not change over the security's life.

2. Select a margin (i.e., a spread above the reference rate).

3. Discount the cash flows found in (1) by the current value of the reference rate plus the margin selected in (2).

4. Compare the present value of the cash flows as calculated in (3) to the price. If the present value is equal to the security's price, the discount margin is the margin assumed in (2). If the present value is not equal to the security's price, go back to (2) and select a different margin.

For a floater selling at par, the discount margin is simply the quoted margin. Similarly, if the floater is selling at a premium (discount), then the discount margin will be below (above) the quoted margin.

Practitioners use the spread measures presented above to gauge the potential return from holding a floater. Much like conventional yield measures for fixed-income securities, the yield or margin measures discussed here are, for the most part, relatively easy to calculate and interpret. However, these measures reflect relative value only under several simplifying assumptions (e.g., reference rates do not change).

One of the key difficulties in using the measures described in this chapter is that they do not recognize the presence of embedded options. As discussed, there are callable/putable floaters and floaters with caps and/or floors. However,

---

5. When the floater's adjusted price is greater than 100, the additional increment is negative and represents the interest foregone.

the recognition of embedded options is critical to valuing floaters properly. If an issuer can call an issue when presented with the opportunity and refund at a lower spread, the investor must then reinvest at the lower spread. With this background, it should not be surprising that sophisticated practitioners value floaters using arbitrage-free binomial interest rate trees and Monte Carlo simulations. These models are designed to value securities whose cash flows are interest-rate dependent.

## PRICE VOLATILITY CHARACTERISTICS OF FLOATERS

The change in the price of a fixed-rate security when market rates change occurs because the security's coupon rate differs from the prevailing rate for new comparable bonds issued at par. So, an investor in a 10-year, 7% coupon bond purchased at par, for example, will find that the bond's price will decline below par if the market requires a yield greater than than 7% for bonds with the same risk and maturity. By contrast, a floater's coupon resets periodically thereby reducing its sensitivity to changes in rates. For this reason, floaters are said to more "defensive" securities. This does not mean, of course, that a floater's price will not change.

### Factors that Affect a Floater's Price

A floater's price will change depending on the following factors:

1. time remaining to the next coupon reset date
2. changes in the market's required margin
3. whether or not the cap or floor is reached

We will discuss the impact of each of these factors in the following sections.

#### Time Remaining to the Next Coupon Reset Date

The longer the time to the next coupon reset date, the more a floater's behaves like a fixed-rate security and the greater a floater's potential price fluctuation. Conversely, the shorter the time between coupon reset dates, the smaller the floater's potential price fluctuation.

To understand why this is so, consider a floater with five years remaining to maturity whose coupon formula is the one-year Treasury bill rate (bond-equivalent yield) plus 50 basis points and the coupon is reset today when the one-year Treasury bill rate is 5.5%. The coupon rate will remain at 6% for the year. One month hence, an investor in this floater would effectively own an 11-month instrument with a 6% coupon. Suppose at that time, the market requires a 6.2% yield on comparable issues with 11 months to maturity. Then, our floater would be offering a below market rate (6% versus 6.2%). The floater's price must decline below par to compensate the investor for the sub-market yield.

Similarly, if the yield that the market requires on a comparable instrument with a maturity of 11 months is less than 6%, the floater will trade at a premium. For a floater in which the cap is not binding and for which the market does not demand a margin different from the quoted margin, a floater that resets daily will trade at par.

## Changes in the Market's Required Margin

At the initial offering of a floater, the issuer will set the quoted margin based on market conditions so that the security will trade near par. Subsequently, if the market requires a higher/lower margin, the floater's price will decrease/increase to reflect the current margin required. We shall refer to the margin that is demanded by the market as the *required margin*. For example, consider a floater whose coupon formula is one-month LIBOR plus 40 basis points. If market conditions change such that the required margin increases to 50 basis points, this floater would be offering a below market margin. As a result, the floater's price will decline below par value. By the same token, the floater will trade above its par value if the required margin is less than the quoted margin—less than 40 basis points in our example.

The required margin for a particular issue depends on: (1) the margin available in competitive funding markets, (2) the credit quality of the issue, (3) the presence of any embedded call or put options, and (4) the liquidity of the issue. An alternative source of funding to floaters is a syndicated loan. Consequently, the required margin will be driven, in part, by margins available in the syndicated loan market.

The portion of the required margin attributable to credit quality is referred to as the *credit spread*. The risk that there will be an increase in the credit spread required by the market is called *credit spread risk*. The concern for credit spread risk applies not only to an individual issue, but to a sector or the economy as a whole. For example, credit spreads may increase due to a financial crises (e.g., a stock market crash) while the individual issuer's condition and prospects remain essentially unchanged.

A portion of the required margin reflects the call risk if the floater is callable. Because the call feature imposes hazards on the investor, the greater the call risk, the higher the quoted margin at issuance, other things equal. After issuance, depending on how interest rates and required margins change, the perceived call risk and the margin required as compensation for this risk will change accordingly. In contrast to call risk owing to an embedded call option, a put provision provides benefits to the investor. If a floater is putable at par, all else the same, its price should trade at par near the put date.

Finally, a portion of the quoted margin at issuance will reflect the issue's perceived liquidity. *Liquidity risk* is the threat of an increase in the required margin due to a perceived deterioration in an issue's liquidity. Investors in nontraditional floater products are particularly concerned with liquidity risk.

## Whether or Not the Cap or Floor is Reached

For a floater with a cap, once the coupon rate as specified by the coupon formula rises above the cap rate, the floater then offers a below market coupon rate and the floater will trade at a discount. The floater will trade more and more like a fixed-rate security the further the capped rate is below the prevailing market rate. Simply put, if a floater's coupon rate does not float, it is effectively a fixed-rate security. *Cap risk* is the risk that the floater's value will decline because the cap is reached.

The situation is reversed if the floater has a floor. Once the floor is reached, all else equal, the floater will trade either at par value or at a premium to par if the coupon rate is above the prevailing rate offered for comparable issues.

# Duration of Floaters

We have just described how a floater's price will respond to a change in the required margin, holding all other factors constant. As explained in Chapter 5, the measure used by market participants to quantify the sensitivity of a security's price to changes in interest rates is called *duration*. A security's duration tells us the approximate percentage change in its price for a 100 basis point change in rates. The procedure of computing a security's duration was explained in Chapter 5.

Two measures are employed to estimate a floater's sensitivity to each component of the coupon formula. *Index duration* is a measure of the floater's price sensitivity to changes in the reference rates holding the quoted margin constant. Correspondingly, *spread duration* measures a floater's price sensitivity to a change in the "quoted margin" or "spread" assuming the reference rate remains unchanged.

# Price Volatility of an Inverse Floater

An inverse floater can be created by acquiring a fixed-rate security and splitting it into a floater and an inverse floater. The fixed-rate security from which the floater and inverse floater are created is called the "collateral." The interest paid to the floater investor and inverse floater investor must be such that it is equal to the interest rate paid on the collateral.

Because valuations are additive (i.e., the value of the collateral is the sum of the floater and inverse floater values), durations (properly weighted) are additive as well. Accordingly, the duration of the inverse floater is related in a particular fashion to the duration of the collateral and the duration of the floater. Specifically, the duration of an inverse floater will be a multiple of the duration of the collateral from which it is created.

To understand this, suppose that a 30-year fixed-rate bond with a market value of $100 million is split into a floater and an inverse floater with market values of $80 million and $20 million, respectively. Assume also that the duration of the collateral (i.e, the 30-year fixed-rate bond) is 8. Given this information, we know that for a 100 basis point change in required yield that the collateral's value will change by approximately 8% or $8 million (8% times $100 million). Since the floater and inverse floater are created from the collateral, the combined change in value of the floater and the inverse floater must be $8 million for a 100 basis point change in required yield. The question becomes how do we partition the change in value between the floater and inverse floater. If the duration of the floater is small as explained earlier, then the inverse floater must experience the full force of the $8 million change in value. For this to occur, the duration of the inverse floater must be approximately 40. A duration of 40 will mean a 40% change in the inverse floater's value for a 100 basis point change in required yield and a change in value of approximately $8 million (40% times $20 million).

Effectively, the inverse floater is a leveraged position in the collateral. That is, ownership of an inverse floater is equivalent to buying the collateral and funding it on a floating-rate basis, where the reference rate for the borrowing is equal to the reference rate for the inverse floater. Accordingly, the duration of the inverse floater is a multiple of the duration of the collateral.

## PORTFOLIO STRATEGIES

There are several portfolio strategies that have been employed using floaters. These include: (1) basic asset/liability management strategies; (2) risk arbitrage strategies; (3) betting on changes in the required margin; and (4) arbitrage between fixed- and floating-rate markets using asset swaps. We will briefly describe each of these strategies in turn.

Asset/liability management strategies can be explained most easily using depository institutions. These institutions typically borrow short-term and their objective is to lock in a spread over their short-term funding costs. Not surprisingly, one obvious way to accomplish this objective is to invest in floating-rate products. Naturally, this strategy is not without risks. The floater's coupon rate will likely be capped while the short-term funding may not be. This is known as *cap risk*. Further, the floater's reference rate may not be the same as the reference rate for funding. If this is the case, the institution is exposed to *basis risk*.

Risk arbitrage strategies using floaters are not arbitrage in the true sense of the term. One example of this type of strategy involves money managers using leverage (via repurchase agreements) to invest in agency adjustable-rate passthrough securities that earn a higher spread over their borrowing rate. Of course, this is not a "risk-free" transaction. Like before, the manager will likely be exposed to cap risk if the floater's coupon is capped while the funding rate is not. The manager may also be exposed to basis risk if the two reference rates are mismatched. Finally, there is *price risk* if the floater's risk changes for the worse and the floater must be sold prior to maturity. In this case, the quoted margin will no longer compensate the investor for the security's risks and the floater will sell at a discount to par. No serious investor believes that a risk arbitrage strategy is a reliable source of spread income.

Investors can also speculate on whether a floater's required margin will change. When a floater is issued, the quoted margin contained in the coupon formula will be set so that the floater will be priced at or near par. After the floater enters the secondary market, the quoted margin for a standard floater does not change. So, if the floater's risk does not change and the compensation demanded by the market does not change either, the floater's price will be par on every coupon reset date. In this case, the quoted margin offered by the security and quoted margin required by the market (called the required margin) are the same. If conditions change such that the required spread is greater than (less than) the quoted margin, the floater will trade at discount (premium) to par. Given this background, one obvious strategy money managers pursue is betting on a change in the required margin for a single issue or a sector.

Lastly, some money managers arbitrage between floaters and fixed-rate securities using a so-called *asset swap*. An asset-based swap transaction involves the creation of synthetic security via the purchase of an existing security and the simultaneous execution of a swap. For example, after the Russian debt default and ruble devaluation in August 1998, risk-averse investors sold corporate bonds and fled to the relative safety of on-the-run U.S. Treasuries. Credit spreads widened considerably and liquidity diminished. A contrary-minded floating-rate investor like a financial institution could take advantage of similar circumstances by buying newly issued investment-grade corporate bonds with relatively attractive coupon rates and simultaneously taking a long position in an interest rate swap (pay fixed/receive floating). Because of the higher credit spreads, the coupon rate that the financial institution receives is higher than the fixed-rate paid in the swap. Accordingly, the financial institution ends up with a synthetic floating-rate asset with a sizeable spread above LIBOR. By similar reasoning, investors could buy floaters and use swaps to create a synthetic fixed-rate security.

## CHAPTER 15

# NONCONVERTIBLE PREFERRED STOCK

**Richard S. Wilson**
Consultant

This chapter reviews fixed-rate and variable-rate nonconvertible preferred stock. Preferred stock that is convertible into common shares is discussed in Chapter 50.

## THE ESSENTIAL NATURE OF PREFERRED STOCKS

Preferred stock is a class of stock entitling the holder to certain preferences over the common stock of the issuer. It is an equity-type security and not a debt instrument. These preferred-equity instruments can be traced back to the mid-16th century in England and to before 1850 in the United States. However, they first came into prominence in the 1890s during the formation of the giant trusts and industrial combinations. At first, preferences concerned dividend rights, but later other provisions were added, giving the shares additional features and priorities over the common equity. Preferred shares have some of the characteristics of debt securities (although ranking below debt in the capital structure of a corporation), including priority over common shares in liquidation of the issuer. For the sake of convenience, the term *preferred* will refer to all classes of senior equity securities unless specifically noted.

## PROFILE OF THE PREFERRED STOCK MARKET

Fixed-dividend, adjustable-rate, and auction market and remarketed preferreds are the three main types of nonconvertible preferred stocks. More will be said later about the specifics of these issues; we will review in this space the size and makeup of the public nonconvertible preferred market.

### Issue Types and Issuers

One of the major structural changes in the preferred stock market over the last 20 years is characterized by the trend away from fixed-rate dividends toward variable-rate dividends. Although the total volume of nonconvertible preferred stock issuance in the public markets is greater than a decade ago, the growth has come in variable-rate issues, not the conventional preferreds. Before 1982, the only dividend a public preferred had was fixed-rate—that is, the same dividend applied throughout the life of the issue. In May of that year, Chemical Bank issued the first adjustable-rate preferred stock (ARPS) in the public market. The private market had a few variable-rate issues such as AMAX Inc.'s LIBOR-based stock issued in 1978 and Citibank and Chemical New York Corporation's three-year adjustable-rate shares.

The market's romance with adjustable-rate preferreds did not last long as a better, less volatile mousetrap was invented. Two years later, in 1984, Dutch auction market preferreds appeared. The next year, ARPS issuance started its descent, and auction market and remarketed preferreds became the new hot items. Thus, although the public market before 1982 was 100% fixed-dividend issues, in 1982 only 45% of the volume was conventional preferreds. In 1984, less than 13% of the dollar volume was in fixed-rate shares, and in 1986 only 26%. In 1988, straight-dividend preferreds accounted for less than 16% of total issuance. But in the four years 1989 through 1992, the issuance trend had reversed, with fixed-dividend issues accounting for 60% of issuance. Exhibit 15–1 shows the new issue nonconvertible preferred stock financing volume by dividend type for 1982 through 1992.

The second major structural change of the 1980s has been the shift in the industrial classification of the issuers. Historically, utility companies have been the largest issuers of preferred stock. Prior to 1982, electric, gas, water, and telephone companies accounted for well over half of any one year's volume, and, in some cases, nearly all. However, in 1982 the pattern changed, as less than 44% of the dollar volume came from utility issuers. Because of the lower financing needs of utilities, issuance fell off on an absolute and relative basis. In 1985, utility preferred stock issuance amounted to $655 million, or only 10% out of some $6.5 billion of preferred offerings. In 1987, utility volume was 29% of the total, and in 1992 only 22%.

Of the more than $81 billion raised in the nonconvertible public preferred market during the 1982 to 1992 period, some 62% was from financially oriented companies—banks, thrifts, finance and insurance companies, and investment funds. A number of these were structured, asset-related transactions of special purpose, bulletproof, bankruptcy remote issuer subsidiaries of thrift institutions. This type of issuer was new to the 1980s. In that 11-year period, utilities accounted for 21.3%, and industrial companies a little more than 17%. Exhibit 15–2 shows the financing volume by industry type in the 1982 to 1992 period.

In October 1990, Merrill Lynch's fixed income research reported that the public nonconvertible preferred stock market consisted, in round numbers, of some 1,038 fixed-dividend issues with a par value of $30.3 billion. To this we can add about 360 or so variable-rate issues with a par value of approximately $28 billion. In total, the preferred market approximated 1,400 issues with a par

**EXHIBIT 15-1**

Nonconvertible Preferred Stock Financing Volume by Dividend Type, 1982–1992

| Type of Issue | Total[a] | 1992 | 1991 | 1990 | 1989 | 1988 | 1987 | 1986 | 1985 | 1984 | 1983 | 1982 |
|---|---|---|---|---|---|---|---|---|---|---|---|---|
| Fixed dividend | $33,587.57 | $11,429.70 | $3,295.80 | $3,416.00 | $3,719.60 | $1,122.50 | $2,896.50 | $2,259.63 | $1,066.60 | $463.00 | $1,609.50 | $2,308.74 |
| Number of issues | 368 | 88 | 27 | 28 | 26 | 18 | 41 | 36 | 10 | 11 | 33 | 50 |
| Variable dividend | $48,037.40 | $3,989.00 | $6,740.20 | $1,366.60 | $2,480.20 | $5,977.96 | $5,325.56 | $6,292.50 | $5,483.34 | $3,182.89 | $4,375.94 | $2,823.21 |
| Number of issues | 551 | 36 | 52 | 19 | 21 | 82 | 71 | 83 | 75 | 40 | 48 | 24 |
| Total volume | $81,624.97 | $15,418.70 | $10,036.00 | $4,782.60 | $6,199.80 | $7,100.46 | $8,222.06 | $8,552.13 | $6,549.94 | $3,645.89 | $5,985.44 | $5,131.95 |
| Number of issues | 919 | 124 | 79 | 47 | 47 | 100 | 112 | 119 | 85 | 51 | 81 | 74 |

[a] Dollar figures are in millions.

**EXHIBIT 15-2**

Nonconvertible Preferred Stock Financing Volume by Industry Type, 1982–1992

| Industry Type | Total[a] | 1992 | 1991 | 1990 | 1989 | 1988 | 1987 | 1986 | 1985 | 1984 | 1983 | 1982 |
|---|---|---|---|---|---|---|---|---|---|---|---|---|
| Bank and financial | $41,110.46 | $5,476.90 | $4,317.30 | $1,641.60 | $2,993.80 | $3,999.96 | $4,989.06 | $5,717.50 | $4,258.84 | $2,185.06 | $3,132.23 | $2,398.21 |
| # of issues | 409 | 31 | 28 | 14 | 21 | 49 | 62 | 73 | 54 | 26 | 32 | 19 |
| Investment companies | $9,151.40 | $2,204.00 | $2,995.80 | $1,365.00 | $1,254.60 | $1,332.00 | | | | | | |
| # of issues | 88 | 24 | 25 | 12 | 7 | 20 | | | | | | |
| Utilities | $17,378.28 | $3,353.00 | $1,347.90 | $950.00 | $985.00 | $763.50 | $2,408.00 | $1,649.60 | $655.00 | $1,019.29 | $2,003.25 | $2,243.74 |
| # of issues | 319 | 54 | 23 | 16 | 11 | 16 | 42 | 32 | 13 | 21 | 42 | 49 |
| Industrials and transportation | $13,984.83 | $4,384.80 | $1,375.00 | $826.00 | $966.40 | $1,005.00 | $825.00 | $1,185.03 | $1,636.10 | $441.54 | $849.96 | $490.00 |
| # of issues | 103 | 15 | 3 | 5 | 8 | 15 | 8 | 14 | 18 | 4 | 7 | 6 |
| Total volume | $81,624.97 | $15,418.70 | $10,036.00 | $4,782.60 | $6,199.80 | $7,100.46 | $8,222.06 | $8,552.13 | $6,549.94 | $3,645.89 | $5,985.44 | $5,131.95 |
| # of issues | 919 | 124 | 79 | 47 | 47 | 100 | 112 | 119 | 85 | 51 | 81 | 74 |

[a] Dollar figures are in millions.

value around $58 billion. In comparison, the Federal Reserve System reported that the amount of U.S. corporate bonds outstanding at the end of 1990 was $1.3 trillion. U.S. Treasury debt at the same time was $2.5 trillion. Thus, the preferred market is "small change" when compared to the considerably larger bond markets.

## PREFERRED-STOCK RATINGS

A preferred-stock rating is an indicator or assessment of the issuer's ability to meet the terms of the issue, including dividend payments and sinking-fund requirements, if any, in accordance with the appropriate legal document authorizing such shares. These documents include the certificate of incorporation, the certificate of designation, or the charter, among others. Preferred-stock ratings are issued by three nationally recognized statistical rating organizations (NRSROs). The three NRSROs are Moody's Investors Service, Inc., Standard & Poor's Ratings Group, and Fitch. These are agencies whose ratings are generally accepted by the vast majority of investment professionals and by regulatory authorities.

Rating agencies help to bridge the gap between issuers and investors by issuing preferred-stock quality rating opinions. Because of their independent and unbiased nature, ratings are used by market participants as a factor in the valuation of securities and the assessment of the risk of the particular issue. Investors should be cautioned that although some agencies' preferred-stock ratings may have symbols similar to their debt-rating symbols, preferred ratings should be viewed within the universe of preferred equity, separate and distinct from debt.

Ratings are defined by these firms in their various publications. Investors are urged to read these definitions. It should be remembered they are not "buy," "hold," or "sell" indicators. They do not state whether or not an issue is "cheap" or "dear" among the multitude of preferred issues. They do not point to the direction of the market. Although only a guide to the issuer's ability and willingness to meet the terms of the issue, they are a most important factor in the preferred-stock investment decision.

## THE TERMS OF THE BARGAIN WITH INVESTORS

The agreement or authorizing document between a corporate issuer and the preferred shareowners has numerous provisions governing the rights and duties of the two parties. Similar to a bond indenture, the preferred-stock document sets forth the terms and dividend preferences, redemption and sinking-fund provisions, and rights in liquidation, among other things.

## Preferred-Stock Terms and Features

The chief difference between preferred and common stock lies with the treatment of dividends. Preferred-stock dividends either are fixed rate or variable rate. As mentioned before, the total public preferred market is now about evenly divided between fixed-rate and variable-rate issues. Fixed-rate preferred stock is entitled to dividends at a predetermined rate based on the par value, stated value, or fixed dollar amount per share annually before any dividend can be paid on the issuer's common stock. For example, such dividend may be stated as $2.50 per share ($25.00 par or stated value) or 10.00% based on some predetermined value. In the latter case, if the par value were $25.00, the annual dividend would amount to $2.50 per share; if the par value were $50.00 per share, the annual dividend would be $5.00; and if the par value were $100.00 per share, the annual dividend would be $10.00. Dividends on fixed-rate shares are normally paid quarterly, although there are a few issues with semiannual dividend payments. The amount of the dividend on straight preferred stock is ordinarily limited to that fixed amount or rate of dividend stated in the description of the issue. It is as though the preferred stockholders say to the common stockholders, "Let us have dividends up to the stipulated amount per share before you receive dividends, and, regardless of whether you receive them, we will agree that our dividends shall be limited to the stipulated amount per share. You common shareholders can have dividends in an amount limited only by the financial ability of the company to pay them."

Most fixed-rate shares pay their dividends in cash. However, in the speculative 1980s there appeared preferreds paying dividends in kind. They are known as *PIKs*. This printing-press paper dividend is a device used by weak companies to conserve their limited cash resources to pay higher-ranked security holders. Although some advocates say that PIKs resemble compounding instruments shares—issued on shares—compounding can work in reverse. After all, if the issuer doesn't succeed, the investor will take a greater loss without having received any cash. True, the PIK dividends can be sold, but this is certainly not the same as a cash dividend. Taxable investors also have to pay income taxes on these paper dividends. If the issuer succeeds, the shares get called and the promoters get the gravy. Also, the number of shares received as dividends is calculated on the par or stated value, not the market value of the preferred. If the preferred shares decline in price, the dividend will be worth less. If this were a cash dividend–paying security and the market for the shares declined, an investor, having confidence in the outlook for the company, would at least be able to reinvest the dividends at the reduced market price for a greater number of shares. In the opinion of many observers, investors in speculative-grade securities would do better receiving a cash return, not funny money.

In contrast to fixed-dividend preferreds, there are adjustable-rate preferred stocks (ARPS). In general, these issues have dividends that are adjusted or reset quarterly at a fixed spread (dividend reset spread) above, at, or below the highest of three points on the Treasury yield curve. These benchmark rates are (1) the per annum market discount rate for three-month Treasury bills, (2) the 10-year Treasury constant maturity, and (3) the 20-year or 30-year Treasury constant maturity (TCM), as the case may be. The Treasury constant maturity yields are calculated by the Federal Reserve and relate the yield on a government bond to its maturity. This dividend-setting structure has an advantage as it is not tied to either a short-term or long-term rate. A fixing based on only one rate could prove to be a disadvantage when the shape or slope of the yield curve changes. Most of the dividends are subject to minimum levels called *collars.* The maximum rate is the cap and the minimum rate is the floor.

ARPS are neither money market instruments nor substitutes for short-dated securities. They possess more of the characteristics of equities than of debt. They do not enjoy the "magical drawing power," or "magnetism," of an approaching maturity as is the case with floating-rate debt. Preferred-stock investors needing an investment in a money market type of equity are advised to turn to remarketed preferred stock or auction market preferred, described below.

Some market participants might be under the impression that ARPS should trade around the par level at the dividend adjustment date, no matter what the direction of interest rates is. However, it should be remembered that the dividend determination spreads were set in place when the shares were first issued. Interest-rate levels, the creditworthiness of the issuer, and/or the tax laws could change, with the result that investors may demand a different relationship to the base rate. Securities do not trade in a vacuum but in the marketplace, which constantly scrutinizes relative values. Values are placed on securities, taking into account many factors, including the terms of the particular issue, other alternative investments, market conditions, and investors' perceptions of quality and liquidity, among others.

Auction preferred stock (*APS*), an offshoot of adjustable-rate preferred stock, was first publicly issued in 1984, when the American Express Company offered $150 million of Money Market Preferred Stock (*MMP*). This evolution in the preferred market has been warmly received by market participants. Investment bankers have given proprietary names and acronyms to the many issue varieties. The instrument is designed for corporate cash managers seeking tax-advantaged money market type income. Most of the shares or units of trading are priced at $100,000. A few issues even have shares with stated values as high as $500,000 or even $1 million each. The dividends, most of which are payable every seven weeks (there are some exceptions) and determined by auction bids from current holders and potential buyers, are reflective of current money market conditions (both taxable and tax-exempt) and perceived credit risks.

In addition to auction preferred shares, there are remarketed preferred stocks (RP), which have the dividend rate determined by a remarketing agent. The dividend is set at a rate designed to enable the agent to remarket all of the tendered shares at the original offering price. The remarketed preferred offers the holder the choice of dividend resets and payments every seven days or every

49 days. In some cases, other dividend periods may also be offered. The port-folio manager of "temporarily" idle corporate funds should find these auction and re-marketed issues attractive alternatives to money market debt instruments, including short-term tax-exempts and other types of preferred stocks.

The more frequent dividend-setting mechanism of APS and RP shares, along with the fact that the rate is determined through an auction or remarketing process as opposed to being fixed at a predetermined spread from a base rate, as is the case with adjustable-rate preferreds, allows the dividends (subject to certain minimum and maximum rates) to be based on the current credit standing and perceptions of the issuer as well as conditions in the marketplace. Thus, the price of auction and remarketed preferred shares does not normally fluctuate, as all purchases and sales conducted through the auction or remarketing are at the original issue price. Therefore, an important difference between ARPS and APS/RP stock involves principal protection. ARPS do not provide it, whereas APS/RPs do. The latter issues are designed so that the issuer, not the investor, gen-erally bears the credit risk as well as the risks associated with supply imbalances.

## Nonparticipating Preferred Stock

Almost all preferred stocks in today's public market are nonparticipating. This means that the owners of preferred are entitled to no more than the rate or amount of dividend stipulated in the legal provisions describing the class of stock. A company may become very profitable and realize earnings many times the amounts necessary to pay the regular preferred dividend. However, this does preferred stockholders little good except perhaps to boost the rating for the shares. The big earnings over and above those needed for preferred dividends go to the common stockholders to be reinvested in the firm or to be distributed as common dividends.

In the history of preferreds, there have been instances of participating preferred stocks. The terms have varied, but the general idea may be illustrated by a single provision: After the preferred has received its stipulated dividend and the common has received the same amount of dividend per share as the preferred, funds remaining available for dividend payments are distributed in equal amounts per share between both the common and preferred stocks. From the standpoint of corporate management, such an arrangement is too good for preferred stock because it permits preferred stockholders to have their cake and eat it, too. Their cake is the preference to dividends; the eating of it is partici-pation with common in larger dividends per share.

## Cumulative Preferred Stock

A lopsided deal in favor of corporate management is noncumulative preferred stock. The language would say, in effect, "If the issuer does not pay the preferred dividend in any dividend period, you just forget about it because you are not going to get paid." That would be a very weak preference because management could skip a dividend payment at its discretion. In our financial history, there have been few noncumulative preferred stocks of this type, and most of these have probably been the result of corporate reorganizations.

An example of noncumulative preferred stock was Wabash Railway's 5% Series A shares. Between 1915 and 1926, no dividends (or less than the stated amount) were paid even though earnings were available for payment at times. The company reinvested earnings in plant and equipment. When the Board of Directors later wanted to pay dividends on the Series B preferred and the common shares, the Series A holders brought legal action to obtain back and unpaid dividends, as they were earned even though not paid. In 1930, the Supreme Court decided in favor of the company, holding that, as the earnings were reinvested in plant and equipment and as no dividends were declared, the preferred holders had no right to receive a share of the earnings. Some state statutes (New Jersey for one) provide that preferred dividends are cumulative if there are earnings and no dividends are declared.

There have been a few more issues of noncumulative preferreds where the dividends are paid *only* if earned; if the company records a loss for a year, the dividend is not paid and it is not made up or left to accumulate for payment in future years. The right to the dividend is gone forever and the company has no obligation to make future payment. These are known as *cumulative-to-the-extent-earned* preferreds.

However, although there have been few noncumulative preferreds, they reappeared in 1988 when The Bank of New York Company, Inc., issued a couple of series of fixed/adjustable-rate noncumulative preferreds. Investors thought this relic of the past had gone the way of the dodo bird, but someone saw the need for it. *Barron's* financial weekly, in its April 18, 1988, issue, refers to this type of preferred as "a relic of the horse-and-buggy era, a device of the robber barons." These preferred shares are contingently convertible into common stock with a market value equal to the preferreds' stated value in the event of a dividend omission or a downgrading below investment grade. However, this contingent conversion feature doesn't provide full principal protection, as there is a maximum number of common shares that can be issued for each preferred share. If the common gets low enough in price, the preferred shareholder could take a hit. Of course, the pricing of the shares theoretically takes into account the noncumulative and contingent conversion features, at least at the initial offering.

One must be wary and make sure to read prospectuses for the correct basic data since some electronic news and security information display screens may not have complete information. Even though the issuer may be highly rated, that is not sufficient reason for an investor to let his or her guard down. Highly rated companies have been known to fall from their lofty status. Federal National Mortgage Association issued "aa3" preferred stock in April 1996. This Series

B, 6.50%, $50 stated value stock is noncumulative. Even if the dividend is earned, it doesn't have to be paid. Page 10 of the offering circular states, "Dividends on shares of the Preferred Stock will not be mandatory. Holders of record of Preferred Stock . . . will be entitled to receive, when, as, and if declared by the Board of Directors of the Corporation . . . in its sole discretion out of funds legally available therefore, non-cumulative, quarterly cash dividends which will accrue. . . ."

*Cumulative* means that when a preferred dividend is not paid (whether or not earned) it accumulates, and no dividend may be paid on shares ranking on a parity with or junior to the preferred until all dividend arrearages have been paid on the particular preferred issue. The prohibition of dividend payments on common stock when dividends on preferred stock are in arrears is a serious restriction. Common stockholders like their dividends, and when common dividends are stopped and cannot be resumed until preferred dividend arrearages are paid, they can direct some very sharp questions to management. This dissatisfaction is also expressed in the stock market by lower share prices.

Usually failure to pay preferred dividends results in other financial restrictions on management. It is common to provide that while preferred dividends are in arrears the issuer may not redeem any shares of stock junior to the preferred. Generally, the terms of preferred stocks also provide that when dividends are in arrears, sinking-fund payments on the preferred and on any junior preferred are suspended and no money may be used to redeem preferred or common stock. The company may not purchase any shares of the preferred except through a purchase offer made to all preferred shareholders. Consumers Power Company is an exception because its corporate charter does not contain any restrictions on the repurchase or redemption of its preferred and preference shares while there are arrearages of dividends on such stock.

A thorough study of a preferred stock includes an examination of the terms of any bond issues and bank loans of the issuer and of any class of preferred senior to the one being studied. Sometimes these senior securities have provisions prohibiting payment of dividends on junior securities when the issuer's financial condition falls below standards set in these agreements, such as a minimum current ratio or a minimum amount of surplus available for the payment of dividends. In 1984, Long Island Lighting Company, as part of its revolving credit agreement with 14 banks, agreed to suspend the declaration of preferred stock dividends payable on and after October 1, 1984. Dividends were resumed in 1989 after reaching agreement with the authorities over rate matters and the disposition of the politically sensitive Shoreham nuclear generating plant.

In early 1985, the LTV Corporation sought approval from the holders of its 5% subordinated debentures due January 15, 1988, to the declaration and payment of regular quarterly cash dividends to January 15, 1988, on its preferred stock then outstanding or to be outstanding. The indenture under which the debentures were issued prohibited the payment of dividends and certain other distributions to the aggregate of $15 million plus LTV's accumulated net income subsequent to December 31, 1966. Because of asset write-downs, losses, and expected losses, there would be a deficiency in retained earnings under this provision, which would preclude the payment of dividends. Declaration of dividends due for payment in the first quarter of 1985 was deferred.

In the proxy statement sent to debentureholders, the Company stated the following:

> The Board of Directors and management of the Company strongly recommend that Debentureholders give their approval [to pay cash dividends on the preferred stock]. The Company believes that such approval is in the best interests of Debentureholders and the Company because it would enhance the Company's ability to refinance existing debt and raise additional capital in the market place. The ability to pay preferred dividends will also enhance the Company's ability to issue additional preferred stock instead of debt, which, under certain circumstances, may be more beneficial to both the Company and its debentureholders.

On February 6, 1985, the debentureholders approved the company's request and received a payment of $2.50 per $100 principal amount of debentures outstanding. Preferred dividends were declared on February 7 for payment on March 1; regular declaration and payments continued thereafter on the normal quarterly schedule until they were again omitted in the fall of the year. In July 1986, LTV sought protection from creditors under Chapter 11 of the bankruptcy laws.

## Preference to Assets

At the time a preferred stock is issued, hardly anyone thinks about the possibility that the issuing corporation may be liquidated or reorganized, except perhaps the lawyers who draw up the terms of security issues. They write in provisions about what happens to a preferred stock in the event the issuer is liquidated either voluntarily or involuntarily in financial failure. A simple preference is that after settlement has been made with creditors, the preferred stockholders are entitled to receive the par, stated, or liquidation value of the preferred before any distribution is made to common stock or to any junior preferred issue. In the case of stock without par value, an amount per share is stipulated. In addition, an amount equal to all accumulated and unpaid dividends to the date of liquidation must also be paid. Sometimes preferred holders are entitled to a larger amount in voluntary liquidation than in involuntary liquidation.

For example, Jersey Central Power & Light Company's 7.52% Series K cumulative preferred has an involuntary liquidation value of $100 per share and a voluntary liquidation value of the amount equal to the optional redemption price applicable at the time of liquidation. In the case of Consumers Power Company's $7.76 preference stock, the involuntary liquidation value is $100 per share and the voluntary liquidation value $101.43 a share (the initial offering price).

There are some issues that may participate with the common stock in the event of liquidation. Public Service Electric & Gas Company had a $1.40 cumulative dividend preference common entitling the holder to receive, upon the company's liquidation, twice the amount per share distributed on each share of common. Holders of Southern California Edison's 5% original cumulative participating preferred stock, par value $8⅓, were entitled to the par value in the event of liquidation before payment on preferred, preference, or common stock. It was also entitled to participate with the common stock in any balance remaining after the preferred and preference shares have been paid in full (including dividends) and par ($4⅙) had been paid on the common. Finally, Southern California Gas Co. has an issue of 6%, $25 par value preferred with asset participation rights. In liquidation or dissolution of the company, holders of the outstanding preferred stock would be entitled to receive no more than the par value for their shares and any accrued dividends. However, the subject preferred will receive the $25 par value and accrued and unpaid dividends; then it shall participate on a pro rata basis with the common in the remaining assets after the par value has been paid on the common.

Seldom are corporations voluntarily liquidated, but City Investing Company is one such exception. On June 28, 1985, it called for redemption at the liquidation values plus accrued dividends three series of publicly issued convertible preference stock. Two of the issues were converted by their holders into common shares, as the conversion values were substantially in excess of the redemption price. However, holders of the third issue—$2.875 convertible/exchangeable preference series E—turned their shares in for the $25 redemption price because the conversion worth was only about $17.50 a share.

Wickes Companies and its subsidiary, Gamble-Skogmo, Inc., emerged from reorganization in early 1985. Wickes $8.75 Series A preferred, $100 par value, received 7.459 shares of the new company's common stock. The new common shares were worth $3.53125 per share, or a total of $26.34 per share of old preferred. Gamble-Skogmo's $1.75 preferred ($40 par value) received 4.321 shares of the new Wickes common, and the $1.60 preferred ($35 par value) received 3.779 shares. The total market values of these two distributions were $15.26 and $13.34 a share, respectively. If the company had liquidated instead of reorganizing, the distribution to all security holders probably would have been smaller.

Another example of a distribution to preferred holders of a company coming out of bankruptcy proceedings is Itel Corporation. Itel had an issue of $1.44 preferred with a liquidation price of $15.00 per share. Each 100 shares of preferred (total liquidation value of $1,500) received 38.7 shares of common stock of the newly reorganized company. With the new common initially valued at $7.25 a share, the holder received $280.58 worth of stock, or about 18.70% of the claim.

# Voting Rights

Preferred-stock issuers are inclined toward the view that as long as preferred shareholders receive their dividends regularly, there is no need for them to have voting rights. Generally, preferred shares do not carry standard voting privileges, but in some cases each preferred share has the same voting rights as the common equity. Southern California Edison's preferred issues have varying degrees of voting power. Shares of cumulative preferred stock are entitled to six votes per share, whereas the $100 cumulative preferred has two votes per share. All of these votes may be cumulative in electing directors.

However, when preferred dividends have been in arrears for a certain period (usually four or six dividend payments), it is common practice to give nonvoting stock the right to elect some number of directors. This is *contingent voting stock;* the voting right is contingent upon the preferred stockholders' lack of dividends. In some cases, the preferred class may elect only two directors (e.g., Southern California Edison); in other cases, they may elect a majority of the board. Thus, preferred holders are assured of representation on the board of a company experiencing financial difficulties. This kind of provision has become common because the New York Stock Exchange requires it as a condition for listing nonvoting preferred stocks. Another kind of contingent voting provision gives preferred stockholders one vote per share, the same as common stock, when dividends are in arrears. When arrears of dividends on contingent voting stock have been paid or settled, the conditional voting right ceases. In 1985, preferred holders elected members to the Board of Directors of Eastern Air Lines and Public Service Company of New Hampshire. In Eastern's case, they elected two members of the Board. In the case of Public Service Company of New Hampshire, the preferred stockholders, voting as a class, elected seven members to serve on the Board, while the common shareholders elected six.

The terms of some preferreds state that certain corporate acts must be approved by preferred shareholders voting as a class whenever dividends have been in arrears for some period of time. For example, agreement by two-thirds of the preferred stock voting as a class may be required for approval of such management proposals as (1) increasing the authorized amount of any class or series of stock that ranks ahead of the preferred as to dividends or as to assets upon liquidation, (2) altering the provisions of the issuer's articles of incorporation, or (3) merging or consolidating with another company in such manner as to adversely affect the rights and preferences of the preferred stock. Preferred stock with such a provision is called *vetoing stock* because it can veto action proposed by management. The power to veto ceases when dividend arrears are paid.

# Redemption Provisions

Circumstances often change while a preferred stock is outstanding, and a time may come when an issuer finds it desirable to eliminate the shares from its capitalization. Preferred-stock voting rights might present an obstacle for control of a corporation by its common shareholders. Or it may become economical to refund a preferred stock with bonds to increase earnings for the common stock. Interest is a deductible expense in calculating corporate income subject to income taxes, but preferred dividends are not. Such a refunding would change a nondeductible expense (preferred dividends) to a tax-deductible expense (bond interest). Or an issuer might want to restructure its capitalization. In 1985, Pacificorp and Atlantic Richfield Co. redeemed preferreds for these reasons. The most important reason for a senior security to be redeemed is that financing costs have declined, thereby making it possible for the issuing company to save money through the replacement of high-cost issues with lower-cost issues. Virtually all issuers of preferred stock make provisions for (1) periodic redemption by a sinking fund, (2) redemption of stock in whole or in part by call, or (3) conversion into common stock.

Preferreds without any redemption provisions are quite rare. These are truly perpetual issues because there is no way other than through reorganization that the issuer can retire the stock against the will of the owner. Of course, it could make open market purchases or ask for tenders of the shares, but the stock cannot be involuntarily lost by the investor. There are a few other issues that do not appear to be callable, but they contain sinking-fund features providing for the periodic retirement of the shares.

Nearly all preferreds are redeemable in one way or another. A majority of the outstanding public issues are currently callable at any time, in whole or in part, at the option of the issuer and at preset prices plus accrued and unpaid dividends up to the call date. Generally, the initial call price is par or the offering price plus the annual dividend or rate. The call price is then reduced periodically to par or the initial offering price. For example, Duke Power Company's 7.12% Series Q preferred stock ($100 par value) is callable at $107.12 for its first five years through March 15, 1992, then at $104.75 for the next five years, then at $102.38 for the next five years, and finally at $100.00 on and after March 16, 2002. A few other issues have redemption schedules with call prices declining each year by generally equal amounts.

Most new issues provide some type of deferred call or redemption provision. Some might not be callable under any circumstance for the first 5 to 10 years, whereas others might be currently callable but protected against lower-cost refunding for a certain period. This is similar to provisions found in corporate debt issues. Noncallable is far more absolute than nonrefundable, and yet many investors are confused and treat refunding protection the same as call protection. This could prove to be costly.

Many currently callable issues cannot be called for a certain period if the company sells debt or equity securities ranking equal or superior to the preferred at a lower cost of capital than the outstanding preferred. This is refunding protection; it does not allow the issuer to take advantage of lower money costs on senior issues for a certain number of years following the initial public offering of the stock. However, if the issuer sells junior preferred or common equity prior to the expiration of the refunding protected period, the proceeds may be used to retire or refund the higher-cost preferred.

Commonwealth Edison Company issued 1 million shares of 9.44% cumulative prior preferred stock in June 1970. Less than two years later, it redeemed the shares at $110; just prior to the redemption announcement, the stock was trading at about $119 to $120 a share. The funds for the redemption came from the sale of common stock and common stock purchase warrants, clearly junior securities. The preferred prospectus stated the following:

> Prior to August 1, 1980, none of the shares . . . may be redeemed through refunding, directly or indirectly, by or in anticipation of the incurring of any debt or the issuance of any shares of the Prior Preferred Stock or of any other stock ranking prior to or on a parity with the Prior Preferred Stock, if such debt has an interest cost . . . or such shares have a dividend cost . . . less than the dividend cost . . . of the 9.44% . . . Stock.

The company was sued by some institutional holders, but the judge decided the redemption provision did not prohibit redemption directly out of an issue of common shares. Since then, other companies have done similar redemptions.

In the decision concerning the Florida Power & Light Company's maintenance and replacement fund redemption,[1] the judge stated that

> The terms "redemption" and "refunding" are not synonymous. A "redemption" is simply a call of bonds. A "refunding" occurs when the issuer sells bonds in order to use the proceeds to redeem an earlier issue of bonds . . . The refunding bond issue being sold is closely linked to the one being redeemed by contractual language and proximity in time so that the proceeds will be available to pay for the redemption. Otherwise, the issuer would be taking an inordinate risk that market conditions would change between the redemption of the earlier issue and the sale of the later issue.

This principle can also be applied to preferred stock redemptions.

Sinking-fund provisions for preferred stocks are similar to those of bonds. They provide for the periodic retirement of stock, usually on an annual basis. Often commencing on or after the call or refunding protected period has expired, there are instances where the sinking fund operates before such expiration. A specific number of shares or a certain percentage of the original issue is specified for retirement periodically. Often it will amount to about 2 to 8% of the original number of shares, with 5% being the more common requirement. Commonwealth Edison had an issue of $10.875 preference stock that required all of the shares to be retired at one time at par through the sinking fund on November

---

1. *Lucas et al.* v. *Florida Power & Light Company,* Final Judgement, 77-4009-CIV-SMA, United States District Court, Southern District of Florida, October 31, 1983.

1, 1989, the date the call-protected period terminated. Thus, this issue had another feature that most bonds have—that is, a maturity of sorts. Most sinking funds have provisions allowing the issuer the noncumulative option to increase payments (usually to double the amount at any one time). Sinking-fund payments may be made in shares of stock purchased in the open market or by the call of the required number of shares at the sinking-fund call price, normally par or stated value. There are instances in which a company wishing to retire an entire issue of sinking-fund preferred will call the maximum number of shares allowed for the sinking fund at the lower sinking-fund redemption price and redeem the balance at the normal call price. Failure to make sinking-fund payments is not an act of default, as it would be in the case of debt; the company cannot be placed in bankruptcy.

Many preferred stock market participants refer to issues without sinking funds as perpetual preferreds, but this is a misuse of that term. Non-sinking-fund issues need not be perpetual, yet they do not have a date at which they must be retired. Sinking-fund operations can provide some measure of market support if the issuer can come into the open market and purchase stock at less than the redemption price. However, in periods of lower interest and dividend rates and higher preferred prices, a call below market prices can result in capital losses to investors. Shares to be redeemed for the sinking fund are usually selected randomly by lot and not pro rata, or in proportion, to one's holdings.

An important consideration for insurance companies is a rule by the National Association of Insurance Commissioners allowing qualifying sinking-fund preferred stocks to be valued on the books at cost rather than to be marked to the current market price. This accounting or valuation treatment, at least for regulatory or reserve purposes, reduces the impact of market fluctuations on the company's portfolio to the extent that it utilizes sinking-fund preferreds.

Some preferred issues have purchase funds. These are, to some extent, optional on the part of an issuer because it will have to use its best efforts to retire a portion of the shares periodically if such shares can be purchased in the open market, or through tender, at less than the redemption or liquidation price. If the stock is selling above the applicable price, the purchase fund cannot be put into operation. Again, the purchase fund may provide some market support to the issue in a higher dividend rate environment, but when rates are lower it is inoperative. In the case of Occidental Petroleum's $15.50 cumulative preferred stock issued in connection with the acquisition of Cities Service Company in 1982, Occidental was required to use its best efforts to purchase shares in the open market at or below the liquidation value with the proceeds derived from certain asset sales in excess of $100 million. Any shares so purchased would then be credited against any sinking-fund payments when the sinking fund became operational.

It is important to read prospectuses carefully. Although preferreds are not bonded securities, unlike mortgage debt with its release and substitution-of-property clauses, there have been instances of preferred stock retirement prior to the end of the refunding protected period because of asset sales. A case in point is Crown Zellerbach Corporation's $3.05 cumulative preferred stock, Series B, issued May 19, 1982, at $20 per share. It was protected against refunding before April 15, 1987, and had the normal call schedule starting immediately at $23.05 and declining to $20 a share in 1997. However, it also had a special provision for its retirement prior to April 15, 1997, if the company sold certain assets aggregating at least $100 million in any 12-month period. The redemption premium under this circumstance was one-half the regular redemption premium. It started at $21.52 per share and declined to $20 in 1997. On May 20, 1983, Crown Zellerbach redeemed this stock at the special redemption price of $21.42 a share; the regular call price at that time was $22.85. The proceeds came from the sale of its interests in Crown Zellerbach Canada Ltd. and a small steamship company. In late October 1982, it announced it had a preliminary agreement for the sale of these assets; the use of the proceeds for share redemption should not have come as any surprise to the preferred holders. The shares sold at $21\frac{7}{8}$ at the end of December and rose as high as $23\frac{7}{8}$ in 1983 before the retirement of the stock.

## MULTIPLE ISSUES OF ONE CLASS OF PREFERRED

Some companies may have multiple classes of preferred stock. The terms of the two or more classes are determined separately at the times of their respective issuance. When there is more than one class, investors may wonder which stock is senior to another in claim to dividends, and assets upon liquidation. A senior preferred may receive dividends whereas a junior preferred does not. Other rights and limitations of the two or more classes of preferred may differ. Generally speaking, preferred shares are senior to preference shares. Some companies have only one class of senior equity outstanding, whereas others might have two classes with different priorities. Consolidated Edison has only preferred shares, whereas Consumers Power and a number of other utilities have preferred and preference shares.

Companies using preferred stocks in their capitalizations usually authorize a class of preferred stock with a defined preference as to dividends. This class may be issued in series from time to time; there may be Series A, Series B, and so on, with each series of the same class ranking equally with each other as to dividend preference. It is not uncommon for public utility companies to have six, eight, or more series of one class of preferred outstanding. One series may have one stipulated rate of dividends and another series a different rate. For example, on December 31, 1994, the Southern Company, an electric utility holding company, listed 54 different issues of subsidiary preferred stocks in its annual report. The 50 fixed-dividend preferred issues had $25 par and stated values and $100 par and stated values with dividends ranging from 4.20% to 11.36%. There were also two adjustable rate and two auction rate series. The total outstanding par and stated values was $1.43 billion.

Just as with bonds, the other terms of a class of preferred stock may differ among the series. One series may be voting and another nonvoting. The terms for sinking-fund redemption and for redemption in whole or in part may vary. One series may be convertible and another not. Each series is tailored to conditions in the securities markets at the time of issue.

In the early 1970s, electric utility companies made increased use of preference stock. Some companies were unable to issue preferred shares because of restrictions contained in their preferred-stock agreements or articles of incorporation; they simply could not meet the required earnings tests for issuance of additional preferred stock. As there are usually no similar restrictions on the issuance of shares junior to the preferred, classes of preference shares were authorized and issued. Also, many corporate charters restricted preferred share to $100 par or stated value. To broaden the market for their stock, some utilities offered preference stock with lower par values, such as $10, $20, and $25. The lower prices appealed to many individual and less sophisticated investors because they could buy round lots of 100 shares each instead of odd lots of one to 99 shares. Although primarily of psychological value only to the small investor (100 shares at $25 is the same as 25 shares at $100 each), this allowed companies to take advantage of a pool of capital that was previously not too interested in preferred stocks.

Another device used by some issuers to bring the price of their shares down to a level at which individual investors would buy them is the depositary preferred share. The depositary share represents a fractional interest in a whole preferred share that has been deposited with a bank under legal depositary agreements. It entitles the holder proportionately to all of the rights and preferences of the underlying preferred stock. For example, in 1992 the Bank of New York Company issued 4 million depositary shares at $25 each representing a one-twenty-fifth interest in a share of 8.60% Cumulative Preferred Stock ($6.25 per share stated value). In 1985, Harnischfeger Corporation issued 3 million shares of Series B $3.402 depositary preferred shares at $25.00 a share. Each represented a one-fiftieth ownership in the Series B sinking-fund exchangeable preferred stock (60,000 shares deposited with the depositary bank). The company used this financing method because it did not have enough authorized shares of preferred stock to permit a broad distribution. Only 132,500 shares of authorized but unissued stock were available.

## TAXABILITY OF PREFERRED STOCK DIVIDENDS

Tax laws should always be considered when making investment decisions, and preferred stock is no different. Currently a corporation may exclude from gross income 70% of the qualified dividends received from other *domestic* corporations subject to federal income taxes. It does not matter whether the dividends are from preferred, preference, or common stock. This exclusion is justified on the ground that it mitigates double taxation of dividends paid by one company to another and then paid to the stockholders of the second company. Dividends by one company are paid after its earnings have been taxed under the federal corporate income tax. Then when received by a second company they would be taxed again as income to that company. This 70% exclusion, or dividends-received deduction (DRD), leaves only 30% to be taxed in the hands of a corporate owner of preferred stock. This rule applies only to preferreds of banks, utility holding companies, railroads, and industrial and financial concerns. Dividends from registered investment companies are treated differently, depending on the source of the income used to pay dividends. Closed-end investment companies with portfolios of tax-exempt municipal and state bonds receive tax-exempt interest income, and that tax exemption is passed along with the dividends paid on these shares. Because of this tax-exempt status, there is no dividend-received deduction and no minimum holding period.

For utility operating companies, the deduction is applicable to "new money" issues—those preferreds sold after October 1, 1942, for purposes other than refunding. Preferreds sold before that date and those issued afterward for debt and preferred refunding purposes are "old money" issues, with the dividends-received deduction only 42%. At the end of 1992 there were approximately 100 to 125 utility old money issues and 25 or so "partly new money" issues out of nearly 1,000 fixed-dividend preferred-stock issues outstanding. Partly new money issues are those where only a portion of the proceeds were used for refunding purposes.

In order to qualify for the dividends-received deduction, a corporation must hold the preferred shares at least 46 days. Days on which the stock is held after the dividend is received, as well as before its receipt, are counted for purposes of this minimum holding period. The deduction is increased to 80% for investors holding at least 20% of a dividend-paying corporation (by the dividend payer's voting power and value). For "debt-financed portfolio stock," the dividends-received deduction must be reduced by the percentage related to the amount of debt incurred to purchase the stock.

The effective tax rate on dividends for qualified investors in the 35% marginal corporate tax bracket and a 70% dividends-received deduction is 10.5% (.30 × .35). Taxes are paid on only 30% of the dividends, with the investor keeping 89.5% of the dividend. Exhibit 15–3 summarizes the intercorporate dividends-received deduction for new money and old money stock for corporations in the 35% tax bracket.

Exhibit 15–4 shows the pretax and the after-tax yields at the 35% corporate tax rate for preferred stocks and fully taxable alternative investments such as commercial paper, certificates of deposit, and corporate debts, as well as the pretax yields needed on alternative fully taxable investments in order to equal the preferred's after-tax return. Thus, a preferred with a dividend of 8.00% will provide an after-tax yield of 7.16% under current tax rates and the new money dividends-received deduction. In order to equal these yields, a fully taxable

**EXHIBIT  15–3**

Summary of Intercorporate Dividends-Received Deduction

|                          | New Money  | Old Money   |
|--------------------------|------------|-------------|
| Dividends received       | $1,000.00  | $11,000.00  |
| Dividend exclusion:      |            |             |
|   Percent      | 70.00%     | 42.00%      |
|   Amount       | $700.00    | $420.00     |
| Amount subject to taxes  | $300.00    | $580.00     |
| Marginal tax rate        | 35.00%     | 35.00%      |
| Taxes paid               | $105.00    | $203.00     |
| Effective tax rate       | 10.50%     | 20.30%      |
| Dividends retained:      |            |             |
|   Percent      | 89.50%     | 79.70%      |
|   Amount       | $895.00    | $797.00     |

investment must yield 11.02% (after-tax preferred yield divided by 1 minus the tax rate, or 7.16/.15). A fully taxable instrument with an 8.00% nominal rate yields only 5.20% to a corporate investor in the 35% tax bracket.

Yields on preferreds and most debt instruments are calculated using a day count basis of a 360-day year as the denominator and either the actual number of days or 30-day months as the numerator. When comparing after-tax yields with most other investments, the second column of Exhibit 15–4 is the appropriate one to use. However, some tax-exempt short-term instruments such as variable-rate demand obligations (VRDOs) and unit priced demand adjustable tax-exempt securities (UPDATES), have yields calculated on the basis of the actual number of days per month and actual number of days per year. This basis is called *actual/actual* and overstates the yield for comparison purposes. The auction market and remarketed preferred yields are understated in comparison to these short-term municipals. Therefore, adjustments have to be made to the auction preferred yield to put it on the same footing as the comparable short-term tax-exempt investment.

Instead of multiplying the nominal preferred yield by 89.5% to get the after-tax return, the preferred yield should be multiplied by 90.7% to get the adjusted after-tax basis equivalent for VRDO/UPDATES comparisons. The nominal preferred yield must be grossed up to account for the actual 365-day count instead of 360 days. Thus, an 8.00% dividend is multiplied by the fraction 365/360 resulting in 8 × 1.0139, or 8.1111. This adjusted pretax yield is then multiplied by 89.5 to obtain the adjusted after-tax yield, which in this case is 7.26%, or 90.7% of the 8% nominal rate. These adjusted after-tax yields are found in the table's third column of Exhibit 15–4.

**EXHIBIT 15-4**

Comparison of New Money Preferred and Other Yields

| | Preferred Stock After-Tax Yield Comparison to: | | | Pretax Yield Needed to Equal After-Tax Return on Preferred | |
|---|---|---|---|---|---|
| Nominal Yield | Taxable and Other Debt 30/360 | Short-Term Tax-Exempts Actual/ Actual | After-Tax Yield on a Fully Taxable Investment | Taxable Securities | Tax-Exempt Securities |
| 4.00% | 3.58% | 3.63% | 2.60% | 5.51% | 3.58% |
| 4.50 | 4.03 | 4.08 | 2.93 | 6.20 | 4.03 |
| 5.00 | 4.48 | 4.54 | 3.25 | 6.88 | 4.48 |
| 5.50 | 4.92 | 4.99 | 3.58 | 7.57 | 4.92 |
| 6.00 | 5.37 | 5.44 | 3.90 | 8.26 | 5.37 |
| 6.50 | 5.82 | 5.90 | 4.23 | 8.95 | 5.82 |
| 7.00 | 6.27 | 6.35 | 4.55 | 9.64 | 6.27 |
| 7.50 | 6.71 | 6.81 | 4.88 | 10.33 | 6.71 |
| 8.00 | 7.16 | 7.26 | 5.20 | 11.02 | 7.16 |
| 8.50 | 7.61 | 7.71 | 5.53 | 11.70 | 7.61 |
| 9.00 | 8.06 | 8.17 | 5.85 | 12.39 | 8.06 |
| 9.50 | 8.50 | 8.62 | 6.18 | 13.08 | 8.50 |
| 10.00 | 8.95 | 9.07 | 6.50 | 13.77 | 8.95 |
| 10.50 | 9.40 | 9.53 | 6.83 | 14.46 | 9.40 |
| 11.00 | 9.85 | 9.98 | 7.15 | 15.15 | 9.85 |
| 11.50 | 10.29 | 10.44 | 7.48 | 15.83 | 10.29 |
| 12.00 | 10.74 | 10.89 | 7.80 | 16.52 | 10.74 |

The breakeven or indifference level between preferreds and the pretax yield needed from a fully taxable instrument to match the preferred's net yield is 72.6%. As long as the preferred's pretax yield is greater than 72.6% of the required return from a fully taxable investment, the preferred shares are the more attractive. When it is less than the breakeven rate percent, the alternative investment will provide a greater yield.

Our discussion to this point has centered on corporations and the dividends-received deduction. Of interest is the issuance of *American Depositary Shares* (*ADS*), representing preference shares of British companies. Dividends paid by these companies to American shareholders, whether corporations or individuals, although not eligible for the dividends-received deduction, are considered dividends for federal income tax purposes. Under the income tax treaty between the United Kingdom and the United States, the dividend payments carry an imputed tax credit, which in 1992 equaled one-third of the nominal dividend. In the United Kingdom, it is called the advance corporation tax (ACT). Eligible corporate U.S. holders receive an effective after-tax equivalent of 87% of the nominal dividend as compared with 89.5% for qualified dividends subject to the DRD. Individual investors in the 28% tax bracket effectively keep 96% of the nominal dividend.

The ACT payment or imputed tax credit is designed to lessen the burden of double taxation on qualified holders. Exhibit 15–5 shows how the effective tax rates are calculated for dividends received from British corporations. The United Kingdom imposes a 15% withholding tax on the sum of the nominal dividend and the ACT.

## THE MARKET FOR PREFERREDS

Publicly distributed preferred stocks are marketable in the sense that they may be traded on the stock exchanges and in the over-the-counter market. There is usually a dealer or a stock exchange specialist willing to quote a bid price (what he or she will pay if you want to sell) and an offered price (what he or she will sell it for if you want to buy). But there are marked differences in the market-ability of preferred stocks, and these differences are important to investors who buy and sell these stocks.

Less than half of the publicly issued preferred shares are listed on the New York or the American Stock Exchanges; the rest trade in the over-the-counter market. This is similar to the situation with corporate bonds. The normal unit of trading is 100 shares on the major stock exchanges, but some issues trade in round lots of 10 shares. Investors who wish to buy or sell odd lots (i.e., less

**EXHIBIT 15–5**

Comparison of Dividends with Imputed Tax Credits Received from United Kingdom Corporations

|     | Marginal Tax Rate | Corporation 35% | Individual 28% |
|-----|-------------------|-----------------|----------------|
| (a) | Nominal dividend | $9.00 | $9.00 |
| (b) | Plus imputed tax credit (1/3 of nominal) | 3.00 | 3.00 |
| (c) | Total dividend and ACT credit | $12.00 | $12.00 |
| (d) | Less 15% U.K. withholding tax on (c) above | 1.80 | 1.80 |
| (e) | Dividend paid to eligible U.S. holder | $10.20 | $10.20 |
| (f) | Cash tax outlay to the IRS on (c) above (marginal income tax rate less tax credit for the 15% U.K. withholding tax) | 2.40 | 1.56 |
| (g) | Net after-tax dividend to U.S. holder | $7.80 | $8.64 |
| (h) | Effective tax-free dividend rate (g)/(a) | 86.7% | 96% |

than the standard unit of trading) may pay a fraction more or receive a fraction less per share than a round-lot transaction. These 10-share issues are indicated in the stock exchange transaction tables with the letter $z$ next to the trading volume.

Exchange listings generally improve an issue's marketability, but other factors include the size and the quality ratings. Larger unlisted issues might be more marketable and trade in greater volume than smaller listed issues. The better marketability of larger and higher-rated issues is attributed to the fact that many preferred investors are restricted to what they can hold in their portfolios. There are generally more buyers for shares with these characteristics, and trades can take place far more easily than for small and noninvestment-grade issues. The spread between the bid and the ask prices is often smaller for highly mar- ketable securities because the volume of trading is greater and the trader or specialist will usually have little trouble in selling the shares to a willing buyer at market prices close to the price at which the shares just previously traded. If it looks as though the trader would experience difficulty in quickly moving the shares, the bid price would likely be lower and the ask price would likely be higher.

## SOURCES OF INFORMATION ABOUT PREFERRED STOCKS

The best source of information about a specific preferred stock is the prospectus published at the time it is first issued. Prospectuses contain fairly complete information about the terms of the new preferred issues; however, in many cases (but not all), the information about the operations of the issuers leaves much to be desired. This is due to the shortened prospectus form used by many corpo- rations under the streamlined shelf-registration procedures introduced by the Securities and Exchange Commission in 1982.

Information about preferred stocks is available from many of the sources for common stocks and bonds. Manuals issued by financial publishers provide detailed information about corporate issuers and their securities. They are par- ticularly useful for information about the provisions of preferred stocks that we have examined here. They also publish monthly guides to senior securities, which contain condensed information about many preferred-stock issues. You can compare a number of preferreds quickly by using them. They provide in abbreviated form the ratings, issues, information about the principal terms, cur- rent and historical price data, and shares outstanding, among other things. Also, corporate annual reports will often contain valuable information. In addition, a number of investment brokers provide research about issuers and issues.

The major daily and weekly financial newspapers have stock tables that include trading and dividend data on common and preferred shares. *The New*

*York Times,* and *Investors Business Daily* are two newspapers that have a separate table for listed preferred stocks, quite a convenience for preferred-stock investors.

## SUMMARY

A preferred stock is a peculiar kind of security. It is senior to common stock and junior to debt. Although preferred may have many features similar to debt, it is not debt. Preferred stock is a right of ownership in a company. There are many possible variations in the terms of the different preferred issues. They are distinctly unlike common stock in that dividends not paid usually accumulate and generally must be paid before dividends may be paid on the common. But unlike bonds, failure to pay dividends on preferred is not a default, as is failure to pay bond interest. Although not a default, dividend omissions may result in the imposition of serious financial restrictions upon the issuer. Like bonds, many preferred issues have no voting power as long as dividends are being paid, but they usually gain some limited voting power when dividends are in arrears. A company may have one class of preferred stock and issue it in series with different terms for different series of stock. Preferred stock is peculiar because it has some of the characteristics of bonds and some of the characteristics of common equity. It is also peculiar because the exclusion from taxable income of most of the amount of preferred dividends received by corporations from qualified issuers causes it to be owned very largely by corporate investors rather than individuals.

## CHAPTER 16

# INTERNATIONAL BOND MARKETS AND INSTRUMENTS

Christopher B. Steward, CFA
Vice President
Wellington Management Company, LLP

## INTRODUCTION

The creation of global bonds and the distribution of bond issues over the Internet has increased the globalization of the bond market in recent years, however, international bond investing is hardly a new activity. Cross-border investments in government bonds were common before the first World War. By 1920, Moody's was providing credit ratings on some 50 sovereign borrowers. However, most of these foreign investments ended badly for U.S. investors. Hyperinflation under the German Weimar Republic of the 1920s rendered the Reichsmark worthless. Similarly, during the 1920s U.S. investors saw their foreign investments decline in U.S. dollar terms by 86% in France, 70% in Italy, and 50% in Spain. Interestingly, some of the countries which avoided sharp devaluations during this period (including the U.K., Sweden, and surprisingly, Argentina) have lost much of their value since the collapse of the Bretton Woods system of fixed exchange rates in the 1970s. Between 1930 and 1970, capital controls and domestic regulations sharply curtailed cross-border bond investment. The offshore markets and banks led the way toward greater cross-border investment flows in the early 1980s, prompting governments to introduce domestic market reforms liberalizing capital flows in money, bond, and equity markets. However, some foreign bond markets, such as Italy's, were closed to foreign investors until 1990.[1]

An explosion in international bond trading has occurred over the past 15 years, driven by reductions in capital controls, spectacular technological advances in the dissemination of information, and in computing power to track portfolios and forecast capital market trends. A large rise in debt issuance, pri-

---

1. See Michael Mussa and Morris Goldstein, "The Integration of World Capital Markets," in *Changing Capital Markets: Implications for Monetary Policy* (Federal Reserve Bank of Kansas, 1993) for a more complete discussion.

marily by governments running large budget deficits, has contributed to a five-fold increase in the nominal value of developed county debt outstanding, from $4.6 trillion in 1984 to $25.5 trillion in 1998.[2] Bonds denominated in U.S. dollars are consistently the largest single component of the world bond market, comprising 49% of the total in 1998. The countries that now participate in the European Monetary Union, plus ECU-denominated debt, together would comprise 26% of the world bond market. If Eurodollar bond issues, which are traded offshore, are stripped out, 57% of the world's bonds are traded outside of the U.S. market. The variety of borrowers in the international bond markets has increased dramatically, and financing techniques in these markets now rival the U.S. domestic market in their sophistication. Although the sheer size of the U.S. economy ensures a central role for U.S. bonds in world capital markets, the growth in volume and turnover in international bonds suggests that a general understanding of their characteristics is in order.

This chapter will attempt to provide a broad overview of the instruments, markets, and players in international bond investing. First, the instruments and markets for the U.S.-pay sector of the international bond market are described, including emerging market debt. Then the foreign-pay sectors of the international bond market are described, with emphasis placed on the contribution of currency to returns for U.S. dollar-based investors. The rationale for international bond investing and the impact of including international bonds in a U.S. bond portfolio, are discussed in Chapter 48.

*Do international bonds have a role for U.S. dollar-based investors?* Domestic bonds are often included in diversified portfolios because their price movements are generally less volatile than equities, they pay a known amount of interest at regular intervals, and they mature; that is, with high credit bonds, you are nearly certain to get your money back. U.S. dollar-denominated international bonds behave much like domestic U.S. bonds. But foreign-pay bonds, because of the currency component, are much more volatile. How should foreign-pay bonds be used in diversified portfolios? How should their performance be judged? Does currency hedging eliminate the diversification benefit of holding international bonds? These are some of the questions addressed below.

## THE INSTRUMENTS: EURO, FOREIGN, AND GLOBAL

International bonds are divided into three general categories: domestic, Euro, and foreign, depending on the domicile of the issuer, the nature of the underwriting syndicate, the domicile of the primary buyers, and the currency denomination. Domestic bonds are issued, underwritten, and traded under the currency

---

2. This, and other data on the size of the international bond market is from data published by
   Salomon Brothers, Inc. in *How Big Is the World Bond Market—1998 Data* (April 2000) and
   *Eurobond Market Trends* (various dates).

and regulations of a country's bond market by a borrower located within the country. Eurobonds are underwritten by an international syndicate and traded outside of any one domestic market. Foreign bonds are issued under the regulations of a domestic market and are intended primarily for that country's domestic investors by a foreign-domiciled borrower. Global bonds are a hybrid, designed to trade and settle in both the Euro, and U.S. foreign (or Yankee) markets.

The most decisive influence on the price or yield of a bond is its currency denomination. Thus, for U.S. investors, the pertinent division is between those international bonds that are denominated in U.S. dollars and those denominated in other currencies. Regardless of the domicile of the issuer, the buyer, or the trading market, prices of issues denominated in U.S. dollars (U.S.-pay) are affected principally by the direction of U.S. interest rates, whereas prices of issues denominated in other currencies (foreign-pay) are determined primarily by movement of interest rates in the country of the currency denomination. Thus, analysis of international bond investing must be separated into two parts: U.S.-pay and foreign-pay.

Most U.S.-pay international bonds can be included in a domestic bond portfolio with little change to the management style and overall risk profile of the portfolio. In most cases, a marginal extra effort is all that is required to analyze the credits of a few new unfamiliar issuers and to learn the settlement procedures for Eurodollar bonds. The notable exception in the U.S.-pay area is in emerging market debt, which, as detailed below, can be far more volatile than most other U.S.-pay bonds. The currency component of foreign-pay bonds, however, entails a fair degree of volatility of return and has a far different risk profile than domestic U.S., and U.S.-pay international bonds. The question of currency hedging (either passive, active, or not at all), plus considerations of trading hours, settlement procedures, withholding taxes, and other nuances of trading foreign-pay international bonds, require much greater training and effort to manage them effectively.

## U.S.-PAY INTERNATIONAL BONDS

The U.S.-pay international bond market consists of Eurodollar bonds, which are issued and traded outside any one domestic market, and Yankee bonds, which are issued and traded primarily in the United States. Global bonds are issued in both the Yankee and Eurodollar markets simultaneously, but domestic investors are generally indifferent between global and straight Yankee issues except where liquidity differs. Before examining the instruments in depth, some of the more basic questions regarding U.S.-pay international bonds need to be addressed.

**Why do foreign-domiciled issuers borrow in the U.S.-dollar markets?** First, the U.S. bond market is the largest, most liquid, and most sophisticated of the world's bond markets. By issuing in the U.S. market, foreign entities diversify their sources of funding. Also, as companies have become more global in production and distribution, they have assets and liabilities in many different currencies and hence are less tied to their domestic bond markets. Financial innovations, particularly the advent of the interest-rate and currency swap markets, have greatly expanded the diversity of borrowers, notably in the corporate sector. Companies in need of floating-rate finance have often been able to combine a fixed-coupon bond with an interest-rate swap to create a cheaper means of finance than a traditional floating-rate note. Similarly, when currency swap terms are favorable, a company in need of, say, sterling funds could issue a Eurodollar bond and combine it with a currency swap to create a cheaper source of sterling funds than a traditional UK bond issue.

**Why should U.S. dollar-based investors be interested in U.S.-pay international bonds?** Yankee bonds are SEC registered and trade like any other U.S. domestic bond. The credit quality of issuers in the Yankee market is very high, although the credit quality of new issuers has been declining in recent years. Eurobonds are generally less liquid than Yankee bonds but can sometimes offer more attractive yields and a broader list of available credits. As most international bond issues are rated by the major rating agencies, for a little additional credit work, investors may be able to find a higher yield on a U.S.-pay international bond than on other comparably rated issues, especially where the credit may be less familiar to United States investors.

**What is the difference between a Yankee and a Eurodollar bond?** The primary difference is SEC registration. Yankee bonds are registered with the SEC, and issued, and traded in the United States; Eurodollar bonds are issued outside the United States and traded primarily by foreigners. Eurodollar bonds are issued mostly by corporate issuers; Yankees are issued mostly by high credit-quality sovereign and sovereign-guaranteed issuers. The size of the Eurodollar market, measured at $1.4 trillion in bonds outstanding in 1998, is more than five times the size of the Yankee market of $262 billion. In addition, Yankees are registered securities; Eurodollar bonds are issued in unregistered, or bearer, form. Yankees pay interest semiannually; Eurodollar bonds carry annual coupons.

## Eurodollar Bonds

The eurobond market existed long before the launch of the pan-European currency, also called the euro. In bonds, the prefix "Euro" has come to mean offshore. The Eurodollar banking market began during the cold war as the Soviet Union, wary that the United States might freeze their dollar deposits, preferred to hold their dollar-denominated bank deposits outside the reach of the U.S. authorities. The Eurodollar market grew as banks sought to avoid domestic banking restrictions such as Regulation Q, which set a ceiling on interest levels paid on deposits, and the Glass-Steagall Act, which prohibited banks from engaging in underwriting and brokerage. Restrictions placed on direct investment overseas by U.S. companies in 1968 encouraged companies to raise capital offshore, thus increasing the size of the Eurobond market. However, the most significant growth in the Eurodollar market occurred in the late 1970s as the recycling of large dollar surpluses by OPEC countries (as oil is denominated in dollars) injected huge amounts of liquidity into the market. Balance-of-payments deficits, due in part to higher oil prices, also increased sovereign and sovereign-guaranteed Eurodollar issuance.

Eurodollar bonds are the largest single component of the Eurobond market, which encompasses securities of all different currency denominations. Eurodollar bonds are:

1. Denominated in U.S. dollars

2. Issued and traded outside the jurisdiction of any single country

3. Underwritten by an international syndicate

4. Issued in bearer (unregistered) form

Since Eurodollar bonds are not registered with the SEC, as U.S. domestic new issues are required to be, underwriters are legally prohibited from selling new issues to the U.S. public until the issue has "come to rest" and a seasoning period has expired. An issue is usually considered seasoned 40 days after it has been fully distributed.[3] This seasoning requirement effectively locks U.S. investors out of the primary market. Even though a portion of Eurodollar outstandings end up in U.S.-based portfolios after the seasoning period expires, the lack of participation of U.S. investors in new offerings ensures that the Eurodollar market will remain dominated by foreign-based investors. Although no single location has been designated for Eurodollar market making, London is the de facto primary trading center for all Eurobonds.

The Eurodollar bond market has grown dramatically from its humble beginnings in the early 1960s, although the vast majority of growth has occurred in only the past 10 years. In 1980, the total Eurodollar market was a modest $64 billion. By 1990, the market has grown nearly eight times larger to $524 billion, then it more than doubled again from 1990 to 1998 to a high of $1.4 trillion. Marketability of Eurodollar bonds has improved as the market has grown. In the past, many straight fixed-coupon eurobonds traded infrequently, particularly among the older issues, which were often only $50 million or less in individual issue size. Normal issue size today is $100–500 million or higher. Despite the increase in market size, liquidity will remain somewhat constrained by the popularity of Eurodollar bonds among European retail investors, who are likely to buy bonds and tuck them away until maturity. Since Eurobonds are

---

3. The Securities and Exchange Commission's revised Regulation S reduced the seasoning period from 90 to 40 days. Other changes in SEC regulations, notably Regulation 144A, make the Euromarkets and the U.S. domestic bond markets more fungible.

held in bearer (unregistered) form, details about major holders of Eurodollar bonds are often unreliable, but market participants estimate retail investors are significant players in the eurobond market.

Borrowers in the Eurodollar bond market may be divided into four major groups: sovereign, supranational agency, corporate, and financial. Supranational agencies, such as the World Bank and the European Investment Bank, are consistently among the top borrowers, reflecting their constant need for development financing and their lack of "home" issuance market. Sovereign and sovereign-backed borrowers are also prominent, although the growth in sovereign Eurodollar issuance slowed in the late 1980s as governments either cut back on their external borrowing in favor of their domestic bond markets, or chose to borrow in the nondollar markets to diversify their currency exposure. Fiscal retrenchment in most developed countries and the growth of domestic bond markets have served to reduce the role that sovereign issuers play in the primary Eurobond market. Bank and finance companies continue to dominate the new issuance market, however, corporate issuance has been rising while sovereign issuance has been declining.

The future of the Eurodollar bond market is largely a function of the domestic regulatory environment in the major issuer countries. In the late 1980s, Japanese companies were among the most active Eurodollar borrowers. However, the opening up of the Japanese domestic bond market (thus diminishing the relative attractiveness of issuing in the offshore market) and intense fiscal retrenchment by Japanese companies as the economy fell into a long running recession led to a sharp drop in Japanese Eurobond issuance.

In the short term, the course of the U.S. dollar and U.S. interest rates have the greatest impact on the Eurodollar bond market. The strength in the dollar from 1987 to 1990, particularly against the yen, increased investor appetite for dollar-denominated securities and encouraged dollar bond issuance. Similarly, the dollar's weakness in 1994 and 1995 led to less issuance of Eurodollar bonds by Japanese borrowers. The relative and absolute level of U.S. interest rates also has a substantial impact on Eurodollar bond issuance.

The direction of U.S. interest rates and the value of the dollar will continue to have an impact on the size and liquidity of the Eurodollar bond market. Over the long term, however, the survivability of the market will be decided by the global trend toward financial deregulation. To the extent that national governments continue to dismantle the laws that hobble the development of domestic bond markets, the attraction of Eurodollar bonds, and all Eurobonds, to issuers and investors will diminish. Running counter to this trend, the growth of global bonds (discussed below), which allows for access to a broad array of investors across national and offshore markets, has served to increase the attractiveness of the Eurobond market.

## Yankee Bonds

The other portion of the U.S.-pay international bond market, referred to as the Yankee bond market, encompasses those foreign-domiciled issuers who register with the SEC and borrow dollars via issues underwritten by a U.S. syndicate for delivery in the United States.[4] The principal trading market is in the United States, although foreign buyers can and do participate. Unlike Eurodollar bonds, Yankee bonds pay interest semiannually.

The Yankee market is much older than the Eurodollar market. Overseas borrowers first issued Yankee bonds in the early 1900s, when the U.S. became the world's preeminent creditor nation. The repayment record of these early issues was not good; as much as one-third of the outstanding "foreign" bonds in the United States were in default on interest payments by the mid-1930s. After years of slow growth the market expanded rapidly after the abolition of the interest-equalization tax in 1974.[5] Between 1989 and 1998, total bonds outstanding in the Yankee market more than tripled, from $66 billion to $262 billion, a figure rivaling other sectors of the U.S. corporate market in size.

Supranational agencies and Canadian provinces (including provincial utilities) have historically been the most prominent Yankee issuers, comprising well over half the total market. The corporate sector, which is a major borrower in the Eurodollar bond market, is of only minor importance in the Yankee bond market. The increased use of global bonds, however, has confused the distinction between the Yankee and Eurodollar bond markets. The rankings of top issuers in the Yankee market change, depending upon whether global bonds are included or excluded.

## The Market for Eurodollar and Yankee Bonds

Foreign investors play a major role in the Yankee market, although the market's location in the United States prevents foreigners from having as dominating a presence as they have in the Euromarkets. Prior to 1984, foreign investors had a preference for U.S.-pay international bonds, which include both Yankees and Eurodollar issues, because they were not subject to the 30% withholding tax imposed by the U.S. government on all interest paid to foreigners. When the withholding tax exception was abolished in July 1984, a major advantage of U.S.-pay international bonds over U.S. Treasuries and domestic corporate bonds was removed. The result was a cheapening of Yankees and Euros relative to the U.S. domestic market, but foreign investor support remained strong. U.S.-pay international bonds offer a yield advantage over U.S. government bonds, usually due to the lesser liquidity and credit quality of international issues, and foreign buyers are often more familiar with Yankee and Eurodollar credits than they are

---

4. A small portion of outstanding Yankee bonds are foreign-currency denominated. These are not included in this analysis.

5. The interest equalization tax was imposed on purchases of foreign securities by U.S. residents during the years 1963–1974. The intent and effect of the tax was to discourage foreign borrowing in the United States by increasing the cost of capital. To make returns after the IET competitive with rates on domestic issues, gross rates on foreign borrowings had to be higher than would otherwise have been the case.

with U.S. domestic credits. Finally, Yankee and Eurodollar issuers sometimes compensate for their "foreign" status in the U.S.-pay market by offering bonds with shorter maturities and greater call protection-structures that traditionally appeal to overseas investors.

For these reasons, when foreign buyers seek exposure to U.S.-pay bonds, they often buy U.S.-pay international bonds—Eurodollar or Yankee—instead of domestic issues. The degree of interest of foreign buyers in U.S.-pay securities, or lack thereof, is reflected in narrowing or widening of the yield spread to U.S. Treasury bonds. This is particularly true of Eurodollar bonds, since foreign interest governs this market to a greater extent than the Yankee market, which is more attuned to U.S. investor preferences. The fact that the Eurodollar market and the Yankee market have different investor bases occasionally leads to trading disparities between the two markets. For example, similarly structured Canadian Yankee bonds often trade at lower yields than Canadian Eurodollar bonds because U.S. investors tend to be more comfortable with Canadian credits due to the close proximity of the two countries.

The globalization of the investment world has brought the Yankee and Eurodollar bond markets closer together, and it is not uncommon for investors to arbitrage the two markets when yield disparities appear. The dividing line between the two markets has become increasingly blurred with the advent of the "global bond." The World Bank issued the first global bond in 1989, with a $1.5 billion issue that was placed simultaneously in both the Yankee and the Eurodollar markets. The idea was to create an instrument that had attributes of both a Yankee bond and a Eurodollar bond and thereby do away with the market segmentation that inhibited liquidity and created yield disparities. The success of global bond issues is further evidence of the melding of the Euro and domestic markets that has accelerated as barriers to cross-border capital movements have been lowered.

The global bond market has been primarily utilized by central governments and supranational organizations. However, as many governments have endeavored to increase the depth and liquidity of their domestic bond markets and lower their borrowing requirements through deficit reduction policies, U.S. borrowers have begun to dominate global bond issuance. U.S. agencies, especially the Federal Mortgage Credit Agencies, have become frequent global bond issuers, as have the international development institutions. The OECD has speculated that "on the basis of recent trends, it would appear that the market for global bonds is, for the time being, evolving into an extension of the domestic United States market and an additional source of funds for United States borrowers."[6] According to OECD estimates, global bond offerings grew from $34 billion in 1993 to $102 billion in 1997.[7]

---

6. *Financial Market Trends,* OECD Paris, June 1995, p. 79.
7. *Financial Market Trends,* OECD Paris, Feb. 1998.

Two other recent developments in the offshore market are worthy of mention: the sharp increase in the use of Euro medium-term note (EMTN) programs, and the success of Regulation 144A. The volume of newly arranged EMTN agreements more than doubled to $243 billion in 1994, up from only $18 billion in 1990. EMTNs allow for issuance in different currencies and maturities under one umbrella agreement. Thus borrowers can use EMTNs to tap the markets more quickly and efficiently than with traditional Eurodollar bonds, which require separate documentation for each bond issue. In fact, although EMTNs were originally used only for nonunderwritten private placements, since 1992 EMTNs have been used for underwritten deals as well, further blurring the distinction between EMTNs and traditional Eurobonds. As the majority of all Eurobond issues are swapped into floating-rate debt and market opportunities to obtain favorable swap terms can be fleeting, borrowers appreciate the flexibility of EMTN programs. EMTNs have been used extensively for small illiquid highly structured private issuance competing with private placements. The EMTN market has become more transparent with the publishing of EMTN issues leading a resurgence of more "plain vanilla" EMTN issues.

Regulation 144A was enacted in 1990 to allow professional investors greater liquidity in trading private placement issues[8] while continuing to restrict access by the general public. According to Moody's, annual issuance of 144A paper has risen to $80 billion; roughly 50% from foreign borrowers. Approximately 90% of the issues in 1995 were rated by the major credit-rating agencies. Historically, 144A securities, due to the somewhat smaller issuance size, have been geared more toward buy-and-hold accounts; however, liquidity has been increasing relative to registered securities. Many 144As are issued with registration rights that allow the issuer quick access to capital with the ability to broaden the issue's liquidity by registering with the SEC.

## Bradys, Aztecs, and FLIRBs: The Emerging Markets

Emerging market bonds are often found in global bond portfolios. Most of these bonds are U.S. dollar-denominated; however, local currency instruments, such as Mexican Cetes, are often available to international investors as well. The majority of secondary market trading is in Brady bonds, named after Treasury Secretary Nicholas Brady, who fostered a market-oriented approach to the Latin American debt crisis by repackaging nonperforming bank loans into marketable securities in the late 1980s.

The first Brady agreement was reached with Mexico, and the bonds were issued in March 1990; however, Aztec bonds, a similar privately arranged re-

---

8. Regulation 144A also provided foreign borrowers with greater access to institutional investors by allowing issuers to provide only the documentation required by their home-market regulators rather than undergo the more cumbersome SEC registration process.

structuring of Mexican debt by J.P. Morgan, were issued two years earlier. The Mexican Brady plan offered the commercial banks two options in return for their Mexican loans: a *discount* bond issued at 65% of face value paying a floating market coupon of LIBOR + 13/16, and a *par* bond issued at full face value, but paying a below-market fixed coupon of 6.25%. Both discount and par bonds have their principal repayment backed by zero-coupon U.S. Treasuries plus a rolling interest guarantee covering 18 months of interest payments. The banks were also given a third alternative, allowing them to carry existing loans on their books at face value if they agreed to provide new lending to Mexico of at least 25% of their existing exposure over the next three years. Today, 12 countries have issued Brady bonds, although Latin American countries still dominate the Brady market, with 86% of debt outstanding. The size of the Brady market grew from $30 billion in 1990 to $136 billion in 1995 but has declined since to $104 billion in 1999 due in part to Brady bond debt exchanges where countries replace a portion of their Brady debt by issuing uncollateralized eurobonds.

There is no generally accepted delineation between an emerging and a developed market. Mexico and the Czech Republic, considered by many to be emerging markets, are now members of the OECD. Emerging markets have also become welcome issuers in the Eurobond market. Generally, the distinction is left up to the credit rating agencies, who determine whether a country is investment grade: Moody's Baa3, Standard & Poor's BBB−, or better. Even the credit rating agencies sometimes cannot agree. For example, El Salvador has a split rating of Baa3/BB+, meaning that Moody's regards the credit as investment grade, whereas Standard & Poor's does not.

Needless to say, regardless of currency denomination, the market risk of holding emerging market securities is much higher than the risk of holding developed country credits. The turmoil in the emerging markets triggered by the Russian default in August of 1998 and the Asian financial crisis of the previous year, serve as a vivid reminders of the risks associated with holding emerging market debt. The devaluation of the Thai baht in the July 1997 triggered a sell off in emerging market debt that spread through other South-East Asian markets and, to a lesser extent, Latin American markets as well. Currencies in the region depreciated by 50 to 100% from August to the end of the year with equity prices dropping by 50% in many markets.

The developed country financial markets in the industrial countries largely escaped the turmoil of the 1997 Asian crisis, however, they were severely affected by the Russian default in August 1998. The resulting flight to safety not only damaged emerging market bond prices, but also pushed down yields in the U.S. Treasury market resulting in a sharp widening of U.S. corporate and agency spreads. These movements led to large losses at the well-known hedge fund Long Term Capital Management. The hedge fund had risk positions of approximately $125 billion supported by a capital base of only $4 billion, many of which were in relatively small and illiquid markets. Ultimately, concerns over Long Term Capital Management's solvency threatened to destabilize the global financial markets, leading the Federal Reserve Board to cut interest rates by 75 basis points and the Federal Reserve Bank of New York to intercede between the hedge fund and its creditors.

## FOREIGN-PAY INTERNATIONAL BONDS

From the standpoint of the U.S. investor, foreign-pay international bonds encompass all issues denominated in currencies other than the dollar. A variety of issues are available to the U.S. investor, but in practically all cases the primary trading market is outside the United States. The currency component introduces a significant source of volatility; hence, the most important question facing U.S. investors in foreign-pay international bonds is whether or not to hedge the currency. The theoretical underpinnings of the currency hedge question are explored in detail below, but first the instruments require some explanation. The three types of instruments, just as in the United States bond market, are determined by the domicile of the issuer and the location of the primary trading market: the domestic market; the foreign market (like the Yankee market), where the issuer is domiciled outside of the country of issuance; and the Euro market, which trades outside of any national jurisdiction.

## The Non-U.S. Domestic Markets

Securities issued by a borrower within its home market and in that country's currency are typically termed domestic issues. These may include bonds issued directly by the government; government agencies, sometimes called semigovernments; or corporations. In most countries, the domestic bond market is dominated by government-backed issues. Central governments have directly issued or guaranteed approximately 51% of the world's outstanding bonds. Another 6% of outstandings is accounted for by state (provincial) or local government issues, meaning 57% of the publicly issued bonds outstanding are government credits. The United States has the most well-developed, actively-traded corporate bond market. Other countries have discourage private-sector bond issuance in favor of bank loans or equity financing, or companies themselves have chosen to raise funds in the Euromarkets, where they have had access to a wider investor audience with fewer issuing restrictions. Recent progress in international credit-rating procedures and greater cross-border capital flows have helped to develop domestic corporate bond markets outside the United States and European Monetary Union has spurred the growth of a U.S. style credit market in Europe accessed by a broader range of issuers with an increase in issues with lower credit ratings.

## Bulldogs, Samurais, and other Foreign Bonds

The *foreign bond market* includes issues sold primarily in one country and currency by a borrower of a different nationality. The Yankee market is the U.S.-dollar version of this market. Other examples are the Samurai market, which consists of yen-denominated bonds issued in Japan by non-Japanese borrowers, and the Bulldog market, which is composed of United Kingdom sterling-dominated bonds issued in the United Kingdom by non-British entities. Relative to the size of the domestic bond markets, these foreign bond markets are quite small, and liquidity can be limited. For borrowers, the major advantage of the foreign bond markets is the access they provide to investors in the country in which the bonds are issued. The Samurai market, for example, allows borrowers directly to tap the huge pools of investment capital in Japan. For investors, foreign bonds offer the convenience of domestic trading and settlement, and often additional yield.

## The Offshore Foreign-Pay Market

Securities issued directly into the international ("offshore") markets are called Eurobonds. Eurodollar bonds are the U.S.-pay version; however, Eurobonds can be issued in a variety of currencies including euros, Japanese yen, even South African rand and Czech koruna. These securities are typically underwritten by international syndicates and are sold in a number of national markets simultaneously. They may or may not be obligations of, or guaranteed by, an issuer domiciled in the country of currency denomination, and the issuer may be a sovereign government, a corporation, or a supranational agency. The Eurobond market encompasses any bond not issued in a domestic market, regardless of issuer nationality, or currency denomination. Eurodollar bonds consistently have been the largest sector of this market, although their share of total Eurobond debt outstanding has declined from about 65% in 1984 to about 50% in 1989, and 47% in 1998. The decline of the share of the U.S. dollar in Eurobond issuance can be traced to three general trends: A trend depreciation of the dollar from its peak in 1984, a desire to diversify currency exposure and funding sources as the deutschemark and yen have become more important as reserve currencies, and the liquidity of the swaps and other derivatives markets. Euro-deutschemark and Euroyen bonds are the next largest sectors.[9] As with the foreign bond markets, liquidity of Eurobonds is typically less than the liquidity of domestic government issues.

---

9. Germany's actual market share is probably slightly less than Japan's as Germany doesn't distinguish between foreign and Eurobond issues.

## Components of Return

To the dollar-based investor, there are two components of return in actively managed U.S.-pay bond portfolios: coupon income and capital change. Capital change can result from either interest-rate movements or a change in the perceived creditworthiness of the issuer. In foreign-pay investing, a third component of return must be considered: foreign currency movements. The U.S. investor must couple the domestic or internal price movement with income and then translate the total domestic return into dollars to assess the total return in U.S. dollars.

For the U.S. investor in foreign currency bonds, the prospects for return should not only be viewed in an absolute sense but should also be analyzed relative to returns expected in the U.S. market. The analysis can be separated into three questions.

### What Is the Starting Yield Level Relative to Yield Levels on U.S. Bonds?

Where this spread is positive, the income advantage will, over time, provide a cushion against adverse movements of the foreign bond price relative to U.S. bonds, or against deterioration in the value of the foreign currency. The longer the time horizon, the greater the cushion provided by this accumulating income advantage. If, on the other hand, the starting income level of the foreign currency issue is below that provided by U.S. bonds, this income deficiency must be offset by an appreciating currency or positive internal price movement relative to U.S. bonds to provide comparable returns. This may appear to be a difficult challenge, but the decade of the 1970s as a whole saw the best U.S. dollar total returns accruing to the bond investments with the lowest income levels. This same result was achieved in the 1980s, when Japanese yen bonds had the world's best total returns in U.S. dollar terms despite the fact that yen bonds offered the lowest interest rates of the world's major bond markets. In the 1990s Japanese bonds posted the second highest returns for the decade (behind the UK) with the lowest bond yields. The underlying rationale for this result is that bonds with low yields are denominated in currencies of countries with low inflation rates, which theoretically translates into currency appreciation relative to the U.S. dollar.[10]

### What Are the Prospects for Internal Price Movements Relative to Expectations for U.S. Bond Prices?

This factor can be broadly discussed in terms of changing yield spreads of foreign-pay bonds versus U.S. issues in the same way that changing yield spreads within the domestic U.S. market are discussed in describing changes in

---

10. See Exhibit 48–14 in Chapter 48, which shows the long-term relationship between currency movements and inflation.

relative prices. However, several points should be considered in regard to this analogy. First, in the U.S. market, all bond prices generally move in the same direction, although not always to the same extent, whereas domestic price movements of foreign-pay bonds may move in the direction opposite to that of the U.S. market. Second, although yield spread relationships within the U.S. market may fluctuate broadly, in many cases there is a normal spread that has some repetitive meaning. However, changing economic, social, and political trends between the United States and other countries suggest that there are few normal relationships to serve as useful guidelines.

Third, investors must be aware that similar interest rate shifts may result in significantly different capital price changes. Both U.S. and international investors are very familiar with the concept of duration; that is, that equal yield movements will result in differing price movements depending upon the individual security's current yield, maturity, coupon, and call structure. However, as international bond investors are focused on the spread relationship to the benchmark market (explained in detail below), they often pay less attention to the consequences of duration on similar maturity bonds across markets. For example, the low yield on Japanese long bonds, currently around 1.60%, makes Japanese 10-year bond prices about 30% more sensitive to changes in yield than New Zealand bonds, where yields are above 7.50%. Thus, a 20-basis-point (0.2%) decline in the yield of a 10-year New Zealand fixed coupon government issue starting at a 7.50-percent yield results in a 1.34% price change, whereas the same 20-basis-point move equates to a 1.73% price change for a 10-year Japanese issue with a starting yield of 1.60%. When the more commonly analyzed effects of varying maturities and differing yield changes are added to the impact of different starting yield levels, the resulting changes in relative price movements are not intuitively obvious. For example, the various combinations of starting yield, maturity, and yield change shown in Exhibit 16–1 all result in the same 10% capital price increases.

Finally, changes in credit quality can have dramatic influences on bond prices. The most spectacular recent example is the sharp drop in emerging mar-

**EXHIBIT   16–1**

Impact of Maturity and Starting Yield on Yield and Price Change Relationships

| Starting Yield | Maturity (Years) | Yield Change | Price Change |
|---|---|---|---|
| 7% | 10 | −1.41% | +10% |
| 7 | 5 | −2.40 | +10 |
| 2 | 10 | −1.11 | +10 |
| 2 | 5 | −2.11 | +10 |

ket asset prices in the fall of 1998. However, credit concerns have also influenced developed country debt premia. During the sharp rise in global bond yields in 1994, there was much discussion over whether highly indebted countries such as Italy, Belgium, Sweden, and Canada could find themselves in a "debt trap," where they would not be able to service their existing debt. As can be seen in Exhibit 16–2, the rise in bond yields during 1994 was highly correlated with budget deficits and national debt levels.[11] As the bond market rally got underway in 1995, concerns over the debt trap faded into the background.

### What Are the Prospects for Currency Gain versus the U.S. Dollar?

Winston Churchill reportedly said, "There is no sphere of human thought in which it is easier to show superficial cleverness and the appearance of superior wisdom than in discussing currency and exchange." This demonstrates that the debate as to whether or not foreign currency changes can be predicted and, if

### E X H I B I T    16–2

Budget Deficit and 1994 10-Year Yield Change

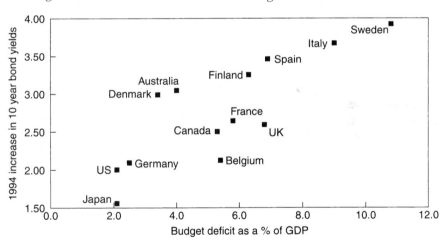

Source: OECD Economic Outlook.

---

11. The debt trap is a condition where the national debt has become so large that a country cannot fully service its existing debt without recourse to new borrowing, which creates a self-perpetuating dynamic of higher future debt service costs and a larger national debt. As the debt grows, the market will demand a higher risk premium, driving up interest rates on new debt and adding further to debt service costs, until credit concerns prompt the market to halt lending altogether and default, or debt restructuring, becomes inevitable. For a more complete discussion of the dynamics of the debt trap, see the *OECD Economic Outlook* no. 58, OECD, Paris (December 1995) pp. 19–23.

so, what factors determine such changes, is an old one. In many ways, this debate is little different from that regarding the predictability of stock market movements or interest rates. Like the stock and bond markets, a number of factors exert a direct influence on foreign exchange rates. The common problems faced by forecasters are whether these factors have already been fully discounted in prices—be they stock, bond, or foreign exchange—and which factor will predominate at any given time. Those factors generally regarded as affecting foreign currency movements include the following:

1. The balance of payments and prospective changes in that balance

2. Inflation and interest-rate differentials between countries

3. The social and political environment, particularly with regard to the impact on foreign investment

4. Relative changes in the money supply

5. Central bank intervention in the currency markets

Part of the reason that exchange rates have become more difficult to forecast is that they are decreasingly governed by end-user transactions. The ratio of foreign-exchange transactions relative to world-trade flows has skyrocketed, from 10:1 in 1983 to more than 60:1 in 1992. The latest estimate of average daily turnover in the foreign exchange markets, based on a 1998 survey conducted by the Bank for International Settlements, is $1.5 trillion.

A common question is whether international bond returns are almost entirely a function of currency movements. Exhibit 16–3[12] shows that for the 15-year period from 1985 to 1999, and for four of the five interim periods, the income component of return proved to be the largest of the three components, as measured by the Salomon Brothers Non-U.S. World Government Bond Index.

Over a shorter time horizon, however, foreign currency or domestic capital changes can be significantly more important. Exhibit 16–4 breaks down the 1985–1999 period into annual returns to demonstrate the influence domestic capital changes and movements in exchange rates can have on total returns over the short term. Domestic capital changes ranged from −10.0% in 1994 to 9.3% in 1993, and currency returns varied from −11.9% in 1997 to 25.5% in 1987. (Recall that negative foreign currency returns for dollar-based investors correspond to a strengthening in the dollar versus other currencies, and vice versa.) The income component of return varied in a much narrower range throughout the period, from a low of 5.1% in 1999 to a high of 8.1% in 1985 and 1991.

For individual countries, of course, the variation in components of return can be much greater. The greatest capital price changes were +15.5% in Italy

---

12. Monthly total returns in Exhibits 16–5 and 16–6 were taken from Salomon Brothers' International Market Indexes, published monthly; particularly the Salomon Brothers' Non-U.S. Dollar World Government Bond Index. The income component of total return was computed from principal local market returns provided by Salomon Brothers.

**EXHIBIT   16–3**

Average Annual Returns of International Bond Index by Components

| | | Contribution to Return | | |
|---|---|---|---|---|
| | Income | Domestic Capital Gain | Foreign Currency | Total Dollar-converted Average Annual Return |
| 1985–87 | +7.6% | +2.2% | +21.7% | +33.8% |
| 1988–90 | +7.9 | −3.0 | −0.2 | +4.5 |
| 1991–93 | +7.8 | +6.6 | −2.6 | +11.9 |
| 1994–96 | +7.0 | +0.2 | +2.2 | +9.7 |
| 1997–99 | +5.7 | +0.1 | −3.3 | +2.3 |
| 1985–99 | +7.2 | +1.2 | +3.2 | +11.9 |

The Salomon Brothers Non-U.S. Dollar World Government Bond Index—Market-weighted in the government bonds of Australia, Austria, Belgium, Canada, Denmark, France, Germany, Italy, Japan, the Netherlands, Spain, Sweden, and the United Kingdom.

in 1982 and −14.8% in Australia in 1994. Currency changes for specific countries ranged from +31.8% in Japan in 1987 to −22.3% in Italy in 1992. The least variable component of return—income—still ranged widely, from 13.5% in Australia in 1990 to just 2.9% in Japan in 1994. These data show clearly that all three factors of return—income, capital change, and currency movement—are important and must be considered both absolutely and relative to U.S. alternatives.

## CONCLUSION

International bonds, both U.S.-pay and foreign-pay, represent a significant portion of the world's fixed-income markets, and an understanding of their characteristics is important for all bond investors. U.S.-pay international bonds generally have very similar characteristics to domestically issued bonds and can offer opportunities to enhance returns in domestic bond portfolios with a little additional credit analysis and education. The risks—and potential returns—however, are much greater in foreign-pay international bonds, which require far more expertise and support to effectively handle the currency, settlement, and custodial risks unique to global bond investing.

U.S.-pay international bonds make up roughly 14% of the U.S.-dollar bond market. Issuance and liquidity in these instruments have increased dramatically in the past decade, although continued growth in the Eurodollar and Yankee bond markets is subject to regulatory policies in the domestic markets as well as the vagaries of the dollar and U.S. interest rates. Foreign investors will continue to have a large presence in the U.S.-pay international bond market.

**E X H I B I T  16–4**

Average Annual Returns of International Bond Index by Components

| | | Contribution to Return | | |
|---|---|---|---|---|
| | Income | Domestic Capital Gain | Foreign Currency | Total Dollar-Converted Average Annual Return |
| 1985 | 8.1% | 2.7% | 21.6% | 35.0% |
| 1986 | 7.4 | 3.6 | 18.1 | 31.4 |
| 1987 | 7.2 | 0.4 | 25.5 | 35.1 |
| 1988 | 7.6 | −0.5 | −4.4 | 2.3 |
| 1989 | 7.7 | −4.9 | −5.7 | −3.4 |
| 1990 | 8.3 | −3.5 | 10.2 | 15.3 |
| 1991 | 8.1 | 5.8 | 1.7 | 16.2 |
| 1992 | 7.9 | 4.8 | −7.3 | 4.8 |
| 1993 | 7.6 | 9.3 | −2.1 | 15.1 |
| 1994 | 7.4 | −10.0 | 9.6 | 6.0 |
| 1995 | 7.1 | 8.5 | 2.9 | 19.6 |
| 1996 | 6.7 | 3.0 | −5.3 | 4.1 |
| 1997 | 6.2 | 2.3 | −11.9 | −4.3 |
| 1998 | 5.7 | 3.3 | 7.9 | 17.8 |
| 1999 | 5.1 | −5.0 | −4.9 | −5.1 |

The Salomon Brothers Non-U.S. Dollar World Government Bond Index—market-weighted in the government bonds of Australia, Austria, Belgium, Canada, Denmark, France, Germany, Italy, Japan, the Netherlands, Spain, Sweden, and the United Kingdom.

Successful utilization of the Eurodollar and Yankee bond markets requires an ongoing familiarity with foreign investor preferences and issuer motivations.

Investors in foreign-pay bonds must consider income levels and prospective price movements both in absolute terms and relative to U.S.-pay alternatives. The outlook for foreign currency changes must also be evaluated. The evidence indicates that over the 1978–1999 period, converted U.S. dollar returns for foreign-pay bonds were somewhat better than returns for U.S. government bonds, although during shorter time periods within that 22-year interval, foreign-pay bonds sometimes provided inferior returns. Although these facts by themselves have little repetitive significance, many of the factors leading to the low correlation in returns between the U.S. and foreign-pay markets can be expected to continue making foreign-pay international bonds an effective diversifier for U.S. dollar-based portfolios.

## CHAPTER 17

# BRADY BONDS

**Jane Sachar Brauer, Ph.D**
First Vice President
Merrill Lynch

**Douglas Chen**
Assistant Vice President
Merrill Lynch

The term *Brady bond* refers to a series of sovereign bonds issued by several developing countries in exchange for their rescheduled bank loans. The term comes from a U.S. government program, which combined U.S. government and official multilateral support in obtaining debt and debt-service relief from foreign commercial bank creditors for those countries that successfully implemented comprehensive structural reforms supported by the International Monetary Fund (IMF) and the World Bank. Typically, a country negotiating a Brady restructuring has significant external debt outstanding and cannot meet its debt repayment schedule when new financing becomes unavailable. By restructuring its debt, the country obtains some debt forgiveness while simultaneously deferring a portion of the principal and interest payments for a few years to allow time for reforms to ripple through the economy and improve its cash flow and balance of payments.

The first Brady agreement with Mexico in 1989–90 was the prototype for other ensuing Brady-type accords. A total of seventeen countries have since taken advantage of the program, with a cumulative face value of $170 billion of Brady bonds issued. The majority of Brady debt has been issued by Latin America, with Brazil, Mexico, Argentina, and Venezuela representing 74% of the current outstanding amounts in the Brady bond market. (See Exhibit 17–1.) Almost all countries with defaulted commercial bank debt from the 1980's have exchanged that debt for Brady bonds or restructured loans. Since then, most countries have been able to improve their financing budget and have subsequently been able to raise more funds in the eurobond market.

The Brady market is unique in two respects. First, the yields are relatively high. In December 1999, for example, they ranged from 8 to 30%. Second, some issues are extremely large and liquid, especially compared to typical sovereign eurobonds. This chapter gives a general background of the evolution of

**E X H I B I T   17–1**

Original Brady/Exchange Issue Amounts (US$ bn)

| Country | Pars | Discounts | Other Brady Debt | Total Brady Debt Issued | Percent of All Bradys |
|---|---|---|---|---|---|
| **Latin America** | | | | | |
| Argentina | 12.67 | 4.32 | 8.47 | 25.45 | 15.0% |
| Brazil | 10.49 | 7.29 | 32.88 | 50.66 | 29.9% |
| Costa Rica | na | na | 0.59 | 0.59 | 0.4% |
| Dominican Republic | na | 0.33 | 0.19 | 0.52 | 0.3% |
| Ecuador | 1.91 | 1.44 | 2.78 | 6.13 | 3.6% |
| Mexico | 22.40 | 11.77 | 2.73 | 36.90 | 21.7% |
| Panama | 0.26 | 0.045 | 2.92 | 3.22 | 1.9% |
| Peru | 0.18 | 0.57 | 4.12 | 4.87 | 2.9% |
| Uruguay | 0.53 | na | 0.54 | 1.07 | 0.6% |
| Venezuela | 7.33 | 1.27 | 9.95 | 18.55 | 10.9% |
| **Non-Latin** | | | | | |
| Bulgaria | na | 1.85 | 3.28 | 5.13 | 3.0% |
| Ivory Coast | na | 0.07 | 1.26 | 1.33 | 0.8% |
| Jordan | 0.49 | 0.16 | 0.09 | 0.74 | 0.4% |
| Nigeria | 2.05 | na | na | 2.05 | 1.2% |
| Philippines | 1.89 | na | 2.32 | 4.21 | 2.5% |
| Poland | 0.90 | 2.99 | 4.02 | 7.90 | 4.7% |
| Vietnam | 0.23 | 0.02 | 0.29 | 0.55 | 0.3% |
| **Total** | **61.34** | **32.11** | **76.43** | **169.88** | **100%** |
| Percent | 36.1% | 18.9% | 45.0% | 100.0% | |

Source: Merrill Lynch

the Brady market, the basic instruments, how they are viewed and how to evaluate them.

# THE BRADY PLAN

The Brady Plan of 1989 grew out of the Less Developed Countries (LDC) debt crisis of 1982–88. In the early 1980's, sluggish growth of industrial countries, rising global interest rates and falling commodity prices triggered a significant economic contraction in developing countries. As a consequence, isolated from the international capital markets and lacking the level of domestic savings needed to service external obligations, most developing countries began to experience severe debt servicing problems. The first strategy adopted to address the crisis was a program of concerted new lending by commercial banks and multilateral organizations combined with structural adjustment efforts by the debtor countries. By 1988, it had become clear that this strategy was less than successful, the LDCs were not emerging out of the debt crisis and a new strategy involving "debt relief" was necessary.

In 1989, the Brady Plan structure, named after former U.S. Treasury Secretary Nicholas Brady, was introduced. It provided debtor countries with debt relief through restructuring their commercial bank debt at lower interest rates or allowing them to write it down, enabling them to exchange that debt for tradable fixed income securities. In return, the developing countries agreed to adopt macroeconomic reforms. Banks were given the choice of mainly debt (face) or debt-service (interest) reduction options. By the late 1980s many banks had written off as much as 25% of the face value of their commercial loans to LDCs. Since commercial banks at that time held these assets at face value, this enabled the banks to participate in a restructuring wherein the LDC obtained some formal debt relief.

The first collateralized restructuring issue, the predecessor to the Brady exchanges was done in March 1988 by Mexico in the form of a $2.6 billion 20-year bond whose principal was fully collateralized with special purpose zero-coupon bonds issued by the United States Treasury. The bank creditors had accepted 30% forgiveness on the face amount of the existing loans in exchange for "Aztec" bonds. The exchange had been done in conjunction with public-sector financing from the IMF, the World Bank, and other official creditor agencies, together with the use of the country's foreign reserves for the purchase of the collateral enhancement. The Aztecs and all succeeding Brady bonds are callable at par; however, the Aztecs were the only bonds issued with a floating rate coupon as high as Libor +1.625%. Within the eight years following the issuance of the Aztecs, Mexico had recovered financially, enough to allow the government to retire the outstanding Aztec bonds by calling them in February 1996.

The first country to reach a Brady agreement was Mexico, in September 1989. The deal covered approximately $48 billion face of the country's eligible foreign debt to commercial banks. In exchange for their illiquid defaulted loans, the banks were given three options, two of which included an exchange of defaulted loans for collateralized bonds. The first option was an exchange for Discount bonds, also known as principal reduction bonds. These bonds required a 35% reduction on the face value of the defaulted loans providing Mexico with debt relief (in terms of the principal amount), though requiring what was then termed a "market" coupon rate of Libor + 13/16. The second option, Par bonds, also known as interest reduction bonds had no reduction in the face value, though they included a below-market coupon of 6.25%, at a time when Libor was over 10%. Both types of bonds included full principal collateral in the form of a special-purpose U.S. Treasury zero coupon bond, similar to the Aztec exchange. The two issues also included a rolling interest guarantee (RIG) covering 18 months worth of interest payments. The third option allowed the banks to carry the full principal amount of their Mexican loans on their books, while requiring the banks to provide additional new lending ("New Money") to Mexico of at least 25% of their existing exposure over a three year period.

The Mexican Brady agreement, which included three basic options: Pars, Discounts, and New Money bonds, set the standard for subsequent Brady accords. Over time the Brady exchanges have become more complex, offering a wider array of possibilities for debt and debt service reduction that would be more advantageous to the debtor countries. These exchanges included increasing the level of debt forgiveness and applying creative ways to account for the past-due interest. An example is Peru, which had a history of approximately twelve years of non-payment on its outstanding debt. For the period of 1984–96, Peru was allowed to accrue interest on its unpaid coupon payments of its outstanding debt at a rate of 2.5% when Libor over that period averaged close to 7.0%. In several of the later Brady Exchange Agreements, the RIG gradually decreased, so much so that in some cases it included a RIG on only one coupon, or in the case of Poland, none. Exhibit 17–2 lists the Brady countries with their respective exchange dates and their current credit rating.

## TYPES OF BRADY BONDS

Countries typically issue several types of Brady bonds covering the outstanding principal amount of their bank loans and one or more bonds covering the past-due interest. The particular bond types are chosen by creditors to provide debt and debt service relief to the sovereign issuer. During the negotiations, creditors were presented with a choice of possible debt restructurings and were given several months in which to choose. At the time of the presentation, all options were equally attractive and produced roughly the same net present value. In their selection, some creditors were constrained by their own internal accounting requirements, while others were able to select the bond that provided the highest present value. Typically, these decisions were mainly influenced by the expectation of the sovereign's spread risk and the movements in the U.S. Treasury markets.

## Collateralized Principal Bonds

Two principal bonds, Pars and Discounts, are 25–30 year registered bullet bonds and represent the largest, most common assets in the Brady bond market. Pars and Discounts represent 45% of the current Brady bond market. Issue size ranges from $90 million to $22.4 billion, and in some cases is larger than the most liquid U.S. Treasury securities. Par bonds were issued at "par" in exchange for the original face value of the rescheduled loans but carry a fixed, below-market interest rate. Discount bonds, on the other hand, carry a floating interest rate,

**E X H I B I T    17–2**

Multilateral Debt Relief Agreements with Commercial Banks

| Country | Official Debt and Debt Service Reduction Agreement Date | % Debt Forgiveness in Exchange Agreement | As of November 1999 | |
|---|---|---|---|---|
| | | | Moody's | S&P |
| Philippines | January-1990/December-1992 | na | Ba1 | BB+ |
| Mexico | March-1990 | 35.0 | Ba1 | BB |
| Costa Rica | May-1990 | na | Ba1 | BB |
| Venezuela | December-1990 | 30.0 | B2 | B+ |
| Uruguay | February-1991 | na | Baa3 | BBB− |
| Nigeria | January-1992 | na | NR | NR |
| Argentina | April-1993 | 35.0 | B1 | BB |
| Jordan | December-1993 | 35.0 | Ba3 | BB− |
| Brazil | April-1994 | 35.0 | B2 | B+ |
| Bulgaria | July-1994 | 50.0 | B2 | B |
| Dominican Republic | August-1994 | 35.0 | B1 | B+ |
| Poland | October-1994 | 45.0 | Baa1 | BBB |
| Ecuador | February-1995 | 45.0 | Caa2 | NR |
| Panama | May-1996 | 45.0 | Ba1 | BB+ |
| Peru | November-1996 | 45.0 | Ba3 | BB |
| Ivory Coast | May-1997 | 50.0 | NR | NR |
| Vietnam | December-1997 | 50.0 | B1 | NR |

Source: The World Bank, Global envelopment Finance: 1999 Analysis and Summary Tables/Merrill Lynch

typically Libor +13/16, but are exchanged for fewer bonds than the original loan amount, or at a discounted face value of the previously rescheduled loans, often ranging between 50 to 65% of the original face.

**Principal and Interest Collateral**
Pars and Discounts generally have principal secured by U.S. Treasury zero coupon bonds[1] which were originally funded by a combination of IMF, World Bank loans and the country's own reserves. In addition, the interest portion of the Pars and Discounts is partially collateralized by securities rated at least AA in amounts sufficient to cover a specified number of months (usually 12 months)

---

1. Collateralized bonds denominated in a currency other than USD may have its principal collateral guaranteed by: Deutschemark Series – Federal Post Office (Bundespost) Zero Coupon Treasury Notes; French Franc Series – Republic of France Compound Interest Bonds; Japanese Yen Series: Japanese Government Bonds; Swiss Franc Series – 30-Year Global Bonds (issued by Swiss Bank Corporation)

of interest on the outstanding principal at a notional rate. The interest guarantee is characterized as a rolling interest guarantee (RIG) because the guarantee rolls forward to the subsequent interest period if not utilized. Both the interest and principal collateral is maintained by an assigned collateral agent and held in escrow at the Federal Reserve Bank of New York. In the event that the country misses an interest payment, the trustee will pay the investor out of the interest collateral until the number of coupon payments guaranteed has been exhausted.

Although the earlier exchanges involved a special-purpose issue of a zero coupon bond by the U.S. Treasury, subsequent issues allowed the sovereign to buy U.S. Treasury strips from the growing open market. Such market transactions required the maturity of the strips to be no longer than that of the Brady bond issued with the restriction that the face value be equal to the principal amount of the Par and Discount bonds. From 1993–94, pre-Brady countries (primarily Argentina and Brazil) accumulated the largest collateral blocks of U.S. Treasury strips. During that period, demand from these Latin American countries had impacted the overall shape and level of the then developing U.S. Treasury strips market.

## Recourse to Collateral

Bondholders do not have recourse to the principal collateral until maturity, at which time the proceeds will be available to pay the full principal amount due. Regarding the recourse to the interest collateral, if the issuer does not make an interest payment within the grace period stipulated in the Brady Exchange Agreement[2], the Collateral agent, at the request of the Fiscal agent, acting upon the instructions of holders of at least 25%[3] of the aggregate principal, will release interest collateral sufficient to cover the interest payable on the bonds.

In August 1999, the Republic of Ecuador failed to make the timely coupon payment on its Brady bond debt. Ecuador was facing its most difficult financial condition in decades.[4] This marked the first time a Brady country had failed to pay on its contractual date. Defaulting on an interest payment does not mean that the sovereign debtor will cease to pay interest on the bond; instead, the country could continue to make payments in arrears after the interest collateral has been depleted, or the country may attempt to re-negotiate the terms of the bond. In the case of Ecuador, the government paid only its non-collateralized Brady debt and asked the collateralized bondholders to tap the interest collateral account for the collateralized coupon payment in order to give the sovereign time to restructure its external debt without defaulting. Instead, the bondholders requested the acceleration of payments, based on a provision stating that the

---

2. This period is typically 15 or 30 days
3. The percentage varies with each Brady Exchange Agreement
4. For 1999, Ecuador's total external debt accounted for over 115% of its GDP.

unpaid balance become immediately due and payable if the debtor fails to meet payments or becomes insolvent, leaving Ecuador in technical default. Subsequently, Ecuador defaulted on its next Brady and eurobond coupon payments.

**Embedded Options**
Aside from the par call feature of Bradys, certain Par and Discount bonds carry "value recovery" rights or warrants, which give bondholders the opportunity to "recapture" some of the debt and debt-service reduction provided in the exchange if the future economic performance and the debt-servicing capacity of the sovereign debtor improves. The rights are a mechanism by which the issuing country shares with its creditors a portion of the incremental revenue generated by, for example, a consistent increase in oil prices or the sovereign's GDP. Often, these warrants are linked to indices of oil export prices, or the country's oil export receipts as in the cases of Mexico, Venezuela, and Nigeria, or the level of a terms-of-trade index in the case of Uruguay.

# Non-Collateralized Brady Bonds

The types of bonds included in a given plan were determined during the debt restructuring negotiations between a consortium of creditors and the debtor country. The bonds often have varying coupon schedules, amortizations, and sometimes include the capitalization of interest. Each plan may also include principal types other than Par and Discount bonds, such as *debt-conversion bonds* (DCBs), *capitalization bonds* (C-Bonds), *front-loaded interest-reduction bonds* (FLIRBs), and the related *new-money bonds* (NMBs). The DCBs, NMBs, and FLIRBs are typically non-collateralized amortizing bearer instruments with a significantly shorter final maturity and average life than the Pars and Discounts. DCBs were exchanged at full face value and carry a floating interest rate, but creditors who chose the DCB option had to commit to extending new funds to the sovereign issuer by buying short-term, floating-rate NMBs. FLIRBs carry collateral-securing interest payments, generally for twelve months, and the guarantee is available for the first five to six years of the life of the bond. C-bonds, also know as *payment-in-kind* (PIK) bonds are capitalizing bonds, which first appeared in the 1994 Brazil Brady plan. In the C-bond exchange agreement, Brazil agreed to an 8% interest accrual rate that initially only paid 4%. The remaining 4% capitalized, for example, increasing the par amount outstanding at the end of the first year to 104% of the original amount.

Past-due interest on several Brady plans have also been consolidated into *past-due interest bonds* (PDIs), *interest due and unpaid bonds* (IDUs), *eligible interest bonds* (EIs), *interest arrears bonds* (IABs), and *floating-rate past-due interest bonds* (FRBs). These instruments generally consist of a non-collateralized, ten or twenty year amortizing floating rate bond. Past-due interest on defaulted loans exchanged for PDI bonds typically capitalize during several of the earlier interest payments periods and then amortize, as is the case in the PDIs issued under the Ecuador, Panama and Peru Brady exchanges.

## Non-Brady Restructured Loans

Perhaps the most speculative segment of this high-risk, high-yielding market has been bank loans (generally non-performing and available only through assignment or participation agreements with extended 21-day settlement periods). Bank loans can be higher yielding than bonds for the same country, since the issuing countries are more cautious about offending bondholders than bank lenders. The principally traded types of bank loans were the "pre-Brady" claims of countries expected to obtain debt and debt service relief under the auspices of the Brady initiative in future negotiations. They were often off-limits to investors.

By the mid-1990's, almost all countries that were eligible to exchange defaulted loans into Brady bonds had done so, though a few countries, such as Algeria, Morocco and Russia, chose not to be a part of the Brady program and opted to exchange their bank loans for new, restructured loans.

In the case of the Russian Federation, it had accepted responsibility for all Soviet-era commercial bank loans taken by the former USSR, but it had no direct legal obligation to service the debt. The Vneshcomenbank loans of the former USSR were restructured into a $20 billion principal loan (Prins) and a $6 billion interest arrears note (IANs). In the aftermath of the Russian financial crisis and the ruble devaluation in August 1998, Russia defaulted on the Prins and subsequently on the IANs. Many investors who were unaware of the seniority class difference between Russian and Soviet-era debt incurred heavy losses. Since legally, the obligor of the restructured loans was not the Russian Federation and no cross default clauses existed, Russia was able to cease payments on the Prins and IANs while it continued to pay on its sovereign eurobond debt without jeopardizing the non-default status of those eurobonds. Currently, Russia is in negotiations with official creditors to restructure and seek debt forgiveness on its defaulted Prins and IANs.

## RETIRING BRADY BONDS: BUYBACKS AND EXCHANGES
### Brady Buybacks

Since the issuance of Brady bonds, many countries sufficiently implemented economic reforms to enable them to access the capital markets in the form of eurobonds. Simultaneously, many countries have been retiring their Brady debt through various forms of buybacks. In the past several years, sovereign issuers of Brady bonds have been able to retire Brady debt through five main approaches:

- The issuer may *exercise the call option* on the bond, as Mexico had done with its Aztec issue. All Brady bonds are callable at par usually on coupon payment dates.

- The sovereign country may *discretely buyback their Brady bonds* in the open market, as did Argentina, Brazil, Mexico, Panama and Poland.

- A sovereign issuer may *initiate a formal Brady exchange* program whereby a price or spread is preset and bids are solicited for an exchange into a new eurobond issue. In 1996, Mexico was the first sovereign country to participate in a large scale Brady to eurobond exchange. At that time, emerging markets were providing extremely high returns, spreads were consistently tightening, and investors were glad to have an opportunity to exchange their collateralized Mexican Par and Discount bonds for a non-collateralized global issue that would outperform if spreads continued to tighten. This set the tone for subsequent formal exchanges that included Argentina, Brazil, Mexico, Panama, Uruguay, Venezuela and the Philippines.

- *Private exchange agreements* have been arranged whereby two to four holders of a sizable block of Brady bonds would agree to an exchange for a sovereign eurobond.

- Brady bonds have also been *accepted as payment in several privatizations*, particularly in Brazil.

Exhibit 17–3 shows the current percentage of the original issue amount of Brady debt that has been retired. So far, Argentina, Mexico, Venezuela, Poland and the Philippines have been the largest buyers of their own Brady bonds, having retired over 30% of the original issued amount. Currently, Latin America still dominates the Brady market, with Argentina, Brazil, Mexico and Venezuela accounting for 73% of the current amount outstanding. (See Exhibit 17–4.)

## Brady Debt Affects the U.S. Bond Market

If a country retires collateralized debt, it may release the collateral associated with the principal amount retired. Since the issuer has a cost of funds which is higher than the return on its invested interest collateral in AA-rated securities, the issuer suffers from a "negative carry" for the life of the bond. In various buybacks and exchange programs, the issuer has been able to gain significant savings on financing costs through retiring its Brady debt. There are restrictions on the timing and size of retiring special purpose zero-coupon bonds used as collateral, however, no restrictions exist on the retirement of open market U.S. Treasury strips. Many of these Brady bond buybacks are often associated with corresponding activity in the U.S. Treasury strips market. As a result, U.S. Treasury investors often have a keen interest in knowing what the Brady countries are doing vis-à-vis retiring collateralized debt. Exhibit 17–5 shows the amount of open market U.S. Treasury strips currently held by each Brady country as principal collateral at the New York Federal Reserve.

**EXHIBIT   17-3**

Percentage of Original Brady Bonds Issued that have been Retired or Amortized as of November 1999

| Country | Pars | Discounts | Other Brady Debt | Total Brady Debt Retired/Amortized |
|---|---|---|---|---|
| **Latin America** | | | | |
| Argentina | 44% | 39% | 18% | 34% |
| Brazil | 63% | 46% | 13% | 28% |
| Costa Rica | 0% | 0% | 0% | 0% |
| Dominican Republic | 0% | 0% | 5% | 2% |
| Ecuador | 10% | 0% | -4% | 1% |
| Mexico | 41% | 54% | 96% | 50% |
| Panama | 25% | 12% | 40% | 38% |
| Peru | 0% | 11% | 8% | 8% |
| Uruguay | 43% | 0% | 20% | 31% |
| Venezuela | 68% | 32% | 22% | 41% |
| **Non-Latin** | | | | |
| Bulgaria | 0% | 16% | 0% | 6% |
| Ivory Coast | 0% | 0% | 1% | 1% |
| Jordan | 0% | 0% | 32% | 4% |
| Nigeria | 0% | 0% | 0% | 0% |
| Philippines | 61% | 0% | 24% | 41% |
| Poland | 17% | 73% | 14% | 36% |
| Vietnam | 0% | 0% | 0% | 0% |
| **Total** | **46%** | **45%** | **18%** | **33%** |

Source: Merrill Lynch

## Brady Bonds Decrease as a Percentage of Foreign Currency Debt

Eurobonds are typically plain vanilla bullet structures and there is some sense by investors that eurobonds are less subject to default risk. Therefore, investors typically do not require as wide of a spread on eurobonds as on Bradys. With tighter eurobond spreads, sovereigns have been able to reduce their cost of funds by occasionally using the proceeds from eurobond issues to retire outstanding Brady debt. The impact of these new issues and buybacks on the composition of external debt can be seen in Exhibit 17-6, which outlines the decline in Brady debt of the major Latin countries as a percentage of outstanding external sovereign debt in the last three years.

## CREDIT RATINGS

When Moody's Investors Service began rating Brady bonds in 1990, it rated Mexico's registered Par and Discount bonds Ba3 even though Mexico had pre-

**E X H I B I T   17–4**

Current Face Amount of Bradys Outstanding (US $bn) as of
November 1999

| Country | Pars | Discounts | Other Brady Debt | Total Brady Debt Outstanding | Percent |
|---|---|---|---|---|---|
| **Latin America** | | | | | |
| Argentina | 7.09 | 2.64 | 6.96 | 16.69 | 14.7% |
| Brazil | 3.87 | 3.95 | 28.45 | 36.27 | 31.9% |
| Costa Rica | na | na | 0.59 | 0.59 | 0.5% |
| Dominican Republic | na | 0.33 | 0.18 | 0.51 | 0.4% |
| Ecuador | 1.71 | 1.43 | 2.90 | 6.05 | 5.3% |
| Mexico | 13.16 | 5.36 | 0.12 | 18.63 | 16.4% |
| Panama | 0.20 | 0.04 | 1.76 | 2.00 | 1.8% |
| Peru | 0.18 | 0.51 | 3.78 | 4.46 | 3.9% |
| Uruguay | 0.30 | na | 0.43 | 0.73 | 0.6% |
| Venezuela | 2.36 | 0.87 | 7.74 | 10.96 | 9.6% |
| **Non-Latin** | | | | | |
| Bulgaria | na | 1.55 | 3.28 | 4.83 | 4.2% |
| Ivory Coast | na | 0.07 | 1.24 | 1.31 | 1.2% |
| Jordan | 0.49 | 0.16 | 0.06 | 0.72 | 0.6% |
| Nigeria | 2.05 | na | na | 2.05 | 1.8% |
| Philippines | 0.74 | na | 1.75 | 2.49 | 2.2% |
| Poland | 0.75 | 0.81 | 3.47 | 5.33 | 4.4% |
| Russia* | na | na | 26.22 | 26.22 | 0.0% |
| Vietnam | 0.23 | 0.02 | 0.29 | 0.55 | 0.3% |
| **Total** | **33.13** | **17.73** | **63.01** | **113.87** | **100%** |
| Percent | 29.1% | 15.6% | 55.3% | 100.0% | |

Though Russia's debt restructuring package of Soviet-era defaulted loans was not an official Brady Exchange, it is
often classified in that category

Source: Merrill Lynch

viously been assigned a ceiling rating of Ba2. Moody's had distinguished other
sovereign bond debt (eurobonds, global bonds) as being senior to Brady bonds.
The one-notch distinction was rationalized because the Brady bonds were perceived as more vulnerable to rescheduling in a potential debt crisis since Brady
bonds had traditionally comprised a significant portion of a country's debt. Also,
the ownership of Brady bonds was concentrated with the original lending banks.
The past rationale was that this concentration, in theory, made Brady bonds
easier to renegotiate. Furthermore, for the approximately 60% of outstanding
Brady bonds that were issued in registered versus bearer form, the bondholders
were also easier to "trace." Moody's also believed that large holders of Brady
bonds could be tempted to submit to re-negotiation of the bonds, rather than
face a significant decline in the market value of their holdings in the event of a
payment crisis.

Since the first Mexican rating, the emerging markets investor base has
changed substantially and many emerging markets countries have returned to
the international capital markets through the issuance of eurobonds. When

**EXHIBIT 17-5**

Brady Bond Principal Collateral Outstanding as of October 30, 1999

| Country | Brady Bond Maturity | Face (US $bn) | US Treasury Strips | Special Issue Gov't Series |
|---|---|---|---|---|
| **Latin America** | | | | |
| Argentina | March-2023 | 9.7 | 3.1 | 6.7 |
| Brazil | April-2024 | 7.8 | 7.8 | — |
| Dominican Republic | August-2024 | 0.3 | 0.3 | — |
| Ecuador | February-2025 | 3.1 | 3.1 | — |
| Mexico | December-2019 | 18.5 | — | 18.5 |
| Peru | March-2027 | 0.6 | 0.6 | — |
| Panama | July-2026 | 0.3 | 0.3 | — |
| Uruguay | February-2021 | 0.3 | 0.3 | — |
| Venezuela | March-2020 | 2.6 | — | 2.6 |
| **Non-Latin** | | | | |
| Bulgaria | July-2024 | 1.6 | 1.6 | — |
| Jordan | December-2023 | 0.6 | 0.6 | — |
| Nigeria | November-2020 | 2.1 | 2.1 | — |
| Philippines | December-2017 | 0.7 | 0.7 | — |
| Poland | October-2024 | 2.3 | 2.3 | — |

Source: Merrill Lynch

**EXHIBIT 17-6**

Percentage of Current Outstanding Brady Debt to Total Outstanding External Sovereign Debt

| | As of November 1999 | December 1998 | December 1997 | December 1996 |
|---|---|---|---|---|
| Argentina | 26% | 34% | 42% | 54% |
| Brazil | 63% | 74% | 78% | 86% |
| Mexico | 33% | 36% | 37% | 45% |
| Venezuela | 60% | 67% | 75% | 84% |

'Includes both Sovereign and Quasi Sovereign Eurobonds
Source: Merrill Lynch

Moody's first rated Brady bonds, the majority of holders were initially the same banks that were owed the defaulted loan, a relatively small and concentrated investor group familiar with the restructuring. In many instances these banks had ongoing financial relationships with the countries involved. Since then, the ownership has changed as trading volume on Brady bonds has soared and holdings by non-banks have become more widespread. By now, many of the same portfolios that hold eurobonds, now also include Brady bonds of the same country. In addition, a sizable number of small investors have also entered the Brady market.

In 1996, Moody's Investors Service revised its approach. Today, like Standard and Poor's, who originally began assigning equal credit ratings to all foreign debt obligations of sovereign countries, Moody's no longer makes a distinction between the credit risk of Brady bonds and sovereign eurobonds of the same issuer. Legally, Brady bonds rank pari passu (equal ranking) with other senior sovereign foreign currency debt obligations of the debtor country. When investing in high-risk securities, investors should take note of the cross default clauses stated in the provisions of the bond agreement.

## ASSESSING VALUE IN BRADY BONDS
### Valuing Collateralized Brady Bonds

A bond with collateral requires a somewhat different method of assessing value than merely calculating yield-to-maturity based on price. Investors can think of a Discount or Par bond as having three components: the U.S. Treasury fully collateralized principal, the collateralized rolling interest guarantee (RIG), and the credit risk remainder of the bond's cash flows. Often, dealers may vary in their measures of the bond's stripped yield (yield-to-maturity without the principal and interest collateral embedded in the bond). The main difference in valuing collateralized Brady bonds has been in the various approaches to valuing the RIG component. In valuing these Brady bonds to assess relative value, we will review two most common methods that allow an investor to more easily compare yields of collateralized and non-collateralized sovereign bonds.

#### The Modified Cash Flow (MCF)
The MCF method is a simple and efficient way to account for the rolling interest guarantee of a bond with interest collateral. Though the interest collateral does not currently cover the later coupons, these coupons still benefit from the RIG as each interest payment is made. The objective of the MCF approach is to simulate the rolling nature of the interest collateral as each successive coupon is paid. This is accomplished by discounting each subsequent coupon beyond the interest collateral at U.S. forward rates as it becomes guaranteed.

Through a continuous manner of discounting and moving forward each coupon by the specified number of periods secured, an investor can simulate the process of selling each coupon for its present value as soon as each successive interest payment becomes guaranteed. The set of proceeds generated from the sales represent the modified cash flows. The investor can now calculate an internal rate of return (IRR) on a collateralized Brady bond using the MCF and a stripped price. The stripped price is the price of the bond less the present value of its collateralized principal (discounted at the Treasury STRIP rate) and the present value of its interest guarantee (discounted using the swap curve to reflect the AA-rate collateral). The stripped yield and stripped spread (the spread off of the U.S. Treasury zero coupon curve) is perceived as a representation of the market's view of that country's level of sovereign risk.

Using these calculated risk values, an investor is able to identify relative value between collateralized Brady bonds and non-collateralized bonds.

### The Implied Probability of Default (IPD)

The IPD method computes the expected present value of each cash flow payment assuming a constant probability of default on each coupon payment given that default can occur at anytime during the life of the bond. If we assign "p" to be the risk neutral default probability, then the probability of defaulting on a future coupon date "n" can be represented as $p*(1 - p)^{n-1}$, conditional on the issuer having paid all previous coupons. The following equation generalizes the IPD valuation of a collateralized Brady bond.

$$\text{Full Price} = \Sigma PV[(1 - p)^n \times \text{Coupon}_n + p(1 - p)^{n-1} \times [\text{Value of RIG}]_n] + [\text{PV of Principal Collateral}]$$

To compute the stripped yield using the IPD approach, an investor would need to solve for the p that equates the value of the bond's cash flows to its price (see above equation). Once the value of p has been determined, the investor can calculate the value of the RIG today, where

$$\text{Present Value of the RIG} = \Sigma PV[p(1 - p)^{n-1} \times [\text{Value of RIG}]_n].$$

The stripped yield is then the discount rate that equates the present value of the bond's cash flows to its stripped price (Full Price − [PV of Principal Collateral] − [PV of the RIG]).

## Valuing Floating Rate Bonds

Unlike most corporate bonds, many Brady bonds amortize and may pay floating rate coupons for some or all of the coupon periods. A common way to compare fixed rate and floating rate coupons is to "swap" the floating rate to a fixed rate, or assume that the floating rate coupon resets based on forward LIBOR, on the LIBOR swap curve or on the Eurodollar futures curve. The computed yield of the resulting cash flows, without the collateral, can then be compared to U.S.

Treasuries to identify cheap bonds (wide stripped spreads) versus rich bonds (tight stripped spreads).

## HIGH YIELDS HAVE ATTRACTED NEW INVESTORS

One key element to investing in Brady bonds is to have an understanding of the supply-and-demand conditions in the market. The debt supply in International Emerging Markets (IEM) comes from a broad range of asset classes, which include Brady bonds, bank loans, eurobond issues, foreign currency-denominated money market instruments, local currency fixed-income instruments, and derivative and structured products (see Exhibits 17–7 and 17–8). Bradys still provide the best combination of high yield, potential price appreciation, and collateralized securities, with the size and liquidity large enough to accommodate the increasingly dominant source of demand—institutional investors. But in this decade, eurobonds will likely surpass Brady bonds as the liquid assets of choice, as buybacks, retirements and large eurobond issues continue the trend begun in the last several years. In addition to cash bonds, active derivatives and repo markets in both Bradys and eurobonds have given institutional investors leverage and enhanced opportunities to express a view or to take advantage of relative mispricings in the market.

In recent years, these attributes have encouraged successive waves of institutional investors to enter emerging markets, especially the Brady market for the first time. Originally, the principal investors in the market were high-net-

EXHIBIT 17–7

Trading Volume Share of Market by Instrument

|  | 2Q 1999 | 1Q 1999 | 1998 | 1997 | 1996 | 1995 | 1994 | 1993 |
|---|---|---|---|---|---|---|---|---|
| Loans | 2.7% | 2.2% | 5.1% | 5.1% | 4.7% | 6.4% | 8.8% | 13.8% |
| Brady Bonds | 38.5% | 37.2% | 36.9% | 40.6% | 50.8% | 57.7% | 60.9% | 51.6% |
| Total Non-Brady Bonds | 31.6% | 23.3% | 24.5% | 22.6% | 10.7% | 7.7% | 5.8% | 8.9% |
| Sovereign Bonds | 22.3% | 16.9% | 17.7% | 15.6% | 6.2% | 4.1% | 2.6% | 4.5% |
| Corporate Bonds | 9.0% | 6.0% | 5.7% | 6.6% | 3.9% | 3.3% | 3.2% | 4.5% |
| Total Local Market Instruments | 19.9% | 32.6% | 28.2% | 25.5% | 24.0% | 21.7% | 19.0% | na |
| Local Currency-denominated | 16.4% | 24.4% | 20.8% | 16.5% | 16.1% | 16.8% | 13.4% | 10.5% |
| US Dollar-denominated | 1.7% | 1.0% | 2.9% | 3.4% | 2.1% | 2.1% | 3.5% | 7.8% |
| Options and Warrants | 7.3% | 4.7% | 5.3% | 6.2% | 8.9% | 6.5% | 5.1% | 2.9% |
| Unspecified / Other | 0.0% | 0.0% | 0.0% | 0.1% | 0.9% | 0.0% | 0.4% | na |
| Total | 100% | 100% | 100% | 100% | 100% | 100% | 100% | 100% |

Source: Emerging Markets Traders Association

**EXHIBIT   17–8**

Trading Volume Share of Market by Region

|  | 2Q 1999 | 1Q 1999 | 1998 | 1997 | 1996 | 1995 | 1994 | 1993 |
|---|---|---|---|---|---|---|---|---|
| Africa | 3.7% | 4.7% | 4.0% | 4.1% | 4.2% | 4.0% | 4.0% | 4.0% |
| Asia | 4.6% | 6.8% | 3.9% | 1.8% | 3.1% | 1.0% | 0.8% | 1.0% |
| Eastern Europe | 10.0% | 9.2% | 20.3% | 14.5% | 11.6% | 11.5% | 6.2% | 4.4% |
| Russia | 6.8% | 4.2% | 16.4% | 11.0% | 7.2% | 5.3% | 2.6% | 1.2% |
| Latin America & Caribbean | 74.6% | 66.3% | 68.1% | 78.4% | 80.5% | 83.4% | 81.7% | 81.9% |
| Argentina | 15.0% | 14.2% | 14.7% | 20.9% | 24.4% | 22.3% | 21.3% | 27.5% |
| Brazil | 38.6% | 28.1% | 30.4% | 30.4% | 27.2% | 32.0% | 21.6% | 13.1% |
| Mexico | 12.0% | 16.4% | 15.3% | 16.6% | 17.9% | 18.6% | 21.7% | 23.5% |
| Venezuela | 5.0% | 3.5% | 4.3% | 5.9% | 7.5% | 7.1% | 14.5% | 14.5% |
| Middle East | 7.0% | 13.0% | 3.6% | 1.1% | 0.4% | 0.2% | 0.1% | 0.1% |

Source: Emerging Markets Traders Association

worth individuals from within the emerging market countries. They were the first to realize that these countries had begun to "turn the corner," and in the late 1980's, they began to repatriate their funds by buying distressed assets. This in turn, triggered a steady recovery in asset values, which was further supported by the subsequent issuance of Brady bonds. The high returns on these assets increasingly attracted institutional interest. The first institutional investors were the more aggressive fund managers (hedge funds, global growth funds, dedicated emerging markets funds, etc.) and broker/dealers (including major Wall Street firms and several of the original lending banks that had participated in the Brady exchange.) Soon after, "crossover" investors from the domestic high-yield bond market (where yields were no longer as attractive) began to view emerging markets as an asset class to include in their portfolios (see Exhibit 17–9). Bonds issued by emerging countries have almost always offered significantly higher yields than the U.S. domestic high yield market. With the upgrade of Poland's Brady bonds to investment grade in 1996, U.S. corporate, Asian and European investors became interested as well. The profile of the IEM market had transformed from sovereign debt ownership concentrated in the hands of few creditor banks and dealers to ownership distributed more widely through actively traded Brady bonds. The performance of the Merrill Lynch Brady Bond Index since June 1990 is shown in Exhibit 17–10. Over the last 9.3 years, it has provided a 15% annual return compared to 13% for the U.S. high yield market.

While the U.S. bond market continued to rally through the mid 1990s, U.S. interest rates had reached a 25-year low, and demand for emerging market assets began to appear from more conservative investors. Insurance companies and pension funds, driven by the need for higher yields, began investing in IEM. With relatively low financing costs, and the sprout of newly formed hedge funds

**EXHIBIT  17–9**

Comparison of Brady Versus U.S. High Yield Index

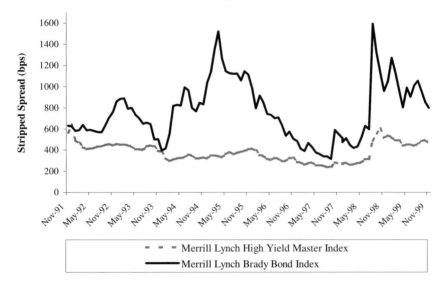

enticed by the large potential of levered returns, emerging markets outperformed with a 41% return in 1996.[5]

As a result of the Asian financial crisis of 1997 followed by the Russian debacle in the summer 1998, capital flows to emerging markets began to diminish. Investors soon reduced their willingness to assume risk as reflected in the flight to quality, as investors deserted higher yielding assets for safer more liquid bonds. The fear of contagion only worsened the financial crisis as developing countries were unable to raise new financing in the international capital markets. With global markets under severe pressure, the hedge fund community collapsed and was forced to liquidate, resulting in massive sell-offs. Liquidity is key in all markets, but especially in one as volatile as emerging markets.

Like all markets, emerging debt markets are cyclical. At the end of the millennium, this market has just come off of a cyclical low point. While other fixed income markets have recovered, some emerging countries have not effectively instituted fiscal reforms, nor do investors feel that they have a process in which to do so. Yet many developing countries have taken the steps needed to become prosperous and some have even become investment grade. Coming from the bottom of a cycle, emerging debt markets as an asset class has the potential

5. As calculated from the Merrill Lynch Extended Emerging Markets Debt Index

# EXHIBIT 17-10

Total Return of Merrill Lynch Brady Bond Index

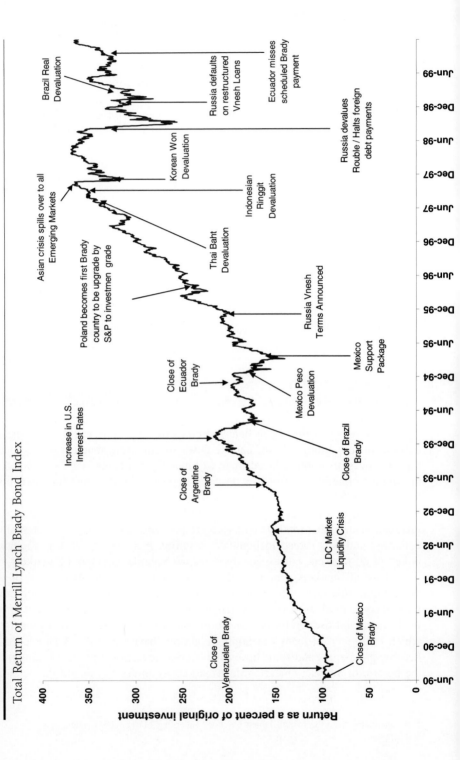

for excellent returns in early 2000. However, several ingredients will be necessary to push to higher levels. One is greater evidence that we will not see a major reversal in global liquidity. Second, is the need for clearer evidence of a rebound in economic activity in Latin America, which still accounts for two thirds of the market's capitalization. And perhaps most important is the market's ability to attract a widening base of crossover investors and eventually increase the pool of dedicated funds.

## CHAPTER 18

# STABLE VALUE INVESTMENTS

**Kenneth L. Walker**
President
T. Rowe Price Stable Asset Management, Inc.

The purpose of this chapter is to discuss stable value investments. In previous editions of this book, the author has presented stable value investing as an investment primarily for 401(k) plans. Today stable value is expanding from its U.S. defined contribution base to include new opportunities in the global arena. We find the concept embedded in Principal Protection Funds for the Japanese retail markets, for the institutional and high net worth markets in both Europe and Japan, and at the retail level in the U.S. for IRA deposits.

## TYPES OF CONTRACTS AND STRATEGIES

The cornerstone of most stable value funds has been the *Guaranteed Investment Contract* (GIC); an obligation of the insurance company, typically issued through the insurer's general account, which provides a fixed rate and fixed maturity. Banks have been active in this market, from time-to-time issuing *Bank Investment Contracts* (BICs) generally as a deposit obligation with a fixed rate and maturity. Alternatives to BICs and GICs exist in response to plan sponsors' desire for added diversification, credit enhancement, and greater control over the underlying assets. Most of these latter structures fall into two broad categories: *separate account contracts* (SACs) offered by insurance companies, where a separate portfolio of assets is owned and managed by the insurance company for the benefit of the plan (or group of plans), and *synthetic investment contracts* (SICs) offered by both insurance companies and banks, where a separate portfolio of securities is owned by the plan and "wrapped" by a third-party financial institution to provide book-value accounting treatment. Characteristics of these contracts are compared in Exhibit 18–1.

Stable value investment contracts[1] differ from traditional fixed income instruments in three ways. First, those issued to qualified plans by insurance com-

---

1. Throughout this chapter, GICs, SACs, and SICs will be referred to as *investment contracts*. However, the term *investment contracts* may have certain regulatory meanings and connotations that are not necessarily applied to BICs, GICs, SACs, and SICs.

**E X H I B I T   18–1**

| Key Points | Separate Account Contracts | Synthetic GICs |
|---|---|---|
| Assets held by | Insurance company in a separate account | Plan in custody account |
| Assets selected by | Issuer | Issuer, plan sponsor, or manager |
| Assets actively managed? | Yes | Yes; for constant duration |
| Assets credit risk borne by | Plan | Plan |
| Credit exposure to issuer | Lower than to general account products | Lower than to general account products |
| Fully benefit-responsive | Yes; benefit liquidations may affect future returns | Yes; benefit liquidations may affect future returns |

panies and banks generally are exempt from registration as a security. Second, the majority of investment contract products enjoy amortized cost (book value) accounting treatment. This accounting basis provides an investment whose principal value remains stable and does not fluctuate with changes in interest rate levels. Third, investment contracts provide an equivalent "put" option at the participant level. The participant can exercise this "put" back to the issuer at any time (for most types of allowable withdrawals) at book value.

Coincident with the introduction of a new generation of SIC stable-value alternatives has been the development of appropriate alternative investment strategies. The buyer/investor now has the opportunity to choose along a risk spectrum from a single security strategy, often referred to as a "buy/hold" SIC, which most closely resembles the fixed-rate GIC, to a more active and diversified strategy, including immunization, constant duration/evergreen, and other "controlled volatility" investment strategies.

The marketplace has witnessed almost 20 years of declining interest rates (see Exhibits 18–2 through 18–5). This decline has produced a positive lag effect for investors in stable value funds as rates declined below the portfolio's blended yield. Should rates trend significantly upward, the positive lag effect in the stable value portfolio could be replaced with a negative one. To guard against the possibility of disintermediation, stable value investment managers employ investment strategies to minimize the effects of significant changes in the yield curve.

## STABLE VALUE INVESTMENT CONTRACTS

The creation of new types of investment contracts has been the next natural step in the evolution of the "GIC" market. The history of every securities market is

**E X H I B I T   18–2**

GIC Returns Compared to Bond Returns

| | Lehman Brothers Intermediate Government/Corporate Index | | | GIC Average Rates (4-Year Maturity) | | |
|---|---|---|---|---|---|---|
| Year | Total Return | (*Yearend*) Yield | Average Maturity | Market High GIC | Market Low GIC | Market Average GIC |
| 1989 | 12.77% | 8.25% | 4.2–4.3 | 9.88% | 8.13% | 8.89% |
| 1990 | 9.16 | 7.94 | 4.2–4.3 | 9.61 | 8.12 | 8.86 |
| 1991 | 14.62 | 5.77 | 4.2–4.3 | 8.24 | 6.05 | 7.61 |
| 1992 | 7.17 | 5.67 | 4.2–4.3 | 7.22 | 5.21 | 6.24 |
| 1993 | 9.79 | 6.59 | 4.2–4.3 | 6.13 | 4.69 | 5.20 |
| 1994 | −1.93 | 7.11 | 4.2–4.3 | 8.12 | 5.10 | 6.84 |
| 1995 | 15.35 | 5.50 | 4.1–4.2 | 8.18 | 5.55 | 6.58 |
| 1996 | 4.05 | 6.22 | 4.2–4.3 | 7.09 | 5.31 | 6.40 |
| 1997 | 7.87 | 5.91 | 4.2–4.3 | 7.09 | 6.07 | 6.52 |
| 1998 | 8.44 | 5.12 | 4.2–4.4 | 6.09 | 4.97 | 5.72 |

Source: GIC rate data obtained from the T. Rowe Price GIC Index. Bond data obtained from Lehman Brothers, *Bond Market Report*.

**E X H I B I T   18–3**

GIC Returns Compared to 90-Day T-Bill Rates

| | GIC Average Rates (2-Year Maturity) | | | | |
|---|---|---|---|---|---|
| Year | Market High GIC | Market Low GIC | Market Average GIC | 90-Day T-Bills | Spread Average |
| 1989 | 9.73% | 7.73% | 8.63% | 8.99% | −0.36% |
| 1990 | 9.26 | 7.57 | 8.40 | 8.42 | −0.02 |
| 1991 | 7.51 | 5.04 | 6.76 | 6.38 | 0.38 |
| 1992 | 6.08 | 4.01 | 5.03 | 3.93 | 1.10 |
| 1993 | 4.93 | 3.97 | 4.27 | 3.19 | 1.08 |
| 1994 | 7.84 | 4.27 | 6.14 | 4.19 | 1.95 |
| 1995 | 7.82 | 5.30 | 6.24 | 6.03 | 0.21 |
| 1996 | 6.67 | 4.97 | 6.02 | 5.31 | 0.72 |
| 1997 | 6.77 | 5.86 | 6.22 | 5.33 | 0.89 |
| 1998 | 5.91 | 4.74 | 5.56 | 5.23 | 0.33 |

Source: GIC rate data obtained from the T. Rowe Price GIC Index. Bond data obtained from Merrill Lynch 90-Day T-Bill Index.

**EXHIBIT 18–4**

GIC Yield Spreads (Three-Year Maturity—Annual Averages)

| Year | Market High GIC | Market Low GIC | High Spread | Low Spread |
|------|------|------|------|------|
| 1989 | 9.85% | 8.01% | 0.65% | −0.02% |
| 1990 | 9.52 | 7.90 | 0.63 | 0.29 |
| 1991 | 7.90 | 5.58 | 0.61 | 0.28 |
| 1992 | 6.75 | 4.60 | 0.58 | 0.18 |
| 1993 | 5.57 | 4.35 | 0.49 | 0.20 |
| 1994 | 8.04 | 4.69 | 0.32 | 0.16 |
| 1995 | 8.06 | 5.42 | 0.30 | −0.19 |
| 1996 | 6.94 | 5.13 | 0.51 | 0.06 |
| 1997 | 6.97 | 5.98 | 0.40 | 0.06 |
| 1998 | 6.01 | 4.92 | 1.01 | 0.18 |

Source: GIC rate data obtained from the T. Rowe Price GIC Index. Yield spreads reflect spreads over equivalent maturity U.S. Treasury issues unadjusted for semiannual versus annualized yields. GIC rates for each year are annual averages.

**EXHIBIT 18–5**

GIC Yield Spreads (1989–1998)

| Maturity (years) | Market High GIC | Market Low GIC | Market Average GIC |
|------|------|------|------|
| 1 | 0.90% | −0.32% | 0.06% |
| 2 | 0.99 | −0.19 | 0.21 |
| 3 | 1.01 | −0.02 | 0.33 |
| 4 | 1.12 | 0.07 | 0.42 |
| 5 | 1.20 | 0.14 | 0.48 |
| 7 | 1.26 | 0.15 | 0.46 |
| 10 | 1.37 | −0.03 | 0.56 |

Source: GIC rate data obtained from the T. Rowe Price GIC Index. Yield spread reflect spreads over equivalent maturity U.S. Treasury issues adjusted for semiannual versus annualized yields. Spreads are annual averages.

characterized by increasing efficiency, better liquidity, and improved risk-management opportunities (e.g., credit and interest-rate risks) at each step in its evolution. The stable value market has been no exception.

A GIC attaches its roots to the Deposit Administration contract and later generation Immediate Participation Guarantee. Unlike those predecessors which were open-ended with a changing interest rate, the GIC, introduced in the mid-

1970s, provided a fixed rate and fixed maturity. When 401(k) plans exploded in popularity in the early 1980s, the GIC became the foundation of the investment spectrum, often representing over 70% of every invested dollar.

In recent years, more diversified structures, including SACs and SICs, have been developed to enhance the diversification profile of the stable value portfolio. The objective of a SAC or SIC is to diversify the credit exposure of the plan away from the unsecured general account or deposit obligation of the issuer. This is accomplished in several ways. In SACs offered by insurance companies, separate accounts holding bonds, mortgages, and other fixed income instruments are established. Assets in such accounts appear to be protected by state laws against liabilities arising out of the insurance company's other business.[2] Often the insurer will pool accounts together into the separate account or, dollar size permitting, a plan may negotiate its own separate account. Securities are selected for the separate account by the insurance company within investment guidelines approved by the plan and the insurance company managing those assets. The insurance company provides a "wrap," which serves to amortize realized and unrealized capital gains in the portfolio, and provides a floor crediting rate and a "guarantee" that if an investing plan has a need for liquidity for normal course withdrawal events, it can liquidate amounts needed to pay participants at book value.

SICs (offered by both banks and insurers) have emerged as another popular alternative. The plan sponsor or the plan's manager selects a portfolio of assets that are purchased and held in custody for the plan.[3] The bank or insurance company provides a zero-floor crediting rate and issues a wrap contract that gives the plan the right to liquidate the securities and receive book value in the event of participant-initiated liquidity needs.

## Separate Account Contracts

The key features of SACs are:

- Contract is typically a modified ("participating") group annuity contract.

- Securities are segregated from other liabilities of the issuer in a separate account.

- Securities are selected and managed by the insurance company.

- Contract earnings rate usually is reset periodically (one-, three-, six-, or 12-month intervals) to reflect:

---

2. The buyer is cautioned to perform independent research to determine the rights of the plan in the event of issuer insolvency. The buyer is also cautioned to research both accounting and ERISA issues as the relate to SACs and SICs. See A.I.C.P.A. Statement of Position 94-4 released in September of 1994 for more information on book-value eligibility.
3. These types of contracts are drafted so that the plan actually owns the securities.

- Gains and losses on individual securities
- Variance in performance from targeted return
- Changes in reinvestment rate
- Securities defaults
- Impact of deposits or withdrawals that alter the ratio of market value to book value or the average yield or duration of the portfolio

- Differences between book value and market value due to the above factors are amortized, typically over the duration of the portfolio, and reflected in future credited rates, resulting in low volatility of returns. (See the Appendix to this chapter for an explanation of crediting rate methodologies.)

## Synthetic Investment Contracts

The key features of SICs are:

- "Wrapped" structure can be either a single-security, immunized strategy or an open-ended (constant-duration) strategy.

- Contract may be fully participating (par), like SACs, where the impact of withdrawals is reflected in credited rates, or the contract may provide that the issuer absorb ordinary participant withdrawal risks (non-par), or the contract may be a hybrid, providing certain levels of par and non-par coverage.

- Securities usually held in a custody account in plan's name

- Securities selected by plan or investment manager with issuer approval

- Various levels of securities cash flow/return risk can be covered by a wrap contract.

## Deciding on the Types of Stable Value Products

Decisions regarding which type(s) of stable value products to use and in what proportions depend on the plan sponsor's objectives and analysis of many factors that relate the characteristics of the products to attainment of these objectives, all within the framework of the existing structure of the fund. For example, high-quality GICs still meet the credit, return, and cash flow needs of many plan sponsors. Single-security SICs may provide credit enhancement and diversification, but the return may be lower than for traditional GICs or other alternatives. Additionally, the plan may have to assume cash flow risks associated with asset-backed and mortgage-backed securities (the two most popular assets used for single security strategies) if not assumed by the wrap provider. Constant-duration SICs provide added diversification and the potential for higher return (due to exposure on the longer end of the yield curve), but typically introduce credit risks if corporate bonds are used.

Decisions are also heavily influenced by the structure of the total investment, which includes contract provisions and investments and how they interrelate. The contract must address questions such as: Does the contract meet all applicable ERISA, tax, and book value accounting requirements? How often is the crediting rate reset, and what method is used to calculate crediting rates? What options do the plan sponsor or investment manager have for terminating the contract, and what are the financial and accounting implications of termination? How are downgraded and defaulted securities handled? What happens in the event of default or breach of contract by the parties?

## TYPES OF SICs

The three predominant strategies that have emerged in the marketplace for SICs as illustrated in Exhibit 18–6, are the single-security, immunized, and constant-duration strategies. The decision as to which strategy is best suited for a fund depends on the particular fund's investment objectives. As illustrated in Exhibit 18–7, returns can differ significantly, depending on market factors, including yield-curve positioning and slope, wrap fees, asset classes utilized, sector allocation, etc.

## Single-Security SIC

A *single-security SIC* usually is structured with one fixed-income security—typically mortgage-backed or asset-backed securities. Because both types of securities provide cash flows from a pool of liquidating collateral, many buyers choose to purchase a form of insurance from the wrapper in order to provide certainty as to the cash flows. Mortgages are subject to prepayment or refinancing and, as such, their cash flows are hard to predict. Asset-backed securities are typically structured around credit card receivables and their cash flows are more predictable. Cash-flow protection at the front end is referred to as *prepayment coverage;* at the tail end it is referred to as *extension coverage.*

Single-security SICs are structured to provide for a final maturity date. The interest rate may be fixed during the investment's life (if prepayment and extension risk coverage are purchased) or can change if no such coverage is purchased to reflect the cash-flow payment behavior of the underlying security(s).

Single-security SICs are often used to provide a future source of cash for benefit payments or reinvestment, or to complement the existing in-force portfolio ladder of traditional GICs.

## Immunized SIC

An *immunized SIC,* like a single-security SIC, has a final maturity date(s). It differs from the single-security SIC because a more highly diversified portfolio of securities are managed and *immunized* to the selected maturity date(s). The contract's maturity date and future payment amount establishes the contract li-

## EXHIBIT 18–6

Features of Principal Types of Stable Value Investments

| Feature | GICs | Single Security SICs* with Extension Coverage Only | Immunized SICs | Constant Duration SICs |
|---|---|---|---|---|
| Credit exposure | 100% to issuer | Securities (Avg-agency). Minimal to SIC issuer. | Securities (Avg-AAA/AA). Minimal to SIC issuer. | Securities (Avg-AAA/AA). Minimal to SIC issuer. |
| Securities types | N/A-issuer general account | Treasuries, Agencies, CMOs, ABSs. | Treasuries, CMOs, ABSs, corporates. | Treasuries, CMOs, ABSs, corporates. |
| Return pattern | Fixed rate | Based on YTM at purchase. Varies, based on changes in securities repayment. | Achieve target rate over investment horizon. Relatively stable crediting rate but will change. Each reset based on performance. | Crediting rate changes. Each reset based on performance. Will track but lag trend in market interest rates. |
| Investment cash flows | Fixed repayment as negotiated in contract | As securities repay, or at contract fixed maturity, whichever occurs first. | Scheduled dates. | No set maturity. Perpetual until payout selected. |
| Investment management | Issuer's general account | Buy-and-Hold. | Periodic rebalancing (more passive than active). Emphasize scenario analysis and horizon returns. | Managed to maintain target duration. Emphasize sector rotation, credit research, quantitative techniques. |
| Deposit types | Lump sum or periodic | Lump sum or periodic. | Lump sum or periodic. | Lump sum or periodic. |

**EXHIBIT 18–7**

Historical Spreads versus U.S. Treasury for GICs and SICs

| | Benchmark | | Spreads-Model Portfolios | | |
| --- | --- | --- | --- | --- | --- |
| | 5 Year Treasury Yields | 5 Year GIC | 5 Year Buy-and-Hold SIC | 5 Year Immunized SIC | Constant Duration SIC |
| 03/31/1994 | 6.23% | 0.58% | 0.50% | 0.75% | 1.07% |
| 06/30/1994 | 6.97 | 0.39 | 0.58% | 0.68% | 0.89% |
| 09/30/1994 | 7.28 | 0.52 | 0.58% | 0.51% | 0.98% |
| 12/31/1994 | 7.83 | 0.54 | 0.74% | 0.65% | 0.68% |
| 03/31/1995 | 7.08 | 0.40 | 0.54% | 0.65% | 0.83% |
| 06/30/1995 | 5.98 | 0.39 | 0.47% | 0.65% | 1.06% |
| 09/30/1995 | 6.01 | 0.42 | 0.49% | 0.56% | 0.91% |
| 12/31/1995 | 5.38 | 0.33 | 0.45% | 0.55% | 1.19% |
| 03/31/1996 | 6.10 | 0.36 | 0.45% | 0.51% | 0.90% |
| 06/30/1996 | 6.47 | 0.50 | 0.48% | 0.67% | 0.92% |
| 09/30/1996 | 6.46 | 0.43 | 0.48% | 0.55% | 1.03% |
| 12/31/1996 | 6.21 | 0.39 | 0.45% | 0.55% | 1.04% |
| 03/31/1997 | 6.77 | 0.39 | 0.43% | 0.46% | 0.89% |
| 06/30/1997 | 6.40 | 0.44 | 0.42% | 0.47% | 0.86% |
| 09/30/1997 | 6.00 | 0.42 | 0.42% | 0.55% | 0.92% |
| 12/31/1997 | 5.71 | 0.51 | 0.57% | 0.61% | 0.86% |
| 03/31/1998 | 5.64 | 0.54 | 0.52% | 0.65% | 0.79% |
| 06/30/1998 | 5.47 | 0.56 | 0.52% | 0.64% | 0.90% |
| 09/30/1998 | 4.23 | 0.80 | 0.87% | 1.06% | 1.68% |
| 12/31/1998 | 4.54 | 1.01 | 1.11% | 0.98% | 1.78% |

Structured Payout SIC Portfolio
   12%–35% Agencies
   35%–52% A-AAA Corporates
    0%–30% Mortgages
    0%–27% ABS

   Effective duration: 4.1–5.2 y
   Average life: 5.0–6.8 y

CDSIC Portfolio
   10%–27% Treasuries
    1%–23% Agencies
   16%–56%54% A-AAA Corporates
   28%–46% Mortgages

   Effective duration: 4.5–5.1
   Average life: 7.4–8.9 years

All SICs gross of wrap and custody fees. For this observation, wrap fees have generally been in the 10-20 basis point range.

Source: GIC rate data obtained from the T. Rowe Price GIC Index. Bond data obtained from Lehman Brothers, *Bond Market Report*.

ability and during the course of the investment term, the manager immunizes the assets to the liability(s) to ensure payment on the future date. The rate is subject to change as the manager rebalances the portfolio to correct for duration drifts and to reflect the amortization of both realized and unrealized gains and losses.

Single-period immunization is typically utilized as a substitute for single-security SICs, BICs, and GICs. Some managers have introduced multi-period immunization which provides for multiple payment dates under an evergreen strategy.

## Constant-Duration SIC

*Constant-duration SICs* do not have a predetermined maturity date. It is an evergreen strategy whose objective is to manage on a total return basis. This open-ended arrangement permits the investment manager to position the portfolio continuously on the longer end of the yield curve which, with a normally positive slope of the curve, should increase investment returns over time. For example, the duration of the Lehman Brothers Aggregate Bond Index, generally in the 4.5–5.5 year range, is a common target duration for a portfolio supporting a constant duration strategy. (Duration of the supporting portfolio is rarely "constant," but will be managed within a narrow range around the target.)

The constant-duration SIC, like other SICs, is available in various structures for providing benefit responsiveness. Generally, four types of liquidity for benefit responsiveness can be negotiated: a "non-participating" feature, where the wrapper absorbs the book-to-market differential if assets are sold; an "advance," where the wrapper advances funds to the plan and is repaid with cash flows arising from income from the assets and/or new contributions; a "participating" feature, where all gains and losses are amortized over the portfolio's duration and reflected in the next crediting-rate reset, and a hybrid, providing certain levels of both non-participating and participating coverage.

## INVESTMENT CONSIDERATIONS

With SACs and constant-duration SICs, the plan sponsor often will depend on an investment manager or consultant to recommend investment guidelines consistent with the plan sponsor's overall investment philosophy and tolerance for risk. Typically, wrap providers are more flexible with respect to managed programs since credit and investment performance risks, as well as potential for higher return, are borne by the plan through the rate-reset mechanism.

To control risks at reasonable levels, investment guidelines generally specify types of permissible investments, credit parameters, and diversification limits by issuer and industry. Generally there is an understanding on the level of risk permitted in the management of assets. This can range from a conservative strategy, where the duration of the portfolio is maintained at the duration of an agreed benchmark index and the average credit quality is high, to a more aggressive strategy, where the duration may be varied within specified ranges around the duration of an index and the average credit quality is lower. Typically, portfolio durations will be maintained within a range of plus or minus 0.5 of the duration of the benchmark index and the average credit quality is AA or higher.

## EMERGING MARKETS

Those wishing to further the concept of stable value investing beyond the domestic 401(k) markets should turn their attention to those countries whose dynamics follow the United States—where defined contribution plans exist or are emerging and where investment climates dictate interest in principal protection. Most notably are the following countries: Canada, Europe, Japan, Latin and South America, and the United Kingdom. As of this writing, Japan and the United Kingdom are most noteworthy.

Japan, with the world's second largest asset base, has two dynamics which encourage stable value investing. First, beginning in late 2000, defined contribution plans will be permitted. Second, investors are conservative by nature. "Principal protection" funds are emerging at the retail level, and one would imagine that they will become a part of the emerging defined contribution plan market.

The United Kingdom too has an asset base and an existing defined contribution platform. As the financial center of Europe, the pool of assets has been estimated to be twice the size of any other European country. While stable value has not to date been on the radar screen, it is getting the product development attention of a number of U.S.-based investment groups.

## FUNDING AGREEMENTS

It would be remiss not to mention the emerging popularity of *Funding Agreements* in both the domestic and non-domestic markets.

In recent years, U.S. domiciled life insurance companies have aggressively pursued the sale of the Funding Agreement as a replacement for the dwindling demand for its cousin, the GIC. The European, Japanese, and domestic markets have been buyers. Within those markets, buyers represent banks, other insurers, pension funds, and high net worth investors. U.S.-based money market funds have used Funding Agreements which provide short "puts" as an eligible sector. The purchase of Funding Agreements has occurred on both a direct basis from the insurer and through the creation of offshore trust, established primarily by investment banking firms. The off-shore trust is more fully described in Exhibit 18–8 below.

**E X H I B I T    18–8**

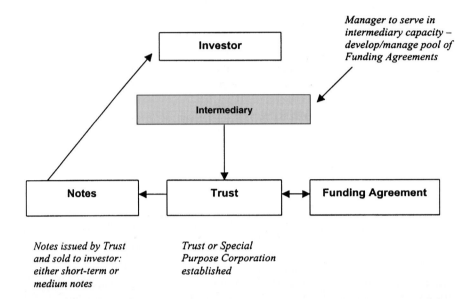

*Manager to serve in intermediary capacity – develop/manage pool of Funding Agreements*

*Notes issued by Trust and sold to investor: either short-term or medium notes*

*Trust or Special Purpose Corporation established*

The investment banking group creates an offshore trust, typically Luxembourg-based or the Cayman Islands-based. The trust sells units, usually as medium term notes, and invests the funds in one or more Funding Agreements. The rate may be either fixed or floating. The buyer receives a note for a specified term, typically five-, seven-, and 10-year maturities. The buyer may elect to maintain the notes in U.S. dollars or swap into another currency.

The popularity of Funding Agreements has been prefaced on its yield premiums to other comparable financial-issued notes, and the introduction of the insurance industry as an eligible, high-quality component of the financial sector.

## SUMMARY

Stable value investing continues to evolve. The alternatives to traditional GICs greatly expand opportunities for better meeting the needs and desires of plan sponsors and participants in managing stable value funds. At the same time, these alternatives create new challenges in understanding and communicating the new structures. Globally, stable value is in its infancy. Rarely has a segment of the financial markets exhibited such rapid and dramatic change. Most practitioners expect continuing developments in the foreseeable future.

**A P P E N D I X**

# Crediting Rate Theory and Methodology

The managed SIC crediting rate is initially set approximately equal to the expected rate of return on the portfolio. The rate is then periodically reset to reflect changes in the portfolio, investment performance, changes in market interest rates, and, for some contracts, benefit payments. While there are at least three mathematically different methods for determining crediting rates, they are all conceptually consistent; that is, the crediting rate is the rate that will amortize differences between book value and market value over the duration of the portfolio. The various methods produce generally consistent crediting rates under most circumstances.

The crediting rate may be reset as frequently as monthly and generally not less than semi-annually. Wrap fees and investment management fees are usually subtracted from the gross crediting rate to arrive at the net rate, which is credited to participant accounts.

Which method is preferred? The issuer and the investment manager usually decide on the crediting-rate method that best meets their needs. All three methods described below are in use, and all produce acceptable results. Method 1, Internal Rate of Return, is the most precise and is generally used for buy-and-hold portfolios and for fixed-term SICs within a few months of final maturity. Methods 2 and 3 are approximations which do not require detailed portfolio cash flows.

## METHOD I—INTERNAL RATE OF RETURN

Using this method, the gross crediting rate is the internal rate of return (or discount rate) that equates projected future inflows of principal and interest to the current book value (present value).

Internal rate of return differs from "weighted average yield-to-maturity," defined as the sum of products of market value times yield-to-maturity for each individual security in the portfolio divided by total market value. In the examples below, the weighted average yield-to-maturity of the sample portfolio is 4.82%, while the internal rate of return is 5.30%. Since the yield curve is positively sloped, IRR is higher than weighted average yield-to-maturity because IRR gives proportionately greater weight to longer maturities.

The IRR formula is:

$$BV = \sum \frac{C_n}{(1 + i)^n}$$

where

$BV$ = Book value
$C_n$ = Cash flow in year n
$n$ = Number of years to receipt of cash flow
$i$ = Crediting rate (IRR)

Calculations for a sample portfolio are shown below.

| Securities | Face Amount | Coupon | Maturity in Years | Current Market Value | Current Market Yield-to-Maturity | Duration |
|---|---|---|---|---|---|---|
| (A) Treasury note | 100.00 | 4.875% | 1.0 | 101.344 | 3.526% | 0.99 |
| (B) Treasury note | 100.00 | 7.500 | 3.0 | 107.156 | 4.966 | 2.75 |
| (C) Treasury note | 100.00 | 7.875 | 5.0 | 108.906 | 5.882 | 4.27 |
| Total market value of portfolio: | | | | 317.406 | 4.821% | 2.71 |
| Book value of portfolio: | | | | 317.406 | | |

| Time in Years | Expected Cash Flows (A) | (B) | (C) | (Book Value) Total Inflows (317,406) |
|---|---|---|---|---|
| 0.5 | 2.4375 | 3.7500 | 3.9375 | 10.1250 |
| 1.0 | 102.4375 | 3.7500 | 3.9375 | 110.1250 |
| 1.5 | | 3.7500 | 3.9375 | 7.6878 |
| 2.0 | | 3.7500 | 3.9375 | 7.6875 |
| 2.5 | | 3.7500 | 3.9375 | 7.6875 |
| 3.0 | | 103.7500 | 3.9375 | 107.6875 |
| 3.5 | | | 3.9375 | 3.9375 |
| 4.0 | | | 3.9375 | 3.9375 |
| 4.5 | | | 3.9375 | 3.9375 |
| 5.0 | | | 103.9375 | 103.9375 |

| | |
|---|---|
| IRR (annualized) of total cash flow on book value if book and market are equal: | **5.30%** |
| IRR if book value is 1% less than market value: | **5.69%** |
| IRR if book value is 1% greater than market value: | **4.91%** |

# METHOD 2—DISCOUNT RATE WHICH EQUATES CURRENT BOOK VALUE TO THEORETICAL FUTURE VALUE

This method begins with a theoretical future market value calculated by taking the current market value of the portfolio and compounding it forward at the average yield-to maturity of the portfolio. The next step is to find the discount rate which equates this future value to the current book value of the portfolio. This is the gross crediting rate, as illustrated by the following formula:

$$i = (MV/BV)^{(1/Dur)} \times (1 + YTM) - 1$$

where

$MV$ = Market value of portfolio
$YTM$ = Dollar-duration weighted yield-to-maturity
$DUR$ = Duration of portfolio.

The yield-to-maturity used in the above formula may be either dollar-duration weighted or dollar weighted. Dollar-duration weighting closely approximates IRR. In a constant-duration portfolio where cash flow is reinvested at longer maturities, dollar-duration weighting gives the best approximation of expected total return. In the case of an immunized portfolio where duration is collapsing, it is preferable to use dollar-weighted yield-to-maturity. In the example below, dollar-duration weighted yield-to-maturity is used. Dollar-duration weighted yield-to-maturity is 5.29%, whereas dollar weighted yield-to-maturity is 4.82%.

Where the terms *yield-to-maturity* and *duration* are used in this discussion, the appropriate measures in the case of mortgages and optionable securities are effective or option-adjusted yield and effective duration.

For the sample portfolios the calculations are as follows:

| Securities | Face Amount | Coupon | Maturity in years | Current Market Value | Current Market Yield-to-Maturity | Duration | Dollar Duration | Dollar Duration Times Yield-to-Maturity |
|---|---|---|---|---|---|---|---|---|
| (A) Treasury note | 100.00 | 4.875% | 1.0 | 101.344 | 3.526% | 0.99 | 100.3306 | 3.5377 |
| (B) Treasury note | 100.00 | 7.500 | 3.0 | 107.156 | 4.966 | 2.75 | 294.6790 | 14.6338 |
| (C) Treasury note | 100.00 | 7.875 | 5.0 | 108.906 | 5.882 | 4.27 | 465.0286 | 27.3530 |
| Total market value of portfolio: | | | | 317.406 | 4.821% | 2.71 | 860.0381 | 45.5244 |
| Book value of portfolio: | | | | 317.406 | | | (a) | (b) |

| | |
|---|---|
| Dollar duration weighted yield to maturity [(b)/(a)] = | 5.29% |
| Calculation of estimated future value: 317.406 * (1.0529)$^{2.71}$ | 365.0.16 |
| Discount rate which equates estimated future value to current book value: | |
| Gross crediting rate if book and market are equal [(365.016/317.406)$^{1/2.71}$ − 1]: | **5.29%** |
| Gross crediting rate if book value is 1% less than market value = | **5.68%** |
| Gross crediting rate if book value is 1% greater than market value = | **4.91%** |

# METHOD 3–DIFFERENCE BETWEEN MARKET VALUE AND BOOK VALUE DIVIDED BY DURATION

For this method the percentage difference between market value and book value is divided by the weighted average duration of the portfolio and added to the current dollar duration weighted (or dollar weighted if appropriate) market yield-to-maturity. This method involves no exponentiation.

The formula is expressed as

$$i = YTM + [(MV - BV)/MV] \times (1/Dur)$$

The calculations for the sample portfolio are as follows:

| Securities | Face Amount | Coupon | Maturity in years | Current Market Value | Current Market Yield-to-Maturity | Duration | Dollar Duration | Dollar Duration Times Yield-to-Maturity |
|---|---|---|---|---|---|---|---|---|
| (A) Treasury note | 100.00 | 4.875% | 1.0 | 101.344 | 3.526% | 0.99 | 100.3306 | 3.5377 |
| (B) Treasury note | 100.00 | 7.500 | 3.0 | 107.156 | 4.966 | 2.75 | 94.6790 | 14.6338 |
| (C) Treasury note | 100.00 | 7.875 | 5.0 | 108.906 | 5.882 | 4.27 | 465.0286 | 27.3530 |
| Total market value of portfolio: | | | | 317.406 | 4.821% | 2.71 | 860.0381 | 45.5244 |
| Book value of portfolio: | | | | 317.406 | | | (a) | (b) |

| | |
|---|---|
| Dollar-duration weighted yield to maturity [(b)/(a)] = | 5.29% |
| Percent difference between market and book divided by weighted average duration: | |
| If book and market are equal | 0.00% |
| If book value is 1% less than market value | 0.37% |
| If book value is 1% greater than market value | −0.37% |
| Gross crediting rate: | |
| If book and market are equal | **5.29%** |
| If book is 1% less than market | **5.66%** |
| If book is 1% greater than market | **4.92%** |

## PART 3

# CREDIT ANALYSIS

## CHAPTER 19

# CREDIT ANALYSIS FOR CORPORATE BONDS*

Jane Tripp Howe, CFA
Director of Credit Research
Freedom Capital Management

Traditionally, credit analysis for corporate bonds has focused almost exclusively on the default risk of the bond—the chance that the bondholder will not receive the scheduled interest payments and/or principal at maturity. This one-dimensional analysis concerned itself primarily with the calculation of a series of ratios historically associated with fixed income investment. These ratios would typically include fixed charge coverage, leverage, and funds flow/total debt. This approach was deemed appropriate when interest rates were stable and investors purchased bonds with the purpose of holding them to maturity. In this scenario, fluctuations in the market value of the bonds due to interest-rate changes were minimal, and fluctuations due to credit changes of the bond issuer were mitigated by the fact that the investor had no intention of selling the bond before maturity. During the past three decades, however, the purpose of buying bonds has changed dramatically. Investors still purchase bonds for security and thereby forgo the higher expected return of other assets such as common stock. However, an increasing number of investors buy bonds to actively trade them with the purpose of making a profit on changes in interest rates or in absolute or relative credit quality. The second dimension of corporate bond credit analysis addresses the latter purpose of buying a bond. What is the likelihood of a change in credit quality that will affect the price of the bond? This second dimension deals primarily with the ratios and profitability trends, such as return on equity, operating margins, and asset turnover, generally associated with common stock analysis. In practice, both dimensions should be applied in corporate bond analysis. In a sense, both dimensions are addressing the same issue—default or credit risk. However, only by using both dimensions of credit analysis will the analyst address the dual purpose of bond holding: security of interest and principal payments and stability or improvement of credit risk during the life of the bond.

---

* The author wishes to thank Richard S. Wilson for his helpful comments and suggestions.

Historically, common stock and bond research areas have been viewed as separate. However, with the development of options theory, the two disciplines are beginning to be viewed as complementary.

The value of the option is a direct function of the company's aggregate equity valuation. As the market value of a company's stock increases, the value of the option increases. Conversely, as the market value of a company's stock declines, so does the value of the option. The practical implication of this theory for corporate bond analysis is that the perceptions of both markets should be compared before a final credit judgment is rendered. For the analyst who believes that there is a higher level of efficiency in the stock market than in the bond market, particular attention should be paid to the stock price of the company being analyzed. Of interest will be those situations in which the two markets are judged to differ substantially.

For example, in early 1981 the market to book values of the major chemical companies ranged from .77 to 2.15. The bond ratings of these same companies ranged from Baa/BBB to Aaa/AAA. The interesting point is not the range of either the market to book values or bond ratings, but rather the fact that although there was some correlation between the market/book ratios and bond ratings, there were instances in which there was little or no correlation. Options theory would suggest that there should be more of a relationship between the two. When the relative valuation of the bond as measured by the rating is low compared with the equity valuation as measured by market/book, one or both markets may be incorrectly valuing the company. Given the evidence that bond-rating changes generally lag behind market moves, it is likely in this case that the bond market is undervaluing the company.

Tracking stocks can benefit the bond analyst in two major ways. First, tracking stock movements are an efficient way of monitoring a large bond portfolio. Second, following the stock price of one company may assist the analyst in following an issuer. For example, analysts should value a company's holdings in other companies to the extent possible. Once a company is public, this is easily accomplished as was the case of Associates and Ford Motor Company. In 1996, Ford Motor Company completed an initial public offering of Associates. Once the IPO was complete, analysts could easily value Ford's interest in Associates simply by looking up the price of Associates common stock.

Significant price movements may indicate a change in credit quality and should be investigated. At the least, an explanation of major stock price movements either by themselves or relative to the stock prices of other companies should be sought with a call to management and a careful reading of related news stories. Sometimes a sharp run up in the price of a stock may indicate an acquisition. Acquisitions are often beneficial for the shareholders of the acquired company because of the premium paid for the stock. However, the effect of an acquisition on a bondholder varies from transaction to transaction. In a favorable scenario, the issuer of the bond is acquired by a higher rated entity. Such was the case in 1997 when AA rated Boeing Company acquired A− rated McDonnell Douglas Corporation. In an unfavorable scenario, the issuer of the bond is either acquired or merged with a lower rated entity and its ratings are lowered. Such was the case with the debt of BBB− rated Ohio Edison after it merged with Centerior Energy and its BB+ rated Cleveland Electric Illuminating and BB rated Toledo Edison operating subsidiaries.

Although there are numerous types of corporate bonds outstanding, three major issuing segments of bonds can be differentiated: industrials, utilities, and finance companies. This chapter will primarily address industrials in its general description of bond analysis, and then discuss the utility and finance issues.

## INDUSTRY CONSIDERATIONS

The first step in analyzing a bond is to gain some familiarity with the industry. Only within the context of an industry is a company analysis valid. For example, a company growing at 15% annually may appear attractive. However, if the industry is growing at 50% annually, the company is competitively weak. Industry considerations can be numerous. However, an understanding of the following eight variables should give the general fixed income analyst a sufficient framework to properly interpret a company's prospects.

Several of these variables should be considered in a global context. For example, it is not sufficient to consider the competitive position of the automobile industry without considering its global competitive position. As trade barriers fall, the need to become globally competitive increases. International competition is also an important factor in an analysis of the paper industry. Although U.S. firms had no plans to significantly increase capacity in the mid to late 1990s, global supply would be affected by capacity increases in several parts of the world, including Southeast Asia and Latin America. Changes in global supply must also be considered in terms of currency-adjusted pricing. Material declines in the currency of a particular country can quickly alter the global economics of an industry. For example, the major decline of the Indonesian rupiah in 1997 and 1998 and the concomitant economic recession in Southeast Asia translated into a material decline in the cash costs of Indonesian produced pulp. As the economic crisis in Southeast Asia worsened, paper producers from that region flooded the global markets with pulp and drove the world pulp price down by over 50%. All paper producers were affected. In this environment, the analyst who focused solely on domestic supply and demand without considering global issues would have concluded that paper prices would increase as a result of strong domestic economic growth and scheduled capacity additions which were below long term demand. Such a parochial viewpoint would have led to the wrong conclusion on the fate of the paper industry.

## Economic Cyclicality

The economic cyclicality of an industry is the first variable an analyst should consider in reviewing an industry. Does the industry closely follow GDP growth, as does the retailing industry, or is it recession-resistant but slow-growing, like the electric utility industry? The growth in earnings per share (EPS) of a company should be measured against the growth trend of its industry. Major deviations from the industry trend should be the focus of further analysis. Some industries may be somewhat dependent on general economic growth but be more sensitive to demographic changes. The nursing home industry is a prime example of this type of sensitivity. With the significant aging of the U.S. population, the nursing home industry is projected to have above-average growth for the foreseeable future. Other industries, such as the banking industry, are sensitive to interest rates. When interest rates are rising, the earnings of banks with a high federal funds exposure underperform the market as their loan rates lag behind increases in the cost of money. Conversely, as interest rates fall, banking earnings outperform the market because the lag in interest change works in the banks' favor.

In general, however, the earnings of few industries perfectly correlate with one economic statistic. Not only are industries sensitive to many economic variables, but often various segments within a company or an industry move counter-cyclically, or at least with different lags in relation to the general economy. For example, the housing industry can be divided between new construction and remodeling and repair. New construction historically has led GDP growth, but repair and remodeling have exhibited less sensitivity to general trends. Therefore, in analyzing a company in the construction industry, the performance of each of its segments must be compared with the performance of the subindustry.

## Growth Prospects

A second industry variable related to economic cyclicality is the growth prospects for an industry. Is the growth of the industry projected to increase and be maintained at a high level, such as in the nursing home industry, or is growth expected to decline, as in the defense industry? Each growth scenario has implications for a company. In the case of a fast-growth industry, how much capacity is needed to meet demand, and how will this capacity be financed? In the case of slow-growth industries, is there a movement toward diversification and/or a consolidation within the industry, such as in the railroad industry? A company operating within a fast growing industry often has a better potential for credit improvement than does a company whose industry's growth prospects are below average. However, barriers to entry and the sustainability of growth must be considered along with growth prospects for an industry. If an industry is growing rapidly, many new participants may enter the business, causing oversupply of product, declining margins, and possible bankruptcies.

The growth prospects of an industry should also be considered in a global context, particularly if a company has international exposure. Frequently, the growth prospects of an industry vary by country. For example, soft drinks are a mature industry in the United States but are a growth industry in other parts of the world.

## Research and Development Expenses

The broad assessment of growth prospects is tempered by the third variable—the research and development expenditures required to maintain or expand market position. The technology field is growing at an above-average rate, and the companies in the industry should do correspondingly well. However, products with high-tech components can become dated and obsolete quickly. Therefore, although a company may be well situated in an industry, if it does not have the financial resources to maintain a technological lead or at least expend a sufficient amount of money to keep technologically current, its position is likely to deteriorate in the long run. In the short run, however, a company whose R&D expenditures are consistently below industry averages may produce above-average results because of expanded margins.

Evaluation of research and development is further complicated by the direction of technology. Successful companies must not only spend an adequate amount of resources on development, they must also be correct in their assessment of the direction of the industry. Deployment of significant amounts of capital may not prevent a decline in credit quality if the capital is misdirected. For example, computer companies that persisted in spending a high percentage of their capital expenditures on the mainframe component of their business suffered declines in credit quality because the mainframe business is declining. Clearly, the risk of misdirected capital exists in the telecommunications area. Currently, there is a high degree of capital investment in the telecommunications industry. The direction of investment varies significantly among companies. For example, some companies, most notably AT&T are investing heavily in cable while others are investing in satellites. A third group believes that the telecommunications infrastructure will become overbuilt and has chosen to buy capacity rather than build it. Still others believe that demand for telecommunications will grow sufficiently fast to absorb all of the new capacity. Although demand for telecommunications is likely to remain high over the foreseeable future, standards, price, and technology will benefit one strategy relative to others. A divergence in credit quality among the fast growing industry will emerge.

## Competition

Competition is based on a variety of factors. These factors vary depending on the industry. Most competition is based on quality and price. However, competition is also derived from other sources, such as airlines operating in bankruptcy that are able to lower their costs by eliminating interest on debt and rejecting high-cost leases and thereby gain a cost advantage.

Increasingly, all forms of competition are waged on an international basis and are affected by fluctuations in relative currency values. Companies that fare well are those that compete successfully on a global basis and concentrate on the regions with the highest potential for growth. Consumers are largely indifferent to the country of origin of a product as long as the product is of high quality and reasonably priced.

Competition within an industry directly relates to the market structure of an industry and has implications for pricing flexibility. An unregulated monopoly is in an enviable position in that it can price its goods at a level that will maximize profits. Most industries encounter some free market forces and must price their goods in relation to the supply and demand for their goods as well as the price charged for similar goods. In an oligopoly, a pricing leader is not uncommon. Philip Morris, for example, performs this function for the tobacco industry. A concern arises when a small company is in an industry that is moving toward oligopoly. In this environment, the small company's costs of production may be higher than those of the industry leaders, and yet it may have to conform to the pricing of the industry leaders. In the extreme, a price war could force the smaller companies out of business. This situation has occurred in the brewing industry. For the past two decades, as the brewing industry has become increasingly concentrated, the leaders have gained market share at the expense of the small local brewers. Many small local brewers have either been acquired or gone out of business. These local brewers have been at a dual disadvantage: They are in an industry whose structure is moving toward oligopoly, and yet their weak competitive position within the industry largely precludes pricing flexibility.

A concern also arises when there is overcapacity in the industry. Often, overcapacity is accompanied by price wars. This has periodically occurred in the airline industry. Generally, price wars result in an industrywide financial deterioration as battles for market share are accompanied by declining profits or losses. In recent years, global overcapacity has increased competition at many levels and removed pricing power. The global automobile industry has been particularly affected by oversupply and lack of pricing power. In 1999, for example, the price of a new automobile in the United States declined.

## Sources of Supply

The market structure of an industry and its competitive forces have a direct impact on the fifth industry vaniable—sources of supply of major production components. A company in the paper industry that has sufficient timber acreage to supply 100% of its pulp is preferable to a paper company that must buy all or a large percentage of its pulp.

The importance of self-sufficiency in pulp has increased over the past few years because of environmental restrictions related to the spotted owl. As a result of the spotted owl situation, over half of the timber provided by the federal forests in the Northwest was removed from the market. The removal caused pulp prices to skyrocket. As a result, companies with low self-sufficiency in the Northwest, such as Boise Cascade, have experienced significant losses in their paper segments. Affected companies were unable to pass along the increased costs because of the commodity nature of the business.

A company that is not self-sufficient in its factors of production but is sufficiently powerful in its industry to pass along increased costs is in an enviable position. Historically, RJR Nabisco has been an example of the latter type of company. However, global deflationary forces have removed pricing power from most companies. In an effort to maintain margins, companies have resorted to efficiencies of production rather than raising prices. This trend is likely to continue.

## Degree of Regulation

The sixth industry consideration is the degree of regulation. The electric utility industry is the classic example of regulation. Nearly all phases of a utility's operations have historically been regulated. However, the industry has a federal mandate to deregulate. Initially, it was thought that deregulation would proceed rapidly. However, the complexity of the process suggests that the deregulation of the electric utility industry will take longer than originally thought. This change in time frame was the result of change in perceptions. Originally, legislators focused on the fact that deregulation would result in lower aggregate rates. More recently, legislators have focused on the fact that the benefit of lower rates will be offset in large part by a loss of control over rates.

The analyst should not be concerned with the existence or absence of regulation per se but rather with the direction of regulation and the effect it has on the profitability of the company. For the electric utility industry, the transition to deregulation will still be largely controlled by the regulatory authorities in a given state. In particular, regulatory commissions will have to deal with the treatment of stranded costs. Stranded costs include such items as generating plants whose cost/KW is above current market costs, and contracts with independent power producers to purchase power at above market prices. Although all electric utilities will transition to deregulation over the next decade, companies whose regulatory authorities assist in the recovery of stranded will be better positioned than companies with unsupportive regulatory authorities. To date, the treatment of stranded cost recovery has varied widely. Some states have allowed the full recovery of stranded costs through a competitive transition charge on consumers' bills, whereas other states have allowed utilities to reduce stranded costs by using gains on the sale of generation to offset stranded costs. In a similar manner, the rate reductions required by the commissions have varied from 0% to 20%.

Other industries, such as the drug industry, also have a high, though less pervasive, degree of regulation. In the drug industry, however, the threat of increased regulation has been a negative factor in the industry for some time. This risk was heightened periodically with the Clinton administration's health care proposals. The anticipation of increased regulation leading to lower profits in the pharmaceutical industry has contributed periodically to a major sell-off in these securities.

## Labor

The labor situation of an industry should also be analyzed. Is the industry heavily unionized? If so, what has been the historical occurrence of strikes? What level of flexibility does management have to reduce the labor force? When do the current contracts expire, and what is the likelihood of timely settlements? The labor situation is also important in nonunionized companies, particularly those whose labor situation is tight. What has been the turnover of professionals and management in the firm? What is the probability of a firm's employees, such as highly skilled engineers, being hired by competing firms?

The more labor intensive an industry, the more significance the labor situation assumes. This fact is evidenced by the domestic automobile industry, in which overcapacity and high unionization have contributed to high fixed costs and cyclical record operating losses.

Many think that the power of unions has weakened over the past decade as membership has declined. Unfortunately for managements negotiating contracts, this decline in power attributable to a decline in membership has been offset in part by the ability of unions to easily disrupt production because of "just-in-time" inventory management. Because corporations inventory small amounts of parts, a strike at a critical parts plant can halt production at an entire corporation in a short time.

Occasionally, analysts concentrate on the per hour wages of the labor force. Such an emphasis is misleading. An evaluation of the labor force should concentrate on work rules because work rules are more important in the overall efficiency of an organization than the wage rates. This is an important factor in the profitability of some automobile supply companies. Although the employees of these companies are generally members of the UAW and receive UAW wages, their work rules are different and their efficiency is generally significantly better than that of captive supply companies. An evaluation of the labor force should also consider the attrition rate of the work force and the requirements to replace workers under certain circumstances. Replacement rules generally are not listed in the popular press because the UAW leadership does not like to emphasize any reduction in membership.

## Accounting

A final industry factor to be considered is accounting. Does the industry have special accounting practices, such as those in the insurance industry or the elec-

tric utility industry? If so, an analyst should become familiar with industry practices before proceeding with a company analysis. Also important is whether a
company is liberal or conservative in applying the generally accepted accounting
principles. The norm of an industry should be ascertained, and the analyst should
analyze comparable figures.

Particular attention should be paid to companies which use an accounting
system other than U.S. GAAP. Reported results should be reconciled with those
which would have been reported under U.S. GAAP. In addition, changes in
GAAP should be scrutinized. For example, most forms of GAAP require that
debt issued in a currency other than the reporting currency should be adjusted
to reflect any changes between the reporting currency and the currency in which
the debt was issued. In this manner, a company in Southeast Asia which issued
debt denominated in U.S. dollars, but whose reporting currency devalued relative
to the dollar would have to write up its U.S. dollar denominated debt to reflect
the change. Such a write up would increase the leverage of the firm. This convention was not used by Indonesian companies because of an accounting change
that was instituted on August 14, 1997, during the early stages of the currency
crisis. On that date, Indonesian regulators ruled that foreign exchange losses
could be capitalized to the extent that the foreign denominated debt was used
to acquire plant and equipment. In essence, the new accounting rules permit
Indonesian companies to write up both their fixed assets and their debt, thereby
offsetting the increase in leverage that would be expected from a material devaluation.

Care should also be taken when dealing with historical data. Frequently,
companies adjust prior years' results to adjust for discontinued operations and
changes in accounting. These adjustments can mask unfavorable trends. For
example, companies that regularly dispose of underperforming segments and
then highlight the more profitable continuing operations may be trying to hide
poor management. In order to fully appreciate all trends, both the unadjusted
and the adjusted results should be analyzed.

Attention to accounting practices should also be paid when mergers and
acquisitions are involved. How much of pro forma results are attributable to
savings that are not yet realized but are allowed in pro forma results? How much
goodwill is generated by the combination? Are any contracts written up because
the acquiring company believes it can improve the historical performance of the
company it acquired? Raytheon wrote up contracts of Hughes Electronics when
it acquired Hughes. Raytheon later had to write down some of these results. A
conscientious analyst will be aware of these accounting entries and determine
whether they reflect a pro forma reality or whether they reflect a too optimistic
assessment of future performance.

## FINANCIAL ANALYSIS

Having achieved an understanding of an industry, the analyst is ready to proceed
with a financial analysis. The financial analysis should be conducted in three

phases. The first phase consists of traditional ratio analysis for bonds. The second phase, generally associated with common stock research, consists of analyzing the components of a company's return on equity (ROE). The final phase considers such nonfinancial factors as management and foreign exposure, and includes an analysis of the indenture.

## Traditional Ratio Analysis

There are numerous ratios that can be calculated in applying traditional ratio analysis to bonds. Of these, eight will be discussed in this section. Those selected are the ratios with the widest degree of applicability. In analyzing a particular industry, however, other ratios assume significance and should be considered. For example, in the electric utility industry, allowance for funds used in construction as a percent of net income as well as the total amount of stranded assets as a percentage of equity are important ratios that are inapplicable to the analysis of industrial or financial companies.

### Pretax Interest Coverage

Generally, the first ratio calculated in credit analysis is pretax interest coverage. This ratio measures the number of times interest charges are covered on a pretax basis. Fixed-charge coverage is calculated by dividing pretax income plus interest charges by total interest charges. The higher the coverage figure, the safer the credit. If interest coverage is less than 1X, the company must borrow or use cash flow or sale of assets to meet its interest payments. Generally, published coverage figures are pretax as opposed to after-tax because interest payments are a pretax expense. Although the pretax interest coverage ratio is useful, its utility is a function of the company's other fixed obligations. For example, if a company has other significant fixed obligations, such as rents or leases, a more appropriate coverage figure would include these other fixed obligations. An example of this is the retail industry, in which companies typically have significant lease obligations. A calculation of simple pretax interest coverage would be misleading in this case because fixed obligations other than interest are significant. The analyst should also be aware of any contingent liabilities such as a company's guaranteeing another company's debt. For example, there has been a dramatic increase in the insurance industry's guaranteeing of other company's debt. Today, this guaranteed debt exceeds the debt of the industry. Although the company being analyzed may never have to pay interest or principal on the guaranteed debt, the existence of the guarantee diminishes the quality of the pretax coverage. In addition, the quality of the guaranteed debt must be considered.

Once pretax interest coverage and fixed-charge coverage are calculated, it is necessary to analyze the ratios' absolute levels and the numbers relative to those of the industry. For example, pretax interest coverage for an electric utility of 4.0 is consistent with a AA rating, whereas the same coverage for a drug company would indicate a lower rating.

Standard & Poor's 1996–1998 median ratios of pretax interest coverage ranges for the senior debt of industrial companies were as follows:

| Rating Classification | Pretax Interest Coverage |
| --- | --- |
| AAA | 12.9 |
| AA | 9.2 |
| A | 7.2 |
| BBB | 4.1 |

## Leverage

A second important ratio is *leverage,* which can be defined in several ways. The most common definition, however, is long-term debt as a percent of total capitalization. The higher the level of debt, the higher the percentage of operating income that must be used to meet fixed obligations. If a company is highly leveraged, the analyst should also look at its margin of safety. The margin of safety is defined as the percentage by which operating income could decline and still be sufficient to allow the company to meet its fixed obligations. Standard & Poor's 1996–1998 median ratios of leverage for the senior debt of industrial companies were as follows:

| Rating Classification | Long-Term Debt/Capitalization |
| --- | --- |
| AAA | 21.4 |
| AA | 29.3 |
| A | 33.3 |
| BBB | 40.8 |

The most common way to calculate leverage is to use the company's capitalization structure as stated in the most recent balance sheet. In addition to this measure, the analyst should calculate capitalization using a market approximation for the value of the common stock. When a company's common stock is selling significantly below book value, leverage will be understated by the traditional approach. In a similar manner, leverage is overstated when a company's equity is selling significantly above book value. However, traditional measures of leverage should not be replaced by market adjusted measures. Market adjusted leverage may appear low when the equity market is at historic highs. However, it should be remembered that high equity values do not generate income to meet fixed charges or repay debt.

Occasionally, stockholders' equity can be negative, as was the case with FMC after it issued significant debt to repurchase its own stock in a leveraged recapitalization. Although FMC's equity was negative after the recapitalization, its stock market capitalization correctly indicated that the equity of FMC was valuable.

The degree of leverage and margin of safety varies dramatically among industries. Finance companies have traditionally been among the most highly leveraged companies, with debt to equity ratios of 10:1. Although such leverage is tolerated in the finance industry, an industrial company with similar leverage would have a difficult time issuing debt.

In addition to considering the absolute and relative levels of leverage of a company, the analyst should evaluate the debt itself. How much of the debt has a fixed rate, and how much has a floating rate? A company with a high component of debt tied to the prime rate may find its margins being squeezed as interest rates rise if there is no compensating increase in the price of the firm's goods. Such a debt structure may be beneficial during certain phases of the interest-rate cycle, but it precludes a precise estimate of what interest charges for the year will be. In general, a company with a small percentage of floating-rate debt is preferable to a similarly leveraged company with a high percentage of floating-rate debt.

The maturity structure of the debt should also be evaluated. What is the percentage of debt that is coming due within the next five years? As this debt is refinanced, how will the company's embedded cost of debt be changed? In this regard, the amount of original-issue discount (OID) debt should also be considered. High-quality OIDs were first issued in sizable amounts in 1981, although lower quality OIDs have been issued for some time. This debt is issued with low or zero coupons and at substantial discounts to par. Each year, the issuing company expenses the interest payment as well as the amortization of the discount. At issuance, only the actual bond proceeds are listed as debt on the balance sheet. However, as this debt payable will increase annually, the analyst should consider the full face amount due at maturity when evaluating the maturity structure and refinancing plans of the company.

The existence of material operating leases can understate the leverage of a firm. Operating leases should be capitalized to give a true measure of leverage. This approach is particularly enlightening in industries such as the airline industry. In the mid 1990s, book leverage of the U.S. carriers was 70% but increased to over 90% when leases were considered. Currently, the difference between book leverage and lease adjusted leverage for the U.S. carriers has declined because of the retirement of on balance sheet debt. However, a difference remains with book leverage of approximately 55% and lease adjusted leverage of approximately 70% as of year end 1999.

A company's bank lines often comprise a significant portion of a company's total debt. These lines should be closely analyzed in order to determine the flexibility afforded to the company. The lines should be evaluated in terms of undrawn capacity as well as security interests granted. In addition, the analyst should determine whether the line contains a Material Adverse Change (MAC) clause under which the line could be withdrawn. For example, a company that has drawn down its bank lines completely and is in jeopardy of activating its MAC clause may have trouble refinancing any debt. In a similar manner, undrawn lines should be evaluated in terms of their capacity to replace commercial paper, if needed. In the event that a company's commercial paper rating is downgraded, the company's access to the commercial paper market may evaporate quickly. In this scenario, the company may be forced to draw on its bank lines to replace its maturing commercial paper. A company whose commercial paper is fully backed by bank lines is in a stronger position than one whose bank lines do not cover its outstanding commercial paper.

**Cash Flow**
A third important ratio is cash flow as a percent of total debt. Cash flow is often defined as net income from continuing operations plus depreciation, depletion, amortization, and deferred taxes. In calculating cash flow for credit analysis, the analyst should also subtract noncash contributions from subsidiaries. In essence, the analyst should be concerned with cash from operations. Any extraordinary sources or uses of funds should be excluded when determining the overall trend of cash flow coverage. Cash dividends from subsidiaries should also be questioned in terms of their appropriateness (too high or too low relative to the subsidiary's earnings) and also in terms of the parent's control over the upstreaming of dividends. Is there a legal limit to the upstreamed dividends? If so, how close is the current level of dividends to the limit? Standard & Poor's 1996–1998 Median Ratios of Funds From Operations/Long-Term Debt for the senior debt of industrial companies were as follows:

| Rating Classification | Funds from Operations/ Total Debt |
|:---:|:---:|
| AAA | 89.7 |
| AA | 67.0 |
| A | 49.5 |
| BBB | 32.2 |

**Net Assets**
A fourth significant ratio is net assets to total debt. In analyzing this facet of a bond's quality, consideration should be given to the liquidation value of the assets. Liquidation value will often differ dramatically from the value stated on the balance sheet. At one extreme, consider a nuclear generating plant that has had operating problems and has been closed down and whose chance of receiving an operating license is questionable. This asset is probably overstated on the balance sheet, and the bondholder should take little comfort in reported asset protection. The issue of overstated values on the balance sheet of an electric utility has been increasingly highlighted as the electric utility industry deregulates and has to explicitly deal with stranded investments. At the other extreme is the forest products company whose vast timber acreage is significantly un-

derstated on the balance sheet. In addition to the assets' market value, some consideration should also be given to the liquidity of the assets. A company with a high percentage of its assets in cash and marketable securities is in a much stronger asset position than a company whose primary assets are illiquid real estate.

The wave of takeovers, recapitalizations, and other restructurings has increased the importance of asset coverage protection. Unfortunately for some bondholders, mergers or takeovers may decimate their asset coverage by adding layers of debt to the corporate structure that is senior to their holdings. While the analyst may find it difficult to predict takeovers, it is crucial to evaluate the degree of protection from takeovers and other restructurings that the bond indenture offers.

In extreme cases, the analyst must consider asset coverage in the case of bankruptcy. This is particularly important in the case of lease obligations because the debtor has the ability to reject leases in bankruptcy. In the case of lease rejections, the resulting asset protection may depend on a legal determination of whether the underlying lease is a true lease or a financing arrangement. Even if the lease if determined to be a true lease, the determination of asset protection is further complicated by a determination of whether the lease relates to nonresidential real property or to personal property. The difference in security (i.e., recovery in a bankruptcy) is significant. Damages under a lease of nonresidential real property are limited to three years of lease payments. Damages under a lease of personal property are all due under the lease.

In addition to the major variables discussed above, the analyst should also consider several other financial variables including intangibles, pension liabilities, the age and condition of the plant, and working capital adequacy.

## Intangibles

Intangibles often represent a small portion of the asset side of a balance sheet. Occasionally, particularly with companies that have or have had an active acquisition program, intangibles can represent a significant portion of assets. In this case, the analyst should estimate the actual value of the intangibles and determine whether this value is in concert with a market valuation. A carrying value significantly higher than market value indicates a potential for a write-down of assets. The actual write-down may not occur until the company actually sells a subsidiary with which the intangibles are identified. However, the analyst should recognize the potential and adjust capitalization ratios accordingly.

## Pension Liabilities

Unfunded pension liabilities can also affect a credit decision. Although a fully funded pension is not necessary for a high credit assessment, a large unfunded pension liability that is 10% or more of net worth can be a negative. Of concern is the company whose unfunded pension liabilities are sufficiently high to interfere with corporate planning. For example, in the late 1980s, a steel company with high unfunded pension liabilities might delay or decide against closing an unprofitable plant because of the pension costs involved. The analyst should also be aware of a company's assumed rate of return on its pension funds and salary increase assumptions. The higher the assumed rate of return, the lower the contribution a company must make to its pension fund, given a set of actuarial assumptions. Occasionally, a company having difficulty with its earnings will raise its actuarial assumption and thereby lower its pension contribution and increase earnings. The impact on earnings can be dramatic. In other cases, companies have attempted to "raid" the excess funds in an overfunded retirement plan to enhance earnings.

In periods of declining interest rates, the analyst must also consider the discount rate companies use to discount their future obligations. Companies generally use the yield of AA corporate bonds as a discount factor. Companies that persist in using a higher rate may be understating their unfunded pension obligations dramatically. General Motors announced in May 1993 that the drop in long-term interest rates could result in a $5 billion increase in its unfunded pension obligations because of a potential drop in its discount rate.

The increases in pension portfolios in the 1990s from rising equity and bonds prices have introduced the possibility that *overfunded* pension funds may contribute to earnings. Specifically, to the extent that a company's pension funds exceed 125% of future obligations, the company may use the excess above 125% to pay other retiree costs.

## Age and Condition of Plant

The age of a company's plant should also be estimated, if only to the extent that its age differs dramatically from industry standards. A heavy industrial company whose average plant age is well above that of its competitors is probably already paying for its aged plant through operating inefficiencies. In the longer term, however, the age of the plant is an indication of future capital expenditures for a more modern plant. In addition, the underdepreciation of the plant significantly increases reported earnings.

The availability of information regarding the average age and condition of plants varies among companies. On one hand, airline carriers readily provide the average age of their fleet and the money each will save as they replace older aircraft with more fuel efficient aircraft that require fewer people in the cockpit. On the other hand, the average age of a plant compared with the industry average is not always available for some companies such as paper companies. Furthermore, management of older plants generally emphasize the capital improvements that have been made to the plants over the years which distort direct comparisons. In this case, it is helpful to carefully read several years of management's explanation of operating results from the annual reports. Often this section will include reports of above average maintenance expense and machines which were out of service for a period of time for maintenance. Such comments indicate that the plants and machines may not be as efficient as initially portrayed.

The Financial Accounting Standards Board Statement Number 33 requires extensive supplementary information from most companies on the effect of changing prices. This information is generally unaudited, and there is still no consensus on the best presentation of such data. However, the supplementary information provision does give the analyst an indication of the magnitude of the effects of inflation on a given company. The effects differ dramatically from industry to industry. At one extreme are the high-technology and financial firms, where the effects are nominal. At the other extreme are the capital intensive industries, where the effects are major.

### Working Capital

A final variable in assessing a company's financial strength concerns the strength and liquidity of its working capital. Working capital is defined as current assets less current liabilities. Working capital is considered a primary measure of a company's financial flexibility. Other such measures include the current ratio (current assets divided by current liabilities) and the acid test (cash, marketable securities, and receivables divided by current liabilities). The stronger the company's liquidity measures, the better it can weather a downturn in business and cash flow. In assessing this variable, the analyst should consider the normal working capital requirements of a company and industry. The components of working capital should also be analyzed. Although accounts receivable are considered to be liquid, an increase in the average days a receivable is outstanding may be an indication that a higher level of working capital is needed for the efficient running of the operation. In addition, companies frequently have account receivable financing, some with recourse provisions. In this scenario, comparisons among companies in the same industry may be distorted.

The state of contraction or expansion should also be considered in evaluating working capital needs. Automobile manufacturers typically need increased working capital in years when automobile sales increase.

## Analysis of the Components of Return on Equity

Once the above financial analysis is complete, the bond analyst traditionally examines the earnings progression of the company and its historical return on equity (ROE). This section of analysis often receives less emphasis than the traditional ratio analysis. It is equally important, however, and demands equal emphasis. An analysis of earnings growth and ROE is vital in determining credit quality because it gives the analyst necessary insights into the components of ROE and indications of the sources of future growth. Equity analysts devote a major portion of their time examining the components of ROE, and their work should be recognized as valuable resource material.

A basic approach to the examination of the components of return on equity is presented in a popular investment textbook by Jerome B. Cohen, Edward D.

Zinbarg, and Arthur Zeikel.[1] Their basic approach breaks down return on equity into four principal components: pretax margins, asset turnover, leverage, and one minus the tax rate. These four variables multiplied together equal net income/stockholders' equity, or return on equity.

$$\left( \frac{\text{Nonoperating pretax income}}{\text{Sales}} + \frac{\text{Operating pretax income}}{\text{Sales}} \right)$$

$$\times \frac{\text{Sales}}{\text{Assets}} \times \frac{\text{Assets}}{\text{Equity}} \times (1 - \text{Tax Rate}) = \text{Net income/Equity}$$

In analyzing these four components of ROE, the analyst should examine their progression for a minimum of five years and through at least one business cycle. The progression of each variable should be compared with the progression of the same variables for the industry, and deviations from industry standards should be further analyzed. For example, perhaps two companies have similar ROEs, but one company is employing a higher level of leverage to achieve its results, whereas the other company has a higher asset-turnover rate. As the degree of leverage is largely a management decision, the analyst should focus on asset turnover. Why have sales for the former company turned down? Is this downturn a result of a general slowdown in the industry, or is it that assets have been expanded rapidly and the company is in the process of absorbing these new assets? Conversely, a relatively high rise in asset-turnover rate may indicate a need for more capital. If this is the case, how will the company finance this growth, and what effect will the financing have on the firm's embedded cost of capital?

The analyst should not expect similar components of ROE for all companies in a particular industry. Deviations from industry norms are often indications of management philosophy. For example, one company may emphasize asset turnover, and another company in the same industry may emphasize profit margin. As in any financial analysis, the trend of the components is as important as the absolute levels.

In order to give the analyst a general idea of the type of ratios expected by the major rating agencies for a particular rating classification, Standard & Poor's medians of key ratios for 1996–1998 by rating category are outlined in Exhibit 19–1. The analyst should use this table only in the most general applications, however, for three reasons. First, industry standards vary considerably. Second, financial ratios are only one part of an analysis. Third, major adjustments often need to be made to income statements and balance sheets to make them comparable with the financial statements of other companies.

The importance of adjusting financial statements to capture differences among firms was highlighted in November 1993 by S&P's introduction of "ad-

---

1. *Investment Analysis and Portfolio Management* (Homewood, IL: Richard D. Irwin, 1977).

**E X H I B I T   19–1**

Three-Year (1996–1998) Medians of Key Ratios by Rating Category

**Adjusted key industrial financial ratios**
**Industrial long-term debt**

| Three-year (1996–1998) medians | AAA | AA | A | BBB | BB | B | CCC |
|---|---|---|---|---|---|---|---|
| EBIT interest conv. (x) | 12.9 | 9.2 | 7.2 | 4.1 | 2.5 | 1.2 | (0.9) |
| EBITDA interest cov. (x) | 18.7 | 14.0 | 10.0 | 8.3 | 3.9 | 2.3 | 0.2 |
| Funds flow/total debt (%) | 89.7 | 67.0 | 49.5 | 32.2 | 20.1 | 10.5 | 7.4 |
| Free oper. cash flow/total debt (%) | 40.5 | 21.6 | 17.4 | 8.3 | 1.0 | (4.0) | (25.4) |
| Return on capital (%) | 30.6 | 25.1 | 19.6 | 15.4 | 12.6 | 9.2 | (8.8) |
| Oper. income/sales (%) | 30.9 | 25.2 | 17.9 | 15.8 | 14.4 | 11.2 | 5.0 |
| Long-term debt/capital (%) | 21.4 | 29.3 | 33.3 | 40.8 | 55.3 | 68.8 | 71.5 |
| Total debt/capital (incl. STD) (%) | 31.8 | 37.0 | 39.2 | 46.4 | 58.5 | 71.4 | 79.4 |

**Industrial commercial paper**

| Three-year (1996–1998) medians | A-1+ | A-1 | A-2 | A-3 |
|---|---|---|---|---|
| EBIT interest cov. (x) | 10.8 | 7.3 | 4.1 | 3.2 |
| EBITDA interest cov. (x) | 14.9 | 11.0 | 7.4 | 5.0 |
| Funds flow/total debt (%) | 72.1 | 54.0 | 37.3 | 23.5 |
| Free oper. cash flow/total debt (%) | 26.9 | 21.7 | 9.8 | 4.4 |
| Return on capital (%) | 25.0 | 20.0 | 17.8 | 13.9 |
| Oper. income/sales (%) | 21.4 | 18.7 | 15.7 | 16.0 |
| Long-term debt/capital (%) | 23.7 | 32.6 | 34.3 | 54.4 |
| Total debt/capital (incl. STD) (%) | 31.6 | 39.1 | 46.1 | 63.8 |

EBITDA—Earnings before interest, taxes, depreciation, and amortization. STD—Short-term debt.

**Glossary**

**Pretax income from continuing operations.** Net income from continuing operations before (1) special items, (2) minority interest, (3) gains or reacquisition of debt, plus income taxes.

**Eight times rents.** Gross rents paid multiplied by capitalization factor of eight.

**Equity.** Shareholders' equity (including preferred stock) plus minority interest.

**Free operating cash flow.** Funds from operations minus capital expenditures and minus (plus) the increase (decrease) in working capital (excluding changes in cash, marketable securities, and short-term debt).

**Funds from operations (or funds flow).** Net income from continuing operations plus depreciation, amoritization, deferred income taxes, and other noncash items.

**Gross interest.** Gross interest incurred before subtracting (1) capitalized interest, (2) interest income.

**Gross rents.** Gross operating rents paid before sublease income.

**Interest expense.** Interest incurred minus capitalized interest.

**Long-term debt.** As reported, including capitalized lease obligations on the balance sheet.

**Operating income.** Sales minus cost of goods manufactured (before depreciation and amortization), selling, general and administrative, and research and development costs.

**Total debt.** Long-term debt plus current maturities, commercial paper, and other short-term borrowings.

**E X H I B I T   19–1**

*(Continued)*

---

**Formulas for Key Ratios**

Pretax interest coverage =

$$\frac{\text{Pretax income from continuing operations} + \text{Interst expense}}{\text{Gross interest}}$$

Pretax interest coverage including rents =

$$\frac{\text{Pretax income from continuing operations} + \text{Interest expense} + \text{Gross rents}}{\text{Gross interest} + \text{Gross rents}}$$

EBITDA interest coverage =

$$\frac{\text{Pretax income from continuing operations} + \text{Interest expense} + \text{Depreciation and amortization}}{\text{Gross interest}}$$

Funds from operations (or funds flow) as a % of total debt = $\dfrac{\text{Funds from operations}}{\text{Total debt}} \times 100$

Free operating cash flow as a % of total debt = $\dfrac{\text{Free operating cash flow}}{\text{Total debt}} \times 100$

Pretax return on permanent capital =

$$\frac{\text{Pretax income from continuing operations} + \text{Interest expense}}{\substack{\text{Sum of (1) the average of the beginning of year and end of} \\ \text{year current maturities, long-term debt, noncurrent deferred} \\ \text{taxes, minority interest, and shareholders' equity and} \\ \text{(2) average short-term borrowings during year per footnotes} \\ \text{to financial statements}}} \times 100$$

Operating income as a % of sales = $\dfrac{\text{Operating income}}{\text{Sales}} \times 100$

Long-term debt as a % of capitalization = $\dfrac{\text{Long-term debt}}{\text{Long-term debt} + \text{Equity}} \times 100$

Total debt as a % of capitalization + short-term debt = $\dfrac{\text{Total debt}}{\text{Total debt} + \text{Equity}} \times 100$

Total debt + 8 times rents as a % of capitalization + short-term debt + 8 times rents =

$$\frac{\text{Total debt} + \text{8 times gross rentals paid}}{\text{Total debt} + \text{Equity} + \text{8 times gross rentals paid}} \times 100$$

---

Source: "Adjusted Key U.S. Industrial Financial Ratios," Standard & Poor's Credit Week, July 28, 1999, pp. 14–20.

justed key industrial financial ratios." In calculating its adjusted ratios, S&P eliminates nonrecurring gains and losses. In addition, S&P includes operating leases in all of its calculations.

Analysts interested in financial ratios for specific industries should consult Standard & Poor's CreditStats Service. This service, introduced in October 1989, presents key financial ratios organized into 53 industry groups as well as ratio analysis by long-term rating category for utility companies.

## Nonfinancial Factors

After the traditional bond analysis is completed, the analyst should consider some nonfinancial factors that might modify the evaluation of the company. Among these factors are the degree of foreign exposure, the quality of management, and ownership. The amount of foreign exposure should be ascertainable from the annual report. Sometimes, however, specific country exposure is less clear because the annual report often lists foreign exposure by broad geographic divisions. If there is concern that a major portion of revenue and income is derived from potentially unstable areas, the analyst should carefully consider the total revenue and income derived from the area and the assets committed. Further consideration should be given to available corporate alternatives should nationalization of assets occur. Additionally, the degree of currency exposure should be determined. If currency fluctuations are significant, has management hedged its exposure?

The internationalization of the bond markets and the ability of countries to issue debt in other countries highlights the importance of understanding the effect of currency risks. For example, many Mexican companies issued U.S. dollar denominated debt in the early 1990s. This issuance positively impacted the financials of these Mexican companies because of the generally lower interest rates available in the United States relative to Mexico. However, when the peso was significantly devalued in December 1994, the ability of some of these companies to meet their U.S. dollar denominated obligations was questioned. Of particular concern were the companies whose revenues were largely denominated in pesos but whose interest expense was denominated in U.S. dollars.

The quality and depth of management is more difficult to evaluate. The best way to evaluate management is to spend time with management, if possible. Earnings progress at the firm is a good indication of the quality of management. Negative aspects would include a firm founded and headed by one person who is approaching retirement and has made no plan for succession. Equally negative is the firm that has had numerous changes of management and philosophy. On the other hand, excessive stability is not always desirable. Characteristics of a good management team include depth, a clear line of succession if the chief officers are nearing retirement, and a diversity of age within the management team.

Ownership of the firm should also be considered. If one family or group of investors owns a controlling interest in a firm, they may be too conservative in reacting to changes in the market. Owners should also be judged in terms of whether they are strategic or financial. Often financial buyers invest for the short to intermediate term, hoping to sell their positions (or the entire company) at a profit. If such a sale involves a leveraged buyout, the credit quality of the bonds is lowered, sometimes dramatically.

## INDENTURE PROVISIONS

An indenture is a legal document that defines the rights and obligations of the borrower and the lender with respect to a bond issue. An analysis of the indenture should be a part of a credit review in that the indenture provisions establish rules for several important spheres of operation for the borrower. These provisions, which can be viewed as safeguards for the lender, cover such areas as the limitation on the issuance of additional debt, sale and leasebacks, and sinking-fund provisions.

Indenture provisions should be carefully analyzed. However, indentures provide little protection in the event of default and therefore are secondary to solid financial analysis. For example, a bondholder will receive little comfort if the company in which he invests is required to grant him security in the company's assets, but the assets are worth less than the company's debt.

The indentures of bonds of the same industry are often similar in the areas they address. Correlation between the quality rating of the senior debt of a company and the stringency of indenture provisions is not perfect. For example, sometimes the debt test is more severe in A securities than in BBB securities. However, subordinated debt of one company will often have less restrictive provisions than will the senior debt of the same company. In addition, more restrictive provisions are generally found in private placement issues. In analyzing a company's indenture, the analyst should look for the standard industry provisions. Differences in these provisions (either more or less restrictive) should be examined more closely. In this regard, a more restrictive nature is not necessarily preferable if the provisions are so restrictive as to hinder the efficient operation of the company.

Bond indentures should be analyzed in conjunction with the covenants of bank lines. Frequently, bank lines can be more restrictive than bond indentures. The analyst should focus on the most restrictive covenants.

Outlined below are the provisions most commonly found in indentures. These provisions are categorized by industry because the basic provisions are fairly uniform within an industry. A general description of the indenture is found in a company's prospectus. However, notification is generally given that the indenture provisions are only summarized. A complete indenture may be obtained from the trustee who is listed in the prospectus.

Careful attention should be paid to the definitions in indentures as they vary from indenture to indenture. Frequently, the definitions of terms specify carve-outs, or excluded items, that are material. For example, the definition of consolidated net assets may carve out or exclude changes resulting from unfunded pension liabilities.

# Utility Indentures

### Security

The security provision is generally the first provision in a utility indenture. This provision specifies the property upon which there is a mortgage lien. In addition, the ranking of the new debt relative to outstanding debt is specified. Generally, the new bonds rank equally with all other bonds outstanding under the mortgage.

This ranking is necessary, but it has created difficulty for the issuing companies because some mortgage indentures were written more than 40 years ago. Specifically, because all bondholders must be kept equal, companies must often retain antiquated provisions in their indentures. Often these provisions hinder the efficient running of a company due to structural changes in the industry since the original writing of the indenture. Changes in these provisions can be made, but changes have occurred slowly because of the high percentage of bondholders who must approve a change and the time and expense required to locate the bondholders. Occasionally, a company may retire certain old issues in order to eliminate a covenant that has not been included in recent offerings.

In November 1992, Illinois Power executed a new mortgage to replace over time its 1943 mortgage. Illinois Power plans to complete the defeasance or retirement of all of its old mortgage obligations and thereafter be bound by the provisions of its new mortgage. Illinois Power executed the new mortgage in order to give it more flexibility in terms of issuing first mortgage debt as well as to facilitate its separation of generation and transmission and distribution assets. Other companies are likely to follow the pattern of Illinois Power. More utility companies have elected to completely retire their first mortgage and issue replacement unsecured debt which will allow them the flexibility to separate and/or sell assets.

The security provisions of first mortgage indentures must be carefully scrutinized because of the disaggregation in the industry. Particular attention must be paid to the release and substitution clause of the security provisions. In general, the release and substitution clause specifies the conditions under which collateral for the first mortgage bonds may either be released from the indenture or other collateral may be substituted. In the context of disaggregation, holders of first mortgage bonds must pay attention to the ability of a company to remove assets from under its mortgage indenture. Some companies require that removal of assets be made at fair market value, while other indentures are silent on this point. Bondholders need to evaluate the degree to which they are protected from having valuable transmission and distribution assets released from the mortgage while retaining higher risk generation assets including overvalued nuclear assets. In addition, the ability of an issuer to effectively remove assets through the use of purchased money mortgages should be evaluated.

### Issuance of Additional Bonds

The "Issuance of Additional Bonds" provision establishes the conditions under which the company may issue additional first mortgage bonds. Often this provision contains a debt test and/or an earnings test. The debt test generally limits the amount of bonds that may be issued under the mortgage to a certain percentage (often 60%) of net property or net property additions, the principal amount of retired bonds, and deposited cash. The earnings test, on the other hand, restricts the issuance of additional bonds under the mortgage unless earnings for a particular period cover interest payments at a specified level.

Although both of these tests may appear straightforward, the analyst must carefully study the definitions contained in the tests. For example, net property additions may be defined as plant that has operating licenses. This was a particular concern during the 1980s. During that time, there was a great deal of nuclear construction, but operating licenses were slow to be granted. As a result, there was a significant backlog of construction work in progress (CWIP) that had to be financed, but which was not operational for some time. This situation presented problems for companies whose indentures required net plant additions to be licensed and/or used and useful assets. In the extreme case, a company may find itself unable to issue bonds under the mortgage indenture.

In a similar circumstance, a company whose regulatory commission requires a substantial write-down related to nuclear construction may find itself unable to meet a debt test for several years if the write-down is taken in one quarter.

The potential for such write-downs has become more visible since the implementation of SFAS 90. SFAS 90 requires utilities to record a loss against income for any portion of an investment in an abandoned plant for which recovery has been disallowed. It further requires all costs disallowed for ratemaking purposes to be recognized as a loss against income as soon as the loss becomes probable with respect to disallowances of new plant costs resulting from a cap on expenditures. These losses may be reported by either restating financial statements for prior fiscal years or by recording the cumulative loss the year SFAS 90 is adopted.

The application of FAS 71 may similarly affect electric utilities. Continued use of FAS 71 requires that (1) rates be designed to recover specific costs of regulated service and (2) it is reasonable to assume that rates are set to continue to recover such costs. In the current environment of a transition to deregulation, utilities may be required to partially or totally write down assets that are to be recovered in rates. Such write-downs may affect these companies' ability to issue first mortgage bonds. In the extreme, should regulators base interim stranded cost recovery on average prices in a region, as was suggested in February 1997 by the New Hampshire Public Utility Commission, the affected utilities would become ineligible for regulatory accounting and be required to book substantial write-offs. Occasionally, the writedown of assets and the concomitant inability to issue first mortgage debt can be offset by a quasi-reorganization. Under this accounting treatment, the company is allowed to write up certain assets to partially or totally offset the writedown of other assets. In this manner, the increased leverage (and negative retained earnings) that would result from a writedown of assets will be largely offset. This method was employed by Illinois Power in the fourth quarter of 1998. During the fourth quarter of 1998, Illinois Power wrote off its remaining investment in its Clinton nuclear station for a total charge of $1.2 billion. During the same quarter, Illinois Power increased the value of its fossil generation assets by approximately $1.4 billion.

**Maintenance and Replacement Fund**

The purpose of a maintenance and replacement fund (M&R) is to ensure that the mortgaged property is maintained in good operating condition. To this end, electric utility indentures generally require that a certain percentage of gross operating revenues, a percentage of aggregate bonded indebtedness, or a percentage of the utility's property account be paid to the trustee for the M&R fund. A major portion of the M&R requirement has historically been satisfied with normal maintenance expenditures. To the extent there is a remaining requirement, the company may contribute cash, the pledge of unbonded property additions, or bonds.

The rapid escalation of fuel costs during the 1970s has greatly raised the required levels of many M&R funds that are tied to operating revenues. This situation precipitated a number of bond calls for M&R purposes. Bonds can still be called for this purpose, but investors are more cognizant of this risk and are less likely to pay a significant premium for bonds subject to such a call. Furthermore, M&R requirements are slowly being changed toward formulas that exclude the large portion of operating income attributable to increases in fuel costs or exclude M&R Funds altogether. Finally, a number of companies have indicated that they have no intention of using M&R requirements for calling bonds because of the original intent of the provision and also because of the disfavor such an action would generate among bondholders. However, the intent of companies in this regard would certainly be secondary if a call for M&R requirements were ordered by a commission.

**Redemption Provisions**

The redemption, or call, provision specifies during what period and at what prices a company may call its bonds. Redemption provisions vary. Refunding is an action by a company to replace outstanding bonds with another debt issue sold at a lower interest expense. (Refunding protection does not protect the bondholder from refunding bonds with equity or short-term debt.) The refunding protection is a safeguard for bondholders against their bonds being refunded at a disadvantageous time.

Declines in long-term interest rates have motivated corporate treasurers to investigate all methods of redeeming high-coupon debt. For example, some indentures allow bonds to be called in the event of municipalization or in the event that the majority of assets are sold to a government agency. Careful attention to these possibilities is required to avoid an untimely redemption. An example of an aggressive interpretation of the redemption provision occurred in 1995 when Texas-New Mexico Power (TNP) announced that it was calling $29 million of its 11.25% first mortgage bonds at par with its proceeds from the sale of assets to Southwestern Public Service Company (SPS). The 11.25% bonds could not be called for property release purposes. However, the bonds could be called in the event "any municipal or governmental body exercises any right it may have to order the sale of all or any part of the Trustee Estate." TNP asserted that it sold its Texas Panhandle properties to SPS because eminent domain proceedings were threatened. Holders of the called bonds litigated that call and a settlement was reached which provided additional funds to the bondholders.

### Sinking Fund

A sinking fund is an annual obligation of a company to pay the trustee an amount of cash sufficient to retire a given percentage of bonds. This requirement can often be met with actual bonds or with the pledge of property. In general, electric utilities have 1% sinking funds that commence at the end of the refunding period. However, there are several variations of the sinking fund provision with which the analyst (and bondholder) should be familiar because they could directly affect the probability of bonds being called for sinking fund purposes. Some companies have nonspecific, or funnel, sinkers. This type of sinker often entails a 1 or 1.5% sinking fund applicable to all outstanding bonds. The obligation can be met by the stated percentage of each issue outstanding, by cash, or by applying (or funneling) the whole requirement against one issue or several issues.

### Other Provisions

In addition to the provisions discussed above, the indenture covers the events of default, modification of the mortgage, security, limitations on borrowings, priority, and the powers and obligations of the trustee. In general, these provisions are fairly standard. However, differences occur that should be evaluated.

Indentures of electric utilities must be scrutinized as part of the analysis during the deregulation process. In specific, attention must be paid to the ability of a company to remove assets from under its mortgage indenture. Some companies require that removal of assets must be made at fair market value, while other indentures are silent on this point. In addition, some companies may effectively remove assets through the use of purchased money mortgages.

# Industrial Indentures

Many of the provisions of an industrial indenture are similar to those of a utility's indenture, although specific items may be changed. In general, there are five indenture provisions that have historically been significant in providing protection for the industrial bondholder.

### Negative Pledge Clause

The negative pledge clause provides that the company cannot create or assume liens to the extent that more than a certain percentage of consolidated net tangible assets (CNTA) is so secured without giving the same security to the bondholders. This provision is important to the bondholders because their security in the specific assets of the company establishes an important protection for their investment. The specific percentage of CNTA that is exempted from this provision ts referred to as exempted indebtedness, and the exclusion provides some flexibility to the company. The amount of exempted indebtedness can vary widely.

### Limitation on Sale and Leaseback Transactions

The indenture provision limiting sale and leaseback parallels the protection offered by the negative pledge clause, except that it provides protection for the bondholder against the company selling and leasing back assets that provide security for the debtholder. In general, this provision requires that assets or cash equal to the property sold and leased back be applied to the retirement of the debt in question or used to acquire another property for the security of the bondholders.

### Sale of Assets or Merger

The sale of assets or merger provision protects the bondholder in the event that substantially all of the assets of the company are sold or merged into another company. Under these circumstances, the provision generally states that the debt be retired or be assumed by the merged company. It should be noted that the merged company that assumes the debt may have a different credit rating.

### Dividend Test

The dividend test provision establishes rules for the payment of dividends. Generally, it permits the company to pay dividends to the extent that they are no greater than net income from the previous year plus the earnings of a year or two prior. Although this provision allows the company to continue to pay dividends when there is a business decline, it assures the bondholders that the corporation will not be drained by dividend payments.

The dividend or restricted payment test also established parameters for the payment of dividends from operating subsidiaries to the holding company. The degree to which payments are allowed varies widely. Clearly, if an issuer is the holding company, a bondholder would favor a lenient restricted payment test because the holding company debt would benefit from the flexibility to upstream funds from the operating subsidiaries. On the other hand, if the issuer is the operating subsidiary, a bondholder would favor more stringent control over the ability of the holding company to upstream funds.

### Debt Test

The debt test limits the amount of debt that may be issued by establishing a maximum debt/assets ratio. This provision is generally omitted from current public offerings. However, there are numerous indentures outstanding that include this provision. In addition, private placements often include a debt test. When present, the debt test generally sets a limit on the amount of debt that can be issued per dollar of total assets. This limitation is sometimes stated as a percentage. For example, a 50% debt/asset limit restricts debt to 50% of total assets.

## Financial Indentures

### Sinking-Fund and Refunding Provisions

Like industrial indentures, indentures for finance issues specify sinking fund and refunding provisions. In general, finance issues with a short maturity are non-callable, whereas longer issues provide 10-year call protection. Occasionally, an issue can be called early in the event of declining receivables. Sinking funds are not as common in finance issues as they are in industrial issues, although they are standard for some companies.

### Dividend Test

Perhaps the most important indenture provision for a bondholder of a finance subsidiary is the dividend test. This test restricts the amount of dividends 'that can be upstreamed from a finance subsidiary to the parent and thereby protects the bondholder against a parent draining the subsidiary. This provision is common in finance indentures, but it is not universal. (One notable exception is International Harvester Credit, now Navistar.)

### Limitation on Liens

The limitation on liens provision restricts the degree to which a company can pledge its assets without giving the same protection to the bondholder. Generally, only a nominal amount may be pledged or otherwise liened without establishing equal protection for the bondholder.

### Restriction on Debt Test

The debt test limits the amount of debt the company can issue. This provision generally is stated in terms of assets and liabilities, although an earnings test has occasionally been used.

## UTILITIES

Historically, utilities have been regulated monopolies. These companies generally operate with a high degree of financial leverage and low fixed-charge coverage (relative to industrial companies). These financial parameters have been historically accepted by investors due to the regulation of the industry and the belief that there is minimal, if any, bankruptcy risk in those securities because of the essential services they provide. The changing structure of the electric utility industry brought about by significant investment in nuclear generating units and their inherent risk as well as the transition to deregulation has changed this belief. Initially, the faltering financial position of General Public Utilities precipitated by the Three Mile Island nuclear accident and the regulatory delays in making a decision regarding the units highlighted the default risk that exists in the industry. More recently, the defaults of several Washington Public Power Supply System issues, the restructuring of Tucson Electric Company, and the bankruptcies of Public Service Company of New Hampshire and El Paso Electric Company and the transition to deregulation reemphasized the default risk. In addition, the industry is faced with the acid rain issue and increased uncertainty in construction costs and growth rates. In 1985, Standard & Poor's developed more conservative financial benchmarks for a given rating to reflect the increased risk in the industry. In 1993, S&P categorized the electric utilities into three groups to reflect their business risk profiles. More recently, in October 1997, S&P revised its analysis with respect to first mortgage bonds. In its refinement, S&P placed more weight on the ultimate recovery of principal in the event of distress. The revision resulted in numerous one notch upgrades and several two notch upgrades for the first mortgage debt of electric utilities. These revisions were appropriate given the fact that first mortgage bonds may receive full recovery even in bankruptcy if they are fully collaterized as was the case with the Public Service Company of New Hampshire. Most recently, the rating agencies have addressed the differences between the transmission and distribution business and the generation business in terms of the business risk of each of these segments.

## Segments within the Utility Industry

There are three major segments within the utility industry: electric companies, gas companies, and telephone companies. This chapter will deal primarily with the electric utilities. A working knowledge of all three utility segments is increasingly important as the electric and gas segments converge and the electric companies increasingly use their access to homes and business to develop telecommunication businesses.

## Nonfinancial Factors

Although financial factors are important in analyzing any company, nonfinancial factors are particularly important in the electric utility industry and may alter a credit assessment. The six nonfinancial factors outlined below are of particular importance to the utility industry.

The importance of nonfinancial factors led S&P to revise its financial ratios for electric utilities to explicitly take these nonfinancial factors into consideration. Specifically, in October 1993, S&P divided the electric utility universe into three groups according to business profile. These business profiles are: above average, average, and below average. Accordingly, the median financial parameters in the Financial Analysis section are segmented according to business risk as well as rating category. As disaggregation occurs in the electric utility business, the financial parameters will be further segmented with the more risky generation assets demanding less leverage and higher interest coverage for a given rating than the less risky transmission and distribution operations.

Regulation is perhaps the most important variable in the electric utility industry because regulatory commissions largely determine how much profit an electric utility generates. All electric companies are regulated, most by the state or states in which they operate. If a company operates in more than one state, the analyst should weigh the evaluation of the regulatory atmosphere by revenues generated in each state.

The evaluation of regulatory commissions is a dynamic process. The composition of commissions changes because of retirements, appointments, and elections. The implications of personnel changes are not clear until decisions have been made. For example, it is not always the case that elected commissioners are pro-consumer and appointments by a conservative governor are pro-business. Several brokerage firms can assist in evaluations of commissions.

In addition, the Federal Energy Regulatory Commission (FERC) regulates interstate operations and the sale of wholesale power. Currently, FERC regulation is considered to be somewhat more favorable than that of the average state regulatory commission.

Utilities that are constructing or operating nuclear reactors are also subject to the regulation of the Nuclear Regulatory Commission (NRC). The NRC has broad regulatory and supervisory jurisdiction over the construction and operation of nuclear reactors. Importantly, the NRC approves licensing of nuclear reactors as well as the transfer of licenses.

There is potential for more Federal regulation of electric utilities in the near term with respect to both deregulation and PUHCA (the Public Utility Holding Company Act). If Federal legislation is passed with respect to deregulation, it is unlikely to affect existing state initiatives. Rather, any Federal legislation would likely extend the general attributes of existing states initiatives to states which have failed to deregulate, such as Florida. Many utilities would support the repeal of PUHCA in order to allow them more flexibility in mergers and acquisitions. PUHCA is likely to eventually be repealed because it has largely become antiquated. However, the timing of PUHCA repeal is political.

Utilities may be affected by the decisions of state commissions even if the commissions are located in a different state. For example, California has imposed significant penalties on long-term purchases of coal-fired energy by publicly owned California utilities. Therefore, non-California utilities that have historically sold coal-fired energy to California may find their energy priced too high.

Regulation is best quantified by recent rate decisions and the trend of these decisions. Although a company being analyzed may not have had a recent rate case, the commission's decisions for other companies operating within the state may be used as a proxy. Regulatory commissions are either appointed or elected.

In either case, the political atmosphere can have a dramatic effect on the trend of decisions.

The regulators determine innumerable issues in a rate decision, although analysts often mistakenly focus only on the allowed rate of return on equity or the percentage of request granted. For example, a commission might rule that an electric utility must reduce rates by 10%. However, if the commission allows the utility to accelerate its depreciation, the negative effect on the cash flow of the company from the rate reduction may be largely offset, particularly if the company had been or was expected to exceed its allowed ROE. The commissions also determine how much of construction work in progress (CWIP) is allowed into the rate base. A company may appear to have a favorable allowed ROE but be hurt by the fact that only a small portion of the company's capital is permitted to earn that return, and the CWIP earns nothing. Allowance of CWIP in the rate base was of critical importance during the 1980s because of the high construction budgets for nuclear generating plants and the length of time these plants are under construction. Some companies have had more than half of their capital in CWIP that is not permitted to earn a return.

The importance of whether CWIP is allowed in the rate base is highlighted by the financial distress and January 1988 bankruptcy filing of Public Service Company of New Hampshire (PSNH). PSNH's Seabrook Nuclear Unit I was virtually complete in 1986. However, licensing delays and New Hampshire's statutory prohibition of CWIP in the rate base were major contributing factors in the bankruptcy filing.

In addition, regulators have a high degree of control over the cash flow of a company through the allowance or disallowance of accounting practices and the speed with which decisions are made on cases.

Regulation by state commissions, the FERC, and the NRC is most visible. However, regulation by congressional action also has potential financial impact. For example, pollution associated with generation has been regulated since the 1970s. At that time, passage of acid rain legislation mandated the reduction of sulfur dioxide and nitrogen oxide emissions. More regulations were added in 1990 with the passage of the Clean Air Act which mandated more stringent standards. In order to meet the standards, utilities (essentially those with coal fired generation) were required to either install scrubbers or switch to low sulfur coal. In addition, the regulations required that utilities install the best available technology to reduce pollution when a plant undergoes a major overhaul or when capacity is added. As part of the legislation, the EPA was designated as the principle permitting body. In November 1999, the EPA sued seven utilities alleging that the utilities refurbished certain plants without adequately upgrading the pollution control systems. The utilities in question have countered by stating that the EPA has mistaken routine maintenance for refurbishment and that they meet current pollution standards. It is likely that the utilities and the EPA will reach a settlement that is far below the $250/KW that it could cost the utilities to upgrade their plants. The final outcome of the suit is less important than the fact that regulation is an integral part of the analysis of utilities.

The source of a company's energy is a second important variable. For many years, a company with a high nuclear exposure was viewed less favorably than a company with natural gas or coal units. Nuclear generation was out of favor because of several factors: licensing requirements, high capital costs, and decommissioning expenses. The disrepute of nuclear generation has reversed somewhat as capital costs have been written down and pollution issues of coal generation have escalated. In fact, there is a likelihood that the licenses of several nuclear plants will be extended. Each fuel must be evaluated in the context of the overall cost of running a plant. The energy source variable relates to a third variable—the growth and stability of the company's territory. Although above-average growth is viewed positively in an industrial company, it may be viewed negatively with respect to an electric utility. An electric utility with above-average growth may face construction earlier than its competitors.

Slow growth is not necessarily positive if it places a utility in a position of excess capacity. The increase in cogeneration and the mergers executed in order to better match supply and demand can place a utility at risk. This could result if Utility A were selling power to Utility B. If the expiration of the contract coincides with Utility B's ability to purchase power for less and results in Utility B's nonrenewal of the contract, Utility A could be negatively affected unless it can sell the power to a third utility. The issue of growth has been complicated by deregulation and the requirement in many states for disaggregation of generation from transmission and distribution as well as the requirement that customers be allowed to choose their supplier. In this new era, utilities engaged in generation must be able to match supply and demand for power.

A fourth variable, whether or not a company is a subsidiary of a holding company, should also be considered. Holding company status permits nonutility subsidiaries, but these subsidiaries (even if successful) will not necessarily improve the overall credit quality of the company. This depends on the regulatory atmosphere. Furthermore, when there are several electric utility subsidiaries, the parent is more likely to give relatively large equity infusions to the relatively weak subsidiaries. The stronger subsidiary may have to support the other subsidiaries. Finally, holding companies should be analyzed in terms of consolidated debt. Although a particular subsidiary may have relatively strong financial parameters, off balance sheet financing may lower the overall assessment.

The current era of deregulation has contributed to a significant increase in international and nonutility investments. Companies which are active in this area emphasize the potential equity returns of these businesses. However, the analyst must carefully analyze the ability of the holding company to downstream funds to these operations and potentially reduce the overall credit quality of the entity.

A final nonfinancial factor is the rate structure of a utility. An electric utility with a comparatively low rate structure is generally in a stronger position politically to request rate increases or to request a rate freeze than one with rates higher than national averages, and particularly one with rates higher than regional averages.

The competitive position of an electric utility is increasingly important as the reality of retail wheeling increases. Those companies with high overall rates, and particularly those with high commercial rates, may find themselves losing customers as access to transmission and distribution lines increases.

In addition, those utilities with high stranded investments are vulnerable to competition. In the transition period to deregulation, many utilities have negotiated rates with their large industrial customers in order to retain them as customers. This negotiation is only a short-term solution if a utility's embedded costs are higher than those of utilities who have access to their service territory. At best, negotiated rates for industrial customers will buy time for utilities with high costs to lower their costs to make them more in line with the rates of their competitors.

## Financial Analysis

The changing competitive nature of the electric industry resulting from deregulation requires that the traditional evaluation of an electric utility be modified. Although historic ratio analysis should still be conducted, an electric company should be also evaluated in the context of its new competitive situation. Is new generation being constructed in its territory that produces energy at a lower cost than the established generation? How does the company plan to expend its excess cash flow? In an era of consolidation, will the company be acquired or be an acquirer? Will the company remain in generation or sell its generation and deal solely with transmission and distribution?

There are four major financial ratios that should be considered in analyzing an electric utility: leverage, pretax interest coverage, cash flow/spending, and cash flow/capital.

Leverage in the electric utility industry is high relative to industrial concerns. This degree of leverage is accepted by investors because of the historical stability of the industry. The expected ranges for AA, A, BBB, and BB companies are outlined below. No electric utility companies are currently rated AAA by Standard & Poor's. The ratios discussed below apply to electric utilities which still retain both their generation and transmission and distribution assets. However, as the process of deregulation accelerates, many companies in the electric utility industry will decide (or be required) to either be in generation or wires (transmission and distribution). As a result of these changes, traditional ratios will no longer be applicable to many electric utilities. After a utility has divested either its generation or wires, the analyst will be required to use benchmark ratios that apply to either generation or transmission and distribution companies.

| | Total Debt / Total Capitalization | | | |
|---|---|---|---|---|
| Business Position | AA | A | BBB | BB |
| Average average | 47% | 52% | 59% | 65% |
| Average | 42 | 47 | 54 | 60 |
| Below average | — | 41 | 48 | 54 |

In calculating the debt leverage of an electric utility, long-term debt/ capitalization is standard. However, the amount of short-term debt should also be considered because this is generally variable-rate debt. A high proportion of short-term debt may also indicate the possibility of the near-term issuance of long-term bonds. In addition, several companies guarantee the debt of subsidiaries (regulated or nonregulated). The extent of these guarantees should be considered in calculating leverage. Subsidiary debt is likely to become an increasingly important factor over the next few years as utilities invest in international utility operations through subsidiaries.

Benchmark leverage figures for a given rating will differ materially from the above figures if a utility engaged solely in generation is being considered. In this case, leverage of 35 to 45% would be consistent with an "A" rating because of the higher level of risk involved. In a similar manner, higher leverage of 55 to 65% would be consistent with an "A" rating for a utility that is engaged exclusively in the less risky transmission and distribution business.

Fixed-charge coverage for the electric utilities is also low relative to coverage for industrial companies. Standard & Poor's expected ranges for coverage are as follows:

| | Pretax Interest Coverage (x) | | | |
|---|---|---|---|---|
| Business Position | AA | A | BBB | BB |
| Above average | 4.0x | 3.25x | 2.25x | 1.75 |
| Average | 4.5 | 4.0 | 3.0 | 2.0 |
| Below average | — | 5.0 | 4.0 | 2.75 |

These ranges are accepted by investors because of the stability of the industry. However, due to the changing fundamentals of the industry as discussed above, perhaps less emphasis should be placed on the exact coverage figures and more on the trend and quality of the coverage.

A third important ratio is net cash flow/spending. This ratio should be approximated for three years (the typical electric company's construction forecast). The absolute level as well as the trend of this ratio gives important insights into the trend of other financial parameters. An improving trend indicates that construction spending is probably moderating, whereas a low net cash flow/ spending ratio may indicate inadequate rates being approved by the commissions and a heavy construction budget. Estimates for construction spending are published in the company's annual reports. Although these are subject to revision, the time involved in building a generator makes these forecasts reasonably reliable. In 1985, Standard & Poor's deemphasized this ratio primarily due to its volatility. Although it will still be considered, Standard & Poor's now emphasizes funds from operations/total debt as a preferable indicator of cash flow adequacy. Over the past several years, less emphasis has been placed on the net cash flow/capital expenditures ratio because the majority of electric utilities have generated positive cash flow after capital expenditures. This positive cash flow has been the result of three factors. First, the aggregate electric utility industry has surplus energy and therefore new construction has been minimal. In fact, the majority of new generation over the past several years has been constructed by nontraditional independent power producers. Second, interest rates have declined significantly and electric utilities have enjoyed lower interest expense as they have refinanced maturing debt at lower interest rates. Third, the electric utility industry has lowered its operating expenses in preparation for deregulation.

Standard & Poor's benchmarks for net cash flow/capital expenditures and for funds from operations/total debt are as follows:

| | Net Cash Flow / Capital Expenditures (%) | | | |
|---|---|---|---|---|
| Business Position | AA | A | BBB | BB |
| Above average | 90% | 70% | 45% | 30% |
| Average | 110 | 85 | 60 | 40 |
| Below average | — | 105 | 80 | 60 |

| | Funds from Operations / Total Debt (%) | | | |
|---|---|---|---|---|
| Business Position | AA | A | BBB | BB |
| Above average | 26% | 19% | 14% | 11% |
| Average | 32 | 25 | 19 | 13 |
| Below average | — | 34 | 29 | 20 |

In calculating cash flow, the standard definition outlined above should be followed. However, AFUDC should also be subtracted, and any cash flow from nonregulated subsidiaries should be segregated and analyzed within the total context of the company. The regulatory commissions take divergent views on non-utility subsidiaries. Some commissions do not regulate these subsidiaries at all, whereas other commissions give inadequate rate relief to an electric utility with a profitable nonutility subsidiary under the premise that the company should be looked at as a whole. In the extreme, the latter view has encouraged companies to sell or spin off some subsidiaries.

## FINANCE COMPANIES

Finance companies are essentially financial intermediaries. Their function is to purchase funds from public and private sources and to lend them to consumers and other borrowers of funds. Finance companies earn income by maintaining a positive spread between what the funds cost and the interest rate charged to customers. The finance industry is highly fragmented in terms of type of lending and type of ownership. This section will briefly outline the major sectors in the industry and then discuss the principal ratios and other key variables used in the analysis of finance companies.

## Segments within the Finance Industry

The finance industry can be segmented by type of business and ownership. Finance companies lend in numerous ways in order to accommodate the diverse financial needs of the economy. Five of the major lending categories are (1) sales finance, (2) commercial lending, (3) wholesale or dealer finance, (4) consumer lending, and (5) leasing. Most often, companies are engaged in several of these lines rather than one line exclusively. Sales finance is the purchase of third-party contracts that cover goods or services sold on a credit basis. In most cases, the sales finance company receives an interest in the goods or services sold. Commercial finance is also generally on a secured basis. However, in this type of financing, the security is most often the borrower's accounts receivable. In factoring, another type of commercial lending, the finance company actually purchases the receivables of the company and assumes the credit risk of the receivables.

Dealer or wholesaler finance is the lending of funds to finance inventory. This type of financing is secured by the financed inventory and is short-term in nature. Leasing, on the other hand, is intermediate to long-term lending—the lessor owns the equipment, finances the lessee's use of it, and generally retains the tax benefits related to the ownership.

Consumer lending has historically involved short-term, unsecured loans of relatively small amounts to individual borrowers. In part because of the more lenient bankruptcy rules and higher default rates on consumer loans, consumer finance companies have dramatically expanded the percentage of their loans for second mortgages. The lower rate charged to individuals for this type of loan is offset by the security and lower default risk of the loan.

There are numerous other types of lending in addition to those described above. Among these are real estate lending and export/import financing.

The ownership of a finance company can significantly affect evaluation of the company. In some instances, ownership is the most important variable in the analysis. There are three major types of ownership of finance companies: (1) captives, (2) wholly-owned, and (3) independents.

Captive finance companies, such as General Motors Acceptance Corporation, are owned by the parent corporation and are engaged solely or primarily in the financing of the parent's goods or services. Generally, maintenance agreements exist between the parent and the captive finance company under which the parent agrees to maintain one or more of the finance company's financial parameters, such as fixed-charge coverage, at a minimum level. Because of the overriding relationship between a parent and a captive finance subsidiary, the financial strength of the parent is an important variable in the analysis of the finance company. However, captive finance companies can have ratings either above or below those of the parent.

A wholly owned finance company, such as Associates Corporation of North America prior to its IPO and spin off from Ford, differs from a captive in two ways. First, it primarily finances the goods and services of companies other than the parent. Second, maintenance agreements between the parent and the subsidiary are generally not as formal. Frequently, there are indenture provisions that address the degree to which a parent can upstream dividends from a finance subsidiary. The purpose of these provisions is to prevent a relatively weak parent from draining a healthy finance subsidiary to the detriment of the subsidiary's bondholders.

Independent finance companies are either publicly owned or closely held. Because these entities have no parent, the analysis of this finance sector is strictly a function of the strengths of the company.

## Financial Analysis

In analyzing finance companies, several groups of ratios and other variables should be considered. There is more of an interrelationship between these ratios and variables than for any other type of company. For example, a finance company with a high degree of leverage and low liquidity may be considered to be of high investment quality if it has a strong parent and maintenance agreements. Variables should be viewed not in isolation but rather within the context of the whole finance company/parent company relationship.

### Asset Quality

The most important variable in analyzing a finance company is asset quality. Unfortunately, there is no definitive way to measure asset quality. However, there are several variables which in the aggregate present a good indication of asset quality.

Diversification is one measure of portfolio quality. Is the portfolio diversified across different types of loans? If the company is concentrated in or deals exclusively in one lending type, is there geographic diversification? A company that deals exclusively in consumer loans in the economically sensitive Detroit area would not be as favorably viewed as a company with broad geographic diversification. Accounting quality is also an important factor in assessing portfolio quality. The security for the loans is also an important variable in portfolio quality. The stronger the underlying security, the higher the loan quality. The analyst should be primarily concerned with the level of loans compared with levels of similar companies and the risk involved in the type of lending. For example, the expected loan loss from direct unsecured consumer loans is higher than for consumer loans secured by second mortgages. However, the higher fees charged for the former type of loan should compensate the company for the higher risk.

Numerous ratios of asset quality such as loss reserves/net charge-offs, net losses/average receivables, and nonperforming loans/average receivables give good indications of asset quality. However, finance companies have a high level of discretion in terms of what they consider and report to be nonperforming loans and what loans they charge off. Therefore, unadjusted ratios are not comparable among companies. In addition, companies periodically change their charge-off policies. For example, in April 1990, ITT Financial Corporation liberalized its charge-off policy for consumer loans by changing to a modified recency basis from a present contractual basis. (Under a recency basis, delinquencies are measured from the date of last payment, regardless of payment history.) ITT reduced the implications of this change by eliminating "curing" activities under which the terms of the contractual loan are modified.

In spite of the drawbacks of the asset quality ratios, they are useful in indicating trends in quality and profitability. Of these ratios, loss reserves/net chargeoffs is perhaps the most important ratio in that it indicates how much cushion a company has. A declining ratio indicates that the company may not be adding sufficient reserves to cover future charge-offs. Such a trend may lead to a future significant increase in the reserves and therefore a decrease in earnings as the increase is expensed. Net losses/average receivables and nonperforming loans/ average receivables are other indicators of asset quality. An increasing ratio indicates a deterioration in quality. Declines may be exacerbated by an overall contraction or slow growth in the receivables. On the other hand, because of different accounting treatments, a stable net losses/average receivables ratio under deteriorating economic conditions may indicate a delay in loss recognition. Consideration should also be given to the age of receivables. In recent years, some finance companies have dramatically increased their lending over a short period of time and reported material improvement in their overall financial parameters. These results have been misleading in some cases where the dramatic improvement has been driven by inadequate reserves. Often the dramatic improvement has been followed by increased losses as the portfolio ages.

## Leverage
Leverage is a second important ratio used in finance company analysis. By the nature of the business, finance companies are typically and acceptably more highly leveraged than industrial companies. The leverage is necessary to earn a sufficient return on capital. However, the acceptable range of leverage is dependent on other factors such as parental support, portfolio quality, and type of business. The principal ratio to determine leverage is total debt to equity, although such variations as total liabilities to equity may also be used. In a di-

versified company with high portfolio quality, a leverage ratio of 5 to 1 is acceptable. On the other hand, a ratio of 10 to 1 is also acceptable for a captive with a strong parent and maintenance agreements. The analyst should always view the leverage of a finance company in comparison with similar companies.

## Liquidity

The third important variable in finance company analysis is liquidity. Because of the capital structure of finance companies, the primary cause of bankruptcies in this industry is illiquidity. If for some reason a finance company is unable to raise funds in the public or private market, failure could quickly result. This inability to raise funds could result from internal factors, such as a deterioration in earnings, or from external factors such as a major disruption in the credit markets. Whatever the cause, a company should have some liquidity cushion. The ultimate liquidity cushion, selling assets, is only a last resort because these sales could have long-term, detrimental effects on earnings. The traditional liquidity ratio is cash, cash equivalents, and receivables due within one year divided by short-term liabilities. The higher this ratio, the higher the margin of safety. Also to be considered are the liquidity of the receivables themselves and the existence of bank lines of credit to provide a company with short-term liquidity during a financial crisis. In general, the smaller and weaker companies should have a higher liquidity cushion than companies with strong parental backing who can rely on an interest-free loan from the parent in times of market stress.

Liquidity considerations were heightened with the implementation of the SEC's rule 2a-7 in June 1991. This rule limits to 5% of assets the amount of medium-grade securities that a money market fund can purchase. As a result, companies whose commercial paper was downgraded to medium-grade are excluded to a large extent from the commercial paper market. A company can avoid a liquidity crisis stemming from lack of access to the commercial paper market by retaining bank lines to back up their commercial paper. Westinghouse Credit was able to replace its commercial paper with bank financing in 1992, despite down-grades, because of the adequacy of its bank lines.

## Asset Coverage

A fourth important variable in the analysis of finance companies that is related to the three variables discussed above is the asset coverage afforded the bondholder. In assessing asset protection, the analyst should consider the liquidation value of the loan portfolio.

A definitive assessment of the value of assets is difficult because of the flexibility finance companies have in terms of valuing assets. A finance company can value real estate assets on a number of bases. For example, a finance company that plans to liquidate its commercial real estate portfolio over twelve months in a depressed real estate environment will value its assets much lower than if it planned to systematically sell the same assets over a three-to five-year period. Westinghouse Credit's $2.6 billion write-off in the fourth quarter of 1992 demonstrates this difference.

### Earnings Record

The fifth variable to be considered is the finance company's earnings record. The industry is fairly mature and is somewhat cyclical. The higher the annual EPS growth, the better. However, some cyclicality should be expected. In addition, the analyst should be aware of management's response to major changes in the business environment. The recent easing of personal bankruptcy rules and the fact that personal bankruptcy is becoming more socially acceptable have produced significantly higher loan losses in direct, unsecured consumer loans. Many companies have responded to this change by contracting their unsecured personal loans and expanding their portfolios invested in personal loans secured by second mortgages.

### Management

The sixth variable to be considered is the finance company's management. This variable is difficult to assess. However, a company visit combined with an evaluation of business strategies and credit scoring methodologies will provide some insight into this variable.

### Size

A final factor related to the finance company or subsidiary is size. In general, larger companies are viewed more positively than smaller companies. Size has important implications for market recognition in terms of selling securities and of diversification. A larger company is more easily able to diversify in terms of type and location of loan than is a smaller company, and thereby to lessen the risk of the portfolio.

In addition to an analysis of the financial strength of the company according to the above variables, the analyst must incorporate the net effect of any affiliation the finance company has with a parent. If this affiliation is strong, it may be the primary variable in the credit assessment. The affiliation between a parent company and a finance subsidiary is straightforward; it is captive, wholly-owned, or independent. However, the degree to which a parent will support a finance subsidiary is not as straightforward. Traditionally, the integral relationship between a parent and a captive finance subsidiary has indicated the highest level of potential support. However, it is becoming increasingly clear that a wholly-owned finance subsidiary can have just as strong an affiliation. For example, General Electric Credit Corporation (GECC) finances few or no products manufactured by its parent, General Electric Company. However, General Electric receives substantial tax benefits from its consolidation of tax returns with GECC. Additionally, General Electric has a substantial investment in its credit subsidiary. Therefore, although there are no formal maintenance agreements between General Electric and GECC, it can be assumed that General

Electric would protect its investment in GECC if the finance subsidiary were to need assistance. In other instances, it may be that the affiliation and maintenance agreements are strong but that the parent itself is weak. In this case, the strong affiliation would be discounted to the extent that parent profitability is below industry standards.

In addition to affiliation, affiliate profitability, and maintenance agreements, the analyst should also examine any miscellaneous factors that could affect the credit standing of the finance company. Legislative initiatives should be considered to determine significant changes in the structure or profitability of the industry.

## THE RATING AGENCIES AND BROKERAGE HOUSES

There is no substitute for the fundamental analysis generated by the fixed income analyst. The analyst has many sources of assistance, however. The major sources of assistance are the public rating agencies and brokerage houses that specialize in fixed income research.

## Rating Agencies

Four rating agencies provide public ratings on debt issues: Standard & Poor's Corporation, Moody's Investors Service, Fitch, and Duff & Phelps.

Standard & Poor's (S&P) and Moody's are the most widely recognized and used of the services, although Duff & Phelps and Fitch are frequently cited. Fitch was revitalized in 1989 by a new investor group. S&P and Moody's are approximately the same size, and each rates the debt securities of approximately 2,000 companies. If a company desires a rating on an issue, it must apply to the rating agency. The agency, in turn, charges a one-time fee. For this fee, the issue is reviewed periodically during the life of the issue, and at least one formal review is made annually.

All of the rating agencies designate debt quality by assigning a letter rating to an issue. Standard & Poor's ratings range from AAA to D, with AAA obligations having the highest quality investment characteristics and D obligations being in default. In a similar fashion, Moody's ratings extend from Aaa to C, and Fitch's from AAA to D. Duff & Phelps' ratings currently extend from AAA to CCC.

Public ratings are taken seriously by corporate managements because a downgrade or an upgrade by a major agency can cost or save a corporation thousands of dollars in interest payments over the life of an issue. In the event of downgrade below the BBB− or Baa3 level, the corporation may find its bonds ineligible for investment by many institutions and funds, by either legal or policy constraints. Corporations therefore strive to maintain at least an investment-grade rating (Baa3 or higher) and are mindful of the broad financial parameters that the agencies consider in deriving a rating.

Many factors promote the use of agency ratings by investors, bankers, and brokers. Among these strengths are the breadth of companies followed, the easy access to the ratings, and the almost universal acceptance of the ratings. On the other hand, the ratings are criticized for not responding quickly enough to changes in credit conditions and for being too broad in their classifications.

The slow response time of the agencies to changes in credit conditions is certainly a valid criticism. There are few instances in which the lag is significant in terms of a dramatic change, but the market generally anticipates rating changes. The rating agencies have become increasingly sensitive to this criticism and have been quicker to change a rating in light of changing financial parameters. On the other hand, the agencies recognize the financial impact of their ratings and their obligation to rate the long-term (as opposed to the short-term) prospects of companies. They therefore have a three-to five-year perspective and deliberately do not change a rating because of short-term fluctuations.

The major rating agencies have addressed this criticism by creating "watch lists" of companies whose credit ratings are under surveillance for rating changes. These potential changes can be either positive or negative. The rating agencies have also expanded their evaluation of companies to indicate the credit trend of the companies.

Investors who are concerned that the ratings are too broad in their classifications have several options among the brokerage-house services that offer more continuous ratings.

## Brokerage-House Services

Numerous brokerage houses specialize in fixed income research. Generally, these services are available only to institutional buyers of bonds. The strength of the research stems from the in-depth coverage provided, the statistical techniques employed, and the fine gradations in rating. On the other hand, the universe of companies that these firms follow is necessarily smaller than that followed by the agencies.

## CONCLUSION

This chapter has emphasized a basic method for analyzing corporate bonds. A format for analysis is essential. However, analysis of securities cannot be totally quantified, and the experienced analyst will develop a second sense about whether to delve into a particular aspect of a company's financial position or to take the financial statements at face value. All aspects of credit analysis, however, have become increasingly important as rapidly changing economic conditions and globalisation change the credit quality of companies and industries.

CHAPTER **20**

# CREDIT CONSIDERATIONS IN EVALUATING HIGH-YIELD BONDS

Jane Tripp Howe, CFA
Director of Credit Research
Freedom Capital Management

## INTRODUCTION

Many analysts shy away from the analysis of high-yield bonds. Perhaps their reticence is a function of the security's lack of a rating or of a rating that is "below investment grade" and therefore publicly documented as having varying degrees of investment risk or elements of speculation. Although the comfort of an investment-grade rating is missing or its assignment is often enough to prohibit the security's inclusion in a portfolio, the potential rewards of this area of credit analysis are well worth the time invested.

The analysis of high-yield bonds, or junk bonds as they are unfortunately nicknamed, is similar to the complete analysis of any other corporate bond, but the emphasis of the analysis must change. Both high-yield and junk bonds are securities that trade primarily on their creditworthiness, as opposed to the level of interest rates. However, an important difference exists between junk and high-yield securities. Both classifications generate high yields. Although the yield of junk bonds reflects the poor quality of the underlying issuer, the yield of many high-yield securities reflects a variety of circumstances such as the small size of a firm or the lack of a credit history. Although rating agencies often penalize such a firm by giving it a low rating, the firm may exhibit good credit quality in many areas. It is this difference that presents the challenge to the credit analyst.

The expansion of the high-yield market over the past two decades presents an opportunity for the analyst to identify quality in issues that the majority of analysts have ignored. This process involves in-depth research. Because many high-yield bonds have short histories, the analyst must necessarily make more projections. Overall, the analysis will be heavily weighted to the second dimension of credit analysis discussed in Chapter 19—the aspects that are most commonly associated with the analysis of common stock. In addition, the analyst is often faced with innovative characteristics of the security, such as options exercisable only under certain circumstances. These features must be evaluated within the context of the total valuation process.

The artificial differentiation between bonds and the associated technique of credit analysis stem perhaps from some investors' segmentation of the market, whereby the bond portion is the "safe" area in which no risk should be taken. In this framework, potential rewards from bonds are probably not considered. Recent academic papers and numerous studies generated by the securities industry show the fallacy of such reasoning. These studies suggest that the historical risk/return relationship is consistent with what is expected from capital market theory: Although high-yield bonds have greater risk than Treasury securities and high-grade corporate bonds, they have provided higher returns.

If this is the case, why have these credits been historically so carefully ignored by most analysts? There are four major reasons for this inefficient behavior. First, institutional and legal constraints are often imposed on money managers, confining investments to "investment-grade" securities (i.e., those rated BBB− or higher by the rating agencies). Interestingly, these same money managers often buy the equity of a company whose debt they would not buy. Second, the high-yield market has been well developed for only a few years. Previously, the high-yield market lacked liquidity and stability. Portfolio managers hesitated to invest in this market for portfolios that required liquidity. Third, diversification in the low-grade market has historically been difficult. Until recently, the market has been heavily weighted in the railroad industry, as potential issuers relied primarily on bank financing and private placements. Finally, the lack of significant buyers restricted young growth companies from issuing public debt. High-yield securities were therefore associated with junk securities and the behavior was reinforced.

The analysis of high-yield bonds is essentially the same as the complete analysis of investment-grade bonds. However, because of the nature of the company, more time will generally be involved. Extensive market projections are often required, as well as possible explanations for inconsistencies in growth patterns. In addition, the commitment involved in the analysis of high-yield bonds cannot be made to merely analyze a single credit or even several credits. Because the prices of high-yield bonds change more as a function of changes in creditworthiness (nonmarket risk) than as a function of interest-rate changes (market risk), any commitment to high-yield bonds must be made within the context of a portfolio in order to help it benefit from diversification and lowering of specific risk. The analyst must be familiar with a number of industries to accomplish this.

The importance of diversification and its ability to increase expected return per unit of risk is an accepted tenet of portfolio management. Even portfolio managers who invest solely in high-grade securities will lower their risk by diversifying across industries, coupons, and maturities. The addition of a diversified portfolio of high-yield bonds may add more to a portfolio than the generally perceived higher rate of return. A study by Blume and Keim found that lower quality bonds experienced less volatility or risk than high-grade bonds or equities over the period studied, when risk was defined as the standard deviation of monthly returns.[1] Blume and Keim suggest that this result may be explained by the fact that much of the risk associated with high-yield bonds is nonmarket or firm specific and can therefore be eliminated by diversification.

The implications of this result are far reaching. Many investors, particularly institutional investors, are leery of the high-yield bonds because of the added risk they attribute to these bonds. This avoidance behavior is reinforced by the occasional well-publicized default or bankruptcy. The evidence shows, however, that the investor would be better off in terms of return and possible reduction of risk by including a diversified portfolio of high-yield bonds in a total portfolio. The avoidance behavior may in fact enhance yields. It is unfortunate that well-intentioned bureaucrats occasionally seek to protect the public by trying to legislate that certain types of high-yield securities be avoided. They may be increasing the rewards to the investors who do participate in the high-yield market.

As in any other bond analysis, the analyst's purpose is to determine the value of the security. Will the issuing company be able to meet its interest and principal payments? Will the credit quality of the bond change over the life of the issue?

The progression of analysis for a high-yield bond should also be the same as that for any bond as discussed in Chapter 19. The analysis must be rigorous, however, as the margin of safety is generally more narrow. In addition, several areas of analysis should be expanded.

## Competition

The size of a company has important credit implications. It is well known that many "small" firms file for bankruptcy each year. It should be noted, however, that these firms are not the same "small" firms that are issuing high-yield debt. The firms labeled small by investors are generally small only in relation to the giants of the industry. As the rating agencies favor the very large, well-established firms, the "small" firms suffer by comparison.

In an industry where the leader or leaders can set pricing, a small firm could be at a significant disadvantage. In the scenario where the pricing is set, the small firm must have unit costs approaching, equal to, or lower than the pricing leaders. The small firm that is inefficient cannot withstand a prolonged pricing war. The leaders in this case could launch a pricing war to gain market

---

1. Marshall E. Blume and Donald B. Keim, *Risk and Return Characteristics of Lower-Grade Bonds* (Philadelphia: Rodney L. White Center for Financial Research, 1984), p. 4.

share and effectively drive the inefficient producers out of business. In certain circumstances, the small firm may be able to differentiate its product and thereby control a certain segment of the market. However, there is always the threat of competition. The company with a market niche must be monitored to ensure that the niche remains the domain of the company in question.

## Cash Flow

One of the most important elements in analyzing a high-yield security is cash flow. In such an analysis, cash flow/long-term debt is not as important as cash flow/total cash requirements. Does the company have enough cash flow to meet its interest payments and to fund necessary research and growth? Does the company have sufficient cash flow to tide it over during a period of weak economic activity? What borrowing capacity is available? The ability to borrow enabled several large firms such as Chrysler and Ford Motor to meet their debt obligations when these companies were experiencing significant losses. As a result, the companies were granted time to reformulate products and reposition themselves for an upturn in the economy and industry. The smaller firm may not have this advantage. On the other hand, the larger firms, which often have the luxury of expanding borrowings during weak markets, may be trading on their market name long after their credit quality has deteriorated.

The evaluation of cash flow coverage of fixed charges should not be conducted to the exclusion of total fixed-charge coverage. Some high-yield issuers have a high percentage of interest that is paid-in-kind. The identification of a clear path (or lack thereof) for meeting these obligations when they become cash payments is an integral part of an analysis of a high-yield bond. Future asset sales to meet these obligations may not materialize at the anticipated prices. Some high-yield issuers assume that maturities of fixed obligations will be met by new issuance. Although this possibility is likely, there have been instances where the high-yield new issue market is essentially closed to all but the most creditworthy of issuers.

The analyst must particularly focus on cash flow in certain leveraged buyout situations. Although the purchaser may have a specific plan for selling assets to reduce debt and related payments, time may be critical. Can the company meet its cash obligations if the sale of assets is delayed? How liquid are the assets that are scheduled for sale? Are the appraised values of these assets accurate? What financial flexibility does the company have in terms of borrowing capacity? Are indenture covenants being met?

## Net Assets

In analyzing a bond, the analyst must ascertain or at least approximate the liquidation value of the assets. Are these assets properly valued on the balance sheet? Of particular interest may be real estate holdings. For example, in analyzing the gaming companies, a market assessment of land holdings should be included. On the other hand, one should also consider the likelihood of those assets being available for liquidation, if necessary. To whom do they belong? Are they mortgaged or being used as collateral? Assets are occasionally spun off to the equity owners of the company. In such a circumstance, the bondholders may experience a sudden and dramatic deterioration of credit quality. Other bondholders are secured by specific assets such as railroad cars or a nuclear power station. In these circumstances, the value and marketability of the collateral must be ascertained. Collateral by definition must be specific and so must be the analysis. Ten railroad engines may appear to be secure until it is discovered that the engines are not only obsolete but have not been maintained for a number of years.

Particular attention must be paid to the asset protection in a takeover situation. In this instance, assets that originally provided protection for your holdings could be used to secure new debt senior to your holding.

The analyst must also focus on the location of the assets. If the assets are in a foreign country, the analyst should be familiar with that country's laws regarding expatriation of funds. In the extreme case, the analyst should be familiar with that country's laws regarding bankruptcy proceedings. In recent years, some analysts have attributed great value to assets which are not concrete. For example, some analysts attribute a high value per customer or access to such customer. Although this valuation may be valid in the short term, the ability to realize that value depends on rapidly changing variables such as technology. Should a company encounter financial distress, it is likely that the value of these "assets" will decline.

## Management

Management is a critical element in the assessment of any firm. Given enough time, poor management can bankrupt the most prosperous firm. Conversely, good management is essential to the long-term survival of all firms. Many successful firms were started by employees of the leaders in an industry. The high-technology area is an example of this. Often, employees decide to start their own firms for personal profit. Very often the firms are founded by some of the leading engineers or salesmen. While the creative talents and profit motive in these firms may be high, the whole management team must be evaluated. Is there a strong financial manager? Is there a strong marketing manager? Where are the controls? Start-up operations provide high incentives for success. The ownership of a significant portion of the company by management is generally positive. Too often, employees of a large firm relate only to their personal paychecks and not to the overall profitability of the firm.

# Leverage

Companies that issue high-yield bonds are generally highly leveraged. Leverage per se is not harmful and in many circumstances is beneficial to growth. However, the degree of leverage should be evaluated in terms of its effect on the financial flexibility of the firm. As pointed out in Chapter 19, leverage should be calculated on absolute and market-adjusted bases. The most common approach to market adjustment is to calculate a market value for the equity of the firm. To the extent that the common stock is selling below book value, leverage will be understated by a traditional approach. Some firms also adjust the market value of debt in calculating leverage. This approach is interesting, but a consistent approach must be employed when convertibles are considered in the equity equation. The benefit of adjusting the equity side of the leverage equation is clear. As the market values a company's equity upward, the market is indicating a willingness to support more leverage. A similar increase in the market adjustment of a firm's debt may indicate an upward appraisal of creditworthiness or an overall lowering of interest rates. In either case, the company would probably have the opportunity to refinance at a lower cost and thereby increase profitability.

## SPECIAL TYPES OF HIGH-YIELD SECURITIES

In addition to the special circumstances involved in analyzing a high-yield security, the analyst is faced with nontraditional forms of financing. This is not surprising. Over the past fifteen years, the high-yield market has provided the majority of innovative financing. A thorough understanding of the type of security is necessary to complete an evaluation. Some modifications of the security have important implications for the analysis. The modifications and refinements to high-yield securities have been numerous. Several of these modifications are outlined below.

## Exchangeable Variable-Rate Notes (EVRNs)

EVRNs are subordinated, intermediate-term obligations that pay interest quarterly. The interest rate is fixed for a short period. This period is called the "teaser" because the fixed rate is generally set above the rate dictated by the formula. After the fixed-rate period, the rate is adjusted quarterly and is tied to certain benchmarks such as the prime rate or 90-day Treasury bills. Generally, the issuer has the option to exchange the notes for fixed-rate notes with predetermined features such as maturity and call price. Generally, the issuer must exchange the securities after five years.

## Usable Bonds

Usable bonds are securities that are issued with a warrant to purchase the issuing company's common stock. When the warrants are exercised, the bonds can be used at par in lieu of cash. (These bonds are also called synthetic convertibles when they are considered with their respective warrants.) The market value of these securities is sometimes highly correlated to the value of the company's stock and amount of usable bonds outstanding in relation to the amount required for exercise of the warrants.

## Springing Issues

Springing securities are issues that will change one or more of their characteristics if a certain event occurs. One such issue was a note with springing warrants that would be exercisable only if someone tried to acquire the issuer. Another springing security was originally issued as subordinated debt but would become senior indebtedness when an old outstanding debenture had been discharged, as long as the issuing company was able to create the additional senior indebtedness without violating any covenants of a third outstanding issue. In evaluating springing issues, the analyst must determine the likelihood of the issue's changing form and the value of the change.

## Pay-in-Kind Securities

Pay-in-kind securities (PIKs) give the issuer the option to pay interest in either cash or additional securities for a specified period of time. This option gives the issuer flexibility in terms of its cash-flow management. The PIK market has grown significantly in recent years. Many PIK securities are issued in Chapter 11 reorganizations.

In evaluating PIK securities, the analyst must use a discounted cash-flow technique if the security is trading at either a discount or a premium. This approach is required because the value of the payments-in-kind is equal to the current market value of the security.

## Other Issues

In recent years, the assortment of high-yield securities has proliferated. Issues that offer a share of the firm's profits in addition to a stated interest rate, as well as issues backed by commodities, have been floated. Other firms have issued private placements with registration rights.

The variety of financing alternatives is likely to continue to expand. The analyst must evaluate the characteristics of each issue to determine how much, if any, value it adds to the credit. The analysis of low-grade securities often requires additional work. The investor is rewarded for this effort in two ways.

The first benefit is enhanced yield. This yield advantage has been significant. Historically, low-grade securities have yielded 300 to 500 basis points more than comparable Treasury issues. The yield advantage over high-grade corporates has almost been as great. When this advantage is compounded annually, the performance benefit to individuals as well as institutional investors is significant. The advantage is only slightly reduced when default risk is considered. The second benefit of high-yield credit analysis is the likelihood of identifying credits that are improving. These credits will provide not only enhanced yield but also capital appreciation relative to the market. This benefit is familiar to the credit analyst who seeks to identify improving as well as deteriorating credits.

## PERFORMANCE OF HIGH-YIELD SECURITIES AND DEFAULT RISK

Historically, defaults and bankruptcies have been nominal in relation to outstanding U.S. debt. W. Braddock Hickman's study, *Corporate Bond Quality and Investor Experience,* concluded that, on average during the period 1900–1943, 1.7% of all straight public and private debt defaulted.[2,3] More recent studies have found historic default rates of only approximately .5% annually, with several years producing no defaults.

Recently, several default studies have been published. These studies address various time frames between 1970 and 1996. Although the studies vary in their methodologies and definitions of default, the consensus annual default figure is approximately 2–4% of all high-yield issues outstanding.

A recent Moody's study of default rates in the speculative grade securities calculated the weighted average one-year default rate for 1970 to 1992 at 4.58%.[4] This figure was influenced by the high default rates of 8.8% and 9.5% in 1990 and 1991, respectively. Although the level of defaults has declined since 1991, the possibility of another period of high defaults reinforces the need for in-depth credit research.

Any study of defaults must pay particular attention to the industry source of the default. When defaults are analyzed by industry, it becomes evident that close to 50% of the high-yield defaults during 1977–1987 were in the oil and steel industries. This fact clearly emphasizes the potential reward of credit research.

Regardless of how low default rates are in a given year, investors who own defaulted issues will be greatly affected if the defaulted issues represent a

---

2. W.B. Hickman, *Corporate Bond Quality and Investor Experience* (Princeton University Press and the National Bureau of Economic Research, 1958).
3. "Historical Default Rates of Corporate Bond Issues, 1920–1996," *Moody's Special Report,* January 1997.
4. "Corporate Bond Defaults and Default Rates 1970–1992," *Moody's Special Report,* January, 1993.

significant portion of their portfolios. A portfolio must be well diversified to prevent such losses.

In spite of careful analysis, the investor may be faced with a default or bankruptcy. In such a circumstance, analysis must continue. There have been situations where a defaulting issuer has subsequently resumed payments or issued stock to bondholders that eventually was worth more than the original debt.

The potential for defaults in the high-yield area has discouraged some investors from participating in this market. For some investors, this may not have been a rational decision. To fully evaluate the decision whether to participate in the high-yield market, investors must balance the potential for default with the potential for gain.

## BROKERAGE HOUSES AND THE RATING AGENCIES

As with high-grade securities, there is no substitute for sound fundamental analysis. The rating agencies can provide some help. In addition, more in-depth research in this area is being conducted by brokerage firms. Even *The Wall Street Journal,* in response to investors' demand for more information about the high-yield bond market, initiated coverage of junk bonds in 1991.

## CONCLUSION

Analysts often classify themselves according to the type of security they analyze. This classification is misleading. An analyst who understands the principles of accounting and credit analysis should feel equally comfortable with high- or low-grade securities. Analysis will never be a rote process. It is only the good analyst who knows when to delve into a specific area exhaustively and when to quickly assess other areas of a company. This intuitive aspect of credit analysis is particularly important in analyzing low-grade credits. It can usually be developed with experience.

## CHAPTER 21

# INVESTING IN CHAPTER 11 AND OTHER DISTRESSED COMPANIES*

Jane Tripp Howe, CFA
Director of Credit Research
Freedom Capital Management

Investors and analysts often shy away from distressed and Chapter 11 companies. On the surface, this hesitancy is understandable. Most investors would not willingly invest in bankrupt companies, which the Random House Dictionary defines as "at the end of one's resources" or in the state of "utter ruin, failure, depletion, or the like." Most analysts believe that analysis directed at healthy companies is more likely to be profitable. This avoidance of bankrupt and distressed companies is unwise for several reasons. First, investing in Chapter 11 companies can be highly profitable. Many companies use the bankruptcy process to reorganize. Often, reorganization gives companies a new start that can provide rewarding investment opportunities. The key to success is to differentiate between the companies that are truly depleted and those that will reorganize successfully. Second, a total avoidance of bankrupt companies may induce an investor to sell a holding of a bankrupt company at its lowest price. The prices of securities of companies that have filed for Chapter 11 often plummet when the filing is made. These prices often recover somewhat with time. Investors who immediately sell their securities upon news of a filing will suffer a more significant loss than would occur if they were patient.

Sometimes portfolio managers are required to sell securities of firms that file for bankruptcy because of policy guidelines. In this case, portfolio managers should evaluate the specifics of the situation with particular emphasis on the timing and amount of ultimate recovery. Such an evaluation could indicate that the security will be paid in full, including interest within a short time. In such a case, the portfolio manager should present the evaluation to the client in order that the client may consider a modification of his policy.

---

* The author wishes to thank George Putnam III, publisher of *Bankruptcy Datasource,* for his helpful comments and suggestions.

Historically, most investors who owned companies in bankruptcy did so by default. Today, many investors actively invest in companies in reorganization. These investors intend to profit by taking advantage of the substantial inefficiencies in this market. This chapter gives the investor an understanding of the bankruptcy process and outlines a method for evaluating securities in bankruptcy.

The methodology outlined here can also apply to companies that are distressed but have not filed for bankruptcy. In the case of distressed companies, the analyst should value the company as an ongoing business as well as a business that has filed for bankruptcy. With these two valuations in hand, the analyst will be able to weigh the potential benefit/cost of investing in the security.

## THE IMPORTANCE OF A BASIC UNDERSTANDING

Most investors believe that they will never have to deal with a company that has filed for protection under the Bankruptcy Code. Although this may be true for the majority of investors, as long as there are bankruptcies, there will be investors who own the securities of the bankrupt companies. The possibility of owning the securities of one of these companies is increasing as the number of companies filing for protection under the Bankruptcy Code has been increasing in recent years. For example, 129 large public companies had filed for bankruptcy for the first 11 months of 1999 versus 70 companies for all of 1994 as reported in *The 1999 Bankruptcy Yearbook and Almanac*, published by New Generation Research. A basic understanding of bankruptcy analysis is also important in order to evaluate the potential rewards of this market.

## OVERVIEW OF BANKRUPTCY

There are two types of investors who deal with the securities of companies in bankruptcy. The first type is the investor who owns the security by default. This investor purchases the security with the intention of profiting from a healthy company. The second type of investor buys the securities of bankrupt companies after the company has filed for protection. Regardless of how you came to own the security, the analysis of the holding is similar.

Investors who analyze their investment holdings carefully are unlikely to be surprised if one of their investments petitions for bankruptcy protection. The decline of a company into bankruptcy generally takes several years and is often the result of illiquidity and deteriorating operating performance. Although most bankruptcies can be predicted in advance with sound credit analysis, occasionally companies that are financially sound file for protection. For example, Johns Manville was profitable when it declared bankruptcy in August 1982. Manville filed for bankruptcy because of the contingent liabilities arising from claims of individuals who had contracted asbestos-related diseases as well as claims from property owners who incurred costs for the removal of asbestos materials from their property. In a similar manner, Dow Corning Corporation filed for bankruptcy in May 1995 in order to resolve its litigation regarding silicone breast implants. Although bankruptcy filings for nonfinancial reasons are less easy to predict, they should not be complete surprises. The bond market has been cognizant of the contingent liabilities of the tobacco companies for a long time and has priced tobacco debt at higher yields than industrial companies in other businesses with comparable financial parameters. The possible monetization of these contingent liabilities first was announced in April 1997. In November 1998, cigarette makers settled its contingent liabilities with the states' attorney generals for $206 billion in exchange for the end of lawsuits brought by the states over public-health costs connected to smoking. Unfortunately for the tobacco companies, threatened and actual litigation has not ended. The astute analyst should always be mindful of footnotes that outline contingent liabilities.

All companies that file for bankruptcy are governed by the Bankruptcy Reform Act of 1978, which then-President Carter signed into law on November 6, 1978. The Act became law on October 1, 1979. The purpose of the law is twofold: (1) to provide consistency to the companies filing for protection under the law and (2) to provide a framework under which a company can either reorganize or liquidate in an orderly fashion. Perhaps the most important facet of bankruptcy law is the protection it affords companies in distress. Filing for protection triggers the automatic stay provisions of the Code. This provision precludes attempts of creditors to collect prepetition claims from the debtor or otherwise interfere with its property or business. This provision gives the debtor breathing room to formulate a plan of reorganization or to formulate a plan for orderly liquidation. Creditors are necessarily discouraged from racing to the court to dismember the debtor.

The current Bankruptcy Code consists of 15 chapters. Each chapter deals with a different facet and/or type of bankruptcy. For most investors, an understanding of Chapters 7 and 11, which deal with corporate liquidation and corporate reorganization, respectively, is sufficient. Occasionally, an investor will encounter companies which have filed bankruptcy two times (Resorts International) or three times (Braniff). These companies generally refile under Chapter 7 or Chapter 11 of the Bankruptcy Code. However, companies which file twice are informally referred to as "Chapter 22s," while companies which file three times are informally referred to as "Chapter 33s."

## When a Company Files for Protection

When a company files for protection under the bankruptcy law, it can do so either voluntarily or involuntarily. A voluntary petition is filed by the company declaring bankruptcy. In an involuntary bankruptcy, the petition is filed by three or more creditors of the company whose claims are neither contingent nor subject to dispute.

When a company files for bankruptcy, the filing may include only the parent company and exclude one or more subsidiaries. For example, when Town & Country filed for bankruptcy on November 17, 1997, it filed its holding company and structured the pre-negotiated plan of reorganization without causing certain of its operating companies, including Town & Country Fine Jewelry Group, to file for bankruptcy. The entities filed for bankruptcy can have a material effect on the outcome and recoveries in bankruptcy. For example, on December 27, 1996, Marvel Entertainment Group, Inc. filed both a petition for bankruptcy as well as a plan of reorganization to implement a restructuring. On the same date, three intermediate holding companies, Marvel III Holdings, Inc., Marvel (Parent) Holdings, Inc., and Marvel Holdings, Inc. also filed for bankruptcy. In this complicated bankruptcy, there was significant legal action among the bondholders of the holding companies, holders of bank debt, and the Marvel Entertainment Group concerning control of Toy Biz, a profitable entity within the group, and the ability of one group of interests to file a plan for an operating company while not including plans for the holding companies where public debt was outstanding. These cases highlight the importance of analyzing the structure of a company in order to fully understand potential recoveries in bankruptcies.

When a company files for bankruptcy, it files in the appropriate circuit and the appropriate district within that circuit. (There are 11 circuits and 93 districts.) The "appropriate" court cannot necessarily be predicted. Appropriate can mean the court with jurisdiction over the company's headquarters location or perhaps the court with jurisdiction over its principal place of business. Companies have some flexibility in their choice of geographic location for filing. Eastern Airlines, for instance, filed in New York even though its corporate headquarters was in Miami. The airline stated it filed in New York because it had substantial operations in New York, and its financial efforts and lawyers were there. In addition, many of Eastern's creditors were also in New York, which facilitated meetings.

When a company petitions for protection, its petition is accompanied by several items, including basic administrative information and a listing of the 20 largest creditors. These creditors will be contacted by the court and called for a meeting. Other financial information is required within 15 days of filing. Sometimes, the financial information accompanies the filing. Other times, it is delayed. Included in this financial information is a listing of assets and liabilities as of the petition date. This listing represents the company's best estimate of its assets and liabilities. Often, this listing of assets and liabilities can cover several hundred pages.

Significant adjustments are often made to the assets and liabilities by the time a company completes its reorganization process. These adjustments are noticeable when assets are sold during the reorganization process and also when the asset values are compared with estimates of the liquidation value of the assets. This is principally because the values are based on the company as an ongoing business in its prepetition form. Revco's February 1989 sale of 113 sites exemplifies the discrepancy between listed asset values and realizable value. In its February 1989 sale, Revco was enabled (with bankruptcy court approval) to sell 14 sites. What is more significant, however, is the fact that no bids were made on several sites. The difference between listed market value of assets and the liquidation value of these assets can be even more dramatic. For example, in its September 5, 1989, Second Amended Plan of Reorganization, Cardis Corporation estimated that its inventory would be discounted by 52%. Cardis further estimated that its net plant, property, and equipment would be discounted by 23% in a liquidation. In fact, the only asset that will not suffer a discount will be cash.

Although the assets and liabilities filed with the Bankruptcy Court are not precise, they are useful because they give an indication of the overall picture of the company. For example, when Manville filed for protection in 1982, it had more assets than liabilities and was a profitable company. On the other hand, when Worlds of Wonder filed on December 22, 1987, it listed $271.6 million in debts and $222.1 million in assets.

Once a company files for protection under the Bankruptcy Code, the company becomes a "debtor-in-possession." As such, the company continues to operate its business under the supervision of the court. Usually, the debtor-in-possession needs to obtain court approval only for major and unusual transactions (such as the sale of property). Generally, the United States Trustee for the particular district is assigned to the proceeding. The U.S. Trustee's duties are essentially administrative. The appointment of the U.S. Trustee has become fairly routine.

The increasing complexity of bankruptcies has resulted in the increased frequency of a second appointment to a bankruptcy case. This appointment is usually an examiner but can also be a trustee. The requirements for the appointment of an examiner are fairly broad. An examiner can be appointed if the appointment serves the interests of the creditors, equity holders, or other interests. For example, an examiner was appointed in the case of A. H. Robbins because management had shown an inability to follow the bankruptcy rules. An examiner was also appointed in the case of Eastern Airlines, whose slide into bankruptcy was at least partially caused by striking unions. Shortly after Eastern Airlines filed for protection, the unions petitioned the court to have a trustee appointed to run the company. Eastern management petitioned the court to have an examiner appointed rather than a trustee so that it would have more flexibility in running its business. The federal bankruptcy judge in the Eastern case ordered the appointment of a "powerful" examiner, who was given a broad mandate to end the strike. Sometimes, if there are allegations of negligence or mismanagement, then an examiner will be appointed to investigate the allegations and report to the court. Occasionally, a trustee will be appointed by the court to take control of the business if there is gross negligence or mismanagement. This is relatively unusual. A recent case where a trustee was appointed was Sharon Steel, where there were allegations of fraud.

## Proceeding toward a Plan

The purpose in filing for protection under the Bankruptcy Code is to give the debtor time to decide whether it should reorganize or liquidate and time to formulate a plan for the chosen action. The intent generally is to successfully reorganize. The first step in formulating a plan of reorganization is the appointment of committees. Generally, only a committee of unsecured creditors is appointed by the U.S. Trustee. Frequently, this committee is comprised of an elected subcommittee of the 20 largest creditors. The committee represents a particular class of claimants. Its principal function is to help formulate a plan of reorganization that is equitable to all classes and that will be confirmed (approved) by the court and the claimants. The committee approach is necessary because plans are negotiated.

Although only one committee is usual, there has been a growing incidence of multiple committees, each representing a different class of creditors. For example, in the Revco D.S. bankruptcy, there were two committees: the Noteholders Committee and the Unsecured Creditors Committee. In the Allegheny bankruptcy, there were four committees: the Equity Holders Committee, the Secured Creditors Committee, the Unsecured Creditors Committee, and the Sunbeam Corporation Creditors Committee. Often, the existence of multiple committees slows the bankruptcy process as factions can develop that undermine the spirit of cooperation necessary to formulate a plan. Cooperation is necessary because plans of reorganization rarely work under the premise of absolute priority; that is, the most senior classes are paid in full before a less senior class receives anything. The negotiation process inherent in a reorganization generally grants all classes some token distribution in order to obtain their acceptance of the plan. This is the reason why shareholders often receive some percent of the equity of the reorganized company. (The percentage distributed to the equity holders varies considerably. In recent plans of reorganization, equity holders of JPS Textile as well as Eagle-Picher Industries were proposed to receive 0%, while the equity of Sizzler Restaurants will be retained by Collins Food International.)

This is also the reason why secured creditors accept less than a full recovery even if there are sufficient assets in the debtor's estate to satisfy the claim.

There are several theories that explain the high incidence of reorganizations that do not adhere to the absolute priority rule. These include the fact that junior creditors and holders of equity interests can significantly delay the reorganization process unless they are given a distribution in order to obtain their acceptance of the plan. Other plans are confirmed that do not adhere to the rule of absolute priority in order to preserve valuable net operating loss carryforwards that may be lost if a plan is confirmed according to strict absolute priority.

After the committee of unsecured creditors has been appointed, the debtor generally makes specific decisions whether to assume or to reject its executory contracts (contractual commitments entered prior to bankruptcy for the provision of future goods or services). In many bankruptcies, the rejection of high-priced contracts has been beneficial to the debtor. For example, when LTV declared bankruptcy, it was able to reject several high-priced contracts for raw materials. Several debtors have also rejected high-priced labor contracts. For example, in 1984, a bankruptcy judge upheld Continental Airlines' decision to break its labor agreements with its pilots union. The laws have changed for the rejection of labor contracts. Currently, collective bargaining agreements cannot be rejected so easily. Although many executory contracts can be rejected, specific rules may apply to the rejection of certain contracts. For example, Chapter 11 companies may reject leases with the approval of the Bankruptcy Court, only after they have made efforts to sell the sites. This was the case with Revco. After Revco had held an auction for 113 of its sites, the Bankruptcy Court was likely to grant Revco permission to reject the leases of sites for which no bids were received.

## Formulation of a Plan

Once the committees are in place, the formulation of a plan begins. The debtor has the exclusive right to file a plan of reorganization for 120 days. The length of the exclusive period is determined by the court and can be extended or short-ened. (Generally, the exclusive period tends to be longer than 120 days.) No other plan can be filed during this period, but this exclusive period does not stop other parties from formulating and circulating plans among creditors. In the case of Allegheny International, the unsecured creditors formulated a plan during the exclusive period (which had been repeatedly extended) because of their frustration with what they perceived to be lack of progress in the Allegheny bankruptcy. Generally, the first plan of reorganization is not the final plan. It is common to see the first amended and second amended plans of reorganization. (During August 1989, Allegheny International filed its Sixth Amended Plan of Reorganization.) Sometimes, even the debtor knows that its first formulation of a plan is not its final formulation. For instance, Allegheny actually labeled its August 30, 1988 Disclosure Statement "Preliminary." It is important to remember that a plan is commonly amended at least once before it is confirmed. Amended plans often entail significant changes in the funding of the plan, terms of the reorganization securities, and distributions to classes. Investors must be certain that they are working with the most recent plan of reorganization.

Investors must also be aware of plans of reorganization filed by others. For example, in September 1989, four plans of reorganization were filed for Public Service Company of New Hampshire. These plans were filed by (1) Public Service Company of New Hampshire (the debtor), (2) New England Power Company on behalf of itself and New England Electric System, (3) The United Illuminating Company, and (4) Northeast Utilities Service Company. A potential investor in Public Service Company of New Hampshire's securities would have to be familiar with each of these plans.

Historically, bankruptcy courts have allowed competing plans to be filed simultaneously. Recently, however, courts are more active in exercising their authority to determine which plans are distributed. This authority is most notably exercised in the court's extension of the period of exclusivity. The Integrated Resources reorganization exemplifies this new activism. The court refused to consider any plans that competed with the debtors' plan until the court determined whether the debtors' plan was confirmable. Once the debtors' plan was judged nonconfirmable by the court, the court authorized the filing of a competing plan by Steinhardt Management Company.

There are several ways to ensure that the investor is working with the most recent plan. One way is to keep in contact with the debtor. A second way is to subscribe to a bankruptcy service such as *Bankruptcy Datasource* in Boston, which has the advantage of being timely and convenient. A third way is to monitor the docket of the case with the bankruptcy court in which the petition was filed. A docket for a bankruptcy case lists all of the filings made with respect to the case. Therefore, the docket is an excellent source to alert the investor to new filings. Access to dockets varies significantly among bankruptcy courts. If an investor is interested in only one bankruptcy and happens to be located in the city in which the bankruptcy case was filed, monitoring the specific docket can be as simple as walking to the court and xeroxing the docket. More likely, investors will be following numerous bankruptcies filed in a variety of cities. In these circumstances, investors are dependent on the accessibility of the court. Fortunately for investors, electronic access to dockets is becoming more common. In addition, many courts are able to provide the names of copy services that are able to quickly access dockets and related filings and mail them for a fee. Unfortunately, some courts persist in requiring a written request for any document. Access to documents is thus more limited. Although documents are available for viewing, at specific courts documents are not available electronically. Copy services are usually the most expedient way of obtaining documents from such courts. Care must be taken to request all of the relevant exhibits. Frequently, these exhibits present the specifics of the securities to be issued under the plan.

In filing a plan of reorganization, a debtor with one or more subsidiaries must decide if the plan will incorporate substantive consolidation of the subsidiaries. Under substantive consolidation, all of the assets and liabilities of the entities in question are pooled and used collectively to pay debts. Substantive consolidation must be approved by the court. The approval is not granted lightly. In order for substantive consolidation to be granted, proponents must prove that the parent and the subsidiaries in question operated as a single unit. This can be proved by such means as intercompany guarantees and transfers of assets. The issue of substantive consolidation can have important ramifications for the investor. For example, in the case of LTV, the aerospace/defense subsidiary was profitable and had assets in excess of its liabilities. On the other hand, the steel subsidiary was unprofitable at the time of filing and had liabilities significantly in excess of its assets. If LTV was reorganized without substantive consolidation, investors owning the securities guaranteed by the aerospace/defense subsidiary would receive generous distributions. On the other hand, if substantive consolidation was granted, the distributions to these investors would be decreased as the assets of the aerospace/defense subsidiary are pooled to pay the debts of the entire corporation.

In fact, LTV eventually confirmed a plan premised on the substantive consolidation of LTV into five cases: LTV (Parent), LTV Steel, LTV Aerospace, AM General, and LTV Energy. The recoveries of the five cases varied significantly.

## Disclosure Statement

Once a plan of reorganization has been finalized (and generally has been informally approved by the major creditors), the debtor produces and files for approval a disclosure statement about the plan with the court. The disclosure statement provides enough information to allow reasonable investors to make informed judgments. Approval of the disclosure statement is premised on the court's opinion that the disclosure statement contains sufficient information to allow reasonable investors to make informed judgments. Approval of a disclosure statement does not reflect an opinion of the court regarding the plan's merits.

A disclosure statement summarizes the plan. It also contains fairly detailed financial information about the debtor, including the company's five-year pro forma statements, which are required by statute. It also presents a liquidation analysis of the company that supports the company's contention that creditors will receive a higher distribution under the plan than they would if the debtor were to be liquidated. The disclosure statement also provides a brief history of the company, including reasons for filing and significant events since filing. The disclosure statement is generally more understandable and readable than the legal plan.

If the court approves the disclosure statement, the plan and the disclosure statement are mailed to the impaired classes for approval. Holders of claims that are not impaired (i.e., claims that are paid in full or whose interests are not adversely affected by the proceeding) are not entitled to vote because unimpaired classes are conclusively presumed to have accepted the plan. Classes that are entitled to vote are generally given 30 days to do so.

In order for a plan to be accepted, at least two thirds of the amount and more than one half of the number of claims actually voting of each impaired class and at least two thirds of the outstanding shares of each class of interests must accept the plan. Institutional investors may have an advantage in the voting process if their holdings are dispersed over a number of accounts. In this instance, an institutional may effectively "control" a specific class if the number of accounts it represents constitutes more than one half of the number of creditors in a specific class. If the plan is approved by the voting classes, it is sent to the court for confirmation. When the court confirms the plan, it approves the transactions specified in the plan and a date for the reorganization to take effect.

## Cram-Down

It is interesting to note that a plan can be confirmed under the cram-down provisions even if the required number of creditors do not approve the plan. The confirmation of a plan under the cram-down provisions must meet several specific requirements. First, the plan must be shown not to discriminate unfairly against any impaired class. Such a determination includes the requirement that no class shall receive more than 100% of the amount of its claim. In addition, each dissenting class must receive as much as they would be entitled to receive under a liquidation. Often, plans state that the Bankruptcy Court will confirm the plan under the cram-down provisions if all the requirements are met except for the requirement that each class has accepted the plan. Second, a plan must be shown to be fair and equitable to a nonaccepting class. Under the Bankruptcy Code, a plan is fair and equitable to a nonaccepting class if, among other things, it provides that the nonaccepting class either (a) receives property of a present value equal to the allowed amount of such claims, or (b) if the class is to receive property of any lesser value, no class junior to the nonaccepting class receives or retains any property under the plan. Third, the plan must be accepted by at least one impaired class.

## ANALYSIS OF COMPANIES IN REORGANIZATION

There are several different approaches that can be used to invest in the bankruptcy market. Large and aggressive investors buy a substantial block of the debtor's bonds and try to become a significant factor in the reorganization plan. Often these investors pool their resources in vulture funds, which invest in the securities of bankrupt companies. Such funds frequently operate by acquiring large blocks of a particular class of securities and use their leverage in the reorganization process to formulate a plan favorable to their position. Not all such strategies are profitable. In one case, a vulture fund acquired a large percentage of the subordinated debentures of a Chapter 11 company, hoping that it would receive a controlling equity interest in the reorganized company. Unfortunately for the vultures, more than 90% of the equity in the reorganized company was distributed to secured creditors.

## Investing in Individual Securities

Another approach to investing in Chapter 11 companies, more suited to individual investors, is to buy specific securities in a bankrupt company. This approach has the advantage of not requiring a large investment, thereby allowing investors to diversify their investments. It does require a significant commitment to analysis of the company, but has the potential to be extremely profitable.

In buying the securities of a bankrupt company, the investor has the choice of investing for a general improvement in the overall condition of the company or of investing in situations (such as secured bonds) where the return is more quantifiable because of the assets.

## Selecting the Universe

Selection of a universe of potential acquisition candidates is the initial step in investing in bankrupt securities. Thousands of corporations file Chapter 11 petitions yearly. However, many of these filings represent corporations whose securities are inappropriate for individual investment because the securities are not publicly traded or because the corporations are very small. In these cases, the individual investor could have difficulty obtaining sufficient financial information for analysis or purchasing the securities if analysis could be accomplished. Individual investors should confine their universe to companies that are publicly traded and have assets of at least $25 million. Potential candidates fitting this description can be collected from a variety of sources. An individual investor will probably find a sufficient universe from which to select simply by consulting the business section of newspapers. All listed bankruptcies are identified by a symbol. All bankruptcies listed on the New York, American, and the National Association of Securities Dealers Automated Quotations system's over-the-counter have a "vj" preceding the name of the stock. For example, Harnisch-feger Industries was listed on the New York Stock Exchange Composite Transactions as of November 24, 1999, as vjHarnisch. The NASDAQ National Market Issue listings include an additional indication of bankruptcy. These listings are identified by a four- or five-letter symbol. The fifth letter indicates the issues that are subject to restrictions or special conditions. Securities that are in bankruptcy have a "Q" as the fifth letter of their symbol. A reading of the business section of a major newspaper should keep investors current on recent bankruptcy listings.

## OBTAINING FINANCIAL INFORMATION

Perhaps the most difficult aspect of investing in Chapter 11 companies is obtaining financial and trading information. Trading in the securities of small companies that have filed for bankruptcy can present problems if the companies are delisted. (If a company is delisted, its price can often be found on the National Daily Quotation Service Pink Sheets, published by the National Quotation Bureau. The Pink Sheets also provide potential market makers for the issues listed on the sheets.) More importantly, financial information can be difficult to obtain after a filing. Although SEC filing requirements are not suspended for Chapter 11 companies, filing requirements are often neither strictly observed nor enforced. Therefore, a potential investor may want to limit his or her universe of investment candidates to Chapter 11 companies whose filings are current. This is not always necessary, however, if the investor uses other sources of information and invests only in those securities that are clearly undervalued, employing alternative methods of evaluation.

Once a list of potential candidates has been selected, the collection of financial information should begin. For each company, the investor should obtain the most recent annual report, 10-K, and quarterly report. In addition, the investor should obtain the 8-K that reports on the bankruptcy because this document may have useful facts about the filing. These documents will give the investor some indication of how the company has performed historically and perhaps why it declared bankruptcy. (Old copies of *Value Line* are also useful for obtaining historical perspectives on companies.) The investor should also collect information on the company's publicly traded securities. For stock, such data would include current shares outstanding, par value, and current price.

The information that should be gathered for bonds is more substantial. Bond data should include a complete description of the bond, the amount of bonds outstanding including the amount of original-issue discount, price, and security (i.e., the specific assets supporting the bond). If the value of the security is known or can be estimated, this should also be listed. All bonds should be listed in order of seniority. Sometimes the securities data is found in the 10-K. More often, the investor needs to consult the appropriate *Moody's Manual* (industrial, public utility, etc.). These are found in most libraries.

It is also important to stay current on the news items that affect each of the companies being considered. An easy way to accomplish this is to use the internet. Finally, one should attempt to be placed on the mailing list of the companies being considered. This is sometimes difficult, particularly for those who do not own any securities.

## Investing Without a Plan of Reorganization

Perhaps the most important documents for the analysis of bankrupt securities are the most recent plan of reorganization and the accompanying disclosure statement. These documents specify what each class of claimants (including each class of security holders) will receive in a reorganization. If a plan of reorganization has not been filed, investors must speculate on the distributions to the classes. Because it does not lend itself to thorough analysis, investing without a plan of reorganization is not generally recommended for the individual investor. Although investors can make intelligent decisions regarding some of the more senior debt of the Chapter 11 company, the inability to analyze thoroughly causes trouble in the area of common stock. An analysis of distributions for numerous bankruptcies quickly reveals the variance of distributions for similar classes of claimants. This is most noticeable in the distributions made to holders of common equity interests who have received from zero percent to a major portion of the equity in the reorganized company.

Potential distributions to common stockholders can be further complicated if the "new value" principle is applied. This principle contends that the equity holders who contribute new money and/or management expertise to the reorganization should receive a substantial equity position in the reorganized company. Unfortunately for the holders of subordinated debt, the increased distribution to equity holders translates into a decreased equity distribution to them. Although this principle has been applied in some small bankruptcies, it is infrequently applied in the larger cases. This may change. Revco filed a preliminary proposal that grants 55% of the new Revco stock to its stockholders in exchange for $150 million. Under the proposal, secured creditors would have been paid in full, but subordinated debt holders received stock and bonds valued at only 25% of their claims. Occasionally, stock is distributed to less traditional creditors. For example, in BioMedical Waste Systems' October 1997 plan of reorganization, 77% of the stock of the Reorganized Debtor was to be distributed to "Retained Professionals" as well as to the Debtor-in-Possession Lenders. Potential distribution to common stockholders can also be further complicated by the issuance or reservation of options to management.

The valuation of the securities of a debtor that has not filed a plan of reorganization is similar to a liquidation analysis with one important exception. The company is assumed to be an ongoing business, and therefore no substantial discount is applied to the value of its assets. Under this approach, the assets of the company are totaled and the liabilities are systematically subtracted from this total to give an approximation of how many assets are available to repay each class of claimants. Each class is subtracted in order of seniority. For example, the fully secured claims will be among the first to be subtracted. Although this approach is a quick valuation technique, it is imprecise. It can, however, be used even with somewhat dated financials. Furthermore, this methodology can be usefully applied to both a full value and a liquidation value of the company. This application would serve to bracket the value of the company with a worst case (liquidation value) as well as an optimistic case (full valuation). The application of this technique is outlined below.

### Estimated Valuations of Securities

| | | |
|---|---|---|
| Total Assets | | $xxx |
| Less: | Collateralized debt | |
| | Banks | −xxx |
| | Other | −xxx |
| Equals: | Amount remaining for distribution to other creditors | xxx |
| Less: | Amount due to other creditors (in order of seniority) | −xxx |
| Equals: | Amount remaining for distribution to equity holders | xxx |

This approach is generally not applicable to the valuation of common stock simply because the assets are depleted before the common stockholders are eligible for a distribution. In order to estimate a value for common stock, one must make assumptions regarding the plan of reorganization and the percentage of the equity of the reorganized company that the old shareholders will receive. If this approach is used, the valuation of the common stock should follow the methodology presented under "Investing with a Plan of Reorganization."

## Secured Bonds

A major exception to the premise that investors should generally wait until a plan of reorganization is filed relates to secured bonds. When a company petitions for protection, it is subject to the automatic stay provisions of the Bankruptcy Code. These provisions generally disallow the accrual of interest during bankruptcy, except in the case of secured debt. Secured claims are allowed to accrue postpetition interest during bankruptcy to the extent of the value of the collateral. (Although postpetition interest is accrued, the Code does not generally require that it be paid.) Given these provisions, an astute investor could conceivably purchase a secured bond whose collateral exceeds the principal amount of the bond at a substantial discount to par, knowing that eventually the bond will either be reinstated or be paid off at par plus postpetition interest. An example of how this provision of the Bankruptcy Code could have been beneficial to investors is provided by the LTV bankruptcy. When LTV filed for bankruptcy on July 1, 1986, all of its securities declined significantly. The overall decline overlooked the intrinsic value of the Youngstown Sheet & Tube First Mortgage bonds, whose collateral exceeded the value of the bonds. These bonds, therefore, were entitled to the continuation of their interest.

The significant declines in real estate values in the early 1990s have focused attention on secured debt in bankruptcies. Because of the decline, the secured debt of many investors exceeds the value of the underlying collateral. In this scenario, investors have a secured claim only to the extent of their collateral. Any deficiency will be treated as an unsecured claim. These creditors are not entitled to postpetition interest. Given the major difference in treatment of secured versus unsecured claims, the debtor and the creditor frequently have major disputes regarding the value of a property. Generally, the creditor and the proponent of the plan negotiate a value for the collateral. If the creditor and the proponent are unable to negotiate a value, the bankruptcy court determines a value. Sometimes, the debtor satisfies its obligation to a secured creditor by simply transferring the collateral to the creditor. However, even the transfer of collateral in satisfaction of the debt can be complicated by the imposition of high taxes associated with such a transfer. Other times, the creditor holding a secured claim is paid a certain amount and any excess claims are treated as unsecured claims.

An additional exception to the automatic stay provisions relates to certain equipment trust financing. Much airline equipment debt and railroad equipment debt is exempt from the automatic stay provisions of the Code and the power of the court to repossess the equipment due to §§1110 and 1168 of the Bankruptcy Code, respectively. Instead, the court gives the debtor 60 days to reaffirm the lease on the equipment or return the equipment to the lessor. The debtor is unlikely to cancel the lease because the company cannot operate without the equipment represented by the lease. Airlines cannot operate without airplanes! Generally, in cases of §1110 equipment trusts, the debtor assumes the lease and resumes current interest payments, including interest payable during the 60-day period. The fact that a particular equipment certificate is covered under §1110 is not part of the general description of the certificate. The investor must refer to the "Events of Default, Notice, and Waiver" section of the prospectus or indenture of a given issue to ensure that a particular trust certificate is covered.

The value of §1110 was thrown in doubt on March 10, 1998, with a decision by the U.S. District Court for the District of Colorado with respect to a bankruptcy of Western Pacific Airlines. In its decision, the U.S. District Court ruled that §1110 did not in and of itself require the return of aircraft once the default had been cured. The Court ruled that once the default had been cured, the leases should be treated as other leases. The decision has been appealed and the likely outcome of the issue will be a clarification and reinstatement of the rights historically associated with §1110.

Although secured claims are afforded special treatment in bankruptcy, investors must be studious in their appraisal of the underlying collateral and the fundamentals of the debtor. Even leases on airline equipment can be rejected if the bankrupt carrier is forced to liquidate or downsize dramatically.

## Fraudulent Conveyance

Investors cannot rely blindly on the secured status of particular bonds. In some instances, fraudulent conveyance or transfer may become an issue. If fraudulent conveyance is proved, the seniority of debt may be reordered.

Fraudulent conveyance can become an issue when a company is restructured and security interests are granted in the stock or assets of a company. For example, assume that company A acquires company B in a leveraged buyout for $550 million. Before the buyout, company B's capital structure consisted of equity and $300 million in subordinated debt.

Assume further that the transaction was financed by $50 million in equity and $500 million in debt secured by the assets of company B. Company A subsequently filed for bankruptcy within six months of the LBO. At first glance, one would assume that the secured bonds issued by company A would be paid in full with company B's bonds receiving a share in the remaining assets. In fact, company B's bonds could be deemed senior to company A's bonds if it can be proved that a fraudulent conveyance occurred. Fraudulent conveyance can be proven if fraud was involved. It can also be proved if, at the time of the transfer, company B received less than fair or less than reasonably equivalent value for the transfer and either (1) it was insolvent or rendered insolvent by the transfer, (2) its remaining unencumbered property constituted unreasonably small capital, or (3) it is believed that it incurred debts beyond its ability to pay as such debt matured.

## Investing with a Plan of Reorganization

The analysis of companies in bankruptcy that have filed plans of reorganization should be approached in the same systematic way that the analysis of any security is approached. However, there are two important differences. First, the analyst must place more emphasis on pro formas and less emphasis on historical results. This emphasis is necessary because a reorganized company is generally significantly different from the company that filed for protection. Second, the analyst must be a combination equity/fixed income securities analyst. It is not always clear which of the securities of the reorganized debtor are the most attractive. Often, the relative rates of return among old securities are substantially reordered under the plan. The analyst must therefore be willing to value all securities of the debtor and purchase those that offer the highest potential returns.

## Evaluation of the Plan

The first step in analyzing a company in bankruptcy that has filed a plan is to carefully read the plan and determine the distribution each class will receive upon reorganization. This effort should be conducted on a per share or per bond basis. Terms of new securities that are to be issued under the plan should be examined carefully so that they can be valued properly. Often, securities issued in reorganization have unique characteristics. For example, the senior notes proposed under Texas International's April 28, 1989, Plan of Reorganization provided for an initial coupon payment 39 months after issuance. The notes proposed under Delta U.S.'s May 1989 plan provided that interest and principal repayments could be deferred for a specific period if cash flow and rig count, respectively, were below certain levels. Furthermore, an increasing number of issues proposed under plans of reorganization are bonds whose interest may be paid-in-kind at the option of the reorganized debtor.

The analysis of a plan should begin with a listing of each class of creditor, the amount of the claim, the proposed distribution, the proposed distribution per security (where applicable), and the value of the distribution. This part of the analysis could take the form of the hypothetical ABC Incorporated shown in Exhibit 21–1.

Frequently, there are only 6 to 12 classes of creditors. These can be individually listed. Sometimes, as in the case of Dow Corning Corporation, there

### EXHIBIT 21–1

Plan of Reorganization—ABC Incorporated

| Class | Amount of Claim | Total Distribution | Distribution per Security | Valuation per Security |
|-------|-----------------|--------------------|---------------------------|------------------------|
| 1st mortgage bonds | $100 million | $100 million plus pre- and post-petition interest in cash | 100% | 100% |
| Debentures | $100 million | $100 million face value of debentures of reorganized debtor | 100% | 90%[a] |

[a]The amount of discount attributable to the new debentures is a function of coupon, credit considerations, etc.

are over 20 with many subclasses. In these instances, it is wise to itemize only the relevant classes or consolidate the classes to make them more manageable. The classes that should be listed are those that contain publicly traded securities or that receive securities to be publicly traded. By consolidating the proposed distribution in this manner, the investor can easily focus on the relevant securities.

It is also advisable at this point to chart the proposed equity ownership per class. This chart allows the investor to quickly convert changes in the valuation of the company into tangible values. A chart of equity ownership could take the form shown in Exhibit 21–2.

Western Company of North America's equity ownership is fairly straightforward. The only dilution that has to be considered is the possible exercise of employee options. Frequently, the distribution of equity in plans of reorganization is more complex, with warrants and options affecting the fully diluted stock ownership of several classes. In such cases, it is helpful to include additional columns that outline the fully diluted common stock ownership. This chart could take the form of Exhibit 21–3, which outlines the equity ownership proposed under Heck's Second Amended Plan.

## Determining a Price per Share for the Debtor

Once the specifics of the plan of reorganization are known, including potential dilution, the valuation of the company can proceed. In this chapter, Hexcel Corporation will be used for illustration.

Often, disclosure statements provide a valuation or a valuation range for the stock of the reorganized debtor. This valuation is generally provided by the financial advisor to the debtor. The use of the disclosure statement's valuation would speed the valuation process. However, an independent analysis that is

**EXHIBIT 21–2**

Distribution of New Common Stock of Western Company of North America: Second Amended Plan of Reorganization

| Class | Number of Shares | % of Common |
|---|---|---|
| Senior unsecured claims | 8,750,000 | 70.00 |
| Senior subordinated claims | 1,285,438 | 10.28 |
| Junior subordinated claims | 1,120,812 | 8.97 |
| Old preferred stock | 562,500 | 4.50 |
| Old common stock | 406,250 | 3.25 |
| Management incentive compensation plan | 375,000 | 3.00 |
| Total | 12,500,000 | 100.00 |
| Reserved for employee option plans | 956,250 | 7.1 |

Source: Western company of North America's Second Amended Plan of Reorganization and Disclosure Statement dated January 19,1989, *Bankruptcy Datasource,* Boston, MA.

**EXHIBIT 21–3**

Proposed Equity Ownership of Heck's

| | Number of Shares | % of Common | Fully Diluted Number of Shares | % of Common |
|---|---|---|---|---|
| Unsecured claims and PNB | 2,000,000 | 79% | 2,000,000 | 68% |
| Shareholder actions | 22,222 | 1 | 22,222 | 1 |
| Old common | 200,000 | 8 | 260,000 | 9 |
| | 60,000 warrants | | | |
| Key employees | 225,000 warrants | 0 | 225,000 | 7 |
| Hallwood | 294,967 | 12 | 442,451 | 15 |
| | 147,484 warrants | | | |
| Total | 2,517,189 shares | 100% | 2,949,673 | 100% |

Source: Heck's Second Amended Joint Plan of Reorganization and Disclosure Statement dated March 24,1989, *Bankruptcy Dafasource,* Boston, MA.

later compared with the disclosure statement's appraisal is recommended for two reasons. First, an independent analysis may be more accurate. Secondly, an independent analysis that is later compared with the official appraisal will eliminate bias.

Hexcel Corporation was founded in 1946 and incorporated in California in 1948. The company was founded by Roger Steele and Roscoe Hughes who researched a structural business which later became known as honeycomb. Numerous applications were developed for honeycomb by placing the material between various metals which formed light but very strong panels. Throughout its history, Hexcel has been the world leader in the development and manufacture of honeycomb. Historically, commercial and military aircraft have been important markets for Hexcel. Both of these markets grew rapidly in the 1980s and Hexcel expanded to meet the demand. Unfortunately, Hexcel's expansion preceded a downturn in both of these markets. Production rates for the B-2 bomber declined significantly and faced an uncertain future. In addition, deliveries of commercial aircraft declined 45% between 1991 and 1994. In December 1992, Hexcel attempted a restructuring to consolidate its operations to make them more compatible with current demand. These efforts were unsuccessful. Hexcel filed for bankruptcy on December 3, 1993. At the time of its bankruptcy filing, Hexcel faced a liquidity crisis. Although the underlying business was profitable on an operating basis, Hexcel needed liquidity to finance the downsizing of its operations.

Shortly after Hexcel filed for bankruptcy, the company filed a plan of reorganization. Pursuant to the plan, Hexcel would sell certain divisions and continue in three businesses: honeycomb, advanced composites, and reinforced fabrics. The plan would be funded by Mutual Series' acquiring between 32.775 and 41.139% of Hexcel for between $23 and $15 million or $2.00/share. The plan was premised on a reorganized equity value of between $165 and $185 million.

Hexcel's liquidity position improved markedly in August 1994 when the company announced that it had reached an agreement in principle to sell its EMT business to Northrup for approximately $30 million. After the announcement of the EMT sale, the debtor and the equity committee intensified negotiations for Mutual Series to increase its price for the equity of the firm. In October 1994, a new plan was filed which increased the subscription price per share to $4.623.

The analysis of Hexcel as a potential equity investment should begin with an analysis of the debtor's pro forma income statement, balance sheet, and cash flow statements which were provided in the disclosure statement. The projections for EBITDA (in $thousands) and Net Income are listed below:

|        | EBITDA   | Net Income  |
|--------|----------|-------------|
| 1994 E | $16,856  | ($13,726)   |
| 1995 E | $33,112  | 6,650       |
| 1996 E | $40,260  | 11,687      |
| 1997 E | $45,914  | 15,349      |

Clearly, if the debtor's projections were accurate, Reorganized Hexcel would quickly generate net income at a higher level than when Hexcel was a viable entity. However, pursuant to the plan, approximately 18 million fully diluted shares would be outstanding on the Effective Date. Therefore, the P/E ratio on this stock at its initial $4.625/share subscription would be a lofty 13 times on 1995 earnings. At these levels, the shares of Hexcel appeared to be overvalued.

However, before a definitive recommendation of Reorganized Hexcel common stock can be made, industry conditions should be evaluated in order to determine whether the projections are too conservative or too optimistic. This part of the analysis requires an evaluation of the aircraft business. At the time of Hexcel's bankruptcy petition, production of new aircraft was continuing to decline from its 1991 peak and was expected to rebound in a cyclical manner over the next several years. The debtor's projections incorporated such a rebound. However, these projections did not incorporate four secular forces that would likely benefit aircraft manufacturing and concomitantly, Hexcel. These factors were: 1) federal legislation that required all aircraft flying in the U.S. to meet Stage 3 noise requirements by December 31, 1999 and therefore the hushkitting of Stage 2 aircraft; 2) growth in global revenue passenger miles that has averaged twice the annual growth of world GDP over the past 20 or so years and is projected to continue; 3) an aging world aircraft fleet which averaged 25 years in age; and 4) expansion of several forms of financing such as leasing that would assist the industry in its growth and recovery. Taken together, these industry trends suggested that Hexcel's projections were conservative and that Hexcel could easily exceed projections, perhaps by a wide margin.

In fact, Hexcel common stock performed well after it emerged from bankruptcy. As of December 31, 1994, the stock was $4.125 per share. By the end of 1997, Hexcel common stock had increased to $22.25 per share and generated an EBITDA and net income of $137.6 million and $73.6 million, respectively, well ahead of projections made at the time Hexcel emerged from bankruptcy. The improvement in Hexcel was not sustained. By late 1999, Hexcel common stock was trading at about $5 per share. The forces which precipitated the decline in Hexcel stock included restructuring charges associated with writedowns of investments and pricing pressures. The factors which caused the decline in the stock are less important than the fact that the price changes reinforce the requirement that all investments be monitored closely. The analysis outlined above indicated that Hexcel was a potentially good investment in 1994. However, investments must be analyzed on a continuous basis to determine whether they remain a good investment.

## CONCLUSION

The analysis of bankrupt securities involves several variables. The investor must analyze both the plan of reorganization and the pro forma projections of the reorganized company. The analysis should not stop once these two analyses are complete, however. Companies should be monitored in order to keep current on changes in the plan as well as on company prospects. Significant changes in this market can occur quickly. The likelihood of such changes must be factored into the analysis. They also signal the need for diversification in bankruptcy investing. The time element must also be factored into the analysis. Most bankrupt securities do not accrue interest during reorganization. Therefore, the investor must estimate when the company will emerge from bankruptcy to fully estimate (and discount) values. Because most bankrupt companies take at least a year to reorganize and some have taken over seven years (Manville), the time element can be significant.

## CHAPTER 22

# GUIDELINES IN THE CREDIT ANALYSIS OF GENERAL OBLIGATION AND REVENUE MUNICIPAL BONDS

Sylvan G. Feldstein, Ph.D.
Assistant Vice President
Investment Department
Guardian Life Insurance Company

## INTRODUCTION

Historically, the degree of safety of investing in municipal bonds has been considered second only to that of U.S. Treasury bonds, but beginning in the 1970s, ongoing concerns developed among many investors and underwriters about the potential default risks of municipal bonds.

### The First Influence: Defaults and Bankruptcies

One concern resulted from the well-publicized, billion-dollar general obligation note defaults in 1975 of New York City. Not only did specific investors face the loss of their principal, but the defaults sent a loud and clear warning to the municipal bond investors in general. The warning was that regardless of the supposedly ironclad legal protections for the bondholder, when issuers have severe budget-balancing difficulties, the political hues, cries, and financial interests of public employee unions, vendors, and community groups may be dominant forces in the initial decision-making process.

This reality was further reinforced by the new federal bankruptcy law that took effect on October 1, 1979, which makes it easier for municipal bond issuers to seek protection from bondholders by filing for bankruptcy. One byproduct of the increased investor concern is that since 1975, the official statement, which is the counterpart to a prospectus in an equity or corporate bond offering and is to contain a summary of the key legal and financial security features, has become more comprehensive. As an example, before 1975 it was common for a city of New York official statement to be only 6 pages long, whereas for a bond sale in 2000 it was 127 pages long.

## The Second Influence: Strong Investor Demand for Tax Exemption

The second reason for the increased interest in credit analysis was derived from the changing nature of the municipal bond market. It is now characterized by strong buying patterns by private investors and institutions. The patterns were caused in part by high federal, state, and local income tax rates. Tax-exempt bonds increasingly have become an important and convenient way to shelter income. One corollary of the strong buyers' demand for tax exemption has been an erosion of the traditional security provisions and bondholder safeguards that had grown out of the default experiences of the 1930s. General obligation bond issuers with high tax and debt burdens, declining local economies, and chronic budget-balancing problems had little difficulty finding willing buyers. Also, revenue bonds increasingly were rushed to market with legally untested security provisions, modest rate covenants, reduced debt reserves, and weak additional-bond tests. Because of this widespread weakening of security provisions, it has become more important than ever before that the prudent investor carefully evaluate the creditworthiness of a municipal bond before making a purchase.

In analyzing the creditworthiness of a general obligation, tax-backed or pure revenue bond, the investor should cover five categories of inquiry: (1) legal documents and opinions, (2) politics/management, (3) underwriter/financial advisor, (4) general credit indicators and economics, and (5) red flags, or danger signals.

The purpose of this chapter is to set forth the general guidelines that the investor should rely upon in asking questions about specific bonds.

## THE LEGAL OPINION

Popular opinion holds that much of the legal work done in a bond issue is boilerplate in nature, but from the bondholder's point of view the legal opinions and document reviews should be the ultimate security provisions because, if all else fails, the bondholder may have to go to court to enforce his or her security rights. Therefore, the integrity and competency of the lawyers who review the documents and write the legal opinions that usually are summarized and stated in the official statements are very important.

The relationship of the legal opinion to the analysis of municipal bonds for both general obligation and revenue bonds is threefold. First, the lawyer should check to determine whether the issuer is indeed legally able to issue the bonds. Second, the lawyer is to see that the issuer has properly prepared for the bond sale by enacting the various required ordinances, resolutions, and trust indentures and without violating any other laws and regulations. This preparation is particularly important in the highly technical areas of determining whether the bond issue is qualified for tax exemption under federal law and whether the issue has been structured in such a way as to violate federal arbitrage regulations. Third, the lawyer is to certify that the security safeguards and remedies provided for the bondholders and pledged by either the bond issuer or third parties (such as banks with letter-of-credit agreements) are actually supported by federal, state, and local government laws and regulations.

## General Obligation Bonds

General obligation bonds are debt instruments issued by states, counties, towns, cities, and school districts. They are secured by the issuers' general taxing powers. The investor should review the legal documents and opinion as summarized in the official statement to determine what specific *unlimited* taxing powers, such as those on real estate and personal property, corporate and individual income taxes, and sales taxes, are legally available to the issuer, if necessary, to pay the bondholders. Usually for smaller governmental jurisdictions, such as school districts and towns, the only available unlimited taxing power is on property. If there are statutory or constitutional taxing power limitations, the legal documents and opinion should clearly describe how they affect the security of the bonds.

For larger general obligation bond issuers, such as states and big cities that have diverse revenue and tax sources, the legal opinion should indicate the claim of the general obligation bondholder on the issuer's general fund. Does the bondholder have a legal claim, if necessary, to the first revenues coming into the general fund? This is the case with bondholders of state of New York general obligation bonds. Does the bondholder stand second in line? This is the case with bondholders of state of California general obligation bonds. Or are the laws silent on the question altogether? This is the case for most other state and local governments.

Additionally, certain general obligation bonds, such as those for water and sewer purposes, are secured in the first instance by user charges and then by the general obligation pledge. (Such bonds are popularly known as being double barreled.) If so, the legal documents and opinion should state how the bonds are secured by revenues and funds outside the issuer's general taxing powers and general fund.

## Revenue Bonds

Revenue bonds are issued for project or enterprise financings that are secured by the revenues generated by the completed projects themselves, or for general public-purpose financings in which the issuers pledge to the bondholders tax and revenue resources that were previously part of the general fund. This latter type of revenue bond is usually created to allow issuers to raise debt outside general obligation debt limits and without voter approvals. The trust indenture and legal opinion for both types of revenue bonds should provide the investor with legal comfort in six bond-security areas:

- The limits of the basic security
- The flow-of-funds structure

- The rate, or user-charge, covenant
- The priority of revenue claims
- The additional-bonds test
- Other relevant covenants

### Limits of the Basic Security

The trust indenture and legal opinion should explain what the revenues for the bonds are and how they realistically may be limited by federal, state, and local laws and procedures. The importance of this is that although most revenue bonds are structured and appear to be supported by identifiable revenue streams, those revenues sometimes can be negatively affected directly by other levels of government. For example, the Mineral Royalties Revenue Bonds that the state of Wyoming sold in December 1981 had most of the attributes of revenue bonds. The bonds had a first lien on the pledged revenues, and additional bonds could only be issued if a coverage test of 125% was met. Yet the basic revenues themselves were monies received by the state from the federal government as royalty payments for mineral production on federal lands. The U.S. Congress was under no legal obligation to continue this aid program. Therefore, the legal opinion as summarized in the official statement must clearly delineate this shortcoming of the bond security.

### Flow-of-Funds Structure

The trust indenture and legal opinion should explain what the bond issuer has promised to do concerning the revenues received. What is the order of the revenue flows through the various accounting funds of the issuer to pay for the operating expenses of the facility, payments to the bondholders, maintenance and special capital improvements, and debt-service reserves? Additionally, the trust indenture and legal opinion should indicate what happens to excess revenues if they exceed the various annual fund requirements.

The flow of funds of most revenue bonds is structured as *net revenues* (i.e., debt service is paid to the bondholders immediately after revenues are paid to the basic operating and maintenance funds, but before paying all other expenses). A *gross revenues* flow-of-funds structure is one in which the bondholders are paid even before the operating expenses of the facility are paid. Examples of gross revenue bonds are those issued by the New York Metropolitan Transportation Authority. However, although it is true that these bonds legally have a claim to the fare-box revenues before all other claimants, it is doubtful that the system could function if the operational expenses, such as wages and electricity bills, were not paid first.

### Rate or User-Charge Covenants

The trust indenture and legal opinion should indicate what the issuer has legally committed itself to do to safeguard the bondholders. Do the rates charged only have to be sufficient to meet expenses, including debt service, or do they have to be set and maintained at higher levels to provide for reserves? The legal opinion should also indicate whether or not the issuer has the legal power to increase rates or charges of users without having to obtain prior approvals by other governmental units.

## Priority of Revenue Claims

The legal opinion as summarized in the official statement should clearly indicate whether or not others can legally tap the revenues of the issuer even before they start passing through the issuer's flow-of-funds structure. An example would be the Highway Revenue Bonds issued by the Puerto Rico Highway Authority. These bonds are secured by the revenues from the Commonwealth of Puerto Rico gasoline tax. However, under the commonwealth's constitution, the revenues are first applied to the commonwealth government's own general obligation bonds if no other funds are available for them.

## Additional-Bonds Test

The trust indenture and legal opinion should indicate under what circumstances the issuer can issue additional bonds that share equal claims to the issuer's revenues. Usually, the legal requirement is that the maximum annual debt service on the new bonds as well as on the old bonds be covered by the projected net revenues by a specified minimum amount. This can be as low as one times coverage. Some revenue bonds have stronger additional-bonds tests to protect the bondholders. For example, the state of Florida Orlando–Orange County Expressway Bonds have an additional-bonds test that is twofold. First, under the Florida constitution the previous year's *pledged historical revenues* must equal at least 1.33 times maximum annual debt service on the outstanding and to-be-issued bonds. Second, under the original trust indenture, *projected revenues* must provide at least 1.50 times the estimated maximum annual debt service on the outstanding and to-be-issued bonds.

## Other Relevant Covenants

Lastly, the trust indenture and legal opinion should indicate whether there are other relevant covenants for the bondholder's protection. These usually include pledges by the issuer of the bonds to insure the project (if it is a project-financing revenue bond), to have the accounting records of the issuer annually audited by an outside certified public accountant, to have outside engineers annually review the condition of the capital plant, and to keep the facility operating for the life of the bonds.

In addition to the above aspects of the specific revenue structures of general obligation and revenue bonds, two other developments over the recent past make it more important than ever for the investor to carefully review the legal documents and opinions summarized in the official statements. The first development involves the mushrooming of new financing techniques that may rest on legally untested security structures. The second development is the increased use of legal opinions provided by local attorneys who may have little prior municipal bond experience. (Legal opinions have traditionally been written by experienced municipal bond attorneys.)

## Legally Untested Security Structures and New Financing Techniques

In addition to the more traditional general obligation bonds and toll road, bridge, and tunnel revenue bonds, there are now more nonvoter-approved, innovative, and legally untested security mechanisms. These innovative financing mechanisms include lease-rental bonds, moral obligation housing bonds, "dedicated tax-backed" and "structural asset-backed" bonds, take-and-pay power bonds with step-up provisions requiring the participants to increase payments to make up for those that may default, commercial bank-backed letter-of-credit "put" bonds, and tax-exempt commercial paper. What distinguishes these newer bonds from the more traditional general obligation and revenue bonds is that they have no history of court decisions and other case law to firmly protect the rights of the bondholders. For the newer financing mechanisms, the legal opinion should include an assessment of the probable outcome if the bond security were challenged in court. Note, however, that most official statements do not provide this to the investor.

## The Need for Reliable Legal Opinions

For many years, concern over the reliability of the legal opinion was not as important as it is now. As the result of the numerous bond defaults and related shoddy legal opinions in the 19th century, the investment community demanded that legal documents and opinions be written by recognized municipal bond attorneys. As a consequence, over the years a small group of primarily Wall Street-based law firms and certain recognized firms in other financial centers dominated the industry and developed high standards of professionalism.

Now, however, more and more issuers have their legal work done by local law firms, a few of whom have little experience in municipal bond work. This development, along with the introduction of more innovative and legally untested financing mechanisms, has created a greater need for reliable legal opinions. An example of a specific concern involves the documents the issuers' lawyers must complete so as to avoid arbitrage problems with the Internal Revenue Service. On negotiated bond issues, one remedy has been for the underwriters to have their own counsels review the documents and to provide separate legal opinions.

## THE NEED TO KNOW WHO *REALLY* IS THE ISSUER

Still another general question to ask before purchasing a municipal bond is just what kind of people are the issuers? Are they conscientious public servants with clearly defined public goals? Do they have histories of successful management of public institutions? Have they demonstrated commitments to professional and fiscally stringent operations? Additionally, issuers in highly charged and partisan environments in which conflicts chronically occur between political parties or among political factions or personalities are clearly bond issuers to scrutinize closely and possibly to avoid. Such issuers should be scrutinized regardless of the strength of the surrounding economic environment.

### For General Obligation and Tax-Backed Bonds

For general obligation bond issuers, focus on the political relationships that exist among chief executives such as mayors, county executives, and governors, and among their legislative counterparts. Issuers with unstable political elites are of particular concern. Of course, rivalry among politicians is not necessarily bad. What is undesirable is competition so bitter and personal that real cooperation among the warring public officials in addressing future budgetary problems may be precluded. An example of an issuer that was avoided because of such dissension is the city of Cleveland. The political problems of the city in 1978 and the bitter conflicts between Mayor Kucinich and the city council resulted in a general obligation note default in December of that year.

### For Revenue Bonds

When investigating revenue bond issuers, it is important to determine not only the degree of political conflict, if any, that exists among the members of the bond-issuing body, but also the relationships and conflicts among those who make the appointments to the body. Additionally, the investor should determine whether the issuer of the revenue bond has to seek prior approval from another governmental jurisdiction before the user-fees or other charges can be levied. If this is the case, then the stability of the political relationships between the two units of government must be determined.

An important example involves the creditworthiness of the water and electric revenue bonds and notes issued by Kansas City, Kansas. Although the revenue bonds and notes were issued by city hall, it was the six-member board of public utilities, a separately elected body, that had the power to set the water and electricity rates. In the spring of 1981, because of a political struggle between a faction on the board of public utilities and the city commissioners (including the city's finance commissioner), the board refused to raise utility rates as required by the covenant. The situation came under control only when a new election changed the makeup of the board in favor of those supported by city hall.

In addition to the above institutional and political concerns, for revenue bond issuers in particular, the technical and managerial abilities of the staff should be assessed. The professional competency of the staff is a more critical factor in revenue bond analysis than it is in the analysis of general obligation bonds. The reason is that, unlike general obligation bonds, which are secured in the final instance by the full faith and credit and unlimited taxing powers of the issuers, many revenue bonds are secured by the ability of the revenue projects to be operational and financially self-supporting.

The professional staffs of authorities that issue revenue bonds for the construction of nuclear and other public power-generating facilities, apartment complexes, hospitals, water and sewer systems, and other large public works projects, such as convention centers and sports arenas, should be carefully reviewed. Issuers who have histories of high management turnovers, project cost overruns, or little experience should be avoided by the conservative investor, or at least considered higher risks than their assigned commercial credit ratings may indicate. Additionally, it is helpful, although not mandatory, for revenue bond issuers to have their accounting records annually audited by outside certified public accountants so as to provide the investor with a more accurate picture of the issuer's financial health.

## ON THE FINANCIAL ADVISOR AND UNDERWRITER

Shorthand indications of the quality of the investment are (1) who the issuer selected as its financial advisor, if any, (2) its principal underwriter if the bond sale was negotiated, and (3) its financial advisor if the bond issue came to market competitively. Additionally, since 1975 many prudent underwriters will not bid on competitive bond issues if there are significant credit-quality concerns. Therefore, it is also useful to learn who was the underwriter for the competitive bond sales as well.

Identifying the financial advisors and underwriters is important for two reasons.

## The Need for Complete, Not Just Adequate, Investment Risk Disclosures

The first reason relates to the quality and thoroughness of information provided to the investor by the issuer. The official statement, or private placement papers if the issue is placed privately, is usually prepared with the assistance of lawyers and a financial advisor or by the principal underwriter. There are industrywide disclosure guidelines that are generally adhered to, but not all official statements provide the investor with complete discussions of the risk potentials that may result from either the specific economics of the project or the community settings and the operational details of the security provisions. It is usually the author of this document who decides what to emphasize or downplay in the official statement. The more professional and established the author is in providing unbiased and complete information about the issuer, the more comfortable the investor can be with information provided by the issuer and in arriving at a credit-quality conclusion.

## The Importance of Firm Reputation for Thoroughness and Integrity

By itself, the reputation of the issuer's financial advisor and/or underwriter should not be the determinant credit-quality factor, but it is a fact the investor should consider, particularly in the case of marginally feasible bond issues that have complex flow-of-funds and security structures. The securities industry is different from other industries, such as real estate, in that trading and investment commitments are usually made over the phone with a paper trail following days later. Many institutional investors, such as banks, bonds funds, and property and casualty insurance companies, have learned to judge issuers by the company they keep. Institutions tend to be conservative, and they are more comfortable with financial information provided by established financial advisors and underwriters who have recognized reputations for honesty. Individual investors and analysts would do well to adopt this approach.

## GENERAL CREDIT INDICATORS AND ECONOMIC FACTORS IN THE CREDIT ANALYSIS

The last analytical factor is the economic health or viability of the bond issuer or specific project financed by the bond proceeds. The economic factors cover a variety of concerns. When analyzing general obligation bond issuers, one should look at the specific budgetary and debt characteristics of the issuer, as well as the general economic environment. For project-financing, or enterprise, revenue bonds, the economics are primarily limited to the ability of the project to generate sufficient charges from the users to pay the bondholders. These are known as pure revenue bonds.

For revenue bonds that rely not on user charges and fees but instead on general purpose taxes and revenues, the analysis should take basically the same approach as for the general obligation bonds. For these bonds, the taxes and revenues diverted to the bondholders would otherwise go to the state's or city's general fund.

As examples of such bonds, both the New York State Municipal Assistance Corporation for the City of New York Bonds (MAC), secured by general New York City sales taxes and annual state-aid appropriations, and the state of Illinois

Chicago School Finance Authority Bonds, secured by unlimited property taxes levied within the city of Chicago, are bonds structured to appear as pure revenue bonds; but in essence they are not. They both incorporate bond structures created to bail out the former, New York City, and the latter, Chicago's board of education, from severe budget deficits. The creditworthiness of these bonds is tied to that of their underlying jurisdictions, which have had portions of their taxing powers and general fund revenues diverted to secure the new revenue-type bailout bonds. Besides looking at the revenue features, the investor therefore must look at the underlying jurisdictions.

## For General Obligation Bonds

For general obligation bonds, the economic concerns include questions in four specific areas: debt burden, budget soundness, tax burden, and the overall economy.

### Debt Burden

In relation to the debt burden of the general obligation bond issuer, some of the more important concerns include the determination of the total amount of debt outstanding and to be issued that is supported by the general taxing powers of the issuer as well as by earmarked revenues.

For example, general obligation bonds issued by school districts in New York State are general obligations of the issuer and are also secured by state-aid payments due the issuer. If the issuer defaults, the bondholder can go to the state comptroller and be paid from the next state-aid payment due the local issuer. An example of another earmarked-revenue general obligation bond is the State of Illinois General Obligation Transportation, Series A Bond. For these state general obligations, debt service is secured by gasoline taxes in the state's transportation fund.

The debt of the general obligation bond issuer includes, in addition to the general obligation bonds outstanding, leases and "moral obligation" commitments. Additionally, the amount of the unfunded pension liabilities should be determined. Key debt ratios that reveal the burden on local taxpayers include determining the per capita amount of general obligation debt as well as the per capita debt of the overlapping or underlying general obligation bond issuers. Other key measures of debt burden include determining the amounts and percentages of the outstanding general obligation bonds as well as the outstanding general obligation bonds of the overlapping or underlying jurisdictions to real estate valuations. These numbers and percentages can be compared with most recent year medians, as well as with the past history of the issuer, to determine whether the debt burden is increasing, declining, or remaining relatively stable.

### Budgetary Soundness

Concerning the budgetary operations and budgetary soundness of the general obligation bond issuer, some of the more important questions include how well the issuer over at least the previous five years has been able to maintain balanced budgets and fund reserves. How dependent is the issuer on short-term debt to finance annual budgetary operations? How have increased demands by residents for costly social services been handled? That is, how frugal is the issuer? How well have the public-employee unions been handled? They usually lobby for higher salaries, liberal pensions, and other costly fringe benefits. Clearly, it is undesirable for the pattern of dealing with the constituent demands and public-employee unions to result in raising taxes and drawing down nonrecurring budget reserves. Last, another general concern in the budgetary area is the reliability of the budget and accounting records of the issuer. Are interfund borrowings reported? Who audits the books?

It should be noted that by the turn of the century, E-commerce and Internet usage are steadily growing among American consumers. Many states, counties, and city governments over the past 50 years have derived substantial revenues from sales taxes that currently are not applied to Internet sales. In some jurisdictions, over 20% of an issuer's revenues may come from local sales taxes. How the growth of the Internet impacts this revenue source is uncertain at this time, but at some future date could be a significant negative for the budgets of at least some issuers as well as for their bonds secured by these taxes.

## Tax Burden

Concerning the tax burden, it is important to learn two things initially. First, what are the primary sources of revenue in the issuer's general fund? Second, how dependent is the issuer on any one revenue source? If the general obligation bond issuer relies increasingly upon a property tax, wage and income taxes, or a sales tax to provide the major share of financing for annually increasing budget appropriations, taxes could quickly become so high as to drive businesses and people away. Many larger northern states and cities with their relatively high income, sales, and property taxes appear to be experiencing this phenomenon. Still another concern is the degree of dependency of the issuer on intergovernmental revenues, such as federal or state revenue sharing and grants-in-aid, to finance its annual budget appropriations. Political coalitions on the state and federal levels that support these financial transfer programs are not permanent and could undergo dramatic change very quickly. Therefore, a general obligation bond issuer that currently has a relatively low tax burden but receives substantial amounts of intergovernmental monies should be carefully reviewed by the investor. If it should occur that the aid monies are reduced, as has been occurring under many federal legislative programs, certain issuers may primarily increase their taxes, instead of reducing their expenditures to conform to the reduced federal grants-in-aid.

## Overall Economy

The fourth and last area of general obligation bond analysis concerns the issuer's overall economy. For local governments, such as counties, cities, towns, and school districts, key items include learning the annual rate of growth of the full value of all taxable real estate for the previous 10 years and identifying the 10 largest taxable properties. What kinds of business or activity occur on the respective properties? What percentage of the total property tax base do the 10 largest properties represent? What has been the building permit trend for at least the previous five years? What percentage of all real estate is tax-exempt, and what is the distribution of the taxable ones by purpose (such as residential, commercial, industrial, railroad, and public utility)? Last, who are the five largest employers? Concerning the final item, communities that have one large employer are more susceptible to rapid adverse economic change than communities with more diversified employment and real estate bases. For additional information that reveals economic health or decline, one must determine whether the population of the community over the previous 10 years has been increasing or declining by age, income, and ethnicity and how the monthly and yearly unemployment rates compare with the national averages as well as with the previous history of the community.

For state governments that issue general obligation bonds, the economic analysis should include many of the same questions applied to local governments. In addition, the investor should determine on the state level the annual rates of growth for the previous five years of personal income and retail sales and how much the state has had to borrow from the Federal Unemployment Trust Fund to pay unemployment benefits. This last item is particularly significant for the long-term economic attractiveness of the state because under current federal law, employers in states with large federal loans in arrears are required to pay increased unemployment taxes to the federal government.

## For Revenue Bonds

### Airport Revenue Bonds

For airport revenue bonds, the economic questions vary according to the type of bond security involved. There are two basic security structures.

The first type of airport revenue bond is one based upon traffic-generated revenues that result from the competitiveness and passenger demand of the airport. The financial data on the operations of the airport should come from audited financial statements going back at least three years. If a new facility is planned, a feasibility study prepared by a recognized consultant should be reviewed. The feasibility study should have two components: (1) a market and demand analysis to define the service area and examine demographic and airport use trends and (2) a financial analysis to examine project operating costs and revenues.

Revenues at an airport may come from landing fees paid by the airlines for their flights, passenger facility charges ("PFC's"), concession fees paid by restaurants, shops, newsstands, and parking facilities, and from airline apron and fueling fees.

Also, in determining the long-term economic viability of an airport, the investor should determine whether or not the wealth trends of the service area are upward; whether the airport is dependent on tourism or serves as a vital transfer point; whether passenger enplanements and air cargo handled over the previous five years have been growing; whether increased costs of jet fuel would make other transportation such as trains and automobiles more attractive in that particular region; and whether the airport is a major domestic hub for an airline, which could make the airport particularly vulnerable to route changes caused by schedule revisions and changes in airline corporate management.

The second type of airport revenue bond is secured by a lease with one or more airlines for the use of a specific facility such as a terminal or hangar. The lease usually obligates them to make annual payments sufficient to pay the expenses and debt service for the facility. For many of these bonds, the analysis of the airline lease is based upon the credit quality of the lessee airline. Whether or not the lease should extend as long as the bonds are outstanding depends on the specific airport and facility involved. For major hub airports, it may be better not to have long-term leases because without leases, fees and revenues can be increased as the traffic grows, regardless of which airline uses the specific facility. Of course, for regional or startup airports, long-term leases with trunk (i.e., major airline) carriers are preferred.

### "Dedicated Tax-Backed" and "Structured/Asset-Backed" Bonds

More recently, states and local governments have issued increasing amounts of bonds where the debt service is to be paid from so-called "dedicated" revenues such as sales taxes, tobacco settlement payments, fees, and penalty payments. Many are structured to mimic the asset-backed bonds that are common in the taxable market. The "assets" providing the security for the municipal bonds are the "dedicated" revenues instead of credit-card receivables, home equity loans, and auto loan repayments that are commonly used to secure the taxable asset-backed bonds.

Additionally, the municipal bonds are usually subject to some form of annual legislative appropriation and result from statutes specially created to pledge the identified taxes and revenues and allow for the bond sales. In the good economic times of the late 1990s many investors as well as the rating agencies have tended to blur the credit distinctions between these bonds and the issuer's own general obligation bonds. In fact, many such bonds carry higher credit ratings than the underlying general obligation bonds because the "coverage" on the former appears to be so high. In most instances, the general obligation bonds are legally backed by specific state constitutional provisions, whereas, the dedicated tax and structured/asset-backed bonds are recent legislative creations and have not been tested yet in stressful budgetary, economic, and political environments.

### Highway Revenue Bonds

There are generally two types of highway revenue bonds. The bond proceeds of the first type are used to build specific revenue-producing facilities such as toll roads, bridges, and tunnels. For these pure enterprise revenue bonds, the bondholders have claims to the revenues collected through the tolls. The financial soundness of the bonds depends on the ability of the specific projects to be self-supporting. Proceeds from the second type of highway revenue bond generally are used for public highway improvements, and the bondholders are paid by earmarked revenues such as gasoline taxes, automobile registration payments, and driver's license fees.

Concerning the economic viability of a toll revenue bond, the investor should ask a number of questions.

1. What is the traffic history, and how inelastic is the demand? Toll roads, bridges, and tunnels that provide vital transportation links are clearly preferred to those that face competition from interstate highways, toll-free bridges, or mass transit.

2. How well is the facility maintained? Has the issuer established a maintenance reserve fund at a reasonable level to use for such repair work as road resurfacing and bridge painting?

3. Does the issuer have the ability to raise tolls to meet covenant and debt-reserve requirements without seeking approvals from other governmental actors such as state legislatures and governors? In those few cases where such approvals are necessary, the question of how sympathetic these other power centers have been in the past in approving toll-increase requests should be asked.

4. What is the debt-to-equity ratio? Some toll authorities have received substantial nonreimbursable federal grants to help subsidize their costs of construction. This, of course, reduces the amount of debt that has to be issued.

5. What is the history of labor-management relations, and can public-employee strikes substantially reduce toll collections?

6. When was the facility constructed? Generally, toll roads financed and constructed in the 1950s and 1960s tend now to be in good financial condition because the cost of financing was much less than it is today. Many of these older revenue bond issuers have been retiring their bonds ahead of schedule by buying them at deep discounts to par in the secondary market.

7. If the facility is a bridge that could be damaged by a ship and made inoperable, does the issuer have adequate use-and-occupancy insurance?

Those few toll revenue bonds that have defaulted have done so because of either unexpected competition from toll-free highways and bridges, poor traffic projections, or substantially higher than projected construction costs. An example of one of the few defaulted bonds is the West Virginia Turnpike Commission's Turnpike Revenue Bonds, issued in 1952 and 1954 to finance the construction of an 88-mile expressway from Charleston to Princeton, West Virginia. The initial traffic-engineering estimates were overly optimistic, and the construction costs came in approximately $37 million higher than the original budgeted amount of $96 million. Because of insufficient traffic and toll collections, between 1956 and 1979 the bonds were in default. By the late 1970s with the completion of various connecting cross-country highways, the turnpike became a major link for interstate traffic. The bonds became self-supporting in terms of making interest coupon payments. It was not until 1989 that all the still-outstanding bonds were finally redeemed.

Concerning the economics of highway revenue bonds that are not pure enterprise type but instead are secured by earmarked revenues, such as gasoline taxes, automobile registration payments, and driver's license fees, the investor should ask the following questions.

- Are the earmarked tax revenues based on state constitutional mandates, such as the state of Ohio's Highway Improvement Bonds, or are they derived from laws enacted by state legislatures, such as the state of Washington's Chapters 56, 121, and 167 Motor Vehicle Fuel Tax Bonds? A constitutional pledge is usually more permanent and reliable.

- What has been the coverage trend of the available revenues to debt service over the previous 10 years? Has the coverage been increasing, stable, or declining?

- If the earmarked revenue is gasoline tax, is it based on a specific amount per gallon of gasoline sold or as a percentage of the price of each gallon sold? With greater conservation and more efficient cars, the latter tax structure is preferred because it is not as susceptible to declining sales of gasoline and because it benefits directly from any increased gasoline prices at the pumps.

- What has been the history of statewide gasoline consumption through recessions and oil shocks?

## Hospital Revenue Bonds

Two unique features of hospitals make the analysis of their debt particularly complex and uncertain. The first concerns their sources of revenue, and the second concerns the basic structure of the institutions themselves.

During the past 35 years, the major sources of revenue for most hospitals have been (1) payments from the federal (Medicare) and combined federal-state (Medicaid) hospital reimbursement programs and (2) appropriations made by local governments through their taxing powers. It is not uncommon for hospitals to receive at least two thirds of their annual revenues from these sources. How well the hospital management markets its service to attract more private-pay patients, how aggressive it is in third-party collections, such as from Blue Cross and HMOs, and how conservatively it budgets for the governmental reimbursement payments are key elements for distinguishing weak from strong hospital bonds.

Particularly for community-based hospitals (as opposed to teaching hospitals affiliated with medical schools), a unique feature of their financial structure is that their major financial beneficiaries, physicians, have no legal or financial liabilities if the institutions do not remain financially viable over the long term. An example of the problems that can be caused by this lack of liability is found in the story of the Sarpy County, Nebraska, Midlands Community Hospital Revenue Bonds. These bonds were issued to finance the construction of a hospital three miles south of Omaha, Nebraska, that was to replace an older one located in the downtown area. Physician questionnaires prepared for the feasibility study prior to the construction of the hospital indicated strong support for the replacement facility. Many doctors had used the older hospital in downtown Omaha as a backup facility for a larger nearby hospital. Unfortunately, once the new Sarpy hospital opened in 1976, many physicians found that the new hospital could not serve as a backup because it was 12 miles further away from the major hospital than the old hospital had been. Because these physicians were not referring their patients to the new Sarpy hospital, it was soon unable to make bond principal payments and was put under the jurisdiction of a court receiver.

The above factors raise long-term uncertainties about many community-based hospitals, but certain key areas of analysis and trends reveal the relative economic health of hospitals that already have revenue bonds outstanding. The first area is the liquidity of the hospital as measured by the ratio of dollars held in current assets to current liabilities. In general, a five-year trend of high values for the ratio is desirable because it implies an ability by the hospital to pay short-term obligations and thereby avoid budgetary problems. The second indicator is the ratio of long-term debt to equity, as measured in the unrestricted end-of-year fund balance. In general, the lower the long-term debt to equity ratio, the stronger the finances of the hospital. The third indicator is the actual debt-service coverage of the previous five years, as well as the projected coverage. The fourth indicator is the annual bed-occupancy rates for the previous five years. The fifth is the percentage of physicians at the hospital who are professionally approved (board certified), their respective ages, and how many of them use the hospital as their primary institution.

For new or expanded hospitals, much of the above data is provided to the investor in the feasibility study. One item in particular that should be determined for a new hospital is whether the physicians who plan to use the hospital actually live in the area to be served by the hospital. Because of its importance in providing answers to these questions, the feasibility study must be prepared by reputable, experienced researchers.

## Housing Revenue Bonds

For housing revenue bonds, the economic and financial questions vary according to the type of bond security involved. There are two basic types of housing revenue bonds, each with a different type of security structure. One is the housing revenue bond secured by *single-family* mortgages, and the other is the housing revenue bond secured by mortgages on *multifamily* housing projects.

Concerning single-family housing revenue bonds, the strongly secured bonds usually have four characteristics.

- The single-family home loans are insured by the Federal Housing Administration (FHA), Federal Veterans Administration (VA), or an acceptable private mortgage insurer or its equivalent. If the individual home loans are not insured, then they should have a loan-to-value ratio of 80% or less.

- If the conventional home loans have less than 100% primary mortgage insurance coverage, an additional 5–10% mortgage-pool insurance policy or its equivalent would be required. The private mortgage insurer should be of high quality in terms of company capitalization and in terms of conservative underwriting standards and limits.

- In addition to a debt reserve with monies equal at least to six months of interest on the single-family housing revenue bonds, there is a mortgage reserve fund equal at least to 1% of the mortgage portfolio outstanding.

- The issuer of the single-family housing revenue bonds is in a region of the country that has stable or strong economic growth as indicated by increased real estate valuations, personal income, and retail sales, as well as low unemployment rates.

In the 1970s, state agency issuers of single-family housing revenue bonds assumed certain prepayment levels in structuring the bond maturities. In recent years, most issuers have abandoned this practice but investors should review the retirement schedule for the single-family mortgage revenue bonds to determine whether or not the issuer has assumed large, lump-sum mortgage prepayments in the early year cash-flow projections. If so, how conservative are the prepayment assumptions, and how dependent is the issuer on the prepayments to meet the annual debt-service requirements?

It should be noted that over the last five years issuers have adopted structures similar to those in the taxable mortgage-backed securities market that incorporate prepayment assumptions. In tax-exempt single-family housing bonds these are usually the Planned Amortization Class (PAC) structures.

State issuing agencies usually have professional in-house staffs that closely monitor the home mortgage portfolios, whereas the local issuers do not. Finally, many state issuing agencies have accumulated substantial surplus funds over the years that can be viewed as an additional source of bondholder protection.

For multifamily housing revenue bonds, there are four specific, though overlapping, security structures. The first type of multifamily housing revenue bond is one in which the bonds are secured by federally insured mortgages. Usually, the federal insurance covers all but the difference between the outstanding bond principal and collectible mortgage amount (usually 1%), and all but the *nonasset* bonds (i.e., bonds issued to cover issuance costs and capitalized interest). The attractiveness of the federal insurance is that it protects the investor against bond default within the limitations outlined. The insurance protects the bondholders regardless of whether the projects are fully occupied and generating rental payments.

The second type of multifamily housing revenue bond is one in which the federal government subsidizes, under the HUD Section 8 program, all annual costs (including debt service) of the project not covered by tenant rental payments. Under Section 8, the eligible low-income and elderly tenants pay only 15 to 30% of their incomes for rent. Because the ultimate security comes from the Section 8 subsidies, which normally escalate annually with the increased cost of living in that particular geographic region, the bondholder's primary risks concern the developer's ability to complete the project, find tenants eligible under the federal guidelines to live in the project, and then maintain high occupancy rates for the life of the bonds. The investor should carefully review the location and construction standards used in building the project, as well as the competency of the project manager in selecting tenants who will take care of the building and pay their rents. In this regard, state agencies that issue Section 8 bonds usually have stronger in-house management experience and resources for dealing with problems than do the local development corporations that have issued Section 8 bonds. It should be noted that the federal government has eliminated appropriations for new Section 8 projects. Since 1995 the federal government has restricted automatic rent increases under the Section 8 program. This has introduced financial pressure.

The third type of multifamily housing revenue bond is one in which the ultimate security for the bondholder is the ability of the project to generate sufficient monthly rental payments from the tenants to meet the operating and debt-service expenses. Some of these projects may receive governmental subsidies (such as interest-cost reductions under the federal Section 236 program and property tax abatements from local governments), but the ultimate security is the economic viability of the project. Key information includes the location of the project, its occupancy rate, whether large families or the elderly will primarily live in the project, whether or not the rents necessary to keep the project financially sound are competitive with others in the surrounding community, and whether or not the project manager has a proven record of maintaining good service and of establishing careful tenant selection standards.

A fourth type of multifamily housing revenue bond is one that includes some type of private credit enhancement to the underlying real estate. These credit enhancements can include guarantees or sureties of an insurance company, securitization by the Federal National Mortgage Association (FNMA), or a bank letter of credit.

Other financial features desirable in all multifamily housing bonds include a debt-service reserve fund, which should contain an amount of money equal to the maximum annual debt service on the bonds, a mortgage reserve fund, and a capital repair and maintenance fund.

Another feature of many multifamily housing revenue bond programs, particularly those issued by state housing agencies, is the state moral obligation pledge. Several state agencies have issued housing revenue bonds that carry a potential state liability for making up deficiencies in their one-year debt-service reserve funds, should any occur. In most cases, if a drawdown of the debt reserve occurs, the state agency must report the amount used to its governor and state budget director. The state legislature, in turn, may appropriate the requested amount, although there is no legally enforceable obligation to do so. Bonds with this makeup provision are called moral obligation bonds.

The moral obligation provides a state legislature with permissive authority—*not mandatory authority*—to make an appropriation to the troubled state housing agency. Therefore, the analysis should determine (1) whether the state has the budgetary surpluses for subsidizing the housing agency's revenue bonds; and (2) whether there is a consensus within the executive and legislative branches of that particular state's government to use state general fund revenues for subsidizing multifamily housing projects.

### Industrial Revenue Bonds

Generally, industrial revenue bonds are issued by state and local governments on behalf of individual corporations and businesses. The security for the bonds usually depends on the economic soundness of the particular corporation or business involved. If the bond issue is for a subsidiary of a larger corporation, one question to ask is whether or not the parent guarantees the bonds. Is it obligated only through a lease, or does it not have any obligation whatsoever for paying the bondholders? If the parent corporation has no responsibility for the bonds, then the investor must look very closely at the operations of the subsidiary in addition to those of the parent corporation.

For companies that have issued publicly traded common stock, operating data are readily available in the quarterly (10-Q) and annual (10-K) financial reports that must be filed with the Securities and Exchange Commission. For privately held companies, financial data are more difficult to obtain.

In assessing the economic risk of investing in an industrial revenue bond, another question to ask is whether the bondholder or the trustee holds the mortgage on the property. Although holding the mortgage is not an important economic factor in assessing either hospital or low-income, multifamily housing bonds where the properties have very limited commercial value, it can be an important strength for the holder of industrial development revenue bonds. If the bond is secured by a mortgage on a property of either a fast-food retailer, such as McDonald's, or an industrial facility, such as a warehouse, the property location and resale value of the real estate may provide some protection to the bondholder, regardless of what happens to the company that issued the bonds.

Of course, the investor should always avoid possible bankruptcy situations regardless of the economic attractiveness of the particular piece of real estate involved. The reason is that the bankruptcy process usually involves years of litigation and numerous court hearings, which no investor should want to be concerned about.

### Lease-Rental Bonds

Lease-rental bonds are usually structured as revenue bonds, and annual payments, paid by a state or local government, cover all costs including operations, maintenance, and debt service. It should be noted that many Certificate of Participation Bonds, or COPs, are similar in security structure in that they too are dependent on the annual legislative appropriation process. The public purposes financed by these bond issues include public office buildings, fire houses, police stations, university buildings, mental health facilities, and highways, as well as office equipment and computers. In some instances, the payments may come from student tuition, patient fees, and earmarked tax revenues, and the state or local government is not legally obligated to make lease-rental payments beyond the amount of available earmarked revenues. However, for many lease-rental bonds, the underlying lessee state, county, or city is to make payment from its general fund subject to annual legislative appropriation. For example, the Albany County, New York, Lease Rental South Mall Bonds were issued to finance the construction of state office buildings. Although the bonds were technically general obligations of Albany County, the real security came from the annual lease payments made by the state of New York. These payments were annually appropriated. For such bonds, the basic economic and financial analysis should follow the same guidelines as for general obligation bonds.

### Public Power Revenue Bonds

Public power revenue bonds are issued to finance the construction of electrical generating plants. An issuer of the bonds may construct and operate one power plant, buy electric power from a wholesaler and sell it retail, construct and operate several power plants, or join with other public and private utilities in jointly financing the construction of one or more power plants. This last arrangement is known as a joint-power financing structure. Although there are revenue bonds that can claim the revenues of a federal agency (e.g., the Washington Public Power Supply System's Nuclear Project No. 2 Revenue Bonds, which if necessary can claim the revenues of the Bonneville Power Administration) and many others that can require the participating underlying municipal electric systems to pay the bondholders whether or not the plants are completed and operating (i.e., the Michigan Public Power Agency Revenue Bonds), the focus here is how the investor determines which power projects will be financially self-supporting without these backup security features.

There are at least five major questions to ask when evaluating the investment soundness of a public power revenue bond.

- Does the bond issuer have the authority to raise its electric rates in a timely fashion without going to any regulatory agencies? This is particularly important if substantial rate increases are necessary to pay for new construction or plant improvements.

- How diversified is the customer base among residential, commercial, and industrial users?

- Is the service area growing in terms of population, personal income, and commercial/industrial activity so as to warrant the electrical power generated by the existing or new facilities?

- Are rates competitive with neighboring IOUs? This is a significant credit factor resulting from the competitive provisions contained in the Energy Policy Act of 1992.

- What are the projected and actual costs of power generated by the system, and how competitive are they with other regions of the country? Power rates are particularly important for determining the long-term economic attractiveness of the region for industries that are large energy users.

- How diversified is the fuel mix? Is the issuer dependent on one energy source such as hydro dams, oil, natural gas, coal, or nuclear fuel?

Concerning electrical generating plants fueled by nuclear power, the aftermath of the Three Mile Island nuclear accident in 1979 has resulted in greater construction and maintenance reviews and costly safety requirements prompted by the Federal Nuclear Regulatory Commission (NRC). The NRC oversees this industry. In the past, although nuclear power plants were expected to cost far more to build than other types of power plants, it was also believed that, once the generating plants became operational, the relatively low fuel and maintenance costs would more than offset the initial capital outlays. However, with the increased concern about public safety brought about by the Three Mile Island accident, repairs and design modifications are now expected to be made even after plants begin to operate. Of course, this increases the ongoing costs of generating electricity and reduces the attractiveness of nuclear power as an alternative to the oil, gas, and coal fuels.

### Resource Recovery Revenue Bonds
A resource recovery facility converts refuse (solid waste) into commercially salable energy, recoverable products, and a residue to be landfilled. The major revenues for a resource recovery bond usually are the tipping fees per ton paid by those who deliver the garbage to the facility for disposal; revenues from steam, electricity, or refuse-derived fuel sold to an electric power company or

another energy user; and revenues from the sale of recoverable materials such as aluminum and steel scrap.

Resource recovery bonds are secured in one of two ways or a combination thereof. The first security structure is one in which the cost of running the resource recovery plant and paying the bondholders comes from the sale of the energy produced (steam, electricity, or refuse-derived fuel) as well as from fees paid by the haulers, both municipal and private, who bring the garbage to the facility. In this financing structure, the resource recovery plant usually has to be operational and self-supporting for the bondholders to be paid. The second security structure involves an agreement with a state or local government, such as a county or municipality, that contractually obligates the government to haul or to have hauled a certain amount of garbage to the facility each year for the life of the facility and to pay a tipping fee sufficient to operate the facility. The tipping fee must include amounts sufficient to pay bondholders whether or not the resource recovery plant has become fully operational.

When deciding to invest in a resource recovery revenue bond, one should ask the following questions. First, how proven is the system technology used in the plant? *Mass burning* is the simplest method, and it has years of proven experience. In mass burning, the refuse is burned with very little processing. Prepared fuels and shredding, the next most proven method, requires the refuse to be prepared by separation or shredding so as to produce a higher quality fuel for burning. More innovative approaches require the most detailed engineering evaluations by qualified specialists. Second, how experienced and reliable are the construction contractors and facility operators (vendors)? Third, are there adequate safeguards and financial incentives for the contractor/vendor to complete and then maintain the facility? Fourth, what are the estimated tipping fees that will have to be charged, and how do they compare with those at nearby landfills? In 1994 the U.S. Supreme Court in the *Carbone* decision struck down "flow control" ordinances which had been used to require all garbage within a local region to be delivered to designated plants regardless of economically attractive alternatives. As a result of *Carbone* the competitiveness of the tipping fee will be a critical credit factor. Fifth, is the bondholder protected during the construction stage by reserves and by fixed-price construction contracts? Sixth, are the prices charged for the generated energy fixed, or are they tied to the changing costs of the fuel sources such as oil and gas in that particular marketplace?

Because of the uniqueness of the resource recovery technology, there are additional questions that should be asked. First, even if the plant-system technology is a proven one, is the plant either the same size as others already in operation or a larger scale model that would require careful investor review? Second, if the system technology used is innovative, is there sufficient redundancy, or low-utilization assumptions in the plant design to absorb any unforeseen problems once the plant begins production? Last, in addition to the more routine reserves (such as debt, maintenance, and special capital improvement reserves) and covenants (such as covenants that commercial insurance be placed on the facility and that the contractor pledge to maintain the plant for the life of the bonds) there should also be required yearly plant reviews by independent consulting engineers. The vendor should be required to make the necessary repairs so that the facility will be operational for the life of the bonds.

For resource recovery revenue bonds that have a security structure involving an agreement with a local government, additional questions for the investor to ask are the following: Is the contractual obligation at a fixed rate, or is the tipping fee elastic enough to cover all the increasing costs of operations, maintenance, and debt service? Would strikes or other *force majeure* events prevent the contract from being enforceable or preclude the availability of an adequate supply of garbage? Last, the investor should determine the soundness of the budgetary operations and general fund reserves of the local government that is to pay the tipping or service fee. For these bonds, the basic economic analysis should follow the same guidelines as for general obligation bonds.

### Student Loan Revenue Bonds

Student loan revenue bonds are usually issued by state agencies or not-for-profit organizations and are used for purchasing new guaranteed student loans for higher education or existing guaranteed student loans from local banks.

The student loans are 100% guaranteed. They are guaranteed either directly by the federal government—under the Federal Insured Student Loan (FISL) program for 100% of principal and interest—or by a state guaranty agency under a more recent federal insurance program, the Federal Guaranteed Student Loan (GSL) program. This latter program provides federal reimbursement for a state guaranty agency on an annual basis for 100% of the payment on defaulted loans up to approximately 5% of the amount of loans being repaid, 90% for claims in excess of 5% but less than 9%, and 80% for claims exceeding 9%. The federal commitments are not dependent on future congressional approvals. Loans made under the FISL and GSL programs are contractual obligations of the federal government.

Although most student loans have federal government support, the financial soundness of the bond program that issues the student loan revenue bonds and monitors the loan portfolio is of critical importance to the investor because of the unique financial structure of a student loan portfolio. Although loan repayments from the student or, in the event of student default, repayments from the guaranty agency are contractually insured, it is difficult to precisely project the actual loan repayment cash flows. The reason is that the student does not begin repaying the loan until he or she leaves college or graduate school and all other deferments, such as military service, have ended. Before the student begins the loan repayments, the federal government pays the interest on the loans under prescribed formulas. Therefore, the first general concern of the investor should be to determine the strength of the cash-flow protection.

The second general concern is the adequacy of the loan guaranty. Under all economic scenarios short of a depression, in which the student loan default rate could be 20% or greater, the GSL sliding federal reinsurance scale of 100–90–80 should provide adequate cash-flow and bond default protection as long as the student loan revenue bond issuer effectively services the student loan repayments, has established and adequately funded loan-guaranty and debt-reserve funds, employs conservative loan-repayment assumptions in the original bond-maturity schedule, and is required to call the bonds at par if the student loan repayments are accelerated. This latter factor presents a reinvestment risk for the bondholder.

There are eight specific questions for the investor to ask:

- What percentage of the student loans are FISL-and GSL-backed?

- Has a loan-guarantee fund been established and funded? Usually, a fund that is required to have an amount equal to at least 2% of the loan principal outstanding is desirable.

- Is the issuer required to maintain a debt-reserve fund? Usually, for notes, a fund with at least six-months interest, and for bonds, a fund with a one-year maximum annual debt-service, are desirable.

- If the bond issuer has purchased portfolios of student loans from local banks, are the local lenders required to repurchase any loans if there are either defaults or improperly originated loans?

- What in-house capability does the issuer have for monitoring and servicing the loan repayments?

- What is the historical loan-default rate?

- How are the operating expenses of the agency met? If federal operating subsidies are received under the "Special Allowance Payment Rate" program, what are the rate assumptions used? In this program, the issuer receives a supplemental subsidy, which fluctuates with the 91-day U.S. Treasury bill rate.

- If a state agency is the issuer, is it dependent on appropriations for covering operating expenses and reserve requirements?

## Water and Sewer Revenue Bonds

Water and sewer revenue bonds are issued to provide for a local community's basic needs and as such are not usually subject to general economic changes. Because of the vital utility services performed, their respective financial structures are usually designed to have the lowest possible user charges and still remain financially viable. Generally, rate covenants requiring that user charges cover operations, maintenance, and approximately 1.2 times annual debt-service and reserve requirements are most desirable. On one hand, a lower rate covenant provides a smaller margin for unanticipated slow collections or increased operating and plant maintenance costs caused by inflation. On the other hand, rates that generate revenues more than 1.2 times the annual debt-service and reserve requirements could cause unnecessary financial burdens on the users of the water and sewer systems. A useful indication of the soundness of an issuer's operations is to compare the water or sewer utility's average quarterly customer billings to those of other water or sewer systems. Assuming that good customer service is given, the water or sewer system that has a relatively low customer billing charge generally indicates an efficient operation and therefore strong bond-payment prospects.

Key questions for the investor to ask include the following:

- Has the bond issuer, through local ordinances, required mandatory water or sewer connections? Also, local board of health directives against well water contamination and septic tank usage can often accomplish the same objective as the mandatory hookups.

- Does the issuer have to comply with an EPA consent decree and thereby issue significant amounts of bonds?

- What is the physical condition of the facilities in terms of plant, lines, and meters, and what capital improvements are necessary for maintaining the utilities as well as for providing for anticipated community growth?

- For water systems in particular, it is important to determine if the system has water supplies in excess of current peak and projected demands. An operating system at less than full utilization is able to serve future customers and bring in revenues without having to issue additional bonds to enlarge its facilities.

- What is the operating record of the water or sewer utility for the previous five years?

- If the bond issuer does not have its own distribution system but instead charges other participating local governments that do, are the charges or fees based upon the actual water flow drawn (for water revenue bonds) and sewage treated (for sewer revenue bonds) or upon gallonage entitlements?

- For water revenue bonds issued for agricultural regions, what crop is grown? An acre of oranges or cherries in California will provide the grower with more income than will an acre of corn or wheat in Iowa.

- For expanding water and sewer systems, does the issuer have a record over the previous two years of achieving net income equal to or exceeding the rate covenants, and will the facilities to be constructed add to the issuer's net revenues?

- Has the issuer established and funded debt and maintenance reserves to deal with unexpected cash-flow problems or system repairs?

- Does the bond issuer have the power to place tax liens against the real estate of those who have not paid their water or sewer bills? Although the investor would not want to own a bond for which court actions of this nature would be necessary, the legal existence of this power usually provides an economic incentive for water and sewer bills to be paid promptly by the users.

Additional bonds should be issued only if the need, cost, and construction schedule of the facility have been certified by an independent consulting engineer and if the past and projected revenues are sufficient to pay operating expenses and debt service. Of course, for a new system that does not have an operating history, the quality of the consulting engineer's report is of the uppermost importance.

## RED FLAGS FOR THE INVESTOR

In addition to the areas of analysis described above, certain red flags, or negative trends, suggest increased credit risks.

## For General Obligation Bonds

For general obligation bonds, the signals that indicate a decline in the ability of a state, county, town, city, or school district to function within fiscally sound parameters include the following:

- Declining property values and increasing delinquent taxpayers
- An annually increasing tax burden relative to other regions
- An increasing property tax rate in conjunction with a declining population
- Declines in the number and value of issued permits for new building construction
- Actual general fund revenues consistently falling below budgeted amounts
- Increasing end-of-year general fund deficits
- Budget expenditures increasing annually in excess of the inflation rate
- The unfunded pension liabilities are increasing
- General obligation debt increasing while property values are stagnant
- Declining economy as measured by increased unemployment and declining personal income

## For Revenue Bonds

For revenue bonds, the general signals that indicate a decline in credit quality include the following:

- Annually decreasing coverage of debt service by net revenues

- Regular use of debt reserve and other reserves by the issuer
- Growing financial dependence of the issuer on unpredictable federal and state-aid appropriations for meeting operating budget expenses
- Chronic lateness in supplying investors with annual audited financials
- Unanticipated cost overruns and schedule delays on capital construction projects
- Frequent or significant rate increases
- Deferring capital plant maintenance and improvements.
- Excessive management turnovers
- Shrinking customer base
- New and unanticipated competition

## CHAPTER 23

# HIGH-YIELD ANALYSIS OF EMERGING MARKETS DEBT

**Allen A. Vine**
International Emerging Markets Specialist
Global High Yield Securities Research
Merrill Lynch

## INTRODUCTION

The distinct strength of high-yield investors is fundamental orientation and ability to translate credit quality into relative pricing. Few markets in the world today can make this activity more rewarding than international emerging markets (IEM). The similarities between high-yield analysis commonly applied to domestic issuers and the type of analysis required for emerging markets, in our view, position U.S. high-yield investors as among the best prepared to take full advantage of the many opportunities emerging markets present. We are not suggesting speculation. Rather, we are suggesting a thorough and conservative analysis of the fundamentals, committed conclusions, and exploitation of market inefficiencies. Toward this end, this chapter examines the variables that determine values in emerging markets and issues of sovereign, technical, and fundamental analysis.

For purposes of this chapter, we define emerging markets as all of Latin America, Eastern Europe, Russia, and Asia (with the exception of Japan). Major product categories available to high-yield investors in emerging markets include Brady bonds, newly issued bonds, tradable performing loans, local currency instruments, and derivatives. Brady bonds are restructured bank loans of governments. They are described in detail in Chapter 17 but the key characteristics include large size, relatively high liquidity, and generally high volatility. Newly issued bonds refer to Eurobond and Yankee obligations of governments, quasi-sovereigns, and corporations, which are primarily dollar-denominated, but also include a growing issuance in currencies such as the Deutsche mark and the yen. Tradable performing loans can offer high yield but are generally the least liquid market instrument with many logistical difficulties in terms of settlement. Local currency instruments include domestic treasuries, bank certificates of deposit, and bonds. These instruments can provide yields substantially in excess of those on hard currency instruments of the same issuer, but they carry full currency risk. Derivatives include a range of options, forwards, and warrants. In light of the high market volatility, these instruments tend to be expensive but can provide very high returns.

## BACKGROUND ON EMERGING MARKETS

The value of emerging markets debt fell sharply in February 1994 after two years of rapid appreciation. Events that followed, including the Mexican financial crisis and the subsequent collapse of the Latin American markets in 1995, have all contributed to a profound discomfort still being experienced by many investors. The sustained high volatility throughout the period, especially the episodes of extreme over- and undervaluation, have all exposed the vast complexity of IEM and the need for a new set of effective tools to deal with it. Perhaps as a result of these conditions, U.S. high-yield investors have continued to largely stay away from emerging markets despite the tight domestic spreads and the still attractive valuation of many IEM issuers. Notwithstanding the likelihood of continued high volatility in emerging markets for the foreseeable future, our view of market dynamics leads us to propose that (1) already in the medium term, U.S. high-yield investors have *no* choice but to develop expertise in emerging markets, (2) these markets offer *unique* profit potential, and (3) tools exist to effectively assess the relative risk of these markets and to transform them into a more stable trading environment.

### No Choice

Emerging markets have now become an indelible part of the global capital arena. First, because of the sheer size. The total amount of the outstanding Brady bonds alone now exceeds $155 billion. With bank debt and the new sovereign and corporate Euro and Yankee issues, the total market size exceeds $500 billion. Second, because of future issuance. The significant capital needs of emerging economies position them as potentially the largest issuers of debt and equity for the foreseeable future. Third, assessment of relative values. A growing number of money managers around the world now view emerging markets as part of the global investment continuum. In valuing domestic issuers, they look abroad for comparison of credit fundamentals and prices. Also, the increasing speed and freedom of international capital flows are creating an environment in which domestic bond values in any country can be affected by a reaction of investors to developments in another nation halfway around the world.

### A Unique Opportunity

Emerging markets today present an unmatched profit potential. Inefficient markets have always offered significant rewards to those willing to brave them. Yet, only a few periods in history can rival conditions today, when in the space of merely five years two-thirds of the world became one big marketplace for investors willing to explore. Reforms in Latin America and Asia, the opening of Russia and Eastern Europe, and privatizations in Western Europe have produced a multitude of new investment opportunities. Direct and portfolio equity investment, debt, local instruments, and derivatives from over 20 countries have now become a part of the investment continuum. However, the international financial community has just begun developing analytical tools adequate to evaluate these opportunities. It has just entered into what is likely to be a long maturation cycle for the emerging markets, whereby a more systematic risk analysis

**E X H I B I T   23–1**

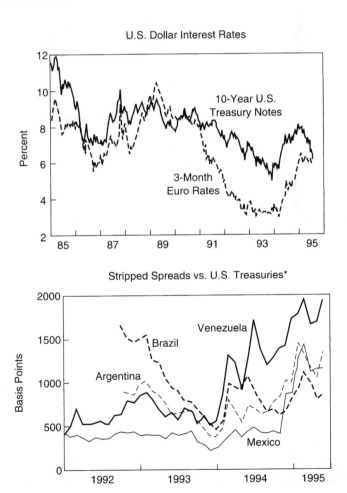

will replace speculations and theories that often drove pricing in the past (see Exhibit 23–1).

## Improved Credit Quality

It can be argued today that the emerging markets boom of the 1990s is qualitatively different from the numerous speculative bubbles that first elated and then crushed investors in the past. While not minimizing the structural problems yet to be addressed by emerging countries, we believe that fundamentally many situations have improved substantially from a decade ago. Going forward, these countries' firm commitment to market reforms suggests a high probability of continued and accelerating fundamental improvement.

## THE VALUE TRIANGLE

The key question to be addressed with regard to any new market is how values are determined. This may sound like an obvious point, yet many people were surprised in early 1995 to learn that it mattered whether a company was located in Mexico, even if that company could have been rated double-A were it located in the United States. In addition, understanding the factors that drive values in a given market is essential to evaluating whether a particular analytical approach can be successful.

Three factors determine values of emerging markets debt: (1) cross-border/ sovereign risk, (2) global capital formation/technical conditions, and (3) fundamental quality of individual issuers.[1] While solid empirical data are not available to assign exact percentages to each category, we estimate that at *present* cross-border risk accounts for 50% of how prices are determined, domestic yields and capital availability account for 30%, and issuer-specific fundamentals represent 20%. Clearly, these percentages vary from country to country and in times of high market volatility.

We emphasize *at present* because the change in relative weightings of each category signifies maturation of the market. For example, it is arguable that in the period from 1992 through 1993, strong technical conditions accounted for over 50% of how values were determined, sovereign risk for less than 40%, and fundamental risk for less than 10% (see Exhibit 23–2). As a result of losses dealt to investors since 1994, these proportions have changed to reflect more of the fundamental risk. We anticipate that this adjustment will continue. Importantly, the increasing role of fundamentals in the determination of values plays directly to the analytical strengths of high-yield investors.

---

1. Factors (1) and (2) apply in the case of sovereign issuers. For issuers that do not have the explicit full faith and credit of the sovereign, such as banks, corporates, and quasi-sovereigns, factors (1), (2), and (3) apply.

**EXHIBIT   23–2**

The Value Triangle

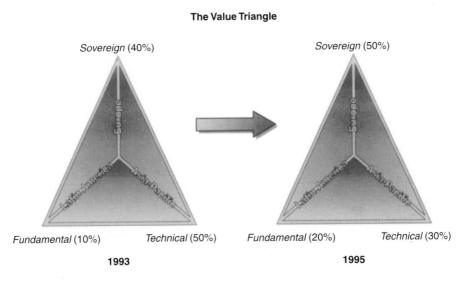

**The Value Triangle**

Sovereign (40%)                    Sovereign (50%)

Fundamental (10%)    Technical (50%)    Fundamental (20%)    Technical (30%)

**1993**                        **1995**

## ANALYSIS OF CROSS-BORDER RISK

Cross-border risk (CBR) embodies all issues that arise as a consequence of investing in a foreign country. Political and social stability, economic conditions, legal and regulatory environment, and bilateral relations are all elements of CBR. A subset of CBR commonly used in the market for analysis of foreign investments is sovereign risk, which includes most key components of CBR. We define *sovereign risk* as a probability of default and pricing volatility which arise as a consequence of actions by a foreign government. There are two components of sovereign risk: (1) *willingness* to pay, which historically has been driven by ideological considerations, and (2) *ability* to pay, which is driven by economic considerations. The conceptual difference between the two defines the degree to which each can be analyzed and predicted.

*The issue of willingness to pay has been rare, but hard to predict.* History indicates that attempts to forecast credit events driven strictly by political considerations of foreign governments have not been successful. Fortunately, such events have happened rarely. In this century, there have been only four major cases of sovereign default motivated primarily by politics and/or ideology. In 1917, the Bolshevik government of Russia repudiated foreign obligations of the czar. In 1934, Hitler repudiated much of Germany's obligations under the Versailles treaty. Japan followed a similar path in 1941, as did communist China in 1949. In all of these cases, extreme internal conditions and/or ideological considerations were at the core of a country's unwillingness to honor obligations.

*The issue of ability to pay is predominant, but predictable.* The majority of events wherein a country failed to service debt were caused by economic inability to pay, which was then followed by a political act of default. Although history is replete with sovereign defaults, most of them could have been predicted and many were. The following are recent examples:

- The 1980s debt crisis in Latin America was caused primarily by the countries' economic inability to pay, which became apparent well before Mexico set in motion a chain of defaults.

- High volatility in pricing of Venezuelan debt in 1994 was due to the country's economic difficulties.

- The Mexican debacle in 1995 had its origin in the country's poor economic policies.

Again, the distinction we draw is between *unwillingness* to pay as the sole cause of default and *inability* to pay, which leads to default. The former is generally unpredictable. The latter can be predicted effectively.

*Cash flow is a good predictor.* Sovereign investment analysis is different from pure political or economic analysis of a country in one key dimension. With investments, at issue is not the *absolute* creditworthiness of a country, although it is obviously important, but the country's creditworthiness *relative* to other sovereign issuers. Thus, an adequate system for analysis of sovereign risk must provide a solid basis for establishing relative value of countries. Such a system needs to incorporate quantitative indicators that can be applied consistently to *all* issuers and that lend themselves to a *meaningful* qualitative interpretation. We propose such indicators to be foreign exchange reserves, exports, and the balance of payments (see Exhibit 23–3).

## Foreign Exchange Reserves

Foreign exchange (FX) reserves represent the money with which investors get paid. In high-yield terms, their function is similar to earnings before interest, taxes, depreciation, and amortization (EBITDA). Some of the analytical tests that can be performed on this indicator are discussed below.

### Percentage of Reserves Obtained through Exports versus Foreign Investment

A country that obtains a high percentage of FX reserves through foreign investment perpetuates its dependence on capital inflows while limiting its ability to deleverage.

Dependence on foreign capital inflows is likely to be symptomatic of an undeveloped or uncompetitive industrial base and/or low domestic saving rates, whereby domestic spending outstrips investment, as was the case with Mexico prior to devaluation. Prices on debt of countries with this characteristic will

**EXHIBIT 23-3**

Analysis of Sovereign Risk

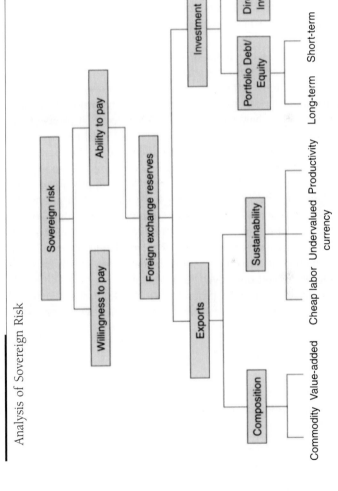

likely become more volatile going forward relative to countries that derive a higher percentage of FX generation from exports.

### Proportion of Portfolio to Direct Investment within the Foreign Investment Category

*Portfolio* investment tends to be short term and can leave a country as fast as it comes in. *Direct* investment tends to be long term and has an added benefit of improving productivity in a country's private sector. Therefore, countries with a higher proportion of direct to portfolio investment should present a more stable credit profile over the longer term.

### Proper Sterilization of Flows of Foreign Capital by the Central Bank

A large change in FX reserves that is not sterilized by the central bank poses high risks to the long-term prospects of an economy. For example, assume a significant capital inflow into a country. Unless the central bank sells an amount of assets to domestic banks matching the FX reserves it received, the inflow will increase money supply and possibly fuel inflation. To persuade domestic banks to buy its assets, the central bank would likely need to raise interest rates. Rising real interest rates make the country more attractive to foreign investors and could induce further capital inflows. This can lead to appreciating currency, which could hamper exports. A deteriorating trade balance can produce a current account deficit. If the government then resorts to devaluing currency to boost exports and curtail inflow, it risks a loss of confidence of international investors. This problem is magnified when a high percentage of the inflow is short-term portfolio investment. Given the complex nature of sterilizations, their success usually can be judged only over the long term.

Ratio tests that can be performed with FX reserves include FX reserves to debt service and months of imports of goods, services, and interest covered by FX reserves.

## Exports

Exports are a "blood test" for an economy. The analysis of exports can provide perhaps the most meaningful insight into the state of a country's economy and its long-term outlook.

1. Exports are a key source for building FX reserves. In high-yield terms, it is similar to operating income. A country for which exports represent a high percentage of FX generation is generally a lower and more stable credit risk than a country that relies primarily on capital inflows. Also, export revenues can provide an opportunity to deleverage.

2. Analysis of the *composition* and *sustainability* of exports can provide reliable insight into the economic *and* political fundamentals of a country.

## EXHIBIT 23–4

Foreign Exchange Reserves

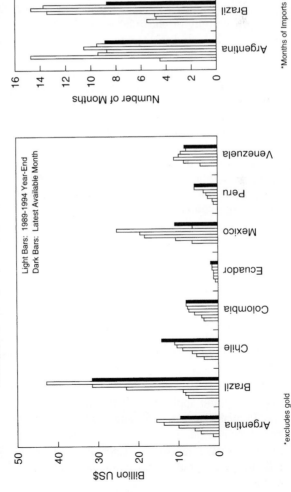

### International Reserves, Billions US$*

Light Bars: 1989–1994 Year-End
Dark Bars: Latest Available Month

Billion US$

50
40
30
20
10
0

Argentina · Brazil · Chile · Colombia · Ecuador · Mexico · Peru · Venezuela

*excludes gold

### International Reserves, Import Coverage Ratio*

Light Bars: 1989–1994 Year-End
Dark Bars: Latest Available Month

Number of Months

16
14
12
10
8
6
4
2
0

Argentina · Brazil · Chile · Colombia · Ecuador · Mexico · Peru · Venezuela

*Months of Imports of goods, services, and income; excludes gold

*Composition* addresses whether a country exports value-added goods or commodities. Reliance on commodities with prices subject to sharp fluctuations adds to the volatility of a country's credit profile. One example would be a contrast between Mexico and Brazil. The bulk of Mexico's exports through the 1970s was oil. When in the early 1980s oil prices declined while interest rates rose and many developed economies went into recession, most Mexican issuers, including the sovereign, encountered great difficulty paying debt. Brazil, however, enjoyed a developed export sector that was well integrated into many major economies of the world. At least partly as a result, there were almost no defaults in the Brazilian private sector in the 1980s, and Brazilian corporate issuers could have continued to service debt were it not for the exchange controls imposed by the government.

*Sustainability* addresses whether a country exports because of high productivity or cheap labor and/or undervalued currency. One of the key points of the Uruguay round of the General Agreement on Tariffs and Trade (GATT) was an implied message from the developed countries that they can no longer afford to allow their developing counterparts to compete primarily on the basis of undervalued currency or cheap labor. With high labor and social costs, the developed world has no choice but to seek productivity as a means to competitiveness. Therefore, those countries that have invested in productivity should outperform in terms of exports.

3. *Purchasing power parity* (PPP) is a useful way to reconcile inflation to export competitiveness. Closed economies and high inflation have been a common characteristic of many developing countries. Inefficient domestic enterprises and import restrictions endemic to such economies have generally produced high inflation. In the absence of foreign exchange controls, a country with high inflation would need to devalue its currency to regain competitiveness and/or raise interest rates to attract foreign capital. A depreciating currency is disadvantageous to foreign investors because (1) it makes it more difficult for domestic issuers to raise the same amount of hard currency with their local currency earnings, and (2) it reduces the value of returns on local financial instruments. Conversely, rising real interest rates can lead to appreciation of the currency through capital inflows, which can hamper exports through an unfavorable exchange rate. In general, knowledge and application of the interrelationships implicit in PPP should enable investors to anticipate changes in a country's interest and exchange rate policies on the basis of inflation and trade balance data. (See the discussion of fundamental valuation later in this chapter.)

EXHIBIT 23-5

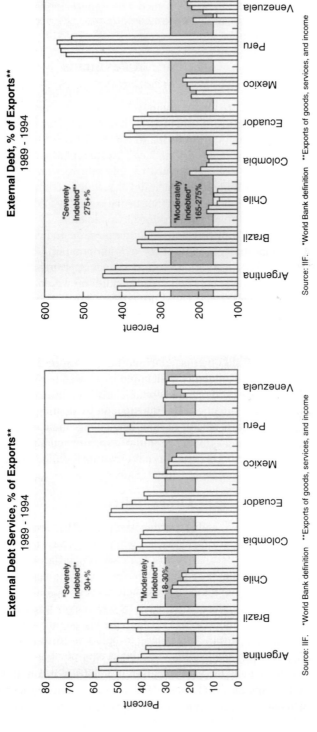

**External Debt Service, % of Exports\*\***
1989 - 1994

"Severely Indebted\*\* 30+%"

"Moderately Indebted\*\* 18-30%"

Argentina Brazil Chile Colombia Ecuador Mexico Peru Venezuela

Percent

Source: IIF.    \*World Bank definition    \*\*Exports of goods, services, and income

**External Debt, % of Exports\*\***
1989 - 1994

"Severely Indebted\*\* 275+%"

"Moderately Indebted\*\* 165-275%"

Argentina Brazil Chile Colombia Ecuador Mexico Peru Venezuela

Percent

Source: IIF.    \*World Bank definition    \*\*Exports of goods, services, and income

Ratio tests that can be performed with exports include total external debt/ exports, and total debt service/exports.

## Balance of Payments

Balance of payments (BOP) presents the overall picture. Defined as exports − imports + capital inflows − capital outflows + change in exchange reserves, the BOP contains important information such as the *current account* (CA) and the composition of foreign capital flows. Since the Mexican financial crisis in early 1995, the investor community has placed great emphasis on the current account balance. Although it is certainly alarming to see a country running a large CA deficit, that alone should not be the basis for judging a country's credit quality because of different natures of CA deficits. Analysis of two other components in the BOP can provide for a more complete evaluation: (1) the composition of imports—proportions of consumption, intermediate and capital goods—and (2) how the deficit is financed—with short- or long-term portfolio money or direct investment. The credit condition of a country that imports primarily capital goods financed with long-term money (e.g., Asian tigers) would be generally stronger than that of a country that imports primarily consumption goods financed with short-term money (e.g., Mexico in 1994).

An added benefit of looking at the BOP is the ability to gauge in broad terms a country's liquidity, that is, credit lines with the International Monetary Fund, World Bank, and other official creditors, and access to global capital markets. Finally, the BOP contains what could be viewed as a leading indicator of a country's credit quality: the flight capital. Consisting primarily of the money of a country's wealthy residents, and often difficult to identify, flight capital empirically has been a good predictor of imminent changes in a country's political and economic conditions. In the discussion of fundamental valuation, we present a formula that captures flight capital as a forecasting tool.

## Other Indicators

Inflation, money supply, and gross domestic product are among other useful indicators available to investors. However, when using these indicators, it is important to keep in mind their handicaps. For example, inflation can be a short-term indicator. Countries that are forced to perform a balancing act between bringing down inflation and keeping the trade deficit in check will likely have intermittent success with both. Judging credit quality by one or even three months worth of inflation or trade data may result in missing the big picture. Gross domestic product, another potential indicator, needs to be adjusted to reflect compositional differences between countries and thus lacks easy comparability in many cases. Overall, the short-term nature and/or lack of comparability of most economic indicators in IEM require that to be useful they must be viewed against the backdrop of a long-term fundamental judgment on a country.

## LIMITATIONS OF SOVEREIGN ANALYSIS

In considering IEM, we believe it is *essential* to differentiate between events that can and cannot be predicted. In general, past evidence suggests that many integral components of sovereign risk do not lend themselves to effective prediction. Such components include political stability, short-term economic policies, and outcomes of major policy initiatives. And it is precisely the events that cannot be anticipated effectively, such as devaluations, that have historically had the greatest impact on market values.

Even if cultural differences are excepted from credit analysis, the number of remaining variables is considerable. Key among them is how a country secures money to pay debt. If it relies mostly on capital inflows, the question is whether its creditors will continue lending. If it primarily earns money through exports, an analysis of its industrial base is needed, though predicting competitiveness and economic cycles is less than a precise science. Finally, assuming a sound assessment on the ability to raise funds is achievable, local political judgment needs to be considered. For example, it is unlikely that the Mexican government expected the violent reaction it received to the devaluation in December 1994. Thus, a government's miscalculation of how others may react to its actions can bring a country to the brink of collapse, even if such an event may not be warranted by the country's credit fundamentals.

A phenomenon worth mentioning in this context is the value of promises. The American public is among the more skeptical electorates in the world. Domestic politicians are commonly afforded limited trust and campaign promises are generally not expected to be totally fulfilled. This skepticism has been in sharp contrast to the firm trust the market has placed in foreign politicians on numerous occasions, no matter how counterintuitive their pronouncements seemed. Recent evidence suggests that this trust was misplaced in many cases, and predictions made on the basis of such promises were equally misplaced, e.g. the well-known pledge of the Mexican government not to devalue the peso.

The fact that sovereign predictions of the past have had a wide margin for improvement has not deterred many current experts from undertaking to forecast exactly what will happen where and when. Often, these forecasts impact or even drive the short-term pricing of securities, but inevitably, reality catches up. Once again, Mexico is a good example. In 1994, despite a skyrocketing current account deficit, dwindling FX reserves, rising political instability, and other loud indicators of trouble, the predicting consensus was that Mexico would become investment grade in 1995. The reality could not have been more different. Investors who were paying attention to the country's fundamentals got out in time. Those who believed in promises and predictions were less fortunate.

Going forward, to succeed in emerging markets, we believe it is critical for investors to recognize (1) the great number of variables that compose sovereign risk, (2) the very limited ability of *anyone* to predict accurately most of these variables, and (3) even less ability to predict their interplay. As a consequence, we view selecting a group of fundamental indicators that are quantifiable, comparable from country to country, and that lend themselves to a meaningful qualitative interpretation as the optimal way for assessing sovereign risk.

## ANALYSIS OF CAPITAL FORMATION/TECHNICAL CONDITIONS

*Technicals can drive the market.* Technical factors play a principal role in determining values in IEM. In fact, it is arguable that the significant flow of portfolio investment to emerging markets in 1992–1993 was driven primarily by the strong technical pressures on U.S. institutional investors. At their peak, these pressures created a market in which the concept of sovereign risk was often ignored, flexible accounting practices and spotty financial disclosure were dismissed as "cultural differences," and bankruptcy protection was barely contemplated. This environment allowed many IEM issuers to enter the U.S. bond market at the same spreads, or even tighter, than domestic high-yield issuers. Ultimately, the minimal absolute yields, strong correlation with U.S. Treasuries, and the lack of a fundamental basis behind prices created a situation where a mere 25-basis-point increase in interest rates by the Federal Reserve in February 1994 caused a precipitous drop in all emerging market values.

Despite a substantial improvement in the general credit quality of emerging markets, significant risk remains. Because of the magnitude and nature of this risk, we believe a large percentage of emerging market issuers should *not* be priced in terms of spread to Treasuries, but in terms of *absolute yield,* like domestic high-yield issuers. Pricing off the U.S. Treasuries curve in 1993 led to yield compression well in excess of fundamental improvement in emerging markets, causing some investors large losses in 1994. Losing sight of the absolute yield level and whether that level reflects the fundamental risk of an issuer will inevitably lead to losses again as the U.S. Federal Reserve adjusts its policies. Once again, capital formation and technical conditions *are* an indelible part of the forces that determine values. However, in certain circumstances, investors may be better served playing these forces directly, rather than through emerging markets debt. (In the 1970s, commercial banks might have been better off betting directly that oil prices would continue to go up, rather than betting that oil prices would continue to go up and thus Mexico's credit quality would continue to improve.) Cognizance of absolute yield can be an effective means for keeping a perspective on the fundamental risk and avoiding technical traps.

## Establishing the Appropriate Absolute Yield Level

The lack of a long track record, limited liquidity, high volatility, and a number of other risks do not allow us at this time to provide a precise recipe for how to establish the appropriate absolute yield level for the emerging market issuers. However, we can suggest two benchmarks. The first one is the general risk profile of a portfolio. Baskets dedicated to quality assets are not suitable for a large percentage of IEM issues. The second benchmark can be calculated through the application of the classic arbitrage theory, described in detail in the section on fundamental valuation. The argument there is that, in equilibrium, the following parity should hold:

$$R_{external\ bond} = R_{domestic\ bond} - Currency\ hedge \pm \frac{Material\ difference\ in}{asset\ characteristics}$$

Where

$R_{external\ bond}$ = Yield on a foreign currency-denominated debt of an entity A

$R_{domestic\ bond}$ = Yield on a domestic currency-denominated debt of an entity A

Material difference in asset characteristics = Collateral, duration, guarantees, structure, etc.

At present, the second benchmark is still largely a conceptual point for the same reasons that a precise recipe on how to establish the appropriate absolute yield level does not exist. However, the grasp of interrelationships implicit in this formula is positively key to understanding the forces that drive values in emerging markets. Incidentally, flight capital, which we view as the leading indicator of a country's credit quality, is captured in this formula. We believe that when the parity described above can be calculated with precision, a new level of stability and efficiency in IEM will emerge.

## A New Dimension of Technical Complexity

An added complexity of emerging markets is attributable to participation by a large number of investors from different parts of the world, mainly Asia and Europe. This has had the effect of materially altering the way values are determined. American investors derive relative value of emerging markets debt primarily on the basis of comparing it to U.S. domestic debt and in relation to U.S. Treasury rates. Investors from other parts of the world derive relative value of IEM debt primarily on the basis of comparing it to *their* own domestic debt and treasury rates. As a result, a change in local conditions in any one of the large investing countries may prompt a buying/selling spree in emerging markets, regardless of whether a fundamental change occurred with any of the issuers. Theoretically, a proper recommendation to address this issue would be to suggest a global portfolio approach, whereby investors would look at markets as a continuum—the United States, Europe, Asia, Latin America—on the basis of credit quality. Realistically, it may not be feasible for anyone to maintain awareness of so many variables and to continuously formulate correct judgments as these variables change. Therefore, a feasible solution comes back to developing a fundamental view on the countries, which should enable investors to wait out technical storms.

Another angle on the same problem is the pricing of new issues. For example, in August 1995, Mexico was able to price a sovereign yen deal almost 180 basis points tighter than its Eurobond deal of a few weeks earlier. This tightening of spread was *not* a result of a material improvement in the credit quality of Mexico in the period between the two deals. Rather, it reflected the fact that the Japanese treasury bonds yielded 1.91% in the week when the yen deal was priced versus 6% for the European LIBOR rate at the time of the Eurobond transaction. Yet, Mexico presents the same fundamental risk to all investors, regardless of the currency in which the debt is held; that is, all investors will see the same FX reserves, inflation, trade and other data as they pertain to the country. Logically, because an issuer presents the same fundamental risk to all investors, the real interest rate charged on its debt should also be the same in efficient markets, regardless of the currency in which the debt is issued. In reality, market efficiency is yet to be achieved in IEM. Because of differences in technical conditions among the United States, Europe, and Asia and differences in investing criteria among investor bases, investors may see inefficiencies in the pricing of new deals as issuers access countries with the most favorable technical conditions. While this is clearly advantageous for issuers, it is not advantageous for investors who may end up *not* being compensated fairly for the intrinsic issuer risks they assume.

Conceptually, technical conditions in a country are largely a product of the country's monetary policy, which in turn is usually reflective of the country's economic cycle. When a country's central bank lowers domestic cost of capital, the goal generally is to stimulate the domestic economy, not to provide cheap capital for foreign issuers. Domestic investors who opt for foreign securities in search of yield, and who reflexively benchmark that yield by the domestic yield curve, may set themselves up for losses as the economic cycle and technical conditions change in their countries. That is why we strongly urge investors to keep in mind absolute yield and not feel compelled to translate every move in treasuries into pricing of emerging markets debt. The absolute yield should reflect an issuer's fundamental risk. The parity that can help investors establish the appropriate absolute yield level was introduced earlier and is discussed in detail in the section on fundamental valuation. We believe that as emerging markets evolve, developed markets integrate further, and fundamentals become the driving force in valuation of IEM debt, the discrepancies in pricing described above will diminish.

## Technicals Can Produce Excess in Secondary Trading

There are two patterns worth mentioning here. First, the "lumping effect," wherein bad news in one country drags down market values in all others. This effect was particularly common while Mexico was the bellwether, since at the time it seemed reasonable that a problem with the "best" should be extrapolated onto the rest. Recent advances in fundamental analysis are making this pattern less prevalent as investors begin to differentiate better between issuers. Second is the "pendulum effect." For example, bad news in a country leads to a sell-off of its securities. This sell-off is often accompanied by the taking of short positions by traders expecting more bad news, which may lead to overselling and price declines in excess of the significance of the news. Then, the pendulum may swing the other way as traders begin to cover their shorts, giving impetus to price appreciation. Of course, what goes down precipitously can come up sharply as well. As a result, investors may see wild swings in prices, until a new equilibrium is found.

On the negative side, these swings have contributed to the staggering losses dealt to many investors in emerging markets. As recently as in the first three months of 1995, some investors saw the value of their IEM portfolios decline by more than 30%. On the positive side, these swings provided many extraordinary trading opportunities for investors who either had the ability to hang on or held a fundamental view on the countries. By mid-June 1995, emerging markets were up almost 40% from the lows of March 1995.

### Rumors Are Not Your Friends

On Friday, May 26, 1995, right before the Memorial Day weekend in the United States, the emerging markets were hit with speculation that Mexico was about to default. In the wake of the debacle earlier in the year, a concern that "things look darkest right before they go pitch black" sent traders and investors heading for the exit, and prices of Latin American instruments dove south. However, a close analysis of the situation showed that there was no new material information released that week to indicate any change in the credit condition of Mexico. The entity that was discussing default was Aeromexico, the country's beleaguered trunk airline. Our recommendation for dealing with such situations is to inquire first whether any new *material* information has become available that would change an issuer's outlook.

### New Players, New Risks

The high returns available in emerging markets have attracted many different types of investors. Highly consequential to market volatility have been hedge funds. Armed with significant capital access and a diverse arsenal of trading strategies, these institutions have demonstrated repeatedly the ability to affect markets and even countries. With regard to IEM, declining interest rates in the United States, Europe, and Japan in 1992 and 1993 made available to hedge funds an unprecedented amount of cheap capital. At the same time, tight liquidity in emerging markets enabled them to move markets by merely shifting capital or using derivatives. Subsequently, an increase in U.S. interest rates in February 1994 caused significant losses to many hedge funds, and their ability to influence markets was subsequently curtailed at least temporarily. Nonetheless, fundamental investors need to keep in mind that any future price storms may be caused artificially. Once again, a determination for whether material new information was released to alter the outlook for issuers can help investors make the right decision.

## ISSUES OF FUNDAMENTAL RISK

A large number of emerging markets issuers are not sovereign but are either quasi-sovereign or private. Quasi-sovereigns include issuers with some form of government ownership but *not* the explicit full faith and credit of the sovereign. Privately owned entities include banks and industrial and service companies. There are obvious reasons why additional credit analysis is required for corporates and banks and compelling reasons why it is required for quasi-sovereigns.

### Quasi-Sovereigns; What You See May Not Be What You Get

At present, fundamental analysis is rarely applied to quasi-sovereigns because of the argument, "the government owns them." Yet, unless the government provides an explicit guarantee for an entity's debt, it should not be assumed that in a case of financial difficulty it will definitely compensate debt holders. Another danger comes from privatizations. Although they are generally good for a country's economy, they may be bad for bondholders because the privatized entity may present greater credit risk as a stand-alone entity than when evaluated as part of the government structure. Specifically, a key risk that arises as a result of privatizations is access to hard currency. A good example would be utilities that earn revenues in domestic currency and rely on the government to supply them with hard currency. Once privatized, they may face difficulty competing and generating sufficient revenues to cover their debt service. Importantly, the ill-defined legal and regulatory frameworks and the general lack of precedents regarding effective bankruptcy protection in foreign countries suggest the absence of an effective exit strategy for investors if a government sells its stake in a quasi-sovereign and that entity does not prove viable on a stand-alone basis.

### Banks Are Difficult to Value

To assess credit quality of a bank, an analysis of its asset quality and duration of its assets and liabilities is required. Banks generally do not disclose who they lend to and how they finance loan portfolios, so neither piece of information is generally available (or reliable when available) in emerging markets. As a result, there is often little indication of trouble with a bank until it is too late, and when it is too late, there are generally no assets to compensate investors. In this context, banks that are not explicitly sovereign but that have government ownership are particularly risky because they are often forced by the government to finance state-run companies, some of which may be insolvent. In the end, such banks may accumulate loan portfolios of poor quality, while their own debt still does not have a sovereign guarantee and investors may have difficulty getting their money back.

## Corporates Present a Favorable Risk-Return Relationship

Corporates are the only product in emerging markets for which the extent of risk can be assessed with a reasonable degree of certainty. Traditional credit analysis of industry cycle, competitiveness, revenue composition, cost structure, and capitalization can be performed with most emerging market companies just as effectively as with domestic issuers. In addition, a majority of foreign corporate issuers fall into the same industry categories that dominate the domestic U.S. high-yield market: telecommunications, oil and gas, steel, paper, bottling, building materials, and so on. As a result, U.S. domestic industry expertise clearly applies. This is especially true for industries like oil, paper, and steel, which have product prices generally determined in the global marketplace. The ability to analyze key variables that exist with corporates is in sharp contrast to the situation with sovereigns and quasi-sovereigns. Going forward, this characteristic should make corporates increasingly attractive to fundamental investors vis-à-vis sovereign debt.

### Sovereign Credit Quality Still Dominates the Pricing of Corporates

Presently, sovereign instruments account for the largest portion of IEM trading. This is reasonable, given the dominant size of Brady bonds outstanding in the marketplace. Also, information flow related to countries and the number of analysts following sovereigns far exceeds information flow and the number of analysts following corporates. As a result of these conditions, fundamentals still play a small role in determining the bond prices of IEM corporate issuers. Rather, these prices often reflect more of sovereign risk, and there tends to be high correlation between prices of sovereign and corporate debt (see Exhibit 23–6). Great opportunities often arise as a consequence of this.

Corporates can present better credit quality than the countries where they are located. While conditions in a country are clearly important, there are compelling reasons why some corporate issuers can and should trade through the sovereign ceiling. These reasons exist *only* when there is a low probability that the sovereign will impose foreign exchange controls and *mainly* when a company earns a high percentage of its external debt service through hard currency exports. In the absence of FX controls, a company with a high percentage of export earnings in its revenue mix, low leverage, and competitive cost structure can present a more attractive credit profile than its home country. One such example is YPF in Argentina, which in addition to export earnings, low leverage,

## EXHIBIT  23-6

Price Correlation of Latin American Eurobonds and Corporates to Brady
Bond Index 1992–First Half 1995

|          | Euro/Brady Correlation | Corporate/Brady Correlation |
|----------|:----------------------:|:---------------------------:|
| 1992     | 0.998 | 0.997 |
| 1993     | 0.984 | 0.980 |
| 1994     | 0.905 | 0.830 |
| 1995*    | 0.939 | 0.920 |
| 1992–1995* | 0.957 | 0.964 |

*First six months
Source: Merrill Lynch Strategy.

and an improving cost structure has assets in the United States worth over \$700 million. The combination of these attributes, at present, arguably makes YPF a better credit risk than Argentina. Thus, provided the country's government does not impose currency controls, a corporation can often present a better credit risk than the sovereign if it commands a more stable and diversified hard currency revenue base, lower leverage, and assets in a stable, developed country. Keeping this thought in mind should allow fundamental investors to identify and exploit multiple market inefficiencies that are bound to arise when sovereign events depress the prices of premier corporates.

## FUNDAMENTAL VALUATION

The increased use of forward and option products in IEM is making the classic arbitrage pricing theory increasingly applicable to these markets. Key economic relationships implied in the theory are as follows:[2]

- The interest rate parity (IRP) relationship, also referred to as the law of one price, links national money market rates to foreign exchange rates and states that the difference in national interest rates for securities of similar risk and maturity should be equal to but opposite in sign to the forward exchange rate discount or premium.

- The purchasing power parity (PPP) relationship states that a country with higher inflation will have a depreciating currency.

---

2. For a more detailed discussion of the concepts presented here, see David K. Eiteman and Arthur I. Stonehill, *Multinational Business Finance* (Reading, MA: Addison-Wesley, 1989), pp. 71–78, 105–109.

- The Fisher effect states the nominal interest rates in each country are equal to the required real rate of return to the investor plus compensation for expected inflation. Consequently, in equilibrium, the difference in expected inflation between two countries must equal the difference in nominal interest rates.

- The International Fisher effect (IFE) describes the theoretical difference in nominal interest rates across national boundaries. The difference is linked to expectations of relative real interest rates and inflation. For example, investors in foreign securities must be rewarded with a higher interest rate to offset the expected rate of depreciation of the foreign currency when they attempt to convert principal and interest back into the home currency.

On the basis of these relationships, with regard to establishing the appropriate absolute yield level for IEM securities, we propose for the following to hold in theory:

$$R_{external\ bond} = R_{domestic\ bond} - Currency\ hedge \pm \frac{Material\ difference\ in\ asset}{characteristics\ (IRP)}$$

$$Currency\ hedge = Forward\ discount/Premium$$

$$Forward\ discount/Premium = Domestic\ anticipated\ inflation$$
$$- Foreign\ anticipated\ inflation\ (PPP)$$

Where

$R_{external\ bond}$ = Yield on a foreign currency-denominated debt of an entity A

$R_{domestic\ bond}$ = Yield on a domestic currency-denominated debt of an entity A

Material difference in asset characteristics = Collateral, duration, guarantees, structure, etc.

## The Concept

A country presents the same fundamental risk regardless of the currency denomination of its debt; that is, local and foreign investors will see the same inflation, trade, and currency reserve data for the country regardless of what type of security they own. Therefore, in theory, the real rate of return on debt of the same issuer in any currency should also be the same, adjusted for currency risk and differences in product characteristics.

The product characteristics component includes duration, guarantees, collateral value, convertibility risks, taxes, put/call options, and so on. Most of these characteristics cannot be valued with a reasonable degree of precision in emerging markets today due to the lack of product comparability, limited liquidity, and other factors. Yet, we believe that eventually most of these characteristics will become quantifiable, introducing a new measure of efficiency to IEM.

The currency risk component represents a microcosm of many key risks confronting investors in the emerging markets. It is through currency that the state of a country's economy relative to other economies can be established. Under the PPP, a depreciating currency signals future inflation. Under a derivative of the IFE, a depreciating currency may also signify such pressures as excessive imports and substantial capital outflows. The former is usually an effect and a cause of serious imbalances in an economy. The latter may primarily comprise the money of foreign investors or of a country's wealthy residents. In the first case, the outflow will likely be a lagging indicator; in the second case, it is likely to be a leading indicator. It either case, capital outflows are likely to be the result of rising political instability or other causes that convey the loss of investor confidence. In all cases, most of the causes under PPP and IFE deal with fundamental risks, which must be equally reflected in values of both local and foreign currency debt instruments.

The practical significance of using currency as a microcosm for fundamental risks is that the cost of a currency hedge subtracted from the rate of return on local currency instruments can provide investors with the first indication of what the required absolute yield level for the hard currency debt of the same issuer should be. This level then needs to be adjusted for different characteristics of debt instruments and risks that do not exhibit themselves through currency fluctuations. As was mentioned above, at present this is not entirely feasible. However, when it does become feasible, investors will have a solid benchmark by which to check whether they are being compensated adequately for the risks they take investing in a foreign country and which will help them avoid technical traps.

## FINANCIAL DISCLOSURE, CONTRACTS, AND BANKRUPTCY

The key purpose of accounting and its main difference from bookkeeping is the ability to achieve a more precise matching of revenues and expenses. Unlike U.S. GAAP, accounting standards in Latin America generally have been so flexible that a host of manipulative practices have been possible, and the numbers produced under these standards have left much to be desired. An example of this flexibility can be found in the treatment of capital expenditures: Companies in Latin America are able to expense or capitalize at their discretion and are not required to follow a consistent practice from year to year. With regard to Asia, there have been few corporate issuers but enough to exhibit equally lacking accounting standards. While this is understandable given the recent entry of these countries into the international capital markets, we believe it is critical for investors to demand more consistent accounting practices from the emerging market issuers if credit analysis is to become valid and the markets more stable.

In general, the value of contracts has not been high in emerging markets, and there are few signs of this changing. Recent noteworthy examples of a "respectful" treatment of contracts include China's decision to change the location of the largest McDonald's in the world from its premier spot in Beijing to another location in 1994 and, in August 1995, the cancellation of a multibillion dollar Enron project in India. This disregard for binding agreements at the government level can generally be found at other levels of society as well. The basic concept here is that a contract or a pledge mean different things in different places, with very limited enforcement available to the injured parties in most cases.

In terms of financing, "a dollar borrowed is a dollar earned" may not be so much the attitude to raising capital today, but neither is responsible conduct. For example, one of the first news items out of Mexico in January 1995 was a decision by Grupo Sidek not to service a part of its debt, which was later reversed. Had it not been reversed, the cross-default covenant could have put most of the company's debt in default. Given the company's eagerness not to pay, it is not clear how the investors would have gotten their money back.

A bankruptcy code exists in the majority of emerging countries. Its value to investors has been very limited in the past and is likely to remain so at least in the foreseeable future. In looking at IEM companies, high-yield investors need to keep in mind that traditional liquidation analysis generally does not apply. Just as with quasi-sovereigns, the ill-defined legal and regulatory frameworks and the general lack of precedents when investors received effective bankruptcy protection should indicate that liquidation will remain an unlikely option for some time. As a result, instead of doing an EBITDA multiple-asset valuation, a more practical approach may be to try to figure out what kind of package a bankrupt company will offer investors in return for the defaulting securities. Evidence to date indicates that these packages have *not* been generous, which should be all the more reason to scrutinize company-specific risks beforehand and *not* expect protection under the law.

In order to scrutinize company-specific risks, investors need financial information. It would seem intuitive that issuers that are new to the market, be it sovereign or corporate, would go an extra mile in trying to get investors comfortable with their credit profiles. However, IEM issuers from countries with a great deal of uncertainty, who are not subject to the U.S. jurisdiction, have been allowed to get away with no or minimal disclosure. By getting away, we mean trading at the same spreads or tighter than domestic U.S. issuers. Many arguments have been used to justify this situation, including cultural sensitivity. It may be the case that in the initial stages of market opening it was somehow reasonable for the emerging market issuers to feel uncomfortable with the "prying" analysts. However, if anything, the Mexican debacle has demonstrated vividly the absolute legitimacy of requests for better disclosure. It is arguable that if information about Mexican FX reserves and other pertinent economic data had been released on a consistent basis, the market might have been better prepared for the action, and great losses might have been avoided. Therefore, we believe that the time of justifying inadequate disclosure has passed. At present, a number of Brazilian companies are preparing financial statements in the U.S. GAAP. Major Russian companies have retained U.S. accounting firms to do the same in advance of their attempts to enter global capital markets. Long-established German automobile manufacturer Daimler Benz recently announced plans to have U.S. GAAP financials as well. The concept here is that if an issuer has no reason to withhold information, "cultural sensitivity" should not prevent it from providing investors with accurate financial statements and straight answers to legitimate questions.

## SUMMARY

We believe the following can be done to succeed in emerging markets: (1) assessment of cross-border/sovereign risk with emphasis on quantifiable variables such as foreign exchange reserves, exports, and the balance of payments; (2) analysis of what part technicals play in determining prevailing bond values; (3) complete credit analysis of quasi-sovereign and corporate issuers; and (4) evaluation of bond values on the basis of absolute yield, not spread to treasuries. In the case of new issues, quality of structure, distribution, and ability of underwriters to support their deals need to be taken into consideration. In terms of corporate issuers, we believe that investors will find optimal values in companies with an export business generating sufficient hard currency to service a high percentage of the company's foreign debt, adequate liquidity to weather an economic downturn, and familiar industry fundamentals so that qualified credit analysis can be performed. A select group of corporate issuers can and should trade through the sovereign ceiling.

## APPENDIX

# Framework for Analysis

Below, we provide a list of questions and issues that we believe investors need to feel comfortable with before making an investment decision on sovereign, quasi-sovereign, and private issuers in emerging markets. This list is not exhaustive but is meant as a general guide.

## A. Sovereign Analysis

1. Amount of foreign exchange (FX) reserves a country has. Coverage ratios:
   - FX reserves/debt service.
   - Months of imports of goods, services, and interest covered by FX reserves.

2. Percentage of FX reserves obtained through exports versus investment.

3. Effectiveness of a country's central bank in sterilizing capital flows.

4. Composition of investment: official creditors; direct versus portfolio capital; short or long term.

5. Trade balance (exports − imports). Coverage ratios:
   - Total external debt/export revenues.
   - Total debt service/export revenues.

6. Composition of exports: commodities versus value-added goods.

7. Sustainability of exports: Is the driving force behind exports cheap labor, undervalued currency, or productivity?

8. Impact of inflation on the value of currency and export competitiveness; application of the purchasing power parity.

9. Composition of imports: proportions of consumption, intermediate and capital goods.

10. How the imports are financed: portfolio/direct investment; if portfolio investment, short- or long-term (imports include goods, services, and debt service).

11. Interrelationship between inflation and the current account: Is a country striving to achieve low inflation while trying to maintain export competitiveness?

12. Capital flows: Do local residents keep money in domestic banks, "under the mattress" in local currency, or invest in hard currency instruments—a leading indicator? Does a country attract direct investment—a less-leading indicator? Does a country attract portfolio investment (short or long term)—an ambiguous indicator?

13. Impact of capital flows on the value of currency and export competitiveness.

14. Political and social stability in a country: unemployment; law and order; cooperation between the branches of government; fiscal prudence; distribution of wealth.

15. History of honoring debt obligations.

16. Respect for foreign investors and international law.

17. Relationship with the United States.

## B. Technical Analysis

1. Domestic interest rates in the United States, Germany, and Japan.

2. Domestic yield levels in secondary markets in the United States, Europe, and Japan.

3. Availability of capital and receptiveness of international investors to emerging market issuers.

4. The size of forward calendar in domestic markets of the United States, Europe, and Japan.

5. Absolute yield levels on domestic and emerging market securities in secondary markets.

6. Domestic interest rates in emerging market countries.

7. What accounts for the difference between domestic yields and yields in developed markets for the same emerging market issuers?

8. Are the yields on emerging market issuers driven by fundamental changes in the quality of issuers or changes in treasury rates in the United States, Europe, or Japan?

9. What happens to prices of the outstanding emerging market issues when the Federal Reserve in the United States or central banks in Germany or Japan change short-term rates? By how much will the change in prices of emerging market issues exceed the change in prices of domestic debt?

10. At times of high-market volatility, what percentage of price movements can be accounted for by fundamental news about the issuer? Could the changes have been caused by rumors, large capital movements by certain players, or trading strategies of certain market participants?

## C. Fundamental Analysis

1. All standard questions about industry cycle, competitiveness, revenue base, cost structure, and capitalization.

2. Percentage of export earnings in the revenue mix.
   • Are exports a product of cheap currency, cheap labor, or productivity?

3. Percentage of foreign currency costs in the cost structure.

4. Percentage of foreign currency debt in the capitalization.

5. Ability to get through an economic downturn.
   • Internal liquidity.
   • Banking relationships, access to capital markets.
6. Past payment history.
7. Quality of financial disclosure.

## PART 4

# MORTGAGE-BACKED AND ASSET-BACKED SECURITIES

## CHAPTER 24

# MORTGAGES AND OVERVIEW OF MORTGAGE-BACKED SECURITIES

**Frank J. Fabozzi, Ph.D., CFA, CPA**
Adjunct Professor of Finance
School of Management
Yale University

**Chuck Ramsey**
CEO
Mortgage Risk Assessment Corp.

A mortgage loan is a loan secured by the collateral of some specified real estate property, which obliges the borrower to make a predetermined series of payments. The mortgage gives the lender (the *mortgagee*) the right of foreclosure on the loan if the borrower (the *mortgagor*) defaults. That is, if the borrower fails to make the contracted payments, the lender can seize the property in order to ensure that the debt is paid off.

The types of real estate properties that can be mortgaged are divided into two broad categories: residential and nonresidential properties. The former category includes houses, condominiums, cooperatives, and apartments. Residential real estate can be subdivided into single-family (one- to four-family) structures and multifamily structures (apartment buildings in which more than four families reside). Nonresidential property includes commercial and farm properties.

The market where these funds are borrowed is called the *mortgage market.* This sector of the debt market is by far the largest in the world. The mortgage market has undergone significant structural changes since the 1980s. Innovations have occurred in terms of the design of new mortgage instruments and the development of products that use pools of mortgages as collateral for the issuance of a security. Such securities are called *mortgage-backed securities.* When a mortgage is used as collateral for the issuance of a security, the mortgage is said to be *securitized.*

Some mortgage-backed securities are backed implicitly or explicitly by the U.S. government. These securities are not rated by commercial rating companies. However, for the wide range of mortgage-backed securities that do not carry an implicit or explicit government guarantee, the securities are rated using the same rating systems as for corporate bonds.

In this chapter, our focus is on the structure of the mortgage market, the risks associated with investing in mortgages, and the different types of mortgage design. We then provide an overview of mortgage-backed securities. Later chapters discuss these securities in much more detail.

## PARTICIPANTS IN THE MORTGAGE MARKET

In addition to the ultimate investor of funds, there are three groups involved in the mortgage market: mortgage originators, mortgage servicers, and mortgage insurers.

### Mortgage Originators

The original lender is called the *mortgage originator.* Mortgage originators include commercial banks, thrifts, mortgage bankers, life insurance companies, and pension funds. The three largest originators for all types of residential mortgages are commercial banks, thrifts, and mortgage bankers, originating more than 95% of annual mortgage originations.

Originators may generate income for themselves in one or more ways. First, they typically charge an *origination fee.* This fee is expressed in terms of points, where each point represents 1% of the borrowed funds. For example, an origination fee of two points on a $100,000 mortgage represents $2,000. Originators also charge application fees and certain processing fees.

The second source of revenue is the profit that might be generated from selling a mortgage at a higher price than it originally cost. This profit is called *secondary marketing profit.* Of course, if mortgage rates rise, an originator will realize a loss when the mortgages are sold in the secondary market. Finally, the mortgage originator may hold the mortgage in its investment portfolio.

A potential homeowner who wants to borrow funds to purchase a home will apply for a loan from a mortgage originator. Upon completion of the application form, which provides financial information about the applicant, and payment of an application fee, the mortgage originator will perform a credit evaluation of the applicant. The two primary factors in determining whether the funds will be lent are the *payment-to-income* (PTI) ratio and the *loan-to-value* (LTV) ratio.

The PTI, the ratio of monthly payments (both mortgage and real estate tax payments) to monthly income, is a measure of the ability of the applicant to make monthly payments. The lower this ratio, the greater the likelihood that the applicant will be able to meet the required payments.

The difference between the purchase price of the property and the amount borrowed is the borrower's down payment. The LTV is the ratio of the amount of the loan to the market (or appraised) value of the property. The lower this ratio, the more protection the lender has if the applicant defaults and the property must be repossessed and sold.

After a mortgage loan is closed, a mortgage originator can do one of three things: (1) hold the mortgage in its portfolio, (2) sell the mortgage to an investor who wishes to hold the mortgage or who will place the mortgage in a pool of mortgages to be used as collateral for the issuance of a mortgage-backed security, or (3) use the mortgage as collateral for the issuance of a mortgage-backed security.

When a mortgage originator intends to sell the mortgage, it will obtain a commitment from the potential investor (buyer). Two federally sponsored credit agencies and several private companies buy mortgages. As these agencies and private companies pool these mortgages and sell them to investors, they are called *conduits*. The two agencies, the Federal Home Loan Mortgage Corporation and the Federal National Mortgage Association (discussed further below), purchase only *conforming mortgages*. A conforming mortgage is one that meets the underwriting standards established by these agencies for being in a pool of mortgages underlying a security that they guarantee. Three underwriting standards established by these agencies in order to qualify as a conforming mortgage are (1) a maximum PTI, (2) a maximum LTV, and (3) a maximum loan amount. If an applicant does not satisfy the underwriting standards, the mortgage is called a *nonconforming mortgage.* Loans that exceed the maximum loan amount are called *jumbo mortgages*.

Mortgages acquired by the agency may be held as investments in their portfolio or securitized. The securities offered are discussed in Chapter 25. Private conduits typically will securitize the mortgages purchased rather than hold them as an investment. Both conforming and nonconforming mortgages are purchased. Examples of private conduits are the Residential Funding Corporation, Countrywide Home Loans, GE Capital Mortgage Services, Prudential Home, Bank of America, First Nationwide, and Chase Mortgage Finance Corporation. When evaluating mortgage-backed securities issued by private conduits, the commercial rating companies assess the underwriting standards and procedures of the originator.

## Mortgage Servicers

Every mortgage loan must be serviced. Servicing of a mortgage loan involves collecting monthly payments and forwarding proceeds to owners of the loan, sending payment notices to mortgagors, reminding mortgagors when payments are overdue, maintaining records of principal balances, administering an escrow balance for real estate taxes and insurance purposes, initiating foreclosure proceedings if necessary, and furnishing tax information to mortgagors when applicable.

Servicers include bank-related entities, thrift-related entities, and mortgage bankers. The servicer receives a servicing fee. This fee is a fixed percentage of the outstanding mortgage balance. Consequently, the revenue from servicing declines over time as the mortgage balance amortizes.

Servicers play a critical role for mortgage-backed securities and asset-backed securities.[1] In rating securities that do not have explicit or implicit government guarantees, the commercial rating companies assess the quality of the operations of the servicer.

## Mortgage Insurers

When the lender makes the loan based on the credit of the borrower and on the collateral for the mortgage, the mortgage is said to be a *conventional mortgage.* The lender may require the borrower to obtain mortgage insurance to insure against default by the borrower. It is usually required by lenders on loans with loan-to-value (LTV) ratios greater than 80%. The amount insured will be some percentage of the loan and may decline as the LTV ratio declines. While the insurance is required by the lender, its cost is borne by the borrower, usually through a higher mortgage rate.

There are two forms of this insurance: insurance provided by a government agency and by a private mortgage insurance company. The federal agencies that provide this insurance to qualified borrowers are the Federal Housing Administration (FHA), the Veterans Administration (VA), and the Rural Housing Service. Private mortgage insurance can be obtained from a mortgage insurance company such as Mortgage Guaranty Insurance Company and PMI Mortgage Insurance Company.

Another form of insurance may be required for mortgages on property that is located in geographical areas where the occurrence of natural disasters such as floods and earthquakes is higher than usual. This type of insurance is called *hazard insurance.*

When mortgages are pooled by a private conduit and a security is issued, additional insurance for the pool is typically obtained to enhance the credit of the security. This is because the major commercial rating agencies of such se-

---

1. For a discussion of the role of servicers, see Galia Gichon, "The Role of Servicers," in *The Handbook of Commercial Mortgage-Backed Securities,* eds. Frank J. Fabozzi and David P. Jacob (New Hope, PA: Frank J. Fabozzi Associates, 1996).

curities require external credit enhancement for the issuer to obtain a particular investment-grade rating. The credit rating of the mortgage insurer is an important factor considered by commercial rating companies. The factors that the commercial rating agencies assess to judge the credit quality of a pool of mortgages are the credit quality of the individual mortgages, the credit rating of the mortgage insurer, the underwriting standards and procedures of the originator, and the quality of the operations of the servicer.

## ALTERNATIVE MORTGAGE INSTRUMENTS

There are many types of mortgage loans from which a borrower can select. We review several of the more popular mortgage designs here.

The interest rate on a mortgage loan (called the *contract rate*) is greater than the risk-free interest rate, in particular the yield on a Treasury security of comparable maturity. The spread reflects the higher costs of collection, the costs associated with default, which are not eliminated despite the collateral, poorer liquidity, and uncertainty concerning the timing of the cash flow (which we explain later). The frequency of payment is typically monthly, and the prevailing term of the mortgage is 20–30 years, although in recent years an increasing number of 15-year mortgages have been originated.

## Level-Payment, Fixed-Rate Mortgage

The basic idea behind the design of the level-payment, fixed-rate mortgage is that the borrower pays interest and repays principal in equal installments over an agreed-upon period of time, called the *maturity* or *term* of the mortgage. Thus, at the end of the term, the loan has been fully amortized. Each monthly mortgage payment for a level-payment mortgage is due on the first of each month and consists of the following:

1. Interest of $\frac{1}{12}$th of the fixed annual interest rate times the amount of the outstanding mortgage balance at the beginning of the previous month

2. A repayment of a portion of the outstanding mortgage balance (principal)

The difference between the monthly mortgage payment and the portion of the payment that represents interest equals the amount that is applied to reduce the outstanding mortgage balance. The monthly mortgage payment is designed so that after the last scheduled monthly payment of the loan is made, the amount of the outstanding mortgage balance is zero (i.e., the mortgage is fully repaid).

To illustrate a level-payment mortgage, consider a 30-year (360-month), $100,000 mortgage with a 9.5% mortgage rate. The monthly mortgage payment would be $840.85.[2] Exhibit 24–1 shows how each monthly mortgage payment is divided between interest and repayment of principal. At the beginning of month 1, the mortgage balance is $100,000, the amount of the original loan. The mortgage payment for month 1 includes interest on the $100,000 borrowed for the month. The interest rate is 9.5%, so the monthly interest rate is 0.0079167 (.095 divided by 12). Interest for month 1 is therefore $791.67 ($100,000 times 0.0079167). The $49.18 difference between the monthly mortgage payment of $840.85 and the interest of $791.67 is the portion of the monthly mortgage payment that represents repayment of principal. This $49.18 in month 1 reduces the mortgage balance.[3]

The mortgage balance at the end of month 1 (beginning of month 2) is then $99,950.81 ($100,000 minus $49.19). The interest for the second monthly mortgage payment is $791.28—the monthly interest rate (0.0079167) times the mortgage balance at the beginning of month 2 ($99,950.81). The difference between the $840.85 monthly mortgage payment and the $791.28 interest is $49.57, representing the amount of the mortgage balance paid off with that monthly mortgage payment. Notice in Exhibit 24–1 that the last monthly mortgage payment is sufficient to pay off the remaining mortgage balance. When a loan repayment schedule is structured in this way, so that the payments made by the borrower will completely pay off the interest and principal, the loan is said to be *fully amortizing*. Exhibit 24–1 is then referred to as an *amortization schedule*.

As Exhibit 24–1 clearly shows, *the portion of the monthly mortgage payment applied to interest declines each month, and the portion applied to reducing the mortgage balance increases*. The reason for this is that as the mortgage

---

2. The formula for obtaining the monthly mortgage payment is

$$MP = MB_0 \left[ \frac{i(1 + i)^n}{(1 + i)^n - 1} \right]$$

where

$MP$ = monthly mortgage payment ($)
$n$ = number of months
$MB_0$ = original mortgage balance ($)
$i$ = simple monthly interest rate (annual interest rate/12)

For our hypothetical mortgage:

$n = 360$
$MB_0 = \$100,000$
$i = .0079167(= .095/12)$

$$MP = \$100,000 \left[ \frac{.0079167(1.0079167)^{360}}{(1.0079167)^{360} - 1} \right] = \$840.85$$

3. Slight differences are due to rounding.

**EXHIBIT  24–1**

Amoritization Schedule for a Level-Payment, Fixed-Rate Mortgage
(Mortgage Loan: $100,000; Mortgage Rate: 9.5%; Monthly Payment: $840.85; Term
of Loan: 30 Years [360 Months])

| Month | Beginning Mortgage Balance | Monthly Mortgage Payment | Interest for Month | Principal Repayment | Ending Mortgage Balance |
|---|---|---|---|---|---|
| 1 | $100,000.00 | $840.85 | $791.67 | $49.19 | $99,950.81 |
| 2 | 99,950.81 | 840.85 | 791.28 | 49.58 | 99,901.24 |
| 3 | 99,901.24 | 840.85 | 790.88 | 49.97 | 99,851.27 |
| 4 | 99,851.27 | 840.85 | 790.49 | 50.37 | 99,800.90 |
| 5 | 99,800.90 | 840.85 | 790.09 | 50.76 | 99,750.14 |
| 6 | 99,750.14 | 840.85 | 789.69 | 51.17 | 99,698.97 |
| 7 | 99,698.97 | 840.85 | 789.28 | 51.57 | 99,647.40 |
| 8 | 99,647.40 | 840.85 | 788.88 | 51.98 | 99,595.42 |
| 9 | 99,595.42 | 840.85 | 788.46 | 52.39 | 99,543.03 |
| 10 | 99,543.03 | 870.85 | 788.05 | 52.81 | 99,490.23 |
| ... | ... | ... | ... | ... | ... |
| ... | ... | ... | ... | ... | ... |
| ... | ... | ... | ... | ... | ... |
| 98 | 92,862.54 | 840.85 | 735.16 | 105.69 | 92,756.85 |
| 99 | 92,756.85 | 840.85 | 734.33 | 106.53 | 92,650.32 |
| 100 | 92,650.32 | 840.85 | 733.48 | 107.37 | 92,542.95 |
| 101 | 92,542.95 | 840.85 | 732.63 | 108.22 | 92,434.72 |
| 102 | 92,434.72 | 840.85 | 731.77 | 109.08 | 92,325.64 |
| 103 | 92,325.64 | 840.85 | 730.91 | 109.94 | 92,215.70 |
| 104 | 92,215.70 | 840.85 | 730.04 | 110.81 | 92,104.89 |
| 105 | 92,104.89 | 840.85 | 729.16 | 111.69 | 91,993.20 |
| 106 | 91,993.20 | 840.85 | 728.28 | 112.57 | 91,880.62 |
| ... | ... | ... | ... | ... | ... |
| ... | ... | ... | ... | ... | ... |
| ... | ... | ... | ... | ... | ... |
| 209 | 74,177.40 | 840.85 | 587.24 | 253.62 | 73,923.78 |
| 210 | 73,923.78 | 840.85 | 585.23 | 255.62 | 73,668.16 |
| 211 | 73,668.16 | 840.85 | 583.21 | 257.65 | 73,410.51 |
| 212 | 73,410.51 | 840.85 | 581.17 | 259.69 | 73,150.82 |
| ... | ... | ... | ... | ... | ... |
| ... | ... | ... | ... | ... | ... |
| ... | ... | ... | ... | ... | ... |
| 354 | 5,703.93 | 840.85 | 45.16 | 795.70 | 4,908.23 |
| 355 | 4,908.23 | 840.85 | 38.66 | 802.00 | 4,106.24 |
| 356 | 4,106.24 | 840.85 | 32.51 | 808.35 | 3,297.89 |
| 357 | 3,297.89 | 840.85 | 26.11 | 814.75 | 2,483.14 |
| 358 | 2,483.14 | 840.85 | 19.66 | 821.20 | 1,661.95 |
| 359 | 1,661.95 | 840.85 | 13.16 | 827.70 | 834.25 |
| 360 | 834.25 | 840.85 | 6.60 | 834.25 | 0.00 |

balance is reduced with each monthly mortgage payment, the interest on the mortgage balance declines. Because the monthly mortgage payment is fixed, a larger part of the monthly payment is applied to reduce the principal in each subsequent month.

What was ignored in the amortization is the portion of the cash flow that must be paid to the servicer of the mortgage. The servicing fee is a specified portion of the mortgage rate. The monthly cash flow from a mortgage loan, regardless of the mortgage design, can therefore be decomposed into three parts:

1. The servicing fee

2. The interest payment net of the servicing fee

3. The scheduled principal repayment

For example, consider once again the $100,000 30-year level-payment, fixed-rate mortgage with a contract rate of 9.5%. Suppose the servicing fee is 0.5% per year. Exhibit 24–2 shows the cash flow for the mortgage with this servicing fee. The monthly mortgage payment is unchanged. The amount of the principal repayment is the same as in Exhibit 24–1. The difference is that the interest is reduced by the amount of the servicing fee. The amount of the servicing fee, just like the amount of interest, declines each month because the mortgage balance declines.

## Adjustable-Rate Mortgage

An adjustable-rate mortgage (ARM) is a loan in which the contract rate is reset periodically in accordance with some designated reference rate.

Outstanding ARMs call for resetting the contract rate either every month, six months, year, two years, three years, or five years. In recent years, ARMs typically have had reset periods of less than one year. The contract rate at the reset date is equal to a reference rate plus a spread. The spread is typically between 125 and 200 basis points, reflecting market conditions, the features of the ARM, and the increased cost of servicing an ARM compared to a fixed-rate mortgage.

### Reference Rate

Two categories of reference rates have been used in ARMs: (1) market-determined rates and (2) calculated rates based on the cost of funds for thrifts. Market-determined rates have been limited to Treasury-based rates. The reference rate will have an important impact on the performance of an ARM and how it is priced.

Cost of funds for thrifts indexes are calculated based on the monthly weighted average interest cost for liabilities of thrifts. The two more popular indexes are the Eleventh Federal Home Loan Bank Board District Cost of Funds Index (COFI) and the National Cost of Funds Index, the former being the most popular.

**EXHIBIT  24–2**

Cash Flow for a Mortgage with Servicing Fee
(Mortgage Loan: $100,000; Mortgage Rate: 9.5%; Servicing Fee: 0.5%; Monthly
Payment: $840.85; Term of Loan: 30 Years [360 Months])

| Month | Beginning Mortgage Balance | Monthly Mortgage Payment | Net Interest for Month | Servicing Fee | Principal Repayment | Ending Mortgage Balance |
|---|---|---|---|---|---|---|
| 1 | $100,000.00 | $840.85 | $750.00 | $41.67 | $49.19 | $99,950.81 |
| 2 | 99,950.81 | 840.85 | 749.63 | 41.65 | 49.58 | 99,901.24 |
| 3 | 99,901.24 | 840.85 | 749.26 | 41.63 | 49.97 | 99,851.27 |
| 4 | 99,851.27 | 840.85 | 748.88 | 41.60 | 50.37 | 99,800.90 |
| 5 | 99,800.90 | 840.85 | 748.51 | 41.58 | 50.76 | 99,750.14 |
| 6 | 99,750.14 | 840.85 | 748.13 | 41.56 | 51.17 | 99,698.97 |
| 7 | 99,698.97 | 840.85 | 747.74 | 41.54 | 51.57 | 99,647.40 |
| 8 | 99,647.40 | 840.85 | 774.36 | 41.52 | 51.98 | 99,595.42 |
| 9 | 99,595.42 | 840.85 | 749.97 | 41.50 | 52.39 | 99,543.03 |
| 10 | 99,543.03 | 870.85 | 746.57 | 41.48 | 52.81 | 99,490.23 |
| . . . | . . . | . . . | . . . | . . . | . . . | . . . |
| . . . | . . . | . . . | . . . | . . . | . . . | . . . |
| . . . | . . . | . . . | . . . | . . . | . . . | . . . |
| 98 | 92,862.54 | 840.85 | 696.47 | 38.96 | 105.69 | 92,756.85 |
| 99 | 92,756.85 | 840.85 | 695.68 | 38.65 | 106.53 | 92,650.32 |
| 100 | 92,650.32 | 840.85 | 694.88 | 38.60 | 107.37 | 92,542.95 |
| 101 | 92,542.95 | 840.85 | 694.07 | 38.56 | 108.22 | 92,434.72 |
| 102 | 92,434.72 | 840.85 | 693.26 | 38.51 | 109.08 | 92,325.64 |
| 103 | 92,325.64 | 840.85 | 692.44 | 38.47 | 109.94 | 92,215.70 |
| 104 | 92,215.70 | 840.85 | 691.62 | 38.42 | 110.81 | 91,104.89 |
| 105 | 92,104.89 | 840.85 | 690.79 | 38.38 | 111.69 | 91,993.20 |
| 106 | 91,993.20 | 840.85 | 689.95 | 38.33 | 112.57 | 91,880.62 |
| . . . | . . . | . . . | . . . | . . . | . . . | . . . |
| . . . | . . . | . . . | . . . | . . . | . . . | . . . |
| . . . | . . . | . . . | . . . | . . . | . . . | . . . |
| 209 | 74,177.40 | 840.85 | 556.33 | 30.91 | 253.62 | 73,923.78 |
| 210 | 73,923.78 | 840.85 | 554.43 | 30.80 | 255.62 | 73,668.16 |
| 211 | 73,668.16 | 840.85 | 552.51 | 30.70 | 257.65 | 73,410.51 |
| 212 | 73,410.51 | 840.85 | 550.58 | 30.59 | 259.69 | 73,150.82 |
| . . . | . . . | . . . | . . . | . . . | . . . | . . . |
| . . . | . . . | . . . | . . . | . . . | . . . | . . . |
| . . . | . . . | . . . | . . . | . . . | . . . | . . . |
| 354 | 5,703.93 | 840.85 | 42.78 | 2.28 | 795.70 | 4,908.23 |
| 355 | 4,908.23 | 840.85 | 36.81 | 2.05 | 802.00 | 4,106.24 |
| 356 | 4,106.24 | 840.85 | 30.80 | 1.71 | 808.35 | 3,297.89 |
| 357 | 3,297.89 | 840.85 | 24.73 | 1.37 | 814.75 | 2,483.14 |
| 358 | 2,483.14 | 840.85 | 18.62 | 1.03 | 821.20 | 1,661.95 |
| 359 | 1,661.95 | 840.85 | 12.46 | 0.69 | 827.70 | 834.25 |

The Eleventh District includes the states of California, Arizona, and Nevada. The cost of funds is calculated by first computing the monthly interest expenses for all thrifts included in the Eleventh District. The interest expenses are summed and then divided by the average of the beginning and ending monthly balance. The index value is reported with a one-month lag. For example, June's Eleventh District COFI is reported in July. The contract rate for a mortgage based on the Eleventh District COFI is usually reset based on the previous month's reported index rate. For example, if the reset date is August, the index rate reported in July will be used to set the contract rate. Consequently, there is a two-month lag by the time the average cost of funds is reflected in the contract rate. This obviously is an advantage to the borrower when interest rates are rising, and a disadvantage to the investor. The opposite is true when interest rates are falling.

The National Cost of Funds Index is calculated based on all federally insured S&Ls. A median costs of funds is calculated rather than an average. This index is reported with about a one and one-half month delay. The contract rate is typically reset based on the most recently reported index value.

### Features of Adjustable-Rate Mortgages

To encourage borrowers to accept ARMs rather than fixed-rate mortgages, mortgage originators generally offer an initial contract rate that is less than the prevailing market mortgage rate. This below-market initial contract rate, set by the mortgage originator based on competitive market conditions, is commonly referred to as a *teaser rate*. At the reset date, the reference rate plus the spread determines the new contract rate. For example, suppose that one-year ARMs are typically offering a 100-basis-point spread over the reference rate. Suppose also that the reference rate is 6.5%, so that the initial contract rate should be 7.5%. The mortgage originator might set an initial contract rate of 6.75%, a rate 75 basis points below the current value of the reference rate plus the spread.

A pure ARM is one that resets periodically and has no other terms that affect the monthly mortgage payment. However, the monthly mortgage payment, and hence the investor's cash flow, are affected by other terms. These are due to (1) periodic caps and (2) lifetime rate caps and floors. Rate caps limit the amount that the contract rate may increase or decrease at the reset date. A lifetime cap sets the maximum contract rate over the term of the loan.

## Balloon Mortgage

In a *balloon mortgage,* the borrower is given long-term financing by the lender, but at specified future dates the contract rate is renegotiated. Thus, the lender is providing long-term funds for what is effectively a short-term borrowing, how short depending on the frequency of the renegotiation period. Effectively, it is a short-term balloon loan in which the lender agrees to provide financing for the remainder of the term of the mortgage. The balloon payment is the original amount borrowed less the amount amortized. Thus, in a balloon mortgage, the actual maturity is shorter than the stated maturity.

## "Two-Step" Mortgage

Akin to the idea of a balloon loan with a refinancing option for the borrower is a fixed-rate mortgage with a single rate reset at some point prior to maturity. Unlike a refinancing option, this rate reset occurs without specific action on the part of the borrower.

Unlike in balloon mortgages, the rate reset on the two-step mortgage does not consist of a repayment of the initial loan and the origination of a new one; thus, a 30-year two-step mortgage has a 30-year final maturity, rather than the shorter final maturity of a balloon mortgage. Essentially, then, the two-step mortgage is an adjustable-rate mortgage with a single reset.

## Graduated Payment Mortgage

With a *graduated payment mortgage* (GPM), both the interest rate and the term of the mortgage are fixed, as they are with a level-payment mortgage. However, the monthly mortgage payment for a GPM is smaller in the initial years than for a level-payment mortgage with the same contract rate but larger in the remaining years of the mortgage term. Origination of GPMs has faded in popularity in recent years with the growing popularity of the other mortgage instruments discussed in this section.

The terms of a GPM plan include (1) the mortgage rate, (2) the term of the mortgage, (3) the number of years over which the monthly mortgage payment will increase (and when the level payments will begin), and (4) the annual percent increase in the mortgage payments.

The monthly mortgage payments in the earlier years of a GPM are generally not sufficient to pay the entire interest due on the outstanding mortgage balance. The difference between the monthly mortgage payment and the accumulated interest (based on the outstanding mortgage balance) is added to the outstanding mortgage balance, so that in the earlier years of a GPM there is *negative amortization.* The higher-level mortgage payments in the later years of the GPM are designed to fully amortize the outstanding mortgage balance, which is by then greater than the original amount borrowed.

## Growing Equity Mortgage

A *growing equity mortgage* (GEM) is a fixed-rate mortgage whose monthly mortgage payments increase over time. Unlike a GPM, there is no negative amortization. The initial monthly mortgage payment is the same as for a level-payment mortgage. The higher monthly mortgage payments are applied to paying off the principal. As a result, the principal of a GEM is repaid faster. For example, a 30-year $100,000 GEM loan with a contract rate of 8.125% might call for an initial monthly payment of $742.50 (the same as a level-payment 8.125% 30-year mortgage loan). However, the GEM payment would gradually increase, and the GEM might be fully paid in only 15 years. Pools of GEMs have been securitized.

## Tiered-Payment Mortgage

Another mortgage design with a fixed rate and a monthly payment that graduates over time is the *tiered-payment mortgage* (TPM). The initial monthly mortgage payments are below that of a traditional mortgage, as with a GPM. However, unlike a GPM, there is no negative amortization because withdrawals are made from a buydown account to supplement the initial monthly payments to cover the shortfall of interest. The buydown account is established at the time the loan is originated by the borrower, lender, or a third party such as a relative or business associate.

## Fixed/Adjustable-Rate Mortgage Hybrids

Another type of mortgage loan structure that has experienced growing popularity is *the fixed/adjustable-rate mortgage hybrid.* Typically, these mortgages are originated with fixed rates for their first 5, 7, or 10 years, after which the interest rate on the loan begins floating, with contractual characteristics similar to those of current ARM structures. For instance, a hybrid structure may have a fixed rate for five years, and thereafter have a floating rate that resets every six months at a margin over the six-month CD index. Like many other ARMs the coupon is subject to both periodic and lifetime limitations on the rate change. Other fixed/ARM hybrids turn into one-year Treasury ARMs or monthly Eleventh District COFI ARMs after their fixed period. In many cases, the first coupon reset is not subject to any periodic caps that may apply to later coupon resets, and instead is subject only to the lifetime cap.

## PREPAYMENT RISK

The investor in a mortgage grants the homeowner the option to prepay the mortgage in whole or in part at any time. Typically, no penalty is imposed on the homeowner for prepaying the mortgage. That is, the loan is repaid at par value at any time. (We will discuss mortgages with prepayment penalties later.) Any amount paid in excess of the contractual mortgage payments is called a *prepayment.* For example, suppose the monthly mortgage payment is $800 and the mortgage balance is $110,000. Any mortgage payment in excess of $800 would be a prepayment. The prepayment could be sufficient to pay off the mortgage completely. Or the prepayment could be less than the remaining mortgage balance. In our example, a mortgage payment of $2,800 would mean a prepayment of $2,000. The mortgage balance would then be reduced by that amount. The effect of this partial prepayment is to reduce the mortgage's life. A partial prepayment of a mortgage is called a *curtailment.*

Because of the right granted to the homeowner to prepay, called the *prepayment option,* an investor in a mortgage cannot be certain of the cash flow. A 30-year mortgage could turn out to have a maturity of one year or a maturity of 30 years. The uncertainty about the cash flow due to the prepayment option granted the homeowner is called *prepayment risk.*

An investor is exposed to prepayment risk for an individual mortgage and for a pool of mortgages. Consequently, any security backed by a pool of mortgages exposes an investor to prepayment risk.

Prepayments occur for one of several reasons. First, homeowners prepay the entire mortgage when they sell their home. The sale of a home can result from (1) a change of employment that necessitates moving, (2) the purchase of a more expensive home ("trading up"), or (3) a divorce in which the settlement requires sale of the marital residence, among other reasons. Second, in the case of homeowners who cannot meet their mortgage obligations, the property is repossessed and sold. The proceeds from the sale are used to pay off the mortgage in the case of a conventional mortgage. For an insured mortgage, the insurer will pay off the mortgage balance. Third, if property is destroyed by fire or another insured catastrophe occurs, the insurance proceeds are used to pay off the mortgage. Finally, the borrower will have an incentive to refinance the mortgage when the current mortgage rate falls by a sufficient amount below the contract rate after taking into account refinancing costs.

The key in analyzing an individual mortgage or a pool of mortgages is the projection of prepayments. All primary dealers and several vendors have developed prepayment models. While a discussion of these models is beyond the scope of this chapter, suffice it to say that there is not one prepayment model for all of the mortgage designs that we reviewed in the previous section. While a good deal of data on the prepayment activity of certain types of mortgage designs is available, the same cannot be said of some of the newer mortgage designs.

Prepayment risk also has implications for the performance of a mortgage. The performance is similar to that of a callable bond, a fact that should not be surprising, given that a mortgage is nothing more than a callable security. Specifically, the investor in a mortgage is exposed to negative convexity when interest rates decline below the loan's contract rate. In addition, the investor is exposed to reinvestment risk.

## DEFAULT RISK

Default or credit risk is the risk that the homeowner/borrower will default. For FHA, VA, and RHS insured mortgages, this risk is minimal. For privately insured mortgages, the risk can be gauged by the credit rating of the private insurance company that has insured the mortgage. For conventional mortgages without private insurance, the credit risk depends on the borrower. In recent years, the market for securities backed a pool of nonconforming mortgage loans that are not backed by a government agency has grown dramatically. An understanding of default risk is critical to investors in such securities.

One of the key characteristics of a mortgage loan that affects defaults is the LTV ratio at origination. This ratio is called the *original LTV*. The higher the original LTV or, equivalently, the less equity the borrower has in the property, the higher the probability of default. This finding was supported by studies of default rates.[4]

Unfortunately, looking at the original LTV underestimates the level of delinquencies because of the mismeasurement of the amount of equity that borrowers have in their home. Such mismeasurement is due to two factors. First, there may be a decline in the value of a home. Second, the homeowner can remove some equity via second mortgages or home equity lines of credit.

A study by Bendt, Ramsey, and Fabozzi examined not just the original LTV and its impact on default rates but also the *current LTV*.[5] The current LTV considers the loan value to the estimated current market price. Looking at the current LTV for a mortgage pool takes into account the effects of changing property values on the distribution of LTVs. Almost all original LTVs did not exceed 80% in a large pool of nonconforming mortgage loans (100,000 plus) they analyzed, and none were above 90%. Adjusted for declines in property values, however, nearly 40% had current LTVs above 80%, and about 15% had current LTVs above 90%.

The Bendt-Ramsey-Fabozzi study also examined defaults, taking into consideration second mortgages. They found that borrowers with second mortgages behind their first mortgage become delinquent twice as often as borrowers without second mortgages. Even adjusting for the higher LTVs, which take into account second mortgages, borrowers with second mortgages had higher delinquency rates compared to borrowers with the same LTV without any seconds. On average, they found that delinquency rates were about 25% higher—possibly because the combined monthly payments on a first and second mortgage would be higher than the same-size first mortgage.

---

4. See Robert Van Order, "The Hazards of Default," *Secondary' Mortgage Markets* (Fall 1990), pp. 29–32; Helen F. Peters, Scott M. Pinkus, and David 3. Askin, "Default: The Last Resort," *Secondary Mortgage Markets* (August 1984), pp. 16–22; and Scott Brown, et al. *Analysis of Mortgage Servicing Portfolios* (New York: Financial Strategies Group, Prudential-Bache Capital Funding, December 1990). The last study analyzed FHA/VA loans as well as conventional loans.

5. Douglas L. Bendt, Chuck Ramsey, and Frank J. Fabozzi, "The Rating Agencies' Approach: New Evidence," in *Whole-Loan CMOs,* eds. Frank J. Fabozzi, Chuck Ramsey, and Frank Ramirez (New Hope, PA: Frank J. Fabozzi Associates 1995).

Empirical studies also suggest there is a seasoning effect for default rates. That is, default rates tend to decline as mortgage loans become seasoned.[6] The reason for the seasoning effect on default rates is twofold. First, since a borrower typically knows shortly after moving into a home whether or not he or she can afford to make the mortgage payments, default rates are higher in the earlier years. Second, the longer a borrower remains in a home, the lower the LTV ratio (i.e., the greater the equity in the home), and therefore the incentive to default declines.

Van Order examined several characteristics of the borrower that he hypothesized would affect default rates. For example, as explained earlier in this chapter, the payment-to-income (PTI) ratio is a measure of the burden of the mortgage payments. It is expected that the higher this ratio at origination, the greater the probability of default. Van Order found that the probability of default increased only slightly the higher this burden. As he notes, this conclusion is only tentative because his sample did not include many observations with high PTIs. None of the other borrower characteristics appeared to significantly affect default rates.

## PREPAYMENT PENALTY MORTGAGES

The majority of mortgages outstanding do not penalize the borrower from prepaying any part or all of the outstanding mortgage balance. In recent years mortgage originators have begun originating *prepayment penalty mortgages* (PPMs). The major originators are Countrywide Home Loans, Bank of America, and First Nationwide.

The laws and regulations governing the imposition of prepayment penalties are established at the federal and state levels.[7] Usually, the applicable laws for fixed-rate mortgage are specified at the state level. As of the second quarter of 2000, only the following states did not permit prepayment penalties on fixed-rate mortgages with a first lien: Alaska, Iowa, New Jersey, New Mexico, and Vermont. There are nine states that do permit prepayment penalties but restrict the type of penalty. For some mortgage designs such as adjustable rate and balloon mortgages, there are federal laws that override state laws. Specifically, imposition of prepayment penalties for alternative mortgage designs by state-regulated entities is governed by the Alternative Mortgage Transactions Parity Act of 1982.

---

6. For conventional mortgage loans, the maximum default rate appears to be three to four years after origination. For FHA/VA mortgage loans, it seems to be two to three years after origination.

7. For a discussion of these laws and regulations, see Anand K. Bhattacharya and Paul C. Wang, "Prepayment Penalty MBS," forthcoming in Frank J. Fabozzi (ed.), *The Handbook of Mortgage-Backed Securities: Fifth Edition* (New York, NY: McGraw Hill Publishing Company, 2001). The information in this section draws from that chapter.

The basic structure of a PPM is as follows. There is a specified time period where prepayments are not permitted. This time period is called the *lockout period*. Typically, this period is either three years or five years. Depending on the structure, a certain amount of prepayments may be made during the lockout period without the imposition of a prepayment penalty. The common prepayment penalty structure is one that allows partial prepayments up to 20% of the original loan amount in any consecutive 12-month period without a prepayment penalty. When a prepayment penalty is imposed, it is typically as follows:[8]

- If there is a three-year lockout period, the prepayment penalty is the lesser of 2% of any prepayment amount within three years that is greater than 20% of the original mortgage, or six months of interest on the portion of the prepayment amount that exceeds 20% of the original principal balance.

- If there is a five-year lockout period, the prepayment penalty is six months interest on any prepayment amount in the first five years that is greater than 20% of the original principal balance.

For example, suppose that a borrower with a PPM with a mortgage rate of 8.5%, original principal balance of $150,000, and a lockout period of five years refinances within the first five and prepays the entire balance. The prepayment penalty will be six months of interest on the amount prepaid in excess of the 20% of the original principal balance. Since 80% of the original principal balance of $150,000 is $120,000 and interest for one year at 8.5% is $10,200 (8.5% times $120,000), the prepayment penalty is six-month's interest, $5,100.

The motivation for the PPM is that it reduces prepayment risk for the lender during the lockout period. It does so by effectively making it more costly for the borrower to prepay. In exchange for this reduction in prepayment risk, the lender will offer a mortgage rate that is less than that of an otherwise comparable mortgage loan without a prepayment penalty.

## OVERVIEW OF MORTGAGE-BACKED SECURITIES

We close this chapter with an overview of mortgage-backed securities. There is one basic product a *mortgage pass-through security*—and two derivative *products—collateralized mortgage obligations* and *stripped mortgage-backed securities*. Mortgage-backed securities can be created in which the underlying mortgages are one- to four-family residential mortgages. Or the underlying mortgages can be created by other property types. Five major property types backing such securities are office space, retail property, industrial facilities, multifamily hous-

---

8. The prepayment penalty structures are explained in Bhattacharya and Wang, "Prepayment Penalty MBS."

ing, and hotels. These securities are called *commercial mortgage-backed securities.*

Securities guaranteed by the full faith and credit of the U.S. government or a government-sponsored enterprise are commonly referred to as *agency mortgage-backed securities.* Those securities that do not carry such a guarantee are referred to as *nonagency mortgage-backed securities.*

We will illustrate the creation of mortgage-backed securities using Exhibits 24–3 through 24–6. It is assumed that the underlying mortgages are one- to four-family residential mortgages. Exhibit 24–3 shows 10 mortgage loans (each loan depicted as a home) and the cash flows from these loans. For simplicity, we will assume that the amount of each loan is $100,000 so that the aggregate value of all 10 loans is $1 million. The cash flows are monthly and consist of three components: (1) interest, (2) scheduled principal repayment, and (3) prepayments.

An investor who owns one of the mortgage loans shown in Exhibit 24–3 faces prepayment risk. For an individual loan, it may be difficult to predict prepayments. If an individual investor purchased all 10 loans, then the investor might be better able to predict prepayments. In fact, if there were 500 mortgage loans in Exhibit 24–3 rather than 10, the investor might be able to use historical prepayment experience to improve predictions about prepayments. But an investor would have to invest $1 million to buy 10 loans and $50 million to buy 500 loans, assuming each loan is for $100,000.

## Mortgage Pass-Through Securities

Suppose, instead, that some entity purchases all 10 loans in Exhibit 24–3 and pools them. The 10 loans can be used as collateral for the issuance of a security, with the cash flow from that security reflecting the cash flow from the 10 loans, as depicted in Exhibit 24–4. Suppose there are 40 units of this security issued. Thus, each unit is initially worth $25,000 ($1 million divided by 40). Each unit would be entitled to 2.5% (1/40) of the cash flow. The security created is called a *mortgage pass-through security,* or simply a *pass-through.*

Let's see what has been accomplished by creating the pass-through. The total amount of prepayment risk has not changed. However, now with an amount of less than $1 million, the investor can be exposed to the total prepayment risk of all 10 loans rather than face the risk of an individual mortgage loan.

So far, this financial engineering has not resulted in the creation of a totally new instrument since an individual investor could have accomplished the same outcome by purchasing all 10 loans. In addition to being able to acquire a proportionate share of all 10 loans with less than $1 million by buying a pass-through, the liquidity of a pass-through is greater than individual loans. Moreover, by selling a pass-through, the investor can dispose of all 10 loans rather than having to dispose of each loan one by one. Thus, a pass-through can be

**EXHIBIT 24–3**

Ten Mortgage Loans

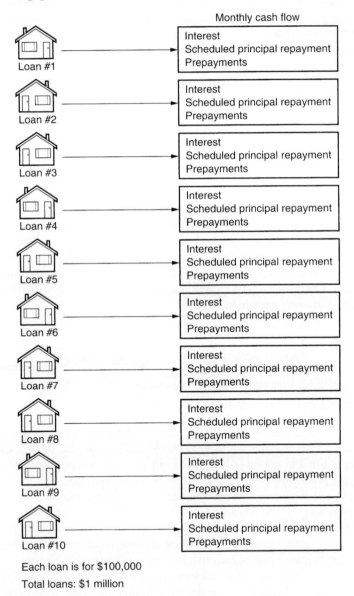

Each loan is for $100,000
Total loans: $1 million

**EXHIBIT  24–4**

Creation of a Pass-Through Security

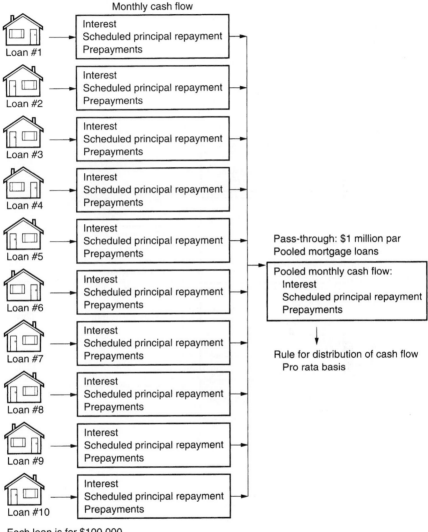

Each loan is for $100,000

Total loans: $1 million

**EXHIBIT   24–5**

Creation of a Collateralized Mortgage Obligation

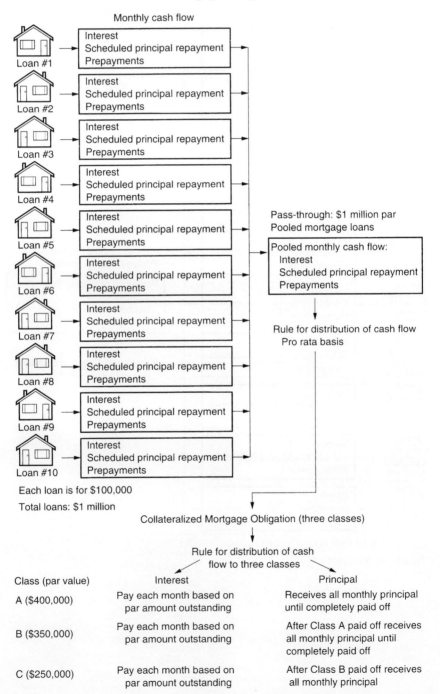

**EXHIBIT 24–6**

Creation of a Stripped-Mortgage-Backed Security

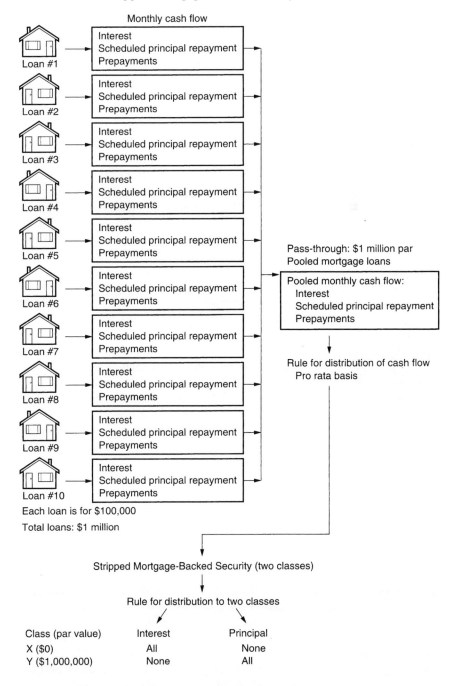

viewed as a more transactionally efficient vehicle for investing in mortgages than is the purchasing of individual mortgages.

## Collateralized Mortgage Obligations

An investor in a pass-through is still exposed to the total prepayment risk associated with the underlying pool of mortgage loans. Suppose that instead of distributing the monthly cash flow on a pro rata basis, as in the case of a pass-through, the distribution of the principal (both scheduled and prepayments) are done on some prioritized basis. How this is done is illustrated in Exhibit 24–5.

Exhibit 24–5 shows the cash flow of our original 10-mortgage loan and the pass-through. Also shown are three classes of bonds, the par value of each class, and a set of rules indicating how the principal from the pass-through is to be distributed to each. Note the following. The sum of the par value of the three classes is equal to $1 million. While not shown in the exhibit, for each of the three classes, there will be units representing a proportionate interest in a class. For example, suppose that for Class A, which has a par value of $400,000, there are 50 units of Class A issued. Each unit would receive a proportionate share (2%) of what is received by Class A.

The rule for the distribution of principal shown in Exhibit 24–5 is that Class A will receive all principal (both scheduled and prepayments) until that class receives its entire par value of $400,000. Then, Class B receives all principal payments until it receives its par value of $350,000. After Class B is completely paid off, Class C receives principal payments. The rule for the distribution of cash flow in Exhibit 24–5 indicates that each of the three classes will receive interest based on the amount of par value outstanding.

The mortgage-backed security that has been created is called a *collateralized mortgage obligation* (CMO). The collateral for a loan may be either one or more pass-throughs or a pool of mortgage loans that have not been securitized. In the latter case, when the underlying mortgages are not guaranteed by an agency, the CMO structure is referred to as a *whole-loan CMO* or a *non-agency CMO*. The ultimate source for the CMO's cash flow is the pool of mortgage loans.

Let's look at what has been accomplished. Once again, the total prepayment risk for the CMO is the same as the total prepayment risk for the 10 mortgage loans. However, the prepayment risk has been distributed among the three classes of the CMO. Class A absorbs prepayments first, then Class B, and then Class C. The result of this is that Class A will effectively be a shorter-term security than the other two classes; Class C will have the longest maturity. Institutional investors will be attracted to the different classes given the nature of their liability structure and the effective maturity of the CMO class. Moreover, the uncertainty about the maturity of each class of the CMO is far less than the uncertainty about the maturity of the pass-through.

Thus, by redirecting the cash flow from the underlying mortgage pool, classes of bonds have been created that are more attractive to institutional investors to satisfy asset/liability objectives than a pass-through. In theory, a CMO is not a new market instrument since it simply represents the redirecting of the cash flow. However, it is a more transactionally efficient instrument for distributing prepayment risk.

The CMO we depicted in Exhibit 24–5 has a simple set of rules for prioritizing the distribution of principal. Today, much more complicated CMO structures exist. The purpose is to provide certain CMO classes with less uncertainty about prepayment risk. However, this can occur only if the reduction in prepayment risk for such classes is absorbed by other classes in the CMO structure.

## Stripped Mortgage-Backed Securities

Consider once again the 10 mortgage loans in Exhibit 24–3. In the CMO, there was a set of rules for prioritizing the distribution of the principal payments amongst the various classes. In a stripped mortgage-backed security, the principal and interest are divided among two classes unequally. For example, one class may be entitled to receive all of the principal and the other class all of the interest. This is depicted in Exhibit 24–6. This distribution for the interest and principal is the most common type of stripped mortgage-backed securities. The class that receives all the interest is called the *interest-only*, or *IO*, class. The class that receives all the principal is called the *principal only*, or *PO*, class. The IO class receives no principal payments.

The PO security is purchased at a substantial discount from par value. The return an investor realizes depends on the speed at which prepayments are made. The faster the prepayments, the higher the investor's return. In the extreme case, if all homeowners in the underlying mortgage pool decide to prepay their mortgage loans immediately, PO investors will realize the entire principal immediately. At the other extreme, if all homeowners decide to remain in their homes for the life of the mortgage and make no prepayments, the return of principal will be spread out over the life of the underlying mortgages, which would result in a lower return for PO investors.

Let's look at how the price of the PO would be expected to change as mortgage rates in the market change. When mortgage rates decline below the coupon rate, prepayments are expected to speed up, accelerating payments to the PO holder. Thus, the cash flow of a PO improves (in the sense that principal repayments are received earlier). The cash flow will be discounted at a lower interest rate because the mortgage rate in the market has declined. The result is that the PO price will increase when mortgage rates decline. When mortgage rates rise above the coupon rate, prepayments are expected to slow down. The cash flow deteriorates (in the sense that it takes longer to recover principal repayments). Couple this with a higher discount rate, and the price of a PO will fall when mortgage rates rise.

An IO has no par value. In contrast to the PO investor, the IO investor wants prepayments to be slow. The reason is that the IO investor receives interest only on the amount of the principal outstanding. When prepayments are made, less dollar interest will be received as the outstanding principal declines. In fact, if prepayments are too fast, the IO investor may not recover the amount paid for the IO. This occurs despite the fact that the interest is guaranteed by a government agency.

Let's look at the expected price response of an IO to changes in mortgage rates. If mortgage rates decline below the coupon rate, the prepayments are expected to accelerate. This would result in a deterioration of the expected cash flow for an IO. While the cash flow will be discounted at a lower rate, the net effect typically is a decline in the price of an IO. If mortgage rates rise above the coupon rate, the expected cash flow improves, but the cash flow is discounted at a higher interest rate. The net effect may be either a rise or fall for the IO. Thus, we see an interesting characteristic of an IO: Its price tends to move in the same direction as the change in mortgage rates: (1) when mortgage rates fall below the coupon rate and (2) for some range of mortgage rates above the coupon rate. Both POs and IOs exhibit substantial price volatility when mortgage rates change. The greater price volatility of the IO and PO compared to the pass-through is due to the fact that the combined price volatility of the IO and PO must be equal to the price volatility of the pass-through.

What may be confusing is why stripped mortgage-backed securities are created. We explained the motivation for the creation of pass-throughs and CMOs but not for a stripped mortgage-backed security. For now, it is sufficient to say that when properly used the risk/return characteristics of these instruments make them attractive for purposes of hedging a portfolio of pass-throughs and hedging other assets such as mortgage servicing rights.

## Real Estate-Backed Asset-Backed Securities

In other chapters in this part of the book, asset-backed securities are described. These securities are backed by loans or receivables. In the U.S. capital market, an artificial distinction is made between mortgage-backed securities and asset-backed securities. Technically, mortgage-backed securities are part of the asset-backed securities market, where the underlying collateral is a first mortgage lien on the real estate property.

There are asset-backed securities backed by loans in which the underlying collateral is real estate. The two primary examples are home equity loans and manufactured housing loans. These two asset-backed securities are discussed in Chapters 30 and 31, respectively.

CHAPTER **25**

# MORTGAGE PASS-THROUGHS

**Lakhbir S. Hayre, D. Phil.\***
Managing Director
Salomon Smith Barney, Inc.

**Cyrus Mohebbi, Ph.D.**
Managing Director
Prudential Securities, Inc.

**John M. Mawe**
Director
Prudential Securities, Inc.

## INTRODUCTION

Imagine an investor looking at alternative bonds investments. One option is a 10-year Treasury. Another is a U.S. government-guaranteed GNMA 7.5 (pronounced "Ginnie Mae") pass-through with a 10-year average life yielding 140 basis points over Treasuries.

On quoted yield alone, the GNMA 7.5 looks most attractive, and may in fact be the right investment to make. However, to make an informed decision, an investor needs to understand several factors unique to mortgage pass-through securities which could result in a realized yield much different from quoted yield. While neither bond has any credit risk, a Treasury has a very different cash flow profile from a GNMA pass-through.

This chapter will introduce the mortgage pass-through, the most basic form of mortgage-backed security ("MBS"). The first section describes the history and issuers of pass-throughs. The second section describes mechanics of how to calculate MBS cash flows and introduces basic valuation tools, prepayment risk and how to quantify prepayment effect on maturity and yield. The last section looks at relative value analysis and total rate of return—focusing on some unique considerations for MBS evaluation.

Many investors shy away from investing in pass-throughs, fearing that dealers and other market participants have much better information. As the market enters the 21$^{st}$ century, the exact opposite is becoming true. Information cost continues to decrease—both investors and dealers have access to the same data. Combined with the fact that investors can trade with multiple dealers and the

Dr. Hayre was employed by Prudential Securities, Inc. when this chapter was written.

result is that often investors can estimate market movements as well as or better than dealers. In summary, dealers used to know more than investors; this may no longer be true.

## ORIGINS OF MBS PASS-THROUGHS

For portfolio managers looking for fixed-rate investments offering greater yield than available in the U.S. treasury market, two options are available.[1] First, the investor can take on credit risk by investing in securities not guaranteed by the U.S. government. Also, or alternatively, the investor can accept securities where the timing of principal repayment is uncertain. Corporate debt, for example, is priced with additional yield to compensate the investor for the default risk of the issuer, and will provide call premiums if the bonds can be repaid on dates other than the maturity date.

Similar to portfolio managers, loan originators face similar risks when projecting returns on their assets. Consumer mortgages, for example, can default or prepay at any time, with considerable yield impact on the originator's portfolio. As in the pricing of corporate debt, originators compensate themselves for accepting these risks by charging borrowers a higher rate of interest.[2] In addition, originators look to buying and selling portions of their portfolios to diversify their risks. When originators sell their mortgages, they are said to engage in secondary market transactions.

The secondary market for whole loans, or unsecuritized mortgages, existed long before the creation of mortgage pass-through securities. The secondary whole-loan market helped to reduce imbalances between lenders in capital-deficit areas and capital surplus-areas. Even though the servicing often remained with the originator of the mortgage, buyers of whole loans faced many of the legal complications and paperwork of mortgage ownership. More importantly, there was little liquidity in the whole-loan market, and buyers ran the risk of potential losses if forced to sell their mortgages quickly. The extensive details, paperwork and cost involved in these types of transactions prevented many small buyers from entering the market. The introduction of the mortgage pass-through created a means of buying and selling mortgages that was more convenient and in many ways more efficient than the whole-loan market. Pass-through certificates represent pro rata shares of the interest (after subtraction of a servicing fee) and principal cash flow from a pool of mortgages. The cash flow from the

---

1. An investor or portfolio manager will often also look to alternatives in the derivative markets such as swaps and other synthetic devices to enhance yield. The use of hedging to leverage a portfolio yield is often also employed. Both topics are beyond the scope of this chapter.

2. If possible, an originator may also try to charge a borrower a fee for prepaying the mortgage—a "prepayment penalty". In most states, the ability to charge prepayment penalities on first mortgages is limited or prohibited. As a result, the sole means of compensation for risk is in the rate.

mortgages are "passed through", after subtraction of a service fee, to the holder of the pass through securities on a monthly basis, typically with a delay. The payments made to the investor consist of scheduled principal and interest and any unscheduled payments of principal (resulting from prepayments and defaults) that may occur.[3]

The great majority of pass-throughs has been issued by three agencies that were created by Congress to increase liquidity in the secondary mortgage markets and thus increase the supply of capital available for residential housing loans. The Federal National Mortgage Association (FMNA or "Fannie Mae"), the oldest of these agencies, was established by the federal government in 1938 to help solve some of the housing finance problems brought on by the Depression. FNMA's original mandate allowed it to buy Federal Housing Administration (FHA) and Veterans Administration (VA) loans from lenders. In 1968, Congress divided the original FNMA into two organizations: the current FNMA and the Government National Mortgage Association (GNMA, or "Ginnie Mae"). GNMA remains a government agency within the Department of Housing and Urban Development (HUD), helping to finance government-assisted housing programs. FNMA became a private corporation rechartered by Congress with a mandate to establish a secondary market for conventional mortgages, that is loans not FHA insured or VA guaranteed. Established in 1970, the Federal Home Loan Mortgage Corporation (FHLMC, or "Freddie Mae") initially was a government-chartered corporation owned by the 12 Federal Home Loan Banks and the federally insured savings institutions, which in turned owned stock in the Federal Home Loan Banks. In 1989, as part of the Financial Institutions, Reform Recovery and Enforcement Act (FIRREA), FHMLC became a private corporation much like FNMA. Like FNMA, FHLMC seeks to enhance liquidity for residential mortgage investments, primarily by assisting in the development of secondary markets for conventional mortgages.

The creation of the pass-through by the government achieves two objectives of making investing in MBS more attractive: 1) credit risk is eliminated through the government's implicit guaranty (explicit for GNMA's), and 2) the cash flow profile is made more predictable through aggregation of a large number of loans and though creation of a single fixed rate bond (vs. various rates

---

3. This chapter will focus exclusively on agency pass-throughs. As discussed below, the timing of principal prepayment on an agency pass-through is solely a function of the prepayment rate on the underlying mortgage pool. By comparison, many mortgage and other assets are regularly securitized into bond form and sold to investors, often in a single class (vs. tranched) form. It is common to refer to any single class deal as a "pass-through". Potential investors should be careful to realize that referring to such deals as pass-throughs ignores an often complex set of rules for application of collections. While beyond the scope of this chapter, the reader should recognize that non-agency "pass-throughs" may require additional analysis beyond prepayment estimation.

on the underlying mortgages). Although any of these loans can prepay at any time, the impact to the overall certificate is minor. Also, market players can apply statistical models to a large number of loans and thereby better estimate monthly prepayments.

## Growth in Pass-Through Issuance

The first pass-throughs were issued by GNMA in 1970. FHLMC issued its first pass-throughs in 1971. FNMA, which traditionally financed its mortgage purchases through debenture offerings, began issuing pass-throughs at the end of 1981. Exhibit 25-1 shows the yearly volume for pass-through issuance from 1985 to 1998. Notice the dramatic urge in pass-through issuance during the major refinancing episodes of 1993 and 1998.

Issuance has shown a major increase since 1985 partly because a larger proportion of mortgage originations is now securitized. After their experiences of the early 1980s, mortgage lenders are now more likely to sell their fixed-rate mortgages in order to avoid losses if rates rise. The increased participation of agency and private issuers in this market has facilitated the increase in mortgage securitization.[4]

The growth in pass-through issuance has occurred not only in absolute terms, but also relative to other sectors of the fixed income market. Exhibit

**E X H I B I T   25-1**

Pass-Through Issuance from 1985–1998

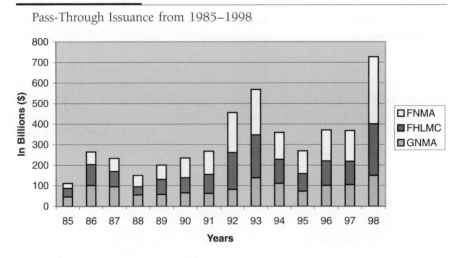

---

4. Mortgages not eligible for purchase by the three agencies are often securitized by issuers in private "jumbo" deals, named for the balances of the loans in the pools—predominantly above agency limits. Such deals were often counted in pass-through issuance statistics but are now predominantly issued as private CMO's.

25–2 shows the sizes of the pass through, Treasury, corporate and the agency markets from year-end 1990 to year-end 1998. As Exhibit 25–2 shows, the pass-through market is now comparable to the corporate market in size and is substantially larger than the agency market.

## Comparison of GNMA, FNMA and FHLMC Pass-Throughs

Although all pass-throughs basically have the same structure—cash flows from the mortgages in the pool are passed through to the security holders after subtraction of a servicing fee—there are a number of generally minor differences among the pass-throughs issued by the three agencies. Exhibit 25–3 gives basic information about the GNMA, FNMA, and FHLMC pass-through programs.

The following are some of the important features of the agency pass-through programs:

### Guarantees
GNMA pass-throughs are guaranteed directly by the U.S government as to timely payment of interest and principal. FNMA and FHLMC pass-throughs carry agency guarantees only; however, both agencies can borrow from the U.S. treasury, and it is not likely that the U.S government would allow the agencies to default. FNMA guarantees the timely payment of interest and principal on all its securities. FHLMC guarantees the timely payment of interest and principal on its Gold program, originated in 1990, but on it's 75-day program it guarantees the timely payment of interest and the ultimate (within one year) payment of

**EXHIBIT  25–2**

Sizes of the Pass-Through, Treasury, corporate, and Agency Markets: Year-End 1990 through Year-End 1998

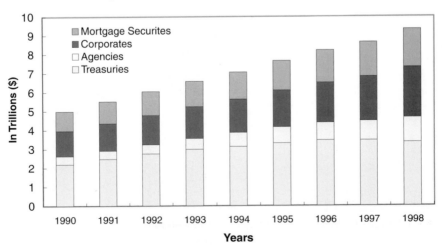

# EXHIBIT 25-3

Characteristics of GNMAs, FNMAs, and FHLMCs[a]

| | GNMA | FNMA | FHLMC 75-day | FHLMC Gold |
|---|---|---|---|---|
| Types of mortgage | FHA/VA | Conventional (some FHA/VA) | Conventional (some FHA/VA) | Conventional (some FHA/VA) |
| Main payment types | Level payment | Level payment | Level payment | Level payment |
| | Graduated payment | ARM | ARM | Balloon |
| | ARM | Balloon | Balloon | |
| | | | Tiered payment | |
| Maximum loan size | $219,849[b,c] | $252,700 | $252,700 | $252,700 |
| Mortgage age at securitization | New origination | New or seasoned | New or seasoned | New or seasoned |
| Main term | 30- and 15-year (some 40-yr. project loans) | 30-, 20-, and 15-year fixed | 30- and 15-year fixed | 30-, 20-, and 15-year fixed |
| | | 7-year balloons | 7- and 5-year balloons | 7- and 5-year balloons |
| | | 30-year ARMS | 30-year ARMS | |
| Mortgage coupon Allowed (%) over pass-through rate | GNMA I: 0.50 GNMA II: 0.50–1.50 | 0.25–2.50, range 2.00 | Cash: 0–2.00, range 1.00 Swap: 0–2.50 | Cash: 0.50–1.00 Swap: 0–2.50 |
| Delays (days): | | | | |
| Stated | 45 (GNMA II: 50) | 55 | 75 | 45 |
| Actual | 14 (GNMA II: 19) | 24 | 45 | 14 |

[a] Data current as of December, 1999.
[b] Maximum FHA loan size is $121,296.
[c] GNMA limit for VA Interest Rate Reduction Refinancing Loans (RRL) is $200,000.

principal. From the investor's point of view, because of the guarantees, a default is essentially equivalent to a prepayment.

**Payment Delay**
Pass-throughs pay interest after a specified delay. For example, interest for the month of August would be paid September 15 for Gold GNMAs (September 20 for GNMA II pass-throughs), on September 15 for Gold FHLMCs (October 15 for 75-day FHLMCs) and on September 25 for FNMAs. On these dates, the security holder would also receive any principal payments made by the mortgage holder made during the month of August. The delay is said to be 45 days from GNMAs and Gold FHLMCs, 55 days for FNMAs, and 75 days for 75-day FHLMCs. However, because interest for the month of August would be paid on September 1 if there were no delay, the actual delays are 14, 24, and 44 days, respectively.

**Pool Composition**
GNMA pools consist of VA- and FHA- insured mortgages that are assumable, whereas FNMA and FHLMC pools generally consist of conventional loans that are not assumable. FNMA and FHLMC pools also tend to be much larger than GNMA pools and hence are less regionally concentrated.

**Liquidity**
The growth in the size of the pass-through markets has led to greater liquidity with FNMA's and FHLMCs now generally as liquid as GNMAs. Bid-ask spreads for the major coupons (currently in the 6.0 to 8.0% range) are generally about 1/8 of a point, which is similar to Treasuries and less than most corporates. Thus, liquidity for the major coupons is comparable to that for Treasuries and greater than that for most corporates. Exhibit 25–4 shows total pass-through issuance by the three agencies for coupons from 6.5% to 13% (only 30 year securities are included). Also shown is the amount outstanding. Two points are clearly indicated by Exhibit 25–4. First, the market for high-premium securities (with coupons of 10% or higher) has virtually disappeared because of the massive refinancings of high-coupon mortgages. Second, although historically GNMA played the largest role in the secondary market, today FNMA and FHLMC have much larger annual issuance and their amounts outstanding approach or surpass the outstanding GNMAs.

## MODELING MBS CASH FLOWS

MBS pass-through cash flows differ from typical bonds in two respects. First, distributions are made monthly as opposed to semi-annually. Second, and of greater significance, the investor receives not only a monthly coupon, but also some amount of principal, the amount of which varies from month to month.

**EXHIBIT 25–4**

Total Pass-Through Issuance for Major 30-Year Coupons (Data as of November, 1999)

### Original Amounts

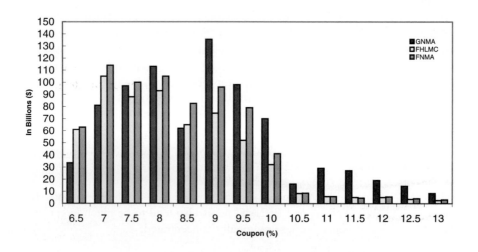

### Oustanding Amounts

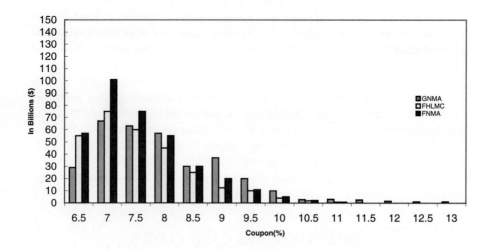

Predicting the amount and timing of this principal payment is the key to proper valuation of the MBS.

Before moving to prepayment prediction, let us first establish the framework for MBS cash flow projections. As a "pass-through" security, the money collected on the underlying pool of mortgages is distributed each month to the investor. Except for a small servicing fee paid to the servicer (usually about 50 bps annually), all of the money collected is distributed each month. The minimum amount of information needed to project cash flows are:

Balance—The balance of the MBS is usually expressed as both an original face amount, and a current factor, ie, $50 million original face with a factor of .80000 would equate to $40 million outstanding.

Coupon—The annual coupon rate for the security. This rate is set at the time the MBS is issued and does not change.

Remaining term—The remaining number of months to maturity. The remaining term is calculated as the weighted average of all the underlying mortgages in the pool. The remaining term, on average, will decrease by one each month.

WAC—The weighted average of underlying mortgage note rates in the pool. If WAC is not available, it is typical to assume 50 bps above the coupon. Assuming a 50 bps servicing fee, that assumption would calculate the minimum WAC of the pool. Generally, the WAC initially will be higher at the time of issuance and drift towards the minimum over time, as mortgages with higher rates prepay.

Using these four pieces of information, the scheduled cash flows for the MBS can be derived. The scheduled monthly principal amortization is calculated assuming each dollar of MBS is one loan having a rate equal to the WAC and term equal to the remaining term of the MBS.

Note that the scheduled principal payment is a function of the WAC, not the coupon, as the MBS amortizes along the schedule of the underlying mortgages. The coupon rate determines only the interest paid to the investor.

## Prepayment and Cash Flow Behavior

The timing and amounts of the cash flows received from a pass-through are greatly affected by the prepayment of the mortgages in the underlying pool. This makes the choice of a projected prepayment rate critical in evaluating and pricing an MBS. Prepayment rates tend to fluctuate with interest rates and other economic variables and depend on mortgage characteristics such as coupon and age. There is also a strong seasonal effect on prepayment, which reflects the well-known seasonal variations in housing turnover. This section addresses the prepayment conventions and models used in pricing and trading MBSs, as well as the effect of prepayments on pass-through cash flows.

## Prepayment Models and Conventions

***Twelve-Year Prepaid Life***     At one time, the standard approach to prepayments was 12-year prepaid life, which assumes no prepayments for the first 12 years of the pass-through life and then full prepayment at the end of the 12th year. This was based on FHA data that showed that on average mortgages terminated in their 12th year. It is now generally realized that the 12-year prepaid life assumption can often give misleading results; prepayment rates tend to vary with interest rates and mortgage characteristics and are higher for premium coupons than for discounts. This method is now rarely used in the pricing and trading of MBSs, although quoted mortgage yields are sometimes based on it.

***Conditional Prepayment Rate (CPR)***     A commonly used method is to assume a conditional prepayment rate (CPR) for a pool of mortgages. If one thinks of the pool as consisting of a large number of $1 mortgages, then the CPR for a period is the percentage of mortgages outstanding at the beginning of the period that terminate during that period. The CPR is usually expressed on an annualized basis, whereas the term single monthly mortality (SMM) or constant monthly prepayment (CMP) refers to monthly prepayment rates.

For example, if a pool of mortgages is prepaying at a constant rate 1% per month, then 1% of the outstanding balance, after subtraction of the scheduled principal, will be prepaid in each month. Thus, if the outstanding principal balance at the beginning of the month is $100,000 and the scheduled principal payment is $1,000, then the SMM of 1% means that 1% of 99,000 (the remaining balance after the scheduled principal payment), or $990, will be prepaid that month. (Because the scheduled principal payments for a 30-year mortgage are generally small until the latter part of the mortgage term, one can as a good approximation, multiply the outstanding balance by the SMM to obtain the amount of principal prepayment.)

The effective annual prepayment rate, or CPR, corresponding to a given monthly prepayment rate is almost, but not quite, equal to 12 times the monthly rate. For a 1% monthly rate, the CPR is 11.36%. The reason that the annual rate is less than 12% is that the monthly prepayment rate of 1% is being applied to a decreasing principal balance each month. Hence, a 1% SMM in month 10, say, means less principal prepayment in dollar terms than a 1% SMM in month 1. (See the appendix in this chapter for a formula for converting a monthly rate to an annual rate and vice versa.)

***FHA Experience***     Once FHA experience was a widely used prepayment model. However, it is not often used today. FHA experience projects the prepayment rate of a mortgage pool relative to the historical prepayment and default experience of FHA-insured, 30-year mortgage loans. FHA periodically publishes a table of 30 numbers that represents the annual survivorship rates of FHA-insured mortgages. The table indicates probability of survival of a mortgage and reports the percentage of mortgages expected to terminate for any given policy year.

A mortgage pool's prepayment rates are expressed as a percentage of FHA experience. For example, if a pool of mortgages prepays at 100% FHA, then in each mortgage year the loans in the pool will terminate at the rate given by FHA statistics. A rate of 200% FHA means that the mortgages terminate twice as fast as 100% FHA experience would predict, and 50% FHA means that the mortgages terminate half as fast as 100% FHA experience would predict.

The major advantage of FHA experience over CPR is that it reflects the effect of age on prepayments and in particular the low prepayment level typical of newer mortgages. Its major disadvantages are its complexity and the fact that periodic updates of the FHA data mean that the prepayment rates implied by a given percentage of FHA experience also change periodically.

***Public Securities Association (PSA) Model***    The current industry standard is the Public Securities Association (PSA) prepayment model, which was developed to describe mortgage prepayment behavior by combining the information in the FHA survivorship schedules with the simplicity of the CPR method. The PSA benchmark (denoted 100% PSA) assumes a series of CPRs that begins at 0.2% in the first month and increases by 0.2% thereafter, until leveling 30 months after mortgage origination, when the CPR is 6% as shown in Exhibit 25–5.

Interpreting multiples of PSA is simpler than interpreting multiples of FHA. For example, a projected prepayment rate of 200% PSA means that the CPR in any month will be twice the CPR corresponding to 100% PSA; thus for 200% PSA, the CPR will be 0.4% in month 1, 0.8% in month 2, and so on until it levels off at 12% in month 30. Exhibit 25–6 illustrates this for 50% PSA, 100% PSA, and 150% PSA. Note that to predict cash flows using the PSA prepayment model on a pass-through less than 30 months old requires an assumption of age to know the starting point for the PSA ramp.

***Economic Prepayment Models***    Many major Wall Street firms have developed econometric models that project prepayment rates as a function of specified economic and mortgage variables. In the most general case, an econometric prepayment model will project SMMs for each remaining month of the mortgage security. This vector of monthly prepayment rates will reflect seasonal and age variation in prepayments, as well as changing patterns of housing turnover and refinancing over time for a given pool of mortgages. For trading and sales purposes, however, using a vector of monthly prepayments is sometimes impractical. Hence, the vector is usually presented as an equivalent averaged CPR or percentage of PSA. For example the Prudential Securities Prepayment Model calculates the PSA rate that produces the same weighted average life as the vector of monthly prepayment rates. Using econometric models is often pref-

**E X H I B I T  25–5**

FHA and PSA Prepayment Models

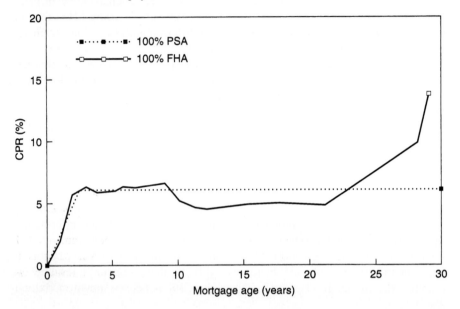

**E X H I B I T  25–6**

Multiples of PSA

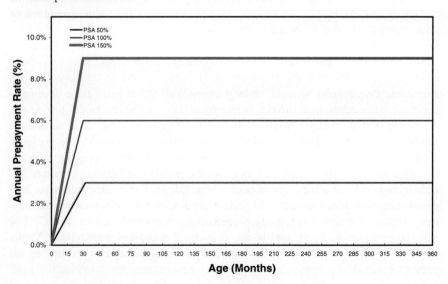

erable to using recent prepayment levels as a means of choosing a projected CPR or PSA rate because changing economic factors may have made recent prepayment levels an unreliable indicator of future prepayments.

***Effect of Prepayments on Cash Flows***   Exhibit 25–7 shows the cash flows generated by the pool of mortgages backing a new current-coupon GNMA at various prepayment rates. At a zero prepayment level, the monthly dollar cash flows from the mortgage loans are constant. Notice however, that the composition of principal, interest, and servicing that constitute each of the monthly cash flows changes as the mortgages amortize. As principal payments increase and the remaining principal balance declines, the dollar amount of interest due declines proportionately. Servicing fees, like interest payments, are calculated based on the remaining principal balance of the mortgage loan. For the current-coupon GNMA in the Exhibit 25–7(a), the servicing fee is 50 basis points of interest. Pass-through investors will experience the effect of a decrease in servicing fees (as the remaining principal balance declines) in terms of slightly increasing monthly dollar cash flows.

At more realistic prepayment levels, the cash flows are more concentrated early in the pass-through term. Exhibit 25–7 (b) shows the cash flows at a prepayment rate of 50%—PSA historically a slow speed for current-coupon GNMA prepayment levels. The principal paydowns increase for the first two and one half-years, as the prepayment rate increases according to the PSA pattern until month 30. The prepayment rate then remains constant at 3% per year. Note that the total amount of principal received by the pass-through investor is fairly constant after the first two years. At an assumed prepayment rate of 50% PSA, the increase in the scheduled principal payment each period offsets the decline in prepaid principal, which is approximately a constant percentage of the remaining principal balance.

Exhibit 25–7(c) shows the cash flows at a prepayment rate of 120% PSA, an average prepayment speed for a current coupon. Again the amount of principal increases for the first two and one-half years, as the prepayment rate increases for 30 months before leveling off at 7.2% (1.20 × 6%) per year after month 30. The total principal payments gradually decrease after month 30, because at 120% PSA the principal balance has declined to the point at which the scheduled principal payments are much less significant than they are at 50% PSA.

Exhibit 25–7(d) shows the cash flow at prepayment rate of 200% PSA, which is considered to be fast by historical standards for a current coupon. The prepayment rate levels off at 12% per annum after month 30, and the principal paydown is concentrated in the early years.

The outstanding principal balances at 0%, 50% and 120% and 200% PSA are shown in Exhibit 25–8. These reflect the principal prepayment pattern shown Exhibit 25–7.

**E X H I B I T   25–7**

Current-Coupon GNMA Cash Flows at Various Prepayment Rates

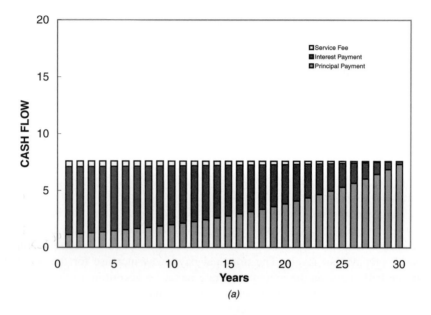

*(a)*

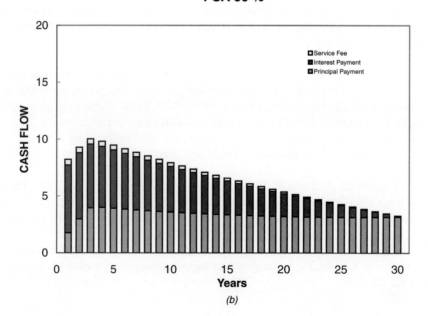

*(b)*

**E X H I B I T   25–7**

(*Continued*)

## PSA 120 %

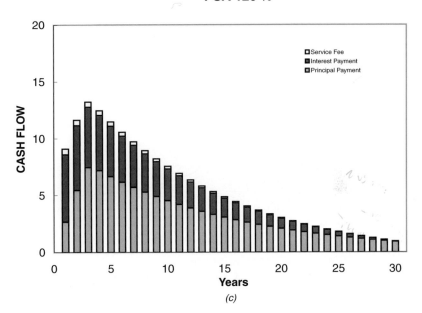

(c)

## PSA 200 %

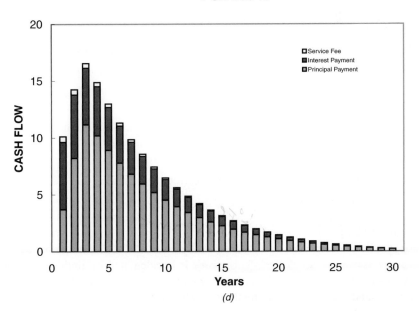

(d)

**E X H I B I T   25–8**

Oustanding Balances of a Current-Coupon GNMA at Various Prepayment Rates

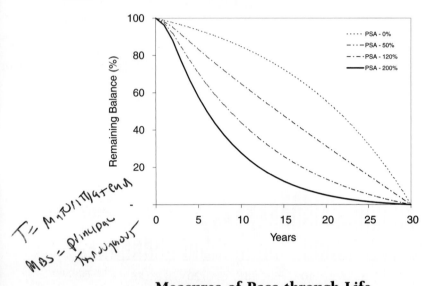

_(handwritten notes in left margin:)_ T = Maturity at end / MBS = Principal Throughout

## Measures of Pass-through Life

A pass-through is a self-amortizing security that returns principal throughout its term. In comparing pass-throughs (or any MBS) with other bonds, such as a Treasury that returns all it as principal at maturity, it is necessary to determine some reasonable measure of the investment life of the pass-through.

The selection of a reasonable measure of mortgage life is important. Measures of investment life are used in several ways when assessing the investment value:

• They suggest the effective span of time during which a mortgage security provides a stated yield or return.

• They suggest how to compare the mortgage security to other, more familiar bond investments; in particular, they suggest the maturity on the Treasury yield curve against which to compare a pass-through.

• They can indicate the pass-through's volatility in a shifting interest-rate environment.

**Average Life**   _(handwritten:)_ Life of Investment

Average life or weighted-average life (WAL) is defined as the weighted-average time to the return of a dollar of principal. It is calculated by multiplying each portion of principal received by the time at which it is received, and then the summing and dividing by the total amount of principal. (See the appendix for the mathematical formula for average life.) For example, consider a simple an-nual-pay, four-year bond with a face value of $100 and principal payments, as in Exhibit 25–9. As the exhibit illustrates, each time point at which principal is returned is weighted by the percentage of principal returned at that time point, so that the average life in this example could be calculated as shown in Exhibit 25–9.

Average life is commonly used as the measures of investment life for MBSs, and the yield of an MBS is typically compared against a Treasury with maturity close to the average life of the MBS.

Exhibit 25–10 plots the average life of a new current-coupon GNMA at prepayment speeds of 50% PSA, 120% PSA and 200% PSA. The exhibit shows that the average life of an MBS depends heavily on the prepayment rate. An interesting graphical interpretation of average life is obtained if one thinks of the principal payments as weights, with each weight equal to the amount of principal. The average life is the point at which the weights on each side of the point are exactly balanced. In other words, if in Exhibit 25–10 the horizontal axis were a seesaw, then the seesaw would have to be balanced at the average life for it not to tilt to one side.

Exhibit 25–11 shows the variation of average life with respect to coupon and prepayment rate. Specifically, it indicates that, for a given remaining term and prepayment rate, the average life of an MBS increases with the coupon. This is true because a higher coupon means that the interest portion is a higher percentage of the monthly payments in the early years of the mortgage term, with the principal payments begin more concentrated toward the later years.

## Macaulay Duration

An alternative to average life as a measure of investment life is duration. Du-ration, or Macaulay duration (named after Fredrick Macaulay, who introduced

**E X H I B I T    25–9**

Calculation of Average Life

| Time | Principal | Time × Principal |
|------|-----------|------------------|
| 1 year | $40 | 1 year  × $40 =  40 |
| 2 | 30 | 2 years ×  30 =  60 |
| 3 | 20 | 3 years ×  20 =  60 |
| 4 | 10 | 4 years ×  10 =  40 |
|  | $100 | 200 |

$$\text{Average Life} = \frac{\text{Sum of (Time} \times \text{Principal)}}{\text{Total Principal}} = 200/10 = 2 \text{ years}$$

**E X H I B I T   25–10**

Average Life of a New Current-Coupon GNMA at 50%, 120%, and 200% PSA.

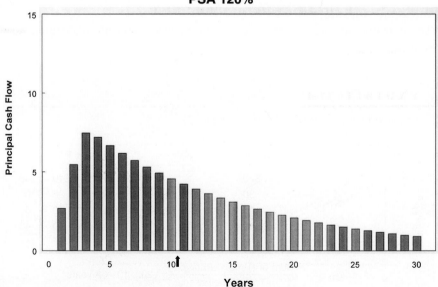
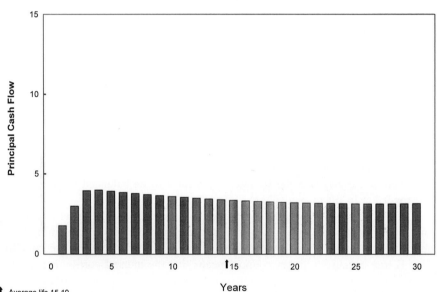

Average life 15.19

Average life 10.97

### EXHIBIT  25–10

*(Continued)*

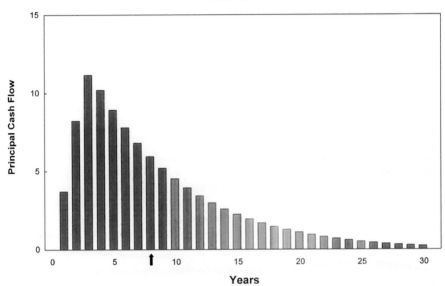

PSA 200 %

Average life 8.19

### EXHIBIT  25–11

Average Life of New GNMA 6s, 9s and 14s

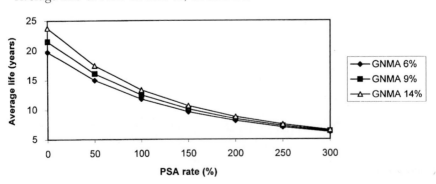

the concept in 1938), is defined as the weighted-average time to return of a dollar of price. It is calculated by multiplying the present value of each cash flow by the time at which it is received, summing and then dividing by the price. (See the appendix for the mathematical formula for Macaulay duration.) Exhibit 25–12 illustrates the calculation of Macaulay duration for an annual-pay, four-year bond with cash flows of $30 each year and an assumed discount rate of 8%.

This example shows that one can obtain Macaulay duration if, in the formula for average life, the total principal is replaced by the price and the principal payments at each point in time are replaced by the present values of the cash flows. Thus, Macaulay duration can be thought of as the average life of a dollar of price of the security.

Macaulay duration is often considered to be a better measure of investment life than average life. It considers the total cash flow, not just the principal component. Thus, it can be applied to derivative MBSs such as CMO residuals and interest-only STRIPS, that have no principal payments. It also recognizes the time value of money by giving greater weight to earlier cash flows.

Exhibit 25–13 shows the Macaulay durations of a new current-coupon GNMA at prepayment rates of 50% PSA, 120% PSA and 200% PSA. A comparison of Exhibit 25–10 and Exhibit 25–13 shows that the later cash flows are less significant in the calculation of duration than in the calculation of average life.

Macaulay duration (or a slight variation on it called "modified duration," which is defined later) is often used as a measure of the volatility of price with respect to changes in yield. This is appropriate as long as the cash flows are not a function of interest rates. However, the flows of an MBS depend on prepayments, which are driven to a large extent by interest rates. In the case of interest

## E X H I B I T  25–12

Calculation of Macaulay Duration

| Cash | Time | Present Value at 8% | Present Value × Time |
|------|------|---------------------|----------------------|
| $30  | 1    | $27.78              | $27.78               |
| 30   | 2    | 25.72               | 51.44                |
| 30   | 3    | 23.81               | 71.43                |
| 30   | 4    | 22.05               | 88.20                |
|      |      | Price = $99.36      | 238.85               |

$$\text{Duration} = \frac{\text{Sum of (Time} \times \text{Present Values)}}{\text{Price}} = 238.5/99.36 = 2.4 \text{ years}$$

**EXHIBIT  25–13**

Macaulay Duration for a New Current-Coupon GNMA at 50%, 120%, and 200% PSA

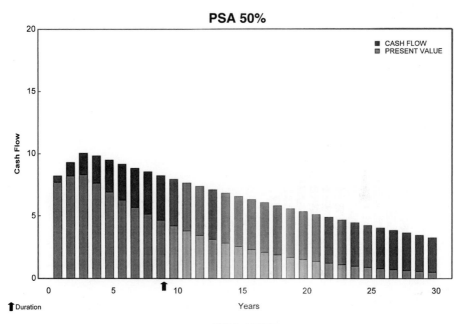

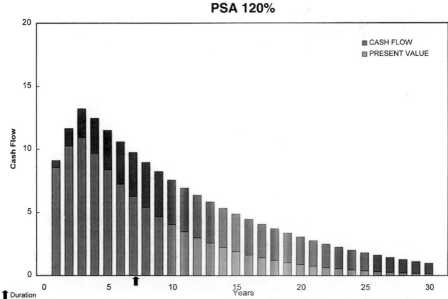

**E X H I B I T   25–13**

(*Continued*)

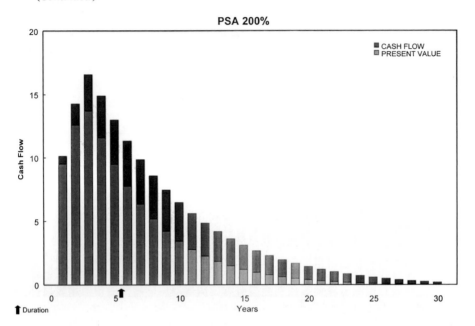

rate-dependent cash flows, great care must be taken in using Macaulay duration as a measure of price volatility.

## Price and Yield Behavior

This section will examine how the price and yield to-maturity of pass-through securities vary as interest rates vary. As discussed earlier, the cash flows from an MBS are affected by changes in interest rates because of the resulting changes in prepayment levels. This makes the price and yield characteristics of an MBS more complex than those of a standard fixed income security such as a Treasury.

### Calculation of Yield-to-Maturity

The yield-to-maturity, or yield of security is defined as the discount rate that makes the present value of the security's cash flows equal to its current price. (See the appendix for a mathematical formula for calculating yield.) For a non-callable bond, the calculation of yield is straightforward, given the price, coupon, and timing of cash flows. Even for a standard callable bond, one can calculate a yield to call or estimate the probability of calls at different points in time.

*Treasuries non Callable*

However, for an MBS there is a separate call option on each dollar of mortgage because in general a homeowner can prepay part or all of a mortgage at any time. Furthermore, because mortgages are self-amortizing, the amount redeemed if a homeowner "exercises a call" will depend on the original term, coupon, and age of the mortgage.

To calculate a yield for an MBS, a prepayment rate must be specified for each remaining month of the MBS's term. Once the prepayment rate has been chosen, cash flows can then be obtained for each month, and the yield (and other security characteristics, such as average life) can be calculated. The necessity of specifying a prepayment rate introduces an element of subjectivity into the calculation of an MBS's yield; there is no consensus on the projected payment rate of an MBS and hence no consensus on the yield.

An earlier approach to prepayment was to assume a 12-year prepaid life, but this method is not used today. MBSs are now usually priced at a specified CPR or percentage of PSA. The CPR or percentage of PSA to be used for a given MBS should be chosen using relevant mortgage characteristics and economic variables.

Exhibit 25–14 shows the projected yields to maturity of various GNMAs plotted against average lives. These are calculated using prepayment projections from the Prudential Securities Prepayment Model. This graph can be thought of as a GNMA yield curve. For comparison, the graph also shows the Treasury curve and an agency yield curve based on the averages of the yields of selected agencies of various maturities. Pass-throughs have essentially the same credit quality and liquidity as agencies, so the pass-through spread over the agencies can be thought of as compensation for prepayment uncertainty and for the relative complexity of pass-throughs compared with agencies.

**Mortgage Yield and Bond-Equivalent Yield**
Mortgage pass-through cash flows typically are paid monthly. The yield calculated from these monthly cash flows is called the mortgage yield; it implicitly assumes monthly compounding of interest. To make the yield of an MBS comparable to semi-annual pay Treasuries or corporates, the mortgage yield must be converted to a semi-annual compounding basis, or bond-equivalent yield. (See the appendix for the mathematical formula for bond-equivalent yield.) The bond-equivalent yield is higher than the mortgage yield because monthly compounding generates a higher annual yield than semi-annual compounding. Hence, to be equivalent to the mortgage yield, the semi-annual yield must be higher.

**Price Behavior as Interest Rates Vary**
The prepayment of principal affects price in different ways for different coupon mortgage securities. Discount coupon securities—those with coupons rates lower than the current coupon rate—trading below par benefit from the early return of principal at par. On the other hand, premium securities trading above

**E X H I B I T   25–14**

GNMA, Agency, and Treasury Yield Curves

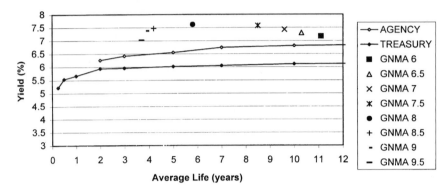

| GNMA coupon | 6.5 | 7 | 7.5 | 8 | 8.50 | 9 |
|---|---|---|---|---|---|---|
| Remaining term (years-months) | 29-08 | 29-09 | 29-10 | 29-06 | 28-00 | 28-00 |
| Price | 95-13 | 97-29+ | 100-02 | 101-27 | 103-13 | 105-02 |
| Projected prepayment rate (% PSA) | 97 | 119 | 145 | 180 | 191 | 251 |
| Average life (years) | 11.415 | 10.46 | 9.479 | 8.038 | 7.043 | 5.614 |
| Yield-to-maturity (bond equivalent) | 7.239 | 7.392 | 7.557 | 7.712 | 7.829 | 7.765 |

| GNMA coupon | 9.5 | 10 | 10.5 | 11 | 11.5 | 12 |
|---|---|---|---|---|---|---|
| Remaining term (years-months) | 25-00 | 17-04 | 16-11 | 13-01 | 12-07 | 13-06 |
| Price | 107-04 | 108-07+ | 109-22 | 111-06 | 114-12 | 116-14 |
| Projected prepayment rate (% PSA) | 282 | 295 | 316 | 363 | 380 | 379 |
| Average life (years) | 4.902 | 4.219 | 3.974 | 3.234 | 3.084 | 3.189 |
| Yield-to-maturity (bond equivalent) | 7.555 | 7.488 | 7.393 | 6.797 | 5.974 | 5.873 |

*12/13/99

par experience a negative effect from early principal prepayment. As an extreme example, if a premium MBS is bought for a price of 105 and a full prepayment of principal is made the next month, 100 is received for 105 paid a month earlier.

Exhibit 25–15 shows closing prices on December 7, 1999 for GNMA, FNMA, and FHLMS pass-throughs. Note that the slope of the graph is less steep for the higher-premium coupons. The price compression in premium–

## EXHIBIT 25–15

Prices of Pass-Through Securities

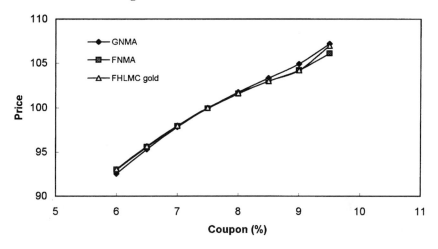

coupon mortgage securities can be explained by the fact that prepayments tend to increase the further the coupon is above the current coupon. The higher the coupon rate on the underlining security, the greater is the likelihood that the homeowner will refinance at the lower prevailing mortgage rates. Exhibit 25–15 indicates that in the opinion of the market, the extra coupon interest earned from the FNMAs and FHLMCs with higher coupons is partially canceled by faster expected prepayment levels.

Changes in the prevailing level of interest rates affect the prepayment rates of mortgage securities. As interest rates increase, prepayments tend to slow down, and as interest rates decrease, prepayments tend to increase. The interaction of interest-rate and prepayment-rate changes on the price of an MBS can be illustrated by looking at projected price paths when interest rates change. Exhibit 25–16 shows the projected price of GNMA 7.5 and 9.5 as interest rates change, assuming the yield spread to the Treasury curve remains constant. (A more complicated method of calculating price change as interest rates change will be described later, but it is useful to first understand the basic price/yield relationship described here.)

As interest rate increase, the slowdown in prepayments has an adverse price effect on the GNMA 7.5 which is priced below par. As interest rates continue to rise, prepayments on the GNMA 7.5 bottom out and become relatively insensitive to interest rates, and its price behavior is similar to that of a Treasury or corporate security. For the GNMA 9.5, which is priced above par, the slowdown in prepayments is beneficial. It reduces the size of the price decline if rates increase 100 basis points. If rates continue to increase, any further

**EXHIBIT  25–16**

Projected Price Paths of GNMA 6.5s and 8.5s

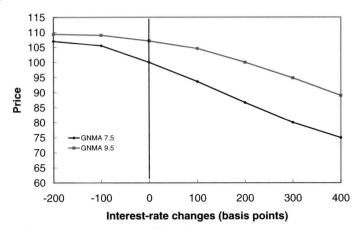

slowdown in the prepayment rate for the GNMA 9.5 is minor, and the GNMA 9.5 like the GNMA 7.5, behaves like a Treasury or corporate security. If interest rates decline, there is a sharp increase in projected prepayment rates for the GNMA 9.5 and consequently very little price appreciation for interest-rate declines of up to 200 basis points. However if rates decline further, prepayments level off, and there is more price appreciation. For the GNMA 7.5, the drag on price appreciation does not occur unless interest rates decline by over 100 basis points. The GNMA 7.5 then becomes a premium security, and there is a sharp increase in prepayments. If interest rates continue to decline, prepayments on the GNMA 7.5 begin to level off, and its price behavior is like that of the GNMA 9.5.

**Yield Behavior as Interest Rates Vary**
Exhibit 25–17 illustrates the effect of various interest-rate changes on the yields-to-maturity of GNMA 7.5 and GNMA 9.5 when price is held constant.

As interest rate increase and prepayments slow down, the yield on the discount GNMA 6.5 decreases slightly, while the yield on the premium GNMA 9.5 increases sharply and then levels off. As interest rates decrease and prepayments accelerate, there is a sharp drop in the yield of the GNMA 9.5 and a slight rise in the yield of the GNMA 6.5. The yield fluctuations are much less for the GNMA 6.5, which is priced near par, than for the premium GNMA 9.5.

**Prepayment Volatility**
In general, prepayment volatility is greatest for MBSs whose underlying mortgages have coupons between 100 and 300 basis points above current mortgage

**EXHIBIT  25–17**

Projected Yields-to-Maturity for GNMA 7.5s and 9.5s

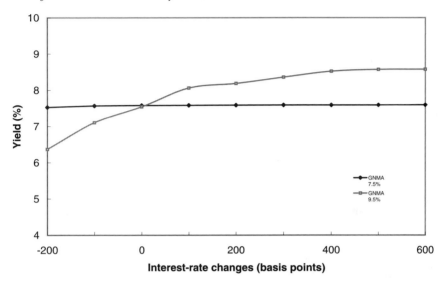

rates. At the lower end of this range, a decrease in the rates may trigger a surge in refinancings, while at the upper end, an increase in interest rates may slow down prepayments substantially. The effect of prepayments on yield will depend on the magnitude of the MBS price discount or premium; for an MBS priced at par, with no payment delay, the yield-to-maturity does not depend on the level of prepayments. Exhibit 25–18 illustrates the yield and average-life volatility of several GNMA coupons if interest rates decline or increase by 50 basis points when price is held constant. For all five coupons in Exhibit 25–18, average life increases with interest rates. The GNMA 6.5 has the highest prepayment volatility and thus experiences the largest increase in average life as mortgage rates rise. Note that higher premium coupons experience less average life change than those priced close to par. The yield change of the GNMA 7.5 is slight because it is priced close to par.

**Option-Adjusted Spread—Stochastic Valuation of Mortgage Securities**
The volatility of a mortgage security's yield and average life typically works against the investor who owns the mortgage security. That is, the actual yield realized on the security has a high probability of being less than the yield projected on the basis of a single prepayment forecast. In essence, homeowners exercise their options to prepay their mortgages at the time least favorable to the investor. For example, if the rates fall, prepayments increase, which means

**E X H I B I T   25–18**

Yield and Average-Life Volatility of GNMAs

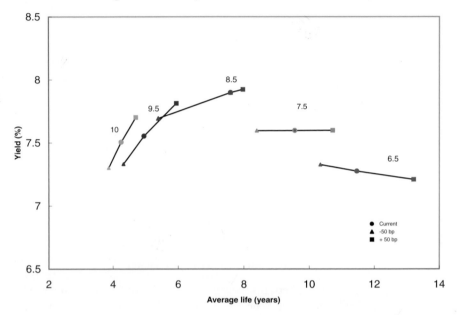

that the homeowner calls away a portion of the investor's principal, and that principal can only be reinvested at a lower rate.

In an attempt to measure this risk, various option models have been developed. The approach most commonly used is the option-adjusted spread (OAS) model. In this approach, the cost of the homeowner's prepayment option is calculated in terms of a basis-point penalty that must be subtracted from the expected yield spread on the security. The OAS method involves simulating hundreds of future interest rate paths and calculating the average impact on the security's expected yield spread. (OAS is not precisely comparable to yield spread because a different discounting method is used. OAS discounts the cash flow in each period by a yield based on the forward Treasury rate plus a constant, i.e., the OAS. In a yield-spread calculation, the cash flows are all discounted by a single yield, i.e., the security's yield-to-maturity. Hence, OAS is a spread added to the entire Treasury curve, whereas yield spread is a spread added to a single point on the Treasury curve.)

Because OAS takes into account the option component of a mortgage security, it will change less than a security's yield spread as interest rates change. In a flat yield curve, one can think of the OAS/yield spread relationship as

$$OAS = Yield - Option\ cost$$

This relationship helps to explain the fact that during market rallies yield spread on current coupon mortgages often widen. As rates fall, the option cost on a current coupon increases. That is, it moves closer to being in the money. Traders and investors adjust for this increased option cost by demanding wider spreads, which in turn keeps the OAS relatively unchanged.

## Duration and Convexity: Modified and Effective Durations

Earlier, Macaulay duration was defined as a commonly used measure of maturity for MBS. Macaulay duration, or a slightly adjusted version known as a "modified duration,"[5] is often used as a measure of the sensitivity of price to small changes in yields. This is based on the fact that if cash flows are not dependent on interest rates, then modified duration is equal to the rate of percentage change of price with respect to change in yield.

For an MBS, however, a key characteristic is the dependence of cash flows, via prepayment, on interest rates. This can make Macaulay or modified duration an inadequate or misleading measure of price sensitivity. To examine the price effect for changes in interest rates, an "effective duration" is often calculated as an alternative measurement of price sensitivity. Effective duration incorporates the changes in prepayment levels that may occur as a result of interest-rate change. (See the appendix for a mathematical definition of effective duration.)

The calculation of effective duration involves the use of our OAS model because we assume that the OAS on the security remains unchanged as interest rates move. This requirement means that the yield on the security may change by a different amount than the change in the reference Treasury curve. In essence, effective duration measures the percentage change in the price of the security for a small change in the Treasury curve. The effective durations in this report are based on a 25-basis-point parallel shift in the Treasury curve.

Exhibit 25–19 illustrates the calculation of effective duration for the GNMA 9.5. The GNMA 9.5 had underlying mortgages several hundred basis points above prevailing mortgage rates and hence had high prepayment volatility.

The exhibit shows the expected price change for a 25-basis-point parallel shift in the yield curve when OAS is held constant. For an upward shift in the curve, the simulated interest-rate paths from the OAS calculation will be higher on average, and hence prepayment speeds will be slower than in the case of a constant prepayment speed. Because premium pass-throughs such as the GNMA 9.5s benefit from slower speeds, the price decline under the constant OAS scenario is less than under the constant prepayment scenario used to calculate modified duration. In a similar fashion, faster prepayments will restrain the expected price rise in the premium GNMA 9.5 when the curve shifts. In the example in Exhibit 25–20, the GNMA 9.5 is projected to have an effective duration, or price volatility, of 2.4% per 100 basis points. This means that at current interest-

---

5. Formally, Modified duration = Macaulay duration$/(1 + y/200)$ where $y$ is the bond equivalent yield.

**EXHIBIT 25–19**

Calculation of Effective Duration

|  | Interest-Rate Change (Basis Points) | | |
|---|---|---|---|
|  | -25 | 0 | 25 |
| Pricing yield (%) | 7.305 | 7.555 | 7.805 |
| Projected prepayment rate (%PSA) | 297 | 282 | 264 |
| Price at 282% PSA | 108.0625 | 107.1250 | 106.1875 |
| Price at projected prepayment rate | 107.7656 | 107.1250 | 106.5000 |

Modified duration = Price volatility assuming no change in prepayments

3.50% = -100/Price x Change in price/Change in yield = -1/107.1250 x (106.1875-108.0625)/.50

= 3.50% per 100 bp change is yield

Effective duration = Price volatility assuming no change in OAS

2.36% = -100/Price x Change in price/Change in yield = -1/107.1250 x (106.5000 - 107.7656)/.50

= 3.36% per 100 bp change in yield

**EXHIBIT 25–20**

Modified and Effective Durations for GNMAs

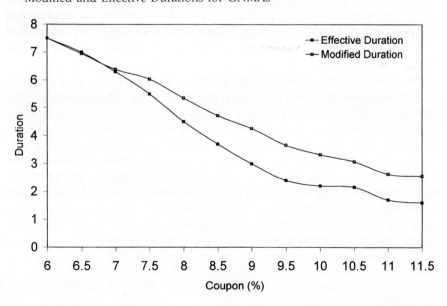

rate levels, a one-basis-point change in Treasury yields will lead to a percentage change in the price of 0.024%. This is much lower than the price volatility of 3.5% per 100 basis points given by the traditional modified calculation, which does not take into account changes in prepayments.

The example of Exhibit 25–20 indicates that while the usual duration calculation may be adequate for discount or high-premium MBSs whose prepayment levels are unlikely to change much for small changes in interest rates, it can be inadequate or even misleading for low-premium coupons, which have high prepayment volatility. An effective-duration calculation is more appropriate in such cases. This is borne out by historical studies that have shown that the price volatilities do tend to follow the pattern suggested by effective durations.

Exhibit 25–20 shows modified and effective durations for several GNMA securities. The effective durations are calculated by using 25 basis points moves in interest rates each direction. The exhibit indicates that modified duration over-estimates the price volatility of low-premium coupons. This has important implications for hedging strategies. Hedge ratios based on the use of Macaulay or modified duration to estimate price volatility will fail for mortgage coupons with high prepayment volatility. (This has been a painful lesson for many participants in the MBS markets.) It is important to look at changes in both yield and prepayment rates when calculating price volatility; effective duration provided a means for doing this. Another useful analytic tool in this context is convexity, which measures the rate of change of price volatility.

### Convexity

In mortgage analysis, considerable attention is given to the concept of convexity and in particular to the so-called negative convexity of MBSs. Convexity refers to the curvature of the price/yield curve. (See the appendix for a mathematical definition of convexity.) In other words, convexity is the rate of change of duration, that is, price volatility. If one considers duration to be the speed of price changes, then the convexity can be thought of as acceleration. The projected price paths shown in Exhibit 25–16 illustrate positive, zero and negative convexity.

A straight line has zero convexity. Thus, because the price/yield curve of the GNMA 7.5 in Exhibit 25–16 is essentially a straight line at the no change point on the horizontal axis, then the GNMA 7.5 has almost zero convexity at prevailing interest rates. This means that for small equal changes in interest rates, the price of the GNMA 7.5 will increase or decrease approximately the same amount.

Discount and high premiums MBSs, like Treasuries, tend to have positive convexity. Positive convexity implies that for small, equal, and opposite changes in interest rates, if rates decline the price increase will be more than the price decrease. This means that the rate of decrease in price slows down as interest rates increase; that is, the curve has a downward "bulge" in the middle. When interest rates rise by several hundred basis points, the GNMA 7.5 will become a deep-discount coupon and have positive convexity.

Negative convexity means that the price/yield curve flattens as interest rates decline. This is characteristic of slight-premium MBSs for which increasing prepayments place a drag on price increases as interest rates decline. Thus, for small equal changes in rates, the price is likely to decline more than it will increase. Exhibit 25–16 shows that at prevailing interest rates the GNMA 9.5 has a high degree of negative convexity whereas the GNMA 7.5 has a large convexity if interest rates decline by between 100 to 200 basis points. On the other hand, if rates rise by 100 to 200 basis points, the GNMA 9.5 will then have positive convexity. Hence negative convexity is a characteristic of low-premium MBSs.

***Calculation of Convexity***  Convexity can be estimated by considering small positive and negative shifts in yield curve (while holding OAS constant) and calculating the changes in price in both cases. Exhibit 25–21 illustrates the calculation of the convexities of a GNMA 9.5 using 25 basis point changes in interest rates.

The GNMA 9.5 has negative convexity. This can be explained by considering the likely magnitudes and effects of prepayment changes for the coupons. The GNMA 9.5 has high prepayment volatility; the increasing prepayment as interest rates decline puts a drag on price increases. The benefits of a slowdown in prepayments if interest rates increase are not sufficient to offset this price compression.

Exhibit 25–22 shows the convexities of various GNMA pass-throughs based on prices and prepayment projections. It can be seen that convexity reaches a low point at the 8 coupon and then starts increasing again. This happens because high-premium coupons, like deep-discounts, have low prepayment volatility and, hence, less negative convexity.

## EXHIBIT  25–21

Calculation of Convexity

| Change in Rate (Basis Points) | GNMA 9.5 Projected Prepayment Rate | Yield | Price | |
|---|---|---|---|---|
| -BP25 | 297 | 7.225 | 107-24 | 107.7500 |
| 0 | 282 | 7.555 | 107-04 | 107.1250 |
| 25 | 264 | 7.814 | 106-14 | 106.4375 |

Convexity = 100/Price x (Change in price if rates go down) - (Change in price if rates go up)/(Change in rates)$^2$

$$-0.9 \quad \frac{100/\text{Price} \times (107.75-107.125) - (107.1250 - 106.4375)}{(.25)^2} \qquad = -0.9 \text{ for GNMA } 9\frac{1}{2}$$

**EXHIBIT 25–22**

Convexities of GNMA Pass-Throughs

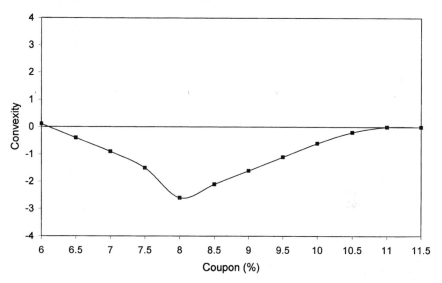

*Investment Implications of Convexity*   Positive convexity is generally a desirable characteristic in a fixed income security. However, this does not mean securities with negative convexity, such as low-premium pass-throughs, should be avoided. The market may have adjusted the prices of such securities to compensate investors for the negative convexity, making their yields sufficiently high so that they offer better value than many securities with positive convexity.

Another point that should be kept in mind is that for a given security, convexity changes with interest rates. In other words, negative convexity is a "local" property of low-premium pass-throughs; if there are substantial changes in interest rates, the low premium pass-through will become a discount or high-premium pass-through and may then have positive convexity. This is a relevant consideration if one plans to hold the security for a year or more, when the length of the holding period makes large interest-rate changes possible. The total return incorporates such factors as initial price and convexity (through the change in the price over the period) and hence will give a good indication of the value of the security.

## A Comment on the Units Used to Measure Duration and Convexity

Traditionally, duration has been measured in units of years, and convexity in (years)$^2$. This is so because Macaulay duration, which is a measure of investment life, is measured in years. Modified duration, which is used as a measure of price volatility, is closely related to Macaulay duration and therefore is also measured in years. The units of convexity result from the fact they have been defined as a weighted (the weights being the present values of the cash flows) average of the squares of the times-to-receipt of all the cash flows. However, years and (years)$^2$ are not appropriate measures of price volatility and convexity. As discussed previously, duration (or effective duration) is the percentage change in the price for a given change in yield. In the example in Exhibit 25–19, the price volatility of the GNMA 9.5 was 2.4% per 100 basis points, or 0.024% per basis point. The appropriate units for duration when it is used as a measure of price volatility are change per basis point or per 100 basis points.

Convexity is the rate of change of price volatility. The convexity of the GNMA 9.5 in Exhibit 25–21 was −.9. Analysis of the calculation in Exhibit 25–21 shows that this can be expressed as −.9% per 100 basis points. In other words, the price volatility, expressed as a percentage price change per 100 basis points, increases by −.9 for each 100-basis-point change in yield.

## RELATIVE VALUE

MBS pass-throughs are priced on a yield spread basis to U.S. treasury bonds of similar life. Like treasuries, agency pass-throughs are perceived to have no default risk, and like treasuries, pay a fixed rate of interest and enjoy a great deal of liquidity in secondary trading. On average, MBS pass-throughs are priced to yield a spread above treasuries—typically in the 100 to 200 basis point range. This is illustrated in Exhibit 25–23.

The bulk of the additional spread earned on MBS pass-throughs is due to prepayment risk. As mentioned earlier, corporate bonds are priced to yield returns greater than Treasuries to compensate investors for credit risk (probability IF principal is repaid). Agency pass-throughs, by comparison are priced to yield returns greater than treasuries to compensate investors for prepayment risk (WHEN principal is repaid). Note that not all all of the spread on an agency pass-through is due to prepayment risk. Agency pass-throughs have very small liquidity and credit premium—the bulk of the yield spread is paid to compensate the investor for prepayment risk.[6]

The prepayment risk plays an important role in not only absolute yield, but also in relative value. It is typical for investors to compare bond returns on a spread to treasury basis. A 7.5% GNMA may have an average life of 10 years, but theoretically could prepay completely tomorrow or extend out many years beyond the 10 year assumed average life. Investors will look at a wide range of

---

6. Since MBS pass-throughs are also used as collateral for CMO's (see chapter 26, market makers will model and compute net proceeds from hypothetical CMO deals to determine the "creation value" of certain pass-through CMO issue. This creation value, coupled with supply (or lack thereof), can affect demand (and price) of agency pass-throughs.

**E X H I B I T    25–23**

Average Spread 30-Yr Mortgages

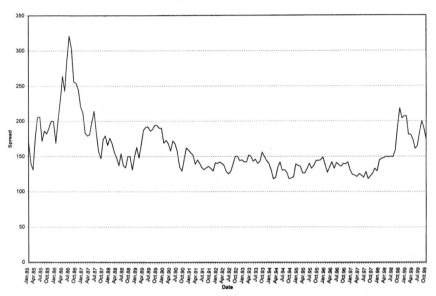

speeds, yields and spreads under those speeds to see how the bond performs vs Treasuries.

Another issue relating to mortgage prepayments is reinvestment risk. Assume an investor with a ten year investment horizon knows that she can buy a 6% yielding 10 year Treasury. Alternatively, she can buy a bond that matures in 9 years, knowing that she will have to reinvest the principal paid in year nine for one year. If she buys the second bond, she is implicitly trading some other aspect of the bond (generally yield) for accepting the reinvestment risk. This is the topic of the next section.

## Total Holding-period Returns

Fixed income securities are generally priced and traded by yield-to-maturity. However, from the inventor's point of view, yield-to-maturity can be an unsatisfactory measure of the likely return from the security for two important reasons:

- The yield-to-maturity assumes that all the cash flows are reinvested at a rate equal to the yield.

- It assumes that the security is held until maturity, thus ignoring the capital gain or loss from selling the security at the end of holding period.

The total return (or the horizon or holding-period return) measures the actual return over a specified holding period. This return is composed of three elements.

- The cash flows from the security during the holding period.

- The reinvestment income from the cash flows from the time each cash flow is received to the end of the holding period for specified levels of reinvestment rates that prevailed during the holding period.

- The gain or loss from selling the security at the end of the period. The proceeds from the sale are equal to the price at the end of the period multiplied by the amount of principal still outstanding at the time, plus any accrued interest.

### Calculation of Total Return

Exhibit 25–24 illustrates the calculation of the total return from holding a new GNMA for six months. The security is purchased on May 14 at a price of 100-14, that is $100^{14}\!/_{32}$ or $100.4375 is paid for each $100 of face value, with settlement on June 16. The security is sold on December 10 for a price of 100-17, with settlement on December 16. Because the security is actually transferred between the buyer and the seller and cash is exchanged on the settlement dates, these dates should be used as the beginning and the end of the holding period. The first cash flow is received on July 15 and constitutes interest and principal for the month of June. The sixth and final cash flow is received on December 15. All cash flows (including reinvestment income) are assumed to be reinvested each month at a reinvestment rate of 3%. A prepayment rate of 120% PSA is assumed.

With these assumptions, the actual return from holding the security over the six months is 3.570% or, stated as an annual rate, 7.140%. The effective annual return, with a six-month compounding frequency, is 7.267%. The corresponding bond-equivalent (semi-annual compounding) rate of return is 7.140%.

### Assumptions Used in Calculating Total Returns

The calculation of a projected rate of return over a holding period requires assumptions about the value of three major determinations of the holding-period return: prepayments rates, reinvestment rates, and the selling price at the end of the holding period. The question of prepayment assumptions was addressed in the prepayment behavior and cash flow section. Here the other two assumptions are discussed.

***Reinvestment Rates***   There are several approaches for determining appropriate reinvestment rates. The calculation in Exhibit 25–24 uses a constant reinvestment rate of 3% with monthly rollover of accumulated cash flows. This method

**E X H I B I T    25–24**

Calculation of Total Return for a GNMA 7

Buy:   $1 million face of GNMA 7s, with a remaining term of 29 years–9 months
       on May 14 at 100-14.
       Settlement is June 16.
Amount paid:                       $1MM × 100-14 = $1,004,375
                        + 15 days of accrued interest = $   2,917
                                            Total    $1,007,292

**Cash Flows**

| Date | Remaining Balance | Interest | Scheduled Principal | Prepaid[a] Principal | Reinvestment[b] Income | Total Cash Flow |
|------|-------------------|----------|---------------------|----------------------|------------------------|-----------------|
| 7/15 | 998,266 | 5,833 | 758 | 976 | 1 | 7,568 |
| 8/15 | 996,404 | 5,824 | 762 | 1,100 | 20 | 7,706 |
| 9/15 | 994,280 | 5,812 | 765 | 1,359 | 40 | 7,976 |
| 10/15 | 991,999 | 5,800 | 770 | 1,511 | 59 | 8,140 |
| 11/15 | 989,439 | 5,787 | 773 | 1,787 | 82 | 8,429 |
| 12/15 | 986,846 | 5,771 | 777 | 1,816 | 100 | 8,464 |
| Totals: | 986,846 | 34,827 | 4,605 | 8,549 | 302 | 48,283 |

Sell:  Remaining $986,846 face value of GNMA 7 on December 10 for settlement
       on December 16.

                       Remaining balance × Price = $992,089
Sale proceeds:         +15 days of accrued interest = $   2,878

                                        Total    $994,967

Total return over holding period = $\dfrac{\text{Sale proceeds} - \text{Price paid} + \text{Total cash flows}}{\text{Price paid}}$

$$= \frac{994{,}967 - 1{,}007{,}292 + 48{,}283}{1{,}007{,}292}$$

$$= 0.3570 \text{ or } 3.570\%$$

Total return of an annualized basis = 3.570% × (12/6) = 7.140%

Effective annual return with six-month compounding frequency

$$= \left(1 + \frac{.0714}{12/6}\right)^{12/6} - 1 = 7.26\%$$

Total return on a semiannual compounding basis

$$= 2\left[\left(1 + \frac{7{,}267}{100}\right)^{12/6} - 1\right] = 7.140\%$$

[a] Constant prepayment rate of 120% PSA is assumed.
[b] Assumed reinvestment rate is 3%

is similar to assuming that all cash flows are deposited in a short-term cash or money market account. Under this method, the money market reinvestment rate can be allowed to change over the course of the holding period in line with projected changes in the yield level used in calculating the selling price of the security. For example, if the initial reinvestment rate is 3%, and it is assumed that yield levels will increase by 100 basis point over the holding period, then the reinvestment rate could be allowed to increase gradually to 4% over the holding period.

A second approach that is sometimes used is to reinvest each cash flow from the time it is received to the end of the holding period at a rate chosen according to the length of the reinvestment period. For example, if a cash flow is received one year before the end of the holding period, it may be reinvested at the one year Treasury rate, rather than at a short-term money market rate. However, this assumes that the end of the holding period is known from the start. In practice, an investor does not generally know the exact time at which the security will be sold.

A third approach is to assume all cash flows are reinvested in securities of the same type and to assume a reinvestment rate close to the yield of the security. However, this approach raises questions about the meaning of the holding-period return because at the end of the period some of the cash flow received is tied up in new securities.

**Selling Price at the Holding Period**    Choosing the price of an MBS at the end of the holding period is perhaps the assumption most open to question. In the example in Exhibit 25–24, a known horizon selling price was assumed for illustrative simplicity. The standard approach in calculating projected returns is to assume a given change in yield levels and then calculate the price at the end of the holding period by discounting future cash flows at the assumed horizon yield. However, in projecting prepayment and reinvestment rates and in comparing the total return of an MBS with a Treasury, assumptions must be made about the relationship between changes in the yield levels of MBSs and changes in interest rates in general. A common assumption is a parallel shift in interest rates, so that short-term, MBS, and Treasury yields all change by the same amount. It is important to realize that this is just an assumption, and that yield spreads of MBSs to Treasuries may widen or narrow. A more recent approach that has become popular is to hold the OAS of the security constant throughout the holding period.

As this discussion suggests, the calculation of a holding-period return requires important assumptions about reinvestment rates and yields used to calculate the redemption value at the end of the period. This is true for all securities, not just MBSs. However, for MBSs there is the additional assumption concerning the projected return, so it is important that these assumptions be understood when evaluating securities on a total-return basis over a holding period.

## Variations of Total Returns with Holding Period And Rate Changes

Exhibit 25–25 shows the total returns for one-year and five-year holding periods under various interest rate changes for a GNMA 7.5 and GNMA 9.5. A parallel shift in the Treasury curve and a constant OAS is assumed. The initial reinvestment rate is assumed to be 6.46% with all cash flows reinvested monthly. Interest rates are assumed to change uniformly over the year for the one-year horizon and a rate of 100 basis points per year for the five-year horizon.

As indicated in Exhibit 25–25, the one-year returns depend on interest-rate changes to a greater degree than do the five-year returns. There are two reasons for this:

- The coupon and reinvestment income constitutes a much larger proportion of the total return over the five-year holding period, thus reducing the importance of the change in price of the security due to changes in interest rates.

- A larger proportion of the principal will pay down over the five-year period, because of both scheduled payment and prepayments. This also reduces the importance of price changes, particularly in a declining interest rate environment when prepayments will be high.

The lackluster performance of both securities over the five-year period in the declining interest-rate scenarios is explained by the second point. The high

**EXHIBIT   25–25**

One-Year and Five-Year Holding-Period Returns for GNMA 7.5s and 9.5s

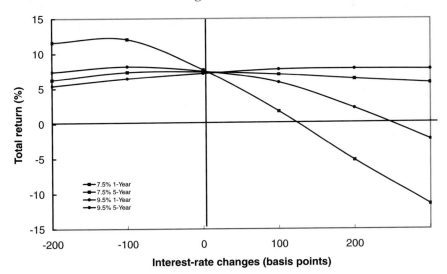

prepayment levels result in a low remaining balance at the time of the sale. This reduces the benefits from price appreciation, which in any case has become compressed by the high prepayments (as illustrated in Exhibit 25–16).

Over the one-year holding period, the GNMA 7.5, like other fixed income securities, perform poorly if interest rates increase, and performs well if interest rates decline (although there is some effect of price comparison and high prepayment if interest rates decline by 200 basis points). The GNMA 9.5 does slightly better than the GNMA 7.5 if rates increase, due to the benefits of a slowdown in prepayments for the premium GNMA 9.5. In the declining-interest-rate scenarios, the high prepayment and the resulting price compression cause the GNMA 9.5 return to increase much more slowly than the GNMA 7.5 return after interest rates have declined by more than 100 basis points.

## SUMMARY

The mortgage pass-through market is a firmly entrenched segment of the bond market, and offers investors returns between 100 and 200 basis points over comparable Treasuries with comparable credit risk. To earn these returns, an investor must be willing to invest effort to understand both the quantitative aspects and the macro-economic variables affecting mortgage value.

This chapter has attempted to describe both the quantitative aspects of mortgage pass-through analysis and the macroeconomic issue of forecasting prepayments. In return for a little extra quantitative analysis, investment in mortgage pass-throughs gives the investor a security that (relative to corporates), requires no ongoing credit analysis.

In addition, the data needed to analyze mortgage pass-throughs, once held only by dealers and specialized research boutiques, can now be obtained more easily through on-line sources. As the cost of computational tools drops and the availability of economic data increases, access to informed decision-making exists for the potential investor. The higher potential returns of mortgage pass-throughs, coupled with increasing availability of data and tools for analysis, makes the mortgage pass-through market an attractive opportunity for investors.

**APPENDIX**

# Mortgage Mathematics

## MORTGAGE CASH FLOW WITHOUT PREPAYMENTS

### Monthly Payment

For a level-payment mortgage, the constant monthly payment is

$$M_n = \frac{B_0 \left(\dfrac{G}{1200}\right)\left(1 + \dfrac{G}{1200}\right)^N}{\left(1 + \dfrac{G}{1200}\right)^N - 1}$$

where

$M_n$ = Monthly payment for month $n$
$B_0$ = Original balance
$G$ = Gross coupon rate (%)
$N$ = Original term in months (e.g., 360)

### Remaining Balance

The remaining balance after $n$ months is

$$B_n = \frac{B_0 \left[\left(1 + \dfrac{G}{1200}\right)^N - \left(1 + \dfrac{G}{1200}\right)^n\right]}{\left(1 + \dfrac{G}{1200}\right)^N - 1}$$

where $B_n$ = Remaining balance at the end of month $n$.

### Principal Payment

The amount of principal paid in month $n$ is given by

$$P_n = \frac{B_0 \left(\dfrac{G}{1200}\right)\left(1 + \dfrac{G}{1200}\right)^{n-1}}{\left(1 + \dfrac{G}{1200}\right)^N - 1}$$

where $P_n$ = Principal paid in month $n$.

## Interest Payment

The amount of interest paid in month $n$ can be written as

$$I_n = \frac{B_0 \left(\frac{G}{1200}\right) \left[\left(1 + \frac{G}{1200}\right)^N - \left(1 + \frac{G}{1200}\right)^{n-1}\right]}{\left(1 + \frac{G}{1200}\right)^N - 1} = B_{n-1}\left(\frac{G}{1200}\right)$$

where $I_n$ = Interest paid in month $n$.

It should be noted that

$$G = S + C$$

where

$S$ = Service fee (%) and
$C$ = Security coupon rate (%), so Servicing Amount $= [S/(C + S)]I_n$.

Therefore, the cash flow to the security holder in month $n$ is given by

$$\text{CF}_n = P_n + I_n - \text{Servicing amount} = P_n + \left(\frac{C}{C + S}\right)I_n$$

## PREPAYMENT MEASURING CONVENTIONS

For a given pool of mortgages, let

$B_n$ = Remaining principal balance per dollar or mortgage at the end of month $n$ if there are no prepayments
$C_n$ = Pool factor (i.e., actual remaining principal balance per dollar of mortgage) at the end of month $n$

Let $Q_n = C_n/B_n$. If one thinks of the pool as consisting of a very large number of SI mortgages, each of which can terminate separately, then $Q_n$ represents the percentage of mortgages remaining at the end of month $n$. Then

Percentage of initial balance that has been prepaid $= 1 - Q_n$

For month $n$, the single monthly mortality, or SMM, stated as a decimal, is given by

SMM = Proportion of $1 mortgages outstanding at the beginning of the month that are prepaid during the month

$$= \frac{Q_{n-1} - Q_n}{Q_{n-1}} = 1 - \frac{Q_n}{Q_{n-1}}$$

For the period from month $m$ to month $n$, the constant SMM rate that is equivalent to the actual prepayments experienced is given by

$$(1 - \text{SMM})^{n-m} = \frac{Q_n}{Q_m}$$

That is,

$$\text{SMM} = 1 - \left(\frac{Q_n}{Q_m}\right)^{1/(n-m)}$$

The conditional prepayment rate, or CPR (also expressed as a decimal), is the SMM expressed as an annual rate, and is given by

$$1 - \text{CPR} = (1 - \text{SMM})^{12}$$
$$\text{CPR} = 1 - (1 - \text{SMM})^{12}$$

The SMM can therefore be expressed as

$$\text{SMM} = 1 - (1 - \text{CPR})^{1/12}$$

## Percentage of PSA

If a mortgage prepays at a rate of 100% of PSA, the CPR for the month when the mortgage is $n$ months old is

$$\text{CPR} = 6\% \times \frac{n}{30} \qquad \text{if } n \leq 30$$
$$= 6\% \qquad \text{if } n > 30$$
$$= 6\% \times \min\left(1, \frac{n}{30}\right) \qquad \text{for any } n$$

For a general prepayment rate of $x$ percent of PSA, for age $n$,

$$\text{CPR} = 6\% \times \frac{x}{100} \times \frac{n}{30} \qquad \text{if } n \leq 30$$
$$= 6\% \times \frac{x}{100} \qquad \text{if } n > 30$$
$$= 6\% \times \frac{x}{100} \times \min\left(1, \frac{n}{30}\right) \qquad \text{for any } n$$

Conversely, if a mortgage of age $n$ months prepays at a given CPR, the PSA rate for that month is given by

$$\% \text{ of PSA} = \text{CPR} \times \frac{100}{6} \times \frac{30}{n} \qquad \text{if } n \leq 30$$
$$= \text{CPR} \times \frac{100}{6} \qquad \text{if } n > 30$$
$$= \text{CPR} \times \frac{100}{6} \times \max\left(1, \frac{30}{n}\right) \qquad \text{for any } n$$

## MORTGAGE CASH FLOW WITH PREPAYMENTS

Let $\hat{M}_n$, $\hat{P}_n$, $\hat{I}_n$, and $\hat{B}_n$ denote the monthly scheduled payment, scheduled principal, interest, and remaining (end-of-month) balance for month $n$ when prepayments are included. Let $\mathrm{SMM}_n$ be the prepayment rate in month $n$, stated as a decimal, and let

$$Q_n = (1 - \mathrm{SMM}_n)(1 - \mathrm{SMM}_{n-1}) \ldots (1 - \mathrm{SMM}_1)$$

The *total scheduled monthly payment* in month $n$ is given by

$$\hat{M}_n = \frac{\hat{B}_{n-1}\left(\dfrac{G}{1200}\right)\left(1 + \dfrac{G}{1200}\right)^{N-n+1}}{\left(1 + \dfrac{G}{1200}\right)^{N-n+1} - 1} = M_n Q_{n-1}$$

The *scheduled principal* portion of this payment is given by

$$\hat{P}_n = \frac{\hat{B}_{n-1}\left(\dfrac{G}{1200}\right)}{\left(1 + \dfrac{G}{1200}\right)^{N-n+1} - 1} = P_n Q_{n-1}$$

The *interest* portion is given by

$$\hat{I}_n = \hat{B}_{n-1}\left(\frac{G}{1200}\right) = I_n Q_{n-1}$$

The *unscheduled principal payment* in month $n$ is written as

$$\mathrm{PR}_n = (\hat{B}_{n-1} - \hat{P}_n)\mathrm{SMM}_n$$

The *remaining balance* is given by

$$\hat{B}_n = \hat{B}_{n-1} - \hat{P}_n - \mathrm{PR}_n = B_n Q_n$$

The total cash flow to the investor is

$$\hat{CF}_n = \hat{P}_n + \mathrm{PR}_n + \left(\frac{C}{C + S}\right)\hat{I}_n$$

## AVERAGE LIFE

Average life assigns weights to principal paydowns according to their arrival dates.

$$\text{Average Life (in years)} = \frac{1}{12} \sum_{t=1}^{N} \frac{(t + \alpha - 1)(\text{Principal}_t)}{\sum_{t=1}^{N} \text{Principal}_t}$$

where

$t$ = Time subscript, $t = 1, \ldots N$
$\text{Principal}_t$ = Principal arriving at time $t$
$N$ = Number of months until last principal cash flow comes in
$\alpha$ = Days between settlement date and first cash flow date, divided by 30 (i.e., the fraction of a month between settlement date and first cash flow date)

## MACAULAY DURATION

Duration assigns time weights to the present values of all cash flows.

$$\text{Maculay duration (in years)} = \frac{1}{12} \sum_{t=1}^{N} \frac{\dfrac{(t + \alpha - 1)C(t)}{(1 + r/1200)^{t+\alpha-1}}}{\displaystyle\sum_{t=1}^{N} \frac{C(t)}{(1 + r/1200)^{t+\alpha-1}}}$$

where

$C(t)$ = Cash flow at time $t$
$r$ = Cash flow yield of mortgage (%)

## CASH FLOW YIELD

To obtain the cash flow yield, equate the present value of the security's cash flows on the settlement date to its initial price $P$ plus its accrued interest $I$.

$$P + I = \sum_{t=1}^{N} \frac{C(t)}{(1 + r/1200)^{t+\alpha-1}}$$

This equation is solved iteratively for $r$. The solution is called the *mortgage yield*.

## BOND-EQUIVALENT YIELD

The interest on a mortgage security is compounded monthly, whereas the interest on bonds such as Treasuries and corporates is compounded semiannually. The compounding frequency is reflected in the yield of a security. Therefore, to make mortgage yields and bond yields comparable, the yield of a mortgage is normally converted to a bond-equivalent yield, that is, a yield based on semiannual compounding of the mortgage's interest payments.

A yield based on monthly compounding can be converted to a bond-equivalent yield and vice versa as follows:

$r$ = Mortgage yield based on monthly compounding (%)

$y$ = Bond-equivalent yield (%)

$$y = 200 \left[ \left( 1 + \frac{r}{1200} \right)^6 - 1 \right]$$

$$r = 1200 \left[ \left( 1 + \frac{y}{200} \right)^{1/6} - 1 \right]$$

## TOTAL RETURN

The total return over a holding period $h$ (percent) is calculated as

$$y_h = \frac{\begin{array}{c} \text{Sales} \\ \text{proceeds} \end{array} - \begin{array}{c} \text{Total} \\ \text{price} \\ \text{paid} \end{array} + \begin{array}{c} \text{Total net cash flow} \\ \text{received during} \\ \text{the holding period} \end{array} + \begin{array}{c} \text{Total reinvestment} \\ \text{income during} \\ \text{the holding period} \end{array}}{\text{Total price paid}} \times 100$$

The bond-equivalent total return rate $y_{BE}$ is given by

$$\left( 1 + \frac{y_h}{100} \right)^{12/h} = \left( 1 + \frac{y_{BE}}{200} \right)^2$$

## MODIFIED DURATION

Modified duration is given by

$$\text{Modified duration} = \frac{\text{Macaulay duration}}{1 + y/200}$$

where $y$ = Bond-equivalent yield (%).

## CHAPTER 26

# COLLATERALIZED MORTGAGE OBLIGATIONS

**Mortgage Research Group***
Lehman Brothers Inc.

## INTRODUCTION

The U.S. mortgage-backed securities (MBS) market has grown significantly in the last 20 years. At the end of 1980, approximately $111 billion MBS were outstanding; by the end of 1999, the amount had grown to more than $2.2 trillion. Much of this growth has come in the form of collateralized mortgage obligations (CMOs) and real estate mortgage investment conduits (REMICs),[1] structures that significantly broadened the investor base for mortgage-backed securities by offering near-U.S. Treasury credit quality, customized performance characteristics, attractive yields across a range of maturities, and a variety of risk/return profiles to fit investors' needs. CMOs currently account for 40% of all fixed-rate mortgage-backed securities outstanding.

Throughout the 1970s and early 1980s, most mortgage-backed securities were issued in pass-through form. Pass-throughs, which are participations in the cash flows from pools of individual home mortgages, have long final maturities and the potential for early partial repayment of principal. These securities primarily appeal to investors willing to accept long and uncertain investment horizons in exchange for relatively high yields and credit quality.

In 1983, a dramatic fall in mortgage rates and a surging housing market caused mortgage originations to double. Much of this production was sold in the capital markets; pass-through issuance jumped from $53 billion in 1982 to $84 billion. To accommodate this surge in supply, financial innovators designed a security that would broaden the existing MBS investor base. In mid-1983, the

---

*The original author of this chapter was Chris Ames. The chapter was updated by Jeffrey K. Mudrick, Vice President, Mortgage Research, Lehman Brothers.

1. Although CMOs and REMICs have different tax and regulatory characteristics for issuers, there is little difference between them for the investor. In practice, the market uses the terms interchangeably, and the term CMO is used generically in this chapter. A detailed discussion of the differences between the two is described later in this chapter.

Federal Home Loan Mortgage Corporation (Freddie Mac, or FHLMC) issued the first CMO, a $1 billion, three-class structure that offered short-, intermediate-, and long-term securities produced from the cash flows of a pool of mortgages. This instrument allowed more investors to become active in the MBS market. For instance, banks could participate in the market more efficiently by buying short-term mortgage securities to match their short-term liabilities (deposits).

The CMO market evolved rapidly, growing in size and complexity. Annual issuance of agency CMOs rose steadily, from $5 billion in 1983 to a peak of $324 billion in 1993. CMO issuance fell from 1994–96 for a variety of reasons. Sharply higher mortgage rates curtailed refinancing activity and resulted in lower MBS collateral issuance. With lower prepayment volatility, many mortgage securities investors chose to hold pass-throughs instead of CMOs. At the same time, bank demand for CMOs softened as lending activity finally began to rise after the credit crunch years of 1991–93. Many of the hedge funds that had been buyers of the more high risk and high-yielding tranches turned to other investments.

Following the 1994–96 downtrend, investor interest in CMOs rebounded sharply in 1997. Agency CMO issuance jumped from $50 billion in 1996 to $150 billion in 1997 and $200 billion in 1998. The resurgence of demand for CMOs was linked to two primary factors: (1) dealers simplified structures to enhance liquidity, and (2) bank demand surged as interest rates descended to all-time lows. Banks, typically buyers of first-call CMO tranches, faced greater requirements for replacement assets as mortgage paydowns accelerated in the 1997–98 prepayment wave. Following the liquidity crisis in the fall of 1998, hedge funds have played a more limited role in CMO issuance, while traditional CMO investors like financial institutions, insurance companies and government sponsored enterprises have remained the primary participants.

Currently, over 40% of all 30-year FHLMC and Federal National Mortgage Association (FNMA) pass-throughs are pledged as collateral for CMOs. More recently, CMOs backed by individual mortgages and issued by nonagency entities (known as whole-loan or private label CMOs) have become a significant market in their own right, and Lehman Brothers' estimate of the balance of whole loan CMOs outstanding as of November 1999 is approximately $280 billion.

The thrust in the CMO market has been the development of innovative structures to meet the needs of institutional investors and broaden the investor base for mortgage-backed securities. For example, demand from traditional corporate bond investors for CMO bonds with insulation from prepayment volatility led to the creation of planned amortization classes (PACs) and targeted amortization classes (TACs). Regulatory pressures on banks and thrifts led to the creation of very accurately defined maturity (VADM) bonds that were guaranteed not to extend past a given date. Growing interest from overseas investors gave rise to floating-rate bonds indexed to the London interbank offered rate

(LIBOR). Increased investor sophistication and technological breakthroughs have created a large market for derivative securities: interest- and principal-only bonds (IOs, POs), inverse floaters, and others. A broad range of products is now available to suit almost any investor preference.

This chapter explains how CMOs are structured and defines the major types of securities available. It also describes the evolving CMO regulatory environment, PAC band drift, the pricing relationship between CMOs and collateral, some valuation techniques employed by CMO investors, and trading conventions.

## PASS-THROUGHS AND WHOLE LOANS: THE BUILDING BLOCKS OF CMOS

In order to develop realistic expectations about the performance of a CMO bond, an investor must first evaluate the underlying collateral, since its performance will determine the timing and size of the cash flows reallocated by the CMO structure. Agency and whole-loan CMOs have distinct collateral, credit, and prepayment characteristics.

### Collateral

Individual home mortgages are the underlying collateral and source of cash flow for CMOs. In the case of agency CMOs, these mortgages are already pooled and securitized in pass-through form. The mortgages backing an agency pass-through are of similar size, age, and underwriting quality and have similar rates. All principal and interest cash flows generated by the underlying mortgages, including any prepayments, are channeled to investors, net of a servicing spread (a small portion of each month's interest payment paid to the institution that collects and distributes the mortgage payments). Pass-through investors share in the cash flows on a pro rata basis.

Whole-loan CMO issuers do not take the interim step of creating a pass-through security from a pool of individual mortgages; instead, they create a structure directly based on the cash flows of a group of mortgages. Whole-loan pools, like agency pass-throughs, usually contain mortgages of similar underwriting quality, age, and rate (the range of ages and rates is often somewhat wider for whole-loan pools than for agency pass-throughs). The most common distinguishing characteristic of whole loans is their size. The agencies accept only mortgages below a certain size (currently $252,700 for FNMA and FHLMC and $219,849 for GNMA); larger loans, known as jumbo loans, make up the primary collateral for whole-loan CMOs.

# Credit

GNMA is a U.S. government agency, and FHLMC and FNMA are government-sponsored enterprises. All three entities guarantee the full and timely[2] payment of all principal and interest due from pass-throughs issued under their names. GNMA securities, like U.S. Treasury securities, are backed by the full faith and credit of the U.S. government. FNMA and FHLMC, although not government agencies, are federally chartered corporations, and the market assumes an implicit U.S. government guarantee backing the agency guarantee. Securities issued by all three entities are called *agency securities.*

Although whole loans do not carry agency guarantees against default, they generally adhere to agency underwriting standards for types of documentation required, loan-to-value ratios, and income ratios. In addition, the rating agencies require significant levels of credit enhancement[3] to obtain a triple- or double-A rating. The combination of collateral quality and structural features make it highly unlikely that investors in senior classes of whole-loan CMOs will sustain credit-related losses.

# Prepayments

Expected prepayment behavior is a critical factor in evaluating CMO collateral. Three collateral characteristics are necessary for evaluating collateral from a prepayment perspective: issuer/guarantor, gross weighted average coupon (WAC), and weighted average loan age (WALA) or weighted average maturity (WAM). The issuer/guarantor is important because of the details known about borrowers within different programs. For example, GNMAs are backed by loans insured by the Federal Housing Administration (FHA) or guaranteed by the Veterans Administration (VA). Borrowers under these programs tend to be less mobile than non-FHA/VA (conventional[4]) borrowers, and therefore GNMA prepayments have been slower and more stable than conventional prepayments. Whole loans, on the other hand, tend to be larger and therefore represent more wealthy or sophisticated borrowers: in falling rate environments, they have prepaid approximately 1.5–2 times faster than comparable coupon conventionals.

---

2. Early FHLMC pass-throughs, known as 75-day delay pass-throughs, carry a guarantee of full and timely payment of interest and eventual payment of principal (after disposal of the foreclosed property). FHLMC CMOs backed by these securities carry the same guarantee as the underlying pass-throughs.

3. Common whole-loan CMO credit enhancements are senior/subordinated structures and third-party pool insurance. These are described in Chapter 22.

4. A conventional mortgage is any mortgage not FHA-insured or VA-guaranteed. In practice, the market uses the term *conventional* to group loans eligible for securitization under FHLMC and FNMA programs since securities from these agencies are usually backed by non-FHA/VA mortgages.

*average coupon of rate*

Gross WAC is the average of the interest rates of the mortgages backing a structure before adjusting for the servicing fee. Since the actual mortgage rate determines a borrower's refinancing incentive, gross WAC is a better indicator of prepayment potential than the net coupon of the collateral. Finally, loan age is important in determining short-term prepayments. The best measure of age is WALA, which tracks the age of the underlying mortgages. If WALA is not available, then taking the original term of the mortgages and subtracting the WAM will give an approximation.

## CMO STRUCTURES

In a CMO, cash flows from one or more mortgage pass-throughs or a pool of mortgages are reallocated to multiple classes with different priority claims. The CMO is self-supporting, with the cash flows from the collateral always able to meet the cash-flow requirements of the CMO classes under any possible prepayment scenario. The CMO creation process is a dynamic one. This chapter describes the most common types of CMO classes, but dealers will frequently tailor bonds to fit investors' specific needs.

The following general points are important for any discussion of CMO structures:

- CMOs issued by FNMA and FHLMC (known collectively as conventional CMOs) carry the same guarantee as conventional pass-throughs, and CMOs issued by GNMA carry the same guarantee as GNMA pass-throughs. Both FNMA and FHLMC are authorized to issue CMOs with GNMA pass-throughs as collateral. The guarantee for a FNMA- or FHLMC-issued CMO backed by GNMA collateral is the same as that for a conventional CMO. Since credit risk is not an issue for agency CMOs, there is no need for credit enhancements in the structures.

- Whole-loan CMOs do not carry government default guarantees and are therefore usually rated by the bond rating agencies. A variety of credit enhancement techniques are employed so that most or all bonds in a structure receive a AAA rating. The most common technique today is the senior/subordinated structure, with senior bonds generally rated AAA and layers of subordinated bonds receiving lower investment- or noninvestment-grade ratings.

- Most CMO classes pay interest monthly, based on the current face amount of the class, even if it is not currently paying down principal.

- Most CMO classes have a principal lockout period during which only interest payments are received. The payment window is the period during which principal payments are received. In most cases, the lockout period and the payment window are not absolute but are affected by prepayments on the underlying collateral.

- CMO classes are structured with specific cash flow profiles and investment terms based on an assumed prepayment rate. This assumed rate, which represents the market's current expectation of future prepayments on the collateral, is known as the pricing speed.

- CMOs can be structured from collateral of any maturity. The examples that follow focus on 30-year collateral, but in the last few years CMOs have been backed by 20- and 15-year fixed-rate and 5-and 7-year balloon collateral, depending on the supply and cost of the collateral and the demand for CMOs with the particular characteristics imparted by the collateral.

CMO structures are of two major types: One provides for the redirection of principal payments only, and the other for redirection of interest as well as principal. Sequential-pay, PAC/companion, and TAC/companion structures redirect principal and are the starting point for all CMOs.

## Sequential-Pay Classes

The primary purpose of the first CMOs was to bring a broader range of maturity choices to the MBS market. These CMOs—called sequential-pay, plain vanilla, or clean structures—reallocate collateral principal payments sequentially to a series of bonds. All initial principal amortization and prepayments from the collateral are paid to the shortest maturity class, or tranche, until it is fully retired; then principal payments are redirected to the next shortest class. This process continues until all classes are paid down. Exhibit 26–1 demonstrates

**EXHIBIT   26–1**

Principal Plows from a Four-Tranche Sequential-Pay Structure ($1 Million 7.5% Pool at 185% PSA)

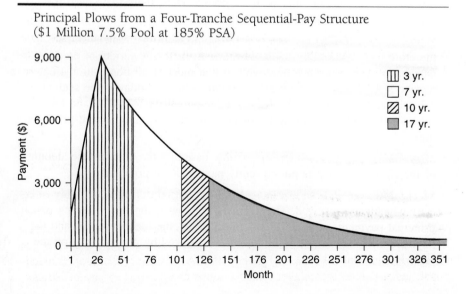

how the principal flows of a $1 million pool of FNMA 7.5s would be distributed in a sequential-pay structure if the collateral prepaid consistently at 185% PSA. In this example, owners of the first class, identified as a three-year class due to its weighted average life of 3.0 years, receive all principal flows from month 1 until month 64, when their principal balance is $0. Investors who own the second class (the seven-year) receive principal flows from month 65 to month 107. Owners of the 10-year class receive principal from month 108 to month 134, and investors in the final class receive the remaining principal flows. The amount of time that each class is outstanding, as well as the months that principal payments begin and end, vary as actual prepayment experience varies from the assumed prepayment rate.

With the creation of the sequential-pay structure, capital market participants with short investment horizons were able to enter the MBS market because they could buy bonds that more closely matched their desired terms. Investors with long-term horizons also benefited because they were insulated from prepayments during the early years of a pool's life.

## Planned Amortization Classes

In 1986, after a period of substantial interest-rate declines and the resulting surge of mortgage refinancing activity and prepayments, issuers began producing prepayment-protected bonds called *planned amortization classes* (PACs). These structures offered substantial protection from the reinvestment risk and weighted average-life volatility associated with prepayments.

PACs have a principal payment schedule (similar to a sinking fund mechanism) that can be maintained over a range of prepayment rates. This schedule is based on the minimum amount of principal cash flow produced by the collateral at two prepayment rates known as the *PAC bands*. For example, if the PAC bands were 95% PSA and 240% PSA, a PAC principal payment schedule could be constructed equal to the shaded area in Exhibit 26–2. The minimum amount of principal produced in the early months follows the principal payment path of the lower band (95% PSA), and after 116 months (where the two lines on the graph intersect), the schedule is constrained by the upper band (240% PSA) because principal has paid off more quickly under this scenario.

The total principal flow available under the PAC schedule determines the original amount of PACs in a structure. (In this example, PACs represent 70% of the structure.) If wider bands are chosen, the derived PAC schedule will be smaller; that is, there will be fewer PACs in the structure.

The PAC schedule is maintained by redirecting cash flow uncertainty to classes called *companions*. In times of fast prepayments, companions support PACs by absorbing principal payments in excess of the PAC schedule. In times of slow prepayments, amortization of the companions is delayed if there is not enough principal for the currently paying PAC. As a result of this support mechanism, faster-than-expected prepayments cause companions to pay off sooner,

Determining the PAC Schedule
Principal Flows from $1 Million 7.5% Pool

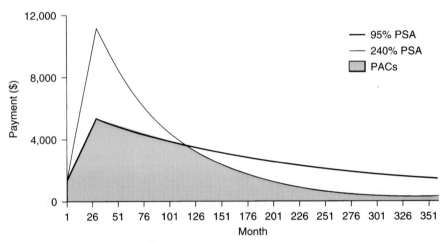

or contract in weighted average life. Conversely, slower-than-expected prepayments cause companions to remain outstanding longer, or extend. Exhibit 26–3 shows how the companions support the PACs at both ends of the protected prepayment range.

Total PAC and companion principal flows can be divided sequentially, much like a sequential-pay structure. Exhibit 26–4 illustrates a possible PAC/companion structure. Exhibit 26–5 shows the WALs of the PACs and companions compared to a sample sequential-pay structure and to the collateral across a range of prepayment rates. In relation to the sequential-pay bonds, the PACs are completely stable at prepayment rates within the bands and less volatile when prepayments fall outside the bands because the companions continue to provide stability. As a result, PACs are generally priced at tighter spreads to the Treasury curve, and companion bonds at wider spreads, than sequential-pay bonds with the same average lives.

Effective PAC bands are important in evaluating PACs. These bands define the actual range of collateral prepayment rates over which a particular PAC class can remain on its payment schedule. An example of this distinction can be seen in the first class of the sample PAC structure. Even though the structure was constructed with bands of 95% to 240% PSA, this class is actually protected from WAL changes over a broader range of prepayment rates: The effective PAC bands are 95% to 288% PSA. All the companions in a structure must be paid off before the WAL of a PAC will shorten, so the earlier PACs in a structure generally have higher upper effective bands than the later PACs since there are

**EXHIBIT 26–3**

PAC/Companion Profile at PAC Band Limits
Principal Flows from $1 Million 7.5% Pool

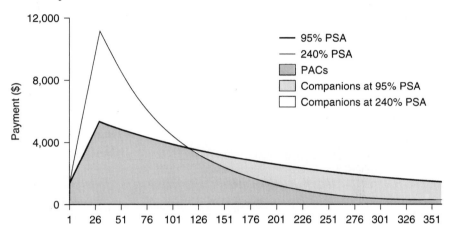

**EXHIBIT 26–4**

PAC/Companion Structure at 185% PSA
Principal Flows from $1 Million 7.5% Pool

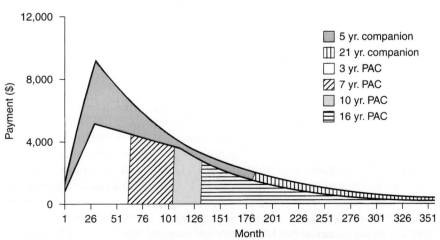

**EXHIBIT  26–5**

Weighted Average Lives of Alternative CMO Structures under Selected Prepayment Assumptions

Backed by 30-Year, 7.5% Pass-Throughs
Pricing Speed: 185% PSA
PAC Bands: 95%-20% PSA

| PSA | 50% | 95% | 185% | 240% | 300% |
|---|---|---|---|---|---|
| Pass-through | 15.4 | 12.2 | 8.3 | 6.9 | 5.9 |
| Sequential-pay | | | | | |
| A | 6.6 | 4.5 | 2.6 | 2.3 | |
| | | 3.0 | | | |
| B | 16.0 | 11.3 | 7.0 | 5.7 | 4.8 |
| C | 20.9 | 15.9 | 10.0 | 8.1 | 6.7 |
| D | 26.3 | 23.3 | 17.1 | 14.2 | 11.9 |
| *PAC / Companion* | | | | | |
| PAC A | 4.3 | 3.0 | 3.0 | 3.0 | 2.9 |
| PAC B | 10.4 | 7.0 | 7.0 | 7.0 | 6.1 |
| PAC C | 14.4 | 10.0 | 10.0 | 10.0 | 8.3 |
| PAC D | 19.1 | 16.2 | 16.2 | 16.2 | 13.6 |
| Companion E | 24.6 | 19.2 | 5.0 | 2.8 | 2.2 |
| Companion F | 29.2 | 28.2 | 21.5 | 6.6 | 4.2 |

more companions outstanding. The effective bands of a PAC will change over time, depending on the prepayment experience of the collateral. As discussed later, most of the time, this change (drift) is small and gradual.

PACs have been structured with varying protection levels and yield trade-offs. The most common variants are Type II/Type III PACs and super/subordinate PACs.

### Type II and Type III PACs

As the CMO marketplace grew more sophisticated, investors sought bonds that would offer some prepayment protection and earn higher cash-flow yields than generic PACs. The resulting innovation was the Type II PAC, structured from companion cash flows in a PAC/companion structure. These bonds have narrower prepayment protection bands than standard PACs, but as long as prepayments stay within the bands, they pay down according to a schedule, much like regular PACs. Because Type II PACs are second in priority to PACs, the remaining companion bonds provide support even if prepayments are outside the bands. If extended periods of high prepayments cause the companions in a structure to be paid off, the remaining Type II PACs become companions to the PACs, with the potential WAL volatility of companion bonds.

Exhibit 26–6 shows the addition of Type II PACs (125% − 220% PSA bands) to the PAC/companion structure illustrated in Exhibit 26–3. The PAC principal flow has not changed, and the Type II PACs are layered on top of the PACs.

Another layer of PACs, with narrower bands, is sometimes created as well. These securities, known as Type III PACs, act as support for PACs and Type II PACs in a structure but retain some stability because of the companions that remain.

### Super/Subordinate PACs

The prepayment experience of 1992–1993 caused many investors to view MBSs as more callable than they had previously thought and to demand significantly higher levels of prepayment protection. In early 1993, Lehman Brothers responded by issuing the first super/subordinated PAC structure. In this structure, standard PACs are divided into super and subordinate (sub-) PACs. By rearranging the cash flow priorities within the total PAC class, the super PACs receive additional prepayment stability from the sub-PACs and therefore have much wider protection bands.

Since both super- and sub-PAC classes are created from the total PAC cash flows and generally have all the structure's companions available to support them, sub-PACs offer more protection from average-life volatility than similar average-life Type II or Type III PACs in the same structure. This relationship can be seen in FHLMC 1499, which has three-year super, sub-, and Type III

**E X H I B I T    26–6**

PAC/Companion Structure With Type II PACs
Principal Flows from $1 Million 7.5% Pool

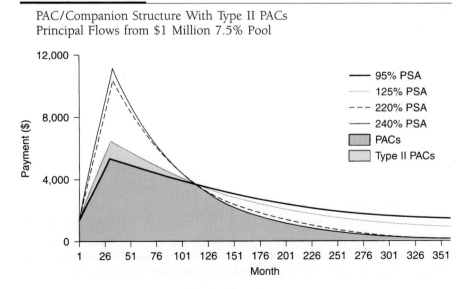

PACs. The effective bands are 70% to 625% PSA on the super PAC, 100% to 250% PSA on the sub-PAC, and 140% to 220% PSA on the Type III PAC. Sub-PACs trade at higher yields than PACs because they can have more average-life volatility at prepayment rates outside their protection bands.

Exhibit 26–7 shows super and sub-PACs in the example PAC/companion structure. The combined principal flows of the super and sub-PACs are equivalent to the original PAC principal flows.

## Targeted Amortization Classes

Targeted amortization classes (TACs) were introduced to offer investors a prepayment-protected class at wider spreads than PACs. Like PACs, TACs repay principal according to a schedule as long as prepayments remain within a range. If the principal cash flow from the collateral exceeds the TAC schedule, the excess is allocated to TAC companion classes. Unlike PACs, TACs do not provide protection against WAL extension if prepayments fall below the speed necessary to maintain the TAC schedule. Therefore, the typical TAC can be viewed as a PAC with a lower band equal to the CMO pricing speed and an upper band similar to that of PACs backed by comparable collateral. In falling/low interest-rate environments, investors are primarily concerned that increasing prepayments will shorten average life due to increasing prepayments. Many investors are willing to forego the protection against extension offered by PACs in exchange for the higher yields of TACs.

**E X H I B I T  26–7**

PAC/Companion Structure With Super and Sub PACs
Principal Flows from $1 Million 7.5% Pool

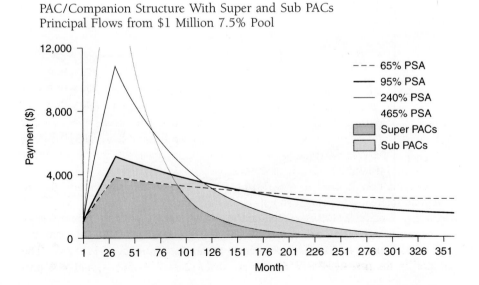

# Companions

*Companion* is a general term in the CMO market for a class that provides prepayment protection for another class. In evaluating companions (also known as *support classes*), it is important to review the rest of the CMO structure; the behavior of a particular companion class is influenced by the class(es) it supports. For instance, if the companion is supporting a TAC, it will have less extension risk than a PAC companion because the TAC is not protected from extension. In addition, other bonds in the structure may affect the companion's potential performance. For example, the presence of Type II PACs in a structure indicates that part of the original companions is being traded in a more stable form, leaving the remaining companions more volatile. Another important consideration for companions is the collateral backing the CMO. If the pass-throughs have a shorter maturity than 30 years, such as 15-year or balloon MBSs, the PACs in the structure will require less extension protection. Therefore, there will be fewer companions in the structure than in a 30-year structure with the same PAC bands, and the companions will have less extension risk. Finally, a class's sensitivity to prepayments should be viewed in a yield or total return context. Because prepayments are paid at par, faster-than-expected prepayments will have a positive effect on a discount bond's yield, and slower-than-expected prepayments will have a positive effect on a premium bond's yield. On a total return basis (see Evaluating CMOs below for details on total return calculation), these generalizations will usually apply as well, although the interaction between prepayments, average life, and reinvestment rate may offset the effects of being repaid at par.

The CMO classes that have been reviewed (sequential-pay, PAC, TAC, and companion) are structures that provide for the redirection of principal payments. The classes that follow address the redirection of interest payments as well. These classes usually rely on one of the above structures to reallocate principal payments.

# Z Bonds

The Z bond is a CMO class with a period of principal and interest lockout. It typically takes the place of a coupon-bearing class at or near the end of a CMO structure. When the CMO is originally issued, the Z bond has a face amount significantly lower than it would have if it were an interest-bearing class. Each month that the Z is outstanding, it generates coupon cash flows, like any other bond in the structure; however, as long as the Z class is not paying out principal, this coupon flow is used to pay down other classes. The Z gets credit for the foregone interest payments through increases to its principal balance, known as *accretion.* Once the classes preceding the Z bond are fully paid down, it begins to receive principal and interest.

The Z bond in Exhibit 26–8 begins with a face amount of $118,000. The coupon in the first month ($118,000 $\times$ 7.5%/12 = $737.50) is paid as a pre-

**EXHIBIT 26-8**

Sample Z-Bond Cash Flows In Sequential-Pay/Z Bond Structure

Backed by 30-Year, 7.5% Pass-Throughs($)

| Month | Beginning Balance | Coupon Accretion | Coupon Cash Flow | Amortiz./ Prepay. | Ending Balance | Total Cash Flows |
|---|---|---|---|---|---|---|
| 1 | 118,000.00 | 737.50 | 0.00 | 0.00 | 118,737.50 | 0 |
| 2 | 118,737.50 | 742.11 | 0.00 | 0.00 | 119,479.61 | 0 |
| 3 | 119,479.61 | 746.75 | 0.00 | 0.00 | 120,226.36 | 0 |
| . | . | . | . | . | . | 0 |
| . | . | . | . | . | . | 0 |
| 131 | 265,245.57 | 1,657.78 | 0.00 | 0.00 | 266,903.35 | 0 |
| 132 | 266,903.35 | 1,668.15 | 0.00 | 0.00 | 268,571.50 | 0 |
| 133 | 268,571.50 | 1,678.57 | 0.00 | 47.44 | 270,202.63 | 47.44 |
| 134 | 270,202.63 | 0.00 | 1,688.77 | 3,131.55 | 267,071.08 | 4,820.31 |
| 135 | 267,071.08 | 0.00 | 1,669.19 | 3,099.51 | 263,971.57 | 4,768.70 |

payment to the first class in the structure, and the Z bond accretes that amount. The accretion amounts increase as the principal amount (on which coupon cash flows are calculated) grows. In month 133, the final sequential-pay class receives its last principal payment, which includes $1,678.57 from the Z coupon. The collateral has produced an additional $47.44 in principal cash flows that month, and since the Z is the only outstanding class, it receives the principal payment. The Z bond balance has grown to $270,203. Since the Z is the only remaining class from month 134 on, it receives all principal and interest payments generated by the collateral.

In a simple sequential-pay/Z bond structure, the Z accelerates the principal repayments of the sequential-pay bonds. As a result, restructuring a sequential-pay bond as a Z allows for larger sequential-pay classes with the same WALs as the original classes. Since a portion of the principal payments of these sequential-pay bonds is coming from the Z coupon flows (which do not vary until the Z begins amortizing), average-life volatility is decreased in the sequential-pay classes. In fact, in the sample structure, all bonds including the Z have less average-life volatility when the Z is introduced to the structure (see Exhibit 26-9). The Z's impact is clearest in the scenario where prepayments fall from 185% PSA to 95% PSA: The change in average life is 10% to 23% lower for all bonds than in the basic sequential-pay structure.

Although the Z structure appears to have reduced uncertainty across the board, it is important to look at the effective durations of the bonds as well.

**EXHIBIT  26–9**

Weighted Average Lives of Alternative Sequential-
Pay Structures under Selected Prepayment
Assumptions

Backed by 30-Year, 7.5% Pass-Throughs
Pricing Speed: 185% PSA

| PSA | 95% | 185% | 240% |
|---|---|---|---|
| *Sequential-Pay* | | | |
| A | 4.5 | 3.0 | 2.6 |
| B | 11.3 | 7.0 | 5.7 |
| C | 15.9 | 10.0 | 8.1 |
| D | 23.3 | 17.1 | 14.2 |
| *Sequential-Pay/Z* | | | |
| A | 4.2 | 3.0 | 2.6 |
| B | 10.1 | 7.0 | 5.9 |
| C | 13.5 | 9.9 | 8.5 |
| Z | 21.5 | 17.0 | 14.8 |

Exhibit 26–10 shows that the durations of the first three sequential-pay bonds do not change substantially when the last class is replaced with a Z. The Z bond, on the other hand, has almost twice the effective duration of the sequential-pay bond that it replaced, moving from 10.2 years to 18.5 years. The price of the Z is highly sensitive to interest-rate movements and the resulting changes in prepayment rates because its ultimate principal balance depends on total accretions credited by the time it begins to pay down. Although WAL volatility has decreased, the price sensitivity of the last class is increased dramatically by making it a Z.

**EXHIBIT  26–10**

Effective Durations of Alternative Sequential-
Pay Structures

Backed by 30-Year, 7.5% Pass-Throughs

| Class | Sequential-Pay | Sequential-Pay with Z |
|---|---|---|
| A | 1.53 years | 1.69 years |
| B | 6.80 | 6.47 |
| C | 8.58 | 8.16 |
| D/Z | 10.19 | 18.47 |

Z bonds offer much of the appeal of zero coupon Treasury strips: There is no reinvestment risk during the accretion phase. In addition, Z bonds offer higher yields than comparable WAL Treasury zeros.

## Accretion-Directed Classes

In the falling interest-rate environment that has characterized most of the CMO era, many structures have been developed to protect investors from higher-than-anticipated prepayments. *Accretion-directed* (AD) bonds are designed to protect against extension in average life if rates rise and prepayments are lower than expected. These bonds, also known as *very accurately defined maturity* (VADM) *bonds,* derive all their cash flows from the interest accretions of a Z class. Because there is no deviation in Z accretions until the Z bond begins to pay down, VADMs do not extend even if there are no prepayments. VADMs are also protected from prepayment increases because the Z bonds that support them tend to be the last classes to begin repaying principal.

## Floaters and Inverse Floaters

The first floating-rate CMO class was issued by Shearson Lehman Brothers in 1986. These classes are created by dividing a fixed-rate class into a floater and an inverse floater. The bonds take their principal paydown rules from the underlying fixed-rate class. A floater/inverse combination can be produced from a sequential-pay class, PAC, TAC, companion, or other coupon-bearing class. The coupon of the floater is reset periodically (usually monthly) at a specified spread, or margin, over an index. Typical indices include LIBOR, the Federal Home Loan Bank 11th District Cost of Funds Index (COFI), and various maturities of the constant maturity Treasury (CMT) series. The coupon of the inverse floater moves inversely with the index. Floaters and inverses have caps and floors that set the maximum and minimum coupons allowable on the bonds. These caps and floors may be explicit (e.g., a floater cap of 10%) or implicit (a floater's floor would equal the floater's margin if the underlying index fell to 0%) and may either be constant throughout the life of the bond or change according to a predetermined schedule.

Floaters are usually designed to be sold at par; their caps and margins are dictated by the option and swap markets and by expectations about the performance of the underlying fixed-rate CMO class. Floaters have many natural buyers, such as banks, which prefer the limited interest-rate risk that an adjustable-rate security provides. Since inverse floater coupons move in the opposite direction from their index, investors generally require higher yields for inverses than for floaters or the underlying fixed-rate classes. To increase the yield, cap, and initial coupon, inverses are often structured with multipliers in the coupon formulas that magnify movements in the underlying index.

Exhibit 26–11 shows how a floater and an inverse can be created from a fixed-rate bond. Both floater and inverse have coupon formulas tied to COFI; the floater coupon adjusts at COFI + 65 basis points with a 10% interest-rate cap, and the inverse coupon, which has a multiplier of 2, adjusts at 21.20 − 2 × COFI with a 2.50% floor. In this example, the floater class is twice the size of the inverse floater. When a multiplier greater than 1 is used to set the inverse floater's coupon, the face amount of the inverse must be smaller than the floater to keep the weighted average of the two coupons equal to the fixed-rate bond coupon.

## Interest- and Principal-Only Strips

Any pool of coupon-bearing collateral can be stripped into interest-only (IO) and principal-only (PO) segments and sold separately. Exhibit 26–12a illustrates the interest cash flows for 7.5% collateral at various prepayment rates. The total amount of interest flow varies depending on the prepayment rate. Since interest cash flows exist only if principal remains outstanding, IOs benefit from slowing prepayments. POs represent a stream of principal payments purchased at a discount. If prepayments rise, discounted principal flows are received at par earlier than expected, improving the security's performance. Exhibit 26–12b illustrates principal cash flows from the collateral. Here the total flows will always equal the face amount of the collateral, but the prepayment rate affects the timing and value of the flows. IOs are bearish securities and usually have negative durations

---

**E X H I B I T   26–11**

Creating a Floater and Inverse

$120MM 5-Year, 7.5% Companion Becomes. . .
$80MM 5-Year Companion COFI Floater (Coupon = COFI + 65 bp, 10% Cap)
$40MM 5-Year Companion COFI Inverse (Coupon = 21.20% − 2 × COFI, 2.50% Floor)

| | Coupon | | Wt. Avg. |
| | | | |
| COFI Index | Floater | Inverse | Coupon |
|---|---|---|---|
| 0.00% | 0.65% | 21.20% | 7.50% |
| 2.00 | 2.65 | 17.20 | 7.50 |
| 4.00 | 4.65 | 13.20 | 7.50 |
| 6.00 | 6.65 | 9.20 | 7.50 |
| 8.00 | 8.65 | 5.20 | 7.50 |
| 9.35 | 10.00 | 2.50 | 7.50 |
| 10.00 | 10.00 | 2.50 | 7.50 |
| 12.00 | 10.00 | 2.50 | 7.50 |

**EXHIBIT  26–12**

A.  Interest Flows from $1 Million 7.5% Pool

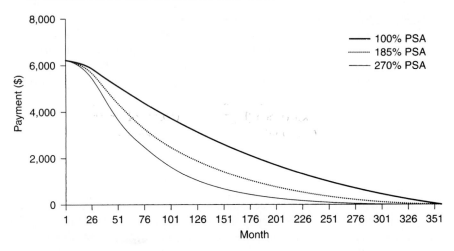

B. Principal Flows from $1 Million 7.5% Pool

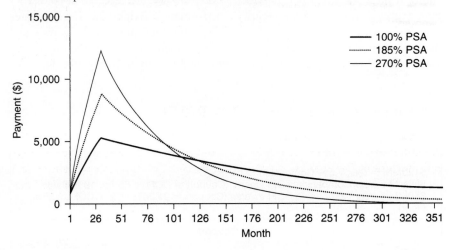

(their prices rise as rates rise); POs are bullish securities with long positive durations.

The same principles for stripping pools of collateral can be applied to individual CMO classes or to blocks of classes within a single structure. CMO strips may represent 100% of the interest or principal flows; or, more commonly, only a portion of the interest may be stripped, resulting in an IO and a reduced-coupon fixed-rate bond. For example, if a dealer is structuring a PAC class with a 7.5% coupon but investors are more willing to buy the class if it has a 7% coupon, a 50-bp PAC IO can be stripped from the class and sold separately.[5] Structurers may also strip part of the coupon flows from the entire block of collateral before dividing it into classes. This method produces an IO-ette security and is employed to lower the coupons on all bonds in a structure.

Strips made from CMO bonds require more analysis than regular IOs and POs. In the above example, since the IO has been stripped from a PAC class, it will be insulated from cash flow changes as long as prepayments remain within the PAC bands. Only if the PAC begins to pay down principal early will the holder of the PAC IO experience the negative effects of prepayments. An investor should look to the underlying class that defines the rules for principal paydown. Since prepayments are the primary consideration in evaluating stripped securities, the behavior of the underlying class plays a significant role in the overall analysis.

Another type of strip results from the creation of whole-loan CMOs. For agency CMOs, the coupon of the collateral (the pass-throughs) is fixed; for whole-loan CMOs, the collateral coupon is a weighted average of all the individual mortgage coupons (which may vary by 100 bps or more). As loans prepay, the weighted-average coupon (WAC) of the collateral can change. To be sure that all fixed-rate bonds in a structure receive their allotted coupons, issuers often split off part of the principal or interest cash flow from individual mortgages in a pool, leaving a block of collateral with a stable WAC. These strips of principal or interest are combined into WAC POs or WAC IOs and trade much like trust POs and IOs.

## PAC BAND DRIFT

Effective PAC bands change (drift) over time, even if prepayments remain within the initial bands. Band drift results from the interaction of actual prepayments and the current PAC bands, and the resulting changes in collateral balance and relative PAC and companion balances. The band drift of a particular PAC can be viewed under three scenarios: when prepayments are within the current ef-

---

5. Until recently, all REMIC IO classes had to be sold with some small amount of principal, called a *nominal balance*. To generate the cash flows for bonds with this structure, the nominal balance is amortized and prepaid according to the type of bond. Since the balance is small, the coupon is extremely large. IOs sold this way tend to have multiple-digit coupons (e.g., 1183%) and high dollar prices (e.g., 3626-12). Alternatively, IOs may be based on a notional balance. Here, the IO tranche has no principal balance and its coupon flows are calculated on the declining balance of the underlying principal-bearing tranche. No principal cash flows are paid to the IO holder. This procedure results in MBS-like coupons (7.5%, 8%, etc.) or in basis-point coupons (e.g., 100 bps) and below-par prices. These two techniques result in equivalent investment amounts and cash flows. The difference in prices (3626-12 versus 18-02, for example) does not denote any relative value difference between IOs priced with one method or the other.

fective bands, when prepayments are above the current upper band, and when prepayments are below the current lower band.

If prepayments are within the bands, the currently paying PAC will pay on schedule. Any additional prepayments will go to the currently paying companion. Over time, both upper and lower bands will drift up. This happens because any prepayment within the bands is also lower than the upper band and higher than the lower band. From the point of view of the upper band, prepayments have been slower than expected and more companions are available to absorb high prepayments in the future. Thus, the upper band rises. From the point of view of the lower band, prepayments have been faster than expected and less collateral is outstanding to produce principal flows. If prepayments slow to the original lower band, there may not be enough principal coming in to pay the PACs on schedule, and they will extend. Thus, the lower band rises as well. For most prepayment rates within the bands, the upper band will rise at a faster rate than the lower, so prepayments within the bands tend to cause the bands to widen over time.

If prepayments are above the current upper band, the PAC will continue to pay on schedule until all companions are retired. If the fast prepayments are only temporary, there will probably be little impact on the bands. If prepayments remain above the upper band, however, the upper and lower bands will begin to converge. This happens because there are fewer companions available to absorb fast prepayments and less collateral outstanding to generate principal cash flows if prepayments slow. The bands will converge once all companions have been retired, and the PAC will pay like a sequential-pay class from that point.

If prepayments are below the current lower band, the currently paying PAC will not be able to pay according to its schedule since there will be no other principal flows coming into the structure that can be redirected to the PAC. This is typically a temporary situation because the lower band is usually substantially lower than the base prepayment rate expected from simple housing turnover and because most PACs have priority over all subsequent cash flows until they are back on schedule. Prepayments below the current lower band cause the upper band to rise (more companions are available to absorb faster prepayments in the future) and may cause the lower band to rise slightly (since most PACs have catch-up features, a higher future prepayment rate is necessary to put the PAC back on schedule).

Most band drift is small and gradual. Large changes to PAC bands will occur only if prepayments are significantly outside the bands, or if they remain near either of the bands for a long period of time. Effective bands represent the range of prepayment rates that the collateral can experience for its remaining life and still maintain the payment schedule for a specific PAC. Temporary movements outside the bands will not affect PAC cash flows as long as companion cash flows and principal balances are available to support them.

## CMO STRUCTURING EXAMPLE

In this section, we follow a structurer through the process of creating a multiclass CMO. Diagrams (not drawn to scale) are included to illustrate the structures.

The structurer begins with a block of collateral—in this case FNMA 7.5s (Exhibit 26–13a). If the market expects interest rates and prepayments to be stable, the structurer may construct a sequential-pay CMO (Exhibit 26–13b). If investors are concerned about rates rising and prepayments slowing (e.g., extension risk), the structurer may produce the last class as a Z bond (Exhibit 26–13c). This allows him to apply the Z coupon flows as principal payments to the early sequential-pay classes or to create VADMs that offer the strongest extension protection (Exhibit 26–13d). If the collateral is priced at a premium, the structurer may strip some interest cash flows before creating the rest of the classes. This allows the creation of discount or par bonds. Exhibit 26–13e shows the FNMA 7.5s after a 50-bp IO-ette is stripped and sold separately. The remaining collateral now has a 7% coupon and can be structured in any way that the original 7.5s could have been.

If the market expects high interest-rate and prepayment volatility, the structurer will likely create PAC/companion or TAC/companion CMOs. Exhibit 26–13f illustrates the initial allocation of cash flows to PACs and companions. Once the amount of principal that can be attributed to PACs or companions is identified, these classes go through the sequential-pay structuring process to create PACs and companions of various average lives (Exhibit 26–13g). Individual classes from any of these structures can be further divided. If a foreign bank wants to purchase a LIBOR-based floater with a relatively high margin and a five- year average life, for example, the structurer can produce a bond with the desired characteristics from the five-year companion class (Exhibit 26–13h) that will offer a higher yield than noncompanion tranches. At the same time, the structurer will look at the inverse floater market to determine yield and coupon (set by adjusting the multiplier) for the resulting LIBOR inverse floater. On the PAC side, there may be an investor who wants to purchase a seven-year PAC with a 6% coupon (and therefore a lower price) as protection from the risk of high prepayments on premium-priced bonds. If so, the structurer can split the seven-year PAC into a 150-bp PAC 10 and a 6% PAC (Exhibit 28-14i). These are a few examples of the flexibility in the structuring process. The customizable nature of many CMO classes is a key to the popularity of these bonds.

## REGULATORY DEVELOPMENTS AFFECTING CMOS

When FHLMC issued the first CMO in 1983, multiclass mortgage securities were subject to various regulatory constraints. For example, federal tax law treated payments from a multiclass trust as equity dividends. Unlike debt pay-

**EXHIBIT 26–13**

CMO Structuring Example
FNMA 7.5% Collateral

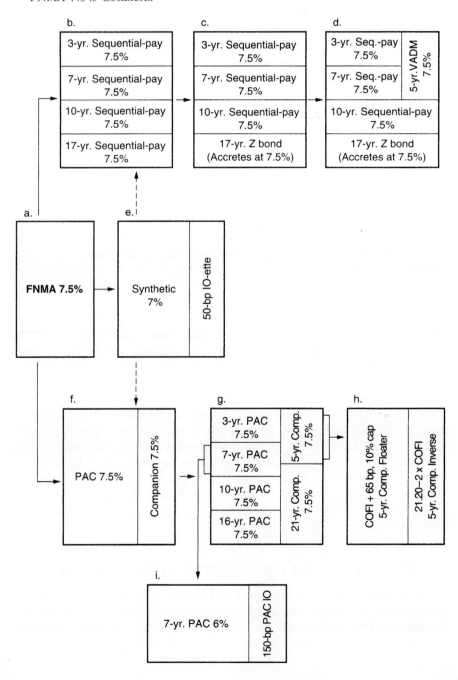

ments, dividend payments are not tax deductible. Therefore, the issuer who established a multiclass trust was unable to claim a tax deduction for interest paid to security holders to offset taxes on interest received from the underlying collateral. The resulting double taxation—interest income was taxed at both the trust and investor level—made the transaction economically impractical.

The CMO avoided this problem because it was an offering of collateralized debt. Therefore, tax deductions for interest paid to certificate holders offset the tax liability on interest received from the underlying collateral. However, CMOs were subject to other constraints to ensure that they were treated as debt instead of equity for tax purposes. Issuers had to maintain a portion of residual interests, record CMOs as liabilities in their financial statements, and satisfy minimum capital requirements. Issuers also had to include a call provision, forcing them to price longer maturity bonds at a wider spread to the Treasury curve. In addition, issuers had to structure a mismatch between receipts on the underlying mortgages and payments to the CMO bondholders; generally they passed monthly collateral payments through to bondholders on a quarterly basis. These constraints made it difficult to issue CMOs efficiently.

Toward the end of 1985, issuers overcame some of these obstacles by issuing CMOs through an owner's trust. This mechanism allowed issuers to sell their residual interests and remove the debt from their books. The owner's trust, however, was not conducive to a liquid market because residual buyers became personally liable for the CMO: If the cash flow from the collateral was insufficient to pay regular interest holders, residual owners had to cover the shortage. As a result, issuers could sell residual interests only to investors capable of meeting ongoing net worth tests. Although these tests were different for each transaction, they all effectively limited potential buyers to institutional investors with adequate net worth.

The 1986 Tax Reform Act addressed these problems by defining a new issuance vehicle: the real estate mortgage investment conduit (REMIC). To qualify for REMIC status, a multiclass offering can have multiple classes of regular interests but only one class of residual interest. The legislation defines a regular interest as a fixed principal amount with periodic interest payments or accruals on the outstanding principal balance. Buyers of regular interests are taxed as holders of debt obligations. A residual interest consists entirely of pro rata payments (if any). Buyers of residual interests are taxed based on the taxable income of the REMIC. Taxable income is the excess collateral and reinvestment income over REMIC regular interest and servicing expenses.

REMIC legislation was a milestone in the development of multiclass mortgage securities because it allowed issuers to adopt whatever structure best exploited particular economic, financial, or accounting considerations. For tax purposes, all conduits qualifying for REMIC status are treated equally whether they structure a multiclass mortgage transaction as a borrowing collateralized by mortgages or as a sale of the underlying mortgages. In either case, only the investors and residual holders are subject to tax, not the conduit itself. REMIC legislation also allows issuers to sell the entire residual class, and since 1987 it has permitted issuers to sell floating-rate classes. This flexibility has allowed issuers to develop new products, particularly since repeated interest-rate declines since 1982 have led investors to seek products with either improved call protection or higher risk/reward opportunities.

Following a five-year phaseout of all previous structures that ended in 1991, all issuers of multiclass mortgage securities must now use REMICs. However, from the investor's perspective, there is little difference between CMO and REMIC products; in either case, the investor is buying multiclass mortgage securities. Consequently, the terms *CMO* and *REMIC* are often used interchangeably, even though they are crucially different tax vehicles from the issuer's perspective.

Until 1988, private issuers (primarily investment bankers and home builders) accounted for almost the entire supply of multiclass mortgage securities. These issuers generally used agency collateral to obtain the highest ratings from the nationally recognized rating agencies. However, the credit quality of the issuer was also important insofar as cash flows from the underlying collateral might be insufficient to cover obligations to all bondholders. Therefore, issuers had to take extra measures, such as overcollateralizing the bonds or buying insurance, to obtain high investment-grade credit ratings.

In 1988, FHLMC and FNMA gained full authorization to issue REMICs. Their REMICs automatically obtained government agency status, regardless of the underlying collateral. Therefore, FHLMC and FNMA were not subject to the credit-enhancing constraints imposed on private issuers, giving them a crucial market advantage. Agency CMOs jumped from only 2% of total CMO issuance in 1987 to 33% in 1988 and 83% in 1989. In 1992, agencies issued 85% of CMOs.

By 1988, regulatory and market developments had stimulated demand for multiclass mortgage securities. In July 1988, the Basle Committee on Banking Regulations and Supervisory Practices set forth risk-based capital guidelines to ensure the fiscal stability of the international banking infrastructure by requiring minimum capital levels as a percentage of assets–loans made and securities purchased—weighted according to risk classification. Since agency-issued REMICs offer high yields in relation to their 20% risk weighting, they became increasingly popular with banks and thrifts. Less volatile REMIC products, such as floaters and short and intermediate maturity PACs and TACs, were most appropriate since banks and thrifts needed to match assets with liabilities of similar maturities.

Since about 1988, insurance companies have looked to the REMIC market for assets to offset intermediate to long-term liabilities. Given the poor performance of real estate holdings and commercial mortgages, insurance companies needed to diversify their portfolios, and REMICs offered an attractive alternative because of their credit quality and spread levels. At year-end 1993, life insurance companies implemented their own risk-based capital requirements, which provided an additional incentive to hold mortgages in securitized form.

## EVALUATING CMOS

The most common way to communicate the value and performance expectations of a CMO bond is the yield table, showing cash flow yields under a series of prepayment rate assumptions. Computer models that produce yield tables take price(s) and prepayment rates as inputs (and index levels, in the case of floaters and inverse floaters), and calculate yields and spreads, average lives, durations, and payment windows for each prepayment assumption. With this information, the investor can determine the level of prepayment protection offered by the bond, the average life volatility for given changes in collateral prepayment rates, the impact of prepayments on yields, and the time over which principal is likely to be received. Exhibits 26–14 and 26–15 are yield tables for the three-year sequential-pay and PAC bonds in the earlier examples. The yield changes for the sequential-pay bond under each prepayment scenario, but the PAC yield is stable from 95% PSA to 285% PSA. The average life and duration of the PAC are more stable at prepayment rates outside the PAC bands as well. The payment windows show when the bonds will begin to pay principal and when the final payment will occur under each prepayment scenario. Finally, a comparison of the two tables shows that in the base case the sequential-pay bond is being offered at nearly double the spread of the PAC to compensate investors for its additional average-life volatility.

Total return scenario analysis may also be used to evaluate CMOs. It addresses two drawbacks of the cash-flow yield approach: Many investors do not expect to hold their securities to maturity, and the reinvestment assumption in the cash flow yield analysis—that all cash flows are reinvested at the security's yield—is usually unrealistic. Total return calculations cover a specific investment period and make an assumption about the bond's price at the end of the period (the horizon). They further assume a reinvestment rate and prepayment rate for the period to generate cash flows. Total return is the change in market value of the bond (reflecting price changes and principal paydown) plus the cumulative value of all cash flows and reinvestment proceeds as of the horizon date, divided by the initial market value. Although total return scenario analysis involves several assumptions, it is often a desirable addition to the yield tables, especially if the investment period is expected to be relatively short.

Option-adjusted spread (OAS) analysis is another relative value measurement tool used by fixed income market participants. Based on multiple interest-rate simulations and the resulting prepayments predicted by a prepayment model, the cash flows of a callable bond are analyzed to calculate the average spread to the Treasury spot curve implied by the security's current price. Since this

## EXHIBIT 26-14

Yield Table for 3-Year Sequential-Pay Class (Price—104-04)

| | | | | Base Case | | | | |
|---|---|---|---|---|---|---|---|---|
| PSA | 35% | 95% | 135% | 185% | 200% | 240% | 285% | 335% |
| Yield(%)/Spread(bp) | 6.79/105 | 6.37/111 | 6.13/127 | 5.86/140 | 5.79/133 | 5.61/114 | 5.42/143 | 5.24/125 |
| Avg. life (yr.) | 7.85 | 4.54 | 3.64 | 3.00 | 2.86 | 2.57 | 2.33 | 2.13 |
| Mod. dur. (yr.) | 5.54 | 3.67 | 3.06 | 2.60 | 2.49 | 2.27 | 2.08 | 1.92 |
| Windows (yr.) | 0.1–14.7 | 0.1–8.6 | 0.1–6.7 | 0.1–5.3 | 0.1–5.1 | 0.1–4.4 | 0.1–3.9 | 0.1–3.5 |
| Benchmark Tsy. | 7-yr. | 5-yr. | 4-yr. | 3-yr. | 3-yr. | 3-yr. | 2-yr. | 2-yr. |

**EXHIBIT 26-15**

Yield Table for 3-Year PAC (Price—106-04)

| | | | | | Base Case | | | | |
|---|---|---|---|---|---|---|---|---|---|
| **PSA** | 35% | 95% | 135% | 185% | 200% | 240% | 285% | 335% |
| Yield(%)/Spread(bp) | 6.04/78 | 5.31/85 | 5.18/72 | 5.18/72 | 5.18/72 | 5.18/72 | 5.18/72 | 5.13/67 |
| Avg. life (yr.) | 5.07 | 3.00 | 3.00 | 3.00 | 3.00 | 3.00 | 3.00 | 2.92 |
| Mod. dur. (yr.) | 4.04 | 2.62 | 2.62 | 2.62 | 2.62 | 2.62 | 2.62 | 2.56 |
| Windows (yr.) | 0.1–9.3 | 0.1–5.2 | 0.1–5.2 | 0.1–5.2 | 0.1–5.2 | 0.1–5.2 | 0.1–5.2 | 0.1–4.7 |
| Benchmark Tsy. | 5-yr. | 3-yr. | 3-yr. | 3-yr. | 3-yr. | 3-yr. | 3-yr. | 3-yr. |

process nets out the impact of prepayments (partial calls) of MB Ss, OAS allows direct comparisons among MBSs and other callable and noncallable fixed income securities. Using current OAS to calculate the horizon price of a CMO is a common method in total return analysis. This allows the investor to avoid making a direct horizon price assumption and incorporates more information (such as the shape of the yield curve) into the analysis.

## THE CMO/COLLATERAL PRICING RELATIONSHIP

Because of strong investor demand for CMOs, a large percentage of newly issued pass-throughs and jumbo mortgages has gone into CMO structures in recent years. Investor preference for structured mortgage securities has led to a highly efficient pricing relationship between the CMO and collateral sectors.

The source of the CMO/collateral pricing relationship is the interplay between the yield curve and spreads on collateral and CMOs. Exhibit 26–16 shows the projected yields and payment windows of each bond in a four-class, sequential-pay CMO and the yield of the collateral. Each bond's yield is quoted as a spread to the on-the-run Treasury with a maturity closest to the bond's average life. In this example, the three-year CMO class has a lower yield than the collateral. The seven-year yield is about equal to, and the 10- and 17-year yields are higher than, the yield of the collateral. When the yield curve is positively sloped, earlier classes are generally offered at lower yields than later classes. Assuming that spreads remain constant, a steepening of the yield curve results in a greater difference between the yields of shorter and longer classes.

**E X H I B I T    26–16**

Yields on Collateral and Sequential-Pay CMO Tranches

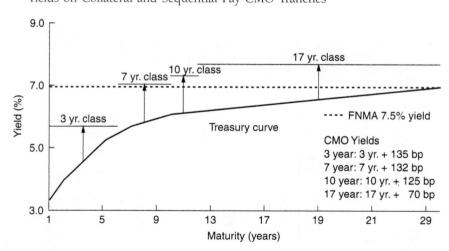

By definition, the price of an individual CMO bond represents the present value of the bond's projected cash flows, using the bond's yield as the discount rate. Therefore, the cash flows of any class with a lower yield than the collateral will be priced using a lower discount rate than the single discount rate used to price all the collateral cash flows. This means that this portion of the pass-through's cash flows will have a higher value when structured as part of a CMO. Likewise, the cash flows of bonds with yields higher than the collateral yield will be priced with a higher discount rate than the collateral, leading to lower valuations in relation to collateral cash flows.

Over time, as CMOs are created using a particular collateral type and coupon, supply and demand forces cause the collateral spread to tighten and/or the spreads of the CMO classes to widen until there is no profit in issuing the CMO. If collateral is too expensive (rich) to make the creation of CMO bonds economic, CMO issuance will slow until pass-through spreads widen and/or CMO spreads tighten. Because of temporary changes in market preference for structured products, collateral can trade at levels too rich to create CMOs. However, in equilibrium, it is rare for CMOs to trade rich to collateral, since collateral spreads will quickly tighten as more CMOs are issued.

## CMO TRADING AND CLEARING

Generally, CMO bonds are offered on the basis of a yield (more accurately, a spread over the yield of a benchmark Treasury) and a prepayment assumption. A price is calculated from this information and is agreed upon by both parties to the trade. The CMO market convention is corporate settlement (three business days after the trade date) unless the CMO is a new issue. In the case of a new issue, the settlement date for all the CMO classes is usually one to three months

**E X H I B I T   26–17**

Payment Delays for CMO Issuers and Collateral Types

| CMO Issuer | Collateral Type | Payment Delay |
|------------|-----------------|---------------|
| GNMA | GNMA | 15 days after the record date |
| FHLMC | FHLMC 75-day | 45 days after the record date* |
| FHLMC | FHLMC Gold | 15 days after the record date |
| FHLMC | GNMA | 25 days after the record date |
| FNMA | FNMA | 25 days after the record date |
| FNMA | GNMA | 15 days after the record date |
| Nonagency | Whole loans | 25 days after the record date** |

*Record date is the last calendar day of each month.

**May vary by issuer.

after the CMO is initially offered for sale. This period allows dealers to accumulate the collateral that will back the CMO. Whether the CMO bond is a new offering or a previously traded security, interest begins accruing on the first day of the settlement month. An exception to this rule is that most floating-rate CMO bonds begin accruing interest on the previous month's payment date so that they more closely resemble floating-rate notes.

Because of their credit quality, most CMOs can be used in repurchase and reverse repurchase agreements.

Most agency CMO trades are cleared through electronic book-entry transfers such as Fedwire, a clearing system maintained by the Federal Reserve. This system also handles monthly principal and interest payments, which are paid to the investor who holds the security on the record date (generally the last calendar day of the month). Whole-loan CMO trades are cleared through physical delivery or electronic book entry, depending on the issuer. Most MBSs pay with a delay—the cash flows earned during one month are paid out a fixed number of days after the end of the month to give mortgage servicers time to collect payments. Exhibit 26–17 identifies payment delays for the various combinations of CMO issuers and collateral types.

## CONCLUSION

A consistent theme in the CMO market throughout the past decade has been innovation in response to investor needs. As the CMO market has grown more liquid, larger structures have become feasible, providing the flexibility to develop new products. These products have refined the distribution of prepayment uncertainty and risk/reward opportunities to meet the increasingly specialized needs and objectives of investors. The range of options in the CMO market will continue to grow as both originators and investors adapt to a continually changing marketplace.

## CHAPTER 27

# NONAGENCY CMOS

**Frank J. Fabozzi, Ph.D., CFA**
Adjunct Professor of Finance
School of Management
Yale University

**Anthony B. Sanders, Ph.D.**
Professor of Finance and Galbreath Distinguished Scholar
The Ohio State University

**David Yuen, CFA**
Susquehanna Advisors Group

**Chuck Ramsey**
CEO
Mortgage Risk Assessment Corp.

All the cash flow structures found in agency CMOs are also applicable to non-agency or whole-loan CMO structures. The major additional element in structuring nonagency CMOs is credit enhancement. The investor in a whole-loan CMO is exposed to both prepayment risk and credit risk. Other elements include compensating interest payments, weighted average coupon dispersions, and clean-up call provisions. In this chapter, we will discuss various credit enhancement structures, compensating interest payments, clean-up call provisions, and the impact of coupon dispersions. In addition, we will discuss the PSA standard default assumption benchmark and whole-loan prepayment behavior.

## CREDIT ENHANCEMENTS

Four nationally recognized statistical rating organizations rate whole-loan CMOs: Standard & Poor's Corporation, Moody's Investors Service, Fitch IBCA, and Duff & Phelps Credit Rating Company. The primary factors these rating organizations consider in assigning a rating are the type of property (single-family residences, condominiums), the type of loan (fixed-rate level payment, adjustable rate, balloon), the term of the loans, the geographical dispersion of the loans, the loan size (conforming loans, jumbo loans), the amount of seasoning of the loan, and the purpose of the loan (purchase or refinancing). Typically, a double-A or triple-A rating is sought for the most senior tranche. The amount of credit enhancement necessary depends on rating agency requirements.

There are two general types of credit enhancement structures: external and internal. We will describe each type below.

## External Credit Enhancements

External credit enhancements come in the form of third-party guarantees that provide for first loss protection against losses up to a specified level, for example, 10%. The most common forms of external enhancements are: (1) a corporate guarantee; (2) a letter of credit; (3) pool insurance; and (4) bond insurance.

Pool insurance policies cover losses resulting from defaults and foreclosures. Policies are typically written for a dollar amount of coverage that continues in force throughout the life of the pool. However, some policies are written so that the dollar amount of coverage declines as the pool seasons as long as two conditions are met: (1) the credit performance is better than expected, and (2) the rating agencies that rated the issue approve. The three major providers of pool insurance are GEMICO, PMI Mortgage Insurance Corp., and United Guarantee Insurance. Since only defaults and foreclosures are covered, additional insurance must be obtained to cover losses resulting from bankruptcy (i.e., court mandated modification of mortgage debt), fraud arising in the origination process, and special hazards (i.e., losses resulting from events not covered by a standard homeowner's insurance policy).

Bond insurance provides the same function as in municipal bond structures. The major insurers are FGIC, AMBAC, and MBIA. Typically, bond insurance is not used as primary protection, but to supplement other forms of credit enhancement.

A CMO issue with external credit support is subject to the credit risk of the third-party guarantor. Should the third-party guarantor be downgraded, the CMO issue itself could be subject to downgrade even if the structure is performing as expected. For example, in the early 1990s, mortgage-backed securities issued by Citibank Mortgage Securities Inc. were downgraded when Citibank, the third-party guarantor, was downgraded. This is the chief disadvantage of third-party guarantees. Therefore, it is imperative that investors perform credit analysis on both the collateral (the loans) and the third-party guarantor.

External credit enhancements do not materially alter the cash flow characteristics of a CMO structure except in the form of prepayment. In case of a default resulting in net losses within the guarantee level, investors will receive the principal amount as if a prepayment has occurred. If the net losses exceed the guarantee level, investors will have a shortfall in the cash flow.

## INTERNAL CREDIT ENHANCEMENTS

Internal credit enhancements come in more complicated forms than external credit enhancements and may alter the cash flow characteristics of the loans even in the absence of default. The most common forms of internal credit enhancements are reserve funds (cash reserve funds or excess servicing spread accounts) and senior/subordinated structures.

### Reserve Funds

Reserve funds come in two forms, cash reserve funds and excess servicing spread accounts. Cash reserve funds are straight deposits of cash generated from issuance proceeds. In this case, part of the underwriting profits from the deal are deposited into a hypothecated fund which typically invests in money market instruments. Cash reserve funds are typically used in conjunction with letters of credit or other kinds of external credit enhancements. For example, a CMO may have 10% credit support, 9% of which is provided by a letter of credit and 1% from a cash reserve fund.

Excess servicing spread accounts involve the allocation of excess spread or cash into a separate reserve account after paying out the net coupon, servicing fee, and all other expenses on a monthly basis. For example, suppose that the gross weighted average coupon (gross WAC) is 7.75%, the servicing and other fees is 0.25%, and the net weighted average coupon (net WAC) is 7.25%. This means that there is excess servicing of 0.25%. The amount in the reserve account will gradually increase and can be used to pay for possible future losses.

The excess spread is analogous to the guarantee fee paid to an agency, except that this is a form of self-insurance. This form of credit enhancement relies on the assumption that defaults occur infrequently in the initial stages of the loans but gradually increase in the following two to five years. This assumption is consistent with the PSA's Standard Default Assumption (SDA) curve that we will describe later in the chapter.

### Senior/Subordinated Structure

The most widely used internal credit support structure is by far the senior/subordinated structure. The subordinated class is the first loss piece absorbing all losses on the underlying collateral, thus protecting the senior class. For example, a $100 million deal can be divided into two classes: a $92.25 million senior class and a $7.75 million subordinated class. The subordination level in this hypothetical structure is 7.75%. The subordinated class will absorb all losses up to $7.75 million, and the senior class will start to experience losses thereafter. So, if there $5 million of losses, the subordinated class will realize this loss. Thus, it would realize a 64.5% loss ($5/$7.75). If, instead, there is $10 million of losses, the subordinated class will experience $7.75 million of losses or a 100% loss, and the senior class will experience a loss of $2.25 million ($10 million minus $7.75 million) or a 2.4% loss ($2.25/$92.25). Exhibit 27–1 is a loss severity table showing various percentage losses in principal on both senior and subordinated classes at different loss levels.

The subordinated class holder would obviously require a yield premium to take on the greater default risk exposure relative to the senior class. This setup is another form of self-insurance wherein the senior class holder is giving up yield spread to the subordinated class holder. This form of credit enhancement does not affect cash flow characteristics of the senior class except in the form of prepayment. To the extent that losses are within the subordination level, the senior class holder will receive principal as if a prepayment has occurred. Exhibit 27–2 shows the average life of both classes at 165 PSA before any default assumption for a hypothetical $100 million structure with a 7.75% subordination level.

Almost all existing senior/subordinated structures also incorporate a shifting interest structure. A shifting interest structure redirects prepayments disproportionally from the subordinated class to the senior class according to a specified schedule. An example of such a schedule would be as follows.

The rationale for the shifting interest structure is to have enough insurance outstanding to cover future losses. Because of the shifting interest structure, the subordination amount may actually grow in time, especially in a low default and fast prepayment environment. This is sometimes referred to as "riding up the credit curve."

Using the same example of our previous $100 million deal with 7.75% initial subordination and assuming a cumulative principal paydown of $16 million ($6 million of regular repayments and $10 million of prepayments) by year five and no losses, the subordination will actually increase to 9.5%. The subordinated class principal balance will be reduced by the pro rata share of regular repayments (7.75% of $6 million) and none of the prepayments to $7.29 million. The senior class principal balance will be reduced by the pro rata share of regular repayments (92.25% of $6 million) and all of the $10 million prepayments to

**EXHIBIT 27–1**

Loss Severity Table. $100 Million Deal, 7.75% Subordination

| Loss Amount (millions) | Senior Class | Subordinated Class |
|:---:|:---:|:---:|
| $5.00 | 0.00% | 64.50% |
| $7.75 | 0.00% | 100.00% |
| $10.00 | 2.40% | 100.00% |
| $20.00 | 13.30% | 100.00% |

## EXHIBIT 27–2

Average Life for Senior/Subordinated Structure Assuming No Defaults and 165 PSA

| Structure<br>Gross WAC<br>New WAC<br>WAM (months) | 8.13%<br>7.50%<br>357 | Average Life |
|---|---|---|
| *No shifting interest* | | |
| Senior class | 92.25% | 8.77 |
| Subordinate class | 7.75% | 8.77 |
| *With shifting interest* | | |
| Senior class | 92.25% | 8.41 |
| Subordinate class | 7.75% | 13.11 |
| *With shifting interest* | | |
| Senior class | 84.50% | 7.98 |
| Subordinate class | 15.50% | 13.11 |

## EXHIBIT 27–2a

Example of a Shifting Interest Structure

| Months | Percentage of Prepayments<br>Directed to Senior Class |
|---|---|
| 1–60 | 100 |
| 61–72 | 70 |
| 73–84 | 60 |
| 85–96 | 40 |
| 97–108 | 20 |
| 109+ | pro rata |

$76.71. The new subordination level will increase to 9.5% ($7.29/$76.71). Exhibit 27–3 shows the new subordination levels, given various combinations of prepayments and losses. Holding net loss at zero, the faster the prepayments, the higher the subordination grows. Even in the case of losses, fast prepayments can sometimes offset the effect of principal losses to maintain the initial subordination.

While the shifting interest structure is beneficial to the senior class holder from a credit standpoint, it does alter the cash flow characteristics of the senior class even in the absence of defaults. As Exhibit 27–2 indicates, a 7.75% subordination with the shifting interest structure will shorten the average life of the

### E X H I B I T   27–3

Subordination Level $100 Million Deal, 7.751% Subordination, 5 Years Out (in millions)

| Regular Paydown | Prepayment | Loss | Size of Senior Class | Size of Sub. Class | Sub. Level |
|---|---|---|---|---|---|
| $6 | $10 | $0 | $76.71 | $7.29 | 9.50% |
| $6 | $20 | $0 | $66.71 | $7.29 | 10.93% |
| $6 | $40 | $0 | $46.71 | $7.29 | 15.61% |
| $6 | $10 | $2 | $76.71 | $5.29 | 6.90% |
| $6 | $20 | $2 | $66.71 | $5.29 | 7.93% |
| $6 | $40 | $2 | $46.71 | $5.29 | 11.33% |
| $6 | $10 | $5 | $76.71 | $2.29 | 2.99% |
| $6 | $20 | $5 | $66.71 | $2.29 | 3.43% |
| $6 | $40 | $5 | $46.71 | $2.29 | 4.90% |

senior class to 8.41 years at the same 165 PSA, assuming no default. The size of the subordination also matters. A larger subordinated class redirects a higher proportion of prepayments to the senior class, thereby shortening the average life even further. A 15.5% subordination in the same example shortens the average life to 7.98.

It may be counterintuitive that the size of the subordination should affect the average life and cash flow of the senior class more than the credit quality. This is because the size of the subordination is already factored into the rating. The rating agency typically requires more subordination for lower credit quality loans to obtain a triple-A rating and less subordination for better credit quality loans. From a credit standpoint, the investor may be indifferent between a 5% subordination on a package of good quality loans and a 10% subordination on a package of lower quality loans as long as the rating agency gives them the same rating. However, the quality of the underlying loans will determine the default rate and therefore the timing of the cash flow.

## COMPENSATING INTEREST

An additional factor to consider, which is unique to whole-loan CMO structures, is compensating interest. Mortgage pass-throughs and CMOs pay principal and interest on a monthly basis (with the exception of some early quarterly-pay CMOs), and principal paydown factors are also calculated only once a month. While homeowners may prepay their mortgage on any day throughout the month, the agencies guarantee and pay the investors a full month of interest as if all the prepayments occur on the last day of the month. Unfortunately, this guarantee does not apply to whole-loan mortgages and, consequently, not to whole-loan CMOs. If a homeowner pays off a mortgage on the 10th day of the month, he or she will stop paying interest for the rest of the month. Because of the payment delay (for example, 25 days) and the once-a-month calculation of principal paydown, the investor will receive full principal but only 10 days of interest on the 25th of the following month.

This phenomenon is known as payment interest shortfall or compensating interest and is handled differently by different issuers and services. Some issuers will only pay up to a specified amount, and some will not pay at all. The economic value of compensating interest depends on the level of prepayment and the types of CMO tranches. Generally, the faster the prepayment and the higher the coupon tranche, the higher the economic value of compensating interest.

## WEIGHTED AVERAGE COUPON DISPERSION

The pooling standard on whole loans is looser than that on agency deals. Therefore, most whole-loan CMOs have wider gross coupon and maturity dispersions given any WAC and WAM. While the agency would strip off variable amounts of servicing and guarantee fees to bring the net coupon of a pool down to 50 bps increments, whole loans have fixed servicing fees, and the net coupons can vary. Using Exhibits 27–4 and 27–5 as examples, an agency CMO may contain four pools with gross coupons of 8.7%, 8.6%, 8.5%, and 8.4% to yield a GWAC of 8.55%. Seventy bps are stripped off the first pool to yield an 8% net coupon. Sixty bps will be stripped off the second pool to also yield an 8% coupon. Fifty bps and 40 bps will be stripped of the third and four pools, respectively. Since all the pools have net coupons of 8%, the weighted average net coupon is also 8%. Conversely, a whole-loan CMO containing four pools with the exact

**EXHIBIT   27–4**

Agency CMO

| Pools | GWAC | Net Coupon | IO-ette (bps) | Stripped-Down Coupon |
|---|---|---|---|---|
| 1 | 8.70% | 8.00% | 100 | 7.00% |
| 2 | 8.60% | 8.00% | 100 | 7.00% |
| 3 | 8.50% | 8.00% | 100 | 7.00% |
| 4 | 8.40% | 8.00% | 100 | 7.00% |
| Average | 8.55% | 8.00% | 100 | 7.00% |

**EXHIBIT 27-5**

Whole Loan CMO

| Pools | GWAC | Servicing (bps) | Net Coupon | WAC IO (bps) | Stripped-Down Coupon |
|---|---|---|---|---|---|
| 1 | 8.70% | 55 | 8.15% | 115 | 7.00% |
| 2 | 8.60% | 55 | 8.05% | 105 | 7.00% |
| 3 | 8.50% | 55 | 7.95% | 95 | 7.00% |
| 4 | 8.40% | 55 | 7.85% | 85 | 7.00% |
| Average | 8.55% | 55 | 8.00% | 100 | 7.00% |

GWACs will have a constant servicing fee of 55 bps. The net coupons on these four pools will then be 8.15%, 8.05%, 7.95%, and 7.85% to yield the same weighted average net coupon of 8%.

To create fixed-rate (e.g., 7% coupon) tranches from the whole-loan CMO regardless of which pool prepays, a WAC IO (weighted average coupon interest only) tranche must be created to absorb the variability of net coupons on the underlying pools. The WAC IO tranche will receive a weighted average coupon of 100 bps off the whole deal. The WAC IO is equivalent in structure to an IO strip or IO-ette in an agency deal. However, as soon as prepayments start to occur, the WAC IO strip may change. Hypothetically and intuitively, Pools 1 and 2, with the higher WACs, prepay first. Exhibit 27–6 shows that this will leave the WAC IO strip with only 90 bps of coupon, one-tenth less in cash flow going forward. This is extremely important in the analysis of WAC IO since whole loan CMOs tend to have wider WAC dispersion.

## CLEAN-UP CALL PROVISIONS

All whole-loan CMO structures are issued with a "clean-up" call provision. The clean-up call provides the servicers or the residual holders (typically the issuers)

**EXHIBIT 27-6**

Whole-loan CMO After Paydown

| Pools | GWAC | Servicing (bps) | Net Coupon | WAC IO (bps) | Stripped-down Coupon |
|---|---|---|---|---|---|
| 3 | 8.50% | 55 | 7.95% | 95 | 7.00% |
| 4 | 8.40% | 55 | 7.85% | 85 | 7.00% |
| Average | 8.45% | 55 | 7.90% | 90 | 7.00% |

the right, but not the obligation, to call back all the outstanding tranches of the CMO structure when the CMO balance is paid down to a certain percentage of the original principal balance. The servicers typically find it more costly than the servicing fee to service the CMO when the balance is paid down to a small amount. For example, suppose a $100 million CMO was originally issued with a 10% clean-up call. When the entire CMO balance is paid down to $10 million or less, the servicer can exercise the call to pay off all outstanding tranches like a balloon payment, regardless of the percentage balance of the individual tranches.

The call provision, when exercised, shortens the principal payment window and the average life of the back-end tranches of a CMO. This provision is not unique to whole-loan CMO structures. It is mandatory, however, for all whole-loan CMO structures, while agency CMOs may or may not have clean-up calls. Typically, FHLMC CMOs have 1% clean-up calls, and FNMA CMOs do not have clean-up calls.

## ASSESSING PREPAYMENT RATES OF NONAGENCY CMOS

Prepayments speeds on nonagency CMOs vary from very sensitive to interest rate changes to independent of interest rates changes. Whole loan CMOs, such as the Residential Funding Mortgage Securities (RFMSI) 1997-S5, are very sensitive to interest rate changes (see Exhibit 27–7). Home equity loans (such as The Money Store Home Equity Trust 1996-D) tend to be less sensitive to interest rate changes. Shared appreciation mortgage deals (in the United Kingdom) appear to be independent of interest rate changes. Hence, it is impossible to make a blanket statement regarding nonagency CMO prepayment speeds.

To highlight the differences across nonagency CMOs in terms of prepayment, we will begin with whole loans. As an example, we will use the Residential Funding RFMSI 1997-S5 deal (see Exhibit 27–8). Like agency mortgages, whole loans exhibit the same seasonality traits (as can be seen by the seasonal spikes as the beginning of the seasoning curve). After the initial ramp-up occurs, the whole loans are quite sensitive to interest rate changes. After 15 months of loan seasoning, a decline in interest rates sent the CPR from 11% to 37% which lead to a dramatic change in CMO prices.

In contrast to the RFMSI 1997-S5 deal, the home equity loan deal (TMSHE 1996-D) has a considerably different prepayment seasoning curve. The prepayments begin at significantly higher levels and do not exhibit the sensitivity to interest rate changes that the whole loans exhibit. The WAC on the RFMSI 1997-S5 deal is 8.16% which contracts sharply with the 11.75% WAC on the TMSHE 1996-D home equity loan deal. The weighted-average LTV for both the whole loan and home equity loan deals are approximately the same.

The third deal presented in Exhibit 27–8 is the FirstPlus Financial 125 LTV 97-1. As the name implies, this home equity loan product allows the household to borrow up to 125% of the appraised value of the dwelling. An attractive

**E X H I B I T   27-7**

Prepayment Seasoning Curve for Whole Loans

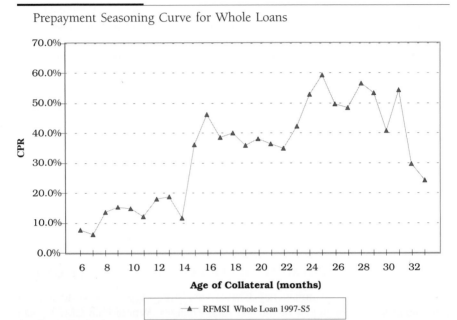

*Source:* Bloomberg Financial

feature of the 125 LTV loan product is that prepayment speeds should be lower than prepayment speeds on other home-equity loans and nonconforming whole loans. One of the reasons for the lower prepayment speeds on the 125 LTV loan is the degree of prepayment protection. Most of the 125 LTV loans have significant prepayments associated with them.

The prepayment speeds on the Residential Funding whole loan portfolio approaches 60% CPR after two years. (The dramatic increase in the prepayment speed on the whole loans in month 14 was a sudden decline in mortgage rates.) The Money Store home equity loan portfolio is in the 30 to 40% CPR range after two years, while the FirstPlus 125 LTV loan portfolio has settled in the low 20% CPR range. While the historical prepayment speeds on the 125 LTV portfolio are higher than the 14% that some analysts expected after two years, the speeds are considerably less than those of whole loans and traditional home equity loans.

## Credit Risk on Alternative Loan Products

As pointed out in the previous section, the 125 LTV loan portfolios have a lower prepayment speed than whole loans and other lower LTV home equity loan products. We would expect that high LTV loan-backed transactions would have

**E X H I B I T   27–8**

Prepayment Seasoning Curves for Whole Loans, Home Equity Loans and
125 LTV Loans.

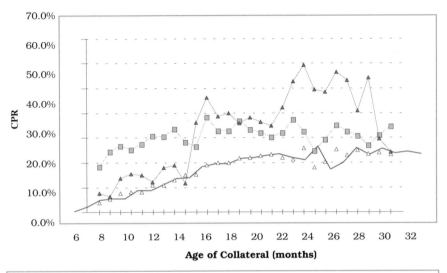

*Source:* Bloomberg Financial

the highest default rates and that standard "A-quality" jumbo MBSs would have
the lowest. Unfortunately, default data are somewhat difficult to obtain for these
products; however, we can use historical 90-day delinquencies as a proxy for
default.

In Exhibit 27–9, we compare the historical 90-day delinquencies on whole
loan, lower LTV home equity loans and 125 LTV loans. As expected, the "A"-
quality jumbo delinquencies are very low. What is somewhat surprising is that
the lower LTV home equity loans from The Money Store have almost a linear
growth in delinquencies that reach 12% after two years. The FirstPlus 125 LTV
loans have a 90-day delinquency rate that is increasing with time as well; however, it is just above 2% of the portfolio after two years which is substantially
less than The Money Store's experience. This appears to support the wisdom of
lending larger amounts to high-quality borrowers, and points out the risks in
lending even small amounts at lower LTVs to lesser-quality ones.

## PSA STANDARD DEFAULT ASSUMPTION BENCHMARK

With the increase in whole-loan CMO issuance, the Public Securities Association introduced a standardized benchmark for default rates. The PSA standard

**E X H I B I T   27–9**

90-days Delinquencies for Whole Loans, Home Equity Loans and
125 LTV Loans

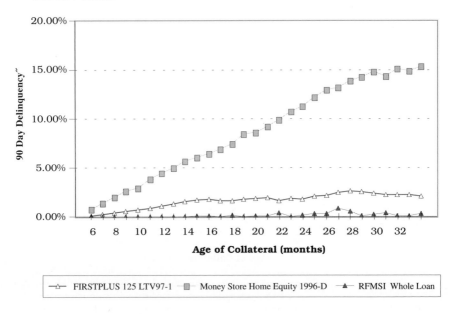

*Source:* Bloomberg Financial

default assumption (SDA) benchmark gives the annual default rate for a mortgage pool as a function of the seasoning of the mortgages. An example of the
PSA SDA benchmark, or 100 SDA, is as follows:

1.  The default rate in month 1 is 0.02% and increases by 0.02% up to
    month 30, so that in month 30 the default rate is 0.60%.

2.  From month 30 to month 60, the default rate remains at 0.60%.

3.  From month 61 to month 120, the default rate declines linearly from
    0.60% to 0.03%.

4.  From month 120 on, the default rate remains constant at 0.03%.

This pattern is illustrated in Exhibit 27–10.

As with the PSA prepayment benchmark, multiples of the benchmark are
found by multiplying the default rate by the assumed multiple. For example,
200 SDA means the following pattern:

•  The default rate in month 1 is 0.04% and increases by 0.04% up to month
   30, so that in month 30 the default rate is 1.20%.

•  From month 30 to month 60, the default rate remains at 1.20%.

**E X H I B I T   27–10**

PSA Standard Default Assumption Benchmark (100 SDA)

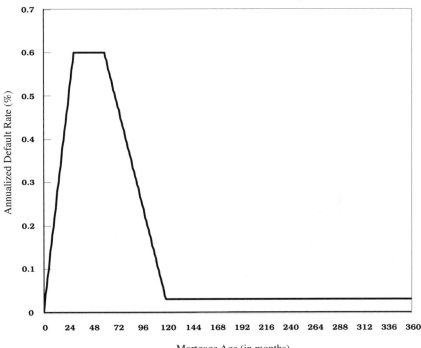

Mortgage Age (in months)

- From month 61 to month 120, the default rate declines from 1.20% to 0.06%.

- From month 120 on, the default rate remains constant at 0.06%.

A 0 SDA means that no defaults are assumed.

The foreclosure experience for the RFMSI 1997-S5 deal is presented in Exhibit 27–11. As with the PSA SDA standard in Exhibit 27–10, the foreclosure experience for the RFMSI 1997-S5 deal shows a positive ramping from month 8 out to month 33. The SDA speed for this deal is faster than the 100 SDA, with foreclosure rates reaching almost 0.9% in month 32 (while the 100 SDA peaks at 0.6% in month 31). According to history, the foreclosure rate for RFMSI 1997-S5 should flatten out for 30 months and then decline to 0.03% after ten years of total aging.

## PREPAYMENT AND DEFAULT RESISTANT MORTGAGES

Thus far, we have examined whole loans, home equity loans and 125 LTV loans. Each of these mortgages has a different sensitivity for prepayment and default.

**E X H I B I T   27–11**

Historical Foreclosure on REFMSI 1997-S5 Deal

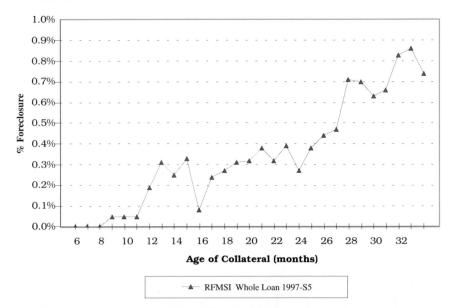

—▲— RFMSI Whole Loan 1997-S5

The whole loans are very senstitive to interest rate changes, while the home equity loans have the greatest sensitivity to 90-day deliquency risk.

An interesting alternative to these loan products is the shared appreciation mortgage (SAM) which has been issued in the United Kingdom for several years. The UK SAM (originated primarily by Bank of Scotland) has some interesting features that make it resistant to both prepayment and default. To begin with, the UK SAM is usually made to households that are free and clear on their property (or have a subsantial equity cushion). For example, consider a household with a dwelling that is currently appraised at $200,000 and has no mortgage outstanding. The lending instituion will give the borrower $50,000 today in exchange for the borrower repaying the $50,000, plus 75% of any appreciation in property value when the borrower sells the dwelling, refinances, or dies. There is no periodic mortgage payment due, so the likelihood of default is zero. In terms of prepayment, there is little risk of refinancing risk (although the likelihood of prepayment due to death is not trivial).

Despite being resistant to both default and prepayment (due to refinancing), there are very few CMOs or passthroughs based on the SAM product. This is somewhat surprising given that consumer demand for the SAM is quite strong. It is the investment banks that are unwilling to create the secondary market product. The primary reason for this resistance is a lack of information about future housing prices. As housing price indices improve, the popularity of SAMs should increase as well.

## CHAPTER 28

# COMMERCIAL MORTGAGE-BACKED SECURITIES*

Anthony B. Sanders, Ph.D.
Professor of Finance and Galbreath Distinguished Scholar
The Ohio State University

## INTRODUCTION

Commercial mortgage-backed securities (CMBS) represent an interesting departure from residential MBS. With residential MBS, the underlying collateral is loans on residential properties (1 to 4 units). With CMBS, the underlying collateral is loans on retail properties, office properties, industrial properties, multifamily housing, and hotels. Unlike residential mortgage loans, commercial loans tend to be "locked out" from prepayment for 10 years. Counterbalancing the reduction of prepayment risk for CMBS is the increase in default risk.

Both CMBS and real estate investment trusts (REITs) have grown tremendously since 1995 as investors' tastes for new real estate-related products have increased. Investment banks were able to apply what they have learned from residential MBS and apply it (with some interesting twists) to the commercial real estate loan market. Not only is the U.S. market continuing to expand, but also CMBS is growing at an ever-increasing rate in Europe (albeit at a much smaller scale). This chapter focuses on the interesting twists that make CMBS such a fascinating product.

## THE CMBS DEAL

A CMBS is formed when an issuer deposits commercial loans into a trust. The issuer then creates securities in the form of classes of bonds backed by the commercial loans. As payments on the commercial loans (and any lump-sum repayment of principal) are received, they are distributed (passed through) to the bondholders according to the rules governing the distribution of proceeds.

---

* This chapter is reprinted with permission from Frank J. Fabozzi (ed.), *Investing in Asset-Backed Securities* (New Hope, PA: Frank J. Fabozzi Associates, 2000).

## Bond Passthrough Rates

An example of a recent CMBS deal can be used to highlight the distribution of cash flows to the bondholders and the rules governing the distribution. The GMAC 1999-C3 deal, underwritten jointly by Deutsche Bank and Goldman Sachs, is summarized in Exhibit 28–1. The balance of the bonds as of the cutoff date (9/10/99) is $1,152,022,048. The gross weighted-average coupon (WACg) is 7.90% and the net weighted-average coupon (WACn) is 7.79%. The weighted-average maturity (WAM) is 117 months

The bonds are sequential-pay. The passthrough rate for class A-1-a is 6.97% and fixed. The passthrough rates for classes A-1-b, A-2, B, C, G, H, J, K, L, M, and N are equal to the lesser of the fixed passthrough rate and net WAC of the mortgage pool. For example, the A-1-b bondholders will receive the lesser of the fixed passthrough rate (7.27%) and the net WAC (7.79%). Passthrough rates for classes D, E, and F are equal to the WAC of the mortgage pool.

Class X is an interest-only class. Class X receives the excess of the net WAC received from the pool over the weighted-average passthrough rate paid to the sequential-pay bonds. Class X's notional balance equals the outstanding balance of the sequential-pay bonds.

## CMBS Ratings and Subordination Levels

The rating agencies play a critical role in the CMBS market. The role of the rating agency is to provide a third-party opinion on the quality of each bond in the structure (as well as the necessary level of credit enhancement to achieve a desired rating level). The rating agency examines critical characteristics of the underlying pool of loans such as the *debt service coverage ratio* (DSCR) and the *loan-to-value ratio* (LTV). If the target ratios at the asset level are below a certain level, the credit rating of the bond is reduced. Subordination can be used at the structure level to improve the rating of the bond. For example, suppose that a certain class of property requires a DSCR of 1.50× to qualify for an A rating; if the actual DSCR is only 1.25×, additional subordination can be added at the deal level to bring the rating to an A rating.

The credit ratings for the bonds in the GMAC 1999-C3 deal are presented in Exhibit 28–1. Fitch rated the first three bonds (A-1-a, A-1-b, and A-2) AAA Moody's rated the same bond classes as Aaa. The B through F bonds have progressively lower ratings. The subordination levels decline with the bond ratings: 27% subordination for the AAA bond down to 10.5% for the BBB–bond. The subordination levels continue to drop for the C bond (17.5%) through the N bond (0%).

## Prioritization of Payments

The highest-rated bonds are paid-off first in the CMBS structure. Any return of principal caused by amortization, prepayment, or default is used to repay the

**EXHIBIT 28–1**

Bonds for GMAC 1999-C3 Deal

| Bond | Moody Rating | Fitch Rating | Original Amount | Subordination Original | Coupon | Coupon Type |
|------|--------------|--------------|-----------------|------------------------|--------|-------------|
| A-1-a | Aaa | AAA | $50,000,000 | 0.2700 | 0.0697 | Fixed |
| A-1-b | Aaa | AAA | $190,976,000 | 0.2700 | 0.0727 | Fixed |
| A-2 | Aaa | AAA | $600,000,000 | 0.2700 | 0.0718 | Fixed |
| B | Aa2 | AA | $51,840,000 | 0.2250 | 0.0754 | Fixed |
| C | A2 | A | $57,601,000 | 0.1750 | 0.0779 | Fixed |
| D | A3 | A− | $20,160,000 | 0.1575 | 0.0779 | WAC-0b |
| E | Baa2 | BBB | $37,440,000 | 0.1250 | 0.0779 | WAC-0b |
| F | Baa3 | BBB− | $23,040,000 | 0.1050 | 0.0779 | WAC-0b |
| G | NA | NA | $57,601,000 | 0.0550 | 0.0697 | Fixed |
| H | NA | NA | $8,640,000 | 0.0475 | 0.0697 | Fixed |
| J | NA | NA | $11,520,000 | 0.0375 | 0.0697 | Fixed |
| K | NA | NA | $14,400,000 | 0.0250 | 0.0697 | Fixed |
| L | NA | NA | $11,520,000 | 0.0150 | 0.0697 | Fixed |
| M | NA | NA | $5,760,000 | 0.0100 | 0.0697 | Fixed |
| N | NA | NA | $11,524,048 | 0.0000 | 0.0697 | Fixed |
| X | NA | NA | $1,152,022,048n | NA | 0.0053 | WAC/IO |
| R | NA | NA | $0r | NA | 0 | |

Source: Charter Research.

highest-rated tranche first and then the lower-rated bonds. Any interest received on outstanding principal is paid to all tranches. However, it is important to note that many deals vary from this simplistic prioritization assumption.

For example, consider the GMAC 1999-C3 deal. The bonds that are rated AAA by Fitch (classes A-1-a, A-1-b, and A-2) are the Senior Certificates. Classes B through M are organized in a simple sequential structure. Principal and interest are distributed first to the class B and last to the class N. Unfortunately, the Senior Certificates are not as simple in their prioritization.

The loans underlying the GMAC 1999-C3 are divided into two groups. Group 2 consists of the multifamily loans and Group 1 consists of the remaining loans (retail, office, warehouse, and so on). In terms of making distributions to the Senior Certificates, 61% of Group 1's distribution amount is transferred to Group 2's distribution amount. Group 1's distribution amount is used to pay:

1. Interest on bond classes A-1-a, A-1-b, and the portion of interest on the Class X on components A-1-a and A-1-b pro rata

2. Principal to the Class A-1-a and A-1-b in that order

Loan Group 2's distribution amount is used to pay:

**1.** Interest on Class A-2 and the portion of interest on the Class X components from A-2 to N pro rata

**2.** Principal to the Class A-2

In the event where the balances of all the subordinated classes (Class B through Class M) have been reduced to zero because of the allocation of losses, the principal and interest will be distributed on a pro rata basis to Classes A-1-a, A-1-b, and A-2.

Loan default adds an additional twist to the structuring. Any losses that arise from loan defaults will be charged against the principal balance of the lowest rated CMBS bond tranche that is outstanding (also known as the *first loss piece*). For the GMAC 1999-C3 deal, losses are allocated in reverse sequential order from Class N through Class B. After Class B is retired, classes A-1-a, A-1-b, and A-2 bear losses on a pro-rata basis. As a consequence, a localized market decline (such as a rapid decline in the Boston real estate market) can lead to the sudden termination of a bond tranche. Hence, issuers seek strategies that will minimize the likelihood of a "microburst" of defaults.

As long as there is no delinquency, the CMBS tranches are well behaved. Unfortunately, delinquency triggers intervention by the servicer (whose role will be discussed later in the chapter). In the event of a delinquency, there may be insufficient cash to make all scheduled payments. In this case, the servicer is supposed to advance both principal and interest. The principal and interest continue to be advanced by the servicer as long as these amounts are recoverable.

## Call Protection

In the residential MBS market, the vast majority of mortgages have no prepayment penalties. In the CMBS market, the vast majority of mortgages have some form of prepayment penalty that can impact the longevity and yield of a bond. Call protection can be made at both the loan level and in the CMBS structure. At the loan level, there exist several forms of call protection: prepayment lockout, yield maintenance, defeasance, and prepayment penalties.

*Prepayment lockout* is where the borrower is contractually prohibited from prepaying the loan during the lockout period. The lockout is the most stringent form of call protection since it removes the option for the borrower to prepay before the end of the lockout period. The prepayment lockout is commonly used in newer CMBS deals.

Under *yield maintenance*, the borrower is required to pay a "make whole" penalty to the lender if the loan is prepaid. The penalty is calculated as the difference between the present value of the loan's remaining cash flows at the time of prepayment and principal prepayment. Yield maintenance was a common form of call protection in older CMBS deals but it is less common in newer deals.

*Defeasance* is calculated in the same manner as yield maintenance. However, instead of passing the loan repayment and any penalty through to the investor, the borrower invests that cash in U.S. Treasury securities (strips/bills) to fulfill the remaining cash flow structure of the loan. The Treasuries replace the building as collateral for the loan. The expected cash flows for that loan remain intact through to the final maturity date. Like yield maintenance, it was more popular with older CMBS deals and is less common in newer deals.

With *prepayment penalties*, the borrower must pay a fixed percentage of the unpaid balance of the loan as a prepayment penalty if the borrower wishes to refinance. The penalty usually declines as the loan ages (e.g., starting with 5% of the outstanding principal in the first year, 4% in the second year, etc., until the penalty evaporates).

Exhibits 28–2 and 28–3 examine the largest 20 loans underlying the GMAC 1999-C3 deal. In terms of call protection, each of the loans is locked-out. The average lockout has about 114 months remaining. Hence, the loans underling this CMBS deal have just less than 10 years of prepayment protection.

**E X H I B I T    28–2**

The Twenty Largest Loans Underlying the GMAC 1999-C3 Deal

| | Name | Location, MSA | Category | Loan Amount |
|---|---|---|---|---|
| 1 | Biltmore Fashion | Phoenix, Arizona | Retail | $80,000,000 |
| 2 | Prime Outlets | Niagara Falls, New York | Retail | $62,835,426 |
| 3 | Equity Inns | Various | Hotel | $46,511,317 |
| 4 | One Colorado | Pasadena, California | Retail | $42,628,093 |
| 5 | Comerica Bank | San Jose, California | Office | $33,640,510 |
| 6 | 120 Monument | Indianapolis, Indiana | Office | $28,955,362 |
| 7 | 125 Maiden | New York, New York | Office | $28,500,000 |
| 8 | Texas Development | Houston, Texas | Apartment | $26,926,701 |
| 9 | Sherman Plaza | Van Nuys, California | Office | $25,984,904 |
| 10 | Alliance TP | Various | Apartment | $24,888,157 |
| 11 | Bush Tower | New York, New York | Office | $23,000,000 |
| 12 | County Line | Jackson, Mississippi | Retail | $20,990,264 |
| 13 | Sherwood Lakes | Schereville, Indiana | Apartment | $20,162,442 |
| 14 | Laurel Portfolio | Various | Apartment | $17,950,331 |
| 15 | Sweet Paper | Various | Warehouse | $17,420,000 |
| 16 | Sheraton Portsmouth | Portsmouth, New Hampshire | Hotel | $15,949,087 |
| 17 | Trinity Commons | Fort Worth, Texas | Retail | $15,242,981 |
| 18 | Village Square | Indianapolis, Indiana | Apartment | $14,993,950 |
| 19 | Golden Books | Fayetteville, North Carolina | Warehouse | $14,493,350 |
| 20 | Air Touch | Dublin, Ohio | Office | $13,992,523 |

Source: Charter Research.

**EXHIBIT  28–3**

Loan Characteristics for the Twenty Largest Loans Underlying the GMAC 1999-C3 Deal

| | Name | Coupon | Maturity | Current Occupancy | DSCR | LTV | Lockout |
|---|---|---|---|---|---|---|---|
| 1 | Biltmore Fashion | 7.68% | 07/01/09 | 96.00% | 1.43 | 60.40% | 114 |
| 2 | Prime Outlets | 7.60% | 05/01/09 | 96.00% | 1.36 | 72.70% | 109 |
| 3 | Equity Inns | 8.37% | 07/01/09 | NA | 1.90 | 49.50% | 114 |
| 4 | One Colorado | 8.29% | 07/01/09 | 91.00% | 1.25 | 72.30% | 114 |
| 5 | Comerica Bank | 7.55% | 05/01/08 | 99.00% | 1.43 | 65.20% | 32 |
| 6 | 120 Monument | 8.09% | 06/01/09 | 100.00% | 1.23 | 74.40% | 113 |
| 7 | 125 Maiden | 8.12% | 09/01/09 | 97.00% | 1.31 | 73.80% | 116 |
| 8 | Texas Development | 7.44% | 05/01/09 | NA | 1.34 | 72.00% | 114 |
| 9 | Sherman Plaza | 7.68% | 08/01/09 | 95.00% | 1.24 | 68.40% | 115 |
| 10 | Alliance TP | 7.32% | 08/01/09 | NA | 1.19 | 86.40% | 112 |
| 11 | Bush Tower | 7.99% | 08/01/09 | 97.00% | 1.27 | 46.00% | 115 |
| 12 | County Line | 7.91% | 08/01/09 | 98.00% | 1.39 | 84.00% | 115 |
| 13 | Sherwood Lakes | 6.99% | 02/01/08 | 94.00% | 1.32 | 76.70% | 94 |
| 14 | Laurel Portfolio | 7.37% | 05/01/09 | NA | 1.22 | 73.60% | 112 |
| 15 | Sweet Paper | 8.26% | 06/01/09 | NA | 1.25 | 71.40% | 113 |
| 16 | Sheraton Portsmouth | 8.53% | 05/01/09 | 71.00% | 1.28 | 72.50% | 116 |
| 17 | Trinity Commons | 7.93% | 08/01/09 | 97.00% | 1.44 | 68.80% | 115 |
| 18 | Village Square | 7.80% | 10/01/07 | 97.00% | 1.28 | 79.30% | 93 |
| 19 | Golden Books | 8.50% | 08/01/09 | 100.00% | 1.69 | 67.40% | 119 |
| 20 | Air Touch | 7.98% | 08/01/09 | 100.00% | 1.20 | 77.70% | 117 |

*Notes:* A * in the Prepay Lockout column denotes that yield maintenance is used in conjunction with Prepay Lockout.
Source: Charter Research.

In addition to call protection at the loan level, call protection is available in structural form as well. Since CMBS bond structures are sequential-pay, lower-rated tranches cannot pay down until the higher-rated tranches are retired. This is the exact opposite of default where principal losses hit the lowest-rated tranches first.

## Timing of Principal Repayment

Unlike residential mortgages that are fully amortized over a long time period (say, 30 years), commercial loans underlying CMBS deals are often *balloon loans*. Balloon loans require substantial principal payment on the final maturity date although the loan is fully amortized over a longer period of time. For example, a loan can be fully amortized over 30 years but require a full repayment of outstanding principal after the tenth year. The purpose of a balloon loan is to keep the periodic loan payment of interest and principal as low as possible.

Balloon loans pose potential problems for investors due to the large, lump-sum payment that must be refinanced. If there is a change in the quality of the underlying asset (e.g., a decline in the real estate market, increased competition leading to a decline in lease rates, etc.), there is a danger that the loan will not be refinanced; this can result in default. In order to prevent this type of loan failure at the balloon date from occurring, there are two types of loan provisions: the internal tail and the external tail.

The *internal tail* requires the borrower to provide evidence that an effort is underway to refinance the loan prior to the balloon date (say, 1 year prior to the balloon date). The lender would require that the borrower obtain a refinancing commitment before the balloon date (say, 6 months prior to the balloon date). With an *external tail,* the maturity date of the CMBS deal is set to be longer than that of the underlying loans. This allows the borrower more time to arrange refinancing while avoiding default on the bond obligations. The servicer advances any missing interest and scheduled principal in this buffer period.

## THE UNDERLYING LOAN PORTFOLIO

There are two sources of risk relating to the underlying loan portfolio. The first risk is prepayment risk and the second risk is default/delinquency risk.

### Diversification

A factor that is often considered when analyzing the risk of a CMBS deal is the diversification of the underlying loans across space. The reasoning for what is termed "spatial diversification" is that the default risk of the underlying pool of loans is lessened if the loans are made on properties in different regions of the country. Rather than have the entire portfolio of loans being subject to an idiosyncratic risk factor (e.g., the decline in oil prices and the collapse of the Houston real estate market), the portfolio can spread its risks across numerous economies. Thus, a collapse of the Houston real estate market (which may lead to higher defaults on commercial loans) will be less of a concern if the commercial property markets in Chicago, Kansas City, New York, and Seattle remain strong.

The strategy of spatial diversification can be seen in Exhibit 28–4. Approximately 22% of the loans underlying the GMAC 1999-C3 are on properties in California, 14% on properties in Texas, and 11% on properties in New York. The remaining loans are spread out among other states such as New Hampshire, Missouri, Illinois, and Mississippi. Thus, the GMAC 1999-C3 deal has achieved a significant degree of spatial diversification. Although a 22% concentration factor for California is still quite large, it is considerably less than a 100% concentration-factor (which is often referred to as a "pure play" strategy). Furthermore, California, Texas, and New York represent the states where most of the commercial loans are being originated.

**EXHIBIT 28–4**

Aggregate Loan Amounts by State for GMAC 1999-C3 Deal

| State | Loan Amount | No. of Loans | % of Pool |
|-------|-------------|--------------|-----------|
| California | $257,522,410 | 33 | 22.35% |
| Texas | $162,355,125 | 26 | 14.09% |
| New York | $130,070,471 | 7 | 11.29% |
| Arizona | $99,942,794 | 5 | 8.68% |
| Indina | $68,623,516 | 5 | 5.96% |
| Ohio | $44,982,528 | 5 | 3.90% |
| Mississippi | $23,067,864 | 2 | 2.00% |
| New Jersey | $22,983,973 | 5 | 2.00% |
| Other | $342,473,371 | 50 | 29.73% |
| Total | $1,152,022,052 | 138 | 100.00% |

Source: Charter Research.

In addition to spatial diversification, CMBS pools can be diversified across property types. Rating agencies tend to give lower levels of credit-enhancement to deals that contain diversification across property types since a pool that is diversified across residential, office, industrial, and retail will likely avoid the potential of a national glut in one of the sectors (such as the retail market).

The degree of property type diversification can be seen in Exhibit 28–5. Approximately 90% of the loans are on retail, apartments, and office properties with retail having the largest percentage (30.44%). As a consequence, the

**EXHIBIT 28–5**

Aggregate Loan Amounts by Property Type for GMAC 1993-C3 Deal

| Property Type | Loan Amount | No. of Loans | % of Pool |
|---------------|-------------|--------------|-----------|
| Apartment | $259,779,802 | 39 | 22.55% |
| Office | $322,053,844 | 36 | 27.96% |
| Retail | $350,683,062 | 34 | 30.44% |
| Warehouse | $99,126,075 | 15 | 8.60% |
| Hotel | $105,832,139 | 8 | 9.19% |
| Other | $14,547,130 | 6 | 1.26% |
| Total | $1,152,022,052 | 138 | 100.00% |

Source: Charter Research.

GMAC 1999-C3 deals have reduced the risk of default by not being heavily concentrated in only one of the property groups.

The loan characteristics of the pool underlying the GMAC l999-C3 pools are presented in Exhibit 28–6. The hotel properties are viewed as being the most risky given that they have the highest coupon (8.50%), the highest DSCR (1.65×), and the lowest LTV (58.93%). The apartment properties are viewed as the safest risk with the lowest coupon (7.62%), the lowest DSCR (1.29×), and the highest LTV (76.51%). As can be seen in Exhibits 28–5 and 28–6, 90% of the underlying loans are in the three least-risky property types: apartment, office, and retail.

## Cross-Collateralization

Diversification of the underlying collateral is one way of reducing default risk. Another way to reduce default risk is to use cross-collateralization. *Cross-collateralization* means that the properties that serve as collateral for the individual loans are pledged against each loan. Thus, the cash flows on several properties can be used to make loan payments on a property which has insufficient funds to make a loan payment. This "pooling" mechanism reduces the risk of default. To add some additional enforcement penalties to the cross-collateralization mechanism, the lender can use cross-default which allows the lender to call each loan within the pool, when any one defaults.

## Loan Analysis

There are several products available that provide analysis of the underlying collateral for CMBS deals. An example of a package that allows for the analysis of the CMBS deal and the underlying collateral is Conquest, an on-line service

**E X H I B I T    28–6**

Characteristics for Loans Underlying the GMAC 1999-C3 Deal by Property Type

| Property Type | Coupon | Due | Current Occupancy | DSCR | LTV | Prepay Lockout |
|---|---|---|---|---|---|---|
| Apartment | 7.62% | 06/29/09 | 92.92% | 1.29 | 76.51% | 113 |
| Office | 7.79% | 04/03/09 | 96.17% | 1.33 | 67.84% | 107 |
| Retail | 7.95% | 09/19/09 | 95.21% | 1.36 | 69.77% | 116 |
| Warehouse | 8.13% | 06/27/09 | 99.56% | 1.42 | 68.28% | 115 |
| Hotel | 8.50% | 12/31/08 | 75.18% | 1.65 | 58.93% | 109 |
| Other | 7.83% | 05/13/09 | 95.11% | 1.54 | 67.00% | 113 |

Source: Charter Research.

provided by Charter Research in Boston. Conquest provides for a detailed examination of each loan in the underlying portfolio. In addition to simply describing the loan data (DSCR, LTV, loan maturity, prepayment lock type, etc.), Conquest provides default risk (delinquency) analysis as well. Using vendors such as Torto Wheaton, Conquest forecasts the growth in net operating income and value for each property in the underlying portfolio.

Torto Wheaton, for example, provides 10-year forecasts of net operating income and value by geographic area (MSA) property type (office, industrial, retail, and apartments). These forecasts are updated quarterly. Torto Wheaton provides five scenarios ranging from best to worst cases. Given these five scenarios, the user is able to examine the future path of debt service coverage and loan to value for each loan in the pool. Thus, the user is able to examine default and extension risk tendencies on a loan-by-loan basis. This information is aggregated to the deal level so that changes in the riskiness for each of the underlying loans is reflected in the cash flows for each tranche at the deal level.

## Stress Testing at the Loan Level

Stress testing the collateral in a CMBS deal is important from both the underwriter and investor perspective. By allowing the forecasts on net operating income and value to be varied over time, underwriters and investors can better understand the default risk and extension risk likelihoods and how these in turn impact CMBS cash flows.

For CMBS markets, stress tests must be performed in a manner that is consistent with modern portfolio theory. While diversification across property type and economic region reduces the default risk of the underlying loan pool, the effects of diversification are negated if the stress test ignores the covariance between the properties. For example, there should be some degree of common variance across all properties (reflecting general economic conditions). Furthermore, there should be some degree of common variance across property type and economic regions.

The Torto Wheaton approach of generating five forecast paths by property type and geographic location permits the construction of a distribution of future outcomes for property value and net operating income growth for the loan pool. Based on Torto Wheaton forecasts, the user can determine the degree to which the portfolio is diversified (by reducing the variance of the distribution of future outcomes). An index of diversification can be created that allows users to compare the degree of diversification across different CMBS deals. Thus, stress testing the underlying properties can be measured in the aggregate by how much the diversification index is changed.

In addition to being able to create a diversification index, the user can construct a default risk/extension risk index as well. As the underlying loans are stressed, a distribution of outcomes in terms of default and extension risk can be obtained. This would allow users to compare CMBS deals not only for the diversification of the underlying loan portfolio, but compare CMBS deals for sensitivity to the stress test.

## Historical Aspect on Loan Performance

While a detailed analysis of loan performance models is beyond the scope of this chapter, it is important to recognize that CMBS deals are not free of prepayment, default, and delinquencies. In Exhibit 28–7, the historical default and prepayment information for deals with a cutoff date in 1994 (from the Conquest database) are presented. As one can see, there is a wide range in terms of the ratio of performing loans to original loans in the pool. The KPAC 1994-M1 deal has the lowest performing loan ratio of 11.48%. On the other hand, the DLJ 1994-MF 11 has a performing loan ratio of 98.72%. The average performing loan ratio is 46.34% for the 13 deals from 1994.

It should be noted that the average performing loan ratio of 46.34% could be explained, in part, by underlying loan maturity. On average, 20.58% on the loans underlying deals from 1994 matured. Mortgage prepayments account for approximately 30.33% of the original loans terminating. Foreclosures, defaults, and real estate owned (REO) comprise only 2.50% of the 13 deals from 1994. Interestingly, the DLJ CMBS deals have a very high performance loan ratio

**E X H I B I T   28–7**

Historical Default and Prepayment for CMBS Deals with Cutoff Dates in 1994

| Deal | Loans | Performing | Matured | Prepaid | Bankrupt | Fore. | REO* |
|------|-------|-----------|---------|---------|----------|-------|------|
| ASC 1994-C3 | 40 | 21 | 3 | 13 | 0 | 3 | 0 |
| ASC 1994-MD1 | 9 | 7 | 1 | 1 | 0 | 0 | 0 |
| ASFS 1993-2 | 30 | 19 | 4 | 5 | 1 | 1 | 0 |
| ASFS 1994-C2 | 39 | 6 | 26 | 7 | 0 | 0 | 0 |
| CLAC 1994-1 | 89 | 37 | 33 | 19 | 0 | 0 | 0 |
| CSFB 1994-CFB1 | 63 | 21 | 8 | 34 | 0 | 0 | 0 |
| DLJ 1993-MF 17 | 42 | 38 | 0 | 3 | 0 | 0 | 0 |
| DLJ 1994-MF 11 | 78 | 77 | 0 | 1 | 0 | 0 | 0 |
| KPAC 1994-M1 | 61 | 7 | 13 | 41 | 0 | 0 | 0 |
| MCFI 1994-MC1 | 44 | 9 | 9 | 26 | 0 | 0 | 0 |
| MLMI 1994-M1 | 80 | 32 | 28 | 20 | 0 | 0 | 0 |
| SASC 1994-C1 | 185 | 67 | 51 | 53 | 0 | 0 | 14 |
| SASC 1995-C1 | 142 | 30 | 21 | 71 | 0 | 5 | 15 |

Source: Charter Research.

**EXHIBIT   28-8**

Percentage Disposition of Loans Underlying 1994 CMBS Deals

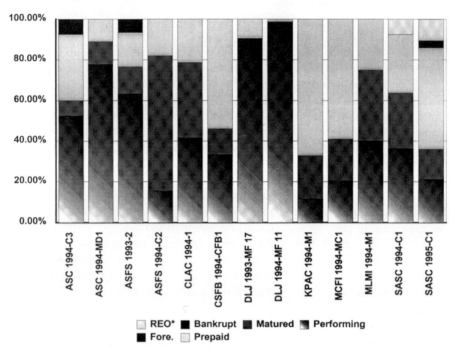

(90% and 98%) with few loan maturities and prepayments (and no defaults or foreclosures).

Despite the historical performance of these deals, analysts must be careful about projecting these results for current deals. Prepayment lockouts, which are more popular now than they were in 1994, will be more effective in determining prepayments than simple yield maintenance provisions. Also, longer-term mortgage loans will extend the duration of the underlying loan pool (keeping the performance loan ratio higher for a longer period of time). Finally, improvements in underwriting and the investor's ability to understand the underlying collateral should improve default and foreclosure risk over time.

## CREATING A CMBS MODEL

As mentioned before, there are a number of CMBS models available in the marketplace. Whether someone chooses one of the "one size fits all" models or designs a customized model tailored to specific needs, there are several key features that should be in a CMBS model.

1. An econometric model of historical loan performance using logit or proportional hazards model. This permits a better understanding of property and loan attributes that predict default and prepayment.

2. If default does occur, empirical estimates of loss severity by property type and state are needed.

3. Database of actual *NOI and Value volatility* by property type and geographic location (see the discussion of Torto Wheaton earlier in this chapter). This step permits the construction of default risk indicators.

4. Monte carlo simulation of interest rates and NOI paths to estimate foreclosure frequency and prepayment risk.

5. Finally, the deal structure (and waterfalls) should interface cleanly with loan-by-loan simulations.

A CMBS model with these features should be able to capture the critical elements of pricing, risk and return.

## THE ROLE OF THE SERVICER

The servicer on a CMBS deal plays an important role. The servicer collects monthly loan payments, keeps records relating to payments, maintains escrow accounts, monitors the condition of underlying properties, prepares reports for trustee and transfers collected funds to trustee for payment.

There are three types of servicers: the subservicer, the master servicer and the special servicer. The *subservicer* is typically loan originator in a conduit deal who has decided to sell the loan but retain the servicing. The subservicer will then send all payments and property information to the *master servicer*. The master servicer oversees the deal and makes sure the servicing agreements are maintained. In addition, the master servicer must facilitate the timely payment of interest and principal. When a loan goes into default, the master servicer has the responsibility to provide for servicing advances.

Unlike the subservicer and the master servicer, the *special servicer* enters the picture when a loan becomes more than 60 days past due. Often, the special servicer is empowered to extend the loan, restructure the loan and foreclose on the loan (and sell the property). This critical role is of great importance to the subordinated tranche owners because the timing of the loss can significantly impact the loss severity, which in turn can greatly impact subordinated returns. Thus, first-loss investors usually want to either control the appointment of the special servicer or perform the role themselves. This creates a potential moral hazard problem since the special servicer may act in their own self-interest and potentially at the expense of the other tranche holders.

## INNOVATIONS IN THE CMBS MARKET: "BUY-UP" LOANS

A recent innovation in the CMBS market is the "buy-*up*" loan. Most participants in the mortgage market are familiar with the "buy-*down*" loan in the residential market. With a buydown loan, a borrower pays "points" upfront to reduce the mortgage interest rate. The resulting loan, having a lower interest rate, is less sensitive to prepayment and has a greater duration than a higher interest rate loan. The buy-up loan in the commercial mortgage market is the exact opposite, but with a twist.

Consider a borrower who approaches a commercial mortgage lender for a $1 million loan. They agree on an 8.00% interest rate with the loan being fully amortized over 30 years (using monthly amortization). The resulting monthly mortgage payment would $7,337.65. The DSCR for the loan (based on annual NOI of $100,000) is 1.14× while the LTV is 71.40%. (See Exhibit 28–9.)

Suppose that the rating agency requires additional loan subordination (or gives a lower rating) if the loan in question has an LTV in excess of 65%. However, the subordination level would be reduced (and/or the rating increased) if the loan has an LTV of 65% or less. With a buy-up loan, the monthly payments of $7,337.65 are discounted at an interest rate of 9.00% (instead of 8.00%) resulting in a present value of the loan being $911,936.30. Although the DSCR remains the same, the LTV declines to 64.9%, thus qualifying the loan for lower subordination levels (and/or a higher rating).

The problem facing the rating agency is selecting the correct LTV. Clearly, for the purpose of correctly identifying default risk; the LTV should be used that is based on the actual amount disbursed to the borrower, not the present value of the mortgage payments. The definition of LTV caused some problems when buy-up loans were first used since it was unclear which definition of LTV the lender was using. Once the rating agencies recognized there were multiple definitions of LTV, the lenders began to report both LTVs.

Technically, the difference between the amount disbursed to the borrower ($1,000,000) and the present value of the buy-up loan ($911,936.30) is the buy-

**EXHIBIT   28–9**

A Comparison of A Standard Loan and a Buy-up Loan

|  | Standard | Buy-up |
| --- | --- | --- |
| NOI (annual) | $100,000.00 | $100,000.00 |
| Loan size | $1,000,000.00 | $911,936.30 |
| Amount to borrower | $1,000,000.00 | $1,000,000.00 |
| Loan term | 360 | 360 |
| Mtg rate | 8.00% | 9.00% |
| Monthly payment | $7,337.65 | $7,337.65 |
| DSCR | 1.14 | 1.14 |
| LTV–PV of loan | 71.4 | 64.9 |
| LTV–amt to borrower | 71.4 | 71.4 |

up premium. The documents on a CMBS deal containing buy-up loans will most likely say that the buy-up loan is locked out; furthermore, in case of prepayment, the borrower would owe both the buy-up loan amount and the buy-up premium. The higher interest rate on the buy-up loan (with its lockout provision) means that there is more interest for an IO class.

## SUMMARY

The purpose of this chapter is to provide a broad overview of the CMBS market from the point of view of a sample CMBS deal. Although CMBS deals tend to be prepayment insensitive, bonds (or tranches) will still be somewhat sensitive to interest rate changes since lockouts usually dissolve after 10 years. Default risk is a concern with CMBS and the underlying collateral needs to be examined on a loan-by-loan basis. Products currently available make this task much more tractable.

## CHAPTER 29

# SECURITIES BACKED BY AUTOMOBILE LOANS

**W. Alexander Roever, CFA**
Managing Director, Head of Asset Backed Research
Banc One Capital Markets, Inc.

**John N. McElravey**
Director, Asset-Backed Research
Banc One Capital Markets, Inc.

**Glenn M. Schultz, CFA**
Director
Banc One Capital Markets, Inc.

## INTRODUCTION

Since the earliest days of the asset-backed securities (ABS) market, auto finance companies have relied on securitization as an economical and reliable source of funding. At the same time, fixed income investors have embraced ABS backed by retail auto loans and leases for many reasons, including the securities' high credit quality, stable average lives, and generally strong relative value characteristics. This confluence of securitization's popularity with issuers and the attractiveness of the resulting securities to investors has made the auto sector a staple of the ABS market.

The auto sector has consistently been one of the ABS market's largest segments. Between 1985 and 1999, over $240 billion of publicly traded ABS backed by auto loans and leases were issued. Over the same period, auto ABS grew at an annualized rate exceeding 30%, reaching total outstandings of $90 billion at year-end 1998 and accounting for nearly 14% of all outstanding public ABS.

This chapter serves as an introduction to this important segment of the ABS market. Included in this analysis is an overview of the collateral characteristics and behavior of auto loans and leases and an exploration of the structural aspects of these securities. The final section of the chapter addresses the relative value characteristics of auto ABS.

# AUTO LOAN BACKED SECURITIES

Compared to the traditional means of financing their operations, securitization has proven an attractive funding alternative for many banks and auto finance companies. Historically, most of these firms have been "balance sheet lenders," meaning they financed their operations using various forms of on-balance sheet debt such as bank loans, commercial paper and corporate bonds. When it relies on these kinds of financing alone, a firm's revenue and profitability are constrained by its capacity to leverage the assets on its balance sheet. This competitive paradigm favored larger, well-capitalized lenders with strong credit profiles because they had access to large amounts of money at relatively low costs of funds. Smaller lenders, and others of lesser credit quality were competitively disadvantaged in this scheme, since their size and greater costs of funds restricted their ability to grow their businesses.

The advent of securitization transformed the competitive landscape of auto finance. Smaller firms often use securitization because it provides a steady source of funding that can be used to fuel asset creation, increase managed assets, and potentially increase profitability. This access to funding can lower the competitive barriers that constrain many lenders. Better still, through the use of various structuring techniques and means of credit enhancement, even a small, non-investment-grade lender can create an investment-grade-rated security and achieve all-in financing costs comparable to high grade corporate debt.

At the same time, securitization appeals to many well-capitalized, investment-grade-rated lenders, who use it mainly for the greater financial flexibility it creates.

## The Auto Finance Industry

The auto finance industry is populated by several types of firms, most of which have relied on securitization to varying degrees. The different types of firms tend to present varied risk profiles with respect to the loans they securitize and their ability to function as servicers for their securitizations.

### Banks

Banks have historically originated more auto loans than any other type of lender, but have generated a proportionately lesser volume of ABS. From 1985 through the second quarter of 1999, banks originated about 20% of auto ABS issuance. From an investor's perspective, bank-originated ABS generally provide an attractive risk profile both in terms of the banks' as servicers and the collateral quality.

Banks typically originate auto loans through two channels. *Direct* loans are made by the bank itself, typically through its branch network. These loans are usually underwritten to conservative standards with respect to both the obligor's ability and willingness to repay the loan and the terms of the loan (e.g., loan-to-value ratio, loan maturity, coupon). In contrast, *indirect* loans are made by auto dealers who are customers of the bank. The bank requires that these loans and their obligors meet certain underwriting standards that owing to the competitive nature of indirect lending, are often not as stringent as the bank's direct loan criteria. Still, most indirect pools tend to experience relatively low levels of delinquencies and defaults.

As ABS servicers, banks have several attractive qualities. Chief among these is the continuity of servicing banks can offer. Most banks that originate auto ABS use securitization as one of several funding sources, and still have significant auto loan exposure on their balance sheets. This exposure encourages them to sustain good underwriting practices and to maintain effective servicing operations. Also, if the auto market deteriorates or if a bank's auto lending operation becomes troubled, banks generally have diversified sources of revenue and liquidity with which to support continued servicing operations. This is not necessarily true of all types of lenders.

### Captive Finance Companies

Captive finance companies are the finance subsidiaries of auto manufacturers. Since 1985, captives have originated about half of all auto ABS. Nearly all auto loans originated by captives are sourced through the manufacturers' franchised dealer networks. Although the bulk of their issues are supported by loans to high-quality obligors, the captives' primary business purpose is to promote and support the sales of their parents' manufacturing operations. For this reason, some incentive exists for captives to price loans aggressively in order to promote sales. As such, pools originated by captives may experience higher delinquencies and losses than similar pools originated by other types of lenders.

But like banks, captives tend to use securitization on a limited basis, and retain a significant portion of their assets on balance sheet. According to the Federal Reserve, captives continue to own over 20% of all outstanding auto loans. As with the banks, these significant holdings promote strong underwriting and servicing. Furthermore, since the captives are an integral part of the parents' operations, the parents have a vested interest in promoting their finance subsidiarys' viability and continued access to funding.

### Finance Companies

Finance companies are independent firms where auto lending may be either the only business or one of several. *Monoline* finance companies focus exclusively on auto finance. Between 1985 and the second quarter of 1999, monolines accounted for about 28% of auto ABS issuance. These specialized firms have been among the biggest beneficiaries of securitization since most are themselves rated below investment grade, and the ABS markets offer relatively cheap funding.

Many monolines originate loans to credit-impaired borrowers. Some monolines focus on marginally weaker obligors, while others concentrate their operations at the absolute bottom of the credit spectrum. These independent and typically non-investment-grade companies can present greater servicing risks than other types of finance companies because of their comparatively limited sources of cash and their often heavy reliance on securitization. If these firms are unable to fund themselves through securitization or have their credit restricted due to greater-than-expected losses or for other reasons, their quality of servicing may be threatened, exposing ABS holders to greater risk. Continuity of servicing is particularly important in servicing non-prime and sub-prime obligors, with whom any servicing disruption is likely to result in a significant increase in losses.

*Multiline* finance companies are independent financial institutions for which auto finance is one of several business lines. This segment of the auto ABS market is relatively small and generally consists of consumer finance companies that have diversified into auto lending as an extension of their overall business strategy. Some are focused on lending to credit-impaired borrowers, while others target niches at the upper end of the market. For several reasons, multilines are often perceived as more stable than monolines. Among these reasons are the financial strength created by their diversified business mix, their demonstrated ability to service a variety of asset types, and access to funding sources besides securitization.

## Auto ABS Are Often Categorized By Obligor Type

There is a tendency within the auto sector to segment the market by obligor quality. Descriptive labels such as "prime," "non-prime," and "sub-prime" and quality grades such as A, B, C and D are commonly used in describing the credit quality of the underlying assets. Unfortunately, these terms are very subjective, and their meaning often varies from one lender to another. As a result, there can be some disagreement among lenders over what constitutes a prime, non-prime or sub-prime borrower. What one lender considers a prime quality loan might be considered non-prime by another lender.

The absence of clear and consistent credit quality delineation makes the task of assessing collateral quality more challenging. Exhibit 29–1 attempts to better define the most common collateral labels. In a perfect world, it might be possible to judge pool quality by comparing some objective quality measure such as average credit scores. (Credit scoring models like those produced by Fair, Isaac & Co. (FICO) evaluate several obligor-specific factors and assign a score to each obligor. Some of these factors are delinquency and default history, prior bankruptcy, and number and usage of credit lines.) Although credit scores are widely used by auto lenders, data regarding scores are rarely made available to ABS investors.

In the absence of objective collateral quality measures, a pool's weighted average coupon (WAC), or alternatively its weighted average annualized percentage rate, can be used as an indicator of average obligor quality. Assuming

**EXHIBIT 29-1**

Making Sense of Obligor Quality

| Borrower Quality | Prime | | Non-Prime | | Sub-Prime | |
|---|---|---|---|---|---|---|
| Borrower Grade | A+ | A | A− | B | C | D |
| FICO Scale[1] | 900    720 | 660 | 620 | 600 | 500 | 400 |
| Credit History | Good credit, No Derogatories | | Very minor, explainable problems | Moderate, perhaps recurring problems | Serious, recurring problems | Severe problems, demonstrated unwillingness to pay |
| Typical Weighted Average Collateral Coupon | 8 to 12% | | | 12 to 16% | 16 to 20% | 20% or greater (up to state usury limits) |
| Typical Pool Delinquency Rate | < 2.5% | | | < 5% | < 10% | < 20% |
| Typical Pool Cumulative Foreclosure Rate | < 3% | | | < 6% | < 20% | < 40% |
| Typical Pool Cumulative Losses | < 2% | | | < 4% | < 10% | > 10% |

[1] FICO scores are a product of Fair, Isaac & Co. and are based on predictive data available in individual credit bureau reports. The scores shown are intended as general indicator of obligor credit quality and are based on research conducted by Banc One Capital Markets. The scores presented are not endorsed by Fair, Isaac & Co. Different lenders can have varing interpretations of credit scores.

that lenders appropriately price the risk of loss into their loans, pools with higher WACs should be riskier than identical pools with lower WACs. As such, it is possible to use WACs as an indicator of collateral quality in order to decompose the industry by originator and obligor type, as in Exhibit 29–2. Between 1985 and the second quarter of 1999, prime, non-prime and sub-prime collateral respectively accounted for 66%, 28% and 6% of total issuance. Captive finance companies were responsible for over half of all issuance, and were the largest issuers of both prime and non-prime ABS. Monolines have accounted for approximately three-quarters of all public market sub-prime issuance.

## Comparing Collateral Performance

To help put the differences between obligor quality and lender type in perspective, it is helpful to look at some actual examples. The next three exhibits compare key collateral characteristics, delinquency, and net loss information for 1996

**EXHIBIT 29–2**

| Market Segmentation by Issuer Type: | | | |
|---|---|---|---|
| | Prime <12% | Non-Prime 12% to 16% | Sub-Prime >16% | As % of Auto ABS Issuance |
| Banks | 20% | 24% | 2% | 20% |
| Captives | 58% | 44% | 0% | 50% |
| Monolines | 21% | 33% | 79% | 28% |
| Multilines | 1% | 0% | 18% | 2% |
| Total | 100% | 100% | 100% | 100% |

| Market Segmentation by Obligor Type: | | | |
|---|---|---|---|
| | Prime <12% | Non-Prime 12% to 16% | Sub-Prime >16% | Total |
| Banks | 67% | 32% | 1% | 100% |
| Captives | 76% | 24% | 0% | 100% |
| Monolines | 50% | 32% | 18% | 100% |
| Multilines | 40% | 0% | 60% | 100% |
| As % of Auto ABS Issuance | 66% | 28% | 6% | 100% |

Analysis through 1999: Q2

vintage transactions for representative lenders. Lender A is a bank with a prime portfolio. Lender B is a captive, also with a prime portfolio. Lender C is a monoline finance company specializing in non-prime obligors, and Lender D is a monoline specializing in the sub-prime sector of the market.

A comparison of the collateral pool (Exhibit 29–3) reveals that the prime pools (A and B) have higher average contract balances, a higher percentage of new vehicles, and lower interest rates than the non-prime and sub-prime pools. The lower coupon on the captive pool relative to the bank pool is likely a reflection of the lower concentration of used vehicles and the presence of *subvented loans*.[1] The higher average interest rates on pools C and D reflect the greater probability of obligor delinquency or default.

Exhibits 29–4 and 29–5 illustrate actual static delinquency and loss performance for each of the lenders. Not surprisingly, Lender A experienced the best performance, closely followed by Lender B. Lender C's experience was notably worse than A's or B's, and Lender D's collateral performance was poorer still.

## Structure and Auto Loan ABS

In any securitization, the structure is used both to protect against various risks and to provide economic funding for the issuer. Structural techniques used must protect ABS investors from risks that may arise outside the securitization (external risks) and from risks inherent to the securitization (internal risks). In both

**EXHIBIT   29–3**

Collateral Pool Comparison, 1996 Vintages

|                                      | Lender A  | Lender B  | Lender C   | Lender D   |
|--------------------------------------|-----------|-----------|------------|------------|
| Lender Type:                         | Bank      | Captive   | Finance Co. | Finance Co. |
| Obligor Type:                        | Prime     | Prime     | Non-Prime  | Sub-Prime  |
| Average Original Contract Size:      | $15,269   | $13,160   | $9,669     | $12,501    |
| Average Original Loan Term (mo.):    | $53       | $52       | $52        | $55        |
| Percent New/Used:                    | 54%/45%   | 66%/33%   | 22%/77%    | 13%/86%    |
| WAC:                                 | 9.20%     | 8.50%     | 13.20%     | 20.50%     |

---

1. Subvention is the subsidization of financing terms, most often by captive finance companies, usually undertaken to increase the unit volume of sales.

**EXHIBIT 29-4**

Serious Delinquencies and Loan Age

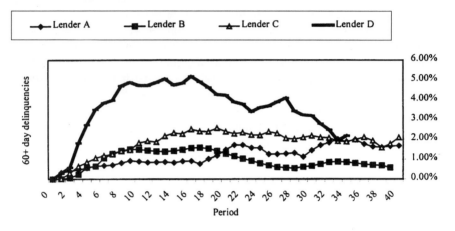

**EXHIBIT 29-5**

Cumulative Losses and Loan Age

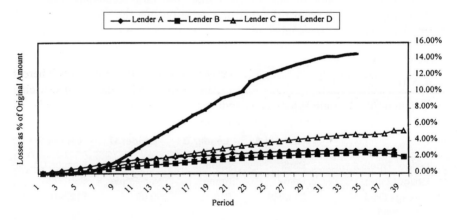

cases, credit rating agencies are intimately involved so as to ensure that the techniques employed adequately address the risks that are present, and are consistent with the ratings issued.

**External Risks**

Because repayment of the ABS depends on the availability of cash flow from the collateral, it is essential to legally segregate the collateral for the exclusive benefit of the ABS owners. To do this, the collateral must be isolated from the bankruptcy or insolvency risk of the lender or other entities involved in the securitization. This is usually achieved through the legal transfer of the loans from the originating firm, or the seller, to one or more bankruptcy-remote Special Purpose Entities (SPE). An SPE is a limited-purpose legal vehicle (e.g., corporation, limited liability corporation, business trust), separate and distinct from the originator, that is designed to protect the collateral from claims of the seller's creditors if the seller enters bankruptcy. Ideally, an SPE will be restricted in its ability to incur debt, pledge its assets, and merge or reorganize.

The transfer of auto loans from the seller to the SPE should be accomplished through one or more "true-sales": arm's-length transactions that transfer ownership of the collateral from the seller to the SPE. Alternatively, if the seller is an FDIC-insured bank or is itself a bankruptcy-remote entity, the transfer may take the form of a grant of a first priority perfected security interest in loans. Under the Uniform Commercial Code (UCC) of most states, both the sale and the grant of a security interest in the auto loans can be perfected either through the possession of the original loan documents, or the filing of UCC financing statements. Because it is usually the quicker and cheaper alternative, collateral transfers are typically perfected by filing UCC statements. Counsel for the seller will render legal opinions addressing the perfection of these transfers among the various parties.

To ensure that the requirements of the rating are met, rating agencies will conduct a review of legal documentation involving these transfers, including the legal opinions and other documents.

### Internal Risks

Structural techniques are also used to protect ABS investors from risks inherent to the transaction such as collateral risk (delinquency and default) and servicing risk. A primary responsibility of the credit rating agencies is to determine levels of credit enhancement that will mitigate these risks to a degree consistent with the ratings they issue. Rating agencies will conduct a review of the originator's underwriting criteria, the servicer's collection capabilities, the performance of the loan portfolio over time with regard to delinquencies and defaults, the transaction structure, and any pertinent legal issues. Each of these factors plays a role in the calculation of the credit enhancement levels.

The quality of the originator's underwriting criteria and its ability to service the portfolio are key elements in a transaction's rating. The rating agency's due diligence of a company will include a review of its history, management's experience in auto lending and its policies and procedures, the business plan and strategy for the firm's growth, and its capital structure and financial strength. Three to five years of operating history are preferred by the agencies; however, firms with less operating history, but more experienced management, may be able to pass muster.

The underwriting standards of the originator are one of the critical pieces of the rating agency review. The make-up and consistency of the lending process is closely scrutinized, including key underwriting criteria, the use of credit scoring models, whether loans are originated in a central location or at the branch level, and the terms and conditions of the loan. In addition, the servicing capabilities of the company are an important consideration because good servicing can improve a transaction, and poor servicing can harm an otherwise sound transaction. The elements of a servicer analyzed by the rating agencies include the firm's ratio of accounts to collectors, collection methods, and the ability and speed with which the firm liquidates repossessed inventory.

Despite the emphasis on the ability of the originator/servicer in the due diligence process, the agencies will often assume that the servicer will go bankrupt during the life of the transaction and not be available to service the portfolio. This is especially true for monoline finance companies or small lenders engaged in the non- or sub-prime market segments. As a result, the provisions for transferring servicing to a back-up servicer will be reviewed closely. For some transactions, (including those from small or relatively inexperienced issuers), an investment grade back-up servicer may need to be named at the outset.

In conjunction with their analysis of the seller/servicer, the agencies also perform an extensive collateral analysis. Using a combination of the issuer's own history, pool-specific factors, and industry experience, the agencies will determine a base-case level of expected losses. Some of the specific characteristics evaluated on a pool basis include the proportion of used cars relative to new cars, geographic concentrations, advance rates (i.e., loan size relative to MSRP or other measure), average loan maturity and seasoning. Other factors are also considered, including the average level and dispersion of loan coupons, loan prepayment speeds, and expected delinquencies, (particularly with respect to their impact on excess spread, an important source of credit enhancement). Based on their evaluation, the rating agencies will size the credit enhancement to absorb a multiple of base-case losses.

Exhibit 29–6 illustrates the typical multiples required for various ratings. For example, a transaction with expected losses of 2% could require between 8 and 12% credit enhancement, with the exact level influenced by several fac-

**EXHIBIT 29-6**

Credit Enhancement as a Multiple of Expected Losses

| Rating | Minimum Loss Multiples |
|--------|------------------------|
| AAA | 4–6 × Base-Case Losses |
| AA | 3–4.5 × |
| A | 2–2.5 × |
| BBB | 1.5–2.5 × |
| BB | 1.5–2 × |

Source: Banc One Capital Markets, Inc.

tors. These might include the form of credit enhancement, the availability of excess spread, or the presence of collateral performance triggers that can increase enhancement levels or accelerate prepayment in the event of collateral deterioration.

As with other types of ABS, credit enhancement can take several forms. Overcollateralization, subordination, and the use of spread accounts are all common, as are monoline insurance policies.

In addition to protecting investors from risk, structures are also designed to minimize the issuer's cost of funds. The two most common structures used in auto ABS are passthrough certificates and pay-through securities. Passthrough certificates are usually issued from a *grantor trust*. Grantor trusts are extremely limited in their ability to reinvest cash collections, and therefore pass principal and coupon received from the collateral to the certificate holders shortly after collection. Because grantor trusts are restricted from issuing multiple senior interests, they can only issue one class of senior BAS. However, grantor trusts can issue subordinate interests, and therefore can issue multiple classes of ABS, each with a different level of priority.

By time-tranching ABS, issuers can often achieve a lower cost of funds than is attainable with a passthrough structure. This type of pay-through structure most often relies on the use of an *owner trust,* which can issue multiple classes of both senior and subordinate bonds.

## AUTO LEASE ABS

Although leasing has been a part of auto finance for decades, its popularity exploded during the 1990s, when captive finance companies began to aggressively promote leasing. Consumers responded to these promotions, drawn either by the cost savings of leasing relative to purchasing a vehicle or by the opportunity to lease a luxury vehicle for the same cost as owning a more standard model. In 1998, 32% of all retail new car and truck purchases made were financed via lease, up from only 7.3% in 1990.[2]

Retail leases differ from loans in several fundamental respects. In a typical loan-financed vehicle purchase, a customer wanting a new vehicle from a dealer will typically finance the purchase with a combination of his own cash and money borrowed from a lender (Exhibit 29–7). In exchange for the loan, the lender gets a pledge of future repayment and, though the title will typically be issued in the customer's name, the lender will perfect a security interest in the vehicle by filing the appropriate documents with the state's department of motor vehicles.

A closed-end lease transaction differs from a loan-financed purchase in that the buyer of the vehicle is not the customer who will use the vehicle. Rather, the owner is a bank or finance company that purchases the vehicle contingent

---

2. Source: CNW Marketing/Research, Bandon, OR.

**E X H I B I T   29–7**

A Loan Financed Auto Sale

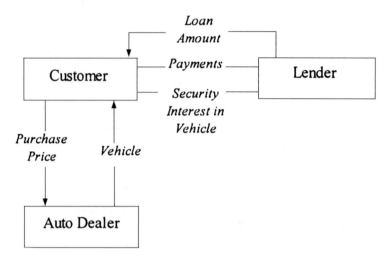

on the customer's agreement to lease the vehicle for some defined period (Exhibit 29–8). At the end of the lease period the customer (and if not the customer, then the dealer) will have the option to purchase the vehicle at a predetermined (residual) value. If neither the lessee nor the dealer exercise their options, then the lessor will continue to own the vehicle until it is re-leased or sold.

For the customer, the cost advantage of leasing arises mainly from the lower monthly payment. Scheduled lease payments are based on the portion of

**E X H I B I T   29–8**

A Lease Financed Auto Sale

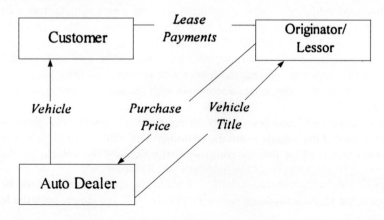

the vehicle to be used during the lease term, or equivalently, the value of the vehicle in excess of the residual. In contrast, loan payments are based on the entire value of the vehicle, less the down payment. The lessee also realizes other savings from the elimination of a down payment and a substantial reduction in sales taxes. Rather than pocketing the savings generated by leasing, many consumers choose to upgrade to more expensive vehicles.

Like the auto lending side of the business, leasing is populated by a variety of firms including captives, independent finance companies, and banks and other depository institutions. Captives dominate the market for auto leases, accounting for over 40% of new lease originations (exhibit not on here). This dominance is partly driven by competition in the auto industry, and the use of subvention programs by manufacturers to promote auto sales. The goal of these programs is to lower the monthly payments faced by consumers, and may involve techniques like offering leases with artificially high residual values. This creates risk for the leasing company because it increases the likelihood that a vehicle's residual value will be greater than its fair market value at lease-end, thereby exposing the lessor to a loss equal to the difference. While subvention may increase the lessor's risk of residual loss at lease-end, for captives this risk is offset by increased sales at the manufacturer level and the dealer networks' unmatched ability to dispose of used vehicles.

Lacking these advantages, banks, independent finance companies, and other firms rarely engage in subvention. Instead, these lessors are focused on the return earned on their leases. This bias leads them to greater conservatism in setting their residual values. The most commonly used resource for forecasting residual values is the *Automotive Lease Guide* (ALG). Historically, ALG values have proven to be less than actual wholesale used car prices, making ALG values a fairly conservative standard. However, lessors are not required to use ALG values, and in a competitive leasing environment they may be incented to set residual values above ALG values to lower the lessee's monthly payments.

## Structure and Auto Leases ABS

Like auto loan ABS, auto lease securitizations are subject to external and internal risks that are addressed through various structural techniques. While many of these risks are the same as those faced in auto loan transactions, auto lease ABS also face several unique challenges.

### External Risks

Perhaps the single most significant obstacle faced by would-be securitizers arises from the need to insulate the securitization from risks relating to the bankruptcy or insolvency of the lessor. In the closed-end lease scenario described earlier, the lessor's assets resulting from the lease are the lease contract and the underlying vehicle. In the event of the lessor's bankruptcy, these assets would be fair game for the lessor's creditors. In order to securitize the leases, both the leases and titles to the vehicles need to be held by a bankruptcy-remote, special purpose entity. However, since title to a motor vehicle can only be transferred following a time-consuming process that typically requires the payment of retitling fees and/or transfer taxes on each vehicle, retitling existing portfolios of leased vehicles can become a prohibitively expensive exercise. Without a cost-effective means of transferring isolated leases and the related vehicles, it becomes practically impossible for auto lease securitization to take place.

An answer to the problems posed by the retitling of leased vehicles is the *titling trust*. A titling trust is a special purpose, bankruptcy-remote entity formed by lease originators to purchase leases directly from dealers as new leases are executed (Exhibit 29–9). Title to the leased vehicles is held by the titling trust, and the originator is removed from the chain of title. Although the originator is removed from the line of title, it retains a beneficial interest in all leases and related vehicles in the titling trust. When the originator decides it is ready to complete a securitization, it can allocate a beneficial interest in a specified pool of titling trust assets to a securitization trust. This beneficial interest in a specified pool within the titling trust is the asset supporting the issuance of auto lease backed ABS. Ownership of the actual leases and vehicles remains with the titling trust. The securitization trust acquires no claim on any assets of the titling trust other than those in its specified pool. Exhibit 29–10 presents a simplified example of how a securitization using a titling trust works.

While titling trusts have proved a workable solution for newly originated leases, they generally have not eliminated the retitling problems of existing lease portfolios. The combination of the time needed to construct titling trust, ensure that the trusts are in compliance with the laws of every state in which they operate, and actually fill the trust with newly originated leases have limited the development of auto lease backed securitization.

**E X H I B I T   29–9**

A Lease Financed Auto Sale to a Titling Trust

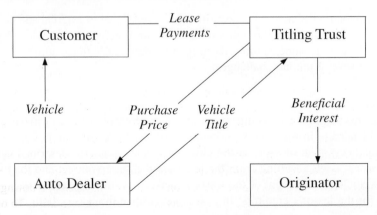

**EXHIBIT  29–10**

Simplified Securitization Using a Titling Trust

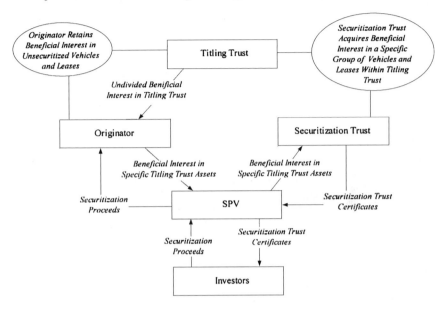

Another type of risk attendant with auto leases is vicarious tort liability. In several states, the owner of a vehicle is liable for damages caused by individuals who operate the vehicle with the owner's permission. This also applies to lessors, who can be liable for damages caused by lessees. In the case of a securitization, this risk can be limited by requiring lessees to maintain the appropriate insurance coverages, naming the titling trust to the insurance policies of originator, and allowing the titling trust to do business only in states that waive liability for lessors.

One other special risk faced in auto lease backed transactions is posed by the indirect nature of the securitization trust's relationship to the assets. Since the securitization trust has neither direct ownership nor a perfected security interest in the leases and vehicles, it is possible that the holder of a perfected lien on the assets could have a higher priority claim than the trust. In practice, minor claims such as tax liens and mechanics' liens filed against the owner can and do arise, but these can be mitigated and are often inconsequential on a portfolio basis. Of more concern are liens that may arise under the Employee Retirement Income Security Act of 1974 (ERISA). If the originator has unfunded pension liabilities, ERISA gives the Pension Benefit Guaranty Corporation the authority to put a lien on the company's assets, which theoretically could be extended to cover assets in a titling trust. This claim would have priority over the interest of the securitization trust. For this reason, a downgrade of the ABS could occur if a substantial pension liability were to arise. To offset this possibility, auto lease securitization documents often contain warranties by the originators that they will keep their pension plans funded, or may contain triggers that lead to credit enhancement increases if pension liabilities reach a specified level.

### Internal Risks

Like auto loans, leases are subject to default and delinquency. When evaluating potential lease transactions, rating agencies will scrutinize the leases for delinquency and default risk in a manner nearly identical to auto loans. However, lease residuals introduce a significant dimension of credit risk that is not present with auto loans, and are an important focus of rating agencies in determining the necessary level of credit enhancement.

Lease residuals can be a source of problems for would-be securitizers. Difficulties arise with residuals because originators, seeking to finance their lease portfolios via securitization, must finance both the leases and the residual value. The problem posed by securitizing the residual values is that they are not, strictly speaking, receivables since their value can only be realized at the end of the lease term, once the vehicle has been sold. Many of the complications of auto lease securitization arise from attempts to securitize the vehicle's residual value. However, these problems are not insurmountable.

Two main factors affect the level of residual risk. The first of these is the rate at which vehicles are turned in at lease-end. Since, on a close-end lease, both the lessee and the dealer usually have the option to purchase the vehicle at lease end, the lessor is only exposed to a potential residual loss if these options remain unexercised. The turn-in rate measures the percentage of vehicles coming off lease that are returned to the lessor. Industry-wide, approximately 22% of vehicles coming off lease are purchased by lessees, 28% by dealers, and the remaining 50% are returned to the lessor.[3] While this represents an industry baseline, many factors can contribute to higher turn-in rates including:

- *Vehicle depreciation:* All else being equal, turn-in rates will be higher if the market value of the vehicle is less than the residual value. For this reason, the strength of the used car market can have a significant impact on turn-in rates and residual value losses.

- *Duration of the lease:* Turn-in rates are generally higher for leases under three-years in length. In these cases, residual values are generally high. Given a choice between paying a large lump sum to purchase the vehicle, or leasing a new vehicle at the same payment, most lessees choose to continue leasing.

- *Manufacturers' marketing strategies:* If a manufacturer changes the styling of a model during a lease, it is common for turn-in rates to increase, as les-

---

3. 1999 Used Car Marketing Report, ADT Automotive, Inc.

sees tend to want to exchange old models for newer ones. Likewise, even if the model styling remains the same, aggressive pricing on the part of the manufacturer can lead to higher turn-in rates, particularly if the new vehicle prices are near, or less than the residual value.

- *Customer satisfaction:* All else being equal, models that require greater maintenance, or that have been subject to one or more manufacturer recalls, are more likely to be turned in.

The second factor affecting residual risk is the difference between the residual value and the market value of turned-in vehicles. If the market value is greater than the residual value, then there will be no residual losses. Risk arises because this is not always the case. Even the most conservative lessors can be exposed to the volatility of used vehicle prices.

Residual risks can be mitigated in several ways. First, the lessor can attempt to underwrite the leases conservatively, so that the residual value is more likely to be less than the expected future value of the vehicle. In a pool of leases, this practice should result in fewer vehicles being returned to the lessor, since lessees or dealers are more likely to buy the vehicle if the market price is greater than the residual value. In turn, this should result in recoveries in excess of residual values on returned vehicles. But from the originator's point of view, this strategy can be non-competitive since it will probably require the lessee to make higher monthly payments, making the lease relatively less attractive compared with those of its competitors.

Leasing companies can also mitigate residual risk through proactive lease termination plans. Under these plans the lessor will, shortly before the scheduled lease maturity, attempt to get the customer to re-lease or trade-in the vehicle. When employed successfully, this strategy can significantly reduce the return rate on vehicles and significantly reduce residual risk. Some lessors are able to achieve early termination on over 80% of their leases.

Residual value insurance is another method sometimes used by lessors to protect against residual risk. These policies typically pay the lessor 80% to 90% of the difference between the residual value and the market value of a vehicle.

Although these mitigation strategies help to limit residual value related losses on average, the variability of expected losses remains substantial. The combination of residual value risk with default and delinquency risk results in auto lease transactions having substantially higher credit enhancement requirements than auto loan transactions. Although the degree will vary on a case-by-case basis, some real-life examples exist which demonstrate the magnitude of the difference. During 1999, Honda issued both auto lease and loan ABS. The initial enhancement level, net of excess spread, for the senior bonds on the lease transaction totaled 14.00%, compared to 5.75% for its loan transaction. Similarly, during 1998, Toyota issued a lease transaction with initial senior enhancement level of 14.00% (Toyota Auto Lease Trust 1998-C), which compares to the 5.00% initial senior enhancement level on a 1999 vintage loan transaction (Toyota Auto Receivables 1999-A Owner Trust).

## RELATIVE VALUE ANALYSIS OF AUTO ABS

Several factors affect the perception of relative value in the auto ABS market, and are applicable to both loan and lease transactions. The first of these factors is issuer and collateral type. Over the life of an ABS, an originator/servicer with a strong credit profile is less likely than a weaker servicer to encounter problems that could interfere with its ability to effectively service loans. All else being equal, ABS supported by stronger servicers should garner higher prices because there is less risk of a servicing interruption, and therefore greater certainty that collateral collections will be made and applied in a timely fashion. Likewise, since collections from sub-prime collateral can be more unpredictable than with other collateral types, and because this uncertainty reflects greater risk, ABS supported by sub-prime loans usually must offer greater yield than otherwise comparable bonds.

Another factor affecting relative value is the structure of the securitization and its effect on the cash flow profile of the bond. Automobile ABS are structured as either a grantor trust or an owner trust. The profile of expected repayments implied by each type of trust affects relative value significantly.

In a grantor trust, principal and interest are passed through to the investors on a pro-rata basis. While ABS issued from grantor trusts may be tranched into senior and subordinate bonds, no time tranching is allowed. Grantor trust ABS are repaid over the life of the securitization and as a result have wide payment windows. In contrast to the grantor trust, an owner trust structure provides for maturity tranching. The tranching of the owner trust allows the issuer to create bonds designed to satisfy investors' maturity preferences and alters the timing of the cash flows received by the bond holder.

When assessing relative value, investors must determine the merits of wide window structures (grantor trusts) versus tighter window structures (owner trusts). Wide window auto ABS do not "roll down" the curve as fast as tight window auto ABS.[4] Consequently, investors usually require a higher spread for a wide window bond as compensation for the lack of price appreciation caused by the slower rolldown. This spread differential between wide window and tight window ABS will increase as the yield curve steepens, and decrease as it flattens.

Another factor to consider when contemplating value is the effect of prepayments on the average life of the bond. Unlike some other types of ABS and MBS, auto loan and lease prepayments are relatively unaffected by changes in interest rates. For this reason, auto ABS usually exhibit greater convexity than MBS and many other types of ABS.

One reason for the insensitivity of this collateral relative to interest rates is that the price of many vehicles depreciates faster than the underlying loan pays down. This can create a situation where the remaining loan balance is either

---

4. "Roll down" refers to the shortening of average life as a bond matures when the yield curve is positively sloped.

greater than the market value of the vehicle or greater than the amount another lender is willing to advance against the vehicle. Another factor limiting prepayments is that a large change in interest rates is needed to generate monthly savings worthy of the effort and cost necessary to refinance a loan.

Still, auto loan and, to a lesser degree, lease collateral do have prepayment variability unrelated to changes in interest rates. Common reasons for prepayment include the sale of the vehicle, repayment from insurance following an accident, and liquidation of the vehicle following default. In addition to these reasons, leases may also be subject to early repayment as a result of early termination programs employed by the manufacturer.

## Prepayment

Most auto ABS are priced using *Absolute Prepayment Speed* (ABS) scale. The ABS scale represents the percentage of the original number of loans that prepay during a given month. An ABS of 1.0% indicates that 1% of the original number of loans are prepaid per month. Although the characteristics of loans can vary greatly within a given pool, as a practical matter an assumption is made that each pool consists of homogenous loans, and the original pool balance is often used as a proxy for the number of loans in the pool.

The difference between the ABS and *Conditional Payment Rate* (CPR), a prepayment metric used for many other ABS types, is that CPR is calculated by comparing actual monthly prepayments measured in dollars to the current outstanding balance.[5] Exhibit 29–11 compares ABS to CPR assuming a constant 1.5% ABS scale, and illustrates that a constant ABS rate implies a continuously rising CPR.

Over the life of a pool, factors such as collateral or obligor type may affect the rate of prepayment, causing it to differ from expectation. However, actual ABS prepayment speeds for most auto loan pools remain fairly close—within 50 basis points—to their estimated speeds at pricing. Exhibit 29–12 provides an example of the difference between actual and estimated prepayment rates

---

5. An approximate ABS to CPR conversion can be performed as follows:

   1. Convert the ABS into a SMM using as follows:

   $$SMM = (100 \times ABS)/[100 - ABS (M - 1)]$$
      where:

   SMM = Single Monthly Mortality rate. The percentage difference between a pool's balance at the beginning of the month less scheduled principal payments, and its balance at the end of the month
      M = Months from origination

   2. Compute the annual CPR using the SMM:

   $$CPR = 1 - (1 - SMM)^{12}$$

**E X H I B I T   29–11**

Approximate CPR Equivalent of 1.5 ABS

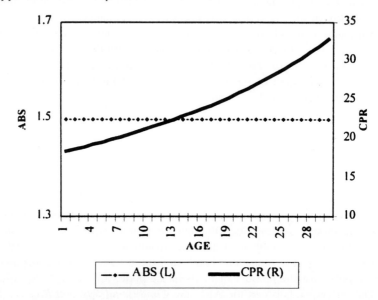

**E X H I B I T   29–12**

Static Prepayment Profiles for Auto Loans

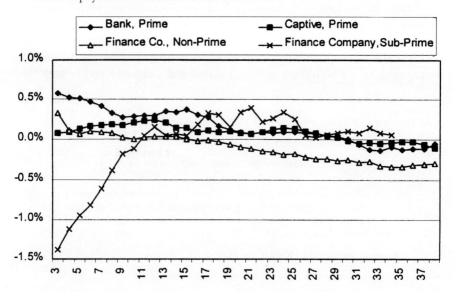

from 1996 transactions for a variety of issuer and collateral types. Because prepayment speeds are relatively stable, the average life variability of these transactions is muted (Exhibit 29–13).

## Tools for Relative Value Analysis

Static spread analysis (also known as "Z-Spread" or "zero volatility option adjusted spread analysis") can be used to compare the bullet equivalency of different structures. Static spread analysis views the cash flows of an amortizing structure as a series of zero coupon cash flows. The static spread is the constant spread over the spot curve that equates the projected cash flow to the current price of the bond plus the accrued interest.

Exhibit 29–14 provides a graphic illustration of static spread analysis. With a normal, upwardly sloping yield curve, the cash flows occurring earlier than the Treasury benchmark are undervalued, while the cash flows occurring later than the Treasury benchmark are overvalued when discounted at the yield to maturity. Static spread analysis provides a framework through which the spread of amortizing securities can be normalized and compared. If the static spread is less than the nominal spread, then a greater proportion of the cash flows are overvalued given the shape of the curve and timing of the cash flows. Conversely, if the static spread is greater than the pricing benchmark, then a greater proportion of the cash flows are undervalued given the shape of the curve and the timing of the cash flows.

Exhibit 29–14 suggests that changes in the shape of the curve affect the valuation of cash flows. For example, a flattening of the yield curve led by the short end of the curve decreases the extent to which the earlier cash flows are

## EXHIBIT 29–13

Effect on Average Life of Differences Between Expected and Realized Prepayment Speeds

| | | Change in A/L at Varying Speeds (ABS) | | | | |
| --- | --- | --- | --- | --- | --- | --- |
| Class | Original A/L at 1.5% ABs | 1.00% | 1.25% | 1.50% | 1.75% | 2.00% |
| A1 | 0.20 | 0.0 | 0.0 | 0.0 | 0.0 | 0.0 |
| A2 | 0.98 | 0.2 | 0.1 | 0.0 | −0.1 | −0.2 |
| A3 | 2.08 | 0.4 | 0.2 | 0.0 | −0.2 | −0.3 |
| A4 | 3.25 | 0.4 | 0.2 | 0.0 | −0.3 | −0.6 |

*AutoNation Receivables Corporation, Series 1999-A*

Average life numbers are expressed in years.

## EXHIBIT 29-14

Comparing Nominal and Static Spreads

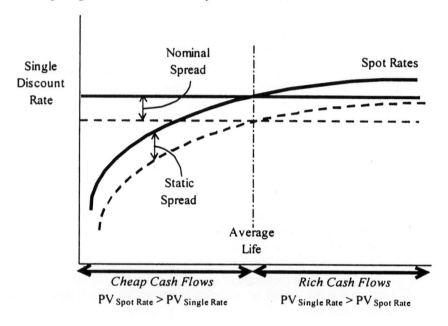

undervalued. Similarly, a steepening of the curve led by the short end increases the extent to which the earlier cash are undervalued. This in turn affects both spreads and expected total returns of wide window securities relative to those with tighter payment windows.

Exhibit 29–15 compares nominal and static spreads on two auto ABS with similar average lives issued by Chase Manhattan Bank. The first, Chase Manhattan Auto Grantor Trust, Series 1996-B class A (CMGT), features a wide payment window and is currently paying down principal. The second, Chase Manhattan Auto Owner Trust, Series 1996-C Class A3 (CMAOT), has a tight payment window and is locked out from receiving principal until the last few months of its life. For continuity, both bonds were priced using the same benchmark Treasury. The exhibit shows that CMGT is priced to a nominal spread of +77 basis points and a static spread of +71 basis points. Given that the static spread is less than the nominal spread, we can conclude that the cost of the payment window is +6 basis points and that the bond is priced rich relative to the benchmark Treasury. In contrast, CMAOT is priced to a nominal spread of +69 basis points and a static spread of +69 basis points. Since the spreads are identical, we can conclude that the pricing benchmark is accurate, the cost of the window is zero, and the bond is fairly priced given the shape of the curve and timing of the cash flows.

**EXHIBIT  29–15**

Static Spread Comparison

| Description: | CMGT 1996-B | CMAOT 1996-C |
|---|---|---|
| Class: | A | A3 |
| Type: | Grantor Trust | Owner Trust |
| Coupon: | 6.61% | 5.95% |
| Pricing speed: | 1.5 ABS | 1.5 ABS |
| Average life: | 1.28 years | 1.22 years |
| Yield to maturity: | 6.31% | 6.23% |
| Nominal spread: | +77 basis points | +69 basis points |
| Static spread | +71 basis points | +69 basis points |

Pricing and analysis as of 10/7/97

**EXHIBIT  29–16**

Total Return Horizon Analysis

| | No Change | Steepen 20 bp | Flatten 20 bp |
|---|---|---|---|
| **CMGT 1996-B, A** | | | |
| Yield at Horizon | 6.30% | 6.30% | 6.30% |
| Avg. Life at Horizon | .90 | .90 | .90 |
| Horizontal Total Return | 6.12% | 6.12% | 6.12% |
| **CMAOT 1996-C, A3** | | | |
| Yield at Horizon | 6.22% | 6.02% | 6.42% |
| Avg. Life at Horizon | .50 | .50 | .50 |
| Horizon Total Return | 6.16% | 6.22% | 6.11% |
| Return Difference | +.04% | +.10% | −.01% |

Another relative value tool that can be used in addition to static spread analysis is forecasting total return. The two major components of total return are price appreciation and coupon income. In a positively sloped yield curve environment, the price appreciation associated with rolling down the yield curve contributes to the investor's expected horizon return. In the auto ABS sector, investors must assess the total return trade-off between higher-yielding wide window bonds and lower-yielding tight window bonds. Exhibit 29–16, shows that CMGT does not roll down the curve as fast as CMAOT. At the end of the 12-month horizon, the CMAOT has rolled down the curve 0.72 years (its beginning average life less its average life at the horizon). The CMGT 1996-B only rolls down the curve 0.38 years due its wide window. Despite an 8 bp yield advantage, CMGT under performs the CMAOT in the "no change" scenario.

The expected shape of the yield curve at the end of the horizon also determines relative performance between wide window and tight window auto ABS. Exhibit 29–16 also illustrates this point. Under a yield curve steepening scenario from fed funds to the one-year Treasury, the horizon total return of CMGT remains unchanged because the bond does not roll into the steeper part of the curve. However, since CMAOT does roll down the curve, the horizon total return increases as the yield curve steepens. Conversely, when the yield curve flattens from fed funds to the one-year Treasury, the expected horizon total return of the CMAOT declines and the total return advantage is shifted to the wide window CMGT.

## CONCLUSION

When evaluating auto ABS, investors must consider several qualitative and quantitative factors that we have outlined in this chapter. Qualitative factors which affect a transaction's relative attractiveness include the issuer/servicer's business type (bank, captive, etc.), its underwriting and servicing standards, its obligor mix (prime, non-prime, or sub-prime), its credit enhancement, and its structure. These factors contribute to a unique pricing structure in the auto ABS market depending upon investors' perception of the cost or value associated with each.

Quantitative factors such as differing cash flow profiles and the shape of the yield curve also influence relative value. Quantitative tools for determining relative value include static spread and total return analysis. Static spread analysis allows investors to compute the bullet equivalent spread of an amortizing security by normalizing spreads and allowing for direct comparisons between securities with different cash flow profiles. Likewise, total return and scenario analysis can be used to determine relative value.

By blending both qualitative and quantitative analysis, investors can identify and profit from the opportunities that exist in one of the most dynamic and mature sectors of ABS market.

CHAPTER **30**

# SECURITIES BACKED BY CLOSED-END HOME EQUITY LOANS*

**R. Russell Hurst**
Director
First Union Securities, Inc.

## INTRODUCTION

This chapter provides investors with an understanding of the U.S. home equity loan (HEL) securitization market and the tools that an investor will need in order to identify and understand the investment opportunities in the HEL market. To gain a firm understanding of HEL asset-backed securities (ABS), an investor must know the fundamental characteristics of the loans, the structure and its characteristics that may affect the credit protection of the security purchased, the credit standing and economic motive of all parties to a transaction, and the legal concepts used to achieve bankruptcy remoteness and sale treatment by the seller/originator.

## WHAT IS THE U.S. HOME EQUITY LOAN TODAY?

In the early 1990s, HEL referred to a traditional second lien mortgage with the proceeds primarily used for home improvement, college education, or debt consolidation. Although second mortgage HELs are still originated, more than 95% of the current nonprime HEL product described above is a first lien mortgage product. A simple but important distinction between HEL mortgage products and other similar securitized nonprime nonconforming mortgage products is that the proceeds from a HEL mortgage are not used to purchase a new home but to refinance an existing mortgage. The payment behavior of nonprime purchase money mortgages and home improvement loans (HILs) differ from HELs primarily due to the circumstances of the borrowers. The proceeds of an HEL loan

---

* This chapter is reprinted with permission from Frank J. Fabozzi (ed.), *Investing in Asset-Backed Securities* (New Hope, PA: Frank J. Fabozzi Associates, 2000).

may be used in part to finance home improvements but most likely will not be used in its entirety for that purpose. The prepayment behavior of HELs is closely related to the characteristics of the borrower. HELs are typically used to

- Consolidate consumer debt in a lower-rate, tax-deductible form
- Monetize equity in the home
- Reduce a homeowner's monthly mortgage payment by extending the loan's term
- Finance home improvements
- Finance temporary liquidity needs such as for education or medical expenses

The traditional second mortgage is still included in the HEL category, but HELs now commonly refer to first lien mortgages to borrowers with some combination of impaired credit history and/or debt-to-income ratios that exceed agency guidelines. These borrowers are commonly referred to as *nonprime* or *B* and *C borrowers*. The originators of HELs use proprietary credit scoring techniques to grade each borrower on their ability to repay debt with letter gradations from A to D. The criteria vary by company, and each company has made some disclosure of the characteristics of each class of borrower. The nuances of underwriting standards among home equity lenders is useful when trying to differentiate the quality of one pool of collateral from another. The underwriting guidelines by credit class of borrower in Exhibit 30–1 are fairly representative of the collateral in the market.

As the credit profile of the borrower becomes increasingly risky or complex, a greater reliance is placed on the equity in the property mortgaged. This equity improves the chances of fully recovering the full principal value of the loan in foreclosure as well as the foreclosure costs including lost interest. An incrementally higher rate is also charged to financially weaker borrowers, which helps to ensure a higher return on a portfolio of nonprime HELs.

The U.S. economy has enjoyed six consecutive years of low inflation, low interest rates and sustained growth, all of which have had a favorable effect on property values in the United States. In addition to contributing to the growth in the HEL market, these factors have reduced the severity of losses in this market. Another, often overlooked, aspect of this market is that bankruptcy law in the United States does not allow a bankruptcy election more than once every seven years. This places the lender in a powerful position with regard to the borrower and may partly explain why bankruptcies are acceptable to this group of lenders. Thus, bankruptcy law is a great motivator for the borrower to make payments and serves to shorten the foreclosure period, thereby reducing the cost of foreclosure (time value of money).

**EXHIBIT 30–1**

Representative Home Equity Underwriting Guidelines

| Grade | Quality | Credit History and Ratios |
|-------|---------|---------------------------|
| A | Good | • No late payment on mortgages<br>• Maximum of two or three late payments on revolving credit and no more than three 30-day late payments on installment debt; perhaps one 60-day late payment<br>• Chapter 7 or 13 bankruptcy must be discharged for one to three years with credit reestablished for two years<br>• Maximum debt-to-income ratio of 45%<br>• Maximum loan-to-values ranging from 85% to 95% |
| B | Satisfactory | • Maximum of three or four 30-day late payments on mortgage payments in the past 12 months<br>• For nonmortgage debt, pattern of 30 delinquencies and limited 60-day delinquencies with isolated 90-day delinquency<br>• Bankruptcies acceptable with one to two years reestablished credit<br>• Maximum debt-to-income ratio of 50%<br>• Maximum loan-to-value of 85% |
| C | Fair | • Maximum 210 total days delinquent with limited 60-day and isolated 90-day delinquencies on mortgage debt<br>• Discretionary with cross section of 30-, 60-, and 90-day delinquencies<br>• Bankruptcies acceptable with one to two years reestablished credit<br>• Maximum debt-to-income ratio of 55%<br>• Maximum loan-to-value of 80% |
| D | Poor | • No more than 120-day mortgage or rent delinquency in the past 12 months and property not in foreclosure<br>• Delinquent or charged-off receivables<br>• Bankruptcies acceptable if discharged or dismissed<br>• Maximum debt-to-income ratio of 60%<br>• Maximum loan-to-value of 65% |

Source: First Union Securities, Inc.

The most prevalent forms of HELs include the following:

• *Closed-end HELs,* where the loan amount and term to maturity are set at origination and bear a fixed rate, constitute most of the market.

• *Adjustable-rate, closed-end HELs* (HEL ARMs) have a set term to maturity and usually have both periodic and lifetime caps. The loans generally allow for the accretion of interest to the principal while the interest rate is at the cap. The additional principal is repaid from future payments when the interest rate is reset or when the rate recedes from the capped level. If the interest rate remains at the cap for the life of the loan, there is usually a provision to extend the maturity. The loans are structured in a manner that renders this extension risk as highly improbable.

- *Home equity lines of credit* (HELOCs) are open-end, revolving loans, where the borrower receives an HEL line of credit that can be partially or completely drawn down and partially or completely paid back over time. HELOCs carry floating rates, usually with high lifetime caps and no interim caps. Because of the open-end, revolving structure of the HELOC collateral, which is similar to that of credit cards, these loans are not discussed in this chapter.

## BASIC STRUCTURE

HELs are financial assets or receivables originated by a bank, a finance company, or other financial institution. HELs are then sold to a bankruptcy-remote special-purpose vehicle (SPV). Certain conditions must be met to achieve a "true sale," and reputable counsel provides legal opinions that confirm these conditions, such as the arm's length requirement and the transfer of the legal title to the asset, have in fact been met.

HEL issues usually take the form of a real estate mortgage investment conduit (REMIC), which allows cash flows to be redirected to create several tranches of certificates with expected average lives at many points on the yield curve. REMICs were created as a new issuance vehicle by the Tax Reform Act of 1986 to solve many of the problems experienced with collateralized mortgage obligations (CMOs) that used a multiclass trust structure. The first passthrough was issued in 1970, followed by the first CMO in 1983. As the moniker implies, CMOs were technically debt instruments rather than passthrough certificates and were successful in avoiding tax liability to the issuing trust. Issuers had to maintain a portion of residual interests, record CMOs as liabilities in their financial statements, and satisfy minimum capital requirements. The CMO structure also created a mismatch between the monthly receipts on the collateral and the quarterly payments on the bonds. In 1985, use of the owner trust structure solved some of these problems by allowing the sale of the residual interest to others and removal from the issuer's balance sheet. The new residual interest holder then became liable for interest rate shortfalls on any of the owner trust tranches. Buyers for the residuals were scarce and as a result the market for this type of CMO was not liquid.

REMICs changed all this. To qualify for REMIC status, a multiclass offering can have multiple classes of *regular interests* but only one class of *residual interest*. The legislation defines a "regular interest" as a fixed principal amount with periodic interest payments or accruals on the outstanding principal balance. Buyers of regular interests are taxed as holders of debt obligations and the buyers of the residual interest pay taxes on the earnings, if any, of the trust. Due to its flexibility in meeting investor demand, the CMO and HEL markets have used the REMIC structure almost exclusively since 1991.

Following these guidelines, the trust issues either debt or passthrough certificates (a ratable equity interest in the pool or some portion of the pool), the proceeds of which are used to buy the pool of assets to be securitized. To facilitate the selling of certificates or debt to the market, some combination or variation of the following provides credit enhancement:

- *Excess spread:* Revenue less expenses of the trust.

- *Reserve account:* Excess spread captured and held in the trust as some predetermined or calculated level to pay any cash flow shortfalls in the trust.

- *Subordinated protection:* The amount by which the collateral value exceeds any class of liability.

- *Senior/subordinated structures:* Certain classes of securities have a senior claim to others on the cash flow of the trust. The purest form of this structure is referred to as *sequential,* where any principal payments received by the trust are used to fully pay down the principal of the most senior class prior to any of the junior classes. All classes receive principal payments sequentially according to their rank of claim to the cash flow of the trust. The lowest-ranking class will be the last to receive a principal payment as well as the last to have its principal fully retired. This is commonly referred to as the *waterfall.* Any amount left over is referred to as the *residual* and flows to the equity holder. A minimal amount of true equity is provided at the formation of the SPV and is necessary to comply with certain legal and tax requirements of the trust. The residual can be, and often is, separated from the true equity in the trust and retained by the seller/servicer. Retention of this amount by the seller/servicer provides a primary motivation to maximize the cash flow in the trust (i.e., accelerate collections and minimize losses) so that the value of the residual is realized.

- *Third-party guarantee:* This can take the form of bond insurance, a letter of credit, or a corporate guarantee of all or any class of a securitization. The motivations vary but the result is a better economic execution for the issuer, which may have to provide less collateral to the trust or may achieve a better pricing on insured bonds than an uninsured funding execution. The issuer may not have access to the market by any other means. Firms active in the guaranty of HEL transactions include Capital Markets Assurance Corp. (CapMac), Financial Guaranty Insurance Co. (FGIC), Mortgage Bond Insurance Associates (MBIA), Financial Security Assurance (FSA), and Capital Guaranty Assurance (CGA).

The most important basic feature of an asset-backed security that should not be underemphasized or overlooked when viewing the home equity securitization market for investment purposes is the true sale of the assets into a bankruptcy-remote SPV (the issuer). This issue as it relates to the recent economic hard times and bankruptcy of sellers/servicers will be discussed in more detail later. From a pure credit perspective, these structures have survived bankruptcy, minimal degradation of servicing cash flow, and there is some evidence that retained residual interests are providing the proper motivation, even in bankruptcy, for the seller/servicer to continue servicing and collections in an efficient manner. In this regard, having tested the structure is a positive for the market and should provide an additional level of comfort to the investor.

Not surprisingly, because growth in the HEL market followed the growth in the mortgage-backed securities (MBS) market, many of the features are patterned after those used in the MBS market and are aimed at smoothing prepayment volatility such that payment windows for each class are shortened. This will reduce the risk that the investment will experience a shorter or longer average life than expected. The most common structures are discussed below.

- Senior/subordinated with up to 10 fixed-rate senior tranches with different average lives ranging out to 10 years. This is a lesser number of fixed-rate subordinated tranches with different average lives and backed by a fixed-rate pool of HELs. There is also a larger longer service average life floating-rate tranche backed by a floating-rate pool of HELs.
- Senior/subordinated with some combination of fixed, floating, HEL, and HIL collateral
- Single class with 100% surety bond
- Senior/subordinated with 100% surety bond on a subordinate piece

Exhibit 30–2 illustrates the principal paydown of The Money Store 98-B home equity securitization and the total collateral cash flow and its allocation to principal payment and the expenses of the program.

Exhibit 30–3 illustrates the total collateral cash flow of The Money Store 98-B home equity securitization and its allocation to principal payment and the expenses of the program. This exhibit illustrates the excess spread concept.

An increasingly important structural feature for analyzing the cash flow expectations of HEL securitizations is the step-down provision. Due to the senior/subordinated structure, where all excess spread and principal payments are used to repay the senior tranche(s), subordinated tranche protection increases as a percentage of total certificate outstandings. This increased percentage protection is more than necessary to support the rating of the senior tranches. Step-downs were created as a method to redirect some of the excess spread cash flow to the subordinated tranches while protecting the rating on the senior ranking tranches throughout the life of the transaction.

Step-downs allow the redirection of a portion of the excess spread to subordinated tranches as long as the collateral is performing within the parameters described later. If the deal deteriorates due to higher-than-expected losses,

**EXHIBIT  30-2**

HEL Principal Paydown—The Money Store 98-B

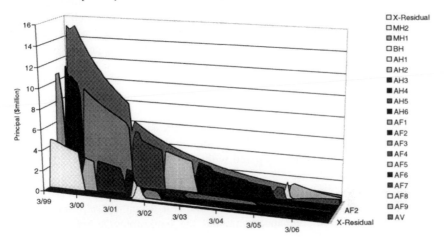

Source: First Union Securities, Inc.

**EXHIBIT  30-3**

The Money Store 98-B HEL Cash Flow

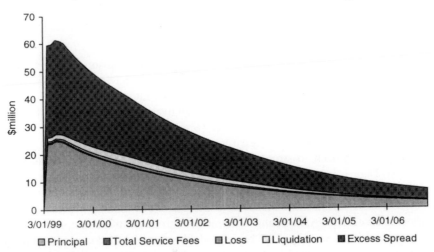

Source: First Union Securities, Inc.

the redirection of cash flows, or step-down, would not be allowed until the conditions were met. If step-down conditions are not met and the collateral exceeds the collateral quality triggers, cash flow would be redirected to the senior tranche until the collateral met the predetermined conditions. The step-down is set to occur usually 3–4 years from the date the deal was issued and requires the collateral pool outstandings to exceed a certain percentage of the original collateral balance, usually 50%, as well as meet certain asset quality tests as of a certain date. Failure to meet the step-down tests would alter the cash flow assumptions on which the senior, mezzanine, and subordinated tranches were priced, resulting in a shorter average life for the senior and mezzanine tranches and a longer average life for the subordinated tranches. The closer an issue comes to failing the tests should be an uncertainty properly priced into the spread of that issue compared with other issues that clearly will not fail the test.

In summary, structural protections include the excess spread at the first layer of protection, subordination, cash collateral accounts, step-down provisions, third-party credit enhancement, and the bankruptcy remoteness of the issuer. In general, ratings from two or three of the rating agencies for the typical HEL securitization will range from AAA for the senior tranches to as low as B− for the most subordinated tranche. In 1998, 42% of all HEL securitizations were floating rate. All of the HEL structures shift credit volatility to the subordinated tranches in varying degrees and ensure in all but the most extreme cases that the senior AAA tranches have sufficient credit protection to remain rated AAA while outstanding. Slower prepayments generate additional credit support. When prepayments slow, the absolute value of the excess servicing spread remains higher for a longer time.


## RATING AGENCY APPROACH

Rating agencies assign a AAA rating to an HEL transaction so that an investor, from a credit perspective, will regard that security as having the same credit worthiness as any other AAA at that moment. The rating agencies are looking to achieve a certain rating consistency across all fixed-income sectors at all rating grades. Moody's Investors Service, Inc. (Moody's), and Standard and Poor's Corp. (S&P) were the first to rate structured transactions.

S&P's approach to structured finance began with a study of defaults in the Great Depression and resulted in a worst-case economic scenario on which it based its cash flow stress scenarios. If a transaction could withstand a number of iterations of this worst-case scenario and survive simulated depression scenarios, it deserved a AAA rating. The model introduced the concept of default frequency and loss severity. This basic model has been applied in modified form to each class of ABS rated by S&P. The result for all ABS, including the HEL sector, is that a AAA will survive 3–5 times historical losses. S&P constructs a prime pool for residential mortgages. As the characteristics of the prime pool differ from the pool to be securitized, penalties are assessed to default frequency and loss severity assumptions used in the cash flow scenarios. Lesser-quality pools require a greater amount of credit loss protection for the senior tranche to achieve a AAA rating than that required for the prime pool. Factors considered in analyzing the mortgage pool include historical level of delinquencies, loss severity, lien type, loan type, number of loans, geographical concentration, quality of borrower and step-downs. The IBCA Fitch and the Duff and Phelps models followed an approach similar to that of S&P in developing their cash flow models.

Moody's started out on a somewhat different route toward the same end. By looking at historical defaults for each rating level, Moody's thought that Aaa structured financed issues should have the same probability of default as a Aaa corporate and so on for each rating grade. Taking this approach to its logical extreme, Moody's studied the Great Depression as well as other recessions in the twentieth century and observed how the collateral being securitized behaved in stressful economic situations. This resulted in the identification of a positive correlation between collateral performance and economic events, allowing Moody's to use a Monte Carlo model to generate a worst-case loss distribution for the collateral pool. Moody's then quantified the loss protection needed for that pool to achieve Aaa loss protection (approximately three standard deviations from the expected loss). Aa transactions provided enough protection to cover 2.5 standard deviations, and single A covered 2.0 standard deviations. Although Moody's approach is similar, the data available for this type of analysis have greatly improved for each asset class (and for the other forms of derivatives in the structure, such as swaps). This approach is also called the *expected value approach*. Currently, Moody's sets credit enhancement levels so that the annual change in yield on the rated security, due to defaults in the collateral pool and

**EXHIBIT 30–4**

Yield Change Limits for Moody's Rated HEL Transactions

| Rating | Yield Change (bps) |
|--------|--------------------|
| Aaa | 0.06 |
| Aa2 | 1.30 |
| A2 | 9.00 |
| Baa2 | 27.00 |
| Ba2 | 106.00 |
| B2 | 231.00 |

Source: Moody's Investor Service, Inc.

other credit events that would cause a loss of cash flow to the trust, is equivalent to the target levels in Exhibit 30–4.

## HEL COLLATERAL PERFORMANCE

Exhibits 30–5 and 30–6, taken from First Union Securities home equity prepayment model, show that collateral performance has been excellent and is well within the worst-case parameters set by the rating agencies. Loss information on HEL product is presented by year of origination (vintage) to avoid any understatement of losses because of new issue volume. Exhibit 30–5 shows that net losses are low the first year after origination and increase rapidly for the next two years. From the peak in the 36th month, the losses recede for two years before percentage net losses increase again.

By examining the loss curve of each issue, an investor can decide, on a relative basis, whether the spread received is appropriate for the collateral's risk profile. Loss curves differ by issuer and vintage because of the targeted niche borrower, underwriting guidelines and, in some cases, servicing and collection.

It is particularly useful to look at cumulative HEL collateral losses by year of origination for the entire HEL universe as shown in Exhibit 30–6.

**E X H I B I T   30–5**

Annualized HEL Net Loss Rate by Vintage

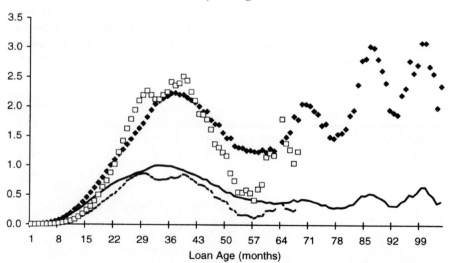

ARM: Adjustable-rate mortgage.

Source: First Union Securities, Inc.

**EXHIBIT 30–6**

Cumulative HEL Losses by Vintage

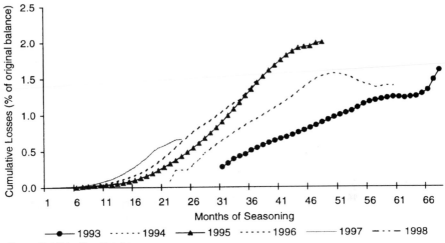

Source: First Union Securities, Inc.

HELs originated in 1993 and 1994 have had significantly better loss experience than the product originated in 1995–1998. In all likelihood, this is the result of the increased competition and market growth during the latter period. Lower interest rates and aggressive origination by brokers also explain why a lower-quality product was originated. It is also useful to compare cumulative loss curves by year of origination for the same issuer to see if the loss experiences on collateral pools originated in the same year differ dramatically from each other.

An increase in 60-day delinquencies, sustained for more than a month or two, is a good predictor of increased losses and whether a certain collateral pool is beginning to deteriorate. If the pool is in fact deteriorating, the increase in 60-day delinquencies will be followed by an increase in 90-day delinquencies and finally an increase in losses.

Loss curve analysis of the collateral pool is fundamental to understanding whether the probability of default has increased or decreased since the origination of the transaction. In most cases, the subordinated protection increases as the senior bonds pay down (see Exhibit 30–7).

There has *not* been a performance downgrade of a public HEL issue since the inception of the asset-backed market. However, variations in collateral performance will cause issues of the same average life to trade at different spreads to the Treasury market. This is also true for insured transactions though to a lesser degree than for senior/subordinated transactions.

**E X H I B I T   30–7**

Seasoned HEL Transaction Comparison

|  | ContiMortgage 1997-1 A4 | Advanta 1993-1 A1 | Saxon 1997-3 AF1 |
|---|---|---|---|
| Weighted Average Coupon |  |  |  |
| Original | 11.556 | 10.340 | 10.094 |
| Current | 11.360 | 10.092 | 10.044 |
| Certificate Coupon |  |  |  |
| Original | 6.680 | 5.950 | 5.816 |
| Current | 6.680 | 5.950 | 5.097 |
| Servicing Fee |  |  |  |
| Original | 1.500 | 0.500 | 0.534 |
| Current | 0.500 | 0.500 | 0.533 |
| Net Annualized Losses |  |  |  |
| Original | 0.000 | 0.000 | 0.000 |
| Current | 1.480 | 0.440 | 0.040 |
| Net Excess Spread |  |  |  |
| Original | 3.376 | 3.890 | 3.744 |
| Current | 2.700 | 3.202 | 4.374 |
| Level of Credit Enhancement Class A |  |  |  |
| Original | 11.500 | 100.000 | 9.230 |
| Current | 23.116 | 100.000 | 17.474 |
| Original Rating | Aaa | Aaa | Aaa |
| Current Reading | Aaa | Aaa | Aaa |

Note: All numbers are stated as percentages.

Source: First Union Securities, Inc.

## HEL PREPAYMENT EXPERIENCE

Prepayments are extremely important to determining the value of any mortgage-backed investment. Exhibit 30–8, from First Union Securities prepayment model, shows the prepayment of the rated universe of HEL product from 1994 to 1998.

The prepayment of HEL product has proved to be much more stable than that of the MBS market and has resulted in securitization with less negative

## EXHIBIT 30-8

Aggregate Historical CPR versus Model CPR

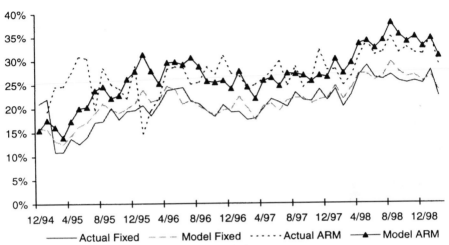

ARM: Adjustable-rate mortgage; CPR: Conditional prepayment rate.
Source: First Union Securities, Inc.

convexity. Investor acceptance of HEL prepayment characteristics contributed to market growth in 1997–1998. From a credit perspective, prepayments will accelerate the retirement of the senior-most tranches and increase the subordinated protection available to classes of the same rank when measured as a percentage of current outstandings. Due to B and C borrowers' limited refinancing opportunities, refinancing rates must fall 200 bps–300 bps to significantly increase prepayments due to refinancing in the HEL market versus the 25 bps–50 bps that move the private MBS market. Examination of this data shows that HEL product originated prior to 1997 has had the highest prepayment experience. HELs originated in 1996 and earlier had higher coupons than current HEL product. Coupons originated as of this writing are lower because of a lower absolute level of interest rates. Intense competition in the market for product and market share has also accelerated prepayments.[1]

## SEPARATING HEL CREDIT RISK FROM THE MARKET PRICING OF THAT RISK

For HEL securitizations, credit risk includes collateral performance, cash flow allocations, asset-quality triggers, access to established reserves, sufficiency of

1. For greater detail on HEL prepayment behavior, see James S. Anderson and Webster Hughes, *Prepayment Models and Home Equity Analysis,* First Union Securities, Inc., Asset-Backed/ Quantitative Research, October 1998.

any subordinated tranche protection, credit worthiness of any third-party guarantor or substitute credit provider, legal integrity of the structure, and administrative risk.

The bankruptcy of a servicer does not, as a stand-alone event, increase the
credit risk of any particular HEL investment. It does raise the concern that the
servicing of the collateral may become less efficient while being transferred to
a back-up servicer and that collections may be less efficient and result in slower
collections due to a significantly pared down servicing operation or the lack of
economic incentive if the servicing is allowed to remain with the bankrupt entity
while it is reorganized or sold to a third party. This is appropriately referred to
as *administrative risk*.

Insured transactions provide solid protection from administrative risk. Insurers become insiders, use covenant protection to a greater degree than for
senior/subordinated structures and promise timely payment of principal and interest as scheduled. For an HEL passthrough, interest due on the outstanding
principal will be paid to certificate holders when due, and payment of any principal amount after the collateral is fully depleted (the only time principal is
"due" in a passthrough). Although there is no promise to pay if collections slow
down, the insurers, to protect their own interests, have teams of auditors that
continually review collateral performance and the servicing process. The insurers
stand ready to take control of collateral if covenants are breached and the result
is to significantly reduce administrative risk in the insured transaction. The insurers are in the business of insuring investment-grade or better transactions and
are heavily regulated by the rating agencies as to capital sufficiency. Insured
transactions, without the insurance, would result in a senior tranche rating of
AA or A and investment grade or better for the subordinated tranches. Insured
transactions provide multiple levels of protection to the investor.

Without a fundamental change in credit risk, HEL credit spreads are affected by the market pricing of that risk. Supply and demand drives the market
pricing of credit risk between sectors and includes the market's reaction to world
events, the health of the U.S. economy, capital flows around the world, or the
market's reaction to headline risk within a sector.

## HEADLINE RISK AND HARD TIMES

The public and private asset-backed market has been largely free of event risk.
The distinction between event and headline risk is important. *Event risk* in the
corporate market represents an event that when announced has immediate credit
rating implications for a company's outstanding debt or the debt of an industry,
which, in most cases, would result in a downgrade (or an upgrade) of the company or companies affected by the event. The most obvious example would be
mergers and acquisitions. *Headline risk* may immediately affect the credit spread
of a security but does not have immediate upgrade or downgrade implications.

None of the recent bankruptcy announcements by sellers/servicers in the HEL market have resulted in the downgrading of the related HEL securitizations.

Since its inception, the ABS market has had a remarkable track record of credit stability. Exhibit 30–9 shows that over the five-year period 1994–1998 no asset-backed security rated by Moody's has defaulted in the public or private market at any rating level. In fact, that statement holds true for the asset-backed market since inception. Moody's first downgrade of a public asset-backed security occurred in February 1998, then again in April 1998 when it downgraded the lower-rated B-1 and B-2 tranches of BankAmerica Manufactured Housing Contract 1996-1. Prior to 1997, only three ABS had been downgraded by Moody's. In 1997, Moody's downgraded four tranches of three private nonprime automobile transactions (Aegis, Autoflow and AJ Acceptance). In 1998, Aegis was downgraded further, as well as a private LSI nonprime auto tranche, and three private securities backed by charged-off credit card accounts issued by Commercial Financial Services (CFS). The undetected fraud in the CFS SMART transactions will result in the first ABS default. Even in this situation, collections on the receivables continue and payments to certificate holders continue. Technically, in a senior/subordinated structure, a default will only occur when pass-through payments fail to make a payment while a certificate balance is still outstanding. This can only occur when current pay collateral is fully depleted.

At this juncture, investors have become conditioned to the headline risk present in the HEL market. Some investors regard headline risk spread widening as a buying opportunity. A pattern has emerged whereby announcements have been made by sellers/servicers in financial difficulty that they are either seeking a strategic partner, seeking to restructure or sell certain parts of their operations, plan to reduce growth, or plan to eliminate or decrease their most costly source of loan origination (in most cases, third-party broker originated product). A few

**E X H I B I T    30–9**

Credit Stability of ABS versus Comparable Corporates (as of June 30, 1998)

| Original Rating | Average 5-Year Default Rate | | Percent Downgraded after 5 Years | | Percent Upgraded after 5 Years | |
|---|---|---|---|---|---|---|
| | CORP | ABS | CORP | ABS | CORP | ABS |
| Aaa | 0.10% | 0.00% | 28.40% | 0.00% | 0.00% | 0.00% |
| Aa | 0.40% | 0.00% | 28.90% | 0.00% | 5.50% | 12.80% |
| A | 0.50% | 0.00% | 20.80% | 0.70% | 10.20% | 11.60% |
| Baa | 1.70% | 0.00% | 17.80% | 1.90% | 20.90% | 4.10% |
| Ba | 11.40% | 0.00% | 23.50% | 5.70% | 17.90% | 0.00% |

ABS: All public and private asset-backed securities rated by Moody's; CORP: All public corporate bonds rated by Moody's.

Source: Moody's Investors Services, Inc. and First Union Securities, Inc.

months after this announcement, sellers/servicers that did not find a partner or alternate sources of financing have announced bankruptcy. Significant headline risk announcements by sellers/servicers are summarized in Exhibit 30–10.

These events will affect the liquidity and pricing of all HEL product. Some issues, with strong sellers/servicers or those owned by investment-grade parents, and insured issues will recover to a normalized spread more quickly than those with servicers experiencing some form of financial stress. In reality, investors prefer not to own a HEL issue when the servicer files for bankruptcy, not because

**E X H I B I T   30–10**

1998/1999 Headline Risk Announcements

| | |
|---|---|
| Aames Financial | Third-quarter 1998 earnings down more than 95%, with much of the reduction attributed to losses on hedging positions. Servicing operation might be sold. Has exited the securitization market. |
| Amresco | Announced $50 million–$60 million loss for 1998 and major reorganization and closing of its wholesale and retail operations |
| Cityscape | Filed for bankruptcy in October 1998. |
| ContiFinancial | Made first-quarter 1999 announcement that it is seeking a strategic partner following a large loss in the third quarter of 1998 and announcement of major restructuring. |
| FirstPlus | Announced $82 million third-quarter 1998 loss. Reduced staff more than 50%. Eliminated wholesale division. Terminated agreement to sell servicing operation to Superior Bank. Proposed merger with Life Financial canceled. Did no securitizations in the fourth quarter. Sold U.K. operations and its conforming loan business. Filed for bankruptcy the first week of March 1999. |
| IMC Mortgage | Third-quarter 1998 earnings down more than 80% from last year. Had severe liquidity problems. Completed previously announced agreement with Greenwich Street Capital Partners to purchase 95% interest in company and assume control in February 1999. |
| IndyMac | Announced fourth-quarter 1998 loss and laid off 280 employees. Reducing servicing portfolio. Exiting manufactured housing business. |
| Southern Pacific | Wrote down earnings during the summer. Sought to raise capital through whole loan sales. Sought strategic partner and then filed for bankruptcy in October 1998. |
| United Companies | Major reorganization announced in the fourth quarter and announced it was looking for a partner. Filed for bankruptcy the first week of March 1999. |

Source: First Union Securities, Inc.

there is an immediate risk of downgrade or default (there is not), but because the investor prefers not to have to deal with the spread widening that accompanies the announcement (i.e., the headline risk).

For an issue sponsored by a seller/servicer that has just filed for bankruptcy, the spread widening is less severe for insured issues. At this point, the market goes through a discovery period with regard to the affected issues and trading in these issues may be light to nonexistent. For the insured issues, investors are uncertain whether the insurer will require that the servicing be transferred to the backup servicer and whether servicing continues smoothly with no discernible slowdown in collections or confusion surrounding the transfer. Liquidity should return to the market for these issues, albeit at a modestly wider spread.

For senior/subordinated structures, the discovery and return to liquidity in the market will take longer and, in the case of Southern Pacific's senior/subordinated issues, has taken 3–6 months. In this case, the bankruptcy court allowed Southern Pacific to retain a substantial of amount of its servicing in an effort to maximize the value of residuals held by the bankruptcy estate. Despite pared-down operations, the retention of the residual by the bankruptcy estate has apparently provided the necessary motivation for Southern Pacific to continue servicing the affected issues in an efficient manner. As a result, some investors have returned cautiously to the market for these securities and currently view the available spreads as cheap. The failure of a servicer/seller should worry the investor to the extent it causes a deterioration in the performance of the collateral. This could be the result of a lost economic incentive for diligent collection of payments or rapid resolution of problem loans. This collateral degradation, if sustained, fundamentally changes the credit protection afforded the issuer and the investor should be compensated for this uncertainty.

In some senior/subordinated issues, backup servicers were not required and the concept of a special servicer was not contemplated. For most commercial mortgage-backed securities, a special servicer is paid a fee and a success fee for collecting seriously delinquent loans or loans in foreclosure. The documents of an HEL issue do not allow a step-up in servicing fees as an incentive for another servicer to step in and take over servicing. As a result, provisions such as these are now being incorporated into some of the new senior/subordinated deals in the market. The insurers have long used the two-tier fee concept.

In a perverse way, all of this has been a positive for the HEL market. The experience of seller/servicer bankruptcy, together with the maintenance of existing ratings, has satisfactorily tested the structural safeguards put in place in HEL transactions and validated the principal tenet of asset securitizations—that the deals are isolated from the insolvency of the issuer. This should result in a higher confidence level in the transactions and in further modification, or fine-tuning, of the documentation used in future transactions.

## CHAPTER 31

# Securities Backed by Manufactured Housing Loans*

**James S. Anderson**
Managing Director
First Union Securities, Inc.

**Kristina L. Clark**
Analyst
First Union Securities, Inc.

## INTRODUCTION

This chapter provides investors with an overview of the manufactured housing industry, as well as the collateral underlying manufactured housing asset-backed securities (ABS). For investors already familiar with manufactured housing ABS, we discuss current issues in the industry and their impact on ABS as well as introduce a source of higher-level analytics and surveillance.

The manufactured housing industry has undergone dramatic changes since the late 1970s and early 1980s. Government regulations and advances in home design have greatly improved product quality and safety. Competitive financing and changes in consumer demand have led to a shift in sales from smaller, less expensive single-section homes to larger, more expensive multisection homes (see Exhibit 31–1). New manufactured homes are being designed to resemble more closely traditional site-built homes, offering amenities such as vaulted ceilings, fireplaces, and walk-in closets. Manufacturers have been working with land developers and dealers to change the negative stereotype of "trailer parks" by promoting the construction of "manufactured housing communities," which include swimming pools, clubhouses, and recreational facilities.

As the manufactured housing industry evolved and demand for such accommodations increased, loans providing underlying financing became more common collateral for securitization. As with other ABS classes, manufactured housing ABS are subject to the growing pains of the underlying industry, and

---

\* This chapter is reprinted with permission from Frank J. Fabozzi (ed.), *Investing in Asset-Backed Securities* (New Hope, PA: Frank J. Fabozzi Associates, 2000).

**E X H I B I T   31–1**

Average Size and Sales Price of Manufactured and Site-Built Homes

| ($) | 1992 | 1993 | 1994 | 1995 | 1996 | 1997 |
|---|---|---|---|---|---|---|
| Manufactured Homes | | | | | | |
| *Total* | | | | | | |
| Average Sales Price | 28,400 | 30,500 | 33,500 | 36,300 | 38,400 | 41,100 |
| Average Square Footage | 1,255 | 1,295 | 1,330 | 1,355 | 1,380 | 1,420 |
| Cost per Square foot | 22.63 | 23.55 | 25.19 | 26.79 | 27.83 | 28.94 |
| *Single Section* | | | | | | |
| Average Sales Price | 20,600 | 21,900 | 23,900 | 26,700 | 28,200 | 29,000 |
| Average Square Footage | 1,035 | 1,065 | 1,085 | 1,115 | 1,120 | 1,125 |
| Cost per Square Foot | 19.90 | 20.56 | 22.03 | 23.95 | 25.18 | 25.78 |
| *Multisection* | | | | | | |
| Average Sales Price | 37,200 | 39,600 | 42,900 | 45,900 | 47,300 | 49,500 |
| Average Square Footage | 1,495 | 1,525 | 1,565 | 1,585 | 1,600 | 1,615 |
| Cost per Square Foot | 24.88 | 25.97 | 27.41 | 28.96 | 29.56 | 30.65 |
| Site-Built Homes | | | | | | |
| Average Sales Price | 144,100 | 147,700 | 154,100 | 158,700 | 166,200 | 176,200 |
| Land Price | 36,025 | 36,925 | 38,525 | 39,675 | 41,550 | 44,050 |
| Price of Structure | 108,075 | 110,775 | 115,575 | 119,025 | 124,650 | 132,150 |
| Average Square Footage | 2,095 | 2,095 | 2,115 | 2,115 | 2,125 | 2,150 |
| Cost per Square Foot | 51.59 | 52.88 | 54.65 | 56.28 | 58.66 | 61.47 |

Source: Manufactured Housing Institute.

although the manufactured housing industry has come a long way, increased competition and a loosening of credit standards pose a continuing challenge to pool performance.

Fortunately for investors, the issuers in this industry are not novice securitizers. Companies such as Green Tree (now wholly owned by Conseco, Inc.), Oakwood Homes Corp., Vanderbilt Mortgage and Finance, Inc., and GreenPoint Credit Corp. (with the recent addition of Bank of America Corp.'s manufactured housing operation) have extensive experience securitizing this industry. By the end of 1998, much of the industry had reorganized and refocused. The credit crunch in the third quarter of 1998 and less-than-stellar performance from 1995–1996 collateral pools have forced the industry to change, and the result has been a clearer focus on borrower and collateral quality.

## WHAT IS A MANUFACTURED HOUSE?

According to the Department of Housing and Urban Development (HUD), manufactured houses are single-family homes constructed on a chassis at a factory and shipped in one or more sections to a housing site, then installed on a sem-ipermanent foundation. Single-section manufactured homes are typically 12–14 feet wide and 40–64 feet long. Multisection homes are created by joining two or more single sections along their length or by stacking them to create addi-tional stories.

Manufactured housing is generally less expensive (15–40%) and smaller than comparable site-built housing. In 1997, the average manufactured home had 1,420 square feet of living space and cost $41,100 compared with the av-erage site-built home (2,150 square feet costing $132,150, excluding land). Al-though commonly referred to as mobile homes, most manufactured homes are permanent residences. Transporting a manufactured home can cost $2,000–$6,000, depending on the size of the home and the location.

There has been a shift in sales from smaller, less expensive single-section homes to larger, more expensive multisection homes (see Exhibit 31–2).

## MANUFACTURED HOUSING LOAN PRODUCTS

Manufactured homes can be purchased separately or with land. In a land and home purchase, the unit is permanently affixed to the site, and the entire property is taxed as real estate. Loans for land and home purchases typically have more financing options and more closely resemble mortgages for traditional site-built homes. The number of land and home contracts has increased in recent years along with the growth in popularity of more expensive multisection homes. This trend has had a positive impact on loan pools as historical performance shows consumers who borrow to purchase the home and the land are more reliable than consumers who borrow to purchase only the home.

Homes purchased separately are typically financed through a retail install-ment sales contract or a personal property loan. Typically, a UCC filing on the home (similar to the documentation for an automobile loan) takes the place of a deed of trust. These loans are commonly referred to as chattel loans. Histor-ically, terms for a chattel loan were 15–20 years with a 10% down payment.

**E X H I B I T   31–2**

Manufactured Housing Loan Characteristics

|  | Single Section | Multisection | U.S. Average Site Built |
|---|---|---|---|
| Loan Rate versus Conventional (bps) | 338 | 288 |  |
| Average Loan Term (months) | 200 | 240 | 360 |
| Average Monthly Payment ($) | 260 | 406 | 831 |

Source: Green Tree Financial Corp.

Recently, however, lenders have begun offering terms of 25–30 years with as low as a 5% down payment in an effort to increase market share.

## WHO ARE THE BORROWERS?

Although the characteristics of a typical manufactured housing buyer have been changing since the late 1980s and early 1990s, two population segments show particular growth. The first segment consists of retirees and baby boomers. A total of 27% of the heads of manufactured housing households are retired, and occupants older than 70 years account for 21% of all manufactured housing residents (see Exhibit 31–3). Manufactured housing combined with home health-care has become for some a favorable alternative to nursing home care.

The second growth segment is Generation X as they move into the first-time home-buying market. Because rents have been rising for the past decade, manufactured housing offers a strong alternative to apartments in addition to substantial cost savings in relation to site-built homes.

For both segments, the average annual income is $21,500 with 21% exceeding $40,000. The average household net worth is $58,000 with 27% exceeding $100,000.

In the late 1980s and the early 1990s, interest rates for manufactured housing loans for lower-income borrowers were as high as 14%. These exorbitant rates negated cost savings from choosing manufactured housing instead of site-built homes, further inhibiting the industry's growth. Finance companies claimed the high rates reflected the greater risk of delinquency and default as-

### EXHIBIT 31–3

Manufactured Housing Borrower Demographics

| (%) | Single Section | Multisection |
|---|---|---|
| Average Age | | |
| 18–34 | 71.0 | 23.5 |
| 35–54 | 24.2 | 67.9 |
| 55+ | 4.8 | 8.6 |
| Average Years Same Job | | |
| 0–5 | 72.3 | 29.1 |
| 5–10 | 23.4 | 59.5 |
| 10+ | 3.4 | 11.4 |
| Family Income | | |
| $15,000–$25,000 | 64.7 | 12.8 |
| $25,000–$50,000 | 34.5 | 84.6 |
| $50,000+ | 0.8 | 2.6 |

Source: Manufactured Housing Institute.

sociated with manufactured housing borrowers, a stereotype plaguing the industry. Reports at that time disproved the claim and illustrated that average delinquencies on manufactured home loans were significantly less than delinquencies on comparable mortgages. Finance companies have since realized their prejudice and, during the past few years, rates for manufactured housing loans have fallen closer in line with mortgage rates.

Increases in the popularity and acceptance of multisection homes have exposed the industry to higher-credit borrowers than those that sought a single-section home (see Exhibit 31–3). The typical multisection homeowner is older, has a longer employment history, and has a larger income. In contrast, the traditional single-section borrower is younger, has a shorter employment history, and has a smaller income.

## OVERVIEW OF MANUFACTURED HOUSING ABS

Manufactured housing ABS volume has grown dramatically, culminating in a 17% increase in volume from 1997 to 1998. The rapid expansion reflects changing characteristics in the industry. Some of the most prevalent changes include the following:

- Increasing demand for low-cost housing alternatives
- Refinancings due to increased industry competition
- Larger loan balances due to increased desire for larger or multisectional homes
- Longer loan terms to help borrowers manage monthly payments
- Maturing of the industry and its key players
- Industry support provided by government agencies such as HUD

The majority of manufactured housing ABS issuance has been in the public market. As of June 22, 1999, issuance volume had reached a level comparable to total issuance in 1995. At this rate, the asset class will have more than doubled in size in only four years. The asset class has proven its ability to grow in the face of volatility and unsure market conditions as evidenced by record growth despite the tough third quarter of 1998 experienced by all ABS market participants.

Manufactured housing ABS has been a significant portion of total ABS issuance since 1995. Although the aggregate market has seen the emergence of many new asset classes from 1995 to 1998, manufactured housing ABS has remained a consistent 5–6% of the total market. While auto-backed issues and home equities (HEQs) have remained similarly consistent, asset classes such as credit cards and student loans have decreased as a percentage of total issuance.

Although manufactured housing competition continues to increase and more issuers continue to come to market, an overwhelming majority of new issuance still comes from key market players such as Green Tree, Oakwood,

**EXHIBIT  31–4**

Change in Market Share by Key Players

|  | 1996 | 1997 | 1998 | 1999 |
|---|---|---|---|---|
| Green Tree Financial Corp. | 63% | 53% | 47% | 1% |
| Associates | 16% | 8% | 0% | 0% |
| Oakwood Homes Corp. | 8% | 9% | 9% | 8% |
| Vanderbilt Mortgage and Finance, Inc. | 5% | 10% | 8% | 11% |
| Others | 5% | 12% | 11% | 0% |
| BankAmerica Housing Services | 3% | 8% | 13% | 0% |
| Merit | 0% | 0% | 0% | 5% |
| Bombardier Capital Mortgage Securitization Corp. | 0% | 0% | 6% | 2% |
| GreenPoint Credit Corp. | 0% | 0% | 6% | 23% |

Note: GreenPoint acquired BankAmerica Housing Services on Sept. 30, 1998.

Source: *Asset-Backed Alert* and First Union Securities, Inc.

Vanderbilt and GreenPoint. Green Tree, in particular, consistently appears at the top of the league table.

With $4 billion of total manufactured housing ABS volume in 1995, Green Tree accounted for 62% of the asset class's total new issuance that year. Although still the largest issuer of manufactured housing ABS, Green Tree's share of new issuance fell from 53% in 1997 to 47% in 1998 (Exhibit 31–4).

## POOL CHARACTERISTICS

Most loan pools today contain a mixture of single- and multisection manufactured home loans. Placement of the homes also varies with some of the collateral on private lots and others in communities. Loans collateralized by larger homes and those supported by land in addition to the home are generally preferred as collateral rather than a loan on a smaller, unattached unit. Historically in pools, there has been a prevalence of multisection homes as collateral, even when single-section home sales exceeded multisection home sales. Multisection homes accounted for 60.9% of total shipments in 1997, whereas single-section home shipments have slipped since 1995. Issuers tend to place higher-credit collateral in their securitization pools to obtain and sustain tranche ratings. By the end of the first quarter of 1999, multisection homes in securitization pools on average were 67.7% of the underlying collateral.

The majority of loans placed in pools are for new property as opposed to used or secondary market collateral. New homes have constituted 76% or more of total loan pools since 1995. Also evident is a steady increase in used homes as a percentage of the total, which is due to the growth of the secondary market.

Also spurring used homes as acceptable collateral is the increasing quality of manufactured homes over the past five years. With better quality standards supported by manufactured housing manufacturers and government housing agencies, it is reasonable that the newer homes would last longer and depreciation rates would be less than those for homes manufactured and sold a few years ago. As manufactured housing increasingly becomes a more acceptable alternative to site-built homes, secondary market activity should increase and thus more used homes should be financed.

To date, collateral on private lots has been more prevalent than properties situated in communities. This aversion to manufactured housing communities is an offshoot of the old trailer park image. As more upscale communities are tailored for manufactured homes, we expect to see an increase of community-based collateral.

The average life of a typical manufactured housing loan currently ranges from seven to eight years, but this is lengthening. Due to increased demand for larger or multisection homes, loan balances have also been rising. Concurrent with rising financing amounts, borrowers have been demanding longer loan terms to accommodate budgets and to simulate site-built home mortgages. There has also been a heightening of industry competition to meet the requirements of increased business flow. A relaxation of credit underwriting has plagued the industry of late. This issue is discussed in greater detail later in this chapter.

## DRAWING BORROWERS AND THE EFFECT ON SECURITIZATION POOLS

During the mid-1990s as the demand for manufactured housing increased, retailers and financiers began implementing aggressive lending terms to capture greater market share. Higher advance rates, extended loan terms and buy-down programs were used to attract customers and increase underwriting volume. Traditional 15–20-year loan terms were extended to 25–30 years and industry standard down payments of 10–15% were lowered to 5% in some cases. The increase in more expensive multisection home purchases and the availability of "5% down" financing have led to a greater percentage of loans with loan-to-value (LTV) ranges of 95% and higher. The proportion of high-LTV loans has risen on average from 0% to 5% of the total in 1994 to 30–40% in 1998 and 1999, depending on the lender.

Not surprisingly, as a result of looser credit standards, defaults and the number of used and repossessed homes on the market have risen and affected pool performance. To assuage losses, many lenders have switched from wholesale to retail channels to clear repos. In retail disposition, homes are often placed on a consignment basis on a dealer's lots. The dealer receives a commission for the sale of the home and the lender provides financing for the new buyer. Pricing trends suggest many repossessed homes on consignment are sold at or above their true market price. The problem with using retail disposition as a form of loss mitigation is that lenders run the risk of replacing old bad loans with new bad loans. In fact, statistics show consumers with a weak credit history are more likely to purchase repossessed manufactured homes.

With new unit shipments leveling off, many lenders have turned to refinancing as a source of increased volume. Larger loan balances, combined with relatively low interest rates, have created an incentive for many borrowers to refinance. Naturally, this trend in loans appeared within securitization pools and resulted in increasing delinquencies, prepayments, and defaults. Although data shows that borrowers in the high advance rate category typically perform better than the average manufactured housing borrower, some have argued the lack of equity in the home raises the likelihood of default should the borrower run into financial trouble.

In 1997, the manufactured housing financing industry began reorganizing and consolidating. This was accelerated by market volatility in the third quarter of 1998, which hindered many specialty finance companies from securitizing. Reorganization and consolidation have continued as weaker players drop out because of their inability to successfully execute in the market.

## What Happened to Green Tree?

Green Tree Financial Corp., the market's top securitizer for manufactured housing, experienced trouble and controversy related to its collateral and use of gain-on-sale accounting. In 1996, the company was forced to take a $150 million cash charge resulting from the miscalculation of assumptions on loans originated in 1995 and 1996. Although the charge was small in relation to the $26 billion in loans under management, the action highlighted the importance of conservatively measuring the gain on sale of securitized assets. Unfortunately for Green Tree, its trouble did not stop there. As a result of similar prepayment miscalculations, the company revised 1996 and 1997 earnings down $400 million. Lawsuits were brought by shareholders who believed management did not efficiently report troubles in the company. Controversy accelerated when it was revealed that former Chairman Larry Coss' salary was a percentage of reported earnings, an amount that reached $102 million in 1996.

Green Tree has since rebounded from the negative press associated with its gain-on-sale treatment, but an example has been made of the potential problems that can arise from misjudging these calculations.

## Buy-Down Programs

In a buy-down program, the lender offers the borrower a rate lower than the prevailing rate by charging the borrower points in exchange for the lower rate. The points are either added to the loan amount or financed by the lender under

**EXHIBIT 31–5**

An Example of Buy-Down Terms

| Original Loan Amount ($) | Loan Term (years) | Interest Rate | Monthly Payment ($) | Points | Buy-Down Amount ($) |
|---|---|---|---|---|---|
| 50,000 | 20 | 10.00% | 482.51 | 0.0 | 0 |
| 50,000 | 20 | 9.75% | 474.26 | 1.0 | 500 |
| 50,000 | 20 | 9.50% | 466.07 | 2.0 | 1,000 |
| 50,000 | 20 | 9.25% | 457.93 | 3.0 | 1,500 |
| 50,000 | 20 | 9.00% | 449.86 | 4.0 | 2,000 |
| 50,000 | 20 | 8.75% | 441.86 | 5.0 | 2,500 |
| 50,000 | 20 | 8.50% | 433.91 | 6.0 | 3,000 |
| 50,000 | 20 | 8.25% | 426.02 | 7.0 | 3,500 |
| 50,000 | 20 | 8.00% | 418.22 | 8.0 | 4,000 |

Source: First Union Securities, Inc.

a separate agreement. Standard practices in the industry are a 1.0 point charge for every 25 bps reduction in rate. Exhibit 31–5 provides an example of buy-down terms for a 20-year, $50,000 loan with a base rate of 10%. By reducing monthly payments, buy-down programs enable lenders to offer financing to homebuyers who might otherwise not qualify for a manufactured housing loan. The low rate also makes it difficult for competitors to refinance the loan, which decreases the likelihood of prepayment.

Buy-down loans that are securitized result in tighter spreads due to the lower weighted average coupon (WAC). While the likelihood of prepayments is less, this is offset by an increase in potential loss severity. When buy-down loans are sold to a trust, the lender receives the face value of the loan plus any points financed. If a buy-down loan defaults, the sale of the asset must cover the loan amount plus points and liquidation costs. Depending on depreciation and the timing of default, it is likely the necessary recovery amount will exceed the value of the underlying asset.

## ISSUER PROFILES

Throughout late 1998 and 1999, the manufactured housing industry has undergone restructuring and reorganization. Bank of America sold its housing operation to GreenPoint, Green Tree merged with Conseco, Inc., in July 1998 and small players such as United Companies Financial Corp. exited the market. Throughout this process, underwriting standards and dealer networks stood out as keys to industry success. This has brought intense focus on the key industry issuers and how they differentiate themselves.

## Green Tree Financial Corp. (Conseco, Inc.)

Green Tree, founded in 1975, is a diversified finance company with nationwide operations serving the consumer and commercial markets. The company has more than 20,000 independent retail dealer relationships and seven business lines with more than 8,000 employees in more than 200 offices nationwide. The company is known for its well-developed dealer network. With finance receivables in excess of $33 billion, Green Tree is the nation's second largest issuer of asset-backed securities, totaling $13.4 billion in 1998. In July 1998, the company merged with Conseco, a specialist in supplemental health insurance, retirement annuities, and universal life insurance.

Green Tree has been and remains the dominant player in the manufactured housing securitization market. In 1998, the company's securitizations totaling $5.5 billion represented roughly 50% of the manufactured housing securitization market. As a result, Green Tree has played a major role in determining market standards for securitization structures and collateral characteristics. Green Tree also leads the market in structural sophistication and has begun to provide a guaranty on subordinated pieces rather than retaining them.

Green Tree's recovery rate on deals from 1995 through 1998 averaged 56.1%, which ranks in the middle of the industry. Green Tree's deals consist primarily of new units on private lots. Average loans size has trended upward, which parallels the industry overall. WACs have fallen as LTVs have increased, again reflecting overall industry trends.

## Oakwood Homes Corp.

Oakwood Homes, headquartered in Greensboro, N.C., is one of only a few vertically integrated housing companies. Oakwood engages in the production, sale, financing and insuring of manufactured housing units. Founded in 1946, Oakwood (NYSE-OH) is the nation's third largest manufacturer of factory-built homes. With 32 nationwide manufacturing plants and 359 company-owned retail sales centers, Oakwood sells more homes each year than any other retail competitor. Furthermore, the company's financial services business unit completes the sale process by providing customer financing as well as insurance coverage. The company markets its retail businesses under the names Oakwood, Freedom, Victory, Golden West, Schult, Crest, Suburban, and Destiny homes.

Since the issuance of the company's first securitization in 1994, Oakwood has significantly increased its manufactured housing securitization program. With a total of $3.7 billion in securitizations, Oakwood is recognized as a quarterly securitizer and maintains a stable presence in the manufactured housing securitization market. According to the rating agencies, the loans in Oakwood's securitizations are typically of lower credit quality as Oakwood liberally uses the 95% LTV program. In addition, Oakwood's securitizations generally have higher credit support levels than others in this market. Although Oakwood has a relatively high default rate, its recovery rate remains well in excess of other market leaders such as Green Tree. This is attributable to Oakwood's strong dealer network fostered through its vertical integration. This structure allows for increased success with repos, unit trading, secondary market creation, and the avoidance of liquidation through wholesaling, but it may not be enough to sustain collateral troubles over an extended time.

Oakwood announced in mid-June 1999 that earnings for the third quarter, ended June 30, would fall short of analysts' expectations by as much as 50% ($0.55/share). Management also announced a decision to explore strategic alternatives, including a management-led buyout. The earnings shortfall stemmed from "unanticipated softness" in both retail and wholesale sales that, as previously noted, has of late generally affected the industry. Another announcement was made on July 17, 1999 stating that third-quarter earnings will be 65–75% below analysts' estimates. The company's Baa3/BBB-ratings have been placed on negative watch by both Moody's Investor Services, Inc., and Standard & Poor's Corp. Recent troubles, however, have not hindered Oakwood from continuing to access the securitization market.

## Vanderbilt Mortgage and Finance, Inc.

Vanderbilt is the captive finance arm and wholly owned subsidiary of Clayton Homes, Inc. (NYSE-CMH), a vertically integrated manufactured housing company operating in 28 states. Vanderbilt engages in manufacturing, retailing, financing and insuring homes as well as operating manufactured housing communities. As a financial services group, Vanderbilt provides financing and insurance for consumers buying manufactured homes from Clayton-owned retail offices and select independent retail centers. The company's current servicing portfolio contains more than 140,000 loans, totaling more than $3 billion.

Since 1995, Vanderbilt has established itself as a quarterly issuer and has increased its market presence in the manufactured housing securitization market. Historically, the issues have been considered by rating agencies as being at the higher end of the credit spectrum. Average loan maturity is below the norm, reducing depreciation risk, and the company has not been as involved in the 95% LTV program, thus reducing the relative delinquency and loss risk of the pools. In addition, the company does not repurchase defaulted loans from its securitizations, but instead relies on the dealers to perform this task. As a result, losses are absorbed at the dealer level rather than in Vanderbilt's securitizations. In 1998, total issuance of manufactured housing securitizations exceeded $850 million.

Vanderbilt tends to use predominantly community-based loans as opposed to private-lot-based loans in its securitizations. Its weighted average LTVs are lower than Oakwood's, but higher than Green Tree's, reflecting Vanderbilt's middle-of-the-market strategy.

# GreenPoint Credit Corp.

GreenPoint Credit, headquartered in San Diego, is a wholly owned subsidiary of GreenPoint Financial Corp. (NYSE-GPT) specializing in the manufactured housing lending industry. It is the second largest originator and servicer of manufactured housing loans, with annual originations of more than $2.6 billion and a servicing portfolio of more than $10 billion. GreenPoint Credit, with 1,500 employees across a national sales and service network of 45 offices, has relationships with 5,000 dealers.

On November 18, 1998, GreenPoint brought its first manufactured housing securitization to market. The $728 million offering consisted of fixed and floating loans purchased from Bank of America as part of the acquisition of BankAmerica Housing Services. Since the first securitization, GreenPoint has issued two others in 1999 for a total of more than $2.3 billion.

On December 7, 1998, the company announced it had acquired the dealer origination segment of NationsCredit Manufactured Housing Corp.'s manufactured housing business. NationsCredit's business was part of NationsBank prior to its merger with Bank of America. On an annual basis, NationsCredit has originated approximately $400 million through its dealer channel. The purchase provided GreenPoint with access to NationsCredit's dealer business throughout the United States. In addition, the agreement called for a future correspondent relationship in which manufactured housing loans originated through Bank of America's branches will be sold to GreenPoint.

The WAC of the GreenPoint deals is lower than that of its competition's deals. GreenPoint also has had more than 80% of new home collateral for all four deals. Like Vanderbilt, GreenPoint's pool collateral is predominantly located in housing parks or communities as opposed to in private lots. This parallels the trend in the manufactured housing industry toward planned communities built with the help of developers and with full recreational equipment for the community and residents.

# Bombardier Capital Mortgage Securitization Corp.

Bombardier Capital is the financial services arm of global transportation equipment manufacturer, Bombardier, Inc. An international provider of financial solutions, Bombardier Capital offers a full line of lending, leasing, and asset management services to the consumer, inventory, commercial, and industrial markets. The company employs more than 1,100 people at multiple locations in the United States, Canada, and Europe.

Bombardier Capital has been in the manufactured housing business for more 10 years. In 1997, the company launched a manufactured housing retail financing business to provide financing services. The business expanded to double its market share in early 1999 with the purchase of NationsCredit Manufactured Housing's manufactured housing inventory finance portfolio.

Bombardier Capital's portfolio prior to the acquisition encompassed $200 million in assets under management and 540 manufactured housing retailers. The purchased portfolio included floor plan financing loans outstanding of $195 million with approximately 290 retailers at the end of 1998.

The company began to securitize in 1998 and, to date, has issued four securitizations totaling $849.3 million. Almost all of Bombardier Capital's collateral consists of new homes, and weighted average LTVs are lower than much of the competition's.

## MANUFACTURED HOUSING PREPAYMENT MODELS

The Asset-Backed and Quantitative Research groups at First Union Securities have developed prepayment models for a variety of mortgage and mortgage-related asset types.[1] There are two models reflecting differing origination and underwriting criteria for manufactured housing originators and servicers. We have tested each model against all publicly issued ABS and have determined the best fit for each particular collateral group. Below we highlight some of the findings regarding manufactured housing prepayments.

Exhibits 31–6 and 31–7 show the prepayment and delinquency/loss for the universe of manufactured housing ABS. Though the data goes back to 1990, the bulk of the information is from 1993 onward. Note the high original WACs from 1990 to 1992, as well as the repricing of manufactured housing loans since 1993. It is not surprising the life speed of 1994 production shows a higher rate than subsequent years, given the higher WAC of that year's production. Moreover, the 12-month speeds for 1994 and 1995 vintages are somewhat above the total life speed. This reflected the interest rate environment, turnover, and competition.

The 1995 vintage at 4.26% exhibits the highest cumulative net loss of any year. The loss curves in Exhibit 31–7 are interesting in that there is a peak in Year 3, followed by a decline until the loans are seasoned (6–7 years). By this time, the factors (current pool collateral balance) are in the 0.2–0.3 range, possibly indicating adverse borrower selection and burnout in seasoned pools.

In Exhibits 31–8 and 31–9, the historical data on Green Tree shows fairly consistent collateral performance, with prepayments over the past two years oscillating in a fairly narrow range around a 12% constant prepayment rate (CPR); this is consistent with Green Tree's FASB 125 assumption of 200 MHP. The effect of competition and the subsequent rise in prepayments is apparent in Exhibit 31–8. Delinquencies (60+ days) have been between 1.5% and 2.0% over the same time frame, with the peak occurring out about 2.5 years. Annualized net losses peak at Year 3 at just under 2.5%. There is some collateral

---

1. The basic framework of our approach may be found in our October 1998 report *Prepayment Models and Home Equity Analysis.*

**EXHIBIT 31–6**

Prepayments for the Universe of Manufactured Housing Asset-Backed Securities

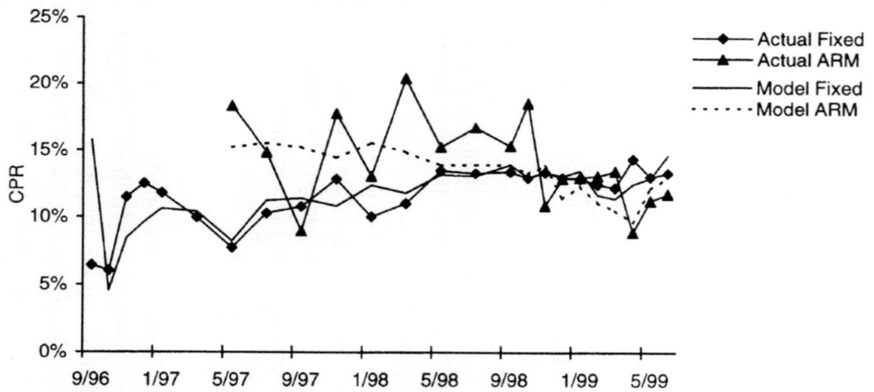


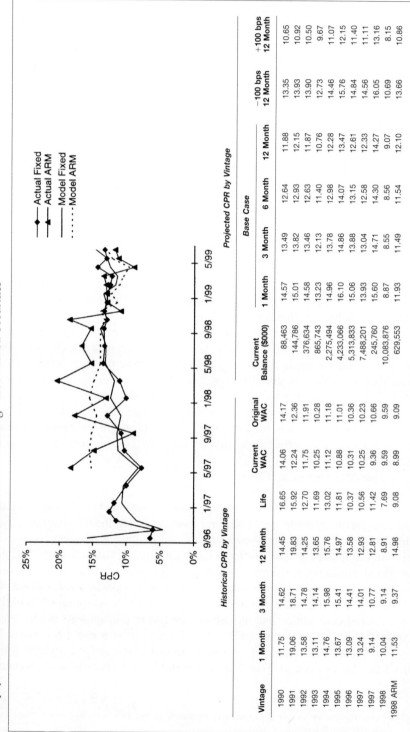

| | Historical CPR by Vintage | | | | | | Projected CPR by Vintage | | | | | | |
|---|---|---|---|---|---|---|---|---|---|---|---|---|---|
| | | | | | | | | Base Case | | | | | |
| Vintage | 1 Month | 3 Month | 12 Month | Life | Current WAC | Original WAC | Current Balance ($000) | 1 Month | 3 Month | 6 Month | 12 Month | −100 bps 12 Month | +100 bps 12 Month |
| 1990 | 11.75 | 14.62 | 14.45 | 16.65 | 14.06 | 14.17 | 88,463 | 14.57 | 13.49 | 12.64 | 11.88 | 13.35 | 10.65 |
| 1991 | 19.06 | 18.71 | 19.83 | 15.92 | 12.24 | 12.36 | 144,786 | 15.01 | 13.82 | 12.93 | 12.15 | 13.93 | 10.92 |
| 1992 | 13.58 | 14.78 | 14.25 | 12.70 | 11.75 | 11.91 | 376,634 | 14.58 | 13.46 | 12.63 | 11.87 | 13.90 | 10.50 |
| 1993 | 13.11 | 14.14 | 13.65 | 11.69 | 10.25 | 10.28 | 865,743 | 13.23 | 12.13 | 11.40 | 10.76 | 12.73 | 9.67 |
| 1994 | 14.76 | 15.98 | 15.76 | 13.02 | 11.12 | 11.18 | 2,275,494 | 14.96 | 13.78 | 12.98 | 12.28 | 14.46 | 11.07 |
| 1995 | 13.67 | 15.41 | 14.97 | 11.81 | 10.88 | 11.01 | 4,233,066 | 16.10 | 14.86 | 14.07 | 13.47 | 15.76 | 12.15 |
| 1996 | 13.09 | 14.41 | 13.58 | 10.37 | 10.31 | 10.36 | 5,313,833 | 15.06 | 13.88 | 13.15 | 12.61 | 14.84 | 11.40 |
| 1997 | 13.24 | 14.01 | 12.93 | 10.56 | 10.25 | 10.23 | 7,488,201 | 13.93 | 13.04 | 12.58 | 12.33 | 14.56 | 11.11 |
| 1997 | 9.14 | 10.77 | 12.81 | 11.42 | 9.36 | 10.66 | 245,760 | 15.60 | 14.71 | 14.30 | 14.27 | 16.05 | 13.16 |
| 1998 | 10.04 | 9.14 | 8.91 | 7.69 | 9.59 | 9.59 | 10,083,876 | 8.87 | 8.55 | 8.56 | 9.07 | 10.69 | 8.15 |
| 1998 ARM | 11.53 | 9.37 | 14.98 | 9.08 | 8.99 | 9.09 | 629,553 | 11.93 | 11.49 | 11.54 | 12.10 | 13.66 | 10.86 |

ARM: Adjustable-rate mortgage; CPR: Constant prepayment rate; WAC: Weighted average coupon.

Source: First Union Securities, Inc.

# EXHIBIT 31-7

Delinquency/Loss for the Universe of Manufactured Housing Asset-Backed Securities

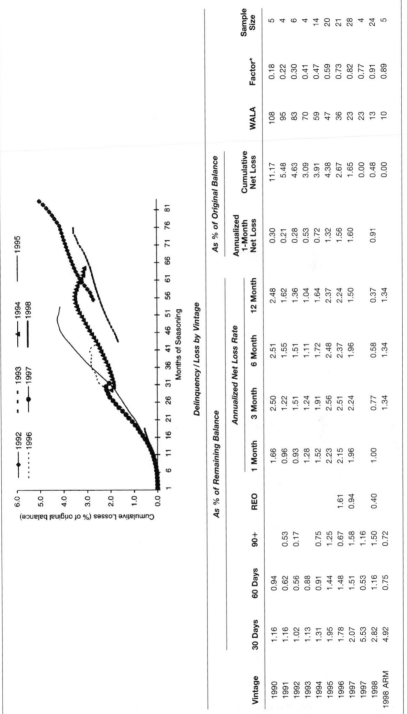

Delinquency/Loss by Vintage

| Vintage | As % of Remaining Balance | | | | Annualized Net Loss Rate | | | | As % of Original Balance | | | | |
|---|---|---|---|---|---|---|---|---|---|---|---|---|---|
| | 30 Days | 60 Days | 90+ | REO | 1 Month | 3 Month | 6 Month | 12 Month | Annualized 1-Month Net Loss | Cumulative Net Loss | WALA | Factor* | Sample Size |
| 1990 | 1.16 | 0.94 | 0.53 | | 1.66 | 2.50 | 2.51 | 2.48 | 0.30 | 11.17 | 108 | 0.18 | 5 |
| 1991 | 1.16 | 0.62 | 0.17 | | 0.96 | 1.22 | 1.55 | 1.62 | 0.21 | 5.48 | 95 | 0.22 | 4 |
| 1992 | 1.02 | 0.56 | | | 0.93 | 1.51 | 1.51 | 1.36 | 0.28 | 4.63 | 83 | 0.30 | 6 |
| 1993 | 1.13 | 0.88 | 0.75 | | 1.28 | 1.24 | 1.11 | 1.04 | 0.53 | 3.09 | 70 | 0.41 | 4 |
| 1994 | 1.31 | 0.91 | 1.25 | | 1.52 | 1.91 | 1.72 | 1.64 | 0.72 | 3.91 | 59 | 0.47 | 14 |
| 1995 | 1.95 | 1.44 | 0.67 | | 2.23 | 2.56 | 2.48 | 2.37 | 1.32 | 4.38 | 47 | 0.59 | 20 |
| 1996 | 1.78 | 1.48 | 1.58 | 1.61 | 2.15 | 2.51 | 2.37 | 2.24 | 1.56 | 2.67 | 36 | 0.73 | 21 |
| 1997 | 2.07 | 1.51 | 1.16 | 0.94 | 1.96 | 2.24 | 1.96 | 1.50 | 1.60 | 1.65 | 23 | 0.82 | 28 |
| 1997 | 5.53 | 0.53 | | | | | | | | 0.00 | 23 | 0.77 | 4 |
| 1998 | 2.82 | 1.16 | 1.50 | 0.40 | 1.00 | 0.77 | 0.58 | 0.37 | 0.91 | 0.48 | 13 | 0.91 | 24 |
| 1998 ARM | 4.92 | 0.75 | 0.72 | | 1.34 | 1.34 | 1.34 | 1.34 | | 0.00 | 10 | 0.89 | 5 |

ARM: Adjustable-rate mortgage; REO: Real estate owned; WALA: Weighted average loan age.

*Factor: Remaining balance compared with the original balance.

Source: First Union Securities, Inc.

**EXHIBIT 31–8**

Green Tree Financial Corp. Aggregate Historical CPR versus Model CPR

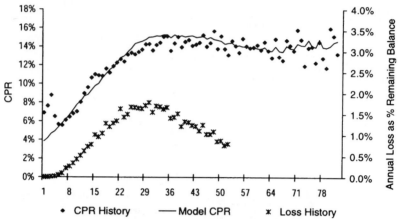

CPR: Constant prepayment rate.

**EXHIBIT 31–9**

Green Tree Financial Corp. Cumulative Losses

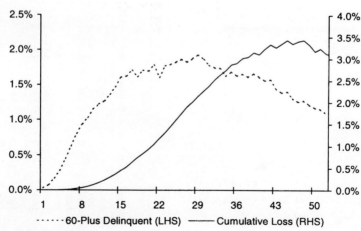

Source: First Union Securities, Inc.

performance tail risk as cumulative net losses rise after Year 5, though thus far exhibiting a much smaller cumulative net loss than the universe as a whole.

Other issuers show a higher base prepayment rate than Green Tree and the manufactured housing universe in general. It seems as if this asset class in general exhibits fairly stable prepayments and therefore better convexity characteristics than other competing mortgage-backed product.

## CONCLUSION

Manufactured housing ABS have been a consistent investment vehicle since 1995. The diverse nature of the underlying collateral allows issuers and underwriters to create securities with favorable convexity characteristics and solid credit support. As with many specialty finance sectors, investors must understand and account for the competitive landscape affecting the origination and ongoing performance of these ABS. The growth of the secondary market, alternative distribution methods, and mortgage-like financing terms continue to draw consumers into this product. As demand for the underlying product remains strong, the asset class should be a viable option for investors.

## CHAPTER 32

# SECURITIES BACKED BY CREDIT CARD RECEIVABLES*

**John N. McElravey**
Director, Asset-Backed Research
Banc One Capital Markets, Inc.

## INTRODUCTION

Credit card asset backed securities (ABS) have been issued in the public debt market since 1987. Over the years, they have become the largest and most liquid sector in the ABS market. Average annual new issuance of credit card ABS since 1990 has been $31.5 billion, with a peak amount of $48 billion in 1996. Because of its liquidity and relatively high credit quality issuers, credit card ABS has become something of a safe haven in times of trouble for ABS investors. Indeed, investors making their first foray into ABS generally dip their toes into credit cards before diving in to the many other asset types available.

The size of the credit card ABS sector corresponds with the growth in the credit card market overall as consumers have come to rely on credit cards as a convenient method of payment for an expanding universe of goods and services, and as a means of accessing credit. In this chapter, we summarize the key structural features of credit card securitizations and provide an overview of the credit card ABS market.

## SECURITIZATION OF CREDIT CARD RECEIVABLES

The earliest credit card securitizations in the late 1980s were executed as a means of diversifying the funding sources for banks active in the credit card market. In the early 1990s, the banking industry faced the imposition of stricter capital standards by regulators. Securitization provided a vehicle to help meet these new standards by reducing balance sheet assets and thereby improving regulatory capital ratios. Securitization also allowed for the entry and growth of specialized credit card banks into the market. These banks, such as MBNA, First

---

* This chapter is reprinted with permission from Frank J. Fabozzi (ed.), *Investing in Asset-Backed Securities* (New Hope, PA: Frank J. Fabozzi Associates, 2000).

USA, and Capital One, were able to access the credit markets directly and achieve funding costs that were more comparable with established bankcard issuers. Much of the increased competition in the credit card market can be traced to these banks, which could not have grown as rapidly as they did without the benefits afforded by securitization.

## BASIC MASTER TRUST STRUCTURE

The structure used for credit card securitization until 1991 was a stand-alone trust formed with a dedicated pool of credit card accounts and the receivables generated by those accounts. Each securitization required a new trust and a new pool of collateral. Since 1991, the master trust has become the predominant structure used in the credit card market (see Exhibit 32–1). As the name implies, the credit card issuer establishes a single trust. This trust can accept numerous additions of accounts and receivables, and can issue additional securities. All of the securities issued by the master trust are supported by the cash flows from all of the receivables contributed to it. The collateral pool is not segregated to support any individual securities.

For the credit card issuer, this structure lowers costs and provides greater flexibility because a new trust need not be established using a unique set of accounts each time additional securities are issued. From the investors' point of view, assessing the credit quality of a new issue requires less effort because there is only one pool of collateral to review. As the collateral pool grows, it

**E X H I B I T   32–1**

Basic Master Trust Structure

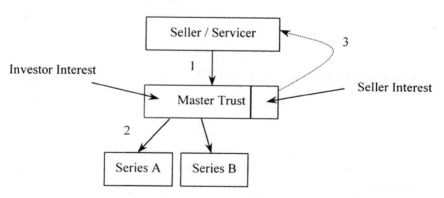

Step 1: Receivables from designated accounts are transferred to the master trust.
Step 2: Pro rata share of charge-offs and cash flows are allocated to investors.
Step 3: Pro rata share of charge-offs and cash flows are allocated to the seller.

becomes more diversified. While the characteristics of the collateral pool can change over time due to changes in interest rates, underwriting criteria, industry competition, and so on, any change in a master trust would be more gradual than would the differences in stand alone pools.

### Investor Interest/Seller Interest

Credit card master trusts allocate cash flow between the ABS investors and the credit card issuer. The "investor interest" is simply the principal amount owed to investors in the ABS. The "seller interest" is a residual ownership interest that the credit card issuer is required to maintain. This seller interest aligns the incentives of the seller with that of the investors because it has a *pari passu* claim on the cash flows. The minimum required seller interest for most master trusts tends to be 7% of outstanding receivables, though the rating agencies allow the minimum required for some trusts to be lower. The seller interest in a master trust is likely to be higher in practice, in some cases much higher, than the minimum. For example, the First Chicago Master Trust II has a seller interest of close to 50%. The actual level of seller interest will be driven by the issuer's strategy with regard to its use of securitization for its funding needs.

The seller interest absorbs seasonal fluctuations in the amount of outstanding receivables, and is allocated dilutions from returned merchandise and ineligible receivables. The seller interest does *not* provide credit enhancement for the ABS. Credit enhancement for the ABS, discussed more fully below, is provided by subordinated securities, which are part of the investor interest, or by other means provided for in the structure of the series.

As an issuer's credit card business grows, accounts that meet the eligibility criteria can be added to a master trust. An account addition normally requires rating agency approval unless it is a relatively small percentage of the current balance (usually 10% to 15%). Sellers are obligated to add accounts if the seller interest falls below its required minimum level. If the seller is unable to add accounts to the trust, then an early amortization event is triggered and investors begin receiving principal payments immediately. The risk of an early amortization gives the seller a powerful incentive to keep the seller interest above the minimum level.

## The Credit Card ABS Life Cycle

Under normal circumstances, the life cycle of credit card ABS is divided into two periods: the *revolving period* and the *amortization period*. We discuss each period below.

### Revolving Period

During the revolving period, investors receive interest payments only. Principal collections on the receivables are used to purchase new receivables or to purchase a portion of the seller interest if there are not enough new receivables generated by the designated accounts. The revolving period is used by an issuer to finance short-term credit card loans over a longer time period. The revolving period is used to maintain a stable average life and to create more certainty for the expected maturity date.

### Amortization Period

After the end of the revolving period, the amortization period begins and principal collections are used to repay ABS investors. The amortization period may be longer or shorter depending on the monthly payment rate of the accounts in the master trust. The payment rate is the percentage of the outstanding receivables balance paid each month. Trusts with lower monthly payment rates will require longer amortization periods. For example, credit card ABS with a five year expected maturity might revolve for 48 months, and then enter amortization for the final 12 months of its life. This part of the credit card ABS life cycle is usually accomplished through one of two mechanisms: *controlled amortization* or *controlled accumulation*.

In a controlled amortization, principal is paid to the ABS investors in equal payments (see Exhibit 32–2). The example assumes one series issued out of the

### E X H I B I T   32–2

Class A Controlled Amortization

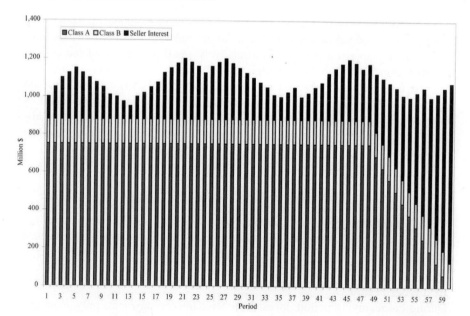

master trust with two classes, a Class A senior certificate and a Class B subordinated certificate. During the four-year revolving period, investors receive only interest payments. Principal collections are used to purchase new receivables. The total amount of receivables varies over time, and these fluctuations are absorbed by the seller interest. At the beginning of year five, the revolving period ends and a controlled amortization begins. Investors receive principal payments in 12 equal installments. Principal collections not needed to repay ABS investors are used to purchase new receivables. Interest payments continue based on the declining principal balance of the ABS. The Class B amount remains fixed during Class A amortization, and the seller interest grows proportionately until the ABS investors are repaid.

In a controlled accumulation, principal collections needed to repay ABS investors are deposited into a trust account each month and held until maturity after the end of the revolving period (see Exhibit 32–3). This example again assumes a simple senior/subordinated structure and a 4-year revolving period. After the end of the revolving period, principal collections are trapped in an account in 12 equal installments to be used to repay the Class A investors. Excess principal collections are used to purchase new receivables. Interest payments to investors during the accumulation period are made based on the original

**E X H I B I T    32–3**

Class A Controlled Accumulation

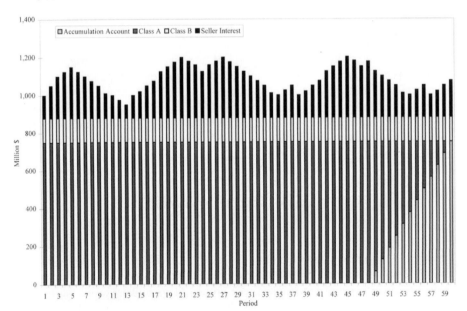

**E X H I B I T   32–4**

Early Amortization Triggers

---

*Seller / Servicer Issues*
1. Failure to make required deposits or payments.
2. Failure to transfer receivables to the trust when necessary.
3. Breach of representations or warranties.
4. Events of default, bankruptcy or insolvency of the seller or servicer.

*Collateral Performance Issues*
5. Three-month average excess spread falls below zero.
6. Seller interest falls below the minimum level.
7. Collateral portfolio balance falls below the invested amount.

*Legal Issues*
8. Trust is reclassified as an "investment company" under the Investment Company Act of 1940.

---

outstanding invested amount. A single "bullet" payment of principal is made at maturity to the ABS investors. This structural device developed as a way to emulate the cash flow characteristics of a corporate bond.

### Early Amortization

Under certain circumstances, such as poor credit performance or a financially troubled servicer, an early amortization of the ABS could occur. Trigger events are put in place to reduce the length of time that investors would be exposed to a troubled transaction. Exhibit 32–4 lists common early amortization trigger events found in credit card master trusts. If an early amortization trigger is hit, then a transaction that is in its revolving period stops revolving and immediately begins to pass principal collections through to the ABS investors. One structural enhancement available to protect investors allows for principal to be passed through on an uncontrolled, or rapid amortization, basis. This mechanism diverts principal due to the seller toward payment of the ABS in order to get investors out more quickly.

## Cash Flow Allocations

### Groups

A credit card master trust may utilize the concept of a "group," which is a structural device used to help allocate cash flow. Within the hierarchy of the master trust, one or more groups may be established, and each series of securities issued to investors will be assigned to a group. At its highest level, the master trust allocates cash on a pro rata basis between the investor interest and seller interest. The investor interest is subdivided further on a pro rata basis at the group level. While many trusts have only one group that encompasses all of the series issued, other trusts may have two or more. In trusts with more than one group, series with similar characteristics could be grouped together. For example, a master trust with two groups could place all of the fixed-rate coupon series in one group and all of the floating-rate coupon series in a second group. The sharing of excess principal or finance charge collections, if called for in the master trust structure, will be determined at the group level.

**Finance Charge Allocations**
The components of the finance charge collected by a master trust include the monthly interest on the account balance, annual or late fees, recoveries on charged-off receivables, interchange,[1] and discounted receivables.[2] When expressed as a percentage of the trust's receivables balance, finance charges are called the *portfolio yield*.

Finance charge collections are allocated by most master trusts pro rata based on the outstanding invested amount of each series. This "floating" allocation adjusts as a series amortizes or accumulates principal collections in a principal funding account. Excess finance charge collections may or may not be shared by series in the same group depending on the structure of the master trust. Some master trusts, such as Discover Card Master Trust, utilize a "fixed" allocation of finance charges. In this structure, the proportion to be allocated to a particular series is fixed at the end of the revolving period and is based on the original principal balance of the series. This structure allows for a greater relative proportion of finance charge collections to go to amortizing series. Such a structure can also be used by an issuer in the event of an early amortization to reallocate a portion of the seller's finance charges to investors to cover any potential shortfall.

Master trusts that allocate finance charges pro rata based on the size of the series invested amount are known as "nonsocialized" master trusts. Finance charges are available to each series to cover its allocated charge-offs, servicing fees, and to pay the coupon to the ABS investors each month. Some nonsocialized master trusts do not share excess finance charges. In other nonsocialized trusts, once all of the expenses are covered, the series included in the same group may share excess finance charges. If excess finance charges are shared

---

1. Interchange is a fee paid to the bank that issues the credit card. It compensates the bank for taking on credit risk and allowing a grace period. Interchange is created when a bank discounts the amount paid to a merchant for a credit card transaction. Interchange is shared by the merchant's bank, the bank issuing the credit card, and visa or MasterCard for clearing the transaction.
2. Some master trusts allow receivables to be added at a discount. The discount typically ranges between 1% and 5%. When the face amount of the receivable is collected, the discounted portion is included as a finance charge collection. This practice can temporarily increase the portfolio yield on the collateral pool.

by the series in a group, then they are distributed to the other series based on need. Any excess finance charges left over are considered excess spread.

The advantage of a nonsocialized master trust is that the risk of early amortization can be isolated at the series level. The disadvantage is that high coupon series are at a relatively greater risk of early amortization if there is a shortfall in finance charge collections. The sharing of excess finance charges helps mitigate, but does not eliminate, this risk. Most master trusts today, such as the Chase Credit Card Master Trust and the Sears Credit Card Master Trust II, are structured as nonsocialized trusts that allow for sharing excess finance charges.

An alternative structure, used by a small number of credit card ABS issuers, is a "socialized" master trust. In such a structure, finance charges are allocated to series within a group based on need. Need is determined by the costs of each series—the coupon, servicing fees, and allocated charge-offs. (Charge-offs are allocated to a series pro rata based on its size within the group.) The expenses for the group are the weighted average of the expenses for each series. Series with higher coupon costs will receive a larger allocation of finance charge collections. The advantage of socialization is that finance charge collections are combined to help support higher cost series, and thus help avoid an early amortization. However, their fates are linked. All series in a group will make payments as expected, or they will all enter early amortization together. Citibank Credit Card Master Trust I and Household Affinity Master Trust I are two prominent examples of socialized master trusts.

**Principal Collections**
Principal collections are allocated on a pro rata basis to each series in the same group based on the size of its invested amount. The allocation of principal to a series is determined by its point in the ABS life cycle. Series that are in their revolving period receive no principal collections. Their principal collections can be reallocated, and may be shared with other series that are amortizing. Sharing principal collections is a structural enhancement that helps to ensure the timely payment of principal to ABS investors. Principal that is not needed to repay investors is reinvested in new receivables.

For a series in its amortization or accumulation period, principal collections allocated to it will be used to repay investors. The allocation of principal is determined by the size of the invested amount of the series at the end of its revolving period. Even though the certificates are amortizing, the allocation percentage to the series will be fixed based on its original invested amount. If the credit card ABS accumulate principal or amortize over 12 months, then $\frac{1}{12}$ of the principal amount of that series will be paid to it. Principal collections in excess of what is necessary for amortization, depending on the structure of the trust, may be shared with other series in the same group as needed to meet their amortization schedules. Otherwise, excess principal is used to purchase additional receivables.

# Credit Enhancement

In order to establish an investment grade rating on credit card ABS, credit enhancement is necessary to absorb losses. The amount of credit enhancement needed will vary from one master trust to another based on the desired rating level and the credit performance of an issuer's credit card portfolio. Early credit card transactions carried letters-of-credit from commercial banks as credit enhancement. However, downgrades of a number of credit enhancers exposed ABS investors to downgrades on their investments. While some issuers still rely on surety bonds, internal forms of credit enhancement have become the norm.

### Excess Spread

*Excess spread* is perhaps the most important measure of the health of a credit card master trust, and as such is a key early amortization trigger. Excess spread is simply the cash flow left over each month after the investor coupon, servicing fees, and charge-offs have been allocated to each series. The calculation of excess spread is straightforward, as shown in Exhibit 32–5, with the values expressed as an annualized percentage of the outstanding receivables balance. If the three-month moving average of excess spread for a particular series in a non-socialized master trust falls below zero, then an early amortization event with regard to that series has occurred. In socialized master trusts, the excess spread for all series in the same group will be equal because they share finance charge collections based on the weighted-average cost of the group. An early amortization trigger based on a decline in excess spread will, therefore, affect all series in the group.

### Cash Collateral Account

A *cash collateral account* (CCA) is a cash reserve account funded at closing and held by the trust. The cash to fund the CCA is usually lent by a third party

**EXHIBIT  32–5**

Excess Spread Calculation

| | |
|---|---|
| Gross Portfolio | 19% |
| Less: | |
| Charge-Offs | 6% |
| Net Portfolio Yield | 13% |
| Less: | |
| Investor Coupon | 6% |
| Servicing Fee | 2% |
| Excess Spread | 5% |

and invested in high-grade, short-term securities. The CCA is used to protect against short falls in cash flow due to rising charge-offs, and any draws on it are reimbursed from future excess spread.

### Collateral Invested Amount

An alternative to a cash reserve is a *collateral invested amount* (CIA), which is a privately placed subordinated tranche of a series. The CIA is placed with a third-party investor, and the investor may or may not require a rating on the CIA. The CIA is an improvement for the issuer over the CCA because this tranche is backed by collateral rather than cash. Like the CCA, the CIA is available to protect against short falls in cash flow due to declining excess spread. The CIA tranche has the benefit of a spread account, which is not available as credit enhancement to other investors. Draws on the CIA also are reimbursed through excess spread.

### Subordination

As credit card ABS have evolved, structures have become more complex. Letters-of-credit have given way to CCAs or CIAs, which in turn have been replaced by some issuers with rated subordinated securities. The subordinated classes also are placed with public ABS investors and tend to be rated in the single-A or triple-B categories. A typical structure might include AAA-rated Class A senior certificates, a single-A rated Class B subordinated tranche, and then a CIA or CCA. More recently, Class C tranches issued to outside investors have been rated at triple-B levels in place of the CIA (see Exhibit 32–6). The Class C tranche is credit enhanced by a spread account that can trap additional cash out of excess spread if certain credit performance triggers are tripped. Using subordinated tranches allows the issuer to monetize a larger portion of its collateral portfolio, and allows it to reach a wider investor audience. Some issuers have developed structures that included ERISA-eligible subordinated classes to improve their overall cost of funding. A number of issuers, including Citibank, First USA, MBNA and Chase, have included certificated C pieces in their credit card ABS transactions.

# Rating Agency Considerations

Rating agency criteria have evolved over time as new structures, such as rated C-pieces, have been introduced. The structural integrity of credit card ABS is tested by stressing the historical performance of critical variables related to the cash flows. The rating agencies generally require three to five years of historical data, and will examine vintage data in order to estimate loss curves and the ultimate level of charge-offs. Once base line performance is determined, then different cash flow stresses are used depending on the desired rating. The key quantitative variables for analyzing credit card securitizations include portfolio

**E X H I B I T   32–6**

Credit Card Series Structure

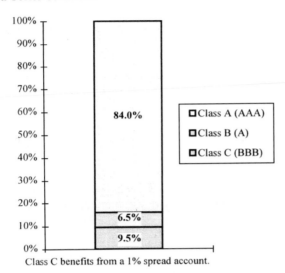

Class C benefits from a 1% spread account.

yield, charge-offs, monthly payment rate, monthly purchase rate, and the investor coupon.[3] Each is discussed below.

- Portfolio yield, as noted above, is a measure of the income generated by the credit card receivables. While portfolio yield is driven largely by the APR on accounts and fees, usage by account holders also plays an important role. All else being equal, a portfolio with proportionately more revolving accounts relative to convenience users will translate into a higher portfolio yield.

- Charge-offs are the credit losses experienced by the portfolio, and are taken by most issuers at about 180 days past due. Peak losses for credit card accounts have been observed at about 24 months of seasoning.

- The monthly payment rate is an important variable in the analysis because high payment rates can be a source of strength and implied credit enhancement. A large proportion of convenience users, while depressing portfolio yield, can sharply increase payment rates. A higher payment rate means that investors will be paid out more quickly during an early amortization.

- Related to the payment rate is the purchase rate, which is the generation of new receivables by the designated accounts. Higher purchase rates mean

3. The methodology and variables used are based on Standard & Poor's rating criteria. The other rating agencies perform a similar analysis when rating credit card ABS.

**E X H I B I T 32–7**

Standard & Poor's Benchmark Credit Card Stress Scenarios

| | AAA-Rating | A-Rating |
|---|---|---|
| Charge-Offs | 3–5× steady-state levels | 2–3× steady-state levels |
| Portfolio Yield (1) | 11%–12% annual rate | 12 annual rate |
| Payment Rate | 45%–55% of steady state level | 50%–60% of steady state level |
| Purchase Rate | 0%–5% annual rate | 0%–5% annual rate |
| Investor Coupon (2) | 15% | 14% |

(1) Based on proposed legislative caps.
(2) Coupon for uncapped floaters.

more receivables are being generated to support outstanding ABS. Bankruptcy of the seller, such as a department store chain, is the main risk with regard to the purchase rate because cardholders may stop using the card.

• Floating-rate ABS generally require more credit enhancement than fixed-rate transactions because the agencies assume in their stress scenarios that market interest rates increase dramatically. Higher funding costs reduce the available excess spread.

The stress tests run by the rating agencies force portfolio yields, payment rates, and purchase rates down sharply at the same time that charge-offs rise. This combination compresses excess spread and causes an early amortization of the transaction. Exhibit 32–7 shows generic stress scenarios for credit card ABS transactions used by Standard & Poor's. The agencies may deviate from these benchmark levels depending on the qualitative factors of the seller's business. Some of the key qualitative elements that go into the rating analysis are new account underwriting, servicing and collections, marketing, card type (private label versus general purpose), geographic diversification, strategic objectives of the firm, account seasoning, and the competitive position of the issuer. These qualitative factors, among others, determine how the generic stress factors will be modified and applied to an individual issuer's credit card portfolio.

## THE CREDIT CARD ABS MARKET

Credit card ABS is the largest and most liquid part of the ABS market. Over the five-year period ending October 22, 1999, total new issuance of credit card ABS has been between $35 billion and $50 billion (see Exhibit 32–8), and there are over $200 billion of credit card ABS outstanding. The large number of issuers and dollar amount outstanding makes this sector a particularly active secondary market. Consequently, spreads for credit card ABS are a benchmark for other ABS sectors. During the past decade, the credit card industry has experienced rapid growth and increasing competition. That dynamic culminated

**E X H I B I T   32–8**

Public Market Credit Card ABS Issuance

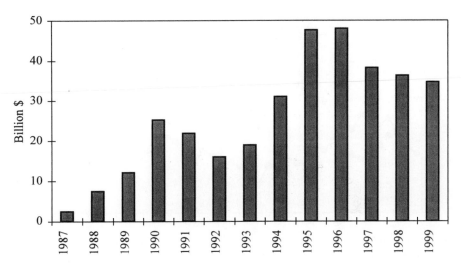

in sharp increases in outstanding receivables in 1995 and 1996, and was reflected in the amount of new credit card ABS issued during that period. However, rapid growth and intense competition also led to problems with asset quality (see Exhibit 32–9). Charge-offs rose steadily and excess spreads dropped from the middle of 1995 through the middle of 1997 as consumer bankruptcy rates reached record levels.

## Industry Consolidation

To better meet their credit underwriting and customer service needs, stronger credit card companies invested heavily in technology, and increased their scale of operations to spread the costs of that investment over more accounts. Many smaller or weaker firms have been unable or unwilling to meet the challenge of the new competitive environment, and have decided to exit the business. As a result, consolidation has been one of the key themes in the credit card business for the past few years. To illustrate, at the start of 1987 there were slightly more than $80 billion of credit card receivables outstanding in the U.S., and the top ten credit card companies had a combined market share of about 40%. At the start of 1999, there were about $445 billion of outstanding credit card receivables, and the top ten credit card companies had a combined market share of 75% (see Exhibit 32–10).

As the credit card industry has consolidated, so has the market for credit card ABS. The three largest credit card issuers accounted for about 58% of credit card ABS outstanding as of year-end 1998, and the top five were respon-

**EXHIBIT 32–9**

Banc One Capital Markets Credit Card Performance Indices

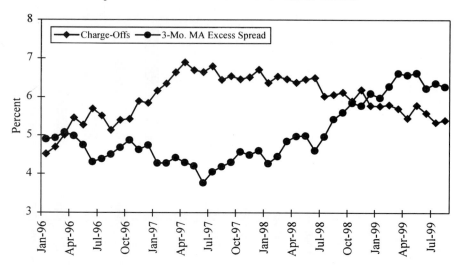

sible for approximately 76%. While consolidation has reduced the number of issuers in the market, the overall credit quality of those that remain has improved. Eight of the top ten sponsors have corporate debt ratings of A2/A or better. From the standpoint of liquidity and issuer quality, this sector is the strongest in the ABS market.

## Credit Card Market Segments

The major issuers of credit card ABS fall into four major categories: commercial banks, consumer finance, independents, and retailers. Following are some examples of the issuers in each of these categories.

- *Commercial Banks:* Bank One, Citibank, Chase, BankAmerica
- *Consumer Finance:* MBNA, Household, Capital One, Providian
- *Independents:* Discover, American Express
- *Retailers:* Sears, Dayton Hudson, World Financial Network, Federated

## General Purpose Cards

The credit card ABS market is divided into two major segments: *general purpose* and *private label*. The larger of the two segments includes transactions sponsored by issuers of general-purpose credit cards. General-purpose credit cards

**EXHIBIT 32–10**

Top Ten General Purpose Credit Card Issuers

| Rank | Sponsor Name | Corporate Ratings (M/S) | Outstanding Receivables[1] ($ bn) | Market Share (%) | Trust Size ($ bn) | Percentage Securitized (%) | Outstanding Securities ($ bn) | As Percent of Market (5) | Series Issued in 1998 | Series Issued in 1999 |
|---|---|---|---|---|---|---|---|---|---|---|
| 1 | Bank One/First USA | Aa3/AA− | 69.86 | 15.7 | 55.74 | 74.9 | 41.77 | 20.8 | 11 | 3 |
| 2 | Citigroup | Aa3/AA− | 69.60 | 15.6 | 51.46 | 70.8 | 36.44 | 18.2 | 9 | 3 |
| 3 | MBNA | Baa2/BBB | 48.90 | 11.0 | 45.02 | 84.2 | 37.92 | 18.9 | 9 | 2 |
| 4 | Discover | Aa3/A+ | 32.80 | 7.4 | 28.11 | 66.4 | 18.65 | 9.3 | 6 | 3 |
| 5 | Chase Manhattan | Aa3/A+ | 32.20 | 7.2 | 21.79 | 81.6 | 17.78 | 8.9 | 7 | 1 |
| 6 | BankAmerica | AA1/AA− | 20.96 | 4.7 | 3.57 | 71.7 | 2.56 | 1.3 | 2 | 0 |
| 7 | Amex | Aa3/A+ | 16.70 | 3.8 | 10.63 | 67.8 | 7.21 | 3.6 | 2 | 1 |
| 8 | Fleet/Advanta | A1/A+ | 15.10 | 3.4 | 9.78 | 34.5 | 3.37 | 1.7 | 1 | 1 |
| 9 | Capital One | Baa3/BBB− | 14.30 | 3.2 | 11.01 | 85.1 | 9.36 | 4.7 | 4 | 0 |
| 10 | Household Bank | A2/A | 14.30 | 3.2 | 9.81 | 55.7 | 5.46 | 2.7 | 1 | 0 |
| | Top Ten Total | | 334.72 | 75.2 | 246.90 | 69.3 | 180.53 | 90.0 | 52 | 14 |
| | ABS Market Total | | 445.00 | | | | 200.50 | | 62 | 16 |

[1] Through December 1998

include both Visa and MasterCard cards issued by commercial banks and consumer finance companies, as well as the independent networks of merchants built by Discover Card and American Express. This group of issuers represents the vast majority of the credit card ABS market. Issuers of general-purpose cards tend to price new ABS at tighter spreads relative to private label issuers. Tiering in that market favors the largest, most frequent issuers with stable credit performance. Citibank and MBNA are generally considered to be the benchmark issuers in this market segment.

## Teaser Rate Cards

In an attempt to gain market share in the face of fierce competition, credit card issuers devised a number of innovations to establish brand loyalty with new customers. Low-price cards, with no annual fee and up-front "teaser" rates, have been used to lure customers away from competitors. These accounts often allow the new customer to transfer existing balances from other, higher rate cards. The teaser rate usually is in effect for 6 to 12 months, and then steps up to a higher rate based on the borrower's credit risk. Balance transfers have been used to great effect, though many borrowers have become adept at rolling balances from one card to another at the end of the teaser rate period. One of the problems with this approach is the potential for adverse selection in the account base. Borrowers with poor credit are more likely to respond to a teaser rate, and may be less likely to roll balances to a new card in the future because they have less credit options.

## Affinity and Co-Branded Programs

One of the uses of the technological investment made by card issuers has been in the customer retention effort. A package of interest rates, credit limits, and other services can be offered to entice customers to stay once the teaser period ends. These packages may come in thousands of possible combinations. The method of mass customization is made possible by the sophisticated computer systems that search for new customers in huge databases, and track the credit performance and profitability of existing customers. Two issuers that practice a mass customization strategy are Capital One and Providian.

Two popular products created by issuers to differentiate themselves in the minds of cardholders and retain them as customers are *affinity* and *co-branded programs*. Affinity cards are issued by a bank in association with a special interest group. This group may be a college alumni association, professional group, or sports team, which receives a fee from the bank. The bank uses its affinity program to attract a certain demographic group to use its card. Co-branded cards are programs that associate a bank's credit card with a particular commercial firm. Customers can earn certain rewards from the commercial firm for making purchases with the card. Earning mileage toward free tickets on airlines is probably one of the most popular bank co-brand programs.

### Private Label Credit Cards

The other, much smaller segment of the credit card market includes private label credit cards, which are sponsored by retailers for use in their own stores. This segment has been dominated by issuance from Sears, which represents about one-third of the private label market. Retail credit card accounts are most often viewed by the sponsor as a means to increase sales, and credit underwriting may not be as stringent as it is for general-purpose credit cards. As a result, charge-offs tend to be higher on private label credit card master trusts than on a typical bank card master trust. On the other hand, APRs and portfolio yields do tend to be higher to compensate for the greater risk in the private label portfolio (see Exhibit 32–11). Because private label transactions tend to be less frequent and somewhat smaller, they tend to price at a concession to the transactions sponsored by general-purpose card issuers. Nevertheless, good value can be found among private label issuers by investors willing to investigate them.

**E X H I B I T   32–11**

BOCM Credit Card Indices—General Purpose versus
Private Label Performance

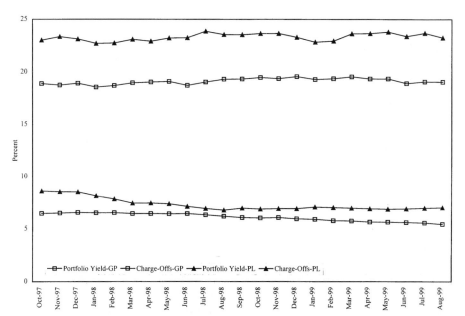

## CONCLUSION

The credit card ABS market is the largest, most liquid asset-backed sector with the greatest investor acceptance. For this reason, it can be viewed as a safe haven for ABS investors in stressful market times. A strong economy, healthy consumer balance sheets, and greater acceptance of credit cards for non-traditional uses have led to a sharp increase in outstanding receivables over the past few years. Meanwhile, the market weathered a deteriorating credit situation from 1995 through 1997, and appears fairly strong as of this writing with falling charge-off rates and rising monthly payment rates. Nevertheless, a growing need for technology and intense competition have led to consolidation in the industry, though there seems to be no less competition as a result. Increasing issuance in the European market should produce a more global credit card ABS market in coming years, and additional innovations are sure to follow. While the unbridled growth of the mid 1990s seems unlikely to be repeated, the credit card ABS market should continue to be the benchmark sector for the foreseeable future.

PART 5

# FIXED INCOME ANALYTICS AND MODELING

## CHAPTER 33

# Characteristics of and Strategies with Callable Securities*

Douglas Johnston
Senior Vice President
Fixed Income Research
Lehman Brothers Inc.

## INTRODUCTION

Recently, volatility has come to be viewed as an asset class in its own right. Next to duration, curve, and spreads, investors realize the importance of having a view on the likely range of yield movements and its impact on security prices. While many money managers do not trade options outright, due to account restrictions, assets with embedded options are accessible, such as mortgage-backed and callable securities. In fact, in April of 1999, both Fannie Mae and Freddie Mac, two large federal agencies, began to issue large, "benchmark" callable structures giving investors highly liquid vehicles to buy or sell volatility.

Callable securities offer opportunities for many fixed income investors. With the callables' exposure to changes in the yield curve and volatility, these securities expand the investment universe and give investors an additional tool to outperform their benchmarks. However, with the anticipation of enhanced yield come commensurate risks. This chapter introduces callable securities and their salient features, discusses the risks due to changes in market variables, and highlights strategies that can be employed to manage those risks and improve portfolio performance.[1]

## WHY CALLABLES?

Callable securities have substantial diversity in structure with call lockouts ranging from a few months to longer than 10 years. Price diversity allows the investor

---

* This chapter is reprinted with permission from Frank J. Fabozzi (ed.), *Perspectives on Fixed Income Portfolio Management: Volume 2* (New Hope, PA: Frank J. Fabozzi Associates, 2000). Special thanks to Andy Sparks for reviewing this chapter and his insightful comments.
1. This chapter was written in 1998. Consequently, the data and illustrations are through 1997.

to choose between discount, par-priced, or premium securities. For indexed investors, not including callables in their asset allocation is equivalent to being short an asset class of sizable market value.

Callable securities make up an asset class that investors can use to enhance returns under appropriate conditions. For example, in 1997 it paid to sell volatility. And similar to mortgage-backed securities, callables performed well with declines in both actual and implied volatility. Using Lehman Brothers' indices, the monthly excess returns of the agency callable sector over duration-matched Treasuries in 1997 was 53 basis points.

Of course returns are not always good. In particular, the rally and flattening of the Treasury and agency curves at the end of 1997 increased the probability that some callable securities would be redeemed. Callable securities are more sensitive to changes in the shape of the yield curve than nominal securities. In addition, the late 1997 spike in implied volatility caused investors to reevaluate the risk premium required to sell volatility. Both effects combined to widen nominal spreads on callable instruments, as reflected in their muted performance in late 1997.

There are risks associated with investing in callable securities. In addition to the usual vagaries of supply and demand, callables have embedded options that are sensitive to changes in the slope of the yield curve. The value of the options is partly a function of forward rates, which are dependent on the spot level of rates and spot yield spreads.

Another risk is volatility, which has two forms. The first is realized volatility. Owners of callable instruments are expressing the implicit view that yields will remain relatively stable, enabling the investor to capture the yield spread over duration-matched noncallable securities. Another way to express this is that callable securities can have negative convexity leading to poor returns in a volatile market. Large swings in rates can necessitate rehedging, leading the investor to lock in lower returns. If these moves in rates are large enough, callable securities will underperform.

Many investors use callable securities within a total return strategy rather than a buy-and-hold strategy; therefore, the second volatility risk is to changes in implied volatility, which is the market forecast of future rate uncertainty. When a position is unwound, the value of the callable security will depend on the new level of implied volatility. If implied volatility were to increase, callable security prices would decline. Therefore, callable investors must have views on the likely range of rates over the investment period and the market's perception of future rate uncertainty at the horizon date.

How much additional return is required to compensate for these risks is the central question for investors. Nominal spreads, and therefore prices, reflect the market's perception of the value of these risks. This chapter introduces investors to callable securities, highlighting the risks and rewards and the tools needed to determine if an investment in callable securities is right for a particular portfolio.

## DISSECTING THE CALLABLE

A callable security gives the issuer the right to redeem the security at predetermined prices at specified times. For example, the traditional five-year security that is noncallable for one year (denoted "5nc1") is redeemable at par at any time starting on the anniversary of its issue date. Different structures may have a schedule of prices for which the issue can be redeemed or specific dates on which the issue may be called.[2] The underlying theme, however, is the same: by purchasing a callable security, the investor gives the issuer the option to buy the security back. Therefore, investors who own callable securities have sold embedded interest rate options and need to be compensated appropriately.

Compensation for selling the embedded option comes in the form of a higher static yield. For example, on 12/5/97, a generic U.S. agency 10nc3 was offered at a yield spread of 94 bp to the 10-year on-the-run Treasury, the 6.125% of 8/15/07. In contrast, a generic 10-year U.S. agency bullet was offered at a nominal yield spread of 32 bp over the 10-year. The additional 62 bp in static yield on the callable was compensation for selling the embedded call options. Determining the fair value of the embedded options and understanding the risks and rewards in selling them is essential for the callable security investor.

A portfolio of a bullet security and an option to buy that security can mimic a callable security. For example, a 10nc3 with only one call date can be separated into a long position in a 10-year bullet and a short position in an option to buy that security starting three years from its issue date. The option is typically referred to as a "3 × 7 option," referring to the option's expiration in three years with an underlying term of seven years.[3]

Returning to our example, the 10nc3 was offered at $100 for a yield of 6.856%. A 10-year bullet with the same coupon and a yield of 6.236% would be priced at $104.57. Thus, the embedded option was sold for a price of $4.57, thereby lowering the cost of the callable security. The relationship between the callable security and the bullet to maturity can be represented as follows:

$$\text{Callable security price} = \text{bullet to maturity price} - \text{value of embedded options}$$

## Types of Callables

One factor that differentiates callable securities is the type of embedded option. One example, that we define as an American callable, is the type that is contin-

---

2. In addition, many callable securities have "notice" periods—a set number of days notice the issuer must give the investor that the security will be called. For example, callable Treasuries are discretely callable on coupon dates with 120 days notice from the issuer.

3. A corresponding option, in the over-the-counter derivatives market, would be a 3 × 7 European style swaption.

uously callable after the noncallable period. The issuer may redeem the bond at the specified price at any time during the call period. Another type is a Bermudan option, which gives the issuer the right to call the bond on specified dates that typically coincide with coupon dates. Finally, issuers have recently begun to structure callable securities with a European style option, a one-time call feature that is a Bermudan option with only one call date.

The most flexible of the options is the American, which gives the issuer maximum flexibility in timing the call decision. Callables with this type of embedded option will be the least expensive. Bermudan options are slightly more restrictive with their schedule of call dates. The European option limits the issuer to only one call date, giving the investor increased call protection. European style callables can be easily synthesized using bullet securities and over-the-counter options.

Bermudan and American options embedded in callable securities actually represent a package of options that are conditional in nature. For example, with a Bermudan callable security, if the issuer calls the issue on the first call date, the remaining options on subsequent coupon dates naturally disappear. A Bermudan or American option cannot be exactly synthesized by selling a strip of options in the derivatives market because the package of individual options would be more expensive than the conditional option that is embedded in the callable security. The complex nature of the embedded option requires a more sophisticated valuation, such as option-adjusted spread (OAS) analysis.[4]

Another important feature of callable securities is the *lockout period,* the period during which the security cannot be called (time to call). Coupled with the time to maturity, the lockout period helps to determine the value of the embedded options. Time to call matters primarily due to the increasing dispersion of possible future rates the farther into the future one looks. For example, the embedded option in a 10-year noncall 6 month (10nc6M) European callable is a six-month European option on a $9\frac{1}{2}$-year security; the embedded option in a 10nc3 European callable is a three-year European option on a seven-year security.

The uncertainty associated with seven-year rates three years hence is larger than the uncertainty associated with $9\frac{1}{2}$-year rates six months from now. This rise in perceived volatility increases the expected payoff of the longer dated option, making the option more expensive. In addition, differences in the lockout period can alter the risk characteristics of the security. In particular, different lockout/maturity structures will expose the investor to different yield spreads and volatilities along the curve. This variation can prove useful for investors who are fine-tuning a curve view along with a view on volatility.

---

4. Term structure models that use a lattice of interest rates are typically employed. Lattices are required to compute the expected value of the security's cash flows based on the evolution of the term structure. The necessary expectation is computed using a risk-neutral probability distribution and the method of iterated expectations called "backward diffusion."

For Bermudan and American style options, the impact of the lockout period is more complicated. The 10nc6M European callable is exposed to the uncertainty in the $9\frac{1}{2}$-year rate 6 months from now. The American and Bermudan style callables are exposed to the uncertainty in the path of forward rates. For example, the Bermudan 10nc6M callable would be exposed to the $9\frac{1}{2}$-year rate 6 months forward, the nine-year rate 1 year forward, and so on including the six-month rate $9\frac{1}{2}$ years forward. In this case, the set of options embedded in the shorter dated lockout contains the options embedded in longer dated lockouts; the option value would be higher for the shorter dated lockout.

## Premiums versus Discounts

In addition to the maturity/lockout structure, investors must consider the relative strikes of the embedded options compared to where forward rates are trading. In other words, investors must consider whether the options are in the money (ITM), at the money (ATM), or out of the money (OTM). By comparing the coupon of the callable security to the par forward rate implied by the issuer's bullet curve, the option can be classified. Premium securities, which trade above par, have embedded options that are in the money and generally trade on a yield-to-call basis given the likelihood that the issue will be called. Discount callables, priced below par with a coupon below the going market rate, have embedded options that are out of the money.

Different options have exposure to different risks. Premium securities are exposed to extension risk. If rates back up, the option is worth less as the security becomes less likely to be called. In effect, this increases the duration of the security, extending the effective maturity beyond what the investor may have expected. Conversely, discount callables trade like bullets to maturity and are exposed to compression risk. If rates rally, the securities will shorten in duration as they become more likely to be called.

A security that is trading near par is usually associated with options that are at the money, which implies that the strike price is close to the forward price of comparable bullets. But this is not necessarily true. For example, new issue European callables are usually priced and callable at par. However, the amount the option is in the money depends on both the nominal spread and the slope of the bullet curve.[5] Flatter curves imply lower forward yields relative to spot yields, which implies that the option will move farther into the money holding

---

5. As a rough approximation, $B = N - (Ym - Yc) \times Tc/(Tm - Tc)$, where $B$ is the number of bp the option is in the money, $N$ is the nominal spread, $Tc$ is the time to call, $Tm$ is the time to maturity, $Yc$ is the bullet yield to the call date, and $Ym$ is the bullet yield to the maturity date. If the nominal spread does not change but the curve flattens instantaneously (i.e., $Ym - Yc$ gets smaller), the option moves farther in the money. Nominal spreads for new issues tend to adjust as the shape of the curve changes.

nominal spreads constant. Investors should compare the coupon they are receiving to forward rates imputed from the issuer's credit curve.

Callable securities are exposed, in varying degrees, to extension and compression risk, which affect performance. As rates decline and the security is called early, the investor receives the principal back instead of continuing to receive the higher coupon. That is, the investor has to reinvest cash flows at a lower market yield than the original stated yield. If the market sells off and rates rise, the investor is holding a longer maturity note at below market rates. The decline in duration as rates rally (or increase as rates rise) is a characteristic of negative convexity (or convexity that is too low relative to duration.) Negative convexity, coupled with the dependence on volatility,[6] is an important reason for the additional spread investors earn on callable securities.

Whether the option is ITM, ATM, or OTM will influence the security's sensitivities to changes in market variables. For example, callable securities that are ATM have the most sensitivity to changes in market rates and implied volatility. This is because the risk characteristics of an option are highest when it is at the money. As the security moves deep into or out of the money, it trades more like a bullet with little optionality. Given the lower uncertainty and hedging costs the investor faces, nominal spreads will tend to tighten to equal duration bullets. Many times investors can find relative value in premium and discount callable securities in the secondary market.

## Nominal Spreads

We next analyze how nominal spreads behave under different market conditions. Shown in Exhibit 33–1 is the nominal spread of the FNMA 8.5 of 2/1/05-00, which was an original $1 billion global 10nc5 issue. The spread is shown to the risk-weighted yield of a bullet portfolio consisting of FNMA 8.35 of 11/10/99 and FNMA 7.875 of 2/24/05. The callable, which was issued at par, quickly became a premium and its effective duration declined rapidly. Originally quoted at a spread over the 10-year Treasury, it began trading to call when yields rallied 100–150 bp.

A close correlation exists between the market level, for which we use the new issue 10-year bullet yield as a proxy, and the nominal spread of the callable. This is because as the option moves farther into the money, the risks associated with the option decline. That is, the option's delta goes to one and its gamma goes to zero, which reduces hedging costs. In addition, model misspecifications,

---

6. In particular, for a simple, one factor model of the short-term interest rate, it can be shown that two securities with equal duration will satisfy the following relation: $\sigma^2 (C_1 - C_2) = \theta_2 - \theta_1$ where $\sigma$ is the volatility of the short rate, $C_i$ is the convexity, and $\theta_i$ is the time value (theta) of the security. Thus, if $C_1 < C_2$ then $\theta_2 < \theta_1$. Securities with negative convexity should have positive carry versus positively convex securities of equal duration, and the spread is proportional to the amount of short rate volatility.

**EXHIBIT   33–1**

Nominal Spread of FNMA 8.5 of 2/1/05-00 to Duration-Matched Bullets, and New Issue 10-year Bullet Yield, January 31, 1995–November 30, 1997

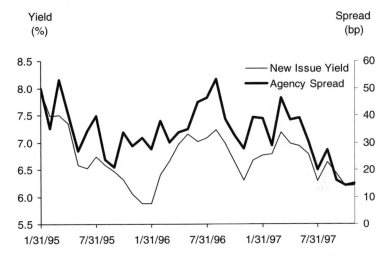

**EXHIBIT   33–2**

General Behavior of Nominal Spreads* for Changes in Market Level

|          | OTM | ATM | ITM |
|----------|-----|-----|-----|
| Rally    | ↑   | ↓   | ↓   |
| Backup   | ↓   | ↓   | ↑   |

* Callable—Duration matched bullet yield.

such as uncertainty in volatility, are less egregious when the option is deep in or out of the money.

In 1997, premium callables performed well versus duration-matched bullets, due to both a decline in implied volatility and a rally-flattening of the yield curve, which caused the securities to trade more securely to call. The general behavior of nominal spreads for different callables and market yield changes is shown in Exhibit 33–2.

## PERFORMANCE AND STRATEGIES

### Sensitivities

One way to analyze the performance of callable securities is to look at their risk due to changes in the underlying variables, such as volatility or yield curve changes. Exhibit 33–3 highlights new issue callables ranging from two-year (noncall 3 months) to 10-year (noncall five-year) as of 12/11/97. A number of statistics are shown starting with the quoted yield to maturity (bid side) at the close of 12/11/97. The forward yields for agency bullets are shown corresponding to the first call date and the remaining maturity. For example, for the 10nc1 callable, the nine-year rate one-year forward was 6.2%, which was 81 bp below the coupon of the new callable issue. Thus, the option embedded in the 10nc1 callable security is fairly deep in the money.

Even though the securities are priced at par, the amount that the options are in the money varies widely and depends on the shape of the issuer's bullet curve. The 2nc1 callable was at the money for the most part, and generally the short-dated lockouts had options that were deeper in the money. For simplicity, we ignored the later dated embedded options beyond the initial call date, which are slightly less in the money given the then upward sloping curve. Options that are trading far from the strike tend to trade at a higher implied volatility (producing what is called the *volatility smile*); therefore, it is important to consider the quoted yield and the reference forward yield.

The option-adjusted duration (OAD) for each security as well as partial durations with respect to key points of the yield curve are shown. Partial durations or key rate durations are computed by shifting a particular sector of the yield curve and examining the price change, holding all other inputs constant. This is a convenient method for determining the risk profile of the different securities and offers more information than the pure OAD, which assumes the curve moves in parallel. For example, the 10nc3 has a fair amount of risk in

**EXHIBIT  33–3**

Indicative Data and Risk Statistics for Selected New Issue Agency Callables, as of Close 12/11/97

|           | 2nc3m  | 2nc1   | 5nc6m  | 5nc2   | 10nc1  | 10nc3  | 10nc5  |
|-----------|--------|--------|--------|--------|--------|--------|--------|
| Yield     | 5.95   | 5.89   | 6.48   | 6.40   | 7.01   | 6.77   | 6.60   |
| Fwd Yld   | 5.86   | 5.89   | 6.01   | 6.08   | 6.20   | 6.27   | 6.33   |
| OADur     | 0.70   | 1.40   | 1.60   | 3.00   | 3.00   | 4.60   | 5.60   |
| PV01 1Y   | −0.21  | −0.56  | −0.29  | −0.02  | −0.46  | −0.05  | −0.04  |
| PV01 2Y   | −0.38  | −0.79  | −0.24  | −0.81  | −0.29  | −0.04  | −0.05  |
| PV01 3Y   | 0.00   | 0.00   | −0.26  | −0.45  | −0.28  | −1.32  | −0.11  |
| PV01 5Y   | 0.00   | 0.00   | −0.88  | −1.65  | −0.48  | −0.87  | −2.42  |
| PV01 10Y  | 0.00   | 0.00   | 0.00   | 0.00   | −1.46  | −2.35  | −3.09  |
| Vega      | −2.91  | −2.30  | −9.30  | −8.96  | −19.50 | −19.62 | −15.70 |

PV01 = price value of 1 bp change.
Vega = price value, in bp, of 1% change in implied volatility.

**EXHIBIT 33-4**

Indicative Data and Risk Statistics for Selected New Issue Agency Bullets, as of Close 12/11/97

| Maturity: | 0.25 yrs. | 0.5 yrs. | 1 yrs. | 2 yrs. | 3 yrs. | 5 yrs. | 10 yrs. |
|---|---|---|---|---|---|---|---|
| Yield | 5.80 | 5.81 | 5.75 | 5.85 | 5.90 | 5.99 | 6.16 |
| OADur | 0.20 | 0.50 | 1.00 | 1.90 | 2.70 | 4.30 | 7.40 |
| PV01 1Y | −0.06 | −0.23 | −0.90 | −0.02 | 0.00 | −0.01 | −0.05 |
| PV01 2Y | 0.00 | 0.00 | 0.00 | −1.78 | −0.03 | −0.01 | −0.02 |
| PV01 3Y | 0.00 | 0.00 | 0.00 | 0.00 | −2.67 | −0.05 | −0.07 |
| PV01 5Y | 0.00 | 0.00 | 0.00 | 0.00 | 0.00 | −4.20 | −0.08 |
| PV01 10Y | 0.00 | 0.00 | 0.00 | 0.00 | 0.00 | 0.00 | −7.12 |

PV01 = price value of 1 bp change.

the 10-year but changes to the three-year also have an impact on performance. This is due to the fact that forward rates partially drive the callable's performance and both the three- and 10-year rates contribute to the seven-year rate three years forward.

To determine the overall price change due to a nonparallel shift in the curve, we multiply each of the partial durations by the amount that sector of the curve moved, in bp, and add the results. Since the partial durations are expressed in basis point price change per basis point yield change, dividing by 100 gives the price change per $100 notional. For example, if the three-, five-, and 10-year rallied by 5 bp, 10 bp, and 15 bp, respectively, the 10nc3 callable would gain about ½ point in price: $[(-5 \times -1.32) + (-10 \times -0.87) + (-15 \times -2.35)]/100 = 0.507$.

Exhibit 33-4 shows comparable statistics for bullet securities. With a modified duration of 4.3 years, the five-year bullet has nearly the same parallel interest rate exposure as the 10nc3 callable security, which has an OAD of 4.6 years. However, examining the partial durations reveals that their exposures to different sectors of the yield curve are very different. In particular, going long the 10nc3 callable versus the five-year bullet expresses a curve flattening view in the three- to 10-year sector of the curve holding all else constant. Duration is useful for describing price changes for relatively small changes in yields over short periods; however, care should be used in extrapolating results.

Exhibit 33-5 shows partial durations for 10nc3 callable securities with different dollar prices, representing discount, par-priced, and premium securities. The discount, with a coupon of 5%, has embedded options that are out of the money. It trades to maturity due to its lower likelihood of being called, and most of the interest rate risk is embedded in the 10-year sector of the curve. This highlights a recurring theme: as rates rise and the callable extends in duration,

**EXHIBIT 33-5**

Partial Durations for 10nc3 Callables as a Function of Dollar Price

| Price: | 90.92 | 100.00 | 104.72 |
|---|---|---|---|
| PV01 1Y | 5.00 | 6.77 | 8.00 |
| PV01 1Y | -0.04 | -0.05 | -0.06 |
| PV01 2Y | -0.04 | -0.04 | -0.07 |
| PV01 3Y | -0.29 | -1.32 | -1.89 |
| PV01 5Y | -0.65 | -0.87 | -0.62 |
| PV01 10Y | -5.03 | -2.35 | -1.24 |

PV01 = price value of 1 bp change.

the investment is lengthening in a bear market compared to a comparable duration bullet. Callables offer an attractive yield over bullets chiefly to compensate investors for this risk. As rates move in either direction, callables underperform equal duration bullets.

The other component of risk highlighted in Exhibit 33-3 is the impact of volatility on callable securities. Vega refers to the change in price, in bp, for a 1% change in implied volatility. In general, callable securities with longer dated lockouts have more exposure to changes in volatility; however, as the lockouts get longer than about three years, the vega exposure of a callable security declines. This is due to mean reversion: interest rates tend to vary randomly but are "pulled" toward a central location, or mean. In other words, when rates are very high there is a better chance they will decline than rise further and vice versa. Mean reversion helps to explain why yields on longer maturity securities are typically less volatile.

## Total Returns and Strategies

Exhibit 33-6 shows the performance of two callable strategies compared to investing in duration-matched bullets. The performance curve for the 10nc5 security was for the FNMA 6.4 of 12/26/07-02 versus the FHLB 6.69 of 9/6/05, both of which have an effective duration of 5.88. Given the coupon of the callable security, the embedded options were close to being at the money. The 10nc3 performance curve illustrates a premium callable, the FNMA 7.49 of 2/7/07-00, versus the FNMA 6.59 of 5/24/01 with a duration of 3.05. The dollar price for the premium callable was 101-29+ (as of 12/22/97) highlighting the fact that the options were in the money by about 120 bp.

Total returns are shown as a three-month annualized return as a function of yield changes, holding all other inputs constant. Although not apparent from the exhibit, the expected payoff from both strategies is near zero. For the 10nc5-ATM strategy, the performance curve is fairly symmetric and is similar to the

**E X H I B I T   33–6**

Total Return Performance for Callables versus Duration-Matched Bullets, As of 12/22/97; 3-month Annualized Return

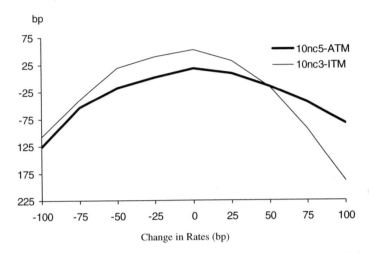

performance of a buy-sell-buy butterfly trade or selling an option straddle. This is typical of a strategy that is short convexity. As discussed in the previous section, being long a callable security versus the duration-matched bullet has a risk profile similar to a barbell versus a bullet.

The 10nc5-ATM has an effective convexity of −48 versus 21 for the bullet, resulting in a net convexity of −69. As the market rallies the position becomes short the market, and the investor would need to purchase additional bullet securities to return to market neutral. This is an important aspect of hedging callable securities. As the market moves, the investor has to decide either to rehedge the position or to take on the market risk due to duration drift. Frequent rehedging can be costly and locks in any losses incurred.

The 10nc3-ITM strategy has an asymmetric performance profile, outperforming the 10nc5-ATM strategy in a bullish environment but faring worse if rates rise significantly. With embedded options that are in the money, the risk of ITM callables is that the option could move closer to being ATM. The duration of the callable changes the most as the option moves closer to being at the money. As yields increase, this exacerbates the duration mismatch that occurs as the callable is lengthening faster than the bullet security. When rates rally, however, the duration of the callable is more stable since its effective duration is already close to that of a bullet to call (1.91 years), which acts as a lower bound.

The underperformance of the 10nc3-ITM strategy in a bearish environment is the reason for the additional 34 bp of annualized return the investor receives over the next three months if the curve remains unchanged. This example shows that callable securities can offer an attractive way for investors to enhance returns according to their views on rates and volatility. Premium callables should be used when the bullish investor believes that rates are unlikely to rally very far. Discount or OTM callables are a better choice when the investor wants to sell volatility but prefers more protection in a bearish environment.

Time, or the expected investment period, also plays a critical role in the decision to buy callables or bullet securities. Exhibit 33–7 shows the performance of the 10nc3-ITM strategy versus the duration-matched bullet for two holding periods. In this example, the returns are not annualized for the three-month holding period to facilitate comparison. As time passes and yields remain stable, the investor is rewarded with the additional spread that callables earn. However, for longer holding periods there is a higher probability of larger rate moves. It is this trade-off that investors must consider carefully. For example, if the investor has the view that rates may well be volatile in either direction over the near term but are likely to remain range bound over the next year, an investment in callable securities can substantially enhance returns.

The performance of callable securities in nonparallel yield shifts is shown in Exhibit 33–8. The flattening and steepening curves are chosen holding one extreme of the yield curve constant with the other end moving by 25 bp. For example, in the BullFlat scenario, the 30-year rallies 25 bp and the short end remains constant. The intermediate points of the curve are interpolated via du-

**EXHIBIT  33–7**

Impact of Time on Returns for 10nc3-ITM Callable versus Duration-Matched Bullet, as of 12/22/97

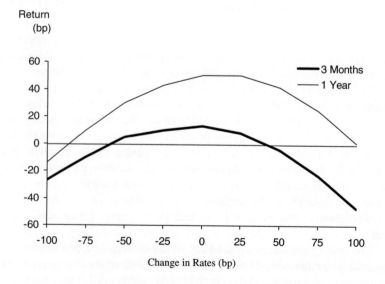

**EXHIBIT 33–8**

Callable Performance Versus Equal Duration Bullets for Nonparallel Curve Shifts, in bp as of 12/22/97

|              | 10nc5-ATM | Net* | 10nc3-ITM | Net* |
|--------------|-----------|------|-----------|------|
| Constant     | 17.6      | —    | 52.0      | —    |
| Dwn 25 bp    | 1.6       | —    | 39.2      | —    |
| Up 25 bp     | 8.4       | —    | 31.6      | —    |
| BullFlat     | 14.0      | 12.4 | 64.4      | 25.2 |
| BullSteep    | 6.4       | 4.8  | 34.8      | −4.4 |
| BearFlat     | 28.4      | 20.0 | 62.8      | 31.2 |
| BearSteep    | −1.2      | −9.6 | 20.0      | −11.6|

Net of parallel shift performance.

ration. Although this picture is not entirely realistic, it shows how the callables will perform in nonparallel shifts to the yield curve.

In general, for any 25 bp twist in the curve, callables tend to outperform with the most improvement in a curve flattening environment. For larger curve twists, callables would underperform. The best environment for the 10nc3-ITM premium callable is a limited bullish flattener; bearish steepeners tend to hurt premium callables the most. This is indicated by net performance of −11.6 bp compared to a parallel 25 bp back-up in rates. Investors who have a limited bullish-flattening view should consider premium callables, whereas investors concerned about a significant steepening of the yield curve within a range-bound scenario should consider discount or at-the-money callables.

## CONCLUSION

Callable securities are an attractive way for investors to express their views on the likely range of rates, market direction, and changes in the slope of the yield curve. Available securities offer a diversity in price and structure that allows investors an opportunity to sculpt the payoff distribution that is most desirable. For example, premium callables, with embedded options deep in the money, are attractive for investors who wish to sell volatility but are concerned about a significant market rally

This chapter introduced callable securities, defined terminology, examined the behavior of nominal spreads, highlighting the risk factors, and looked at the return structure for various callable structures. But this chapter only begins the discussion of evaluating callable securities. Other aspects of investing in callable securities include the impact of changes in implied volatility and the choice of liquid volatility instruments for analyzing callables. Option-adjusted spread analysis is a key tool for analyzing embedded interest rate options and worthy of a discussion on its own. Finally, the pros and cons of different hedging strategies are of paramount importance and must also be explored.

## CHAPTER 34

# VALUATION OF BONDS
# WITH EMBEDDED OPTIONS

**Frank J. Fabozzi, Ph.D., CFA, CPA**
Adjunct Professor of Finance
School of Management
Yale University

**Andrew J. Kalotay, Ph.D.**
President
Andrew J. Kalotay Associates

**George O. Williams, Ph.D.**
Vice President
Fixed Income Research
Lehman Brothers Inc.

In this chapter, we'll examine bonds with embedded options. The method described in this chapter is called the *binomial lattice model*, or simply the *binomial method*. Other methods used to value bonds with embedded options include more complicated lattice models, Monte Carlo methods, and the continuous-time diffusion method. Monte Carlo methods are addressed in the next chapter, while the continuous-time approach is applied to convertible bonds in Chapter 51.[1]

Because the most common type of option embedded in a bond is a call option, our primary focus will be on callable bonds. Although callable bonds are used to illustrate the valuation approach, these methods are applicable to all types of fixed income securities with embedded options.

## IMPLICATIONS OF CALLABLE BONDS

The holder of a callable bond has given the issuer the right to redeem the bond before its maturity date. A mortgage-backed security is also callable because the homeowner has the right to pay off all or part of the mortgage at any time.

---

1. The continuous-time diffusion method is explained in Frank J. Fabozzi and H. Gifford Fong, *Advanced Fixed Income Portfolio Management* (Chicago: Probus Publishing, 1994).

The call option poses two related disadvantages to the holder. First, it exposes the investor to reinvestment risk of principal because the issuer will call only when the current market rate is less than the coupon. For example, if the coupon is 13% and the prevailing market rate is 7%, the issuer will find it economical to call the 13% issue and refund with a 7% issue. In turn, the holder's reinvestment opportunities will be limited to lower rates. Second, the price appreciation potential for a callable bond is restricted. It will trade at a price below that of a comparable optionless bond.

## COMPONENTS OF BONDS WITH EMBEDDED OPTIONS

We develop a valuation framework for a callable bond by decomposing the bond into parts. In effect, the holder of a callable bond has bought an optionless or option-free bond and has sold a call option. In terms of value,

Callable bond value = Optionless bond value − Call option value

It follows that the price of a callable bond will always be less than the price of an otherwise identical optionless bond. This is shown in Exhibit 34–1. The difference between the value of the noncallable bond and that of the callable bond at any given level of interest rates is the value of the embedded call option.

**E X H I B I T   34–1**

Price–Interest Rate Relationship for Callable and Optionless Bonds

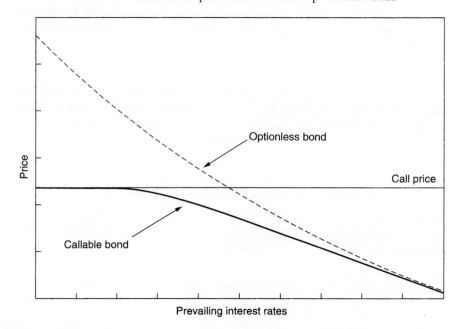

Prevailing interest rates

Typically, there is an initial period of call protection, after which the bond is callable at any time at a premium to par. The call price subsequently declines to par over the remaining life of the bond in a manner specified in the bond's indenture. Thus, we have an American call option whose exercise price varies over time.

The same logic applies to putable bonds; the holder has the right to sell the bond to the issuer at a designated time and price. A putable bond can likewise be broken into two separate parts, an optionless bond and a put option. The value of a putable bond is then

Putable bond value = Optionless bond value + Put option value

## A GENERALIZED MODEL FOR VALUING BONDS WITH EMBEDDED OPTIONS[2]

The previous section provides a useful way to conceptualize a bond with an embedded option. Specifically, the value of a callable bond equals the value of a comparable optionless bond less the value of the call option. This insight led to the first generation of valuation models for bonds with embedded options. These early models attempted to directly estimate the value of the embedded call option, but without explicitly incorporating the shape of the yield curve. Both the level and the shape of the yield curve affect the value of interest-rate-sensitive options.

Instead of relying on an external pricing model, the model presented in this section is based on an internally consistent framework appropriate to bonds with and without embedded options. The difference between the values of a bond with an option and an otherwise identical bond without that option is the value of the option.

As we saw in Chapter 6, instead of discounting all cash flows at the same rate, one should discount each cash flow at its own spot rate. This is equivalent to discounting at a sequence of forward rates. Both the spot and the implied forward rates can be calculated by the bootstrapping method described in Chapter 6. However, we did not discuss how interest-rate volatility affects the value of a bond with embedded options.

## VALUATION OF OPTIONLESS BONDS

We begin with a review of the valuation of optionless bonds. The value of an optionless bond is the present value of its cash flows discounted at the spot rate. One begins with the issuer's non-call-life yield curve. This is obtained by adding

---

2. This section is adapted from Andrew J. Kalotay, George O. Williams, and Frank J. Fabozzi, "A Model for Valuing Bonds with Embedded Options," *Financial Analysts Journal*, May/June 1993, pp. 35–46.

an appropriate credit spread to each on-the-run Treasury issue. The credit spreads tend to increase with maturity.

Consider a hypothetical issuer with the following non-call-life yield curve:

| Maturity (yr.) | Coupon | Market Price |
|:---:|:---:|:---:|
| 1 | 3.50% | 100 |
| 2 | 4.00 | 100 |
| 3 | 4.50 | 100 |

For simplicity, we consider only annual-pay bonds here. The bootstrapping methodology provides the spot rates:

| Year | Spot Rate |
|:---:|:---:|
| 1 | 3.500% |
| 2 | 4.010 |
| 3 | 4.531 |

The corresponding one-year forward rates are:

| | |
|:---|:---:|
| One-year rate today | 3.500% |
| One-year rate one year forward | 4.523 |
| One-year rate two years forward | 5.580 |

Now consider an optionless bond with three years remaining to maturity and a coupon of 5.25%. This bond's value can be determined in either of two ways; both produce the same value. First, the cash flows can be discounted at the zero-coupon or spot rates, as shown below:

$$\frac{\$5.25}{(1.03500)^1} + \frac{\$5.25}{(1.04010)^2} + \frac{\$100 + \$5.25}{(1.04531)^3} = \$102.075$$

The second way is to discount year-by-year at the forward one-year rates:

$$\frac{\$5.25}{(1.03500)} + \frac{\$5.25}{(1.03500)(1.04523)} + \frac{\$100 + \$5.25}{(1.03500)(1.04523)(1.05580)} = \$102.075$$

## BINOMIAL INTEREST-RATE TREE

Exhibit 34–2 shows a binomial interest-rate tree. Each node (vertical column of dots) is one year after the node to its left. Each node is connected to two nodes on its right. The subscript at a particular node specifies the path followed by the one-year rate in reaching that node. *L* represents a path to the lower of the two subsequent one-year rates and *H* represents a path to the higher of the two

**E X H I B I T    34–2**

Three-Year Binomial Interest-Rate Tree

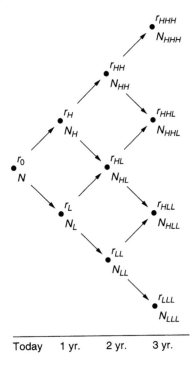

Today    1 yr.    2 yr.    3 yr.

rates. For example, $N_{HH}$ represents a node reached in two years along a path through the higher of the two rates seen after each annual splitting.[3]

Look first at the point denoted by $N$ in Exhibit 34–2. This is the root of the tree and is simply the current one-year rate, which we denote by $r_0$. In creating this tree, we have assumed that the one-year rate will take on one of two equally likely values after each one-year period elapses. We construct the tree so that the logarithm of the one-year rate obeys a binomial distribution with $p = \frac{1}{2}$. In this way, the limiting distribution for the one-year rate is lognormal.

We use the following notation to describe the tree in the first year. Let

$\sigma$ = Assumed volatility of the one-year rate
$r_L$ = The lower one-year rate one year forward
$r_H$ = The higher one-year rate one year forward

The relationship between $r_L$ and $r_H$ is as follows:

---

3. Note that $N_{HL}$ is equivalent to $N_{LH}$ in the second year. Similarly, in the third year $N_{HLH}$, $N_{LHH}$, and $N_{HHL}$ are all equivalent.

$$r_H = r_L\, e^{2\sigma}$$

where $e = 2.71828 \ldots$ , the base of the natural logarithm.

For example, if $r_L$ is 4.074% and $\sigma$ is 10% per year, then

$$r_H = 4.074\% \times e^{2\times 0.10} = 4.976\%$$

In the second year, there are three possible values for the one-year rate, which we will denote as follows:

$r_{LL}$ = The lowest one-year rate two years forward; reached by two successive lower paths

$r_{HH}$ = The highest one-year rate two years forward; reached by two successive higher paths

$r_{HL}$ = The middle one-year rate two years forward; reached by either the upper path followed by the lower path or the lower path followed by the upper path.

The relationship between $r_{LL}$ and the other two rates is as follows:

$$r_{HH} = r_{LL}\, e^{4\sigma} \quad \text{and} \quad r_{HL} = r_{LL}\, e^{2\sigma}$$

For example, if $r_{LL}$ is 4.53%, then with $\sigma$ again being 10%,

$$r_{HH} = 4.53\% \times e^{4\times 0.10} = 6.757\%$$

and

$$r_{HL} = 4.53\% \times e^{2\times 0.10} = 5.532\%$$

Exhibit 34–3 shows the notation for the binomial tree in the third year. The notation has been simplified by letting $r_t$ be the one-year rate $t$ years forward reached by taking the lower path at every juncture.

Two issues must be addressed before we can value bonds using this binomial tree. What does the volatility parameter $\sigma$ in the expression $e^{2\sigma}$ represent? Second, how do we find the value of a bond at each node?

## Volatility and Standard Deviation

The standard deviation of the one-year rate one year forward at any node is approximately $r\sigma$.[4] The standard deviation is a statistical measure of volatility. The volatility is expressed relative to the level of the one-period rate at each node in the tree. For example, if $\sigma$ is 10% and the current one-year rate $r_0$ is

---

4. This can be seen by noting that $e^{2\sigma} \approx 1 + 2\sigma$. Then the standard deviation of the one-period rates one period forward is

$$\frac{r\, e^{2\sigma} - r}{2} \approx \frac{r + 2\sigma r - r}{2} = \sigma r$$

**EXHIBIT   34–3**

Three-Year Binomial Interest-Rate Tree Showing Volatility

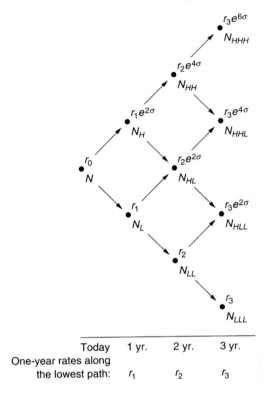

| | Today | 1 yr. | 2 yr. | 3 yr. |
|---|---|---|---|---|

One-year rates along
the lowest path:        $r_1$        $r_2$        $r_3$

4%, then the standard deviation of the one-year rate one year from now is 4% times 10%, which is 0.4% or 40 basis points. If the current one-year rate is 12%, the standard deviation of the one-year rate one year forward would be 12% times 10%, or 120 basis points.

## Determining the Value at a Node

A bond's value at a given node depends on the bond's value at the two nodes to its right. As seen in Exhibit 34–4, finding a bond's value at node $N$ requires knowing its values at nodes $N_L$ and $N_H$. We will discuss how one gets these two values later; as we will see, the process involves starting from the last year in the tree and working backward to get the final solution, so these two values will be known.

Thus, a bond's value at a given node depends on future cash flows. These future cash flows may be separated into the bond's value one period from now

**E X H I B I T    34–4**

Calculating a Value at a Node

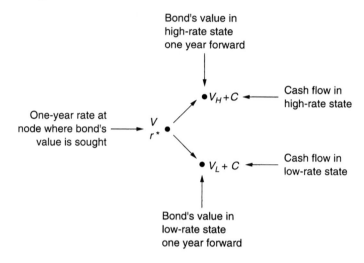

Bond's value in
high-rate state
one year forward

One-year rate at
node where bond's
value is sought

$V_H + C$ — Cash flow in high-rate state

$V_L + C$ — Cash flow in low-rate state

Bond's value in
low-rate state
one year forward

and any cash flow—like the coupon payment—that occurs at that time. The latter is known, but the former depends on which value the one-year rate takes on in the coming year.

Value is expressed in present value terms at a particular time. Here, we are speaking of the present value of expected cash flows. The appropriate discount rate is the one-year rate $r^*$ at $N$, the node in question. If the rate takes the upper path, we discount the sum of the two components at $N_H$: $V_H$ and the coupon $C$. If the rate takes the lower path, we discount the components of value at $N_L$. Because these two outcomes are equally likely, we can simply average. This can be thought of as the average of two separate present values, or as the present value of an average. Thus with

$V_H$ = The bond's value along the upper path
$V_L$ = The bond's value along the lower path
$C$ = The coupon payment

the cash flow along the upper path is $V_H + C$ and that along the lower path is $V_L + C$. These have respective present values $(V_H + C)/(1 + r^*)$ and $(V_L + C)/(1 + r^*)$. Thus, a bond's value at node N is given by

$$V = \frac{1}{2}\left(\frac{V_H + C}{1 + r^*} + \frac{V_L + C}{1 + r^*}\right)$$

## Constructing a Binomial Interest-Rate Tree

We will demonstrate the construction of the tree using the same on-the-run yields as before. Using a volatility $\sigma$ of 10%, we will construct a two-year tree that prices a two-year 4% bond at 100.

Exhibit 34–5 shows a more detailed binomial tree with the cash flow shown at each node. The root rate for the tree, $r_0$, is simply the current one-year rate, 3.5%.

There are two possible one-year rates one year forward—one along the upper path, and one along the lower. They must be consistent with the volatility assumption (that is, their ratio $r_H/r_L$ is $e^{2\sigma}$), and the value of a 4% two-year bond must be 100. We can write down a simple algebraic expression for these two rates, but the formulation becomes increasingly complex beyond the first year. Furthermore, because we may want to implement this procedure on a computer, the natural approach is to find these rates by an iterative process. The steps are described below:

### EXHIBIT 34–5

Find the One-Year Rates for Year 1 Using the Two-Year 4 Percent On-the-Run Issue: First Trial

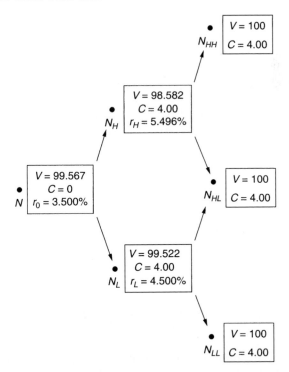

1. Select a value for $r_1$. Recall that $r_1$ is the one-year rate one year forward along the lower path. In this first trial, we arbitrarily selected a value of 4.5%.

2. Determine the corresponding value for the higher one-year rate. As explained earlier, this rate is found from the lower rate by $r_1\ e^{2\sigma}$. Because $r_1$ is 4.5%, the forward one-year rate if rates rise is 5.496% ($= 4.5\% \times e^{2\times0.10}$). This value is reported in Exhibit 34–5 at node $N_H$.

3. Compute the bond's value in each of the two interest-rate states one year from now, using the following steps.

   • Determine the bond's value two years from now. Because we are using a two-year bond, the bond's value is its maturity value of $100 plus its final coupon payment of $4, or $104.
   • Calculate the bond's present value at node $N_H$. The appropriate discount rate is the forward one-year rate along the upper path, or 5.496% in our example. The present value is $98.582 ($= \$104/1.05496$). This is the value of $V_H$ referred to earlier.
   • Calculate the bond's present value at node $N_H$. The appropriate discount rate is the forward one-year rate along the lower path, or 4.5%. The present value is $99.522 ($= \$104/1.045$) and is the value of $V_L$.
   • Add the coupon to both $V_H$ and $V_L$ to get the cash flow at $N_H$ and $N_L$, respectively. In this example, these values are $102.582 along the upper path and $103.522 along the lower.
   • Calculate the present value of the cash flows at $N_H$ and $N_L$ using the assumed value of $r_0$, 3.5%, for $r^*$. Thus

$$\frac{V_H + C}{1 + r^*} = \frac{\$102.582}{1.035} = \$99.113$$

and

$$\frac{V_L + C}{1 + r^*} = \frac{\$103.522}{1.035} = \$100.021$$

4. Calculate the average present value of the two cash flows obtained in the previous step using

$$V = \frac{1}{2}\left[\frac{V_H + C}{1 + r^*} + \frac{V_L + C}{1 + r^*}\right]$$

$$= \frac{\$99.113 + \$100.021}{2} = \$99.567$$

5. Compare the result obtained in step 4 with the target market value of $100. If the two values are the same, then the $r_1$ used in this trial is

the one we seek and is the correct one-year rate to be used in the binomial tree along the lower rate path. If the value found in step 4 is not equal to the target value of $100, our assumed value is not consistent with the yield curve. In such a case, one must repeat the five steps with a different value for $r_1$.

When $r_1$ is 4.5%, the value obtained in step 4 is $99.567 and is smaller than the target value of $100. Therefore, 4.5% is too large, and the five steps must be repeated with a smaller value for $r_1$. It turns out that the correct value for $r_1$ is 4.074%. The corresponding binomial tree is shown in Exhibit 34–6. Steps 1 through 5, using the correct rate, are as follows.

1. Select a value of 4.074% for $r_1$.

2. The corresponding value for the forward one-year rate if rates rise is 4.976% ($= 4.074\% \times e^{2\times0.10}$).

3. The bond's value one year from now is determined from the bond's value two years from now—$104, just as in the first trial. The bond's

**EXHIBIT  34–6**

The One-Year Rates for Year 1 Using the Two-Year 4 Percent On-the-Run Issue

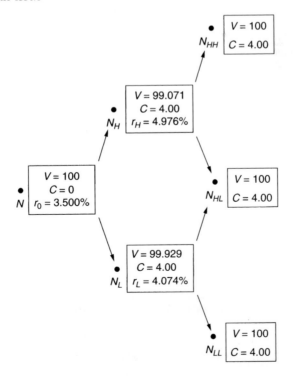

present value at node $N_H$ is $V_H$, or \$99.071 (= \$104/1.04976). The bond's present value at node $N_L$ is $V_L$, or \$99.929 (= \$104/1.04074). With the coupons added in, we have \$103.071 and \$103.929 to discount back to today at 3.5%, giving \$99.586 = \$103.071/1.035 from the upper path and \$100.414 = \$103.929/1.035 from the lower path.

4. The average present value is then (\$99.586 + \$100.414)/2 = \$100.

5. Because the average present value is equal to the observed market price of \$100, $r_1$ or $r_L$ is 4.074% and $r_H$ is 4.976%.

We're not done. Suppose that we want to grow this tree for one more year—that is, we want to determine $r_2$. We will use a three-year on-the-run 4.5% coupon bond to get $r_2$. The same five steps are used in an iterative process to find the one-year rates two years forward. Our objective now is to find the value of $r_2$ that will produce a value of \$100 for the 4.5% on-the-run bond and will be consistent with (1) a volatility assumption of 10%, (2) a current one-year forward rate of 3.5%, and (3) the two possible one-year rates of 4.074% and 4.976% one year from now. The desired value of $r_2$ is 4.530%.

We explain how this is done using Exhibit 34–7, which shows the beginning of the computation. The principal payment at maturity and the final coupon payment for the three-year on-the-run bond appear in the four boxes at the end of the tree. Two years from today, the coupon payment of \$4.50 is seen, but the present values of the future cash flows (from year three) are unknown. This is because the appropriate one-year discount rates are also unknown. One year from today, the coupon is again known, as are the one-year discount rates, but the present values remain unknown because the future cash flows remain unknown.

Exhibit 34–8 is the same as Exhibit 34–7, except that we have filled in the unknown values. As shown in Exhibit 34–8, the desired value of $r_2$ or $r_{LL}$ is 4.530%. Thus the other one-year rates in year two, $r_{HL}$ and $r_{HH}$, are 5.532% and 6.757%, respectively.

To verify that these are the correct one-year rates to be used in year two, work backwards from the four final nodes at the right-hand end of the tree. For example, the present value of the future flows at node $N_{HH}$ is found by discounting at 6.757% the (average) cash flow of \$104.5 found at both of its adjacent nodes, giving \$97.886.

## Valuing an Optionless Bond

Exhibit 34–9 shows the resulting binomial tree that can be used to value any one-, two-, or three-year bond for this issuer. To illustrate its use, consider a 5.25% optionless bond with two years remaining to maturity. Also assume that

**E X H I B I T   34–7**

Information for Deriving the One-Year Rates for Year 2 Using the
Three-Year 4.5 Percent On-the-Run Issue

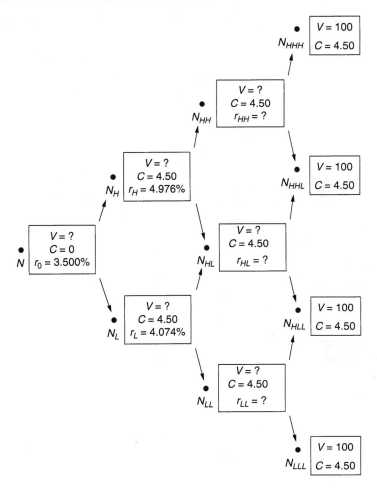

the issuer's yield curve is the one corresponding to the interest rate tree in
Exhibit 34–9. Exhibit 34–10 shows the various values in the discounting process. The bond's value is $102.075.

It is important to note that this value is identical to that found earlier by
discounting at the spot rates or at the forward rates. Because the tree was calibrated to value the on-the-run securities, it will necessarily value any contractual
set of cash flows correctly. This merely serves to demonstrate that this model is
consistent with the standard valuation model for an optionless bond.

**E X H I B I T    34–8**

The One-Year Rates in Year 2 Using the Three-Year 4.5 Percent On-the-Run Issue

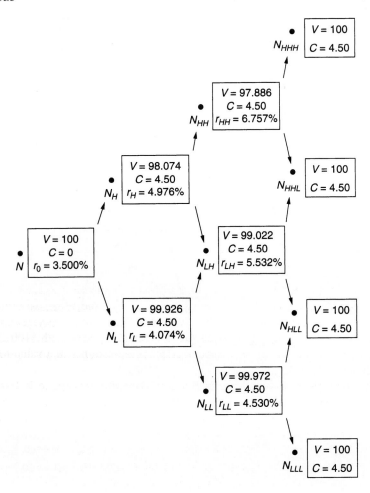

## Valuing a Callable Bond

The binomial interest-rate tree can also be applied to callable bonds. The valuation process is the same as for an optionless bond, with one exception: When the call option can be exercised by the issuer, the bond's value at the node must be changed to reflect the lesser of the call price and the present value of the future cash flows.

Consider a 5.25% bond with three years remaining to maturity that is callable in years one and two at $100. Exhibit 34–11 shows the values at each

**EXHIBIT 34-9**

Binomial Interest-Rate Tree for Valuing up to a Three-Year Bond

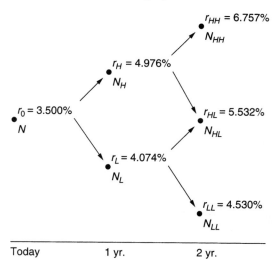

| Today | 1 yr. | 2 yr. |

node of the binomial tree. The discounting process is identical to that shown in Exhibit 34–10, except that at two nodes, $N_L$ and $N_{LL}$, the values from the recursive valuation formula ($101.002 at $N_L$ and $100.689 at $N_{LL}$) exceed the call price ($100) and therefore have been struck out and replaced with $100. These values are carried along in the discounting process, resulting in a value for this callable bond of $101.432.

In this model, the issuer calls the bond when the call price is less than the expected cost of leaving the bond outstanding to the next node, where the option exercise decision will generally be revisited. This option exercise policy means that a bond will be called only when the resulting net present value savings equal the value of the call option. In other words, the option has only exercise value; it has no time value. Actual exercise strategies may involve the sacrifice of some time value and entail tax and accounting considerations.

## Determining the Value of the Call Option

From our discussion regarding the relationship among the value of a callable bond, the value of an optionless bond, and the value of the call option, we know that:

Value of call option = Value of optionless bond − Value of callable bond.

We have just seen how to determine the values of optionless and callable bonds. Their difference is just the value of the call option. In our illustration,

**E X H I B I T   34–10**

Valuing an Optionless Bond with Three Years to Maturity and a Coupon of 5.25 Percent

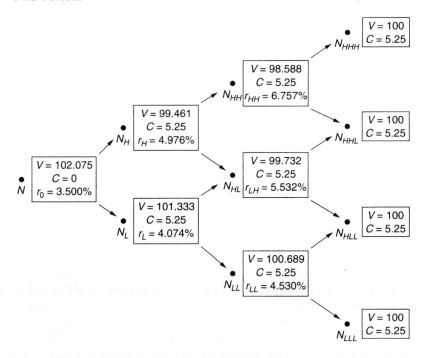

the optionless bond is worth $102.075 and the callable bond is worth $101.432, so the value of the call option is $0.643.

## Extension to Other Embedded Options

The bond valuation framework presented here can be used to analyze putable bonds, options on interest-rate swaps, caps and floors on floating-rate notes, and the optional accelerated redemption granted to an issuer in fulfilling sinking-fund requirements.[5] Consider a putable bond. Suppose that a 5.25% bond with three years remaining to maturity is putable at par ($100) in years one and two. Assume that the appropriate binomial interest-rate tree for this issuer is the one in Exhibit 34–9. Exhibit 34–12 shows the binomial tree with the bond values

---

5. For a discussion of these options in a sinking-fund provision, see Chapter 5 in Richard S. Wilson and Frank J. Fabozzi, *Corporate Bonds: Structures & Analysis* (New Hope, PA: Frank J. Fabozzi Associates, 1996) pp. 188–197. The valuation of these options is explained further in Andrew J. Kalotay and George O. Williams, "The Valuation and Management of Bonds with Sinking Fund Provision," *Financial Analysts Journal,* March/April 1992, pp. 59–67.

**EXHIBIT 34–11**

Valuing a Callable Bond with Three Years to Maturity, a Coupon of 5.25 Percent, and Callable in Years 1 and 2 at 100

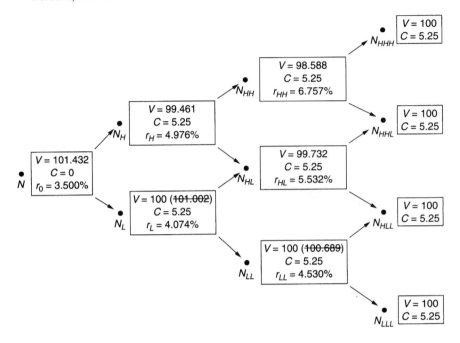

altered at two nodes $(N_{HH}$ and $N_{HL})$ because the bond values at these two nodes are less than \$100, the value at which the bond can be put. The value of this putable bond is \$102.523.

Since the value of a putable bond can be expressed as the value of an optionless bond plus the value of a put option on that bond,

Value of put option = Value of optionless bond − Value of putable bond.

In our example, the value of the putable bond is \$102.523 and the value of the corresponding optionless bond is \$102.075, so the value of the put option is −\$0.448. The negative sign indicates the issuer has sold the option, or equivalently, the investor has purchased the option.

This framework can also be used to value a bond with multiple embedded options. The bond values at each node are altered to reflect the exercise of any options.

## Volatility and the Theoretical Value

In our illustrations, interest-rate volatility has been set at 10%. The volatility assumption has an important impact on the theoretical value of option-bearing

**EXHIBIT  34–12**

Valuing a Putable Bond with Three Years to Maturity, a Coupon of 5.25
Percent, and Putable in Years 1 and 2 at 100

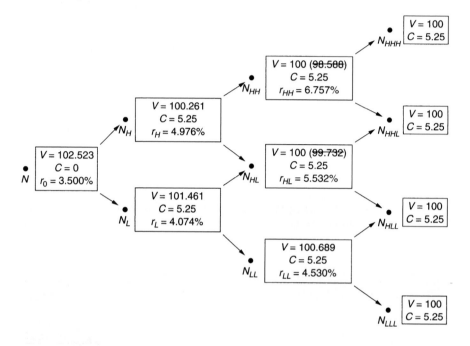

securities: the higher the volatility, the higher the value of any option,[6] including
one embedded in a bond.

For a callable bond, greater volatility increases the value of a call option
and so decreases the value of the bond. At the same time, greater volatility
increases the value of a put option and hence increases the value of a putable
bond.

## Option-Adjusted Spread

This model determines the theoretical value of a bond; this value can then be
compared to the observed market price. For example, if the market price of the
three-year 5.25% callable bond is $101 and the theoretical value is $101.432,
the bond is cheap by $0.432. Bond market participants, however, prefer to think

---

6. This is explained in Chapter 55.

not in dollar terms but rather in terms of a yield spread: A cheap bond trades at a higher spread and a rich bond at a lower spread relative to some basis.

The market convention has been to quote a nominal spread—the difference between the yield-to-maturity on a particular bond and that on a Treasury bond of comparable maturity. This approach can be extended to take into account the entire yield curve, through either a set of spot rates or a set of forward rates.

We can now discuss a discounting spread over the forward-rate curve. In terms of our binomial tree, we seek the constant spread that, when added to all the forward rates on the tree, makes the theoretical value equal to the market price. This quantity is called the *option-adjusted spread* (OAS). It is option-adjusted in that a bond fairly priced relative to an issuer's yield curve will have an OAS of zero whether the bond is option-free or has embedded options.

Returning to our illustration, if the observed market price is $101, the OAS would be the constant spread added to every rate in Exhibit 34–9 that will make the theoretical value equal to $101. In this case, that spread is 23.2 basis points, as can be verified in Exhibit 34–13.

Like the value of an option-bearing bond, the OAS will depend on the volatility assumption. For a given bond price, the higher the interest-rate vola-

**EXHIBIT   34–13**

Demonstration of the Option-Adjusted Spread

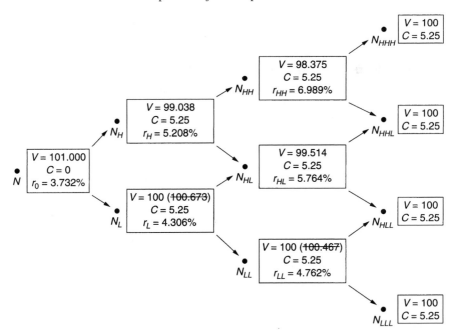

tility, the lower the OAS for a callable bond and the higher the OAS for a putable bond.

## Effective Duration and Effective Convexity

Portfolio managers also want to know the sensitivity of a bond's price to changes in interest rates. As explained in Chapter 5, modified duration is a measure of the sensitivity of a bond's price to changes in the yield-to-maturity and is equivalent to assuming that the yield curve is flat and that future cash flows do not depend on interest rates. Consequently, modified duration is not an appropriate measure for bonds with embedded options whose cash flows can change with changing interest rates. For example, high rates change the cash flows of putable bonds, and low rates change the cash flows of callable bonds.

The correct duration measure—called *effective* duration—quantifies the price sensitivity to small changes in interest rates while simultaneously allowing for changing cash flows. In terms of our binomial interest-rate tree, price response to changing interest rates is found by shifting the tree—or, more appropriately, the yield curve from which the tree is derived—up and down by a few basis points.

Analogous to the discussion in Chapter 5, if $P$ is the value of a bond *including accrued interest*, $P_-$ is the value of the bond if the entire yield curve is shifted down by $\Delta y$ basis points, and $P_+$ is its value when the curve is shifted up by $\Delta y$ basis points, then

$$\text{Effective duration} = \frac{P_- - P_+}{2P_0\Delta y}$$

Let's return to the example of the callable 5.25% three-year bond. Given the yield curve and volatility assumptions we have been using, the central value $P$ is \$101.432. Shifting the yield curve down 10 basis points, refitting the tree, and revaluing the bond gives a value for $P_-$ of \$101.628. Similarly, shifting the curve up 10 basis points gives a value for $P_+$ of \$101.234. Then

$$\text{Effective duration} = \frac{101.628 - \$101.234}{2 \times \$101.432 \times 0.0010}$$

$$= \frac{\$0.394}{\$0.202864}$$

$$= 1.94$$

In the same manner, the standard convexity measure ignores the effects produced by both the shape of the yield curve and the presence of options. The applicable formula for convexity is

$$\text{Effective convexity} = \frac{P_- - 2P + P_+}{2 \times P \times (\Delta y)^2}$$

so that

$$\text{Effective convexity} = \frac{101.628 - 2 \times \$101.432 + \$101.234}{\$101.432 \times 0.0010^2}$$

Using the inserted values based on price to seven decimal places,

$$\text{Effective convexity} = \frac{\$0.0006867}{2 \times \$0.0001014}$$

$$= 3.39$$

## THE CHALLENGE OF IMPLEMENTATION

For use as a practical tool, the basic interest-rate tree requires several refinements. For one thing, the spacing of the node lines in the tree must be much finer, particularly if American options are to be valued. However, the fine spacing required to value short-dated securities becomes computationally inefficient if one seeks to value, say, 30-year bonds. Although one can introduce a time-dependent node spacing, caution is required; it is easy to distort the term structure of volatility. Other practical difficulties include the management of cash flows that fall between two node lines.

## SUMMARY

There are a good number of bonds that are redeemable before maturity: They contain one or more embedded options. This chapter offered a framework for valuing such bonds. Our primary focus was on callable bonds. Callable bonds pose two risks to the investor in a declining-rate environment: There is reinvestment risk of principal, and there is limited upside potential relative to an optionless but otherwise similar bond.

The valuation framework presented here employs a binomial interest-rate tree based on an issuer's noncall life yield curve and an assumed interest-rate volatility. The binomial tree provides the volatility-dependent one-period rates to discount cash flows.

The option-adjusted spread is the constant spread that, when added to the rates in the interest-rate tree, produces a theoretical value for a bond equal to the market price of the bond. It is a means of expressing the difference between the theoretical value and an observed market price as a yield spread.

The archaic modified duration and convexity are inappropriate for a bond with an embedded option because these measures assume a flat yield curve and ignore the presence of any options. The appropriate measures of the response of a bond's price to changes in the yield curve are effective duration and effective convexity.

## CHAPTER 35

# Valuation of CMOs*

**Frank J. Fabozzi, Ph.D., CPA**
Adjunct Professor of Finance
School of Management
Yale University

**Scott F. Richard, DBA**
Portfolio Manager
Miller, Anderson & Sherrerd

**David S. Horowitz, CFA**
Portfolio Manager
Miller, Anderson & Sherrerd

## INTRODUCTION

The traditional approach to the valuation of fixed-income securities is to calculate yield—the yield to maturity, the yield to call for a callable bond, and the cash flow yield for a mortgage-backed security. A superior approach is the option-adjusted spread (OAS) method. Our objective in this chapter is to describe the OAS method and apply it to collateralized mortgage obligations (CMOs).

In this chapter, we describe the theoretical foundations of this technique, the input and assumptions that go into the development of an OAS model, and the output of an OAS model, which in addition to the OAS value includes the option-adjusted duration and option-adjusted convexity. Because the user of an OAS model is exposed to *modeling risk,* it is necessary to test the sensitivity of these numbers to changes in the assumptions.

Valuation modeling for CMOs is similar to valuation modeling for passthroughs, although the difficulties are amplified because the issuer has sliced and diced both the prepayment risk and the interest rate risk into smaller pieces called *tranches.* The sensitivity of the passthrough securities from which the CMO is created to these two risks is not transmitted equally to every tranche.

---

* Updated from Chapter 6 in Frank J. Fabozzi (ed.), *Advances in the Valuation and Management of Mortgage-Backed Securities* (New Hope, PA: Frank J. Fabozzi Associates, 1999).

Some of the tranches wind up more sensitive to prepayment risk and interest rate risk than the collateral, while some of them are much less sensitive.

The objective of the money manager is to figure out how the OAS of the collateral, or, equivalently, the value of the collateral, gets transmitted to the CMO tranches. More specifically, the objective is to find out where the value goes and where the risk goes so that the money manager can identify the tranches with low risk and high value: the ones he or she wants to buy. The good news is that this combination usually exists in every deal. The bad news is that in every deal there are usually tranches with low OAS, low value, and high risk.

## STATIC VALUATION

Using OAS to value mortgages is a dynamic technique in that many scenarios for future interest rates are analyzed. Static valuation analyzes only a single interest rate scenario, usually assuming that the yield curve remains unchanged. Static valuation results in two measures, average life and static spread, which we review below.

## Average Life

The *average life* of a mortgage-backed security is the weighted average time to receipt of principal payments (scheduled payments and projected prepayments). The formula for the average life is:

$$\frac{1(\text{Principal at time 1}) + \cdots + T(\text{Principal at time } T)}{12(\text{Total principal received})}$$

where $T$ is the number of months.

In order to calculate average life, an investor must either assume a prepayment rate for the mortgage security being analyzed or use a prepayment model. By calculating the average life at various prepayment rates, the investor can gain some feeling for the stability of the security's cash flows. For example, a PAC bond's average life will not change within the PAC bands, but may shorten significantly if the prepayment rate exceeds the upper band. By examining the average life at prepayment rates greater than the upper band, an investor can judge some of the PAC's risks. With a prepayment model available, the average life of a mortgage security can be calculated by changing the mortgage refinancing rate. As the refinancing rate rises, the prepayment model will slow the prepayment rate and thus cause the bond's average life to extend. Conversely, if the refinancing rate is lowered, the model will cause prepayments to rise and shorten the average life.

## Static Spread

One of the standard measures in evaluating any mortgage-backed security is the cash flow yield, or simply "yield." The yield spread, sometimes referred to as the *nominal spread,* is found by spreading the yield to the average life on the interpolated Treasury yield curve. This practice is improper for an amortizing bond even in the absence of interest rate volatility.

What should be done instead is to calculate what is called the *static spread.* This is the yield spread in a static scenario (i.e., no volatility of interest rates) of the bond over the entire theoretical Treasury spot rate curve, not a single point on the Treasury yield curve. The magnitude of the difference between the nominal spread and the static yield depends on the steepness of the yield curve: the steeper the curve, the greater the difference between the two values. In a relatively flat interest rate environment, the difference between the nominal spread and the static spread will be small.

There are two ways to compute the static spread. One way is to use today's yield curve to discount future cash flows and keep the mortgage refinancing rate fixed at today's mortgage rate. Since the mortgage refinancing rate is fixed, the investor can usually specify a reasonable prepayment rate for the life of the security. Using this prepayment rate, the bond's future cash flow can be estimated. Use of this approach to calculate the static spread recognizes different prices today of dollars to be delivered at future dates. This results in the proper discounting of cash flows while keeping the mortgage rate fixed. Effectively, today's prices indicate what the future discount rates will be, but the best estimates of future rates are today's rates.

The second way to calculate the static spread allows the mortgage rate to go up the curve as implied by the forward interest rates. This procedure is sometimes called the *zero volatility OAS.* In this case a prepayment model is needed to determine the vector of future prepayment rates implied by the vector of future refinancing rates. A money manager using static spread should determine which approach is used in the calculation.

## DYNAMIC VALUATION MODELING

Because CMOs are simply a regrouping of the cash flows from the underlying passthrough securities, the valuation of CMO tranches follows directly from the valuation of passthrough securities.

## Using Simulation to Generate
## Interest Rate Paths and Cash Flows

A technique known as simulation is used to value complex securities such as passthroughs and CMOs. Simulation is used because the monthly cash flows are path-dependent. This means that the cash flows received this month are determined not only by the current and future interest rate levels, but also by the path that interest rates took to get to the current level.

There are typically two sources of path dependency in a CMO tranche's cash flows. First, collateral prepayments are path-dependent because this month's prepayment rate depends on whether there have been prior opportunities to refinance since the underlying mortgages were issued. Second, the cash flow to be received this month by a CMO tranche depends on the outstanding balances of the other tranches in the deal. We need the history of prepayments to calculate these balances.

Conceptually, the valuation of passthrough securities using the simulation method is simple. In practice, however, it is very complex. The simulation involves generating a set of cash flows based on simulated future mortgage refinancing rates, which in turn imply simulated prepayment rates.

The typical model that Wall Street firms and commercial vendors use to generate these random interest rate paths takes as input today's term structure of interest rates and a volatility assumption. The term structure of interest rates is the theoretical spot rate (or zero coupon) curve implied by today's Treasury securities. The volatility assumption determines the dispersion of future interest rates in the simulation. The simulations should be normalized so that the average simulated price of a zero coupon Treasury bond equals today's actual price.

Each OAS model has its own model of the evolution of future interest rates and its own volatility assumptions. Until recently, there have been few significant differences in the interest rate models of dealer firms and OAS vendors, although their volatility assumptions can be significantly different.

The random paths of interest rates should be generated from an arbitrage-free model of the future term structure of interest rates. By arbitrage-free it is meant that the model replicates today's term structure of interest rates, an input of the model, and that for all future dates there is no possible arbitrage within the model.[1]

The simulation works by generating many scenarios of future interest rate paths. In each month of the scenario, a monthly interest rate and a mortgage refinancing rate are generated. The monthly interest rates are used to discount the projected cash flows in the scenario. The mortgage refinancing rate is needed to determine the cash flow because it represents the opportunity cost the mortgagor is facing at that time.

If the refinancing rates are high relative to the mortgagor's original coupon rate, the mortgagor will have less incentive to refinance, or even a disincentive (i.e., the homeowner will avoid moving in order to avoid refinancing). If the

---

1. A risk-neutral, arbitrage-free model of Treasury yields means that at all future dates the price of any long-term bond equals the expected value of rolling short-term to maturity. For more details, see Fischer Black, Emmanuel Derman, and William Toy, "A One-Factor Model of Interest Rates and its Application to Treasury Bond Options," *Financial Analysts Journals* (January/February 1990), pp. 33–39.

## EXHIBIT 35-1

Simulated Paths of 1-Month Future Interest Rates

| | Interest Rate Path Number | | | | | |
|---|---|---|---|---|---|---|
| Month | 1 | 2 | 3 | . . . | n | N |
| 1 | $f_1(1)$ | $f_1(2)$ | $f_1(3)$ | . . . | $f_1(n)$ | . . . | $f_1(N)$ |
| 2 | $f_2(1)$ | $f_2(2)$ | $f_2(3)$ | . . . | $f_2(n)$ | . . . | $f_2(N)$ |
| 3 | $f_3(1)$ | $f_3(2)$ | $f_3(3)$ | . . . | $f_3(n)$ | . . . | $f_3(N)$ |
| t | $f_t(1)$ | $f_t(2)$ | $f_t(3)$ | . . . | $f_t(n)$ | . . . | $f_t(N)$ |
| 358 | $f_{358}(1)$ | $f_{358}(2)$ | $f_{358}(3)$ | . . . | $f_{358}(n)$ | . . . | $f_{358}(N)$ |
| 359 | $f_{359}(1)$ | $f_{359}(2)$ | $f_{359}(3)$ | . . . | $f_{359}(n)$ | . . . | $f_{359}(N)$ |
| 360 | $f_{360}(1)$ | $f_{360}(2)$ | $f_{360}(3)$ | . . . | $f_{360}(n)$ | . . . | $f_{360}(N)$ |

Notation:
$f_t(n)$ = one-month future interest rate for month $t$ on path $n$
$N$ = total number of interest rate paths

## EXHIBIT 35-2

Simulated Paths of Mortgage Refinancing Rates

| | Interest Rate Path Number | | | | | |
|---|---|---|---|---|---|---|
| Month | 1 | 2 | 3 | . . . | n | N |
| 1 | $r_1(1)$ | $r_1(2)$ | $r_1(3)$ | . . . | $r_1(n)$ | . . . | $r_1(N)$ |
| 2 | $r_2(1)$ | $r_2(2)$ | $r_2(3)$ | . . . | $r_2(n)$ | . . . | $r_2(N)$ |
| 3 | $r_3(1)$ | $r_3(2)$ | $r_3(3)$ | . . . | $r_3(n)$ | . . . | $r_3(N)$ |
| t | $r_t(1)$ | $r_t(2)$ | $r_t(3)$ | . . . | $r_t(n)$ | . . . | $r_t(N)$ |
| 358 | $r_{358}(1)$ | $r_{358}(2)$ | $r_{358}(3)$ | . . . | $r_{358}(n)$ | . . . | $r_{358}(N)$ |
| 359 | $r_{359}(1)$ | $r_{359}(2)$ | $r_{359}(3)$ | . . . | $r_{359}(n)$ | . . . | $r_{359}(N)$ |
| 360 | $r_{360}(1)$ | $r_{360}(2)$ | $r_{360}(3)$ | . . . | $r_{360}(n)$ | . . . | $r_{360}(N)$ |

Notation:
$r_t(n)$ = mortgage refinancing rate for month $t$ on path $n$
$N$ = total number of interest rate paths

refinancing rate is low relative to the mortgagor's original coupon rate, the mortgagor has an incentive to refinance.

Prepayments are projected by feeding the refinancing rate and loan characteristics, such as age, into a prepayment model. Given the projected prepayments, the cash flow along an interest rate path can be determined.

To make this more concrete, consider a newly issued mortgage passthrough security with a maturity of 360 months. Exhibit 35-1 shows $N$ simulated

**EXHIBIT 35-3**

Simulated Cash Flow on Each of the Interest Rate Paths

| Month | Interest Rate Path Number | | | | | | |
|---|---|---|---|---|---|---|---|
| | 1 | 2 | 3 | . . . | n | | N |
| 1 | $C_1(1)$ | $C_1(2)$ | $C_1(3)$ | . . . | $C_1(n)$ | . . . | $C_1(N)$ |
| 2 | $C_2(1)$ | $C_2(2)$ | $C_2(3)$ | . . . | $C_2(n)$ | . . . | $C_2(N)$ |
| 3 | $C_3(1)$ | $C_3(2)$ | $C_3(3)$ | . . . | $C_3(n)$ | . . . | $C_3(N)$ |
| t | $C_t(1)$ | $C_t(2)$ | $C_t(3)$ | . . . | $C_t(n)$ | . . . | $C_t(N)$ |
| 358 | $C_{358}(1)$ | $C_{358}(2)$ | $C_{358}(3)$ | . . . | $C_{358}(n)$ | . . . | $C_{358}(N)$ |
| 359 | $C_{359}(1)$ | $C_{359}(2)$ | $C_{359}(3)$ | . . . | $C_{359}(n)$ | . . . | $C_{359}(N)$ |
| 360 | $C_{360}(1)$ | $C_{360}(2)$ | $C_{360}(3)$ | . . . | $C_{360}(n)$ | . . . | $C_{360}(N)$ |

Notation:
$C_t(n)$ = cash flow for month $t$ on path $n$
$N$ = total number of interest rate paths

interest rate path scenarios. Each scenario consists of a path of 360 simulated one-month future interest rates. Just how many paths should be generated is explained later. Exhibit 35–2 shows the paths of simulated mortgage refinancing rate corresponding to the scenarios shown in Exhibit 35–1. Assuming these mortgage refinancing rates, the cash flow for each scenario path is shown in Exhibit 35–3.

## Calculating the Present Value for a Scenario Interest Rate Path

Given the cash flow on an interest rate path, its present value can be calculated. The discount rate for determining the present value is the simulated spot rate for each month on the interest rate path plus an appropriate spread. The spot rate on a path can be determined from the simulated future monthly rates. The relationship that holds between the simulated spot rate for month $T$ on path $n$ and the simulated future one-month rates is:

$$z_T(n) = \{[1 + f_1(n)][1 + f_2(n)] \ldots [1 + f_{2T}(n)]\}^{1/T} - 1$$

where

$z_T(n)$ = simulated spot rate for month $T$ on path $n$
$f_j(n)$ = simulated future one-month rate for month $j$ on path $n$

Consequently, the interest rate path for the simulated future one-month rates can be converted to the interest rate path for the simulated monthly spot rates as shown in Exhibit 35–4. Therefore, the present value of the cash flow

## EXHIBIT 35-4

Simulated Paths of Monthly Spot Rates

| Month | Interest Rate Path Number | | | | | | |
|---|---|---|---|---|---|---|---|
| | **1** | **2** | **3** | **. . .** | **n** | | **N** |
| 1 | $z_1(1)$ | $z_1(2)$ | $z_1(3)$ | . . . | $z_1(n)$ | . . . | $z_1(N)$ |
| 2 | $z_2(1)$ | $z_2(2)$ | $z_2(3)$ | . . . | $z_2(n)$ | . . . | $z_2(N)$ |
| 3 | $z_3(1)$ | $z_3(2)$ | $z_3(3)$ | . . . | $z_3(n)$ | . . . | $z_3(N)$ |
| t | $z_t(1)$ | $z_t(2)$ | $z_t(3)$ | . . . | $z_t(n)$ | . . . | $z_t(N)$ |
| 358 | $z_{358}(1)$ | $z_{358}(2)$ | $z_{358}(3)$ | . . . | $z_{358}(n)$ | . . . | $z_{358}(N)$ |
| 359 | $z_{359}(1)$ | $z_{359}(2)$ | $z_{359}(3)$ | . . . | $z_{359}(n)$ | . . . | $z_{359}(N)$ |
| 360 | $z_{360}(1)$ | $z_{360}(2)$ | $z_{360}(3)$ | . . . | $z_{360}(n)$ | . . . | $z_{360}(N)$ |

Notation:
$z_t(n)$ = spot rate for month $t$ on path $n$
$N$ = total number of interest rate paths

for month $T$ on interest rate path $n$ discounted at the simulated spot rate for month $T$ plus some spread is:

$$\text{PV}[C_T(n)] = \frac{C_T(n)}{[1 + z_T(n) + K]^{1/T}}$$

where

$\text{PV}[C_T(n)]$ = present value of cash flow for month $T$ on path $n$
$C_T(n)$ = cash flow for month $T$ on path $n$
$z_T(n)$ = spot rate for month $T$ on path $n$
$K$ = spread

The present value for path $n$ is the sum of the present value of the cash flow for each month on path $n$. That is,

$$\text{PV}[\text{Path}(n)] = \text{PV}[C_1(n)] + \text{PV}[C_2(n)] + \cdots + \text{PV}[C_{360}(n)]$$

where $\text{PV}[\text{Path}(n)]$ is the present value of interest rate path $n$.

The option-adjusted spread is the spread, $K$, that when added to all the spot rates on all interest rate paths will make the average present value of the paths equal to the observed market price (plus accrued interest). Mathematically, OAS is the spread $K$ that will satisfy the following condition:

$$\text{Market Price} = \frac{\text{PV}[\text{Path}(1)] + \text{PV}[\text{Path}(2)] + \cdots + \text{PV}[\text{Path}(N)]}{N}$$

where $N$ is the number of interest rate paths.

This procedure for valuing a passthrough is also followed for a CMO tranche. The cash flow for each month on each interest rate path is found according to the principal repayment and interest distribution rules of the deal. In order to do this, a CMO structuring model is needed. In any analysis of CMOs, one of the major stumbling blocks is getting a good CMO structuring model.

## Selecting the Number of Interest Rate Paths

Let's now address the question of the number of scenario paths or repetitions, N, needed to value a CMO tranche. A typical OAS run will be done for 512 to 1,024 interest rate paths. The scenarios generated using the simulation method look very realistic, and furthermore reproduce today's Treasury curve. By employing this technique, the money manager is effectively saying that Treasuries are fairly priced today and that the objective is to determine whether a specific tranche is rich or cheap relative to Treasuries.

The number of interest rate paths determines how "good" the estimate is, not relative to the truth but relative to the OAS model used. The more paths, the more average spread tends to settle down. It is a statistical sampling problem.

Most OAS models employ some form of *variance reduction* to cut down on the number of sample paths necessary to get a good statistical sample.[2] Variance reduction techniques allow us to obtain price estimates within a tick. By this we mean that if the OAS model is used to generate more scenarios, price estimates from the model will not change by more than a tick. So, for example, if 1,024 paths are used to obtain the estimated price for a tranche, there is little more information to be had from the OAS model by generating more than that number of paths. (For some very sensitive CMO tranches, more paths may be needed to estimate prices within one tick.)

## Interpretation of the OAS

The procedure for determining the OAS is straightforward, although time-consuming. The next question, then, is how to interpret the OAS. Basically, the OAS is used to reconcile value with market price. On the left-hand side of the last equation is the market's statement: the price of a mortgage-backed security or mortgage derivative. The average present value over all the paths on the right-hand side of the equation is the model's output, which we refer to as value.

What a money manager seeks to do is to buy securities whose value is greater than their price. A valuation model such as the one described above allows a money manager to estimate the value of a security, which at this point would be sufficient to determine whether to buy a security. That is, the money

---

2. For a discussion of variance reduction, see Phelim P. Boyle, "Options: A Monte Carlo Approach," *Journal of Financial Economics* 4 (1977), pp. 323–338.

manager can say that this bond is 1 point cheap or 2 points cheap, and so on. The model does not stop here, however. Instead, it converts the divergence between price and value into a yield spread measure, as most market participants find it more convenient to think about yield spread than about price differences.

The OAS was developed as a measure of the yield spread that can be used to reconcile dollar differences between value and price. But what is it a "spread" over? In describing the model above, we can see that the OAS is measuring the average spread over the Treasury spot rate curve, not the Treasury yield curve. It is an average spread because the OAS is found by averaging over the interest rate paths for the possible spot rate curves.

## Option Cost

The implied cost of the option embedded in any mortgage-backed security can be obtained by calculating the difference between the OAS at the assumed volatility of interest rates and the static spread. That is,

$$\text{Option cost} = \text{Static spread} - \text{Option-adjusted spread}$$

The reason that the option cost is measured in this way is as follows. In an environment of no interest rate changes, the investor would earn the static spread. When future interest rates are uncertain, the spread is less, however, because of the homeowner's option to prepay; the OAS reflects the spread after adjusting for this option. Therefore, the option cost is the difference between the spread that would be earned in a static interest rate environment (the static spread) and the spread after adjusting for the homeowner's option.

In general, a tranche's option cost is more stable than its OAS in the face of market movements. This interesting feature is useful in reducing the computational expensive costs of calculating the OAS as the market moves. For small market moves, the OAS of a tranche may be approximated by recalculating the static spread (which is relatively cheap and easy to calculate) and subtracting its option cost.

## Other Products of the OAS Models

Other products of the valuation model are option-adjusted duration, option-adjusted convexity, and simulated average life.

### Option-Adjusted Duration
In general, duration measures the price sensitivity of a bond to a small change in interest rates. Duration can be interpreted as the approximate percentage change in price for a 100-basis point parallel shift in the yield curve. For example, if a bond's duration is 4, this means a 100-basis point increase in interest rates will result in a price decrease of approximately 4%. A 50-basis point

increase in yields will decrease the price by approximately 2%. The smaller the change in basis points, the better the approximated change in price will be.

The duration for any security can be approximated as follows:

$$\text{Duration} = \frac{P_- - P_+}{2P_0 \Delta y}$$

where

$P_-$ = price if yield is decreased (per \$100 of par value) by $\Delta y$
$P_+$ = price if yield is increased (per \$100 of par value) by $\Delta y$
$P_0$ = initial price (per \$100 of par value)
$\Delta y$ = number of basis points change used to calculate $P_-$ and $P_+$

The standard measure of duration is modified duration. The limitation of modified duration is that it assumes that if interest rates change, the cash flow does not change. While modified duration is fine for option-free securities such as Treasury bonds, it is inappropriate for mortgage-backed securities, because projected cash flows change as interest rates and prepayments change. When prices in the duration formula are calculated assuming that the cash flow changes when interest rates change, the resulting duration is called *effective duration*.

Effective duration can be computed using an OAS model as follows. First the bond's OAS is found using the current term structure of interest rates. Next the bond is repriced holding OAS constant, but shifting the term structure. Two shifts are used; in one yields are increased, and in the second they are decreased. This produces the two prices, $P_-$ and $P_+$, used in the above formula. Effective duration calculated in this way is often referred to as *option-adjusted duration* or *OAS duration*.

The assumption in using modified or effective duration to project the percentage price change is that all interest rates change by the same number of basis points; that is, there is a parallel shift in the yield curve. If the term structure does not change by a parallel shift, then effective duration will not correctly predict the change in a bond's price.

## Option-Adjusted Convexity

The convexity measure of a security is the approximate change in price that is not explained by duration. *Positive convexity* means that if yields change by a given number of basis points, the percentage increase in price will be greater than the percentage decrease in price. *Negative convexity* means that if yield changes by a given number of basis points, the percentage increase in price will be less than the percentage decrease in price. That is, for a 100-basis point change in yield:

| Type of Convexity | Increase in Price | Decrease in Price |
|---|---|---|
| Positive convexity | X% | less than X% |
| Negative convexity | X% | more than X% |

Obviously, positive convexity is a desirable property of a bond. A pass-through security can exhibit either positive or negative convexity, depending on the prevailing mortgage rate relative to the rate on the underlying mortgage loans. When the prevailing mortgage rate is much higher than the mortgage rate on the underlying mortgage loans, the passthrough usually exhibits positive convexity. It usually exhibits negative convexity when the underlying coupon rate is near or above prevailing mortgage refinancing rates.

The convexity of any bond can be approximated using the formula:

$$\frac{P_+ + P_- - (P_0)}{2P_0(\Delta y)^2}$$

When the prices used in this formula assume that the cash flows do not change when yields change, the resulting convexity is a good approximation of the standard convexity for an option-free bond. When the prices used in the formula are derived by changing the cash flows (by changing prepayment rates) when yields change, the resulting convexity is called *effective convexity*. Once again, when an OAS model is used to obtain the prices, the resulting value is referred to as the *option-adjusted convexity* or *OAS convexity*.

### Simulated Average Life

The average life reported in an OAS model is the average of the average lives along the interest rate paths. That is, for each interest rate path, there is an average life. The average of these average lives is the average life reported in an OAS model.

Additional information is conveyed by the distribution of the average life. The greater the range and standard deviation of the average life, the more the uncertainty about the tranche's average life.

## ILLUSTRATIONS

We use three deals to show how CMOs can be analyzed using the OAS methodology: a plain vanilla structure, a PAC/support structure, and a reverse pay structure.

## Plain Vanilla Structure

The plain vanilla sequential-pay CMO bond structure in our illustration is FHLMC 1915. A diagram of the principal allocation structure is given in Exhibit 35–5. The structure includes eight tranches, A, B, C, D, E, F, G, and S, and two residual classes. Tranche F is a floating-rate bond, and tranche S is an inverse floating-rate IO. Tranches D, E, and G are special "exchangeable bonds" which allow for the combination of tranches F and S. The focus of our analysis is on tranches A, B, and C.

**EXHIBIT 35–5**

Diagram of Principal Allocation Structure of FHLMC 1915

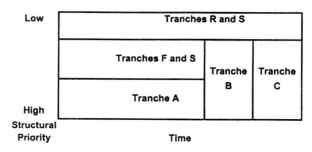

The top panel of Exhibit 35–6 shows the OAS and the option cost for the collateral and the five classes in the CMO structure. The OAS for the collateral is 51 basis points. Since the option cost is 67 basis points, the static spread is 118 basis points (51 basis points plus 67 basis points). The weighted-average OAS of all the classes (including the residual) is equal to the OAS of the collateral.

At the time this analysis was performed, March 10, 1998, the Treasury yield curve was not steep. As we noted earlier, in such a yield curve environment the static spread will not differ significantly from the traditionally computed yield spread. Thus, for the three tranches shown in Exhibit 35–6, the static spread is 83 for A, 115 for B, and 116 for C.

Notice that the classes did not share the OAS equally. The same is true for the option cost. The value tended to go toward the longer bonds, something that occurs in the typical deal. Both the static spread and the option cost increase as the maturity increases. The only tranches where there appears to be a bit of a bargain is tranche C. A money manager contemplating the purchase of this last cash flow tranche can see that C offer a higher OAS than B and appears to bear less of the risk, as measured by the option cost. The problem money managers may face is that they might not be able to go out as long on the yield curve as the C tranche because of duration, maturity, and average life constraints.

Now let's look at modeling risk. Examination of the sensitivity of the tranches to changes in prepayments and interest rate volatility will help us to understand the interaction of the tranches in the structure and who is bearing the risk.

We begin with prepayments. Specifically, we keep the same interest rate paths as those used to get the OAS in the base case (the top panel of Exhibit 35–6), but reduce the prepayment rate on each interest rate path to 80% of the projected rate.

As can be seen in the second panel of Exhibit 35–6, slowing down prepayments increases the OAS and price for the collateral. This is because the

**EXHIBIT 35–6**

OAS Analysis of FHLMC 1915 Classes A, B, and C (As of 3/10/98)

| | *Base Case (assumes 13% interest rate volatility)* | | |
| --- | --- | --- | --- |
| | **OAS (in basis points)** | **Option Cost (in basis points)** | **Effective Duration** |
| Collateral | 51 | 67 | 1.2 |
| Class | | | |
| A | 32 | 51 | 0.9 |
| B | 33 | 82 | 2.9 |
| C | 46 | 70 | 6.7 |

| | *Prepayments at 80% and 120% of Prepayment Model (assumes 13% interest rate volatility)* | | | | | |
| --- | --- | --- | --- | --- | --- | --- |
| | **New OAS (in basis points)** | | **Change in Price per $100 par (holding OAS constant)** | | **Effective Duration** | |
| | **80%** | **120%** | **80%** | **120%** | **80%** | **120%** |
| Collateral | 63 | 40 | $0.45 | −$0.32 | 2.0 | 0.6 |
| Class | | | | | | |
| A | 40 | 23 | 0.17 | −0.13 | 0.9 | 0.9 |
| B | 43 | 22 | 0.54 | −0.43 | 3.3 | 2.7 |
| C | 58 | 36 | 0.97 | −0.63 | 7.4 | 6.0 |

| | *Interest Rate Volatility of 9% and 17%* | | | | | |
| --- | --- | --- | --- | --- | --- | --- |
| | **New OAS (in basis points)** | | **Change in Price per $100 par (holding OAS constant)** | | **Effective Duration** | |
| | **9%** | **17%** | **9%** | **17%** | **9%** | **17%** |
| Collateral | 79 | 21 | $1.03 | −$0.94 | 1.4 | 1.1 |
| Class | | | | | | |
| A | 52 | 10 | 0.37 | −0.37 | 0.9 | 0.9 |
| B | 66 | −3 | 1.63 | −1.50 | 3.1 | 2.7 |
| C | 77 | 15 | 2.44 | −2.08 | 6.8 | 6.5 |

collateral is trading above par. Tranches created by this collateral will typically behave the same way. However, if a tranche was created with a lower coupon, allowing it to trade below par, then it may behave in the opposite fashion. The Exhibit reports two results of the sensitivity analysis. First, it indicates the change in the OAS. Second, it indicates the change in the price, holding the OAS constant at the base case.

To see how a money manager can use the information in the second panel, consider tranche A. At 80% of the prepayment speed, the OAS for this class increases from 32 basis points to 40 basis points. If the OAS is held constant, the panel indicates that the buyer of tranche A would gain $0.17 per $100 par value.

Notice that for all of the tranches reported in Exhibit 35–6 there is a gain from a slowdown in prepayments. This is because all of the sequential tranches in this deal are priced over par. If the F and S tranches were larger, then the coupon on tranche A would have been smaller. This coupon could have been made small enough for tranche A to trade at a discount to par, which would have caused the bond to lose in a prepayment slowdown. Also notice that, while the changes in OAS are about the same for the different tranches, the changes in price are quite different. This arises because the shorter tranches have less duration. Therefore, their prices do not move as much from a change in OAS as a longer tranche. A money manager who is willing to go to the long end of the curve, such as tranche C, would realize the most benefit from the slowdown in prepayments.

Also shown in the second panel of the exhibit is the second part of our experiments to test the sensitivity of prepayments: the prepayment rate is assumed to be 120% of the base case. The collateral loses money in this scenario because it is trading above par. This is reflected in the OAS of the collateral which declines from 51 basis points to 40 basis points.

Now look at the four tranches. They all lost money. Additionally, the S tranche, which is not shown in the exhibit, also loses in an increase in prepayments. The S tranche is an IO tranche, and, in general, IO types of tranches will be adversely affected by an increase in prepayments.

Now let's look at the sensitivity to the interest rate volatility assumption, 13% in the base case. Two experiments are performed: reducing the volatility assumption to 9% and increasing it to 17%. These results are reported in the third panel of Exhibit 35–6.

Reducing the volatility to 9% increases the dollar price of the collateral by $1.03 and increases the OAS from 51 in the base case to 79 basis points. This $1.03 increase in the price of the collateral is not equally distributed, however, between the four tranches. Most of the increase in value is realized by the longer tranches. The OAS gain for each of the tranches follows more or less the OAS durations of those tranches. This makes sense, because the longer the duration, the greater the risk, and when volatility declines, the reward is greater for the accepted risk.

At the higher level of assumed interest rate volatility of 17%, the collateral is severely affected. The collateral's loss is distributed among the tranches in the expected manner: the longer the duration, the greater the loss. In this case, tranche F and the residual are less affected.

Using the OAS methodology, a fair conclusion that can be made about this simple plain vanilla structure is: what you see is what you get. The only surprise in this structure is the lower option cost in tranche C. In general, however, a money manager willing to extend duration gets paid for that risk in a plain vanilla structure.

## PAC/Support Bond Structure

Now let's look at how to apply the OAS methodology to a more complicated CMO structure, FHLMC Series 1706. The collateral for this structure is Freddie Mac 7s. A summary of the deal is provided in Exhibit 35–7. A diagram of the principal allocation is given in Exhibit 35–8.

While this deal is more complicated than the previous one, it is still relatively simple compared to some deals that have been recently printed. Nonetheless, it brings out all the key points about application of OAS analysis, specifically, the fact that most deals include cheap bonds, expensive bonds, and fairly priced bonds. The OAS analysis helps a money manager identify how a tranche should be classified.

There are 19 classes in this structure: ten PAC bonds (including one PAC IO bond), three Scheduled bonds, two TAC support bonds, a floating rate support bonds, an inverse floating rate support bond, and two residual bonds. This deal contains no principal-only (PO) tranches.

The deal also includes an IO tranche, IA, which is structured such that the underlying collateral's interest not allocated to the PAC bonds is paid to the IO bond, which causes the PAC bonds to have discount coupons (as shown by the lower coupons of the front PACs in Exhibit 35–7). Unlike a typical mortgage-backed security backed by deep discount collateral, prepayments for the front tranches will be faster because the underlying collateral is Freddie Mac 7s, which was premium collateral at the time this analysis was computed. Thus, with PAC C, the investor realizes a low coupon rate but a much higher prepayment rate than would be experienced by such a low coupon mortgage bond.

Tranches A and B had already paid off all of their principal when this analysis was performed. The other PAC bonds are still available. Tranche IA is a PAC IO. The prepayment protection for the PAC bonds is provided by the support or companion bonds. The support bonds in this deal are tranches LA, LB, M, O, OA, PF, and PS. LA is the shortest tranche (an SCH bond), while the floating rate bonds, PF and PS, are the longest. SCH bonds, as represented by tranches LA and LB, have PSA bands similar to a PAC bond, but they typically have a narrower window of speeds. Also, they are often much less

**EXHIBIT 35-7**

Summary of Federal Home Loan Mortgage Corporation—Multiclass
Mortgage Participation Certificates (Guaranteed), Series 1706

| | | | | |
|---|---|---|---|---|
| Total Issue: | $300,000,000 | Original Settlement Date: | 3/30/94 | |
| Issue Date: | 2/18/94 | Days Delay: | 30 | |
| Structure Type: REMIC CMO | | Payment Frequency: | Monthly; 15th day of month | |
| Issuer | Class: Agency | | | |
| Dated Date: | 3/1/94 | | | |

|  | | | | *Original Issue Pricing* | |
|  | | | | *(225% PSA Assumed)* | |
| Tranche | Original Balance ($) | Coupon (%) | Stated Maturity | Average Life (yrs) | Expected Maturity |
|---|---|---|---|---|---|
| A (PAC Bond) | 24,600,000 | 4.50 | 10/15/06 | 1.3 | 6/15/96* |
| B (PAC Bond) | 11,100,000 | 5.00 | 9/15/09 | 2.5 | 1/15/97* |
| C (PAC Bond) | 25,500,000 | 5.25 | 4/15/14 | 3.5 | 6/15/98 |
| D (PAC Bond) | 9,150,000 | 5.65 | 8/15/15 | 4.5 | 1/15/99 |
| E (PAC Bond) | 31,650,000 | 6.00 | 1/15/19 | 5.8 | 1/15/01 |
| G (PAC Bond) | 30,750,000 | 6.25 | 8/15/21 | 7.9 | 5/15/03 |
| H (PAC Bond) | 27,450,000 | 6.50 | 6/15/23 | 10.9 | 10/15/07 |
| J (PAC Bond) | 5,220,000 | 6.50 | 10/15/23 | 14.4 | 9/15/09 |
| K (PAC Bond) | 7,612,000 | 7.00 | 3/15/24 | 18.8 | 5/15/19 |
| LA (SCH Bond) | 26,673,000 | 7.00 | 11/15/21 | 3.5 | 3/15/02 |
| LB (SCH Bond) | 36,087,000 | 7.00 | 6/15/23 | 3.5 | 9/15/02 |
| M (SCH Bond) | 18,738,000 | 7.00 | 3/15/24 | 11.2 | 10/15/08 |
| O (TAC Bond) | 13,348,000 | 7.00 | 2/15/24 | 2.5 | 1/15/08 |
| OA (TAC Bond) | 3,600,000 | 7.00 | 3/15/24 | 7.2 | 4/15/09 |
| IA (IO, PAC Bond) | 30,246,000 | 7.00 | 10/15/23 | 7.1 | 9/15/09 |
| PF (FLTR, Support Bond) | 21,016,000 | 6.75 | 3/15/24 | 17.5 | 5/15/19 |
| PS (INV FLTR, Support Bond) | 7,506,000 | 7.70 | 3/15/24 | 17.5 | 5/15/19 |
| R (Residual) | — | 0.00 | 3/15/24 | | |
| RS (Residual) | — | 0.00 | 3/15/24 | | |

### *Structural Features*

**Prepayment Guarantee:**     None
**Assumed Reinvestment Rate:**   0%

| **Cash Flow Allocation:** | Excess cash flow is not anticipated; in the event that there are proceeds remaining after the payment of the bonds, however, the Class R and RS Bonds will receive them. Commencing on the first principal payment date of the Class A Bonds, principal equal to the amount specified in the Prospectus will be applied to the Class A, B, C, D, E, G, H, J, K, LA, LB, M, O, OA, PF, and PS Bonds. After all other Classes have been retired, any remaining principal will be used to retire the Class O, OA, LA, LB, M, A, B, C, D, E, G, H, J, and K Bonds. The Notional Class IA Bond will have its notional principal amount retired along with the PAC Bonds. |
|---|---|
| **Redemption Provisions:** | Nuisance provision for all Classes: Issuer may redeem the Bonds, in whole but not in part, on any Payment Date when the outstanding principal balance declines to less than 1% of the original amount. |
| **Other:** | The PAC Range is 95% to 300% PSA for the A–K Bonds, 190% to 250% PSA for the LA, LB, and M Bonds, and 225% PSA for the O and OA Bonds. |

**EXHIBIT 35–8**

Diagram of Principal Allocation Structure of FHLMC 1706 (as of 3/10/98)

protected from prepayment surprises when the bands are exceeded. The LB tranche, for example, is essentially a support bond, once the PSA bands are broken.

The top panel of Exhibit 35–9 shows the base case OAS an the option cost for the collateral and all but the residual classes. The collateral OAS is 60 basis points, and the option cost is 44 basis points. The static spread of the collateral to the Treasury spot curve is 104 basis points.

# EXHIBIT 35–9

OAS Analysis of FHLMC 1706 (as of 3/10/98)

| | Base Case (assumes 13% interest rate volatility) | | |
| --- | --- | --- | --- |
| | OAS (in basis points) | Option Cost (in basis points) | Effective Duration |
| Collateral | 60 | 44 | 2.6 |
| Class | | | |
| C (PAC) | 15 | 0 | 0.2 |
| D (PAC) | 16 | 4 | 0.6 |
| E (PAC) | 26 | 4 | 1.7 |
| G (PAC) | 42 | 8 | 3.3 |
| H (PAC) | 50 | 12 | 4.9 |
| J (PAC) | 56 | 14 | 6.8 |
| K (PAC) | 57 | 11 | 8.6 |
| LA (SCH) | 39 | 12 | 1.4 |
| LB (SCH) | 29 | 74 | 1.2 |
| M (SCH) | 72 | 53 | 4.9 |
| O (TAC) | 70 | 72 | 3.8 |
| OA (TAC) | 68 | 68 | 5.4 |
| PF (Support Fltr) | 17 | 58 | 1.5 |
| PS (Support Inverse Fltr) | 54 | 137 | 17.3 |
| IA (PAC IO) | 50 | 131 | 0.5 |

**Prepayments at 80% and 120% of Prepayment Model (assumes 13% interest rate volatility)**

| Collateral Class | Base Case OAS | New OAS (in basis points) | | Change in Price per $100 par (holding OAS constant) | | Effective Duration | |
|---|---|---|---|---|---|---|---|
| | | 80% | 120% | 80% | 120% | 80% | 120% |
| Collateral | 60 | 63 | 57 | $0.17 | −$0.11 | 3.0 | 2.4 |
| C (PAC) | 15 | 15 | 15 | 0.00 | 0.00 | 0.2 | 0.2 |
| D (PAC) | 16 | 16 | 16 | 0.00 | 0.00 | 0.6 | 0.6 |
| E (PAC) | 26 | 27 | 26 | 0.01 | −0.01 | 1.7 | 1.6 |
| G (PAC) | 42 | 44 | 40 | 0.08 | −0.08 | 3.5 | 3.1 |
| H (PAC) | 50 | 55 | 44 | 0.29 | −0.27 | 5.5 | 4.7 |
| J (PAC) | 56 | 63 | 50 | 0.50 | −0.47 | 7.3 | 6.4 |
| K (PAC) | 57 | 65 | 49 | 0.77 | −0.76 | 9.1 | 8.1 |
| LA (SCH) | 39 | 31 | 39 | −0.12 | 0.00 | 1.5 | 1.2 |
| LB (SCH) | 29 | 39 | 18 | 0.38 | −0.19 | 1.3 | 1.1 |
| M (SCH) | 72 | 71 | 76 | −0.07 | 0.18 | 5.9 | 4.2 |
| O (TAC) | 70 | 69 | 72 | −0.06 | 0.10 | 4.0 | 3.6 |
| OA (TAC) | 68 | 69 | 71 | 0.07 | 0.15 | 5.8 | 5.3 |
| PF (Support Fltr) | 17 | 26 | 7 | 0.75 | −0.69 | 1.8 | 1.3 |
| PS (Support Inverse Fltr) | 54 | 75 | 49 | 1.37 | −0.27 | 17.6 | 17.2 |
| IA (PAC IO) | 50 | 144 | −32 | 0.39 | −0.32 | 1.0 | −1.2 |

**EXHIBIT 35-9**

*(Continued)*

| | | Interest Rate Volatility of 9% and 17% | | | | | |
| | Base Case OAS | New OAS (in basis points) | | Change in Price per $100 par (holding OAS constant) | | Effective Duration | |
| Collateral Class | | 9% | 17% | 9% | 17% | 9% | 17% |
|---|---|---|---|---|---|---|---|
| Collateral | 60 | 81 | 35 | $0.96 | −$0.94 | 2.9 | 2.5 |
| C (PAC) | 15 | 15 | 15 | 0.00 | 0.00 | 0.2 | 0.2 |
| D (PAC) | 16 | 16 | 16 | 0.00 | 0.00 | 0.6 | 0.6 |
| E (PAC) | 26 | 27 | 24 | 0.02 | −0.04 | 1.7 | 1.7 |
| G (PAC) | 42 | 48 | 34 | 0.21 | −0.27 | 3.3 | 3.3 |
| H (PAC) | 50 | 58 | 35 | 0.48 | −0.72 | 5.1 | 4.9 |
| J (PAC) | 56 | 66 | 41 | 0.70 | −1.05 | 7.1 | 6.6 |
| K (PAC) | 57 | 66 | 44 | 0.82 | −1.19 | 8.9 | 8.4 |
| LA (SCH) | 39 | 47 | 24 | 0.09 | −0.18 | 1.3 | 1.4 |
| LB (SCH) | 29 | 58 | −4 | 0.80 | −0.82 | 1.1 | 1.2 |
| M (SCH) | 72 | 100 | 41 | 1.80 | −1.72 | 5.4 | 4.7 |
| O (TAC) | 70 | 103 | 30 | 2.03 | −1.74 | 3.9 | 3.8 |
| OA (TAC) | 68 | 103 | 30 | 2.40 | −1.98 | 5.8 | 5.4 |
| PF (Support Fltr) | 17 | 51 | −27 | 3.11 | −2.92 | 1.0 | 2.1 |
| PS (Support Inverse Fltr) | 54 | 123 | −5 | 4.85 | −2.85 | 20.7 | 15.6 |
| IA (PAC IO) | 50 | 158 | −70 | 0.45 | −0.48 | 0.8 | 0.2 |

The 60 basis points of OAS did not get equally distributed among the tranches, as was the case with the plain vanilla structure. Tranche LB, the scheduled support, did not realize a good OAS allocation, only 29 basis points, and had an extremely high option cost. Given the prepayment uncertainly associated with this bond, its OAS would be expected to be higher. The reason for the low OAS is that this tranche was priced so that its cash flow yield is high. Using the static spread as a proxy for the spread over the Treasury yield curve, the 103 basis point spread for tranche LB is high given that this appears to be a short-term tranche. Consequently, "yield buyers" probably bid aggressively for this tranche and thereby drove down its OAS, trading off "yield" for OAS. From a total return perspective, however, tranche LB should be avoided. It is a rich, or expensive, bond. The three longer supports did not get treated as badly as tranche LB; the OAS for tranches M, O, and OA are 72, 70, and 68 basis points, respectively.

It should be apparent from the results of the base case OAS analysis reported in the top panel of Exhibit 35–9 where the cheap bonds in the deal are. They are the long PACs, which have a high OAS, a low option cost, and can be positively convex. These are well-protected cash flows.

Notice that the option cost for tranchees IA and PS are extremely high. These two tranches are primarily IOs. An investor who purchases an IO has effectively sold an option, and this explains the large option cost. As long as volatility is low, the owner of the IO will be able to collect the premium, because the realized option cost will be less than that implied by the model.

The next two panels in Exhibit 35–9 show the sensitivity of the OAS and the price (holding OAS constant at the base case) to changes in the prepayment speed (80% and 120% of the base case) and to changes in volatility (9% and 17%). This analysis shows that the change in the prepayment speed does not affect the collateral significantly, while the change in the OAS (holding the price constant) and price (holding OAS constant) for each tranche can be significant. For example, a faster prepayment speed, which decreases the time period over which a PAC IO bondholder is receiving a coupon, significantly reduces the OAS and price. The opposite effect results if prepayments are slower than the base case.

Tranche H, a premium priced medium-term PAC, benefits from a slowing in prepayments, as the bondholder will receive the coupon for a longer time. Faster prepayments represent an adverse scenario. The PAC bonds are quite well-protected. The long PACs will actually benefit from a reduced prepayment rate because they will be earning the higher coupon interest longer. So, on an OAS basis, our earlier conclusion that the long PACs were allocated a good part of the deal's value holds up under our first stress test.

A slowdown in prepayments helps the support tranche LB and a speedup hurts this tranche. A somewhat surprising result involves the effect that the change in prepayments has on the TAC bond OA. Notice that whether the prepayment speeds are slower or faster, the OAS and the price increases. This result arises from the structure of the bond. The prepayment risk of this bond is more prevalent when prepayments increase sharply, and then soon return to the base speed. This phenomenon, known as a "whipsaw," would adversely affect the OA tranche. Without the use of an OAS framework, this would not be intuitively obvious.

The sensitivity of the collateral and the tranches to changes in volatility are shown in the third panel of Exhibit 35–9. A lower volatility increases the value of the collateral, while a higher volatility reduces its value. Similarly, but in a more pronounced fashion, lower volatility increases the value of IO instruments, and higher volatility decreases their value. This effect can be seen on the PAC IO tranche IA in Exhibit 35–9.

The long PACs continue to be fairly well-protected, whether the volatility is lower or higher. In the two volatility scenarios they continue to get a good OAS, although not as much as in the base case if volatility is higher (but the OAS still looks like a reasonable value in this scenario). This reinforces our earlier conclusion concerning the investment merit of the long PACs in this deal.

## Reverse PAC Deal

We have stressed that the OAS analysis helps the money manager avoid the traps inherent in examination of a deal on a static basis. The next deal we look at is the Bear Stearns 88-5 deal, a reverse-pay deal. While it is an old deal, it highlights this point. The deal is summarized in Exhibit 35–10. It has four PACs and three support bonds, two of which are TACs. The principal allocation diagram is shown in Exhibit 35–11.

Our focus here is on the PAC bonds. According to the average life reported in Exhibit 35–10, PAC D is the longest bond with an average life of 19.7 years. The next-to-the-longest PAC is PAC C with an average of 10.9 years.

**EXHIBIT 35–10**

Summary of Bear Stearns 88-5 Reverse Pay Deal

| Tranche (type) | Coupon (%) | Average Life (years) | Balance (million) |
|---|---|---|---|
| A (PAC) | 9.125 | 2.4 | $28.7 |
| B (PAC) | 9.250 | 5.9 | 30.1 |
| C (PAC) | 9.625 | 10.9 | 44.4 |
| D (PAC) | 9.800 | 19.7 | 29.8 |
| E (Support TAC) | 9.450 | 1.1 | 5.3 |
| F (Support TAC) | 9.500 | 5.9 | 35.6 |
| G (Support) | 9.750 | 22.2 | 26.1 |

**EXHIBIT  35-11**

Principal Allocation Diagram of Bear Stearns 88-5 Reverse Pay Deal

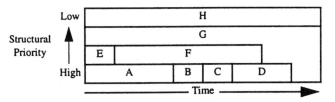

How good is the average life as a proxy for the price sensitivity of a bond? Since the average life is a static measure, it does not take into consideration interest rate volatility. The option-adjusted duration and convexity of PAC C and PAC D are as follows:

|        | Average Life | OA-Duration | OA-Convexity |
|--------|:---:|:---:|:---:|
| PAC C  | 10.9 | 6.3 | −0.22 |
| PAC D  | 19.7 | 5.9 | 0.04 |

PAC C actually has a longer duration then the PAC that follows it because it is a reverse-pay structure. OAS and option-adjusted duration would show the money manager immediately where the risk is. Moreover, it can be seen that PAC C is a negatively convex tranche.

## SUMMARY

CMOs are complex instruments. The valuation model described in this chapter is a sophisticated analytical tool available to analyze CMOs. The product of this valuation model is the option-adjusted spread. The results of this model should be stress-tested for modeling risk: alternative prepayment and volatility assumptions.

OAS analysis helps the money manager to understand where the risks are in the deal and to identify which tranches are cheap, rich, and fairly priced. Compared to a sophisticated analytical tool such as OAS analysis, traditional static analysis can lead to very different conclusions about the relative value of the tranches in a deal. This may lead a money manager to buy the expensive tranches and miss the opportunity to invest in cheap tranches.

CHAPTER **36**

# FIXED INCOME RISK
# MODELING

Ronald N. Kahn, Ph.D.
Managing Director
Barclays Global Investors

Many years ago, bonds were boring. Returns were small and steady. Fixed income risk monitoring consisted of watching duration and avoiding low qualities. But as interest-rate volatility has increased and the variety of fixed income instruments has grown, both opportunities and dangers have flourished. Accurate fixed income risk measurement has become more important and more difficult. The sources of fixed income risk have proliferated and intensified. Exposures to these risks are subtle and complex. Today's fixed income environment requires advanced multifactor techniques to adequately model the many sources of risk influencing the market, and powerful tools to compute exposures to those risks.

Duration is the traditional fixed income risk factor, and measures exposure to the risk of parallel term-structure movements. But term structures not only shift in parallel, they also twist and bend, and these movements tend to increase in magnitude as interest rates rise. In addition to interest-rate volatility, most issues are exposed to various sources of default risk, assessed by marketwide sector and quality spreads. These spreads can depend on maturity and move unpredictably over time. Beyond marketwide sources of default risk, individual issues face specific sources of default risk.

Nominal cash flows and quality ratings no longer suffice to measure risk exposures. Call and put options and sinking-fund provisions can significantly alter an instrument's risk exposures in intricate ways. Mortgage-backed securities are subject to uncertain prepayments, which influence the risk exposures of those instruments. When they are packaged as IOs, POs, or CMOs, the risk exposure accounting becomes even more difficult.

There is no question that building a fixed income risk model is complicated business. Forecasting risk factor covariance and analyzing the Byzantine provisions of today's fixed income instruments require sophisticated methods.

Using a fixed income risk model, however, should be intuitive and straightforward. Bond investors should find the risk factors sensible. Risk analysis results should be precise, but still conform to investor instincts. A good risk model should actually simplify the investment process, quantify risks, and increase investor insight.

Fixed income risk modeling plays a critical role in bond portfolio management, benchmark tracking, immunization, active strategy implementation, and performance measurement and analysis. Benchmark tracking involves comparing the risk exposures of an investment portfolio and a benchmark. Matching those exposures should lead to investment returns that accurately track benchmark returns. Immunization involves comparing the risk exposures of a portfolio and a liability stream. Matching those exposures should immunize the portfolio's liability coverage against market changes. Active strategies involve deliberate risk exposures relative to a benchmark, aimed at exceeding benchmark returns. Performance measurement and analysis involves identifying active bets and studying their past performance so as to measure bond manager skill.

This chapter describes a multifactor approach to risk modeling. This approach consists of two basic components. First, a valuation model identifies and values the many risk factors in the market. The valuation model requires the machinery to estimate exposures to these risk factors, including an option simulation to handle the wide variety of optionable fixed income securities. Second, a risk model examines the historical behavior of these risk factors to estimate their variances and covariances. The presentation here will be general, but this chapter will conclude with evidence of the performance of multifactor risk models based on their specific application to the U.S. bond market.[1]

## THE VALUATION MODEL

The following multifactor valuation model is designed to identify and value risk factors in the market. This model estimates bond prices as

$$PM_n(t) = \sum_T \frac{cf_n(T) \cdot PDB(t, T)}{\exp[\kappa_n(t) \cdot T]} + \xi_n(t) \qquad (36\text{--}1)$$

$$= PF_n(t) + \xi_n(t) \qquad (36\text{--}2)$$

with

$$\kappa_n(t) = \sum_j x_{n,j} \cdot s_j(t) \qquad (36\text{--}3)$$

where

$PM_n(t)$ = bond $n$ market price at time $t$
$Pf_n(t)$ = bond $n$ fitted price at time $t$

---

1. For a more detailed description of this application to the U.S. bond market, see Ronald N. Kahn, "Risk and Return in the U.S. Bond Market: A Multifactor Approach," in *Advances and Innovations in the Bond and Mortgage Markets,* ed. Frank J. Fabozzi (Chicago: Probus Publishing, 1989).

$$\text{cf}_n(T) = \text{bond } n \text{ option-adjusted cash flow at time } T$$
$$\text{PDB}(t, T) = \text{price at } t \text{ of default-free pure discount bond maturing at } T$$
$$x_{n,j} = \text{bond } n \text{ exposure to factor } j$$
$$s_j(t) = \text{yield spread due to factor } j \text{ at time } t$$
$$\xi_n(t) = \text{bond } n \text{ price error at time } t$$
$$\kappa_n(t) = \text{bond } n \text{ total yield spread at time } t$$

The characteristics of the market as a whole are the term structure, represented here by the default-free pure discount bond prices $\text{PDB}(t, T)$, and the marketwide factor yield spreads $s_j(t)$. The bond-specific exposures include the option-adjusted cash flows $\text{cf}_n(T)$ and the exposures $x_{n,j}$. These depend upon any call or put options or sinking-fund provisions embedded in bond $n$. The final bond-specific component of this model is the price error $\xi_n(t)$. This model clearly enumerates how a bond's total exposure to the various factors determines its price. The estimated values [$\text{PDB}(t, T)$, $s_j(t)$, $\xi_n(t)$] result from fitting this model to actual trading prices at time $t$.[2] All these values change unpredictably over time.

The yield-spread factors $s_j$ correspond to the nonterm-structure sources of risk and return identified by the model. Most of these are sources of default risk. For example, each corporate bond sector might have its own yield spread, measuring the default risk common to all AAA-rated members of the sector. Each quality rating would also have its own yield spread, measuring the additional default risk common to issues rated lower than AAA.

Beyond the factors that measure default risk, there are other factors that capture risk and return in bond markets. Benchmark factors measure the uncertain liquidity premiums afforded heavily traded issues. A current-yield factor measures the market's assessment at time $t$ of the advantage of receiving return in the form of capital gains instead of interest, providing a possible tax advantage. A perpetual factor, appearing in markets containing perpetual bonds, measures the market's assessment at time $t$ of the advantage or disadvantage of owning perpetual bonds.

Observed corporate bond yield spreads tend to increase with maturity, quantifying the market's perception of the increase in default risk over time. For investors, any change in the dependence of spreads upon maturity constitutes a source of return risk. Because these spreads appear to increase linearly with duration, a duration spread can measure the extent of this increase with duration at any given time. A risk model can then measure how this dependence changes over time.

So far, this analysis has concentrated on the estimated marketwide factors of value. Estimates of these factors rely on option-adjusted cash flows, however.

---

2. For more details, see Ronald N. Kahn, "Estimating the U.S. Treasury Term Structure of Interest Rates," in *The Handbook of U.S. Treasury and Government Agency Securities: Instruments, Strategies and Analysis,* Revised Edition, ed. Frank J. Fabozzi (Chicago: Probus Publishing, 1990).

Hence, the next section will describe the option adjustment procedure in more detail.

## Option Adjustments

Estimating the values [PDB($t$, $T$), $s_j(t)$, $\xi_n(t)$] requires market prices, cash flows, and yield-spread factor exposures. However, because embedded options alter the nominal cash flows, the final step in the valuation model involves adjusting the nominal bond cash flows accordingly.

Bonds can include call and put options and sinking-fund provisions. Mortgage-backed securities include prepayment options. These securities are portfolios containing a nonoptionable security and an option. For callable and sinkable bonds and mortgages, the issuer retains the option, and so the portfolio is long a nonoptionable security and short the option:

$$\text{Optionable bond} = \text{Nonoptionable bond} - \text{Option} \qquad (36\text{–}4)$$

and

$$PF_n(t) = PFN_n(t) - PFO_n(t) \qquad (36\text{–}5)$$

where

$PFN_n$ = bond $n$ nominal fitted price
$PFO_n$ = bond $n$ option fitted price

For putable bonds, the purchaser owns the put option, so the portfolio is long both the nonoptionable security and the option.

Viewed in this portfolio framework, the key aspect of option adjustment involves modeling the embedded option. A detailed description of option modeling is beyond the scope of this chapter, but basically it is a three-step procedure.

First, choose a model that describes the stochastic evolution of future interest rates. This model will describe the drift and, more importantly, the interest rate volatility, of either the short interest rate or the entire term structure. It will describe a set of possible future interest-rate paths.

Second, impose a no-arbitrage condition to fairly price bonds of different maturities. This step will determine the probability weight, for valuation purposes, of each possible future interest-rate path and generate a current set of bond prices. A properly tuned model will generate prices consistent with observed bond prices.

Third, impose relevant option decision rules to apply the model to the particular option of interest. These decision rules will depend on the specific option covenants as well as the behavioral model governing the corporation or the individual mortgage holder. Imposing these rules will lead to estimated cash flows and a price for the option. The portfolio property described in Equation (36–4) dictates how the option cash flows adjust the optionable bond cash flows.

## Option Adjustment Example[3]

To see this work in practice, consider a simple example of a callable zero-coupon bond. The bond nominally pays $V$ dollars at maturity $M$:

$$\text{PFN}_n(t) = V \cdot \text{PDB}(t, M) \tag{36-6}$$

However, the traded security includes an embedded option for the issuer to call the bond at strike price $K$ and time $T$, with $t < T < M$. The option model estimates the call option value as

$$\text{PFO}_n(t) = -K \cdot Y \cdot \text{PDB}(t, T) + V \cdot X \cdot \text{PDB}(t, M) \tag{36-7}$$

where $X$ and $Y$ are cumulative distribution functions.[4] Equation (36–7) resembles the Black–Scholes stock option formula,[5] although $X$ and $Y$ are not necessarily cumulative normal distributions. They do, however, act as probabilities and range between zero and one.

Now consider the interpretation of Equation (36–7): The option involves paying the amount $KY$ at time $T$, to receive $VX$ at the later time $M$. With this interpretation, and with the portfolio property (Equation 36–4), the adjusted price and cash flows for the callable security are

$$\text{PF}_n(t) = V \cdot \text{PDB}(t, M) - [-K \cdot Y \cdot \text{PDB}(t, T)$$

$$+ V \cdot X \cdot \text{PDB}(t, M)]$$

$$= K \cdot Y \cdot \text{PDB}(t, T) + V \cdot (1 - X) \cdot \text{PDB}(t, M) \tag{36-8}$$

$$\text{cf}_n(T) = K \cdot Y \tag{36-9}$$

$$\text{cf}_n(M) = V \cdot [1 - X] \tag{36-10}$$

As Equations (36–9) and (36–10) show, the probabilities $X$ and $Y$ adjust the nominal cash flows. An out-of-the-money option has $X$, $Y$, and PFO all equal to zero, and the option-adjusted cash flows reduce to the nominal cash flows. For this callable bond example, as $X$ and $Y$ increase, the option will shorten the nominal cash flows. More complicated options involve more cash flows (a set of $T_1, \ldots, T_N$), more probabilities, and perhaps even more complicated numerical procedures to estimate the probabilities; but, in principle, the adjustment procedure is the same.

Remember that the true option-adjusted cash flows are still not certain. The option model chooses cash flows $-KY$ and $VX$ to replicate the value and duration of the modeled security. Unfortunately, it is impossible to choose these

---

3. This section covers more details of the option adjustment process for the benefit of mathematically inclined readers.

4. These cumulative distribution functions correspond to the valuation probability—the martingale probability associated with the stochastic interest-rate model.

5. Fischer Black and Myron Scholes, "The Pricing of Options and Corporate Liabilities," *Journal of Political Economy,* May–June 1973.

cash flows to also replicate the convexity of the modeled security. The discrepancy between the convexity of the modeled security and the convexity of the replicating cash flow—the "excess convexity" of the option—is greatest when the option is at-the-money and approaches zero elsewhere. Fortunately, this discrepancy affects risk modeling only in second order, at worst—it affects only convexity, not duration. An additional yield-spread factor—an additional $s_j$—can account for the discrepancy.

Given a procedure for estimating these option-adjusted cash flows at time $t$, a set of market prices at time $t$ will lead to estimates of $\text{PDB}(t, T)$ and $s_j(t)$, according to a procedure designed to minimize overall pricing error. The historical behavior of these market variables will then lead to the risk model itself.

## THE RISK MODEL

Bond prices change over time in response to three general phenomena: shortening bond maturities, shifting term structures, and changing yield spreads. Bonds are risky because the last two phenomena are uncertain. The core of a bond risk model is, therefore, an estimate of the variances and covariances of the term structure and the yield-spread factor excess returns. The next two sections describe how to estimate these marketwide factor excess returns, and a third section describes how to estimate bond-specific risk.

## Term-Structure Factor Returns

Building the risk model requires a history of the behavior of all relevant market factors, which the valuation model provides. How exactly does this work? Consider first the term-structure risk factors: the default-free pure discount bond prices. The price $\text{PDB}(t, T)$ represents the price at time $t$ of $1.00$ paid at time $T$. The return to this factor between $t - \Delta t$ and $t$ is the return to the following strategy:

> Invest $1.00 at time $t - \Delta t$ in $\text{PDB}(t - \Delta t, T)$, a default-free pure discount bond. This bond has a maturity of $T - (t - \Delta t)$. Hold for a period $\Delta t$. Then sell the bond, now with a maturity $T - t$, for price $\text{PDB}(t, T)$.

The excess return to this factor follows by subtracting the risk-free rate of return. This risk-free rate is the return to the strategy:

> Invest $1.00 at time $t - \Delta t$ in the default-free pure discount bond $\text{PDB}(t - \Delta t, t)$ maturing at time $t$. This bond has a maturity of $\Delta t$. Hold for a period $\Delta t$. Then redeem the bond, which has now matured.

The fixed holding period $\Delta t$ is a defining constant of the risk model.

## Yield-Spread Factor Returns

Now consider the returns associated with the yield-spread factors. The excess return to factor $j$ at time $t$ is the return to the following artificial strategy:

> Invest \$1.00 at time $t - \Delta t$ in a portfolio exposed only to factor $j$ and to term-structure risk. The portfolio duration is set to the average market duration over the risk model history. Hold for a period $\Delta t$, *and roll down the term structure over this period.* Sell the portfolio at time $t$.

This strategy is artificial because it assumes a fixed term structure. The excess return to this strategy is the change in yield spread $s_j$ over the holding period, multiplied by the average bond market duration, plus the yield spread multiplied by the holding period $\Delta t$. Duration, the fractional change in price accompanying a change in yield, enters into this formula to convert a change in yield spread into a price return.

## Specific Return

Beyond the general, marketwide sources of risk discussed, individual issues also face specific risk. Factors that influence only one particular issue, or only the bonds of a particular company, generate specific risk and return. For example, LBO event risk constitutes a source of specific risk.[6] In the context of the risk model, specific returns arise because the bond pricing error $\xi_n(t)$ can change randomly over time.

The specific return to bond $n$ at time $t$ is the return to the following strategy:

> Invest \$1.00 at time $t - \Delta t$ in a portfolio long bond $n$, but with all marketwide sources of risk hedged. Hold for a period $\Delta t$, and then sell. The difference in pricing error will generate the specific return $[\xi_n(t) - \xi_n(t - \Delta t)]/[PM_n(t - \Delta t)]$.

The distinction between marketwide sources of risk and specific risk is important because investors can hedge marketwide sources of risk through other instruments exposed to those same risk sources. Specific risk is uncorrelated with marketwide risk.[7]

## Integration

A multifactor risk model identifies the risk factors operating in a given market and then estimates their risk. Each factor generates excess returns over the

---

6. Ronald N. Kahn, "LBO Event Risk," in *Managing Institutional Assets,* ed. Frank J. Fabozzi (New York: Ballinger, 1990).
7. The specific risk of two different issues may be correlated, for example, if one company issued them both.

model's estimation period. The risk model analyzes those return histories to forecast their variances and covariances.

Several difficult questions arise during the course of this analysis. What historical estimation period works best for covariance forecasting? Is covariance stable over time, or does it cycle or trend? These basic questions remain the subject of continual debate.

One particular question about forecasting bond market covariance concerns whether or not covariance depends on the level of rates. Does bond market risk increase as rates increase? Is volatility higher when rates are 16% than when rates are 8%? Academics have speculated that the answer is yes, and historical investigation confirms it for the U.S. bond market.

John Cox, Jonathan Ingersoll, and Stephen Ross[8] have developed a widely accepted model of the term structure, which prices bonds and bond options based on equilibrium arguments. Their model posits the stochastic evolution of the term structure, with interest-rate standard deviation and bond return standard deviation both proportional to the square root of the level of rates. When rates double from 8% to 16%, volatility rises by a factor of 1.4: the square root of 2.0.

Historical investigation can probe the dependence of bond market risk on the level of rates. Exhibit 36–1 illustrates the results of a test comparing the

## EXHIBIT 36–1

Risk versus Level of Rates

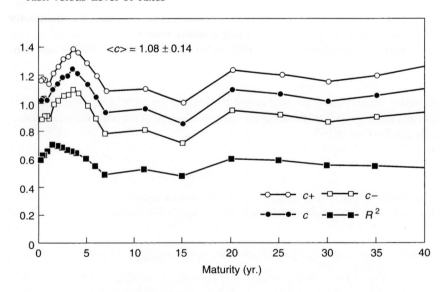

standard deviation of monthly pure discount bond excess returns each year from 1948 to 1988, to the mean five-year spot rate observed each year. This test determined the exponent $c$ of the relationship

$$\text{volatility} \propto (\text{rate})^c$$

If $c = 1$, then volatility is directly proportional to rates; when rates double, volatility doubles. The Cox, Ingersoll, Ross model assumes that $c = \frac{1}{2}$. The empirical results illustrated in Exhibit 36–1 demonstrate that $c = 1.08 \pm 0.14$. Within the standard errors shown in Exhibit 36–1, volatility is directly proportional to rate level. Moreover, as the $R^2$ statistic reveals, the level of rates explains 61% of the observed difference in risk from year to year. The effect is more pronounced in high-rate periods than in low-rate periods. Further study examined the dependence of yield-spread factor risk on the level of the five-year spot rate. Results were mixed, though generally consistent with direct proportionality.

Given the broad empirical and theoretical evidence supporting the dependence of covariance upon rates, forecasts of covariance based on historical data should take this effect into account.

With all this sophisticated risk model machinery now in place and integrated, how well does the resulting risk model perform?

## PERFORMANCE

Multifactor risk modeling involves significant effort. Is this effort justified? Does it significantly differ from the duration approach? How well does the multifactor approach to fixed income risk modeling actually work?

To see how the multifactor approach differs from the duration and convexity approach, consider the performance of a multifactor model in the U.S. bond market. Remember that duration and convexity are both parallel yield-shift concepts. They measure the risk of parallel yield shifts. However, the term structure does not move in parallel.

The risk model views the term structure as a set of pure discount bonds of different maturities, each allowed to move independently. The covariance matrix then describes the extent to which they actually do move together. Exhibits 36–2 and 36–3 illustrate the two predominant, coherent movements of the term structure, as forecast in September 1989 based on the observed term-structure history throughout the 1980s. These *principal components* are the independent, uncorrelated collective movements of the term structure. Exhibit 36–2 illustrates the primary term-structure movement: a nonparallel shift, with short rates more volatile than long rates. A duration-based risk model would assume that a parallel shift completely specified term-structure risk. This nonparallel shift accounts for 95.4% of modeled term-structure risk. Exhibit 36–3 illustrates the secondary term-structure movement: a twist, with short and long rates moving in opposite directions. This twist accounts for an additional 4.1%

**EXHIBIT 36-2**

First Principal Component

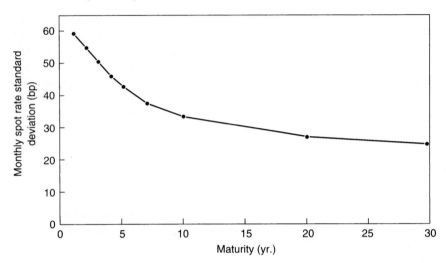

**EXHIBIT 36-3**

Second Principal Component

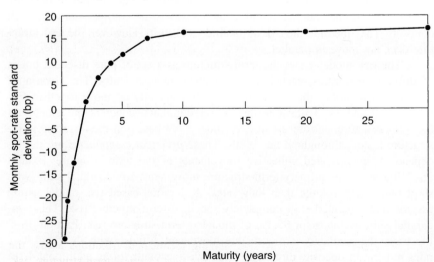

of modeled term-structure risk. These shapes specifically apply to the September 1989 forecast, but they have remained relatively stable from the 1950s into the 1990s, taking the level of rates into account.

To further examine how well multifactor risk modeling performs, the following test compared a simple duration model and a duration plus convexity model with a 10-factor model (pure discount bonds with maturities of 0.25, 0.5, 1, 2, 3, 4, 5, 6, 7, 10, and 30 years) in modeling noncallable U.S. Treasury security returns between January 1980 and October 1986. The noncallable U.S. Treasury market should be the simplest market to model because it requires no factors to account for default risk and no option simulation model. For demonstrating the significant enhancement resulting from the multifactor approach, this is the most difficult test. The results are as follows:

| Model | Number of Factors | Percent of Explained Variance |
|---|---|---|
| Duration | 1 | 75.8 |
| Duration and convexity | 2 | 81.1 |
| First principal components | 1 | 82.4 |
| First two principal components | 2 | 87.0 |
| Full multifactor model | 10 | 88.0 |

The full multifactor model explains significantly more of the observed variance than the simple duration model or even the duration and convexity model. The first two principal components are the optimized first two risk factors. The first principal component model employs just one factor, a nonparallel shift, and outperforms the two-factor duration and convexity model. Of course, one must construct the full multifactor risk model to identify this optimal one-factor model.

This chapter so far has described the construction of a risk model and a test of its overall performance measuring fixed income risk. How, though, does the risk model apply to a particular investment portfolio?

## PORTFOLIO RISK CHARACTERIZATION

Historical analysis captures the inherent riskiness of the factors of value present in the bond market. The riskiness of a particular bond portfolio depends upon its exposure to these sources of risk.

The fraction of a portfolio's present value at each vertex measures the portfolio's exposure to term-structure risk. Two portfolios with identical distributions of present value along the vertices face identical term-structure risk. Of course, these two portfolios have identical durations. However, two portfolios can have identical durations without having identical distributions across the entire set of vertices. Such portfolios will not face identical term-structure risk.

What about yield-spread factor risk? Consider for example the risk associated with the sector yield spread. The fraction of the portfolio in each sector, multiplied by the duration of the bonds in that sector compared to bond market average duration, measures the portfolio's sector risk exposure. Risk exposures for quality factors and other factors follow analogously.

Beyond the marketwide factors of value the model identifies, there are also risk factors associated solely with individual issues. By definition, the specific risk for each issue is uncorrelated with all marketwide factor risk. It may be correlated, though, with the specific risk of other bonds of the same issuer. We can estimate this specific issue risk historically as the realized excess return risk of each specific issue not explained by the model.

Total risk follows from combining the risk exposures that characterize a given portfolio with the variances and covariances of the underlying risk factors that characterize the market, and adding in specific issue risk. This number is the predicted total variance of the portfolio excess return.

Portfolio risk analysis usually involves comparing the portfolio against a benchmark (or liability stream). Comparing risk exposures will quantify the manager's bets in relation to the benchmark. The risk model can then predict how well the portfolio will track the benchmark. For active managers, an optimizer can implement common factor and specific issue bets while still controlling risk. An active manager's utility will usually increase with expected excess return and decrease with expected tracking error. An optimizer can maximize this utility.

## SUMMARY

Today's fixed income markets are characterized by complex instruments and increased volatility. In this environment, bond portfolio management must increasingly rely on sophisticated models to accurately gauge fixed income risk. Building these models requires considerable sophistication. Using them, however, should be straightforward. A good model should simplify the investment process and increase investor insight.

CHAPTER **37**

# OAS AND EFFECTIVE DURATION

**David Audley***
Chief Operating Officer
Research Technology
Merrill Lynch

**Richard Chin***
Fixed-Income Research
Goldman Sachs & Co.

**Shrikant Ramamurthy**
Senior Vice President
Fixed-Income Research
Prudential Securities, Inc.

Bonds with embedded options have uncertain maturities because the decision to exercise the option generally depends on the relationship between the level of interest rates, the exercise price of the option, and the market price of the security. Issuers of callable debt will tend to call their bonds when rates have fallen sufficiently to justify refinancing outstanding debt. However, the exact timing for the exercise of the call option is not always known because the nature of the American-style option allows issuers to exercise their call at any time between the first call date and the final maturity date. This option type is prevalent among corporate, agency, and Treasury securities. The maturities of bonds with embedded put options are known with slightly more certainty because investors will either redeem the bonds on the put date or hold them to final maturity (assuming that there are no other embedded options in addition to the one put option).

The presence of an embedded option complicates the bond-valuation process because the bond's maturity date is uncertain. It is not always clear whether the bond should be analyzed according to its final maturity, first call or put date, or par call date, for example. Consider a 30-year callable utility bond with 5

---

* This chapter was written when David Audley and Richard Chin were employed by Prudential Securities.

years of call protection and a given level of interest-rate volatility. From a price-sensitivity standpoint, does the bond behave more like a 30-year bond, a five-year bond, or an intermediate-maturity bond? From a compensation standpoint, are the yield spread and option-adjusted spread (OAS) commensurate with the level of interest-rate risk? The ability to quantify the price sensitivity of a particular bond is a necessary step in gauging the risk/reward trade-offs inherent in any one bond. Furthermore, the hedging of such bonds requires having the means to calculate a bond's price sensitivity to changes in interest rates.[1]

For a bond with a defined set of cash flows, such as a bullet bond, the price/yield relationship is well understood. Consequently, the bullet bond's modified duration may be calculated easily because the amount and timing of all the cash flows are known with certainty. In this chapter, we will illustrate how the effective duration of an option-embedded bond is simply an extension of the already familiar concept used for bullet bonds. Additionally, the chapter discusses why OAS and effective duration by themselves may not provide sufficient information to completely judge the relative value between two securities.

## THE PRICE/YIELD RELATIONSHIP FOR OPTION-EMBEDDED BONDS

As a starting point in the conceptual analysis of option-embedded bonds, consider the effect an embedded option has on a bond's maturity in the case of extreme interest-rate movements. If interest rates move to either very high or very low levels, the embedded option very likely will or will not be exercised (depending on whether the option is a call or a put) and, therefore, the maturity of a bond should be known with relative certainty. For example, if long-term Treasury rates drop to 2% and stay at that level, callable-bond issuers will probably exercise their options at the earliest possible date, whereas putable bonds will remain outstanding to final maturity as holders will not exercise their put option. On the other hand, if Treasury rates rise to 25% and remain at that level, putable-bond holders will exercise their options as quickly as possible in order to reinvest the proceeds at higher interest rates, whereas callable bonds will remain outstanding until final maturity because issuers will not exercise their call option. These extreme interest-rate-movement scenarios illustrate that the maturity range of most option-embedded bonds is bound by the first option-exercise date and the final maturity date. Because interest-rate movements generally are milder than those described above, the maturity of an option-embedded bond usually lies somewhere between the first option-exercise date and the final maturity date. Therefore, the price sensitivity of an option-embedded bond lies somewhere between that of a bond priced to final maturity and that of a bond priced to the earliest exercise date.

---

1. See Chapter 56.

The following sections describe how the price/yield behavior of a bond with an embedded put or call option may be visualized in relation to the price/yield sensitivities of bonds at either end of the maturity boundaries. We will then extend the analysis to encompass put/call parity, which is helpful in understanding the effects of price/yield sensitivity on duration and OAS. As we will see, the put/call parity relationship inherent in option-embedded bonds is key to understanding the effects of interest-rate volatility on the duration and yield of option-embedded bonds.

## The Price/Yield Relationship of Callable Bonds

A callable bond may be viewed as a portfolio consisting of two positions: a long position in an underlying noncallable bond and a short position in a call option. This relationship is illustrated in the following pricing equation:

$$\text{Callable bond} = \text{Underlying bond} - \text{Call option} \qquad (37-1)$$

From the equation, we can see that if interest rates fall, the price of the underlying bond increases as if it were a bullet bond. However, the magnitude of the overall price increase for the callable bond is limited by a corresponding increase in the value of the call option. If interest rates fall very far, the callable bond's price appreciation will be limited to that of a short-term bond with a maturity that is approximately equal to the option-exercise date.

Exhibit 37–1 shows how the price of a 10-year bond with 3 years of call protection is affected by changes in interest rates. For this bond, the longest possible maturity is the 10-year final maturity and the shortest term to maturity is 3 years, the earliest option-exercise date. Therefore, Exhibit 37–1 also shows price/yield curves for three- and 10-year bullet bonds. At very high yield levels, the callable bond's price/yield curve approaches that of the 10-year bullet bond. This is because the call option's value decreases as interest rates move higher and higher. As the value of the option declines, the price behavior of the callable bond increasingly resembles that of the bullet bond with the same final maturity date as the callable bond. Conversely, if interest rates fall, the callable bond's price/yield curve becomes more like that of the three-year bullet bond because the likelihood of option exercise increases.

## Effect of Volatility on Callable-Bond Pricing

Exhibit 37–1 also indicates that the callable bond's price behavior is a function of interest-rate volatility. As volatility increases from 10% to 20%, the call option's value increases and the price of the callable bond correspondingly decreases. Thus the callable bond's price/yield curve at 20% volatility lies below the bond's price/yield curve at 10% volatility, reflecting a greater degree of negative convexity at the higher volatility levels.

**EXHIBIT 37-1**

Price Behavior of Hypothetical 10-Year Callable Bond with 3 Years of Call
Protection

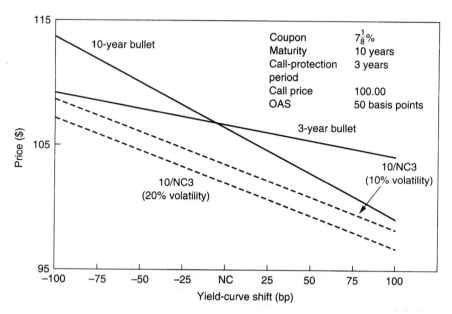

At any given yield level, the vertical distance between the price/yield
curves of the callable bond and the underlying noncallable 10-year bond is a
reflection of the value of the call option. As volatility increases, the option value
also increases, as indicated by the increasing distance between the price/yield
curves.

## The Price/Yield Relationship of Putable Bonds

A putable bond may be viewed as a portfolio of a long position in an underlying
noncallable bond plus a long position in a put option, as shown in the following
relationship:[2]

$$\text{Putable bond} = \text{Underlying bond} + \text{Put option} \qquad (37\text{--}2)$$

The equation illustrates that if interest rates rise, the price of the underlying
bond decreases, but the magnitude of the overall price decrease of the put bond
itself is mitigated by an increase in the value of the put option. If interest rates

---

2. See David Audley and Richard Chin, *Bonds with Embedded Put Options* (New York: Financial
   Strategies Group, Prudential Securities Incorporated, December 1990).

rise sharply, then the price depreciation of the putable bond will be limited to that of a short-term bond maturing on the putable bond's exercise date. Thus the put option cushions the putable-bond holder's downside risk.

Exhibit 37–2 shows the analogous price/yield curves of a 10-year bond with a put option that may be exercised in 3 years at two different levels of interest-rate volatility (10% and 20%). The price/yield curves for the associated three- and 10-year bullet bonds also are shown. As yields increase, the price/yield curve for the putable bond approaches that of the three-year bullet bond due to the growing likelihood of option exercise. Conversely, if interest rates fall, then the price/yield curve of the putable bond approaches that of the 10-year bullet because the economic incentive to exercise the put option decreases.

## Effect of Volatility on Putable-Bond Pricing

As with a callable bond, the shape and level of the price/yield curve for a putable bond is a function of interest-rate volatility. Exhibit 37–2 shows that as volatility increases, the option value increases and, consequently, the price of the putable bond increases. Thus the putable bond's price/yield curve at the 20% volatility level lies above the bond's price/yield curve at 10% volatility.

**E X H I B I T   37–2**

Price Behavior of Hypothetical 10-Year Putable Bond with Put Exercisable in 3 Years

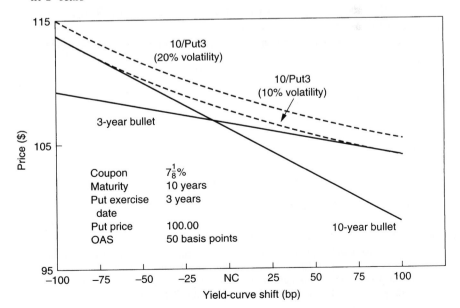

The next section expands on the concept of viewing option-embedded bonds as portfolios of bonds and options by reviewing the concept of put/call parity. Put/call parity is helpful in further understanding the price/yield relationship and relative valuation of option-embedded bonds.

## Put/Call Parity

Put/call parity is an important relationship in option-pricing theory that relates the price of a put option to the price of a call option. As applied to option-embedded bonds, the relationship illustrates that a position in either a callable bond or a putable bond may be viewed in two equivalent ways.[3] We will examine a callable bond first, and then a putable bond.

A callable bond may be viewed as a portfolio consisting of a long position in a bond and a short position in an option (notice that we did not specify the type of option).

For example, a 10-year callable bond with 3 years of call protection may be viewed as a portfolio consisting of a long position in a 10-year bullet bond and a short position in a call option exercisable by the issuer in 3 years. Under the principles of put/call parity, the same callable-bond position may be viewed as a long position in a three-year bullet bond and a short position in a put option, where the issuer has the right to put a seven-year bullet bond to the investor in 3 years. Equation (37–3) reflects the duality of the option embedded in a callable bond.

Long-maturity bullet bond − Call option

$$= \text{Short-maturity bullet bond} - \text{Put option} \quad (37\text{–}3)$$

Similarly, a putable bond may be viewed as a portfolio consisting of a long position in a bullet bond and a long position in an option (notice again that we did not specify the type of option).

For example, a 10-year bond with a put option exercisable in 3 years may be viewed as a portfolio consisting of a long position in a 10-year bullet bond and a long position in a put exercisable in 3 years. (This pricing concept is similar to the one we introduced in the section on price/yield relationships of putable bonds.) Alternatively, the same putable bond may be viewed as a portfolio of a long position in a three-year bullet bond and a long position in a call option that gives the bondholder the right to call a seven-year bullet bond away from the issuer. This pricing relationship is shown in Eq. (37–4).

---

3. See David Audley and Richard Chin, *The Internal Consistency of Option Valuation Models: The Validation of Put/Call Parity* (New York: Financial Strategies Group, Prudential Securities Incorporated, September 11, 1990).

Long-maturity bullet bond + Put option

$$= \text{Short-maturity bullet bond} - \text{Call option} \quad (37-4)$$

Note that Eq. (37–4) may be derived by rearranging Eq. (37–3), which simply reflects the change from a short option position in a callable bond to a long option position in a putable bond.

## EFFECTIVE DURATION

The objective of effective duration is to quantify an option-embedded bond's price sensitivity to changes in interest rates. If we calculate a security's price for a small change in interest rates (e.g., plus or minus 25 basis points), then the percentage change in price for this specified change in rates represents the bond's effective duration.

## Effective-Duration Calculations

An OAS model calculates the value of an option-adjusted spread for a given market price for a security. For small parallel shifts in the yield curve, the prices that correspond to the same OAS are the security's constant-OAS prices.[4] The effective duration is then found from the expression shown in Eq. 37–5.

$$\text{Effective duration} = \frac{10,000}{\text{Price} + \text{Accrued}} \times \frac{(\text{Price up} - \text{Price down})}{(\text{Total shift in yield curve})} \quad (37-5)$$

where

        Price = Market price of security
  Accrued = Accrued interest
  Price up = Constant-OAS security price for downward yield-curve shift
Price down = Constant-OAS security price for upward yield-curve shift
 Total shift = Total range of yield-curve shift (in basis points)

Exhibit 37–3 shows the computation of effective duration.

## Effective Duration of Callable Bonds

Just as the slope of the tangent line to a bullet bond's price/yield curve is a measure of the bond's modified duration, the slope of the tangent line to a callable bond's price/yield curve is a measure of the callable bond's effective

---

4. See David Audley and Richard Chin, *Constant QAS Analysis* (New York: Financial Strategies Group, Prudential Securities Incorporated, May 14, 1990).

**EXHIBIT   37–3**

Effective Duration of FHLMC 7⅝ of 9/9/09 Callable at Par from 9/9/02[a]

| Issuer | FHLMC |
|---|---|
| Coupon | 7.65% |
| Maturity | 9/9/09 |
| Call date | 9/9/02 |
| Call price | 100.000 |
| Price | 99.689 |
| Accrued interest | 0.000 |
| Yield | 7.67 |
| OAS | 89 basis points |

Effective duration using yield-curve shift

$$= \frac{10,000}{Price + Accrued} \times \frac{Price\ up - Price\ down}{Total\ shift\ in\ yield\ curve}$$

$$= \frac{10,000}{99.689} \times \frac{100.862 - 98.522}{50}$$

$$= 4.69$$

[a]Price as of September 2, 1999
Source: Prudential securities

(modified) duration. Exhibit 37–4 illustrates that the slope of the line tangent to the callable bond's price/yield curve (Tangent Line A) is between that of the two reference noncallable bonds. This indicates that a callable bond's effective duration is bounded by the modified durations of the noncallable bonds. As interest rates either move up or down, the slope of Tangent Line A correspondingly approaches that of the appropriate noncallable bond.

### The Effect of Selling Call Options on Duration

Equation 37–1 illustrates how a change in interest rates affects the duration of a callable bond. If the 10-year callable bond in Exhibit 37–4 is viewed as a portfolio of a long position in a 10-year bullet bond and a short position in a call option exercisable in 3 years, the decreasing slope of Tangent Line A as interest rates fall shows that selling a call option decreases a portfolio's duration. Conversely, when rates rise, the call option is not exercised so that, in effect, the option holder (the issuer) has elected to put the bond to the bondholder. In this case, the increasing slope of Tangent Line A indicates that selling a put option increases the portfolio's duration when rates rise. In either case of extreme interest-rate movements (plus or minus 100 basis points in Exhibit 37–4), the duration of the portfolio changes in a way that is adverse to the seller of the

**EXHIBIT   37–4**

Effective Duration of Hypothetical 10-Year Callable Bond with 3 Years of Call Protection

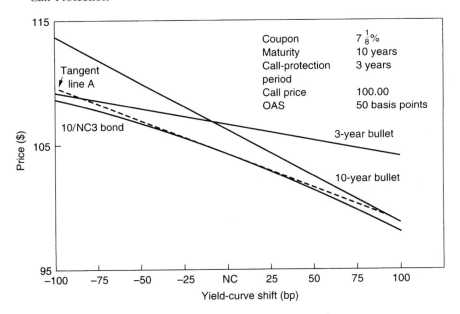

option (the investor). Hence, the portfolio (i.e., the callable bond) is negatively convex.

## Effective Duration of Put Bonds

Exhibit 37–5 illustrates that the slope of Tangent Line A, which is tangent to the putable bond's price/yield curve, also falls between the slopes of curves of the two underlying bullet bonds. Thus, the putable bond's effective duration lies between the durations of the reference bullet bonds. This indicates that, although a putable bond may be priced to the put date, its effective duration is at least as high as that of the comparable bullet bond maturing on or near the put date.

### The Effect of Buying Put Options on Duration

Similar to callable bonds, the effect of interest-rate changes on a putable bond's duration is illustrated by the relationship shown in Eq. 37–2. If the 10-year putable bond shown in Exhibit 37–5 is viewed as a portfolio consisting of a long position in a 10-year bullet bond plus a long position in a put option exercisable in 3 years, the decreasing slope of Tangent Line A when interest rates rise shows that buying a put option decreases a portfolio's duration. Con-

**EXHIBIT 37–5**

Effective Duration of Hypothetical 10-Year Putable Bond with Put
Exercisable in 3 Years

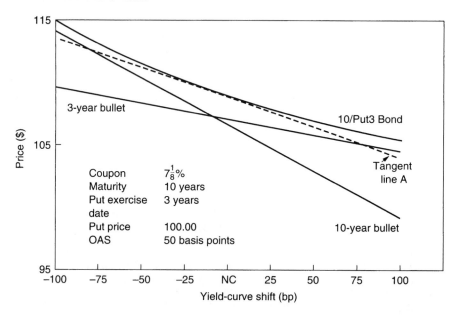

versely, when rates fall, the put option is not exercised, so the holder of the
option (the bondholder) has essentially elected to call the bond. In this case, the
increasing slope of Tangent Line A indicates that purchasing a call option increases the portfolio's duration when rates drop. In either case of extreme
interest-rate movements, the duration of the portfolio changes in a way that
benefits the holder of the option (the investor). Thus the portfolio (i.e., the
putable bond) is positively convex.

## EFFECTIVE MATURITY

Once the effective duration of an option-embedded bond is calculated, it is
possible to construct a bullet bond with a modified duration equal to the effective
duration of the option-embedded bond. This allows an option-embedded bond's
price sensitivity to be expressed in terms of properties that are well understood
for bullet bonds. The option-embedded bond's *effective maturity* is stated in
terms of the maturity of the duration-matched bullet with the same coupon payments and payment dates.[5] Furthermore, if the option-embedded bond has a

---

5. The effective maturity date is found by an iterative process in which the maturity date of the
   duration-matched bullet bond is varied until the modified duration of this bullet bond is equal
   to the original bond's effective duration.

premium call schedule that declines to par over time, then the bullet bond's redemption value on the effective maturity date is equal to the call option's exercise price.

For example, a par-priced, 10-year bond that is callable for the last 7 years at par may have the price sensitivity of a seven-year bullet bond even though the original bond is priced relative to the 10-year Treasury note. Thus the effective maturity of this callable bond is 7 years. Bonds that are more likely to be called, perhaps due to a higher coupon or to an earlier call date, may have shorter effective maturities than bonds that are less likely to be called. Conversely, high- coupon, premium-priced putable bonds, whose put options are less likely to be exercised, may have longer effective maturities than bonds that are more likely to be put, such as deep-discount bonds.[6]

Exhibit 37–6 compares the price/yield curves of a 10-year callable bond with 3 years of call protection and its duration-matched bullet bond. For relatively small changes in interest rates, the price/yield curves are very close to

### EXHIBIT 37–6

Price/Yield-Curve Comparison of Hypothetical 10/NC3 Bond and Its Duration-Matched Bullet Bond

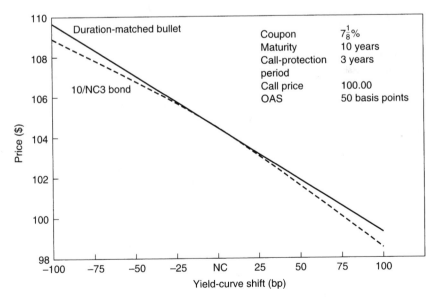

---

6. Although the calculation of effective maturity takes into account the range of possible interest rates in the future, the effective maturity does not strictly equal the expected maturity, which is the probability-weighted maturity. In contrast, the effective maturity is the maturity of the duration-matched bullet.

one another. For larger interest-rate movements, the two price/yield curves begin to diverge as the callable bond's negative convexity begins to dominate.

Exhibit 37–7 displays the effective maturities of a hypothetical 10-year bond, callable at par in 3 years, at two different yield volatilities. Because the value of the call option generally increases with higher volatilities, the negatively convex nature of callable securities is more apparent at 20% volatility than at 10% volatility, as shown by its lower effective maturities. Note, however, that there is a combination of interest-rate shifts and volatilities in which the two effective maturity plots cross each other. This occurs at lower interest-rate levels and reflects the situation in which a higher interest-rate volatility actually increases the likelihood that rates may increase.

## OPTION-ADJUSTED SPREADS

Up to this point, our discussion has centered on using a bond's price sensitivity to interest-rate changes as one measure of risk. Now we'll switch our focus to the other side of the risk/reward equation and consider the OAS an investor receives as compensation for assuming a variety of risks. It is important to note that an OAS value by itself does not provide sufficient information to determine

**EXHIBIT  37–7**

Effective Maturity of 10/NC3 Bond as a Function of Volatility and Yield-Curve Shifts

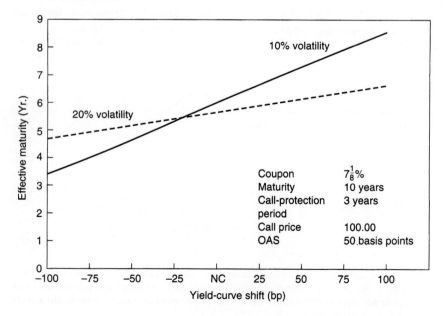

whether a bond is rich or cheap. The OAS and effective duration of one security must be compared with those of another security. In the absence of such a context, it is difficult to assess accurately the relative value between two securities.

For example, a common question that arises about OAS is the point along the maturity spectrum that should be used as a reference point. Should the OAS be viewed as an adjusted yield spread relative to the option-embedded bond's maturity date or its call/put date? Should the OAS of a 10-year callable bond with 3 years of call protection be compared with the spread of a three-year bullet bond or a 10-year bullet bond? Furthermore, if the callable bond has an effective maturity of 7 years, should the OAS be compared to the yield spread of a seven-year bullet bond? Quantitative fixed-income analysts usually say yes to all of the above because OAS is a spread to the curve.

The view that OAS is a spread over the curve is based on the definition of OAS: *OAS is the spread to short-term interest rates that equates the theoretical price of a bond to its market price.*

It can be demonstrated mathematically that the above definition of OAS results in a parallel shift of the entire zero-coupon (spot-yield) curve by an amount equal to the OAS. Thus, in a sense, the OAS is a spread over the entire curve.

A less technical, and perhaps more intuitive, way of viewing OAS as a spread to the curve is to consider the duality of embedded options in terms of put/call parity. For example, callable bonds usually are quoted either on a yield-to-maturity basis or a yield-to-call basis, depending on the level and direction of interest rates. If interest rates are high or moving higher, then the issuer is unlikely to call the bond. By electing not to exercise the call option, the issuer has effectively put the bond to the investor.

Thus, even though a bond is quoted on a yield-to-maturity basis, a corresponding yield-to-call spread exists. Because the OAS is an adjustment to the nominal yield spread, the OAS can be viewed as the result of the appropriate adjustments to *both* the yield-to-maturity and yield-to-call spreads. In this view, the OAS is an adjusted spread to both the maturity date and the call date. The following equations demonstrate this relationship:

$$\text{OAS} = \text{Yield-to-maturity spread} - \text{Call-option value in basis points} \qquad (37\text{--}6)$$

or

$$\text{OAS} = \text{Yield-to-call spread} - \text{Put-option value in basis points} \qquad (37\text{--}7)$$

Moreover, if the option is American-style (i.e., the option can be exercised at any time during a specified period), then the OAS may be viewed as an adjusted yield spread over an entire range of call dates.

In considering which point on the yield curve is most appropriate for comparison of OASs to bullet yield spreads, a common first approximation is that the OAS should be compared to the yield spread of the bullet bond whose final maturity is comparable to the effective maturity of the bond with embedded options. Because OAS and effective maturity are risk/reward measures, it is reasonable to determine whether the particular value of OAS is sufficient compensation for an approximately equivalent amount of risk (when compared to the comparable bullet yield spread). For example, if the OAS of the callable 10-year bond is 100 basis points and the effective maturity is 7 years, it is reasonable to first compare the OAS to the yield spread of a seven-year bullet from the same or very similar issuer. However, this approach serves only as a general rule, and there are other important factors that enter into the determination of relative value.

## Looking Beyond the OAS and Effective Duration Numbers

A common assumption is that comparable bonds with comparable effective durations should have comparable OASs. The result of this view is that bonds with higher OASs are perceived to represent better value. However, a variety of other factors should be considered before rendering a judgment about the relative richness or cheapness between the two securities.

### Effect of Exogenous Factors

The technology embedded within an OAS model may be very sophisticated, but a not-too-commonly discussed point is that OAS models quantify the value of the embedded option only within the context of the model's underlying assumptions. By assuming an interest-rate process and a given randomness in interest rates, the value of the option is calculated. Then the OAS is, roughly speaking, the effective yield spread after adjusting for the value of the embedded option. Consequently, the effective yield spread implicitly reflects the host of other considerations (beyond that of the embedded option) that factor into the marketplace's pricing of the bond.

Exogenous factors such as supply and demand in particular market sectors and current investor preferences can cause one bond to be cheap to another bond on an OAS basis. Just as two comparable bullet securities can trade at different yield spread levels, comparable bonds with embedded options can trade at different OASs relative to each other or relative to equivalent-duration bullets. Thus, although there may be circumstances in which two bonds may trade at approximately the same OAS, there can be fundamental factors causing the bonds to trade at substantially different OASs.

### Effect of Convexity

The comparison of the OAS versus the effective duration of two bonds provides insight into the local price sensitivities of the securities to changes in interest rates only. For relatively small changes in interest rates, two securities with similar effective durations should have similar price sensitivities. However, as interest rates move significantly, the effective durations of the two securities may no longer be comparable, so any convexity dissimilarities between the two securities begin to take effect. See Exhibit 37–6 (price/yield curve comparison between a callable bond and a bullet bond).

The effective duration number (in the absence of other information) does not highlight, for example, the possibility that a 30-year callable bond with an effective maturity of 10 years can still extend out to 30 years if interest rates rise steadily. Conversely, if interest rates decrease significantly, the effective duration continues to decrease so that the price appreciation of the callable bond is even more muted. The bond's negative convexity, which is a result of the bondholder's selling of options, reflects the potential downside of a short-option position in a volatile interest-rate environment.

Generally, the length of the investment horizon and the outlook on interest rates influence the extent to which investors may be concerned about the magnitude of the convexity effect. If the investment horizon is short and if interest rates are viewed as being stable over that time period, an investor may not be very concerned about the convexity effect. On the other hand, if the horizon spans a longer period of time, long-term price performance and convexity become larger issues. In this latter case, investors may need to be compensated for the greater exposure to negative convexity through a higher OAS, even though the two securities being compared currently may have similar effective durations.

Exhibit 37–8 illustrates such a situation in which two comparable securities do not have similar OASs. In this case, two callable FHLMC bonds with similar final maturities have different OASs. At a 15.8% yield volatility[7] the 7⅝s have an OAS of 89 basis points, as compared to the OAS of 85 basis points for the 6.45s.

The difference in OAS can be attributed to several competing factors that act to influence the pricing of these securities. First, securities with shorter effective durations tend to have lower OASs than securities with higher effective durations, simply to reflect the trend observed for bullet securities that yield spreads increase with increasing maturities. (This OAS trend would be most evident for securities that clearly trade either to the maturity date or to the option- exercise date.) On this basis, it can be argued that the 7⅝s should have the lower OAS.

On the other hand, for securities with intermediate effective durations (such as the FHLMC 7⅝s), it is not obvious whether the security will be called or remain outstanding to final maturity. Hence, it can also be argued that as compensation for the greater degree of uncertainty, the 7⅝s should have a higher OAS than do the 6.45s. In the final analysis, the higher OAS of the 7⅝s indicates that the market currently demands greater compensation for the maturity uncertainty than for the duration risk.

---

7. See David Audley and Richard Chin, *Technology and Its Effect on Valuation Metrics #3: Choosing the Correct Volatility for the Valuation of Embedded Options* (New York: Financial Strategies Group, Prudential Securities Incorporated, March 1991).

**E X H I B I T   37–8**

OAS and Effective-Duration Comparison

| Issuer | FHLMC | FHLMC |
|---|---|---|
| Coupon | 7.625% | 6.45% |
| Maturity | 9/9/09 | 4/29/09 |
| Call date | 9/9/02 | 4/29/02 |
| Call price | $100.00 | $100.00 |
| Issue size | $1,000 MM | $3,000 MM |
| Price[a] | $99.689 | $94.389 |
| OAS (15.8% yield volatility) | 89 bp | 85 bp |
| Effective maturity | 6.06 years | 7.06 years |
| Effective duration | 4.69 | 5.32 years |

[a] Prices as September 2, 1999
Source: Prudential Securities

## SUMMARY

Bonds with embedded options and bullet securities can respond very differently to movements in interest rates. Investors may use the analytical concepts of OAS and effective duration to help gauge the relative risk/reward trade-offs across a range of assets to determine relative value. OAS and effective duration can be useful analytical tools, but investors need to recognize that there can be a variety of fundamental and analytical reasons that may cause two comparable securities to trade at widely different OASs.

## CHAPTER 38

# EVALUATING AMORTIZING ABS: A PRIMER ON STATIC SPREAD

**Anthony V. Thompson**
Director of ABS Research
Goldman, Sachs & Co.

## INTRODUCTION

Yield to maturity (YTM) has long been recognized as a fundamental tool for measuring relative value among traditional fixed income securities. Although certain assumptions inherent to YTM can understate or overstate actual return, these inaccuracies are often benign when comparing noncallable securities in a market such as corporates, where cash flows are relatively standardized. This, however, is not always the case within the asset-backed market, where the amortization characteristics can vary significantly from security to security.

A price calculated using yield to maturity assumes a rate of return based on the discounting of a security's interest and principal cash flows at a constant rate. For a corporate bond, the discount rate represents the yield on the Treasury benchmark nearest to maturity, plus a spread. As a measure of relative value, a price based on YTM takes into account only a security's yield, coupon, and final maturity. YTM reflects neither reinvestment nor dispersion of cash flows. When used to compare relative value among traditional corporate bonds, the assumptions inherent to YTM are less significant to the extent that all securities with similar cash flow characteristics are affected equally. However, when comparing bonds with more complex cash flow structures, what YTM offers in simplicity, it sacrifices in accuracy.

## THE DRAWBACKS OF USING AVERAGE MATURITY TO DETERMINE YIELD

Certain securities in the asset-backed market, such as soft bullet credit cards, offer a single payment of principal at maturity, thus imitating the cash flow profile of a corporate bond. However, in other asset-backeds, such as retail auto loans, principal amortizes over the life of the transaction. The market convention for pricing these amortizing securities is to discount all cash flows at a rate based on the Treasury whose maturity is closest to the weighted average maturity of the security's principal cash flows. It is assumed that the impact of discounting longer cash flows at a rate that is too low relative to their maturity will equally offset the discounting of shorter cash flows at a rate that is too high. As we explain below, when cash flows are significantly dispersed, the use of an average maturity becomes an increasingly inaccurate measure of return.

Suppose an investor could own either (a) one bond with a maturity of 18 months, which we will call B18, or (b) equal amounts of two bonds, one with a maturity of 12 months (B12) and the other with a maturity of 24 months (B24), having a combined average maturity of 18 months. Assume all three bonds have the same coupon and are priced at par based on a discount rate of 6%. As shown in Exhibit 38–1, the price of B18 and the combination of B12 and B24 are the same. An investor should therefore be indifferent to choice (a) or (b). This method illustrates one way in which asset-backed securities with multiple principal payments are priced, i.e., based on the yield to average maturity of the underlying principal.

Now suppose the price of B12 combined with B24 was expressed as the sum of the individual prices instead of the average. For purposes of illustration, assume discount rates for B12 and B24 such that, when averaged, they equal 6% (see Exhibit 38–2).

This very simple example shows that the sum of the individual prices of B12 and B24 is 99.96, or .04 lower than when the Average Method is used. There is an explanation for this. In the Average Method, we calculate the price of B12+B24 using a single rate (6%) based on the average maturity of 18 months. Using the Individual Method, we discount B12 and B24 by separate rates, one lower (5.4%) and one higher (6.6%). Because the average of the individual discount rates still equals 6%, one would think that the two prices using either method should still be equal. But they are not. The difference in price can be explained by the effect of compounding. Because the price of the longer security (B24) is more sensitive to the higher rate than B12 is to the

**E X H I B I T   38–1**

Calculation of Price Using Average Method

|              | B18      | B12      | B24      | B12 + B24 |
|--------------|----------|----------|----------|-----------|
| Average life | 18 mos.  | 12 mos.  | 24 mos.  | 18 mos.   |
| Discount rate| 6.0%     |          |          | 6.0%      |
| Price        | 100.00   |          |          | **100.00**|

**E X H I B I T   38–2**

Calculation of Price Using Individual Method

|              | B18     | B12     | B24     | B12 + B24 |
|--------------|---------|---------|---------|-----------|
| Average life | 18 mos. | 12 mos. | 24 mos. | 18 mos.   |
| Discount rate | 6.0%   | 5.4%    | 6.6%    | 6.0%      |
| Price        | 100.00  | 100.12  | 99.73   | **99.96** |

lower rate, their combined price is lower when using the Individual Method. In order for the sum of the prices of the individual bonds to equal the price derived using the Average Method, lower discount rates are needed. The difference between the discount rates can essentially be attributed to the difference between a security's static spread and its nominal spread.

## STATIC SPREAD CREATES A LEVEL PLAYING FIELD

Static spread assumes that a given security represents a portfolio of individual securities, as if each were a zero coupon bond. Rather than discounting all cash flows by the same yield to maturity, the static spread methodology discounts each individual cash flow at a spread plus the spot rate of a zero coupon Treasury with the corresponding duration. The spread at which the sum of the discounted cash flows equals their nominal price is the static spread.

A more practical example further demonstrates how YTM based on average maturity would be misleading when comparing the three securities shown in Exhibit 38–3, each with an average life of 18 months. Security #1 pays a single "bullet" payment of principal in month 18, similar to a corporate bond or soft bullet credit card ABS. Security #2 returns principal in 24 equal installments beginning in month 7, not unlike a credit card ABS with a long controlled amortization period. Security #3 pays principal over 36 months, with a gradually declining amount of principal paid in each successive month. Security #3 approximates a short retail auto ABS. If each security trades at a price to yield of 6% and the yield on the 18-month Treasury benchmark is 5.45%, then the spread (also called the nominal spread) will be 55 bp.

The YTM derived in the example above assumes that each cash flow will be discounted at 6%, a rate based on the average principal maturity (18 months). If the yield curve were positively sloped, the early cash flows would be discounted at too high a rate and the later cash flows discounted at too low a rate. YTM based on an average maturity assumes that the two effects will equally offset each other. However, we know from the previous example that this is not the case.

## EXHIBIT 38–3

Cash Flow Profiles of Three Types of Asset-Backed Securities

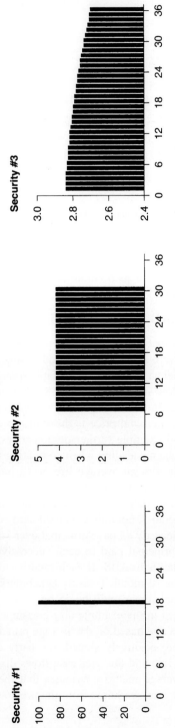

*Principal cash flows shown in black, plotted on left Y axis; interest payments shown in gray, plotted on right Y axis. Months shown on X axis.*

To calculate static spread, assume the hypothetical yield curve shown in Exhibit 38–4. From this curve, a zero coupon curve is derived that will be used to discount each cash flow as if each were a zero coupon bond. The static spreads on the three different securities are shown in Exhibit 38–5.

Why are the nominal spreads for Security #2 and Security #3 higher than the static spreads? Their prices, when based on an average benchmark plus the nominal spread, are effectively too high. This is because the cash flows in Securities #2 and #3, which are received beyond the average maturity, are more sensitive to the average discount rate, which is too low. In order for the lower price of the sum of the individual zero coupon securities to equal the higher price of the securities using average maturity, the spread (i.e., the static spread) used to discount the series of zeros must be lower.

As one would expect, the difference between static spread and nominal spread is most significant in the case of Security #3, where the cash flows are the most dispersed. Conversely, the difference between static spread and nominal spread is the smallest in the case of Security #1, which exhibits relatively less cash flow dispersion.

## E X H I B I T 38–4

Hypothetical Year Yield Curve, Maturities Three Years and Under

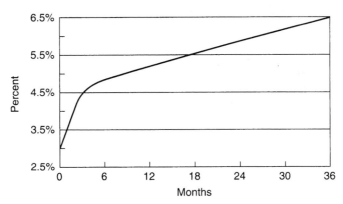

## E X H I B I T 38–5

Comparison of Static and Nominal Spreads

|  | Security #1 | Security #2 | Security #3 |
|---|---|---|---|
| Static Spread | 55 bp | 45 bp | 30 bp |
| Nominal Spread | 55 bp | 55 bp | 55 bp |

# CONCLUSION

As asset-backeds become an increasingly popular substitute for corporate bonds, investors should be aware of the subtle differences used to evaluate these securities. Yield to maturity based on a security's average maturity does not take into account the dispersion of cash flows. This is of little consequence in the corporate bond market, where securities typically have a single payment of principal at maturity. When making relative value comparisons among securities with different amortization profiles, it is more appropriate to use static spread. Static spread assumes that each cash flow is discounted individually at a rate based on the zero coupon Treasury curve. When the yield curve is upwardly sloping, static spreads on amortizing asset-backed securities will generally be lower than nominal spreads; when the yield curve is inverted, the reverse will be true. The amount that a security's static spread differs from its nominal spread will depend on the steepness of the curve and the dispersion of cash flows.

## PART 6

# PORTFOLIO MANAGEMENT

## CHAPTER 39

# BOND MANAGEMENT: PAST, CURRENT, AND FUTURE

**H. Gifford Fong**
President
Gifford Fong Associates

Fixed income management has undergone a remarkable evolution. The range of portfolio strategies has expanded as the technology of portfolio analysis has developed over time. This broadened capability is permitting greater efficiency and effectiveness as well as the introduction of innovative strategies. Perhaps more remarkable is the prospect of a new dimension of fixed income portfolio strategy that dramatically goes beyond the traditional notions of management.

What follows is an overview of the changes that have occurred in fixed income portfolio strategy over the last 20 years. This historical survey will trace the emergence of various quantitative tools that have helped shape the world of modern fixed income portfolio management. After this review, a description of a representative strategy harnessing this technology will be presented.

## TRADITIONAL FIXED INCOME PORTFOLIO STRATEGY[1]

The primary functional areas of modern fixed income management are shown in Exhibit 39–1, which is a triangle with three intersections representing the major strategies. At the bottom left can be found *active management,* made up of rate anticipation and/or sector management. Key to this area are expectations of interest-rate change and/or sector spread (yield difference from Treasury securities). To the lower right can be found *passive management,* where either a buy-and-hold strategy or indexing to a representative market bogey is typical.

Active and passive management can be differentiated on the basis of the kinds of input necessary. For example, traditional active management is "expectationally driven"; that is, the most important set of inputs will be expecta-

---

1. For a more comprehensive discussion of traditional fixed income strategies, see H. Gifford Fong and Frank J. Fabozzi, *Fixed Income Portfolio Management* (Homewood, IL: Dow Jones-Irwin, *1985*).

**E X H I B I T   39-1**

Fixed Income Management

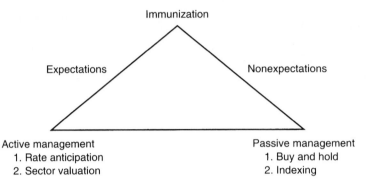

tions of interest-rate and spread relationship changes. Passive management, on the other hand, is based on nonexpectational inputs; in other words, the key inputs are known at the time of the analysis. In the case of indexing, these inputs are the basic characteristics of the market index chosen.

This difference in inputs corresponds to variations in the risk-return characteristics of the alternatives. The greater the expectational inputs are, all other things being equal, the greater the return potential and the associated variability (risk) of the strategy will be. Thus, active management will have the highest expected return but the highest associated risk, and passive management will have the lowest expected return and risk on average. The emphasis in this traditional setting is to seek higher returns by managing the expectations, which in turn increase the expected returns.

In contrast to the expectational nature of active management and nonexpectational nature of passive management, the top of the triangle, *immunization,* represents a hybrid strategy. Under some circumstances, an expectational, high expected risk-return approach may be chosen, or a nonexpectational, minimum-risk posture may be assumed.

## HISTORICAL PERSPECTIVE

Early quantitative tools in the 1970s were first used to support active management. Sensitivity analysis, in which the implications of the expectations on portfolio returns could be evaluated, became a fundamental tool in active strategies. Expected scenarios of interest-rate change could be applied to the current portfolio, and prospective returns could be calculated. This analysis was extended to include insights from evaluating the implications of the expected returns.[2]

---

2. See, for example, John L. Maginn and Donald L. Tuttle, eds., *Managing Investment Portfolios: A Dynamic Process* (Charlottesville, VA: The Institute of Chartered Financial Analysts, 1983), Chapter 9.

This early application represents the quantification of a traditional task that was formerly done informally by the portfolio manager. With this tool, the portfolio manager could pursue a more systematic and structured approach to portfolio decision making. This was not merely a foreign step, but rather an alternative path freeing the time of the portfolio manager. In effect, a computational task became automated so more time could be devoted to tasks that could not be automated. Given the usual demands on the available time of the portfolio manager, this quantitative assistance leveraged the ability of the manager to focus on the expectational inputs that are central to the active management process.

With the approach of the 1980s, new developments encouraged the use of an old concept in a new form—immunization. Originally conceived in the 1930s, the immunization strategy awaited a series of theoretical and empirical developments before it could be put to practical use. So when relatively high interest rates prevailed (in relation to the typical actuarial assumption), and the desire to minimize pension contributions and the growth of new theoretical understanding[3] emerged at the same time, the basis for the use of immunization was laid. Moreover, the tarnished reputation of traditional active management (due to the performance of many portfolio managers in the 1970s) further confirmed the need for a new strategy.

In the 1980s, the further evolution of strategy took the direction of duration-controlled approaches. Given the aversion to unexpected exposure to changes in interest rates, reliance on interest-rate risk control by monitoring the duration of the portfolio became widespread. Out of this trend emerged indexing, which targeted the portfolio duration. Indexing is extremely quantified and minimizes the need for expectational input.

More recently, other targeted-duration strategies have emerged. These, in general, have a duration target different from the popularly followed bond indexes but serve a similar function: limiting or controlling the exposure to interest-rate changes by "targeting" the duration.

This brief history traces the changes in strategy over about the last 20 years. Concurrently, the role of quantitative methods has altered. What started out as a useful means of measuring and monitoring has developed over time as an important source of portfolio strategy.

Early applications were mere alternatives to traditional practice, and allowed the automation of basic tasks. As concern for unconstrained use of expectations increased, quantitative methods provided the means of monitoring and controlling risk exposure, especially the risk of interest-rate change different from a desired duration level. These applications involved the use of quantitative

---

3. Important advances in the nature of immunized portfolios were made in Lawrence Fisher and Roman Weil, "Coping with Risk of Interest Rate Fluctuations: Return to Bondholders from Naive and Optimal Strategies," *Journal of Business,* October 1971; and H. Gifford Fong and Oldrich A. Vasicek, "A Risk Minimizing Strategy for Portfolio Immunization," *The Journal of Finance,* December 1984, provided explicit risk measures for immunized portfolios.

techniques, first to free up the time of the portfolio manager and then to help shape the appropriate policy of the portfolio management process. For example, a targeted duration portfolio removes interest-rate forecasting from the manager's judgment but still allows expectations to be applied in sector and individual bond selection. However, as the use of quantitative methods has increased, the potential for return has decreased. The question now becomes how to expand the horizons of return in the face of qualitative control.

## QUANTITATIVE INNOVATION

Exhibit 39–2 lists representative fixed income applications. Historically, the cornerstone of quantitative analysis has been the measurement of relevant factors providing analytical insight. And historically, the time demands of the traditional process of management could have been better served. More recent developments, such as indexing and immunization, suggest that quantitative innovation supplemented by traditional activities such as investment objective setting and trading can be the principal expedient of portfolio management.

Of the important contributing factors to the return of a fixed income portfolio, duration management has had the greatest impact, followed by sector selection and then individual bond selection.[4] The potential for superior performance from management contribution is therefore severely handicapped if the most important potential source is taken away.

Active duration management may not be appropriate for all investors, but the consequences and merits of the choice should be understood.

For example, targeted-duration strategies are designed to preclude large return departures from the chosen duration level. The choice of the level may be due to a number of considerations (including, importantly, the duration of the liabilities to be funded); however, whatever the level, if there is a consistent and reliable means of adding value through active duration management around the target, the potential for substantial incremental returns is achieved.

Granted, the aversion to unconstrained expectational duration management may still exist. However, if a means of active duration management could operate in a controlled, nonexpectational framework, an interesting alternative would be achieved.

Drawn from modern option valuation theory, an asset allocation analysis can provide a form of active duration management.[5] The objective is to create

---

4. This can be intuitively understood by considering the relative contribution to the variability of portfolio returns from these three sources.
5. A discussion of a specific fixed income application can be found in John L. Maginn and Donald L. Tuttle, eds., *Managing Investment Portfolios,* 2nd ed. (Charlottesville, VA: The Institute of Chartered Financial Analysts, 1990), Chapter 8; the discussion here is based on the theory discussed in H. Gifford Fong and Oldrich A. Vasicek, "Forecast-Free International Asset Allocation," *The Financial Analyst Journal,* March/April 1989, pp. 29–33.

**EXHIBIT   39–2**

Quantitative Applications

| | |
|---|---|
| *Active Management* | |
| Return simulation | Predicts bond and portfolio behavior given alternative interest-rate scenario projections. |
| *Immunization* | |
| Immunization model | Creates and maintains a portfolio that will have an ensured return over a specified horizon, irrespective of interest-rate change. |
| *Passive Management* | |
| Indexing system | Creates and maintains a portfolio that will track the performance of a given bond index with a manageable set of securities. |
| *Individual Security Analysis* | |
| Swap systems | Allows for comparison of individual securities, with the objective of identifying historical price (or basis point spread) relationships. |
| Term-structure analysis | Evaluates the current level of yields by producing spot, discount, and forward-rate structures. Also values Treasury securities. |
| Bond valuation model | Develops a normative value for corporate and mortgage-backed securities, based on the evaluation of those characteristics of the security that contribute to overall price. |
| Contingent-claims model | Evaluates the embedded option in a security without forecasting interest rates. |
| *Other* | |
| Performance attribution system | Calculates the total return for a bond portfolio and attributes the return to its components. |
| Risk analysis report | Calculates option-adjusted average duration, convexity, and yield for a portfolio. |

a synthetic call option on the best performing of the two extremes of the selected duration range. What would result would be a systematic shift within this range based on an active asset allocation between the longest and shortest duration assets.

An option valuation model used for this purpose determines the appropriate proportions of the two duration extremes. The model can systematically shift the portfolio to the highest returning asset from the lowest returning asset.

A synthetic option is thereby created from this active asset allocation—an option that will achieve the returns of the best performer of the two assets. The final portfolio return will be the return of the best-performing asset less the synthetic option cost. This cost, which may be determined at the beginning of the analysis, arises from the return slippage due to the portfolio not using the best-performing asset all of the time. Because there is a gradual shift, there is a "cost" or return differential as compared to the return of the best-performing asset.

In general, the cost will vary with the number of assets, the length of the investment horizon, and the estimated risk of the assets considered (standard deviation of returns and correlation between assets). Although the cost of the strategy can vary depending on the actual outcome of the risk estimates, the strategy will still achieve the desired property of a synthetic call on the best-performing asset class.

Consider the management of an intermediate fixed income portfolio made up of high-grade government and corporate securities. Conventional indexing would target the duration of the index as the duration of the portfolio to be held. Value enhancement would take the form of a sector selection and/or individual security selection. Return differences from the most important management activity, that of active duration management, would be eliminated.

Introducing active duration management using option valuation technology can retain the most important source of management return, without the need for interest-rate forecasting. The portfolio returns would be further enhanced by using a term-structure model to value Treasury securities and a bond valuation model for the balance of the portfolio.

By harnessing the quantitative innovation of option valuation technology, a new dimension of portfolio decision making emerges. Active duration management without the need for interest-rate forecasting is made possible.

What has been described is a strategy applying quantitative innovation in the management of an active intermediate portfolio. Without the additional return potential of this technology, the return prospect would be that of a conservative-duration portfolio. With the technology, the return range can be extended to longer-duration portfolios with the downside cushion of a short-duration portfolio.

Another nonexpectational form of active duration management is tactical asset allocation. This strategy varies the duration of the portfolio based on fair value for the bond market. When the market is considered undervalued, the duration of the portfolio will be lengthened to what is considered normal; and, conversely, when the market is considered overvalued, the portfolio duration is shortened. The key is the determination of what is "fair value"; and here tactical asset allocation differs from an option valuation approach. Expectations are required in the determination of fair value for tactical asset allocation, whereas the option valuation approach does not rely upon asset valuation expectation.

## SUMMARY

A review of the main functional areas of fixed income management reveal a range of risk/return potential. Over time, the popularity of strategy has shifted in recognition of the difficulty of valid and reliable interest-rate forecasts. Recent developments in option valuation technology reintroduce more active strategies, without the need for interest-rate forecasting.

CHAPTER **40**

# THE ACTIVE DECISIONS IN THE SELECTION OF PASSIVE MANAGEMENT AND PERFORMANCE BOGEYS[*]

**Chris P. Dialynas**
Managing Director
Pacific Investment Management Company

The asset allocation decision is perhaps a plan sponsor's most important decision. Within the scope of that decision, the selection of investment managers and performance bogeys are critical. Traditional asset allocation methods are based on studies of relative returns and risk over long periods of time. Performance periods, however, both for the plan itself and the investment manager entrusted with the funds, are based upon relatively short time spans. As such, there is an inherent inconsistency in the investment process.

In this chapter, the active bond management process will be explored and contrasted with the "passive management" option. We will also examine the differences in index composition. Performance references will be made based exclusively on the index composition and the future economic environment. We will see that successful bond management, whether active or passive, depends on good long-term economic forecasting and a thorough understanding of the mathematical dynamics of fixed income obligations. Likewise, selection of a performance bogey depends on similar considerations as well as the liability structure of the plan itself.

## ACTIVE BOND MANAGEMENT

Active management of bond portfolios capitalizes on changing relations among bonds to enhance performance. Volatility in interest rates and changes in the

[*] The author expresses his gratitude to his associate at PIMCO, Mark Kiesel, for his considerable contribution, and to the research department at Lehman Brothers for their effort in providing data. This chapter is reprinted with permission from Frank J. Fabozzi (ed.), *Perspectives on Fixed Income Portfolio Management: Volume 2* (New Hope, PA: Frank J. Fabozzi Associates, 2000).

amount of volatility induce divergences in the relative prices between bonds. Since volatility, by definition, allows for opportunity, the fact that during the first half of 1986 and the second half of 1998 active bond managers as a class underperformed the passive indexes in two of the most volatile bond markets in the past fifty years seems counter-intuitive. What went wrong then? What should we expect in the future?

Active bond managers each employ their own methods for relative value analysis. Common elements among most managers are historical relations, liquidity considerations, and market segmentation. Market segmentation allegedly creates opportunities, and historical analysis provides the timing cue. The timing of strategic moves is important because there is generally an opportunity cost associated with every strategy. Unfortunately, since the world is in perpetual motion and constant evolution, neither market segmentation nor historical analysis is able to withstand the greater forces of change. Both methods, either separately or jointly, are impotent. The dramatic changes in interest rates and the volatility of interest rates experienced in the past few decades implies the world is changing and evolving more quickly. Paradoxically, many active managers are using methods voided by volatility to try to capitalize on volatility.

The mistakes of active bond managers have been costly. As a result, a significant move from active to passive (or indexed) management has occurred. Does this move make sense? To understand relative performance differentials between passive and active managers, we need to dissect the active and passive portfolios and reconstruct the macroeconomic circumstances. We will see that composition of the indexes and the circumstances produced by a dynamic combination that was most difficult to beat in 1986 and in the second half of 1998.

## MARKET INDEXES

While a variety of bond market indexes are popular today, only two have been notable throughout the present business cycle. The Lehman Brothers Government Corporate (LBGC) bond index was the most popular and the Salomon High Grade Long Term Bond Index was the traditional measure. Since the high-grade index sees little use today, our focus will be primarily on the LBGC index and the Lehman Brothers Aggregate Index (LBAG), which includes mortgage securities and became the industry standard in the late 1980s. We will conclude with a comparison of the different indexes and their respective performance expectations given various interest-rate movements, as well as a review of historical performance comparisons.

## The LBGC Index

The LBGC is primarily composed of government and agency securities. The composition of the index is detailed in Exhibit 40–1. It also includes investment grade corporate bonds.

**E X H I B I T   40-1**

LBGC Characteristics

|  | 6/80 | 6/84 | 6/89 | 6/94 | 6/98 | 9/98 | 6/99 | 12/99 |
|---|---|---|---|---|---|---|---|---|
| US Government | 59.0 | 72.3 | 73.3 | 76.8 | 70.0 | 69.7 | 68.0 | 66.0 |
| Corporates | 41.0 | 27.7 | 26.7 | 23.2 | 30.0 | 30.3 | 32.0 | 34.0 |
| Duration | 5.04 | 4.02 | 4.67 | 4.98 | 5.46 | 5.61 | 5.47 | 5.30 |
| Yield-to-Maturity | 10.25 | 13.59 | 8.48 | 7.12 | 5.87 | 5.08 | 6.29 | 6.96 |

The LBGC is constructed such that its composition is representative of the relative distribution of securities in the market exclusive of the mortgage market. Because the government issues the vast majority of debt, it is not surprising that the index holds such a high proportion of government securities. It is noteworthy that, after a period of stability, government debt will represent a smaller proportion of the index. The index must, by definition, "buy" the debt. With the exception of some of the 30-year government bonds issued during this period, virtually all of the government and most agency debt held in the index is noncallable. Because of this, between 1980 and 1989 the index has become increasingly call-protected. We will see that the callable/noncallable distribution is an important distinguishing feature between the index and active managers. The transition from government fiscal deficit to government fiscal surplus during the latter half of the 1990s has reversed the growing influence of noncallable higher-quality debt in the index. In fact, Table 40-1 demonstrates that, in the time intervals evaluated, the distribution of government debt increased from 59% in 1980 to a peak of 76.8% in 1994. It has subsequently declined to 66% in 1999. Similarly, the percentage of corporate bonds decreased and has subsequently increased. These changes in index character have important implications for asset allocation models and relative performance expectations. The distributional changes in sector composition translate into more subtle changes in index callability, quality and sensitivity to the volatility of interest rates and the usual increase in volatility that accompanies significant changes in rates.

## The LBAG Index

The primary difference between the LBGC and the LBAG is the inclusion of mortgage-related securities in the LBAG. A mortgage provides the most uncertain distribution of cash flows among conventional fixed income securities and can exhibit substantial negative convexity. The degree of convexity differential between the LBGC and the LBAG is largely determined by the concentration of mortgages below par. (Convexity is a measure relating to the elasticity of duration with respect to yield changes.) The greater the percentage of mortgages

**EXHIBIT 40–2**

LBAG Characteristics

|  | 6/80 | 6/84 | 6/89 | 6/94 | 6/98 | 9/98 | 6/99 | 12/99 |
|---|---|---|---|---|---|---|---|---|
| US Government | 53.8 | 60.6 | 53.9 | 53.6 | 48.2 | 48.0 | 43.4 | 42.0 |
| Corporates | 36.0 | 23.2 | 19.6 | 17.7 | 21.6 | 21.0 | 22.0 | 22.0 |
| Mortgages | 10.2 | 16.2 | 26.5 | 28.7 | 30.2 | 31.0 | 34.6 | 36.0 |
| Duration | 5.26 | 4.24 | 4.52 | 4.87 | 4.47 | 4.29 | 4.89 | 4.92 |
| Yield | 10.34 | 13.78 | 8.77 | 7.41 | 5.88 | 5.37 | 6.55 | 7.16 |

below par is, the greater the relative convexity of the LBAG will be. Relative index performance expectations along the yield curve spectrum are sensitive to the relative coupon distribution of mortgages in the market at any point in time. That distribution, reported in Exhibit 40–2, will largely influence subsequent duration differences between the indexes and, therefore, subsequent performance differences as well.

## The Salomon Brothers High Grade Index

The Salomon Brothers high-grade, long-term index was a popular bond market bogey during the 1970s and early 1980s. The index is comprised primarily of high-quality long-term (10 years and longer) corporate bonds. Its reported duration approximated 8.5. The performance of the index was very poor during this period of increasing rates and increasing volatility in interest rates. The rate increases were so great that call options were driven well out of the money, reducing the localized cushioning effect normally associated with rate increases. The increase in volatility was tremendous and directly reduced the value of corporate bonds. Naturally, the high-grade index became perceived as too risky and not representative of the market's distribution of bonds. The LBGC was adopted as the market index. Its shorter duration allowed it to better weather the bear market. The LBAG index is most representative of the market and gained popularity during the latter half of the 1980s. Ironically, the shift to shorter and shorter duration market bogeys coincided with a substantial decline in long-term interest rates.

## PERFORMANCE CHARACTERISTICS OF CALLABLE AND NONCALLABLE BONDS

Exhibit 40–3 characterizes the expected performance characteristics of callable and noncallable bonds under different market environments. The market envi-

**EXHIBIT 40–3**

Expected Performance Characteristics of Callable and Noncallable Bonds Under Different Market Environments

| | | | Direction of Interest Rates | | |
|---|---|---|---|---|---|
| | | | Increase in Rates | No Change | Decrease in Rates |
| Volatility Changes | Increase | NC | + | + | ⊕ |
| | | C | Amb+ | − | ⊖ |
| | No Change | NC | i | i | ⊕ |
| | | C | + | i | ⊖ |
| | Decrease | NC | − | −i | +Amb |
| | | C | ⊕ | + | −Amb |

Performance Expectations
Relative to Comparable Duration
Govt. Securities Portfolios

| | | | |
|---|---|---|---|
| i | Income advantage | ⊕ | Big winner |
| ⊖ | Big loser | − | Loser |
| Amb | Ambiguous | NC | Noncallable portfolio |
| + | Winner | C | Callable portfolio |

ronments are described by two parameters: the direction of interest rates and the volatility of rates.

Callable bonds do well in rising rate environments and decreasing volatility environments. Decreases in volatility have the profound direct effect of reducing the value of the call option imbedded within the callable bond. Since the bondholder has effectively sold the option, as its value is reduced by the lower volatility, the total value of the bond increases independent of any interest-rate movement.

Callable bonds do better than noncallable bonds in increasing rate environments because the higher rates cause the option to go out of the money. As the option goes out of the money, its value diminishes and the bond's value increases. The option value decline cushions the bond price decline induced by higher rates, thereby reducing the *market duration* of the bond. The perceived duration of the bond decreases as rates increase, and the callable bond outperforms the noncallable bond, whose duration is relatively inelastic. However, this phenomenon is only true for small changes in interest rates. The callable bond's duration can extend quite substantially with large interest rates causing it to perform very poorly if relative durations are not managed.

Noncallable bonds perform better than callable bonds in decreasing rate and increasing volatility environments. Their effective duration[1] increases in decreasing rate environments because, exclusive of credit-risk considerations, the noncallable bonds are more *convex*[2]; that is, their *rate* of price increase outpaces that of the comparable duration callable bonds. As the volatility of interest rates increases, noncallable bonds will command a premium and, because the noncallable bonds are more convex, they will appreciate exclusively because of their relative convexity advantage.

The call features of the bond universe are summarized in Exhibit 40–4.

**E X H I B I T   40–4**

Call Features of the Bond Universe

| Issue Type | Refunding Protection | Call Protection | Refunding Price | Current Call Price |
|---|---|---|---|---|
| Treasury | Maturity* | Maturity | NA | NA |
| Traditional agency | Maturity | Maturity | NA | NA |
| Traditional industrial | 10 Years | None | Premium | Premium |
| Traditional utility | 5 Years | None | Premium | Premium |
| Traditional finance | 10 Years† | None | Premium | Premium |
| GNMA pass-through | None | None | 100 | 100 |
| FNMA pass-through | None | None | 100 | 100 |
| FHLMC PC | None | None | 100 | 100 |
| CMO | None | None | 100 | 100 |
| Title XI | None‡ | None‡ | 100‡ | ‡100 |
| PAC CMO | Within prepayment range | None outside range | 100 | 100 |
| TAC CMO | Within prepayment range§ | None outside range | 100 | 100 |

*Some 30-year government bonds were issued with 25 years of call protection.
†A decline in receivables may permit an immediate par call.
‡Default negates any refunding or call protection.
§Call protected within a prespecified range of prepayment rates on the collateral.

---

1. In this instance, effective duration refers to the expected percentage price change in the market. It is not used here in a volatility adjusted duration context.
2. Convexity is the measure of how a bond's price change as yields change differs relative to the price change expected from its duration. Convexity is a measure of duration elasticity.

# A LOOK AT MARKET VOLATILITY

It is helpful to examine the volatility of the bond market to make inferences about performance attributes. Exhibit 40–5 displays the volatility of the bond market as described by the six-month moving average of the 12-month standard deviation of total return on 30-year U.S. Treasury bonds.

Unprecedented, high volatility had been experienced in the bond market during the 1980s. Not only was volatility high, but the degree of variation in volatility was high as well. It is *volatility change* that influences the changes in the value of options, which, in turn, causes relative performance differences between callable and noncallable portfolios. The 1990s experienced a period of lower absolute volatility but percentage changes in the volatility of volatility remained high.

# A LOOK AT INTEREST RATES

The most important piece of the puzzle is the direction of interest rates. Exhibit 40–6 depicts the movement of rates for the period February 1977 to December 1999. We observe dramatic changes in the absolute level of rates. As such changes occur, the relative values of callable and noncallable bonds change. Lower rates work to the advantage of noncallable bonds, and higher rates to the advantage of callable bonds. With extreme increases in rates, ironically, U.S. Government non-callable bonds perform best. This is generally because of the importance of liquidity and credit considerations of corporate bonds (credit risk is also an option the investor sells with the purchase of a corporate bond) and the fact that their duration change is influenced exclusively by interest rates since there are few embedded options. Virtually all callable bonds suffer the joint problem of effective duration variability based upon both interest rates and volatility.

## A Look at Recent History

The volatility of the bond market increased from about 4% in 1976 to about 20% in 1982. It averaged about 8% during the 1990s. In the period from 1976 to 1982, the volatility of return on thirty-year Treasury bonds ranged between 2% and 20%. In the period from 1982 to 1986, volatility was never less than 7%. Over the complete period from 1976 to 1986, average volatility tripled. Volatility declined substantially after 1986 and hit a low of about 6% in 1992. It ranged from 6–12% for the balance of the 90s. Therefore, as we can see from the graph, volatility levels rose and then fell, but the volatility of volatility remains. The information from 1976–1986 alone would favor bond portfolios containing the *fewest* callable securities. However, all else equal, we would prefer noncallable portfolios during the period from 1976 to 1982 and callable ones

EXHIBIT 40-5

Not sure about this!

## Volatility
6-Month Moving Average, 12-Month Standard Deviation of TR on 30-Year Treasury

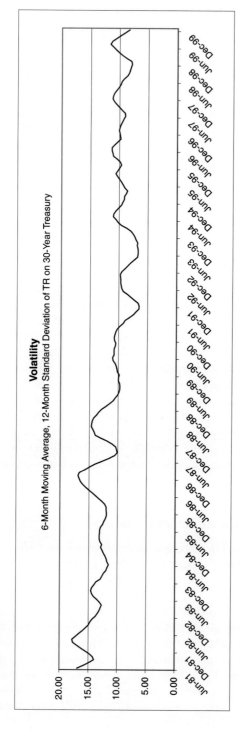

| Period | Volatility | Relative Benchmark Performance |
|---|---|---|
| 1990-1992 | Declined | LBAG outperforms LBGC |
| 1992-1995 | High volatility in wide range | LBGC outperforms LBAG |
| 1995-1997 | Rangebound, volatility of volatility calm | LBAG outperforms LBGC |
| 1997-1999 | Increased; sharp pick-up in late '98 | LBGC outperforms LBAG |
| 2nd Half 1998 | Increased sharply | LBGC outperforms LBAG |
| 2nd Half 1999 | Declined | LBAG outperforms LBGC |

## Change in Volatility

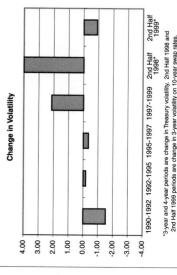

1990-1992  1992-1995  1995-1997  1997-1999  2nd Half 1998*  2nd Half 1999*

*3-year and 4-year periods are change in Treasury volatility. 2nd Half 1998 and 2nd Half 1999 periods are change in 3-year volatility on 10-year swap rates.

Not sure about this!

## 30-Year Treasury Yields

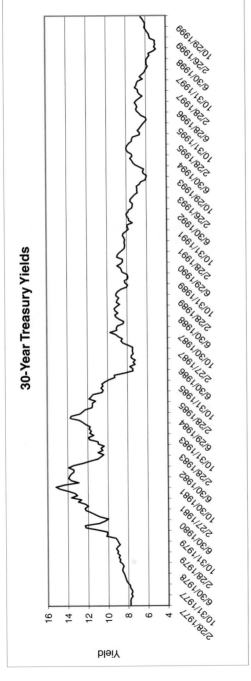

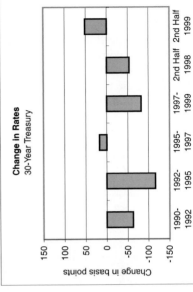

**Change in Rates**
30-Year Treasury

| Period | Rates | Relative Benchmark Performance |
|---|---|---|
| 1990-1992 | Gradual decline | LBAG outperforms LBGC |
| 1992-1995 | Lower and volatile | LBGC outperforms LBAG |
| 1995-1997 | Modestly higher | LBAG outperforms LBGC |
| 1997-1999 | Down | LBGC outperforms LBAG |
| 2nd Half 1998 | Sharp fall | LBGC outperforms LBAG |
| 2nd Half 1999 | Significant increase | LBAG outperforms LBGC |

during the 1982–1986 period. Subsequently, all else equal, we would prefer callable portfolios during the dramatic reduction in volatility. In essence, non-callable portfolios "buy" volatility and callable portfolios "sell" volatility.

Yields on long-term government bonds increased from 8% in 1976 to 14.5% in 1982. In the 1982–1986 period, rates dropped from 14.5% to 7.25%. The 1986–1989 period was one within which rates increased from 7.25% to 8.625%. The range in rates from 1976 to 1982 was 8% to 14.5%. The range for the period was 7.25% to 14.5%. Rates changed from 7.25% to 10.00% during

**EXHIBIT  40–7**

Historical Review: LBAG vs. LBGC

---

**1976–1982**

Interest-rate change from 8% to 14.5% moved the call features out of the money. However, the change in interest rates is so large that the duration of callable bonds increased substantially. This, combined with a substantial increase in volatility, led to the outperformance of noncallable portfolios.

**1982–1986**

The steep decline in interest rates and the virtually unchanged level of high volatility favored noncallable over callable portfolios by a wide margin. The options became in-the-money and shortened the duration of the callable portfolio, revealing the dramatic effects of negative convexity.

**1976–1986**

While interest rates declined only modestly, the tremendous increase in volatility served to make the option more valuable. A countervailing effect of callable issues' income advantage did not offset their decrease in principal value created by the option over short investment horizons.

**1986–1989**

During the first half of this period, the increase in interest rates swamped the increase in volatility. Callable bonds outperformed noncallables during this subperiod. During the second half of the period rates declined and volatility declined. The drop in rates dominated and callables performed best. There were ambiguous results for the full period. Rates increased modestly and volatility was largely unchanged.

**1990–1992**

Intermediate interest rates declined gradually throughout the period. Despite the Gulf War and a US recession in 1991, volatility declined causing callable bonds to outperform non-callable bonds. The relatively range-bound path of interest rates helped the LBAG outperform the LBGC during the period. While the Fed Funds rate was lowered 525 basis points from 8.25% in June of 1990 to 3.00% in September of 1992, ten-year Treasury rates remained primarily in a 6¾% to 8¼% range. As a result, mortgage repayments remained benign. Fortunately, the LBAG started the decade with solid convexity due to a mortgage pool that was the least negatively convex in June of 1990 than at any point in the 1990s (65% of the GNMA mortgage universe traded at or below par).

**E X H I B I T   40-7**

(*Continued*)

---

**1992–1995**

Interest rates moved down and then up and then down again in this highly
volatile period which was marked by a US recovery and the Fed's aggressive
monetary stance against inflation. By June of 1992, only 3.5% of the GNMA
mortgage universe was priced at or below par. The negative convexity of the
mortgage universe during this timeframe caused the LBGC to sharply
outperform the LBAG as interest rates fell and volatility increased from 1992-
1993. Throughout 1994, the Fed was vigilant in its fight against inflation
causing volatility to remain high. Long-term interest rates moved up in 1994
but then fell in 1995 once inflation was no longer a threat to the US
economy. The LBGC continued to lead the LBAG near the end of this period
due to its longer duration.

**1995–1997**

Ten-year interest rates remained range-bound between 5½% and 6 ½%.
Volatility remained calm. The LBAG outperformed the LBGC due to the
range-bound nature of interest rates during the period and a more positively
convex mortgage universe (by June of 1996, 52% of the GNMA mortgage
universe was priced at or below par).

**1997–1999**

This period was marked by the Asian Contagion, the IMF's bailout of Russia,
the LTCM crisis and a liquidity scare which lead to the decade's low in
interest rates, rising risk premiums, soaring volatility and widening credit
spreads. Mortgage prepayments surged and the mortgage universe became
its most negatively convex ever in the decade with only 3% of the GNMA
mortgage universe trading at or below par by December of 1998. The Fed
lowered by Fed Funds rate to 4.75% and ten-year Treasury rates approached
4½% by the end of 1998. The LBGC outperformed the LBAG throughout this
period due to a sharp rise in volatility.

**1999**

Interest rates moved up sharply throughout 1999 as the Fed took away its
75bp of easing in 1998 by tightening 75bp in 1999, taking the Fed Funds
rate back up to 5.50%. Ten-year Treasury rates soared almost 2% to end the
decade at 6.44%. While interest rates rose, volatility came down. Fears of a
Y2K induces liquidity crush were contained by the Fed's aggressive actions.
The LBAG outperformed the LBGC due to a shorter duration and callable
bonds outperformed non-callable bonds as volatility declined.

---

the latter period. We would naively expect portfolios containing callable securities to do best during the first period, portfolios containing noncallable bonds
to do best during the middle period, and portfolios containing callable bonds to
excel during the latter period. Of course, these inferences assume constant conditions in credit, volatility, and yield-curve shape.

Thirty-year interest rates subsequently fell to 6% in 1993 but increased
substantially to 8% in 1994. The 1994 rate increase was coincident with a dra-

matic increase in volatility from about 6 to 12%—a 100% increase. Interest rates subsequently fell to a low of about 5% in 1998 but rebounded to 6½% in 1999—a 30% increase representing a price change of −20 points on a thirty-year bond.

The performance differences between callable and noncallable bonds for these periods are summarized in Exhibit 40–7.

## A Review of The Second Half of 1998

The latter half of 1998 is one of the most interesting intervals in recent bond market history. Let us review the vital statistics of the respective indexes.

**Lehman Brothers Aggregate Index**

|  | Duration | % Government | % Corporate | % Mortgage | % Callable | % ≤ 7-Yr. | % Mortgages Below Par |
|---|---|---|---|---|---|---|---|
| 6/98 | 4.47 | 48.2 | 21.6 | 30.2 | 8.1 | 80.9 | 17.2 |
| 9/98 | 4.29 | 43.3 | 17.5 | 39.2 | 8.0 | 79.8 | 3.0 |
| 12/98 | 4.44 | 46.3 | 23.0 | 30.7 | 7.9 | 79.6 | 6.4 |

**Lehman Brothers Government/Corporate Index**

|  | Duration | % Government | % Corporate | % Mortgage | % Callable | OAD % ≤ 7-Yr. | % Mortgages Below Par |
|---|---|---|---|---|---|---|---|
| 6/98 | 5.46 | 70.0 | 30.0 | 0.0 | 11.8 | 72.3 | 0.0 |
| 9/98 | 5.61 | 69.7 | 30.3 | 0.0 | 11.6 | 70.5 | 0.0 |
| 12/98 | 5.58 | 68.0 | 32.0 | 0.0 | 11.6 | 70.2 | 0.0 |

|  | 30-Yr. | 10-Yr. | Change In Volatility | Change In |
|---|---|---|---|---|
| 6/98–9/98 | −66 bp | −104 bp | +20 bp* | −55 bp Steeper |
| 9/98–12/98 | +136 bp | +24 bp | +380 bp* | −146 bp Flatter* |

*Change in UDS swaption volatility (3-yr. Option on 10-yr. Swap rates)

**Performance**

|  | 6/98–9/98 | 9/98–12/98 | 6/98–12/98 |
|---|---|---|---|
| LBAG | 4.23 | 0.34 | 4.58 |
| LBGC | 4.95 | 0.13 | 5.08 |
| LBGC–LBAG | +72 bp | −21 bp | +50 bp |

A series of events, including a Russian default on its debt and the dissolution of Long-Term Capital Management Hedge Fund, resulted in a tremendous increase in volatility and incredible decline in interest rates and a coincident but unprecedented increase in liquidity premiums. This set of circumstances favored the LBGC over the LBAG in all respects except yield curve exposure. However, the combination of substantially lower rates and substantial increased volatility swamped the yield curve effort. For example, MBS underperformed Treasuries by −180 basis points in the third quarter of 1998 alone as interest rates fell and prepayments surged. The call-protected LBGC outperformed the LBAG by 1.01% through 9/98 and by 0.78% through 12/98.

## The Exclusion of Treasury Inflation Protected Securities

Treasury Inflation Protected Securities (TIPS) are bonds issued by the U.S. government. TIPS provide a fixed coupon that is added to the rate of inflation to render a static return expectation. In 1999, these securities represented 7% of the U.S. Treasury's issuance of debt. They were originally included in the Lehman Brothers indexes and subsequently excluded. Presumably, this exclusion is a result of the difficulty in computation of durations. This, however, is not a robust reason. Arguably, the calculation of the duration of mortgage securities is even more uncertain.

A consistent application of the standard that the index contains that which is sold would suggest that TIPS should be included in the indexes. It seems appropriate to include these securities and extraordinary to exclude them. For our purposes, it is important to understand that the addition of these securities to the indexes would alter the investment dynamics. The indexes would:

1. Increase direct exposure to real interest rates

2. Increase quality

3. Increase call protection

4. Become less volatile

5. Cause the risk parameter of the LBGC and the LBAG to diverge

The inclusion of TIPS, while complicating the dynamics, would be an appropriate and necessary choice given the volume of supply of these securities.

### The Budget Surplus Trend

The recent trend toward continued fiscal budget surpluses will have a profound influence on the risk parameters of the respective indexes. The LBGC index will contain a lower percentage of government securities. The LBGC will become less call-protected and its quality will diminish both absolutely and relative to the LBAG. We should expect the LBGC to become dominated by corporate securities and to find that its volatility sensitivity merge with the LBAG and its credit sensitivity to diverge from the LBAG.

## THE IMPLICIT FORECASTS OF VOLATILITY AND INTEREST RATES

Most active bond managers are sector managers, or sector rotators. They hold portfolios composed of a high proportion of nongovernment securities. These portfolios are short the call options or, viewed alternatively, long portfolios of callable bonds. Few managers seem to have anticipated the magnitude of the change in interest rates and the profound increase in realized volatility that occurred during the 1980s. Both of these forecast errors were important detractors from performance. Even those managers who correctly forecasted the changes in interest rates terribly underestimated the combined impact of increased volatility and declining rates on the value of the option. Thus, their selection of bonds was inconsistent with their forecast.

Bond management necessarily requires an interest-rate forecast, a volatility forecast, and a set of analytical models that calculate the future value of individual securities and portfolios of securities based upon those forecasts. It is the confluence of volatility movement and interest-rate movement that largely affects bond values.[3]

Similarly, the decision to move from active to passive management, or from passive to active, is necessarily predicated upon an implicit forecast of interest rates, volatility, and perceived investment manager consciousness. Moreover, the choice of index as a bogey for active managers or as a source of investment value contains within it an implicit forecast of both interest rates and volatility. Bogey selection may be a plan sponsor's most important decision. The plan sponsor should be careful interpreting statistical data. The pack mentality in the industry may distort the fundament economics of investment risk.

The choice of indexes today (long government rates at 6.75%) is a choice, as is generally the case, of buying or selling convexity and duration. Convex portfolios, such as the LBGC, hold a high percentage of noncallable bonds. Portfolios with little convexity, such as the Lehman Brothers Aggregate Index (LBAG) hold many callable bonds. Thus, the durations of convex portfolios change inversely with market rates, whereas the durations of nonconvex portfolios may, perversely, change in the same direction as rates.

Simply stated, in today's world, the LBGC is a more convex portfolio than the LBAG[4]. However, the fact that a high proportion of mortgages securities in

---

3. See Chris P. Dialynas and David H. Edington, "Bond Yield Spreads Revisited," *Journal of Portfolio Management, Fall 1992,* for a rigorous discussion.
4. The importance of coupon concentration in the relative performance of these two indexes is explained in the next section.

the LBAG are at a discounted price provides for a reasonably convex portfolio over relatively short interest rate changes. Moreover, the percentage of corporate bonds in the LBGC index has increased rendering it less convex. The approximate 10% duration differential between the two indexes is an important issue. As such, the LBGC yields less than the LBAG and is much more sensitive to changes in interest rates. However, if rates decline substantially, the LBAG index will underperform the LBGC by a significant margin because its duration will not increase and may actually decrease and it starts with a lower duration. The LBAG will outperform the LBGC in a mild bear market but will run into problems in an extreme bear market within which volatility also increases. Exhibit 40–8 compares the expected performance characteristics of the LBGC and LBAG.

## Implicit Forecasts

The LBAG portfolio seeks yield in place of convexity. The style is one that does well in stable yield environments. In Exhibit 40–9, we can observe relative bogey performance. The LBAG index is the higher-yielding, less convex index. The respective duration proxies are missing so it is hard to be completely precise. However, for the first half of 1986, second half of 1988, first half of 1993, first half of 1995, and the second half of 1998, volatilities increased dramatically. We would expect, duration assumed constant, the LBAG to underperform the LBGC and, in fact, it happened.

Portfolios described in terms of both duration and convexity have greater explanatory power because risk parameters are more fully defined. Implicit within a move to passive management and the selection of a bogey is both a volatility and an interest-rate forecast. The move to passive management reinforces Say's Law, which holds that supply creates its own demand. Passive investment portfolios have done well in spite of their main investment criterion: Buy that which is produced independent of price or value considerations. Passive management relies upon the market forces to ensure that asset values are appropriately priced. Passive, narrow indexes, such as the LBGC, have even done very well at times because of the circumstances—radically lower rates and increased volatility, both of which benefited call-protected portfolios. The past is prologue: today's investment choice will be judged by tomorrow's circumstances.

The compositional and structural differences between the narrow and aggregate indexes are much more similar today than they were in September 1998. Previously, while compositionally distinct, their structural similarities caused highly correlated performance results. (See Exhibits 40–9 and 40–10.) The performance characteristics of the two indexes in September 1998 differed to a degree that had been previously experienced infrequently. In fact, the aggregate index, with very few securities below par (3%) was at the risk of experiencing

# EXHIBIT 40-8

Comparison of the Expected Performance of the LBGC and LBAG

| Interest Rates | UNCH | Rise | Fall | UNCH | UNCH | Rise | Rise | Fall | Fall |
|---|---|---|---|---|---|---|---|---|---|
| Volatility | UNCH | UNCH | UNCH | Rises | Falls | Rises | Falls | Rises | Falls |
| Index That Performs Best | LBAG | LBAG | LBGC | LBGC | LBAG | Ambiguous (LBAG)* | LBAG | LBGC | Ambiguous (LBGC)* |

*Interest-rate movements are usually the prevailing force. The index in parentheses would therefore dominate unless the interest-rate movement was very small and the volatility movement great.

**EXHIBIT  40–9**

Index Performance (%) (Six-Month Periods)

| End Date | LBGC | LBAG | AG-GC Difference | Ratio GC to AG% |
|---|---|---|---|---|
| Dec-78 | 0.99 | 1.26 | 0.27 | 78.57 |
| Jun-79 | 6.62 | 6.50 | −0.12 | 101.85 |
| Dec-79 | −4.05 | −4.29 | −0.24 | 94.41 |
| Jun-80 | 8.22 | 8.44 | 0.22 | 97.39 |
| Dec-80 | −4.77 | −5.29 | −0.52 | 90.17 |
| Jun-81 | 0.70 | 0.15 | −0.55 | 466.67 |
| Dec-81 | 6.51 | 6.09 | −0.42 | 106.90 |
| Jun-82 | 6.41 | 6.84 | 0.43 | 93.71 |
| Dec-82 | 23.20 | 24.13 | 0.93 | 96.15 |
| Jun-83 | 4.82 | 4.91 | 0.09 | 98.17 |
| Dec-83 | 3.03 | 3.29 | 0.26 | 92.10 |
| Jun-84 | −1.02 | −1.68 | −0.66 | 60.71 |
| Dec-84 | 16.42 | 17.11 | 0.69 | 95.97 |
| Jun-85 | 10.56 | 10.95 | 0.39 | 96.44 |
| Dec-85 | 9.72 | 10.05 | 0.33 | 96.72 |
| Dec-86 | 5.14 | 5.70 | 0.56 | 90.18 |
| Jun-87 | −0.44 | −0.17 | 0.27 | 258.82 |
| Dec-87 | 2.74 | 2.93 | 0.19 | 93.52 |
| Jun-88 | 4.60 | 4.98 | 0.38 | 92.37 |
| Dec-88 | 2.85 | 2.77 | −0.08 | 102.89 |
| Jun-89 | 9.23 | 9.20 | −0.03 | 100.33 |
| Dec-89 | 4.58 | 4.89 | 0.31 | 93.66 |
| Jun-90 | 2.42 | 2.82 | 0.40 | 85.82 |
| Dec-90 | 5.73 | 5.96 | 0.23 | 96.14 |
| Jun-91 | 4.25 | 4.47 | 0.22 | 95.08 |
| Dec-91 | 11.38 | 11.04 | −0.34 | 103.08 |
| Jun-92 | 2.49 | 2.71 | 0.22 | 91.88 |
| Dec-92 | 4.87 | 4.57 | −0.30 | 106.58 |
| Jun-93 | 7.79 | 6.89 | −0.90 | 113.06 |
| Dec-93 | 3.01 | 2.67 | −0.34 | 112.73 |
| Jun-94 | −4.34 | −3.87 | 0.47 | 112.14 |
| Dec-94 | 0.66 | 0.99 | 0.33 | 66.67 |
| Jun-95 | 11.80 | 11.44 | −0.36 | 103.15 |
| Dec-95 | 6.66 | 6.31 | −0.35 | 105.55 |
| Jun-96 | −1.88 | −1.21 | 0.67 | 155.37 |
| Dec-96 | 4.88 | 4.90 | 0.02 | 99.59 |
| Jun-97 | 2.74 | 3.09 | 0.35 | 88.67 |

**EXHIBIT 40–10**

Index Returns (%) (Two-Year Periods)

| End Date | LBGC | LBAG | AG-GC Difference | Ratio GC To AG |
|----------|------|------|------------------|----------------|
| Dec-97   | 6.83 | 6.36 | −0.47 | 107.39 |
| Jun-98   | 4.17 | 3.93 | −0.24 | 106.11 |
| Dec-98   | 5.09 | 4.58 | −0.51 | 111.14 |
| Jun-99   | −2.28 | −1.37 | 0.91 | 166.42 |
| Jun-1980 | 11.81 | 11.92 | 0.11 | 99.08 |
| Jun-1982 | 8.70 | 7.51 | −1.19 | 115.85 |
| Jun-1984 | 31.45 | 32.25 | 0.80 | 97.52 |
| Jun-1986 | 55.29 | 55.94 | 0.65 | 98.84 |
| Jun-1988 | 12.50 | 14.02 | 1.52 | 89.16 |
| Jun-1990 | 20.33 | 21.03 | 0.70 | 96.67 |
| Jun-1992 | 25.84 | 26.24 | 0.40 | 98.48 |
| Jun-1994 | 11.50 | 10.33 | −1.17 | 111.33 |
| Jun-1996 | 18.01 | 18.19 | 0.18 | 99.01 |
| Jun-1998 | 19.91 | 19.55 | −0.36 | 101.84 |
| Oct-1999 | 2.16 | 2.94 | 0.78 | 73.47 |

a gradual, unpredictable lengthening in duration as the high percentage of low-duration premium mortgages are prepaid and refinanced with current coupon longer duration mortgages. This lengthening would occur quite independently of any changes in interest rates and as long as rates do not drop considerably. A big drop in rates will most likely cause the LBAG duration to decrease, and its performance would lag behind the performance of the LBGC substantially. The differential would probably exceed most market participants' expectations.

In fact, since September 1998, interest rates on 10-year bonds have risen from 5% to 6.25% in June 2000. The LBAG duration lengthened from 4.29 to approximately 5. Meanwhile, the duration of the LBGC dropped to 5.4 from 5.61. Therefore, today, in June 2000, absent very large changes in interest rates, we should expect the two indexes to perform very similarly. Duration differences between the bogeys will dominate performance considerations if interest rate changes are large.

Those who are required to select a performance bogey for their fund have a difficult choice. The bogey performs the role of directing the risk of the assets. The choice involves a trade-off between a bogey that (1) replicates the proportional distribution of bonds in the market, (2) has risk characteristics complementary to the liability structure of the assets, and (3) has a relatively neutral market bias associated with it. Unfortunately, no bogey satisfies all of these requirements, and the trade-offs can be costly. It is important to fully understand what the bogey represents to insure the robustness of the asset allocation decision.

The choices are difficult. Ultimately, correct macroeconomic forecasts will dominate the active/passive choice. Will volatility increase or diminish and when? Will rates go up or down and when? What influences volatility? How do interest rates and volatility changes trade off? When does the volatility/interest-rate forecast favor one index over the other? These are the tough questions you should be asking your active manager or your passive index.

## THE IMPORTANCE OF COUPON CONCENTRATION IN RELATIVE LBGC/LBAG PERFORMANCE

The LBAG and LBGC have exhibited a high historical correlation. The high correlation was violated during the second half of 1998. It is important to understand why the high correlation existed and why it diverges to better understand tomorrow's expected correlation.

It was previously noted that the major distinction between the LBGC and the LBAG is the inclusion of mortgages in the LBAG. As such, we must determine whether these securities' options were at the money, in the money, or out of the money to establish their effect on portfolio convexity. The simplest framework we can utilize to evaluate the effect on convexity is a pricing framework. Mortgages selling at a discount exhibit positive convexity and higher durations, whereas other mortgages exhibit low or negative convexity and lower durations.

Exhibit 40–11 shows the percentage of outstanding GNMAs priced at or below par for selected time periods. We observe that in 1982 all mortgages were at par or a discount. In 1984, most mortgages were at a discount. The situation differed in June 1986 in that very few mortgages were priced at a discount. The bear market into 1988 caused most mortgages to be at a discount. The bull market in 1998 caused most mortgages to be at a premium. Today, most mortgages are at a discount but only a modest discount. A bear market will cause more mortgages to be discounted and improve the convexity of the index.

Exhibit 40–12 provides combined coupon distribution data of GNMA, FHLMC, and FNMA mortgage pass-throughs. The greater percentage of discount mortgage securities will cause the durations of the two indexes to converge. In a modest bull market, the LBAG index duration will decline and it will increase in a bear market. A radical bull or bear market in interest rates will magnify these phenomenons. The opposite response will occur within the LBGC index. As such, at prevailing yield levels the relative performance differentials between the indexes will be meaningful given some meaningful level of interest rate volatility.

Lower yields will increase performance differentials as index character diverges; higher yields will mitigate expected performance differentials because index character will merge.

**EXHIBIT 40-11**

Percentage of
Outstanding GNMAs
Priced at or Below Par

| Date | Percentage |
|------|-----------|
| 6/78 | 96.8 |
| 6/80 | 97.4 |
| 6/82 | 97.1 |
| 6/84 | 95.7 |
| 6/86 | 34.9 |
| 6/88 | 83.0 |
| 6/90 | 65.1 |
| 6/92 | 3.5 |
| 6/94 | 58.7 |
| 6/96 | 52.2 |
| 6/98 | 13.1 |
| 6/90 | 37.1 |
| 12/99 | 77.7 |

**EXHIBIT 40-12**

GNMA Pass-Through Prices

| Coupon | 6/30/98 | 9/30/98 | 12/31/98 | % of Market |
|--------|---------|---------|----------|-------------|
| 5.5 | 97.47 | 97.25 | 96.63 | 0.35% |
| 6.0 | 97.47 | 100.34 | 99.13 | 6.79% |
| 6.5 | 99.78 | 102.16 | 101.00 | 23.43% |
| 7.0 | 101.56 | 103.16 | 102.31 | 27.98% |
| 7.5 | 102.72 | 103.59 | 103.00 | 19.16% |
| 8.0 | 103.65 | 104.16 | 103.88 | 12.33% |
| 8.5 | 105.56 | 105.63 | 105.88 | 3.64% |
| 9.0 | 107.06 | 106.63 | 106.72 | 3.37% |

**Prices of 10-Year Treasury Securities**

| | 6/30/98 | 9/30/98 | 12/31/98 |
|------|---------|---------|----------|
| Treasury | 101.34 | 109.36 | 100.80 |

# THE IMPORTANCE OF CHANGES IN THE SHAPE OF YIELD CURVE

Changing yield-curve shapes represent the other important first-order determinant of relative performance differentials. The indices are represented by various distributional holdings along the yield curve. Distributional differences between the LBGC and the LBAG,[5] and bond managers' portfolios will be important when yield-curve shapes are frequently variable and/or when changes in shape are of substantial magnitude. Generally speaking, the LBAG index contains a set of cash flows heavily weighted in the intermediate portion of the yield curve relative to the LBGC. Therefore, yield curve steepening favors the LBAG and flattening yield curves favor the LBGC; cetaris paribas. Yield-curve shape changes also change expected returns relative to those expected a priori because of the effects upon duration, call and put option values, prepayment behavior, and other more subtle effects.

The yield-curve effect is not included in this analysis. The difficulty in bond investment analysis is extremely complex when yield-curve shape changes are included. These complexities, including the potential correlation between interest rates and volatility, are beyond the scope of this chapter. Professional bond portfolio managers must understand these uncertain linkages if they hope to succeed.

# INDEX CONSCIOUSNESS

The extraordinary increased volatility of interest rates during the 1970s and 1980s and the reduction in volatility in the 1990s has resulted in considerable volatility in returns. Durational differences between portfolios result in substantially different returns when interest rates are volatile. The historical return differences between the LBGC and the Salomon High Grade Index illustrate this point. Many market participants were apparently surprised by the amount of price volatility that their bond portfolios experienced in the 1960s and 1970s. In an effort to control portfolio return variability relative to the "market," some bond managers have adopted portfolio constraints wherein the durational risk relative to the market index is bound. The movement to this new investment strategy helped control variability but nullifies the relative advantages achievable through expert macroeconomic analysis and interest-rate forecasting. The movement to this policy is an admission of a flawed investment theory, risk aversion, and/or an uncertain conviction in forecasting of quantitative capability. This chapter has emphasized the importance of the contribution of good interest-rate and volatility forecasts with consistent period-dependent asset selection.

---

5. Changes in the shape of the yield curve directly affect mortgage values. Coupon distribution relative to prevailing interest rates will influence the LBAG asset distribution along the yield curve.

# SOME IMPORTANT MISCELLANEOUS COMMENTS ABOUT INDEXES

In 1986, the author was perplexed by the peculiar behavior of the plan sponsor community. The well-educated community requires and understands rigorous modern finance statistical methods. A compelling risk/reward statistical argument resulted in the transition from the Long Salomon Bond Index to the LBGC just after interest rates hit a historical high. At the time, the high interest rates caused, oddly enough, the durational difference (risk) of long bonds and 10-year bonds to approach each other. The subsequent transition to the LBAG occurred shortly thereafter, resulting in a further reduction in duration and call protection at a time when interest rates were very high.

Presently, there is a movement to a "core-plus" concept represented by the Lehman Universal Index (LUNV). This more closely coincides with the end of one of the most remarkable growth decades in U.S. history. A move to the LUNV implies a further reduction in (1) duration, (2) call protection, and (3)

## EXHIBIT 40–13

Important Macroeconomics and Microeconomics Phenomena

|  | Micro | Macro |
|---|---|---|
| 1. Salomon Long Index → LBGC | Substitution of issuance of intermediate debt in lieu of longer bonds. | More risky capital structure |
| 2. LBGC → LBAG | Financing of mortgage industry from banking industry to longer-term investors. Securitization of asset markets. | Cheaper cost of debt to consumers. Results in more robust housing industry, consumer demand and household leverage. Potential moral hazard risk in loan origination. |
| 3. LBAG → LUNV | Financing of emerging market and high yield debt market. | Reduces cost of debt to highly leveraged producers. Encourages more debt and leverage. Increases risk of plan assets and reduces value of bond portfolio as deflationary hedge. |

quality. The author remains skeptical of the "historically blind" but, empirically rigorous, approach of the herd. A study of financial history over longer periods of time reveals gradual transitions to greater risk followed by abrupt periods of wealth destruction and risk aversion. It is because all agents in the process—especially plan sponsors and investment managers—are judged over relatively short time periods. However, that decision-making is dominated by studies subjugated by recent data. These short periods are incongruent with the life of the plans.

Important macroeconomic and microeconomic phenomena result from the choices plan sponsors make with respect to bogeys. Exhibit 40-13 illustrates the point. The herd move from one bogey to another initially results in shifting demand curves for a sector that is soon followed by a shift in the supply curve. The demand curve shift reinforces the asset allocation realignment as prices of the newly added asset class are bid up. When more and more of the herd enter, assets are bid up ever more—further reinforcing the original statistical analysis and creating a more powerful updated statistical study. Eventually, supply catches up to the fresh demand resulting in a more leveraged economy and a reduced quality of plan assets. Present U.S. Treasury debt retirement will accelerate the transition to lower quality holdings.

## CHAPTER 41

# MANAGING INDEXED AND ENHANCED INDEXED BOND PORTFOLIOS*

**Kenneth E. Volpert, CFA**
Principal and Senior Portfolio Manager
The Vanguard Group, Inc.

## OVERVIEW OF DOMESTIC BOND MANAGEMENT

Domestic bond management can be likened to a sailing regatta. The index is the lead boat, since it does not have expenses and transaction costs to contend with, and all managers (including index fund managers) are the other boats, trying to make up the distance and pass the index boat. Strategies that may be used to make up the difference and pass the lead boat comprise a wide spectrum of styles and approaches. Exhibit 41–1 displays the major elements of these approaches.

### Pure Bond Index Matching

*Pure bond indexing* is the lowest risk (and lowest expected return) approach to bond management versus a specific benchmark. This approach essentially guarantees that returns will lag behind the index boat by the cost difference (expenses plus transaction costs). Pure bond index matching attempts to fully replicate the index by owning all the bonds in the index in the same percentage as the index. Hence, this approach is also called the *full replication approach*. In the bond market, however, such an approach is very difficult to accomplish and very costly to implement. Many bonds in the index were issued years ago, and are consequently illiquid. Many bonds were also issued when interest rates were

---

* Reprinted from Chapter 12 in Frank J. Fabozzi (ed.), *Managing Fixed Income Portfolios* (New Hope, PA: Frank J. Fabozzi Associates, 1997).

The author wishes to achknowledge the professional and personal contribution of Irwin E. Jones, who retired from the business in 1996. Irwin introduced the author to the bond indexing business in 1986. Irwin's highest integrity, his inquisitive nature, his professional mentoring role, and his personal friendship have deeply affected the author. Thank you Irwin!

**EXHIBIT 41-1**

Bond Management Risk Spectrum

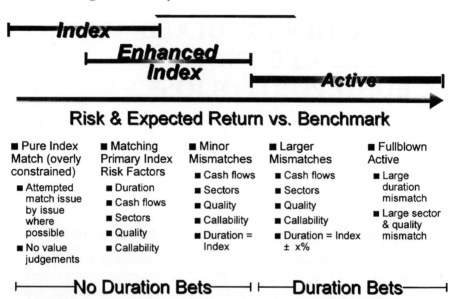

Risk & Expected Return vs. Benchmark

- Pure Index Match (overly constrained)
  - Attempted match issue by issue where possible
  - No value judgements

- Matching Primary Index Risk Factors
  - Duration
  - Cash flows
  - Sectors
  - Quality
  - Callability

- Minor Mismatches
  - Cash flows
  - Sectors
  - Quality
  - Callability
  - Duration = Index

- Larger Mismatches
  - Cash flows
  - Sectors
  - Quality
  - Callability
  - Duration = Index ± x%

- Fullblown Active
  - Large duration mismatch
  - Large sector & quality mismatch

├————No Duration Bets————┤ ├————Duration Bets————┤

significantly different from current rates. Today's holders may be unwilling to incur a gain or loss by selling their bonds to an index fund.

On March 31, 2000, the Lehman Brothers Aggregate Bond Index contained 142 Treasury issues, 890 federal agency issues, 3,649 corporate issues, 161 asset-backed issues, 250 commercial mortgage-backed securities, and 474 broadly categorized mortgage issues (essentially hundreds of thousands of mortgage pools). Full replication is feasible (although not desirable for reasons to be mentioned later) in the Treasury market, but cannot be reasonably implemented in the agency, mortgage or corporate markets. Thousands of the agency and corporate issues are locked away in long-term bond portfolios and could only be purchased from these investors by paying extremely high prices. For this reason, full replication of a broad bond index (including corporates and mortgages) is very inefficient, if not impossible.

## Enhanced Indexing/Matching Primary Risk Factors

The *enhanced bond indexing/matching primary risk factors approach* involves investing in a large sample of bonds such that the portfolio risk factors match the index risk factors. The result is a portfolio that, when fully implemented, will have higher average monthly tracking differences (standard deviation of tracking differences) than the full replication (i.e., pure index matching) approach, but it can be implemented and maintained at much lower cost resulting in net investment performance that is much closer to the index. Returning to the regatta analogy, the portfolio boat stays on the same "tack" as the index boat, but "trims its sails" to run a little more efficiently. Staying on the same "tack" means that the sails are set to take the portfolio boat in the same direction as the index boat, thereby being exposed to the same winds and elements. "Trimming the sails" means that the little details of the sail position and sail shape are performed better and executed more efficiently than on the index boat. The risk factors that need to be matched are duration, cash flow distribution, sector, quality, and call exposure (more on this later). This approach is considered a form of enhanced indexing because the return is enhanced (more on this later) relative to the full replication indexing approach.

## Enhanced Indexing/Minor Risk Factor Mismatches

The *enhanced bond indexing/minor risk factor mismatches approach* allows for minor mismatches in the risk factors (except duration) to tilt the portfolio in favor of particular areas of relative value (sector, quality, term structure, call risk, etc.). Because the mismatches (and impact on tracking) are very small, this is still considered enhanced indexing. These additional enhancements are essentially "sail trimming" strategies designed to make up additional distance versus the index boat, while staying on the same tack, and being exposed to the same elements.

## Active Management/Larger Risk Factor Mismatches

The active management/larger risk factor mismatches approach is a conservative approach to active management. The manager will make larger mismatches in the risk factors to attempt to add greater value. This approach may also make small duration bets. In most cases, the management fee and transaction costs are significantly higher than for pure or enhanced indexing, yet the net investment return is usually lower. The addition of these additional costs is the reason why a typical index portfolio often outperforms the average active manager in performance universes. Since this strategy has higher costs (higher expenses and transaction costs), the manager will moderately "change tack" to seek greater winds elsewhere, resulting in increased manager risk (i.e., greater risk of deviating from the "market" return and structure).

## Active Management/Full-Blown Active

The *active management/full-blown active approach* is an aggressive active style where large duration and sector bets are made, and where significant value-added (or lost) relative to an index can be experienced. Above-average performance consistency is difficult to find in this group of managers, so investors who choose this management style need to look deeper than just at recent performance to discern the good from the bad. This approach may significantly change the "course" relative to the index boat and may risk significant tracking and portfolio structure variations from the index boat in the hope of adding much greater return.

## WHY INDEX BOND PORTFOLIOS?

There are several reasons for indexing: broad diversification, competitive performance, low cost, consistent relative performance, market performance predictability, time-tested, and redirection of focus on asset allocation. Each reason is discussed below.

### Broad Diversification

Broad bond index portfolios provide excellent diversification. The Lehman Brothers Aggregate Bond Index, which is designed to capture the entire U.S. investment-grade bond market, has over 5,500 issues and more than $5.5 trillion in market value as of March 31, 2000. A large bond index portfolio designed to replicate this Index may have 500 or more issues, resulting in significant issuer diversification benefits. Most active portfolios have much heavier specific issuer concentrations, resulting in significant exposure to issuer event (credit) risk.

In addition, an index portfolio designed to match the Lehman Brothers Aggregate Bond Index will have exposure to not only Treasury and agency sectors, but also to mortgages, industrials, electric and telephone utilities, finance, dollar-denominated foreign, and asset-backed sectors. Such a portfolio will also have broad exposure to the yield curve with holdings from one year to over 30 years to maturity. These sources of diversification result in a portfolio with lower risk for a given level of return than is available from less diversified portfolios.

### Competitive Performance

Since index portfolios have lower management fees and lower transaction costs (resulting from significantly lower portfolio turnover), it is not surprising that they usually outperform the average active portfolio in most universes. After all, a broad index is by design a representation of the whole pie of investment alternatives. Therefore, the sum of all active managers should equal the index in composition. Also, the sum of the investment performance of all active managers (grossed up for the higher management fees and transaction costs) should also equal the index in performance. In the mutual fund market, where the bond index expense ratio advantage is about 0.8% per year, the largest bond index portfolio (managed against the Lehman Brothers Aggregate Bond Index) outperformed over 80% of its Lipper Group over 1 year, and 90% over 3, and 5 years ending 12/31/99. In the large institutional market, where the expense advantage of indexing is lower, index portfolios outperformed 60–75% of actively managed portfolios over the same period (depending on the universe chosen).

## Low Cost

The primary reason for competitive performance of index funds is lower cost. This lower cost takes two forms: (1) lower management fees and (2) lower transaction costs associated with lower portfolio turnover rates. This lower cost advantage is durable and predictable—year after year. Don Phillips, President of Morningstar, summarizes the impact of higher costs: "if you pay the executive at Sara Lee more, it doesn't make the cheesecake less good. But with mutual funds (investment management), it comes directly out of the batter." Indeed it does!

## Consistent Relative Performance

Exhibit 41–2 shows the performance for the largest bond index mutual fund against its Lipper universe (Intermediate Government) for calendar years starting

### EXHIBIT 41–2

Annual Performance Consistency Analysis
Index Portfolio versus Lipper Intermediate Government

|      | Index Portfolio Return | Lipper Rank | Total in Group | Percent Outperformed |
|------|------------------------|-------------|----------------|----------------------|
| 1989 | 13.65                  | 4           | 25             | 84                   |
| 1990 | 8.65                   | 15          | 26             | 42                   |
| 1991 | 15.25                  | 5           | 24             | 79                   |
| 1992 | 7.14                   | 4           | 32             | 88                   |
| 1993 | 9.68                   | 12          | 50             | 76                   |
| 1994 | −2.66                  | 27          | 77             | 65                   |
| 1995 | 18.18                  | 13          | 98             | 87                   |
| 1996 | 3.54                   | 24          | 120            | 80                   |
| 1997 | 9.41                   | 16          | 123            | 87                   |
| 1998 | 8.58                   | 22          | 123            | 82                   |
| 1999 | −0.76                  | 25          | 124            | 80                   |

in 1989. In fairness, this portfolio has approximately 40% in corporates (the other 60% is U.S. Treasury and agency securities, and agency mortgage-backed securities), so a comparison against a government universe is not entirely appropriate. The only year where the portfolio outperformed less than 50% of the universe was 1990 (42%). For all the other years the portfolio outperformed between 65% to 88% of the competition in its maturity and quality category with the average over the full 11 years at 77%. The primary reason (approximately 67% of the advantage) for this consistent outperformance is the significantly lower expenses and transaction costs incurred by the portfolio.

## Market Performance Predictability

A properly managed broad bond index portfolio can be assured of performing in line with the market as a whole. Therefore, regardless of the direction the market takes, the investor can be assured of the performance of a diversified broad index (the "market").

## Time Tested

Bond index portfolios have been successfully managed since the early 1980s—through rising and falling interest rate cycles as well as through increasing and declining credit spread cycles. Through all these market changes, bond indexing has proven to provide a more than competitive return with low to moderate risk.

## Redirects Focus to Most Important Decision—Asset Allocation

Perhaps the most significant reason to index bonds is that it enables investors to concentrate on the more important asset allocation decision. Very often, limited decision-making time and effort is wasted on the hope of adding 20–40 basis points on the bond portion of a portfolio, when existing misallocation of assets to stocks or international investments are resulting in hundreds of basis points of underperformance for the entire portfolio. Indexing helps facilitate more effective use of limited decision-making resources available to most investors.

## WHICH INDEX SHOULD BE USED?

A bond index is defined by a set of rules (characteristics) that are then applied to all issues in the marketplace. The rules include maturity, size, sector, and quality characteristics. The issues that fit the rules are then combined, as if in a portfolio, with each issue's weight determined by its relative market value outstanding.

For indexing, the broader the Index (for a given level of risk) the better the benchmark. The broadest U.S. bond index is the Lehman Brothers Aggregate Bond Index (essentially identical to the Salomon Broad Investment Grade Index and the Merrill Lynch Domestic Master Index). At March 31, 2000, the Lehman Brothers Aggregate Bond Index had more than 5,500 issues representing a market value of over $5.5 trillion. Exhibit 41–3 shows that the composition of the Aggregate Bond Index was 32% Treasury bonds, 9% agency bonds, 25% corporate, asset-backed, and commercial mortgage-backed, and 34% mortgage-backed securities. The option-adjusted duration (a duration number that reflects the possibility of bonds being called by the issuer) was 4.9, with an average maturity of 8.9, making it the broadest domestic intermediate investment grade index available. Sub-indices of the Lehman Brothers Aggregate Bond Index can be created that result in different risk/return profiles. For example, a corporate-only index can be replicated for those who do not want as much quality as exists in the Lehman Brothers Aggregate Bond Index; or a one- to five-year government/corporate Index can be created, for those who would rather have a short duration portfolio.

## Market Value Risk

Generally, the longer the maturity of the bond portfolio, the higher its yield, assuming a "normally" sloped yield curve. The total return on a bond is made up of the coupon (or income) component and the principal (or price change) component. Since the yield curve (which impacts the principal component of total return) is highly unlikely to remain unchanged, the longer bond portfolio will not necessarily have a higher total return. Exhibit 41–4 shows the one-year total return of different maturity securities (short: 3 years; intermediate: 7 years;

**EXHIBIT 41–3**

Lehman Brothers Aggregate Bond Index Composition (As of 3/31/2000)

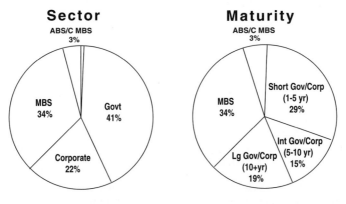

### E X H I B I T   41–4

Market Value Risk

| High Interest Rate Environment | | | | 1 Year Return (Income + Price Return) | |
| --- | --- | --- | --- | --- | --- |
| Coupon | Maturity | Price | Duration | Rates Rise 1% | Rates Fall 1% |
| 12 | 3 year | 100 | 2.5 | 9.6 | 14.5 |
| 12 | 7 year | 100 | 4.6 | 7.5 | 16.8 |
| 12 | 20 year | 100 | 7.5 | 4.9 | 20.0 |

| Low Interest Rate Environment | | | | 1 Year Return (Income + Price Return) | |
| --- | --- | --- | --- | --- | --- |
| Coupon | Maturity | Price | Duration | Rates Rise 1% | Rates Fall 1% |
| 6 | 3 year | 100 | 2.7 | 3.3 | 8.8 |
| 6 | 7 year | 100 | 5.6 | 0.5 | 11.8 |
| 6 | 20 year | 100 | 11.6 | −4.7 | 18.6 |

and, long: 20 years) in both high-rate and low-rate environments, assuming yields rise or fall 1%. Clearly, as the maturity or duration of the portfolio lengthens, the greater the market value risk. In addition, the lower the yield environment, the greater the market value risk, especially for the intermediate-term and long-term portfolios. This is the result of (1) the portfolio's duration increasing as interest rates decrease and (2) the portfolio's lower yield to maturity which provides less of a cushion to offset principal losses. Therefore, for investors who are risk averse in terms of their principal, the short-term or intermediate-term index as a benchmark may be more appropriate than the long index.

## Income Risk

Many investors invest for income, spending only the income distributed by an investment without dipping into principal. Foundations and retirees invest for a stable and hopefully growing income stream that they can depend on for current and future consumption. Exhibit 41–5 shows the income stream (distributed mutual fund income) from a $10,000 investment in a short (three-year), intermediate (seven-year), and long (20-year) mutual fund over the last 15 years, assuming equivalent growth rates for the portfolios. It's obvious that if stability and durability of income are the primary concerns, than the long portfolio is the least risky and the short portfolio is the most risky.

## Liability Framework Risk

Pension funds and financial institutions invest to finance future liabilities. Long-term liabilities (like active retired lives liabilities) require investments in long-

**EXHIBIT   41–5**

Income Risk

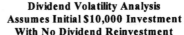

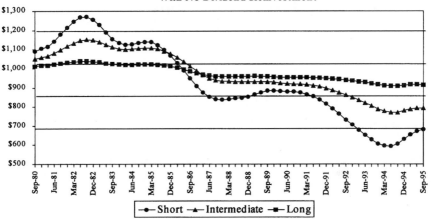

term assets to minimize risk, resulting in both a portfolio and a liability stream that is equally sensitive to interest-rate changes. A portfolio that invests in short bonds may look less risky on an absolute return basis, but it is actually much riskier (because of its mismatch with long liabilities) when the portfolio market value is compared to the present value of the pension liability (the difference is the surplus or deficit). The "surplus" risk will be minimized on a fully funded plan against small changes in market rates when the duration of the portfolio is matched (or immunized) to the duration of the liability.

Exhibit 41–6 contains a summary comparison showing that the investment with the lowest market value risk has the highest income or liability risk. Likewise, the investment with the highest market value risk has the lowest income or liability risk. Clearly, the risk framework chosen depends on whether the investment objective is principal preservation or income durability.

## PRIMARY BOND INDEXING RISK FACTORS

Effective bond indexing does not require full replication, nor is it desired. What is required is matching the primary risk factors of the benchmark index in a credit diversified portfolio. Exhibit 41–7 lists the primary risk factors that apply to the government, corporate, and mortgage sectors, accompanied by an explanation of these primary risk factors.

**E X H I B I T   41–6**

Bond Market Risk Summary

| NAV Type | Market Value Risk | Income or Liability Risk | Average Maturity | Current Duration | Portfolios |
|---|---|---|---|---|---|
| Stable Dollar NAV | Lowest | Highest | 30–90 Days | 0.1 | Money Market Portfolios |
| Variable NAV | Low | High | 2–4 Years | 2.5 | Short-Term Portfolios |
| | Medium | Medium | 7–10 Years | 5.0 | Intermediate-Term Portfolios |
| | High | Low | 15–25 Years | 10.0 | Long-Term Portfolios |

**E X H I B I T   41–7**

Primary Bond Index Matching Factors

| | Government | Corporate | MBS |
|---|---|---|---|
| Modified Adjusted Duration | X | X | |
| Percent Value of Cash Flows | X | X | |
| Precent in Sector and Quality | | X | |
| Duration Contribution of Sector | | X | |
| Duration Contribution of Credit Quality | | X | |
| Sector/Coupon/Maturity Cell Weights | | X | X |
| Issuer Exposure Control | | X | |

## Modified Adjusted Duration

The modified adjusted duration (or option-adjusted modified duration) is a simple single measure of interest rate risk of the portfolio. It's a great place to start, but is entirely too rough of a measure to adequately track an index. The portfolio duration will give the manager a rough approximation of the price change observed if interest rates rise or fall (in a parallel fashion) immediately by 1%. If rates rise by 1%, a five-year duration portfolio will experience an approximate 5% decline in value ((+1% yield change) × (five-year portfolio duration) × (−1)). If the yield curve does not move in a parallel fashion, then the duration is of limited value. For obvious reasons, it is important to match the duration of the portfolio to the duration of the benchmark index.

# Present Value Distribution of Cash Flows

A more accurate way to capture yield curve risk is by matching the cash flow distribution of the index. Yield curve changes are composed of parallel shifts, curve twists (e.g., short rates down, intermediate rates unchanged, long rates up), and curve butterfly (e.g., short and long rates down, intermediate rates up) movements. By decomposing the index (and portfolio) into a stream of future payments and discounting each payment to the present value and summing these values, one calculates the index (and portfolio) market value. By matching the percent of the portfolio's present value that comes due at certain intervals in time (each vertex) with that of the benchmark index, the portfolio will be largely protected from tracking error (versus the benchmark) associated with yield curve changes. Since the portfolio duration is equal to the benchmark index duration (duration is the sum of all vertices (Exhibit 41–8), of the percent of present value multiplied by the vertex (time)), this method will guard against parallel changes in yield. Since all points in time (vertices) are closely matched in percent, any local term structure movements (non-parallel changes) will not affect tracking (these yield change risks are essentially immunized). For callable se-

**E X H I B I T   41–8**

Cash Flow Distribution Analysis

| Time | Percent of Value | Duration Contribution | Percent of Duration |
|------|------------------|-----------------------|---------------------|
| 0 | 2.6 | 0.00 | 0.0 |
| 0.5 | 5.7 | 0.03 | 0.6 |
| 1 | 8.1 | 0.08 | 1.6 |
| 1.5 | 10.2 | 0.15 | 3.1 |
| 2 | 11.8 | 0.24 | 4.8 |
| 3 | 13.0 | 0.39 | 7.9 |
| 4 | 10.5 | 0.42 | 8.5 |
| 5 | 7.6 | 0.38 | 7.7 |
| 6 | 5.7 | 0.34 | 6.9 |
| 7 | 4.6 | 0.32 | 6.5 |
| 8 | 4.4 | 0.35 | 7.1 |
| 9 | 4.0 | 0.36 | 7.3 |
| 10 | 2.8 | 0.28 | 5.7 |
| 12 | 2.3 | 0.28 | 5.6 |
| 15 | 2.7 | 0.41 | 8.2 |
| 20 | 2.4 | 0.48 | 9.7 |
| 25 | 1.1 | 0.28 | 5.6 |
| 30 | 0.5 | 0.15 | 3.0 |
| 40 | 0.0 | 0.00 | 0.0 |
| Total | 100.0 | 4.93 | 100.0 |

curities, the cash flows need to be distributed to the vertices in accordance with the probability of call. A 10-year bond that is highly likely to be called in three years should have cash flows that are primarily allocated to the three-year vertex.

## Percent in Sector and Quality

The yield of the index is largely replicated by matching the percentage weight in the various sectors and qualities, assuming that all maturity categories are fully accounted for by the replicating portfolio. Exhibit 41–9 shows the Lehman Brothers Aggregate Bond Index weights in the various sectors and qualities as of 9/30/96.

## Duration Contribution of Sector

The best way (without excessively constraining the process) to protect a portfolio from tracking differences associated with changes in sector spreads (industry

### EXHIBIT 41–9

Sector and Quality Distribution Analysis

| Sector | Percent of PV | Duration | Duration Contribution | Percent of Duration |
|---|---|---|---|---|
| Treasury | 31.2 | 5.55 | 1.73 | 35.1 |
| Agency | 9.6 | 4.69 | 0.45 | 9.1 |
| Industrial | 9.2 | 6.55 | 0.60 | 12.2 |
| Utility | 1.5 | 5.84 | 0.09 | 1.8 |
| Finance | 6.3 | 4.49 | 0.28 | 5.7 |
| Canadian | 1.0 | 5.98 | 0.06 | 1.2 |
| Sovereign | 1.3 | 5.15 | 0.07 | 1.3 |
| Foreign Corporate | 2.2 | 5.45 | 0.12 | 2.4 |
| Supranational | 0.8 | 4.65 | 0.04 | 0.8 |
| GNMA | 8.5 | 4.12 | 0.35 | 7.1 |
| FNMA | 14.1 | 4.00 | 0.56 | 11.4 |
| FGLMC | 11.6 | 4.00 | 0.46 | 9.4 |
| Asset-Backed | 1.3 | 3.07 | 0.04 | 0.8 |
| CMBS | 1.5 | 5.22 | 0.08 | 1.5 |
| Total | 100.0 | 4.93 | 4.93 | 100.0 |
| Quality | | | | |
| AAA | 79.3 | 4.74 | 3.76 | 76.2 |
| AA | 4.2 | 5.12 | 0.22 | 4.4 |
| A | 9.6 | 5.73 | 0.55 | 11.2 |
| BAA | 6.9 | 5.91 | 0.41 | 8.3 |
| Total | 100.0 | 4.93 | 4.93 | 100.0 |

risk) is to match the amount of the index duration (Exhibit 41–9) that comes from the various sectors. If this can be accomplished, a given change in sector spreads will have an equal impact on the portfolio and the index.

## Duration Contribution of Quality

Similarly, the most effective way to protect a portfolio from tracking differences related to changes in quality spreads (leverage/economic risk) is to match the amount of the index duration that comes from the various quality categories. This is particularly important in the lower-rated categories, which are characterized by larger spread changes.

## Sector/Coupon/Maturity Cell Weights

The call exposure of an index is a difficult factor to replicate. The convexity value (convexity measures how a bond's duration changes as yield levels change) alone is inadequate since it measures expected changes in duration over a small change in yield levels. In addition, the change in convexity can be very different as yield levels change. Managers who attempt only to match the index convexity value often find themselves having to buy or sell highly illiquid callable securities to stay matched and, in the process, generate excessive transaction costs. A better method of matching the call exposure is to match the sector, coupon, and maturity weights of the callable sectors. By matching these weights, the convexity of the index should be matched. In addition, as rates change, the changes in call exposure (convexity) of the portfolio will be matched to the index, requiring little or no rebalancing.

In the mortgage market, call (prepayment) risk is very significant. The volatility in the option-adjusted duration of the Lehman Brothers Mortgage Index, which measures the extent of the call exposure of the mortgage market, is shown in Exhibit 41–10. Also shown in the exhibit is the Mortgage Bankers Refinancing Index (inverted), which measures the extent of mortgage refinancing occurring in the market. Clearly, the greater the refinancing activity, the shorter the index duration due to the greater likelihood that the higher coupons (issues priced above par) will be refinanced with lower coupon securities. For this reason, matching the coupon distribution of the mortgage index is critical. The best risk management is accomplished by matching the index weights in a multidimensional matrix of the maturity (balloon, 15-year, 30-year), sector (FNMA, FGLMC, GNMA), coupon (50 basis point increments), and seasoning (new, moderate, and seasoned). This level of detail is easily accomplished in a large portfolio (more than $1 billion in assets), but more difficult to accomplish in smaller portfolios.

**E X H I B I T   41–10**

Mortage Call Exposure Analysis

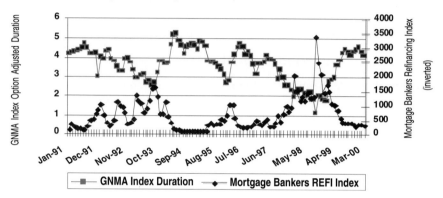

## Issuer Exposure

If the major risk factors described above are matched, but with too few issues, there remains significant risk that can still be diversified away. "Event" risk, a risk widely watched in the late 1980s, when there was significant corporate leveraging taking place (LBOs), is the final primary risk factor that needs to be measured and controlled. Issuer exposure, like sector and quality, needs to be measured in more than percentage terms only, versus the index benchmark. Setting percent of market value limits without regard to issuer duration risk and issuer index weights is not adequate. Immediately after a negative credit event, the spread widens. Therefore, the best measure of the issuer event risk impact on a portfolio is the impact on portfolio market value of that spread widening. This can be measured by calculating how much of the portfolio duration ("duration contribution") comes from the holdings in each issuer. This calculation should also be figured for the index. The basis point impact on tracking of a spread-widening event will be the spread change (of the issuer) multiplied by the difference in duration contribution (portfolio − index) multiplied by (−1).

Exhibit 41–11 contains an example of this analysis. Issuer XXX Corp has an equal percent weight to the Index, but its duration contribution is 0.16 greater. If an event occurred that would widen XXX Corp spreads by 100 basis points, the portfolio would suffer an unfavorable tracking difference of 16 basis points versus the index (100 basis point spread change × 0.16 duration contribution overweight × −1). If the same 100 basis points widening were to occur to XYZ Corp bonds, the tracking difference would be a favorable 8 basis points (100 basis point spread change × −0.08 duration contribution underweight × −1), even though the percent weight is matched to the index. For effective index fund management, duration contribution exposure limits (versus the index) need to be set at the issuer level.

**E X H I B I T   41–11**

Issuer Exposure Comparison—Percent of Market Value versus Duration Contribution

|  | Portfolio | | |
|---|---|---|---|
|  | Percent of Market Value | Duration | Duration Contribution |
| XXX Corp | 4 | 8 | 0.32 |
| ZZZ Corp | 4 | 4 | 0.16 |
| XYZ Corp | 4 | 2 | 0.08 |

|  | Index | | | Portfolio-Index | |
|---|---|---|---|---|---|
|  | Percent of Market Value | Duration | Duration Contribution | Percent Difference | Contribution Difference |
| XXX Corp | 4 | 4 | 0.16 | 0 | 0.16 |
| ZZZ Corp | 4 | 4 | 0.16 | 0 | 0.00 |
| XYZ Corp | 4 | 4 | 0.16 | 0 | −0.08 |

# BOND INDEX ENHANCEMENTS

## Details, Details, Details

As in sailing, speed (returns versus the benchmark) comes from paying close attention to the details, not simply from "watching the wind" (interest rates). Portfolio managers can "trim" their portfolio sails to more efficiently compete in the investment management race. The trimming strategies include: (1) lower costs, (2) issue selection, (3) yield curve positioning, (4) sector and quality positioning, and (5) call exposure positioning.

## Why Enhancements are Necessary

Since the index does not incur expenses or transaction costs, enhancements are necessary just to provide a net return equal to the index. A primary source of return shortfalls besides expenses is the transaction costs associated with portfolio growth.

Exhibit 41–12 shows the transaction costs and resulting tracking error associated with single contribution growth versus multiple contribution growth. In the example, the single contribution portfolio had tracking error of 18 basis points associated with investing net cash flow. In the multiple contribution portfolio the tracking error is a significantly higher 41 basis points, even though the

**EXHIBIT 41-12**

Why Enhancements are Necessary
Analysis of the Tracking Impact of Growth
Single Contribution versus Multiple Contributions

| | Portfolio Market Value | Contribution | Trans. Cost ($ at 18bp) | New Portfolio Value | Tracking Error from Trans Cost (bp) | Cumulative Tracking Error from Trans Cost (bp) |
|---|---|---|---|---|---|---|
| **Single Contributions** | $ — | $250,000,000 | $450,000 | $249,550,000 | 18.0 | 18.0 |
| **Multiple Contributions** | $ — | $50,000,000 | $90,000 | $49,910,000 | 18.0 | 18.0 |
| | $49,910,000 | $50,000,000 | $90,000 | $99,820,000 | 9.0 | 27.0 |
| | $99,820,000 | $50,000,000 | $90,000 | $149,730,000 | 6.0 | 33.1 |
| | $149,730,000 | $50,000,000 | $90,000 | $199,640,000 | 4.5 | 37.6 |
| | $199,640,000 | $50,000,000 | $90,000 | $249,550,000 | 3.6 | 41.2 |
| | | $250,000,000 | $450,000 | | | |

dollar cost of transaction costs is the same ($450,000). Therefore, portfolios with high growth rates will suffer additional negative tracking error, making enhancements necessary simply to stay equal to a no-growth or slow-growth portfolio.

Exhibit 41–13 shows in graphical form the cumulative adverse tracking impact resulting from portfolio growth for Treasury, government/corporate, and corporate portfolios. The greater the growth rate and/or the less liquid the market, the greater the adverse impact on tracking error.

## Lower Cost Enhancements

One of the simplest but most overlooked forms of enhancements is to keep costs down. Costs that impact portfolio performance are expenses/management fees and transaction costs.

Enhanced indexers work hard to add an incremental 10 to 30 basis points per year to portfolio returns, yet in the mutual fund arena, the average bond fund expense ratio is 80 basis points greater than the lowest index portfolio expense ratio. As a result, returns of such funds are significantly lower. Even in the indexing arena, expenses vary by large margins. Simply shopping around for the index fund with the lowest expenses, provided the net return is competitive with other index funds, is a simple way to enhance returns. For a plan sponsor with outside index managers, having the existing manager and one or two other reputable indexers re-bid the business every few years will make sure the expenses are as low as possible.

**E X H I B I T    41–13**

Why Enchancements are Necesary
Return Impact of Transaction Costs Over 1 Year

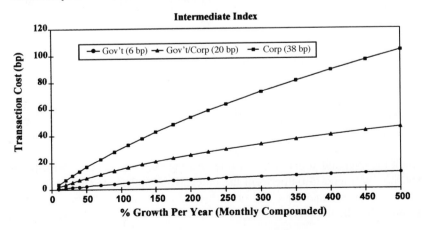

The other major cost factor is transaction costs. Since bond index funds have low annual turnover (about 40%) versus active portfolios (generally over 100%), transaction costs are significantly lower for index portfolios. In addition, the development of a competitive trading process will further reduce the transaction cost impact. It's obvious when seeking bids to include many brokers in the bidding process. For rapidly growing portfolios, where most of the transactions are offerings, an effective competitive trading process is essential. Since there is no central exchange for corporate bonds, an efficient system of evaluating real-time offerings of target issuers from many different brokers to compare relative value, will yield significant transaction cost savings, hence further enhancing the returns.

## Issue Selection Enhancements

For U.S. Treasury securities, the primary tool for selecting cheap bonds is comparing actual bond prices to the theoretical "fitted" price. The theoretical curve is derived that will minimize the pricing errors of all Treasury issues in the market, subject to various curve-smoothing rules. Each actual bond's yield is then compared to the bond's "fitted" yield (calculated using the theoretical curve). Bonds yielding more than the "fitted" yield are cheap, and those yielding less are rich. Another useful supplement is an analysis of the recent history of the bond yield versus the fitted yield. This analysis will indicate whether a cheap bond has been getting cheaper or richer.

Corporate issue selection enhancements come primarily from staying clear of deteriorating credits, and owning (generally overweighted versus the index) improving credits. The greater the manager's confidence in the ability of the credit analyst of the firm to add value via issuer selection, the larger can be the maximum issuer exposure limit (see "Primary Index Risk Factors—Issuer Exposure" section of this chapter). If the manager does not believe the firm's credit analyst can add value via issuer selection, the greater will be the diversification among issuers.

## Yield Curve Enhancements

Various maturities along the term structure are consistently overvalued or undervalued. For example, the 30-year Treasury region tends to be consistently overvalued, resulting in an inverted yield curve from 25 to 30 years. Likewise, the high-coupon callable bonds maturing in 2009–2012 tend to be consistently undervalued. Strategies that overweight the undervalued maturities and underweight the overvalued maturities, while keeping the same general term structure exposure, will tend to outperform the index. This analysis is similar to looking for the maturities that have the more favorable "roll down" characteristics—meaning that the near-term passage of time may result in the bond rolling down the yield curve and, therefore, it will trade at a lower yield resulting in potential price appreciation. Cheap parts of the curve tend to have favorable "roll down," while rich parts of the curve (e.g., 30-year area) tend to have little or no "roll down" opportunities.

## Sector/Quality Enhancements

Sector and quality enhancements take two primary forms: (1) ongoing yield tilt toward short duration corporates and (2) periodic minor over or underweighting of sectors or qualities.

The ongoing yield tilt enhancement (also called "corporate substitution") strategy recognizes that the best yield spread per unit of duration risk is available in short-term corporates (under 5 years). A strategy that underweights 1–5 year government bonds and overweights 1–5 year corporates will increase the yield of the portfolio with a less than commensurate increase in risk. Exhibit 41–14 shows the rolling 12-month return differential of the Lehman Brothers 1–5 Year Corporate Index versus the Lehman Brothers 1–5 Year Treasury Index.

The persistent return enhancement is obvious for all periods except the brief spread widening periods of 1990–91, 1998, and early in 2000. The primary reason the strategy is effective is that the yield advantage of short corporates requires a significant corporate spread widening move over a one-year period for short corporates to perform as poorly as short Treasuries. Exhibit 41–15 shows the spread increases that would be required to break-even with equal risk Treasury securities over a one-year holding period for corporates of varying

**EXHIBIT    41–14**

Lehman 1–5 year Corporate Index versus Lehman 1–5 year Treasury Index

### Rolling 12-month Total Return Difference

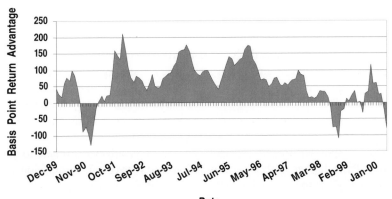

*Date*

**EXHIBIT  41–15**

Breakeven Spread Widening Analysis—Corporates vs. Treasuries
Assumes One Year Holding Period

| Maturity | Wide Spreads | Breakeven additional Widening | Moderate Spreads | Breakeven additional Widening | Narrow Spreads | Breakeven additional Widening |
|---|---|---|---|---|---|---|
| 2 year | 120 | 155 | 80 | 105 | 40 | 55 |
| 3 year | 130 | 81 | 90 | 59 | 50 | 37 |
| 5 year | 140 | 46 | 100 | 34 | 60 | 23 |
| 10 year | 150 | 25 | 110 | 19 | 70 | 13 |
| 30 year | 200 | 18 | 150 | 14 | 100 | 10 |

maturities and spreads levels. With the passage of time, the duration of corporate bonds shorten, and the yield spread over comparable Treasury securities generally narrows (positive credit curve spread). These two risk reducing and return enhancing forces, when combined with the yield spread advantage, provide compelling reasons to overweight short corporates. Even at narrow spreads, significant protection is available in maturities under five years. A two-year corporate with a yield spread of 40 basis points, can widen by 55 basis points versus a comparable Treasury security over the next year before it performs as poorly as the comparable Treasury security. Clearly, as the maturities increase, the spread widening protection decreases.

The risks involved in the strategy are recessionary spread widening risk and issuer default risk. The recessionary spread widening risk tends to be short lived and quickly overcome by the increased yield advantage of the strategy. The issuer default risk can be minimized by broad issuer diversification (50 or more issuers) and by credit analyst oversight.

The periodic over- or underweighting of sectors and qualities is a scaled back version of active "sector rotation." The primary way this can be implemented on a cost effective basis is to allow new cash flow (net new portfolio growth) to facilitate the mismatching. For example, if spreads are narrow going into the fourth quarter and the manager expects some widening, new money may be invested primarily in Treasury securities, resulting in a gradual reduction in the corporate exposure versus the index. Once the corporate spread widening materializes, Treasury securities (with low transaction costs) can be sold and corporates overweighted. Expected first quarter asset growth will eventually bring the corporate weighting back in line with the Index. A strategy of outright selling of corporates to buy Treasury securities is always difficult to justify because of the higher corporate transaction costs involved, in addition to the yield "penalty" associated with Treasury securities.

## Call Exposure Enhancements

The option-adjusted duration of a callable bond is the average of what the model duration is, if rates rise and fall marginally. These durations (under rising and falling rates) can be quite different for bonds that are trading at a price where the bond changes from trading to maturity, to trading to call (or visa versa). The result is a situation where the actual performance of a bond could be significantly different than would be expected given its beginning of period option-adjusted duration.

Generally, the greater the expected yield change, the greater the desire to have more call protection. With regard to near-term yield changes: (1) for premium callable bonds (bonds trading to call), the empirical duration (observed price sensitivity) tends to be less than the option-adjusted duration, resulting in underperformance during declining rates and (2) for discount callable bonds (bonds trading to maturity), the empirical duration tends to be greater than the option-adjusted duration, resulting in underperformance in rising rates. Any large deviations from the index exposure to call risk should recognize the potential significant tracking implications and the market directionality of the bet.

## MEASURING SUCCESS

Common sense dictates that "you can't manage what you can't measure." Managers know this to be true, yet so often find themselves without the tools necessary to measure the extent of their bets and the value added or lost from those bets. Measuring the extent of the bets was covered earlier in this chapter. This section will discuss how to measure whether any value has been added and from what bets.

## Outperform Adjusted Index Returns

Returning to the sailing theme, how is the portfolio sailboat doing versus the index sailboat? Is the portfolio making any ground against the index? To evaluate relative performance, the portfolio returns need to be adjusted for each of the following: (1) pricing, (2) transaction costs of growth and rebalancing, and (3) expenses. Pricing is a critical factor that needs to be considered, especially in enhanced indexing where deviations versus the index are small and pricing errors can hide valuable information. If a Lehman Brothers Index is the benchmark, then the portfolio needs to be re-priced with Lehman Brothers prices. Small differences in either the time of pricing or the pricing matrix, may result in large differences (among pricing services) in periodic returns over short measurement periods. Over longer periods, these pricing differences will average zero, but for value-added measurement purposes, periodic pricing accuracy is critical.

Since the index does not have transaction costs associated with asset growth, principal reinvestment, or income reinvestment, accurate adjustments need to be made to portfolio returns to account for these differences. A simple way to account for this is to maintain a trading log with implied transaction costs as a percent of total portfolio assets. The periodic summation of these implied costs will provide a good estimate of tracking error drag associated with growth and income reinvestment.

Finally, an adjustment for expenses is required. As was discussed earlier, keeping low expenses is a simple way to enhance returns. Nevertheless, portfolio returns should be "grossed up" by these expenses to put the portfolio on equal footing with the index for measurement purposes.

Exhibit 41–16 shows the monthly *adjusted* tracking of the largest bond index (enhanced) mutual fund. This portfolio is managed against the Lehman Brothers Aggregate Bond Index. If the sources of enhancements are multiple and of a controlled nature, it's expected that the average tracking difference would be small and usually positive. During periods of extreme market stress or spread volatility (i.e. the Asian crisis of 1998), the enhancement strategies may result in increased tracking differences. As shown, the monthly tracking differences are small (between +13 basis points and −4 basis points) and mostly positive. Exhibit 41–17 shows a rolling 12-month summation of the monthly *adjusted* tracking differences. An enhanced indexing strategy that has good risk management and diversified enhancements should be able to consistently perform above the index. Falling below the index return over 12 months most likely would be the result of either not matching the index risk properly, of the enhancement strategies not being adequately diversified, or of significant market stresses (three or more standard deviation events) adversely affecting the enhancement strategies.

**EXHIBIT   41–16**

Consistent Positive Tracking

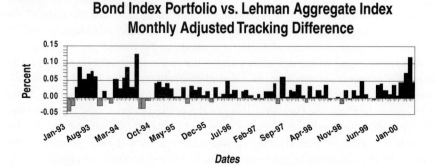

**EXHIBIT  41–17**

Consistent Positive Tracking

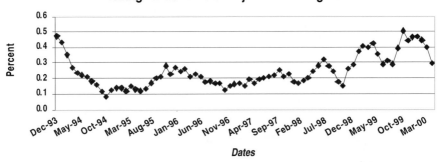

## Low and Stable Monthly Tracking Differences

The other measure of success, from an indexing standpoint, is how closely the portfolio is exposed to the same risk factors of the index. This can be measured by evaluating the rolling 12-month standard deviation of *adjusted* tracking differences of the portfolio versus the index. Exhibit 41–18 is an example from the same bond index mutual fund managed against the Lehman Brothers Aggregate Bond Index. If a portfolio is properly exposed to the index risk factors, the standard deviation will be low and stable, as shown. Periods of excess market stress and spread volatility may result in higher standard deviations of tracking differences but the increases should be roughly in proportion to the spread volatility increase.

## Consistently Positive Information Ratios

A good way to evaluate enhanced indexing success uses a measure called the information ratio. This ratio measures the amount of value added versus the index relative to the risk taken versus the index. This ratio can be calculated by dividing the trailing twelve month adjusted (for expenses, transaction costs of growth, and pricing) tracking difference (the value added versus the index) by the annualized trailing 12-month standard deviation of monthly adjusted tracking errors (the risk taken versus the index). An effective, and diversified, enhanced indexing strategy should be able to keep this ratio between a value of one and three over most periods. Exhibit 41–19 is an example of consistent positive information ratio from this same mutual fund example.

**EXHIBIT  41–18**

Consistently Low Tracking Error

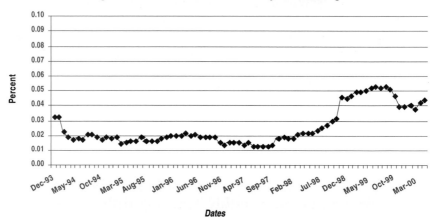

## Bond Index Portfolio vs. Lehman Aggregate Index
### Trailing 12-Month Standard Deviation of Adjusted Tracking Difference

**EXHIBIT  41–19**

Consistent Positive Information Ratio

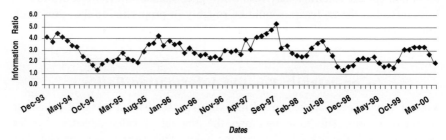

## Bond Index Portfolio vs. Lehman Aggregate Index
### Trailing 12-Month Information Ratio

## Detailed Performance Attribution

To accurately measure the success of risk factor management and the enhancement strategies, the manager needs excellent performance attribution tools. The
performance attribution analysis should be able to attribute tracking error to term
structure factors, sector bets, quality bets, and issue selection across sectors and
qualities.

The term structure attribution should be analyzed at the portfolio level versus the index. The sector and quality attribution (allocation and issue selection) should be analyzed at the sector and sub-sector levels (detailed sector and maturity categories) with the ability to drill down to issue level detail. Issue performance should be risk adjusted (versus Treasury equivalent returns) with sub-sector, sector, and portfolio returns rolled up from the security level. This level of attribution will provide the manager with the tools to measure with precision the risk matching and return enhancing strategies, with the result being "winning the race" against the index and against most managers.

## CHAPTER 42

# GLOBAL CORPORATE BOND PORTFOLIO MANAGEMENT

**Jack Malvey, CFA**
Managing Director
Lehman Brothers

## INTRODUCTION

Corporate bonds constitute the most fascinating, diverse, and rapidly growing subset of the global debt capital markets. By 2010, corporate bonds will represent about a third of the global debt capital markets as fiscally-prudent major governments shrink their reliance on the debt markets and as larger and more-mature technology firms pursue the classic funding migration from near-total reliance on equity to some use of the debt capital markets. This shift in the composition of the global debt capital markets, coupled with an already-begun transition from "government bond only" index benchmarks to "government plus corporate and securitized debt benchmarks," will fuel an even greater need for corporate bond expertise in global bond portfolio management. Without mastery of the global corporate asset class, superior portfolio performance will become impossible for competitive asset managers. This chapter provides readers with a brief guide to methodologies that may help portfolio managers meet this formidable yet exciting challenge.

Globally, there are more corporate bonds outstanding than commonly supposed (approximately $10.0 trillion in 2000). The label, "corporate," actually understates the scope of this burgeoning asset class. As commonly traded and administered within the context of an overall debt portfolio, the "corporate asset class" actually encompasses more than pure corporate entities. Instead of the title "corporate asset class," this segment of the global bond market really should be classified as the "credit asset class," including any non-MBS, CMBS, and ABS issuers (i.e., sovereigns and government-controlled entities with taxable issues) thought to have more credit risk than the U.S. government.

Unlike many of the newly invented securitized and derivative structures introduced during the late 20th century, corporate debt securities have a long history. Over the 19th and 20th centuries, thousands of organizations with different credit "stories" have sold debt to sustain their operations and to finance their expansion. These debt-issuing organizations range from 19th century rail-roads, early 20th century utilities, Canadian provinces like Ontario, development banks like the Asian Development Bank, and sovereigns like Brazil, Italy, Poland, and Malaysia, to firms throughout the Americas, Europe, Asia, and Oceania; their credit quality spans from impeccable Aaa's to defaulted D's. These borrowers use dozens of different types of debt instruments (first mortgage bonds, debentures, equipment trust certificates, subordinated debentures, medium-term notes, floating rate notes, private placements, and preferred stock) in multiple currencies (dollars, yen, euros, Swiss francs, and pounds) at any maturity ranging from one year to even a thousand years. Occasionally, these debt structures carry embedded options, which may allow for full or partial redemption prior to maturity at the option of either the borrower or the investor. Sometimes, the coupon payment floats with short-term interest rates or resets to a higher rate after a fixed interval or a rating change.

Investors buy corporate bonds because of the greater long-term performance, despite the assumption of credit risk. Except near and during recessions and periods of unusual technical stress like the "Great Spread Sector Crash" of August 1998 and the "U.S. yield curve inversion double cross" of January to March 2000, corporate bonds (almost always priced at a higher yield than the government securities of equivalent duration)[1] usually outperform U.S. Treasury securities and other higher-quality "spread sectors" like U.S. Agencies, mortgage-backed securities, and asset-backed securities. Since the inception of the Lehman indices in 1973, investment-grade corporates (9.06%) have outperformed U.S. Treasuries (8.76%) by 30 bp per year on average through March 31, 2000 as shown in Fig. 42–1 (absolute returns of key Lehman indices from 1973). During the 1990s, this advantage leaped to 84 bp per year over U.S. Treasuries, and U.S. high-yield corporate debt generated an additional 311 bp per year over U.S. investment-grade corporate debt in the 1990s. On a relative basis (standardized for the duration differences among asset classes), Fig. 42–2 shows investment-grade corporates (45 bp) and high-yield corporates (350 bp) with a compelling advantage over U.S. Treasuries and even MBS (20 bp) during the 1990s.

Global corporate bond portfolio management presents a complex challenge. Each day, hundreds of corporate bond portfolio managers face thousands of choices in the primary (new issue) and secondary markets. In addition to tracking primary and secondary flows, investors must keep tabs on ever-variant issuer fundamentals (acquisitions, earnings, ratings, etc.). Figure 42–3 illustrates the magnitude of this information-processing challenge. From a set of 5,000 different issuers, investors can assemble $4 \times 10$ (55) different combinations of

---

1. This difference between the corporate yield and government yield of equivalent-duration securities is referred to as the spread.

# EXHIBIT 42-1

## Total Nominal Returns (%) Lehman Brothers Fixed Income Indices 1973 through March 31, 2000

| | Pan-European Aggregate (EUR) (a) | Euro-Aggregate (EUR) (b) | U.S. $-Denom. Universal | U.S. Aggregate | U.S. Trsy | U.S. Agcy | U.S. MBS | U.S. ABS | U.S. Inv-Grd. Corporate | Global Sovereign (a) | Global High-Yield (a) | U.S. High-Yield Corporate | EMG |
|---|---|---|---|---|---|---|---|---|---|---|---|---|---|
| 1973 | | | | | 3.51 | | | | 1.51 | | | | |
| 1974 | | | | | 7.05 | | | | -5.86 | | | | |
| 1975 | | | | | 8.07 | | | | 16.70 | | | | |
| 1976 | | | | 15.60 | 11.82 | 13.00 | 16.31 | | 19.34 | | | | |
| 1977 | | | | 3.04 | 2.67 | 3.05 | 1.89 | | 3.16 | | | | |
| 1978 | | | | 1.39 | 2.06 | 1.25 | 2.41 | | 0.35 | | | | |
| 1979 | | | | 1.93 | 5.73 | 5.14 | 0.13 | | -2.10 | | | | |
| 1980 | | | | 2.71 | 5.61 | 5.20 | 0.65 | | -0.29 | | | | |
| 1981 | | | | 6.25 | 9.24 | 9.73 | 0.07 | | 2.95 | | | | |
| 1982 | | | | 32.62 | 27.84 | 26.72 | 43.04 | | 39.20 | | | | |
| 1983 | | | | 8.36 | 7.05 | 8.32 | 10.13 | | 9.27 | | | 5.84 | |
| 1984 | | | | 15.15 | 14.47 | 14.53 | 15.79 | | 16.62 | | | 9.70 | |
| 1985 | | | | 22.10 | 20.91 | 18.12 | 25.21 | | 24.06 | | | 25.64 | |
| 1986 | | | | 15.26 | 15.61 | 13.76 | 13.43 | | 16.53 | | | 17.45 | |
| 1987 | | | | 2.76 | 2.00 | 3.37 | 4.29 | | 2.56 | | | 4.89 | |
| 1988 | | | | 7.89 | 6.99 | 7.28 | 8.72 | | 9.22 | | | 12.53 | |
| 1989 | | | | 14.53 | 14.38 | 13.33 | 15.35 | | 14.09 | | | 0.83 | |
| 1990 | | | | 8.96 | 8.54 | 9.71 | 10.72 | | 7.05 | | | -9.59 | |
| 1991 | | | | 16.00 | 15.29 | 15.42 | 15.72 | | 18.51 | | | 46.08 | |
| 1992 | | | | 7.40 | 7.21 | 7.31 | 6.95 | 7.35 | 8.69 | | | 15.75 | |
| 1993 | | | | 9.75 | 10.68 | 10.51 | 6.84 | 7.95 | 12.16 | | | 17.12 | 38.73 |
| 1994 | | | | -2.92 | -3.38 | -3.32 | -1.61 | 0.13 | -3.93 | | | -1.03 | -13.44 |
| 1995 | | | | 18.47 | 18.35 | 18.27 | 16.80 | 13.43 | 22.25 | | | 19.17 | 23.85 |
| 1996 | | | | 3.63 | 2.70 | 3.30 | 5.35 | 5.05 | 3.28 | | | 11.35 | 28.33 |
| 1997 | | | | 9.65 | 9.57 | 9.70 | 9.49 | 7.41 | 10.23 | | | 12.76 | 13.18 |
| 1998 | | 7.51 | | 8.69 | 10.03 | 8.85 | 6.96 | 7.76 | 8.57 | | | 1.87 | -11.60 |
| 1999 | 0.23 | -1.74 | 0.17 | -0.82 | -2.56 | -0.94 | 1.86 | 1.81 | -1.96 | -4.36 | 10.45 | 2.39 | 23.07 |
| **2000** | | | | | | | | | | | | | |
| January | -0.48 | -0.39 | -0.34 | -0.33 | 0.26 | -0.29 | -0.87 | -0.04 | -0.35 | -2.06 | -0.50 | -0.43 | -0.58 |
| February | 0.66 | 0.60 | 1.27 | 1.21 | 1.50 | 1.15 | 1.16 | 0.75 | 0.93 | -0.48 | 2.14 | 0.19 | 4.91 |
| March | 1.66 | 1.44 | 1.17 | 1.32 | 1.99 | 0.38 | 1.09 | 0.80 | 0.85 | N/A | -0.07 | -2.10 | 2.79 |
| **YTD** | **2.26** | **1.65** | **2.11** | **2.21** | **3.79** | **1.84** | **1.38** | **1.52** | **1.43** | **-2.53** | **1.55** | **-2.34** | **7.21** |
| **YTD Annualized** | **14.01** | **6.67** | **13.03** | **8.95** | **15.37** | **7.45** | **5.60** | **6.17** | **5.79** | **-15.66** | **9.59** | **-9.47** | **29.24** |
| Mean (1973-March 31, 2000) | | | | 9.22 (c) | 8.76 (c) | 8.94 (c) | 9.52 (c) | 5.82 (d) | 9.06 | | | 10.58 (e) | 13.67 (e) |
| Mean (1973-1979) | | | | 5.49 (c) | 5.84 (c) | 5.63 (c) | 5.19 (c) | | 4.73 | | | | |
| Mean (1980-1989) | | | | 12.76 | 12.41 | 12.03 | 13.67 | | 13.42 | | | 11.00 (e) | |
| Mean (1990-1999) | | | | 7.88 | 7.64 | 6.70 | 7.91 | 6.36 (d) | 8.48 | | | 11.59 (e) | 14.59 (f) |
| Std. Dev. (1973-March 31, 2000) | | | | 8.08 (c) | 6.93 (c) | 6.81 (c) | 9.74 (c) | 4.16 (d) | 10.14 | | | 12.57 (e) | 18.71 (f) |
| Std. Dev. (1973-1979) | | | | 6.77 (c) | 3.46 (c) | 5.18 (c) | 7.48 (c) | | 9.55 | | | | |
| Std. Dev. (1980-1989) | | | | 9.33 | 7.83 | 6.90 | 12.84 | | 11.78 | | | 8.43 (e) | |
| Std. Dev. (1990-1999) | | | | 6.64 | 7.01 | 6.70 | 5.65 | 4.10 (d) | 8.16 | | | 15.21 (e) | 20.01 (f) |
| Compounded Annual Return (1973-00) | | | | 9.23 (c) | 8.96 (c) | 8.97 (c) | 9.31 (c) | 6.28 (d) | 8.78 | | | 9.49 (e) | 14.90 (f) |
| Compounded Annual Return (1973-79) | | | | 5.33 (c) | 5.53 (c) | 5.53 (c) | 4.99 (c) | | 4.37 | | | | |
| Compounded Annual Return (1980-89) | | | | 12.43 | 12.17 | 11.64 | 13.06 | | 12.90 | | | 10.73 (e) | |
| Compounded Annual Return (1990-00) | | | | 7.81 | 8.13 | 7.67 | 7.57 | 6.28 (d) | 7.99 | | | 8.70 (e) | 14.90 (f) |

(a) Returns reported on an unhedged basis
(b) Index introduced in July 1998
(c) Index introduced in 1976
(d) Index introduced in 1992
(e) Half-year number in 1983; High-Yield Index introduced on 7/1/83
(f) Index introduced in 1993; Expanded beyond Latin America in 1997

# EXHIBIT 42-1

*(Continued)*

| Year | Global Treasury (ex-U.S.) Unhedged | Hedged | ARMs | Inv.-Grade 144A | Eurodollar | High-Yield Corporate Loan | Municipal | Global Reits | S&P500 |
|---|---|---|---|---|---|---|---|---|---|
| 1973 | | | | | | | | | -14.77 |
| 1974 | | | | | | | | | -26.39 |
| 1975 | | | | | | | | | 37.16 |
| 1976 | | | | | | | | | 23.84 |
| 1977 | | | | | | | | | -7.18 |
| 1978 | | | | | | | | | 6.56 |
| 1979 | | | | | | | | | 18.44 |
| 1980 | | | | | | | -8.92 | | 32.42 |
| 1981 | | | | | | | -10.23 | | -4.91 |
| 1982 | | | | | | | 40.87 | | 21.41 |
| 1983 | | | | | | | 8.05 | | 22.51 |
| 1984 | | | | | | | 10.55 | | 6.27 |
| 1985 | | | | | | | 20.02 | | 32.16 |
| 1986 | | | | | | | 19.32 | | 18.47 |
| 1987 | 34.73 | 9.30 | | | 1.35 | | 1.51 | | 5.23 |
| 1988 | 2.17 | 8.93 | | | 9.12 | | 10.16 | | 12.54 |
| 1989 | -2.13 | 4.19 | | | 13.54 | | 10.79 | | 32.81 |
| 1990 | 15.66 | 3.69 | | | 8.84 | | 7.29 | | -4.79 |
| 1991 | 16.05 | 10.89 | | | 16.49 | | 12.14 | | 31.97 |
| 1992 | 3.02 | 8.42 | | | 8.17 | | 8.81 | | 7.61 |
| 1993 | 13.77 | 13.82 | 6.99 | | 10.30 | 0.63 | 12.29 | | 10.10 |
| 1994 | 5.33 | -4.71 | 0.01 | | -2.41 | 7.56 | -5.17 | | 1.52 |
| 1995 | 21.47 | 17.33 | 11.72 | | 16.91 | 8.39 | 17.45 | | 37.62 |
| 1996 | 6.73 | 12.07 | 6.70 | | 4.09 | 8.31 | 4.43 | | 22.96 |
| 1997 | -4.01 | 10.39 | 7.19 | 0.97 | 7.78 | 8.44 | 9.19 | | 33.36 |
| 1998 | 18.22 | 11.96 | 7.10 | 5.79 | 8.59 | 4.66 | 6.48 | 5.20 | 28.58 |
| 1999 | -6.47 | 2.52 | 4.89 | -1.17 | -0.63 | 11.17 | -2.08 | 13.20 | 21.04 |
| **2000** | | | | | | | | | |
| January | -3.05 | -0.01 | 0.27 | -0.04 | -0.50 | 1.22 | -0.43 | -1.16 | -5.02 |
| February | -1.54 | 0.67 | 0.78 | 1.05 | 0.84 | -0.79 | 1.18 | -0.28 | -1.89 |
| Mar. 1-31 | 3.27 | 1.35 | 0.61 | 0.73 | 1.00 | -0.27 | 2.19 | 2.17 | 9.78 |
| **YTD** | **-1.42** | **2.02** | **1.66** | **1.75** | **1.34** | **0.14** | **2.92** | **0.70** | **2.29** |
| **YTD Annualized** | **-5.75** | **8.20** | **6.69** | **7.08** | **5.42** | **0.57** | **11.84** | **2.84** | **9.30** |
| Mean (1973-March 31, 2000) | 8.80 (a) | 7.77 | 5.66 | 1.83 | 7.39 (a) | 6.18 | 8.38 | 5.08 (c) | 14.60 |
| Mean (1973-1979) | | | | | | | | | 5.38 |
| Mean (1980-1989) | 11.59 (a) | 7.47 | | | 8.00 (a) | | 10.21 | | 17.89 |
| Mean (1990-1999) | 8.98 | 8.44 | 6.23 | | 7.81 | 7.64 | 7.09 | | 19.00 |
| Std. Dev. (1973-March 31, 2000) | 11.64 (a) | 5.76 | 3.60 | 2.91 | 6.02 (a) | 3.91 | 11.12 | 5.77 (c) | 16.75 |
| Std. Dev. (1973-1979) | | | | | | | | | 22.71 |
| Std. Dev. (1980-1989) | 20.15 (a) | | | | | | 14.85 | | 12.97 |
| Std. Dev. (1990-1999) | 9.55 | 6.48 | 3.48 | | 6.29 | 3.31 | 6.74 | | 14.58 |
| Compounded Annual Return (1973-00) | 7.89 (a) | 8.08 | 6.24 | 3.11 | 7.54 (a) | 6.17 | 8.28 | 5.52 (c) | 13.60 |
| Compounded Annual Return (1973-79) | | | | | | | | | 3.22 |
| Compounded Annual Return (1980-89) | 10.44 (a) | 7.46 | | | | | 9.83 | | 17.23 |
| Compounded Annual Return (1990-00) | 7.20 | 8.25 | 6.24 | | 7.44 | 6.17 | 7.83 | | 17.33 |

(a) Index introduced in 1987
(b) Index introduced on 7/1/97
(c) Index introduced in October 1997; Global Reits returns reported on an unhedged basis

Source: Standard & Poor's and Lehman Brothers Fixed Income Research

# E X H I B I T 42-2

## Excess Returns 1990 through March 31, 2000

| | 1990 | 1991 | 1992 | 1993 | 1994 | 1995 | 1996 | 1997 | 1998 | 1999 | 1990s Average | Cumulative Total 1990-1999 | 1990s Sharpe Ratio | Mar. 1-31 2000 | YTD 2000 |
|---|---|---|---|---|---|---|---|---|---|---|---|---|---|---|---|
| U.S. Inv.-Grade Corp. | -177 | 229 | 97 | 80 | 58 | 114 | 120 | -29 | -220 | 177 | 45 | 449 | 0.30 | -134 | -227 |
| U.S. High Yield | -515 | 1,660 | 552 | 671 | 258 | 57 | 769 | 344 | -777 | 479 | 350 | 3,498 | 0.56 | -413 | -496 |
| Eurodollar | N/A | N/A | N/A | N/A | N/A | 52 | 70 | -58 | -74 | 85 | 15 | 75 ** | 0.20 | -71 | -115 |
| Emerging Markets | N/A | N/A | N/A | 2,489 | -1,209 | 857 | 2,293 | 439 | -1,619 | 2,248 | 785 | 5,499 ** | 0.47 | 104 | 408 |
| U.S. MBS | 115 | 9 | -104 | -98 | 97 | -44 | 79 | 122 | -84 | 113 | 20 | 204 ** | 0.16 | -69 | -79 |
| U.S. ABS | N/A | N/A | 72 | 116 | 54 | 43 | 70 | -12 | -83 | 137 | 50 | 397 ** | 0.64 | -45 | -25 |

**Excess Return:**

**Definition:** Incremental return which removes yield curve effects embedded in nominal total returns, isolating the reward ("excess return") earned for the assumption of credit and volatility ri:

**Methodology:** Each non-Treasury bond in an index is hedged against interest-rate moves using similar-duration U.S. Treasury bonds. The nominal return
of the hedging Treasury bonds (the credit-risk-free benchmark) is subtracted from the total return of each hedged bond to form the bond's excess return.
The individual performance differentials are then market-value weighted to arrive at an overall excess return for each asset class.

For the Global Treasury Index, excess returns are relative to U.S. Treasury bonds on a currency-hedged basis.
For the Euro-Aggregate and Pan-European Indices, excess returns are reported in euro and are calculated over comparable-duration like-currency government bonds.

**Forecast Methodology:**

**2000:** Excess return forecasts equal the option-adjusted spread (OAS) with adjustments for expected spread movement

**Decade:** Excess return forecasts equal ten times the current OAS less the product of the probability of underperformance and the average amount of underperformance for the 1990s

**Sharpe Ratio:** average excess return/standard deviation of returns.

**E X H I B I T   42–3**

The Global Portfolio Management Challenge: Enormous Information
Processing Problem

## Optimize Per Investment Constraints From:

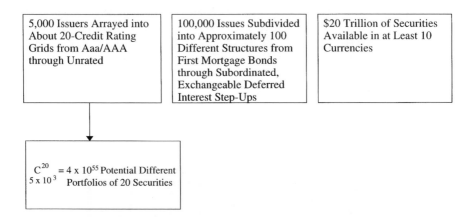

| 5,000 Issuers Arrayed into About 20-Credit Rating Grids from Aaa/AAA through Unrated | 100,000 Issues Subdivided into Approximately 100 Different Structures from First Mortgage Bonds through Subordinated, Exchangeable Deferred Interest Step-Ups | $20 Trillion of Securities Available in at Least 10 Currencies |

$$C^{20}_{5 \times 10^3} = 4 \times 10^{55} \text{ Potential Different Portfolios of 20 Securities}$$

20-bond portfolios. The number of potential portfolio combinations of 20 bonds expands to the infinity neighborhood with the inclusion of additional variables like rating (20 choices), issues (100,000), and currencies (at least 20). Incredibly, the number of potential combinations of this 20-bond corporate portfolio exceeds the neutrons in the known universe. In turn, this begs the question of whether corporate portfolio "optimization" is truly achievable given the current state of technology. Although "perfect optimization" may prove elusive, the "optimization goal" remains a worthy pursuit for asset managers.

Despite this apparent limitation on the perfection of corporate portfolio optimization, broad demand exists for corporate debt. Investors in corporate debt consist of individuals in the pursuit of high yields; central banks aiming to extract a higher yield and return on their considerable holdings of fixed-income assets; commercial banks arbitraging the difference between the higher yields on floating-rate notes and their lower cost of funding; mutual funds attempting to maximize both yield and total return; insurers and state pension funds seeking to fund their projected long-term liabilities; "pure" total-return maximizers competing against each other on a monthly, quarterly, and annual basis to satisfy their clients (public or private pension fund plan sponsors) or risk their loss; and hedge funds staking out leveraged long or short positions in credits with short-term potential for major spread movements. Portfolio investment choices are driven also by the existing security population of the corporate market (sector, issuer, structure, and currency), by the psychology of the portfolio managers (overall risk tolerance, shortfall risk aversion and internal politics of the investment-management institution), and by the state of market liquidity.

Borrowers and investors intersect mainly through dealers, in both the classic telephone form and increasingly through "e-market techniques" such as web sites and e-mails. Each day, a few dozen corporate bond dealers convey information about secondary positions and new issue offerings from any of the thousands of corporate borrowers, to the hundreds of corporate bond portfolio managers. Through their investment banking and syndicate operations, dealers also advise issuers on when and how to sell new debt. Through their fixed-income research, sales, and trading arms, dealers relay investment recommendations to portfolio managers.

As shown in Fig. 42–4, the task of global corporate bond portfolio management is to process all of this rapidly-changing information about the corporate bond market (issuers, issues, dealers, and competing managers), and to construct the portfolio with the best return for a given risk tolerance. This discipline combines the excitement and qualitative tools of equity analysis with the quantitative precision of fixed-income analysis.

## CORPORATE RELATIVE-VALUE ANALYSIS

Corporate bond portfolio management represents a major subset of the multi-asset global portfolio management process illustrated in Fig. 42–5. After setting

**E X H I B I T   42–4**

Global Credit Sector Asset Allocation Methodology

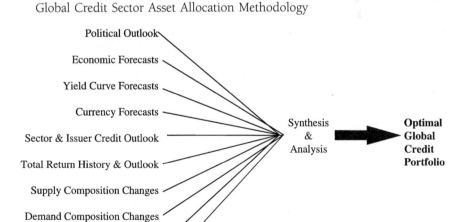

**E X H I B I T   42–5**

Global Portfolio Management Process

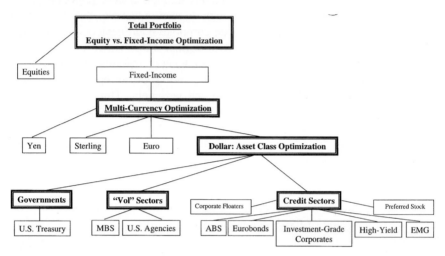

the equity/fixed income allocation, currency allocation (in this case, dollars were selected for illustration convenience), and distribution among fixed-income asset classes, bond managers are still left with a lengthy list of questions pertinent to the construction of the optimal corporate portfolio.

Should U.S. investors add dollar-denominated Eurobonds of non-U.S. issuers? Should European portfolio managers buy fixed-rate U.S. industrial paper and swap into floating-rate notes? Should Japanese mutual funds own euro-denominated telecommunications debt, swapped back into dollars or yen? Should U.S. insurers buy perpetual floaters issued by British banks and swap back into fixed-rate coupons in dollars? When should investors fade the corporate sector and increase allocation to governments, pursue the "strategic upgrade trade" (sell Baa/BBBs and buy higher-rated A corporate debt), rotate from industrials into utilities, switch from consumer cyclicals to non-cyclicals, overweight airlines and underweight telephones, and deploy a credit derivative (i.e., short the high-yield index to hedge their portfolios)? To respond to such questions, investors need to begin with an analytical framework (relative-value analysis), and to develop a strategic outlook for the global corporate market.

Economists have long debated the concept and measurement of "value." But fixed-income practitioners, perhaps because of the daily pragmatism enforced by the markets, have developed a consensus about the definition of value. In the bond market, "relative value" refers to the ranking of fixed-income investments by sectors, structures, issuers, and issues in terms of their expected performance[2] during some future interval.

For the day trader, relative value may carry a maximum horizon of a few minutes. For the dealer, relative value may extend from a few days to a few months. For a large insurer and most investors operating in the global corporate market, relative value usually spans a multi-year horizon. Accordingly, "relative-value analysis" refers to the methodologies used to generate such rankings of expected returns.

Within the global corporate market, "classic" relative-value analysis is a dialectical process combining the best of top-down and bottom-up approaches as exhibited in Fig. 42–6. This process blends the macro input of chief investment officers, strategists, economists, and portfolio managers with the micro input of credit analysts and quantitative analysts. The goal of this methodology is to pick the sectors with the most potential upside, populate these favored sectors with the best representative issuers, and select the structures of the designated issuers at the yield curve points that match the investor's outlook for the benchmark curve.

**E X H I B I T   42–6**

Credit Sector Portfolio Management Process: "Classic," Dialectical Relative Value Analysis

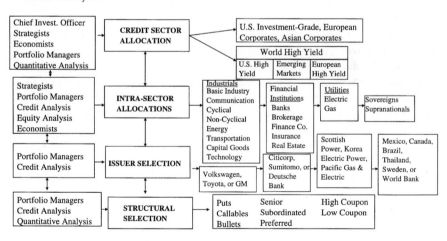

_____

2. Performance (return) may be measured in absolute nominal return, typically the sum of price movement and accrued coupon for some interval. Alternatively, performance (return) may be characterized as the "excess return" of a corporate sector and corporate security vs. government securities of identical duration. Most professional managers now think in terms of both nominal and excess returns for the corporate asset class.

For many corporate investors, the use of classic relative-value analysis has been sufficient to ensure a measure of portfolio success. Although sector, issuer, and structural analyses remain the core of superior relative-value analysis, the increased availability of information and technology has transformed the analytical process into a complex discipline. To assist their endeavors, corporate portfolio managers have far more data on the total returns (nominal and excess as described in footnote 2) of sectors, issuers, and structures, quantity and composition of new-issue flows, distribution of product demand by investor classes, aggregate credit-quality movements, multiple sources of credit analyses on individual issuers, spreads, and the details of their index benchmark.

## RELATIVE VALUE METHODOLOGIES

This section reviews the main relative value methodologies used in the pursuit of optimization of corporate bond portfolio performance.

### Total Return Analysis

Corporate relative-value analysis begins with a detailed dissection of past returns and a projection of expected returns. Capital markets have regular rhythms. For instance, the economic cycle is the major determinant of overall corporate spreads. During recessions, the escalation of default risk widens spreads (which are risk premiums over underlying, presumably default-free government securities) and reduces corporate returns relative to Treasuries. Conversely, economic prosperity reduces bankruptcies, tightens corporate spreads, and boosts corporate returns relative to Treasuries. This cyclical ebb and flow of nominal, quality (Baa yields minus Aaa yields), and percent yield spreads (corporate yield over Treasury yield) is illustrated in Figs. 42–7 to 42–9 from 1919 (start of this series by Moody's) through March 30, 2000.

Thanks to the development of corporate indices (effectively databases of prices, spreads, issuer, and structure composition), analyses of monthly, annual, and multi-year total returns have uncovered numerous patterns (i.e., seasonality, election-cycle effects, and auction effects) in the global corporate market. Admittedly, these patterns do not always re-occur. But an awareness and understanding of these total-return patterns are essential to optimizing portfolio performance.

Total return analysis also justifies portfolio objectives and constraints. After years of admonitions by various academics, market analysts, and consultants, total return data was used to justify the relaxation of credit-quality constraints for many corporate portfolios during the 1990s.

### Primary Market Analysis

Supply is often a misunderstood factor in the tactical relative-value calculus. Prospective new supply induces many traders, analysts, and investors to advocate

30-Year Baa Industrial Spreads 1919 through March 31, 2000

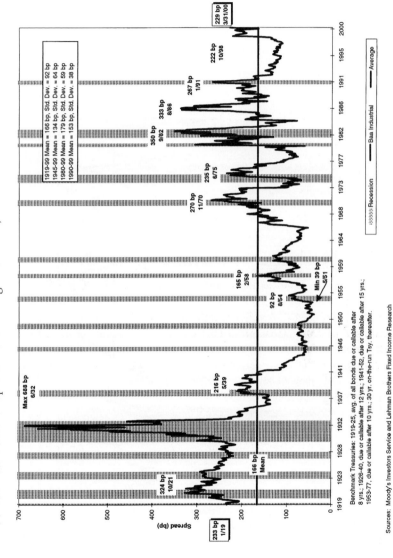

Benchmark Treasuries: 1919-25, avg. of all bonds due or callable after
8 yrs.; 1926-40, due or callable after 12 yrs.; 1941-52, due or callable after 15 yrs.;
1953-77, due or callable after 10 yrs.; 30 yr. on-the-run Tsy. thereafter.

Sources: Moody's Investors Service and Lehman Brothers Fixed Income Research

30-Year Industrial Quality Spreads (Baa-Aaa) 1919 through March 31, 2000

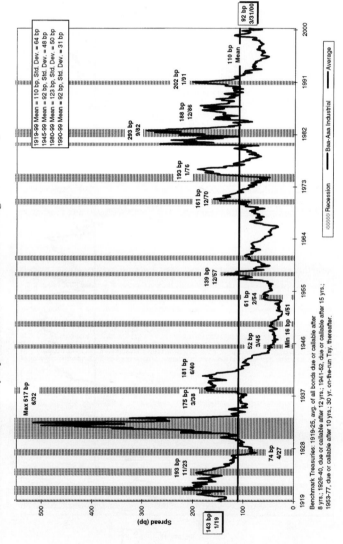

Benchmark Treasuries: 1919-25, avg. of all bonds due or callable after
8 yrs.; 1926-40, due or callable after 12 yrs.; 1941-52, due or callable after 15 yrs.;
1953-77, due or callable after 10 yrs.; 30 yr. on-the-run Tsy. thereafter.

Sources: Moody's Investors Service and Lehman Brothers Fixed Income Research

# EXHIBIT 42–9

## 30-Year Baa Industrial Percent Yield Spread 1919 through March 31, 2000

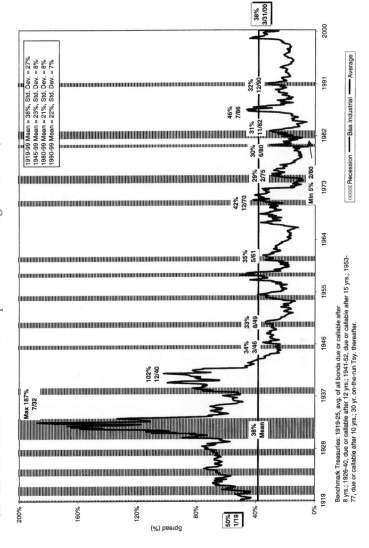

Benchmark Treasuries: 1919-25, avg. of all bonds due or callable after 8 yrs.; 1926-40, due or callable after 12 yrs.; 1941-52, due or callable after 15 yrs.; 1953-77, due or callable after 10 yrs.; 30 yr. on-the-run Tsy. thereafter.

Sources: Moody's Investors Service and Lehman Brothers Fixed Income Research

a defensive short-term portfolio stance to the overall corporate market as well as toward individual sectors and issuers. Yet the premise, "supply will hurt spreads" is more cliche than fact. During the 1990s, origination surges (most notably during the first quarter) were associated with market-spread contraction and strong relative returns for corporates. In contrast, sharp supply declines (like the third quarter of 1998 and the first quarter of 2000 when spreads widened as supply shriveled due to poor technical conditions) were accompanied frequently by spread expansion and a major decline in both relative and absolute returns for corporates. This was most conspicuous during the August to October 1998 interval, when the new-issuance calendar evaporated in the face of the "Great Spread-Sector Crash."

In the investment-grade corporate market, heavy supply often helps spreads and returns as new primary valuations validate and enhance secondary valuations. When primary origination declines sharply, secondary traders lose reinforcement from the primary market and tend to raise their bid spreads. Counter to intuition and cliche, relative corporate returns often perform best during periods of heavy supply. For example, November 1998 marked both the then all-time record for new corporate origination as well as the single best month ever for corporate spread contraction.

Given their immediate focus on the deals of the day and week, portfolio managers often overlook market-structure dynamics in making portfolio decisions. Because the pace of change in market structure is gradual, market dynamics have less effect on short-term tactical investment decision-making than on long-term strategy.

The composition of the global corporate bond market shifted markedly during the 1980s and 1990s. Medium-term note (MTN) origination now dominates the front end of the corporate curve. Rule 144A bonds (quasi-private placement bonds) have captured a growing share of sovereign, non-U.S. corporate issuers (selling dollar denominated debt in the U.S.), high yield, and emerging-market debt. Structured notes and index swaps heralded the introduction of derivative instruments into the mainstream of the corporate market. The high-yield corporate sector was mainstreamed as just another asset class after having been stress-tested in 1989 to 1990. Global origination became a more popular technique for agencies, supranationals, sovereigns, Canadians, and some large corporate borrowers.

Although the growth of derivatives and high-yield instruments stood out during the 1990s, the globalization of the corporate market has been the most striking long-term development. The rapid growth of the Eurobond market since 1975, the introduction of many non-U.S. issuers into the dollar markets during the 1990s, and the birth of the euro on January 1, 1999 led to the proliferation of truly transnational corporate portfolios.

Partially offsetting this proliferation of issuers, the global corporate market became structurally more homogeneous (intermediate bullets) during 1990s for three reasons. First, there was a continued shift away from utility issuers who had preferred long-dated maturities to fund long-term capital assets. Second, new origination was less costly at the front of persistently steep yield curves in the U.S., Europe, and Asia. Third, the emergence and tremendous growth of the swap market made intermediate origination more convenient.

The trend toward bullet securities does not pertain to the high-yield market, where callables remain the structure of choice. With the hope of credit-quality improvement, many issuers expect to refinance prior to maturity at lower rates.

There are three strategic portfolio implications for this structural evolution. First, scarcity value must be considered in corporate relative-value analysis. The dominance of bullet structures translates into scarcity value for structures with embedded call and put features. This aspect is not captured by option-valuation models.

Second, long-dated maturities will decline as a percentage of outstanding corporate debt. This shift will lower the effective duration of all outstanding corporate debt and reduce aggregate sensitivity to interest-rate risk. For asset/liability managers with long horizons, this shift of the maturity distribution suggests a rise in the value of long corporates and helps to explain the warm reception afforded initially to most new "century offerings" (100-year maturities) in the early and mid-1990s.

Third, the use of corporate derivatives will escalate rapidly. The maturation of corporate bond derivatives, whether on a stand-alone basis or embedded in structured notes, will give rise to new strategies for investors and issuers.

## Liquidity and Trading Analysis

Short-term and long-term liquidity influence portfolio management decisions. Citing lower expected liquidity, some investors are often reluctant to purchase smaller-sized issues (less than $1.0 billion), equipment trust certificates, Rule 144A's, private placements, MTNs, and non-local corporate issuers. Other investors (especially insurers) gladly exchange a potential liquidity disadvantage for incremental yield. For investment-grade issuers, these liquidity concerns frequently are exaggerated.

As widely lamented since 1998, the corporate liquidity function is not continuous. Liquidity varies with the economic cycle, credit cycle, shape of the yield curve, supply, and the season. As in all markets, stark shocks, like a surprise wave of defaults or a major correction in equities, can desiccate corporate debt liquidity. In reality, these transitory bouts of liquidity volatility mask an underlying trend towards stable liquidity across the global corporate asset class. With a gentle push from regulators, the global corporate asset class is well along in converting from its historic "over-the-counter" domain to a fully transparent, equity/U.S. Treasury-style marketplace. New technology has fostered the late 1990s' formation of ECN's (electronic communication networks), essentially electronic trading exchanges. In turn, corporate bid/ask differentials generally have trended lower for very large, brand-name corporate issues. This powerful twin combination of technological innovation and competition promise the rapid development of an even more liquid and efficient global corporate market during the early 21$^{st}$ century.

During the last decade of the 20$^{th}$ century, secondary corporate trading was spurred by multiple catalysts: the great refunding blitzes of the early 1990s and the late 1990s; the resulting multiplier effect of record origination as most new issues were sold partially on swap against existing issues; the market volatility triggered by the 1990–1991 recession, the "Great Spread Sector Crash" of August 1998, and the ensuing rebound beginning in November 1998; a variety of secular sector swings (such as buying U.S. bank debt in the early 1990s and coping with the "Asian Contagion" of 1997–1998); the effects of the descent of the U.S. yield curve as investors sought call protection in bullets, some defense against possible yield curve rides in put structures in 1994, and short-term yield maximization in high-coupon callables in 1992 and 1993; the cyclical steepening of the U.S. yield curve in the early 1990s, which facilitated the expansion of dealer inventories to take advantage of the "positive carry trade" and the flattening of the U.S. yield curve in 1997 and 1999, which induced some dealers to stock lower inventory; the inversion of the U.S. Treasury curve in 2000; the entrance of new dealers into the corporate bond market, especially from the ranks of commercial banks; the conversion of some total-return managers to an equity-style approach; and the declaration by some insurers to embrace a total-return style approach.

## Secondary Trade Rationales

Capital market and issuer expectations constantly change. Recession may arrive sooner rather than later. The yield curve may steepen rather than flatten. The auto and paper cycles may be moving down from their peaks. Higher oil and natural gas prices may benefit the credit quality of the energy sector. An industrial may have announced a large debt-financed acquisition, earning an immediate ratings rebuke from the agencies. A major bank may plan to repurchase 15% of its outstanding common stock (great for shareholders, but leading to higher financial leverage for debtholders). In response to such daily information flows, portfolio managers amend their portfolios. To understand trading flows and the real dynamics of the corporate market, investors should consider the most common rationales to trade and not to trade. There are dozens of rationales to execute secondary trades in the pursuit of portfolio optimization. Several of the most popular are discussed below.

### Yield/Spread Pickup Trades

These trades account for the most common secondary transactions across all sectors of the global corporate market. Based on our observation, 60% of all secondary swaps reflect investor intentions to add additional yield within the duration and credit-quality constraints of a portfolio. If five-year, A2/A GMAC paper trades at 100 bp, 5 bp more than five-year, A1/A+ Ford Motor Credit at 95 bp, then some investors will deem the rating differential irrelevant and swap into GMAC for a spread gain of 5 bp per annum. This "yield-first psychology" mirrors the institutional yield needs of long-term asset/liability managers. Despite the passage of more than two decades, this investor bias towards yield maximization also may be a methodological relic left over from the era prior to the introduction and market acceptance of total-return indices in the mid-1970s. There is empirical support for the effectiveness of "yield-first psychology." Baa corporates (9.85%) outperformed A-rated securities (9.04%) by 81 bp from 1973 through March 2000 according to Lehman indices. But this tactic is not without risk. As measured by the standard deviation of total return, Baa returns (11.43%) have been considerably more volatile than A's (10.27%). In general, yield/spread maximization works reasonably during periods of economic growth.

**Credit-Upside Trades**
"Credit-upside trades" are closely related to yield/spread maximization transactions. In the illustration of the GMAC and Ford Motor Credit trade described above, some investors may swap based on their view of potential credit-quality improvement for GMAC. For example, a one-notch upgrade of GMAC paper to A1/A+ might produce a five-bp contraction in its five-year spread to 95 bp, the same value as Ford Motor Credit paper. This would produce relative outperformance for holders of GMAC paper compared to Ford Motor Credit paper. Credit-upside trades are particularly popular in the crossover sector (securities with ratings between Ba2/BB to Baa3/BBB- by either rating agency). After sustaining portfolio damage from descents and spread expansions, subsequent recoveries by "crossover rebound" stories like Chrysler, McDonnell Douglas, Transco Energy, K-Mart, and Korea produced exceptional relative returns for holders.

**Credit-Defense Trades**
"Credit-defense trades" become more popular with the gathering of economic storm clouds. Recessions increase the probability of corporate defaults. High-yield corporates will underperform investment-grade corporates during periods of economic distress. Within these asset classes, Baa's will lag A's and BB's will trail B's. Secular sector transformations, especially in this exciting yet more uncertain internet age, often generate valuation confusion and induce defensive repositioning by investors. In anticipation of greater competition, some investors reduced their portfolio exposures in the mid-1990s to sectors like electric utilities and telecommunication firms. And as some Asian currencies and equities swooned in mid-1997, some portfolio managers cut their allocation to the Asian debt market. Unfortunately because of yield-maximization needs and a general reluctance to realize losses by some institutions (i.e., insurers), many investors tend to react more slowly to credit-defense propositions. Ironically once a credit

sours sufficiently to invoke the wrath of the rating agencies, internal portfolio guidelines often dictate security liquidation immediately after the loss of single-A or investment-grade status. This is usually the worst possible time to sell a security, as it maximizes the harm incurred by the portfolio.

### New Issue Swaps

"New-issue swaps" contribute to secondary turnover. Because of perceived superior liquidity, many portfolio managers prefer to rotate their portfolios gradually into more current and usually larger sized on-the-run issues. This disposition, reinforced by the usually superior market behavior of newer issues in government markets, has become a self-fulfilling prophecy for many corporate issues. In addition, some portfolio managers buy certain new issues to generate sufficient commissions to pay vendors through soft dollars. Rarely, an underwriter may insist on cash-only purchases for "hot" transactions. As a result of these practices, investors usually pay for their new-issue purchases through some combination of cash and swap of an existing security in their portfolio.

### Sector-Rotation Trades

"Sector-rotation trades," within corporates and among fixed-income asset classes, became more popular during the 1990s, but do not rival similar activity in the equity market. With the likely development of enhanced liquidity and lower trading transaction costs across the global bond market in the early $21^{st}$ century, sector-rotation trades should become more prevalent in the corporate bond asset class. Such intra-asset class trading already has played a major role in differentiating performance among corporate bond portfolio managers. For example, as soon as the Fed launched its preemptive strike against inflation in February 1994, some investors correctly exchanged fixed-rate corporates for floating rate corporates. In 1995, the specter of U.S. economic weakness prompted some investors in high-yield corporates to rotate from consumer-cyclical sectors like autos and retailing into consumer non-cyclical sectors like food, beverage, and healthcare. The anticipation of slower U.S. economic growth in 1998 induced a defensive tilt by some asset managers away from other cyclical groups like paper and energy. The resurrection of Asian and European economic growth in 1999 stimulated increased portfolio interest in cyclicals, financial institutions, and energy debt. Inter-currency (U.S. dollar, euro, sterling, yen) maximization of credit-risk positioning is still relatively rare. But the increased use of asset-swapping techniques (exchanging fixed cash flows for floating cash flows and trading coupon payments in one currency for another), as well as the migration from local currency index benchmarks to multicurrency index benchmarks should boost inter-currency sector rotation during the coming decade.

### Curve Adjustment Trades

"Curve-adjustment trades" are undertaken to reposition overall portfolio duration. For most corporate investors, their portfolio duration resides within a range from 20% below to 20% above the index duration. If corporate investors could have predicted yield curve movements perfectly in 1994 and 1995, then they would have lowered their portfolio duration at the beginning of 1994 and extended their duration in late 1994. The reverse pattern prevailed in 1998 (extend duration), 1999 (reduce duration), and 2000 (cut duration, especially for maturities beyond 20 years). Although most fixed-income investors prefer to reconfigure the duration of their aggregate portfolios in the more-liquid Treasury and MBS markets, strategic portfolio duration tilts also can be implemented in the corporate market.

### Structure Trades

These trades also gain appeal with movements in volatility and the shape of the yield curve. As shown during the second quarter of 1995, the rapid descent of the U.S. yield curve contributed to underperformance of callable structures. With curve stabilization during the third quarter of 1995, investors were more willing to trade into an extra 35 bp of spread for high-quality callables compared to bullets of stellar quality and less put off by the possible cost of negative convexity. The sharp downward rotation of the U.S. yield curve during the second half of 1997 also contributed to poor relative performance by put structures. The yield sacrifice for protection against higher interest rates instead constrained total return as rates fell. The plunge in U.S. interest rates and escalation of yield-curve volatility during the second half of 1998 again restrained the performance of callable structures compared to bullet structures. The upward rebound in U.S. interest rates and the fall in interest-rate volatility during 1999 contributed to relative outperformance of callable structures.

### Cash Flow Reinvestment

"Cash flow reinvestment" needs force investors into the secondary market on a regular basis. During 1999, the sum of all coupon, maturity, and partial redemptions (via tenders, sinking funds, and other issuer prepayments) equaled approximately 80% of all new gross origination in the U.S. dollar bond market. Before the allocation of any new savings to the bond market, investors had sufficient incoming portfolio cash to absorb most new bond supply. Some portfolio cash flows arrive during interludes in the primary market, and sometimes the composition of recent primary supply may not be compatible with portfolio objectives. In these periods, corporate portfolio managers must shop the secondary market to remain fully invested or replicate for brief intervals the composition of index targets through the use of financial futures.

### Bias for Activity

Bias for activity affects passive (indexers) and active managers as well as dealers. Referring to the overall capital markets, the late Fisher Black characterized some of this activity as "noise trading." Dealers closely monitor the aging of their security inventories. Stale positions, usually on the books for more than

90 days, are justifiably viewed with suspicion by risk managers. Ancient holdings may be worth less than their marks, otherwise, they would have been purchased by investors. Accordingly, all corporate traders seek to limit their stale positions. At the same time in their quest for portfolio optimization, indexers rebalance their portfolios to conform with the ever-shifting composition of indices, and active managers surf among primary and secondary flows for the slightest glimmer of incremental value. This sum of dealer activity, indexer realignments to cut tracking error, and active managers searching for valuation nuances breeds a natural bias for activity in the global corporate market.

## Trading Constraints

Asset managers also should review their main rationales for not trading. Some of the best investment decisions are to hold onto a corporate security instead of trading it away based on mercurial development with little fundamental substance. Conversely, some of the worst investment decisions are to hold onto a corporate security because of stale views or anachronistic portfolio constraints. The best portfolio managers retain very open minds, constantly self-critiquing both their successful and unsuccessful methodologies.

## Portfolio Constraints

Collectively, these inhibitions are the single biggest contributor to the persistence of market inefficiency across the global corporate market. Some U.S. state pension funds cannot purchase corporate securities with ratings below A3/A- and Rule 144A's under administrative and legislative guidelines. Some pension funds also have limitations on their ownership of MTNs and non-U.S. corporations. Regulators have limited the exposure of U.S. insurers to high-yield corporates. Meanwhile, many European and Asian investors are restricted to issues rated at least single-A and sometimes Aa3/AA- and above, manufactured originally in annual-pay Eurobond form. Globally, many commercial banks must operate exclusively in the floating-rate realm: all fixed-rate securities, unless swapped, are ineligible for portfolio investment.

## "Story" Disagreement

Traders, salespersons, sell-side analysts and strategists, and buy-side portfolio managers rely on dozens of trade rationales that potentially will benefit portfolio performance. The "Credit Story" is by far the most important rationale. The proponents of a secondary trade may make a persuasive argument, but the portfolio manager may be unwilling to accept the "shortfall risk" if the investment recommendation does not pan out. For example in early 1998, analysts and investors alike were divided equally on short-term prospects for better valuations of Asian sovereign debt. After a very disappointing 1997 for Asian debt performance, Asia enthusiasts had little chance to persuade pessimists to buy Asian debt at the outset of 1998. Technically, such lack of market consensus in the corporate market usually signals an investment with great outperformance potential. Indeed, most Asian debt issues recorded exceptional outperformance over the full course of 1998 and 1999.

### Buy-and-Hold

Although many long-term asset/liability managers claim to have become more total-return focused in the 1990s, accounting constraints (cannot sell positions at a loss compared to book cost or take too extravagant a gain compared to book cost) often limit the ability of these investors to transact. Effectively, these investors (mainly insurers) remain traditional "buy-and-hold" investors. And some active bond managers have converged to quasi-"buy-and-hold" investment programs at the behest of consultant recommendations to curb portfolio turnover. In the aftermath of the "Asian Contagion of 1997–1998," this disposition toward lower trading was reinforced by the reduction in market liquidity provided by more wary bond dealers.

### Administrative Burdens

Asset management marketing, compliance, and accounting demands soared during the 1990s. Many asset management firms spend almost 50% of their schedule on these administrative chores. In turn, some investors are burdened with multiple functions: analysis, portfolio management, and marketing. In particular, portfolio managers with heavy marketing obligations to existing and potential clients may be limited in their capability to react to short-term valuation anomalies in the corporate bond market.

### Seasonality

Secondary trading slows at month ends, more so at quarter ends, and the most at the conclusion of calendar years. Dealers often prefer to reduce their balance sheets at fiscal year-end (November 30, December 31, or March 31 (Japan)), and portfolio managers take time to mark their portfolios, prepare reports for their clients, and chart strategy for the next investment period. During these intervals, some of the most compelling secondary offerings can languish.

## Spread Analysis

By custom, some segments of the high yield, and EMG markets still prefer to measure value by bond price or bond yield rather than spread. But for the rest of the global corporate market, nominal spread (the yield difference between corporate and government bonds of similar duration) has been the basic unit of both price and relative-value analysis for more than two centuries.

For comparability with the "vol" sectors (mortgage-backed securities and U.S. Agencies), many U.S. practitioners also prefer to cast the valuations of investment-grade corporate securities in terms of option-adjusted spreads (OAS). However, given the rapid reduction of corporate structures with embedded options during the 1990s (see structural discussion below), the use of OAS in primary and secondary pricing has diminished within the investment-grade corporate asset class. Moreover, the standard one-factor binomial models of the 1990s do not account for credit spread volatility. Perhaps incorrectly, OAS valuation has seen only limited extension into the higher risk realms of the quasi-equity, high-yield corporate and EMG debt-asset classes.

Starting in Europe during the early 1990s and gaining momentum during the late 1990s, swap spreads have emerged as the common denominator to measure relative value across fixed- and floating-rate note structures. During the next decade, the U.S. investment-grade and high-yield markets eventually may switch to swap spreads to be consistent with Europe and Asia.

Other U.S. corporate spread calculations have been proposed, most notably off the U.S. Agency benchmark curve. These proposals emanate from the assumption of persistent U.S. budgetary surplus and significant liquidation of outstanding U.S. Treasury securities during the first decade of the 21$^{st}$ century. History teaches that these assumptions unfortunately may prove to be faulty. The inevitability of economic cycles (at least to all non-members of the "New Paradigm School") and the potential for U.S. tax cuts will probably temper the realized reduction in U.S. Treasury debt by 2010. Moreover, the U.S. Treasury appreciates the significance of a well-defined yield curve for the global capital markets. Although some practitioners may choose to derive corporate-agency spreads for analytical purposes, this practice is unlikely to become standard market convention.

Given the market's ability to price any corporate debt instrument in multiple spread guises (nominal, OAS, swap, and possibly even over U.S. Agencies), investors should develop a rigorous understanding of the strengths and weaknesses of each spread tool. Investors should also understand how best to use spread tools for valuation decision-making.

The most common technique for analyzing spreads among individual securities and across industry sectors is mean-reversion analysis. Buy this "cheap" sector or issuer because the spread used to be much tighter. Sell this "rich" sector or issuer because the spread used to be much wider. Mean-reversion analysis can be instructive as well as misleading. The mean is highly dependent on the interval selected, and there is no market consensus on the appropriate interval. "Persistence" frequents the corporate bond market. Cheap securities, mainly a function of credit clouds, often tend to become cheaper, while rich securities, usually high-quality issues, tend to remain on the rich side.

Quality-spread analysis examines the spread differentials between low and high-quality credits. Corporate debt managers have long benefited from the over-weighing of lower-quality debt at the outset of an upward turn in the economic cycle. Over the long run, incremental portfolio yield does generate higher portfolio return. Over short intervals from one month to even a couple of years, this additional yield advantage from lower-quality debt may not fully compensate asset managers for the assumption of higher credit risk. Accordingly, asset managers should consider the "upgrade trade" to high-quality corporate securities at cyclical quality spread troughs based on the premise that subsequent economic/credit cycle deterioration will produce wider spreads and at least brief periods of relative underperformance for lower-quality credits. The "upgrade trade" should also be deployed in anticipation of periodic bouts of technical turbulence, usually associated with events like equity corrections, central bank tightenings, and yield curve inversions.

Dating from the early 20th century, "percent yield spread" analysis (the ratio of corporate yields to government yields for securities of similar duration) is another popular technical tool with some investors. This methodology has serious drawbacks that undermine its usefulness. Percent yield spread is more a derivative than an explanatory or predictive variable. The usual expansion of corporate percent yield spreads during low-rate periods like 1997 and 1998 over-states the risk as well as the comparative attractiveness of corporate debt. The typical contraction of corporate percent yield spreads during upward shifts of the benchmark yield curve does not necessarily signal an imminent bout of underperformance for the corporate asset class. Effectively, the absolute level of the underlying benchmark is merely a single factor among many factors (de-mand, supply, profitability, defaults, etc.) that determine the relative value of the corporate asset class. These other factors can offset or reinforce any insights derived from percent yield spread analysis.

## Structure Analysis

Structural decision-making became less influential in corporate bond portfolio management during the 1990s. The Asian and European corporate bond markets almost exclusively feature intermediate bullets. The U.S. corporate and the global dollar-bond markets have moved to embrace this structurally-homogeneous European bullet standard. Plenty of structural diversity still resides within the U.S. high yield and EMG debt markets. However, portfolio decisions in these speculative-grade sectors understandably hinge much more on pure credit differentiation than the structural diversity of the issue-choice set.

Still, structural optimization can enhance risk-adjusted returns of corporate portfolios. Leaving credit aside, issue structure analysis and structural allocation decisions usually hinge on yield curve and volatility forecasts as well as inter-pretation of option-valuation model outputs (see the discussion below). In the short run and assuming no change in the perceived creditworthiness of the issuer, yield curve and volatility movements will largely influence structural perform-ance. However, investors should also take into account long-run market dynam-ics that affect the composition of the market and, in turn, corporate index bench-marks.

Specifically, callable structures have become a rarer species in the U.S. investment-grade corporate bond market. Thanks to an almost continuously positively-sloped U.S. term structure during the 1990s and the yield curve's intermittent declines to approximately three-decade lows in 1993, 1997, and 1998, the composition of the public U.S. corporate bond market converged toward its intermediate-bullet Eurobond and euro-denominated cousins. Bullets climbed from 24% of Lehman's investment-grade corporate index at the start of 1990 to 68% on March 31, 2000 (principal value basis). Over this decade-long interval, callables declined at a remarkable rate from 72% to just a 25% index share. Sinking-fund structures, once the structural mainstay of natural-gas pipelines and many industrial sectors, are on the "structural endangered species list," with a drop from 32% of the public bond market in 1990 to only 2% as of March 31, 2000. Despite several brief flurries of origination in the mid-1990s and the late-1990s introduction of callable/putable structures, put market shares fell from 5% in 1990 to 3% by March 31, 2000. Pure corporate zeros are in danger of extinction with a fall from 4% market share in 1990 to negligible by 2000.

## Bullets

Front-end bullets (one- to five-year maturities) have great appeal to the growing cadre of "barbellers" (use corporates at the front of the curve and Treasuries in longer maturities) and asset swappers (institutions who convert short bullets into floating-rate products). Short high-quality corporate securities also have gained favor in the late 1990s, with certain central banks and supranationals charged with extracting a higher long-term performance from their fixed-income assets. Intermediate corporates (five- to 12-year maturities), especially in the 10-year neighborhood, have become the most popular segment of the U.S. and European investment-grade and high-yield corporate markets. Fifteen-year maturities are comparatively rare and have been favored by banks that occasionally uncover arbitrages in the asset-swap market. Because 15-year structures take five years to roll down a positively-sloped yield curve, these structures hold less appeal for many investors. In contrast, in positively sloped yield curve periods, 20-year structures are favored by many investors. Spreads for these structures are benched off the 30-year Treasury. With a positively-sloped yield curve, the 20-year structure provides higher yield than a 10-year or 15-year security and less vulnerability (lower duration) than a 30-year security.

The 30-year maturity is the most popular form of long-dated security in the global corporate market. In 1992, 1993, late 1995, and 1997, there was a minor rush to issue 50-year (half-centuries) and 100-year (centuries) securities in the U.S. corporate bond market. These longer-dated securities provide investors with extra positive convexity for only a modest increase in modified-adjusted duration. In the wake of the "Asian Contagion" and especially the "Great Spread-Sector Crash" of August 1998, the cyclical increases in risk aversion and liquidity premiums sidelined both issuer and investor appetites for the fresh issuance of these ultra-long maturities. The inversion of the U.S. yield curve in January 2000, which looks destined to persist for an extended period, further dampens investor demand and issuer ability to place fresh long-dated corporate origination.

## Callables

Typically after a five-year or 10-year wait (longer for some rare issues), corporate structures are callable at the option of the issuer at any time. Call prices usually are set at a premium above par (par + the initial coupon) and decline linearly on an annual basis to par by 5 to 10 years prior to final scheduled maturity. The ability to refinance debt in a potentially lower-interest rate environment is extremely valuable to issuers. Conversely, the risk of earlier-than-expected retirement of an above-current market coupon is bothersome to investors. To place callables, issuers pay investors an annual spread premium (about 30 bp to 40 bp for high-quality issuers) for being short the call option. Like all security valuations, this call premium varies through time with capital market conditions. Given the higher chance of exercise, this call option becomes much more expensive during low rate and high volatility periods. During the 1990s, this call premium has ranged from approximately 20 bp to 50 bp for investment-grade issuers. Callables significantly underperform bullets during rapid yield curve descents. When the bond market rallies, callable structures often do not fully participate given the upper boundary imposed by call prices. Conversely, callable structures outperform bullets in bear bond markets as the probability of early calls diminishes.

## Sinking Funds

This structure allows an issuer to execute a series of partial calls (annually or semi-annually) prior to maturity. There is also usually a provision to retire an additional portion of the issue on the sinking fund date, typically ranging from one to two times the mandatory sinking fund obligation. Historically, especially during the early 1980s, keen total return investors favored the collection of sinking fund structures at sub-par prices. These discounted sinking funds retained the price upside during interest rate rallies (provided the indicated bond price remained below par). Given the issuers' requirement to retire at least annually some portion of the issue at par, the price of these sinking fund structures did not fall as much compared to callables and bullets when interest rates rose.

## Putables

Conceptually, put structures are simpler than callables. Yet in trading circles, put bond valuations often are the subject of much debate. American-option callables grant issuers the right to call an issue at any time at the designated call price after expiration of the non-callable or non-redemption period. Put bonds typically provide investors with a one-time, one-date put option (European option) to demand full repayment at par. Less frequently, put bonds include a second or third put option date. A very limited number of put issues afford investors the privilege to put such structures back to the issuers at par in the case of rating downgrades (typically to below investment-grade status).

Thanks to falling interest rates, issuers shied away from new put structures as the 1990s progressed. Rather than incur the risk of refunding the put bond in 5 years or 10 years at a higher cost, many issuers would prefer to pay an extra 10 bp to 20 bp for the privilege of issuing a longer-term liability.

Put structures provide investors with a partial defense against sharp increases in interest rates. Assuming that the issuer still has the capability to meet its sudden obligation, put structures triggered by a credit event enable investors to escape from a deteriorating credit. Perhaps because of its comparative scarcity, the performance and valuation of this defensive structure has been a challenge for many asset managers. Unlike callable structures, put prices have not conformed to expectations formed in a general volatility-valuation framework. Specifically, the volatility implied by the price of corporate put structures has ranged between 4% and 9% during the 1990s, well below the 10% to 20% volatility range associated with callable structures. Unless put origination spurts, allowing for greater liquidity and the creation of more standardized trading conventions for this rarer structural specimen, this asymmetry in implied volatility between putable and corporate structures will persist. Meanwhile, this structure should be favored as an outperformance vehicle only by those investors with a decidedly bearish outlook for interest rates.

## Corporate Curve Analysis

The rapid growth of credit derivatives since the mid-1990s has inspired a groundswell of academic and practitioner interest in the development of more rigorous techniques to analyze the term structure (1 to 100 years) and credit structure (Aaa/AAA through B2/B's; defaulted high-yield securities trade on a price rather than a spread basis) of corporate spread curves.

Credit curves, both term structure and credit structure, are almost always positively sloped. In an effort to moderate portfolio risk, many asset managers choose to assume credit risk in short-and-intermediate maturities and to substitute less-risky government securities in long-duration portfolio buckets. Accordingly, the application of this so-called "credit barbell strategy" diminishes demand for longer-dated credit debt instruments by many total return, mutual fund, and bank portfolio bond managers. Fortunately for corporate issuers that desire to issue long maturities, insurers and pension plan sponsors often meet long-term liability needs through the purchase of corporate debt with maturities that range beyond 20 years.

Default risk increases non-linearly as creditworthiness declines. The absolute risk of issuer default in any one year remains quite low through the investment-grade rating categories (Aaa/AAA to Baa3/BBB-). But investors constrained to high-quality investments often treat downgrades like quasi-defaults. In some cases like a downgrade from single-A to the Baa/BBB category, investors may be forced to sell securities under rigid portfolio guidelines. In turn, investors justifiably demand a spread premium for the increased likelihood of potential credit difficulty as rating quality descends through the investment-grade categories.

Credit spreads jump sharply in the high-yield rating categories (Ba1/BB+ through D). Default risk, especially for weak single B's and CCC's, becomes a major possibility. The corporate market naturally assigns higher and higher risk premia (spreads) as credit and rating risk escalate.

In particular, the investment-grade corporate market has a fascination with the slope of issuer credit curves between 10-year and 30-year maturities. Like the underlying Treasury benchmark curve, corporate spread curves change shape over the course of economic cycles. Typically, spread curves steepen when the bond market becomes more wary of interest rate and general credit risk. Spread curves also have displayed a propensity to steepen when the underlying benchmark curve flattens or inverts. This loose spread curve/yield curve linkage reflects the diminished appetite for investors to assume both curve and credit risk at the long end when higher total yields may be available in short-and-intermediate credit products.

## Credit Analysis: Cornerstone of Corporate Portfolio Analysis

In the continuous quest to seek credit upgrades and issuer/issue spread contractors and, more importantly, to avoid credit downgrades and the issuer/issue spread expanders, superior credit analysis has been and will remain the most important determinant of the relative performance of corporate bond portfolios. Unfortunately, investors and dealers periodically must relearn the hard way that fundamental credit analysis does not have any easy shortcuts and does not succumb readily to model magic. Often, to the disadvantage of their corporate portfolio performance, many institutional investors have under-invested in internal credit research. Credit screening tools tied to equity valuations, relative spread movements, and the Internet (intelligent agents tracking all related news on portfolio holdings) can provide helpful supplements to classic credit research and rating agency opinions. But some credit models, relying exclusively on variables like interest-rate volatility and binomial processes imported from option-valuation techniques, are not especially helpful in ranking the expected credit performance of credits as diverse as IBM, British Gas, Pacific Gas & Electric, Pohang Iron & Steel, Sumitomo, and Argentina.

Credit analysis is both non-glamorous and arduous for many top-down portfolio managers and strategists, who focus primarily on macro variables. Genuine credit analysis encompasses actually studying issuers' financial statements and accounting techniques, interviewing issuers' management, evaluating industry issues, reading indentures and charters, and developing an awareness of (not necessarily concurrence with) the views of the rating agencies about various industries and issuers. A superior credit evaluation process must take these factors into account.

Unfortunately, the advantages of such analytical rigor may clash with the rapid expansion of the universe of global bond credits. At the beginning of 2000, there were approximately 5,000 different credits scattered across the global corporate bond market.

With continued privatization of state enterprises, new entrants to the high-yield club, and expected long-term growth of the emerging-debt markets, the global roster of issuers could swell to 7,500 by 2010. The sorting of this expanding roster of global corporate issues into outperformers, market performers, and underperformers demands the establishment and maintenance of a formidable credit-evaluation function by asset managers. Anything less would be a prescription for portfolio credit casualties.

## Asset Allocation/Sector Rotation

Sector rotation strategies have long played a key role in equity portfolio management. In the corporate bond market, "macro" sector rotations among industrials, utilities, financial institutions, and non-local issuers like Yankees (non-U.S.-domiciled issuers of dollar-denominated debt into the U.S. market) also have a long history. During the last quarter of the 20th century, there have been major variations in investor sentiment toward these four major corporate bond sectors. Utilities endured market wariness about heavy supply and nuclear exposure in the early-to-mid 1980s. U.S. and European financial institutions coped with investor concern about asset quality in the late 1980s and early 1990s. Similar investor skittishness affected demand for Asian financial institution debt in the late 1990s. Industrials embodied severe "event risk" in the mid-to-late 1980s, recession vulnerability during 1990 to 1992, and a return of event risk in the late 1990s amid a general boom in corporate mergers and acquisitions. As well, Yankees were exposed to periodic market reservations about the implications of sovereignty for Quebec, political risk for various sovereigns (i.e., Russia), and the effects of the "Asian Contagion" during 1997 and 1998.

In contrast, "micro" sector rotation strategies have a briefer history in the corporate bond market. A detailed unbundling of the four main corporate sectors into their sub-components (shown in Fig. 42–10 along with average monthly returns and Sharpe ratios) was not available from corporate index providers until 1993 in the U.S. and until 1999 in Europe. Beginning in the mid-1990s, these "micro" sector rotation strategies in the corporate asset class have become much more influential as portfolio managers gain a greater understanding of the relationships among intra-corporate sectors.

## U.S. Investment-Grade Corporate Index Average Monthly Returns by Industry Classification During the 1990s

| | Average | Std Dev | Sharpe Ratio |
|---|---|---|---|
| **Investment-Grade Corp Index** | 0.59 | 0.52 | 1.14 |
| **Industrial** | 0.60 | 0.55 | 1.10 |
| Basic Industry | 0.62 | 0.51 | 1.21 |
| Chemicals | 0.59 | 0.51 | 1.16 |
| Metals | 0.62 | 0.53 | 1.17 |
| Paper | 0.66 | 0.53 | 1.25 |
| Capital Goods | 0.60 | 0.56 | 1.08 |
| Aerospace | 0.62 | 0.64 | 0.97 |
| Building Materials | 0.61 | 0.53 | 1.15 |
| Conglomerates | 0.62 | 0.52 | 1.17 |
| Construction Machinery | 0.62 | 0.63 | 0.98 |
| Packaging | 0.61 | 0.63 | 0.98 |
| Environmental | 0.43 | 0.52 | 0.83 |
| Communications | -0.24 | 1.28 | -0.18 |
| Media-Cable | 0.67 | 0.82 | 0.82 |
| Media-Noncable | 0.60 | 0.64 | 0.93 |
| Telecommunications | 0.58 | 0.61 | 0.96 |
| Consumer Cyclical | 0.61 | 0.56 | 1.09 |
| Automotive | 0.67 | 0.64 | 1.04 |
| Entertainment | 0.69 | 0.58 | 1.19 |
| Gaming | 0.43 | 0.55 | 0.77 |
| Home Construction | 0.33 | 0.80 | 0.42 |
| Lodging | 0.55 | 0.52 | 1.05 |
| Retailers | 0.58 | 0.47 | 1.23 |
| Services | 0.43 | 0.39 | 1.12 |
| Textile | 0.53 | 0.56 | 0.95 |
| Consumer Noncyclical | 0.58 | 0.56 | 1.04 |
| Beverage | 0.55 | 0.57 | 0.97 |
| Consumer Products | 0.61 | 0.58 | 1.04 |
| Food | 0.60 | 0.54 | 1.11 |
| Health Care | 0.52 | 0.56 | 0.93 |
| Pharmaceuticals | 0.55 | 0.56 | 0.98 |
| Supermarkets | 0.59 | 0.48 | 1.22 |
| Tobacco | 0.64 | 0.57 | 1.11 |
| Energy | 0.61 | 0.52 | 1.17 |
| Independent Energy | 0.62 | 0.59 | 1.06 |
| Integrated Energy | 0.61 | 0.51 | 1.19 |
| Oil Field Services | 0.64 | 0.54 | 1.17 |
| Refining | 0.65 | 0.47 | 1.39 |
| Technology | 0.56 | 0.54 | 1.03 |
| Transportation | 0.66 | 0.55 | 1.19 |
| Airlines | 0.75 | 0.59 | 1.26 |
| Railroads | 0.62 | 0.58 | 1.05 |
| Services | 0.63 | 0.49 | 1.29 |
| Other | -0.48 | 1.02 | -0.47 |
| **Utility** | 0.59 | 0.54 | 1.10 |
| Electric | 0.58 | 0.52 | 1.11 |
| Natural Gas | 0.62 | 0.52 | 1.19 |
| Nat. Gas Distributors | 0.58 | 0.62 | 0.94 |
| Nat. Gas Pipelines | 0.63 | 0.51 | 1.23 |
| Other | -0.59 | 1.51 | -0.39 |
| **Finance** | 0.62 | 0.52 | 1.18 |
| Banking | 0.60 | 0.49 | 1.22 |
| Brokerage | 0.60 | 0.42 | 1.41 |
| Finance Companies | 0.56 | 0.40 | 1.41 |
| Captive | 0.58 | 0.42 | 1.36 |
| Non-Captive | 0.55 | 0.38 | 1.44 |
| Consumer | 0.54 | 0.41 | 1.32 |
| Diversified | 0.55 | 0.36 | 1.54 |
| Insurance | 0.58 | 0.56 | 1.03 |
| Life Insurance | -0.32 | 1.14 | -0.28 |
| P & C Insurance | -0.43 | 1.24 | -0.35 |
| REITS | 0.28 | 0.68 | 0.41 |
| Other | 0.54 | 0.44 | 1.21 |
| **Yankee** | 0.59 | 0.54 | 1.09 |
| Canadians | 0.63 | 0.57 | 1.12 |
| Corporates | 0.60 | 0.51 | 1.19 |
| Supranationals | 0.60 | 0.57 | 1.05 |
| Sovereigns | 0.52 | 0.60 | 0.87 |

Sharpe Ratio = average return/standard deviation of returns

Source: Lehman Brothers Fixed Income Research

Figure 42–11 illustrates the main factors bearing on sector rotation and issuer selection strategies. For example, an actual or perceived change in rating agency philosophy toward a sector and an amendment in profitability expectations for a particular industry represent just two of many factors that can influence relative sectoral performance.

Common tactics to enhance corporate portfolio performance are also highlighted in Fig. 42–11. In particular, seasonality stands out. The annual rotation toward risk aversion in the bond market during the second half of most years contributes to a "fourth-quarter effect" (underperformance of lower-rated corporates, B's in high yield and Baa's in investment grade compared to higher-rated corporates). A fresh spurt of market optimism greets nearly every New Year (2000 was the first exception since 1986 thanks to the inversion of the U.S. Treasury curve); lower-rated corporates outperform higher-quality corporates (the "first-quarter effect"). This pattern suggests a very simple and popular portfolio strategy: underweight low quality and possibly even corporate product by the mid-third quarter of each year and then overweight lower-quality and corporate product by the late fourth quarter of each year.

## CONCLUSION

As prescribed in capital market theory, investors should be rewarded for the assumption of incremental risk. Reality conforms to theory in the global bond

### EXHIBIT   42–11

Some Outperformance Methodologies

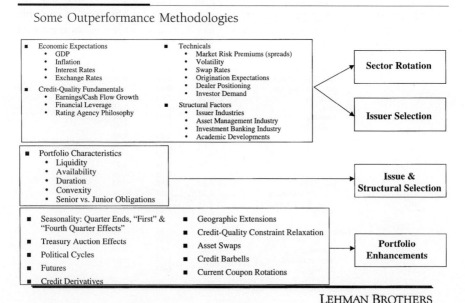

market. Credit products like corporate bonds provide higher long-term returns than government securities.

Global bond management philosophy has evolved rapidly over the past two decades. The arrival of the euro in 1999 curbed the use of currency strategies. Major portfolio duration bets (more than 10% above or below the duration of an index benchmark) have become less common by asset managers because of duration-timing disappointments in the mid-to-late 1990s. In conjunction with the demonstrably higher long-term returns of corporates and an ongoing migration from "government-only index benchmarks" to "government plus corporate and securitized index benchmarks," this reduction in currency and curve timing has propelled investor interest in global corporate portfolio optimization as a path to more consistent overall portfolio outperformance in an increasingly-competitive asset management industry.

Moreover, bond investors may have little choice in using more corporate bonds in the early 21$^{st}$ century. Thanks to the bulging U.S. government surplus, U.S. government debt has rapidly shrunk as a share of the U.S. bond market. U.S. corporates may well move from about 23% of the bond market investment choice as of early 2000 to 33% by 2010. The same trends also are in place in Europe.

Corporate bond portfolio management requires more work and asset management firm infrastructure than other fixed-income asset classes. There are thousands of credit choices, dozens of security forms, and multiple structures, and the evolution of the global corporate asset class will accelerate during the early 21$^{st}$ century. Although destined to become more structurally homogeneous with intermediate bullets as the instrument of choice, this asset class will become more heterogeneous in terms of credit quality (lower-quality credits) and geography (more European, Asian, and emerging-market corporates). Over this interval, the eventual arrival of real-time corporate indices as well as improved analytics will lead to a proliferation in the use of credit derivatives to enhance risk-adjusted returns. The long-run portfolio returns should justify this considerable effort. As a result, corporate debt is unlikely to relinquish its return leadership within the global bond realm during the early 21$^{st}$ century.

## CHAPTER 43

# MANAGEMENT OF A HIGH-YIELD BOND PORTFOLIO*

**J. Thomas Madden, CFA**
Executive Vice President
Federated Investors

**Joseph Balestrino, CFA**
Senior Vice President
Federated Investors

## INTRODUCTION

High-yield bonds are usually defined as bonds rated less than Baa (Moody's) or BBB (Standard & Poor's) or securities of equivalent quality. Such bonds may be called "lower rated" or, more cavalierly, "junk." High-yield bond management is, first and last, the balancing of risk and return. Any investment in subordinated debt of issuers rated less than Baa/BBB with debt to capitalization ratios in the 7:10 to 10:10 range bears significant risk. (Adjusted for intangible assets, some high-yield deals have negative equity.) Issuers may default, postpone payments, force exchanges, or tender for or call debt, depriving the holder of the high coupon. But in return for accepting such risks, investors are paid annual yields that well exceed yields on U.S. Treasury bonds.

Studies of the high-yield market that focus only on default rates, annual or cumulative, without considering returns on specific portfolios, are of little help in evaluating the attractiveness of the market. Such analyses are like describing the risks of a professional football career without ever mentioning the players' salaries. The high-yield bond market studies that address return as well as risk, from the earliest to most recent, provide a strong rationale for high-yield bond investing.

The objective of this chapter is to discuss some of the practical aspects of high-yield bond management in a diversified portfolio. This chapter focuses on

---

* Reprinted from Chapter 20 in Frank J. Fabozzi (ed.), *Managing Fixed Income Portfolios* (New Hope, PA: Frank J. Fabozzi Associates, 1997).

the game rules of successful high-yield investment. The ultimate objective is to achieve excess returns—largely in the form of a cash stream—for assuming risk and to compound the investment over time at attractive rates. The portfolio management process we will describe has evolved over more than two decades. It has been successful in creating superior results for mutual funds, but applies equally well to separate accounts management. We begin by examining portfolio objectives.

## DEFINITION OF PORTFOLIO OBJECTIVE

Any portfolio management process is driven by the definition of portfolio objectives. High-yield bonds may be used as components of larger portfolios (for example, as a subset of bond portfolios to boost overall fixed income return) or as substitutes for common stock investments in equity portfolios. The approach we describe assumes a client who desires superior total return on a pure portfolio of lower rated debt. Inclusion of such a portfolio within a larger investment strategy is a separate and complex topic beyond the scope of this chapter. How should such a high-yield portfolio be managed? The first step is the definition of the available universe from which the portfolio can be assembled.

By definition, a portfolio can be assembled only from the universe of buyable securities. Although in excess of 3,000 issuers have used the market in the last decade, perhaps 200 to 250 issues normally trade in the secondary market. The available universe is augmented by new issues. One evaluation a manager must make early on is to consider whether the new issue market is "cheap" or "rich" relative to the secondary market. That is, are new issues higher or lower in yield relative to risk than similar issues in the secondary market?

After defining the array of possible holdings, the portfolio manager moves to create the portfolio. In order to make this process successful, experience teaches some "rules of the road," which we examine next.

## SUMMARY OF HIGH-YIELD INVESTMENT STRATEGY

### Low Cash Position

We manage high-yield portfolios on a fully invested basis; that is, cash positions are held below 10% of our portfolios. The cash versus market decision is a separate portfolio issue and departs from the most basic reason to own lower rated debt, which is to benefit from the positive net yield spread over reasonable holding periods. We believe that significantly raising or lowering cash within a high-yield portfolio, based on assertions that the high-yield market is cheap or rich relative to higher quality bonds, departs from this primary objective.

## Target Securities Rated Single or Double B

Our objective here is to purchase stable to improving credits in the middle range of the lower rated sector. These may be nonrated, but of comparable quality. Recent empirical results suggest that single and double B rated portfolios have provided attractive net returns versus investment-grade bond portfolios over long holding periods.

## High Degree of Diversification

Diversification provides the primary method of risk management in the high-yield portfolio, as in any investment portfolio. Our portfolios typically hold 1% to 3% in a single issuer and never over 5% of total portfolio assets per issuer. All academic studies suggesting superior returns assume, in effect, a degree of diversification comparable to the market as a whole. Though we have demonstrated in our portfolios the added value of security selection over time, one large incorrect bet can damage results severely. The portfolio discipline should prevent such bets.

Investors may also want to think about percentage ownership of an issue—in the extreme case, the manager who owns an entire issue is not likely to find much of a trading market. Investors must balance the control that a large position provides in times of trouble with ongoing liquidity. We try to own less than 15% of any given issue, for example, no more than $15 million of a $100 million deal. Today, with liquidity at a premium, much smaller positions are the rule in our portfolios.

Diversification doesn't mean owning a sector of the high-yield market even if that sector has unattractive fundamentals in relation to high leverage or is unanalyzable. As part of our "critical factor" analysis, which we describe more fully later, we ask whether industry fundamentals are congenial to use of high-yield debt. For example, we have for many years sharply limited investments in airline issuers, believing that deregulation of the airlines and subsequent industry consolidation implies constant margin pressure and volatile cash flows, both broadly unfavorable conditions for high leverage. Further, we systematically avoided financial intermediaries (Southmark, Integrated Resources, savings and loans) because analysis of balance sheets appeared difficult if not impossible. Portfolio diversification should never force mechanical investment in unattractive industry sectors.

## Intensive Fundamental and Credit Review of Each Issuer

Issuer analysis is worthy of a full-blown separate discussion. The following merely outlines important areas. The analysis should always focus on sources of cash, because cash is ultimately what pays debt service. Fundamental analysis of high-yield issuers begins with examination of an issuer's dominant lines of business and its position relative to competition, as well as industry trends and cyclicality. The seasonality, volatility, and profitability of operations are considered in light of the impact of these variables on operating cash flow before noncash charges, interest, and taxes, often referred to as earnings before interest, taxes, and depreciation or amortization (EBITDA). This is cash flow available for interest, principal repayments, property and equipment expenditures, and working capital additions. EBITDA projection is the heart of high-yield bond analysis.

We prefer to invest in operating companies whose dominant products or services have proprietary or semiproprietary characteristics against an industry backdrop of high-capacity utilization, because these attributes favor stable pricing, higher margins, and more predictable cash flow. We also prefer issuers with strong brand names or product franchises for similar reasons.

Accounting practices are scrutinized. A smaller or less well known accounting firm is typically a flag for possible trouble. Similarly, a recent change in accountants should be questioned.

Balance-sheet analysis includes an evaluation of working capital requirements, estimated asset values, and the separability of assets or operations for sale. In effect, the analyst should ask: How much cash does this company need to invest in inventories, receivables, and other current assets to grow its business? What could it sell to raise cash if things go wrong? Would such sales be easy or difficult? If asset sales are built into the financing, as with RJR Nabisco in the late 1980s, the realism of expectations about price and timing are crucial. Evaluation of intangibles like goodwill can lead to a more realistic view of the balance sheet.

Debt structure may include floating- versus fixed-rate debt; examination of the schedule of debt amortization, and contingencies affecting that schedule is critical. Bank line availability and public marketability of the company's equity are considered. Here, the analyst should ask how appropriate the structure is to the company's business plan. Is too much debt repayable too soon? If zero-coupon bonds are used, what happens when they "go cash-pay"? How much does debt repayment depend on asset disposition instead of cash from the operating cycle? Can the company borrow more from its banks?

Also important are environmental and legal issues, union contracts (if applicable), and contingent liabilities, including self-insurance and underfunding of pension and other liabilities. The prior experience of Mid-American Waste Systems shows the critical nature of good analysis of nonfinancial risk.

Overt judgments about management are of critical importance: character, experience, past performance, knowledge of the business, ability to state its business plan clearly, and degree of management equity ownership are evaluated. We like deals where management has significant personal wealth at stake below the subordinated debt.

Willingness to assume risk and ability to manage in financially risky circumstances are not always coupled. Management's motivation for underwriting a transaction should be examined. Is the deal "ego driven" or based on financial opportunity? Is the business forecast on which the transaction is based realistic or "pie in the sky"? These analytical elements form the backdrop for calculation of cash interest, total interest, and debt service coverages. Most of our holdings cover cash interest 2.0 to 2.5 times, when EBITDA—earnings before depreciation, amortization, interest, and taxes—is divided by annual charges. With such narrow margins, stability of cash flow is critical. Our forecasts have a time frame of no longer than two years. Experience teaches that outlooks beyond the two-year area are guesses, not analyses.

## Market Analysis

Our objective in market analysis is to understand risks associated with indenture covenants; call, exchange, and sinking fund provisions; interest rate resets, and other elements of the issue's structure and provisions. In addition, the investment banker creating and distributing the deal should be examined both from the standpoint of (1) due diligence, and (2) sale/trading commitment and capability. Both issues deserve careful consideration. With newer forms of financing that include zero-coupon, pay-in-kind, and other deferred interest bonds (DIB), careful attention is paid to calculation of internal rate of return, security ranking, put characteristics, reset characteristics, and other structural elements.

Additionally and critically, market analysis also includes evaluation of the record of the underwriter, with attention to historical effectiveness of due diligence on past issues, support for issues in the secondary market, knowledge of investment bankers, responsibility for the issue, and overall corporate strategy of the underwriter toward the high-yield market. Federated Investors, Inc., has found specific consideration of these issues to be critical, as high-yield investment banking and trading performance varies sharply among firms and over time. A separate section discussing the analysis of investment bankers follows later.

## Critical Factor Determination

The objective here is to identify those specific aspects of the deal that have the largest impact on risk and return. Results of sector, fundamentals, and market analysis are evaluated to determine the most important issues determining bond performance (Critical Factor Identification). We have learned that in successful high-yield bond management, the ultimate challenge is to analyze what's important to an investment outcome, not every attribute of the issuer. This is the Pareto principle, or "80/20" rule, applied to high-yield analysis. No matter what the process is termed, we believe it is crucial to rank order analytical insights to focus attention on those that carry most weight for the issuer's performance. In the early 1980s, for many high-yield issuers, the critical factor was the trend in oil prices. Today, it may well be the impact of a recession on an issuer's major operations. Analyze the critical, not the trivial.

## Simple Sell Disciplines

With this approach, we strive to sell issues when yields improve to an effective BB to BBB equivalent or when issuer fundamentals appear to be deteriorating. We strive to be early sellers: our rule is "first sale, best sale."

## ANALYZING THE HIGH-YIELD INVESTMENT BANKING PROCESS

The investment banker is critically important in the creation of a successful high-yield issue. While issuer objectives for a high-yield transaction are important, it's the investment banker as intermediary who typically structures and engineers the transaction in its final form.

Ideally, the banker has performed extensive due diligence on the issuer, thought carefully about how the high-yield financing will fit the issuer's business and financing objectives, and helped the issuer plan the role of the deal in the issuer's overall strategy. What will the size of the issue be? What term will apply? Will the coupon be fixed, floating, adjustable, or increasing? Will the issue be a single financing or complex and multilayered? Will the issue convert to common stock? Will warrants for common stock be attached, or is there some other form of equity kicker required to make the deal a success? What will the call and refunding provisions be? What covenants will be included in the indenture? Will the transaction be protected against event risk—that is, the releveraging of the enterprise at some later date with an adverse effect on current creditors? Will financing covenants be included? (For example, pledges as to minimum levels of interest coverage or net worth.) These examples are but a fraction of the issues the investment banker deals with when negotiating between high-yield buyers and the issuer.

The intelligent high-yield buyer will attempt to test the investment banking process within the analysis. Conversations with underwriters may cast light on the thoroughness of the due diligence. Questions to management may illuminate the appropriateness of the deal and its structure. For example, the high-yield buyer should ask whether the valuation process makes sense if assets are being acquired with bond proceeds: Have peak cycle operating earnings been discounted, with allowance for the down cycle? How does the equity market value similar businesses? Do competitors think the deal is fair, or is the issuer going to overpay? If cost savings will help repay the debt, are such savings realistic? Are capital expenditures being unrealistically reduced? A reasonable approach may be for the high-yield investor to stand in the shoes of the banker and then ask how he or she might have put the transaction together. Seen from the "sell side," the transaction may appear to change form. The presence of obscure covenants may become clear and the likelihood of developments adverse to the high-yield buyer may be clearly discerned. One additional rule of thumb: a thick, overly complex, poorly organized offering circular may signal an overly complex and poorly organized financing.

Evaluation of the deal and its structure is only part of the buyer's analysis. The buyer must also consider the history and reputation of the investment banker. Among questions the buyer should ask are: What continuing commitment, if any, will the banker have to the deal after it is placed? Does the investment banker have a record of supporting high-yield transactions in the secondary market—will it bid in the secondary market for its own deals? If a transaction runs into trouble, will the banker actively work to restructure the deal or will it leave this task to bondholders and their attorneys and advisors?

Perhaps more broadly, the high-yield buyer should consider what appear to be the investment banker's general objectives for its high-yield operation. In the 1980s, to many observers, some Wall Street firms appeared to participate in the market on a deal-by-deal basis. These firms seemed to examine each transaction on its own merits without a sustained commitment to the market. Other firms lacked commitment to the high-yield market at the most senior level. High-yield market observers recognize that the policy toward lower rated debt at these firms was a cause of much disagreement and rancor with high personnel turnover. More recently, major firms have confined their high-yield efforts to a highly successful leveraging of their historical client base, focusing intelligently on industries with stable cash flow characteristics. Senior managers of one such firm have stated emphatically their intent to transact as principals, not on an agency basis, in their high-yield activities. Their well-articulated strategy focuses on diversified equity investment by the firm for its own account using high-yield bonds as one financing tool. This firm's high-yield debt issuance has been favorable for both buyers and sellers.

The successful high-yield manager will be both thoughtful regarding the difference between high-yield investment banks and knowledgeable about their track records in the market, since continuity and consistency have been scarce commodities. In the current climate, the focus appears largely transactional. High-yield issuers switch investment bankers on a deal-by-deal basis. Corporate finance and sales and trading units swap personnel like professional sports franchises. Several well-known high-yield broker/dealers have experienced severe illiquidity as a result of over-aggressiveness in bridge financing transactions.

Thoughtful assessment of all of these issues as they bear on a specific purchase candidate is critical. Again, a useful analytical technique is to place oneself in the shoes of the issuer and its corporate finance advisor. Failure to address the history, intent, and objectives of the high-yield investment banker is a hallmark of incomplete analysis.

In the next section, we discuss issues concerning problem credits. Though it is certainly among the least attractive aspects of high-yield investments, an alert and aggressive approach to problem credits presents an area of added value provided by a high-yield manager.

## ISSUES OF PROBLEM CREDITS

Most investors in high-yield bond portfolios will eventually encounter the complex problems of deteriorating credits. Various well-publicized studies of high-yield default experience suggest that between 1% and 2% of a representative high-yield portfolio will default in any given year. Several recent studies have looked at cumulative default experience for high-yield portfolios, and although the results may differ to some extent, all such studies show a tendency for high-yield issues to become more susceptible to credit problems with the passage of time. Hence, any effective approach to the management of lower rated bond portfolios must include a specific strategy for deteriorating and defaulted deals.

### Early Detection and Sale Is the Best Defense

Our approach begins with the doctrine of "first sale, best sale." The mathematical advantage of taking a small loss on a position, selling that position with accrued interest, and reinvesting proceeds in a more attractive high-yield bond is instantly apparent when compared with holding a security through a work-out period of one to two years, during which the investment stops paying interest. Use of present value analysis in making the decision to exit a troubled issue at a loss is frequently helpful. Proceeds of a bond sale, even at a deep discount, can be reinvested at currently very high yield and immediately begin compensating for the difference between today's price and some hoped-for higher value in the future.

A full description of methods for detecting deteriorating credit worthiness is beyond the scope of this chapter. However, several major causes of such deterioration are summarized below.

#### Secular Deterioration in the Issuer's Principal Product or Service

Energy and energy services companies' inability to escape collapsing oil prices in the early 1980s provides a clear-cut example. Only a handful of such companies with high leverage could avoid debt service problems as oil prices plummeted from in excess of $30.00 per barrel to an eventual low of $7.00–$8.00 per barrel over the period 1981–1985. Early perception of the macro premise that the demand for hydrocarbons was elastic should have spurred high-yield managers to wholesale elimination of energy-related bonds from portfolios.

### Inadequate Financing Controls

It is imperative for any issuer operating with high leverage to have a clear and timely way to monitor cash. Among the causes for the Chapter 11 filing of Revco Drug Stores were inadequate management accounting and inventory control systems. Rapid growth through acquisition by Northern Pacific similarly led to inventory management problems. This area should rank high among analyst concerns.

### Initial or Second Stage Overleveraging

The problem of high-yield financings by Robert Campeau (Federated-Allied Stores) and by the Thompson family (Southland) are straightforward results of overpaying for operating assets.

Given that perpetuals went out of style during Napoleon's time, one way to look at determining whether growth in earnings or cash flow and exit valuation are important in realizing the return on debt claim is to look at how long it would take to recover your investment from internally generated cash flow. The assumption here is that most lenders will not rent their money for longer than 20 or 30 years.

### Fraud and Criminal Activity by Management

The most difficult cause of a deteriorating credit to detect or avoid comes from malfeasance in the management of highly leveraged companies. Issuers like Saxon Industries, Flight Transportation, ZZZZ Best, and Wedtech are examples of high-yield transactions where managements systematically defrauded creditors while misleading investment bankers and accountants. The importance of thorough due diligence by high-yield underwriters cannot be overemphasized. Further, any suspicions by analysts or managers should be highlighted and discussed routinely. A sense of unease may provide the best signal to sell. Visits to production facilities and other operating assets financed by the issue should also be emphasized. A refusal by management to accommodate such visits is a danger signal.

# Restructuring the Troubled Issuer

This section proposes a few summary observations derived from practical experience. The sharp rise in corporate debt use has been accompanied by deterioration in the rights and remedies of creditors. Recent changes in bankruptcy statutes provide growing flexibility for the troubled debtor. Leveraging of investment-grade bond issuers like R. J. Reynolds has incorporated the deliberate exploitation of weak indenture covenants in older investment-grade bond offer-

ings. High-yield borrowers have become, in the last 15 years, ever more ready
to propose out-of-court exchanges of new securities for old, usually involving
reductions in claims and attempted preservation of large equity stakes by underperforming managements or investors. One example, blocked eventually by
bondholders, was Marvel Group. Over the last several years these trends have
been met by increased militancy on the part of high-yield bondholders. Some
attributes of successful restructurings are set forth below; these appear to be
increasingly embraced by high-yield creditors.

## Out-of-Court Exchanges Must Be Guided by the Intent of the Bankruptcy Statutes

In brief, this means that a company that fails to pay as agreed must sacrifice its
equity to preserve creditor wealth. A high-yield company that cannot service its
debt belongs to its senior and subordinated lenders. Restructurings that seek to
escape this outcome are increasingly unsuccessful. Much time and energy can
be saved in negotiations with issuers if all sides understand that an out-of-court
proposal, which is inferior to the likely outcome of a court-supervised reorganization, is likely to be a nonstarter.

## Aggressive, Concerted Action by Bondholders Is a Necessity

The successful high-yield bond manager must be prepared to intervene early
and forcefully in a deteriorating situation. Uncovering the list of issue holders
and conferencing on the intent and objectives of the creditor group is paramount.
Any negotiation with a troubled issuer is likely to be more efficient and successful when a large percentage of bondholders are negotiating within a united
front. Knowledge of the general purpose and mechanisms of the bankruptcy
laws and the ability by bondholders to retain top quality legal advisors are
critical. The reader can immediately grasp the advantages of scale and institutional resources in a reorganization negotiation. The small-scale bondholder is
disadvantaged compared to the institutional high-yield manager in a difficult
negotiation with troubled issuers. Legal fees and travel expenses in a restructuring can mount quickly.

  Further, the bondholder group must be alert to the prospect for restoring
the investment through litigation, not only against the issuer, but also against
parties involved in the initial transaction, such as managements and boards of
directors, as well as individuals. Accounting firms should also be scrutinized.
The rise of lawsuits involving fraudulent conveyance is one example of a growing interest in a variety of litigation strategies. One seminar on this topic listed
breach of covenant litigation, RICO liabilities, direct liability, and the class action lawsuit among important considerations for creditors. The effective high-
yield manager needs to understand such concepts as equitable subordination,
constructive trust, and lender liability in order to successfully integrate with other
bondholders and litigators. Note again the disadvantage suffered by the odd-lot

bondholder and stand-alone money manager or investment advisor in this increasingly complex arena.

The importance of an aggressive and forceful approach in troubled negotiations, in or out of bankruptcy court, can be scarcely overemphasized. The insolvent or illiquid debtor is aided by the passage of time during which he is failing to pay debt service. Protracted negotiations over minor details and less important issues is an effective debtor strategy, as is dividing the creditor group and conducting separate negotiations with group members. Most effective resolutions are likely to result from the appointment of leadership among creditors and the delegation of authority to negotiate to those leaders.

## The Importance of Not Liquidating at the Bottom

Given the complexity of troubled debt negotiations, along with the expense and time involved in moving such negotiations forward successfully, the student of high-yield management may wonder whether a quick sale of the defaulted issue may not prove the better alternative. While each investment must be individually analyzed, strong empirical evidence exists suggesting the perils of early sale of defaulted bonds. One of the most powerful conclusions from the Hickman study is the high return enjoyed by investors who purchased corporate bonds at deeply depressed levels in the trough of the Great Depression. Prices of high-yield bonds following the initial announcement of grave financial difficulties appear to overly discount the impact of such problems.

Exceptions to this rule exist of course, but such exceptions typically emanate from deals that financed assets of very limited economic usefulness (for example, the ultralarge and slow-steaming container ships of McLean Industries). Another exception is where the business is acquired for a price well in excess of the economic value of its operating units (e.g., Southland, Federated-Allied). But in many instances aggressive negotiations may be handsomely rewarded. A rule of thumb that has prevailed since the early years of this century is that the subordinated debt of troubled issuers ultimately provides a worth of approximately 40 cents on the dollar. This outcome is suggested in the Hickman report as well as in several studies by Edward Altman of New York University. Money managers use this benchmark to begin consideration of restructuring outcomes.

## CONCLUSION

Seeing an erroneous obituary in 1897, Mark Twain quipped to a correspondent that the report of his death had been greatly exaggerated. A similar exaggeration was the widely reported demise of the high-yield market in the late 1980s—in the year 2000, this market is a primary financing source for thousands of growing businesses, with dozens of major financial institutions, banks, and brokers alike issuing and trading lower rated debt. But the practical rules for successful high-yield money managers have altered little in the past several decades. Thorough diversification, careful credit and market analysis, early sales when trouble approaches, and aggressive, prompt action when restructuring is required, all will apply in the coming millenium as they did in the 1990s, 1980s, and, we suspect, the more distant past.

## CHAPTER 44

# BOND IMMUNIZATION: AN ASSET/LIABILITY OPTIMIZATION STRATEGY*

Frank J. Fabozzi, Ph.D., CFA, CPA
Adjunct Professor of Finance
School of Management
Yale University

Peter F. Christensen
Managing Director
ComTech, Incorporated

The purpose of this chapter is to review the mechanics and applications of the bond immunization strategy. In the first section, we define immunization as a duration-matching strategy, and then compare it to maturity-matching as an alternative approach to locking in rates. To hedge the reinvestment risk present in maturity-matching, we then explain the single-period immunization strategy and the rebalancing procedures that accompany it. Following single-period immunization, we discuss multiperiod immunization and its applications for the pension, insurance, and thrift markets. Finally, we review variations on the strategy, including combination matching, contingent immunization, immunization with futures, and immunization with options.

## WHAT IS AN IMMUNIZED PORTFOLIO?

Single-period immunization is usually defined as locking in a fixed rate of return over a prespecified horizon, such as locking in a 10% return for a five-year period. It can also be defined as generating a minimum future value at the end of a specified horizon, such as generating $100 million from a $70 million investment five years earlier. With multiperiod immunization, the horizon over which rates are locked in is extended to include multiple periods (such as a

---

* The previous version of this chapter, appearing in the fifth edition, was coauthored with Anthony LoFaso.

schedule of monthly payouts to retirees of a pension plan). Multiperiod immunization is a duration-matching strategy that permits funding of a fixed schedule of multiple future payouts at a minimum cost (such as funding a $500 million schedule of payouts at a cost of $200 million).

The actuary generally credited with pioneering the immunization strategy, F. M. Reddington, defined immunization in 1952 as "the investment of the assets in such a way that the existing business is immune to a general change in the rate of interest." [1] He also specified a condition for immunization: The average duration of assets must be set equal to the average duration of the liabilities. He thought that by matching the durations of assets and liabilities he would then immunize a portfolio from the effects of small changes in interest rates. By matching durations on both sides of the balance sheet, he felt that assets and liabilities would be equally price-sensitive to changes in the general level of interest rates. For any change in yield, both sides of the ledger should be equally affected; therefore, the relative values of assets and liabilities would not be changed.

Much later, Lawrence Fisher and Roman Weil defined an immunized portfolio as follows:[2]

> A portfolio of investments is immunized for a holding period if its value at the end of the holding period, regardless of the course of rates during the holding period, must be at least as large as it would have been had the interest rate function been constant throughout the holding period.
>
> If the realized return on an investment in bonds is sure to be at least as large as the appropriately computed yield to the horizon, then that investment is immunized.

Fisher and Weil demonstrated that to achieve the immunized result, the average duration of the bond portfolio must be set equal to the remaining time in the planning horizon, and the market value of assets must be greater than or equal to the present value of the liabilities discounted at the internal rate of return of the portfolio.

Before reviewing the logic of this portfolio strategy, let's look at maturity-matching as an early approach to locking in a current level of interest rates.

## MATURITY-MATCHING: THE REINVESTMENT PROBLEM

Suppose that an investor wishes to lock in prevailing interest rates for a 10-year period. Should he or she buy 10-year bonds?

1. F. M. Reddington, "Review of the Principle of Life-Office Valuations," *Journal of the Institute of Actuaries,* vol. 78, 1952, pp. 286–340.
2. Lawrence Fisher and Roman Weil, "Coping with the Risk of Interest-Rate Fluctuations: Returns to Bondholders from Naive and Optimal Strategies," *Journal of Business,* October 1971, pp. 408–431.

By purchasing 10-year bonds and holding them to maturity, an investor can be certain of receiving all coupon payments over the 10-year period as well as the principal repayment at redemption (assuming that no default occurs). These two sources of income are fixed in dollar amounts. The third and final source of income is the interest earned on the semiannual coupon payments. "Interest on coupon" is not fixed in dollar amounts; rather it depends on the many interest-rate environments at the various times of payment.

A reinvestment problem occurs when the reinvestment of coupon income occurs at rates below the yield-to-maturity of the bond at the time of purchase. Note from Exhibit 44–1 that as interest rates shift instantaneously and remain at the new levels for a 10-year period, the total "holding period" return on a 9% par bond due in 10 years will vary considerably. The initial effect will appear in the value of the asset. The immediate result will be a capital gain if rates fall (or loss, if rates rise).

As the holding period increases after a change in rates, the interest-on-coupon component of total return begins to exert a stronger influence. At 10 years, we note that interest on coupon (reinvestment income) exerts a dominance over capital gain (or loss) in determining holding period returns.

Intuitively, we know that these relationships make sense. Capital gains appear instantly, whereas changes in reinvestment rates take time to exert their effect on the total holding-period return on a bond.

If rates were to jump immediately from 9% to 15% and a capital loss were to appear today, at what point will that capital loss be made up because the reinvestment of coupon payments is occurring at a higher (15%) rate? As illustrated in Exhibit 44–2, the two "offsetting forces" of market value and reinvestment return equally offset at 6.79 years. This is the duration of the 10-year, 9% bond. To earn the original 9% target return (the yield-to-maturity at the time of purchase), it is necessary to hold that bond for the period of its duration—6.79 years in our example. If we wish to lock in a market rate of 9% for a 10-year period, we would select a bond with a duration of 10 (not a maturity of 10 years). The maturity for such a par bond in a 9% yield environment is roughly 23 years.

From Exhibit 44–1, we note that regardless of the immediate, one-time interest-rate shift, we are still able to earn a 9% total return if our holding period is 6.79 years—the duration of the bond. By targeting the duration of a portfolio rather than specific maturities to the prescribed investment horizon of 6.79, we see the equal offsets of capital gain with lower reinvestment return occurring in the portfolio. This principle of duration-matching together with rebalancing procedures that are used over time allow us to lock in rates and minimize the reinvestment risk that is associated with the maturity-matching strategy.

## SINGLE-PERIOD IMMUNIZATION

The most straightforward approach to funding a single-period liability five years from today is to purchase a five-year, zero-coupon bond maturing on the liability

# EXHIBIT 44-1

Total Return on a 9% Noncallable $1,000 Bond Due in 10 Years and Held through Various Holding Periods

| Income Source | Interest Rate at Time of Reinvestment | Holding Period in Years | | | | | |
|---|---|---|---|---|---|---|---|
| | | 1 | 3 | 5 | 6.79[a] | 9 | 10 |
| Coupon income | 5% | $ 90 | $270 | $450 | $611 | $ 810 | $ 900 |
| Capital gain or loss | | 287 | 234 | 175 | 100 | 39 | 0 |
| Interest-on-interest | | 1 | 17 | 54 | 105 | 191 | 241 |
| Total return | | $378 | $521 | $679 | $816 | $1,040 | $1,141 |
| (and yield) | | (37.0%) | (15.0%) | (11.0%) | (9.0%) | (8.5%) | (8.2%) |
| Coupon Income | 7 | $ 90 | $270 | $450 | $611 | $ 810 | $ 900 |
| Capital gain or loss | | 132 | 109 | 83 | 56 | 19 | 0 |
| Interest-on-interest | | 2 | 25 | 78 | 149 | 279 | 355 |
| Total return | | $224 | $404 | $611 | $816 | $1,108 | $1,225 |
| (and yield) | | (22.0%) | (12.0%) | (10.0%) | (9.0%) | (8.6%) | (8.5%) |
| Coupon income | 10 | $ 90 | $270 | $450 | $611 | $ 810 | $ 900 |
| Capital gain or loss | | 0 | 0 | 0 | 0 | 0 | 0 |
| Interest-on-interest | | 2 | 32 | 103 | 205 | 387 | 495 |
| Total return | | $ 92 | $302 | $553 | $816 | $1,197 | $1,395 |
| (and yield) | | (9.0%) | (9.0%) | (9.0%) | (9.0%) | (9.0%) | (9.0%) |
| Coupon income | 10 | $ 90 | $270 | $450 | $611 | $ 810 | $ 900 |
| Capital gain or loss | | -112 | -95 | -75 | -56 | -18 | 0 |
| Interest-on-interest | | 2 | 40 | 129 | 261 | 502 | 647 |
| Total return | | $ 20 | $215 | $504 | $816 | $1,294 | $1,547 |
| (and yield) | | (2.0%) | (6.7%) | (8.5%) | (9.0%) | (9.7%) | (9.8%) |

[a] Duration of a 9% bond bought at par and due in 10 years.

**E X H I B I T   44–2**

"Offsetting Forces" Principle (9% Coupon, 30-Year Maturity Bond, Rates Rise Instantly from 9% to 15%, Reinvestment Rate Is 15%)

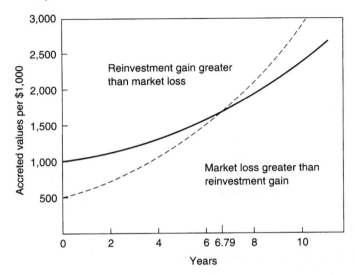

payment date. Regardless of future fluctuations in interest rates, the bond, or portfolio of bonds, will be price insensitive (or immune) to changes in rates as the zero-coupon securities mature at par on the payment date. Because zero coupons have durations equal to their maturities, the five-year, zero-coupon bonds both cash-match and duration-match the single-period liability payment.

If zero-coupon bonds have insufficient yield, a portfolio of *coupon-bearing* Treasury, agency, and corporate bonds can be immunized to fund the same single-period payment only if three conditions are met: (1) the duration of the portfolio of coupon bonds must be set equal to the five-year horizon; (2) the market value of assets must be greater than the present value of liabilities; and (3) the dispersion of the assets must be slightly greater than the dispersion of the liabilities. That is,

1. $\text{Duration}_{Assets} = \text{Duration}_{Liabilities}$

2. $\text{PV}_{Assets} > \text{PV}_{Liabilities}$

3. $\text{Dispersion}_{Assets} > \text{Dispersion}_{Liabilities}$

Immunization requires that the average durations of assets and liabilities are set equal at all times. Unfortunately, simple matching of durations is not a sufficient condition.

Consider both a $200,000 par-value zero-coupon, five-year bond in a 9% rate environment and a $1 million five-year single-period liability. Obviously the durations of both the assets and liabilities are matched because they are both zero-coupon, five-year obligations. However, a $200,000 par-value zero-coupon, five-year bond (with a market value of $128,787) cannot realistically compound to $1 million in five years. The required annual rate to compound to $1 million in five years is almost 67%. In a 9% rate environment, $643,937 is required in market value of assets to compound to $1 million in five years.

Therefore, a second condition for immunization is necessary; the market value of assets must be greater than or equal to the present value of liabilities, using the internal rate of return (IRR) of the assets as the discount factor in present-valuing the liabilities. The assets, when compounded at the "locked-in" immunized rate of 9%, will grow to equal or exceed the future-value immunized target of $1 million in this example.

To meet a target duration of 6.79 a portfolio could be constructed as either (1) a barbell of roughly equal amounts of bonds with zero and 13 duration, (2) an even ladder of equal amounts of bonds with zero through 13 duration, or (3) a bullet of only 6.79 durations. Because the duration calculation assumes a parallel shift in the yield curve, the barbell structure incorporates the greatest amount of yield-curve risk by concentrating cash flows on both ends of the curve. If the yield curve is positive or inverted, the barbell structure will violate the assumption of a flat curve more than the even ladder or bullet structure. On the other hand, the bullet structure, by concentrating cash flows at a single maturity point, incorporates a flat slope over the relevant range on the yield curve.

For single-period immunization, a bullet maturity structure with tight cash flows around the liability date is generally preferred to an even ladder or bar-belled portfolio because of the reduced risk exposure to the yield curve becoming steeper or twisting. In fact, to eliminate the risk of pathological shifts in yields, the investor could tighten the cash flows still further and purchase a zero-coupon bond to cash-flow-match the single-period liability. Short of that, a bullet structure is the least risky and the barbell the most risky.

Therefore, for immunization the third condition of controlling the degree of barbelling must be incorporated into the process of structuring a portfolio. The measure used to control the barbelling is dispersion—a measure of the variance of cash flows around the duration, (D), of a bond. The mathematical formula for dispersion is as follows:[3]

$$\text{Dispersion} = \frac{\sum(t_i - D)^2 \text{PV(CF}_i)}{\sum \text{PV(CF}_i)}$$

---

3. This measure, commonly referred to as $M^2$, was first developed in H. Gifford Fong and Oldrich Vasicek, "A Risk Minimizing Strategy for Multiple Liability Immunization," *Journal of Finance*, December 1984, pp. 1541–1546.

The dispersion of a zero-coupon bond therefore is zero, whereas the dispersion of a 30-year current-coupon U.S. Treasury bond can exceed 100.

## REBALANCING PROCEDURES

As time passes, the single-period immunized portfolio must be rebalanced so that the duration of the portfolio is always reset to the remaining life in the planning period to ensure the offsetting effects of capital gains with reinvestment return. This rebalancing procedure requires that the coupon income, reinvestment income, matured principal, and proceeds from possible liquidation of longer bonds be reinvested into securities that maintain the duration equal to the remaining life in the planning period. Because of the multiple rebalancings required throughout the planning period, the bond portfolio is continually maintained in a duration-matched state and therefore should achieve its target return in spite of periodic shifts in rates.

An immunized bond portfolio, therefore, can be constructed once a time horizon is established. Because duration is inversely related to both the prevailing yields and the coupon rate, it may not be possible to immunize a portfolio beyond a certain number of years using only coupon-bearing securities. For example, when bond market yields reached their historic highs in 1981, it was not possible to immunize a bullet liability beyond seven years in the taxable markets with current-coupon securities. In an 8% rate environment, the maximum lock-up period would be closer to 12 years. However, the use of zero-coupon securities with long maturities and durations can allow the investor the opportunity to lengthen the planning period over which he or she can lock in rates.

The actual targeted return on an immunized portfolio will depend on the level of interest rates at the time the program is initiated. Though bond values may, for example, decline as interest rates rise, the future value of the portfolio (or security) based on the new higher reinvestment rate and lower principal value should still correspond to the original targeted yield. As we demonstrate later in an actual simulation of an immunized portfolio, duration is the key to controlling the equal offset of reinvestment income with asset value as interest rates fluctuate.

The important point to remember is this: *The standard deviation of return on an immunized portfolio will be much lower over a given horizon than that on a nonimmunized portfolio—whether measured around a sample mean or promised yield.* With interest-rate risk minimized (when held over an assumed time horizon), the performance of the immunized portfolio is virtually ensured, regardless of reinvestment rates.

## MULTIPERIOD IMMUNIZATION

In the discussions so far, we have documented how the three conditions are required to create a single-period immunized portfolio. These conditions can be extended to create an immunized portfolio that will satisfy the funding requirements of multiple-period liabilities, such as the monthly payouts to the retired-lives portion of a pension plan.

If a liability schedule were composed of 30 annual payments, it would be possible to create 30 single-period immunized portfolios to fund that schedule. If we then analyzed the overall duration of the 30 asset portfolios, it would equal the duration of the liabilities. As long as the dispersions of assets and liabilities are closely matched and the asset value is greater than the present value of liabilities, then the liability schedule should be fully funded and the portfolio immunized.

Calculating the duration of multiperiod liabilities is not as straightforward as calculating the duration of a single-period liability, where the remaining time in the planning horizon is the liability duration. With multiple payout periods, the liability duration is derived by using, as the discount factor, the internal rate of return (IRR) on the assets. Of course, the IRR of the assets is not determinable unless we know the precise portfolio, its duration, and its dispersion.

As a result of this simultaneity problem, the construction of an immunized portfolio is an iterative process whereby an IRR guess for the portfolio is advanced; the durations and dispersion of the liabilities are then calculated based on the IRR guess; an optimal immunized portfolio is simulated to match the duration and dispersion estimates; the portfolio IRR is then compared with the estimated IRR; and, if they differ, a new IRR estimate is advanced and the procedure repeated.

In the absence of strict cash matching it is anticipated that some liabilities will be met through a combination of asset cash flows *and* asset sales. In this regard, immunization introduces an element of market risk into the asset/liability equation that is only minimally present under a dedicated strategy.

The degree to which market risk can be limited and the cost savings of immunization thereby justified on a risk-adjusted basis depends in large part on one's ability to characterize correctly the price response of the bonds in the portfolio to changes in interest rates. This issue is especially critical when bonds containing embedded options—such as mortgages and callable corporates—are part of the asset mix and is best resolved by appealing to option-adjusted bond analytics for the relevant bond durations. The immunization simulation above, which assumed that all bond cash flows were fixed, is justified in part by the degree of call protection on the callable corporates selected; but the inclusion of bonds with more call risk would require more finely tuned analysis.

## Rebalancing Procedures for Multiperiod Portfolios

Just as with a single-period immunized portfolio, a multiperiod portfolio must be rebalanced whenever one of the three conditions is violated. If, for example, the asset and liability durations were to wander apart over time, then the portfolio must be rebalanced to return it to a duration-matched state.

In a multiperiod portfolio, the durations will tend to wander whenever a liability payment comes due. An extreme example might be a $10 million bullet liability due in one month (almost zero duration) and a $10 million bullet liability due in 10 years. The average duration of the two liabilities will be about 5.

One month from now, the one-month liability will be extinguished and the remaining liability will be 9 years and 11 months. As the asset portfolio has a duration of roughly 5 to match what was an average duration liability of 5, the sudden shift in liability duration from 5 to approximately 10 will cause a major duration mismatch and will need to be rebalanced.

## APPLICATIONS OF THE IMMUNIZATION STRATEGY

As indicated in Exhibit 44–3, the major applications of the immunization strategy have been in the pension, insurance, banking, and thrift industries.

The pension market has made widespread use of both single-period and multiperiod immunization. Single-period immunization is generally employed as an alternative to the purchase of a guaranteed investment contract (GIC) from an insurance company. Both vehicles seek to lock in today's prevailing rates over a finite planning horizon. Immunization has the advantage of liquidity, as the portfolio is composed of marketable securities. GICs are privately written contracts between plan sponsor and insurance company and are not generally traded in the secondary market.

The additional benefit of an immunized portfolio is that the portfolio manager can take advantage of market opportunities in structuring and rebalancing these portfolios by including securities in the portfolio that are attractive on a relative-value basis. Investors can actively position portfolios in sectors and cred-

## EXHIBIT  44–3

Applications for Immunization

|  | Market | | |
| --- | --- | --- | --- |
|  | **Pension** | **Insurance** | **Banking and Thrift** |
| *Single period* | Asset strategy (GIC alternative) |  |  |
| *Multiperiod* | Funding retired-live payouts | Funding GIC and structured settlements | GAP management Matched growth |
|  | Single premium buyouts Portfolio insurance | Portfolio insurance | Portfolio insurance |

its they perceive to be cheap or upgrade candidates. By actively positioning the immunized portfolio, investors can add incremental value to the portfolios and potentially outperform the illiquid GIC over a fixed planning horizon.

The pension market has also made widespread use of multiperiod immunization. Multiperiod immunization is generally employed to fund a schedule of expected benefit payouts to the retired-lives portion of a defined benefit plan. As explained in the next chapter on cash flow matching, by matching the duration of an immunized portfolio with corresponding liabilities, the plan sponsor can lock in prevailing rates, raise its actuarial interest-rate assumption, and reduce cash contributions to the pension fund.

The insurance market has also made widespread use of the multiperiod immunization strategy for its fixed-liability insurance products such as GICs and structured settlements. Because GIC, structured settlement, and single-premium buyout assets and liabilities are generally segmented from general account assets and liabilities, the entire line of business can be immunized to minimize the interest-rate risk and lock in a spread. Again, these portfolios can be actively positioned to take advantage of market opportunities.

Lastly, banks and thrifts have made extensive use of the multiperiod immunization strategy to assist in the management of their asset/liability gap and to ensure future duration-matched growth of assets and liabilities. *Technical Bulletin 13* (TB-13) mandated for the thrift industry that the interest sensitivity of a company's assets be similar to the interest sensitivity of its liabilities. For those thrifts whose durations are not closely matched, their capital requirements will be increased.

## VARIATIONS TO IMMUNIZATION

There are several variations or enhancements to the immunization strategy, including combination-matching; contingent immunization; immunization with futures, options, mortgages, or swaps; and stochastic duration matching.

The most popular variation of the immunization strategy is *combination-matching,* also called *horizon-matching.* A combination-matched portfolio is one that is duration-matched with the added constraint that it be cash-matched in the first few years, usually five years. The advantages of combination-matching over immunization are that liquidity needs are provided for in the initial cash-flow-matched period. Also, most of the positive slope or inversion of a yield curve tends to take place in the first few years. By cash flow matching the initial portion, we have reduced the risk associated with nonparallel shifts of a sloped yield curve.

The disadvantages of combination-matching over immunization are that the cost is slightly greater and the swapping discretion is constrained. The freedom to swap a combination-matched portfolio is partially hampered not only because the asset durations must be replaced in a swap but also because the cash flows in the initial five-year period must be replaced as well.

A variant strategy to immunization is *contingent immunization.* The contingent immunization strategy is a blend of active management with immunization such that a portfolio is actively managed with a lower floor return ensured over the horizon.[4]

The floor return, or safety net, is a rate set below the immunized rate, allowing managers discretion to actively position their portfolios. If managers incorrectly position their portfolios and the market moves against them, the portfolios can still be actively managed. If the market continues to move against the portfolios and the floor return is violated, then managers must commit to immunized portfolios to ensure the floor return over the remainder of the horizon.

Contingent immunization requires an abrupt change in management strategy at the moment the floor return is violated. With dynamic asset allocation (portfolio insurance), the change in strategy is gradual. In this instance, managers gradually shift out of risky assets into riskless assets to avoid violating minimum return requirements. An actively managed bond portfolio or equity portfolio is the risky asset. An immunized portfolio, with duration matched to the holding period, can serve as the riskless asset. Overall, the performance of the portfolio of risky and riskless assets replicates the performance that would be obtained were a put option added to the risky portfolio. This synthetic put gives the portfolio maximum upside potential consistent with a prespecified level of protection on the downside.

Immunized portfolios can also be created with the use of futures contracts to replicate the interest sensitivity of an immunized duration. In this form, a desired portfolio can be selected without regard to a target duration, and futures contracts can then be used to replicate the price sensitivity of an immunized portfolio at the desired duration.

Options can also be used with immunized portfolios to enhance returns over a specified horizon. Through the use of covered call writing or long put or call positions, managers can enhance returns over a specified horizon.

Finally, CMO PAC bonds are sometimes used in immunized portfolios to enhance returns. Though they are mortgage derivatives, their cash flows are certain across a wide band of interest-rate scenarios (prepayment speeds). As such, they can enhance performance as long as their use is actively monitored.

## CONCLUSION

Bond immunization is an important risk-control strategy used by the pension fund, insurance, banking, and thrift industries. In today's volatile markets, it is imperative that all asset/liability gaps be intentional. Immunization provides the tools to measure the interest-rate risk position an institution or a fund is taking with respect to its liabilities; it also provides the tools to minimize that risk when a minimum gap is desired.

---

4. See Martin L. Leibowitz and Alfred Weinberger, "The Uses of Contingent Immunization," *Journal of Portfolio Management,* Fall 1981, pp. 51–55.

## CHAPTER 45

# DEDICATED BOND PORTFOLIOS

**Frank J. Fabozzi, Ph.D., CFA, CPA**
Adjunct Professor of Finance
School of Management
Yale University

**Peter F. Christensen**
Managing Director
ComTech, Incorporated

Dedication is a popular and important portfolio strategy in asset/liability management. The dedicated bond portfolio, as it is frequently called, is a strategy that matches monthly cash flows from a portfolio of bonds to a prespecified set of monthly cash requirements of liabilities. Cash matching or prefunding these liabilities leads to the elimination of interest-rate risk and defeasance of the liability. Applications for the dedicated strategy include pension benefit funding, defeasance of debt service, municipal funding of construction take-down schedules, structured settlement funding, GIC matching, and funding of other fixed insurance products.

## THE NEED FOR A BROADER ASSET/LIABILITY FOCUS

For financial intermediaries such as banks and insurance companies, there is a well-recognized need for a complete funding perspective. This need is best illustrated by the significant interest-rate risk assumed by many insurance carriers in the early years of their guaranteed investment contract (GIC) products. A large volume of compound interest (zero-coupon) and simple interest (annual pay) GICs were issued in three- through seven-year maturities in the positively sloped yield-curve environment of the mid-1970s. Proceeds from thousands of the GIC issues were reinvested at higher rates in longer 10- to 30-year private placement, commercial mortgage, and public bond instruments. At the time, the

The authors are grateful for the assistance of Anthony LoFaso for his constructive comments and contributions to the chapter.

industry expected that the GIC product would be very profitable because of the large positive spread between the higher "earned" rate on the longer assets and the lower "credited" rate on the GIC contracts.

By pricing GICs on a spread basis and investing the proceeds into mismatched assets, companies gave little consideration to the rollover risk they were assuming in volatile markets. As rates rose dramatically in the late 1970s and early 1980s, carriers were exposed to extreme disintermediation as GIC liabilities matured and the corresponding assets, with 20 years remaining to maturity, were valued at only a fraction of their original cost.

As a result of this enormous risk exposure, insurance carriers were induced to adopt a broader asset/liability focus to control the interest-rate risk associated with writing a fixed-liability product. Dedication and immunization (described in Chapter 44) have become popular matching strategies to control this market risk.

Similarly, in funding pension liabilities there is also a need for a broad asset/liability focus. Since the future investment performance of a pension fund is unpredictable, actuaries generally incorporate conservative investment return assumptions in the calculation of annual funding requirements. This conservative approach requires current contributions at much greater levels than the amounts needed under more realistic (higher) investment return assumptions. Such oversized contributions diminish both corporate cash flow and current profits for the sponsoring entity.

Through use of the dedication strategy to fund the relatively well-defined, retired-lives portion of the pension liability, some of this conservative margin can be eliminated. In the process, the plan sponsor may elect to reduce its current contributions to the pension fund or offer more generous benefits to plan participants, without increasing the current level of funding.

## CASH FLOW MATCHING FOR PENSION FUNDS

The most popular application of the dedicated strategy has been to fund the payout obligations of the retired-lives portion of a pension plan. In the following simulation developed in November 1992, we illustrate, in detail, the mechanics of this strategy as it applies to pension funds.

## Determining the Liabilities

The first step in establishing a dedicated bond portfolio is to determine the schedule to be funded. For pension funds, usually it is the expected benefit payouts to a closed block of current retirees. Since the benefit payouts to active employees cannot be projected with great accuracy, they are generally not included in the analysis. Since active employees and future retirees are not included in the closed block, the schedule of benefit payments declines over time due to mortality experience. The second column of Exhibit 45–1 illustrates the annual schedule of benefit payouts that are expected to be paid to current retirees.

The forecast payouts are based on the known benefit payouts at retirement for each employee and a number of variables, including expected cost-of-living increases. As shown in Exhibit 45–1, the payouts over the 35-year time horizon for the retired employees total $283,758,000.

In addition to funding the retired-lives payouts, the dedicated strategy is frequently applied to a somewhat broader universe of participants that includes retirees plus terminated vested participants. Terminated vested participants are former employees who are vested in the pension plan and are entitled to benefit payouts commencing sometime in the future. Since these benefit amounts are relatively fixed, they can be readily match-funded. A retired plus terminated vested liability schedule is illustrated in the last column of Exhibit 45–1.

Several pension plans have extended the dedication strategy to include the funding of "anticipated retiree" pension obligations. That is, in addition to funding the retired and terminated vested liabilities, the cash flow-matched design is used to offset liabilities associated with active employees aged 50 and greater. Since these benefit payments are not fixed until the employee actually retires, the various mortality, termination, and benefit assumptions must be reviewed periodically to ensure that actual experience tracks the forecast.

Instead of a downward-sloping liability schedule, the profile of expected benefit payouts for this broad population of plan participants would increase dramatically in the first 10 to 15 years, level off for a brief period, and then begin a downward slope. The benefit schedule peaks because the active participants who will be joining the retired population over the next 10 to 15 years are generally greater in number and have higher salaries (due to inflation) compared with the population of retirees, which declines due to mortality. The percentage reduction in actuarial liability and hence in contribution requirements associated with the anticipated retirees, is frequently larger than that for the currently retired population because a higher discount rate applied to larger and longer liabilities results in a bigger savings.

Similarly, one can apply the dedication strategy to insurance company funding, where a liability schedule can represent monthly projections of fixed payouts for products such as GICs, single-premium buyouts, or structured settlements. Once that schedule is derived, the procedures for match-funding an insurance product line are similar to those for creating a dedicated portfolio for a pension fund.

## Setting Portfolio Constraints

With the liability schedule determined, the next step in instituting a dedicated portfolio is to specify portfolio constraints on sector, quality, issuer, and lot sizes.

EXHIBIT 45-1

Schedule of Expected Benefit Payouts

| Year | Retired-Lives Liabilities Dollar Payout | Retired-Lives plus Terminated Vested Dollar Payout |
|---|---|---|
| 1992[a] | 1,250,000 | 2,000,000 |
| 1993 | 15,000,000 | 24,000,000 |
| 1994 | 14,916,015 | 24,519,000 |
| 1995 | 14,427,473 | 25,021,000 |
| 1996 | 13,445,985 | 25,523,000 |
| 1997 | 12,435,248 | 26,190,000 |
| 1998 | 11,754,199 | 26,809,000 |
| 1999 | 11,384,959 | 27,459,000 |
| 2000 | 11,028,026 | 28,026,000 |
| 2001 | 10,654,684 | 28,630,000 |
| 2002 | 10,408,523 | 29,221,000 |
| 2003 | 10,355,190 | 29,780,000 |
| 2004 | 10,236,214 | 30,294,000 |
| 2005 | 9,953,126 | 30,576,000 |
| 2006 | 9,670,039 | 30,312,000 |
| 2007 | 9,302,164 | 29,758,000 |
| 2008 | 8,748,308 | 29,196,000 |
| 2009 | 8,621,160 | 28,684,000 |
| 2010 | 8,209,594 | 27,992,000 |
| 2011 | 7,893,578 | 27,209,000 |
| 2012 | 7,435,436 | 26,535,000 |
| 2013 | 6,993,713 | 25,714,000 |
| 2014 | 6,579,349 | 24,996,000 |
| 2015 | 6,145,834 | 24,008,000 |
| 2016 | 5,732,824 | 23,121,000 |
| 2017 | 5,322,551 | 22,189,000 |
| 2018 | 4,983,398 | 21,076,000 |
| 2019 | 4,615,526 | 19,986,000 |
| 2020 | 4,257,221 | 28,826,000 |
| 2021 | 3,892,088 | 17,701,000 |
| 2022 | 3,537,881 | 16,589,000 |
| 2023 | 3,216,510 | 15,437,000 |
| 2024 | 2,934,788 | 14,319,000 |
| 2025 | 2,659,900 | 13,211,000 |
| 2026 | 2,385,026 | 12,098,000 |
| 2027 | 2,123,504 | 10,982,000 |
| 2028 | 1,337,297 | 9,869,000 |
| Total | $283,758,000 | |

[a] Partial year @ $15 million.

To identify the cheapest portfolio possible that funds the fixed schedule of liabilities, the portfolio manager may wish to constrain the optimal or least-cost solution to a universe of government and corporate securities rated single-A or better by one rating agency, as illustrated in Exhibit 45–2. In the simulation that follows, a *minimum* of 20% of the portfolio is constrained to be in U.S. Treasury securities, and a 30% *maximum* is set for the bank and finance, industrial, utility, and telephone sectors; a 30% *maximum* is established collectively for Yankee, Canadian, and World Bank issues; and no Euro or PAC bonds (CMOs) are allowed in this example.

As a general rule, mortgages are not desirable instruments for dedicated portfolios because uncertain prepayment rates cause uncertainty in monthly cash flows from mortgage securities. Nevertheless, some portfolio managers allow

## EXHIBIT 45–2

Portfolio Constraints

|  | Minimum | Maximum |
|---|---|---|
| Quality[a] |  |  |
| Treasury | 20% | 100% |
| Agency |  | 100 |
| AAA | 0 | 100 |
| AA | 0 | 100 |
| A | 0 | 50 |
| BBB | 0 | 0 |
| Sector |  |  |
| Treasury | 20% | 100% |
| Agency |  | 100 |
| Industrial | 0 | 30 |
| Utility | 0 | 30 |
| Telephone | 0 | 30 |
| Bank and finance | 0 | 30 |
| Canadian |  |  |
| Yankee | 0 | 30 |
| World Bank |  |  |
| Euros | 0 | 0 |
| Concentration |  |  |
| Maximum in one issue |  | 10% |
| Maximum in one issuer |  | 10 |
| Call Constraints on Corporate |  |  |
| Securities | Noncallable only |  |
| Lot Size |  |  |
| Conditional minimum | $2,000,000 (par) |  |
| Increment | $1,000,000 (par) |  |
| Maximum | Unlimited |  |

[a] Single-A split-rated securities allowed.

PACs because PAC cash flows are call-protected within a relatively wide band of prepayment speeds.

As seen in the protracted bull markets of the early 1990s, even wide-band PACs have become "busted" as prepayment speeds have pierced through their upper bands. As this occurs, the previously cash flow-matched portfolio becomes mismatched, compromising the integrity of the dedicated portfolio. Though the PACs can be swapped out as prepayment speeds approach the upper or lower limits of their bands, there is usually a cost associated with that swap; frequently, the plan sponsor is required to "pay in" additional funds to the program to purchase call-protected instruments. It is for these reasons that mortgages in general and PACs in particular are rarely used in the dedicated design.

It is also worth noting that the use of corporate securities, although providing higher yields, carries credit and call risks. If corporate securities are used in a dedicated portfolio, care must be taken to select call-protected securities that have a low probability of a credit downgrade. Although downgrades are always undesirable, the actual integrity of the cash flow match is still preserved with a downgrade (or even a series of downgrades) as long as the issuer does not default.

It is only when the coupon or principal payments are not made on time or in full that the cash flow match breaks down and the portfolio must be restructured.

Note also from Exhibit 45–2 that constraints on lot size are emphasized. Round-lot solutions (in lots of $2 million or more) are strongly preferred since the actual execution of the portfolio may be accomplished more efficiently without the added costs of odd-lot differentials. Also, as the dedicated portfolio is swapped or reoptimized over time, additional odd-lot premiums on the sale of such assets are avoided.

## The Reinvestment Rate

Since the timing of cash receipts does not always exactly match the timing of cash disbursements, surplus funds must be reinvested at an assumed reinvestment rate until the next liability payout date. This reinvestment or rollover rate is vital because it is often preferable to prefund future benefit payments with higher-yielding securities rather than to purchase lower-yielding issues that mature closer to the liability payment dates. The more conservative the reinvestment rate, the greater the penalty for prefunding future benefit payouts and, therefore, the tighter the cash flow match. The more aggressive the reinvestment rate, the greater the prefunding in optimal portfolios but the greater the risk of not earning that aggressive short-term reinvestment rate in a future period and experiencing a shortfall of cash. Though the current actuarial rates (investment return assumptions) range from 5% to 8%, the simulation that follows assumes a short-term reinvestment rate of only 3%.

## Selecting the Optimal Portfolio

Once the liability schedule, the portfolio constraints, and the reinvestment rate(s) are specified, an optimal (least-cost) portfolio can be structured for defeasance of the expected benefit payouts. The optimal portfolio is illustrated in Exhibit 45–3.

Assembling a dedicated portfolio that has a high probability of attaining its funding objectives over time requires restricting the universe of available issues. The fund manager must avoid questionable credits and, most important, avoid issues that may be called prior to maturity, have large sinking-fund call risk, or have significant prepayment risk. Retirement of issues prior to their stated maturity, whether through default or call, jeopardizes the funding of the liability schedule. As a result, most current coupon-callable bonds and non-PAC CMO bonds are not appropriate for matched portfolios.

The logic used to select the optimal or least-cost portfolio varies among purveyors of the cash flow-matching service. Three methods are used to identify an "optimal" portfolio. In order of sophistication, they are stepwise solutions, linear programming, and integer programming. Of the three, integer programming is the most technically advanced and is able to identify the lower-cost round-lot solution.

## The Cash Flow Match

Exhibit 45–4 summarizes the cash flow match inherent in the dedicated portfolio in our example. Note that, in every year, the cash flow from the maturing principal when added to the coupon income from all securities in the portfolio and the reinvestment income will almost precisely equal the liability requirements specified by the actuary in Exhibit 45–1. Since almost all cash flow is paid out each month to fund the liability payment, the portfolio has very little cash to reinvest each period and hence assumes very little reinvestment risk. The plan can therefore lock in a rate of over 7.83%—the rate prevailing at the time of this writing—regardless of the future course of rates.

In this simulation, the computer model has controlled reinvestment risk by structuring relatively small surplus positions in most years. However, the model sometimes prefunds distant payouts by reinvesting the proceeds of high-yielding, shorter-maturity issues at the low reinvestment rate. This is frequently preferable to purchasing bonds with longer maturities and better matching characteristics, but with lower yields to maturity. Note from Exhibit 45–4 that the larger amount of prefunding in the years 2021 and 2022 is due to the lack of high-yielding call-protected issues in subsequent years.

## Pricing the Bonds

Notice in Exhibit 45–4 that neither prices nor yields appear in the analysis. A dedicated portfolio is concerned only with cash flows. As long as all coupon

# EXHIBIT 45-3

Proposed Optimal Dedicated Portfolio

| Par ($000) | Moody | S&P | Security | Coupon | Maturity | Market | | | Duration | | Market Value ($000) |
| | | | | | | Price | Yield | WAL | Nominal | Effective | |
|---|---|---|---|---|---|---|---|---|---|---|---|
| 5,000 | GOV | GOV | United States | 5.000 | 12/31/1993 | 101.266 | 3.849 | 1.1 | 1.08 | 1.08 | 5,154 |
| 5,500 | GOV | GOV | United States | 7.625 | 12/31/1994 | 106.078 | 4.604 | 2.1 | 1.92 | 1.93 | 5,986 |
| 5,500 | GOV | GOV | United States | 11.500 | 11/15/1995 | 117.406 | 5.186 | 3.0 | 2.48 | 2.50 | 6,765 |
| 5,000 | AGN | AGN | Federal Home L | 8.600 | 11/13/1996 | 104.406 | 7.312 | 4.0 | 3.23 | 3.27 | 5,432 |
| 4,500 | GOV | GOV | United States | 8.875 | 11/15/1997 | 111.750 | 6.118 | 5.0 | 3.93 | 4.01 | 5,223 |
| 4,500 | GOV | GOV | Resolution FDG | 0.000 | 10/15/1998 | 67.753 | 6.676 | 5.9 | 5.74 | 5.91 | 3,049 |
| 3,000 | Aaa | AAA | Southern RY CO | 8.350 | 12/15/1999 | 105.411 | 7.356 | 7.1 | 5.18 | 5.30 | 3,263 |
| 3,500 | A3 | A | Shearson Lehma | 9.875 | 10/15/2000 | 106.992 | 8.637 | 7.9 | 5.49 | 5.61 | 3,769 |
| 2,000 | A3 | A | Westpac BKG CO | 9.125 | 8/15/2001 | 101.854 | 8.813 | 8.8 | 5.86 | 5.99 | 2,080 |
| 1,000 | A3 | A+ | Firemans PD MI | 8.875 | 10/15/2001 | 103.392 | 8.327 | 8.9 | 6.11 | 6.25 | 1,040 |
| 1,500 | A3 | A | Skandinaviska | 8.450 | 5/15/2002 | 99.302 | 8.558 | 9.5 | 6.18 | 6.34 | 1,551 |
| 2,000 | A3 | A | Westpac BKG CO | 7.875 | 10/15/2002 | 93.878 | 8.809 | 9.9 | 6.61 | 6.79 | 1,895 |
| 3,500 | Aa2 | AA- | National West M | 9.375 | 11/15/2003 | 108.579 | 8.178 | 11.0 | 6.70 | 6.85 | 3,960 |
| 3,500 | A2 | A- | Svenska Handel | 8.350 | 7/15/2004 | 97.306 | 8.719 | 11.7 | 7.10 | 7.26 | 3,504 |
| 5,000 | A3 | A | Shearson Lehma | 11.625 | 5/15/2005 | 119.891 | 8.950 | 12.5 | 6.74 | 6.86 | 6,277 |
| 3,500 | Aaa | AAA | General Elec | 7.875 | 12/1/2006 | 100.378 | 7.829 | 14.1 | 8.14 | 8.33 | 3,635 |
| 4,000 | Aa1 | AA | Bell Tel CO PA | 7.375 | 7/15/2007 | 89.569 | 8.640 | 14.7 | 8.29 | 8.47 | 3,677 |
| 5,000 | A2 | A | K Mart Corp | 6.000 | 1/1/2008 | 80.752 | 8.893 | 10.6 | 6.94 | 7.08 | 4,145 |
| 4,000 | A3 | AA- | Berkley W R CO | 9.875 | 5/15/2008 | 111.226 | 8.554 | 15.5 | 7.92 | 8.07 | 4,641 |
| 5,000 | Aa1 | AAA | General RE | 9.000 | 9/12/2009 | 104.713 | 8.467 | 16.8 | 8.66 | 8.83 | 5,308 |

EXHIBIT 45-3

(Continued)

| Par ($000) | Moody | S&P | Security | Coupon | Maturity | Market | | | Duration | | Market Value ($000) |
|---|---|---|---|---|---|---|---|---|---|---|---|
| | | | | | | Price | Yield | WAL | Nominal | Effective | |
| 4,500 | A2 | A | May Dept Store | 10.625 | 11/1/2010 | 117.564 | 8.677 | 18.0 | 8.66 | 8.81 | 5,302 |
| 5,000 | A1 | A+ | Hillenbrand In | 8.500 | 12/1/2011 | 99.225 | 8.582 | 19.1 | 8.98 | 9.16 | 5,149 |
| 4,500 | A3 | A- | Norsk Hydro | 9.000 | 4/15/2012 | 102.500 | 8.729 | 19.4 | 9.17 | 9.34 | 4,641 |
| 500 | Aaa | AAA | General Elec | 8.125 | 5/15/2012 | 99.184 | 8.209 | 19.5 | 9.32 | 9.52 | 514 |
| 5,000 | AGN | AGN | Financing Corp | 0.000 | 12/27/2013 | 16.618 | 8.676 | 21.1 | 20.25 | 22.25 | 831 |
| 4,000 | AGN | AGN | Financing Corp | 0.000 | 12/27/2014 | 15.217 | 8.691 | 22.1 | 21.21 | 23.56 | 609 |
| 4,000 | A3 | A- | NCNB Corp | 10.200 | 7/15/2015 | 111.389 | 9.010 | 22.7 | 9.14 | 9.29 | 4,586 |
| 5,000 | Aa2 | AA | Southern Ind G | 8.875 | 6/1/2016 | 99.740 | 8.901 | 23.6 | 9.43 | 9.61 | 5,183 |
| 3,000 | AGN | AGN | Financing Corp | 0.000 | 11/30/2017 | 11.808 | 8.711 | 25.1 | 24.01 | 27.87 | 354 |
| 3,500 | AGN | AGN | Financing Corp | 0.000 | 9/26/2018 | 11.036 | 8.701 | 25.9 | 24.80 | 29.25 | 386 |
| 3,000 | AGN | AGN | Federal Natl M | 0.000 | 10/9/2019 | 10.281 | 8.634 | 26.9 | 25.80 | 31.16 | 308 |
| 3,500 | A2 | A | Ford Hldgs | 9.375 | 3/1/2020 | 105.244 | 8.860 | 27.3 | 9.98 | 10.18 | 3,746 |
| 5,000 | A3 | A | Dayton Hudson | 9.700 | 6/15/2021 | 109.229 | 8.810 | 28.6 | 9.90 | 10.10 | 5,657 |
| 5,000 | A3 | AA- | Berkley W R Co | 8.700 | 1/1/2022 | 97.752 | 8.916 | 29.1 | 10.05 | 10.27 | 5,043 |
| 2,500 | GOV | GOV | Resolution FDG | 0.000 | 10/15/2024 | 7.519 | 8.271 | 31.9 | 30.66 | 40.31 | 188 |
| 3,000 | GOV | GOV | Resolution FDG | 0.000 | 10/15/2025 | 7.000 | 8.241 | 32.9 | 31.63 | 41.30 | 210 |
| 1,500 | GOV | GOV | Resolution FDG | 0.000 | 10/15/2026 | 6.520 | 8.211 | 33.9 | 32.59 | 42.28 | 98 |
| 139,000 | Aa2 | AA+ | | 6.942 | 16.0 years | 86.213 | 7.835 | 15.8 | 7.14 | 7.37 | 123,160 |

**EXHIBIT 45–4**

Proposed Dedicated Portfolio: Yearly Cash Flow Summary
(Amounts in $000)

| Period Ending | Beginning Balance | Maturing Principal | Coupon Income | Reinvestment Income | Cash Flow Available | Liability Schedule | Ending Balance |
|---|---|---|---|---|---|---|---|
| 12/31/1992 | 0 | 0 | 2,740 | 8 | 2,748 | 1,250 | 1,498 |
| 12/31/1993 | 1,498 | 5,000 | 9,661 | 176 | 16,335 | 15,000 | 1,335 |
| 12/31/1994 | 1,335 | 5,500 | 9,399 | 169 | 16,403 | 14,916 | 1,487 |
| 12/31/1995 | 1,487 | 5,500 | 8,979 | 192 | 16,158 | 14,427 | 1,730 |
| 12/31/1996 | 1,730 | 5,000 | 8,347 | 190 | 15,268 | 13,446 | 1,822 |
| 12/31/1997 | 1,822 | 4,500 | 7,917 | 186 | 14,424 | 12,435 | 1,989 |
| 12/31/1998 | 1,989 | 4,500 | 7,517 | 197 | 14,204 | 11,754 | 2,450 |
| 12/31/1999 | 2,450 | 3,500 | 7,502 | 202 | 13,654 | 11,385 | 2,270 |
| 12/31/2000 | 2,270 | 4,000 | 7,222 | 212 | 13,703 | 11,028 | 2,675 |
| 12/31/2001 | 2,675 | 3,500 | 6,846 | 226 | 13,247 | 10,555 | 2,692 |
| 12/31/2002 | 2,692 | 4,000 | 6,482 | 232 | 13,406 | 10,409 | 2,998 |
| 12/31/2003 | 2,998 | 4,000 | 6,231 | 210 | 13,439 | 10,366 | 3,072 |
| 12/31/2004 | 3,072 | 4,000 | 5,873 | 243 | 13,188 | 10,236 | 2,952 |
| 12/31/2005 | 2,952 | 5,500 | 5,260 | 277 | 13,989 | 9,953 | 4,036 |
| 12/31/2006 | 4,036 | 4,000 | 4,939 | 218 | 13,193 | 9,670 | 3,523 |
| 12/31/2007 | 3,523 | 4,500 | 4,634 | 245 | 12,902 | 9,302 | 3,600 |
| 12/31/2008 | 3,600 | 4,500 | 4,111 | 261 | 12,471 | 8,748 | 3,723 |
| 12/31/2009 | 3,723 | 5,000 | 3,899 | 215 | 12,836 | 8,621 | 4,215 |
| 12/31/2010 | 4,215 | 4,500 | 3,449 | 199 | 12,363 | 8,210 | 4,153 |

**EXHIBIT 45-4**

*(Continued)*

| Period Ending | Beginning Balance | Maturing Principal | Coupon Income | Reinvestment Income | Cash Flow Available | Liability Schedule | Ending Balance |
|---|---|---|---|---|---|---|---|
| 12/31/2011 | 4,153 | 5,000 | 2,970 | 182 | 12,305 | 7,894 | 4,412 |
| 12/31/2012 | 4,412 | 5,000 | 2,323 | 277 | 12,011 | 7,435 | 4,576 |
| 12/31/2013 | 4,576 | 5,000 | 2,100 | 173 | 11,849 | 6,994 | 4,855 |
| 12/31/2014 | 4,855 | 4,000 | 2,100 | 181 | 11,136 | 6,579 | 4,557 |
| 12/31/2015 | 4,557 | 4,000 | 2,100 | 226 | 10,883 | 6,146 | 4,737 |
| 12/31/2016 | 4,737 | 5,000 | 1,470 | 254 | 11,461 | 5,733 | 5,729 |
| 12/31/2017 | 5,729 | 3,000 | 1,248 | 200 | 10,177 | 5,323 | 4,855 |
| 12/31/2018 | 4,855 | 3,500 | 1,248 | 194 | 9,797 | 4,983 | 4,814 |
| 12/31/2019 | 4,814 | 3,000 | 1,248 | 185 | 9,247 | 4,616 | 4,632 |
| 12/31/2020 | 4,632 | 3,500 | 1,084 | 246 | 9,462 | 4,257 | 5,205 |
| 12/31/2021 | 5,205 | 5,000 | 677 | 253 | 11,135 | 3,892 | 7,243 |
| 12/31/2022 | 7,243 | 5,000 | 217 | 377 | 12,837 | 3,538 | 9,299 |
| 12/31/2023 | 9,299 | 0 | 0 | 281 | 9,581 | 3,217 | 6,364 |
| 12/31/2024 | 6,364 | 2,500 | 0 | 208 | 9,072 | 2,935 | 6,137 |
| 12/31/2025 | 6,137 | 3,000 | 0 | 205 | 9,342 | 2,660 | 6,682 |
| 12/31/2026 | 6,682 | 1,500 | 0 | 211 | 8,393 | 2,385 | 6,008 |
| 12/31/2027 | 6,008 | 0 | 0 | 182 | 6,190 | 2,124 | 4,066 |
| 12/31/2028 | 4,066 | 0 | 0 | 123 | 4,189 | 1,337 | 2,852 |
| Total | | 139,000 | 139,794 | 7,817 | | 283,758 | |

payments are made in a timely fashion and every bond matures on schedule, the liabilities specified by the actuary will be funded. Though credit ratings on some bonds in a portfolio may deteriorate over time and their market prices drop markedly, the integrity of the dedicated design is preserved as long as cash flow payments are complete and punctual.

Prices and yields enter the analysis only in determining the initial cost of the optimal portfolio as seen in Exhibit 45–3. In this simulation, all bonds were priced as of November 6, 1992.

## The Savings to the Pension Plan

As illustrated in Exhibit 45–5, using the current actuarial investment rate assumption of 5%, the plan must have on hand $159,818,000 in order to fully fund the $283,758,000 of payouts to retired lives. On the basis of the November 6, 1992, pricing, the portfolio can, with a yield of 7.83%, fully fund the same $283,758,000 in liability payouts with an initial investment of only $123,160,000. Purchase of this portfolio would generally give the actuary the comfort level necessary to increase the assumed actuarial investment rate on the retired-lives portion of the fund. In many cases, this increase may go all the way to the funding rate of 7.83%.

By raising the assumed rate from 5% to 7.83% on the retired portion of the plan, the plan sponsor has reduced the present value of the accumulated plan benefits by $36,658,000. This long-term actuarial gain or potential savings of $36.7 million represents a 23% reduction from the higher present value required under a 5% actuarial assumption.

Increasing the assumed rate on the retired-lives portion of the pension fund decreases the present value of the funds promised as future payouts, thus reducing the actuarial liability. Reductions in actuarial liability usually translate

**EXHIBIT  45–5**

Reduced Funding Requirements

|  | Percent | Dollar Amount |
|---|---|---|
| 1. Total liabilities | — | $283,758,000 |
| 2. Present value of total liabilities at | 5.00 | 159,818,000 |
| 3. Portfolio cost (market value) at | 7.83 | 123,160,000 |
| 4. Potential savings (2–3) | — | 36,658,000 |
|     Percent savings (4/2) | 22.94 | — |
|     Percent savings (4/3) | 29.76 | — |

into reductions in the current contribution requirements. The reduction in current contribution due to the dedicated strategy can be substantial.

In our example, the reduction in actuarial liability is $36.7 million. This amount cannot be realized in the form of a reduced contribution all in the first year. Pensions and tax legislation require that the gain be spread over 10 to 30 years. With all other factors remaining constant, the reduction in pension contribution might amount to a couple million dollars per year for each of the next 10 years. However, since every pension plan is different, and different actuarial cost methods treat gains differently, the actual savings to a plan may be of a different magnitude than represented by this example.

## Reoptimizing a Dedicated Bond Portfolio

It was originally thought that once a dedicated portfolio was structured, it should be passively managed, that is, left untouched as assets roll off in tandem with liabilities. Active management techniques can, however, be applied to dedicated portfolios. In addition to bond-for-bond swapping and active sector positioning of the portfolio, a cash-matched solution can be entirely reoptimized on a periodic basis.

For example, a portfolio that was "optimized" last year, in last year's rate environment, is not an optimal portfolio in today's rate environment, with a new yield curve, new yield spreads, and new available issues. As seen in Exhibit 45–6, a new least-cost portfolio can be created one year later to fund the same liability schedule with the same portfolio constraints. Since the new optimal portfolio will be less expensive than the old, a cash take-out can be generated by selling off a portion of the original portfolio and replacing the cash insufficiencies with a new combination of securities. When the take-out is significant, such trades are usually executed.

The take-out generated by the computer solution can be guaranteed if the reoptimization is executed through a dealer firm. Frequently, money managers and third-party software vendors work in conjunction with dealer firms to obtain

**EXHIBIT   45–6**

Take-Out from Reoptimizations

|  | Market Value (000) | Average Rating | Take-Out (000) |
|---|---|---|---|
| Original dedicated portfolio | $100,000 | Aaa/AA+ | — |
| Reoptimized dedicated portfolio (marked to market 1 year later) | 99,400 | Aaa/AA+ | $600 |

a trader-priced database and guaranteed take-outs. On the other hand, if a reoptimization is simulated on a database of matrix (computer-derived) prices, the takeout may disappear when market prices are obtained in the actual execution.

Note that the new optimal portfolio will always be cheaper than the original portfolio. If the computer is not able to find a portfolio that is cheaper than the original, it will select the original portfolio again, establishing that it is still the optimum.

## Active Management of Dedicated Portfolios

In addition to the use of comprehensive reoptimizations to add value, bond swaps can be undertaken to pick up yield or to swap out of an undesirable credit. To preserve the integrity of the dedicated portfolio, however, the cash flows associated with the bond being sold must be replaced with those from the bond (or bonds) being purchased. Thus bonds with identical coupons and maturities, or bonds with higher coupons and similar maturities, can be swapped. Bonds with similar coupons and slightly earlier maturities can also be swapped provided an additional cash pay-up is not required.

In addition to swapping, an active manager might add significant value by actively positioning a new dedicated portfolio in cheap sectors of the market. As spreads change, the optimized portfolio will automatically overweight the newly cheapened sectors of the market and underweight the rich ones.

For example, suppose that an existing $100 million dedicated portfolio could be reoptimized, using the same set of constraints, into a $99.4 million portfolio with a $600,000 take-out. Suppose further that the portfolio manager believes that corporate spreads will widen over the next few months. The manager might desire to temporarily upgrade the portfolio from the current average rating of double-A, await the anticipated spread changes, and then reverse the trade at a later date.

In this situation the optimal strategy is to spend the $600,000 take-out to buy a higher-quality portfolio. Rather than minimize cost, the portfolio can be optimized to maximize the quality rating, subject to the constraint of spending the full $100 million and cash flow-matching every liability payment. As shown in Exhibit 45–7, the average rating of the portfolio is increased by two rating categories, from double-A to agency.

Similarly, if rates are expected to rise, the portfolio could be positioned as short as possible by minimizing duration. In Exhibit 45–8, the duration of the portfolio has been shortened by almost 0.5 with a cash flow match maintained. Alternatively, if rates are expected to fall, the $600,000 surplus in the portfolio could be used to maximize duration.

## ROLE OF MONEY MANAGER AND DEALER FIRM

Both money managers and dealer firms have played important roles in managing and executing cash flow-matched portfolios. There are advantages to selecting

**EXHIBIT   45–7**

Maximize Quality

|  | Market Value (000) | Average Rating | Take-Out (000) |
|---|---|---|---|
| Original dedicated portfolio | $100,000 | Aaa/AA+ | — |
| Reoptimized dedicated portfolio (minimum cost) | 99,400 | Aaa/AA+ | $600 |
| Reoptimized dedicated portfolio (maximum quality) | 100,000 | Treasury/Agency | — |

**EXHIBIT   45–8**

Minimize Duration

|  | Market Value (000) | Duration | Percent Decrease |
|---|---|---|---|
| Original dedicated portfolio | $100,000 | 5.4 | — |
| Reoptimized dedicated portfolio (minimum cost) | 99,400 | 5.4 | — |
| Reoptimized dedicated portfolio (minimum duration) | 100,000 | 4.9 | 8.3 |

a money manager over a dealer firm (and vice versa) in implementing the dedicated strategy. For example, all portfolio optimizations require a database of bonds that is both priced and sized by traders. Most money managers have access only to matrix pricing (computer-derived pricing), which is generally reliable for corporate securities within a range of plus or minus 30 basis points. When an optimizer is applied to a matrix-priced database of bonds, the optimizer will find the least-cost solution by identifying bonds that are cheap (due to mispricing) and will select them in large blocks for the optimal solution. Since the computer-derived solution is not executable at the cheap levels specified in the database, the "least-cost" solution is not optimal when executed at market rates.

Dealer firms and software vendors with dealer connections are best positioned to simulate, structure, and execute an optimal portfolio due to the accurate pricing and sizing in their databases. However, because dealer firms are not fiduciaries, money managers are best suited to make the active management decisions about sector positioning, call protection, credit decisions, and spread forecasts. In addition, money managers are best suited to oversee the execution of reoptimizations with dealers.

In short, both dealers and money managers can add value to the process of structuring and reoptimizing dedicated portfolios.

## CONCLUSION

Dedication is an important portfolio investment strategy for controlling interest-rate risk and for locking in prevailing market rates. For insurance companies with fixed liability products such as GICs or structured settlements, cash flow matching and horizon matching (duration matching with cash matching of early payouts) has been a popular approach to lock in a spread (or profit) on the entire line of business.

For pension funds, the motivation has been to control market risk by fully funding or defeasing the more quantifiable retired liabilities of a plan and locking in a market rate that is well in excess of the actuarial investment return assumption. By raising the actuarial rate to today's market levels on the dedicated portion of the plan, the plan sponsor may be able to reduce pension contributions (pension expense) and thereby increase corporate cash flow and reported earnings.

The plan sponsor can also eliminate most funding risk (market risk) from a significant part of a plan's liability and eliminate market value fluctuations when reporting surplus asset (or unfunded liability) positions associated with that liability.

## CHAPTER 46

# MANAGING MARKET RISK PROACTIVELY AT LONG-TERM INVESTMENT FUNDS*

**Lang Gibson**
Vice President
Fixed Income Strategy Research
First Union Securities, Inc.

## INTRODUCTION

While risk management has taken center stage among regulators, accountants, and practitioners, long-term investment funds (LTIFs) have been slower than financial institutions to utilize risk management for either defensive or proactive purposes. This is perhaps largely due to budget constraints, a lower level of sophistication, and downsized investment staffs. Further, some LTIFs continue to view their assets in isolation from their liabilities while they remain rooted in historical performance measurement and optimization methodologies. Nevertheless, other LTIFs rigorously analyze sources of risk in the present portfolio and which investments will provide effective ways to reduce future risk and enhance future return.

Armed with their staunch asset allocation culture, LTIFs are positioned better than any entity to allocate capital on a risk-adjusted basis. LTIF assets can be optimally allocated to fund their long-term liabilities. Liabilities (or spending profiles for foundations and endowments) are simply negative cash flows projected with some degree of confidence to occur at different points in the future. They can be analyzed similar to a portfolio of zero-coupon bonds, and the analogy to the asset/liability management (ALM) process of a bank or insurance company can be a model. As such, the same practices used to allocate capital daily on a risk-adjusted basis in financial institutions may be applied to

---

* This chapter is adapted from Chapter 14 in Frank J. Fabozzi (ed.), *Managing Fixed Income Portfolios* (New Hope, PA: Frank J. Fabozzi Associates, 1997).

LTIFs on a monthly basis. LTIF ALM differs from bank and insurance company ALM by requiring less fixed income immunization and more equity-like investments to match the variability of uncertainty in liability projections.

LTIFs bear risk at two levels: the residual risk between the asset benchmarks and projected liabilities (Level I) and the residual risk between the actual securities and the benchmarks (Level II). Level I risk (balance sheet level) should be measured and optimized on a risk-adjusted basis quarterly or annually and after market shocks; in contrast, Level II risk (manager level) should be monitored on a more frequent basis. This chapter focuses on the asset/liability optimization process as well as risk management tools allowing fund managers to better allocate risk at both the balance sheet and manager levels. Risk management tools permit a decomposition of risk, an ability to find potential hedges, and an ability to detect key drivers of portfolio profit and loss on a correlated basis.

## BEST PRACTICE MODERN ASSET/LIABILITY MANAGEMENT

The market has witnessed an interesting evolution in the 1990s in methodologies for integrating liabilities into the asset allocation framework. Traditional ALM, or linear forms of risk forecasting such as immunization, dedication, and optimization using linear programming was state-of-the-art for institutions at the beginning of the decade. At the same time, the foundation for the new modern ALM (MALM), which includes non-linear forms of risk forecasting such as VAR and Monte Carlo simulation was being laid in the trading side of financial institutions.

Some financial managers are now transferring this same technology to other applications. Currently, best practice for commercial bank end-users is GAAP earnings at risk (GEAR), VAR, and simulation to forecast potential ranges of short-term profit and loss. LTIFs are just beginning to use a combination of VAR and simulation for their longer holding periods. Some insurance companies are making progress transitioning from immunization and optimization to more robust VAR and simulation models. All are taking direct account of volatilities and correlations among instruments.

MALM can allow a line manager to price products and balance risk for reward based on the marginal impact to capital of the managers' potential actions. The VAR framework lends itself well to any financial institution that is concerned about how its liabilities will correlate with its asset portfolio over a short horizon period. Currently, most institutional managers are concerned about protecting their capital base by instituting defensive forms of risk management controls. But many are beginning to learn that risk management can also be used proactively to allocate capital more efficiently. The focus here is MALM for investment funds, but these principles can be applied equally well to banks and insurance companies, where their liability structures should bear directly on the asset risk allocations.

## Importance of Benchmarking Against Liabilities

LTIFs should optimize their asset allocation as correlated with their liabilities before they begin monitoring and controlling manager level risks. Most studies show that 80% to 98% of risk and returns come from market sectors as opposed to individual security selection. In the case study to follow, we create strategies to link fixed income benchmarks more closely to projected liability cash flows, which has the result of freeing up risk capital to be applied towards higher returning assets. LTIFs today rarely incorporate the risk profile of their liabilities into their benchmarking profile. Even more rarely do they compare the risk/ return profile of the economic surplus to that of corporate equity. For instance, if a company plan sponsor's return on equity (ROE) target is 15%, what should the pension surplus target be? The answer is most likely greater than the return one would expect from a fully immunized balance sheet.

In the case study to follow, the asset/liability model determines the optimal mix of benchmarks on a risk-adjusted basis and demonstrates expected surplus risk. The appropriate mix of benchmarks is not only a function of the case study plan sponsor's risk appetite but also the liabilities, which define the riskless portfolio. In a perfectly immunized portfolio, the surplus risk and return would be that of the risk-free rate for any funding ratio. But for particularly low funding ratios, anything other than perfect cash flow matching exacerbates surplus risk, which is extremely sensitive to less than perfect negative correlations. To achieve returns superior to statutory guaranteed rates, an expected return reasonably higher than the risk-free rate is desired. Perfect cash flow matching would not be achievable in any case, as the case-study pension fund prefers to outsource investing to external managers, whose mandate is to outperform market benchmarks.

## Pension Funds versus Banks and Insurance Companies

Pension surplus volatility should probably be quite higher than the capital volatility of banks and insurance companies, who cannot rely on a corporate plan sponsor to make regular contributions. Bank and insurance company balance sheets more closely resemble a fixed income arbitrage book with tremendous leverage and little spare capital available for higher returning assets (their returns come mostly from pricing credit and insurance risk efficiently). On the other hand, pension funds usually have a larger surplus and thus significantly more funds that need not be linked directly to liabilities. Nevertheless, in both instances, the unmatched assets are roughly equal to capital (surplus). Whereas an insurance company's capital may represent 5% of assets, the same amount allocated to equities, a pension fund's surplus may represent 40% of assets, more or less the same amount allocated to equities.

## Matching and Linking Strategies

In the analysis to follow using a hypothetical pension fund, we will demonstrate how plan sponsors can free up risk capital and apply it towards more profitable areas by benchmarking their assets to correlate better with their liabilities. Matching fixed income assets to pension liabilities has always found appeal, because many view pension funds as existing solely to pay out benefits. In the mid 1980s, full dedication and immunization were popular until plan sponsors decided that asset performance mattered more than pension surplus performance and that higher returns could be achieved in the stock markets. Today, MALM has revived the popularity of matching, or at least more pronounced linking of assets to liabilities, particularly through the study of the correlations of one to the other.

The case-study U.S. defined benefit pension fund currently benchmarks its fixed income allocation against the JP Morgan bond indices in the major countries. These indices currently have durations of 3.5 to 5.4 years, which gives an illusory sense of conservatism because of the lower level of absolute risk in shorter durations. But the average pension fund liabilities are significantly longer than five years in duration. Therefore, shorter term benchmarks actually increase surplus volatility, because there is a correlation imbalance between the more volatile liability stream and the less volatile benchmark. The lower negative correlations between the short duration benchmarks and long duration liabilities exacerbate this imbalance. Consequently, we should introduce longer duration indices into the hypothetical fund's reinvestment set. Longer duration indices such as EFFAS can best link the fund's assets to liabilities to minimize duration mismatch risk and free up risk capital for equity-like investments, which more closely match the variability of the uncertainty in liability projections. Further, a wider range of benchmark duration profiles allows a manager to more efficiently match asset and liability cash flow distributions.

## Short- versus Long-Term Risk Forecasting

A focus on shorter term risk control can protect an LTIF's economic surplus (capital). If the focus is only on long-term risk control (i.e., simulation), an unforeseen short-term loss could make it difficult for the fund to recover in the long term. By optimally allocating risk in the short term, the fund can maintain a high enough expected return to build a long-term cushion against losses in both the long and short term. Further, because accounting rules usually force funds to revalue liabilities annually and manager performance is typically measured even more frequently, funds should incorporate at least one year holding periods into their risk forecasting. Conversely, long-term risk forecasting assumes that shareholders, employees, and management are not concerned with short-term fluctuations in the capital markets and liability pricing. If short-term performance is unacceptable, however, it is difficult to console management and shareholders with reassurance that 40 or 60 years in the future the fund will be able to meet its liabilities.

## LIABILITY RISK AND PRICING

### Forecasting Liability Risk

LTIF liabilities can be viewed similarly to a portfolio of Treasury strips with similar volatility and correlation characteristics. The major risk in the short term is interest rate, or market, risk. In longer term forecasts used for simulating future contributions out 10 to 40 years, a larger portion of risk arises from the uncertainty in timing and amount of cash flows. Exhibit 46–1 shows fading confidence in methodologies for valuing plan sponsor liabilities. Among the four methodologies for representing pension liabilities, we represent the hypothetical fund's liabilities by the accumulated benefit obligation (ABO). The present asset

**E X H I B I T   46–1**

How a Plan Sponsor Might Express Pension Obligations

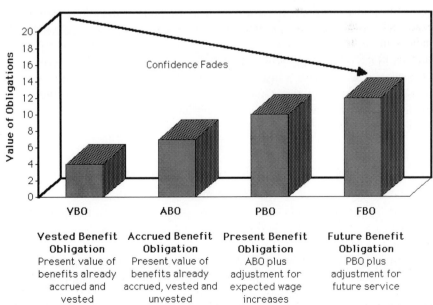

| Vested Benefit Obligation | Accrued Benefit Obligation | Present Benefit Obligation | Future Benefit Obligation |
|---|---|---|---|
| Present value of benefits already accrued and vested | Present value of benefits already accrued, vested and unvested | ABO plus adjustment for expected wage increases | PBO plus adjustment for future service |

Source: GTE and Morgan Stanley Joint Research

portfolio should only be compared to the present liabilities, the ABO. ABO reflects economic reality and FAS 87 requires plan sponsors to use the ABO in computing their funding status. Therefore, liabilities, as defined by ABO, should be targeted for risk management and hedging purposes. Only underfunding as defined by ABO may result in a balance sheet entry as an unfunded pension liability.

FAS 87 does however recognize an additional measure of a defined benefit's liability—the projected benefit obligation (PBO), which projects salary increases between now and retirement. But the PBO is not an appropriate measure of the benefits that the employer has guaranteed. FAS 87 requires corporations to use the projected method in computing the pension expense reported in their income statements. This figure may help analysts value a firm as a going concern. The actual pension benefit guarantee does exceed the ABO because the pension plan plays an important part in the implicit long-term contract between employers and employees. However, it does not follow that what could happen in the future, the PBO, is the correct measure of the liabilities or should be targeted for hedging. Finally, since we are concerned about risk in the short term, future service and wage inflation as captured in the future benefit obligation (FBO) is insignificant.

## Pricing the Liabilities

Best practice for incorporating LTIF liabilities into the optimization process is to discount the liability cash flows at the appropriate Treasury zero-coupon strip yields. Both the FASB and the SEC have endorsed this methodology for pricing liabilities. Exhibit 46–2 depicts the hypothetical pension's discounted ABO cash flows. The distribution for sponsors with younger employees would be more skewed to the right; sponsors with older employees and/or lump sum payments at retirement would have a distribution skewed to the left. Volatilities, correlations, and returns are a direct function of the zero-coupon rates. So the ALM model is set up similar to an asset portfolio funded by a 30-year yield curve of zero-coupon strips.

## Deriving Liability Volatilities, Correlations, and Expected Returns

For the hypothetical fund, we use an equally-weighted five-year lookback period to calculate volatilities and correlations for the liability zero-coupon proxies. The return history is the total returns of both the Datastream constructed Constant Maturity Treasury bonds (CMT) up to 12 years duration and our own generated CMT zero-coupon strips out to 30 years duration. Returns are interpolated from the spot Treasury strip yield curve.

**EXHIBIT   46–2**

Distribution of Projected Pension Liability Cash Flows

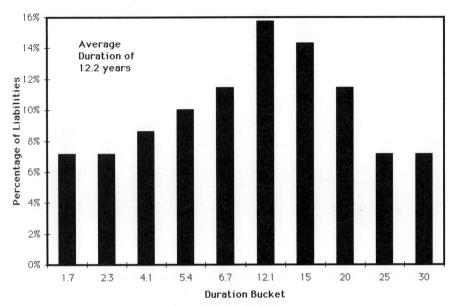

## BENCHMARKS VERSUS LIABILITIES
### Risk/Return Relationship

Exhibit 46–3 depicts the expected risk and return characteristics of the fund's universe of possible benchmarks against the liability zero-coupon strip proxies. The curve representing the liabilities is similar to a yield curve but instead of maturity, the horizontal axis represents volatility. Consequently, we may compare the risk profiles of both equity and fixed income securities using the same measure, volatility. As expected, a range of domestic fixed income indices (EF-FAS) cluster along the line representing the liabilities. Morgan Stanley (MS) equity indices have the most risk with a wide range of expected returns. The four U.S. equity indices clearly outperform the other indices and the liabilities. Finally, the Goldman Sachs Commodity Index (GSCI) has a slightly higher risk-adjusted return profile than the liabilities.

### Volatility, Correlation, and VAR Assumptions

We have chosen a forecast of volatilities and correlations based on historic observations because of the two drawbacks for the alternatives. First, a scenario,

**E X H I B I T    46–3**

Expected Return and Risk Benchmarks versus Fund Liabilities

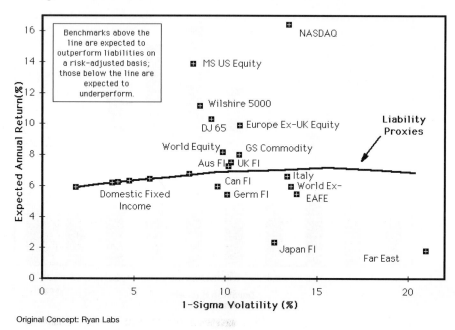

Original Concept: Ryan Labs

or deterministic, approach would be too arbitrary. Second, research shows that a "market-implied" approach (i.e., deducing from option market prices the volatilities they imply) does not give better forecasts. Furthermore, liquid option contracts do not exist on all of the benchmark indices and liability proxies. We have chosen parametric VAR using a multiplicative factor that depends on the confidence level, as the indices are fairly normally distributed. The lookback period for monthly returns is December 31, 1991 to September 30, 1996. VAR figures are annualized at a two standard deviation (2-sigma) confidence level of 95%. The parametric VAR format represents a plus or minus band within which the asset will likely fluctuate on 19 out of 20 periods.

## Generating Expected Returns

The hypothetical pension fund chose the present market to represent expected one-year returns, as it believes current yields and foreign exchange rates are a better predictor of future returns than the forwards, historical averages, or its own predictions. Estimating returns is a subjective process; no one model can predict them with any significant degree of accuracy. Expected returns are estimated in the following fashion:

- Fixed income and liability proxies: current yields in each market and spot exchange rates
- Equities: Capital Asset Pricing Model (CAPM)
- Commodities: forecast for energy prices (47% of GSCI)

## The Fund's Current Benchmark Strategy

With a 60/40 allocation of fixed income/equity, the fund's base case portfolio has an allocation similar to many funds. Its funding ratio is 1.43 (100% assets/ 70% liabilities), which implies a leverage factor for the pension surplus of 3.33. As pictured in Exhibit 46–4, the expected return of the surplus is 8.7%. The relatively high 2-sigma yearly surplus VAR of 41.2% is due to the implicit surplus leverage and small degree of linking. A forward-looking Sharpe ratio is consequently 0.08. (This ratio is an ex-ante version of the traditional ex-post Sharpe ratio and is equal to the portfolio return minus three-month Libor divided by 2-sigma VAR.) An "asset-only" view of risk would exhibit significantly lower risk for the fund due to the low correlations among domestic and un-hedged foreign assets. Importantly, the low −0.51 correlation of the assets to liabilities exacerbates the true pension risk, surplus risk. A perfectly immunized portfolio would have a correlation of −1.00.

## THE EFFICIENT FRONTIER
### Generating Efficient Allocations

Asset allocation models seek to optimize the risk/return trade-off. We calculate portfolio VAR, or risk, and expected return using the universe of benchmarks

### E X H I B I T  46–4

Base Case Balance Sheet

| Assets: | Base-60/40 |
|---|---|
| Fixed Income-percent | 60 |
| Equity-percent | 40 |
| Commodities-percent | 0 |
| **Liabilities (percent of assets)** | **70** |
| 2-Sigma Surplus VAR | 41.2% |
| Expected Return | 8.7% |
| A&L Correlation | −0.51 |
| Sharpe Ratio | 0.08 |

and liabilities depicted in Exhibit 46–3 to generate the efficient frontier curve shown in Exhibit 46–5. Along the frontier, the optimization algorithms maximize expected return for each level of VAR (risk). The lowest risk portfolios suggest linking strategies to minimize the risk between assets and liabilities by maximizing the negative correlation between the two. Interestingly, the three lowest risk strategies include a barbell strategy for linking. The mid-points on the curve force a duration linking strategy by joining the EFFA-9.7 benchmark with the liabilities' 12.2-year average duration.

This is a good example of where reasoned judgment is needed to override the duration assumption used in constructing the benchmarks. Since duration assumes a parallel yield curve shift and only small movements in rates, we override this assumption by matching the liability cash flow proxies to the full range of EFFAS buckets in the proposed allocations below.

As VAR increases along the efficient frontier, the fixed income/equity blend migrates from a 97/3 mix (7.5% VAR) to a 25/75 mix (40% VAR). Apart from a fixed liability structure and no short-sale assumption, the model is unconstrained so that we do not force a non-optimal allocation. Consequently, only a few assets are chosen in each portfolio. In the higher VAR portfolios, the model is forced to choose more volatile equities to achieve a higher expected

**EXHIBIT 46–5**

The Efficient Frontier of Possible Benchmarking Strategies

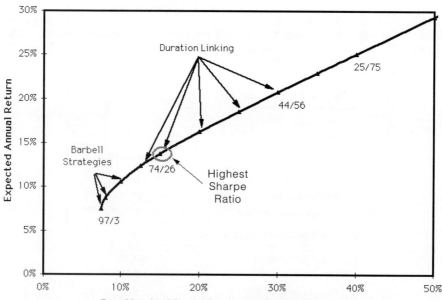

return. The most efficient portfolio is the 74/26 portfolio with 15% VAR and 13.7% expected return (0.55 forward Sharpe ratio). We would probably not choose this exact portfolio because of its low diversification with only three benchmarks suggested.

## Correlations and Efficiency

Exhibit 46–6 depicts the correlation between assets and liabilities and forward Sharpe ratios for all points along the frontier. Starting at the lowest VAR port-folios, the forward Sharpe ratio is particularly sensitive to small changes in correlations. Progressing through the most efficient portfolio of 15% VAR (74/ 26), declining correlations are associated with weakening Sharpe ratios as higher volatile and lower correlated equities enter the picture. Interestingly, the model never picks GSCI commodities despite its low correlation to fixed income and equities and attractive 8% return. The reason is that the GSCI's 0.06 correlation with liabilities exacerbates balance sheet risk. For such positive correlations to liabilities, the model will only pick extremely high returning assets. U.S. equities

**E X H I B I T   46–6**

A Weakening Correlation of Assets to Liabilities from less Linking Results in a Declining Sharpe Ratio Over Most of the Efficient Frontier

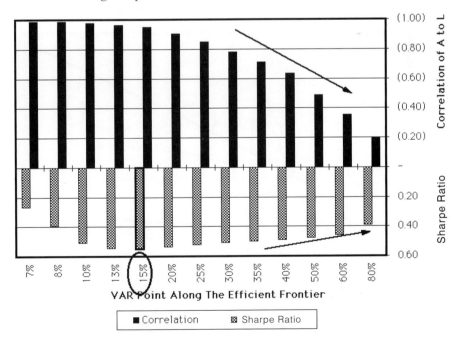

are chosen at higher volatilities because of their superior returns and sufficiently negative correlations to liabilities vis-à-vis the GSCI's positive correlation to liabilities.

# EFFICIENT BENCHMARK ALLOCATIONS

## Proposed Portfolios

Finally, we want to use reasoned judgment to propose optimal benchmark allocations for the hypothetical pension fund. The present and alternative portfolios are presented together against the same efficient frontier in Exhibit 46–7. The first thing to notice is that the present portfolio (base case) is exceedingly far from the frontier. Although the portfolio seems to have the right fixed income allocation, its risk is exacerbated by the particular type of fixed income allocation it has chosen. First, the 30% allocation to the JPM four-year duration index actually exacerbates risk because the liabilities have an average duration of 12.2 years. It is like matching the long bond to a six-year maturity bond—the two points on the yield curve have a low correlation and different volatilities. Second, despite their lower correlations, unhedged foreign bonds are quite volatile and

**E X H I B I T   46–7**

Alternative Benchmarking Strategies versus the Efficient Frontier

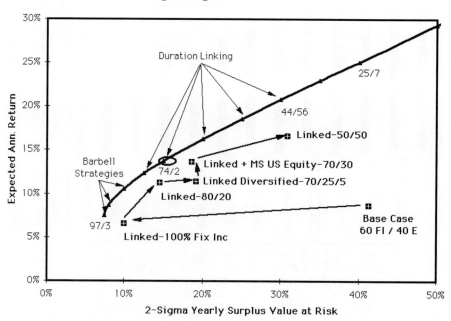

have a low risk-adjusted return profile—generally, passive foreign exchange is expected to have a zero Sharpe ratio on average over the long run.

To improve the base case portfolio's efficiency, we first place the fund close to the frontier at a low VAR point. We then suggest alternative allocations of increasing return and VAR along the frontier. The actual allocations and risk/return characteristics for each strategy compared to the base case are presented in Exhibits 46–8 and 46–9. All six strategies match asset with liability fixed income cash flows out to six-years duration. Altering allocations between the nine-and-seven-tenths-year duration bucket and the various equity indices account for the greatest part of different risk/return characteristics among the six portfolios.

The lowest risk portfolio is the fully linked strategy because it results in the highest negative correlation (-0.98) between assets and liabilities. Its 6.6% expected return on surplus is unacceptable to the pension manager, because it is significantly lower than the company level 15% ROE target. The Linked-80/20 mix quadruples the Sharpe ratio with only a 20% reallocation out of fixed income into U.S. equity. Moving on, the diversified portfolio moves the fund slightly away from the efficient frontier, but provides a hedge against a breakdown in correlations. That is to say, more correlations have to breakdown in a diversified portfolio to dangerously increase risk. A full 30% allocation to MS U.S. equity maximizes portfolio efficiency as measured by the Sharpe ratio. At the expense of significantly higher risk, the 50/50 strategy pushes expected surplus return beyond the company's 15% ROE target.

## EXHIBIT 46–8

Alternative Benchmark Allocations and Risk/Return Summary: U.S. Pension Fund ALM Study

| Assets | Base-60/40 | Linked | L-80/20 | L+Diversif | L+MSUS | L-50/50 |
|---|---|---|---|---|---|---|
| Fixed Income (percent) | 60 | 100 | 80 | 70 | 70 | 50 |
| Equity (percent) | 40 | 0 | 20 | 25 | 30 | 50 |
| Commodities (percent) | 0 | 0 | 0 | 5 | 0 | 0 |
| Liabilities (percent of assets) | 70 | 70 | 70 | 70 | 70 | 70 |
| 2-SD Surplus VAR | 41.2% | 9.9% | 14.5% | 19.2% | 18.6% | 30.9% |
| Expected Return | 8.7% | 6.6% | 11.3% | 11.4% | 13.7% | 16.6% |
| A&L Correlation | −0.51 | (0.98) | (0.95) | (0.90) | (0.91) | (0.74) |
| Sharpe Ratio | 0.08 | 0.11 | 0.40 | 0.31 | 0.44 | 0.36 |

**E X H I B I T   46–9**

Alternative Benchmark Allocations—Line Item Detail: U.S. Pension Fund ALM Study

| Benchmark | Base-60/40 | Linked | L-80/20 | L+Diversif | L+MSUS | L-50/50 |
|---|---|---|---|---|---|---|
| **Fixed Income** | | | | | | |
| US-4 | 30 | | | | | |
| Aus-4 | 5 | | | | | |
| Can-4.6 | 5 | | | | | |
| Germ-4.4 | 5 | | | | | |
| Italy-3.6 | 5 | | | | | |
| Jap-6 | 5 | | | | | |
| UK-5.4 | 5 | | | | | |
| EFFA-1.6 | 0 | 3 | 3 | 3 | 3 | 3 |
| EFFA-3.3 | 0 | 4 | 4 | 4 | 4 | 4 |
| EFFA-4.6 | 0 | 7 | 7 | 7 | 7 | 7 |
| EFFA-5.9 | 0 | 14 | 14 | 14 | 14 | 14 |
| EFFA-9.7 | 0 | 72 | 52 | 42 | 42 | 22 |
| **Equity/Commodity** | | | | | | |
| MS World | 5 | | | | | 5 |
| MS EAFE | 5 | | | | | |
| MS Ex-UK | 5 | | | 5 | | 5 |
| MS Ex-US | 5 | | | | | |
| MS Far East | 5 | | | | | |
| DJ-65 | 0 | | | 5 | | 5 |
| NASDAQ | 0 | | 5 | 5 | | 10 |
| Wilshire | 0 | | 5 | 5 | | 5 |
| MS US | 15 | | 10 | 5 | 30 | 20 |
| GSCI | 0 | | 0 | 5 | | |
| **Liabilities** | | | | | | |
| Liab-1.7 | −5 | −5 | −5 | −5 | −5 | −5 |
| Liab-2.3 | −5 | −5 | −5 | −5 | −5 | −5 |
| Liab-4.1 | −6 | −6 | −6 | −6 | −6 | −6 |
| Liab-5.4 | −7 | −7 | −7 | −7 | −7 | −7 |
| Liab-6.7 | −8 | −8 | −8 | −8 | −8 | −8 |
| Liab-12.1 | −11 | −11 | −11 | −11 | −11 | −11 |
| Liab-15 | −10 | −10 | −10 | −10 | −10 | −10 |
| Liab-20 | −8 | −8 | −8 | −8 | −8 | −8 |
| Liab-25 | −5 | −5 | −5 | −5 | −5 | −5 |
| Liab-30 | −5 | −5 | −5 | −5 | −5 | −5 |

The following analytics allow the manager to make a trade-off between the desire to minimize future contributions and to maximize returns.

## IMPACT OF CORRELATIONS ON EFFICIENCY

Exhibit 46–10 depicts how correlations (top bars) impact portfolio efficiency (bottom bars). The transition to a −0.98 correlation afforded by the 100% fixed income strategy improves the Sharpe ratio only modestly. Strategies trading into higher returning equity produce significantly higher Sharpe ratios since the efficient frontier slope is comparatively steep at 0.5. A 0.5 slope means that, at the margin, we get half the increase in expected return as the increase in VAR. Such an advantageous risk/return trade-off between fixed income and equities is not possible in all markets. For instance, many European stock markets have not historically compensated investors for higher volatility. Consequently, their efficient frontier curves are practically flat. Many practitioners believe that Eur-

**E X H I B I T   46–10**

The Sharpe Ratio Increases with Optimal Correlations between Assets and Liabilities

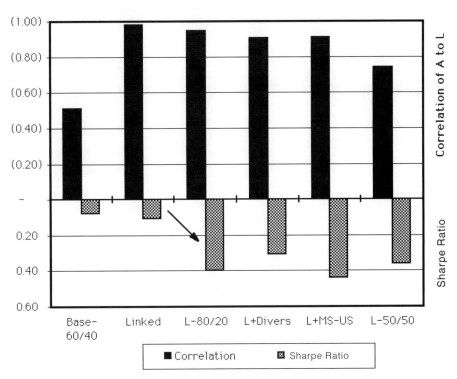

opean equities may outperform fixed income on a risk-adjusted basis in the future. So they may be willing to withstand the possibility of higher equity volatility to benefit from this expected outperformance.

## Surplus Drawdown Risk

Exhibit 46–11 demonstrates surplus drawdown risk for high levels of confidence to capture the extreme tails of distributions. Maximum expected drawdown is both a function of expected return and VAR. The proposed allocations quite significantly minimize the fund's downside risk. Even the 6-sigma probability downside of the riskiest alternative, the 50/50 allocation, ensures that the surplus will not decline more than 33% over the next year.

## Fixed Income Duration

Although modified duration as a risk measure has a number of deficiencies, the concept is intuitive for most managers and accounts for 92% of bond price

**EXHIBIT 46–11**

Proposed Benchmarking Strategies Significantly Minimize Surplus Drawdown Risk from Base Case

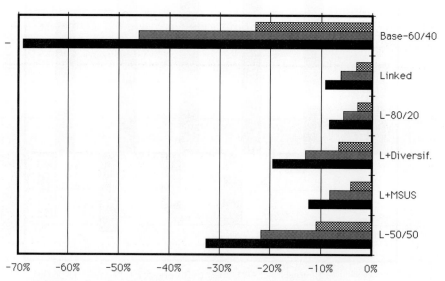

Maximum Surplus Drawdown For Three Levels of Confidence

⊠ 2-Sigma        ▨ 4-Sigma        ■ 6-Sigma

variance on average. Since modified duration does not have the same economic meaning for equity as it does for fixed income, we isolate the fixed income portion of the balance sheet to stress test surplus duration. We cannot assign a modified duration number to equities because this liberty would assume perfect correlations between equities and liabilities.

Exhibit 46–12 depicts surplus duration for the current portfolio versus the average of the linked portfolios over a wide range of parallel yield curve shifts. Linking clearly minimizes surplus duration over the full range of interest rate shocks. For instance, a 300 basis point decline in rates decreases the current portfolio's surplus value by 42% versus the linked portfolios' 8%. To marry VAR concepts with duration, a normal distribution curve of long bond returns is overlaid. We see that 68% of the expected distribution (1-sigma) falls within a 77 basis point change in rates, while a full 99% (3-sigma) falls within 231 basis points. Only extreme markets would push yields further than a 3-sigma move.

# CONTRIBUTION TO RISK

## Liabilities

A position's contribution to risk is the percentage of the portfolio's total cor-related risk attributable to that portion. The contribution to risk for each position

**E X H I B I T    46–12**

Linking Minimizes Pension Surplus Duration

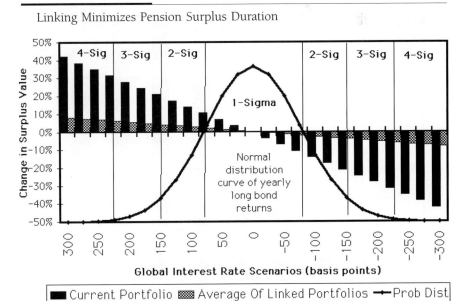

adds up to 100% and measures changes in portfolio risk for small allocation changes. Exhibit 46–13 is a graphical risk report depicting the contribution to risk for each of the pension fund's liability proxies in a hypothetical portfolio of equally weighted asset benchmarks.

## EQUALLY WEIGHTED FIXED INCOME SECTORS

The contribution to risk is a function of volatilities, correlations and position weightings. Consequently, Exhibit 46–13 shows a distribution more skewed to the right than the cash flow's more bell shaped distribution shown in Exhibit 46–2, which represents strictly weightings. Clearly, most of the fund's risk lies in the higher duration liability proxies.

## Fixed Income Benchmarks

We equally weight the benchmarks to allow us to more easily measure relative contribution to risk for each sector. In so doing, we may better understand how the optimization model tries to minimize VAR. In Exhibit 46–14 we isolate and sort the fixed income benchmarks as they contribute to total portfolio VAR. The overseas bond markets grouped to the left clearly represent risk-enhancing sec-

**E X H I B I T   46–13**

Contribution to Risk of Liabilities

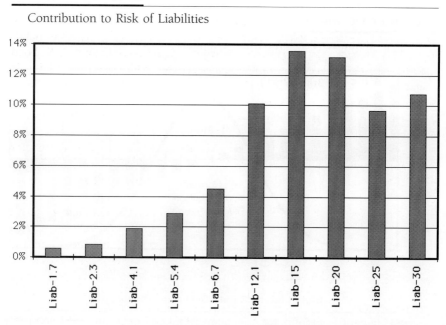

**E X H I B I T   46–14**

Contribution to Risk of Equally Weighted Fixed Income Sectors

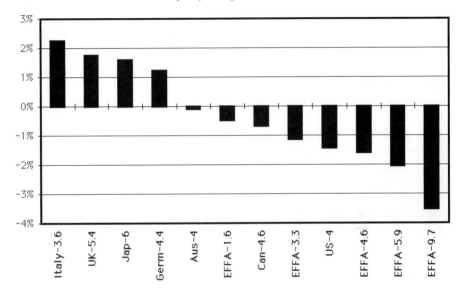

tors due to the high volatility component of their foreign exchange rate risk which represents on average two-thirds of foreign fixed income risk.

Negative contribution to risk bars represent potential risk-reducing sectors. The largest risk-reducing sector is the EFFA-9.7 index. To link assets to liabilities, the manager can increase the allocation to the risk-reducing U.S. bond sectors, which are most strongly correlated with the liabilities. As linking is augmented, the manager would reduce surplus VAR up to the point that U.S. bonds represent more risk than the liabilities. Then U.S. bonds would become a risk-enhancing sector and begin to dominate the portfolio. Further, as Canadian bond returns are strongly correlated with U.S. bond returns, we see that they also provide a risk-reducing opportunity for the manager. Varying correlations among sectors could significantly alter these relationships. We will demonstrate the effect of changing correlations and volatilities over time for key sectors later in this chapter.

Remembering that all sectors are equally weighted notionally, sectors within 0.5% contribution to risk represent risk-minimizing sectors (also called "best hedges" by Robert Litterman of Goldman Sachs). These sectors are the least correlated with the portfolio and represent a market-neutral position relative to the portfolio. The best example is the Australian four-year duration bonds (Aus-4), whose bar in Exhibit 46–14 is hardly visible. The JPM Aus-4 index contributes significantly less market exposure than its four-year duration or notional size would imply. The pension manager could allocate more here without significantly contributing to surplus risk.

## Equities and Commodities

Exhibit 46–15 is a risk report showing the contribution to risk of equally weighted equity and commodity sectors. A function of its extreme volatility and high absolute correlations, Far Eastern equity contributes by far the most risk to the surplus despite its equal notional weighting with the other benchmarks. Importantly, commodities qualify as a risk-enhancing sector. Although the GSCI has a low correlation with the other assets, its positive correlation to liabilities does not have the risk-reducing qualities of U.S. fixed income securities' negative correlation to liabilities. The MSCI U.S. equity index represents a risk-minimizing sector. Consequently, the most efficient portfolios along the efficient frontier represent large allocations to this sector. The U.S. markets generate substantially less risk than foreign equity sectors due to the latter's foreign exchange rate volatility.

## Diversified Portfolio (70/30)

Based on the information garnered from the equally weighted portfolio in Exhibit 46–15 and the optimization process, we can make sense of the diversified

**EXHIBIT   46–15**

Contribution to Risk of Equally Weighted Equity and Commodity Sectors

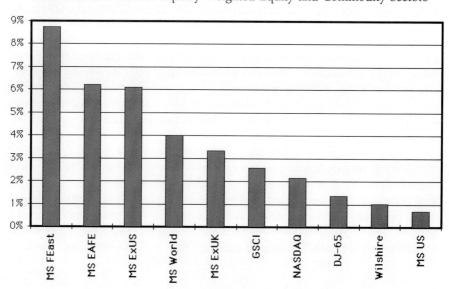

portfolio's risk/return attributes. This is depicted in the Exhibit 46–16 risk report. The comparatively efficient U.S. equities and commodities market represent
a fairly flat distribution of risk-enhancing surplus risk. By far, the largest risk-
reducing sectors continue to be U.S. bonds (EFFAS). EFFA-9.7 is the largest
risk-reducing position, as it represents 42% of the benchmark notional allocation
and has a high negative correlation with the liabilities, the portfolio's dominant
risk. Consequently, marginal allocations to U.S. bonds would still have a risk-
reducing impact on surplus VAR.

## STRESS TESTING VAR ON HEAT MAPS

Once the largest risk exposures have been identified, the manager needs to identify "worst-case" market scenarios by shocking risk exposures on a heat map
risk report. Heat maps demonstrate aggregate surplus VAR under worst-case
correlation and volatility scenarios and provide a road map for shifting VAR
exposure. The manager can use the heat map report to determine how large his
surplus VAR can grow during periods of strengthening volatility and rising correlations. For instance, consider the largest benchmark risk exposure, the DJ65.
The heat map for this exposure is shown in Exhibit 46–19.

　　To forecast future market shocks, we can analyze historical data, such as
the 1987 and 1989 stock crash and the 1994 bond route, or derive deterministic
scenarios. The heat map shown in Exhibit 46–19 depicts a scenario where the

**E X H I B I T  46–16**

Contribution to Risk of Diversified Portfolio Assets

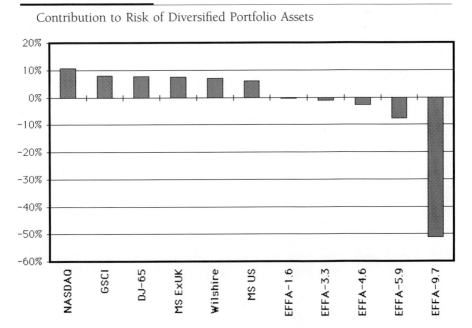

**E X H I B I T   46–17**

Key Drivers—Diversified Portfolio Liabilities 19.2% 2-Sigma Yearly VAR

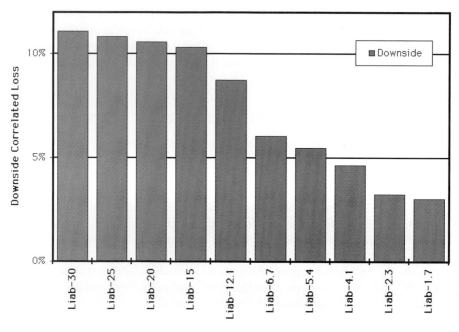

**E X H I B I T   46–18**

Key Drivers—Diversified Portfolio Benchmarks 19.2% 2-Sigma Yearly VAR

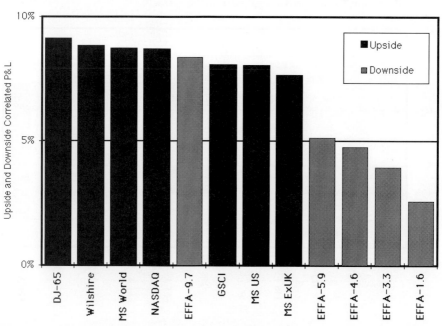

**EXHIBIT  46–19**

Heat Map of DJ65 Against Diversified Portfolio Initial 19.2% Yearly
2-Sigma VAR

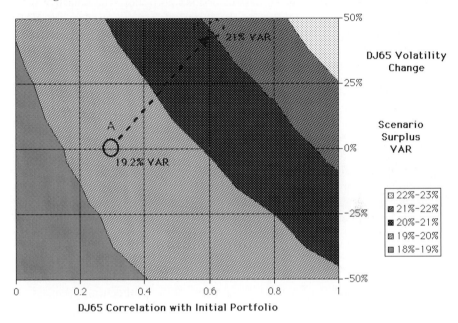

**EXHIBIT  46–20**

Two-Sigma Pension Shortfall Risk (99.93% Confidence) Uncorrelated Assets
and Liabilities: Linked 70/30 Portfolio

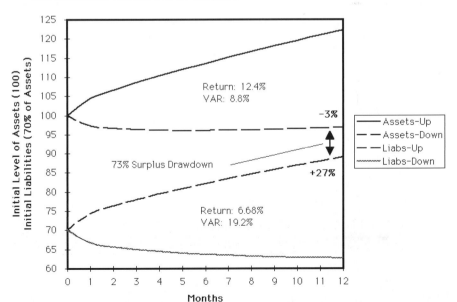

correlation of the DJ65 with the initial portfolio increases from 0.24 to 0.60 and its volatility increases by 45%. Such a scenario would push surplus VAR from point A (19.2% VAR) towards the northeast corner at point B (21% VAR). The increase in VAR is far greater in less diversified portfolios. The objective is to provide an alternative to relying on the historical data captured in the VAR calculation's five-year return history. By stress testing VAR, a manager has a complete picture of risk with which he can plan contingencies for possible market shocks before they happen or hedge them out altogether.

## REGULATORY AND LITERATURE GUIDANCE

Most risk management literature and regulatory guidance are preemptive and offer little advice on how to make money using proactive risk allocation techniques. While such "risk directives" have traditionally been aimed at sell-side institutions, newer literature has focused more specifically on buy-side institutions. For instance, the "Risk Standards for Institutional Investment Managers," published in November 1996 by the Risk Standards Working Group, promises

**E X H I B I T  46–21**

Projected Surplus Return and Risk (2-Sigma: 95% Confidence) of Linked 70/30 Portfolio

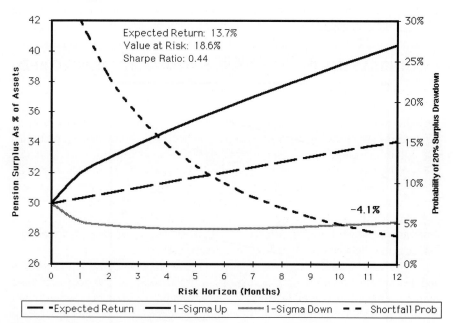

**EXHIBIT  46–22**

Risk Standards Working Group

Management

• Independent risk oversight
• Clearly defined organizational structure
• Adequate education, systems, and resources

Measurement

• Valuation procedures
• Valuation reconciliation
• Risk/return attribution
• Risk-adjusted return
• Stress testing
• Back testing

Oversight

• New activities review

to encourage LTIFs and their external managers to update and apply the Working Group's recommended risk policies, practices, and procedures.

## MODEL ASSUMPTIONS THAT SHOULD BE MONITORED

The major assumption in the ALM model is that historical volatility and correlations may not represent the future. All forecasting models that rely on history, no matter how complex, have this problem. Further, the analysis demonstrates how stress testing allows a manager to check that actual market conditions are within the range of assumptions made by parametric VAR.

With any optimization model, there is always the problem that the model will pick an unrealistic combination of instruments to maximize return and minimize volatility. The combination of instruments may have worked in the past, but it is highly unlikely that the same results will happen in the future. Most importantly, we must diversify the benchmarks and monitor and control the residual risk between the liabilities and the assets.

We can be fairly confident in the correlations between the fixed income indices and the liability proxies, because fixed income correlations are more stable over time. It is the correlation of equities and commodities to bonds and liability proxies which must be most closely monitored. Market shocks increase this correlation and thus total portfolio risk. Further, volatility tends to go through cycles—some years, equity and bond volatility is high, and others it is not. So volatility levels must also be monitored.

Both volatility and correlations for individual risk positions can be shocked on a heat map. The purpose of demonstrating worst-case risk scenarios is to prepare the manager's actions before a market shock. Specifically, a pension fund manager could forewarn his board of potentially needed accelerated contributions from the plan sponsor. In the eventuality that the plan sponsor cannot make these contributions, the board may decide to minimize the pension surplus risk today via increased linking, hedging, or other risk-minimizing strategy.

## CONCLUSION

Through the use of state-of-the-art ALM techniques, we have shown how the risk and return characteristics of asset benchmarks correlated to LTIF liabilities can be optimized efficiently for a range of risk appetites. For a hypothetical pension fund, we have analyzed a number of alternative allocations to demonstrate how surplus return can be balanced for risk to maximize future pension performance. Although focusing on the management of Level I risks (balance sheet level), we have analyzed useful risk management tools to permit a decomposition of risk. Such tools may be implemented in risk reports to monitor and manage Level I and Level II risk (manager level).

Much has already been written on applying risk management and VAR to short-term investors, such as commercial and investment banks. Hopefully, long-term investment funds can benefit from the risk management techniques and VAR extensions presented in this chapter.

## CHAPTER 47

# IMPROVING INSURANCE COMPANY PORTFOLIO RETURNS

Kevin Edward Grant, CFA
Portfolio Manager
Fidelity Management and Research

The investment utility function for a corporation is quite different from that of a pension fund or other purely investment-oriented entity. The principal difference lies in the breadth of business activities. A corporation's performance is consolidated with all business lines, creating a much more complex investment decision-making process. Pension funds adjust their portfolios in the best economic interests of the beneficiaries alone; their decisions are focused on economic factors related only to assets and liabilities.

Insurance companies and other diversified corporations operate in a highly interrelated and regulated environment; results are consolidated with business lines and are reported on a GAAP/statutory basis. This complicates the pure asset/liability economic decision-making process, requiring that corporatewide financial performance be considered. A strategic asset move may enhance investment returns but severely limit flexibility to write new insurance business. Reactions by regulators and rating agencies further complicate the process. The insurance company portfolio manager has to consider the reaction of these overseers: The proper economic decision in a pure asset/liability framework may create a temporary distortion in financial ratios and a downgrade by the rating agencies that could impair the insurance company's ability to write new business.

Thus, an insurance company portfolio manager seeking to improve portfolio investment performance has to solve a very complex problem with many conflicting objectives. At first blush, the manager's objective may appear to be to maximize total return; however, it could just as easily be to minimize risk. More realistically, though, an insurance company portfolio manager's objectives involve a complex risk/return function that includes not only asset/liability man-

The author wishes to acknowledge the considerable contributions of Charles Melchreit, CFA, and David Canuel for their assistance in preparing the exhibits and sharing their insights.

agement but also statutory regulations, accounting treatment, rating agencies, claims-paying abilities, new business potential, and ultimately the corporation's value to its shareholders.

## SPECIAL CONSIDERATIONS FOR INSURANCE COMPANY PORTFOLIOS

The insurance company portfolio management process is not one of academic purity, with no transaction costs or taxes, with continuous prices, and with arbitrage-free markets. The capital gain/loss decision, for example, involves more than just the judgment that the asset to be purchased is better than the one to be sold. There may be insurance underwriting losses that could reduce the company's ability to take losses on the portfolio. Executing a bond swap that involves a capital loss or gain has tax and statutory implications that must be viewed in light of both the corporation's overall financial position and the portfolio's assets and liabilities. Rules requiring some bonds to be carried at market rather than book value create another set of distortions and incentives, particularly when the liabilities are carried at book and the assets at market. The key to managing around the distortions is to reduce unexpected transactions: In highly active bond management strategies, many transactions result from volatility. Active strategies require transactions, and the extent of those transactions is a positive function of volatility rather than the corporation's objectives.

The most effective approach for insurance company portfolio managers is to take a long-term view of value. This doesn't mean buy and hold, which some people interpret as buy and ignore. Rather, it means buy and incubate: Construct a portfolio that you expect will provide superior returns in many economic scenarios, and seek opportunities to improve the portfolio with asset swaps. The key is to develop the analytical tools that will identify long-term value and measure risk. The approach is not active management; rather, it's attentive management.

## DON'T BUY AND HOLD, BUY AND INCUBATE

The recommended approach is to look at the assets and liabilities in a wide variety of long-run economic scenarios. The cheap bonds enhance the risk/return characteristics of the portfolio in all scenarios, whereas the rich bonds enhance the risk/return characteristics in only a few. The cheap ones should be held until they become rich. This happens much more slowly than price volatility may suggest. This realization gives the portfolio manager a tremendous advantage over the market. The manager can wait; the players showing bids and offers cannot. If you take a long-term view, you are never forced to transact.

# EXISTING APPROACHES TO ASSET/LIABILITY MANAGEMENT

Fixed income portfolio management techniques have improved dramatically in the past few years. These include asset/liability techniques, which attempt to construct portfolios and control risk, and immunization, which attempts to continuously match the present value of assets to liabilities as interest rates change. The belief is that if present values (prices) are always matched, as time passes assets can be sold at their present values to fund the liabilities.

Immunization uses differential calculus to parameterize the elasticity of price to interest-rate changes. The first derivative, the modified duration, is simply the percentage change in present value (price) relative to a basis point change in interest rates. Thus, if the modified durations of the assets and liabilities are equal, as rates change their present values will change by equal proportions. This assumes that the interest-rate change on all the assets and liabilities is identical; that is, the yield curve shifts in parallel.

In general, immunization models use linear programming optimization programs to find the least-cost solution (maximize the dollar-duration-weighted internal rate of return) of the assets while matching the assets' and liabilities' modified durations. As time passes and rates change, the portfolio will become mismatched and rebalancing will become necessary. Rebalancing is most frequent when volatility is high.

Several refinements have improved immunization technology over the past few years, including the development of convexity. This is simply the second derivative of the price-yield equation; that is, it is the rate of change in modified duration due to a change in yield. Incorporating convexity into simple immunization reduces the amount of rebalancing. A convenient accidental feature of the computation is that it's a summary of the dispersion of cash flows. Matching the convexities of assets and liabilities reduces the mismatch of cash flows. Other researchers have approached cash flow dispersion mismatches more directly with other measures that have the same results as matching convexity.

Matching D3 (the sensitivity of convexity to rate changes), D4, and so on, gradually will reduce risk and rebalancing in matched portfolios. However, they have diminishing importance. When more derivatives are matched than there are cash flows, only one feasible solution exists, a dedicated portfolio having no interest-rate risk. Until this point, however, yield-curve risk remains and rebalancing is required.

Exhibit 47–1 lists several bonds and an assumed five-year bullet liability. The asset weightings were derived with the immunization model previously described. In this case, only the duration was matched. Only two bonds were required to match the liability within reasonable tolerances ($\pm 0.5\%$): the U.S. Treasury 6.50% and the Thailand 8.70%.

Exhibit 47–2 shows the relative present-value movement of the optimal portfolio versus the liability. Under parallel yield-curve shifts, the portfolio is

**E X H I B I T   47–1**

First-Pass Immunization Noncall Assets Only[a]

| Security | Coupon | Maturity | PV or Price | Yield | Duration | Dollar Allocation |
|---|---|---|---|---|---|---|
| Liability | | 8/15/1994 | 65.772 | 8.50% | 4.83 | ($100.00) |
| U.S. Treasury | 6.500 | 2/15/1990 | 99.250 | 7.96 | 0.50 | $ 27.51 |
| Thailand | 8.700 | 8/1/1999 | 100.000 | 8.70 | 6.51 | 72.49 |
| U.S. Treasury | 14.250 | 11/15/1991 | 114.688 | 7.15 | 1.93 | 0.00 |
| U.S. Treasury | 8.625 | 1/15/1995 | 104.031 | 7.70 | 4.30 | 0.00 |
| U.S. Treasury | 9.125 | 5/15/2018 | 113.688 | 7.91 | 10.87 | 0.00 |
| Ford Motor Credit | 8.000 | 8/1/1994 | 100.000 | 8.00 | 4.00 | 0.00 |
| Bowater | 9.000 | 8/1/2009 | 100.000 | 9.00 | 9.12 | 0.00 |
| GMAC | 8.250 | 8/1/1996 | 100.000 | 8.25 | 5.17 | 0.00 |
| Total assets | | | | 8.50% | 4.85 | $100.00 |

[a] Duration matched within 0.5% tolerance; convexity is not matched; all figures as of 8/3/89.

**E X H I B I T   47–2**

Effects of Yield-Curve Shifts on Immunized Portfolio (as of 8/3/89)

| Yield Curve | Present Values | | | |
|---|---|---|---|---|
| | Liability | Treasury 6.5% of '90 | Thailand 8.7% of '99 | Overfunded (Underfunded) |
| Unchanged[a] | ($100.00) | $27.51 | $72.49 | $0.00 |
| +100 BP | (95.26) | 27.37 | 67.92 | 0.04 |
| −100 BP | (105.00) | 27.65 | 77.52 | 0.17 |
| Steeper 50 BP[b] | (99.80) | 27.54 | 71.73 | (0.53) |
| Flatter 50 BP[c] | (100.20) | 27.48 | 73.30 | 0.59 |

[a] Treasury yield curve:
   2-year 7.53%
   3-year 7.58
   4-year 7.54
   5-year 7.56
   7-year 7.64
   10-year 7.74
   30-year 7.83

[b] Steeper curve pivots counterclockwise around the 5-year. The 3-month rate falls 25 basis points, and the 30-year rate rises 25 basis points.

[c] Flatter curve pivots in the opposite direction.

matched fairly well and actually becomes modestly overfunded. When the yield curve steepens, the account is underfunded. It's overfunded when the curve flattens. Exhibit 47–2 examines only instantaneous rate changes. Exhibit 47–3 examines the effects of time and rate changes on the portfolio. The reason mismatches are more dramatic in six months is that the assets' and liabilities' durations decay at different rates. The portfolio becomes mismatched simply because time passes. Transactions to rebalance the portfolio are necessary to maintain the match. Immunization requires frequent rebalancing due to the passage of time, without regard to value.

Immunization provides an easy way of controlling overall interest-rate risk. However, it falters because it is a static approach to dynamic yield-curve risks. Immunization exhibits several weaknesses:

1. It requires transactions. Those transactions are a result of the mathematics, not of value or opportunities in the market.

2. It overwhelmingly focuses on matching instantaneous price changes, whereas it should be concerned with the future value of the liability.

3. Transactions are a function of volatility and time, not value. This creates unpredictable capital gains and losses, which may not be appropriate for the corporation as a whole.

**E X H I B I T   47–3**

Effects of Yield-Curve Shifts and Time on Immunized Portfolio (as of 2/3/90)

| Yield Curve | Liability | Present Values | | | Overfunded (Underfunded) |
|---|---|---|---|---|---|
| | | Treasury 6.5% of '90 | Thailand 8.7% of '99 | Cash | |
| Unchanged[a] | ($104.39) | $27.70 | $72.49 | $4.06 | ($0.14) |
| +100 BP | (99.95) | 27.69 | 68.04 | 4.06 | (0.16) |
| −100 BP | (109.04) | 27.71 | 77.33 | 4.06 | 0.06 |
| Steeper 50 BP[b] | (104.31) | 27.70 | 71.74 | 4.06 | (0.80) |
| Flatter 50 BP[c] | (104.46) | 27.70 | 73.24 | 4.06 | 0.53 |

[a] Position becomes underfunded in unchanged rate scenario because liability rolls down the yield curve faster than the asset. Starting Treasury curve:      2-year 7.53%
　　　　　　　　　　　　　　　　　　　　　　　　　　　3-year 7.58
　　　　　　　　　　　　　　　　　　　　　　　　　　　4-year 7.54
　　　　　　　　　　　　　　　　　　　　　　　　　　　5-year 7.56
　　　　　　　　　　　　　　　　　　　　　　　　　　　7-year 7.64
　　　　　　　　　　　　　　　　　　　　　　　　　　　10-year 7.74
　　　　　　　　　　　　　　　　　　　　　　　　　　　30-year 7.83
[b] Steeper curve pivots counterclockwise around the 5-year. The 3-month rate falls 25 basis points, and the 30-year rate rises 25 basis points.
[c] Flatter curve pivots in the opposite direction.

**4.** The computations assume parallel yield-curve shifts. This has been a rarity, as Exhibit 47–4 illustrates.

**5.** Only simply structured bonds may be used in an immunized portfolio. Bonds with variable cash flows (e.g., callables, putables, mortgage-backed securities) don't fit the model and can't be used, regardless of their value.

**6.** Immunization assumes reinvestment into the same security. This may not be appropriate.

Several ad hoc approaches are available to reduce transactions and yield-curve risk. Specifically, option technology attempts to broaden the universe of assets.

|          | 6/30/87 | 12/31/87 | 6/30/88 | 12/31/88 | 6/30/89 |
|----------|---------|----------|---------|----------|---------|
| 3-month  | 5.87    | 5.85     | 6.75    | 8.36     | 8.26    |
| 6-month  | 6.13    | 6.47     | 7.02    | 8.66     | 8.14    |
| 1-year   | 6.65    | 7.10     | 7.42    | 9.00     | 8.09    |
| 2-year   | 7.47    | 7.78     | 7.99    | 9.27     | 8.14    |
| 3-year   | 7.72    | 8.01     | 8.15    | 9.27     | 8.11    |
| 4-year   | 7.91    | 8.26     | 8.31    | 9.28     | 8.12    |
| 5-year   | 8.01    | 8.40     | 8.41    | 9.26     | 8.07    |
| 7-year   | 8.24    | 8.68     | 8.65    | 9.30     | 8.14    |
| 10-year  | 8.37    | 8.86     | 8.80    | 9.24     | 8.16    |
| 20-year  | 8.68    | 9.06     | 8.99    | 9.28     | 8.29    |
| 30-year  | 8.49    | 8.98     | 8.88    | 9.08     | 8.05    |

**E X H I B I T   47–4**

Yield Curves

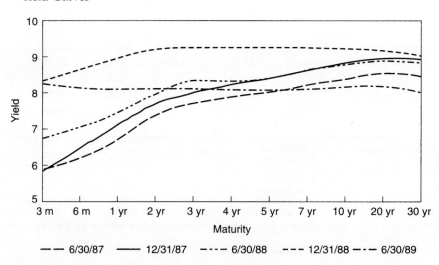

## Option Valuation and Immunization

Improvements in option valuation models have helped expand the asset classes that may be included in immunized portfolios. Option-adjusted, effective, or implied durations are often substituted for modified durations. These sensitivity measures are unstable, however, and inclusion of option-related assets in an immunized portfolio may introduce risks with which the immunization model is not equipped to deal. Maximizing an option-adjusted yield while matching effective duration may seem like a reasonable approach—until risk is closely examined. Exhibit 47–5 incorporates callable corporate bonds and pass-throughs into the immunization problem. Exhibit 47–6 shows the performance of the optimal portfolio in several scenarios. Over the six-month period, the portfolio became heavily underfunded in all but one scenario. The degree of underfunding was worse than for a portfolio of noncall securities. It's clear that the immunization model obscured risks inherent in the new securities.

Incorporating option technology into immunization technology has all the weaknesses of pure immunization and adds risks that neither approach is capable of evaluating fully. In fact, because effective durations are unstable, incorporating option technology into immunization may exacerbate the need for rebalancing and unexpected transactions. The term *immunization* is a misnomer; there are always bets in immunized portfolios, known and unknown. The immunization model has the capacity to neither identify nor quantify those risks.

## THE WISH LIST FOR PORTFOLIO MANAGEMENT

The ideal portfolio construction methodology would allow the portfolio manager to

1. Explicitly specify risk/return preferences and build them into the portfolio.

2. Never transact unless he or she wishes to (the manager should transact only when there is an opportunity to improve the risk/return profile of the portfolio and when it is in the corporation's overall best interest; transacting should be the portfolio manager's option, not the market's or the model's).

3. Always fund liabilities in any economic scenario (at the very least, the manager should be able to specify precisely what risks of underfunding liabilities he or she wishes to assume).

4. Most importantly, achieve long-run return objectives within the chosen risk and transaction tolerances.

Immunization and most other common asset/liability approaches have none of these characteristics. The total-return approach, however, begins to satisfy many of these needs.

# EXHIBIT 47-5

First-Pass Immunization Including Callable and Putable Assets[a]

| Security | Coupon | Maturity | Call/Put Date | Call/Put Price | PV or Price | Yield | Effective Duration | Dollars |
|---|---|---|---|---|---|---|---|---|
| Liability | | 8/15/1994 | — | — | 64.453 | 8.92 | 4.82 | $100.00 |
| UST | 6.500 | 2/15/1990 | — | — | 99.250 | 7.96 | 0.50 | 21.36 |
| Thailand | 8.700 | 8/1/1999 | — | — | 100.000 | 8.70 | 6.51 | 0.00 |
| UST | 14.250 | 11/15/1991 | — | — | 114.688 | 7.15 | 1.93 | 0.00 |
| UST | 8.625 | 1/15/1995 | — | — | 104.031 | 7.70 | 4.30 | 0.00 |
| UST | 9.125 | 5/15/2018 | — | — | 113.688 | 7.91 | 10.87 | 0.00 |
| Ford Motor Credit | 8.000 | 8/1/1994 | — | — | 100.000 | 8.00 | 4.00 | 0.00 |
| Bowater | 9.000 | 8/1/2009 | — | — | 100.000 | 9.00 | 9.12 | 41.57 |
| GMAC | 8.250 | 8/1/1996 | — | — | 100.000 | 8.25 | 5.17 | 0.00 |
| GNMA | 8.000 | 1/31/2018 | — | — | 94.813 | 8.95 | 5.94 | 0.00 |
| GNMA | 9.500 | 1/31/2019 | — | — | 100.906 | 9.43 | 4.98 | 0.00 |
| GNMA | 10.500 | 7/31/2018 | — | — | 104.219 | 9.38 | 2.55 | 37.07 |
| Xerox[b] | 9.200 | 7/15/1999 | 7/15/1996 | 100.00 | 99.551 | 9.36 | 5.97 | 0.00 |
| Household Finance[b] | 8.875 | 7/5/1999 | 7/5/1996 | 100.00 | 98.934 | 9.03 | 5.73 | 0.00 |
| ITT[c] | 8.250 | 8/1/2001 | 8/1/1996 | 100.00 | 100.000 | 8.25 | 5.47 | 0.00 |
| American General[c] | 8.125 | 8/15/2009 | 8/15/1996 | 100.00 | 99.150 | 8.29 | 7.13 | 0.00 |
| Total assets | | | | | | 8.92% | 4.84 | $100.00 |

[a]All figures as of 8/3/89; duration matched with 0.5% tolerance; convexity is not matched but is constrained to exceed 0.
[b]Callable.
[c]Putable.

**EXHIBIT  47–6**

Effects of Yield-Curve Shifts and Time on Immunized Portfolio
(as of 2/3/90)

| | Liability | UST 6.5% of '90 | Bowater 9.0% of '09 | GNMA 10.5% | Cash | Overfunded (Underfunded) |
|---|---|---|---|---|---|---|
| Unchanged[a] | ($104.60) | $21.50 | $41.59 | $34.97 | $6.13 | ($0.42) |
| +100 BP | (100.15) | 21.50 | 38.04 | 34.28 | 5.77 | (0.57) |
| −100 BP | (109.24) | 21.51 | 45.67 | 34.98 | 6.58 | (0.50) |
| Steeper 50 BP[b] | (104.51) | 21.51 | 40.82 | 35.01 | 6.07 | (1.11) |
| Flatter 50 BP[c] | (104.67) | 21.50 | 42.37 | 34.91 | 6.18 | 0.30 |

[a] Position becomes underfunded in unchanged rate scenario because liability rolls down the yield curve faster than the assets. Starting Treasury curve:
2-year 7.53%
3-year 7.58
4-year 7.54
5-year 7.56
7-year 7.64
10-year 7.74
30-year 7.63

[b] Steeper curve pivots counterclockwise around the 5-year. The 3-month rate falls 25 basis points, and the 30-year rate rises 25 basis points.

[c] Flatter curve pivots in the opposite direction.

# TOTAL RETURN IN THE ASSET/LIABILITY/REGULATORY/GAAP/TAX WORLD

By examining the total returns of securities in various scenarios, many real-world constraints may be considered explicitly. Reinvestment assumptions, tax effects, regulatory restrictions, and GAAP treatment may be included in the analysis.

The total-return approach involves a lot of modeling and specification by the portfolio manager. It forces the manager to think explicitly about risk. Total return approaches examine the behavior of securities in different interest-rate environments, allowing the portfolio manager to specify tolerance for loss versus liability in each scenario and then construct a portfolio that provides superior performance over the investment horizon. The portfolio manager must specify the following:

1. An objective (he or she can maximize expected total return, maximize it in only one scenario, or minimize risk at some minimum total return level)

2. Likely and unlikely economic scenarios (the manager must specify the level of key economic variables, for example, the yield curve and credit spreads)

3. Tolerances for losses in each scenario

4. Various portfolio parameters, such as diversification

Models must be developed for the assets to be included:

1. For corporate bonds, all the characteristics of call and put options, sinking funds, and credit risk must be modeled.

2. For mortgage-backed securities and their various derivatives, cash flow and prepayment models must be developed. A good prepayment model may involve an econometric model with coefficients for economic refinancing, prepayment burnout, seasoning effects, and the lags in these variables.

3. Any other securities that the manager wishes to include must be modeled: for example, floating-rate notes, futures and options, swaps, and dynamic strategies.

Exhibit 47–7 shows several interest-rate scenarios specified by a portfolio manager, the assigned subjective probability, and the manager's tolerance for loss versus his liability. Exhibit 47–8 lists several assets and their modeled total return in each scenario specified by the portfolio manager. The data in Exhibits 47–7 and 47–8 are then optimized and the results reported in Exhibit 47–9. The results suggest how the manager should structure the portfolio to satisfy the risk-return objectives. As long as the specified scenarios sufficiently incorporate the actual yield-curve movement, the portfolio should not require rebalancing. However, if the manager perceives a change in value in the market, he or she has the option of taking advantage of it. The manager can also tilt the portfolio by adjusting the probabilities assigned to each scenario.

The main weakness of the total-return approach is its complexity. The investment organization must commit people, computers, and research to develop the models and educate users.

## Long-Term Arbitrage

Market makers and traders are by definition short-term-oriented. They reduce their risk and increase their return by keeping their inventory turnover high. This creates opportunities that often persist. Total-return models are useful tools in identifying these opportunities.

Exhibit 47–10 shows an application of total-return approaches to arbitrage. The axes of the matrix list several bonds: Each column represents a bond that may be purchased; each row represents one that may be sold. The contents of the matrix are swap suggestions where the purchased combination of bonds will outperform the one sold in each scenario.

**EXHIBIT 47–7**

Yield Curves

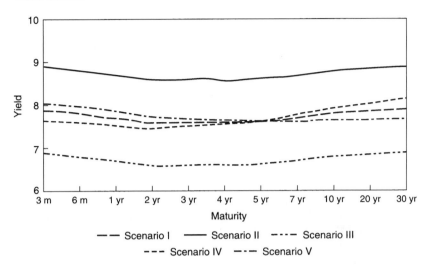

| | | Horizon Interest Rates | | | |
|---|---|---|---|---|---|
| **Scenario** | **3-Month** | **2-Year** | **10-Year** | | **Loss Tolerance Probability vs. Liability** |
| I | 7.89 | 7.53 | 7.74 | 20% | 0.00% |
| II | 8.89 | 8.53 | 8.74 | 15 | −0.10 |
| III | 6.89 | 6.53 | 6.74 | 10 | 0.00 |
| IV | 7.64 | 7.41 | 7.90 | 30 | 0.00 |
| V | 8.04 | 7.65 | 7.58 | 25 | −0.10 |

## PROBABILITY DISTRIBUTIONS: THE NEXT FRONTIER

A particularly burdensome task involved in total-return modeling is the specification of scenarios. Generally, only a small number of scenarios are specified, and it's easy to miss some important ones. This creates a potential for incomplete analysis.

One solution is to use mathematical simulations to create many scenarios. The ideal simulation is a stochastic process that simulates movement of the entire yield curve, both its position and shape. With a large number of simulated total returns, return distributions may be examined.

Exhibit 47–11 shows total-return distributions for several securities in many scenarios. They have clearly very different risk/return characteristics.

## EXHIBIT 47-8

Pro Forma Total Returns for Specified Assets[a]

| Security | Coupon | Maturity | Scenario Total Return | | | | |
|---|---|---|---|---|---|---|---|
| | | | I | II | III | IV | V |
| Liability | — | 8/15/1994 | 8.77% | −0.10% | 18.08% | 8.61% | 8.93% |
| UST | 6.500 | 2/15/1990 | 7.95 | 7.89 | 8.02 | 7.97 | 7.94 |
| Thailand | 8.700 | 8/1/1999 | 8.87 | −3.41 | 22.23 | 8.31 | 9.46 |
| UST | 14.250 | 11/15/1991 | 7.24 | 4.26 | 10.27 | 7.56 | 6.92 |
| UST | 8.625 | 1/15/1995 | 7.89 | 0.13 | 16.03 | 7.71 | 8.06 |
| UST | 9.125 | 5/15/2018 | 7.93 | −11.92 | 31.76 | 2.64 | 13.42 |
| Ford Motor Credit | 8.000 | 8/1/1994 | 8.07 | 0.81 | 15.67 | 8.23 | 7.91 |
| Bowater | 9.000 | 8/1/2009 | 9.01 | −8.04 | 28.64 | 6.52 | 11.54 |
| GMAC | 8.250 | 8/1/1996 | 9.42 | −1.21 | 18.65 | 8.27 | 8.64 |
| GNMA | 8.000 | 1/31/2018 | 8.95 | −3.19 | 21.08 | 7.13 | 10.74 |
| GNMA | 9.500 | 1/31/2019 | 8.42 | −1.27 | 16.04 | 8.22 | 10.43 |
| GNMA | 10.500 | 7/31/2018 | 9.35 | 3.69 | 11.86 | 9.25 | 9.35 |
| Xerox | 9.200 | 7/15/1999 | 9.24 | −1.83 | 20.69 | 8.88 | 9.63 |
| Household Finance | 8.875 | 7/15/1999 | 9.10 | −2.15 | 20.73 | 8.71 | 9.51 |
| ITT | 8.250 | 8/1/2001 | 8.43 | −0.47 | 19.33 | 8.28 | 8.67 |
| American General | 8.125 | 8/15/2009 | 8.61 | −3.44 | 23.36 | 7.59 | 9.83 |

[a] Liability return assumes an initial discount rate of 8.50%; one-year horizon.

# EXHIBIT 47-9

Suggested Portfolio for Specified Assets and Risk/Return Objectives[a]

| Security | Coupon | Maturity | Weight | Scenario Total Return | | | | |
|---|---|---|---|---|---|---|---|---|
| | | | | I | II | III | IV | V |
| Liability | — | 8/15/1994 | -100% | 8.77% | -0.10% | 18.08% | 8.61% | 8.93% |
| UST | 6.500 | 2/15/1990 | 0.0 | 7.95 | 7.89 | 8.02 | 7.97 | 7.94 |
| Thailand | 8.700 | 8/1/1999 | 0.0 | 8.87 | -3.41 | 22.23 | 8.31 | 9.46 |
| UST | 14.250 | 11/15/1991 | 0.0 | 7.24 | 4.26 | 10.27 | 7.56 | 6.92 |
| UST | 8.625 | 1/15/1995 | 0.0 | 7.89 | .13 | 16.03 | 7.71 | 8.06 |
| UST | 9.125 | 5/15/2018 | 0.0 | 7.93 | -11.92 | 31.76 | 2.64 | 13.42 |
| Ford | 8.000 | 8/1/1994 | 0.0 | 8.07 | 0.81 | 15.67 | 8.23 | 7.91 |
| Bowater | 9.000 | 8/1/2009 | 0.0 | 9.01 | -8.04 | 28.64 | 6.52 | 11.54 |
| GMAC | 8.250 | 8/1/1996 | 0.0 | 8.42 | -1.21 | 18.65 | 8.27 | 8.64 |
| GNMA | 8.000 | 1/31/2018 | 0.0 | 8.95 | -3.19 | 21.08 | 7.13 | 10.74 |
| GNMA | 9.500 | 1/31/2019 | 0.0 | 9.42 | -1.27 | 16.04 | 8.22 | 10.43 |
| GNMA | 10.500 | 7/31/2018 | 29.6 | 9.35 | 3.69 | 11.86 | 9.25 | 9.35 |
| Xerox | 9.200 | 7/15/1999 | 70.4 | 9.24 | -1.83 | 20.69 | 8.88 | 9.63 |
| Household Finance | 8.875 | 7/15/1999 | 0.0 | 9.10 | -2.15 | 20.73 | 8.71 | 9.51 |
| ITT | 8.250 | 8/1/2001 | 0.0 | 8.43 | -0.47 | 19.33 | 8.28 | 8.67 |
| AGC | 8.125 | 8/15/2009 | -0.0 | 8.61 | -3.44 | 23.36 | 7.59 | 9.83 |
| Total asset return | | | 100.0% | 9.27% | -0.19% | 18.08% | 8.99% | 9.55% |
| Assets–liabilities return spread | | | | 0.50% | -0.09% | 0.00% | 0.38% | 0.62% |
| Maximum permitted loss | | | | 0.00% | -0.10% | 0.00% | 0.00% | -0.10% |
| Scenario probability | | | | 20% | 15% | 10% | 30% | 25% |
| Expected gain | | | 36% | | | | | |

[a] Selected portfolio maximizes expected total return in five probability-weighted scenarios, subject to the loss constraints enumerated in Exhibit 47–7. The investment horizon is one year.

# EXHIBIT 47–10

## Total-Return Arbitrage Matrix[a]

| Return Advantage[a] | | | GN30N 7.50 | GN30N 8.00 | GN30N 8.50 | GN30N 9.00 | GN30N 9.50 | GN30N 10.00 | GN30N 10.50 | FN30N 8.00 | FN30N 8.50 | FN30N 9.00 | FN30N 9.50 | FN30N 10.00 | FH30N 8.50 |
|---|---|---|---|---|---|---|---|---|---|---|---|---|---|---|---|
| 0 BP | GN30N | 7.50 | 100.0 | .0 | .0 | .0 | .0 | .0 | .0 | .0 | .0 | .0 | .0 | .0 | .0 |
| 0 BP | GN30N | 8.00 | .0 | 100.0 | .0 | .0 | .0 | .0 | .0 | .0 | .0 | .0 | .0 | .0 | .0 |
| 0 BP | GN30N | 6.50 | .0 | .0 | 100.0 | .0 | .0 | .0 | .0 | .0 | .0 | .0 | .0 | .0 | .0 |
| 0 BP | GN30N | 9.00 | .0 | .0 | .0 | 100.0 | .0 | .0 | .0 | .0 | .0 | .0 | .0 | .0 | .0 |
| 0 BP | GN30N | 9.50 | .0 | .0 | .0 | .0 | 100.0 | .0 | .0 | .0 | .0 | .0 | .0 | .0 | .0 |
| 0 BP | GN30N | 10.00 | .0 | .0 | .0 | .0 | .0 | 100.0 | .0 | .0 | .0 | .0 | .0 | .0 | .0 |
| 23 BP | GN30N | 10.50 | .0 | .0 | .0 | .0 | .0 | .0 | .0 | .0 | .0 | 24.4 | .0 | .0 | .0 |
| 0 BP | FN30N | 8.00 | .0 | .0 | .0 | .0 | .0 | .0 | .0 | 100.0 | .0 | .0 | .0 | .0 | .0 |
| 0 BP | FN30N | 8.50 | .0 | .0 | .0 | .0 | .0 | .0 | .0 | .0 | 100.0 | .0 | .0 | .0 | .0 |
| 0 BP | FN30N | 9.00 | .0 | .0 | .0 | .0 | .0 | .0 | .0 | .0 | .0 | 100.0 | .0 | .0 | .0 |
| 0 BP | FN30N | 9.50 | .0 | .0 | .0 | .0 | .0 | .0 | .0 | .0 | .0 | .0 | 100.0 | .0 | .0 |
| 0 BP | FN30N | 10.00 | .0 | .0 | .0 | .0 | .0 | .0 | .0 | .0 | .0 | .0 | .0 | 100.0 | .0 |
| 0 BP | FH30N | 8.50 | .0 | .0 | .0 | .0 | .0 | .0 | .0 | .0 | .0 | .0 | .0 | .0 | 100.0 |
| 0 BP | FH30N | 9.00 | .0 | .0 | .0 | .0 | .0 | .0 | .0 | .0 | .0 | .0 | .0 | .0 | .0 |
| 0 BP | FH30N | 9.50 | .0 | .0 | .0 | .0 | .0 | .0 | .0 | .0 | .0 | .0 | .0 | .0 | .0 |
| 9 BP | FH30N | 10.00 | .0 | .0 | .0 | .0 | .0 | .0 | .0 | .0 | .0 | .0 | .0 | 66.4 | .0 |
| 0 BP | FH30N | 10.50 | .0 | .0 | .0 | .0 | .0 | .0 | .0 | .0 | .0 | .0 | .0 | .0 | .0 |
| 15 BP | GN30S | 8.00 | .0 | .0 | .0 | .0 | .0 | .0 | .0 | 12.7 | 63.1 | .0 | .0 | .0 | .0 |
| 13 BP | GN30S | 8.50 | .0 | .0 | .0 | .0 | .0 | .0 | .0 | .0 | 63.5 | .0 | .0 | .0 | .0 |
| 13 BP | GN30S | 9.00 | .0 | .0 | .0 | .0 | .0 | .0 | .0 | .0 | 17.7 | 29.7 | .0 | .0 | .0 |
| 0 BP | GN15N | 8.00 | .0 | .0 | .0 | .0 | .0 | .0 | .0 | .0 | .0 | .0 | .0 | .0 | .0 |
| 6 BP | GN15N | 8.50 | .0 | .0 | .0 | .0 | .0 | .0 | .0 | 9.8 | 7.4 | .0 | .0 | .0 | .0 |
| 23 BP | GN15N | 9.00 | .0 | .0 | .0 | .0 | .0 | .0 | .0 | .0 | 23.1 | .0 | .0 | .0 | .0 |
| 0 BP | FH15N | 8.00 | .0 | .0 | .0 | .0 | .0 | .0 | .0 | .0 | .0 | .0 | .0 | .0 | .0 |
| 0 BP | FH15S | 8.50 | .0 | .0 | .0 | .0 | .0 | .0 | .0 | .0 | .0 | .0 | .0 | .0 | .0 |
| 0 BP | FH15S | 8.00 | .0 | .0 | .0 | .0 | .0 | .0 | .0 | .0 | .0 | .0 | .0 | .0 | .0 |
| 0 BP | UST | 7.88 | .0 | .0 | .0 | .0 | .0 | .0 | .0 | .0 | .0 | .0 | .0 | .0 | .0 |
| 95 BP | UST | 8.25 | .0 | .0 | .0 | .0 | .0 | .0 | .0 | 10.7 | .0 | .0 | .0 | .0 | .0 |
| 101 BP | UST | 9.88 | .0 | .0 | .0 | .0 | .0 | .0 | .0 | 16.4 | 77.8 | .0 | .0 | .0 | .0 |
| 0 BP | UST | 8.00 | .0 | .0 | .0 | .0 | .0 | .0 | .0 | .0 | .0 | .0 | .0 | .0 | .0 |

Number of simulations evaluated = 13

Maximum allowable underperformance = 0 BP

One-year horizon scenarios:

   ±200
   ±150
   ±100
   ±50
   No change
   Steeper 50, 100
   Flatter 50, 100

[a] The column headed "Return Advantage" indicates the expected return pickup over the one-year horizon. The row headed GN30N 10.50 shows that we can expect to pick up 23 BP of total return if we sell the new GNMA 30-year 10.5% and buy a portfolio composed of 24.4% FNMA, 30-year 9.0s, 72.6% new FHLMC 30-year 10.5s, and 2.9% Gnome 8.5s.

The arbitrage is evaluated over 13 scenarios encompassing a sufficient range of curve shifts and twists. The optimization finds the portfolio that shows the highest expected return advantage but that does not underperform the target security in any scenario.

## E X H I B I T   47–10

(*Continued*)

| FH30N 9.00 | FH30N 9.50 | FH30N 10.00 | FH30N 10.50 | GN30S 8.00 | GN30S 8.50 | GN30S 9.00 | GN15N 8.00 | GN15N 8.50 | GN15N 9.00 | FH15N 8.00 | FH15S 8.50 | FH15S 9.00 | UST 7.88 | UST 8.25 | UST 8.88 | UST 8.00 |
|---|---|---|---|---|---|---|---|---|---|---|---|---|---|---|---|---|
| .0 | .0 | .0 | .0 | .0 | .0 | .0 | .0 | .0 | .0 | .0 | .0 | .0 | .0 | .0 | .0 | .0 |
| .0 | .0 | .0 | .0 | .0 | .0 | .0 | .0 | .0 | .0 | .0 | .0 | .0 | .0 | .0 | .0 | .0 |
| .0 | .0 | .0 | .0 | .0 | .0 | .0 | .0 | .0 | .0 | .0 | .0 | .0 | .0 | .0 | .0 | .0 |
| .0 | .0 | .0 | .0 | .0 | .0 | .0 | .0 | .0 | .0 | .0 | .0 | .0 | .0 | .0 | .0 | .0 |
| .0 | .0 | .0 | .0 | .0 | .0 | .0 | .0 | .0 | .0 | .0 | .0 | .0 | .0 | .0 | .0 | .0 |
| .0 | .0 | .0 | .0 | .0 | .0 | .0 | .0 | .0 | .0 | .0 | .0 | .0 | .0 | .0 | .0 | .0 |
| .0 | .0 | .0 | 72.6 | .0 | .0 | .0 | .0 | .0 | .0 | .0 | 2.9 | .0 | .0 | .0 | .0 | .0 |
| .0 | .0 | .0 | .0 | .0 | .0 | .0 | .0 | .0 | .0 | .0 | .0 | .0 | .0 | .0 | .0 | .0 |
| .0 | .0 | .0 | .0 | .0 | .0 | .0 | .0 | .0 | .0 | .0 | .0 | .0 | .0 | .0 | .0 | .0 |
| .0 | .0 | .0 | .0 | .0 | .0 | .0 | .0 | .0 | .0 | .0 | .0 | .0 | .0 | .0 | .0 | .0 |
| .0 | .0 | .0 | .0 | .0 | .0 | .0 | .0 | .0 | .0 | .0 | .0 | .0 | .0 | .0 | .0 | .0 |
| .0 | .0 | .0 | .0 | .0 | .0 | .0 | .0 | .0 | .0 | .0 | .0 | .0 | .0 | .0 | .0 | .0 |
| 100.0 | .0 | .0 | .0 | .0 | .0 | .0 | .0 | .0 | .0 | .0 | .0 | .0 | .0 | .0 | .0 | .0 |
| .0 | 22.1 | .0 | .0 | .0 | .0 | .0 | .0 | .0 | .0 | .0 | .0 | .0 | .0 | .0 | .0 | .0 |
| .0 | 100.0 | .0 | 11.5 | .0 | .0 | .0 | .0 | .0 | .0 | .0 | .0 | .0 | .0 | .0 | .0 | .0 |
| .0 | .0 | .0 | 100.0 | .0 | .0 | .0 | .0 | .0 | .0 | .0 | .0 | .0 | .0 | .0 | .0 | 0 |
| .0 | .0 | .0 | .0 | .0 | .0 | .0 | .0 | .0 | .0 | 24.2 | .0 | .0 | .0 | .0 | .0 | .0 |
| .0 | .0 | .0 | .0 | .0 | .0 | .0 | .0 | .0 | .0 | .0 | 36.5 | .0 | .0 | .0 | .0 | .0 |
| .0 | .0 | .0 | .0 | .0 | .0 | .0 | .0 | .0 | .0 | .0 | 52.6 | .0 | .0 | .0 | .0 | .0 |
| .0 | .0 | .0 | .0 | .0 | .0 | .0 | 100.0 | .0 | .0 | .0 | .0 | .0 | .0 | .0 | .0 | .0 |
| .0 | .0 | .0 | .0 | .0 | .0 | .0 | .0 | .0 | .0 | 82.8 | .0 | .0 | .0 | .0 | .0 | .0 |
| .0 | .0 | .0 | .0 | .0 | .0 | .0 | .0 | .0 | .0 | .0 | 76.9 | .0 | .0 | .0 | .0 | .0 |
| .0 | .0 | .0 | .0 | .0 | .0 | .0 | .0 | .0 | .0 | 100.0 | .0 | .0 | .0 | .0 | .0 | .0 |
| .0 | .0 | .0 | .0 | .0 | .0 | .0 | .0 | .0 | .0 | .0 | 100.0 | .0 | .0 | .0 | .0 | .0 |
| .0 | .0 | .0 | .0 | .0 | .0 | .0 | .0 | .0 | .0 | .0 | .0 | 100.0 | .0 | .0 | .0 | .0 |
| .0 | .0 | .0 | .0 | .0 | .0 | .0 | .0 | .0 | .0 | .0 | .0 | 100.0 | .0 | .0 | .0 | .0 |
| .0 | .0 | .0 | .0 | .0 | .0 | .0 | 27.9 | .0 | .0 | 61.4 | .0 | .0 | .0 | .0 | .0 | .0 |
| .0 | .0 | .0 | .0 | .0 | .0 | .0 | .0 | .0 | .0 | 5.7 | .0 | .0 | .0 | .0 | .0 | .0 |
| .0 | .0 | .0 | .0 | .0 | .0 | .0 | .0 | .0 | .0 | .0 | .0 | .0 | .0 | .0 | 100.0 | |

## E X H I B I T   47–11

Total Return Distributions: GNMAs and 5-Year Treasury

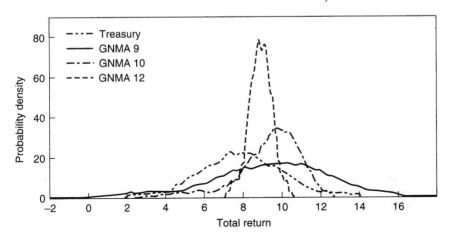

Total return distributions help us to delineate clearly the risk/return character-istics of securities.

## CONCLUSION

Total-return models are effective approaches to portfolio management for com-plex organizations. They allow their users to explicitly incorporate the realities of their businesses.

## CHAPTER 48

# INTERNATIONAL BOND INVESTING AND PORTFOLIO MANAGEMENT

**Christopher B. Steward, CFA**
Vice President
Wellington Management Company, LLP

**Adam M. Greshin, CFA**
Principal
Scudder Kemper Investments

## INTRODUCTION

The communications revolution has had a profound impact on the world at large, but it is the capital markets that have come closest to fulfilling Marshal McLuhan's vision of a "global village." International capital markets enjoy practically instantaneous communication on a scale that was nearly unimaginable a decade ago. Faxes, market information systems such as Reuters and Bloomberg, and most recently the internet, have created a seamless flow of investment information that functions as well across borders as it does across the street. This increased flow of information, combined with the removal of capital controls in most developed markets during the 1980s, has resulted in a dramatic increase in cross-border investment flows. Between 1981 and 1994, holdings of foreign assets by the G7 countries grew 3.4 times to $10.1 trillion, a compound annualized growth rate of 12%.[1] At the same time, household savings have been increasingly invested with professional fund managers through mutual funds and pension funds. By one estimate, U.S. and European fund managers alone control over $8 trillion in assets.[2] Reduced transactions costs and greater liquidity in the asset markets, especially in the derivatives markets, has enabled these professional investors to shift large amounts of capital across borders more freely. These flows can quickly overwhelm national authorities, as, in 1992, George

---

1. *OECD Economic Outlook,* no. 58, Paris (December 1995).
2. Michael Mussa and Morris Goldstein, "The Integration of World Capital Markets," in *Changing Capital Markets: Implications for Monetary Policy* (Federal Reserve Bank of Kansas, 1993).

Soros's Quantum hedge fund was able to force a devaluation of the British pound in a matter of days. A market-forced devaluation of the British pound in 1967 required several years of speculative pressure. Financial leverage can also threaten the stability of the global financial markets as the near collapse of the hedge fund Long Term Capital Management in the fall of 1998 illustrated.[3]

Institutional investors have been active in the international bond markets for a long time, but the amount of institutional assets invested in international bonds is tiny relative to the available pool of assets. Only 7% of the assets of the world's 300 largest pension funds are estimated to be invested in foreign bond and equity securities.[4] Retail investment in international bonds, primarily through mutual funds, is a much more recent phenomenon. In 1995, Lipper Analytical Services, which tracks U.S. Mutual Funds, counted 157 funds in its General World Income category with total net assets of 20 billion.

Questions remain as to the appropriateness of international bonds in U.S. dollar portfolios, particularly in light of the volatility in the foreign exchange markets in the past two decades. The advent of European Monetary Union in 1999 also led some investors to question the viability of global bonds as an asset class. Should international bonds be a core holding in U.S. portfolios, or should they be used on an occasional basis when foreign interest rate and currency levels appear attractive? This chapter will examine the reasons for investing in international bonds and will touch on some of the more interesting issues in constructing a global bond portfolio. First, the historical data regarding the return enhancement and diversification, or risk-reduction, benefits of international bond investments are examined. Next, the impact of including foreign-pay international bonds in a U.S. bond portfolio is discussed. Finally, techniques for management of foreign-pay international bond portfolios are addressed, with emphasis on the question of whether or not to hedge currency exposures.

## THE RATIONALE FOR INTERNATIONAL BOND INVESTING

Risk and return are the universal yardsticks applied to any potential investment as rational investors are always seeking the highest return for the lowest level of risk. Wall Street firms hire Ph.D. mathematicians to seek out correlations between markets that can be exploited to either tailor risk management products (such as exotic options or structured notes) or to uncover anomalies that can be used for arbitrage. Under the standard Markowitz mean-variance framework, any asset class with a less than perfect correlation to another will provide some diversification benefit in reducing portfolio risk. Many investors are attracted to

---

3. See Mussa and Goldstein.
4. See "A Review of Financial Market Events in Autumn 1998," October 1999 report from the Bank of International Settlements Committee on the Global Financial System.

international bonds by the higher returns that they have historically provided, the components of which will vary among income, domestic price change, and foreign currency change. However, for some investors, the potential for a reduction in the risk or volatility of return to a portfolio invested solely in U.S. fixed income securities will be more important.

In analyzing the case for international bonds, there is no a priori reason why one rationale for international bond investing should receive more emphasis than another. The relative emphasis on these rationales is properly a function of the investment objectives of the investor, and these objectives should be reflected in the guidelines for and composition of an international bond portfolio. To certain investors, especially those with long-term time horizons, return enhancement may be paramount, and the impact of international bonds on interim volatility of returns is relatively unimportant. For these investors, embarking on a program of international bond investing is not appropriate unless international bonds can be expected to improve the rate of return. To others, particularly investors with shorter time horizons who have been concerned by the occasional roller-coaster ride in the U.S. fixed income markets, the attraction of international bonds may be their potential for reducing the volatility of overall portfolio returns.

## Superior Rates of Return

A very powerful fundamental argument can be made for the inclusion of international equities as a separate asset class in domestic portfolios. Since many areas of the world are growing more rapidly than the United States and are experiencing higher rates of investment spending and productivity growth, a portfolio of foreign equities should, over time, provide a higher return than a portfolio of U.S. equities. No such strong fundamental arguments exist, however, for international bonds. Whatever their currency denomination, all bonds are influenced by the same factors: coupon income, interest-rate movements, and changes in credit risk. Unlike equities, which can theoretically rise in price indefinitely, bond prices are effectively capped, as their yields will never fall to zero.[5] The addition of currency exposure allows for significantly greater returns but also greater losses, as currency movements are notoriously difficult to forecast.

There have been long periods (throughout much of the late 1960s and 1970s and again from 1985–1987) when international bonds provided superior returns to U.S. instruments, and long periods (from 1981 to 1984 and from 1988 to 1989) when the reverse was true. In the former case, foreign bonds benefited both from higher yields than in the United States and strengthening currencies. This, coupled with the higher unanticipated inflation rates in the United States

---

5. In Japan, bond yields fell to a historical low of 0.8% as overnight interest rates were cut to zero.

compared with other industrialized countries, led to lackluster domestic U.S. bond returns relative to those abroad. The 1985–1987 period is most memorable for the downward spiral in the U.S. dollar, which produced windfall currency gains for holders of foreign-pay instruments. In the 1981–1984 period, U.S. bonds benefited from income streams much higher than in other markets coupled with an improvement in the inflation outlook, which resulted in generous capital gains as interest rates declined. In 1988 and 1989, renewed confidence in the U.S. dollar and lower-than-expected inflation in the U.S. economy led to the superior performance of U.S. bonds relative to most foreign-pay alternatives.

These results strongly suggest that potential returns from international bonds relative to U.S. bonds must be carefully analyzed by the three components: income advantage, expected relative domestic price movements, and prospective currency changes.

The best case for ongoing observance of international bonds lies in the continual array of opportunities and risks provided by the constant shifting of international exchange rate and interest rate relationships. The range of starting yields is continuously changing; some foreign rates provide a yield advantage against a U.S. interest rate bogey, and others provide a disadvantage. At any time, different countries will be at different points in their economic and interest rate cycles. Similarly, foreign currency relationships are continuously shifting, sometimes moving with interest rates and sometimes moving against them. Over time, it should be possible to capitalize on these shifting relationships, which will, in the aggregate, supply a greater number of opportunities than any one individual and relatively homogeneous market could. This rationale is an opportunistic and selective one, which has at its heart the cyclicality of economic behavior worldwide.

In the analysis that follows, the eight foreign bond markets in the Salomon Smith Barney World Bond Market Performance Index[6] are analyzed in relation to the U.S. market. Included are the government bond markets of Australia, Canada, France, Germany, Japan, Netherlands, Switzerland, and the United Kingdom. The analysis focuses on the 1978–1999 period due to the availability of reliable data and a sufficient amount of time for interest rate and currency cycles to work their way through the markets.

A comparison of the eight foreign bond markets with the U.S. market shows that over the 1978–1999 period, U.S. bonds provided a slightly inferior rate of return of 9.35% compared to a 10.10% rate of return produced by a

---

6. Exhibits 48–1 through 48–8, and 48–10 through 48–12, use the Salomon Smith Barney World Bond Market Performance Index (WBMPI) through 1995 and the World Government Bond Index (WGBI) thereafter. The WBMPI differs from the WGBI in that it has only 9 countries (plus ECU denominated bonds), compared with the WGBI's 14. The WBMPI also includes Euro and foreign bonds, whereas the WGBI includes only domestic government debt. For the analysis of individual country returns, we look only at the domestic government debt component of the WBMPI. Returns for Australia are from October 1984.

market-weighted index of foreign-pay bonds. The superior performance of the international bond index during this period is largely a function of the time period chosen, since there is no a priori reason to expect international bond returns, over the long run, to be any better or worse than domestic returns. Furthermore, the result is largely influenced by the very strong Japanese returns, which represents roughly one third of the market-weighted index. Without Japan the index would have produced a return only 10 basis points higher than that of the United States.

Exhibit 48–1 shows total returns from nine bond markets in U.S. dollar terms over the 1978–1999 period. It is interesting to note that foreign-exchange movements added to returns in half the countries, and it subtracted from returns in the other half. Also note that domestic returns were higher than U.S. domestic returns in less than half the markets studied. Japan was the best-performing bond market in U.S. dollar terms during that period due primarily to the strength of the yen. The United States ranked third toward the top of the range of returns. Switzerland lagged behind the other countries due to its historically low yields, which more than counteracted the 1% per annum appreciated of the Swiss franc versus the U.S. dollar over the 22 year period.

The total return figures in Exhibit 48–1 mask significant disparities in annualized total returns among bond markets. In Exhibit 48–2, the 1978–1999 period is broken down into annual return data for a better look at short-run changes. Notice the large disparity between the best- and worst-performing bond

**E X H I B I T   48–1**

International Bond Market Annualized Rates of Return—1978–1999

| | | | Components of Return | |
| --- | --- | --- | --- | --- |
| | Total Return in U.S. Dollars | Return vs. U.S. | Total Domestic Return | Foreign Exchange Change |
| Australia | 6.81% | −2.54% | 8.01% | −1.11% |
| Canada | 9.04 | −0.31 | 10.45 | −1.28 |
| France | 8.90 | −0.45 | 10.59 | −1.53 |
| Germany | 7.47 | −1.88 | 7.14 | 0.31 |
| Japan | 11.40 | 2.05 | 7.19 | 3.93 |
| Netherlands | 8.10 | −1.25 | 7.96 | 0.13 |
| Switzerland | 5.68 | −3.68 | 4.66 | 0.97 |
| United Kingdom | 10.73 | 1.38 | 11.63 | −0.80 |
| United States | 9.35 | — | 9.35 | — |
| International index | 10.10 | 0.74 | 8.63 | 1.35 |

**EXHIBIT 48–2**

U.S. Bonds and Non-U.S. World Index (Unhedged) vs. Best and Worst Performing Markets

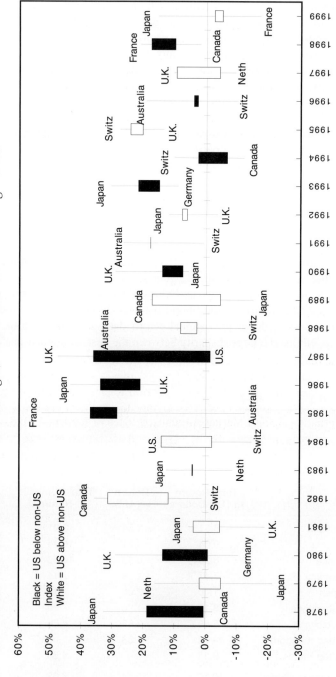

markets in each year. The smallest difference in total returns was recorded in 1995, when the 27.8% return in Switzerland was 14.2%, better than the 13.6% return in the United Kingdom. The largest difference in returns appeared in 1985, when France had a 52.7% return and Australian bonds lost 12.4%—a 65% return differential. These wide disparities are far greater than the return differentials in Exhibit 48–1, which have been smoothed out with the passage of time. Also note that the range of variation among bond market returns, and between the U.S. bond market and the non-U.S. government bond index, was much narrower in the 1990s than it was in the 1980s. Exhibit 48–2 also shows that it is unusual for countries to appear in the best or worst column in consecutive years. Japan was the best performing market in 1992–93 but was also the worst performing market in 1989–90. Switzerland was the best performer in both 1994 and 1995. All of the countries except Germany had at least one year at the top of the performance ranking. This reinforces the idea mentioned earlier that value added from opportunistic international bond investing can be great, but over time government policies and market forces tend to correct the economic disparities that lead to large short run gains or losses.

The rates of return experienced by each of the nine countries have no necessary repetitive significance. The 1978–1999 period was unique in many respects. In the late 1970s an acceleration in U.S. inflation and a widening gap in economic growth between the United States and Europe caused U.S. interest rates to rise relative to those in Europe and Japan. The second oil shock in 1979 was the reason for the strong performance of the United Kingdom's bond market from 1979 to 1980 and the negative returns in Japan and Germany, two oil-importing countries. The 1981–1984 period was characterized by strong relative returns of U.S. and Canadian bonds due to high income levels and renewed confidence in the dollar. Japanese bonds also performed well due to Japan's success at combating global inflation and the emergence of the yen as the world's strongest currency. The 1985–1986 period experienced one of history's great bond market rallies, with interest rates retreating from the record levels reached earlier in the decade. The dollar's decline from its 1984 peak meant that foreign bond markets were once again in favor among U.S. investors. The 1988–1989 period witnessed a return to dollar strength and declining interest rates in the United States relative to other countries. The political liberalization of Eastern Europe in 1989 had a negative impact on European bond markets as interest rates rose to reflect the unanticipated growth and inflation potential of a more integrated European market. In the early 1990s, concerns over the political fate of European Monetary Union, which led to the United Kingdom and Italy suspending their participation in the European Monetary System, and the eventual widening of the currency fluctuation bands from $2\frac{1}{4}$ to 15% caused significant European bond and currency market volatility.

More recently, in the late 1990s, global bond yields were able to decline to extremely low levels as the major industrialized countries were able to reduce inflation rates substantially, to less than 1% in many European countries and

Japan. Bond yields fell below 1% in Japan, 4% in Germany and 5% for the U.S. 30-year bond. Volatility in the global bond markets, however, remained high as the impact of emerging market crises in 1997 and 1998 was felt in the developed markets. The strength of the U.S. dollar in the late 1990s also served to reduce global bond returns to unhedged U.S. dollar-based investors.

Exhibit 48–3 shows the contribution of currency movements to returns. The 1978–1999 period has been divided into 4 subperiods to illustrate the impact of a shorter time horizon on foreign currency returns. For each of the periods, the impact of currency on return has been much higher than for the 22-year period as a whole. This is not surprising given the wide swings in foreign currency values that can occur in the short term. Over time, as the economic imbalances that caused the currency movements have adjusted, currency prices have readjusted toward previous levels. However, it should be remembered that looking at changes over a long period can mask significant shorter-term volatility. For example, the U.S. dollar appreciated a modest 3.5% against the yen during calendar 1995, yet, at one point the dollar had fallen by as much as 20% from year-end 1994 levels. A similar caveat should be mentioned in regard to analysis of cyclical data. Applying a long-term average to a study of the cycles of the sun would lead one to conclude that dusk is the normal state, when night and day account for the vast majority of the hours in a day.

A second challenge involving foreign currency exposure relates to the fact that foreign currency adds to the volatility of foreign bond returns. On a market-by-market basis, this has been true. Exhibit 48–4 and 48–5 show the standard deviation of monthly total returns in nine bond markets in both local currency and dollar-denominated terms. The data are presented for the 1978–1999 period and are also broken down into 4 segments. For the 22-year period as a whole,

**E X H I B I T    48–3**

Average Annual Contribution of Foreign Currency Changes to International Bond Returns

|                      | 1978–99 | 1978–83 | 1984–89 | 1990–95 | 1996–99 |
| -------------------- | ------- | ------- | ------- | ------- | ------- |
| Australia            | −1.11%  |         | −1.42%  | −0.98%  | −3.15%  |
| Canada               | −1.28   | −2.13%  | 1.19    | −2.68   | −1.54   |
| France               | −1.53   | −9.18   | 6.24    | 2.83    | −7.02   |
| Germany              | 0.31    | −4.31   | 8.25    | 2.83    | −7.45   |
| Japan                | 3.93    | 0.51    | 8.25    | 5.72    | 0.19    |
| Netherlands          | 0.13    | −4.92   | 8.18    | 2.97    | −7.59   |
| Switzerland          | 0.97    | −1.52   | 5.86    | 5.00    | −7.92   |
| United Kingdom       | −0.80   | −4.59   | 1.75    | −0.60   | 0.94    |
| International index  | 1.35    | −2.09   | 6.37    | 3.50    | −3.80   |

**EXHIBIT  48–4**

Annualized Standard Deviations of Monthly Domestic Local Bond Market
Total Returns

| Local Currency | 1978–99 | 1978–83 | 1983–89 | 1990–95 | 1996–99 |
|---|---|---|---|---|---|
| Australia | 7.1% | | 7.7% | 7.8% | 4.8% |
| Canada | 10.1 | 13.1% | 8.7 | 10.6 | 4.6 |
| France | 5.7 | 5.7 | 5.8 | 6.5 | 3.7 |
| Germany | 5.0 | 6.8 | 4.0 | 4.9 | 3.0 |
| Japan | 5.9 | 5.8 | 6.2 | 6.5 | 4.3 |
| Netherlands | 4.9 | 6.5 | 3.7 | 4.9 | 3.4 |
| Switzerland | 4.0 | 4.6 | 2.5 | 4.7 | 3.3 |
| United Kingdom | 8.9 | 11.7 | 8.4 | 8.3 | 4.8 |
| United States | 8.9 | 11.8 | 9.5 | 6.8 | 3.9 |
| International index | 4.8 | 5.8 | 4.8 | 4.8 | 2.8 |

**EXHIBIT  48–5**

Annualized Standard Deviations of Monthly Bond Market Total Returns
Converted to U.S. Dollars

| U.S. Dollars | 1978–99 | 1978–83 | 1984–89 | 1990–95 | 1996–99 |
|---|---|---|---|---|---|
| Australia | 14.2% | | 19.0% | 11.0% | 10.3% |
| Canada | 12.1 | 15.2% | 10.9 | 12.0 | 7.4 |
| France | 12.7 | 13.7 | 14.3 | 11.7 | 8.2 |
| Germany | 13.8 | 16.2 | 15.4 | 11.8 | 8.2 |
| Japan | 15.5 | 17.1 | 16.4 | 14.0 | 12.9 |
| Netherlands | 13.1 | 14.8 | 14.9 | 11.4 | 8.2 |
| Switzerland | 14.0 | 16.2 | 15.4 | 11.9 | 9.9 |
| United Kingdom | 15.4 | 17.6 | 18.2 | 13.3 | 8.1 |
| United States | 8.9 | 11.8 | 9.5 | 6.8 | 3.9 |
| International index | 11.6 | 13.2 | 13.7 | 9.7 | 7.3 |

the volatility of returns in the United States was greater than the volatility of
local currency returns in any other market except Canada. Exhibit 48–4 also
reflects the fact that volatility has decreased in some countries and increased in
others. When foreign exchange movements are factored in, the volatility of foreign bond returns in U.S. dollar terms increases substantially, as shown in Exhibit 48–5. Thus, for the 1978–1999 period, and for each of the subperiods, the

United States had the lowest standard deviation of return when all returns were converted to U.S. dollars.

The additional volatility associated with foreign currency instruments has led to the development of *currency-hedged* investments, which neutralize the currency component of international bonds while maintaining exposure to local bond price movements. This will be addressed later in the chapter. As discussed in the next section, although foreign exchange rate movements greatly increase the volatility of individual market returns, the overall impact of the currency movements on a diversified international bond portfolio in far less. Importantly, as Exhibit 48–5 shows, the standard deviation of the unhedged International Index in US. dollar terms, although higher than the U.S. market, is lower than that of most of the individual markets. This is because the correlations of return between the individual foreign markets and currencies are less than perfect.

## Diversification

A second rationale for international bond investing is diversification. The inclusion of foreign bonds in a portfolio should reduce the risk or volatility of returns of a portfolio otherwise invested solely in U.S. fixed income securities. This is because foreign bond markets do not move with, or are not perfectly correlated with, the U.S. bond market. Intuitively this is obvious. The dynamics of the business cycle, and the role of monetary policy in dealing with the business cycle, differ by country. Institutional or structural forces, government financing practices, and tradition mean that the role of buyers and sellers varies among fixed income markets. The trend of inflation, a country's tolerance of inflation, and the sources of inflationary pressure differ among countries, as does the impact of inflation on the trend and structure of interest rates. Finally, a host of geopolitical, foreign policy, and societal forces ensure that the movements of foreign bond prices are not perfectly correlated. Consequently, when foreign currency bonds are added to a portfolio of U.S. fixed income securities, the price movements often offset each other, and the overall volatility of returns can be reduced.

Some investors were concerned that the diversification benefits of global bond investing would be substantially diminished by European Monetary Union (EMU). But, in fact, the economies of continental Europe were already very closely tied together before EMU with most European central banks following the interest rate policies of the German Bundesbank for several years before the move to a single currency. Thus, the impact on diversification of a global bond portfolio caused by EMU has been a small one. EMU, however, has created a much more robust credit market in Europe as issuers and investors, no longer confined to their home markets, have access to a larger, more liquid pan-European bond market. Corporate bond issuance has increased sharply in Europe, and seems likely to continue, building toward a broader range of credits and instruments similar to those available in the U.S. bond market.

Exhibit 48–6 shows the correlation coefficients of monthly changes in total returns (bond prices plus income) in local currency terms among nine major bond markets over the 1978–1999 period. The bond market with the highest correlation to the U.S. market is Canada's—not a surprising occurrence in view of the bilateral relationships between the two economies. The lowest correlations are between Japanese bonds and some of the European bond markets, which once again is reasonable in view of the lesser interdependence between these economies. In most cases, the correlation among the continental European bond markets is higher than that between those markets and the United States, reflecting the high degree of interdependence between the European economies, and the convergence toward European Monetary Union.

Exhibit 48–7 shows the correlation coefficients of monthly domestic total returns between the United States and foreign markets broken down into 4 time periods. In most cases the degree of correlation or interdependence rose over the 22-year period or remained roughly unchanged. This is one more statistical manifestation of the degree to which the world is getter smaller, and of the increased synchronization of economic behavior resulting from freer global capital movements. Increased bond market correlation also reflects the more uniform impact on the industrialized countries of a number of significant economic events during the period, notably the second oil shock in 1979–1980, which led to inflation and higher interest rates in all industrialized countries; the global recession that ended in 1982; the economic expansion throughout the remainder of the 1980s; and the crash and quick recovery of global stock markets from 1987 to 1988 and 1998–1999. The economic policy coordination that began in the postwar era with Bretton Woods accelerated rapidly in the 1970s and 1980s. To the extent that this trend continues, increased interdependence among bond markets is to be expected. For reasons discussed above, however, international bond price trends should remain less than perfectly correlated.

Exhibit 48–8 shows the correlation coefficients of monthly total returns converted to U.S. dollars for the 1978–1999 period overall, again broken down into 4 segments. A comparison of Exhibits 48–7 and 48–8 shows that the impact of currency movements on the correlation of returns with the United States over the 22 years resulted in substantially smaller correlations for all countries. In the German bond market, changes in the deutschemark/U.S. dollar exchange rate markedly reduced the domestic bond market correlation coefficient from .51 to .33. Over shorter periods, where exchange rate movements are more marked, domestic total return and converted U.S. dollar total return correlations can diverge more substantially. For example, in the 1984–1989 period, the correlation coefficient of German bond market returns with U.S. returns was .47 in local currency terms and only .21 in U.S. dollar terms. Similarly, the correlation coefficient between Japanese and U.S. returns in 1984–1989 was reduced from .44 to .21 when the currency factor was added.

Exhibits 48–7 and 48–8 lead to the conclusion that while local bond price movements among countries are becoming more correlated, currency volatility

# EXHIBIT 48–6

Correlation Coefficients of Domestic Total Returns in Foreign Bond Markets, 1978–1999 (Based on Monthly Data)

| 1978–99 | US | Australia | Canada | France | Germany | Japan | Holland | Switzerland | UK |
|---|---|---|---|---|---|---|---|---|---|
| US | 1.00 | | | | | | | | |
| Australia | 0.36 | 1.00 | | | | | | | |
| Canada | 0.71 | 0.26 | 1.00 | | | | | | |
| France | 0.36 | 0.26 | 0.39 | 1.00 | | | | | |
| Germany | 0.51 | 0.29 | 0.50 | 0.60 | 1.00 | | | | |
| Japan | 0.37 | 0.17 | 0.31 | 0.32 | 0.49 | 1.00 | | | |
| Holland | 0.52 | 0.31 | 0.47 | 0.67 | 0.84 | 0.42 | 1.00 | | |
| Switzerland | 0.34 | 0.23 | 0.32 | 0.43 | 0.55 | 0.35 | 0.57 | 1.00 | |
| UK | 0.40 | 0.31 | 0.39 | 0.40 | 0.45 | 0.33 | 0.46 | 0.37 | 1.00 |

**E X H I B I T   48–7**

Correlation Coefficients between U.S. and Foreign Bond Market Domestic Total Returns (Based on Monthly Data)

|  | 1978–99 | 1978–83 | 1984–89 | 1990–95 | 1996–99 |
|---|---|---|---|---|---|
| Australia | 0.36 |  | 0.03 | 0.68 | 0.60 |
| Canada | 0.71 | 0.76 | 0.83 | 0.51 | 0.76 |
| France | 0.36 | 0.13 | 0.51 | 0.49 | 0.62 |
| Germany | 0.51 | 0.54 | 0.47 | 0.51 | 0.62 |
| Japan | 0.37 | 0.34 | 0.44 | 0.43 | 0.25 |
| Holland | 0.52 | 0.56 | 0.49 | 0.53 | 0.62 |
| Switzerland | 0.34 | 0.35 | 0.36 | 0.46 | 0.20 |
| UK | 0.40 | 0.40 | 0.34 | 0.49 | 0.65 |

**E X H I B I T   48–8**

Correlation Coefficients between U.S. and Foreign Bond Market Total Returns Converted to U.S. Dollars (Based on Monthly Data)

|  | 1978–95 | 1978–83 | 1984–89 | 1990–95 |
|---|---|---|---|---|
| Australia | .11 |  | −.04 | .42 |
| Canada | .64 | .68 | .71 | .49 |
| France | .29 | .25 | .27 | .38 |
| Germany | .33 | .42 | .21 | .33 |
| Japan | .26 | .31 | .21 | .26 |
| Netherlands | .36 | .48 | .20 | .35 |
| Switzerland | .28 | .38 | .16 | .26 |
| United Kingdom | .34 | .44 | .18 | .39 |
| International index | .40 | .50 | .25 | .44 |

has continued to reduce the correlation among international bond markets as measured in U.S. dollar terms. This supports the use of international bonds for portfolio diversification.

Another driving force behind the increased correlation of global bond markets has been the convergence of inflation rates at relatively low levels. As Exhibit 48–9 shows, G7 inflation rates rose into double digits following the 1973 and 1979 OPEC oil price shocks. Bond investors, who had misjudged the inflationary impact during the first OPEC oil price shock in 1973, drove bond prices sharply higher to keep real yields positive. The deflationary policies pur-

**EXHIBIT 48–9**

G7 Inflation Rates (1974–1999, year-on-year changes, smoothed)

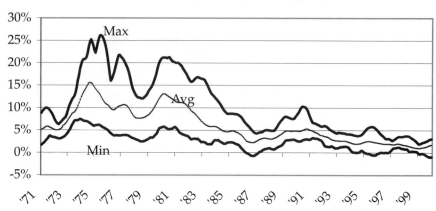

sued by the Federal Reserve under Chairman Volker, especially the shift to targeting money supply growth rather than interest rates, also pushed short-term interest rates into uncharted territory. Hence, by 1980, both bond yields and inflation were at extraordinarily high levels, providing opportunities for exceptional bond market returns as central banks waged war on inflation. As might be expected, past inflation rates have a strong influence on bond yields. Studies have shown that markets have long memories and that bond yields are more impacted by inflation averages of a fairly long duration, roughly 10 years or so, than by shorter term inflation experience.

Since the beginning of European Monetary Union on January 1, 1999, the eleven countries of the Euro zone have shared a single monetary policy set by the European Central Bank (ECB). In the late 1990s, in the lead up to European Monetary Union (EMU), most European central banks began to closely follow the monetary policy established by the Bundesbank. The convergence of short term interest rates was due in large part to the approach of the date for EMU itself. However, the convergence of bond yields was influenced just as much by an improvement in economic fundamentals as inflation rates throughout Europe converged upon very low levels as countries tightened fiscal policy to meet the tight budget deficit constraints mandated for entry into EMU.

## THE IMPACT OF INTERNATIONAL BONDS ON A U.S. BOND PORTFOLIO: THE CASE FOR INTERNATIONAL BOND INVESTING

The above analysis demonstrates that a market-weighted portfolio of foreign-pay bonds over the 22-year period from 1978 to 1999 had a U.S. dollar average annual total return of 10.10%, slightly higher than the 9.35% average annual return of a U.S.-pay portfolio. Over shorter periods of time, however, foreign-pay bonds occasionally offered better returns, and occasionally worse. Volatility in the individual foreign markets and the aggregate markets in an international index measured in U.S. dollar terms was shown always to be greater than U.S. bond volatility, due to fluctuations in exchange rates. Finally, the correlation of foreign-pay bonds with U.S. bonds was shown to be relatively low, supporting the diversification benefits of international bonds in a U.S. portfolio. Given these risk/return characteristics, it is possible to examine the impact of foreign bonds on a U.S. fixed income portfolio.

Exhibit 48–10 shows a comparison of the compound rates of return of three portfolios: an international bond index market-weighted in the eight foreign markets studied above; the U.S. bond market; and two diversified portfolios. One portfolio is assumed to be invested 80% in the U.S. market average and 20% in the international index; the second has a 70% U.S. weighting.

For the period as a whole, the U.S. bond market underperformed the international index by a margin of 75 basis points (0.75%) per annum. The U.S. portfolio return was augmented by 15 basis points when a 20% commitment to the international bond index was made, as illustrated by portfolio 1. In portfolio 2, the return was boosted by 23 basis points through a 30% commitment to international bonds. The results are magnified if the period is divided into four segments. In 1984–1989, and again in 1990–1995, international bonds outperformed U.S. bonds by a large margin, and a 20% commitment to the international bond index added 30 basis points to total return in the 1984–1989 period and 56 basis points to total return in the 1990–1995 period. From 1978 to 1983 and 1986–1999, U.S. bonds had better returns than the international index, and the net result of a 20% commitment to international bonds subtracted only 2 basis points from returns in the 1978–1983 period, but 42 basis points in the

**E X H I B I T    48–10**

Compound Annual Rates of Return

|  | 1978–99 | 1978–83 | 1984–89 | 1990–95 | 1996–99 |
|---|---|---|---|---|---|
| International index | 10.10% | 6.09% | 15.78% | 13.77% | 2.74% |
| United States | 9.35 | 6.20 | 14.26 | 10.96 | 4.85 |
| Portfolio 1 (80% United States, 20% international index) | 9.50 | 6.18 | 14.56 | 11.52 | 4.43 |
| Portfolio 2 (70% United States, 30% international index) | 9.58 | 6.17 | 14.72 | 11.80 | 4.22 |

1996–1999 period. The 30% allocation to international bonds in portfolio 2 magnifies the over or underperformance relative to U.S. bond returns by a factor of roughly 1.5. Exhibit 48–10 is intuitively obvious from a total return standpoint. International bonds will add to the total returns of a U.S.-based portfolio when the foreign bond markets or currencies outperform the U.S. market, and they will be a drain on returns when the reverse is true.

Exhibit 48–11 shows the effect of international diversification on the standard deviation of a portfolio. Despite the substantially higher volatility of the international bond index relative to the U.S. market, a weighting in international bonds can lower the overall volatility of a U.S. portfolio because the correlation between U.S. bonds and international bonds is relatively low. Over the 1978–1999 period, a 20% weighting in international bonds added 15 basis points to total return while lowering the annual standard deviation of the portfolio from 8.89% to 7.56%. A 30% allocation to international bonds results in an even lower standard deviation of 7.23%. This supports the theory that international bonds have some diversification characteristics. Even during the 1978–1983 and 1996–1999 periods, when international bonds had a lower return and higher volatility than U.S. bonds, a 20% weighting in international bonds resulted in a reduction in portfolio annualized standard deviation of 16% and 11% relative to the U.S. bond portfolio at a cost of 2 and 42 basis points in foregone return.

During shorter periods of time, or during different time periods, the internationally diversified portfolio may have a higher volatility than the U.S. market average. For example, in the 1986–1989 period, coinciding with strong returns in the foreign bond markets and sharp fluctuation in exchange rates, international bonds increased portfolio volatility slightly, but added 95 basis points to total return. During this period, correlations of returns to the U.S. market remained relatively low although somewhat higher than in previous periods. However, the fluctuations of the currency markets added significantly to

**EXHIBIT   48–11**

Annualized Standard Deviations of Monthly Returns (in U.S. Dollars)

|  | 1978–99 | 1978–83 | 1984–89 | 1990–95 | 1996–99 |
|---|---|---|---|---|---|
| International index | 11.62% | 13.17% | 13.66% | 9.66% | 7.26% |
| United States | 8.89 | 11.83 | 9.50 | 6.79 | 3.91 |
| Portfolio 1 (80% United States, 20% international index) | 7.56 | 9.93 | 8.13 | 5.83 | 3.48 |
| Portfolio 2 (70% United States, 30% international index) | 7.23 | 9.32 | 7.88 | 5.66 | 3.54 |

the volatility (and return) of foreign bonds relative to U.S. bonds, which were enjoying a period of relative stability. The net effect was that a combination of 20% international bonds and 80% U.S. bonds was slightly more volatile than a U.S. portfolio.

The trade-off between low correlations of international returns with U.S. returns but higher volatility compared with U.S. returns also explains why most long-run studies of the appropriate mix of international bonds in an overall portfolio is in the 20 to 40% range. This is illustrated in Exhibit 48–12 using the data from Exhibits 48–10 and 48–11. A portfolio of 100% U.S. government bonds resulted in a return of 9.35% and a standard deviation of 8.89%. As international bonds were initially added to the portfolio, volatility declined and returns increased. A portfolio of 64% U.S. bonds and 36% international bonds had the lowest overall volatility; 19% lower than the volatility of the U.S. market with 27 basis points of additional return. Beyond this point, an investor could still have added to total returns by increasing the portfolio weighting in international bonds, but only at the cost of higher overall portfolio volatility. At the upper end of this range, the higher volatility of foreign bonds in U.S. dollar terms relative to U.S. bonds, despite the low correlation of foreign bonds and U.S. bonds, meant that the combined volatility of foreign and U.S. bonds was higher than for U.S. bonds alone.

**E X H I B I T    48–12**

Historical Risk/Return Trade-Off of International Diversification (1978–1999 Monthly Data)

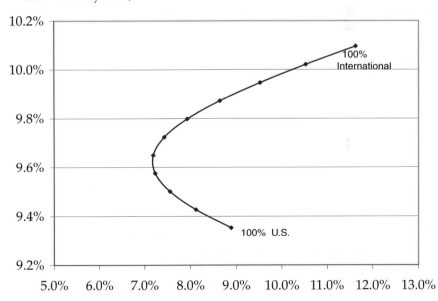

As discussed above, the rationale behind foreign-pay bond investing is twofold: the opportunity for superior returns resulting from changes in relative interest rates and exchange rates, and a reduction in long-term portfolio volatility for a given return. The objectives and requirements of each different portfolio will determine which of these considerations has greater sway over the decision to invest overseas. Although return enhancement and lower volatility are both important considerations in portfolio management, the evidence suggests that the potential for enhanced returns through active management should be the primary motive for international bond investing since the reduction in volatility of a combined U.S. and foreign portfolio is relatively small.

## ACTIVE INTERNATIONAL BOND MANAGEMENT

Thus far, the discussion has centered on passive allocations to either hedged or unhedged foreign-pay international bonds. But what of active international bond management? There is little question that, with the benefit of hindsight, a strategy of active international bond investing over the 22-year period from 1978 to 1999 could have provided enhanced returns to a U.S. dollar-based investor. Exhibit 48–2 showed the best- and worst-performing bond markets for each of the 22 years. In only one of the 22 years, 1984, was the U.S. market the best performer. In 1987, for example, a U.S. investor could have realized almost a 50% return enhancement by investing in United Kingdom bonds. Although choosing the best market is always difficult, *any* of the foreign bond markets in 1987 would have provided more attractive returns in dollar or local currency terms than the U.S. market. Against the U.S., the unhedged international bond index outperformed in 10 years, underperformed in 10 years, and had the same total return in 2 years, with an annualized outperformance of 0.74%. The crucial question, of course, is whether, without such hindsight, a portfolio manager can provide incremental return through active international investing without incurring a commensurate degree of risk. The wide disparity of returns in Exhibit 48–2 illustrates the significant opportunities in foreign-pay bonds but also points to the pitfalls of adopting an inappropriate investment strategy.

At the heart of the case for active international bond management is the ability to profit from inefficiencies in international markets. Inefficiencies arise from capital controls, restricted information flows, or simply differences in how market participants use similar information. Differences in tax treatment by countries, legal impediments that restrict the free flow of capital across borders, and differences in national character and institutions all create disparities in national investment postures. Although there is evidence to suggest that the international bond and currency markets are becoming more efficient, they are still a long way from the efficiency of the U.S. market, which benefits from the homogeneity of rules and regulations governing the investment community. In the international markets, the availability of information, particularly with regard to central bank policies, is much improved over earlier years, but a variety of impediments prevent market information from being used in a similar fashion.

A classic example of the inefficiency of international bond markets arising from differences in investment objectives is the case of Switzerland. For years, the Swiss capital markets benefited from the country's reputation as a safe haven from the Cold War, and from strict secrecy laws that emphasized anonymity. The demand among private investors for Swiss franc-denominated assets and bank accounts meant Swiss interest rates were far lower than they otherwise would have been had investors been making the same analytical decisions regarding Swiss bonds as they were making regarding other international bonds. This is one reason for the unattractive total returns on Swiss bonds. This is one reason for the unattractive total returns on Swiss bonds in the 1978–1989 period. In the late 1980s, as the Cold War wound down and the secrecy laws that attracted dubious cash to Switzerland came under fire, Swiss interest rates rose to levels more in line with economic fundamentals.

The foreign exchange markets do compensate over time for inefficiencies noticeable in various domestic bond markets, but in the short term currencies can actually magnify total return discrepancies. Economic theory teaches that interest rate differentials and currency changes reflect differential inflation rates so that currency changes equal the difference in income factors. Historically, high-inflation countries, such as Australia, with generous domestic bond returns due to high nominal income streams, have experienced a loss in the value of their currency relative to moderate-inflation countries with lower domestic nominal bond returns. Exhibit 48–13 shows that there has been a strong correlation between the change in exchange rates relative to the dollar since the demise of fixed exchange rates in the early 1970s and changes in the price level relative to the United States. The currencies of Japan, Germany, Switzerland, and the Netherlands, whose price levels grew during the 24-year period only 60 to 80% as much as in the United States, all appreciated significantly against the U.S. dollar, from 100 to 240%.

Over shorter periods of time, however, foreign exchange movements often act counter to what theory would dictate. This is most apparent in the huge total return differentials in Exhibit 48–2. A myriad of special factors determine exchange rate movements in the short term; inflation differentials is only one of these factors. Official foreign exchange intervention and different perceptions of political forces are among the many factors that distort fundamental exchange rate relationships. In view of these inefficiencies and the investment opportunities they present, active international bond investment can use active currency management to add incremental value to a U.S.-based portfolio.

## THE TOOLS OF ACTIVE MANAGEMENT

Of the three components of international bonds returns: income, capital change, and currency, only income in local currency terms, and hence the initial margin

**EXHIBIT 48-13**

Exchange Rates and Inflation Relative to U.S. 1972–1999

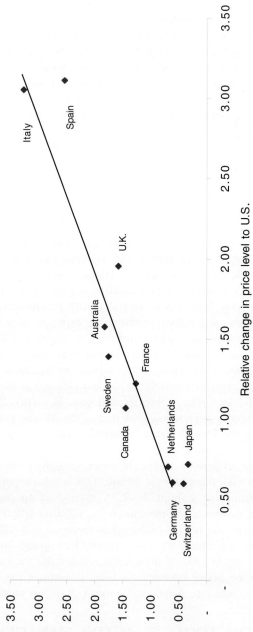

Change in Exchange Rates 1971-1999

Relative change in price level to U.S.

over the income bogey provided by U.S. alternatives, are known with certainty. However, even this income cushion will be subject to change as exchange rates fluctuate; and the shorter the investment time horizon, the less important the yield relationship with U.S. bonds. Yield spreads are measured in annual terms, so that a 2% yield advantage of Australian bonds over U.S. bonds shrinks to a mere 0.5% cushion if the investment time horizon is three months. A margin of 50 basis points is practically insignificant in the international bond markets in light of the potential volatility in currencies and relative interest rates that can occur over three months.

A simple, long-term strategy of investing in the highest-yielding international bond markets normally is not appropriate for total-return-oriented investors. This is true for two reasons. First, high interest rates usually reflect domestic economic imbalances, such as inflation (real or perceived) or strong growth in the money supply, which can lead to an erosion in local bond prices. Second, high yields often are necessary to compensate investors for an expected decline in the relative value of the local currency. Those countries with the highest income streams—such as Australia, the United Kingdom, and Canada—have experienced a weakening of their currencies versus the U.S. dollar. Over shorter periods of time, when foreign exchange movements and bond prices are not directly linked to domestic economic fundamentals but are a response to managed rates, a yield-oriented investment strategy may be appropriate. This proved to be the case in 1988 in Australia, where high yields and a strengthening currency led to generous converted U.S. dollar returns.

The factors that have a bearing on currency fluctuation, the second component of return, have been reviewed earlier. By and large, they relate to fundamental economic and political trends.[7] From a practical viewpoint, there are two main problems in using these factors to project currency movements. One relates to the analyst's ability to accurately perceive trends not already reflected in the present currency price. The second relates to the interaction of these factors and the ability to project which factors will dominate. As pointed out earlier, the component of return provided by currency changes for an international bond index over long time periods has not been large. In Exhibit 48–1, the currency contribution to the index's total return for the 1978–1999 period was shown to be 1.35% per annum. As can be seen in Exhibit 48–2, currency becomes increasingly important, however, as the time period is shortened; and changes can be even more significant for individual markets. Thus the international bond investor must be willing to make judgments on foreign exchange.

The third component of return, domestic price movements, must be analyzed both absolutely and relative to expected U.S. movements. There are sub-

---

7. For a complete discussion of the fundamental and technical factors influencing exchange rates, see Michael Rosenberg, *Currency Forecasting: A Guide to Fundamental and Technical Models of Exchange Rate Determination* (Burr Ridge, IL: Irwin, 1993) and Roger G. Clarke and Mark P. Kritzman, *Currency Management: Concepts and Practices* (Charlottesville, VA: The Research Foundation of the Institute of Chartered Financial Analysts, 1996).

stantial differences between various markets regarding the extent of government influence on the level of interest rates. However, the common key variables affecting interest rate movements are generally viewed to be the following:

1. Monetary policy, particularly with regard to exchange rates
2. The level and direction of domestic inflation rates
3. Demand for funds, which is often related to real GNP growth
4. Supply of funds
5. Fiscal policy and budget deficits
6. Social and political developments

These variables must be analyzed to assess their likely impact on the direction of interest rates in each country. As in the United States, this analysis must distinguish between movements in short rates and long terms, which most often are in the same direction but not usually of equal magnitude. When the potential shape and movement of the yield curve in each country is projected, judgments on the appropriate maturity structure can be made.

Gone are the days when interest rate projections could be made on a country-by-country basis, with no regard to the impact of international economic developments on domestic bond prices. In the early 1980s, for example, domestic economic trends and apparent government desires would have suggested lower interest levels in a number of foreign economies, but record-high US. interest rates precluded lower rates abroad without precipitating even further foreign exchange deterioration versus the U.S. dollar. In 1989, the surging deutschemark forced many European countries to keep short-term rates high relative to Germany to guard against currency volatility in the closely aligned European economies. This divergence of policy objectives led to intense pressures within the European Monetary System, which resulted in the United Kingdom and Italy leaving the EMS in 1992 and the widening of the fluctuation bands from $2\frac{1}{4}\%$ to 15% in 1993. Today, few projections of foreign interest rate levels are made without reference to expectations for German, Japanese, and United States interest rate levels. In fact, some systems, such as J. P. Morgan's RiskMetrics™, use correlations between markets to arrive at a measure of value at risk for global bond portfolios.

Clearly, then, international bond portfolio management requires ongoing economic analysis and judgment to assess the prospective exchange rate and domestic price components of return. It is important to distinguish between these two components when making judgments about prospective total returns. Whereas the income component of return is predictable, exchange rates and domestic bond prices will change, and they may not change in the same direction and with the same magnitude. Active international investment requires separate judgments to be made about the attractiveness of each country's interest rates and currency. There may be times when a bond market is attractive for interest-rate reasons and unattractive for currency reasons. Whereas one option in such a scenario would be to avoid foreign-pay investment until currency risk is deemed appropriate, another option would be to purchase the foreign bond and eliminate the foreign exchange risk by hedging the currency exposure in the forward currency markets. Currency-hedged bond investments are examined later in the chapter.

## MANAGING AN INTERNATIONAL BOND PORTFOLIO

The foregoing analysis detailing the advantages of including foreign-pay international bonds in a domestic bond portfolio still leaves many questions unanswered about how such a portfolio should be structured. Should the portfolio be global, or international (excluding the United States)? If it is international, can U.S. bonds be held opportunistically, or not at all? Can the portfolio invest in emerging markets? Can it use features and options? For currencies, or for interest rates also? Should the portfolio be completely hedged? Should proxy hedging (hedging a cash bond exposure in one currency with a short derivatives position in another currency) be allowed? Should duration or maturity limitations be imposed? Should a maximum country allocation be imposed? If so, on an absolute basis or relative to a benchmark?

### Guidelines and Benchmarks

As a global bond portfolio can be many things, a clear set of guidelines is essential for effective management. As part of the guidelines, the selection of an appropriate benchmark is desirable. Many benchmark indexes are available for global bond markets with subindexes in many permutations: ex-U.S., currency-hedged, G7 only, 1–3 year, 3–5 year, 7–10 year, emerging markets. Brady bonds, and so on. Although some clients may only wish to outperform a U.S. benchmark, an international benchmark should be selected for both measuring performance and quantifying risk.

The benchmark, with its weightings and durations for each market, serves as the baseline portfolio and the performance bogey. The portfolio manager may choose to over- or underweight a particular market based upon a favorable or unfavorable outlook in one of three ways. Hold a smaller (or even zero) percentage in the portfolio than is contained in the index; reduce the duration of the holdings in that country to below the duration of the index; or hedge out the currency risk back into dollars or into another currency expected to provide better performance or some combination of the above. Many investment managers now measure portfolio tracking error, or the expected volatility of return relative to the benchmark. Some clients have begun to include tracking error targets in investment guidelines.

Exhibit 48–14 displays the composition of two of the most widely used global government bond indices: the Salomon Brothers World Government Bond Index and the J. P. Morgan Global Government Bond Index.

**E X H I B I T    48–14**

Comparison of J. P. Morgan and Salomon Smith Barney Non-U.S.
Government Bond Indexes (December 1999)

| | J. P. Morgan Global Government Bond Index—Excluding U.S. | | Salomon Smith Barney Non-U.S. World Government Bond Index | |
|---|---|---|---|---|
| Country | Weight | Duration | Weight | Duration |
| Japan | 31.76% | 6.11 | 36.49% | 5.77 |
| Germany | 8.96 | 5.08 | 10.81 | 4.99 |
| France | 8.47 | 5.49 | 10.29 | 5.39 |
| U.K. | 6.48 | 6.95 | 8.07 | 7.01 |
| Italy | 7.97 | 5.26 | 11.06 | 4.84 |
| Holland | 2.74 | 5.41 | 3.58 | 5.10 |
| Belgium | 2.77 | 5.20 | 3.34 | 5.22 |
| Spain | 3.59 | 5.17 | 4.50 | 4.97 |
| Canada | 2.61 | 5.68 | 3.94 | 5.67 |
| Denmark | 1.35 | 4.58 | 1.65 | 4.58 |
| Australia | 0.69 | 4.66 | 0.85 | 4.34 |
| Austria | — | — | 1.19 | 5.61 |

As you can see, the two indexes differ somewhat in the weightings they
give to different markets. The largest difference is in the weight given to Japan,
which accounts for 36.5% of the Salomon index but only 32.1% of the J. P.
Morgan index. The J. P. Morgan index also has a duration of almost one-third
of a year longer than the Salomon Brothers index in both Japan and Italy. The
reason for these differences is that the Salomon index is market-weighted, based
on the total outstandings of each bond market, whereas the J. P. Morgan index
purports to use only actively traded bonds within each market. Of the universe
of non-U.S. fixed income domestic government securities, J. P. Morgan considers
only 60% to be "investable," that is, tradeable and redeemable for cash and not
appealing exclusively to domestic investors for tax or regulatory reasons. Thus,
care should be taken to select a benchmark that most closely matches the objectives of the client or fund.

The selection of a benchmark is only part of establishing an appropriate
set of guidelines. The guidelines should also be explicit on what markets or
securities may be purchased (by region, credit rating, etc.), any maturity or
credit-quality targets or constraints, the use of derivatives in either foreign
exchange or interest rate instruments, hedging policy, and so on.

## Portfolio Allocation: Selecting Markets

Actively managed portfolios (i.e., those not attempting to replicate the performance of an index) need a discipline for deciding which markets to over- or underweight within the portfolio at any one time. Loosely speaking, international bonds trade within four blocs: the dollar bloc (the United States, Canada, Australia, and New Zealand); the European bloc; Japan (which stands alone); and the emerging markets. The European bloc is subdivided into two groups: the euro zone markets which share a common currency (Germany, France, Holland, Belgium, Luxembourg, Ireland, Austria, Italy, Spain, Finland, and Portugal) and the non-euro zone markets. The U.K. often trades more on its own, influenced by both the euro zone and the U.S. as well as its own economic fundamentals.

The trading bloc construct is useful because each bloc has a benchmark market that greatly influences price movements in the other markets. Investors are often more focused on the spread level of, say, Denmark to Germany, than the absolute level of yields in Denmark. Since the beginning of European Monetary Union in 1999 the euro zone markets have traded in a much tighter range. Investors have focused on generating excess returns in the rapidly developing European corporate bond market since European Monetary Union as the scope for playing inter-country spreads has diminished. Generally speaking, when bond markets are rallying, spreads within each bloc tend to narrow, much as corporate bond spreads tend to tighten in the United States when yields on Treasuries are falling. In Europe, the peripheral markets tend to outperform the core markets in a bond market rally, much like a high beta stock will outperform during a stock market rally. However, just like high beta stocks in the equity market, peripheral bond portfolio managers tend to add risk relative to the benchmark (lengthen duration, overweight higher-yielding markets) if they are bullish and to reduce risk if they are bearish.

As bond markets within each trading bloc tend to trade in a similar fashion, international bond portfolio managers can try to outperform the index without incurring excessive additional risk by over- and underweighting selected markets within a bloc while keeping their bloc-by-bloc allocations close to the benchmark. International bond portfolio managers can also sometimes outperform their benchmarks by investing in markets outside of the index (provided that such investments are permissible under the portfolio's guidelines). For example, one of the best performing bond markets in dollar terms for 1995 was Finland, which at the time was not contained in either the Salomon or J. P. Morgan government bond indexes. The downside of this strategy can be seen in those portfolios that had a significant exposure to emerging markets during the 1997 and 1998 emerging market crises.

## CURRENCY-HEDGED BOND INVESTMENT

Foreign-pay bonds incorporate three kinds of risks: interest rate and credit risk, which are a part of all fixed income securities; and currency risk, which is unique to foreign currency-denominated securities. Once the decision is made to purchase foreign-pay bonds, the investor must decide whether the expected return from the foreign currency component of the bond is sufficient to compensate for the additional volatility inherent in a foreign currency instrument. The decision whether or not to adopt an open foreign currency position is easier to make if incremental return is the sole reason for international bond investing. However, international bonds also have important diversification benefits that result from both foreign interest-rate and currency exposure. Because foreign currency movements are a major factor behind the lower correlation of foreign-pay bonds with domestic bonds, a decision to eliminate currency risk based on a pessimistic foreign currency projection will almost certainly increase the correlation of the non-dollar bond returns with the U.S. returns relative to the correlation of unhedged returns with the U.S. returns. While highly correlated, the volatility of hedged bonds, especially a diversified group of hedged bonds, may be sufficiently lower than the U.S. markets to provide a significant diversification benefit (see Exhibit 48–15).

## Mechanics of Currency-Hedged Bond Investing

To purchase a foreign-pay bond, two separate transactions must be made. The bond must be purchased, and then the currency in which the bond is denomi-

**EXHIBIT 48–15**

Risk-Adjusted Returns

|  | Non-US WGBI | US | Non-US WGBI Hedged | 50% Hedged | S&P 500 |
|---|---|---|---|---|---|
| **1985–1999** |  |  |  |  |  |
| Return | 11.91% | 8.89% | 8.68% | 10.40% | 18.93% |
| Volatility | 10.7% | 4.9% | 3.6% | 6.4% | 14.9% |
| Sharpe | 0.55 | 0.58 | 0.74 | 0.68 | 0.86 |
| **1985–1989** |  |  |  |  |  |
| Return | 18.83% | 11.81% | 8.98% | 13.98% | 20.38% |
| Volatility | 13.6% | 6.0% | 4.0% | 8.3% | 17.6% |
| Sharpe | 0.83 | 0.71 | 0.35 | 0.77 | 0.73 |
| **1990–1994** |  |  |  |  |  |
| Return | 11.36% | 7.51% | 6.18% | 8.84% | 8.69% |
| Volatility | 8.9% | 4.4% | 3.7% | 5.4% | 12.4% |
| Sharpe | 0.69 | 0.53 | 0.27 | 0.67 | 0.28 |
| **1995–1999** |  |  |  |  |  |
| Return | 5.90% | 7.41% | 10.94% | 8.48% | 28.55% |
| Volatility | 8.3% | 4.1% | 2.9% | 4.8% | 13.8% |
| Sharpe | 0.07 | 0.50 | 1.94 | 0.65 | 1.68 |

nated must be purchased to pay for the bond. If the decision is made to hedge the foreign currency component of the bond, a simultaneous sale of the currency purchased is transacted through the forward currency market.[8] In practice, the forward sale of a currency entails no money changing hands between the currency dealer and the investor. Instead, a sale price for the currency at some point in the future is agreed upon, and the investor commits to deliver the currency at that future point and at that price. The currency dealer commits to delivering dollars in return. In other words, the investor has locked in a sale price for the foreign currency, thereby eliminating practically all exposure to currency volatility in the interim.

Currency exposure can be fully hedged using a series of forward exchange contracts matching each of the coupon payments and the final principal repayment when the foreign bond matures. Currency hedges rarely match the maturity of the underlying bonds mostly because investors rarely purchase a bond with the intention of holding it to maturity, but also because the liquidity of the forward currency markets beyond one or two years is fairly limited. The most common practice is to use rolling forward contracts from one month to one year in duration, which may be renewed at the expiration date. Rolling forward contracts are not perfect hedges because the price of the bond is difficult to predict at some point in the future, but the amount of residual foreign exchange exposure generally is quite small and has little impact on total return.

Hedged foreign bond investment reduces the currency volatility involved with international investing. Two components of return, income and currency gain or loss, become known quantities.[9] The only unknown is the local price change of the foreign bond. An investor can compare the foreign-pay bond yield combined with the known currency gain or loss embodied in the forward discount or premium with yields available on straight domestic bonds. This differential can then be incorporated into projections for foreign interest rate changes relative to domestic interest rate changes. If expected foreign bond market returns are greater than both the yield give-up (if any) required to buy the foreign bond and the forward currency discount (if any), then the hedged foreign bond is an attractive investment from a total return point of view. A simple example illustrates this relationship.

Assume that 10-year yields on United Kingdom (U.K.) bonds are 7.0% and 10-year U.S. bond yields are 6.0%. Further assume that the spot rate for sterling is 1.600 dollars per one pound sterling and that the three-month forward

---

8. Several currency-hedging alternatives, including currency swaps or options, are available, although the forward markets combine the most widely used for hedged global bond investing.
9. For a more detailed analysis of forward currency contracts and the foreign exchange markets, see Roger M. Kubarych, *Foreign Exchange Markets in the United States*. Rev. ed. (Federal Reserve Bank of New York, 1983).

rate is 1.595 dollars per pound—a 0.33% discount over three months.[10] The hedged U.K. bond return over a three-month period is as follows:

$$\text{Income} + \begin{array}{c}\text{Forward discount} \\ \text{or premium}\end{array} + \begin{array}{c}\text{U.K. bond} \\ \text{price change}\end{array}^{11}$$

$$= 7\% + (-0.33\%) + \text{U.K. bond price change}$$
$$= 1.42\% + \text{U.K. bond price change}$$

The 1.42% known return from income and currency in U.K bonds can then be compared to the 1.50% known income return from the U.S. bonds (6%/4) over three months. The differential of 0.08% must be made up by price appreciation of the U.K. bond relative to the U.S. bond. If the U.K. bond appreciates by more than 0.08% on a relative basis, the currency-hedged investment earns a superior return.

Currency-hedged international bond investment reduces the decision to buy foreign-pay bonds to a projection of relative interest rate spreads. If foreign interest rates are expected to decline relative to U.S. rates sufficiently to offset the net of the income advantage or disadvantage versus the hedge gain or cost, then hedged investment will augment total returns regardless of the course of the U.S. dollar over the holding period. The cost of the currency hedge generally is of only minor import in making total return projections, particularly over the

---

10. The discount or premium for the currency in the forward market is closely aligned with the yield spread on Eurodeposits of the same duration as the forward contract. In this example, three-month Eurosterling deposits are assumed to be 6.8%, and three-month Eurodollar deposits are 5.5%. The discount is computed as follows:

$$\text{Spot rate} \times 1 + \frac{(\text{Eurodollar rate} - \text{Eurosterling rate})}{4}$$

$$= 1.600 \times 1 + \frac{(.055 - .068)}{4}$$

$$= 1.600 \times .99675$$

$$= 1.5948$$

Therefore, $1.5948/1.6000 = .9967$ or a discount of .0033.

11. These three components are not really additive since currency gain or loss should be applied to the income and local price change as well. Nonetheless, both these effects generally are quite small. More specifically, the actual formula is as follows:

$$\begin{array}{c}\text{Forward discount} \\ \text{or premium}\end{array} + (\text{Income} + \text{U.K. bond price change}) \times 1 + \frac{(\text{forward discount or premium})}{100}$$

short term.[12] In the above example, U.K. 10-year interest rates have to decline only 2 basis points relative to U.S. rates to compensate for the cost of the hedge, an insignificant movement considering the lack of correlation between U.K. and U.S. local bond markets.

## Rolling Hedged Yields

When currency-hedged investment first became popular in the mid-1980s, reference occasionally was made to computing so-called rolling hedged yields on foreign bonds as a basis of comparison with U.S. bond yields. Rolling hedged yields are computed by adding the *annualized* discount or premium for the currency hedge to the yield-to-maturity of the foreign bond for an "all-in yield." In the above example using a U.K 10-year bond, the rolling hedged yield is calculated as follows:

Yield-to-maturity of foreign bond + Annualized discount or premium

$$= 7.0\% + -(0.33\% \times 4) = 7.0\% - 1.3\%$$
$$= 5.7\%$$

The rolling hedged yield of 5.7% of the U.K. bond could then be used as a measure of relative value versus the 6.0% yield available in the United States.

Looking at international bonds on a rolling hedged yield basis in effect separates the bond and the currency decision. Many would argue that this provides a more robust portfolio management process as it allows for a better direct comparison of various foreign bond markets with the short-term interest rate component subtracted from the bond return and attributed to the currency return.[13] If bond markets are compared using nominal rather than rolling hedged yields, there is a bias toward investing in those bond markets with the highest nominal yields regardless of the outlook for the currency. For example, although

---

12. Occasionally, hedge costs can be fairly high, particularly when short-term interest rates in the United States are low relative to foreign rates. In December 1989, three-month Eurosterling deposits were 15.2% and three-month Eurodollar deposits were 8.5%. A three-month sterling hedge back into dollars would have cost 1.7%. Nonetheless, this is relatively unusual and generally coincides with a time when the yield advantage of the foreign bond in question exceeds the U.S. rate by a large amount. In December 1989, 10-year U.K. government bonds yielded 10.5%, and U.S. Treasuries yielded 7.9%.

13. As we just demonstrated, the cost of hedging a foreign currency exposure is determined by short-term interest rate differential between the two countries. When foreign short-term interest rates are higher, hedging foreign currency exposures implies a cost; when foreign rates are lower, the hedge produces income. This means that the expected return on a currency where local interest rates are low should be higher than that of a high interest rate country to justify maintaining an unhedged currency position. Thus, this short-term interest rate differential is more properly attributed to the currency hedge decision than the country or bond decision.

Japanese bond yields were the lowest in the Salomon Smith Barney World Government Bond Index at the end of 1988 with a yield of 1.65% compared with 4.26% for the non-Yen WGBI, the Japanese bond market was the top performing bond market in 1999. In local currency terms, the Japanese bond market rose 4.8% against a loss of 0.8% for the overall index. In currency hedged terms, the Japanese bond market returned 10.4%, an additional 5.6% gained through currency hedging. If comparing bond yields on a nominal basis, a portfolio manager may have underweighted Japan, while on a rolling hedged basis, Japan was the highest yielding bond market in the index with a yield of 6.7% compared with an average rolling hedged yield of 6.1% for the WGBI.[14]

The problem with using rolling hedged yields as yield-to-maturity equivalents is that rolling hedged yield calculations assume that the cost of the hedge (i.e., the discount or premium) will not change over the life of the bond. This is almost assuredly not the case. Hedge costs vary directly with U.S. and foreign short-term interest rate spreads. When the currency hedge is rolled out after each expiration date, the new hedge cost will reflect the prevailing short-term interest rate spread, which may be very different from what it was when the hedge was last rolled. A rolling hedged yield is better used as a measure of the shape of the foreign yield curve relative to the U.S. yield curve than as a measure of prospective total returns.[15]

To restate, with currency-hedged investment, the cost of the hedge and the income advantage or disadvantage of the foreign bond is known from the outset. The investor is left with the decision of whether the foreign bond market will have better local price appreciation relative to the U.S. market and whether the expected marginal appreciation will be enough to compensate for any income or hedge costs that may accompany the foreign bond purchase. Analyzing bonds in this way also forces a separation of the currency decision from the bond decision.

## Hedged versus Unhedged Foreign Bonds

The ability to participate in foreign interest-rate cycles without the added volatility of currency movements is appealing from both a theoretical and a practical standpoint. Many analysts and portfolio managers have argued that currency-hedged investing is a priori superior to unhedged investing because of the former's more favorable risk/return characteristics over the long term. There is

---

14. Currency hedged returns in the Salomon Smith Barney World Government Bond Index are calculated using one-month forward foreign exchange contracts. The rolling hedged yield was calculated by annualizing the one-month forward foreign exchange rate premium.
15. This is true because hedge costs are a function of relative short rates, and the yield spread between two 10-year bonds is a function of relative long rates. High-rolling hedged yields reflect more positively shaped foreign yield curves, which, taken alone, say little about prospective total returns.

some theoretical justification to this argument for dollar-based investors. If forward exchange rates, which govern hedge costs, accurately reflect the expected average movement of foreign currencies versus the dollar (i.e., forward rates do not include an embedded risk premium or discount), then hedged foreign bond returns will be equivalent to unhedged returns over time. Research tends to support this theory, although, as was mentioned earlier, total return comparisons between foreign and domestic bonds, hedged or unhedged, are somewhat beholden to the time period chosen. For example, for the period 1985–1999, the Salomon Non-U.S. World Government Bond Index returned 11.91% in U.S. dollar terms, 3.2% more than the hedged Non-U.S. World Government Bond Index. However, if we exclude the first three years of the index, 1985–1987 when the dollar was declining sharply against all currencies from its 1984 peak and currencies contributed more than 23% on average to index returns, the picture changes dramatically. Over the last 12 years of the index, 1988–1999, the unhedged Non-U.S. World Government Bond Index underperformed the hedged index by 1.2%.

The currency component of investing in unhedged foreign-pay international bonds accounts for much of the volatility in total return. Investing in international bonds on a hedged basis reduces the return in most periods, but also substantially reduces the return volatility. As can be seen in Exhibit 48–15, over the 15-year history of the WGBI, hedged international bonds returned far less than unhedged international bonds and even lagged the U.S. component of the WGBI slightly. However, the volatility of the hedged non-U.S. index was one third that of the unhedged index, and three quarters that of the U.S. component. To compare returns on a risk-adjusted basis, we can use the Sharpe ratio.[16] Despite the higher return of the unhedged index, its risk-adjusted return is lower than the hedged index and the U.S. bond component alone of the 1985–1999 period. A 50% hedged portfolio offers a compromise in that its return is virtually midway between the return of the unhedged index and the U.S. bond component with substantially lower volatility than the unhedged index giving it a higher Sharpe ratio than either the unhedged index or U.S. component. The S&P 500 index is also included for comparison. In the last five years, the S&P 500 has experienced extraordinarily strong returns of nearly 30% per annum. However, in the 1985–1989 and 1990–1995 periods, equity market returns were in line with international bond returns, and often less attractive on a risk-adjusted basis.

The advantage of using a partially hedged benchmark versus a fully hedged or fully unhedged benchmark are illustrated in Exhibit 48–16. The 50% hedged portfolio offers better diversification with some small reduction in return

---

16. The Sharpe ratio is used to compare portfolio returns on a risk-adjusted basis; here we are using it to compare asset class returns. The Sharpe ratio divides the portfolio return in excess of the risk free rate by the portfolio's volatility. The formula is $S = (R_p - RFR)/\sigma_p$.

**E X H I B I T   48–16**

Exchange Rates and Inflation Relative to U.S. 1972–1995

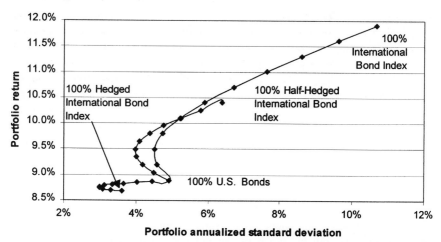

when a modest allocation to international bonds is added to U.S. bond portfolios. A half-hedged benchmark also offers other advantages to a fully hedged or fully unhedged benchmark. The chief benefit is that it eliminates the asymmetric constraints on taking active currency views on the U.S. dollar. When managed against an unhedged benchmark, a portfolio manager can hedged foreign currency positions when the dollar is expected to strengthen, but when the dollar is expected to weaken the portfolio can hold no more foreign currency than the 100% contained in the benchmark without adding leverage to the portfolio.[17]

## CONCLUSION

International bonds have historically provided both superior returns and a risk-reduction benefit when added to portfolios of U.S. Treasuries. Active management of an international bond portfolio offers the possibility of further enhancing returns as market inefficiencies and varying economic cycles result in imperfectly correlated bond market movements. However, a thorough understanding of capital flows, economic fundamentals, and local market structure is required to anticipate changes in bond and currency prices and to outperform the international index over time.

Some investors have turned to currency-hedged international bond investment to participate in foreign interest rate cycles without taking currency risk.

---

17. For a full discussion of the benefits of utilizing a partially hedged benchmark see the currency discussion in the research monograph *The International Equity Commitment*, by Steve Gorman, AIMR 1998.

Hedged investment is appropriate when the prospects for foreign bond markets are attractive relative to the prospects for U.S. bonds, irrespective of potential currency movements. Although hedged international bonds have a greater correlation with U.S. bonds due to the lack of currency fluctuation, evidence suggests that hedged bonds can reduce the volatility of a U.S.-based portfolio and occasionally augment portfolio returns. A half-hedged, or partially-hedged benchmark provides both diversification and return potential while providing additional scope for deriving gains from active currency management.

In the long run, there is no a priori reason to expect international bonds, hedged or unhedged, to provide superior returns relative to U.S. bonds. To the extent that governments continue to remove the remaining barriers to world capital flows, fixed income returns and interest-rate volatility in the major markets can be expected to converge. In the meantime, the variance of monetary, fiscal, and political trends and policies among countries suggest that, from time to time, particular markets will offer better investment value than the U.S. market.

CHAPTER **49**

# INTERNATIONAL FIXED INCOME INVESTING: THEORY AND PRACTICE

**Michael R. Rosenberg, Ph.D.**
Managing Director
Global Head of FX Research
Deutsche Bank

In a recent Greenwich Associates study of institutional bond buying in the United States, two emerging trends appeared significant to the future direction of the fixed income investment business. According to the study, the primary trend emerging among U.S. bond buyers is the increasing globalization of bond portfolios. The secondary trend, which is directly related to the primary trend, is the greatly increased use of risk management instruments to deal with the risk and volatility of U.S. portfolio managers' increasingly diversified international bond portfolios.

These trends toward globalization and the more sophisticated use of risk management tools are growing at an increasingly rapid pace among European and Japanese investors as well and have caused a need for more detailed information on the theory and practice of global bond portfolio management. The purpose of this chapter is to address that need by critically analyzing the case for international fixed income diversification from a risk/return and active-management standpoint, and by providing internationally minded investors with the basic tools to actively manage their global bond portfolios.

The chapter is divided into six sections. The first section examines the contribution that international bonds can make to the risk/return profile of a broadly diversified portfolio. Contrary to the generally accepted notion that substantial risk reduction opportunities are available, the evidence suggests that only a modest reduction in portfolio risk can be achieved through international diversification on an unhedged basis. The second section analyzes whether a stronger case can be made for international diversification on a hedged basis. Once again, contrary to the growing belief that hedged diversification guarantees investors less risk without sacrificing portfolio return, it can be demonstrated that if transaction costs and other fees associated with hedging are taken into consideration, international diversification on a currency hedged basis may prove to be more expensive than not hedging at all.

The third section focuses on whether there are unique "free-lunch" strategies that investors can exploit. One favorite strategy has been to favor markets that offer relatively high yields. We show that high-yield strategies can prove to be quite risky and are by no means a free lunch.

The fourth section attempts to salvage the case for international fixed income investment by directing the focus away from purported free-lunch strategies and toward tactical asset allocation considerations. Sizable differences in total return exist among the domestic and overseas markets that, if exploited, can substantially enhance the total-return prospects of an otherwise purely domestic bond portfolio. Thus, domestic investors will profit by viewing foreign bonds not as a *separate* asset class for *all* seasons, but as a *tactical* asset for *selected* seasons.

The fifth section provides internationally minded investors with general guidelines for setting up and constructing a global bond portfolio. The sixth and final section provides both a general framework for designing an active global bond portfolio strategy and a disciplined approach to assess the key decision criteria—the currency, market, and bond selection decisions—that global bond investors must address.

# THE CASE FOR INTERNATIONAL FIXED INCOME DIVERSIFICATION

Proponents of international fixed income diversification quite often point to reams of charts and tables that purport to show significant risk-reduction possibilities from combining U.S. and foreign bonds in a passively managed diversified portfolio. Unfortunately, our research does not corroborate that evidence. Although portfolio risk reduction is possible through international diversification, our research indicates that the extent of risk reduction from passive management is fairly modest.

Exhibit 49–1 plots the cumulative total returns on U.S. and foreign dollar-denominated bonds from March 1973 (the beginning of floating exchange rates) to December 1995. U.S. bonds are represented by the Merrill Lynch Domestic Master Index, which includes government and corporate debt and, since 1975, mortgage securities. The foreign bond market performance index splices two international bond indexes together: the InterSec Research Non-North American Bond Index from 1973 to 1984 and the Salomon Brothers World Bond Index from 1985 to 1995, both measured in U.S. dollar terms. Note that in Exhibit 49–1 the performance of the U.S. and overseas markets differed widely over interim periods: The foreign markets were stronger in the late 1970s, the U.S. market was stronger in the early 1980s, and the foreign markets regained superiority during 1985–95. Over the entire period, the evidence shows that the

Total Return Performance of the Non-U.S.$ and the U.S. Bond Market since 1973 (in U.S. Dollar Terms)

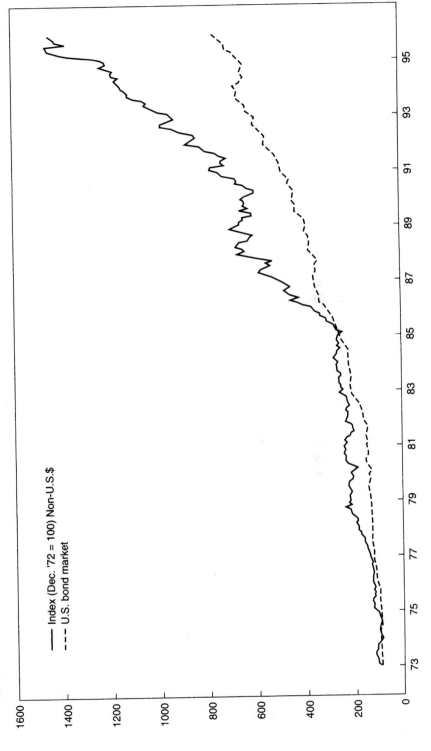

—— Index (Dec. '72 = 100) Non-U.S.$
- - - U.S. bond market

average annualized return in U.S. dollar terms was 12.2% on foreign bonds and 9.2% per annum on U.S. domestic bonds. We attribute that disparity to sampling error over the time period chosen for study. In the long run, there is no a priori reason why the expected return on foreign bonds in U.S. dollar terms should be higher or lower than the expected return on U.S. domestic bonds. Indeed, as Exhibits 49–2 and 49–3 show, the cumulative returns on U.S. and foreign bonds were the same over the 1973–85 period, and were also quite similar over the 1988–94 period.

The evidence shows that the volatility of foreign bond market returns in U.S. dollar terms has been considerably greater than the volatility of U.S. domestic bond market returns. Between March 1973 and December 1995, the standard deviation of monthly returns was 12.2% on foreign bonds in U.S. dollar terms, whereas it was 6.1% on U.S. domestic bonds. The roughly 100% difference in volatility was due entirely to the impact of the dollar's volatility; in fact, foreign bond market returns in local currency terms were, on average, less volatile than U.S. bond market returns.

Although foreign bonds in U.S. dollar terms were more volatile than U.S. domestic bonds, it was still possible to combine foreign bonds with U.S. domestic bonds in a diversified bond portfolio to reduce overall portfolio risk, because the returns on U.S. and foreign bonds are not highly positively correlated. The evidence shows that the average correlation of monthly U.S. and foreign bond returns for the 1973–95 period was only 0.34.

Exhibit 49–4 shows how much portfolio risk could have been reduced through passive international diversification on an unhedged basis. This graph demonstrates how an investor could have varied the allocation of an internationally diversified bond portfolio between dollar and nondollar bonds from March 1973 to December 1995 to achieve a certain level of return for a given level of risk. For example, if a U.S. investor had committed 100% of his or her funds to the U.S. domestic bond market, the average annual return would have been 9.2% and the annualized standard deviation of monthly returns would have been 6.1%. Allocating 10% of his or her funds to foreign bonds and leaving the balance in U.S. domestic bonds would have yielded a slightly higher annual return of 9.6%, with a portfolio standard deviation of 6.0%. That constitutes a 0.1% reduction in portfolio volatility from the 100% U.S. allocation case. At that allocation, overall portfolio risk would have been minimized. Any commitment to foreign bonds beyond 10% would have increased portfolio risk.

The extent of risk reduction from passive international fixed income diversification appears quite modest, so much so that it hardly seems worthwhile. In fact, one major U.S. pension consultant, after examining the historical evidence, concluded that "nondollar bond investment is a diversification opportunity that U.S. investors can afford to pass up, especially those with smaller funds and limited resources for the conduct of their investment program.

Total Return Performance: U.S. & Foreign Bonds 1973–1985 (in U.S. Dollar Terms)

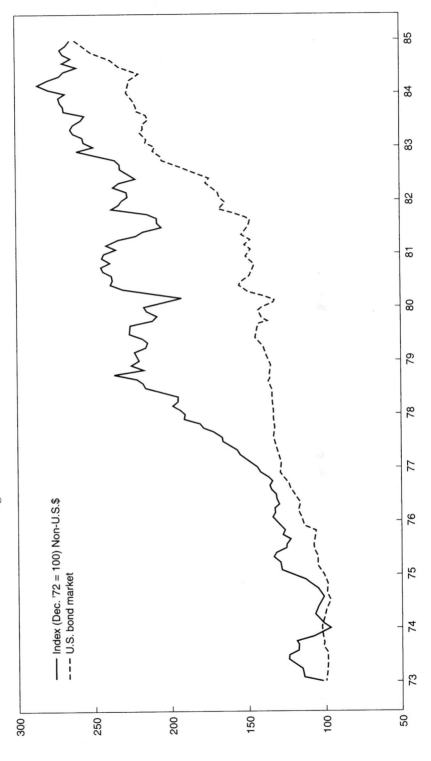

—— Index (Dec. '72 = 100) Non-U.S.$

- - - U.S. bond market

Total Return Performance: U.S. & Foreign Bonds 1988–1995 (in U.S. Dollar Terms)

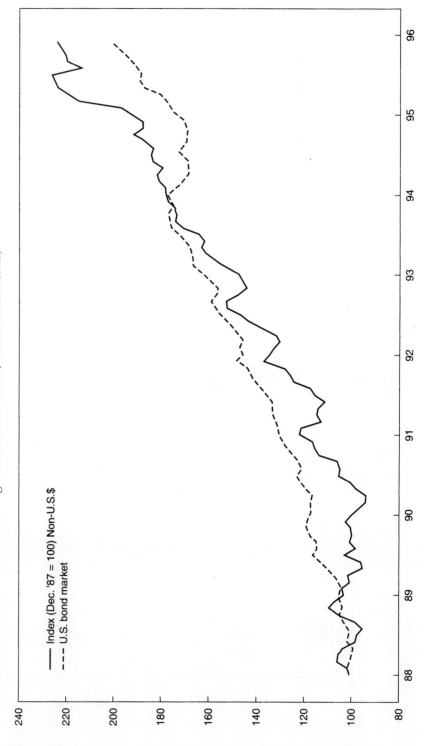

**EXHIBIT 49–4**

Risk/Return Profile of Passively Managed International Fixed Income Portfolios (1973–1995)

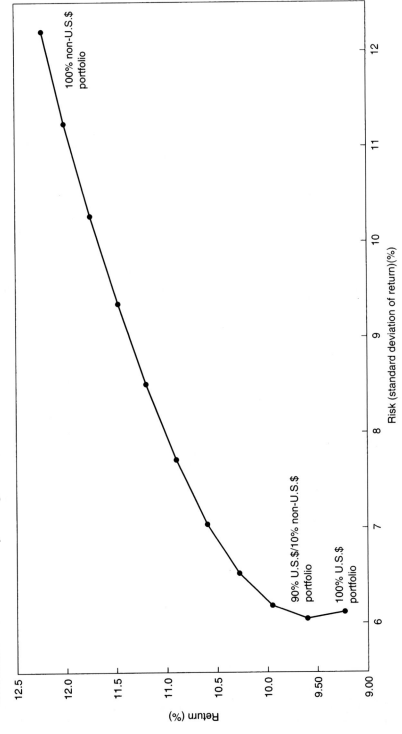

# WHY THERE IS NO FREE LUNCH IN CURRENCY-HEDGED FOREIGN BONDS

In order to salvage the case for nondollar bonds, a number of analysts have argued for hedged rather than unhedged foreign bonds in U.S. portfolios. Those analysts contend that because currency volatility adds to the volatility of a foreign bond portfolio, hedging away currency risk in the forward exchange market should render hedged foreign bonds less volatile than unhedged foreign bonds. At the same time, currency hedging should not involve any loss of long-term expected return, assuming no risk premium is embedded in forward exchange rates. Taken together, a policy of purchasing hedged foreign bonds should offer greater risk reduction with no loss of expected return compared to traditional unhedged international diversification. That assessment has led a number of observers to conclude that hedged foreign bonds offer U.S. investors a free lunch.

Had U.S. investors bought the idea of currency-hedged foreign bonds during the 1978–87 period, they would indeed have received a free lunch, as the historical evidence clearly shows (see Exhibit 49–5a). The return on hedged nondollar bonds (11.0% per annum) over the 1978–87 period closely matched the return on unhedged nondollar bonds (10.9% per annum), but the monthly annualized standard deviation of return on hedged foreign bonds was significantly lower than the comparable volatility of unhedged foreign bonds (5.9% vs. 13.6%). As Exhibit 49–5a shows, had U.S. investors diversified into nondollar bonds, they could have reduced portfolio risk by purchasing either hedged or unhedged nondollar bonds, but the extent of available risk reduction was much more dramatic for diversification into hedged nondollar bonds. In the case of unhedged nondollar bond diversification, the modestly lower overall portfolio risk was due to the low average monthly correlation between U.S. and unhedged foreign bonds (0.42). In contrast, in the case of hedged nondollar bond diversification, the dramatically lower overall portfolio risk was due largely to the low volatility of hedged foreign bonds (5.9%) compared to U.S. bond market volatility (10.6%).

Although the historical evidence indicates that a free lunch existed during the 1978–87 period, we were never comfortable with the idea that this free lunch would persist indefinitely. After all, one of the first basic principles we learn in introductory economics courses is that there is no such thing as a free lunch. We questioned the validity of the free-lunch hypothesis, largely because it cannot hold for all investors. Exhibit 49–5b looks at the risk/return trade-off that would have faced Japanese fund managers had they invested in hedged nonyen bonds during the 1978–87 period. The evidence clearly shows that hedged nonyen bonds fared poorly compared to yen domestic bonds in terms of both risk and return, which is opposite to the case for U.S. investors. The reason is fairly straightforward: U.S. domestic bonds were more volatile than their foreign counterparts over the 1978–87 period, whereas Japanese domestic

**EXHIBIT   49–5**

(*a*) Historical Risk/Return Trade-Off: U.S. Domestic Bonds versus Hedged andUnhedged Nondollar Bonds (Annualized Monthly Returns and Standard Deviations)
(*b*) Historical Risk/Return Trade-Off: Yen Bonds versus Hedged and Unhedged Nonyen Bonds (Annualized Monthly Returns and Standard Deviations)

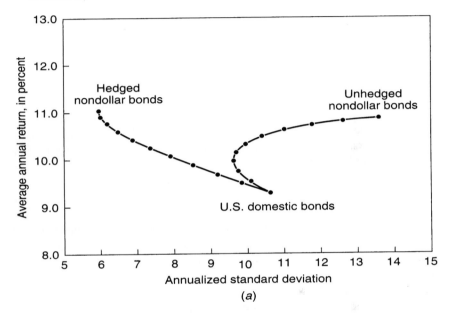

(*a*)

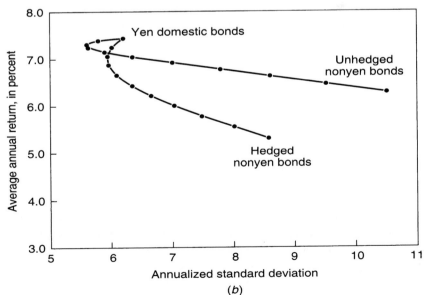

(*b*)

bonds were less volatile than their foreign counterparts. However, there is no reason why either of those trends must persist.

In fact, we attributed the lower average volatility of hedged foreign bonds relative to U.S. bonds to two factors that we felt would not likely recur in the future: (1) institutional rigidities such as capital flow restrictions and heavily regulated capital markets in a number of key overseas financial centers, which may have limited their volatility, at least artificially, and (2) monetary policies in the late 1970s and early 1980s in the United States that were more unstable than in Germany or Japan, which accentuated the U.S. bond market's volatility.

Indeed, changes on both counts are now taking place that are contributing to a worldwide convergence in bond market volatilities. Regarding the first point, we are presently witnessing a major liberalization and deregulation of many of the overseas markets. Regarding the second point, we see growing evidence of a convergence of world inflation rates and macroeconomic policies. As a result, the evidence now shows that had U.S. investors shifted funds from U.S. to hedged foreign bonds over the more recent 1988–1995 period, they would have had to sacrifice considerable return in order to achieve any meaningful reduction in portfolio risk (see Exhibit 49–6). In other words, the free lunch that was available in 1978–87 is now gone.

Theoretically, it is more reasonable to assume not only that long-term expected returns should be the same across markets, but that their expected risks should be the same as well. If we make the assumption that both the expected returns and expected volatilities will be the same on U.S. and hedged foreign bonds, it can be shown that it makes no difference in terms of long-term risk reduction whether or not a foreign bond portfolio is hedged.

Consider the assumptions outlined in Exhibit 49–7. The table shows that the return on U.S. bonds and unhedged foreign bonds was 9.3% per annum over the 1973–85 period. We also show the historical volatilities of U.S. and unhedged foreign bonds (10.6% and 13.6%, respectively) for the 1973–85 period. Now let's make the assumption that the return on hedged foreign bonds and the volatility of hedged foreign bonds just matches the U.S. historical average return and volatility. It is really not important to this exercise which level of volatility is assumed as long as the volatilities of U.S. and hedged foreign bonds are assumed to be the same. Finally, lets assume that the average historical correlations between U.S. bonds and hedged and unhedged foreign bonds will continue to prevail. Note that the monthly correlation of U.S. bond returns with unhedged foreign bond returns was 0.42, which was significantly lower than the 0.54 correlation of U.S. bond returns with hedged foreign bond returns. This is because currency fluctuations reduce the co-movement of U.S. and foreign bonds. This suggests that although unhedged foreign bonds will tend to be more volatile than their hedged counterparts, because of currency volatility, unhedged foreign bonds have the upper hand over hedged foreign bonds because they are more efficient diversifiers when a combined U.S.–foreign bond portfolio is created.

EXHIBIT 49–6

U.S. vs. Hedged Foreign Bonds: Historical Risk/Return Trade-Offs—1978–87 and 1988–95

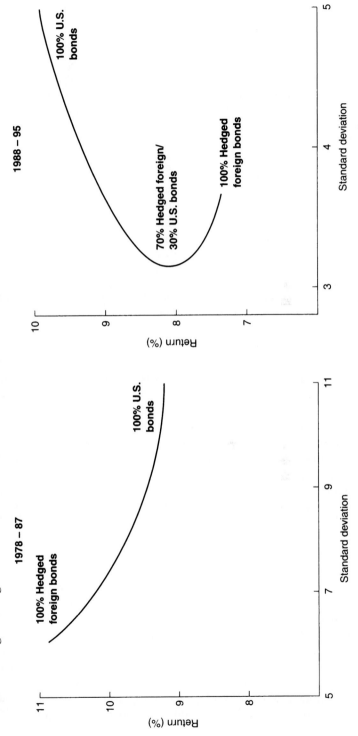

## EXHIBIT 49-7

Theoretical Long-Run Expected Returns, Standard Deviations, and Correlations for U.S. Domestic, Hedged Nondollar, and Unhedged Nondollar Bonds

|  | Expected Return | Expected Standard Deviation | Correlation with U.S. Bonds |
|---|---|---|---|
| U.S. domestic bonds | 9.3[a] | 10.62[a] | 1.00[a] |
| Hedged nondollar bonds | 9.3 | 10.62 | 0.54[a] |
| Unhedged nondollar bonds | 9.3 | 13.57[a] | 0.42[a] |

[a] Historic average.

If these assumptions are plausible, then the diversification benefits derived from portfolio combinations of U.S. and hedged foreign bonds can be shown to be the same as those derived from portfolio combinations of U.S. and unhedged foreign bonds. This is demonstrated in Exhibit 49–8: Whichever diversification route is taken, the same minimum risk portfolio results. Hedged foreign bonds have an advantage over their unhedged counterparts in that they are less volatile, but unhedged foreign bonds have an advantage over their hedged counterparts in that they are more efficient diversifiers. When combined with U.S. bonds, both advantages cancel each other out, such that hedged and unhedged foreign bonds offer the same long-term risk-reduction benefits.

That analysis leads to what I humbly term *Rosenberg Proposition I.*

### Rosenberg Proposition I

*In a world free of transaction costs, the amount of risk reduction available from international bond diversification in the long run is independent of whether or not currency risk is hedged.*

Followers of finance theory will recognize this to be a paraphrase of the famous Modigliani–Miller proposition that the value of the firm is independent of its capital structure (debt/equity mix). The conclusion from Rosenberg Proposition I is that hedged international fixed income diversification offers no advantage over unhedged international fixed income diversification in the long run. Unfortunately, the story does not end there; there are transaction costs and other fees associated with continuously hedging a foreign bond portfolio. Exhibit 49–9 lists the extra costs and fees associated with always hedging an otherwise passively managed foreign bond portfolio. Those include (1) the execution costs of buying and selling forward exchange (in terms of bid-ask spreads); (2) additional settlement costs in the form of custodial fees; and (3) additional man-

**EXHIBIT   49–8**

Alternative Paths to Achieve the Minimum Risk Portfolio through Diversified Combinations of U.S. and Hedged/Unhedged Foreign Bonds

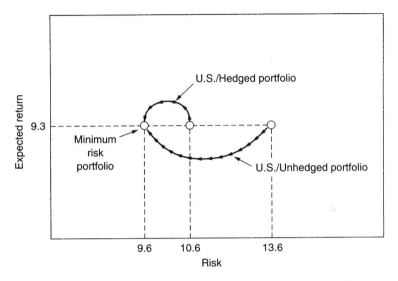

**EXHIBIT   49–9**

Additional Costs Associated with Managing a Continuously Hedged Foreign Bond Portfolio

|  | Cost in Basis Points |
| --- | --- |
| Execution costs | 5 |
| Settlement costs | 5 |
| Management fees | 10–20 |
| Total | 20–30 |

Source: Roger G. Clarke and Mark P. Kritzman, *Currency Management: Concepts and Practices* (AIMR, 1996).

agement fees, because a continuously hedged foreign bond portfolio, unlike a passively managed unhedged foreign bond portfolio, requires constant rollover of short-term hedges. Clarke and Kritzman estimate the additional cost to be 20–30 basis points if the forward hedges are rolled over on a monthly basis. Those additional costs and fees must then be subtracted from the expected return on hedged foreign bonds, and the resulting net return can then be compared to U.S. and unhedged foreign bond market returns. If we factor that lower expected return into the theoretical diversification exercise described in Exhibit 49–8, it becomes evident that the unhedged foreign bond diversification route will yield a higher expected return for the same level of risk than the hedged foreign bond diversification route.

That leads to what I have termed *Rosenberg Proposition II.*

### Rosenberg Proposition II

*In a world where transaction costs and management fees are not insignificant, hedged foreign bonds will be a more expensive means than unhedged foreign bonds to achieve risk reduction.*

Thus, our findings suggest that from a long-term perspective, instead of offering a free lunch, currency hedging may prove to be a more expensive lunch than if one never hedged at all. This does not mean that we do not favor hedging at all. What it does mean is that we favor hedging only on a selective basis when conditions warrant it. Pursuing an alternative policy of continuously hedging will prove to be a costly means to achieve guaranteed long-term risk reduction.

## WHY THERE IS NO FREE LUNCH IN HIGH-YIELD FOREIGN BONDS

Ever-eager to build a case for international fixed income diversification, a number of analysts have suggested that investors may be able to earn excess returns by overweighting high-yield markets and underweighting low-yield markets in a diversified international bond portfolio. The rationale for implementing such a strategy is to exploit what appears to be persistent departures from uncovered interest-rate parity. The theory of uncovered interest-rate parity (UIP) states that the return on high-yield markets should match the return on low-yield markets when the returns are expressed in a common currency. UIP will be valid if high-yielding markets have depreciating currencies and low-yielding markets have appreciating currencies, with the loss or gain on the exchange rate offsetting, on average, the yield differential between the high- and low-yielding markets.

While sensible in theory, the UIP hypothesis does not hold up to empirical verification. Indeed, the evidence shows that currencies with relatively high interest rates normally do not depreciate as much as interest-rate differentials predict, while currencies with relatively low interest rates do not rise in value as much as interest-rate differentials anticipate. If such departures from UIP can be counted on to persist in the future, investors would, over time, be able to earn higher average returns by overweighting the high-yield bond markets.

The problem with adopting a strategy that favors the high-yield markets is that it can be extremely risky. While it is true that most empirical studies find evidence of persistent departures from UIP in the past, one cannot guarantee that the departures from UIP will continue in the future. There is no agreement among economists as to what led to the departures from UIP in the past. Several analysts contend that high-yield markets offer higher average returns because they are perceived to be riskier assets. Other analysts contend that the market-place systematically overpredicts the potential weakness of high-yield "soft" currencies and at the same time overpredicts the potential strength of the low-yield "hard" currencies. Still others contend that interest-rate differentials be-tween high- and low-yielding markets embody, in part, the market's anticipation of a possible dramatic event that may upset the currency markets. If that dramatic event fails to take place during the sample period that UIP is tested, high-yield markets may appear to offer higher average returns than low-yield markets over that period. A dramatic event, such as a speculative attack, normally has a small probability of occurring, but as long as there is some possibility of a crisis occurring, this possibility will be reflected in yield spreads. Over a sufficiently long period, a speculative attack may eventually take place, thereby validating UIP as a long-run proposition. But over short- and even medium-term horizons when no such attack takes place, it may appear that yield spreads overpredict the underlying weakness of high-yield currencies.

Consider the case of the ERM collapse in 1992–93 and the subsequent weakness in many of the European currencies versus the deutsche mark. Prior to the ERM collapse, the cumulative return on high-yield European currencies substantially exceeded the cumulative return on DM-denominated investments. For example, in the case of the Italian lira, the cumulative return on lira money market investments, when expressed in DM terms, far exceeded the cumulative return on deutsche mark money market investments over the January 1987 to August 1992 period (see Exhibit 49–10). That outperformance was due largely to a comfortably wide yield spread between Italian and German money market investments that was not completely offset by the lira's modest depreciation versus the deutsche mark over that period. Italian investments offered a large yield pickup over German investments because the market perceived that there was significant risk in owning lira assets and that at some point a dramatic event might cause the lira to come under heavy downward pressure versus the deutsche mark. Since no dramatic event took place over the January 1987 to August 1992 period that upset the lira/DM crossrate, the cumulative return on lira-denominated investments far exceeded the cumulative return on deutsche mark-denominated investments over that period.

However, market perceptions about the potential riskiness of lira invest-ments eventually proved to be correct. The lira came under heavy downward pressure in September 1992 and was first devalued and then permitted to float freely. The lira remained under heavy downward pressure for the next 2½ years, with the net decline in the lira far exceeding the Italian–German yield spread. In fact, as shown in Exhibit 49–10, the cumulative excess returns available on lira denominated assets were completely erased in 1992–95.

To put it simply, what goes around comes around—UIP appears to be valid over very long-run periods, although significant departures will exist over

**EXHIBIT 49–10**

Total Return Performance of Italian and German Money-Market Investments
(In Deutsche mark Terms)

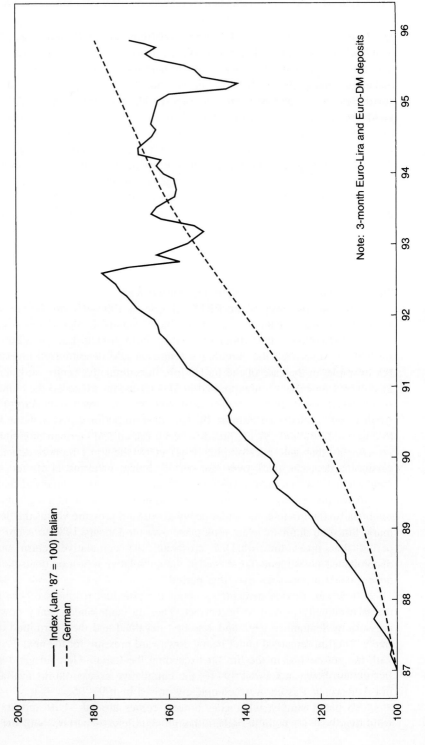

Index (Jan. '87 = 100) Italian
German

Note: 3-month Euro-Lira and Euro-DM deposits

short- and medium-term periods. This example demonstrates that one should be skeptical of strategies that purportedly guarantee investors a free lunch. The foreign exchange and international bond markets are among the most actively traded markets in the world. It is highly unlikely that these markets could be so inefficient as to generate unexploited profit opportunities from purported free-lunch strategies.

## THE CASE FOR ACTIVE MANAGEMENT

If a strong case cannot be made for currency-hedged foreign bonds or high-yield foreign bonds, can the case for international fixed income diversification be salvaged? The answer to that question is an emphatic yes. If we are to build a case for nondollar bonds, we must admit that, in terms of reducing portfolio risk, the benefits of passive international fixed income diversification are limited, whether or not the underlying foreign currency exposure is hedged. Instead, the case for international fixed income diversification needs to be directed away from risk-reduction considerations and toward total-return-enhancement considerations. Foreign bonds offer U.S. investors a unique opportunity to enhance the return on their U.S. fixed income portfolios, but that return enhancement opportunity is available only through successful active management, not through purported free-lunch strategies. It is widely recognized that the differences in total-return performance among the competing subsectors of the U.S. domestic bond market are relatively small when compared to the sizable differences in performance that exist between the U.S. and overseas markets. If U.S. fund managers can exploit such differences by correctly shifting their portfolios from U.S. to foreign bonds and then back when conditions warrant, there will be great interest in the use of foreign bonds, not as a separate asset class for all seasons, but as a tactical asset for selected reasons.

One way of measuring the total-return opportunity set available to international investors is to examine the total-return spread between the best- and worst-performing markets over time. The difference between the best and worst performers gives some indication of the return that could have been earned if an investor had correctly underweighted the weak markets and overweighted the strong markets. Another way of measuring the total-return opportunity set is to examine the total-return spread between the strongest market and the investor's homebase market.

Exhibit 49–11 shows the total-return spread between the best- and worst-performing markets over the 1973–95 period, as well as the U.S. domestic bond market's total return over the same period. On average, there has been a 33% per annum difference (that is, 3300 basis points) in total return performance between the strongest- and weakest-performing markets during that period. That suggests that there have been substantial opportunities to increase total return by correctly overweighting the strong markets and underweighting the weak.

## EXHIBIT 49-11

Total Return Performance of Major Gov't. Bond Markets in U.S. Dollar Terms
Best, Worst, and U.S. Market Total Returns

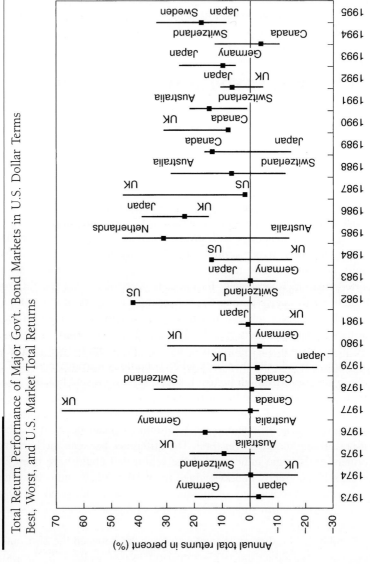

The U.S. domestic bond market was the best-performing market only twice, in 1982 and 1984. On four occasions—1977, return performance 1978, 1987, and 1990—it was at or near the bottom of the international bond total return performance list. On average, the spread between the best-performing market and the U.S. market has been about 15% per annum. Thus, U.S. investors who could correctly forecast relative market performance could have significantly enhanced their total-return performance had they taken a global perspective in their bond investment decisions.

If U.S. bond investors accept the notion that the tactical use of foreign bonds can help boost the performance of their domestic portfolios, then we should expect to see a growing number of U.S. fund managers selectively adding foreign bonds in an aggressive manner to help them outperform their domestic benchmark, such as the Merrill Lynch Domestic Master Index or the Lehman Government Corporate Bond Index. In fact, we believe that the way the international fixed income investment game is played in the U.S. will change radically in the coming years, from a dedicated international bond management strategy that treats foreign bonds as a *separate* asset class to one that treats foreign bonds as a tactical asset to help domestic-oriented investors outperform their domestic benchmark and competition. To get an idea of how U.S. fund managers may use foreign bonds on a tactical basis, let's consider the following exercise.

Consider a hypothetical U.S. domestic bond fund that establishes internal investment policy guidelines in the following manner: The fund will allocate 20% of its portfolio to foreign bonds and the remainder to U.S. domestic and corporate bonds when it is believed that the dollar is trending lower. When it is believed that the dollar is trending higher, the fund will allocate 100% to U.S. domestic bonds (see Exhibit 49–12). To determine whether the dollar's trend is up or down, a simple trading rule is followed. If the dollar's trade-weighted value on a monthly average basis lies below its 12-month moving average, the dollar's trend is considered to be down, and vice versa. Hence the crossover of the 1- and 12-month averages in the dollar's value is used as the criterion to adjust the domestic/foreign mix. Exhibit 49–13 shows that the dollar has had

**E X H I B I T   49–12**

Investment Policy Guidelines—Hypothetical U.S. Domestic Bond Portfolio

| *Recommended Allocation to Domestic and Foreign Bonds* | | |
|---|---|---|
| | **Bearish on the Dollar** | **Bullish on the Dollar** |
| U.S. domestic bonds | 80% | 100% |
| Foreign bonds | 20 | 0 |

**EXHIBIT 49–13**

Long-Run Trend in the U.S. Dollar Index

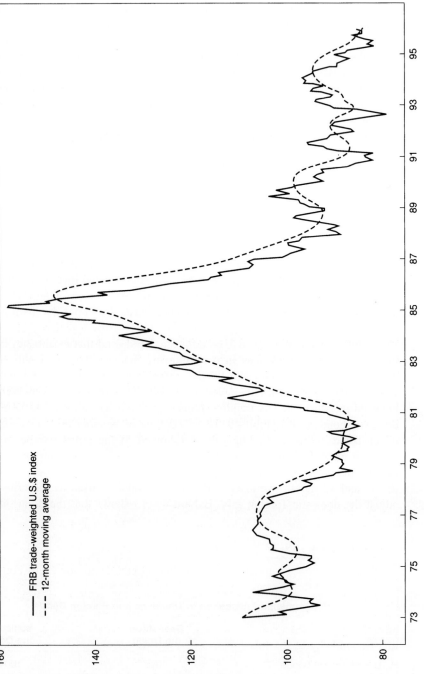

several major cycles in the past 23 years. The 1- and 12-month moving average trading rule defines those broad cycles fairly clearly, although several moving average crossovers have proved to be false signals.

We have simulated the total-return outcome (excluding transaction costs) that could have been achieved had a U.S. bond manager followed our trading rule over the 1973–95 period. Exhibit 49–14 shows the cumulative differences in total return performance between the Merrill Lynch Domestic Master Index and the active domestic/foreign bond strategy. It is assumed that a U.S. bond manager starts out owning 100% of the Merrill Lynch Domestic Master Index; then, when the trading signal indicates the dollar is heading lower, the manager cuts that position to 80%, with the remaining 20% allocated to the foreign bond index. When the trading signal indicates the dollar is headed higher, the foreign bond position is liquidated, returning the portfolio to the original 100% domestic bond allocation. Implementing that active domestic/foreign bond strategy on an ongoing basis for the period 1973–95 yielded a total return of 10.7% per annum, which amounts to a 150-basis-point per annum total-return pickup over the 9.2% per annum return on the Merrill Lynch Domestic Master Index for the same period. The 10.7% per annum return also compares favorably to the 9.9% average annual return that could have been earned on an 80% U.S./20% foreign *passively* managed global bond portfolio (see Exhibit 49–15).

The preceding analysis was conducted for illustrative purposes only. In no way are we suggesting we have uncovered a new free-lunch trading strategy. The analysis simply highlights the importance of taking an active management approach to international fixed income investment and shows why total-return enhancement issues will eventually dominate risk-reduction considerations in decisions about involvement in the overseas bond markets. The next two sections provide internationally minded investors with general guidelines for setting up and constructing a global bond portfolio and a comprehensive framework for designing an active global bond portfolio strategy.

## GENERAL GUIDELINES FOR CONSTRUCTING A GLOBAL BOND PORTFOLIO

Managing a global bond portfolio is more complex than managing a domestic bond fund. Variations in government regulations, market practices, settlement procedures, yield conventions, and secondary market liquidity mean that the international investment manager must be thoroughly knowledgeable about numerous institutional details. Moreover, transaction costs in the form of commissions, taxes, bid-ask spreads, custody fees, and settlement charges differ widely among markets, so the international investment manager must have a thorough understanding of trading, regulatory, and accounting practices as well. Finally, and perhaps most important, the international fixed income strategy process requires that the investment manager evaluate the complex interaction of currency

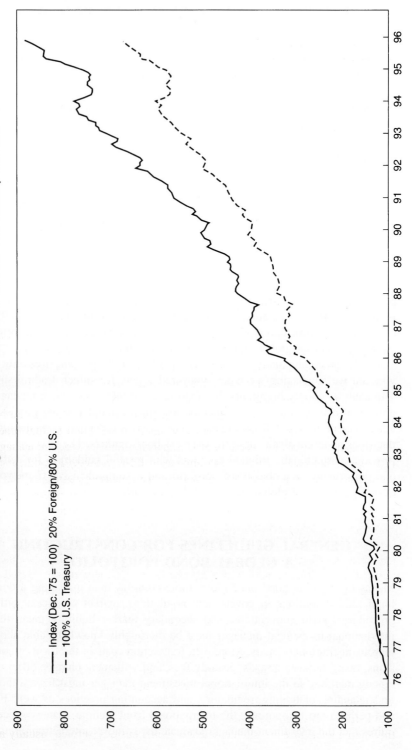

**EXHIBIT 49-14**

Total Return Performance of an Actively-Managed Global Bond Portfolio vs. a 100% U.S. Treasury Portfolio

Index (Dec. '75 = 100) 20% Foreign/80% U.S.

100% U.S. Treasury

**EXHIBIT  49–15**

Total Returns of Alternate Strategies

| Strategy | Total Return per Annum |
|---|---|
| Active 80/20—100/0 mix | 10.7% |
| Passive 80/20 mix | 9.9% |
| 100% U.S. passive | 9.2% |

movements, interest-rate changes, inter- and intramarket yield-spread developments, and yield-curve shifts in all of the major markets.

The investor's first step in setting up an international bond portfolio is to determine financial objectives. Some managers seek to maximize total return, whereas others seek to maximize income. Time horizons also differ widely among investment managers; some global bond investors may select a short-term time horizon to capture short-run swings in exchange rates or interest rates, whereas others may adopt a longer term to capture broad trends in currency and bond market movements. Management styles also differ regarding the level of portfolio turnover and the use of derivative products. Finally, investors with different base currencies may face different constraints on the investments they can make in other currencies.

The U.S. institutional investor market for nondollar bonds can be broken down into 11 investor types: (1) dedicated international bond mutual funds, (2) internationally dedicated accounts of U.S. pension funds, (3) active managers of U.S. domestic bond portfolios, (4) high-yield (junk) domestic bond funds, (5) the treasury departments of U.S. banks, (6) the treasury/cash management departments of U.S. corporations, (7) international property and casualty insurance companies, (8) global equity funds, (9) individuals, (10) hedge funds, and (11) general investment managers.

In the initial stages of setting up an international bond portfolio, the investment manager should draw up a delegation-of-authority list that indicates which foreign markets and credits will be approved for purchase. Based on an assessment of country and credit risk, as well as an assessment of tax and liquidity considerations, an approved list of issuers should be drawn up. Names can be added and dropped as conditions warrant.

For example, a risk-averse fund manager may choose to invest only in government and government-guaranteed issues. Another manager may approve the purchase only of AAA and AA corporate issues, and so forth. The delegation -of-authority list should also detail what percentage of the fund's assets can be assigned to any single credit.

Once it is clear which markets and credits will be approved for purchase, the international investor should select a global custody service (usually a large international bank with an extensive overseas branch and correspondent banking network) to arrange for the delivery and settlement of traded securities and foreign exchange, the collection of coupon income, the reclamation of any coupon tax due the investor because of double-taxation treaties, the maintenance of cash balances in various markets on deposit, the receipt of comprehensive and timely reports on portfolio activities, and the valuation of total assets under management. It would be wise for the investment manager to set up an internal bond operations unit to review all trade details (e.g., price, settlement date, and accrued interest), specify delivery instructions, and contact the global custody service to arrange for settlement and safe custody.

Once those housekeeping duties are fulfilled, the international investment manager should attend to the establishment of portfolio management guidelines for the distribution of the global bond fund's assets. Those self-imposed asset allocation guidelines should assign minimum, normal, and maximum positions that can be held in any single currency block or market. The purpose of the guidelines is to underscore the desire for diversification yet provide ample latitude for active management. For example, Exhibit 49–16 highlights the asset distribution guidelines for a hypothetical global bond fund. The guidelines define the proportion of the portfolio's funds that can be assigned to the major currency blocks: U.S. dollar, Canadian dollar, German mark, French franc, Japanese yen, British pound, and Australian/New Zealand dollars.

The weights chosen as "normal" should reflect the approximate relative current market value of each of the major markets in the total world bond market, or perhaps even better, the relative liquidity and tradeability of each market. If investors use a widely followed external benchmark for performance evaluation, such as the Merrill Lynch Global or Salomon Brothers World Bond Index, they might want to use the benchmark's fixed weights as the normal

**E X H I B I T   49–16**

Asset Allocation Guidelines for Structuring a Global Bond Portfolio (Percent Breakdown)

| Currency Block | Minimum Position | Normal Position | Maximum Position |
|---|---|---|---|
| U.S.$ | 23.5 | 47.0 | 73.5 |
| Yen | 11.5 | 23.0 | 46.0 |
| DM, Dfl, SFr | 6.5 | 13.0 | 33.0 |
| Sterling | 3.5 | 7.0 | 25.0 |
| FFr, ECU | 2.0 | 4.0 | 20.0 |
| C$ | 2.0 | 4.0 | 20.0 |
| A$, NZ$ | 1.0 | 2.0 | 10.0 |

weights. The normal weights shown in Exhibit 49–16 are the market capitalization weights of all the key markets in the Merrill Lynch Global Government/ Eurobond Index as of April 1989 (see Exhibit 49–17).

By assigning minimum and maximum guidelines in the manner shown in Exhibit 49–16, the investment manager places certain operational constraints on the asset allocation decisions. Within the limits defined by these guidelines, the investment manager is free to allocate funds among currencies and markets. Those markets and/or currencies expected to perform relatively favorably should be assigned portfolio weights in the normal-maximum range, whereas those markets and/or currencies expected to perform relatively poorly should be assigned weights in the minimum-normal range. The stronger an investor's conviction about currency and interest-rate trends, the more the assigned weight may lean toward the extreme end of the min-norm or norm-max range. Because the risk of being wrong must be factored into each investment decision, in times of uncertainty there is likely to be a tendency for the recommended portfolio weights to move closer to the market norm. That is consistent with the risk-averse behavior of most individual investors and portfolio managers.

## A FRAMEWORK FOR FORMULATING INTERNATIONAL FIXED INCOME STRATEGY

This section describes a unique framework to assist investors in their formulation of a global bond portfolio strategy. The framework revolves around a strategy table, depicted in Exhibit 49–17, that highlights the key decision criteria that global bond investors must address. The strategy table breaks down the global fixed income investment process into three key decision criteria—currency, market, and bond selection. Each of those decision criteria can and should be treated separately in a forecasting context, but they need to be integrated in a portfolio construction context. In the analysis that follows, we show how to accomplish this integration process.

The strategy table shows how an investor's desired exposure to the individual currencies, markets, maturity categories, sectors, and market durations compares with the broad market capitalization and individual maturity category, sector, and duration weights of the Merrill Lynch Global Government/Eurobond Index. The recommended portfolio weights are in standard type and the weights of the Merrill Lynch Global Bond Index are shown in boldface. How far investment managers will allow their portfolio stances to deviate from market capitalization weights will depend not only on their confidence about the general direction that currencies and interest rates may take, but on their outlook for yield-curve slope and sector-spread changes as well. We begin our analysis by focusing on the factors that determine an investor's optimal net currency position. We then focus on those factors that determine the level of exposure to interest-rate risk that an investor will desire across a wide range of markets. We

# EXHIBIT 49–17

International Fixed Income Strategy Table—Recommended Asset Mix (Percent Breakdown)

| | Currency Decision | | Market Decision | | | Bond Selection Decision — Maturity Structure | | | | | Bond Selection — Sector Breakdown | | | Portfolio Risk | |
| --- | --- | --- | --- | --- | --- | --- | --- | --- | --- | --- | --- | --- | --- | --- | --- |
| Currency Block | Net Currency Position | Currency Hedge | Gross Currency Position | Cash Equivalent | Bonds | 1–3 Years | 3–5 Years | 5–7 Years | 7–10 Years | Long | Government | Euro/Foreign | Portfolio Duration | Currency Risk | Interest-Rate Risk |
| U.S.$ | 49 | 0 | 49 | 24 | 25 | 0 | 0 | 0 | 21 | 4 | 25 | 0 | 3.3 | 1.04 | 0.76 |
|  | **47** |  | **47** |  | **47** | **17** | **9** | **5** | **5** | **11** | **41** | **6** | **4.5** |  |  |
| C$ | 6 | 0 | 6 | 2 | 4 | 2 | 0 | 0 | 2 | 0 | 4 | 0 | 2.3 | 1.50 | 0.77 |
|  | **4** |  | **4** |  | **4** | **1** | **1** | **1** | **0** | **1** | **3** | **1** | **4.5** |  |  |
| A$/NZ$ | 8 | 0 | 8 | 0 | 8 | 4 | 0 | 0 | 4 | 0 | 8 | 0 | 3.8 | 4.00 | 5.07 |
|  | **2** |  | **2** |  | **2** | **1** | **1** | **0** | **0** | **0** | **1** | **1** | **3.0** |  |  |
| Yen | 20 | 0 | 20 | 8 | 12 | 0 | 0 | 0 | 12 | 0 | 12 | 0 | 4.5 | 0.87 | 0.80 |
|  | **23** |  | **23** |  | **23** | **5** | **5** | **5** | **7** | **1** | **20** | **3** | **4.9** |  |  |
| European STG | 7 | 0 | 7 | 4 | 3 | 0 | 0 | 0 | 0 | 3 | 3 | 0 | 4.1 | 1.00 | 0.73 |
|  | **7** |  | **7** |  | **7** | **1** | **2** | **2** | **1** | **1** | **6** | **1** | **5.6** |  |  |
| DM, DFI and SF | 8 | 0 | 8 | 0 | 8 | 2 | 0 | 0 | 4 | 2 | 8 | 0 | 5.7 | 0.62 | 0.80 |
|  | **13** |  | **13** |  | **13** | **2** | **3** | **3** | **3** | **2** | **8** | **5** | **4.4** |  |  |
| FFr, ECU | 2 | 0 | 2 | 0 | 2 | 2 | 0 | 0 | 0 | 0 | 2 | 0 | 8.8 | 0.50 | 1.00 |
|  | **4** |  | **4** |  | **4** | **1** | **1** | **0** | **2** | **0** | **3** | **1** | **4.4** |  |  |
| Total | 100 | 0 | 100 | 38 | 62 | 10 | 0 | 0 | 43 | 9 | 62 | 0 | 3.9 |  | 0.84 |
|  | **100** |  | **100** |  | **100** | **38** | **22** | **16** | **18** | **16** | **82** | **18** | **4.6** |  |  |

Note: Recommended portfolio weights are shown in standard type and the weights of the Merrill Lynch Global Government/Eurobond index are shown in boldface.

conclude by showing how to combine currency and bond investment decisions in the portfolio construction process.

## Currency Decision

In a global bond portfolio context, currency and interest-rate decisions should be treated separately. In the strategy table, the currency and market decisions are clearly separated, with currency hedging driving a wedge between the two key decision criteria. By means of the currency hedge, an investor can simultaneously overweight (underweight) a market and underweight (overweight) the underlying currency.

The purpose of the currency decision section of the strategy table is to draw an investment manager's attention to his or her portfolio's net currency position or exposure. A portfolio's net currency exposure in a particular market equals the actual gross allocation to that market, adjusted for any currency hedges. From the strategy table, this is shown simply as

Net currency position = Gross currency position − Currency hedge

The net currency position of a global bond portfolio will be tilted in favor of one currency depending on the portfolio manager's opinion about the trend in exchange rates. To get a quick reading of how far each currency bet deviates from market norms, we introduce a summary risk measure called *currency risk*, which we define as the ratio of the portfolio's (recommended) net currency position to the benchmark index's market capitalization weight (see Exhibit 49–18). A reading above 1.0 for the currency risk measure indicates a willingness to bear more currency risk than that to which a global bond market performance index would be exposed.

By undertaking currency exposure that exceeds or falls short of market norms, investors are making relative value judgments, namely, whether one cur-

**EXHIBIT 49–18**

Calculation of Currency Risk

| Currency Decision | Portfolio Risk |
|---|---|
| Net Currency Position | Currency Risk |
| 49 | 1.04 |
| 47 | |
| Currency risk = $\dfrac{\text{Net currency position}}{\text{Market capitalization weight}}$ | |

rency will do better or worse than another. In the aggregate, the composite currency risk of a global bond portfolio must equal 1.0, with those currencies enjoying a currency risk objective greater than 1.0 offset by those currencies with a currency risk objective less than 1.0.

The decision to set a currency risk objective at any particular level for any single currency depends on your outlook and conviction regarding the future path of exchange rates. There are essentially three inputs that investors need to determine their own optimal net currency exposures: (1) the projected change in currency values, (2) the projected local returns in each bond market, and (3) the levels of short-term forward premiums, which are known at the outset. To help explain how an investor can set optimal net currency exposures, let's assume a two-bond-market world consisting of the U.S. and German markets, where each makes up 50% of the global bond market. We will wish to have a 25% minimum exposure to each currency and a 75% maximum exposure. With two markets and the use of forward currency hedges, an investor can create four asset categories. (In an $N$-market world, an investor can create $N^2$ asset categories.) Those asset categories are listed in Exhibit 49–19, along with their projected total returns for a given investment horizon expressed in U.S. dollar terms.

Given the four asset categories shown in Exhibit 49–19, there are two asset categories that allow an investor to have a net exposure to dollars: U.S. dollar bonds and German bonds hedged into dollars. Likewise, there are two categories that allow an investor to have a net exposure to deutsche marks: German bonds and U.S. dollar bonds hedged into deutsche marks. If an investor wanted to make a currency bet in favor of the dollar (i.e., have a dollar currency risk objective greater than 1.0), two conditions would have to be met:

1. The projected return on U.S. bonds must exceed the projected return on German bonds (unhedged) in U.S. dollar terms; that is

**EXHIBIT  49–19**

Asset Choices in a Two-Market World

| Asset Choices | Projected Total Return in U.S. Dollar Terms |
|---|---|
| U.S. Dollar Bonds | $R_{U.S.}$ |
| German Bonds | $R_G + DM$ |
| German Bonds Hedged into U.S.$ | $R_G + FP_{DM}$ |
| U.S. Dollar Bonds Hedged into DM | $R_{U.S.} - FP_{DM} + DM$ |

$R_{U.S.}$ = U.S. local bond market return
$R_G$ = German local bond market return
$FP_{DM}$ = Short-term forward premium on deutsche marks
 DM = Appreciation / depreciation of DM versus U.S. dollar

$$R_{\text{U.S.}} > R_G + \text{DM}$$

2. The projected return on German bonds hedged into U.S. dollars on a rolling basis must exceed the projected return on German bonds (unhedged) in U.S. dollar terms; that is

$$R_G + \text{FP}_{\text{DM}} > R_G + \text{DM}$$

If either of those conditions is not met, an investor would do better by making a currency bet in favor of the deutsche mark, either by buying DM bonds outright or by buying U.S. bonds hedged into deutsche marks. Let's assume that both conditions are met, and thus, in terms of setting strategy, we adopt a U.S. dollar currency risk objective equal to 1.5 and a deutsche mark currency risk objective equal to 0.5. Because an overweight net U.S. dollar position can be detained by being long U.S. dollar bonds or by being long German bonds hedged into U.S. dollars, it becomes evident that a variety of gross currency position/hedging schemes can satisfy those single-currency risk objectives. This is demonstrated in Exhibit 49–20.

A net U.S. dollar currency position of 75% (i.e., a currency risk objective equal to 75%/50% = 1.5) can be arrived at by having a gross currency position or allocation in U.S. bonds of 75%; by having a 50% allocation to U.S. bonds and a 25% allocation to German bonds hedged into U.S. dollars; by having a

**E X H I B I T   49–20**

How a Variety of Gross Allocation/Hedging Schemes Can Satisfy a Single-Currency Risk Objective[a]

| Market | Currency Decision | | Market Decision | Portfolio Risk |
|---|---|---|---|---|
| | Net Currency Position (%) | Currency Hedge (%) | Gross Currency Position (%) | Currency Risk |
| U.S. | 75.0 | +50.0 | 25.0 | 1.5 |
| | 75.0 | +37.5 | 37.5 | 1.5 |
| | 75.0 | +25.0 | 50.0 | 1.5 |
| | 75.0 | +12.5 | 62.5 | 1.5 |
| | 75.0 | 0.0 | 75.0 | 1.5 |
| Germany | 25.0 | −50.0 | 75.0 | 0.5 |
| | 25.0 | −37.5 | 62.5 | 0.5 |
| | 25.0 | −25.0 | 50.0 | 0.5 |
| | 25.0 | −12.5 | 37.5 | 0.5 |
| | 25.0 | 0.0 | 25.0 | 0.5 |
| Total | 100.0 | 0.0 | 100.0 | 1.0 |

Assumption: U.S. and Germany make up 50% of the world bond market.

25% allocation to U.S. bonds and a 50% allocation to hedged German bonds; and so forth. Is there a difference in terms of total-return outcome between choosing one particular gross allocation/hedging scheme over another, when the net currency exposure is the same? The answer is "sometimes." Remember that the decision to have an overweight U.S. dollar position depends upon the following:

$$R_{U.S.} > R_G + DM \qquad \text{Acquire U.S. dollar bonds}$$

and

$$R_G + FP_{DM} > R_G + DM \qquad \text{Acquire hedged German bonds}$$

If both conditions are satisfied, the appropriate method to obtain an overweight dollar position will depend on the relationship between $R_{U.S.}$ and ($R_G + FP_{DM}$). If the projected return on U.S. dollar bonds exceeds the projected return on hedged German bonds, that is, if

$$R_{U.S.} > R_G + FP_{DM}$$

then the optimal allocation will be a 75% exposure (our maximum required exposure) in U.S. bonds with nothing hedged. If the projected return on hedged German bonds exceeds the projected return on U.S. dollar bonds, that is, if

$$R_{U.S.} < R_G + FP_{DM}$$

then the optimal allocation will be a 25% exposure in U.S. dollar bonds (our minimum required exposure) and a 50% exposure in German bonds hedged into U.S. dollars. If the projected return on U.S. dollar bonds equals the projected return on hedged German bonds, that is, if

$$R_{U.S.} = R_G + FP_{DM}$$

then all gross allocation/hedging schemes will yield the same expected return, and thus, everything else being equal, investors who seek a certain currency risk objective will be indifferent as to allocation schemes.

In the final analysis, either the allocation/hedging scheme is irrelevant, or the optimal allocation scheme is actually a corner solution, where nothing or everything is hedged.

## Market Decision

The purpose of the market decision section of the strategy table is to draw an investment manager's attention to his or her gross currency position, or to the total allocation to each market and how that allocation is divided between cash and bonds. To get a more complete reading of a global bond portfolio's price sensitivity to changes in interest rates, we introduce a summary risk measure we call *interest-rate risk*. We define interest-rate risk in a given market as the ratio of the recommended gross currency position to the market capitalization weight multiplied by the ratio of the recommended portfolio duration to the market's average duration (see Exhibit 49–21).

By defining interest-rate risk in this manner, we highlight the fact that a global bond portfolio can achieve greater exposure to an anticipated interest-rate decline in a particular market in two ways: (1) by increasing the size of either the gross currency position or allocation relative to market norms, leaving the portfolio's duration unchanged, or (2) by raising the portfolio's duration relative to the market's average duration, leaving the gross allocation unchanged. Likewise, a global bond portfolio can achieve a reduced exposure to an anticipated interest-rate rise in a particular market both by cutting back the size of either the gross currency position or allocation relative to the market norm, and by lowering the duration of the existing holdings relative to the market's average duration. For an entire portfolio, the composite interest-rate risk is a weighted average of the interest-rate risks of the individual markets.

The decision to set an interest-rate-risk objective at any particular level for an individual market or for an entire multimarket portfolio depends on opinions regarding the future trend in interest rates. A reading above 1.0 for interest-

**EXHIBIT 49–21**

Calculation of Interest-Rate Risk

| Currency Block | Market Decision | | Portfolio Risk |
|---|---|---|---|
| | Gross Currency Position | Portfolio Duration | Interest-Rate Risk |
| U.S.$ | 49 | 3.3 | 0.76 |
| | 47 | 4.5 | |
| C$ | 6 | 2.3 | 0.77 |
| | 4 | 4.5 | |
| A$/NZ$ | 8 | 3.8 | 5.07 |
| | 2 | 3.0 | |
| Yen | 20 | 4.5 | 0.80 |
| | 23 | 4.9 | |
| STG | 7 | 4.1 | 0.73 |
| | 7 | 5.6 | |
| DM | 8 | 5.7 | 0.80 |
| | 13 | 4.4 | |
| FFr | 2 | 8.8 | 1.00 |
| | 4 | 4.4 | |

$$\text{Interest-rate risk} = \frac{\text{Gross currency position}}{\text{Market capitalization weight}} \times \frac{\text{Portfolio duration}}{\text{Market duration}}$$

rate risk indicates a willingness to bear more interest-rate risk than that to which a global benchmark index would be exposed.

An investor can obtain a desired interest-rate risk through a variety of gross allocation/duration schemes simply by altering the gross currency position and the portfolio's average duration in an inverse manner. To see that more clearly, assume that an investor wishes to have an overweight exposure to a projected decline in U.S. bond yields equal to 1.5 times the U.S. market's average exposure to yield changes; that is, the investor desires a U.S. bond interest-rate risk equal to 1.5. Assume that the U.S. bond market makes up 50% of the world bond market and that the average duration of the U.S. bond market is four years.

As illustrated in Exhibit 49–22, a variety of gross allocation/duration schemes can satisfy the 1.5 interest-rate risk for the U.S. bond market. For example, a 75% allocation to U.S. bonds, with the average duration of the U.S. bond holdings equal to four years (75%/50% × 4.0/4.0 = 1.5) satisfies the 1.5 interest-rate risk objective, or a gross allocation of 50% to U.S. bonds, with the average duration of the U.S. bond holdings equal to six years (50%/50% × 6.0/4.0 = 1.5) achieves this objective, and so forth.

If a variety of gross allocation/duration schemes generate the same interest-rate risk, is there a difference in terms of total-return outcome between one particular allocation scheme and another? As was true in the case of currency risk, the answer is "sometimes." The interest-rate risk as we defined it relies on duration being a reliable proxy measure of the price sensitivity of a bond portfolio to a given change in yield. Duration is widely viewed as a reliable measure of interest-rate risk if it is assumed that the yield curve is flat and that any yield changes that do occur are small and uniform across the entire yield curve, that is, parallel. If those conditions are met, then it does not matter which gross allocation/duration scheme is adopted, because the total-return outcome

**EXHIBIT 49–22**

How a Variety of Gross Allocation/Duration Schemes Can Satisfy a Single Interest-Rate-Risk Objective[a]

| Market | Gross Currency Position | Portfolio Duration | Interest-Rate Risk |
|--------|------------------------|--------------------|--------------------|
| U.S.   | 25.0                   | 12.0               | 1.5                |
|        | 37.5                   | 8.0                | 1.5                |
|        | 50.0                   | 6.0                | 1.5                |
|        | 62.5                   | 4.8                | 1.5                |
|        | 75.0                   | 4.0                | 1.5                |

Assumption: (1) U.S. makes up 50% of the world bond market; (2) U.S. bond market average duration = four years.

from the competing allocation schemes will be the same. If the yield curve is assumed to be fiat (with yields unchanged) the same standstill yield will be earned along the entire maturity/duration spectrum. Thus, a small-allocation/long-duration scheme will yield the same return as a large allocation/short duration scheme.

However, if the assumption of a flat yield curve is relaxed, the standstill yield on various gross allocation/duration schemes will differ. Consider an unchanging, upward-sloping yield curve where the standstill yield on long-duration bonds exceeds the standstill yield on short-duration notes. In that instance, the standstill yield on a small-allocation/long-duration scheme will exceed the standstill yield on a large-allocation/short-duration scheme, even though both allocation schemes generate the same interest-rate risk. Thus, investors who expect an upward-sloping yield curve to exhibit little change should use small-allocation/long-duration schemes to meet interest-rate risk objectives. The opposite would be the case for a downward-sloping yield-curve environment.

Now consider the implications of a large parallel shift of a flat or upward-sloping yield curve. As was true in the case of an unchanging upward-sloping yield curve, the return on small-allocation/long-duration schemes will once again exceed the return on large-allocation/short-duration schemes, because small-allocation/long-duration schemes offer greater positive convexity than do large-allocation/short-duration schemes. Thus, assuming yield changes are large and yields move in a parallel fashion, the greater positive convexity of small-allocation/long-duration schemes will lead to greater upside performance in a declining-yield environment and less downside risk in a rising-yield environment.

Let's now consider the possibility of nonparallel shifts. If the yield curve flattens because short-term interest rates rise relative to long-term interest rates or steepens because short-term interest rates decline relative to long-term interest rates, then the relative performance of competing gross allocation/duration schemes may differ considerably, even though they may generate the same interest-rate risk. In the case of a flattening yield curve, small-allocation/long-duration schemes should outperform large-allocation/short-duration schemes, whereas in the case of a steepening yield curve the opposite should be true.

## The Bond Selection Decision

When nonparallel shifts of the yield curve are anticipated, neither duration nor our summary measure of interest-rate risk may be adequate indicators of a bond portfolio's price sensitivity to changes in interest rates. In such cases, it may be more important to manage the maturity structure of the portfolio correctly than to get the portfolio's duration or interest-rate risk right. Therefore, in any bond investment decision, the summary measure of interest-rate risk—which considers only the gross allocation and the portfolio's relative duration—must be supplemented by comparing the portfolio's recommended maturity structure to the maturity mix of the benchmark index. That is why the strategy table breaks down the bond selection decision into component sources of bond investment risk. The bond selection section of the strategy table draws an investment manager's attention not only to his or her portfolio's average duration and how that compares to market norms, but also to the portfolio's maturity structure and how that compares with the maturity mix of the benchmark index and to the portfolio's sector breakdown (governments versus Euros) and how that compares to market norms.

## Tying the Pieces Together

In the preceding sections, we described the steps that investors should take in formulating their currency, market, and bond selection decisions. The strategy table helps investors formulate a global investment decision process by allowing them to assess just how far their currency, market, and bond selection decisions deviate from market norms. In this section, we show how those individual decision criteria can be integrated into the construction of a global bond portfolio.

An investor begins the process of assigning portfolio weights by setting out desired currency and interest-rate risk objectives for each market, with allowances made for any maturity or sector adjustments if changes are expected in yield-curve slope or intramarket spread. How far the bets on currency and interest-rate risk will be allowed to deviate from market norms will depend on the investor's outlook and conviction regarding the future direction of exchange rates and interest rates.

The precise assignment of portfolio weights across currencies and markets must satisfy both the currency risk and the interest-rate risk objectives. The problem for portfolio managers is that a variety of portfolio schemes can jointly satisfy any set of currency and interest-rate risk objectives. That is shown in Exhibit 49–23, which plots a range of currency risk and interest-rate risk measures between 0 and 1.5 for the U.S. dollar and the U.S. bond market on the horizontal axes and various gross currency positions or allocations consistent with those risk objectives on the vertical axis. Given a U.S. dollar currency risk objective of 1.5, for example, it is evident that a variety of gross allocation/ hedging schemes can satisfy that objective—for example, a 75% allocation to U.S. dollar bonds with nothing hedged satisfies it, as does a 50% allocation to U.S. dollar bonds with an additional 25% coming from hedged foreign bonds, and so forth. Likewise, a variety of gross allocation/duration schemes can satisfy an interest-rate risk objective of 1.5—for example, a 75% U.S. allocation, with the portfolio's duration equal to the market's average duration, or a 50% U.S. allocation, with the portfolio's duration equal to 1.5 times the market's average duration, and so forth. As the shaded area in the graph indicates, a variety of allocations to the U.S. dollar bond market, coupled with selective currency

**E X H I B I T   49–23**

Integrating Currency and Market Decisions

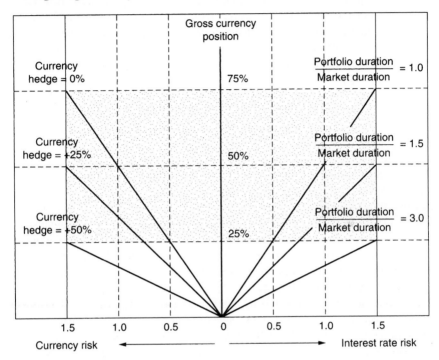

hedges and adjustments to portfolio duration, can jointly satisfy both the 1.5 currency risk objective and 1.5 interest-rate risk objectives. Which gross allocation/hedging/duration scheme should be selected in constructing a global bond portfolio? The answer is fairly straightforward: the optimal allocation scheme is one that maximizes portfolio return while satisfying the investor's currency and interest-rate risk objectives.

There are two important steps in deriving the optimal allocation scheme: the gross allocation/hedging decision and the gross allocation/duration decision. As we previously discussed, under certain assumptions it makes no difference which gross allocation hedging/duration scheme is selected to satisfy a desired set of currency and interest-rate risk objectives, because they all should yield the same return. However, once those assumptions are relaxed, certain allocation schemes may yield higher expected returns than others, even though they may satisfy the same currency and interest-rate risk objectives.

The best way to describe how an optimal portfolio allocation can be selected from a range of competing risk allocation schemes is through a simple illustration. As before, let's assume a universe consisting of the U.S. and German bond markets, where each makes up 50% of the global bond market. We wish to have a 25% minimum exposure to each currency and market and a 75% maximum exposure. Let's assume that, given our assessment and conviction of likely currency changes and local market return outcomes, we adopt a U.S. dollar currency risk objective equal to 1.5 and a deutsche mark currency risk objective of 0.5. Let's assume further that interest-rate risk objectives of 1.0 are sought for both the U.S. and German bond markets. The projected local market returns for the U.S. ($R_{U.S.}$) and German ($R_G$) bond markets are shown in Exhibit 49–24 along with the known 6% short-term forward premium on deutsche marks ($FP_{DM}$).

It is expected that the returns earned on U.S. and German bonds in local currency terms will amount to 10% and 5%, respectively. For now, let's assume that those returns will be invariant to the particular gross allocation/duration scheme selected; that is, we assume flat total-return curves for both markets.

Given the 6% short-term forward premium on deutsche marks, the projected return on German bonds hedged into U.S. dollar terms is 11% (5% + 6% = 11%). Assuming that the dollar is projected to rise by 5% against the deutsche mark over the investment horizon, the projected return on unhedged German bonds in U.S. dollar terms will be equal to zero (5% − 5% = 0%). As shown in the total-return analysis section of Exhibit 49–25, assuming flat U.S. and German total-return curves and a minimum 25% exposure to both the U.S. market and the German bond market on an unhedged basis, the desired currency risk and interest-rate risk objectives are satisfied, and total return is maximized by having a 25% allocation to U.S. bonds and a 50% exposure to German bonds hedged into U.S. dollars. That follows from the analysis de-

**EXHIBIT   49–24**

Projected Total Returns on U.S. and Hedged German Bonds under Hypothetical Alternative Allocation Schemes

| Asset Allocations | | Projected Total Return When U.S. and German Total-Return Curves are Flat | | | | Projected Total Return When German Total-Return Curve is Upward Slopping | |
| --- | --- | --- | --- | --- | --- | --- | --- |
| U.S. | Germany | $R_{U.S.}$ | $R_G$ | $FP_{DM}$ | $R_G + FP_{DM}$ | $R'_G$ | $R'_G + FP_{DM}$ |
| 25.0% | 75.0% | 10% | 5% | 6% | 11% | 5% | 11% |
| 37.5 | 62.5 | 10 | 5 | 6 | 11 | 6 | 12 |
| 50.0 | 50.0 | 10 | 5 | 6 | 11 | 7 | 13 |
| 62.5 | 37.5 | 10 | 5 | 6 | 11 | 8 | 14 |
| 75.0 | 25.0 | 10 | 5 | 6 | 11 | 9 | 15 |

# EXHIBIT 49–25

Asset-Weighted Total-Return Analysis

| Assumptions | Total Return from U.S. Assets + | | Return from Unhedged German Assets + | | Return from Hedged German Assets = | | Total Return |
|---|---|---|---|---|---|---|---|
| | Asset Weight | Total Return (%) | Asset Weight | Total Return (%) | Asset Weight | Total Return (%) | (%) |
| U.S. and Germany | .250 | (10) | .25 | (5-5) | .500 | (11) | 8.00 |
| have flat total-return | .375 | (10) | .25 | (5-5) | .375 | (11) | 7.88 |
| curves | .500 | (10) | .25 | (5-5) | .250 | (11) | 7.75 |
| | .625 | (10) | .25 | (5-5) | .125 | (11) | 7.63 |
| | .750 | (10) | .25 | (5-5) | 0 | (11) | 7.50 |
| Germany has an | .250 | (10) | .25 | (5-5) | .500 | (11) | 8.00 |
| upward-sloping | .375 | (10) | .25 | (6-5) | .375 | (12) | 8.50 |
| total-return curve | .500 | (10) | .25 | (7-5) | .250 | (13) | 8.75 |
| | .625 | (10) | .25 | (8-5) | .125 | (14) | 8.75 |
| | .750 | (10) | .25 | (9-5) | 0 | (15) | 8.50 |

scribed earlier, when we noted that hedged German bonds would be preferred over U.S. dollar bonds outright if

$$R_G + FP_{DM} > R_{U.S.}$$

whereas U.S. dollar bonds outright would be preferred over hedged German bonds if

$$R_{U.S.} > R_G + FP_{DM}$$

Given that the projected return on hedged German bonds equals

$$R_G + FP_{DM} = 0.05 + 0.06 = 0.11$$

whereas the projected return on U.S. dollar bonds outright equals

$$R_{U.S.} = 0.1$$

it is clear that

$$R_G + FP_{DM} > R_{U.S.}$$

Thus, the optimal allocation should be a corner solution in favor of hedged German bonds.

In this example, the specific allocation scheme that maximized total return was determined by focusing only on the optimal gross allocation/hedging scheme, because all the competing gross allocation/duration schemes must yield the same return if flat total-return curves are assumed. However, if we relax the assumption that the projected local returns on U.S. and German bonds are invariant to the particular gross allocation/duration scheme selected, a different total-return ranking among the competing allocation schemes will arise. Consider the case where, as before, the U.S. local bond market return (10%) is invariant to the gross allocation/duration scheme selected, but the German total-return curve is positively sloped; that is, the projected return on small-allocation/long-duration schemes will yield a higher projected return than large-allocation/short-duration schemes, even though the same interest-rate risk objective is satisfied. In Exhibit 49–24, the projected local return on German bonds ($R_G'$) is shown to vary from 5% for large-allocation (75%)/short-duration schemes to 9% for small-allocation (25%)/long-duration schemes. As shown in the total-return analysis section of Exhibit 49–25, the desired currency risk and interest-rate risk objectives are satisfied and total return is maximized by having a U.S. dollar bond allocation equal to 50–62.5% and a hedged German bond allocation of 12.5–25.0%. This more balanced allocation contrasts to the corner solution allocation (a 25% U.S. dollar bond allocation and a 50% allocation to hedged German bonds) in the previous example, because even though hedged German bonds have a higher expected return than U.S. dollar bonds under all allocation schemes, that is,

$$R_G' + FP_{DM} > R_{U.S.}$$

smaller hedged German bond allocations (with larger portfolio durations) have a comparative advantage over larger hedged German bond allocations (with smaller portfolio durations) in an upward-sloping total-return-curve environment. Thus, investors would do better to exploit the higher projected returns on such schemes. Although the projected 10% return on U.S. dollar bonds is lower than the projected returns on hedged German bonds (11%–15%) for all allocations shown, the portfolio weight assigned to U.S. dollar bonds (50.0%–62.5%) turns out to be larger than the 25% U.S. dollar bond allocation when flat U.S. and German bond total-return curves were assumed. The allocation to U.S. dollar bonds is larger because the currency risk and interest-rate risk objectives can both be satisfied with a higher expected return if a small rather than a large hedged German bond allocation is chosen.

## CONCLUSION

A global bond portfolio's currency and interest-rate exposure will be dictated by the investment manager's currency risk and interest-rate risk objectives. Although various portfolio weighting schemes simultaneously can satisfy both risk objectives, they may yield quite different returns. The analysis presented here reveals how a portfolio manager can find the particular weighting scheme that both maximizes total return and satisfies the investor's currency risk and interest-rate risk objectives.

## PART 7

# EQUITY-LINKED SECURITIES AND THEIR VALUATION

## CHAPTER 50

# Convertible Securities and Their Investment Characteristics

**Chris P. Dialynas**
Managing Director
Pacific Investment Management Company

**Sandra Durn**
Senior Vice President/Portfolio Manager
Pacific Investment Management Company

**John C. Ritchie, Jr., PhD.**
Professor of Finance
Temple University

## INTRODUCTION

Convertible securities are fixed income securities that permit the holder the right to exchange that security for the common stock of the issuing corporation under pre-specified conditions. The terms at which the debt security can be exchanged for the issuer's common stock are set forth in the security's indenture. The option to convert is solely at the discretion of the debt holder and will only be exercised if the holder finds such an exchange desirable.

Convertible securities typically contain other embedded options. The most common is an option providing the issuer the right to call the issue at its discretion in accordance with the terms set forth in the indenture. Many convertible securities also contain "put" provisions, which enable the holder to redeem the bond prior to maturity. Because of the multiple embedded options in a convertible security, the valuation of these securities is not a simple task. Valuation methods for convertible securities have advanced significantly in recent years with the development of option pricing theory for both equity options and interest-rate options and with the tremendous advances in computer technology. Even so, the valuation of convertible securities remains very complex.

In this chapter, the fundamental characteristics of convertible securities, the convertible universe, risk and return characteristics, and the basic principles of how convertibles can be valued are described.

The authors wish to thank Yuri Garbuzov of PIMCO for considerable technical assistance.

## GENERAL CHARACTERISTICS OF CONVERTIBLES

Convertible bonds are often subordinated debentures. Conceptually, this means that the claims of "senior" creditors must be settled in full before any payment will be made to holders of subordinated debentures in the event of insolvency or bankruptcy. Senior creditors typically include holders of all other long-term debt issues and bank loans. Subordinated debentures have a priority over preferred and common stock. Structurally, a convertible bond is very similar to a straight corporate bond with an attached warrant. Exhibit 50–1 details the similarity. Convertible preferred stocks are equity type securities which offer a priority to dividend payments over common stock as well as higher payments and that offer the opportunity to share in corporate growth, albeit at a slower rate than the common.

The value of a convertible security is related to many variables including changes in the price of the underlying stock, changes in interest rates, credit quality, and changes in the volatility of both the stock and the volatility of interest rates. The ideal convertible bond renders a bond-like return if the return on the underlying issuer's stock is minimal or negative and an equity-like return if the underlying stock's return is quite positive. Naturally, a bond-like return, if held to maturity, is determined by the coupon payments, the earnings on the reinvested coupons and the return of principal. So, the convertible provides the investor with the "better of" return profile. (See Exhibit 50–2.)

**E X H I B I T   50–1**

Factors Affecting a Convertible's Valuation

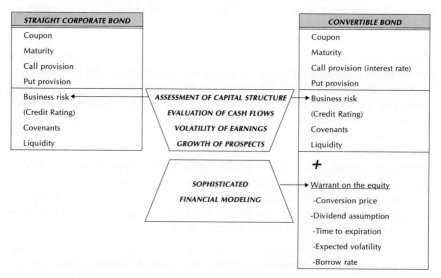

**E X H I B I T   50–2**

Convertible Securities: The Best of Two Worlds

*THE BASIC CONVERTIBLE STRUCTURE*

| STRAIGHT BOND | OPTION | CONVERTIBLE |

*PURCHASE CONVERTIBLES WITH*
*ASYMMETRIC RISK / REWARD PROFILES*

- Upside Participation

- Downside Protection

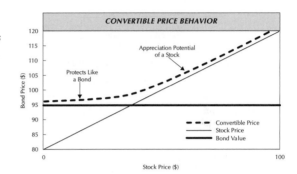

The yield on convertible bonds is lower than the yield on the more senior debt of the same issuer. The cumulative yield sacrificed represents a payment for the conversion privilege. Normally, the convertible bond yield will exceed the dividend yield of the stock. However, the cost of the stock, when purchased through the conversion rights, will exceed the price at which the common stock could have been purchased by the premium paid. The premium will vary upon issuance but will approximate 25% for a well-balanced convertible bond.

The final maturity of convertible bonds may vary. Historically, most convertibles were issued with maturities of 25 to 30 years. More recently, convertible bonds have been issued with intermediate type maturities of 5 to 10 years. This change implies that the investment value, or bond floor, of the convertible bond universe is currently more stable than in the past, all other factors constant. However, it also implies that the option period is much shorter. In addition, most bonds issued have issuer call provisions which serve to further truncate the option period, to the investor's detriment.

There are many varieties of convertible securities in the market. The main factor distinguishing the various types of securities is the degree of equity-like association. Exhibit 50–3 briefly describes some of the issue types in the market and their relative bond/equity exposure. The analytical convention of this chapter is primarily directed to traditional convertible bonds.

Convertible bonds are issued in many countries and denominated in many currencies. Rather than dwell on detail, we will generalize by region to approx-

## EXHIBIT 50-3

Convertible Securities A Range of Investment Alternatives

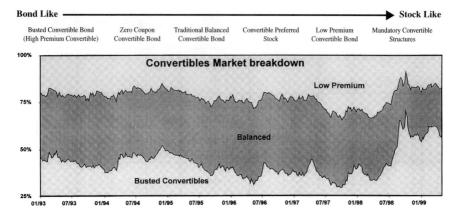

Source: Lehman Brothers Convertibles Research

imate the size of the respective markets. Exhibit 50–4 summarizes the historical issuance of domestic convertible bonds as well as the present distribution of convertible bonds in the three foreign primary markets.

Because a bond is issued in a particular country does not mean that the bond is necessarily issued in the local currency. In fact, many foreign bonds are dollar denominated. With the introduction of the Euro, a number of Asian corporations have issued Euro-denominated bonds.

Convertible bonds have been issued by companies engaged in a variety of businesses along a broad range of credit worthiness. Exhibit 50–5 provides a glimpse of the change in profile of the universe with respect to quality, and time.

## ADVANTAGES AND DISADVANTAGES TO ISSUING FIRMS

Convertible issues offer two basic potential advantages to the issuer. The issuance of convertible bonds offers the advantage of lower interest cost and less restrictive covenants relative to a nonconvertible bond issue. In other words, the investor pays for the right to participate in future favorable price changes in the underlying common stock by accepting a lower yield and a less restrictive debt agreement.

The required yield to sell a convertible relative to that of a nonconvertible issue varies over time and with the particular deal structure and credit quality. A nonconvertible issue will require a yield to maturity that is higher than that offered by a convertible issue. This is true in spite of the fact that convertibles are typically subordinated debt issues. The rating agencies have usually rated convertible issues one class below that of a straight debenture issue. Absent

**EXHIBIT 50-4**

Convertible Market Size

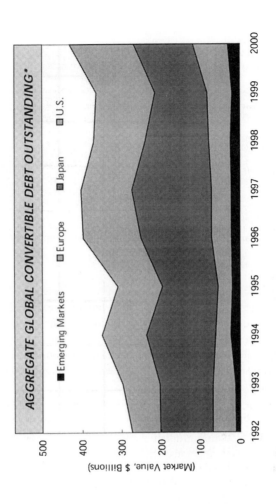

AGGREGATE GLOBAL CONVERTIBLE DEBT OUTSTANDING*

■ Emerging Markets   □ Europe   ■ Japan   □ U.S.

(Market Value, $ Billions)

**THE GLOBAL CONVERTIBLE MARKET HAS EXPERIENCED STEADY GROWTH**

**THE MARKET NOW EXCEEDS $400 BILLION**

* SOURCE: Credit Suisse First Boston

**E X H I B I T   50–5**

The Distribution of Credit Quality Changes with Time

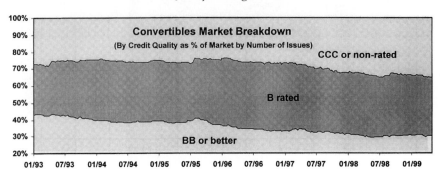

Source: Lehman Brothers Convertibles Research

covenants to the contrary, the convertible debt holder is exposed to the risk of expropriation that comes with the issuance of additional new debt. The interest-cost-savings to a firm will be highly related to market uncertainty for the issuer and its common stock. Paradoxically, to some extent the greater the uncertainty, the lower the interest costs. This happens because the increased uncertainty results in an increase in the option value.

The issuer of a convertible bond is confronted with capital structure uncertainty. Normally, the firm will choose between debt and equity capital. The decision to issue a convertible bond is a hybrid, uncertain capital structure decision. At the outset, the issue is a debt issue. The issuer can thus expense interest costs. In contrast, dividend payments cannot be expensed. However the firm does incur greater interest costs relative to revenues, increasing the riskiness of the firm. In fact, in the extreme, the issuer is faced with the worst of two worlds. If the firm's business prospects sour, the choice of a convertible bond rather than equity will have proven to be a bad one because bankruptcy risk will have increased considerably. If, on the other hand, the business booms and the common stock price accelerates substantially, the firm's convertible bonds will be converted to equity and existing shareholders' share of the growth is diluted. Obviously, the issuance of a straight debt issue would have been preferred in this case. The choice of a convertible bond is a bet by the firm that its business is more stable than that implied by the market's assessment of firm-specific volatility. The firm incurs lower marginal financing costs and fewer restrictions while accepting the possibility of having to "pay-up" in common stock in the future.

The following example illustrates the complexity of capital structure decisions. Assume a high quality (AA rated) company knows its business is slowing. Management believes earnings will fall. A convertible bond issue will not materially affect the company's rating. Management decides to issue the convertible because it does so at an implied premium to its stock price and at reduced interest costs. Price/earnings multiples need to expand considerably for dilution to occur. The cost of capital is reduced because of the convertible bond issuance.

Naturally, corporate finance decisions are made at time of issue and are not plain and simple. The firm's ability to access the capital market, the float in its stock, and its specific tax situation are among many considerations that complicate the financial structure decisions. The bottom line is that the company usually knows more about its particular financial attributes than the market. Thus, corporate financing decisions may provide important signals to the market.

## ADVANTAGES TO THE INVESTOR

An investor purchasing a convertible security receives the advantages of a more senior security: the safety of principal (prior claim to assets over equity security holders) and relative income stability at a known interest rate. Furthermore, if the common stock of the issuer rises in price, the convertible instrument will usually also rise to reflect the increased value of the underlying common stock. Upside potential can be realized through sale in the secondary market of the convertible bond without conversion into the stock. In contrast, if the price of the underlying common stock declines in the market, the bond can be expected to decline no lower in price than where it yields a satisfactory return on its value as a straight bond. A convertible offers the downside protection that bonds can offer during bad economic times, while allowing one to share in the upside potential for the common stock of a growing firm. As we will see later in this chapter, the empirical price of the Rite Aid 5.25 9/15/02 behaved precisely as convertible theory would predict for quite a while and then, not at all. Hewlett-Packard bonds, of very high quality, have performed as predicted throughout their tenure.

Convertible bonds typically offer higher current yield than do common stocks. If the dividend yield on the underlying common stock surpassed the current yield on the convertible bond, conversion would tend to become more attractive. All else equal, increases in the dividend yield are detrimental to the value of the convertible bond.

Convertible bonds may be a particularly attractive asset class for investors whose ability to take equity risk is constrained. Many investors face discrete equity market risk allocation constraints. Because convertible bonds are in fact bonds, they may be an ideal asset for a constrained investor who desires more equity risk. They offer downside protection afforded by the bond and the upside potential of the equity risk. This investor may construct a bond portfolio with an "equity kicker" component through the use of convertible securities.

## DISADVANTAGES TO THE INVESTOR

The investor pays a premium to bond value for the conversion privilege by accepting a significantly lower yield than that offered by nonconvertible bonds of equivalent quality. If anticipated corporate growth is not realized, the purchaser will have sacrificed current yield and may well see the market value of the convertible instrument fall below the price paid to acquire it. A substantial rise in the price of the underlying common stock is usually necessary to offset the yield sacrifice. Convertible bonds offer an insurance policy to the investor at a relatively cheap price. However, if the price of the stock is very stable, then there is little use for the insurance, and the price of the option may be too much.

The investor must be cognizant of the potential inverse association between the convertible bond's yield spread and the issuer's stock price. The fact that the yield spread may widen as the stock price falls and contract as the stock price increases renders an elasticity to the bond that is independent of interest rates and the attached warrant. For some convertible bonds this means that the bond's price may fall as much or more than the stock falls (excepting the limit case). As with all bonds, a strict fundamental credit analysis is a prerequisite to the purchase of convertible bonds.

## ALTERNATIVE FORMS OF CONVERTIBLE FINANCING

Exhibit 50–6 lists six convertible types and notes how each differs from a traditional convertible. The wide variety of convertibles issued increases investor alternatives, meeting a variety of portfolio objectives.

## TYPES OF CONVERTIBLE INVESTORS

The following are brief descriptions of some of the types of convertible investors typically found in the market.

> *Defensive equity managers*—Some managers of common stock portfolios may wish to be defensive at times. Convertible securities offer the possibility of being defensive through their downside protection, while still pursuing the growth potential associated with common-stock investment.
>
> *Equity managers seeking income*—Some portfolio managers may desire a higher level of income than currently being provided by common stocks, while maintaining the potential of sharing in the growth of the firm through the embedded warrant on the underlying equity. Some growth potential is sacrificed because convertibles typically sell at a premium to the underlying equity value.
>
> *Convertible specialists*—There are investment mangers who specialize in the management of convertible securities.
>
> *Bond portfolio managers*—Some bond portfolio managers are willing to sacrifice income to obtain a limited exposure to the growth potential and risks associated with an option on the underlying common stock.

**EXHIBIT 50–6**

| Convertible Structure | Distinctive Characteristics |
|---|---|
| High Coupon | Premium greater<br>Income greater<br>More bond-like<br>Sacrificing equity participation |
| Puttable Securities | Reduces credit risk<br>Shortens bond life<br>Sacrifice yield |
| Callable Securities | Force conversion<br>Reduce effective option period due to *either* changes in interest rates or changes in the stock price |
| Exchangeable Securities | Bond of an issuing company exchangeable into the equity of another company<br>Permits exchange of credit risk with equity risk |
| Zero Coupon | Greater credit risk<br>More interest rate exposure per maturity<br>Lower premium<br>Lower bond floor |
| Premium Redemption Price | Advertised yield to maturity realized only if bond held to maturity |

*Arbitrageurs and hedgers*—These investors are "hedged" (i.e., they short common stock against their long convertible bond position and hope to profit from changes in valuation and volatility). These investors tend to participate in the in-the-money part of the universe.

*Insurance companies*—Insurance companies are required to reserve capital as a function of portfolio risk. Because stocks are riskier than bonds, the capital requirements are greater. Often times, insurance companies will invest in convertible bonds to achieve a greater exposure to the equity market without increasing capital requirements. Insurance companies tend to participate in the at-the-money part of the universe.

## ANALYSIS OF CONVERTIBLE SECURITIES

The following factors must be considered when evaluating convertible securities:

1. The appreciation in price of the common stock that is required before conversion could become attractive as measured by the *conversion premium*

2. The prospects for growth in the price of the underlying stock

3. The downside price risk in the event that the conversion privilege proves valueless. The ultimate credit quality of the issuer. This analysis helps define the stability of the bond floor

4. The probability of greater than anticipated volatility in the price of the underlying common stock

5. Special provisions and covenants

## AN ILLUSTRATIVE ANALYSIS

We will illustrate how to analyze convertibles using three convertible issues. Information about each issue is provided in Exhibit 50–7.

A few basic definitions are in order before explaining the analysis. The convertible security contract will state either a *conversion ratio* or a *conversion price*. A conversion ratio directly specifies the number of shares of the issuing firm's common stock that can be obtained by surrendering the convertible security. Alternatively, the conversion ratio may be expressed in terms of a conversion price—the price paid per share to acquire the underlying common stock through conversion. The conversion ratio may then be determined by dividing the stated conversion price into the par value of the security. For example, if the conversion price were $20, a holder of such a bond would receive 50 shares of common stock in conversion, assuming a typical par value of $1,000 for the bond.

In some cases, the security contract may provide for changes in the conversion price over time. For example, a conversion price of $20 might be specified for the first five years, $25 for the next five years, $30 for the next five years, and so on. This means that a holder of the instrument will be able to obtain fewer shares through conversion each time the conversion price increases. For example, 50 shares can be obtained when the conversion price is $20, but only 40 shares when the conversion price rises to $25. Such a provision forces investors to emphasize early conversion if they intend to convert, and the provision would be reasonable if corporate growth generally leads to a rising value for the common stock over time.

One of the issues analyzed is a zero-coupon bond (the Hewlett-Packard bonds). In general, zero-coupon convertible bonds have 20 years to maturity, they are issued at a fraction of par value, and redemption at 100% of par provides yield. Most of these bonds have 3 to 5 years of call protection and offer an option to put the bond back to the issuer at the first call date and a couple of dates after. Call and put strike prices for the same dates are matched at accreted values. Zero-coupon bonds do not have any yield advantage over underlying equities and their premium is determined by the value of the embedded equity put option with a sliding up strike price (at the first put date the strike is lower than that at maturity).

**EXHIBIT 50–7**

| | Rite Aid | Hewlett-Packard | Winstar Communications |
|---|---|---|---|
| **Issue Information** | | | |
| Conversion Ratio | 27.672 | 5.43 | 1.0079 |
| Coupon/Dividend | 5.25% | 0% | 7% |
| Maturity | 09/15/02 | 10/14/17 | 03/15/10 |
| First Call Date | 09/15/00 | 10/14/00 | 03/20/01 |
| First Call Price | 102.10 | 59.03 | 51.75 |
| First Put Date | — | 10/14/00 | — |
| First Put Price | — | 59.03 | — |
| Provisional Call Hurdle | — | — | — |
| Redemption Value | 100 | 100 | 50 |
| Issue Price | 100 | 53.785 | 50 |
| Issue Size, Par | $650,000,000 | $2,000,000,000 | $200,000,000 |
| Conversion Restrictions | None | None | None |
| **Market Information** | | | |
| Bond Price (Bid/Ask) | 100.00/100.50 | 63.375/63.625 | 59.125/59.875 |
| Stock Price | $25.438 | $100.50 | $51.75 |
| Spread | 135 bp | 80 bp | 550 bp |
| Implied Volatility for Long-Term Stock Options | 40% | 38% | 65% |
| Credit Rating (Moody's/S&P) | Baa2/BBB- | Aa3/AA | NA/CCC- |
| Last-Quarter Stock Dividend | $0.115 | $.16 | — |
| Short Rebate Rate for Stock Borrowing | 0.30% | 0.30% | 1.60% |
| **Valuation Results** | | | |
| Fair Bond Value | 101.95 | 63.69 | 61.17 |
| Parity | 70.39 | 54.57 | 52.16 |
| Percent Premium to Bid | 42% | 16% | 13% |
| Delta | 37% | 58% | 81% |
| Bond Floor | 94.45 | 54.75 | 37.25 |
| Breakeven Time | 12.20 years | — | 1.91 years |
| Yield to Maturity | 5.25% | 2.51% | 4.86% |
| Yield to Call | 6.97% | −5.52% | −1.27% |
| Yield to Put | — | −5.52% | — |
| Effective Duration | 1.5 | 0.6 | 0.8 |

## Conversion Premium

The market conversion price of a convertible instrument represents the cost per share of the common stock if obtained through the convertible instrument. For example, the market conversion price of $38.66 calculated for the Rite Aid 5¼% convertible bond is obtained by dividing the market price of the convertible bond (1,019.50) by the number of common shares that could be obtained by converting that bond (27.672 shares). Because the market conversion price is higher than the current market price of a common share, the bond is selling at a conversion premium, represented by the excess cost per share to obtain the common stock through conversion.

The *conversion premium ratio* shows the percentage increase necessary to reach a parity price relationship between the underlying common stock and the convertible instrument. *Conversion parity* is that price relationship between the convertible instrument and the common stock at which neither a profit nor a loss would be realized by purchasing the convertible, converting it, and selling the common shares that were received in conversion, ignoring commissions.

When the price of the common stock exceeds its conversion parity price, one could feel certain that the convertible security would fluctuate directly with changes in the market price of the underlying common stock. In other words, gains in value of the underlying common stock should then be able to be realized by the sale of the convertible instrument, rather than conversion and sale of the stock itself. The market conversion price, incidentally, is the parity price for a share of common stock obtainable through the convertible instrument.

There is usually, although not always, some conversion premium present on convertible instruments, which reflects the anticipation of a possible increase in the price of the underlying common stock beyond the parity price. Professional arbitrageurs are constantly looking for situations in which the stock can be obtained more cheaply by buying the convertible instrument than through direct purchase in the market. For example, assume that a bond is convertible into 20 shares and can be purchased for $1,000. If the common stock was currently selling at $55 a share, an arbitrageur would buy the convertible and simultaneously short sell the common stock. The arbitrageur would realize a gross profit (before transaction costs) of $100 calculated as follows:

| | |
|---|---|
| Short sale of $20 shares at $55/share | $1,100 |
| Less purchase cost of bond | 1,000 |
| | $ 100 |

The demand by arbitrageurs for the convertible would continue until the resultant rise in the price of the convertible no longer made such actions profitable.

## Yield Sacrifice

At the time of this analysis, nonconvertible bonds of equivalent quality to the convertible issued by Rite Aid offered a yield to maturity of 7.20%, or 195 basis points higher than the yield to maturity offered by the convertible. The yield sacrifice suggested by this would have to be overcome by an equivalent rise in the price of the underlying common stock, assuming the bond was held to maturity, or the investor would have been better advised to purchase the non-convertible instrument. This differential is possibly misleading in this case, as the sacrifice relative to the current yield is significantly less. The current yield would seem more significant if the rise in the common stock were realized well before maturity.

In the final analysis, it is the price appreciation potential for the underlying common stock and the quality of the bond floor that are most important.

## Downside Risk Potential

The floor price for a convertible is estimated as that value at which the instrument would sell in the market to offer the yield of an equivalent nonconvertible instrument. Rite Aid bonds were rated BBB by Standard & Poor's Corporation in June 1999, and the yield paid by BBB bonds was used as the basis for estimating the required market yield for present value calculations for the nonconvertible bond.

The floor price of the Rite Aid bonds is the sum of the present values of the cash flows (discounting at 7.21%) that would be generated by a nonconvertible 5$\frac{1}{4}$% bond maturing in 3 years and 3 months. The floor price is $94.45 for Rite Aid bonds. A similar calculation for the Hewlett Packard bonds renders a bond floor of $54.75. The investor put option for this issue, effective in 16 months on 10/14/00, provides for a high, stable bond floor despite the long maturity.

The analysis suggests a 5.45% (5.55/101.95) downside risk for the Rite Aid bonds, and a 13.54% (8.625/63.69) downside risk for the Hewlett Packard bonds.

The bond floor, representing the insurance inherent to a convertible bond, is very important. However, one should not place too much emphasis on the estimated floor prices. The calculations assume that current yield levels will continue, and this may well not be correct. If instead, if market yields rise to higher levels and the conversion privilege proves worthless, the price of the bonds could fall below the estimated floor price. On the other hand, if market yield levels fall, the loss would not be as great as suggested. In fact, if interest rates fall enough, the bond may actually be called independent of any movement on the price of the stock. More importantly, normally an investor should not be purchasing convertibles (remember the yield sacrifice) unless an investor believes the probability is relatively high that the market price of the underlying common stock will be more volatile than implied by the bond and that the price will rise and eventually exceed the parity price for that common stock.

## Breakeven Time

*Breakeven time* represents the number of years it will take for the favorable income differential over the common stock offered by the convertible instrument to equal the total dollar conversion premium paid to acquire the convertible instrument on a per share basis. For example, the breakeven time for the Rite Aid convertible bonds is 12.2 years, calculated as follows:

| | |
|---|---|
| Interest paid on each $1,000 bond at | 5.25% |
| Stock dividend yield | |
| 4 × 0.115/25.438 | 1.81% |
| Favorable bond differential | 3.44% |
| Percent premium [(100-70.39)/70.39]) | 42% |
| Breakeven time equals percent premium | |
| Divided by bond yield advantage (42%/3.44) | 12.2 years |

Breakeven time is a crude method for measuring the value of a convertible security. It is a measure of the amount of time it takes to pay for the option premium but ignores the actual value of the equity option. All else equal, we expect that the more volatile the underlying stock, the greater the premium and breakeven time.

The deficiency of "breakeven time" as a valuation variable is readily gleaned from Exhibit 50–7. By most conventional rules of thumb, a 12.2 year breakeven time for the Rite Aid bonds would render it unattractive. (Historically, five years or less until breakeven was required for consideration in the "attractive" category.) However, we see that the RAD bonds are theoretically valued at 101.95, yet are offered at only 100.50. The investor should consider many things when evaluating convertible securities including a dynamic scenario analysis and the quality of the inputs into a theoretical model. Scenario analysis of these securities is presented in Exhibit 50–7. The inputs of the valuation theoretic are designated in dashed boxes in Exhibit 50–7.

## Scenario Analysis

The theoretical scenario analysis in Exhibit 50–8 illustrates many of the convertible's attributes discussed earlier in this chapter. The analysis is "dynamic" in the sense that the yield spread of the bond and the volatility of the stock are both integrally related to the movement of the stock. Price movements of the stock are assumed independent of the market interest rate charges. For example, we can see that the return of the bond varies over the annual period and is varying in the same direction of the stock. Conceptually, the RAD bonds epitomize a classical convertible bond. The investment value (bond floor) is extremely stable and the bond participated in the portion of the upside of the equity

**E X H I B I T   50–8**

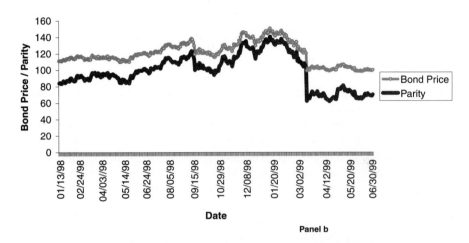

**Panel a**

## Rite Aid Convertible Bond Performance

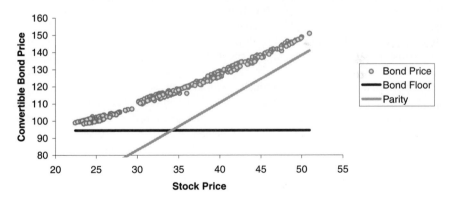

**Panel b**

## Rite Aid Convertible Bond Price versus the Stock Price

**Source: PIMCO Analytics**

movement. The participation is somewhat muted because the price of the stock has rendered the option component slightly out of the money.

In Exhibit 50–8, we observe actual historical price behavior of the RAD bond and stock for the period through June 1999. In Panel a, we see the historical point premium between the bond and its parity. We note that there is always a positive premium (will always be positive unless the bond is not immediately convertible). Moreover, as expected, the premium narrows as parity increases and expands as parity decreases.

The empirical information in Panel b portrays the theoretically perfect convertible. The price of the bond travels with the stock as stock prices increase and falls at a slower and slower rate as the stock falls. Finally, it hits its bond value and stops falling even though the stock continues to fall. The Hewlett Packard bonds exhibit a very similar historical pattern (see Exhibit 50–9). The HWP bonds are conceptually nice because of the high credit quality and because the put option period is near which serves to create a strong, stable bond floor. It should be noted, however, the HWP bonds are trading to the call/put date.

The scenario analysis for the HWP zero is interesting because, contrary to the RAD bond, it is slightly in the money. As a consequence, the bond floor is further away. The HWP's local performance (within a 25% move of the stock) is symmetric. However, given a substantial move in the stock price of greater than 25%, a strong asymmetry between stock and bond performance is to be expected. Most convertible bonds should outperform the delta adjusted underlying equity when large price changes (high volatility) occur because the value of the option exceeds the premium paid. There are instances when a convertible security may fare poorly when the stock falls sharply. Empirically, Winstar Communications 7% Preferred is such a security.

Winstar Communications 7% Preferred is a low quality, long-term security in a very volatile competitive industry. Convertible securities issued by speculative companies can, as noted above, be very valuable but can also perform very poorly at times. The Winstar convertible preferred is one such security. During the Fall of 1998, the bond was issued at $50 in a very volatile market at a credit spread of 9% which implied a 23.45 bond floor. The collapse in the market value of Winstar Communications common stock from 40 in March 1998 (time of issue of the preferred) to 15 in October 1998 implied a change in the total firm value from $2 billion to $750 million. This abrupt valuation change caused the perception of the credit risk of the Preferred to increase dramatically. The implied credit spread of 15% has subsequently declined to 6% as the stock price has recovered to 50 (August 1999). The extreme volatility in the credit spread implies a very unstable investment value. Given the security's long maturity and the improved credit perception, the investment value has increased from 23.45 to 37.25. We can see the extremely poor convertible dynamics in both the theoretical construct as well as in the empirical data. Despite this poor set of dynamics, there may be other compelling investment merits of the Winstar

**EXHIBIT  50–9**

Panel a

## Hewlett-Packard Convertible Bond Performance

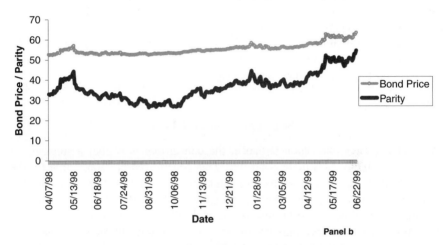

Panel b

### Hewlett-Packard Convertible Bond Price versus the Stock Price

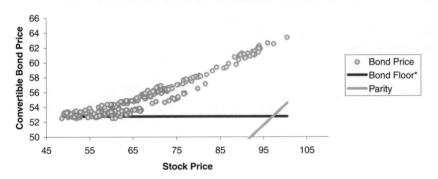

\* Bond floor here is calculated for the beginning of the period shown and is lower than its
current level.  See discussion on the bond in the text.

**Source: PIMCO Analytics**

Preferred. The investor must, however, be able to predict, *a priori,* the probable value of the convertible given a particular scenario for the common stock.

The importance of credit quality and credit analysis to convertible bond portfolio management cannot be overstated. Rite Aid 5¼ of 2002, our model convertible bond, experienced a substantial change in its investment value. The company started experiencing financial problems in Fall 1999. There were fraud allegations and management changes accompanying poor financial results. The credit spread gapped wider while simultaneously the equity value tumbled. The convertible bond price fell from 100 in March 1999 to 50 in June 2000. As investors viewed the credit to be distressed and highly speculative, the meaning of a "bond floor" was called into question.

## Separate Asset Class

We noted earlier that, upon issuance, the convertible is neither a stock nor a bond. Most likely, it is more bond-like. This generalized opinion is true for the issuer and the investor alike. Neither buyer nor seller know. It is only after the fact that one can conclude about its ultimate character. Because this is true and because not all stocks go up together (nor do they change at a constant rate), the correlation of the performance of the convertible bond universe to bonds and stocks varies considerably but predictably; neither stock nor bond. Convertible securities should be considered a separate asset class. Exhibit 50–10 provides

### EXHIBIT 50–10

Risk Reward Statistics

Convertibles have produced attractive risk-adjusted returns

Performance summary of Broad Market Indices for the Period January 1988 through June 1999*

|  | Annualized Return | Standard Deviation | Sharpe Ratio** |
|---|---|---|---|
| Merrill Lynch All U.S. Convertible Index | 13.95% | 9.46% | 0.89 |
| S&P 500 | 19.28% | 13.06% | 1.05 |
| Russell 2000 | 14.13% | 16.43% | 0.52 |
| Merrill Lynch Government and Corporate Bond Master Index | 8.57% | 4.45% | 0.69 |
| Lehman Brothers Aggregate Bond Index | 8.59% | 4.17% | 0.74 |

\* Merrill Lynch All US Converts Index return data are available from January 1988.
\*\* Sharpe ratio = (Total Return − Risk Free Rate)/Standard Deviation, where we used average return on 3-month Tbills for the reporting period (5.52%).
Source: PIMCO

such statistical data. In Exhibit 50–11 a modest 20% allocation of convertibles to a portfolio containing a mix of the S&P 500 and the Lehman Brothers Aggregate Bond Index is shown to exert a substantial improvement in the efficient frontier.

The investor in a convertible bond has a great advantage over the holder of a non-convertible corporate bond of the same issuer. Management of many companies have engaged in leveraged stock-buy back programs at the expense of the debt holders and to the benefit of stockholders and option holders (like management itself). Similarly, although not likely, capital structure changes initiated by management that reduce leverage tend to help bond holders. Convertible bonds tend to increase in value as the issuer's credit quality improves, all else equal. Because convertible bondholders participate in both bond and

**EXHIBIT   50–11**

Efficient Frontier for Lehman Aggregate and Merrill Lynch
All Converts Portfolio, January 1988–June 1999

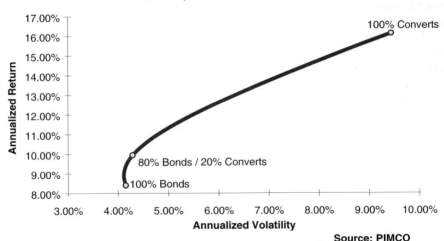

Source: PIMCO

Addition of corporate bonds to fixed-income portfolio can benefit an investor for the following reasons:

- Convertibles allow investors to get exposure to companies which often do not have straight-debt issues
- Upside potential, or in general, return profiles on fixed-income and convertible instruments issued by the same company, are quite different
- Provide investors mechanism to purchase cheap equity market insurance

Due to these three factors, a portfolio with an allocation to convertibles (1) benefits from diversification (correlation between components less than 1), and (2) allows for better use of portfolio manager's security-selection skills.

stock movements, the investors cannot be a target of management. Ultimately, the effect of a change in capital structure upon the value of the convertible will depend upon the success of the initiative and the relative changes in the price of the equities, the quality of the bonds and the "state" of the convertible at the time of the initiative.

## Call Risk

In June 1999, the RAD was callable in one year on 9/15/00 at a call price in excess of the market price of the convertible. The call risk was not high. However, the call will limit the potential gain on the convertible if the stock moves substantially to the upside. In June 2000, with the call out of the money and the yield high on the bond, the probability of call is about zero.

The convertible of HWP offered call protection through 10/14/00. The low premium, and the put provision are attractive elements of this convertible. However, because of the probable call, the price of the common, and the zero coupon, there is a negative yield on the bond. This convertible is in the money and trading to its call date. As such, there is on a modest amount of premium and the bond will trade to stock closely on the upside.

## Putable Convertibles

Some convertibles offer a put option, adding a possible further attractive feature to the instrument. For example, the Hewlett Packard convertibles are putable to the corporation on October 14, 2000 at 59.03, offering downside protection. However the yield to the 2000 put is $-5.52\%$.

## Dilution of the Conversion Privilege

A large common stock split or stock dividend could markedly dilute the value of the conversion privilege, unless adjustment of the number of shares received in conversion is made. For example, assume that a bond is convertible into 20 shares and that the company undergoes a 2-for-1 stock split. Recognizing this, the conversion privilege is typically protected by terms in the bond indenture providing for a pro rata adjustment of the conversion price and/or the conversion ratio so that the exchange ratio would increase to 40 shares after the stock split.

## DURATION MANAGEMENT

Duration is a measure of the sensitivity of the price of a bond to changes in interest rates. Embedded options complicate the calculation of duration; particularly when there are multiple embedded options as is the case with convertible bonds.

The importance of duration to convertible bond management varies as a function of the price of the equity relative to the conversion price. The greater this ratio, the less the importance of duration management. At low ratios, convertible bonds approach straight corporate bond status and duration management is most important. Effective duration calculation, which accounts for the effect of the embedded options, is the important bond management metric for duration management.

## VALUATION OF CONVERTIBLES

An investor in a convertible security effectively owns a nonconvertible fixed income security and a call option on the issuer's common stock. The value of a convertible security is therefore the sum of these two values, disregarding any other options that may be embedded in the convertible security (e.g., the issuer's right to call the issue).

The value of a convertible bond disregarding the conversion feature is called its *straight value*. This is found by discounting the cash flow for the bond at a yield equal to the yield to maturity of an equivalent nonconvertible bond.

The value of a convertible bond, if it is converted immediately into the common stock of the issuer, is called its *conversion value*. This value is found by multiplying the conversion ratio by the current market price of the common stock. The conversion value for RAD is 70.39 (27.672 × 25.458) and 54.57 for HWP.

The minimum value of a convertible bond is the *greater* of its straight value and conversion value. Arbitrage ensures that this will occur. For example, suppose that the straight value of the Rite Aid issue is 94.45 when its conversion value is 100 and that the issue is trading at 94.45. Investors would buy the issue for 94.45 and convert it for 27.67 shares worth 35.14 each, resulting in a riskless arbitrage profit of 5.55. Suppose, instead, the straight value is 94.45 at the time of the conversion value is 70.39 but the issue is trading at 70.39. In this case, investors would be buying a bond offering a higher-than-market yield with a "free" equity option.

A convertible bond will trade at a premium above the minimum value just described because of the value of the option the security holder has. It is usually very difficult to infer precise values because the convertible bonds are generally subordinate to the senior debt and the covenants in the indenture are different. The option component always has a value even if it is way out of the money.

Exhibit 50–12 shows the typical price response of a convertible bond at different stock price levels. The solid line in the exhibit shows the conversion value. The dashed curve is the actual price of the convertible bond. At any common stock price, the difference between the actual price and the minimum price is the value of the option.

Determining the worth of the option to buy the common stock embedded in a convertible bond is complicated. Here is where equity option pricing models

**E X H I B I T   50–12**

Convertible Bond Price versus Stock Price

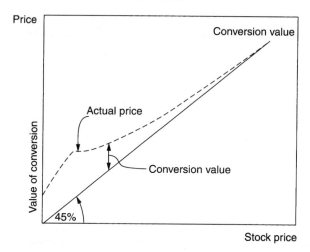

are typically used. The Black-Scholes option pricing model might be used for a quick approximation of the value of the equity option. A more comprehensive model that takes into consideration the many nuances embedded within a convertible bond was utilized to derive the matrix of theoretical valuations shown in Exhibit 50–13 for its RAD bonds. This exhibit includes many of the important valuation measures and portfolio management variables that were discussed in this chapter and are quite important to convertible bonds. The information contained in Exhibit 50–13 is the result of an advanced, comprehensive analysis of convertible bonds and is a necessary information set for convertible bond management.

## SUMMARY

Some fixed income securities are convertible into common stock, offering the basic advantages of a senior security (bond or preferred stock), while allowing the holder to participate in potential corporate growth. The investor pays for the conversion privilege by accepting a significantly lower yield than could be obtained by purchasing nonconvertible bonds or preferred stocks. A convertible, moreover, usually sells at a premium over the value of the underlying common stock. If the anticipated growth in the value of the common stock is not realized, the purchaser will have sacrificed yield and, in some instances, may well see the value of the convertible instrument fall sharply.

**EXHIBIT   50–13**

Rite Aid 5¼ 9/15/02

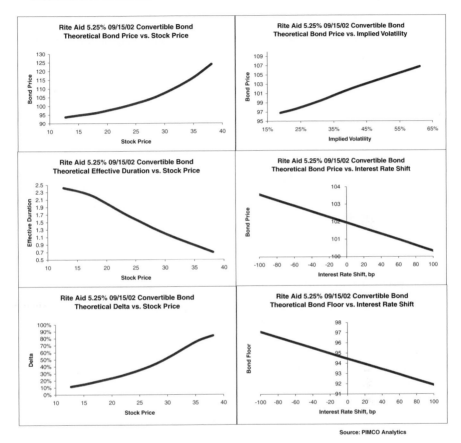

Source: PIMCO Analytics

Dated 9/15/99

There are three distinct areas of analysis that should be undertaken when evaluating a convertible security:

1. The quality of the security should be assessed in the same way as for other nonconvertible senior securities. This requires assessing the ability of the issuing company to meet the fixed charges mandated by the issue under reasonably conceived adverse economic circumstances.

2. The growth potential for the underlying common stock must be evaluated, because that growth potential offers the basis for generating

the added yield necessary to offset the yield sacrifice incurred at the time of purchase and provides a return that makes purchase attractive.

3. A rigorous quantitative and scenario analysis of the convertible security must be performed to insure expectational consistency of the security to portfolio objectives.

## CHAPTER 51

# CONVERTIBLE SECURITIES AND THEIR VALUATION

**Mihir Bhattacharya***
Managing Director
Deutsche Banc Alex. Brown

Convertible debentures and convertible preferred shares, or more generally *equity-linked securities,* span the space from common stock on the one hand to straight (non-convertible) debt on the other. While the majority of newly issued convertible securities combine a balance of the common stock and straight debt attributes, some are close proxies for common stock and others skewed towards straight debt. Some new issues may have maturity of as short as 3 years, as in the case of convertible notes and mandatorily convertible securities, while traditional convertible preferred shares are perpetual (i.e., the issuer is not ever required to repay the par or the principal amount of the security). Over time, a convertible security that may have started out as very close to straight debt may become very much like common stock due to price appreciation in the common stock into which it is convertible. The reverse is also true as the price of the underlying common stock declines.

Convertible securities have greatly evolved with the increasing market volatility of the past decade. This chapter will examine the products that comprise the asset class, the size of the market and its evolution, motivations for their issuance and purchase, and their structural aspects. A substantial part of the chapter will focus on valuing and hedging these securities colloquially known as *convertibles* or *converts.* Passing reference will be made to convertible markets in Europe and Japan.

The essential features of convertible products, and notable exceptions thereto, are as follows:

• A convertible security may be converted, generally at any time until its maturity date, into the underlying common stock. Exception: some converts may have an initial non-conversion period of 6 to 12 months.

---

* In the earlier editions of this *Handbook,* this chapter was co-authored with Yu Zhu. I remain grateful for his comments and insight.

- The vast majority of convertibles are convertible into the shares of the issuer. The rest are convertible into shares of another publicly traded entity. These latter securities are called *exchangeables.*

- The conversion right rests with the holder. Exception: in some mandatorily convertible securities, investors are not given a conversion option. They receive the applicable shares mandatorily at maturity.

- Almost all converts have a redemption feature that allows the issuer to redeem them prior to maturity. Exception: most recent mandatorily convertibles are non-redeemable.

- Although convertible at any time, their holders are likely to exercise the conversion right only in response to a redemption notice by the issuer—also known as the *issuer call* or simply, the *call.* In other words, virtually all conversions occur only when forced by the issuer. Exceptions: (a) when there is a high dividend paying underlying stock that is also illiquid e.g. Real Estate Investment Trust Stocks; (b) in the presence of material market friction, such as, restrictions on conversion or a high cost for hedging the convert; and (c) when the underlying stock price is above the *critical stock price,* discussed in further detail below.

- Upon conversion, the issuer will usually satisfy its obligation by transferring to the holder the specified number of shares of the underlying security per convertible. This is called a *physical settle.* Exception: sometimes the issuer may have the right, specified in the prospectus for the convertible, to satisfy its obligation by paying the holder the cash value of the underlying securities. This is known as the *cash settle option.* Depending on the liquidity of the underlying stock, a cash-settled convert may fetch a slightly lower price than would a physical settled convert due to the cost incurred by arbitrage and hedge fund investors in covering their stock short position. (As a rule, these investors short the underlying stock against a long position in the convert.)

- A convertible's current yield or yield to maturity usually exceeds the yield of the underlying security.

- The price of a convertible security is at least equal to the value of the shares into which it is convertible, that is, its *conversion value.* In other words, a convertible should trade at a non-negative premium to its conversion value. Exceptions may occur under the following conditions: (a) when there are restrictions on the holders' conversion right; (b) when the underlying stock is illiquid; (c) in anticipation of forced conversion leading to a loss of the accrued coupon, a currently redeemable, deep in-the-money, convertible may trade at a discount to its conversion value; and (d) in the case of cash settled convertible, which may cause additional transaction costs for arbitrage fund and hedge fund investors.

- Convertible debentures are almost always issued as subordinated debentures. Thus they are the least senior debt security, senior only to preferred shares—of both the convertible and non-convertible type—and common stock. When issued as either subordinated convertible debenture or convertible preferred they are accompanied with virtually no restrictive covenants. Exceptions occur: (a) infrequently in the U.S., when they are issued as senior subordinated securities, and on rare occasions as senior debentures with a corresponding level of covenants; (b) in Europe, where most converts are senior unsubordinated debentures.

- Convertibles have a pre-specified maturity and a pre-specified number of shares per convertible, i.e. a fixed *conversion ratio*. Exceptions include: (a) a handful of mandatorily convertibles the maturities of which may be extended by a year at the option of the issuer; (b) the "PHONES" convertible product (described below) the maturity of which may be extended by as long as 30 years; (c) the number of shares received upon conversion of a mandatorily convertible security is not fixed, but is a function of the underlying share price on the settlement date. However, the number of shares to be received is bounded by pre-specified maximum and minimum limits; (d) some Japanese bank converts, among others, have a *reset* or *refix* clause whereby the conversion ratio is adjusted upwards, and the conversion price adjusted downwards if the underlying stock price does not exceed pre-specified trigger prices.

Higher volatilities in the equity and debt markets during the past decade, combined with the evolving sophistication of issuers and investors, have changed the convertible market in several key ways. Increased debt market volatility has driven home the point of the *duration risk* inherent in any security with a fixed income component, including converts. The increased volatility of the spreads (over Treasury or other interest rate benchmarks) has heightened investor sensitivity to the reliability of the *fixed income floor* or *bond value* of the convert. And the volatile equity market with its sustained upward trend has greatly contributed to the shortening of the maturities of new issue converts. As a result of conversion forcing redemptions, the effective life of an average convert now tends not to exceed the first redemption date. Thus issuers, when faced with the cost benefit analysis of a longer term convertible financing on the balance sheet, with its attendant higher coupon versus a lower coupon for a shorter dated convertible, are generally choosing the latter. Investors, too, are more aware of the value of the redemption feature embedded in the convertible, a feature which may be viewed as the investor selling back an option to the issuer. Investors increasingly demand a market price for this feature.

Convertibles have equity and interest rate options, and occasionally, currency options, embedded in them. Issuers and investors are becoming even more aware that option valuation is driven by, among other factors: (a) equity volatility; (b) interest rate volatility; and (c) spread volatility. In some situations the embedded options may easily be separated and valued. However, in the vast majority of cases, they interact with each other and so prove difficult, if not impossible, to separate. Investors should be aware of the inherent danger of attempting to value the embedded options as if they were separable options.

We will employ the contingent claims approach to the valuation of convertible securities. After reviewing the evolution of convertible markets in the past decade and describing the products and recent innovations, we will discuss the general attributes of a convertible and the traditional valuation method. We will then introduce the modern valuation method and discuss the impact of the various inputs to the model. Finally, we will discuss the applications of the model and decisions faced by issuers and investors.

## EVOLUTION IN THE CONVERTIBLE MARKETS

The convertible market was viewed until relatively recently as a source of funds for firms of marginal equity story and/or a high risk profile (i.e. a high probability of default), firms unable to obtain financing from more established markets. Convertibles have now evolved into an asset class for investors in which the largest single issue raised $3.18 billion for an A1/A+ (investment grade) rated issuer.[1] Several very large firms have raised more than $ 1 billion each, some through overnight transactions with very little marketing effort, a fact that indicates the impressive reach of the convert market. To understand better this evolution and its future direction, it will prove useful to segment the market for this asset class into its distinct distribution channels.

## Convertible Market Segments

The first, and by far the largest, segment of the convertible market is the "publicly issued" convertible market. This segment includes all flavors of convertible securities issued either as registered under the Securities Act of 1933 ("SEC registered") or under Rule 144A institutional private placement ("144A issue"). Issues in this segment are of least $50 million each; smaller issues do not generate liquid secondary market trading. Trading of smaller issues is infrequent, with wide bid-offer spreads; consequently, these issues will usually fail to attract the notice of managers of large institutional portfolios, which are the "anchor

---

1. Bell Atlantic Financial 4.25% exchangeable note maturing on 9/15/2005, issued in August 1998, pegged to the value of Cable and Wireless Communication plc (CWZ) ordinary shares. Upon conversion, the issuer has the option to deliver the CWZ ordinary shares or its cash equivalent.

buyers" of almost all new issues.[2] The present chapter will, therefore, focus on the publicly traded convertibles, though the economic and valuation logic apply to the other segments as well.

The second segment of the convertible market consists of convertibles issued by "small cap" and "micro cap" issuers. For this segment, the equity market capitalization, i.e. the number of shares outstanding multiplied by the price per share, is less than $350 million. Typically, convertible issues in this group range in size from $10 million to $45 million, underwritten and distributed by smaller investment banks. These issues may be either SEC registered or issued under Rule 144A. Though they are structured so as to permit secondary trading, and they do trade, albeit infrequently, these issues are distinct from those in the next segment, called the "privately placed" or "Rule 144" or "Regulation D" issues.

This third segment of the convertible market consists of highly structured and individually negotiated transactions, wherein the issuer and a single investor or handful of investors draw up the terms and conditions of the investment and the structure of the convertible security to be exchanged. This "private invest-ment" is not available to investors at large. The specific one-off, non-market features and covenants of privately placed issues may include: (a) very high conversion premium in exchange for a high coupon or preferred dividend; (b) an extended period of non-conversion; (c) conversion into restricted stock which cannot immediately be monetized upon conversion; (d) a resetting of the con-version premium and/or coupon or preferred dividend based on balance sheet/income statement/cash flow target ratios for specific time periods; (e) debt cov-enant restrictions; (f) seniority in the event of bankruptcy, merger or acquisition; and (g) provisions for voting and control issues. The typical buyers of the pri-vately placed, illiquid convertible transactions are leveraged buyout funds, private equity funds, and the like. These buyers provide strategic capital infusion to distressed firms, firms needing added capital to restructure or to grow through acquisitions, and firms not otherwise ready for, or unwilling to pursue, public market transactions. Private equity investors tend to have long holding period horizons, and have bullish projections about the future stock market performance of the firm. Secondary market liquidity is therefore of less concern to them. These privately placed convertibles are a component in the menu of "mezzanine financing products" in the non-investment grade sector.

---

2. Although convertible bonds may be listed on the New York Stock Exchange (NYSE) or the American Stock Exchange (AMEX), they are most frequently traded in the over-the-counter (OTC) markets. As a result, the price levels reported in the press may not be representative of the current market price indications. SEC registered convertible preferreds usually trade on the NYSE and AMEX. 144A convertible preferreds trade on the OTC market until they are registered or are "seasoned" at which time they are listed and trade on the NYSE or AMEX.

Another very large privately placed segment for equity-linked products are the equity derivative departments of investment banks, the investment arms of insurance companies, and other financial institutions. Regulatory or contractual obligations do not allow the direct sale of the restricted common shares, which include equity stakes by the officers of a firm, holdings by affiliates, often venture capital firms or private equity firms, and non-core equity stakes received as a part of merger or acquisition by an individual or another entity. Equity derivative departments of investment banks employ equity-linked structures, such as collars or trust backed convertibles (see below) which they buy on their own account and forward up to approximately 80% of the value of the shares, depending on the specific structure, to the seller. They then hedge and/or trade the position for their own account to mitigate the risk of the long position or to sell down the position.

## Convertible Products Range

Convertible products[3] may be divided into three categories, based on their seniority in the balance sheet and the tax treatment of the preferred dividend. These categories are (a) convertible debt products; (b) convertible preferred products of the mandatory and the non-mandatory type; and (c) hybrid products which are preferred shares from a financial reporting perspective, but are structured so as to be tax deductible, and thus to reduce the net cost to the issuer.

### Convertible Debt Products

*Convertible debt products* are almost always issued as subordinate debt in the United States. The coupons of these products are tax deductible and the issuer is accorded no equity credit from the rating agencies.[4] The products in this category include:

• *Traditional Convertible Debt:* Typical maturities are 5, 7 or 10 years, with a 20% to 25% conversion premium, and a non-redemption period (*hard non-call*) of three years. The bond is issued at par, matures at par, and has a

---

3. For the balance of this chapter, unless otherwise noted, we will use the term "convertible" for exchangeables as well. As may be expected, exchangeables are used to monetize stakes that an entity, be it a firm or an individual, owns in the shares of another publicly traded common stock.

4. Equity credit from rating agencies is outside the scope of this chapter. Suffice it to say that rating agencies have repeatedly indicated that, with the exception of common shares, which (by definition) are accorded 100% equity credit, they do not adhere to a formulaic approach to assigning ratings for securities or corporate issuers. Nonetheless, one of the rating agencies has indicated the general range of equity credit that may be expected for a list of financial instruments. See Libby Bruch, "Integration of Rating Scales and Re-evaluation of Equity Credit," *Standard & Poor's CreditWeek,* February 24, 1999, 9–11.

fixed conversion ratio[5] and hence a fixed conversion price during its life. Basic variations include a higher conversion premium with a higher associated coupon, or a stock price trigger based conditional redemption (also known as a *provisional call* or a *soft call protection*).[6] The combination of an initial period of hard non-call followed by a soft call is often used to trade-off against a lower coupon and/or a higher conversion premium. As a rule, the greater the volatility of the underlying stock, and the higher its growth expectations, the greater the variation from the basic structure.[7] Reset or refix convertibles are issued when the outlook for the firm or for the firm's primary economic domicile country, or both, is unfavorable. Such has been the case for Japan for most of the 1990s and for other Asian countries in the latter half of the decade; hence the development of the reset converts there. The conversion price is revised downward if some stock price triggers are not met. The reset clause lowers the risk to the investor and transfers it to the issuer.[8]

- *Zero Coupon Convertible Debt:* Also known as LYON,[9] this product is a zero coupon, putable, redeemable, convertible debenture with 15 to 20 years maturity; with one day puts at accreted value on every fifth anniversary of the issue date; and with a hard non-call until the first put date. Thereafter, the issue is unconditionally redeemable at any time at the accreted value. The debenture is issued at a discount to par, calculated as the semi-annually compounded yield to maturity of the security. For example, a 5% yield to

---

5. Conversion ratios for all converts are adjusted for stock splits and special situations, such as special dividends or distributions, as specified in the prospectus for each convert.

6. A "two-year hard plus one year 130% provisional" means that the convert is not redeemable in the first two years from issue date. It is conditionally redeemable in the third year only if the stock price is at least 30% above the conversion price for at least 20 out of 30 consecutive trading days. After the third year, the convert is redeemable unconditionally. Provisional triggers usually range from 120% to 150%.

7. For example, Amazon.com issued a $1.25 billion, 10-year maturity convertible debt in January 1999 with a coupon of 4.75%, and conversion premium of 27%. Amazon.com is a very volatile stock with strong name recognition as a market leader in the internet sector. It was able to issue the convert after a one-day marketing and increase the issue size from an initially announced $500 million to a finally executed $1.25 billion based on investor demand. The structure provided no hard call protection. Instead, it had a three-year "150% provisional redemption with investment premium makewhole." This means that if the 150% trigger condition were satisfied during the first 3 years, then the issuer may force conversion. However, the issuer would then simultaneously have to pay the investor a cash amount of $212.60 [=$1,000.00 less ($1,000.00 divided by 1.27)] per bond. The net effect upon conversion is as if the investor purchased Amazon.com common stock on the date of issue of the convert.

8. To our knowledge, no publicly traded reset converts have been issued in the U.S. market in the last 15 years, although some small private issues for microcap firms have been executed in recent years.

9. Liquid Yield Option Note is a service mark of Merrill Lynch & Co.

maturity, 20-year LYON will be issued at a price of 37.243% of par, which is the present value of $100 discounted at 2.5% for 40 periods. The initial conversion premium ranges in most cases from 15% to 25%. The conversion ratio established at issue remains constant during the life of the security. As a result, since the bond value is accreting towards par while the conversion ratio is fixed, the resulting conversion price rising continuously rises.[10] Attractive features of this security from the perspective of the issuer include:

- Conservation of cash and the option to deploy it at the (higher) internal rate of return of the issuer
- Tax deduction on the accrued interest
- Upon conversion, the per bond equity addition to the balance sheet is comprised of the initial issue price plus the accrued interest amount
- Upon conversion, there is no re-capture (by the Treasury) of the accrued tax deduction
- This product is, all else being equal, the most debt-like of all equity-linked securities and has the highest effective conversion price
- It signals to the market that the issuer is unwilling to sell equity at the spot price but only willing to sell it at the high effective conversion premium

The trade-offs to investors for the rising conversion price lies in the higher option value in the 5 years of hard non-call; a higher accretion rate; and the option to put the security back to the issuer at accreted value at the stated intervals.[11] Among the typical variations in the structure are higher conversion premiums for highly rated issuers and/or high volatility-high expected growth stocks, sometimes in conjunction with a first put in year 3 with a corresponding hard non-call also for 3 years. Earlier variations had non-symmetric first put and call dates, or had a provisional call in place of a hard non-call.

- *Original Issue Discount Convertible Debt:* This structure (called the *OID convert*) combines aspects of the preceding two structures in that a small

---

10. Continuing with the numerical illustration, assuming that the stock price of the underlying share to be $45.00 per share, and the initial conversion premium of 25%, the initial conversion price is equal to $45.00 × 1.25 = $56.25 per share. The conversion ratio per bond accreting at 5% and 20-year maturity will be the issue price divided by the initial conversion price 6.621 shares (=372.43/56.25). In five years, the bond will accrete to $476.74 which is the issue price compounded at 2.5% for 10 semi-annual periods. The effective conversion price will then be $72.00 per share (=476.74/6.621 shares).

11. The puts are sequential European type and can be either *hard puts* or *soft puts*. In the former, the put is paid in cash. In the latter, it can be satisfied in cash or shares equal to the value of the put amount, or combination, at the option of the issuer. Earlier versions had an equal value of a new straight debt security as a third alternative; this alternative has been dropped due to ambiguities regarding the valuation of the new debt security.

part of the yield to maturity is paid in the form of cash coupon, and the balance accretes. As is to be expected, all else being equal, the yield to maturity in this structure straddles those of the preceding two structures. The conversion price is also rising but at a rate lower than that for the zero coupon structure; the tax deduction associated with the accrued interest is therefore also lower. Maturity for this product is 5 to 7 years with a typical hard non-call protection of three years. The security is not putable.

- *Premium Redemption Convertible Debt:* This is simply another variation of the OID convert. The only difference between this variation and the OID is that the latter is issued at below par and accretes to par at maturity, while the former is issued at par and accretes in exactly the same manner to some number above par. This structure is very common for converts issued out of Europe and Asia, where regulations may require the issuance of bonds at par.

- *Step-Up Convertible Debt:* This product follows a common structure in the non-investment grade debt (*high yield*) market, wherein the security pays no coupon for a period of up to 5 years. The coupon then steps up to a higher level than what it would have been if it were current coupon paying from the start. Adapted for the convertible market, this security pays a low cash coupon for the first 3 years, which is also the hard non-call period. The coupon then steps up for the balance of the life of the convert that ranges from another 4 to 7 years. The effective conversion price rises continuously until the last low-coupon payment date, and stays constant at its higher level thereafter until maturity. As might be expected, the absolute levels of the coupons in step-up convertibles are much lower than those in the high yield market due to the inclusion of the conversion option. Interest is expensed at the rate of the yield to maturity, which is higher than the cash coupon during the low coupon period, but lower than the cash coupon rate in the later period. The incentive for the issuer to redeem this security prior to the higher coupon kicking in is therefore very strong.

- *Negative Yield Convertible Debt:* Since 1998, the interest rates on Japanese Government debt denominated in yen has been particularly low and stands at 1.10% as of 9/1/99. Dividend yields on Japanese equity is traditionally very low. Under this scenario, if a yen denominated, zero coupon, low conversion premium, unsubordinated convertible debt with an effective maturity of 5 years were to be issued with hard non-call also of 5 years, its theoretical value would most likely be a few points above par. To make it equitable to both issuer and investor, such a convert is issued at 1% to 5% above par yet it matures at par thereby resulting in a negative yield to maturity security. A few of these are presently in the market with more likely if the current environment continues. Compared to the traditional Japanese converts issued with 2.5% conversion premiums which tended to be very cheap to the investor, the pricing of the embedded options of negative yield convertibles is more even-handed.

### Convertible Referred Products

*Convertible preferred products* are senior only to the issuer's common stock. The preferred dividend is not tax deductible, and hence is a costly source of funding on an earnings per share basis. Convertible preferreds are mostly issued therefore when the firm needs equity credit from the rating agencies; when it is unable or unwilling to issue debt due to leverage test ratios imposed on them by other classes of senior securities; or when the firm does not pay taxes due to accumulated losses. These products are viewed as "permanent" or long-term financing, and provide the issuer with the ability to skip payment of preferred dividends without triggering default. Hence they are generally accorded up to 50% equity credit from the rating agencies.[12,13] Withholding taxes and the low bond floor resulting from the perpetual maturity are the primary reasons why these structures are not commonly used in Europe. The products in this category may be further sub-divided into those that redeem at par if not converted, that is, without impairment to the original investment and those that convert mandatorily into a formula number of common shares at maturity. In the latter case, investors may lose part of their initial investment if the stock price falls below that on the date of issue.

*Non-mandatorily convertible preferred shares* include:

• *Perpetual Maturity Convertible Preferred Shares:* This is the preferred share counterpart of the Traditional Convertible Debt described above in that it has a fixed conversion price, it is a very easy to understand structure, and has been a staple of the convertible market for several decades. The main differences are its perpetual maturity and lower seniority; consequently the dividend on the convertible preferred will be higher than the coupon on an otherwise identical convertible debt. The higher rate on the preferred results from the fact that both the benchmark interest rate, the 30-year U.S. Treasury in this case, and the credit spread corresponding to this longer maturity

---

12. While skipping preferred dividends does not result in default, it does tend to severely depress the stock price. Restrictions on common dividend payments and board seats to preferred shareholders and other remedies may be imposed on the firm until the arrears in preferred dividends are paid. Consequently, the option to skip preferred dividends, although embedded in the structure, is resorted to only when the firm is in financial distress.

13. Issuance of traditional preferred shares, in most cases, are viewed as helping prevent a ratings downgrade but not necessarily help in a ratings upgrade. Since mandatorily convertible securities, by structure, are certain to convert into common shares within 3 to 5 years, they are viewed more akin to common shares, and therefore may be accorded up to 85% equity credit. This applies to all flavors of mandatorily convertible securities—preferred, exchangeable debt, or hybrid tax deductible preferred.

is higher, and the two together form the base rate. The dividend rate on the convertible preferred is determined by adjusting downward from this higher base rate for the embedded equity option.[14,15]

- *Dated Convertible Preferred:* Again a convertible adaptation from the high yield market, this product has a maturity of 10 to 12 years; thus it matches or is outside the typical maturity of high yield debt which is 10 and sometimes 12 years. If not converted, a dated convertible preferred must be redeemed at par at maturity. In all other aspects it is similar to the perpetual maturity convertible preferred. Rating agencies are understandably less likely to accord any equity credit due to this product's debt-like redemption at maturity feature. This structure is infrequent in the U.S.; it is, however, always used by non-investment grade issuers faced with covenant restriction limits.

- *Step-Up Convertible Preferred:* This product is analogous to the step-up convertible debt, but with perpetual maturity.

***Mandatorily convertible preferred shares*** in essence transfer the downside risk of the stock to the investor in exchange for a higher preferred dividend. This category of converts include:

- *Capped Common:* Also known as PERCS,[16] the capped common is essentially a combination of purchasing a common share and writing a 30 to 60% out-of-the-money call (relative to the spot price on the date of issue). Investors have no conversion option at any time during the life of the security, which is typically 3 years; the issuer, however, may redeem this convertible at any time provided the preferred dividend due until the maturity date is paid in its entirety. The call option premium is packaged in the form of quarterly preferred dividends. This packaging of a common options strategy, known as the *buy-write* strategy, allows convertible funds to invest in them. Were these three-year convertible securities unbundled, the charter of convertible funds would generally prohibit such investment. The investor in the capped common realizes all of the stock price appreciation from the price at issue up to the cap level; anything beyond that goes to the issuer. On the other hand, the investor loses part of her principal to the extent the stock price is lower than the issue price at maturity. In a rising equity market, the issuer has almost always exercised the call option and, hence ex-post, this product has under-performed the common stock from an investor perspec-

---

14. This logic applies to all converts.
15. A variation of this security allows the issuer the option to exchange the convertible preferred for an otherwise identical convertible subordinated debenture of maturity 10 years from the original date of issue. Issuer will usually exercise this option when it returns to tax paying status.
16. The Preferred Equity Redemption Cumulative Stock (PERCS) is a service mark of Morgan Stanley Dean Witter.

tive. Consequently, its popularity has declined considerably. Rating agencies may generally be expected to accord equity credit of up to 85%.

- *Modified Capped Common:* A variation on the above, the modified capped common may be viewed as a PERC with some downside protection to the investor, in the form of an embedded put the investor purchases from the issuer. Microsoft Corporation issued $1 billion of this security in 1996 with a cap of 28% on the upside but without any downside risk to the investor— that is, with no hit to the principal. The embedded put purchased by the investor was a three-year at-the-money put on a high volatility stock, and hence was very expensive. The net preferred dividend to the investor was accordingly low.[17]

- *Traditional Mandatorily Convertible Preferred:* Although invented recently, in 1993, this structure has been so frequently used to raise funds in the convertible market that it is already viewed as a "traditional" product and has spawned a host of acronyms.[18] Typically, it is issued at the same price as the underlying stock price; matures in 3 to 5 years, most frequently three-year maturity; and has a conversion premium in the 20% to 22% range. It is easiest to view this security (popularly known as a *mandatory*) as a traditional convertible with a three-year maturity that is share settled, packaged with an embedded at-the-money put purchased by the issuer from the investor. The number of shares received by the investor at maturity depends on the share price on the maturity date.[19] This security's popularity has stemmed from the high equity credit from rating agencies; the transfer of risk to the investor in the event of a drop in the share price; and the traditional convertible features on the upside. Because the issue is settled in shares, the question of credit risk of the issuer with respect to payment of par is irrelevant. Only the credit risk with respect to the payment of the preferred dividends remains. Consequently, the structure is relatively insensitive to the creditworthiness of the issuer. The preferred dividend for a mandatory ranges from 6.25 % to 8.50%, depending on the dividend yield on the underlying common shares. The most frequent preferred dividend is 6.50% to

---

17. Microsoft Corp. Series A 2.75% Convertible Preferred issued on 12/17/96 maturing on 12/15/99; CAT at 28%.
18. The service marked acronyms, followed in parenthesis by their respective investment banks, include: DECS (Salomon Smith Barney), PRIDES (Merrill Lynch), ACES (Goldman Sachs), PEPS (Morgan Stanley Dean Witter), SAILS (Credit Suisse First Boston), and PIES (Lehman Brothers).
19. Assuming a spot stock price of $100 a share, the mandatory will also be issued at $100. If the conversion premium is 20%, the minimum conversion ratio is the issue price divided by the conversion price = $100.00/120.00 = 0.8333 shares per mandatory. If the stock price at maturity is at or above $120 the investor receives 0.8333 shares. If the stock price is at $100 or below, he receives one share that is the maximum number of shares per preferred. So, in the event that the stock price is $65 at maturity, the investor has a hit to the principal of $35 per share. If the stock price is between $100 and $120, the investor receives between 0.8333 and 1.0 shares so as to be worth the initial investment of $100.

7.00% for a 21% conversion premium on a three-year mandatory on a non-dividend paying stock.

- *Modified Mandatorily Convertible Preferred:* A variation on the preceding structure, the modified mandatory convertible preferred provides the investor with downside protection for the first 10% to 15% from the spot price, in exchange for a lower preferred dividend. In effect, the net put component of the package purchased by the issuer is 10% to 15% out-of-the-money. Hence the put premium is lower, and this is translated as a lower preferred dividend. The maximum number of shares is 1.111 for a 10% out-of-the-money put case, rather than the one share in the at-the-money put case of the traditional mandatory. The equity credit accorded is identical. Daimler-Benz issued DM 993 million (US$ 585 million) worth of this structure in 1997.

Mandatorily and modified mandatorily exchangeable securities (wherein the underlying stock is different from the issuer's common stock) can be issued as debt securities. Such securities constitute a major portion of all mandatory securities, and were the primary motivation for invention of this structure. When a mandatorily convertible security is issued on the issuer's own stock, it is deemed as a forward sale of the common and hence is not tax deductible. Specialized structures, the specific details of which are outside the scope of this chapter, are crafted in compliance with the applicable tax code in order to achieve effective tax deductability. The next sub-section briefly outlines these hybrid products.

**Hybrid convertible products:** This category consists of structures which are treated as preferred shares for financial reporting purposes, but their distributions are tax deductible. The development of hybrid convertible preferreds closely followed the invention of the MIPS, QUIPS[20] in the fixed rate non-convertible preferred market. The essential structure in this category is as follows: a Trust[21] issues convertible preferred shares to investors and simultaneously uses the proceeds to purchase convertible subordinated debt from the issuer. The convertible subordinated debt will be the sole asset of the Trust. The coupon from the issuer to the Trust exactly mirrors the preferred dividend paid by the Trust. Upon conversion by the investors, the Trust in turn converts the convertible debentures and passes through the shares to the investors.

- *Trust Non-mandatory Preferred:* The maturity of this product ranges from 15 to 30 years and equals the life of the Trust; its cash distributions and maturity mirrors that of the convertible debenture purchased by the Trust

---

20. Monthly Income Preferred Shares (MIPS) and Quarterly Income Preferred Shares (QUIPS) are service marks of Goldman Sachs. Trust Originated Preferred Securities (TOPRS) is a service mark of Merrill Lynch and is more descriptive of the structure.
21. The Trust is set up as a closed end fund under the Investment Company Act of 1940.

from the issuer. Investors are generally not sensitive to the structural difference between these securities and the traditional perpetual convertible preferred. Rating agency equity credit may be equal to that of the traditional perpetual convertible preferred, though recent discussions that might lead this product to be viewed as being closer to debt.

- *Trust Mandatory Preferred and Modified Mandatory Preferred:* This product is similar to its non-tax deductible counterpart, except for the complexities involved with the Trust and the forward purchase contract between the investor and the issuer which is required to ensure mandatory conversion at the end of the life of the Trust, typically 3 years. This Trust structure is also employed when the entity selling the shares is not a SEC registrant but rather as an individual or an investment or venture capital partnership. Should the creditworthiness of the corporate issuer be less than acceptable, or if the seller is not a SEC registrant, preferred dividends due the investors over the life of the security are escrowed in the Trust in the form of Treasury strips with maturities matching the scheduled preferred dividend payment dates. On the date of issue, proceeds from the sale of the Trust mandatory preferred to the investors, less the cost of the Treasury strips and Trust administration costs are forwarded to the issuer. The underlying shares are simultaneously escrowed in the Trust so as to create a bankruptcy remote Trust with an implied AAA credit rating.[22]

  - *Zero Premium Exchangeable Debt:* This product is a 1999 invention with the acronym "PHONES".[23] It is a 30-year zero conversion premium security issued at the same price as the underlying share into which it is exchangeable. It is redeemable by the issuer at any time, and convertible by the investor at any time, though there may be an initial non-conversion period. However, if the security were to be converted by the investor in the initial 30-year maturity period, the conversion ratio will be 0.95 implying a 5% penalty for voluntary conversion. The security is extendible for a further 30 years, subject to certain minimal conditions, at which time the conversion ratio becomes one share. The investor receives a pass-through of the dividend paid by the underlying share plus a fixed interest component. Any increase in the dividend paid by the share is deemed return of principal and deducted from the residual "par value" which is initially equal to the original issue price. Investors are liable for taxes on income deemed as received at the issuer's subordinated straight debt rate,

---

22. "Treasury stock method" is applicable to Trust mandatory converts as opposed to the "if converted" method applicable to most other convertible structures. In addition to the advantageous tax deductions resulting to issuers, this structure is particularly attractive to them because they receive equity credit immediately upon issuance of the mandatory, yet e.p.s. dilution is postponed to the third year as the incremental new shares are recognized only upon settlement of the mandatory at the end of the third year.
23. Participating Hybrid Option Note Exchangeable Securities (PHONES) is a service mark of Merrill Lynch.

which considerably exceeds the interest paid by the issuer. In exchange, the investor's basis for the share will rise with time. Zero premium exchangeable debt, at its most basic level, is a tax advantaged way for the issuer to monetize its holding of the underlying shares without actually transferring ownership of the shares. It thus potentially allows the issuer to defer the capital gains tax for as long as 60 years while enjoying a much larger interest deduction than cash coupon paid (9% imputed rate versus 1.75% actual cash coupon rate in one instance). Given the substantial tax advantage it provides the issue it is attractive for the issuer. However, due to its material tax liability for a taxable investment entity, this product is most likely to appeal to tax sheltered investment vehicles of the equity income type, to tax sheltered index funds and to off shore hedge funds.[24] Many investors do not consider this security to be a convertible as it lacks any meaningful convexity.

Exhibit 51–1 provides a schematic of the terminal payoff diagrams for the major convertible securities. Similar payoff diagrams can be drawn for the other convertible products.

## Convertible New Issues

The publicly traded U.S. equity-linked new issue market has jumped in size from $12 billion in 1992 to $38 billion in 1998 and demonstrates a wide diversity in issue sizes and products.[25] In addition to the Bell Atlantic Financial 4.25% exchangeable note in which in a single transaction $3.18 billion was raised,[26] 46 other convertible issues, each of at least $500 million, collectively raised another $38.75 billion during the 1996 to June 1999 period. In that same period, 198 unrated convertibles were also issued, collectively raising $31.5 billion. The size of the median transaction was $125 million.

What determines the amount and type of capital market financing selected by issuers? One key factor is the economic cycle, and by implication the equity market and bond market environments. In 1991 and 1992, U.S. firms undertook

---

24. The two transactions to date were for (i) Comcast Corp. exchangeable into AT&T Corp., issued in March 1999 raising $718 million. It paid 1.75% coupon in addition to the 1.60% dividend on AT&T stock. The issue was redeemed in its entirety four months later; and (ii) Tribune Company exchangeable into America Online, Inc. (AOL) in April 1999 raising $1.256 billion. The security paid 2% coupon while AOL pays no dividend.

25. This only includes equity-linked securities that meet all of the following criteria: (a) the issue is publicly traded, including registered and Sec. 144A securities; (b) (i) the underlying common stock is primarily or solely traded in the U.S. and regulated by U.S. regulators; or (ii) if the primary exchange is not the U.S., the equity-linked security is substantially marketed to U.S. investors (for example, Bell Atlantic Corporation's $2.455 billion exchangeable into Telecom Corporation of New Zeland issued in February 1998); and (c) gross proceeds from the issue is $50 million or larger.

26. See note 1.

**EXHIBIT 51-1**

Equity-Linked Product Payoff Diagram

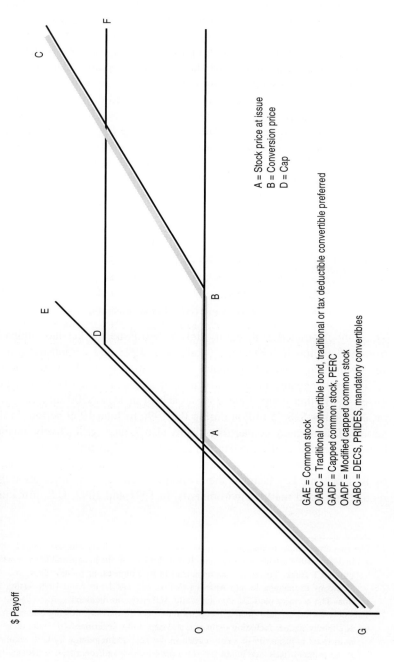

$ Payoff

A = Stock price at issue
B = Conversion price
D = Cap

GAE = Common stock
OABC = Traditional convertible bond, traditional or tax deductible convertible preferred
GADF = Capped common stock, PERC
OADF = Modified capped common stock
GABC = DECS, PRIDES, mandatory convertibles

substantial restructuring of their balance sheets in order to lower the leverage added in the 1980s. To this end, convertible preferreds issued in those two years included: (a) $2.3 billion from Ford Motors Co.; (b) $1.725 billion from General Motors Corp. exchangeable into Electronic Data Systems Corp.; (c) $1.15 from Delta Air Lines, Inc.; and (d) $863 million from Chrysler Corp. With the market recovery in full swing in 1993, the issuance of convertibles hit a then record of $24.7 billion, more than twice the total amount of convertibles issued in 1992.

Convertible preferreds accounted for 39% of the total convert financing in 1993 (see Exhibit 51–2). The interest rate shock of February 1994 caused a substantial derailment of the bond and equity markets leading in turn to a material decline in financing and the subsequent emergence of the mandatory convertible product. As the markets recovered in 1995 and peaked in mid 1998, the tax-deductible mandatory and tax-deductible non-mandatory preferred increased in importance. Issuance of traditional convertible debt has declined substantially in 1998. New issuance came to a virtual halt following the Russian government bond default in mid 1998 and the Asian/emerging market contagion then in full swing. Convertible financing in the first half of 1999 was off significantly from that of the previous year, due to fears of rising interest rates.

In the European sector during this same period, however, convertible issuance spurted far ahead of that in the United States.[27] The difference might be attributed to the introduction of the Euro and the serious restructuring of balance sheets, most notably in France, which accounted for nearly 58% of all convertible issuance. The industry sectors that have been most active in accessing the convert market from 1995–1999 have, predictably, been those making rapid advances in the economy at large. They are the telecommunication, technology, healthcare (including sub-fields of pharmaceuticals, drug delivery, biotechnology), financial services, media, and internet sectors.

Exhibit 51–2 shows the breakdown of new issues between registered and 144A issues.[28] This exhibit indicates the urgency of executing a transaction quickly and the growing importance of mutual funds and QIB's in the investment process. The share and size of investment grade issues is worthy of note. For instance, in 1998 there were 27 investment grade transactions out of a total of

---

27. There were 41 issues raising the equivalent of U.S. $23.8 billion in the first half of 1999 in Europe. This compares with 72 issues raising $28.5 billion for all of 1998. Corresponding numbers in the U.S. were $14.9 billion through 43 issues, and $38.283 billion through 126 issues, respectively.

28. As an alternative to an SEC registered offering which can be sold to any investor, including individual investors or institutions with less than $100 million in net assets, 144A issues can be publicized, sold or resold only to the larger institutional investors and Qualified Institutional Buyers (QIBs). The main reason for the market increase in 144A transactions is that they can be executed quickly without having to undergo the time-consuming registration process. This option is available to SEC registrant firms who are current with respect to filing financial reports with the SEC or those that agree to make the financial reports available to investors.

## EXHIBIT 51-2

U.S. Convertible New Issue Profile

| | 1993 | 1994 | 1995 | 1996 | 1997 | 1998 |
|---|---|---|---|---|---|---|
| Total new issue ($ billion) | $24.7 | $16.1 | $17.3 | $29.6 | $34.6 | $38.3 |
| Total number of issues | 145 | 77 | 79 | 157 | 166 | 126 |
| Investment Grade ($ billion) | $ 6.8 | $ 4.6 | $ 6.3 | $ 9.7 | $14.8 | $18.2 |
| Number of Investment Grade issues | 29 | 16 | 20 | 34 | 36 | 27 |
| Non-investment Grade as % of total new issues | 72% | 71% | 64% | 67% | 57% | 52% |
| Number of Non-investment Grade issues | 116 | 61 | 59 | 123 | 130 | 99 |
| 144A Issues as % of total new issues | 35% | 27% | 42% | 46% | 61% | 61% |
| Number of 144A issues | 39 | 20 | 33 | 82 | 108 | 76 |

*Percent of Gross Proceeds by Product*

| Product | 1993 | 1994 | 1995 | 1996 | 1997 | 1998 |
|---|---|---|---|---|---|---|
| Mandatory Preferred or Debt | 0.0% | 28.0% | 18.6% | 11.3% | 14.2% | 22.6% |
| Capped Common | 5.1% | 10.7% | 3.6% | 5.6% | 0.0% | 0.0% |
| Trust Non-Mandatory Preferred | 2.0% | 6.0% | 6.0% | 20.9% | 14.6% | 13.7% |
| Traditional Convertible Preferred | 39.3% | 14.9% | 7.3% | 11.8% | 8.2% | 10.2% |
| Traditional Convertible Debt | 29.9% | 32.4% | 50.6% | 46.3% | 49.8% | 28.9% |
| Step-Up Convertible Debt | 3.2% | 0.0% | 0.0% | 0.0% | 0.9% | 0.0% |
| OID Convertible Debt | 5.2% | 4.5% | 5.0% | 2.3% | 2.1% | 9.7% |
| Zero Coupon Convertible Debt | 15.3% | 3.5% | 8.9% | 1.8% | 7.7% | 14.2% |
| Miscellaneous | 0.0% | 0.0% | 0.0% | 0.0% | 2.5% | 0.7% |
| Total new issue ($ billion) | $24.7 | $16.1 | $17.3 | $29.6 | $34.6 | $38.3 |

126 transactions, yet these 27 accounted for $18.2 billion, or 47.7% of total new issues by proceeds. Overall, the current supply-demand dynamics in the U.S. suggest a shortage of investment grade or high-end non-investment grade traditional debentures with attractive risk-return attributes. This brings us to the question of who buys converts, and to the considerations of which issues investors should buy and when.

## Investing in Convertible Securities

The most often cited reason to invest in convertibles is that convertibles provide upside participation with downside protection. This is generally true; it does not, however, explain why investors would buy mandatory securities with little or no downside protection. Clearly, investors should be compensated for taking the downside risk. In developing meaningful investment objectives, investors should seek risk-adjusted returns commensurate with their own risk profile. Since convertibles span the space between equities and straight debt, the risk profile of each convertible product should straddle both. Knowledgeable investors will choose from the subset of convertible offerings that match their target risk-reward profile.

Institutional investors in convertible securities include the dedicated convertible funds; equity income funds; insurance companies; fixed income funds seeking to participate in the potential upside in the equity; and convertible arbitrage or hedge funds.[29] Currently, the largest among these is the pool of funds dedicated exclusively to investing in convertibles. These include convertible mutual funds; money managers who manage third party funds such as those from pension funds with specific allocation for convertibles as an asset class; and in-house managed funds earmarked for convertibles. Their common investment objective is to obtain equity exposure with portfolio volatility lower than that of common stocks. They are active money managers and are often measured by holding period returns compared to benchmark indexes such as the Standard & Poor's 500 Index, or the Russell 2000 Index of small stocks, or a risk adjusted benchmark. A subset of managers is measured by the Sharpe ratio.[30] Together with the equity income funds, and the fixed income funds seeking equity upside, they constitute the *outright* accounts. Outright accounts, by their respective char-

---

29. The market making activity of an investment bank's convertible trading desk is also a de facto convertible arbitrage function. Since the activities of a hedge fund and an arbitrage fund, as they pertain to the convertible product, are identical, we will use the terms synonymously.

30. Sharpe ratio is defined as the excess return of the portfolio divided by the risk of the portfolio as measured by the standard deviation of its returns, where portfolio excess return is the realized return of the portfolio minus the return from the riskless asset. It attempts to measure the excess return per unit of risk undertaken by the portfolio manager. The measure can be applied to portfolios or to asset classes. Higher the Sharpe ratio, the better the performance of the portfolio manager or the asset class.

ters, are only allowed to be long the convertibles and may not be allowed to hold the common shares received upon conversion. Neither are they permitted to hedge their convertible positions. That flexibility is left to the convertible arbitrage funds.

With the flood of funds pouring into the market in the past 5 years, largely due to the performance of the equity markets, investors seeking higher returns have channeled substantial amounts into hedge funds whose importance in the converts market has significantly increased. This phenomenon has also occurred in the equity and straight debt markets. Hedge funds are currently estimated to account for 30% to 40% of the funds invested in U.S. convertible markets, and may comprise an even larger percentage of the European market. Due to their high portfolio turnover, convertible arbitrage funds account for a substantial portion of secondary market trading.

No active money manager will invest in a convert unless he or she likes the fundamentals, or the *equity story,* of the underlying stock. Ideal attributes of an issuer, from an investor perspective, include:

- A strong management team with a well articulated business model
- Presence in a growing sector of the economy
- The firm being in the growth phase of its business cycle
- Strong or improving credit
- Credit spread established by an actively traded non-convertible bond by the issuer
- High volatility stock
- Little or no dividend on the common stock
- The ability to undertake the fixed liability without jeopardizing its credit rating

Through a combination of fundamental equity research, credit spread research, and valuation of the convertibles, money managers seek to outperform their benchmarks, and each other. To understand the various valuation approaches, we will look first at the basic characteristics of convertible securities.

## BASIC CHARACTERISTICS OF CONVERTIBLE SECURITIES

The simplest convertible security, namely a traditional convertible bond, can be viewed from a fixed income investor's perspective as a combination of an otherwise identical non-convertible bond plus a call option to exchange the bond for the underlying shares. From the equity oriented investor's viewpoint, it may be viewed as a combination of a long position in the underlying shares, a put option to exchange the underlying shares for an otherwise identical non-convertible bond, and a swap to receive coupons of the convertible bond in exchange for dividends on the underlying shares. This is an immediate implication of the European version of the put-call parity theorem.[31] The introduction of redemption features and other embedded options in the more varied convertible structures discussed above may complicate, but does not invalidate, the basic equivalence concept.

## Value Diagram and Descriptive Measures

The price behavior of a convertible security can be explained by its value diagram such as Exhibit 51–3, which shows how the value of a convertible bond is determined by its debt and equity components.[32] The horizontal axis in the exhibit is the value of the underlying shares and equals the stock price times the conversion ratio. This value is often called the convertible's *parity value,* or simply *parity.* The line ODQ also represents parity. ACDB is the value of the corresponding straight debt, and ACVS represents the value of the convertible bond. Because a convertible bond provides the holder with rights beyond those provided by an otherwise identical non-convertible bond, in that it can be converted into the underlying shares, its value should equal or exceed the larger of the corresponding debt or parity. Accordingly, in the value diagram, ACVS is equal to or above the segment ACD, where bond value exceeds parity, and is equal to or above DQ, where parity exceeds bond value.

Three measures of premium are commonly used in convertible parlance. They are the *conversion premium,* the *points premium,* and the *investment premium.* The vertical distance between ACVS denoting the value of the convertible bond, and the bond floor (or investment value) line ACDB, represents the convertible bond value in excess of its investment value. This is expressed as the *investment premium,* defined as

---

31. See John Cox and Mark Rubinstein, *Option Markets,* Prentice Hall, 1985, 41–43.

32. The value of a convertible in a two-factor valuation model would be represented by a three dimensional surface with the value of the convertible on the y-axis, stock price—the first factor—on the x-axis, and interest rates—the second factor—on the z-axis. The simpler two-dimensional representation above is, therefore, a section of the pricing surface parallel to the x, y plane, at a particular level of interest rate. The term "value" is used for theoretical worth of the security, and "price" is used to denote the consideration paid or required to be paid to transact in the security. For the present, we will assume that price equals value; the situation when the two differ and the resulting implications will be addressed later in the chapter.

**EXHIBIT 51-3**

Convertible Value Diagram

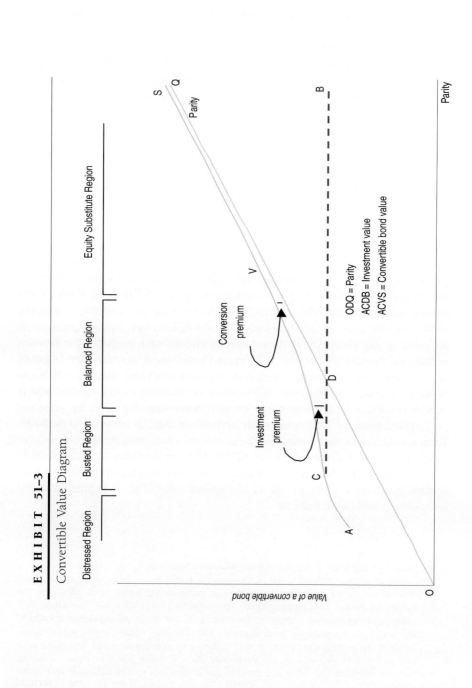

ODQ = Parity
ACDB = Investment value
ACVS = Convertible bond value

Distressed Region    Busted Region    Balanced Region    Equity Substitute Region

Value of a convertible bond

Conversion premium

Investment premium

Parity

Investment Premium = [(Convertible Price/Investment Value) − 1]

$$\times\ 100 \qquad\qquad (51–1)$$

The vertical distance between the convertible bond value ACVS and parity ODQ represents *premium over parity.* This may be stated in *points premium,* defined as the dollar value of the convertible bond minus the dollar value of parity, expressed as a percent of par. For example, if the bond price were $1047.50 and parity were $920, then points premium would be 12.75 points. Alternately, the premium may be stated as the *conversion premium,* defined as

Conversion Premium = [(Convertible Price/Parity) − 1] × 100    (51–2)

The conversion premium is 13.86% in the illustration above. Conversion premium, or simply, the *premium,* is an important and commonly used measure. Together with the investment premium and the notion of the *delta* of the convertible (defined below), the conversion premium helps characterize the change in the value of the convertible with a changing underlying share price.

The ratio of the change in the value of the convertible to the change in the value of the underlying shares, or parity, is called the convertible's *parity delta.* As does the equity call option delta, the parity delta ranges from zero to 1.0, and is the per share delta of the convertible. Therefore, it is also called the *delta,* or the *neutral hedge ratio;* the per share basis is the unstated assumption. At zero delta, the convertible behaves like straight debt, and at 1.0 it behaves like common stock. Therefore, the delta of the convert may be viewed as the correlation of the change in the price of the convert to the price change in the underlying share. A 65% delta means that for small moves in the underlying share price of, say, $0.125, the change in parity = the change in the price per share × the number of shares per convertible = $0.125 × 6.621 = $0.8276. The expected change in the value of the convertible bond, then, is = the change in parity × the hedge ratio = $0.8276 × 0.65 = $0.5380, or 0.0538 bond points. If a holder of the convert wanted to hedge the equity risk, she would in theory have to sell short

conversion ratio × delta = 6.621 × 0.65 = 4.3037 shares per bond
to establish a *delta neutral* position.

The neutral hedge ratio is the tangent to, and the slope of, the convertible bond valuation curve at a particular stock price. For infinitesimal moves up or down in the stock price from this initial level, a hedged portfolio consisting of long the convert and short the shares, as illustrated above, will result in neither a loss nor gain. Larger moves in either direction will lead to gains in the hedged portfolio, because the tangent to the convertible bond valuation curve always touches the curve from below. Thus, for non-infinitesimal stock price changes, the gain arising from the long position in the convert will always be greater than the loss incurred due to the short position in the shares. This feature is termed the *positive convexity* or *positive gamma* of the convert, and hence of the hedged portfolio.[33] A simple explanation of the impact of the positive convexity is that in the event of a large move up, the ex-ante neutral hedged position turns out to be ex-post under-hedged, and hence the profit. The reverse is true in a large down move in share price.

## Stages of a Convertible Security

The price response of a convertible to a change in parity can be conceptually segmented into four stages or regions. These approximate regions are delineated in Exhibit 51–3. They are:

> *Balanced Converts:* In the latter half of the 1990s, an overwhelming majority of new issue convertibles were priced with a 25% conversion premium, while very few were priced at the extreme ends of the new issue range of 10% to 60%. Several factors determine the specific agreed upon conversion premium. Among the more important of these factors is the price response of the new convertibles to changes in the underlying stock price and interest rates. Convertibles with conversion premium of 15% to 40%, and investment premium of 15% to 25%, respond materially to both. Their hedge ratios, or equivalently, their correlation with stock price changes, range from roughly 55% to 80%.[34] Hence converts with these attributes, either upon issuance or subsequently as a result of stock price movements, are called *balanced* convertibles. Their upside/downside participation, or their risk/return tradeoff characteristics appeal to dedicated convertible funds. As dedicated convertible funds are, by charter, more risk averse than equity funds, they account for the bulk of the investment in this phase of a convert. The next sizable investor group during this phase of the convert comprises of equity funds seeking a lower risk alternative to common stock from an issuer with attractive equity fundamentals, an issuer in which they usually already have equity holdings.

> *Equity Substitute Converts:* When the stock price is substantially above the fixed conversion price of a traditional convert, or, in the case of

---

33. Gamma is the second derivative of the convertible value with respect to parity, and is the rate of change of delta with respect to the share price. Gamma of common shares is zero, since its delta is 1.0 by definition, and derivative of a fixed number is zero. In times of high volatility such as what the markets have witnessed in recent years, gamma of each position, and its aggregation to the level of each trader's position and to the level of the firm, is an important measure of risk of the entity's profit/loss potential. A positive gamma is always desirable and negative gamma "a Giffen good."

34. Higher (lower) the credit rating, higher (lower) the delta of a new issue convert. High bond floor makes the convert respond more to interest rates and less to equity. Issues with wide credit spreads have, correspondingly, a lower bond floor and hence it stands to reason that the delta is higher.

an accreting convert, above the then effective conversion price, the convert is deep-in-the-money. Such a convert is referred to as being *equity like,* or as an *equity substitute* if its conversion premium is less than 15%, while its investment premium is higher than 40%. Such a convert will respond sharply to changes in parity, and to a lesser extent to changes in the interest rates or interest spreads, and its delta is usually above 80%. While share price is the prime determinant of the value of a convert in this phase, it cannot be emphasized enough that other factors, such as remaining call protection and stock price volatility, also materially affect its value. The shorter (longer) the remaining call protection, the lower (higher) the conversion premium an investor would be willing to pay.

The more in-the-money the convert, the more its risk/return dynamics mimic those of the underlying shares. While a deep-in-the-money convert increases in value with parity in proportion to its high delta, it also moves down correspondingly, and thus loses its low risk attribute. Clearly, this movement is due to the investor put option to exchange the convert for its redemption price being now deep-out-of-the-money. Investor self selection will cause the dedicated convert funds to sell the security in favor of other balanced converts, and equity income funds to purchase the security. Convertible arbitrage funds and hedge funds are the most active in this phase, as they can leverage the portfolio with a high delta short position in the shares thereby employing little net capital.

*Busted Converts:* If the share price were to decline such that the conversion option were deep-out-of-the-money, and correspondingly, the put option deep-in-the-money, the conversion premium would increase while the investment premium would decline. The conversion premium in this stage is usually larger than 40% and may be as high as 200%, but investment premium is less than 15%. As the conversion option is worth very little, the convertible bond value approaches that of an otherwise equivalent non-convertible bond. Its price falls to a level determined by the relevant yield measures. For traditional converts, those measures are the current yield and the yield to maturity. For the accreting converts, they are the yield to put and/or yield to maturity. Dedicated convert funds exit their positions in these converts, to be replaced by fixed income funds seeking equity participation. The yield give-up in exchange for the deep-out-of-the-money conversion option is relatively minor and, sometimes even negative, due to market inefficiencies in this region. Of course, fixed income funds that traditionally invest in senior or senior-subordinated bonds may be reluctant to buy (pure) subordinated debt that has a lower priority in the event of bankruptcy, as is the case with the majority of convertible bonds. Fixed income funds do not generally buy busted convertible preferreds.

*Distressed Converts:* These converts may be considered a subset of the busted converts, differing in that the stock price has fallen so far as to materially increase the probability of default. The ratings may be lowered, either explicitly by the rating agencies or implicitly by the market, a change reflected in a substantial widening of its credit spread over the Treasury rate. Unlike the other stages, in which the investment value is assumed to be steady (see Exhibit 51–3), in the distressed convert stage the bond floor falls rapidly with the stock price. At this stage, the fixed income funds exit and *special situation funds,* also known as *distress funds* or *vulture funds,* are the primary investors. These funds specialize in assessing the default probability and legal remedies in the event of default. Both the conversion premium and the investment premium are very small to negligible in this stage. Interestingly, the gamma with respect to the stock price is extremely high as small changes in the stock price may change the delta very significantly.

Several important conclusions may be drawn from the above discussion. First, the stages discussed do not have discrete boundaries. For instance, newly issued converts in Europe may have high conversion premiums but a low investment premium, and a delta in the region of 55%. This is due to the very high implied ratings of the converts, in the AAA or AA range, resulting in a high bond floor. Second, convertible securities are not static, in that their price response changes and they may become more equity-like or debt-like with the attendant changes in the risk/return profile. Consequently, analytical tools for fundamental equity research as well as those for valuing fixed income securities and derivatives would be needed to select and manage a portfolio of convertible securities. Third, while the conversion premium is often used as a readily available measure to determine the current stage of the convertible, i.e., whether it is a busted convert or in-the-money or something else, the more appropriate measure is the investment premium. For example, an in-the-money convert with extended period of remaining call protection, on a volatile, low dividend paying underlying stock can trade at substantial conversion premium. However, higher (lower) the investment premium, unambiguously more (less) in-the-money is the convert.

## TRADITIONAL VALUATION METHOD

The traditional valuation method is based on the premise that buying a convertible is the equivalent of buying common stock at a premium, with the premium recouped over time from the difference between the higher income from the convertible coupon and the lower dividend on the underlying stock.[35] *Payback period* or *breakeven period* is the chief quantitative measure employed in assessing the relative attractiveness of the convert versus the common stock. The shorter the payback period, the more attractive the convertible, especially if the payback period is shorter than the call protection period. As we shall see below, the concept of payback period is flawed, yet this concept continues to be used by some equity-oriented investors as an adjunct to their fundamental analysis of the underlying stock. Unfortunately, this measure is not applicable to some of the newer structures, and may even prove misleading. Even within the traditional structures, most convertible new issues in the past decade would fail the payback period test, and yet investors in the new convertibles have done well due to the embedded optionality in highly volatile markets. We will use the following example to explain the traditional valuation method.

*Example*
On March 24, 1998, Clear Channel Communications, Inc. (CCU) issued $575 million of a senior convertible note with 2 5/8% annual coupon and a five-year maturity. Each bond has a par amount of $1,000 and can be converted into 16.1421 (adjusted for a 2:1 split that occurred in July 1998) shares of CCU common stock. On March 26, 1999, the bond was traded at 121 (bond points, in percent of the par amount) with the CCU common stock at $65 1/16. The common pays no dividend.

If an investor purchased one CCU 2 5/8% 4/1/2003 convertible note instead of buying CCU common shares equal to the conversion ratio of the note, she paid a premium of $159.75 (= $1,000 × 121% − $65.0625 × 16.1421), or 15.975 bond points. However, this premium would be compensated for by the cash flow differential between the convertible bond and the underlying shares:

Annual cash flow differential
= Par amount × coupon rate − Parity × dividend yield
= $1,000 × 2.625% − $1,050.25 × 0%
= $26.25

This implies that each year, the bondholder receives $26.25 more income than she would from dividends on the CCU common shares. Thus the payback period is

---

35. Note the difference between this approach and the contingent claims approach which, views the convert as a combination of equity, a put option to exchange into straight debt, and the swap to receive coupons of the convertible for dividends on the underlying shares.

= Premium paid/Annual cash flow differential
= $159.75/26.25
= 6.09 years

Simple derivation leads to the following formula for computing the cash flow payback:[36]

Cash flow payback period
$$= \frac{\text{Conversion Premium}/(1 + \text{Conversion Premium})}{\text{Current yield} - [\text{Dividend yield}/(1 + \text{Conversion Premium})]} \quad (51-3)$$

where current yield refers to the current yield of the convertible. For the CCU convertible note, the conversion premium was 15.211% and the current yield is 2.625%/121 = 2.169%, and the dividend yield on the common was zero. Using these inputs, Eq. (51-3) results in the same payback period of 6.09 years. All inputs for the computation should be in decimals.

An alternate method of calculating payback period, though less defensible, is more commonly used. It is called the *dollar-for-dollar* payback. Under this method, the implicit question asked is: "If I were to invest the same dollar amount in buying the common shares as I would in buying the convertible, what would be the payback period of the premium?"

In the above example, if the same dollar amount were invested in CCU stock, one could buy $1210/$65.0625 = 18.60 shares. The annual cash flow differential would still be the same as before, as would the payback period under this method, on account of the fact that CCU pays no dividends. However, if the stock paid a significant dividend, the latter method would result in a larger payback period.[37] The formula for this latter method can be derived as:

Dollar-for-dollar payback
$$= \frac{\text{Conversion Premium}/(1 + \text{Conversion Premium})}{\text{Current yield} - \text{Dividend yield}} \quad (51-4)$$

The denominator of Eq. (51-4) is called the *yield advantage*. Note that the payback period of over 6 years is longer than the remaining maturity of the CCU convertible bond, which is about 4 years. Is this a valuation anomaly, or is the valuation approach lacking?

While the definitions of paybacks can be refined by using dividend growth rates and discounting the cash flow streams, the basic flaw in the traditional valuation approach lies in its failure to consider the optionality embedded in the

---

36. For convertibles with changing coupons or dividends, such as step-up convertibles, this formula does not apply. The payback period can be calculated by directly using the definition.

37. Consider the Pennzoil-Quaker State Company's 4.95% bonds maturing on 8/15/2008. The bonds are exchangeable into 9.3283 shares of Chevron Corporation (CHV) with the first redemption date on 8/15/2000. On 8/27/99, this bond traded at $1,000.125 with CHV common share at $92.75 and its quarterly dividend at $0.61. The two payback periods in this case are 5.09 and 5.87 years, respectively.

convert, i.e., in its assuming conversion into common stock with absolute certainty. In the case of the traditional convertible, bondholders have the right, but not the obligation, to convert should the stock price not exceed the conversion price, in which event they would receive par at maturity. And the meaning of payback period becomes even more problematic for accreting securities. For example, investors in zero-coupon convertible bonds do not receive current cash income. Thus, the convertible's income advantage would be zero or negative, and its payback period could not be calculated. One may be tempted to substitute the yield to maturity or yield to the next put for the current yield. However, this again implicitly assumes a conversion probability of 100%, and excludes the possibility of default by the issuer.

## CONVERTIBLE VALUATION MODELS

Virtually all valuation models for convertible securities currently in use by market professionals follow the economic framework of the contingent claims analysis pioneered by Fischer Black, Myron Scholes, and Robert Merton.[38] Their seminal papers view an equity warrant as a derivative security, the value of which is established as a function of the value of the underlying primary security, which is common stock. Their approach therefore results in a relative valuation model as opposed to an absolute valuation model. Black/Scholes and Merton demonstrate that, in equilibrium, a hedged portfolio consisting of the warrant and (a specific number of) the underlying shares will, over an infinitesimally short time period, be riskless, and will therefore yield the riskless rate of return. The model that results does not require the expected return of the underlying stock as an input that, heretofore, had been a significant shortcoming of the existing warrant valuation models. This risk neutral valuation, meaning a valuation in which the risk preference of the investor is absent, is undoubtedly the most important innovation in the valuation of derivative securities. Indeed, this development may be among the primary reasons for the spectacular growth of derivative markets for both equity and fixed income.

Structural complexities of the various derivative securities have required the development of specific valuation models depending on the distributional properties of the underlying asset returns. These are extensions and generalizations of the Black/Scholes and Merton contingent claim based relative valuation methodology. Convertible valuation models differ from each other in the number of *stochastic variables* used in their construction.[39] The simpler one-factor model assumes that the stock price, or more correctly, the stock return,

---

38. See Fischer Black and Myron Scholes, "The Pricing of Options and Corporate Liabilities," *Journal of Political Economy,* May–June 1973, 637–659; and Robert C. Merton, "Theory of Rational Option Pricing," *Bell Journal of Economics and Management Science,* 1973, 141–183.

39. A variable whose value changes over time in a non-deterministic or an uncertain way is said to follow a stochastic process.

is the only underlying stochastic variable. All other items that impact the value of a convertible are descriptors and static variables. The more complex two-factor models assume both stock returns and interest rates to be stochastic. Regardless of the number of factors in these models, they share the common basic assumptions of Black/Scholes and Merton:

- Capital markets are perfect; there are no transaction costs and no taxes; all market participants are atomistic price takers; and all investors have the same information.
- Trading is continuous and the markets are arbitrage free.
- Stock prices (and interest rates, in the case of two-factor models) follow specific stochastic processes.

### Descriptors and Variables that Affect Convertible Valuation

Earlier we listed some of the equity story attributes of an ideal issuer of convertibles, from the perspective of investors. Most of these attributes are qualitative and therefore difficult to include in an analytical model, yet they affect the price an investor may be willing to pay. Fundamental equity-oriented fund managers tend to be more receptive to converts from issuers whose stocks have performed very well in the recent past (i.e. stocks with "positive momentum"), and from repeat issuers in the convert market whose prior converts made them money. These qualitative aspects, though important to understand, are again difficult to measure. We shall therefore restrict our attention to quantifiable descriptors, static variables, and stochastic variables or factors.

Descriptors are the attributes of a security that are known with certainty, such as its stated maturity, coupon, call and put schedules. Static variables are inputs that can be estimated, albeit with estimation error. Examples include future dividends and the costs involved in hedging the security. Descriptors and static variables that affect the value of a convertible security include:

- *Spot Price of the Underlying Security:* The higher the stock price, the more the conversion option in-the-money (or less out-of-the-money), and hence the higher the value of the convert as described in Exhibit 51–3.
- *The Dividend Yield of the Underlying Common Stock:* The higher the dividend yield, the lower the value of the convert as a high dividend yield will lower the yield advantage of the convert and hence will lower the attractiveness of the convert as an alternative to the common stock. Looked at another way, a higher dividend restrains the stock price appreciation and the convert's potential to go in-the-money. The same logic holds for the dividend growth rate.
- *Coupon or Preferred Dividend:* The higher the distributions from the convert, the higher the yield advantage and hence the higher the value of the convert.

- *Issuer Redemption:* A longer non-call period increases the value of the convert in two ways. First, the investor enjoys the yield advantage for a longer period. Second, absent a voluntary conversion by the investor, the minimum maturity of the conversion option equals the convert's first redemption date; hence the longer the conversion option, the higher the value of the convert. A hard non-call is worth more to the investor than a soft call of the same maturity.

- *Maturity:* Consider two converts identical in all respects except their maturity dates. The longer maturity convert will have the lower value. This may seem contradictory because we know that the longer the maturity of a call option, the higher will be its value. But while longer maturity does increase the value of the conversion option, it is swamped by the decrease in the value of the bond floor caused by the discounting the cash flow stream at a higher rate over a longer period. Equivalently, the bond's duration increases and its value falls. For deep-in-the-money converts, the impact of increasing rates is smaller because of the negative duration of the conversion option, due to the high likelihood of forced conversion.

- *Investor Put:* Redemption at maturity is the equivalent of an investor put at maturity. A convert with a put prior to maturity will be worth more than one without. The earlier the put date, all else being equal, the higher the convert's value; also, the higher the put price, the higher the convert's value.

- *Liquidity and Hedging Cost:* The more illiquid the convert or its underlying common stock, the lower the value of the convert as even moderate size trades are likely to materially change convert prices, causing sellers to realize less than they otherwise would and buyers to pay more. The cost of borrowing the shares to short against the convert is also likely to be higher. Stock borrow cost effectively has the same impact as an increase in the dividend of the underlying stock. When the convert is illiquid and/or the stock borrow cost excessive, the convert may trade below parity, leading holders voluntarily to exercise their conversion option, which they would normally be loath to do. Even outright investors, in other words, non-hedgers, are affected by liquidity and hedging costs. Investment banks' trading desks are less likely to provide liquidity and respond to the outright investors' sell order, as it would entail holding the position unhedged or under-hedged until another buyer is found. Since less than appropriate hedging increases their risk position, bid/offer spread is wider and/or the transaction sizes are smaller. Most likely, the sell order will be accepted subject to finding the appropriate short position in the stock or executed in stages as new buyers are located. The resulting delay continues the exposure of the seller to market moves even though he has decided to exit the position. Anticipating these conditions, the value of the convert will be lower than it otherwise would. The same logic applies to converts with conversion restrictions, as in the case of some converts issued out of Asia. Restrictions on short sale of common shares also lower the value of the convert.

A cash settled convert generally trades at a discount to physical settled convert, especially when the convert is in-the-money and currently redeemable, or is approaching the end of the call protection period. The magnitude of the discount for a cash settled convert is again a function of the liquidity of the stock. The less liquid the stock, more the stock price is likely to move up as hedgers try to cover their short position during the usual 30-day redemption notice period, and hence greater the discount.

- *Country Risk:* Political risk, exchange rate risk, and fluctuations in the rate of economic growth, together comprise country risk. Most U.S. based dedicated convert funds and fundamental equity-oriented funds do not invest when the country risk is very high, as is the case in the emerging markets. International funds, specific regional funds and, most important, hedge funds account for the bulk of the investment pool, the latter because they can hedge away part of the country risk. Since all the risk cannot be hedged away, converts originating from these countries typically are issued at low premiums and/or their volatility is not fully priced. On the other hand, converts from large multinational firms, especially from the G-7 countries, Switzerland and selected western European countries, are well received due to their usually high credit ratings and low country risk.

Candidate stochastic variables that may, in principle, be used to model the value of a convert include:

- *Stock Price:* This is the most natural explanatory variable, and is part of all convertible valuation models. A single factor model assumes stock price to be the sole stochastic variable, all others being non-stochastic. With assumptions identical to those in Black/Scholes and Merton approach,[40] the model values respond very significantly to the volatility of stock returns, which is assumed to be fixed and is an input to the model. The higher the volatility the higher the probability that the convertible will be in-the-money, thus the higher its value. This positive impact will however be reduced when the convertible is callable.

- *Interest Rates:* Valuation models for bond options have the term structure of interest rates as the main stochastic variable. Since the price dynamics of a convertible are governed in large part by the straight bond and the embedded interest rate options, it stands to reason that two-factor models to price

---

40. The common assumption is that the process governing stock price returns is a geometric Weiner process. Stock returns over time $\Delta t$ are normally distributed with mean $\mu \Delta t$ and variance $\sigma^2 \Delta t$, where $\mu$ and $\sigma^2$ are the instantaneous mean and variance of the stock price returns, respectively.

converts include as the second factor the term structure of interest rates. Yield volatility is an estimated parameter, analogous to stock return volatility in the single factor model discussed above.

As stated earlier, higher interest rates reduce the value of the bond floor of a convert by discounting the convert's cash flows at the higher rate. The impact of interest rates on the embedded options is more complex. An increase (decrease) in the interest rate increases (decreases) the value of the conversion option, and that of the option to put the convert, if there is an investor put feature. From the issuer's perspective, if the convert is out-of-the-money, higher (lower) interest rates will reduce (increase) the value of the issuer's call option, as it would entail financing the redemption value by new debt at a higher (lower) rate. In the case of in-the-money converts, which should in most cases be called as soon as possible, the issuer's incentive for a conversion-forcing call will increase with rising interest rates.

- *Credit Spread:* The lower the credit quality of the issuer as determined by leverage and other measures, the higher the assessed probability of default, and hence the higher the credit spread. For example, a Baa3/BBB-rated issuer may have a credit spread of 210 basis points for a five-year maturity subordinated debt. With the five-year Treasury rate at 5.85%, the total straight debt rate is 5.85 + 2.10 = 7.95%. If the rating were a notch lower at Ba1/BB+, the spread would be about 250 basis points.[41] Thus spreads have the same impact on converts as do interest rates. The credit spread is increasingly viewed as a stochastic variable in its own right and its volatility is tracked very closely.[42] However, it is not generally used as a separate factor due to the current lack of liquid hedging instruments to protect a portfolio from this source of risk.

- *Exchange Rates:* Consider the Bell Atlantic Financial 4.25% bond maturing on 9/15/2005 and exchangeable into 87.287 shares of Cable and Wireless Communications plc (CWZ). Both the coupon and par are US$ denominated. In addition to the equity risk associated with the investor's conversion option into CWZ ordinary shares, a U.S. based investor is exposed to exchange rate risk because CWZ shares are denominated in British Pounds (GBP). With the number of shares per bond fixed at 87.287 shares, any increase in the value of the GBP against the US$ would benefit the investor, and any decline reduce the value of her position. Thus the investor thus has an embedded call on GBP, or equivalently, an embedded put on US$, embedded in the convert.

---

41. The spreads are based on market conditions as of 9/1/1999.
42. The widening of credit spreads globally, despite falling Treasury rates, during the Asian and Russian debt crises of the latter half of 1998 have caused portfolio managers to monitor credit spreads more closely.

Since exchange rates are stochastic, they could be the third factor in the valuation of a convert. Exchange rate volatility would have to be estimated.

- *Value of the Firm:* Finance literature has demonstrated that the value of the firm can be conceived as the underlying asset with common stock, straight bonds, convertibles, indeed, all corporate securities, valued as its derivatives. An equilibrium model which values corporate securities as derivatives of the underlying value of the firm would lead to a consistent valuation paradigm for all corporate securities as opposed to standalone models for each security based on, sometimes, inconsistent assumptions. We will use the Brennan and Schwartz model that is based on the value of the firm and interest rates as the two stochastic factors as our point of departure.[43]

- *Term Structure of Volatility:* The variance of stock returns tends to be correlated with the level of the stock price. At high (low) stock price levels, the volatility is higher (lower). Volatility also changes with time. As a result, some models explicitly consider volatility of stock returns as a stochastic variable rather than an input parameter that is estimated and assumed fixed at all levels of the stock price and time to maturity.

## Choosing Between Multiple Factor Alternatives

Convertibles are complex securities, and do not lead to closed form solutions. Partial differential equations (p.d.e.), subject to several boundary conditions, need to be solved using computationally intensive numerical methods. The number of computations increases exponentially with each additional stochastic variable included in the valuation model. Consequently, even in non-convertible bond option modeling where the interest rates for short maturity and long maturity are two logical stochastic variables, most practitioners employ a single factor model for the short rate and assume the evolution of the long rate in relation to the short rate. The inclusion or exclusion of a stochastic variable, therefore, involves a tradeoff between theoretical elegance and/or incremental gain in accuracy on the one hand, and computational complexity on the other. As a rule, when estimation errors are likely to swamp the computational precision achieved through the inclusion of an additional stochastic variable, it is better to spend more effort in improving the input estimates and to opt for a simpler model.

One-factor models, with the stock returns as the stochastic variable, are the most commonly used models. Two-factor models, with interest rates as the second factor, are gaining in popularity. Virtually all models sacrifice the can-

---

43. Michael J. Brennan and Eduardo S. Schwartz, "Analyzing Convertible Bonds," *Journal of Financial and Quantitative Analysis,* November 1980, 907–929.

didates for a third or fourth factor in favor of computational ease. Credit spreads are bundled together with interest rates, and the two together are assumed to follow a stochastic process. The impact of exchange rates on a convertible with two currencies is similarly addressed by creating a price series of, for example, CWZ stock price in GBP multiplied by the exchange rate of \$ per GBP, and estimating the volatility of the price series thus generated in US\$. As a proxy for the term structure of volatility of stock price returns, volatility is estimated by applying subjective corrections to historical and implied volatilities, and the estimate is assumed to be constant over the life of the security.

Notwithstanding the theoretical elegance of a single valuation model that encompasses all corporate securities, individual valuation models for the various assets are, for several reasons, still more commonly used. Chief among them is that the value of a firm is not a traded asset. Consequently, price observations are rarely, if ever, available, and their distributional properties cannot empirically be established. The complexities of the individual securities, and their correlations with each other, necessitate assumptions that are not always palatable.

## Analytical Valuation Model: An Outline

The interest rate process in the two-factor Brennan/Schwartz model is assumed to follow a stochastic process wherein, over short time interval $\Delta t$, the change in the interest rate $\Delta r$ is approximated by

$$\Delta r = \alpha(\mu_r - r) + r\sigma_r z_r \qquad \alpha > 0 \qquad (51\text{--}5)$$

where $z_r$ is normally distributed with mean of zero and a variance of unity. This is a common assumption in most interest rate models, and is called a mean reverting process. The change in the interest rate has a non-random component represented by the first term of the right hand side of the equation, and a random component by the second term. The non-random component is a function of the current interest rate $r$. The difference between $\mu_r$ the mean of the interest rate process, and $r$ determines the direction of reversion towards the mean, while $\alpha$ is the coefficient or speed of this mean reversion. The random change in the interest rate is a function of the standard deviation of the interest rate process, $r\sigma_r$, and is superimposed on the mean reverting change.

The change in the value of the firm, $\Delta V$, is similarly assumed to be approximated by

$$\Delta V = (V\mu_v - Q(V,t)) + V\sigma_v z_v \qquad (51\text{--}6)$$

where $\mu_v$ is the expected total rate of return on the value of the firm, and $Q(V,t)$ represents the cash distributions paid out to the various securities in the firm and is a function of the value of the firm and of time. The random component of the value of the firm has a standard deviation of $\sigma_v V$, and $z_v$ is a unit normal. Brennan/Schwartz then, by using $dz_r^2 = dt$, $dz_v^2 = dt$, and $dz_r dz_v =$

$\rho dt$ where $\rho$ is the instantaneous correlation between $dz_r$ and $dz_v$, and applying Ito's lemma and the risk neutral valuation argument arrive at the p.d.e. (Eq. (51–7)) that the value of a convertible bond needs to satisfy[44]

$$0.5V^2\sigma_v^2 C_{vv} + r\rho V\sigma_v\sigma_r C_{vr} + 0.5\ r^2\sigma_r^2 C_{rr} + C_r[\alpha(\mu_r - r) - \lambda r\sigma_r]$$
$$+ C_v(rV - Q(V,t)) - rC + cF + C_t = 0 \qquad (51\text{–}7)$$

where $C(V,r,t)$ is the value of the convertible bond. Subscripts of $C$ denote its partial derivatives with respect to $V$, $r$ and $t$; $F$ is the face value of the convert, $c$ is the coupon rate; and $\lambda$ is the market price of interest rate risk. $\lambda$ is the reward for the incremental risk of a portfolio whose return is perfectly correlated with changes in the interest rate. It is a concept very similar to the Sharpe measure.

The Ingersoll (1977) single factor model is also based on the value of the firm. For a firm with only two types of securities, namely, common stock and convertible bonds, the p.d.e. in the case of a non-dividend paying stock thus becomes a special case of Eq. (51–7), and reduces to[45]

$$0.5V^2\sigma_v^2 C_{vv} + Cv[rV - Q(V,t)] - rC + cF + C_t = 0 \qquad (51\text{–}8)$$

Most convertible models currently in use substitute the underlying stock for the value of the firm due to the frequency and accurate recording of trading in common stock. Equation (51–7) then becomes

$$0.5S^2\sigma_s^2 C_{ss} + r\rho S\sigma_s\sigma_r C_{sr} + 0.5\ r^2\sigma_r^2 C_{rr} + C_r[\alpha(\mu_r - r) - \lambda r\sigma_r]$$
$$+ C_s[rS - cF] - rC + cF + C_t = 0 \qquad (51\text{–}9)$$

Finally, a single factor model variation of Eq. (51–9) leads to

$$0.5S^2\sigma_s^2 C_{ss} + C_s[rS - cF] - rC + cF + C_t = 0 \qquad (51\text{–}10)$$

The value of a convertible bond is obtained by solving the p.d.e. selected subject to the boundary constraints applicable for the convertible. These constraints require that the value of the convertible:

a) Be the higher of par or the conversion value at maturity

b) Be less than or equal to its redemption price during the redemption period

c) If putable, be higher than or equal to the put price

d) At other times, be at least as large as its conversion value

The two-factor model (Eq. (51–9)) requires the estimation of several more inputs than does the single factor model (Eq. (51–10)). These additional inputs

---

44. See Brennan/Schwartz, 1980.
45. Jonathan E. Ingersoll, Jr., "A Contingent-Claims Valuation of Convertible Securities," *Journal of Financial Economics*, 1977, 289–322.

are: the yield volatility, $\sigma_r$; the speed of mean reversion, $\alpha$; the market price of interest rate risk, $\lambda$ and the correlation between the interest rate process and the stock price process, $\rho$. All inputs except for the last are estimated by using Treasury bill data and employing standard term structure models. The estimate of $\rho$ is notoriously unstable. In most cases this parameter is, therefore, set to zero.

As an aside, note that the p.d.e. for the Black/Scholes and Merton warrant valuation models is a special case of Eq. (51–10). As previously discussed, only when the convertible is non-redeemable and non-convertible until maturity are its debt and warrant components separable, and the debt plus warrant valuation applicable. An American style conversion adds an interest option in favor of the investor whereby the investor can turn in the convertible bond to satisfy the exercise price, even if the bond component is worth less than the exercise price, which usually equals the bond's par value. This *usable bond* feature of the convert is absent in a bond plus warrant. In the event of exercise prior to maturity, the warrant exercise price is payable in cash and equals the par value, never anything less.

Clearly, the theoretical value of a convertible security will be a function of the particular p.d.e. chosen with Eq. (51–10)) being the most prevalent. In this case, the interest rate is assumed to be an input parameter and several variations are used to compensate for the stochastic interest rate attributes lost in a single factor model.

## Implementing a Convertible Bond Valuation Model

Since convertible valuation is not amenable to closed form solutions, numerical methods need to be employed. Implicit finite-difference method and explicit finite-difference method are commonly used. They are Taylor Series approximations for partial derivatives in partial differential equations. While the implicit finite-difference has better stability properties than does the explicit finite-difference approach, it is computationally more time consuming; explicit finite-difference method is more flexible and more easily understood. A special case of the explicit finite-difference method is the binomial method, by far the most widely used approach for derivative valuations.

Space considerations do not permit us to describe the details of the construction of the binomial tree and the backward induction.[46] We will discuss the interest rate and volatility parameters in detail as they materially affect the value of the convert.

*Interest Rate:* While some use a flat term structure assumption, others estimate the zero coupon yield curve from the on-the-run Treasury securities. A

---

46. Interested readers are referred to Kevin B. Connolly, *Pricing Convertible Bonds*, 1998, John Wiley & Sons.

flat credit spread is the most common, though a term structure of credit spreads is also used. The interest rate input for each node is obtained from the derived zero coupon yield curve.

Note that all the p.d.e.s above use a single interest rate. This makes the resulting models more analytically tractable and the results conform to the put–call parity theorem. However, there is a problem. Consider a convertible that is separable into a bond and a warrant. Using a single interest rate, equal to the Treasury plus the applicable spread in valuing this convertible implies that both the bond component and the warrant component are discounted at the same rate. Warrants and options, however, when traded separately, do not use the credit spread in their valuations because the risk neutral valuation approach of derivatives is independent of the default risk of the associated bond. When the single rate is used, it tends to overvalue the embedded net conversion option. To achieve consistency with the option markets, the Treasury rate alone is used for the optionality and the Treasury rate plus the spread for the coupons and par. In practice, the short equity position in a hedged portfolio earns the short term riskless rate and not the Treasury rate plus the spread rate used to discount the cash flows of the convertible. Note that the put-call parity attribute is then lost.

A further modification of the two interest rates is to use a hedge ratio weighted mix of the Treasury rate and the Treasury rate plus the credit spread. If the convert is deep-out-of-the-money, the probability of conversion is very low and the convert behaves like straight debt; its delta equals zero. Hence all cash flows associated with the convert are discounted at the Treasury rate plus the credit spread. At the other extreme, with the convert is deep-in-the-money, the probability of conversion is very high and the convert behaves like a common stock; its delta equals 1. With a 100% hedge, the probability of loss vanishes and the portfolio should earn the Treasury rate. At intermediate points, the weighted average rate, weighted by the delta at the node, is employed.

*Stock Volatility:* In any contingent claim model, an estimate of the future volatility likely to occur during the life of the contingent claim security is the required input. As we have seen, the higher the volatility, the higher the option value; and the longer the option maturity, the higher the value. Volatility estimation is even more critical for the very long dated options embedded in converts. The following data are collected to estimate volatility:

a) Historical volatility for periods ranging from one month to twelve months, and their trend

b) The implied volatility trends for listed options and *LEAP*s, the latter being equity (and index) options with maturities longer than nine months

c) The implied volatility of any existing converts from the same issuer

d) The implied volatility of converts in the sector

Based on these data and with a downward correction if the common stock and/or convert are not likely to be liquid, a volatility estimate is established.

Very high volatility estimates, if above 50%, are capped in anticipation of volatility reversion towards the market mean volatility.[47]

## Applying the Valuation Model

Obviously, valuation models are most commonly used to establish the theoretical worth of a security at any point in time. If the theoretical value is, say, 104.5, and the security is trading at par, it is said to be 4.5% cheap. This cheapness depends of course on the inputs and the particular valuation model employed. A newly implemented valuation model will therefore be calibrated against market prices of liquid converts to catalog its biases. After this initial calibration, most practitioners are more concerned with the consistency of the model than with its absolute accuracy.

Theoretical rich/cheap analysis is not the sole determinant of an investor's decision to invest in a convert; that decision may depend on several additional analytic criteria. Among them are: the relative value of the convert compared to other candidate converts, scenario analysis, and the risk/expected return profile. We discuss these next.

*Partial Derivatives:* The partial derivatives commonly used in monitoring equity and bond derivative risk/reward profiles are also applicable here. Briefly, in addition to the hedge ratio or delta, $\Delta$, and gamma, $\Gamma$, the measure of convexity discussed above, these partial derivatives are:

- Theta, $\theta$, which measures the time decay of the value of the convertible. Theta moves can be significant for short maturity options, such as during the call notice period, and the period approaching a reset date of a reset convert.

- Kappa, $\kappa$, also known as vega, it measures the change in the value of the convertible for changes in volatility. For high volatility underlying shares, such as those in the internet, technology and telecommunication sectors currently, kappa helps define the aspect of the valuation risk as firms mature and their volatilities decline. Volatility collapse during market corrections or market illiquidity leads to collapse in the premium and the value of convertibles. This occurred during 1994 and again during the Russian and emerging market crises of 1998. Kappa estimates for a portfolio's potential profit/loss for sudden large moves are common in risk reports.

- Rho, $\rho$, which measures the change in the value of the convert due to change in the interest rate. As previously discussed, out-of-the-money con-

47. A more elaborate method for estimating volatility is the generalized autoregressive conditional heteroskedasticity (GARCH) approach, which gives progressively increasing weight to more recent observations of volatility. The weighting scheme is defined by an estimated decay parameter, analogous to the mean revision parameter in interest rate models. See T Bollerslev, "Generalized Autoregressive Conditional Heteroskedasticity," *Journal of Econometrics,* 1986, 307–327.

verts are very sensitive to interest rate and spread changes. This is particularly true for the lower end of the non-investment grade issues where the spreads may easily be 400 basis points or higher for a security with a five-year maturity. Hedging via shorting the underlying stock may not help mitigate the risk of spread widening if it is not related to deterioration of the firm's fundamentals. A case in point is the widening of spread that usually occurs in anticipation of a rate hike by the Federal Reserve Bank.

*Implied Volatility and Implied Credit Spread:* A valuation model is particularly useful in helping investors and issuers select between the disparate aspects of the different convertible structures by boiling down the alternative securities and their particular attributes to a single statistic that establishes their relative value. Such a statistic is the implied volatility of the convert. The volatility input to the valuation model which, in conjunction with all other inputs, yields a theoretical value equal to the convert's market price, is its implied volatility. To establish the richness/cheapness of the convert, its implied volatility is compared with that of comparable converts, and of options on the underlying stock. Higher (lower) the implied volatility richer (cheaper) is the security for the investor. The reverse is true for the issuer of a new issue convertible.

Similarly, the credit spread that yields the market price of the convert is compared with those of comparable converts and straight bonds. Implied credit spread is known as the *option adjusted spread* in the context of non-convertible fixed income securities.

While implied volatility and implied credit spread are very useful metrics, a few words of caution are in order. Estimates of implied volatility and implied credit spread are conditioned on the validity of the other inputs and the valuation model itself. Thus they are "joint estimates" of the parameter being inferred as well as of the rest of the inputs.[48] Furthermore, there is an element of circularity in sequentially estimating the volatility and then the credit spread with the same set of inputs. We also know that the value of a convertible is most sensitive to volatility when the convert is near-the money, and to credit spread when deep-out-of-the-money; it is less sensitive to either when deep-in-the-money. As a result, large estimation errors, and resulting erroneous conclusions, may result if one is not mindful of, and does not control for, the conversion price to stock price ratio.

*Scenario Analysis:* Theoretical values and total returns at different levels of stock price for changing levels of interest rate, or for different holding period horizons, are essential tools for portfolio managers attempting to gauge the future potential risk/rewards in buying a convert versus the buying common stock. Similar analysis is useful when swapping one bond for another.

---

48. We have previously alluded to the biases of any valuation model and will ignore them here.

## EXERCISING THE EMBEDDED OPTIONS

In this section, we discuss the decisions that investors and issuers face with respect to the options embedded in the convert. Clearly, there are some game-theoretic aspects to the anticipatory or responsive actions taken by these parties.

## Investors' Options

*Conversion Option:* When a convert is redeemed by the issuer, it loses the conversion privilege on the last day of the *redemption notice period*, which is generally 15 to 30 calendar days following the redemption notice, with 30 days the norm. Most often, redemption is intended to force the convert into equity. For that to occur, the convert should be in-the-money when the investor turns in the bond. And this raises the question of when during the 30-day period should the investor tender the bond for conversion. Following the redemption notice, if the stock price falls below the effective per share redemption price,[49] the investor can choose to receive the redemption price. Thus, the redemption notice triggers a put, with maturity equal to the number of days in the redemption notice period, during which time the investor has the right to tender the convert and receive the redemption price. As is well known, all long positions in American options have non-negative value. Consequently, under normal circumstances they should not be exercised prematurely. The investor should wait to exercise either option until the moment before the expiration of the redemption period. By then it will be clear whether the convert is in-the-money and hence worth more than the redemption value, in which case it should be tendered for conversion; or whether should be tendered for the redemption value. Investors who choose to exit during the redemption notice period can find ready buyers among convertible arbitrage funds who will usually pay some value for the remaining optionality, less their transaction cost

In the vast majority of cases, conversions occur in response to issuer redemptions. We know that the holder of a typical convertible is net long a conversion, i.e. a call option, and that a call option should never be exercised prior to maturity for stocks that do not pay dividends. For a dividend paying stock, a call should be exercised prior to maturity only in the event that the present value of the dividend stream during the life of the call is greater than the present value of interest likely to be earned on the exercise price. This roughly implies that voluntary conversion of a convertible is rational when the dividend yield on the common exceeds the current yield on the convert, and the yield advantage

---

49. Effective conversion price is defined as the redemption price divided by the conversion ratio. For example, if the bond is redeemable at 103.5 and the conversion ratio is 14.865 shares, the effective conversion price is $1035/14.865 shares = $69.627 per share, although the conversion price is $1000/14.865 shares = 67.272 per share.

becomes negative.[50] These situations seldom arise. Occasionally, voluntary conversion may occur when the stock borrow cost is very large, and thus has the same effect as a negative yield advantage. The voting right of a common share will rarely be the reason to voluntarily terminate the life of the convert and receive the shares.

This brings us to the notion of the *critical stock price*. As the stock price rises, there will come a point at which the yield advantage will turn negative for dividend paying stocks. The stock price level at which the value of the put option exactly equals the absolute value (of the now negative value) of the swap to receive the coupon in place of dividends is called the critical stock price. At this point conversion premium is zero and the investor is indifferent between holding the convert and receiving common stock. If the stock price rises above this level, voluntary conversion will then be optimal. A convert model is able to take these considerations into account and alert the investor should the stock price reach the critical level and the issuer has not yet redeemed the convert. Higher the dividend yield, lower the critical stock price. For most stocks, this point is approximately at 175% of the conversion price.[51]

*Put Option:* In the case of a putable convert, an investor would be expected to exercise the put if the estimated value of the convert immediately following the put date is lower than the put price. The valuation model is useful in establishing the optimal put condition. Some issuers want to know the scenarios under which the convert will be put to them, and can be an important consideration in their choice of financing instrument.

*Change of Control Put Option:* Most converts include an investor put at par, or slightly above par, in the event that a specified percent, usually 51%, of the shares of the underlying stock is acquired by another entity. The put price is payable in cash and has the deterrent effect of a poison pill, particularly if the convert is out-of-the-money. For those trading above the put price, the put exercise results in the loss of the conversion premium in excess of the put price, and the convert is terminated. Quite often, the acquirer's common stock will replace the target firm's common shares according to a specified exchange ratio. This will preserve the conversion option and some, or all, of the conversion premium. The decision rule for investors, as always, is to choose the value-maximizing alternative. Depending on the circumstances, value maximization may or may not entail exercising the change of control put.

## Issuer's Options

*Redemption Option:* The optimal issuer action is to minimize the gain of the convert holder and maximize the benefit to the shareholder. Conceptually, in the

---

50. We say "roughly" because some converts on high dividend yielding stocks have been issued with negative yield advantage. Investors correctly view them as equity with very valuable puts, and hence, as very defensive securities.

51. This explains why following a hard non-call period, a year of provisional call protection at 175% or higher is roughly worth equal to another year of hard call protection.

absence of the redemption notice period, the optimal redemption moment is exactly when parity equals the redemption price. Since the redemption notice period does exist, the optimal decision, and its timing, become a function of the issuer's intent and of whether the convert is in-the-money and by how much. If the issuer is indifferent to whether the issue converts or is redeemed for cash, then the issuer's optimal decision will be to redeem at the earliest opportunity. This situation occurs when the convert constitutes an insignificant component of a large firm's balance sheet. But in all other cases, issuers will be guided by one of the following two objectives:

- *Conversion Forcing Redemption:* The benefits to the shareholder of forcing conversion include saving the interest expense, lower leverage, and an increase in debt capacity due to the additional equity in the balance sheet resulting from the conversion. If the after tax cost of the coupon on the convertible is lower than the dividend yield, or in the case of accreting converts, if the after tax cash flow is positive to the issuer, the issuer may choose to defer redemption. Given the redemption notice period, the issuer needs to allow for a margin of safety such that the probability of the stock's falling below the effective conversion price is at an acceptable level. The greater the risk aversion of the issuer to the adverse effects of non-conversion, the higher will be the cushion, and results in what is known as the *call delay*. The negative impact of a failed attempt at forcing conversion may be severe; and in smaller firms it may lead to financial distress. At the very least, the issuer will have to refinance the redemption value with cash or debt and thereby cause the capital structure to be different than intended. Greater the call delay, higher the value of the convert.

  Empirical studies have documented the existence of call delays, though their average size has declined from higher than 40% in the 1970s to about 20% to 30% today. The call delay is a function of the volatility of the underlying stock, the length of the redemption notice period, and the issuer's risk aversion. Specifically, it is equal to $\sigma\sqrt{t}$, where $t$ is the length in years of the redemption notice period. As a numerical illustration, if $t$ is one month, the short term volatility estimate is 30% per annum, and absent any jumps, the stock is expected to move $0.30 \times \sqrt{(1/12)} = 0.866$, that is, $\pm 8.66\%$ in one month with a probability of 68%. The two standard deviation, or equivalently, a 95% confidence interval implies a call delay of $2 \times 8.66 = 17.32\%$ above the effective conversion price.

- *Debt Refinancing Redemption:* If the issuer does not want conversion to occur, the logic of the call delay also applies here, except that now the stock price has to be below the effective redemption price so as to provide the desired cushion. The issuer's primary reason for redeeming the convert for debt is to minimize equity dilution, and potentially to increase the diluted earnings per share. The cost of debt of matching seniority and maturity is the appropriate benchmark from a cost of capital perspective. This refinancing rate may be lower or higher than the coupon on the convert, depending on the change in the interest rates since the date of the convert's issuance. Nonetheless, the desire to reduce dilution overrides most other considerations.

## LOOKING FORWARD

Over time, the convertible product has evolved considerably in its level of sophistication and product diversity. Yet the amount of issuance in the convert market has not kept up with that in equity and debt markets. A case in point is the high yield market in the U.S. Although a relative newcomer, the high yield market now stands at roughly three to four times the size of the convert market. Perhaps the reason lies in the fact that the performance measurement of investors is still tied to the equity performance benchmarks, causing the funds flow to be relatively limited, in comparison to equity funds. Perhaps the convert market needs new product segments to attract a wider pool of funds and corresponding different benchmarks. Two recent pools of funds that have helped expand the convert market by adding liquidity and efficiency are the convertible hedge funds and the asset swap buyers. We will discuss them next.

*Hedge Funds:* Issuers generally dislike this class of investors as they are seen to exert downward pressure on the stock when they buy the convert and short the stock. As the stock price rises, the hedge ratio tends towards 1.0, and the number of shares to be shorted increases. However, the point overlooked is that hedge funds also support the stock were it to decline. In this event, they would buy back the stock to reduce their hedge ratio and arrive at a lower neutral hedge position. Thus hedge funds contribute towards lowering the volatility of the underlying share. Imagine a situation in which hedging were not permitted. Since most convert portfolio managers are, by charter, prevented from holding common stock following conversion and receipt of the shares they would have to sell their shares. Severe disruptions would, most likely, occur in anticipation of conversion. But his does not currently happen. Upon conversion, the underlying shares tend to decline by about 2% to 3%, but recover within 2 to 4 weeks. This is largely due to the short position in the shares by the hedge portfolios against their holdings of deep-in-the-money converts. In effect, hedging is equivalent to pre-converting over time so that the single day rush to the exits that would have otherwise occurred does not occur. Additionally, hedge funds provide liquidity to dedicated convert and equity funds seeking to exit their positions. And finally, they have contributed significantly to making the convert market more efficient by their more rigorous valuation and pricing of the embedded options.

*Asset Swap Buyers:* These are fixed income portfolios and financial institutions that take the interest rate and credit risks embedded in the convert. Trading desks enter into callable swaps on the underlying convert with a back-to-back redemption feature. If the issuer redeems the convert, the trading desk may redeem the convert from the asset swap buyer. Until then, the cash flows of the convert are passed through; the trading desk retains the equity optionality. This partitioning of the convert also helps provide liquidity to the busted converts, subject to credit quality constraints, and to new issue investment grade converts.

## SUMMARY

Convertible securities are fairly complex, with several interwoven embedded options. Traditional methods of evaluation are often flawed, sometimes even misleading. This chapter describes the products in the convertible asset class, the evolution of the convert market, and the modern analytical valuation approach. This approach, in conjunction with the fundamental equity analysis of the underlying equity security, plays a crucial role in the issuance, trading, and hedging of equity-linked securities. The valuation models discussed in this chapter have become indispensable in convertible investment and portfolio management.

## PART 8

# DERIVATIVE INSTRUMENTS AND THEIR PORTFOLIO MANAGEMENT APPLICATIONS

CHAPTER **52**

# INTRODUCTION TO INTEREST-RATE FUTURES AND OPTIONS CONTRACTS

**Mark Pitts, Ph.D.**
Principal
White Oak Capital Management Corp.

**Frank J. Fabozzi, Ph.D., CFA, CPA**
Adjunct Professor of Finance
School of Management
Yale University

With the advent of options, futures, and forwards on interest-rate instruments, proactive fixed income risk management, in its broadest sense, assumes a new dimension. Investment managers and traders can achieve new degrees of freedom. It is now possible to alter the interest-rate sensitivity of a fixed income portfolio economically and quickly. *Derivative contracts,* known as such because they derive their value from an underlying instrument, offer investment managers and traders risk and return patterns that were previously either unavailable or too costly.

The purpose of this chapter is twofold. First, we explain the basic characteristics of options, futures, and forward contracts. Second, we review the most actively traded and most representative over-the-counter (OTC) and listed contracts. We omit from our discussion the use of futures for hedging; this topic will be explained in more detail in Chapter 56.

## BASIC CHARACTERISTICS OF DERIVATIVE CONTRACTS

### Futures Contracts

A *futures contract* is an agreement between a buyer (seller) and an established futures exchange or its clearinghouse in which the buyer (seller) agrees to take (make) delivery of a specific amount of a valued item such as a commodity, stock, or bond at a specified price at a designated time. For some futures contracts, settlement at expiration is in cash rather than actual delivery.

When an investor takes a position in the market by buying a futures contract, the investor is said to *be long the futures* or have a *long position in the futures.* If, instead, the investor's opening position is the sale of a futures contract, the investor is said to *be short the futures* or have a *short position in the futures.*

Futures contracts based on a financial instrument or a financial index are known as *financial futures.* Financial futures can be classified as interest-rate futures, stock index futures, or currency futures. This chapter focuses on interest-rate futures and includes a description of the most important interest-rate futures contracts currently traded.

To illustrate how financial futures work, suppose that $X$ buys a futures contract and $Y$ sells a futures contract on an 8% five-year Treasury note for settlement one year from now. Suppose also that the price at which $X$ and $Y$ agree to transact one year from now is $100. This is the futures price. This means that one year from now $Y$ must deliver an 8% five-year Treasury note and will receive $100. $X$ will take delivery of an 8% five-year Treasury note and will pay $100.

The profit or loss realized by the buyer or seller of a futures contract depends on the price and interest rate on the delivery date. For example, if the market price of an 8% five-year Treasury note at the settlement date is $110, because rates have declined, the buyer profits, paying $100 for a security that is worth $110. In contrast, the seller loses, because an instrument worth $110 must be delivered in exchange for $100. If interest rates rise on 8% five-year Treasury notes so that the market price is $90, the seller of the futures contract profits and the buyer loses.

When the investor first takes a position in a futures contract, he must deposit a minimum dollar amount per contract as specified by the exchange. As the price of the futures contract fluctuates, the value of the investor's equity in the position changes. At the close of each trading day, any market gain results in an increase in the investor's equity, whereas any market loss results in a decrease. This process is referred to as *marking to market.* Should an investor's equity position fall below an amount determined by the exchange, he must provide additional margin. On the other hand, if an investor's equity increases, he or she may withdraw funds. Consequently, a futures position frequently involves substantial cash flows before the delivery date. Margin is described in more detail later in this chapter.

## Forward Contracts

A *forward contract* is much like a futures contract. A forward contract is an agreement for the future delivery of some amount of a valued item at a specified price at a designated time. Futures contracts are standardized agreements that define the delivery date (or month) and quality and quantity of the deliverable. Futures contracts are traded on organized exchanges. A forward contract is, in contrast, usually nonstandardized, and is traded over the counter by direct contact between buyer and seller.

Although both futures and forward contracts set forth terms of delivery, futures contracts are not intended to be settled by delivery. In fact, generally only a small percentage of outstanding futures contracts are delivered or go to final settlement. However, forward contracts *are* intended to be held to final settlement. Many of the most popular forward contracts, however, settle in cash rather than actual delivery.

Forward contracts may or may not be marked to market. Consequently, there is no interim cash flow on forwards that are not marked to market.

Finally, both parties in a forward contract are exposed to credit risk because either party may default on its obligation. In contrast, credit risk for futures contracts is minimal because the clearing corporation associated with the exchange guarantees the other side of each transaction.

## Options

An *option* is a contract in which the seller of the option grants the buyer of the option the right to purchase from, or sell to, the seller a designated instrument at a specified price within a specified period of time. The seller (or *writer*) grants this right to the buyer in exchange for a certain sum of money, called the *option price* or *option premium.*

The price at which the instrument may be bought or sold is called the *exercise* or *strike price.* The date after which an option is void is called the *expiration date.* An *American option* may be exercised any time up to and including the expiration date. A *European option* may be exercised only on the expiration date.

When an option writer grants the buyer the right to purchase the designated instrument, it is called a *call option.* When the option buyer has the right to sell the designated instrument to the writer, the option is called a *put option.* The buyer of an option is said to be *long the option;* the writer is said to be *short the option.*

Consider, for example, an option on an 8% five-year Treasury note with one year to expiration and an exercise price of $100. Suppose that the option price is $2 and the current price of the Treasury note is $100 with a yield of 8%. If the option is a call option, then the buyer of the option has the right to purchase an 8% five-year Treasury note for $100 within one year. The writer of the option must sell the Treasury note for $100 to the buyer if he or she exercises the option. Suppose that the interest rate on the Treasury note declines and its price rises to $110. By exercising the call option, the buyer realizes a profit, paying $100 for a Treasury note that is worth $110. After considering the cost of buying the option, $2, the net profit is $8. The writer of the option loses $8. If, instead, the market interest rate rises and the price of the Treasury note falls below $100, the call option buyer will not exercise the option, losing the option price of $2. The writer will realize a profit of $2. Thus, the buyer of a call option benefits from a decline in interest rates (a rise in the price of the under-lying fixed income instrument) and the writer loses.

If the option is a put rather than a call, and the interest rate on Treasury notes declines and the price rises above $100, the option buyer will not exercise the option. The buyer will lose the entire option price. If, on the other hand, the interest rate on Treasury notes rises and the note's price falls below $100, the option buyer will profit by exercising the put option. In the case of a put option, the option buyer benefits from a rise in interest rates (a decline in the price of the underlying fixed income instrument) and the option seller loses.

The maximum amount that an option buyer can lose is the option price. The maximum profit that the option writer (seller) can realize is the option price. The option buyer has substantial potential upside return, whereas the option writer has substantial downside risk. The risk/reward relationships for option positions are investigated in Chapter 55.

Options can be written on cash instruments or futures. The latter are called *futures options* and are traded only on the exchanges. Options on cash instruments are also traded on the exchanges, but have been much more successfully traded over the counter. These *OTC*, or *dealer*, *options* are tailor-made options on specific Treasury issues, mortgage securities, or interest-rate indexes. Option contracts are reviewed later in this chapter.

## Differences between Option and Futures (or Forward) Contracts

Unlike a futures or forward contract, an option gives the buyer the *right* but not the *obligation* to perform. The option seller has the obligation to perform. In the case of a futures or forward contact, both the buyer and seller are obligated to perform. In addition, the buyer of a futures or forward contract does not pay the seller to accept the obligation, whereas in the case of an option, the buyer pays the seller an option premium.

Consequently, the risk/reward characteristics of the two contracts also differ. In a futures or forward contract, the long position realizes a dollar-for-dollar gain when the price of the futures or forward increases and suffers a dollar-for-dollar loss when the price of the futures or forward decreases. The opposite holds for a short position. Options do not provide such a symmetric risk/reward relationship. The most a long position may lose is the option premium, yet the long retains all the upside potential. However, the gain is always reduced by the price of the option. The maximum profit the short position may realize is the option price, but the short position has substantial downside risk.

# REPRESENTATIVE EXCHANGE-TRADED INTEREST-RATE FUTURES CONTRACTS

Interest-rate futures contracts can be classified by the maturity of their underlying security. Short-term interest rate futures contracts have an underlying security that matures in less than one year. The maturity of the underlying security of long-term futures exceed one year. Below we describe the specifications of the Treasury futures contracts and Eurodollar CD futures contract.

## The Treasury Bond Futures Contract

The T-bond futures contract is the most successful interest-rate (or commodity) futures contract. Prices and yields on the T-bond futures contract are quoted in terms of a (fictitious) 20-year 6% Treasury bond, but the CBT allows many different bonds to be delivered in satisfaction of a short position in the contract. Specifically, any noncallable Treasury bond with at least 15 years to maturity from the first day of the delivery month, qualifies for delivery. Consequently, there are usually at least 20 outstanding bonds that constitute good delivery.

The T-bond futures contract calls for the short (i.e., the seller) to deliver $100,000 face value of any one of the qualifying Treasury bonds. However, because the coupons and maturities vary widely, the price that the buyer pays the seller depends on which bond the seller chooses to deliver. The rule used by the Chicago Board of Trade is one that adjusts the futures price by a conversion factor that reflects the price the bond would sell for at the beginning of the delivery month if it were yielding 6%. Using such a rule, the conversion factor for a given bond and a given delivery month is constant through time and is not affected by changes in the price of the bond or the price of the futures contract.

The seller has the right to choose which qualifying bond to deliver and when during the delivery month delivery will take place. When the bond is delivered, the buyer is obligated to pay the seller the futures price times the appropriate conversion factor, plus accrued interest on the delivered bond.

Paradoxically, the success of the CBT Treasury bond contract can in part be attributed to the fact that the delivery mechanism is not as simple as it may first appear. There are several options implicit in a position in bond futures. First, the seller chooses which bond to deliver. Thus, the seller has an option to swap between bonds. If the seller is holding bond A for delivery, but bond B becomes cheaper to deliver, she can swap bond B for bond A and make a more profitable delivery. Second, within some guidelines set by the CBT, the seller decides when during the delivery month delivery will take place. She thus has a timing option that can be used to her advantage. Finally, the short retains the possibility of making the wildcard play. This potentially profitable situation arises from the fact that the seller can give notice of intent to deliver for several hours after the exchange has closed and the futures settlement price has been fixed. In a falling market, the seller can use the wildcard option to profit from the fixed delivery price.

The seller's options tend to make a contract a bit more difficult to understand, but at the same time they make the contract more attractive to speculators, arbitrageurs, dealers, and anyone else who understands the contract better than other market participants. Thus, in the case of the Treasury bond futures contract, complexity has helped provide liquidity.

Because of the importance of this contract, it is discussed in more detail in Chapter 54.

## Treasury Note Futures

There are three Treasury note futures contracts: 10-year, five-year, and two-year. All three contracts are modeled after the Treasury bond futures contract and are traded on the CBT. The underlying instrument for the 10-year Treasury note futures contract is $100,000 par value of a hypothetical 10-year, 6% Treasury note. There are several acceptable Treasury issues that may be delivered by the short. An issue is acceptable if the maturity is not less than 6.5 years and not greater than 10 years from the first day of the delivery month. The delivery options granted to the short position and the minimum price fluctuation are the same as for the Treasury bond futures contract.

For the five-year Treasury note futures contract, the underlying is $100,000 par value of a U.S. Treasury note that satisfies the following conditions: (1) an original maturity of not more than five years and three months, (2) a remaining maturity not more than five years and three months, and (3) a remaining maturity of not less than four years and two months. The minimum price fluctuation for this contract is one 64th of a percent. The dollar value of one 64th for a $100,000 par value is $15.625 and is therefore the minimum price fluctuation.

The underlying for the two-year Treasury note futures contract is $200,000 par value of a U.S. Treasury note with a remaining maturity of not more than two years and not less than one year and nine months. Moreover, the original maturity of the note delivered to satisfy the two-year futures cannot be more than five years and three months. The minimum price fluctuation for this contract is one 128th of a percent. The dollar value of one 128th for a $200,000 par value is $15.625 and is therefore the minimum price fluctuation.

## The Treasury Bill Futures Contract

The IMM's futures contract on Treasury bills was the first contract on a short-term debt instrument, and has been the model for most subsequent contracts on short-term debt. The contract is based on three-month Treasury bills with a face value of $1 million.

The contract is quoted and traded in terms of a futures "price," but the futures price is, in fact, just a different way of quoting the futures interest rate. Specifically, the futures price is the annualized futures rate subtracted from 100. For example, a futures price of 92.25 means that Treasury bills are trading in the futures market at a rate of 7.75%. The actual price that the buyer pays the seller is calculated using the usual formula for Treasury bills:

$$\text{Invoice price} = \$1,000,000 \times \left[ 1 - \text{Rate} \times \left( \frac{\text{Days to maturity}}{360} \right) \right]$$

where the rate is expressed in decimal form. As this formula shows, each basis-point change in the interest rate (or each .01 change in the futures price) leads to a $25 change in the invoice price for a 90-day bill. Consequently, the value of a .01 change in the futures contract is always $25.

The Treasury bill futures contract is considerably simpler than the T-bond and T-note futures contracts. First, because all Treasury bills of the same maturity are economically equivalent, there is effectively only one deliverable issue, namely, Treasury bills with three months to maturity. The fact that the three-month bills may be either new three-month bills or older bills that currently have three months of remaining life makes little difference because the new and old issues will trade the same in the cash market. Thus, all the subtleties surrounding conversion factors and most deliverable issues are absent from the Treasury bill futures market. Furthermore, there is little uncertainty or choice involved in the delivery date, because delivery must take place during a very narrow time frame, usually a three-day period. The rules of the exchange make clear well in advance the exact dates on which delivery will take place. Finally, because there are no conversion factors, there is no wildcard play in the Treasury bill futures market.

Although the Treasury bill futures contract is simple and thus may not provide as many speculative and arbitrage opportunities as the more complex long- and intermediate-term futures contracts, it does provide a straightforward means of hedging or speculating on the short end of the yield curve. Because the Treasury bill rate is a benchmark off which other short-term rates may be priced, the bill contract fills a well-defined need of many market participants.

## The Eurodollar Time Deposit Futures Contract

As the Eurodollar and LIBOR sectors of the fixed income market have grown substantially in recent years, so has volume in the IMM's Eurodollar time deposit futures contract. Unlike most other fixed income futures contracts, the Eurodollar contract does not allow actual delivery. Instead, settlement is made in cash. The final settlement price is determined by the three-month Eurodollar deposit rate when trading on the contract is concluded. Although this mechanism does not allow delivery of an actual instrument, the cash flow from a futures position is such that the contract provides a very good vehicle for hedging or speculating on short-term Eurodollar and LIBOR-based debt.

Like the Treasury bill contract, the quoted futures price for Eurodollar time deposits is equal to 100 minus the annualized yield. Also, each .01 change in the futures price (one-basis-point change in yield) carries a value of $25. Settlement on Eurodollar futures takes place on a single day during the delivery month.

The yield on the Eurodollar futures contract is quoted in terms of an add-on, or simple, interest rate. Rates on Eurodollar contracts are thus directly comparable to the rates on domestic CDs or interbank deposits. However, to compare the Eurodollar rate to the Treasury bill rate, one of the rates must be converted so that both rates will be in the same terms.

The Eurodollar futures contract is one of the most heavily traded contracts. It is frequently used to trade the short end of the yield curve, and many hedgers have found the Eurodollar contract to be the best hedging vehicle for a wide range of hedging situations.

## Mechanics of Futures Trading

### Types of Orders

When a trader wants to buy or sell a futures contract, the price and conditions under which the order is to be executed must be communicated to a futures broker. The simplest type of order, yet potentially the most perilous from the trader's perspective, is the *market order.* When a market order is placed, it is executed at the best price available as soon as the order reaches the trading pit, the area on the floor of a futures exchange where all transactions for a specific contract are made. The danger of market orders is that an adverse move may take place between the time the trader places the order and the time the order reaches the trading pit.

To avoid the dangers associated with market orders, the trader can place a *limit order* (or *resting order*) that designates a price limit for the execution of the transaction. A *buy limit order* indicates that the futures contract may be purchased only at the designated price or lower. A *sell limit order* indicates that the futures contract may be sold only at the designated price or higher.

The danger of a limit order is that there is no guarantee that it will be executed at all. The designated price may simply not be obtainable. Even if the contract trades at the specified price, the order may not be filled because the market does not trade long enough at the specified price (or better) to fill all outstanding orders. Nevertheless, a limit order may be less risky than a market order. The trader has more control with a limit order, because the price designated in the limit order can be revised based on prevailing market prices as long as the order has not already been filled.

The limit order is a conditional order: It is executed only if the limit price or a better price can be obtained. Another type of conditional order is the *stop order.* A stop order specifies that the order is not to be executed until the market reaches a designated price, at which time it becomes a market order. A *buy stop order* specifies that the order is not to be executed until the market rises to a designated price (i.e., trades at or above, or is bid at or above, the designated price). A *sell stop order* specifies that the order is not to be executed until the market price falls below a designated price (i.e., trades at or below, or is offered at or below, the designated price). A stop order is useful when a futures trader already has a position on but cannot watch the market constantly. Traders can preserve profits or minimize losses on open positions by allowing market movements to trigger a closing trade. In a sell (buy) stop order, the designated price is less (greater) than the current market price of the futures contract. In a sell (buy) limit order the designated price is greater (less) than the current market price of the futures contract.

There are two dangers associated with stop orders. Because futures markets sometimes exhibit abrupt price changes, the direction of the change in the futures price may be very temporary, resulting in the premature closing of a position. Also, once the designated price is reached, the stop order becomes a market order and is subject to the uncertainty of the execution price noted earlier for market orders.

A *stop-limit order,* a hybrid of a stop order and a limit order, is a stop order that designates a price limit. Thus, in contrast to the stop order, which becomes a market order if the stop is reached, the stop-limit order becomes a limit order if the stop is reached. The order can be used to cushion the market impact of a stop order. The trader may limit the possible execution price after the activation of a stop. As with a limit order, the limit price might never be reached after the order is activated, and therefore the order might not be executed. This, of course, defeats one purpose of the stop order—to protect a profit or limit a loss.

A trader may also enter a *market-if-touched order.* A market-if-touched is like a stop order in that it becomes a market order if a designated price is reached. However, a market-if-touched order to buy would become a market order if the market *falls* to a given price, whereas a stop order to buy becomes a market order if the market *rises* to a given price. Similarly, a market-if-touched order to sell becomes a market order if the market rises to a specified price, whereas the stop order to sell becomes a market order if the market falls to a given price. One may think of the stop order as an order designed to exit an existing position at an acceptable price (without specifying the exact price), and the market-if-touched order as an order designed to enter a position at an acceptable price (also without specifying the exact price).

Orders may be placed to buy or sell at the open or the close of trading for the day. An *opening order* indicates that a trade is to be executed only in the opening range for the day, and a *closing order* indicates that the trade is to be executed only within the closing range for the day.

Futures brokers may be allowed to try to get the best possible price for their clients. The *discretionary order* gives the broker a specified price range in which to fill the order. For example, a discretionary order might be a limit order that gives the broker a one-tick (i.e., one-basis-point or one-32nd) discretion to try to do better than the limit price. Thus, even if the limit price is reached and the order could be filled at that limit, the broker can wait for a better price. However, if it turns out that the market goes in the wrong direction, the broker must fill the order but at no worse than one tick from the limit price. A *not held order* gives the broker virtually full discretion over the order. The not held order may be placed as any of the orders mentioned so far (market, stop, limit, etc.), but if the broker believes that filling the orders is not advisable, he or she need not fill them.

A client may enter orders that contain order cancellation provisions. A *fill-or-kill* order must be executed as soon as it reaches the trading floor or it is immediately canceled. A *one-cancels-other order* is a pair of orders that are worked simultaneously, but as soon as one order is filled the other is automatically canceled.

Orders may designate the time period for which the order is effective—a day, week, or month, or perhaps by a given time within the day. An *open order,* or *good-til-canceled order* is good until the order is specifically canceled. If the time period is not specified, it is usually assumed to be good only until the end of the day. For some orders, like the market order, a specific time period is not relevant, because they are executed immediately.

Upon execution of an order, the futures broker is required to provide confirmation of the trade. The confirmation indicates all the essential information about the trade. When the order involves the liquidation of a position, the confirmation shows the profit or loss on the position and the commission costs.

### Taking and Liquidating a Position

Once an account has been opened with a broker, the futures trader may take a position in the market. If the trader buys a futures contract, he is said to have a long position. If the trader's opening position is the sale of the futures contract, the trader is said to have a short position.

The futures trader has two ways to liquidate a position. To liquidate a position before the delivery date, he must take an offsetting position in the same contract. For a long position, this means selling an identical number of contracts; for a short position, this means buying an identical number of contracts.

The alternative is to wait until the delivery date. At that time, the investor liquidates a long position by accepting the delivery of the underlying instrument at the agreed-upon price, or liquidates a short position by delivering the instrument at the agreed-upon price. For interest-rate futures contracts that do not call for actual delivery (e.g., Eurodollar futures), settlement is in cash at the settlement price on the delivery date.

### The Role of the Clearing Corporation

When an investor takes a position in the futures market, there is always another party taking the opposite position and agreeing to satisfy the terms set forth in the contract. Because of the *clearing corporation* associated with each exchange, the investor need not worry about the financial strength and integrity of the party taking the opposite side of the contract. After an order is executed, the relationship between the two parties is severed. The clearing corporation interposes itself as the buyer for every sale and the seller for every purchase. Thus the investor is free to liquidate a position without involving the other party to the original transaction and without worry that the other party may default. However, the investor *is* exposed to default on the part of the futures broker through which the trade is placed. Thus, each institution should make sure that the futures broker (and specifically the *subsidiary* that trades futures) has adequate capital to ensure that there is little danger of default.

**Margin Requirements**

When first taking a position in a futures contract, an investor must deposit a minimum dollar amount per contract as specified by the exchange. (A broker may ask for more than the exchange minimum, but may not require less than the exchange minimum.) This amount is called the *initial margin,* and constitutes a good faith deposit. The initial margin may be in the form of Treasury bills. As the price of the futures contract fluctuates, the value of equity in the position changes. At the close of each trading day, the position is marked to market, so that any gain or loss from the position is reflected in the equity of the account. The price used to mark the position to market is the settlement price for the day.

*Maintenance margin* is the minimum level to which an equity position may fall as a result of an unfavorable price movement before additional margin is required. The additional margin deposited, also called *variation margin,* is simply the amount that will bring the equity in the account back to its initial margin level. Unlike original margin, variation margin must be in cash. If there is excess margin in the account, that amount may be withdrawn.[1]

If a variation margin is required, the party is contacted by the brokerage firm and informed of the additional amount that must be deposited. A margin notice is sent as well. Even if futures prices subsequently move in favor of the institution such that the equity increases above the maintenance margin, the variation margin must still be supplied. Failure to meet a request for variation margin within a reasonable time will result in the closing out of a position.

Margin requirements vary by futures contract and by the type of transaction; that is, whether the position is an outright long or short, or a spread (a

---

1. Although there are initial and maintenance margin requirements for buying stocks and bonds on margin, the concept of margin differs for futures. When securities are bought on margin, the difference between the price of the security and the initial margin is borrowed from the broker. The security purchased serves as collateral for the loan and interest is paid by the investor. For futures contracts, the initial margin, in effect, serves as good faith money, indicating that the investor will satisfy the obligation of the contract. No money is borrowed by the purchaser. Similarly, the seller of futures borrows neither money nor securities.

long together with a short), and whether the trade is put on as a speculative position or as a hedge. Margins are higher for speculative positions than for hedging positions and higher for outright positions than for spreads. Margin requirements also vary between futures brokers. Exchanges and brokerage firms change their margin requirements as contracts are deemed to be more or less risky, or as it is felt that certain types of positions (usually speculative positions) should be discouraged.

## REPRESENTATIVE EXCHANGE-TRADED FUTURES OPTIONS CONTRACTS

Although futures contracts are relatively straightforward financial instruments, options on futures (or *futures options,* as they are commonly called) deserve extra explanation. Options on futures are very similar to other options contracts. Like options on cash (or spot) fixed income securities, both put and call options are traded on fixed income futures. The buyer of a call has the right to buy the underlying futures contract at a specific price. The buyer of a put has the right to sell the underlying futures contract at a specific price. If the buyer chooses to exercise the option, the option seller is obligated to sell the futures in the case of the call, or buy the futures in the case of the put.

An option on the futures contract differs from more traditional options in only one essential way: The underlying instrument is not a spot security, but a futures contract on a security. Thus, for instance, if a call option buyer exercises her option, she acquires a long position in futures instead of a long position in a cash security. The seller of the call will be assigned the corresponding short position in the same futures contract. For put options the situation is reversed. A put option buyer exercising the option acquires a short position in futures, and the seller of the put is assigned a long position in the same futures contract. The resulting long and short futures positions are like any other futures positions and are subject to daily marking to market.

An investor acquiring a position in futures does so at the current futures price. However, if the strike price on the option does not equal the futures price at the time of exercise, the option seller must compensate the option buyer for the discrepancy. Thus, when a call option is exercised, the seller of the call must pay the buyer of the call the current futures price minus the strike price. On the other hand, the seller of the put must pay the buyer of the put the strike price minus the current futures price. (These transactions are actually accomplished by establishing the futures positions at the strike price, then immediately marking to market.) Note that, unlike options on spot securities, the amount of money that changes hands at exercise is only the difference between the strike price and the current futures price, not the whole strike price. Of course, an option need not be exercised for the owner to take her gains; she can simply sell the option instead of exercising it.

We now turn to the options contracts themselves. We describe two of the most important contracts, the CBT's option on the long-term bond futures contract and the IMM's option on the Eurodollar contract. There are also options on the five-year and 10-year note futures contracts, but because they are both very similar in structure to options on Treasury bond futures, they are not included in this section.

## Options on Treasury Bond Futures

Options on CBT Treasury bond futures are in many respects simpler than the underlying futures contracts. Usually, conversion factors, most deliverables, wildcard plays, and other subtleties of the Treasury bond futures contract need not concern the buyer or seller of options on Treasury bond futures. Although these factors affect the fair price of the futures contract, their impact is already reflected in the futures price. Consequently, they need not be reconsidered when buying or selling an option on the futures.

The option on the Treasury bond futures contract is in many respects an option on an index; the "index" is the futures price itself, that is, the price of the fictitious 20-year 6% Treasury bond. As for the futures contract, the nominal size of the contract is $100,000. Thus, for example, with futures prices at 95, a call option struck at 94 has an intrinsic value of $1,000 and a put struck at 100 has an intrinsic value of $5,000.

In an attempt to compete with the OTC option market, in 1994 the CBT introduced the *flexible Treasury futures options*. These futures options allow counterparties to customize options within certain limits. Specifically, the strike price, expiration date, and type of exercise (American or European) can be customized subject to CBT constraints. One key constraint is that the expiration date of a flexible contract cannot exceed that of the longest standard option traded on the CBT. Unlike an OTC option, where the option buyer is exposed to counterparty risk, a flexible Treasury futures option is guaranteed by the clearinghouse. The minimum size requirement for the launching of a flexible futures option is 100 contracts.

The premiums for options on Treasury bond futures are quoted in terms of points and 64ths of a point. Thus, an option premium of 1-10 implies a price of $1\frac{10}{64}\%$ of face value, or $1,156.25 (from $100,000 \times 1.15625\%$): Minimum price fluctuations are also $\frac{1}{64}$ of 1%.

Although an option on the Treasury bond futures contract is hardly identical to an option on a Treasury bond, it serves much the same purpose. Because spot and futures prices for Treasury bonds are highly correlated, hedgers and speculators frequently find that options on bond futures provide the essential characteristics needed in an options contract on a long-term fixed income instrument.

## Options on Eurodollar Futures

Options on Eurodollar futures fill a unique place among exchange-traded hedging products. These options are currently the only liquid listed option contracts based on a short-term interest rate.

Options on Eurodollar futures (traded on the IMM) are based on the quoted Eurodollar futures price (i.e., 100 minus the annualized yield). Like the underlying futures, the size of the contract is $1 million and each .01 change in price carries a value of $25. Likewise, the option premium is quoted in terms of basis points. Thus, for example, an option premium quoted as 20 (or .20) implies an option price of $500; a premium of 125 or (1.25) implies an option price of $3,125.

Like other debt options, buyers of puts on Eurodollar futures profit as rates move up and buyers of calls profit as rates move down. Consequently, institutions with liabilities or assets that float off short-term rates can use Eurodollar futures options to hedge their exposure to fluctuations in short-term rates. Consider institutions that have liabilities that float off short-term rates. These include banks and thrifts that issue CDs and/or take deposits based on money market rates. Also included are industrial and financial corporations that issue commercial paper, floating-rate notes, or preferred stock that floats off money market rates. Likewise, those who make payments on adjustable-rate mortgages face similar risks.[2] In each instance, as short-term rates increase, the liability becomes more onerous for the borrower. Consequently, the issuers of these liabilities may need a means of capping their interest-rate expense. Although options on Eurodollar futures do not extend as far into the future as many issuers would like. they are effective tools for hedging many short-term rates over the near term. Consequently, an institution with floating-rate liabilities can buy an interest-rate *cap* by buying puts on Eurodollar futures. As rates move up, profits on the put position will tend to offset some or all of the incremental interest expense.

On the other side of the coin, and facing opposite risks, are the purchasers of floating-rate instruments—that is, investors who buy money market deposits, floating-rate notes, floating-rate preferred stock, and adjustable-rate mortgages. Investors who roll over CDs or commercial paper face the same problem. As rates fall, these investors receive less interest income. Consequently, they may feel a need to buy interest-rate *floors,* which are basically call options. As rates fall, calls on debt securities increase in value and will offset the lower interest income received by the investor.

In conclusion, options on Eurodollar futures can be used to limit the risk associated with fluctuations in short-term rates. This is accomplished by buying puts if the exposure is to rising rates, or by buying calls if the exposure is to falling rates.

---

2. To the extent that the interest-rate payment on an adjustable-rate mortgage has an upper and lower bound, the risk to issuers and investors is limited by the nature of the instrument.

## Mechanics of Trading Futures Options

To take a position in futures options, one works with a futures broker. The types of orders that are used to buy or sell futures options are generally the same as the orders discussed for futures contracts. The clearinghouse associated with the exchange where the futures option is traded once again stands between the buyer and the seller. Furthermore, the commission costs and related issues that we discussed for futures also generally apply to futures options.

There are no margin requirements for the buyer of futures options, but the option price must be paid in full when the option is purchased. Because the option price is the maximum amount that the buyer can lose regardless of how adverse the price movement of the underlying futures contract, there is no need for margin.

Because the seller has agreed to accept all of the risk (and no reward other than the option premium) of the position in the underlying instrument, the seller is generally required to deposit not only the margin required for the underlying futures contract but, with certain exceptions, the option price as well. Furthermore, subsequent price changes adversely affecting the seller's position will lead to additional margin requirements.

## OTC CONTRACTS

There is a substantial over-the-counter market for fixed income options and forwards. (Forward contracts are the over-the-counter equivalent of futures contracts.) For example, in the OTC market, one can easily buy or sell options on LIBOR, commercial paper, T-bill, and prime rates. One can buy and sell options on virtually any Treasury issue. One can buy and sell options on any number of mortgage securities. One can buy and sell options with expirations ranging from as short as one day to as long as 10 years. In the OTC market, one can easily take forward positions in three- and six-month LIBOR going out to about 2 years.

In the options market in particular, a natural division has evolved between the OTC market and the listed market. Given the relatively small number of futures contracts, the exchanges' need for standardization, and the synergy created by the futures options contract trading side by side with the underlying futures contract, the exchanges have been most successful with options on futures contracts. Because off-exchange options on futures are prohibited, futures options cannot be traded over the counter. On the other hand, because the OTC market is very good at creating flexible structures and handling a diversity of terms, the OTC market has been more successful than the exchanges in trading options on cash securities and on cash market interest rates.

In the following sections, we discuss the structure of the OTC fixed income derivative markets and their advantages and disadvantages relative to the exchange-traded markets. We also discuss the most important contracts traded in the OTC market. These are options on mortgage securities, options on cash Treasuries, caps and floors on LIBOR, and forward rate agreements on LIBOR.

## The Structure of the OTC Market

As in other OTC markets, there is no central marketplace for OTC fixed income options and forward contracts. A transaction takes place whenever a buyer and seller agree to a price. Unlike an exchange transaction, the terms, size, and price of the contract generally remain undisclosed to other market participants. Accordingly, the OTC market is much less visible than the exchange markets and it is more difficult to ascertain the current market price for a given option or forward contract. Two groups, however, help to alleviate this problem. First, there are the OTC market makers. Market makers in OTC fixed income options and forwards are typically large investment banks and commercial banks. A market maker, by definition, stands ready to buy or sell a given option or forward contract to accommodate a client's needs. To be effective, the market maker must be willing and able to handle large orders and must keep the bid-ask spreads reasonably narrow.

The other group that helps bring order to the OTC market is the brokers. The sole job of the brokers is to bring together buyers and sellers; it is not the brokers' job to take positions in option and forward contracts. The buyers and sellers that the brokers bring together can be market makers or the end users of the contracts. To do their job, the brokers must distribute information about the prices where they see trades taking place and the prices at which they believe further trades can be completed. This information is distributed to potential buyers and sellers over the phone and over publicly available media such as Telerate pages.

Because there is no central market for OTC fixed income options and forwards, there can be no clearinghouse. Consequently, those who position OTC contracts may have to give considerable weight to the creditworthiness of their counterparty. For example, entities that sell options or position forward rate agreements (FRAs) can have potential liabilities equal to several times their net worth. Furthermore, there is no guarantee that these counterparties have effective hedges against their positions, or in fact, that they are hedging at all. Furthermore, financial problems on the part of the counterparty can jeopardize the ability or willingness of the counterparty to make good on the terms of a contract even if it is hedged. Consequently, unlike the exchange-traded markets where one neither knows nor cares who is on the other side of a trade, in the OTC market it is usually very important to know who is on the other side. Creditworthiness can be one of the most important considerations in the trade.

The potential credit problems associated with OTC trades are mitigated in a number of ways. First, some institutions will not buy options from or take either side of an FRA contract with any party other than a major entity with a sound credit rating. Secondly, some institutions require their counterparty to post collateral immediately after the transaction is completed. This collateral serves much the same purpose as initial margin in the futures and futures options market. Finally, some institutions reserve the right to call for additional collateral from their counterparties if the market moves against the counterparty. This is analogous to variation margin in the exchange-traded markets. Although these provisions may not be as good as a central clearinghouse, they are apparently good enough for a very large number of institutions and good enough for a very large market to develop.

Liquidity, in terms of being able to easily close out an existing position, can be a constraint in the over-the-counter market. OTC options and forwards are generally not assignable transactions. Thus, for example, if one sells an option, the contingent liability associated with that option cannot be transferred to a third party without the express permission of the option buyer. If an option seller wants to cover a short option position, often the best strategy is to buy a similar option from a third party to offset the risks of the original option. However, if the credit of the offsetting party is in question, or the offsetting option is not identical, risks will remain for the option seller. The option buyer can face similar problems if closing out the option before expiration. Credit considerations and the fact that the option buyer may not be able to sell an identical option to offset the first option make it more difficult to effectively close out the long option position. Because FRAs involve contingent liabilities for both sides of the transaction, similar problems exist for both buyers and sellers of FRAs.

Some of the problems associated with the OTC market arise from the fact that the contracts are not standardized. However, nonstandardization leads to many benefits as well. As indicated above, OTC contracts can be specified in virtually any terms that are acceptable to both buyer and seller. A potential buyer or seller can thus approach a market maker with whatever structure is needed and in many (but certainly not all) cases obtain the desired structure at a reasonable price. Compared to the very rigid structure of the exchange-traded markets, this is a remarkable advantage.

# The OTC Contracts

## Options on Mortgages

The over-the-counter market for options on fixed income instruments began in the mid-1970s with *standby* commitments. Standbys were essentially put options on mortgages that allowed the holder (usually a mortgage banker) to sell mortgages at a given price during a given period of time. Although standbys were popularized by the Federal National Mortgage Association, other institutions soon got into the business of selling options. Thrift institutions, in particular, soon became sellers of puts, as well as calls, on mortgages. The thrift would typically sell out-of-the-money puts (struck at a yield that seemed attractive relative to current yields) and out-of-the-money calls (often struck at the thrift's cost of the underlying securities). Until the early 1980s, there were no real market makers in the OTC mortgage options market. Thus, a trade typically did not occur until an end-user who wanted to buy an option could be paired with an end-user who wanted to sell the very same option. The intermediary who stood in between these two parties was usually not willing to position one side without the other.

Today, the market for options on mortgages includes many more participants, although the original standby commitments no longer exist. Investment banks and commercial banks now play a major role in the mortgage options market. Many of the large investment and commercial banks are now willing to position mortgage options without having the other side of the trade. This makes the market much more liquid and flexible than it would be otherwise. The end-users of options on mortgages have not changed greatly, but the number of users has increased greatly. Mortgage bankers continue to buy puts on mortgages. Thrifts continue to sell both puts and calls. As some thrifts now play the role of mortgage banker, they too have become buyers of puts on mortgages. Money managers have also become a part of the market, usually as sellers of call options against mortgages in their portfolios.

The market for mortgage options today is composed almost entirely of options on the standard agency pass-through mortgage securities. Options on CMO tranches, IOs, POs, and the like are not a significant part of the OTC mortgage options market. The majority of the options traded are on 30-year mortgages, but options on 15-year products are also readily available. In terms of expiration, trading in mortgage options tends to be concentrated in the shorter expirations, with most of the options expiring within 60 days, and the vast majority expiring within one year. In terms of strike price, most of the trading is in at the money and out of the money options.

Given the willingness of OTC market makers to position options, a client can easily trade options on $25 million of underlying securities with little or no prior notice. Some firms will position $100 million or more of mortgage options on the wire. Thus, the OTC options market can be as liquid as the exchange-traded options markets.

### Options on Treasury Securities

Although not as old as the OTC options market for mortgages, the OTC options market for Treasury securities is now just as large and liquid. As in the mortgage options market, investment banks and commercial banks play major roles as market makers, frequently standing ready to buy or sell options on $100 million (or more) of Treasury securities. Most of the action is in options expiring within 60 days, written at the money or out of the money. Options on Treasuries are concentrated in the on-the-run issues, with most of the remaining business being done in the off-the-run issues.

Except for the mortgage bankers, who have considerably less interest in options on Treasuries, the end-users of options on Treasuries mirror the market for options on mortgages. Thrifts tend to be writers of out-of-the-money puts and calls, and money managers and mutual funds tend to be covered call writers.

## Caps and Floors on LIBOR

The primary OTC options covering the short end of the yield curve are the caps and floors on three- and six-month LIBOR. A cap on LIBOR is, in essence, a series of puts on LIBOR-based debt, whereas a floor on LIBOR is, in essence, a series of calls on LIBOR-based debt.

The buyer of a cap or floor holds most of the rights in the contract, as with other options. The seller of a cap or floor will of course receive an options premium from the buyer but is then obligated to perform on the contract.

To see how these contracts work, consider a five-year, $100 million cap on three-month LIBOR struck at 11%. Such a contract will specify reset dates occurring every three months for a total of 20 resets. The first reset will usually occur immediately or within a couple of weeks of the trade date, and the last reset will usually be about three months before the stated maturity of the contract. To determine what the payoff to the cap buyer will be, on every reset date one compares the three-month LIBOR (taken from a predetermined source) with the 11% strike rate. If the three-month LIBOR is at or below 11%, nothing is owed to the cap buyer. However, if the three-month LIBOR is above 11%, the cap seller must pay the cap buyer the monetary value of the amount by which three-month LIBOR exceeds 11%. In this case, for a 90-day interest accrual period, the value of each basis point is $2,500 (from .0001 × $100,000,000 × 90/360). Thus, for example, if three-month LIBOR on a particular reset date is 11.50%, the cap seller owes the cap buyer $125,000 for that reset. If, on the next reset date, three-month LIBOR is 13%, the cap seller owes the cap buyer $500,000 for that reset. If, on the next reset date, three-month LIBOR is 10.50%, the cap seller owes nothing to the cap buyer for that reset. In most cases, the cap seller pays the cap buyer the amount of money owed for a particular reset at the end of the interest accrual period-in this case, three months after the reset date.

The mechanics of floors are similar, except that the payoff comes when rates fall below a given level, instead of when they rise above a given level. For example, if one buys a $25 million seven-year 6.50% floor on six-month LIBOR, there are a total of 14 reset dates. On each of these reset dates, one compares six-month LIBOR to 6.50%. If six-month LIBOR is above 6.50%, nothing is owed to the buyer of the floor for that reset. However, if six-month LIBOR is below 6.50%, for a 180-day interest accrual period the floor seller owes the floor buyer $1,250 for every basis point by which six-month LIBOR is below 6.50% (from .0001 × $25,000,000 × 180/360).

Like other OTC options markets, the cap and floor market is composed of market makers, end users, and brokers. The market makers are once again the large investment banks and commercial banks. However, there are fewer market makers and generally wider spreads in the cap and floor market than there are in the options market for mortgages or Treasury securities. Nonetheless, there is an active market out to 10 years, particularly for out-of-the-money caps, and to a lesser degree, out-of-the-money floors.

The end user buyers of caps and floors are primarily institutions with risks that they need to cover. For example, institutions that fund short and lend long will tend to have losses as short-term rates rise. Similarly, businesses that fund by rolling over short-term obligations such as commercial paper or by bank borrowings tied to LIBOR or the prime rate will tend to have losses as short-term rates rise. These institutions, which include many thrifts, banks, and finance companies, as well as industrial and construction companies, can protect themselves against rising short-term rates by buying caps. End-user buyers of floors tend to be firms that face losses if rates fall. Such a case might occur, for example, if an institution borrows at a floating rate with a built-in floor. Such an institution may be structured so that floating rates, per se, pose no problem; the problem arises when the floating rate at which they borrow is no longer really floating because the floor has been hit. This institution may buy a floor so that it will receive monetary compensation from the floor seller whenever the floating rate falls below the floor rate, thus covering the risks of lower rates.

The sellers of caps and floors, other than the market makers, are quite varied. In some cases, sellers sell caps or floors outright to bring in premium income. Others sell caps and/or floors to smooth out the cash flows on other fixed income instruments, such as certain derivative mortgage products. In other cases, sellers only implicitly sell the caps or floors. The following example illustrates both kinds of sellers.

When the cap market was developing, it quickly became obvious that there were many natural buyers of caps, but few natural sellers of caps. One successful effort to create sellers of caps occurred when investment bankers, who had many potential buyers of caps, realized that caps could be created as a derivative of the floating-rate note (FRN) market. Issuers of FRNs routinely issue notes reset off LIBOR. Furthermore, there were known buyers of *capped* FRNs; but of course, capped FRNs must have a higher coupon than uncapped FRNs to compensate the FRN buyer for the cap risk. If an issuer sells capped floating-rate notes, the issuer, in effect, buys a cap on LIBOR from the buyer of the FRN. This cap can then be sold to the investment banker, who in turn sells it to cap-buying clients. The deals that took place took exactly this form. The investment bankers underwrote capped FRNs for certain FRN issuers who agreed to make caplike payments to their investment banker. The banker then sold caps to another client but did not incur any market risks, because the two sets of potential payments offset one another. Using part of the proceeds of the sale of the cap, the investment bank agreed to make payments to the issuer to bring the cost of the floating-rate debt down to a level below that of uncapped floating-rate notes. Thus the investment bankers, the issuers of the FRNs, the buyers of the FRNs, and the ultimate cap-buying clients all walked away with a satisfactory transaction.

Such a transaction illustrates how creative financing can be used to create a seller of an instrument when no obvious seller exists. In this example, the issuers of the FRNs are willing to sell caps, given the fact that they, in turn, find someone willing to sell the caps to them. The ultimate seller of caps is the buyer of the capped FRNs. The buyers of the FRNs are, however, only implicit sellers of caps in the sense that they never explicitly have a position in caps on their books.

This example, which is just one of dozens, shows how market makers explicitly and implicitly induce end-users of financial products to buy or sell the instruments that allow the market makers to cover their positions in the OTC market. This is not to say that the market makers are taking advantage of the other parties to their trades. As is often the case, all parties to a transaction can come out ahead.

## Forward Rate Agreements (FRAs)

The FRA market represents the over-the-counter equivalent of the exchange-traded futures contracts on short-term rates. FRAs are a natural outgrowth of the interbank market for short-term funds. However, unlike the interbank market, virtually any creditworthy entity can buy or sell FRAs.

The liquid and easily accessible sector of the FRA market is for three- and six-month LIBOR. Rates are widely quoted for settlement starting one month forward, and settling once every month thereafter out to about six months forward. Thus, for example, on any given day forward rates are available for both three- and six-month LIBOR one month forward, covering, respectively, the interest period starting in one month and ending in four months, and the interest period starting in one month and ending in seven months. These contracts are referred to as $1 \times 4$ and $1 \times 7$ contracts. On the same day, there will be FRAs on three- and six-month LIBOR for settlement two months forward. These are the $2 \times 5$ and $2 \times 8$ contracts. Similarly, settlements occur three months, four months, five months, and six months forward for both three- and six-month LIBOR. These contracts are also denoted by the beginning and end of the interest period they cover.

On each subsequent day, contracts with the same type of structures, that is, contracts with one month, two months, and so on, to settlement date, are offered again. Thus, although on any given day a relatively limited number of structures are widely quoted, new contracts with new settlement dates are offered at the beginning of each day. This is quite different from the futures market, where the same contracts with the same delivery dates trade day after day.

As for other OTC debt instruments, there are market makers and brokers who make the market work. However, unlike the other OTC derivative instruments, in the FRA market the commercial banks are clearly the dominant force among the market makers. This dominance is due to the ability of the banks to blend their FRA transactions into their interbank transactions and overall funding operations. Consequently, many banks are willing to quote on a much wider variety of structures than the standard structures explained above. One can choose maturities other than three- and six-month LIBOR, and one can choose many settlement dates other than at an even number of months in the future.

In most cases, FRAs are written so that no money changes hands until the settlement date. To determine the cash flows on the settlement date, LIBOR taken from some predetermined source is compared to the LIBOR rate specified in the FRA contract. The actual dollar amount that changes hands is the dollar value of the difference between the two rates, *present valued* for a period equal to the maturity of the underlying LIBOR, either three or six months. The rationale behind present valuing is that if an FRA is used to hedge the rate on a deposit (or other short-term instrument), the loss (gain) due to a change in interest rates will be paid (saved) at the maturity of the deposit, not at the issue date. Thus, because cash payments on the FRA are made on the settlement date (which presumably is the same as the issue date of the deposit) the present value of the interest expense (or saving) on the deposit will equal the amount of money actually received or paid on the FRA.

Finally, one peculiarity of the FRA market deserves note. If one *buys* an FRA, one profits from an *increase* in rates, and if one *sells* an FRA, one profits from a *decline* in rates.

## SUMMARY

In this chapter, we have examined several of the most important and representative exchange-traded and OTC interest-rate futures and options contracts. In the next chapter, we discuss the pricing of futures contracts and the applications of futures to portfolio management.

## CHAPTER 53

# PRICING FUTURES AND PORTFOLIO APPLICATIONS

**Frank J. Fabozzi, Ph.D., CFA, CPA**
Adjunct Professor of Finance
School of Management
Yale University

**Mark Pitts, Ph.D.**
Principal
White Oak Capital Management Corp.

One of the primary concerns most traders and investors have when taking a position in futures contracts is whether the futures price at which they transact will be a fair price. Buyers are concerned that the price may be too high and that they will be picked off by more experienced futures traders waiting to profit from the mistakes of the uninitiated. Sellers worry that the price is artificially low and that savvy traders may have manipulated the markets so that they can buy at bargain-basement prices. Furthermore, prospective participants frequently find no rational explanation for the sometimes violent ups and downs that occur in the futures markets. Theories about efficient markets give little comfort to anyone who knows of or has experienced the sudden losses that can occur in the highly leveraged futures markets.

Fortunately, the futures markets are not as irrational as they may at first seem; if they were, they would not be so successful. The interest-rate futures markets are not perfectly efficient markets, but they probably come about as close as any market. Furthermore, there are very clear reasons why futures prices are what they are, and there are methods by which traders, investors, and borrowers will quickly eliminate any discrepancy between futures prices and their fair levels.

In this chapter, we will explain how the fair or theoretical value of an option is determined. We then explain some of the more important portfolio applications of interest-rate futures.

## PRICING OF FUTURES CONTRACTS

There are several different ways to price futures contracts. Fortunately, all lead to the same fair price for a given contract. Each approach relies on the *Law of*

*One Price.* This law states that a given financial asset (or liability) must have the same price regardless of the means by which one goes about creating that asset (or liability). In this section, we will demonstrate one way in which futures contracts can be combined with cash market instruments to create cash flows that are identical to other cash securities.[1] The Law of One Price implies that the synthetically created cash securities must have the same price as the actual cash securities. Similarly, cash instruments can be combined to create cash flows that are identical to futures contracts. By the Law of One Price, the futures contract must have the same price as the synthetic futures created from cash instruments.

## Illustration of the Basic Principles

To understand how futures contracts should be priced, consider the following example. Suppose that a 20-year, 100 par value bond with a coupon rate of 12% is selling at par. Also suppose that this bond is the deliverable for a futures contract that settles in three months. If the current three-month interest rate at which funds can be loaned or borrowed is 8% per year, what should be the price of this futures contract?

Suppose the price of the futures contract is 107. Consider the following strategy:

Sell the futures contract at 107.

Purchase the bond for 100.

Borrow 100 for three months at 8% per year.

The borrowed funds are used to purchase the bond, resulting in no initial cash outlay for this strategy. Three months from now, the bond must be delivered to settle the futures contract and the loan must be repaid. These trades will produce the following cash flows:

| | |
|---|---:|
| *From settlement of the futures contract* | |
| Flat price of bond | 107 |
| Accrued interest (12% for 3 months) | +3 |
| Total proceeds | 110 |
| | |
| *From the loan* | |
| Repayment of principal of loan | 100 |
| Interest on loan (8% for 3 months) | +2 |
| Total outlay | 102 |
| Profit | 8 |

---

1. For other ways to price futures contracts, see Chapter 5 in Mark Pitts and Frank J. Fabozzi *Interest Rate Futures and Options* (Chicago: Probus Publishing, 1990).

This strategy will guarantee a profit of 8. Moreover, the profit is generated with no initial outlay because the funds used to purchase the bond are borrowed. The profit will be realized *regardless of the futures price at the settlement date.* Obviously, in a well-functioning market, arbitrageurs would buy the bond and sell the futures, forcing the futures price down and bidding up the bond price so as to eliminate this profit.

In contrast, suppose that the futures price is 92 instead of 107. Consider the following strategy:

> Buy the futures contract at 92.
>
> Sell (short) the bond for 100.
>
> Invest (lend) 100 for 3 months at 8% per year.

Once again, there is no initial cash outlay. Three months from now a bond will be purchased to settle the long position in the futures contract. That bond will then be used to cover the short position (i.e., to cover the short sale in the cash market). The outcome in three months would be as follows:

| | |
|---|---:|
| *From settlement of the futures contract* | |
| Flat price of bond | 92 |
| Accrued interest (12% for 3 months) | +3 |
| Total outlay | 95 |
| | |
| *From the loan* | |
| Principal received from maturing investment | 100 |
| Interest earned from the three-month investment (8% for 3 months) | +2 |
| Total proceeds | 102 |
| Profit | 7 |

The 7 profit is a pure arbitrage profit. It requires no initial cash outlay and will be realized regardless of the futures price at the settlement date.

There is a futures price that will eliminate the arbitrage profit, however. There will be no arbitrage if the futures price is 99. Let's look at what would happen if the two previous strategies were followed and the futures price were 99. First, consider the following strategy:

> Sell the futures contract at 99.
>
> Purchase the bond for 100.
>
> Borrow 100 for 3 months at 8% per year.

In three months the outcome would be as follows:

*From settlement of the futures contract*

| | |
|---|---:|
| Flat price of bond | 99 |
| Accrued interest (12% for 3 months) | +3 |
| Total proceeds | 102 |

*From the loan*

| | |
|---|---:|
| Repayment of principal of the loan | 100 |
| Interest on the loan (8% for 3 months) | +2 |
| Total outlay | 102 |
| Profit | 0 |

There is no arbitrage profit.

Next, consider the following strategy:

Buy the futures contract at 99.

Sell (short) the bond for 100.

Invest (lend) 100 for 3 months at 8% per year.

The outcome in three months would be as follows:

*From settlement of the futures contract*

| | |
|---|---:|
| Flat price of bond | 99 |
| Accrued interest (12% for 3 months) | +3 |
| Total outlay | 102 |

*From the loan*

| | |
|---|---:|
| Principal received from maturing investment | 100 |
| Interest earned from the three-month investment (8% for 3 months) | +2 |
| Total proceeds | 102 |
| Profit | 0 |

Thus, neither strategy results in a profit. The futures price of 99 is the equilibrium price, because any higher or lower futures price will permit arbitrage profits.

### Theoretical Futures Price Based on Arbitrage Model

Considering the arbitrage arguments just presented, the equilibrium futures price can be determined on the basis of the following information:

- The price of the bond in the cash market.

- The coupon rate on the bond. In our example, the coupon rate was 12% per annum.

- The interest rate for borrowing and lending until the settlement date. The borrowing and lending rate is referred to as *the financing rate*. In our example, the financing rate was 8% per annum.

We will let

$r$ = financing rate
$c$ = current yield, or coupon rate divided by the cash market price
$P$ = cash market price
$F$ = futures price
$t$ = time, in years, to the futures delivery date

and then consider the following strategy that is initiated on a coupon date:

Sell the futures contract at $F$.
Purchase the bond for $P$.
Borrow $P$ until the settlement date at $r$.

The outcome at the settlement date is as follows:

| *From settlement of the futures contract* | |
| --- | ---: |
| Flat price of bond | $F$ |
| Accrued interest | $+ ctP$ |
| Total proceeds | $F + ctP$ |
| | |
| *From the loan* | |
| Repayment of principal of the loan | $P$ |
| Interst on loan | $+ rtP$ |
| Total outlay | $P + rtP$ |

The profit will equal

$$\text{Profit} = \text{Total proceeds} - \text{Total outlay}$$
$$\text{Profit} = F + ctP - (P + rtP)$$

In equilibrium, the theoretical futures price occurs where the profit from this strategy is zero. Thus, to have equilibrium, the following must hold:

$$0 = F + ctP - (P + rtP)$$

Solving for the theoretical futures price, we have

$$F = P + Pt(r - c) = P(1 + t(r - c)) \qquad (53\text{--}1)$$

Alternatively, consider the following strategy:

Buy the futures contract at $F$.
Sell (short) the bond for $P$.
Invest (lend) $P$ at $r$ until the settlement date.

The outcome at the settlement date would be as follows:

| | |
|---|---:|
| *From settlement of the futures contract* | |
| Flat price of bond | $F$ |
| Accrued interest | $+\ ctP$ |
| Total outlay | $\overline{F + ctP}$ |
| | |
| *From the loan* | |
| Proceeds received from maturing of investment | $P$ |
| Interest earned | $+\ rtP$ |
| Total proceeds | $\overline{P + rtP}$ |

The profit will equal

$$\text{Profit} = \text{Total proceeds} - \text{Total outlay}$$
$$\text{Profit} = P + rtP - (F + ctP)$$

Setting the profit equal to zero so that there will be no arbitrage profit and solving for the futures price, we obtain the same equation for the futures price as Equation (53–1).

Let's apply Equation (53–1) to our previous example in which

$r = .08$

$c = .12$

$P = 100$

$t = .25$

Then, the theoretical futures price is

$$F = 100 + 100 \times .25(.08 - .12)$$
$$= 100 - 1 = 99$$

This agrees with the equilibrium futures price we derived earlier.

The theoretical futures price may be at a premium to the cash market price (higher than the cash market price) or at a discount from the cash market price (lower than the cash market price), depending on the value of $(r - c)$. The term $r - c$ is called the *net financing cost* because it adjusts the financing rate for the coupon interest earned. The net financing cost is more commonly called the *cost of carry,* or simply *carry. Positive carry* means that the current yield earned is greater than the financing cost; *negative carry* means that the financing cost exceeds the current yield. The relationships can be expressed as follows:

| Carry | Futures Price |
|---|---|
| Positive $(c > r)$ | Will sell at a discount to the cash price $(F < P)$ |
| Negative $(c < r)$ | Will sell at a premium to the cash price $(F > P)$ |
| Zero $(r = c)$ | Will be equal to the cash price $(F = P)$ |

In the case of interest-rate futures, carry (the relationship between the short-term financing rate and the current yield on the bond) depends on the shape of the yield curve. When the yield curve is upward-sloping, the short-term financing rate will generally be less than the current yield on the bond, resulting in positive carry. The futures price will then sell at a discount to the cash price for the bond. The opposite will hold true when the yield curve is inverted.

## A Closer Look at the Theoretical Futures Price

To derive the theoretical futures price using the arbitrage argument, we made several assumptions. We will now discuss the implications of these assumptions.

***Interim Cash Flows***    No interim cash flows due to variation margin or coupon interest payments were assumed in the model. However, we know that interim cash flows can occur for both of these reasons. Because we assumed no variation margin, the price derived is technically the theoretical price for a forward contract (which is not marked to market at the end of each trading day). If interest rates rise, the short position in futures will receive margin as the futures price decreases; the margin can then be reinvested at a higher interest rate. In contrast, if interest rates fall, there will be variation margin that must be financed by the short position; however, because interest rates have declined, the financing can be done at a lower cost. Thus, whichever way rates move, those who are short futures gain relative to those who are short forward contracts that are not marked to market. Conversely, those who are long futures lose relative to those who are long forward contracts that are not marked to market. These facts account for the difference between futures and forward prices.

Incorporating interim coupon payments into the pricing model is not difficult. However, the value of the coupon payments at the settlement date will depend on the interest rate at which they can be reinvested. The shorter the maturity of the futures contract and the lower the coupon rate, the less important the reinvestment income is in determining the theoretical futures price.

***The Short-Term Interest Rate (Financing Rate)***    In deriving the theoretical futures price, it is assumed that the borrowing and lending rates are equal. Typically, however, the borrowing rate is greater than the lending rate.

We will let

$r_B$ = borrowing rate

$r_L$ = lending rate

Consider the following strategy:

Sell the futures contract at $F$.

Purchase the bond for $P$.

Borrow $P$ until the settlement date at $r_B$.

The futures price that would produce no arbitrage profit is

$$F = P + P(r_B - c) \tag{53--2}$$

Now consider the following strategy:

Buy the futures contract at $F$.
Sell (short) the bond for $P$.
Invest (lend) $P$ at $r_L$ until the settlement date.

The futures price that would produce no profit is

$$F = P + P(r_L - c) \tag{53--3}$$

Equations (53–2) and (53–3) together provide boundaries for the theoretical futures price. Equation (53–2) provides the upper boundary and equation (53–3) the lower boundary. For example, assume that the borrowing rate is 8% per year, or 2% for three months, and the lending rate is 6% per year, or 1.5% for three months. Then, using equation (53–2) and the previous example, the upper boundary is

$$F \text{ (upper boundary)} = \$100 + \$100 \,(.02 - .03)$$
$$= \$99$$

The lower boundary using equation (53–3) is

$$F \text{ (lower boundary)} = 100 + \$100 \,(.015 - .03)$$
$$= \$98.50$$

In calculating these boundaries, we assumed no transaction costs were involved in taking the position. In actuality, the transaction costs of entering into and closing the cash position as well as the round-trip transaction costs for the futures contract must be considered, and do affect the boundaries for the futures contract.

**Deliverable Bond and Settlement Date Unknown**    In our example, we assumed that only one bond is deliverable and that the settlement date occurs three months from now. As explained earlier in this chapter, futures contracts on Treasury bonds and Treasury notes are designed to allow the short position the choice of delivering one of a number of deliverable issues. Also, the delivery date is not known.

Because there may be more than one deliverable, market participants track the price of each deliverable bond and determine which is the cheapest to deliver. The futures price will then trade in relation to the bond that is cheapest to deliver.

The cheapest to deliver is the bond or note that will result in the smallest loss or the greatest gain if delivered by the short futures position.[2]

In addition to the reasons we have already discussed, there are several reasons why the actual futures price will diverge from the theoretical futures price based on the arbitrage model. First, there is the risk that although an issue may be the cheapest to deliver at the time a position in the futures contract is taken, it may not be the cheapest to deliver after that time. Thus, there will be a divergence between the theoretical futures price and the actual futures price. A second reason for this divergence is the other delivery options granted the short position. Finally, there are biases in the CBT conversion factors.

***Deliverable Is a Basket of Securities***    The municipal index futures contract is a cash settlement contract based on a basket of securities. The difficulty in arbitraging this futures contract is that it is too expensive to buy or sell every bond included in the index. Instead, a portfolio containing a smaller number of bonds may be constructed to track the index. The arbitrage, however, is no longer risk-free, because there is the risk that the portfolio will not track the index exactly. This is referred to as *tracking error risk*. Another problem in constructing the portfolio so that the arbitrage can be performed is that the composition of the index is revised periodically. Therefore, anyone using this arbitrage trade must constantly monitor the index and periodically rebalance the constructed portfolio.

## APPLICATIONS TO PORTFOLIO MANAGEMENT

This section describes various ways in which a money manager can use interest-rate futures contracts.

## Changing the Duration of the Portfolio

Money managers who have strong expectations about the direction of interest rates will adjust the duration of their portfolio to capitalize on their expectations. Specifically, if they expect interest rates to increase, they will shorten the duration of the portfolio; if they expect interest rates to decrease, they will lengthen the duration of the portfolio. Also, anyone using structured portfolio strategies must periodically adjust the portfolio duration to match the duration of some benchmark.

---

2. An alternative procedure is to compute the implied (breakeven) repo rate. This rate is the yield that would produce no profit or loss if the bond were purchased and a futures contract were sold against the bond. The cheapest-to-deliver bond is the one with the highest implied repo rate. For a further discussion, see Chapter 54.

Although money managers can alter the duration of their portfolios with cash market instruments, a quick and less expensive means for doing so (especially on a temporary basis) is to use futures contracts. By buying futures contracts on Treasury bonds or notes, they can increase the duration of the portfolio. Conversely, they can shorten the duration of the portfolio by selling futures contracts on Treasury bonds or notes.

## Asset Allocation

A pension sponsor may wish to alter the composition of the pension fund's assets between stocks and bonds. An efficient means of changing asset allocation is to use financial futures contracts: interest-rate futures and stock index futures.

## Creating Synthetic Securities for Yield Enhancement

A cash market security can be synthetically created by using a position in the futures contract together with the deliverable instrument. The yield on the synthetic security should be the same as the yield on the cash market security. If there is a difference between the two yields, it can be exploited so as to enhance the yield on the portfolio.

To see how, consider an investor who owns a 20-year Treasury bond and sells Treasury futures that call for the delivery of that particular bond three months from now. The maturity of the Treasury bond is 20 years, but the investor has effectively shortened the maturity of the bond to three months.

Consequently, the long position in the 20-year bond and the short futures position are equivalent to a long position in a three-month riskless security. The position is riskless because the investor is locking in the price that he or she will receive three months from now—the futures price. By being long the bond and short the futures, the investor has synthetically created a three-month Treasury bill. The return the investor should expect to earn from this synthetic position should be the yield on a three-month Treasury bill. If the yield on the synthetic three-month Treasury bill is greater than the yield on the cash market Treasury bill, the investor can realize an enhanced yield by creating the synthetic short-term security. The fundamental relationship for creating synthetic securities is as follows:

$$RSP = CBP - BFP \qquad (53\text{--}4)$$

where

CBP = cash bond position
BFP = bond futures position
RSP = riskless short-term security position

A negative sign before a position means a short position. In terms of our previous example, CBP is the long cash bond position, the negative sign before BFP refers to the short futures position, and RSP is the riskless synthetic three-month security or Treasury bill.

Equation (53–4) states that an investor who is long the cash market security and short the futures contract should expect to earn the rate of return on a risk-free security with the same maturity as the futures delivery date. Solving equation (53–4) for the long bond position, we have

$$CBP = RSP + BFP \qquad (53–5)$$

Equation (53–5) states that a cash bond position equals a short-term riskless security position plus a long bond futures position. Thus, a cash market bond can be synthetically created by buying a futures contract and investing in a Treasury bill.

Solving equation (53–5) for the bond futures position, we have

$$BFP = CBP - RSP \qquad (53–6)$$

Equation (53–6) tells us that a long position in the futures contract can be synthetically created by taking a long position in the cash market bond and shorting the short-term riskless security. Shorting the short-term riskless security is equivalent to borrowing money. Notice that it was equation (53–6) that we used in deriving the theoretical futures price when the futures was overpriced. Recall that when the futures price was 107, the strategy to obtain an arbitrage profit was to sell the futures contract and create a synthetic long futures position by buying the bond with borrowed funds. This is precisely what equation (53–6) states. In this case, instead of creating a synthetic cash market instrument as we did with equations (53–4) and (53–5), we have created a synthetic futures contract. The fact that the synthetic long futures position was cheaper than the actual long futures position provided an arbitrage opportunity.

If we reverse the sign of both sides of equation (53–6), we can see how a short futures position can be synthetically created.

In an efficient market, the opportunities for yield enhancement should not exist very long. Even in the absence of yield enhancement, however, synthetic securities can be used by money managers to hedge a portfolio position that they find difficult to hedge in the cash market either because of lack of liquidity or because of other constraints.

## Hedging

Hedging[3] with futures involves taking a futures position as a temporary substitute for transactions to be made in the cash market at a later date. If cash and futures prices move together, any loss realized by the hedger from one position

---

3. Hedging is discussed in more detail in Chapter 56.

(whether cash or futures) will be offset by a profit on the other position. When the net profit or loss from the positions are exactly as anticipated, the hedge is referred to as a *perfect hedge.*

In practice, hedging is not that simple. The amount of net profit will not necessarily be as anticipated. The outcome of a hedge will depend on the relationship between the cash price and the futures price when a hedge is placed and when it is lifted. The difference between the cash price and the futures price is called the *basis.* The risk that the basis will change in an unpredictable way is called *basis risk.*

In most hedging applications, the bond to be hedged is not identical to the bond underlying the futures contract. This kind of hedging is referred to as *cross hedging.* There may be substantial basis risk in cross hedging. An unhedged position is exposed to price risk, the risk that the cash market price will move adversely. A hedged position substitutes basis risk for price risk.

A short (or sell) hedge is used to protect against a decline in the cash price of a fixed income security. To execute a short hedge, futures contracts are sold. By establishing a short hedge, the hedger has fixed the future cash price and transferred the price risk of ownership to the buyer of the futures contract. As an example of why a short hedge would be executed, suppose that a pension fund manager knows that bonds must be liquidated in 40 days to make a $5 million payment to the beneficiaries of the pension fund. If interest rates rise during the 40-day period, more bonds will have to be liquidated to realize $5 million. To guard against this possibility, the manager would sell bonds in the futures market to lock in a selling price.

A long (or buy) hedge is undertaken to protect against an increase in the cash price of a fixed income security. In a long hedge, the hedger buys a futures contract to lock in a purchase price. A pension fund manager may use a long hedge when substantial cash contributions are expected and the manager is concerned that interest rates will fall. Also, a money manager who knows that bonds are maturing in the near future and expects that interest rates will fall can employ a long hedge to lock in a rate.

## SUMMARY

In this chapter, we have explored the cash and futures arbitrage and equilibrium futures pricing. The theoretical futures price is determined by the net financing cost, or carry. Carry is the difference between the financing cost and the cash yield on the underlying cash instrument. The basic futures pricing model presented in this chapter must be modified to account for nuances of specific futures contracts. In the next chapter, the basic pricing model is extended to the Treasury bond futures contract.

Some of the important uses of futures contracts by portfolio managers— altering a portfolio's duration, the potential to create synthetic securities with enhanced returns, and hedging—are discussed. Probably the most common application is hedging a portfolio. The details of how to do this with interest rate futures (and futures options) are explained in Chapter 56.

## CHAPTER 54

# TREASURY BOND FUTURES MECHANICS AND BASIS VALUATION*

**David T. Kim**
Tokai Bank

## INTRODUCTION

Since its inception in 1977, the bond futures contract has been the grandfather of the family of financial futures contracts. It is the primary vehicle for hedging an investor's Treasury cash positions and is easily the most liquid Treasury futures contract. It has become so successful, in fact, that it is often the driving force of the Treasury market.

An investor owning or long a bond futures contract can expect the delivery of one of a group of bonds within a certain time. Conversely, an investor who is short that contract is expected to make that delivery. However, the belief that the bond futures contract is simply a substitute for the current cash long bond is potentially a very costly one. The bond future may have the trading characteristics of many different bonds. Depending on the current yield environment, shape of the yield curve, and other factors, some bonds will obviously have a much greater impact on the pricing and consequent movement of the futures contract. One should never assume that only one bond controls its price.

The futures contract is like a large station wagon carrying a group of bonds. The bonds that are most important sit in the front and have the most impact on its direction and speed, but during some instances, the forgotten bonds in the back can grab control of the steering wheel. The true essence of basis pricing is determining how likely certain bonds are to gain control and how long they will drive. Frequently, the car that seemed to be driving straight on the expected route can lurch right through a trader's P and L and sometimes right over the trader. Thus, it is of paramount importance to comprehend fully the different dimensions of the contract and its deliverability options.

---

*The author would like to thank Sole Marittimi and Gene Kim for their helpful comments and suggestions.

# MECHANICS OF THE FUTURES CONTRACT

## Conversion Factor

The Chicago Board of Trade (CBT) was initially a place where participants in the agricultural market (e.g., farmers) went to protect themselves against inclement weather and other factors that could cause wide price and delivery swings. Thus, the CBT made a number of bonds deliverable because it was well-steeped in agricultural futures and wanted to ensure ease in delivering bonds if there was a large open interest at settlement. The conversion factor helps in that regard. In fact, if only one bond were eligible for delivery, the open interest or total number of positions in the bond future would be lower. Because most traders never involve themselves in the delivery process, there can obviously be positions before the last day of trading of that futures contract that are much larger than the deliverable bond.[1] However, such positions would still curtail activity in bond futures because there would be no more delivery games, which would be the antithesis of what the Board desires—the largest volume of trading and positioning possible. Undoubtedly, it is cynical to claim that this was the Board's main reason for allowing a group of bonds to be delivered, because most of the ideas that have come out of basis trading originated far after the contract's introduction. It was most likely an effort to stop a squeeze on any one deliverable bond.

For that reason, the CBT established a delivery factor algorithm to approximately equalize the cost of delivering a host of eligible bonds. Certainly, the factor does not make all bonds equally profitable to deliver. In fact, it is one of the main reasons why they are not. Without a factor system, the contract would simply be a futures contract on the lowest coupon bond with the longest maturity, because this would obviously have the lowest dollar price and, thus, be the cheapest security to deliver.

The factor rate the CBT uses is 6%. That is, when calculating conversion factors (CF), these bonds are all priced to yield 6%. The resulting price is then divided by 100 and rounded off to the nearest ten thousandth (four decimal places). A 25-year bond with a 7% coupon to yield 6% should be priced at $112.86. The conversion factor is simply 1.1286 (price/100). Keep in mind that the CF is roughly the price of the security to yield 6%.

This, however, is not precisely correct. To calculate the CF exactly, one must take the first day of the delivery month of the futures contract as the settlement date and the first day of the last delivery month as its maturity (the contract month that is closest to the maturity without being longer than the maturity). In other words, whatever the length of the bond, one would simply

---

1. The amount outstanding of each issue in the basket of deliverable bonds varies from $3.01 billion of both the 8¾% 5/20 to $18 billion of the 6¼% of the 8/23. The open interest on bond futures is typically between 500,000 and 600,000, whereas the number delivered is much smaller. For the December 1999 contract, only 26,000 contracts were delivered.

round down to the nearest quarter. For example, if the bond were maturing on 5/31/25, the maturity date used to calculate the CF would be 3/01/25. Even though June 1 is an eligible date and only one day from the actual maturity, it falls *after* the bond matures. One must remember to always go back to the last contract month passed. Thus, for both maturity and settlement, there can only be four days used: March 1, June 1, September 1, and December 1, for these are the four contract months for bonds on the CBT. The CF for the 6⅛% of 11/15/27 for the December 2001 contract is determined as follows:

| | |
|---|---|
| Settlement date | 12/01/01 |
| Maturity date | 9/01/27 |
| Priced to yield | 6% (as always) |
| To price | $101.63 |
| CF | 1.0163 |

## Invoice Price

The futures contract trades in increments of $100,000 per contract. Thus, for every contract a trader is long and involved in delivery, he will receive $100,000 par amount of an eligible bond. The one defining characteristic of an eligible bond is that it must be 15 years or longer to maturity or to call. The trader long the futures and short the cash bond must pay, upon being delivered the bond, the following invoice price per contract:

Invoice price = Futures settlement price × Conversion factor
× $1,000 + Accrued interest

Accrued interest is simply the amount of interest earned on a bond from the last coupon payment to the settlement date. The futures settlement price is the official closing price determined by the CBT at the end of each trading day. If one makes delivery after the contract has stopped trading, the settlement price is the price at which the contract stopped trading.

To illustrate the calculation of the invoice price, consider the 7⅛% of 2/15/23 for delivery into the September 2001, contract if delivery is made on September 30, 2001, and the futures settlement price (price at which the contract ceases to trade) is 90⁸/₃₂.

$$CF = 1.1347$$

Futures settlement price = 90.25

Accrued interest per contract[2] = $890.63

Then,

Invoice price = 90.25 × 1.1347 × $1,000 + $890.63
= $92,275

## Implied Repo Rate

Simply looking at the bond with the highest conversion factor will not identify which bond is cheapest to deliver (CTD). It is necessary to take into account that if a bond has a conversion factor greater than one, it is a premium bond, and must be purchased at a premium.

The best instrument with which to gauge cheapness should incorporate the *relative* cost of delivering, and that is precisely what the implied repo rate indicates. The implied repo rate is the return received by going long the basis. This involves buying the cash bond, financing it at the current borrowing or repo rate to term, and then delivering those bonds to satisfy the short futures obligation. Therefore, the bond with the highest implied repo rate is the one that is cheapest to deliver; the higher the implied repo rate, the cheaper the bond is to deliver.

The implied repo rate is simply

$$\frac{\text{Cash in } - \text{ Cash out}}{\text{Cash out}} \times \frac{60}{n}$$

where

$n$ = number of days involved in the trade

We must annualize the return by multiplying the cash flow quotient by $360/n$ because other money market rates are also quoted using this convention.

For the exact return, the formula is as follows:

$$\frac{[(\text{FP} \times \text{CF}) + \text{Ae} + \text{IC} - (\text{Price of bond} + \text{Ab})] \times 360}{\text{d1} \times (\text{Price of bond} + \text{Ab}) - (\text{IC} \times \text{d2})}$$

where

FP = Futures price
Ab = Accrued interest of bond at beginning or inception of trade
Ae = Accrued interest of bond at end of trade (delivery to cover short)
IC = Interim coupon (any coupon that falls between settlement date and delivery date)
d1 = Number of days between settlement and actual delivery
d2 = Number of days between interim coupon and bond delivery

For example, the implied repo rate of the $8\frac{1}{2}\%$ of 2/15/20 with settlement on 7/14/01, delivery on 9/30/01, a futures price of 91, and a bond price of 116.50 is calculated as follows:

---

2. Accrued interest is calculated by simply dividing the coupon rate by 2 and multiplying that quotient by the number of days elapsed since the last coupon payment divided by the total number of days in that six-month period. In this case, the total number of days between the coupon payment on August 15 and the settlement date of September 30 is 46 days. Therefore, the accrued interest is simply $(7.125/2) \times (46/184)$.

$$FP = 91$$

$$CF = 1,2748$$

$$Ae = \frac{8.5}{2} \times \frac{46}{184} = 1.0625$$

$$IC = \frac{8.5}{2} = 4.25$$

$$\text{Bond price} = 119.6875$$

$$Ab = \frac{8.5}{2} \times \frac{149}{181} = 3.499$$

$$d1 = 9/30/94 - 7/14/94 = 78 \text{ days}$$

$$d2 = 9/30/94 - 8/15/94 = 46 \text{ days}$$

Thus, the implied repo rate is

$$\frac{[(91 \times 1.2748) + 1.0625 + 4.25 - (116.50 + 3.499)] \times 360}{78 \times (116.50 + 3.499) - (4.25 \times 46)}$$

$$= .0518 \text{ or } 5.18\%$$

## The Delivery Procedure

The vast majority of people who trade bond futures never involve themselves in the process of delivery because of its complexities. Instead, they either liquidate the futures position completely with an offsetting transaction or roll forward into the next contract, which is more liquid. If an investor is long a future after it has ceased trading, she can expect to be delivered a Treasury bond, and if an investor is short a future after it has stopped trading, she will be required to deliver a Treasury bond to fulfill the obligation required of her position. The short would adhere to the following three-day procedure.

1. *Position Day:* The day in which the CBT is given notice by the futures short that he plans to make delivery of a certain amount of bonds in two business days. This intention can be made any time before 8:00 P.M. central standard time (CST). The first eligible intention day is the second-to-last business day of the month before the delivery month. If the investor has not informed the Board of intention to deliver by the second-to-last day of the delivery month, then the Board automatically assumes that he will be delivering at the end of the month.

2. *Notice Day:* The day in which the CBT is given notice about which particular issue he intends to deliver and then matches the short with the futures long who has had the longest outstanding position. The

Board then informs the long that she will be delivered to the next day. Notice must occur before 2:00 P.M. CST unless it is the last notice day of the month, in which case notice must be made before 3:00 P.M. The party long the futures is notified by 4:00 P.M. which bond she will be receiving.

**3.** *Delivery Day:* The short must have in his account by 10:00 A.M. CST the bonds he has specified he would deliver and must actually deliver them by 1:00 P.M. CST to the long party the Board has assigned to him. The long pays the short the invoice price for that particular bond only after being delivered the bonds.

The short may not promise to deliver a certain bond and then deliver another one; there is a one point per contract penalty for not delivering the bonds specified on notice day. The advantage gained by switching bonds will seldom ever offset the one point penalty.

## THE BASIS

As mentioned earlier, the best measure of what is cheapest to deliver is the implied repo rate. However, this is not the way most people determine which issue is the cheapest or whether the futures contract is over- or undervalued. That is done through following the basis because, computationally, the implied repo rate is considerably more difficult and because the basis is derived from price, which is what traders deal in when they trade cash bonds and futures.

The basis is simply the difference between the cash bond price and the converted futures price. The converted futures price is the product of the futures price and the conversion factor. To place the figure in 32ds, multiply the basis by 32.

$$\text{Basis} = (\text{Bond price} - \text{Futures price} \times \text{Conversion factor}) \times 32$$

A long basis trade involves the purchase of a deliverable cash bond and sale of a factor-weighted amount of futures contracts. Going short the basis means selling a deliverable cash bond and buying a factor-weighted number of futures contracts.

It should be recognized that the basis on the cheapest-to-deliver bond (CTD) must converge to zero by the end of the delivery month. Riskless money could be made if this were not the case. For example, if the basis were still worth something on the last day of the month, a trader could do the following: (1) sell the basis and then effectively "buy" the bond upon delivery and (2) sell the futures position to fulfill his short basis obligation. The trader is synthetically selling the cash bond at a level higher than it is delivered to him. This difference is the positive value of the basis on that last day.

Many people believe that the basis can never be negative. This is simply not true. The *net* basis can never be negative because an option can never have a negative value because it only provides one with the *opportunity* to transact at a certain price, not an obligation. The gross basis may be negative before the delivery month if there is an inverted curve and if the value of the delivery options granted to the short is low. (This is a rare occurrence.) However, during the delivery month, the basis cannot be negative at any time because one could simply buy the basis (buy bonds, sell futures) and subsequently unwind it by selling cash bonds at the higher current market price while being able to buy futures at the same level.

The most famous blunder in basis trading occurred at the end of 1987. In the middle of December, a primary dealer who was long 5,500 December bond futures contracts was delivered $550 million par amount of the 10⅜% 11/15/12 to satisfy the short's obligation. Even though this issue was the cheapest, the basis on the bond was trading in the marketplace at around $10,000 per $1 million. Of course, the dealer congratulated itself on its serendipity. The firm had fallen quite unexpectedly into a cash pool of about $5.5 million. This present was known on Wall Street as the Christmas gift; the deliverer should not have handed those bonds over until the last day because it could have at least made positive carry by holding them, and, conversely, the Wall Street firm could now forgo the cost of being short the cash bonds. That bond was trading in the cash market at approximately $109.30; however, the firm received bonds at an effective cost of $108.30, which is 87²⁵/₃₂ (contract price) multiplied by a conversion factor of 1.2336. As soon as the firm was delivered these bonds, it turned around and sold them back out to complete every trader's fantasy—a huge profit with no risk.

The early delivery in this case was not only excruciatingly painful for the deliverer but also uncommon. However, even discounting this example as a fluke, one might still wonder why anyone would be content in buying the basis and earning a lower return or implied repo rate than could be obtained from simply investing money at current short-term interest rates.[3] The discrepancy exists because the basis long has several deliverability options that could increase his or her return, sometimes dramatically. These options, combined with carry, comprise the value of the basis. Both will be discussed in the next two sections.

## CARRY

*Carry* is a Wall Street term used to describe the amount of money made or lost by holding, or carrying, a bond. The ownership of the bond provides interest

---

3. If we were to look at an implied repo table, we would see that all eligible bonds have a lower return or implied repo rate than the present money market rates.

income, which is offset by the financing charge one must pay to borrow the money to purchase the bond. Obviously, with an upward-sloping yield curve, there is positive carry when one is long a bond whereas an inverted curve burdens the long with negative carry (i.e., a daily loss).

For basis trades, most people calculate carry until the last possible delivery date, which is usually the best time for delivery with a normal yield curve. An inverted curve is more complex, as one has to determine whether the negative carry (money lost by financing a bond purchase, or the bond yield minus the financing or repo rate) is greater than the value of the options.

An ideal example is Paul Volcker's monetarist experiment between 1979 and 1981, when the curve twisted and often was inverted. Initially, traders automatically delivered their bonds on the first eligible delivery date to avoid the negative carry. As time passed, the deliveries began to take place later in the month. This occurred because some traders began to realize that it was advantageous to deliver later in the month, retain the options, and suffer through the negative carry. Early delivery in this scenario should be based solely on whether the exercising of the option is more valuable than the money forgone in financing. Thus, it is crucial to value those options accurately.

However, one should be cautious in dismissing the importance of carry. The simplicity of its calculation can and often does belie its ability to damage a trader's P&L. There is no question that with a certain term repo rate (financing rate to a certain date—in this case, that date is usually the end of the delivery month), figuring the amount of carry for that period is quite easy. However, as any repo desk will attest, those financing rates do not stay very constant and can often swing dramatically.

For example, assume that a bond is currently yielding 8% and the repo rate to the end of the delivery month is 3%. If there are 30 days left, the amount of money made per million by carrying the bond is $4,075.[4] However, if a dealer or a big hedge fund decided to squeeze[5] or tighten an issue in the financing

---

4. A relatively precise and fairly common estimation of carry is as follows:

$$(\text{Coupon rate}/365) - (\text{Repo rate}/360 \times \text{Price}/100)$$

In this case, because the yield is also 8%, the price is 100. Thus, the calculation is $(.08/365) - (.03/360) \times 100/100 = .0001358$. Per million, the carry is $135.84. For 30 days, this totals $4,075.

5. A squeeze in the repo market occurs when there are too many traders short a particular issue and not enough lenders of that security. The most famous example of this was the squeeze of the April and May 1993 two-year notes. Many traders were short the issue during the when-issued period in hopes of purchasing them cheaper during the auction. Unfortunately for them, most were unable to buy them from the Treasury in the auction. Consequently, desperate shorts who needed to make delivery or fail, and effectively lend money at 0% in the finance market, were often willing to lend money at exactly that level. Large regional banks are frequently mentioned as creating a tight repo rate in an issue when they buy a large amount of an issue and keep it in their portfolio instead of lending it out. The Fed has now established a policy that if an issue becomes remarkably or "unnaturally" tight, they will reopen that issue to mitigate the shortage.

market or if there are simply too many shorts in that issue and the rate drops to 2%, then the carry increases quickly to $4,908 per million. On the surface, this does not appear to be a substantial amount, but for a basis position of $500 million, quite an ordinary position for some basis traders, this translates into a difference of $416,500—quite a large payout.

This variability can be avoided by simply locking up, or lending (borrowing), money at the current term rate. In this case, the trader who is short the bonds and has cash available to borrowers could lend money at the fixed rate of 3% for the duration of her expected holding, which appears to be 30 days. Unfortunately, this act of prudence is often overlooked for several reasons. In some cases, the trader may not know how long she will keep the trade alive, or she may predict that the term rate will rise in the future. However, the reason could also be appetite for risk, ignorance, or sloth. Regardless of the motive, this oversight can prove to be very volatile. However, these concerns do not affect the true value of the basis, because one can always be assured of a certain financing rate. The key to rewards lies in valuing the deliverability options.

## OPTIONS

The true essence of determining basis richness or cheapness is in the valuation of the net or option-adjusted basis, which is the gross basis minus carry. This value is comprised of the value of the different deliverability options. The mathematics of calculating those different options is highly complex, not only because of the inherent difficulty associated with valuing any derivative with multiple pricing constraints, but also because many of these constraints, and hence the effect on the option prices, are interdependent. Even if a trader were to correctly value each delivery option, he may not obtain the value of the net basis simply by summing them because some options are mutually exclusive. For example, if the trader exercises the wildcard, he cannot exercise the switching option.

For the sake of clarity, each option will be explained independently. It is beyond the scope of this chapter to derive precise values for each option. Although the following explanations omit the exact mathematical derivations, they should prove helpful in understanding the skeleton of basis valuation. The five different deliverability options are the yield shift option, yield spread option, new-auction option, wildcard option, and switching option.

## Yield-Shift Option

Because the conversion factor is the price of the bond at 6% divided by 100, there is a general bias toward delivering bonds with higher durations when yields are above 6% and with lower durations when yields are below 6%.

The logic behind this idea is rather simple. Consider that the converted cash price equals the bond price divided by the CF. Assuming that there is no severe penalty for high-coupon bonds (that is, they do not trade substantially cheaper), all bonds would be almost equally deliverable if yields are at 6%. However, if rates are below 6% and an investor uses an 6% factor to discount, then he is underestimating the value of the subsequent coupon and principal receipts. Likewise, if the trader uses 6% as the discount rate when rates are above 6%, he is overvaluing those future payments. Now, the low-coupon, long-maturity bonds have a higher CF than they should, and that makes them more attractive to deliver.

For a different perspective, suppose that yields are rising above 6% and are now pushing up against 8%. Obviously, the higher duration bonds drop more in price than the shorter durations when yields rise. Because the CF is constant, the fiat price (price/CF) is lower. The price of the higher duration issue goes down more than the lower duration bond, and this leads to a lower converted price. If yields are moving down through 6% and to almost 5%, for example, then the higher duration bond will rise in price faster. This is not what traders want if they are short because this will increase the converted price. The low-duration bond is preferable because its price rises more slowly in both relative and absolute terms.

It has been proven that when yields are above 6%, it is generally cheaper to deliver bonds with higher duration, and when they are below 6%, it is generally cheaper to deliver bonds with lower duration.

The 6% mark is the general cutoff, but it is not the precise point at which all the breakeven prices of the eligible bonds are equal. This is because the CF truncates the actual maturity of the bond: It is rounded down to the last contract month, and the first deliverable date is used as the settlement date. Also, there is a slight difference because it is assumed that all callable bonds will be called at the first call date, which is obviously not necessarily true. After the bond auction in November 1984, the Treasury discontinued the issuance of callable bonds, which effectively added five years to the maturity of post-1984 bonds in determining the factors.

To see how the cutoff ultimately affects deliverability, consider that if carry is ignored, then the converted cash price (CC) of any given Treasury issue is the price of the bond divided by its conversion factor. That is,

$$CC = \frac{\text{Bond price}}{\text{CF}}$$

Remember that the basis at the end of the delivery month has to be zero. Obviously, the bond price must equal, by that last day, the futures settlement price multiplied by the CE Thus, if one can sell a bond at the market price and buy futures at a price less than the CC, then a profit will be locked in. Also, by definition, the most deliverable bond is the one with the lowest CC price. Exhibit 54–1 shows the group of bonds that we will consider to be the entire eligible basket for delivery.

**EXHIBIT 54-1**

Deliverability Analysis of Yields below 6%

| Issue | Price | Yield | CF | CC |
|-------|-------|-------|-----|-----|
| 8 7/8% 8/17 | 144.843 | 5.00% | 1.3062 | 110.89 |
| 8 1/8% 8/19 | 138.33 | 5.02% | 1.2405 | 111.51 |
| 6 1/2% 11/26 | 120.303 | 5.10% | 1.0659 | 112.87 |
| 6 1/8% 11/27 | 114.304 | 5.15% | 1.0167 | 112.43 |

The bonds are all yielding less than 6%, and thus the market favors those issues with lower durations; clearly, the 8⅞ and 8⅛ have the lowest durations of the four. This can be verified by observing the CCs. The lowest CC, 110.89, belongs to the 8⅞ and the highest CC belongs to the 6⅛, which has the highest duration. However, as Exhibit 54–2 shows, if bond yields rise above 6%, the basket instantly inverts as the higher duration bonds put a sparkle in the deliverer's eye. The 6½ and the 6⅛ are now several points more deliverable than the 11/26 and 27 bonds. In general, one can assume that when yields rise, higher duration issues (low-coupon, long-maturity) become more deliverable, and when yields decline, lower duration issues (high-coupon, short-maturity) become more deliverable.

It is easier to observe this characteristic by simply looking at a graph of converted cash prices versus different bond yields. As shown in Exhibit 54–3, as bond yields rise through 6%, the higher duration 6 has a lower converted or breakeven futures price than the lower duration 8⅞ and the 8⅛, and is thus cheaper to deliver. The converse is also true—the further bond yields fall below 6%, the cheaper the 8⅞ and the 8⅛ is to deliver.

The value of the yield shift option is clearly correlated with the proximity of current rates to the switchover point (the yield level at which it becomes more

**EXHIBIT 54-2**

Deliverability Analysis of Yields Above 6%

| Issue | Price | Yield | CF | CC |
|-------|-------|-------|-----|-----|
| 8 7/8% 8/17 | 118.75 | 7.00% | 1.3062 | 90.91 |
| 8 1/8% 8/19 | 111.641 | 7.02% | 1.2405 | 90.00 |
| 6 1/2% 11/26 | 92.283 | 7.15% | 1.0659 | 86.58 |
| 6 1/8% 11/27 | 87.153 | 7.20% | 1.0167 | 85.72 |

Attractiveness of Market Basket Due to Yield Change

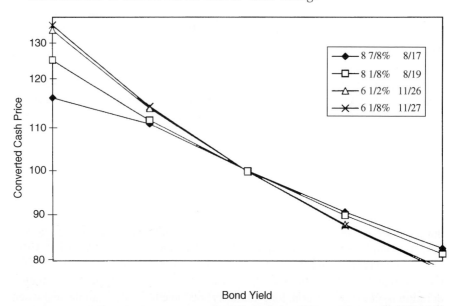

Bond Yield

profitable to deliver opposite duration bonds).[6] If rates are relatively stable and long bond yields are hovering around 8%, the probability of rates breaking through the switchover point is very low, and thus the value of the yield change option is also very low. Conversely, if bond yields are fluctuating wildly around the 6% level, the option can be quite valuable.

One would probably imagine that if yields at the beginning of a delivery month were 8%, for example, and gradually declined 5 basis points every trading day for the next couple of weeks, the value of the option would increase as it slowly approached 6%. This is not necessarily true because, like an ordinary option, the value of the yield-change option suffers from time decay or theta. This is simply the daily decline in an option's value due strictly to the passage of time. The theta as we approach the expiration date of the option (which is, in this case, the eighth-to-the-last business day of the delivery month) does not increase linearly but rather almost exponentially. Therefore, if the aforementioned scenario occurred, the March yield-shift option would approach being worthless while the June yield-shift option would increase in value. This is not

---

6. This point is generally around 6%, but as discussed before, this is not the precise level. In this case, it appears to be closer to 5.98 percent.

only because the June contract still has months before expiration, but also because the rate of time decay is different for the two contract months.

## Yield-Spread Option

The basket of bonds is affected not only by the general yield movements but also by the yield spread between the different bonds in the basket. Clearly, bonds that are more expensive in the cash bond market relative to their neighbors are usually more expensive to deliver. Several factors can affect these yield spreads, including the stripping of a bond, tightening in the repo markets, or simply buying or selling of a certain issue by a fund.

This also explains why the cheapest to deliver (CTD) is not always the bond that is delivered. The CTD is only the cheapest up to a certain point. If everyone who intended to deliver bought the CTD and its price rose, it probably would not remain the cheapest. Exhibit 54–4 shows this clearly.

At the time of this initial writing, for the September 1994 contract, the 11 ¼ was the CTD, followed by the 10 ⅝ and the 11 ¾. Notice how close the implied repo rates of these three issues are. This implies that even a small change in price between the issues can easily change the profitability landscape. If the price of the 11 ¼ increases by only .008% or ⁴⁄₃₂ while the other two bonds stay unchanged, the implied repo rate of the 11 ¼ decreases to 2.72%, which makes the issue the most expensive out of this basket.

Clearly, if the CTD can change with seemingly minor moves, upon large shifts in the yield curve, the basis can move dramatically. Inherent in every basis trade is a yield-curve bet. For example, consider the basis move in late July–early August of 1993. Interest rates were well below 8%, making the lower duration bonds cheaper to deliver, and that was indeed the case with the 11 ¾%

**E X H I B I T   54–4**

Yield-Spread Effects on Implied Repo Rates for the September 1994 Contract

| Issue | Price | Yield | CF[b] | Implied Repo Rate |
|---|---|---|---|---|
| 11 ¼% 2/15/10–15 | 155.52 | 6.45% | 1.3230 | 2.79% |
| 10 ⅝   8/15/10–15 | 148.44 | 6.47 | 1.2634 | 2.75 |
| 11 ¾   11/15/09–14 | 156.30 | 6.21 | 1.3242 | 2.74 |
| 11 ¼[a]   2/15/10–15 | 155.64 | 6.44 | 1.3230 | 2.72[a] |

[a] Former CTD, now most expensive to deliver.
[b] Note that the CF was one priced to yield 8% and was changed to yield 6% beginning with the March 2000 bond future. The analysis, however, is exactly the same.

11/15/14, which was the CTD. The current long bond at the time was the 7 $\frac{1}{8}$% 2/15/23. A trader long that basis would, in effect, be long the 7 $\frac{1}{8}$ and short the 11 $\frac{3}{4}$. This basis was at $^{93}\!/_{32}$ on July 29. By August 10, it had risen all the way to $^{136}\!/_{32}$. Many observers attributed the move to the purchase of large strips, but it had much more to do with the flattening of the curve.

The basis is often market directional: As the market trades up with an even yield move, the basis will increase because of the differing durations. In this case, the rally was coupled with the aforementioned flattening, especially between the 10-year note and the long bond, which flattened from 77.5 bp to 64 bp during that interim. Thus, in this instance, it really was not due to any of the other complicated options but rather a simple yield-curve play.

## New-Auction Option

The new-auction option's value is derived from the possibility that a new bond may be auctioned with a different coupon or maturity than any bond in the current basket and thus be a candidate for the exalted station of cheapest to deliver.

Look at the basket of bonds in Exhibit 54–5. Assuming that the prices and the different bases listed are typical of those currently in the marketplace, the calculations of CC prices are shown in Exhibit 54–5. As can be seen, the 11/27 is the cheapest and the 8/17 is the most expensive.

Let us see how a newly auctioned issue can change the profitability of delivering the new bond. First, understand that bond yields must move from the current yields for the new bond to be attractive. For example, if the CTD is currently the most recently auctioned bond (5 $\frac{1}{8}$% 2/15/30) and bond yields move to 5.23%, the new bond will still have a 5 $\frac{1}{8}$% coupon. Second, realize that if the current environment of rates is well below the 6% level, the probability that a newly auctioned bond becoming the cheapest is very low. This is because this environment favors a low-duration bond. Because of the wide disparity of bond maturity dates in the market basket (from 5/17 to 5/30), it is difficult for a move in the yields to compensate for the difference in the lengths of maturities.

**EXHIBIT  54–5**

Breakeven Prices of the Deliverable Basket

| Issue | Price | Yield | CF | CC(Price/CF) |
|-------|-------|-------|-----|--------------|
| 8 7/8% 8/17 | 144.843 | 5.00% | 1.3062 | 110.89 |
| 8 1/8% 8/19 | 138.33 | 5.02% | 1.2405 | 111.51 |
| 6 1/2% 11/26 | 120.303 | 5.10% | 1.0659 | 112.87 |
| 6 1/8% 11/27 | 114.304 | 5.15% | 1.0167 | 112.43 |

Consider a case in which the newly issued bond is the CTD and there is an auction that would compete with it. These conditions suggest an environment of yields over 6% (remember that over 6%, the CTD usually tracks the highest duration bond). If the current bond is the 7.5% of 2/15/31 (for simplicity's sake, assume that it is the only bond deliverable into the March 2000 contract), and yields decrease to 6.5% before the Feb 2001 auction, the profit scenario would be as follows:

| Issue | Price | Yield | Factor | CC |
|-------|-------|-------|--------|-----|
| 7½% 2/15/23 | 113.13 | 6.5% | 1.2078 | 93.66 |
| 6½   5/15/23 | 100.00 | 6.5 | 1.0683 | 93.60 |

The simple addition of an extra deliverable should not have an impact on the price of the $7\frac{1}{2}$, but notice how this affects the *basis* of the one previously deliverable bond. For example, assume that the basis of that bond was $^{5.5}/_{32}$ before the new bond auction and that the futures price was $94\,^{19}/_{32}$. The newly auctioned bond is more deliverable than the old bond by $^{2}/_{32}[93.66 - 93.60]$. This means that the bond future price will fall by just that amount because that is now the new CC price (remember that CC does not include carry). This would occur as arbitrageurs bought the new bond and sold the futures price down to the CC. If the cash bond prices remained constant and the futures price fell by $^{2}/_{32}$, the basis on that old bond would increase by $^{2}/_{32}$ to $^{7}/_{32}$. Thus, as expected, the investor who is long the basis of the $7\frac{1}{2}$ profits by the introduction of the newly auctioned bond.

Notice that if the new bond does not create a potentially profitable switching opportunity, the trader long that basis loses only the value of the auction option. As with any other option, the largest amount of money an investor can lose is the value of that option, which in this case is worth very little, if anything.

It is evident that the new-auction option is most valuable when yields are above the switchover point and move down or when yields are below the switchover point and rise. The yield increase, however, must produce a coupon that compensates for the extra six months on the next bond auctioned.

The value of the option theoretically ends immediately after the bond auction results are posted, which is around 2:00 P.M. eastern time—approximately an hour after the auction itself. The bond futures price should adjust immediately, or there is ample room for arbitrage. However, one should not be misled into thinking that traders are on the edge of their seats waiting for the auction results to see if there will be a cheaper-to-deliver bond. Clearly, they are aware if there is a potential for the creation of a more profitable delivery, and the future's price will hover accordingly.

Also, reconsider the first instance of yields below 6%. If the auction results in a bond with a lower coupon, then the new bond could prove profitable to deliver if rates rise through 6%. Even though it was the new auction that created the issue, the potential option value would then be attributed to the yield change option, because it was not the auction itself that created the opportunity, but rather the yield shift. However, there also would be no opportunity to switch into the new, cheaper bond if the bond is never created in an auction. Regardless, the categorization is a simple matter of semantics.

# The Wildcard Options

The CF creates tails in one's position. If a trader is long $50 million of the bond basis, he is required to deliver $50 million in eligible bonds. If the bond has a coupon other than 6%, he will have a tail of some sort. For example, the $8\frac{3}{4}\%$ 8/20 has a CF of 1.3197 for the March 2000 contract. Thus, if a trader is long $100 million of this basis, he would be short 1319 contracts. After he delivers the bonds to cover his 1319 short in the futures, he would still be short $31.9 million cash bonds, which is his tail.

This wildcard or late-day option comes into play because of the tail and because the futures markets and cash markets do not trade simultaneously at all times. The CBT stops trading at 2:00 P.M. CST, whereas the cash market is open almost the entire day.[7] The short has until 8:00 P.M. CST to give notice of intention to deliver, but the futures price is stuck at the 2:00 P.M. close. This allows the short to buy the bond tail short after 2:00 if the market dips and allows the short to sell the bond tail long after 2:00 if the market rallies.

Although this option is available on many consecutive days, it does not cover those entire trading days but rather only the six-hour time frame between 2:00 PM. and 8:00 PM. If the short fails to give notice of intent to deliver by 8:00, that day's wildcard option expires worthless.

## Wildcard Call Option

The call is in effect if the hedge ratio is less than one. In this instance, the trader who is long the basis is also long the bond tail, which she will try to sell before delivering. Therefore, if the market rises after the 2:00 futures close, she will be able to sell that tail at a high price although the futures price is frozen at the 2:00 settlement price. However, not all rallies will do. The rally should be looked at as just a rally of the tail, as the remainder is hedged and must be delivered. The size of the tail is obviously very important because the larger it is, the smaller the movement has to be to reach a profitable switching point or strike price. Remember that the tail is simply the CF minus one. The formula for how much it should rally is as follows:

---

7. The only exception is on weekdays between 4:30 P.M. and 5:30 P.M. CST, which is the time between the close of the cash bond market in the United States and its opening in Tokyo, and on the weekends up until 5:30 P.M. CST Sunday.

$$S(\text{call}) = BP + \frac{(BS \times CF)}{1 - CF}$$

where

$S$ = Strike or breakeven price
$BP$ = Bond price at 2:00 P.M. CST
$BS$ = Basis
$CF$ = Conversion factor

**Wildcard Put Option**
This option is in effect if the hedge ratio is greater than one. The short holds an implicit out-of-the-money put option on the bond. A hedge ratio greater than one means that the long basis trader possesses a futures tail that she must cover in the cash market. If the market falls after 2:00, the trader can buy back her cash at a lower price and still use the higher futures close to calculate her invoice price. However, this does not imply that any drop in the cash market will make it profitable to deliver. The strike price is determined by the following formula:

$$S(\text{put}) = BP - \frac{(BS \times CF)}{(CF - 1)}$$

The following illustrates the wildcard put option scenario. Suppose it is 4:25 on a Thursday afternoon. The market has begun to suspect that the Federal Reserve may begin an aggressive tightening campaign due to recent economic strength. Federal Reserve chairman Greenspan tells the New York Economics Club that inflation is expected to be materially worse in the period ahead. The market quickly drops.

The calculation to determine how much it has to drop before the wildcard option is profitable is shown below:

| Issue | Price | Futures Settlement | Basis | CF |
|---|---|---|---|---|
| 8½% 2/20 | 121 8/32 | 94 4/32 | 3 8/32 | 1.2869 |

$$S(\text{put}) = 121.25 - \frac{.1187 \times 1.2869}{1.2869 - 1}$$
$$= 120.717$$
$$= 120\,23/32$$

The issue has to drop $17/32$ ($121\,8/32 - 120\,23/32$) before it is profitable to exercise this option. Certainly, this does not imply that a trader should buy the tail at 164-03. If he thinks the market will decline further, he should wait before purchasing the tail. If the market begins to rise after the initial decline, the trader has missed an opportunity for profit but he has not lost any money. It is the asymmetric profit profile of not being able to lose any money besides the value of that day's wildcard option, which is usually infinitesimally small, and of having a large upside potential that makes this wildcard an option. If the market falls anywhere short of the 164-04 level, it would not be profitable to cover and give notice to deliver.

The wildcard option is enhanced by a few characteristics of the specific bond and the market in general. If the bond's coupon is significantly different from 8%, then the CF will be greatly different from one. This leaves a larger tail with which to cover the basis loss a trader gives up by exercising his option early. It should then be obvious that the smaller the basis at the time of exercise, the easier it is to cover the loss. So if financing rates are close to the bond's yield (i.e., a relatively flat yield curve), the carry is small if positive at all, and thus the wildcard's strike price is not as far out of the money. Lastly, if the market is very volatile, that increases the value of the option because there is a greater potential for price jumps after 2:00 P.M. CST.

The wildcard option in the environment at the time of this writing usually does not come into play very often for a few reasons.

The first is that the market has to rise (or fall) enough to cover the value of the basis. The time frame in which a wildcard option can come into play is from the first notice day, which is two business days before the start of the delivery month, to the day before the last trading day. Also, remember that the theoretical value of the basis must converge to zero by the end of the month. But because the basis stops trading eight days before the end of the month, and because the switching option is usually the most valuable, the basis on that eighth day is usually considerably more than zero. Consequently, it would take a substantial rise (or fall) to cover the value of the remaining basis.

The second reason is that the market generally tends to quiet down after the close of the futures market because of lack of liquidity (which can sometimes be the impetus of precipitous declines and explosive rallies) and lack of interest. The only news that comes out after 2:00 P.M., besides those occasional breaking world events, is the money supply announcement at 3:30 P.M. CST and sometimes a late Johnson Redbook report (a report on retail sales), which is usually released to its subscribers around 1:45 P.M. CST. Money supply is not the earth-shaker it used to be even as recently as 1992,[8] and even though the Redbook reports have found a following, they are not usually impressive enough to move the market substantially. This is partly because both numbers generally have more relevance (in terms of yield) for the short end of the yield curve.

---

8. Financial numbers tend to fall in and out of favor with Wall Street. Money supply, once considered by many to be the preeminent predictor of future economic strength, has been recently frowned upon by some who question its true correlation with the growth rate. As recently as 1989, the release of merchandise trade figures used to move markets like nothing else. It now comes and goes with barely a whisper.

## Switching Option

After the last day of the futures trading, the deliverer has the option to deliver another bond if it becomes more deliverable. In other words, he is looking to switch or change the bond he has currently taken with him "off the board" for a more profitable bond. This option, often referred to as the *end-of the-month option,* is similar to the wildcard option in that much of the potential profitability depends on the futures settlement price being frozen on the last trading day's settlement at 1:00 P.M. while the cash prices are free to fluctuate. Thus, he is guaranteed a fixed invoice price (the price he is paid to deliver those particular bonds) and will only "lose" the value of that basis if he delivers it, and less than that if he delivers a cheaper bond. Like any other option, then, the maximum loss is the value of the net basis or the value of the option premium.

The switching option is different from the wildcard option in that if the trader is positioned in the basis when it goes "off the board" or stops trading, he will guarantee himself either of having to make delivery or of being delivered to. In fact, at 1:00 P.M. on that eighth-to-last business day, he should position himself to face amounts because that is what is required in delivery. Therefore, it is not as if there is a one-week option on the tail, because the tail should be covered when the contracts go off the board. For example, assume that a trader is long $10 million of the 8¾% 5/20 basis and is short 132 contracts against the amount as a factor weight. He must either buy back 32 contracts right before they close or sell $3.2 million 8¾s. No tail means no wildcard.

Return back to Exhibit 54–1, the original basket of deliverable bonds. Because yields are far below the 6% mark, the lower durations are clearly the CTDs. Now assume that the futures stopped trading at 95.50 and yields rise 50 basis points during the seven-day window. This is obviously a hefty change in yields during a relatively short time span. As shown in Exhibit 54–6, however unlikely, the move is both possible and elucidating.

The switching profitability can be easily calculated to determine which issue should be swapped into and delivered. A trader should just follow the

**E X H I B I T   54–6**

Analysis of Deliverability with Yields Rising Roughly 50 Basis Points

| Issue | Price | Yield | CF | CC |
|---|---|---|---|---|
| 8 7/8% 8/17 | 137.635 | 5.50% | 1.3062 | 105.37 |
| 8 1/8% 8/19 | 130.88 | 5.52% | 1.2405 | 105.51 |
| 6 1/2% 11/26 | 112.395 | 5.60% | 1.0659 | 105.45 |
| 6 1/8% 11/27 | 105.159 | 5.75% | 1.0167 | 103.43 |

logical procession of switching by totaling the different cash flows involved and subtracting the value of the old invoice price, that is, the money forgone by switching to another bond.

1. Sell the old (previous) deliverable—Receive money (+).

2. Buy the new (cheaper) deliverable—Expend money (−).

3. Lose potential money on old deliverable—Money forgone (−).

4. Deliver the new bond at new invoice price—Receive money (+).

This analysis is shown in Exhibit 54–7. When calculating the profitability of swapping into different issues after the move in yields, it can be seen that the $6\frac{1}{8}$ is now the most profitable to switch into. The long basis trade in this case has resulted in a whopping $4.84 profit minus the value of the original basis. If the basis minus carry had been greater than $4.84, then the entire trade would not have been profitable.

In the above scenario, every issue provides the opportunity for a profitable switch. If, for example, the $8\frac{1}{8}$'s yield rose to only 5.42% because of large hedge fund buying, and the price fell to $132.33, there would be a loss of $.96 in switching to the $8\frac{1}{8}$. Thus, if this were the case and the $8\frac{1}{8}$ were the only other deliverable bond, the trader should simply keep and deliver the $8\frac{7}{8}$ and just realize the switching option loss. This should illuminate the fact that the yield spread option is extremely important during this end-of-the-month period.

Now view the trade from the basis short's perspective. The trader was hoping to make the premium of the option or the net basis. But the large and sudden drop in yields has netted him ownership of the $6\frac{1}{8}$ and a loss of $4.84 minus the value of the outstanding basis.

Notice that there is no change if the trader stays with the $8\frac{7}{8}$ as expected. This implies that the maximum loss associated with not switching is zero. In other words, it has the same profit profile as an option. If the market rallies, and there exists a profitable swap opportunity, then the basis long owns an implied out-of-the-money call option, and if the market declines and there exists

**EXHIBIT 54–7**

Profitability of Switching Issues to Deliver

| Issue | 1. Sell Old | 2. Buy New | 3. Lose Potential | 4. Deliver New | 5. Net Gain (Loss) |
|---|---|---|---|---|---|
| 8 7/8% 8/17 | +$137.64 | −$137.64 | −$124.74 | +$124.74 | $0.0 |
| 8 1/8% 8/19 | +$137.64 | −$130.88 | −$124.74 | +$118.47 | $0.49 |
| 6 1/2% 11/26 | +$137.64 | −$112.39 | −$124.74 | +$101.793 | $2.30 |
| 6 1/8% 11/27 | +$137.64 | −$105.16 | −$124.74 | + $97.095 | $4.84 |

a profitable swap opportunity, then the trader owns an implied out-of-the-money put option. Both options have implied strikes at where the market must move to execute a profitable swap.

The degree to which the bonds are out of the money depends on the difference in deliverability of the bonds in the basket. If one bond is clearly the most deliverable under almost any circumstance, then both options are considerably out of the money. If the basket is tightly bunched as to profitability, and thus as to possibility of delivery, then the strikes are closer to the current market price. The aforementioned sell off clearly shows that the basis long owns an out-of-the-money call option.

In the case of neither of the two strikes being touched, the basis long loses the premium or the basis. If the basis long does indeed profit from both a market decline and rally, it is, in effect, long a strangle. However, even if it is a true strangle, that is, the out-of-the-money factor is the same for both the put and the call, equal price moves both up and down are still significant because, unlike an ordinary bond strangle, the payoff can often have an asymmetric profitability profile. Therefore, one should be careful to ascertain not only the probability of yields moving to a certain level, but also the profitability once through there.

To fully understand the risk inherent in any basis position, one must not only be able to calculate the profitability of switching but also ascertain at what point the profitable switch can occur. To determine exactly how far out of the money those strike prices are, that is, how much the yield curve has to move to enable a profitable switch (assuming a parallel yield move), one has to first observe the relative dollar durations (DD) of the two issues. Dollar duration is the *dollar* value change per 100-basis-point change in yield, or approximately the present value of a basis point multiplied by 100. It is also the key to determining the profitability of switching because one should be more concerned with the *dollar* amount involved in switching than with the change as a percentage of price, which is what is measured by Macaulay's duration and modified duration.

Clearly, if two bonds are of equal maturity, the bond with the higher coupon will have the higher price. Thus, by definition, the higher coupon bond will often have the higher dollar duration. Thus, if yields decline, the higher coupon bond will jump in price more than the lower coupon bond, and on a yield rise, the lower coupon bond will lose more money. During the switching period, the implication is clear—on a rally, one can sell the higher coupon bond and, with that money, buy the lower coupon. The converse is also true: If yields rise, the higher dollar duration bond will decline in price more and thus make it cheaper to deliver.

Because the price/yield relationship is not linear for larger price moves, convexity can play a major role. Convexity, the second derivative of the price/yield function, simply implies that for equal yield movements, the price will increase more than it will decline. Thus, any formula that measures price change by simply using duration will be inaccurate for large yield shifts. Of course, this problem can be at least partially rectified by simply including convexity in the calculation. For simplicity's sake, we will assume the prices are very good approximations, and thus omit the effect of convexity.

Therefore, the formula to find the strike price of the implied option would simply equal the low and high coupons' DD multiplied by the yield shift. Obviously, only a small yield change is required to make it profitable to switch into another bond if the new bond's basis (BS) is only $\frac{1}{32}$ more expensive than the previous CTD. Consequently, one must also consider the two bonds' basis to determine how much the move must compensate. The following formula gives the strike price:

Basis of high coupon $- (\Delta\,r \times DD_H) =$ Basis of low coupon
$\quad - (\Delta r \times DD_L)$

where

$\Delta r$ = parallel rate change required for the two issues to be equally deliverable

This reduces to

$$BS_H - BS_L = \Delta r(DD_H - DD_L)$$

Solving for $\Delta r$,

$$\Delta r = BS_H - BS_L/DD_H - DD_L$$

The following example shows how to determine the movement required for a profitable switch. Suppose that there are only two deliverable bonds—the $8\frac{7}{8}\%$ of 8/17, which is currently the cheapest, and the $6\frac{1}{2}\%$ of 11/26 which is the potential switching candidate. The yield shift required to make the two issues equally deliverable is calculated as follows.

| Issue | Price | Yield | Dollar duration | CF | Basis |
|---|---|---|---|---|---|
| 8 7/8% 8/17 | 144.84 | 5.00% | 14.95 | 1.3062 | 8/32 |
| 6 1/2% 11/26 | 120.3 | 5.10% | 16.62 | 1.0659 | 14/32 |

$$\Delta r = \frac{^{14}\!/_{32} - {}^{8}\!/_{32}}{16.62 - 14.95} = \frac{(0.437 - .25)}{1.67} = .1419$$

Therefore, a profitable switch can be executed if yields fall more than 11.25 basis points. The further the sell off, the greater will be the profit in switching and delivering the $6\frac{1}{2}$. Also remember, however, that the larger the shift, the greater is the error due to convexity.

# EXHIBIT 54-8

Calendar of Delivery Month

## June 2005

| Sunday | Monday | Tuesday | Wednesday | Thursday | Friday | Saturday |
|---|---|---|---|---|---|---|
| May 29 <br> Yield shift option[b] | May 30 <br> *First Position Day* <br> Wildcard option <br> Yield shift option | May 31 <br> *First Notice Day*[b] <br> Wildcard option <br> Yield shift option | 1 <br> *First Delivery Day* <br> Wildcard option <br> Yield shift option | 2 <br> Wildcard option <br> Yield shift option | 3 <br> Wildcard option <br> Yield shift option | 4 <br> Wildcard option <br> Yield shift option |
| 5 <br> Wildcard option <br> Yield shift option | 6 <br> Wildcard option <br> Yield shift option | 7 <br> Wildcard option <br> Yield shift option | 8 <br> Wildcard option <br> Yield shift option | 9 <br> Wildcard option <br> Yield shift option | 10 <br> Wildcard option <br> Yield shift option | 11 <br> Wildcard option <br> Yield shift option |
| 12 <br> Wildcard option <br> Yield shift option | 13 <br> Wildcard option <br> Yield shift option | 14 <br> Wildcard option <br> Yield shift option | 15 <br> Wildcard option <br> Yield shift option | 16 <br> Wildcard option <br> Yield shift option | 17 <br> Wildcard option <br> Yield shift option | 18 <br> Wildcard option <br> Yield shift option |
| 19 <br> Wildcard option <br> Yield shift option | 20 <br> Wildcard option <br> Yield shift option | 21 <br> *Last Trading Day* <br> Switching option <br> Yield shift option | 22 <br> Switching option | 23 <br> Switching option | 24 <br> Switching option | 25 <br> Switching option |
| 26 <br> Switching option | 27 <br> Switching option | 28 <br> *Last Position Day* <br> Switching option | 29 <br> *Last Notice Day* | 30 <br> *Last Delivery Date* | | |

[a] Yield shift option here also encapsulates the yield spread option. It is in effect much before May 29 as it is the only option affected by a change in the overall yield environment, and this, obviously, can occur considerably before the month of June. The new-auction option is similar in that it is applicable any time before the auction of a new bond. *First notice day* here refers to the first day the basis short can inform the CBT which bond is to be delivered. Some people refer to position day as first notice day.

[b] Do not confuse the terminology.

# CONCLUSION

As stated before, the value of the basis cannot be derived simply by adding all the deliverability options, because some are mutually exclusive and some are interdependent. Accurate valuation is immensely difficult because of the many parameters that must be considered. Among them are market volatility, potential change in the financing rate, time to first and last delivery dates, the shape of the yield curve, whether or not an auction will be held in the interim, yield spreads between the deliverable bonds, and how they all interact with each other. The delivery process and options for the June 2005 contract shown in Exhibit 54–8 should prove helpful in conceptualizing the sequence of events in a delivery month.

A beginning in valuing the basis through a simplified approach is to take the expected value of the futures at the different stages of the delivery process and calculate the value of the basis at each final outcome. One first has to make an assumption about whether the future distribution of bond prices is normal, lognormal, or any other shape. Then, by creating numerous scenarios of yield moves in both directions, one can observe which bond's net basis appears to be cheapest.

## CHAPTER 55

# THE BASICS OF INTEREST-RATE OPTIONS

William J. Gartland, CFA
Vice President
Bloomberg Financial Market

Nicholas C. Letica
Managing Director
Bear Stearns & Co.

As the sophistication and diversity of investors have grown, the need for derivative instruments such as options has increased accordingly. Knowledge of option strategies, once the province of a few speculators, is now necessary for everyone who wishes to maintain a competitive edge in an increasingly technical market. Moreover, the new options technology has been applied with increasing success to securities with optionlike characteristics such as callable bonds and mortgage-backed securities.

In Chapter 52, option contracts were described: exchange-traded options on physical securities, exchange-traded options on futures, and over-the-counter options. In this chapter, we will review how options work, their risk/return profiles, the basic principles of option pricing, and some common trading and portfolio strategies. A more detailed discussion of hedging strategies is provided in Chapter 56.

Throughout most of the discussion, our focus will be on options on physicals. The principles, however, are equally applicable to options on futures or futures options.

## HOW OPTIONS WORK

An *option* is the right but not the obligation to buy or to sell a security at a fixed price. The right to buy is called a *call,* and the right to sell is called a *put;* a call makes money if prices rise and a put makes money if prices fall.

If the owner of an option used the option to buy or to sell the underlying security, we say that the option has been *exercised.* Because the holder is never required to exercise an option, the holder can never lose more than the purchase price of the option—an option is a limited-liability instrument.

An option on a given security can be specified by giving its strike price and its expiration date. The *strike price* is the price on the optional purchase. For example, a call with a strike price of par is the right to buy that security at par. The *expiration date* is the last date on which the option can be exercised: After that, it is worthless, even if it had value on the expiration date. If an option is allowed to expire, it is said to be *terminated*. On or before the expiration date, the option holder may decide to sell the option for its market value. This is called a *pair-off*.

Some options can be exercised at any time until expiration: They are called *American* options. On the other hand, some options can only be exercised at expiration and are called *European* options. Because it is always possible to delay the exercise of an American option until expiration, an American option is always worth at least as much as its European counterpart. In practice there are only a limited number of circumstances under which early exercise is advantageous, so the American option rarely costs significantly more than the European.

The easiest way to analyze a position in a security and options on that security is with a *profit/loss graph*. A profit/loss graph shows the change in a position's value between the *analysis date* ("now") and a *horizon date* for a range of security prices at the horizon.

Suppose a call option struck at par is bought today for 1 point. At expiration, if the security is priced below par, the option will be allowed to expire worthless; the position has lost 1 point. If the security is above par at expiration, the option will be exercised; the position has made 1 point for every point the security is above par, less the initial one-point cost of the option. Exhibit 55–1 shows the resulting profit/loss graph.

Note that if the price of the underlying increases by 1 point, the option purchase breaks even. This happens because the value of the option at expiration is equal to the initial purchase price. A price of 101 is the breakeven price for the call: The call purchase will make money if the price of the underlying exceeds 101 at expiration.

A put is the reverse of a call. Look at Exhibit 55–2, which is the profit/loss graph of a put option struck at par bought for 1 point. At expiration, the put is worth nothing if the security's price is more than the strike price and is worth one point for every point that the security is priced below the strike price. The breakeven price for this trade is 99, so the put purchase makes money if the underlying is priced below 99 at expiration.

## Put/Call Parity

A put and a call struck at the money split up the profit/loss diagram of the underlying security into two parts. Consider the position created by buying a

## EXHIBIT 55–1

Long Call vs. Underlying Security Price
Call Struck at Par, at Expiration, with One-Point Premium

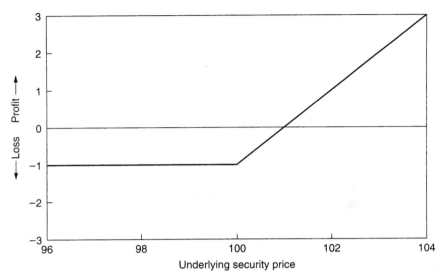

## EXHIBIT 55–2

Long Put vs. Underlying Security Price
Put Struck at Par, at Expiration, with One-Point Premium

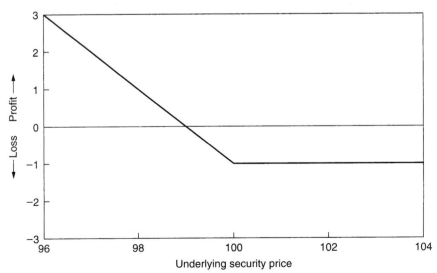

call and selling a put such that the strike price of the two options is equal to the price of the underlying. If the price of the security goes up, the call will be exercised; if the price of the security goes down, the put will be exercised. In either case, at expiration the underlying is delivered at the strike price. So in terms of profit and loss, owning the call and selling the put is the same as owning the underlying.

Exhibit 55–3 divides the profit/loss graph of the underlying security into graphs for a long call and a short put, respectively. The following three facts can be deduced.

$$\text{Long security} = \text{Long call} + \text{Short put} \quad \text{(Exhibit 55–3)}$$

$$\text{Long call} = \text{Long security} + \text{Long put} \quad \text{(Exhibit 55–4)}$$

$$\text{Long put} = \text{Short security} + \text{Long call} \quad \text{(Exhibit 55–5)}$$

This relationship is called *put/call parity;* it is one of the foundations of the options markets. Using these facts, a call can be created from a put by buying the underlying, or a put made from a call by selling the underlying. This ability

**EXHIBIT  55–3**

Long Security = Long call + Short Put

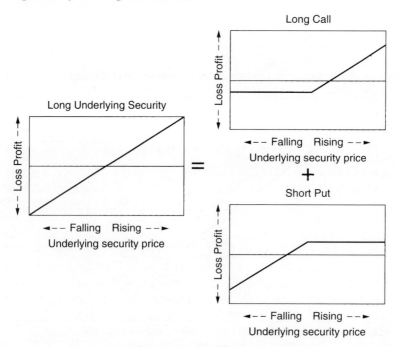

**EXHIBIT 55-4**

Long Call = Long Security + Long Put

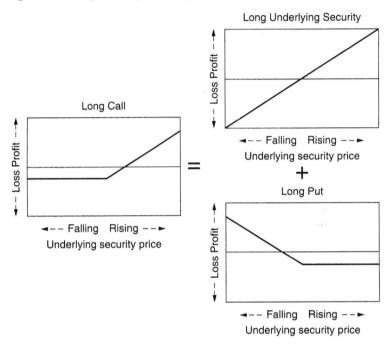

to convert between puts and calls at will is essential to the management of an options position.

## Valuing an Option

The first fact to determine about an option is its worth. There are many option valuation models for each class of options, each of which uses different parameters and returns slightly different values. However, the five main determinants of option value are the price of the underlying, the strike price of the option, the expiration of the option, the volatility of the underlying, and the cost of financing the underlying.

The most apparent component of option value is intrinsic value. The *intrinsic value* of an option is its value if it were exercised immediately. An option with intrinsic value is an *in-the-money* option. When the underlying security trades right at the strike price, the option is called *at the money*. Otherwise, an option with no intrinsic value is called *out of the money*.

**EXHIBIT 55-5**

Long Put = Short Security + Long Call

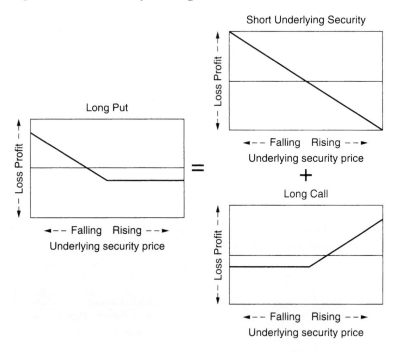

An option may have value over and above its intrinsic value, called *time value*. The intrinsic value is the value of the option if exercised immediately, whereas the time value is the remaining value in the option due to time expiration. Clearly, the more time there is to expiration, the greater the time value.

Exhibit 55-6 graphs the value of an option as time to expiration increases. Exhibit 55-7 compares the value of an option at expiration with the values of options with one and three months to expiration. There is a sharp corner in the graph at the strike price that becomes more pronounced as the time to expiration decreases. This sharp corner makes an at-the-money option increasingly difficult to hedge as expiration approaches.

If the option is out of the money, it has some time value because there is a chance that the option will expire in the money; as it gets further out of the money, this is less likely and the time value decreases.

If the option is in the money, its time value is due to the fact that it is better to hold the option than the corresponding position in the underlying security because if the security trades out of the money the potential loss on the option is limited to the value of the option; as the option gets further in the money, this possibility becomes more farfetched and the time value decreases.

**EXHIBIT 55-6**

Call Option Value vs. Time until Expiration
Three Calls: At the Money, 1 Point in the Money, 1 Point out of the Money

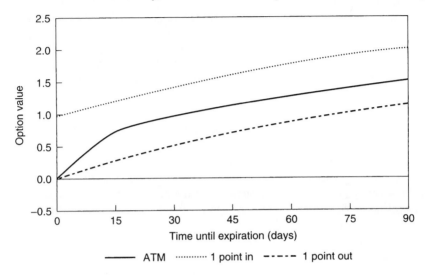

**EXHIBIT 55-7**

Call Option Value vs. Underlying Security Price
Call Struck at Par with 1 and 3 Months to Expiration

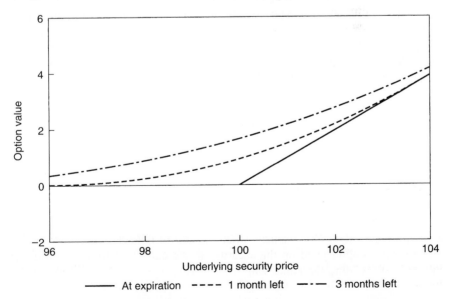

Either way, the time value depends on the probability that the security will trade through the strike price. In turn, this probability depends on how far from the strike price the security is trading and how much the security price is expected to vary until expiration.

*Volatility* measures the variability of the price or the yield of a security. It measures only the magnitude of the moves, not the direction. Standard option pricing models make no assumptions about the future direction of prices, but only about the distribution of these prices. Volatility is the ideal parameter for option pricing as it measures how wide this distribution will be. We discuss volatility in more detail at the end of this chapter.

The higher the volatility of a security, the higher is the price of options on that security. If a security had no volatility, for example, that security would always have the same price at time of purchase of an option as at its expiration, so all options would be priced at their intrinsic value. Increasing the volatility of a security increases the time value of options on that security as the chance of the security price moving through the strike price increases. Increases in the value of an at-the-money option are approximately proportional to increases in the volatility of the underlying. Exhibit 55–8 shows how the price of an option behaves as the volatility of the underlying security increases.

The final factor that influences options prices is the *carry* on the underlying security. Carry is the difference between the value of the coupon payments on a security and the cost of financing that security's purchase price. With the usual upward-sloping yield curve, most securities have a positive carry.

The effect of the carry can be seen by comparing the price of an at-the-money call with an at-the-money put where the underlying security has a positive carry. The writer of the call anticipates the chance of being required to deliver the securities and thus buys the underlying as a hedge; the put writer hedges by selling the underlying. The call writer earns the carry while the put writer loses the carry, so the call should cost less than the put. When the yield curve inverts and short-term rates are higher than long-term rates, carry becomes negative and calls cost more than puts.

By put/call parity, selling an at-the-money call and buying an at-the-money put is equivalent to shorting the underlying security. The cash taken out of the option trade, accounting for transaction costs, compensates the option holder for the carry on the position in the underlying until expiration. This trade is called a *conversion,* and it is frequently used to obtain the effect of a purchase or sale of securities when buying or selling the underlying is impossible for accounting reasons.

Exhibit 55–9 compares the cost of an at-the-money call and put for a range of financing rates. The two graphs intersect where the call and the put have the same value: This happens when the cost of financing the underlying is equal to the coupon yield on the security, so the carry is zero and there is no advantage to holding the underlying over shorting it.

**EXHIBIT 55-8**

Call Option Value vs. Percent Price Volatility
Three Calls: At the Money, 1 Point in the Money, 1 Point out of the
Money; Three Months from Expiration

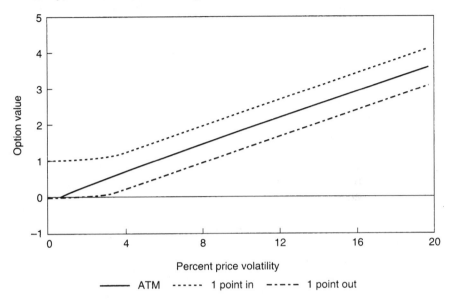

Exhibit 55–10 summarizes the parameters that affect the value of an option and how much raising each parameter affects that value.

## Delta, Gamma, and Theta: Hedging an Option Position

More precise quantitative ways to describe the behavior of an option are needed to manage an option position. Options traders have created the concepts of delta, gamma, and theta for this purpose. Delta measures the price sensitivity of an option, gamma the convexity of the option, and theta the change in the value of the option over time.

For a given option, the *delta* is the ratio of changes in the value of the option to changes in the value of the underlying for small changes in the underlying. A typical at-the-money call option would have a delta of 0.5; that means for a one-cent increase in the price of the underlying the value of the call would increase by 0.5 cents. On the other hand, an at-the-money put would have a delta of −0.5; puts have negative deltas because they decrease in value as the price of the underlying increases (see Exhibit 55–10).

**E X H I B I T   55–9**

Treasury Option Value vs. Financing Rate
Long Call, Long Put Struck at Par, 3 Months to Expiration

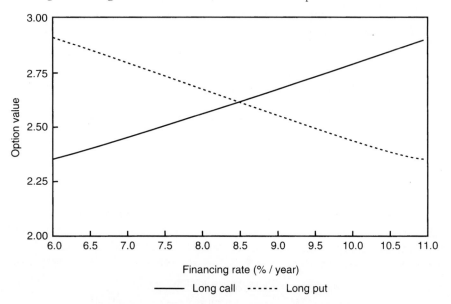

**E X H I B I T   55–10**

The Effect of an Increase of a Factor on Option Values

|                    | Call     | Put      |
|--------------------|----------|----------|
| Underlying price   | Increase | Decrease |
| Strike Price       | Decrease | Increase |
| Carry              | Decrease | Increase |
| Time to expiration | Increase | Increase |
| Volatility         | Increase | Increase |

The standard method of hedging an options position is called *delta hedging,* which unsurprisingly makes heavy use of the delta. The idea behind delta hedging is that for small price moves, the price of an option changes in proportion with the change in price of the underlying, so the underlying can be used to hedge the option. For example, 1,000,000 calls with a delta of 0.25 would for small price movements track a position of 250,000 of the underlying bonds, so a position consisting of 1,000,000 of these long calls and 250,000 of the security sold short would be delta hedged. The total delta of a position shows how much that position is long or short. In the example above, the total delta is

$$0.25 \times 1,000,000 - 1 \times 250,000 = 0$$

so the position is neither long nor short.

Intuitively, the delta of an option is the number of bonds that are expected to be delivered into this option. For example, an at-the-money call has a delta of 0.5, which means that one bond is expected to be delivered for every two calls that are held. In other words, an at-the-money call is equally as likely to be exercised as not. An option that is deeply out of the money will have a delta that is close to 0 because there is almost no chance that the option will ever be exercised. An option that is deeply in the money will almost certainly be exercised. This means that a deeply in the money put has a delta of $-1$ because it is almost certain that the holder of the option will exercise the put and deliver one bond to the put writer.

Put/call parity tells us that a position in the underlying security may be duplicated by buying a call and selling a put with the same strike price and expiration date. Thus, the delta of the call less the delta of the put should be the delta of the underlying. The delta for the underlying is 1, so we get the following equation:

$$\text{delta}(call) - \text{delta}(put) = 1$$

where call and put are options on the same security with the same strike price and expiration date. This says that once the call is bought and the put sold, the bond is certain to be delivered; if the call is out of the money, the put is in the money. Moreover, as the chance of having the underlying delivered into the call becomes smaller, the chance of having to accept delivery as the put is exercised becomes larger. Exhibit 55–11 compares the deltas for a long and a short put.

Making the position delta neutral does not solve all hedging problems, however. This is demonstrated in Exhibit 55–12. Each of the three positions shown is delta neutral, but position 1 is clearly preferable to position 2, which is in turn better than position 3. The difference between these three positions is *convexity*. A position such as position 1 with a profit/loss graph that curves upward has a positive convexity, whereas position 3 has a graph that curves downward and thus has negative convexity.

*Gamma* measures convexity for options; it is the change in the delta for small changes in the price of the underlying. If a position has a positive gamma, then as the market goes up the delta of the position increases and as it declines the delta increases. Such a position becomes longer as the market trades up and shorter as the market trades down. A position like this is called *long convexity* or *long volatility*. These names come from the fact that if the market moves in either direction this position will outperform a position with the same delta and a lower gamma. Exhibit 55–13 shows this phenomenon.

**EXHIBIT 55-11**

Option Delta vs. Underlying Security Price
Long Call, Short Put Struck at Par, 3 Months to Expiration

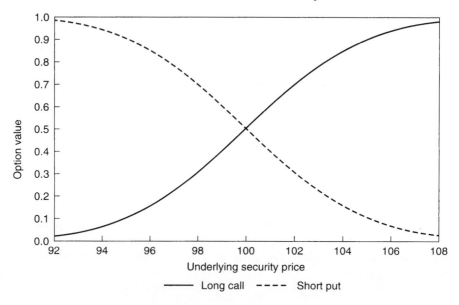

A long option always has a positive gamma. The delta of a call increases from 0 to 1 as the security trades up and the delta of a put increases also, moving from −1 to 0. Exhibits 55–1 and 55–2 show that the profit/loss graph of options curves upward. Because of this, options traders often speak of buying or selling volatility as a synonym for buying or selling options.

A position with a zero gamma is called *flat convexity* or *flat gamma*. Here, a change in the underlying security price does not change the delta of the position. Such a position trades like a position in the underlying with no options bought or sold. If the position has in addition a delta of zero, then its value is not affected by small changes in the price of the underlying security in either direction. Position 2 in Exhibit 55–12 is a profit/loss graph for a position with no delta or gamma.

A position with negative gamma is called *short volatility* or *short convexity*. The profit/loss curve slopes downward in either direction from the current price on the underlying; thus the position gets longer as the market trades down and shorter as the market trades up. Either way, this position loses money if there are significant price movements. Position 3 demonstrates this behavior.

A position that is long volatility is clearly preferable to an otherwise identical position that is short volatility. The holder of the short-volatility position must be compensated for this. In order to create a position that is long volatility it is necessary to purchase options and spend money; moreover, if the market

**EXHIBIT  55–12**

Delta-Neutral Positions with Different Gamma

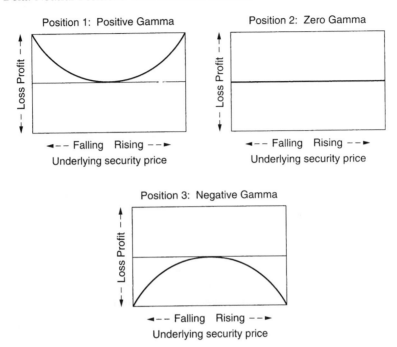

does not move, the values of the options will decrease as their time to expiration decreases, so the position loses money in a flat market.

Conversely, creating a position that is short volatility involves selling options and taking in cash. As time passes the value of these options sold decreases because their time value falls, so the position makes money in a fiat market. Large losses could be sustained in a volatile market, however.

To describe the time behavior of options, there is one last measure called *theta*. The theta of an option is the overnight change in value of the option if all other parameters (prices, volatilities) stay constant. This means that a long option has a negative theta, because as expiration approaches the time value of the option will erode to zero. For example, a 90-day at-the-money call that costs 2 points might have a theta of −0.45 ticks per day.

Exhibit 55–14 shows the effects of different volatility exposures.

## OPTIONS STRATEGIES—REORGANIZING THE PROFIT/LOSS GRAPH

Investors have many different goals; reducing risk, increasing rates of return, or capturing gains under expected market moves. Often, these objectives are simply

### EXHIBIT 55-13

Profit/Loss Diagram with Convexity
Long Security with Flat and Long Convexity

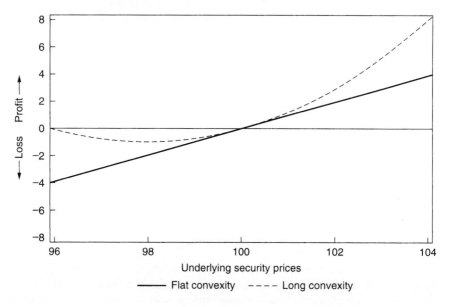

Flat convexity   — — — Long convexity

### EXHIBIT 55-14

Comparison of Different Volatility Positions (All Positions Are Delta Neutral)

|  | Short Volatility | Flat Volatility | Long Volatility |
|---|---|---|---|
| Convexity | Position has negative convexity: gamma < 0 | Position has no convexity: gamma = 0 | Position has positive convexity: gamma > 0 |
| Options purchased | More sold than bought | Sold as many as bought | More bought than sold |
| Time value | Position earns value as time passes: theta > 0 | Position stays flat as time passes: theta = 0 | Position loses value as time passes: theta < 0 |
| Market moves | Position loses money if the market moves in either direction | Position is invariant with respect to market moves | Position makes money if the market moves in either direction |

to rearrange the profit/loss graph of a position in accordance with the investor's expectations or desires. By increasing the minimum value of this graph, for example, the investor reduces risk.

Options provide a precise tool to accomplish this rearrangement. Because it is impossible to replicate the performance of an option position using just the underlying, options allow a much broader range of strategies to be used. The following characteristics of options provide an explanation.

## Directionality

Both a put and a call are directional instruments. A put, for example, performs only in a decreasing market. This property makes options ideal for reducing directional risk on a position. Take, for example, a position that suffers large losses in a downward market and makes a consistent profit if prices rise. By purchasing a put option, some of these profits are given up in exchange for dramatically increased performance if the market declines.

## Convexity

Buying and selling options makes it possible to adjust the convexity of a position in almost any fashion. Because OTC options can be purchased for any strike price and expiration, convexity can be bought or sold at any place in the profit/loss graph. For example, an investor holding mortgage-backed securities priced just over par might anticipate that prepayments on this security would start to increase dramatically if the market traded up, attenuating possible price gains. In other words, the investor feels that the position is short convexity above the market. To adjust the profit/loss graph, calls could be purchased with strike prices at or above the market. This trade sells some of the spread over Treasuries in exchange for increased performance in a rising market.

## Fee Income

An investor who wishes to increase the performance of a position in a stable market can sell convexity by writing options and taking in fees. This increases the current yield of the position, at the cost of increasing volatility risk in some area of the profit/loss graph. A typical example of this is the venerable covered call strategy, where the manager of a portfolio sells calls on a portion of the portfolio, forgoing some profits in a rising market in exchange for a greater return in a stable or decreasing market.

## Leveraged Speculation

Investors with a higher risk/reward profile wish to increase their upside potential and are willing to accept a greater downside risk. In this case, options can be used as a highly leveraged position to capture windfall profits under a very specific market move. A strongly bullish investor might purchase one-point out-of-the-money calls with 30 days to expiration for $\frac{1}{2}$ point. If the market traded up 2 points by expiration the option would then be worth 1 point and the investor would have doubled the initial investment; a corresponding position in the underlying would have appreciated in value by only about 2%. Of course, if the market did not trade up by at least 1 point the calls would expire worthless.

## CLASSIC OPTION STRATEGIES

The following section gives a brief explanation of some of the simplest pure options strategies.

### Straddle

The most pure convexity trade is called a *straddle,* composed of one call and one put with the same strike price. Exhibit 55–15 shows the profit/loss graph of a straddle struck at the money at expiration and with 3 months to expiration.

This position is delta neutral, as it implies no market bias. If the market stays flat, the position loses money as the options' time value disappears by expiration. If the market moves in either direction, however, either the put or

**EXHIBIT 55–15**

Profit/Loss Diagram for a Long Straddle
Struck at Par, at Expiration, and 3 Months Out

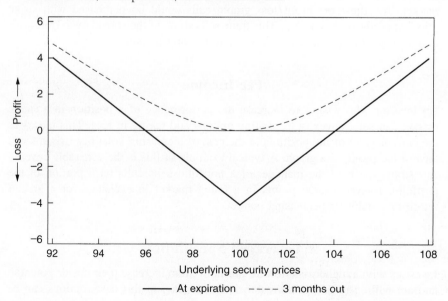

the call will end up in the money and the position will make money. This strategy is most useful for buying convexity at a specific strike price. Investors who are bearish on volatility and anticipate a flat market could sell straddles and make money from time value.

## Strangle

A *strangle* is the more heavily leveraged cousin of a straddle. An at-the-money strangle is composed of an out-of-the-money call and an out-of-the-money put. The options are struck so that they are both equally out of the money and the current price of the security is halfway between the two strikes. The profit/loss graph is found in Exhibit 55–16.

Just like a straddle, a strangle is a pure volatility trade. If the market stays flat, the position loses time value, whereas if the market moves dramatically in either direction the position makes money from either the call or the put. Because the options in this position are both out of the money, the market has to move significantly before either option moves into the money. The options are much cheaper, however, so it is possible to buy many more options for the same money. This is the ideal position for the investor who is heavily bullish on volatility and wants windfall profits in a rapidly moving market.

**E X H I B I T   55–16**

Profit/Loss Diagram for a Long Strangle
Struck at Par, at Expiration, and 3 Months Out

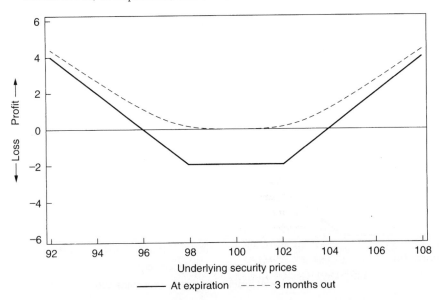

Underlying security prices

—— At expiration    ---- 3 months out

Writing strangles is a very risky business. Most of the time the market will not move enough to put either option much into the money and the writer of the strangle will make the fee income. Occasionally, however, the market will plummet or spike and the writer of the strangle will suffer catastrophic losses. This accounts for the picturesque name of this trade.

## Spread Trades

*Spread trades* involve buying one option and funding all or part of this purchase by selling another. A *bull spread* can be created by owning the underlying security, buying a put struck below the current price, and selling a call above the current price. Because both options are out of the money, it is possible to arrange the strikes so that the cost of the put is equal to the fee for the call. If the security price falls below the put strike or rises above the call strike, the appropriate option will be exercised and the security will be sold. Otherwise, any profit or loss will just be that of the underlying security. In other words, this position is analogous to owning the underlying security except that the final value of the position at expiration is forced to be between the two strikes. Exhibit 55–17 shows the profit/loss graph of this position at expiration and with three months left of time value.

**E X H I B I T    55–17**

Profit/Loss Diagram for a Bull Spread
Struck at Par, at Expiration, and 3 Months Out

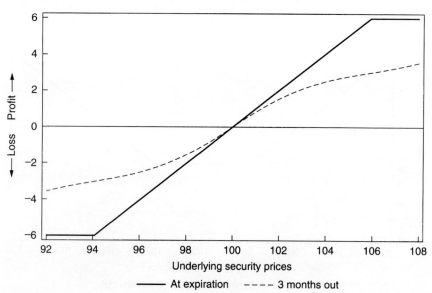

The other spread trade is a *bear spread:* It is the reverse of a bull spread. It can be created by selling a bull spread. Using put/call parity, it can also be set up by holding the underlying security, buying an in-the-money put, and selling an in-the-money call. A bear spread is equivalent to a short position in the underlying, where the position must be closed out at a price between the two strike prices. Exhibit 55–18 shows the profit/loss graph of a bear spread.

## PRACTICAL PORTFOLIO STRATEGIES

The strategies discussed in the previous section are the basic techniques used by speculators to trade options. The usual fixed income investor has a lower risk/reward profile than the speculator and specific objectives that must be accomplished; a floor on rate of return or an increase in current yield, for example. Such investors need a class of strategies different from that needed by speculators; even though the same strategies are often used, the risk is carefully controlled.

### Portfolio Insurance

This is the most obvious and one of the most commonly used options strategies. An investor with a portfolio of securities who fears a decreasing market buys

**EXHIBIT  55–18**

Profit/Loss Diagram for a Bear Spread Struck at Par, at Expiration, and 3 Months Out

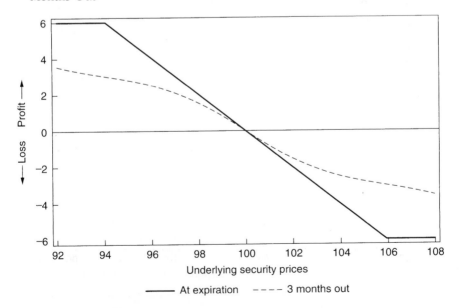

puts on some or all of the portfolio; if the market falls, the puts are exercised, and the securities are sold at the strike price. Alternatively, the investor may keep the underlying security and pair off the in-the-money puts, receiving cash in compensation for the decreased value of the security. Either way, the investor has limited losses on the portfolio in exchange for selling off return in a stable or rising market.

As the strike price of the put increases, so does its cost and the resultant impact on the stable market rate of return. Often, out-of-the-money options are used; the floor on returns is lower because the strike price is lower, but the lower cost of the options means that less return is given up if the market is flat or rises. By put/call parity, such a position is equivalent to holding a call option struck at or in the money.

Another popular strategy is to buy at-the-money options on a portion of the portfolio. This reduces but does not eliminate downside risk: Exhibit 55–19 shows the profit/loss graphs at expiration for positions with different percentages of the portfolio hedged with an at-the-money put. Note that all the graphs intersect at a single point. This is the point where the initial cost of the option is equal to the value of the option at expiration, which is the breakeven price for this trade.

**E X H I B I T   55–19**

Hedged Underlying Security with Puts
Long Puts Struck at Par, at Expiration

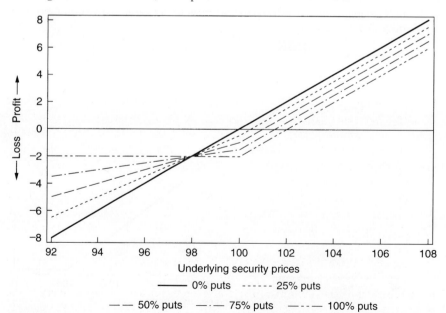

It is not possible to buy options on many classes of securities that may well be held in a portfolio. Perfect insurance for such securities is unattainable, but cross-market hedging will often permit a reduction in downside risk to acceptable levels. This is discussed further in Chapter 56.

## Covered Calls

Writing covered calls is a strategy that sells volatility in return for fees. An investor who holds a portfolio sells calls on some or all of the portfolio in return for fees. If the market stays the same or falls, the investor pockets the option fees. If the market increases until the calls are in the money, the investor is called out by the option holder. In other words, possible gains on the portfolio are sold for fee income.

Often the investor wishes to preserve some upside potential. Just as in the portfolio insurance example, there are two different ways to do this. The calls can be struck out of the money, that is, above the current market price. This strategy allows all gains up to the strike price to be captured. If the bonds in the portfolio are currently trading below the original purchase price, a popular strategy is to sell calls struck at this purchase price. This provides fee income and increased current yield but prevents the possibility that the bonds will be called at a price below the original purchase price and the portfolio will book a capital loss.

Otherwise, calls can be sold on a portion of the portfolio. This allows unlimited price gains to be captured on the remainder. Exhibit 55–20 shows the profit/loss graph of a covered call program where different portions of the portfolio have calls sold against them.

## Buy-Writes and Writing Puts

Buy-writes and writing puts are two very closely related strategies for selling volatility that most investors think of as entirely different. To execute a buy-write, a bond is purchased, and simultaneously a call is written on this bond to the same dealer for the fee income. If the security is trading above the strike price at expiration, the security is called and the investor is left with just the option fee. If the price of the security has fallen, the investor is left holding the security but the total cost of the security is reduced by the fee from the call. By put/call parity, this trade is identical to writing a put struck at the money. In both cases, the investor is delivered the security only if the price of the security is lower than the price of the original sale.

In the MBS market, a buy-write is composed of forward purchases and short calls on forward delivery contracts (standard TBA transactions). If the call is exercised, it offsets the forward sale and the buyer never takes delivery of the security, keeping the fee income. Otherwise, the buyer will receive the security

**EXHIBIT  55–20**

Covered Call Writing Program
Short Calls Struck at Par, at Expiration

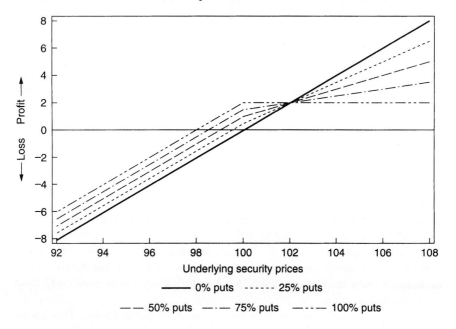

on the forward settlement date for the original forward sale price, although the total price is decreased by the value of the option fee.

Put writing is a more general strategy that applies to all fixed income options markets. The investor writes a put for the fee income and receives the underlying instrument at expiration if the security trades below the strike price. This can be a very effective strategy if carefully structured. An investor may feel that a security offers real value if bought at a certain price below the market. The investor could then write puts struck at that price. If the security falls below the strike, it is delivered at a price that is more agreeable than the current price. Otherwise, the investor simply pockets the fee income.

## Volatility

Volatility plays a key role in the valuation of options and in option strategies. In this section, we focus on methods for estimating volatility.

Statistically, volatility is a measure of the dispersion or spread of observations around the mean of the set of observations. If volatility seems strangely like a standard deviation, then you remember your statistics. When people speak of volatility, all they really are talking about is a standard deviation.

For fixed income securities, volatility is expressed in yield or price units, either on a percentage or on an absolute basis. Price volatilities can be computed for any security. Yield volatilities should be computed only for those securities with a consistent method for computing yield. Given the complexity of calculating a yield on a MBS and the variation of results, the predominant volatility measure in the MBS market is price volatility. The government bond market, where yields are easily calculated, favors yield volatility.

There are two types of volatility: empirical volatility and implied volatility. Each is described below.

## Empirical Volatility

Empirical volatility is the actual, historical market volatility of a specific security. These numbers are typically calculated for various time periods (10 days, 30 days, 360 days) and are usually annualized.[1] Calculating an empirical volatility is nothing more than calculating the standard deviation of a time series. Thus, an absolute volatility is the annualized standard deviation of daily price or yield changes, assuming a normal distribution.

Percentage volatility is the annualized standard deviation of the daily change in the log of prices or yields, assuming a lognormal distribution of prices or yields. Similar to the daily absolute yield changes, the logs of the daily yield changes have a slight bias toward lower yields. The intuitive approach to calculating a percentage volatility is to find the standard deviation of daily *returns,* assuming a normal distribution. This approach is equivalent to the lognormal assumption as long as the distribution can be characterized as being equally normal and lognormal and the changes in prices are taken on a small interval, such as daily.

As previously mentioned, empirical volatility can be measured over various time periods. The most common interval on which the standard deviation is taken is 30 days; other common intervals are 10 days and 360 days. The choice of interval determines how quickly and to what degree an empirical volatility responds to deviations. As the time period shortens, volatility increasingly reflects current conditions but is more unstable as each sample asserts greater influence in the deviation. Conversely, as the interval increases, more of a lag and a smoothing are introduced into the calculation.

The interval used to calculate an empirical volatility should be chosen to match the length of the option contract. This provides the investor with an indication of how volatile the underlying security has been recently and how this relates to the volatility employed to price the option.

---

1. When annualizing a volatility, certain assumptions are inherent to the calculation. To convert from daily to yearly volatility, for example, the daily volatility is multiplied by the square root of the number of business days in the year, approximately 250.

With no industry standard for volatility units, converting between the price and yield expression of absolute or percentage volatility is a useful skill. The path to follow to convert from one unit to the next is shown in Exhibit 55–21. The modified duration of a security provides the link between price and yield volatilities. Modified duration is defined as the percentage change in price divided by the absolute change in yield.

## Implied Volatility

Implied volatility is merely the market's expectation of future volatility over a specified time period. An option's price is a function of the volatility employed, so where an option's price is known the implied volatility can be derived. Although it sounds straightforward, calculating an implied volatility is far more complicated than calculating an empirical volatility, because expectations cannot be observed directly. An option pricing model along with a mathematical method to infer the volatility must be employed. The result of this calculation is a percentage price volatility that can be converted to the various types of volatility measures discussed previously (see Exhibit 55–21).

Owing to the existence and liquidity of fixed income options, proxies for implied volatilities can be derived from Treasuries. Options on Treasury futures listed on the Chicago Board of Trade (CBT) are often the best vehicles for

**E X H I B I T    55–21**

Converting Volatility Measures

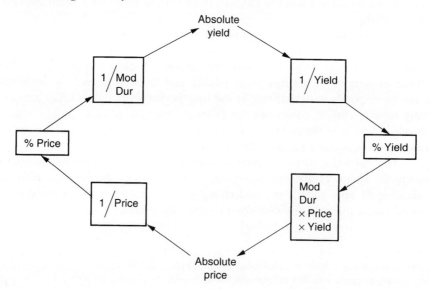

implied volatility calculations. Of these, the bond contract provides the best information necessary to calculate an implied volatility. The resultant implied volatility provides a good indication of the market's expected volatility for the Treasuries with maturities similar to that of the particular bond futures contract in question. The implied volatility on the 20-year bond future contract, for example, is a useful proxy for the market's expected volatility on long-term Treasury securities.

## CONCLUSION

Options are no longer merely toys for speculators and dealers. Any investor with specific goals can use option strategies to tailor the performance of a portfolio. Because it is impossible to obtain the effects of options by using only the underlying securities, a whole new universe of strategic possibilities is opened up. In particular, investors with contingent liabilities cannot create an adequate hedge without the use of options.

Increased liquidity in the options markets and a better understanding of the properties of options make option strategies more accessible to the average investor and allow these strategies to be used for a wider range of securities. In particular, the over-the-counter options markets allow the purchase and sale of options with any desired strike price and expiration date.

In the future, options and option valuation technology will be used increasingly often for cross-market arbitrage trades where securities and options in one market will be used to duplicate securities in another. As options trading removes the arbitrages, the relationships between the various markets will become reinforced.

## CHAPTER 56

# CONTROLLING INTEREST RATE RISK WITH FUTURES AND OPTIONS

**Frank J. Fabozzi, Ph.D., CFA**
Adjunct Professor of Finance
School of Management
Yale University

**Shrikant Ramamurthy**
Senior Vice-President
Prudential Securities, Inc.

**Mark Pitts, Ph.D.**
Principal
White Oak Capital Management Corp.

In Chapter 51 the features and characteristics of interest rate futures and options were explained. In this chapter, our focus is on how these derivative instruments can be used to control the interest rate risk of a portfolio.

## CONTROLLING INTEREST RATE RISK WITH FUTURES

The price of an interest rate futures contract moves in the opposite direction from the change in interest rates: when rates rise, the futures price will fall; when rates fall, the futures price will rise. By buying a futures contract, a portfolio's exposure to a rate increase is increased. That is, the portfolio's duration increases. By selling a futures contract, a portfolio's exposure to a rate increase is decreased. Equivalently, this means that the portfolio's duration is reduced. Consequently, buying and selling futures can be used to alter the duration of a portfolio.

This chapter is adapted from an article by the authors appearing in *Professional Perspectives on Fixed Income Portfolio Management: Volume 1* (New Hope, PA: Frank J. Fabozzi Associates, 2000).

While managers can alter the duration of their portfolios with cash market instruments (buying or selling Treasury securities), using interest rate futures instead of trading long-term Treasuries themselves has the following three advantages:

> *Advantage 1:* Transaction costs for trading futures are lower than trading in the cash market.
>
> *Advantage 2:* Margin requirements are lower for futures than for Treasury securities; using futures thus permits greater leverage.
>
> *Advantage 3:* It is easier to sell short in the futures market than in the Treasury market.

Futures can also be used in constructing a portfolio with a longer duration than is available with cash market securities. For example, suppose that in a certain interest rate environment a pension fund manager must structure a portfolio to have a duration of 15 to accomplish a particular investment objective. Bonds with such a long duration may not be available. By buying the appropriate number and kind of interest rate futures contracts, a pension fund manager can increase the portfolio's duration to the target level of 15.

## General Principles of Interest Rate Risk Control

The general principle in controlling interest rate risk with futures is to combine the dollar exposure of the current portfolio and the dollar exposure of a futures position so that the total dollar exposure is equal to the target dollar exposure. This means that the manager must be able to accurately measure the dollar exposure of both the current portfolio and the futures contract employed to alter the exposure.

There are two commonly used measures for approximating the change in the dollar value of a bond or bond portfolio to changes in interest rates: price value of a basis point (PVBP) and duration. PVBP is the dollar price change resulting from a one-basis-point change in yield. Duration is the approximate percentage change in price for a 100-basis-point change in rates. (Given the percentage price change, the dollar price change for a given change in interest rates can be computed.) There are two measures of duration: *modified* and *effective*. Effective duration is the appropriate measure that should be used for bonds with embedded options. In this chapter when we refer to duration, we mean effective duration. Moreover, since the manager is interested in dollar price exposure, it is the effective *dollar* duration that should be used. For a one basis point change in rates, PVBP is equal to the effective dollar duration for a one-basis-point change in rates.

To estimate the effective dollar duration, it is necessary to have a good valuation model. It is the valuation model that is used to determine what the new values for the bonds in the portfolio will be if rates change. The difference between the current values of the bonds in the portfolio and the new values estimated by the valuation model when rates are changed is the dollar price exposure. Consequently, the starting point in controlling interest rate risk is the development of a reliable valuation model. A reliable valuation model is also needed to value the derivative contracts that the manager wants to use to control interest rate exposure.

Suppose that a manager seeks a *target duration* for the portfolio based on either expectations of interest rates or client-specified exposure. Given the target duration, a target dollar duration for a small basis point change in interest rates can be obtained. For a 50 basis change in interest rates, for example, the target dollar duration can be found by multiplying the dollar value of the portfolio by the target duration and then dividing by 200. For example, suppose that the manager of a $500 million portfolio wants a target duration of 6. This means that the manager seeks a 3% change in the value of the portfolio for a 50 basis point change in rates (assuming a parallel shift in rates of all maturities). Multiplying the target duration of 6 by $500 million and dividing by 200 gives a target dollar duration of $15 million.

The manager must then determine the dollar duration of the current portfolio. The current dollar duration for a 50 basis point change in interest rates is found by multiplying the current duration by the dollar value of the portfolio and dividing by 200. So, for our $500 million portfolio, suppose that the current duration is 4. The current dollar duration is then $10 million (4 times $500 million divided by 200).

The target dollar duration is then compared to the current dollar duration. The difference between the two dollar durations is the dollar exposure that must be provided by a position in the futures contract. If the target dollar duration exceeds the current dollar duration, a futures position must increase the dollar exposure by the difference. To increase the dollar exposure, an appropriate number of futures contracts must be purchased. If the target dollar duration is less than the current dollar duration, an appropriate number of futures contracts must be sold. That is,

If target dollar duration − current dollar duration > 0, buy futures

If target dollar duration − current dollar duration < 0, sell futures

Once a futures position is taken, the *portfolio's dollar duration* is equal to the *current dollar duration without futures* plus the *dollar duration of the futures position*. That is,

portfolio's dollar return = current dollar duration without futures
+ dollar duration of futures position

The objective is to control the portfolio's interest rate risk by establishing a futures position such that the portfolio's dollar duration is equal to the target dollar duration. Thus, portfolio's dollar duration = target dollar duration

Or, equivalently,

target dollar duration = current dollar duration without futures
+ dollar duration of futures position    (56–1)

Over time, the portfolio's dollar duration will move away from the target dollar duration. The manager can alter the futures position to adjust the portfolio's dollar duration to the target dollar duration.

### Determining the Number of Contracts

Each futures contract calls for delivery of a specified amount of the underlying instrument. When interest rates change, the value of the underlying instrument changes, and therefore the value of the futures contract changes. How much the futures dollar value will change when interest rates change must be estimated. This amount is called the *dollar duration per futures contract*. For example, suppose the futures price of an interest rate futures contract is 70 and that the underlying interest rate instrument has a par value of $100,000. Thus, the futures delivery price is $70,000 (0.70 times $100,000). Suppose that a change in interest rates of 50 basis points results in the futures price changing by about $0.03 per contract. Then the dollar duration per futures contract is $2,100 (0.03 times $70,000).

The dollar duration of a futures position is then the number of futures contracts multiplied by the dollar duration per futures contract. That is,

dollar duration of futures position
= number of futures contracts
× dollar duration per futures contract    (56–2)

How many futures contracts are needed to obtain the target dollar duration? Substituting Eq. (56–2) into Eq. (56–1), we get

number of futures contracts × dollar duration per futures contract
= target dollar duration − current dollar duration without futures    (56–3)

Solving for the number of futures contracts we have:

number of futures contracts

$$= \frac{\text{target dollar duration} - \text{current dollar duration without futures}}{\text{dollar duration per futures contract}} \quad (56\text{–}4)$$

Equation (56–4) gives the approximate number of futures contracts that are necessary to adjust the portfolio's dollar duration to the target dollar duration. A positive number means that the futures contract must be purchased; a negative number means that the futures contract must be sold. Notice that if the target dollar duration is greater than the current dollar duration without futures, the numerator is positive and therefore futures contracts are purchased. If the target dollar duration is less than the current dollar duration without futures, the numerator is negative and therefore futures contracts are sold.

## Dollar Duration for a Futures Position

Now we turn to how to measure the dollar duration of a bond futures position. Keep in mind what the goal is: it is to measure the sensitivity of a bond futures position to changes in rates.

The general methodology for computing the dollar duration of a futures position for a given change in interest rates is straightforward given a valuation model. The procedure is the same as for computing the dollar duration of any cash market instrument – shock (change) interest rates up and down by the same number of basis points and determine the average dollar price change.

An adjustment is needed for the Treasury bond and note futures contracts. The pricing of the futures contract depends on the cheapest-to-deliver (CTD) issue.[1] The calculation of the dollar duration of a Treasury bond or note futures contract requires determining the impact of a change in interest rates will have on the price of a futures contract, which in turn affects how the futures price will change. The dollar duration of a Treasury bond and note futures contract is determined as follows:

dollar duration of futures contract

$$= \text{dollar duration of the CTD issue} \times \frac{\text{dollar duration of futures contract}}{\text{dollar duration of the CTD issue}}$$

There is a conversion factor for each issue that is acceptable for delivery for the futures contract. The conversion factor makes deliverable equitable to both the buyer and seller of the futures contract. For each deliverable issue, the product of the futures price and the conversion factor is the adjusted futures price for the issue. This adjusted price is called the *converted price*. Relating this to the equation above, the second ratio is approximately equal to the conversion factor of the cheapest-to-deliver issue. Thus, we can write:

dollar duration of futures contract
    = dollar duration of the CTD issue × conversion factor for the CTD issue

Why did we focus on dollar duration rather than duration? Recall that duration is the approximate percentage change in price. But what is the price of this leveraged instrument? The investor does not put up the full price of the position in order to acquire the position. Only the initial margin need be made in cash or a cash equivalent. Consequently, what is the base investment made by the investor? Rather than debate what should be used as the base investment

---

1. The cheapest-to-deliver issue is the one issue from among all those that are deliverable to satisfy a contract that has the highest return in a cash-and-carry trade. This return is called the implied repo rate.

in order to compute duration, let's simply ask why we are interested in calculating the exposure to changes in rates. As we have emphasized, it is to determine how a futures position will alter the exposure of a portfolio to changes in rates. Once we know how a futures position changes the dollar duration of a portfolio, we can determine for a portfolio its dollar duration. Given the funds invested by the investor in the portfolio, the portfolio's duration can be computed.

## Hedging with Interest Rate Futures

*Hedging with futures* calls for taking a futures position as a temporary substitute for transactions to be made in the cash market at a later date. If cash and futures prices move together, any loss realized by the hedger from one position (whether cash or futures) will be offset by a profit on the other position. *Hedging is a special case of controlling interest rate risk. In a hedge, the manager seeks a target duration or target dollar duration of zero.*

A *short hedge* (or *sell hedge*) is used to protect against a decline in the cash price of a bond. To execute a short hedge, futures contracts are sold. By establishing a short hedge, the manager has fixed the future cash price and transferred the price risk of ownership to the buyer of the futures contract. To understand why a short hedge might be executed, suppose that a pension fund manager knows that bonds must be liquidated in 40 days to make a $5 million payment to beneficiaries. If interest rates rise during the 40-day period, more bonds will have to be liquidated at a lower price than today to realize $5 million. To guard against this possibility, the manager can sell bonds in the futures market to lock in a selling price.

A *long hedge* (or *buy hedge*) is undertaken to protect against an increase in the cash price of a bond. In a long hedge, the manager buys a futures contract to lock in a purchase price. A pension fund manager might use a long hedge when substantial cash contributions are expected, and the manager is concerned that interest rates will fall. Also, a money manager who knows that bonds are maturing in the near future and expects that interest rates will fall can employ a long hedge to lock in a rate for the proceeds to be reinvested.

In bond portfolio management, typically the bond or portfolio to be hedged is not identical to the bond underlying the futures contract. This type of hedging is referred to as *cross hedging*.

The hedging process can be broken down into four steps:

*Step 1:* Determining the appropriate hedging instrument

*Step 2:* Determining the target for the hedge

*Step 3:* Determining the position to be taken in the hedging instrument

*Step 4:* Monitoring and evaluating the hedge

We discuss each step below.

## Determining the Appropriate Hedging Instrument

A primary factor in determining which futures contract will provide the best hedge is the degree of correlation between the rate on the futures contract and the interest rate that creates the underlying risk that the manager seeks to eliminate. For example, a long-term corporate bond portfolio can be better hedged with Treasury bond futures than with Treasury bill futures because long-term corporate bond rates are more highly correlated with Treasury bond futures than Treasury bill futures. Using the right delivery month is also important. A manager trying to lock in a rate or price for September will use September futures contracts because September futures contracts will give the highest degree of correlation.

Correlation is not, however, the only consideration if the hedging program is of significant size. If, for example, a manager wants to hedge $600 million of a cash position in a distant delivery month, liquidity becomes an important consideration. In such a case, it might be necessary for the manager to spread the hedge across two or more different contracts.

## Determining the Target for the Hedge

Having determined the right contract and the right delivery months, the manager should then determine what is expected from the hedge — that is, what rate will, on average, be locked in by the hedge. This is the *target rate* or *target price*. If this target rate is too high (if hedging a future sale) or too low (if hedging a future purchase), hedging may not be the right strategy for dealing with the unwanted risk. Determining what is expected (calculating the target rate or price for a hedge) is not always simple. We'll see how a manager should approach this problem for both simple and complex hedges.

***Risk and Expected Return in a Hedge.***    When a manager enters into a hedge, the objective is to "lock in" a rate for the sale or purchase of a security. However, there is much disagreement about what rate or price a manager should expect to lock in when futures are used to hedge. Here are the two views:

> *View 1:* The manager can, on average, lock in the current spot rate for the security (i.e., current rate in the cash market).
>
> *View 2:* The manager can, on average, lock in the rate at which the futures contracts are bought or sold.

The truth usually lies somewhere in between these two views. However, as the following cases illustrate, each view is entirely correct in certain situations.

***The Target for Hedges Held to Delivery.***    Hedges that are held until the futures delivery date provide an example of a hedge that locks in the futures rate (i.e., the second view). The complication in the case of using Treasury bond futures and Treasury note futures to hedge the value of intermediate- and long-term bonds, is that because of the delivery options the manager does not know for sure when delivery will take place or which bond will be delivered. This is because of the delivery options granted to the short.[2]

To illustrate how a Treasury bond futures held to the delivery date locks in the futures rate, assume for the sake of simplicity, that the manager knows which Treasury bond will be delivered and that delivery will take place on the last day of the delivery month. Suppose that for delivery on the September 1999 futures contract, the conversion factor for a deliverable Treasury issue is 1.283, implying that the investor who delivers this issue would receive from the buyer 1.283 times the futures settlement price plus accrued interest. An important principle to remember is that at delivery, the spot price and the futures price times the conversion factor must converge. *Convergence* refers to the fact that at delivery there can be no discrepancy between the spot price and futures price for a given security. If convergence does not take place, arbitrageurs would buy at the lower price and sell at the higher price and earn risk-free profits. Accordingly, a manager could lock in a September 1999 sale price for this issue by selling Treasury bond futures contracts equal to 1.283 times the par value of the bonds. For example, $100 million face value of this issue would be hedged by selling $128.3 million face value of bond futures (1,283 contracts).

The sale price that the manager locks in would be 1.283 times the futures price. This is the converted price. Thus, if the futures price is 113 when the hedge is set, the manager locks in a sale price of 144.979 (113 times 1.283) for September 1999 delivery, regardless of where rates are in September 1999. Exhibit 1 shows the cash flows for a number of final prices for this issue and illustrates how cash flows on the futures contracts offset gains or losses relative to the target price of 144.979.

Let's look at all of the columns in Exhibit 56–1 and explain the computations for one of the scenarios — that is, for one actual sale price for the $11\frac{1}{4}\%$ Treasury bond. Consider the first actual sale price of 140. By convergence, at the delivery date the final futures price shown in Column (2) must equal the Treasury bond's actual sale price adjusted by the conversion factor. Specifically, the adjustment is as follows. We know that

$$\text{converted price} = \text{Treasury bond's price} \times \text{conversion factor}$$

and by convergence

$$\text{final futures price} = \text{converted price}$$

so that

$$\text{final futures price} = \text{Treasury bond's actual sale price} \times \text{conversion factor}$$

Thus to compute the final futures price in Column (2) of Exhibit 56–1 given the Treasury bond's actual sale price in Column (1), the following is computed:

---

2. These delivery options are explained in Chapter 52.

**EXHIBIT 56–1**

Treasury Issue Hedge Held to Delivery

Instrument to be hedged: $100 million 11¼% Treasury Bonds of 2/15/15
Conversion factor for September 1999 = 1.283
Price of futures contract when sold = 113
Target price = (1.283 × 113) = 144.979
Par value hedged = $100,000,000
Number of futures contracts = 1,283
Futures position = Target = $144,979,000

| (1) | (2) | (3) | (4) | (5) | (6) |
|-----|-----|-----|-----|-----|-----|
| Actual Price for 11.25% T-Bonds | Final Futures Price[1] | Market Value of Treasury Bonds | Value of Futures Position[2] | Gain or Loss from Futures Position[2] | Effective Sale Price[3] |
| 140 | 109.1192518 | 140,000,000 | 140,000,000 | 4,979,000 | 144,979,000 |
| 141 | 109.898675 | 141,000,000 | 141,000,000 | 3,979,000 | 144,979,000 |
| 142 | 110.6780982 | 142,000,000 | 142,000,000 | 2,979,000 | 144,979,000 |
| 143 | 111.4575214 | 143,000,000 | 143,000,000 | 1,979,000 | 144,979,000 |
| 144 | 112.2369447 | 144,000,000 | 144,000,000 | 979,000 | 144,979,000 |
| 145 | 113.0163679 | 145,000,000 | 145,000,000 | −21,000 | 144,979,000 |
| 146 | 113.7957911 | 146,000,000 | 146,000,000 | −1,021,000 | 144,979,000 |
| 147 | 114.5752143 | 147,000,000 | 147,000,000 | −2,021,000 | 144,979,000 |
| 148 | 115.3546376 | 148,000,000 | 148,000,000 | −3,021,000 | 144,979,000 |
| 149 | 116.1340608 | 149,000,000 | 149,000,000 | −4,021,000 | 144,979,000 |
| 150 | 116.913484 | 150,000,000 | 150,000,000 | −5,021,000 | 144,979,000 |
| 151 | 117.6929072 | 151,000,000 | 151,000,000 | −6,021,000 | 144,979,000 |
| 152 | 118.4723305 | 152,000,000 | 152,000,000 | −7,021,000 | 144,979,000 |
| 153 | 119.2517537 | 153,000,000 | 153,000,000 | −8,021,000 | 144,979,000 |
| 154 | 120.0311769 | 154,000,000 | 154,000,000 | −9,021,000 | 144,979,000 |
| 155 | 120.8106002 | 155,000,000 | 155,000,000 | −10,021,000 | 144,979,000 |

[1] By convergence, must equal bond price divided by the conversion factor.
[2] Bond futures trade in even increments of 1/32. Accordingly, the futures prices and margin flows are only approximate.
[3] Transaction costs and the financing of margin flows are ignored.

$$\text{final futures price} = \frac{\text{Treasury bonds actual sale price}}{\text{conversion factor}}$$

Since the conversion factor is 1.283 for the 11¼% Treasury issue, for the first actual sale price of 140, the final futures price is

$$\text{final futures price} = \frac{140}{1.283} = 109.1193$$

Column (3) shows the market value of the Treasury bonds. This is found by multiplying the actual sale price in Column (1) by 100 to obtain the actual sale price per \$1 of par value and then multiplying by the \$100 million par value. That is,

market value of Treasury bonds = (actual sale price/100) × \$100,000,000

For the actual sale price of 140, the value in Column (3) is

$$\text{market value of Treasury bonds} = (140/100) \times \$100,000,000$$
$$= \$140,000,000$$

Column (4) shows the value of the futures position at the delivery date. This value is computed by first dividing the futures price shown in Column (2) by 100 to obtain the futures price per \$1 of par value. Then this value is multiplied by the par value per contract of \$100,000 and further multiplied by the number of futures contracts. That is,

value of futures position
= (final futures price/100) × \$100,0000 × number of futures contracts

In our illustration, the number of futures contracts is 1,283. For the actual sale price of the bond of 140, the final futures price is 109.1193. So, the value shown in Column (4) is

$$\text{value of futures position} = (109.1193/100) \times \$100,000 \times 113$$
$$= \$140,000,062$$

The value shown in Column (4) is \$140,000,000 because the final futures price of 109.1193 was rounded. Using more decimal places the value would be \$140,000,000.

Now let's look at the gain or loss from the futures position. This value is shown in Column (5). Recall that the futures contract was shorted. The futures price at which the contracts were sold was 113. So, if the final futures price exceeds 113, this means that there is a loss on the futures position—that is, the futures contract is purchased at a price greater than for which it was sold. In contrast, if the futures price is less than 113, this means that there is a gain on the futures position—that is, the futures contract is purchased at a price less than for which it was sold. The gain or loss is determined by the following formula:

(113/100 − final futures price/100) × \$100,000 × number of futures contracts

In our illustration, for a final futures price of 109.1193 and 1,283 futures contracts, we have

$$(113/100 - 109.1193/100) \times \$100,000 \times 1,283 = \$4,978,938.1$$

The value shown in Column (5) is \$4,979,000 because that is the more precise value using more decimal places for the final futures price than shown in Exhibit 56–1. The value is positive which means that there is a gain in the futures position. Note that for all the final futures prices above 113 in Exhibit 56–1, there is a negative value which means that there is a loss on the futures position.

Finally, Column (6) shows the effective sale price for the Treasury bond. This value is found as follows:

effective sale price for Treasury bond
  = actual sale price of Treasury bond + gain or loss on futures position

For the actual sale price of $140 million, the gain is $4,979,000. Therefore the effective sale price for the Treasury bond is

$$\$140,000,000 + \$4,979,000 = \$144,979,000$$

Note that this is the target price for the Treasury bond. In fact, it can be seen from Column (6) of Exhibit 56–1 that the effective sale price for all the actual sale prices for the Treasury bond is the target price. However, the target price is determined by the futures price, so the target price may be higher or lower than the cash (spot) market price when the hedge is set.

When we admit the possibility that bonds other than the deliverable issue used in our illustration can be delivered, and that it might be advantageous to deliver other issues, the situation becomes somewhat more involved. In this more realistic case, the manager may decide not to deliver this issue, but if she does decide to deliver it, the manager is still assured of receiving an effective sale price of approximately 144.979. If the manager does not deliver this issue, it would be because another issue can be delivered more cheaply, and thus the manager does better than the targeted price.

In summary, if a manager establishes a futures hedge that is held until delivery, the manager can be assured of receiving an effective price dictated by the futures rate (not the spot rate) on the day the hedge is set.

***The Target for Hedges with Short Holding Periods.*** When a manager must lift (remove) a hedge prior to the delivery date, the effective rate that is obtained is much more likely to approximate the current spot rate than the futures rate the shorter the term of the hedge. The critical difference between this hedge and the hedge held to the delivery date is that convergence will generally not take place by the termination date of the hedge.

To illustrate why a manager should expect the hedge to lock in the spot rate rather than the futures rate for very short-lived hedges, let's return to the simplified example used earlier to illustrate a hedge to the delivery date. It is assumed that this issue is the only deliverable Treasury bond for the Treasury bond futures contract. Suppose that the hedge is set three months before the delivery date and the manager plans to lift the hedge after one day. It is much more likely that the spot price of the bond will move parallel to the converted futures price (that is, the futures price times the conversion factor), than that the spot price and the converted futures price will converge by the time the hedge is lifted.

A one-day hedge is, admittedly, an extreme example. Other than underwriters, dealers, and traders who reallocate assets very frequently, few money managers are interested in such a short horizon. The very short-term hedge does, however, illustrate a very important point: *when hedging, a manager should not expect to lock in the futures rate (or price) just because he or she is hedging with futures contracts.* The futures rate is locked in only if the hedge is held until delivery, at which point convergence must take place. If the hedge is held for only one day, the manager should expect to lock in the one-day forward rate,[3] which will very nearly equal the spot rate. Generally hedges are held for more than one day, but not necessarily to delivery.

***How the Basis Affects the Target Rate for a Hedge.*** The proper target for a hedge that is to be lifted prior to the delivery date depends on the basis. The *basis* is simply the difference between the spot (cash) price of a security and its futures price; that is:

$$\text{basis} = \text{spot price} - \text{futures price}$$

In the bond market, a problem arises when trying to make practical use of the concept of the basis. The quoted futures price does not equal the price that one receives at delivery. For the Treasury bond and note futures contracts, the actual futures price equals the quoted futures price times the appropriate conversion factor. Consequently, to be useful the basis in the bond market should be defined using actual futures delivery prices rather than quoted futures prices. Thus, the price basis for bonds should be redefined as:

$$\text{price basis} = \text{spot price} - \text{futures delivery price}$$

For hedging purposes it is also frequently useful to define the basis in terms of interest rates rather than prices. The *rate basis* is defined as:

$$\text{rate basis} = \text{spot rate} - \text{futures rate}$$

where spot rate refers to the current rate on the instrument to be hedged and the futures rate is the interest rate corresponding to the futures delivery price of the deliverable instrument.

The rate basis is helpful in explaining why the two views of hedges explained earlier are expected to lock in such different rates. To see this, we first define the *target rate basis*. This is defined as the expected rate basis on the day the hedge is lifted. A hedge lifted on the delivery date is expected to have, and by convergence will have, a zero rate basis when the hedge is lifted. Thus, the target rate for the hedge should be the rate on the futures contract plus the expected rate basis of zero, or in other words, just the futures rate. When a hedge is lifted prior to the delivery date, one would not expect the basis to

---

3. Forward rates were covered in Chapter 6.

change very much in one day, so the target rate basis equals the futures rate plus the current difference between the spot rate and futures rate, i.e., the current spot rate.

The manager can set the target rate for any hedge equal to the futures rate plus the target rate basis. That is,

target rate for hedge = futures rate + target rate basis

If projecting the basis in terms of price rather than rate is more manageable (as is often the case for intermediate- and long-term futures), it is easier to work with the target price basis instead of the target rate basis. The *target price basis* is just the projected price basis for the day the hedge is to be lifted. For a deliverable security, the target for the hedge then becomes

target price for hedge = futures delivery price + target price basis

The idea of a target price or rate basis explains why a hedge held until the delivery date locks in a price with certainty, and other hedges do not. The examples have shown that this is true. For the hedge held to delivery, there is no uncertainty surrounding the target basis; by convergence, the basis on the day the hedge is lifted is certain to be zero. For the short-lived hedge, the basis will probably approximate the current basis when the hedge is lifted, but its actual value is not known. For hedges longer than one day but ending prior to the futures delivery date, there can be considerable basis risk because the basis on the day the hedge is lifted can end up being anywhere within a wide range. Thus, the uncertainty surrounding the outcome of a hedge is directly related to the uncertainty surrounding the basis on the day the hedge is lifted (i.e., the uncertainty surrounding the target basis).

The uncertainty about the value of the basis at the time the hedge is removed is called *basis risk*. For a given investment horizon, hedging substitutes basis risk for price risk. Thus, one trades the uncertainty of the price of the hedged security for the uncertainty of the basis. Consequently, when hedges do not produce the desired results, it is customary to place the blame on basis risk. However, basis risk is the real culprit only if the target for the hedge is properly defined. Basis risk should refer only to the unexpected or unpredictable part of the relationship between cash and futures prices. The fact that this relationship changes over time does not in itself imply that there is basis risk.

Basis risk, properly defined, refers only to the uncertainty associated with the target rate basis or target price basis. Accordingly, it is imperative that the target basis be properly defined if one is to correctly assess the risk and expected return in a hedge.

### Determining the Number of Futures Contracts
The final step that must be determined before the hedge is set is the number of futures contracts needed for the hedge. This is called the *hedge ratio*. Usually the hedge ratio is expressed in terms of relative par amounts. Accordingly, a

hedge ratio of 1.20 means that for every $1 million par value of securities to be hedged, one needs $1.2 million par value of futures contracts to offset the risk. *In our discussion, the values are defined so that the hedge ratio is the number of futures contracts.*

Earlier, we defined a cross hedge in the futures market as a hedge in which the security to be hedged is not deliverable on the futures contract used in the hedge. For example, a manager who wants to hedge the sale price of long-term corporate bonds might hedge with the Treasury bond futures contract, but since non-Treasury bonds cannot be delivered in satisfaction of the contract, the hedge would be considered a cross hedge. A manger might also want to hedge a rate that is of the same quality as the rate specified in one of the contracts, but that has a different maturity. For example, it is necessary to cross hedge a Treasury bond, note, or bill with a maturity that does not qualify for delivery on any futures contract. Thus, when the security to be hedged differs from the futures contract specification in terms of either quality or maturity, one is led to the cross hedge.

Conceptually, cross hedging is somewhat more complicated than hedging deliverable securities, because it involves two relationships. First, there is the relationship between the cheapest-to-deliver (CTD) issue and the futures contract. Second, there is the relationship between the security to be hedged and the CTD. Practical considerations may at times lead a manager to shortcut this two-step relationship and focus directly on the relationship between the security to be hedged and the futures contract, thus ignoring the CTD altogether. However, in so doing, a manager runs the risk of miscalculating the target rate and the risk in the hedge. Furthermore, if the hedge does not perform as expected, the shortcut makes it difficult to tell why the hedge did not work out as expected.

The key to minimizing risk in a cross hedge is to choose the right number of futures contracts. This depends on the relative dollar duration of the bond to be hedged and the futures position. Equation (56–4) indicated the number of futures contract to achieve a particular target dollar duration. The objective in hedging is to make the target dollar duration equal to zero. Substituting zero for target dollar duration in Eq. (56–4) we obtain:

$$\text{number of futures contracts} = -\frac{\text{current dollar duration without futures}}{\text{dollar duration per futures contract}}$$

$$(56–5)$$

To calculate the dollar duration of a bond, the manager must know the precise point in time that the dollar duration is to be calculated (because volatility generally declines as a bond matures) as well as the price or yield at which to calculate dollar duration (because higher yields generally reduce dollar duration for a given yield change). The relevant point in the life of the bond for calculating volatility is the point at which the hedge will be lifted. Dollar duration at any other point is essentially irrelevant because the goal is to lock in a price or rate only on that particular day. Similarly, the relevant yield at which to calculate dollar duration initially is the target yield. Consequently, the numerator of Eq. (56–5) is the dollar duration on the date the hedge is expected to be delivered. The yield that is to be used on this date in order to determine the dollar duration is the forward rate.

Let's look at how we apply Eq. (56–5) when using the Treasury bond futures contract to hedge. The number of futures contracts will be affected by the dollar duration of the CTD issue. We can modify Eq. (56–5) as follows:

$$\text{number of futures contracts} = -\frac{\text{current dollar duration without futures}}{\text{dollar duration of the CTD issue}}$$
$$\times \frac{\text{dollar duration of the CTD issue}}{\text{dollar duration per futures contract}}$$
$$(56\text{–}6)$$

As noted earlier, the conversion ratio for the CTD issue is a good approximation of the second ratio. Thus, Eq. (56–6) can be rewritten as

$$\text{number of futures contracts} = -\frac{\text{current dollar duration without futures}}{\text{dollar duration of the CTD issues}}$$
$$\times \text{conversion factor for the CTD issue}$$
$$(56\text{–}7)$$

***An Illustration.***    An example for a single bond shows why dollar duration weighting leads to the correct number of contracts to use to hedge. The hedge illustrated is a cross hedge. Suppose that on 6/24/99, a manager owned $10 million par value of a 6.25% Fannie Mae (FNMA) option-free bond maturing on 5/15/29 selling at 88.39 to yield 7.20%. The manager wants to sell September 1999 Treasury bond futures to hedge a future sale of the FNMA bond. At the time, the price of the September Treasury bond futures contract was at 113. The CTD issue was the 11.25% of 2/15/15 issue that was trading at the time at 146.19 to yield 6.50%. The conversion factor for the CTD issue was 1.283. To simplify, assume that the yield spread between the FNMA bond and the CTD issue remains at 0.70% (i.e., 70 basis points) and that the anticipated sale date is the last business day in September 1999.

The target price for hedging the CTD issue would be 144.979 (from 113 × 1.283), and the target yield would be 6.56% (the yield at a price of 144.979). Since the yield on the FNMA bond is assumed to stay at 0.70% above the yield on the CTD issue, the target yield for the FNMA bond would be 7.26%. The corresponding price for the FNMA bond for this target yield is 87.76. At these target levels, the dollar duration for a 50 basis point change in rates for the CTD issue and FNMA bond per $100 of par value is $6.255 and $5.453, respectively. As indicated earlier, all these calculations are made using a settlement date equal to the anticipated sale date, in this case the end of September 1999. The dollar duration for $10 million par value of the FNMA bond is then $545,300 ($10 million/100 times $5.453). Per $100,000 par value for the CTD issue, the dollar duration per futures contract is $6,255 ($100,000/100 times $6.255).

Thus, we know

$$\text{current dollar duration without futures}$$
$$= \text{dollar duration of the FNMA bond}$$
$$= \$545,300$$

$$\text{dollar duration of the CTD issue} = \$6,255$$
$$\text{conversion factor for CTD issue} = 1.283$$

Substituting these values into Eq. (56–7) we obtain

$$\text{number of futures contracts} = -\frac{\$545,300}{\$6,255} \times 1.283 = -112 \text{ contracts}$$

Consequently, to hedge the FNMA bond position, 112 Treasury bond futures contracts must be shorted.

Exhibit 56–2 uses scenario analysis to show the outcome of the hedge based on different prices for the FNMA bond at the delivery date of the futures contract. Let's go through each of the columns. Column (1) shows the assumed sale price for the FNMA bond and Column (2) shows the corresponding yield based on the actual sale price in Column (1). This yield is found from the price/yield relationship. Given the assumed sale price for the FNMA bond, the corresponding yield can be determined. Column (3) shows the yield for the CTD issue. This yield is computed based on the assumption regarding the yield spread of 70 basis points between the FNMA bond and the CTD issue. So, by subtracting 70 basis points from the yield for the FNMA bond in Column (2), the yield on the CTD issue (the 11.25% of 2/15/15) is obtained. Given the yield for the CTD issue in Column (3), the price per $100 of par value of the CTD issue can be computed. This CTD price is shown in Column (4).

Now we must move from the price of the CTD issue to the futures price. As explained in the description of the columns in Exhibit 56–1, by dividing the price for the CTD issue shown in Column (4) by the conversion factor of the CTD issue (1.283), the futures price is obtained. This price is shown in Column (5).

The value of the futures position is found in the same way as in Exhibit 56–1. First the futures price per $1 of par value is computed by dividing the futures price by 100. Then this value is multiplied by $100,000 (the par value for the contract) and the number of futures contracts. That is,

$$\text{value of futures position}$$
$$= (\text{futures price}/100) \times \$100,0000 \times \text{number of futures contracts}$$

Since the number of futures contracts sold is 112,

**EXHIBIT   56–2**

Hedging a Nondeliverable Bond to a Delivery Date with Futures

Instrument to be hedged: $10 million FNMA 6.25% of 05/15/29
Price of FNMA as of hedge date (6/24/99) = 88.39
Conversion factor for September 1999 = 1.283
Price of futures contract when sold = 113
Target price for FNMA bonds = 87.76
Par value hedged = $10,000,000
Number of futures contracts = 112
Futures position = $12,656,000
Target market value for FNMA bonds = $8,776,000

| (1) | (2) | (3) | (4) | (5) | (6) | (7) | (8) |
|---|---|---|---|---|---|---|---|
| Actual Sale Price of FNMA Bonds | Yield at Sale | Yield of 11.25% Treasury Bond | Price of 11.25% Treasury Bond | Futures Price | Value of Futures Position | Gain or Loss on Futures Position | Effective Sale Price |
| 8,000,000 | 8.027 | 7.327 | 135.813 | 105.85581 | 11,855,850 | 800,150 | 8,800,150 |
| 8,100,000 | 7.922 | 7.222 | 137.031 | 106.80514 | 11,962,176 | 693,824 | 8,793,824 |
| 8,200,000 | 7.818 | 7.118 | 138.234 | 107.74279 | 12,067,193 | 588,807 | 8,778,807 |
| 8,300,000 | 7.717 | 7.017 | 139,422 | 108.66875 | 12,170,899 | 485,101 | 8,785,101 |
| 8,400,000 | 7.617 | 6.917 | 140.609 | 109.59392 | 12,274,519 | 381,481 | 8,781,481 |
| 8,500,000 | 7.520 | 6.820 | 141.781 | 110.50740 | 12,376,829 | 279,171 | 8,779,171 |
| 8,600,000 | 7.424 | 6.724 | 142.938 | 111.40920 | 12,477,830 | 178,170 | 8,778,170 |
| 8,700,000 | 7.330 | 6.630 | 144.094 | 112.31021 | 12,578,744 | 77,256 | 8,777,256 |
| 8,800,000 | 7.238 | 6.538 | 145.250 | 113.21122 | 12,679,657 | −23,657 | 8,776,343 |
| 8,900,000 | 7.148 | 6.448 | 146.391 | 114.10055 | 12,779,261 | −123,261 | 8,776,739 |
| 9,000,000 | 7.059 | 6.359 | 147.531 | 114.98909 | 12,878,778 | −222,778 | 8,777,222 |
| 9,100,000 | 6.972 | 6.272 | 148.656 | 115.86594 | 12,976,985 | −320,985 | 8,779,015 |
| 9,200,000 | 6.886 | 6.186 | 149.766 | 116.73110 | 13,073,883 | −417,883 | 8,782,117 |
| 9,300,000 | 6.802 | 6.102 | 150.875 | 117.59548 | 13,170,694 | −514,694 | 8,785,306 |
| 9,400,000 | 6.719 | 6.019 | 151.984 | 118.45986 | 13,267,504 | −611,504 | 8,788,496 |
| 9,500,000 | 6.637 | 5.937 | 153.078 | 119.31255 | 13,363,005 | −707,005 | 8,792,995 |

* By assumption, the yield on the cheapest-to-deliver issue is 70 basis points lower than the yield on the FNMA bond.
** By convergence, the futures price equals the price of the cheapest-to-deliver issue divided by 1.283 (the conversion factor).
*** Transaction costs and the financing of margin flows are ignored.

value of futures position = (final futures price/100) × $100,0000 × 112

The values shown in Column (6) use the above formula. Using the first assumed actual sale price for the FNMA of $8 million as an example, the corresponding futures price in Column (5) is 105.85581. Therefore, the value of the futures position is

$$\text{value of futures position} = (105.85581/100) \times \$100,000 \times 112$$
$$= \$11,855,850$$

Now let's calculate the gain or loss on the futures position shown in Column (7). This is done in the same manner as explained for Exhibit 56–1. Since the futures price at which the contracts are sold at the inception of the hedge is 113, the gain or loss on the futures position is found as follows:

(113/100 − final futures price/100) × $100,000 × number of futures contracts

For example, for the first scenario in Exhibit 56–2, the futures price is 105.85581 and 112 futures contract were sold. Therefore,

$$(113/100 - 105.85581/100) \times \$100,000 \times 112 = \$800,150$$

There is a gain from the futures position because the futures price is less than 113. Note that for all the final futures prices above 113 in Exhibit 56–2, there is a negative value which means that there is a loss on the futures position. For all futures prices below 113, there is a loss.

Finally, Column (8) shows the effective sale price for the FNMA bond. This value is found as follows:

effective sale price for FNMA bond
= actual sale price of FNMA bond + gain or loss on futures position

For the actual sale price of $8 million, the gain is $800,150. Therefore the effective sale price for the FNMA bond is

$$\$8,000,000 + \$800,150 = \$8,800,150$$

Looking at Column (8) of Exhibit 56–2 we see that if the simplifying assumptions hold, a futures hedge using the recommended number of futures contracts (112) very nearly locks in the target price for $10 million par value of the FNMA bonds.

**Refining for Changing Yield Spread.**   Another refinement in the hedging strategy is usually necessary for hedging nondeliverable securities. This refinement concerns the assumption about the relative yield spread between the CTD issue and the bond to be hedged. In the prior discussion, we assumed that the yield spread was constant over time. Yield spreads, however, are not constant over time. They vary with the maturity of the instruments in question and the level of rates, as well as with many unpredictable and nonsystematic factors.

Regression analysis allows the manager to capture the relationship between yield levels and yield spreads and use it to advantage. For hedging purposes, the variables are the yield on the bond to be hedged and the yield on the CTD issue. The regression equation takes the form:

yield on bond to be hedged $= a + b \times$ yield on CTD issue $+$ error    (56–8)

The regression procedure provides an estimate of $b$, which is the expected relative yield change in the two bonds. This parameter $b$ is called the *yield beta*. Our example that used constant spreads implicitly assumes that the yield beta, $b$, equals 1.0 and $a$ equals 0.70 (because 0.70 is the assumed spread).

For the two issues in question, that is, the FNMA bond and the CTD issue, suppose the estimated yield beta was 1.05. Thus, yields on the FNMA issue are expected to move 5% more than yields on the Treasury issue. To calculate the number of futures contracts correctly, this fact must be taken into account; thus, the number of futures contracts derived in our earlier example is multiplied by the factor 1.05. Consequently, instead of shorting 112 Treasury bond futures contracts to hedge $10 million of the FNMA bond, the investor would short 118 (rounded up) contracts.

The formula for the number of futures contracts is revised as follows to incorporate the impact of the yield beta:

$$\text{number of futures contracts} = -\frac{\text{current dollar duration without futures}}{\text{dollar duration of the CTD issue}}$$
$$\times \text{ conversion factor for the CTD issue}$$
$$\times \text{ yield data}$$

(56–9)

where the yield beta is derived from the yield of the bond to be hedged regressed on the yield of the CTD issue [Eq. (56–8)].

The effect of a change in the CTD issue and the yield spread can be assessed before the hedge is implemented. An exhibit similar to that of Exhibit 56–2 can be constructed under a wide range of assumptions. For example, at different yield levels at the date the hedge is to be lifted (the second column in Exhibit 56–2), a different yield spread may be appropriate and a different acceptable issue will be the CTD issue. The manager can determine what this will do to the outcome of the hedge.

## Monitoring and Evaluating the Hedge

After a target is determined and a hedge is set, there are two remaining tasks. The hedge must be monitored during its life, and evaluated after it is over. Most futures hedges require very little active monitoring during their life. In fact, overactive management poses more of a threat to most hedges than does inactive management. The reason for this is that the manager usually will not receive enough new information during the life of the hedge to justify a change in the hedging strategy. For example, it is not advisable to readjust the hedge ratio every day in response to a new data point and a possible corresponding change in the estimated value of the yield beta.

There are, however, exceptions to this general rule. As rates change, dollar duration changes. Consequently, the hedge ratio may change slightly. In other cases, there may be sound economic reasons to believe that the yield beta has changed. While there are exceptions, the best approach is usually to let a hedge run its course using the original hedge ratio with only slight adjustments.

A hedge can normally be evaluated only after it has been lifted. Evaluation involves, first, an assessment of how closely the hedge locked in the target rate—that is, how much error there was in the hedge. To provide a meaningful interpretation of the error, the manager should calculate how far from the target the sale (or purchase) would have been, had there been no hedge at all. One good reason for evaluating a completed hedge is to ascertain the sources of error in the hedge in the hope that the manager will gain insights that can be used to advantage in subsequent hedges. A manager will find that there are three major sources of hedging errors:

1. The dollar duration for the hedged instrument was incorrect.

2. The projected value of the basis at the date the hedge is removed can be in error.

3. The parameters estimated from the regression (*a* and *b*) can be inaccurate.

Recall from the calculation of duration in Chapter 5 that interest rates are changed up and down by a small number of basis points and the security is revalued. The two recalculated values are used in the numerator of the duration formula. The first problem listed above recognizes that the instrument to be hedged may be a complex instrument (i.e., one with embedded options) and that the valuation model does not do a good job of valuing the security when interest rates change.

The second major source of errors in a hedge—an inaccurate projected value of the basis—is the more difficult problem. Unfortunately, there are no satisfactory simple models like the regression that can be applied to the basis. Simple models of the basis violate certain equilibrium relationships for bonds that should not be violated. On the other hand, theoretically rigorous models are very unintuitive and usually soluble only by complex numerical methods. Modeling the basis is undoubtedly one of the most important and difficult problems that managers seeking to hedge face.

## HEDGING WITH OPTIONS

Hedging strategies using options involve taking a position in an option and a position in the underlying bond in such a way that changes in the value of one position will offset any unfavorable price (interest rate) movement in the other position. We begin with the basic hedging strategies using options. Then we illustrate these basic strategies using futures options to hedge the FNMA bond for which a futures hedge was used earlier in this chapter. Using futures options in our illustration of hedging the bond is a worthwhile exercise because it shows how complicated hedging with futures options is and the key parameters involved in the process. We also compare the outcome of hedging with futures and hedging with futures options.

## Basic Hedging Strategies

There are three popular hedging strategies: (1) a protective put buying strategy, (2) a covered call writing strategy, and (3) a collar strategy. We discuss each strategy below.

### Protective Put Buying Strategy

Consider a manager who has a bond and wants to hedge against rising interest rates. The most obvious options hedging strategy is to buy put options on bonds. This hedging strategy is referred to as a *protective put buying strategy*. The puts are usually out-of-the-money puts and may be either puts on cash bonds or puts on interest rate futures. If interest rates rise, the puts will increase in value (holding other factors constant), offsetting some or all of the loss on the bonds in the portfolio.

This strategy is a simple combination of a long put option with a long position in a cash bond. Such a position has limited downside ask, but large upside potential. However, if rates fall, the price appreciation on the bonds in the portfolio will be diminished by the amount paid to purchase the puts. Exhibit 56–3 compares the protective put buying strategy to an unhedged position.

The protective put buying strategy is very often compared to purchasing insurance. Like insurance, the premium paid for the protection is nonrefundable and is paid before the coverage begins. The degree to which a portfolio is protected depends upon the strike price of the options; thus, the strike price is often compared to the deductible on an insurance policy. The lower the deductible (that is, the higher the strike price for the put), the greater the level of protection and the more the protection costs. Conversely, the higher the deductible (the lower the strike price on the put), the more the portfolio can lose in value; but the cost of the insurance is lower. Exhibit 56–4 compares an unhedged position with several protective put positions, each with a different strike price, or level of protection. As the exhibit shows, no one strategy dominates any other strategy, in the sense of performing better at all possible rate levels. Consequently, it is impossible to say that one strike price is necessarily the "best" strike price, or even that buying protective puts is necessarily better than doing nothing at all.

**EXHIBIT   56–3**

Protective Put Buying Strategy

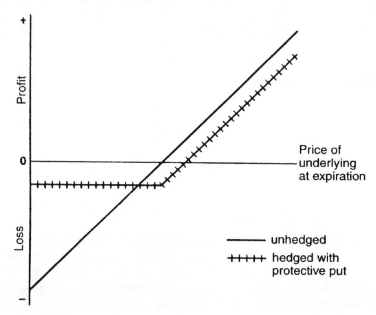

## Covered Call Writing Strategy

Another options hedging strategy used by many portfolio managers is to sell calls against the bond portfolio. This hedging strategy is called a *covered call writing strategy*. The calls that are sold are usually out-of-the-money calls, and can be either calls on cash bonds or calls on interest rate futures. Covered call writing is just an outright long position combined with a short call position. Obviously, this strategy entails much more downside risk than buying a put to protect the value of the portfolio. In fact, many portfolio managers do not consider covered call writing a hedge.

Regardless of how it is classified, it is important to recognize that while covered call writing has substantial downside risk, it has less downside risk than an unhedged long position alone. On the downside, the difference between the long position alone and the covered call writing strategy is the premium received for the calls that are sold. This premium acts as a cushion for downward movements in prices, reducing losses when rates rise. The cost of obtaining this cushion is that the manager gives up some of the potential on the upside. When rates decline, the call options become greater liabilities for the covered call writer. These incremental liabilities decrease the gains the manager would otherwise have realized on the portfolio in a declining rate environment. Thus, the covered call writer gives up some (or all) of the upside potential of the portfolio

**E X H I B I T   56–4**

Protective Put Buying Strategy with Different Strike Prices

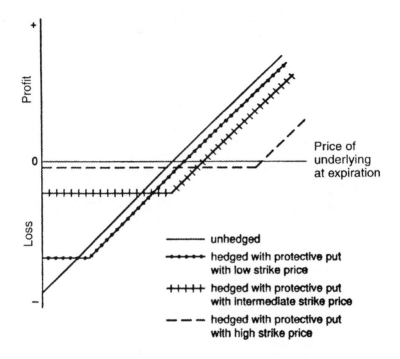

in return for a cushion on the downside. The more upside potential that is forfeited (that is, the lower the strike price on the calls), the more cushion there is on the downside. Exhibit 56–5 illustrates this point by comparing an unhedged position to several covered call writing strategies, each with a different strike price. Like the protective put buying strategy, there is no "right" strike price for the covered call writer.

**Collar Strategy**
There are other hedging strategies using options frequently used by managers. For example, many managers combine the protective put buying strategy and the covered call writing strategy. By combining a long position in an out-of-the-money put and a short position in an out-of-the-money call, the manager creates a long position in a *collar*. Consequently, this hedging strategy is called a *collar strategy*. The manager who uses the collar eliminates part of the portfolio's downside risk by giving up part of its upside potential. A long position hedged with a collar is shown in Exhibit 56–6.

The collar in some ways resembles the protective put, in some ways resembles covered call writing, and in some ways resembles an unhedged position.

**EXHIBIT 56-5**

Covered Call Writing Strategy with Different Strike Prices

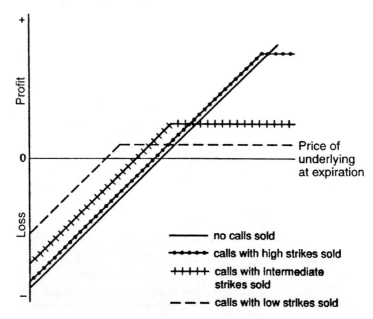

The collar is like the protective put buying strategy in that it limits the possible losses on the portfolio if interest rates go up. Like the covered call writing strategy, the portfolio's upside potential is limited. Like an unhedged position, within the range defined by the strike prices the value of the portfolio varies with interest rates.

### Selecting the "Best" Strategy

Comparing the two basic strategies for hedging with options, one cannot say that the protective put buying strategy or the covered call writing strategy is necessarily the better or more correct options hedge. The best strategy (and the best strike price) depends upon the manager's view of the market. Purchasing a put and paying the required premium is appropriate if the manager is fundamentally bearish. If, instead, the manager is neutral to mildly bearish, it is better to receive the premium on the covered call writing strategy. If the manager prefers to take no view on the market at all, and as little risk as possible, then the futures hedge is the most appropriate. If the manager is fundamentally bullish, then no hedge at all is probably the best strategy.

## Steps in Options Hedging

Like hedging with futures, there are steps that managers should consider before setting their hedges. These steps include:

**E X H I B I T   56–6**

Long Position Hedged with a Collar

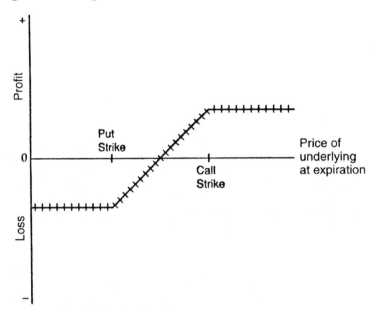

*Step 1: Determine the option contract that is the best hedging vehicle.*
The best option contract to use depends upon several factors. These
include option price, liquidity, and correlation with the bond(s) to be
hedged. In price-inefficient markets, the option price is important because not all options will be priced in the same manner or with the
same volatility assumption. Consequently, some options may be overpriced and some underpriced. Obviously, with other factors equal, it is
better to use the underpriced options when buying and the overpriced
options when selling.

Whenever there is a possibility that the option position may be
closed out prior to expiration, liquidity is also an important consideration. If the particular option is illiquid, closing out a position may be
prohibitively expensive, and the manager loses the flexibility of closing out positions early, or rolling into other positions that may become more attractive. Correlation with the underlying bond(s) to be
hedged is another factor in selecting the right contract. The higher the
correlation, the more precisely the final profit and loss can be defined
as a function of the final level of rates. Poor correlation leads to more
uncertainty.

While most of the uncertainty in an options hedge usually comes
from the uncertainty of interest rates themselves, the degree of corre-

lation between the bonds to be hedged and the instruments underlying the options contracts add to that risk. The lower the correlation, the greater the risk.

*Step 2: Find the appropriate strike price.* For a cross hedge, the manager will want to convert the strike price on the options that are actually bought or sold into an equivalent strike price for the actual bonds being hedged.

*Step 3: Determine the number of contracts.* The hedge ratio is the number of options to buy or sell.

Steps 2 and 3, determining the strike price and the number of contracts, can best be explained with examples using futures options.

## Protective Put Buying Strategy Using Futures Options

As explained above, managers who want to hedge their bond positions against a possible increase in interest rates will find that buying puts on futures is one of the easiest ways to purchase protection against rising rates. To illustrate a protective put buying strategy, we can use the same FNMA bond that we used to demonstrate how to hedge with Treasury bond futures.[4] In that example, a manager held $10 million par value of a 6.25% FNMA bond maturing 5/15/29 and used September 1999 Treasury bond futures to lock in a sale price for those bonds on the futures delivery date. Now we want to show how the manager could use futures options instead of futures to protect against rising rates.

On 6/24/99 the FNMA bond was selling for 88.39 to yield 7.20% and the CTD issue's yield was 6.50%. For simplicity, it is assumed that the yield spread between the FNMA bond and the CTD issue remains at 70 basis points.

### Selecting the Strike Price

The manager must determine the minimum price that he wants to establish for the FNMA bonds. In our illustration we will assume that the minimum price before the cost of the put options purchased is 84.453. This is equivalent to saying that the manager wants to establish a strike price for a put option on the

---

4. As explained in Chapter 52, futures options on Treasury bonds are more commonly used by institutional investors. The mechanics of futures options are as follows. If a put option is exercised, the option buyer receives a short position in the underlying futures contract and the option writer receives the corresponding long position. The futures price for both positions is the strike price for the put option. The exchange then marks the positions to market and the futures price for both positions is then the current futures price. If a call option is exercised, the option buyer receives a long position in the underlying futures contract and the option writer receives the corresponding short position. The futures price for both positions is the strike price for the call option. The exchange then marks the positions to market and the futures price for both positions is then the current futures price.

hedged bonds of 84.453. But, the manager is not buying a put option on the FNMA bond. He is buying a put option on a Treasury bond futures contract. Therefore, the manager must determine the strike price for a put option on a Treasury bond futures contract that is equivalent to a strike price of 84.453 for the FNMA bond.

This can be done with the help of Exhibit 56–7. We begin at the top left hand box of the exhibit. Since the minimum price is 84.453 for the FNMA bond, this means that the manager is attempting to establish a maximum yield of 7.573%. This is found from the relationship between price and yield: given a price of 84.453 for the FNMA bond, this equivalent to a yield of 7.573%. (This gets us to the lower left hand box in Exhibit 56–7.) From the assumption that the spread between the FNMA bond and the cheapest-to-deliver issue is a constant 70 basis points, setting a maximum yield of 7.573% for the FNMA bond is equivalent to setting a maximum yield of 6.873% for the cheapest-to-deliver issue. (Now we are at the lower box in the middle column of Exhibit 56–7.) Given the yield of 6.873% for the CTD issue, the minimum price before the cost of the puts purchased can be determined (the top box in the middle column of the exhibit). A 6.873% yield for the CTD issue gives us a price of 141.136. (This is determined from the characteristics of the CTD issue.) The corresponding futures price is found by dividing the price of the CTD issue by the conversion factor. This gets us to the box in the right hand column of Exhibit 56–8. Since the conversion factor is 1.283, the futures price is about 110

**E X H I B I T   56–7**

Calculating Equivalent Strike Prices and Yields for Hedging with Futures Options

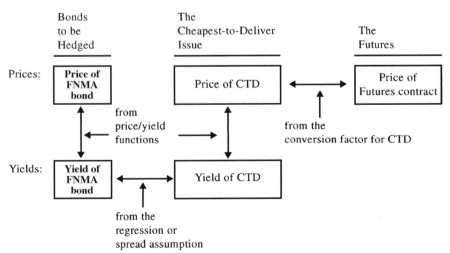

**EXHIBIT  56–8**

## Hedging a Nondeliverable Bond to a Delivery Date with Puts on Futures

Instrument to be hedged: $10 million FNMA 6.25% of 05/15/29
Price of FNMA as of hedge date (6/24/99) = 88.39
Conversion factor for September 1999 = 1.283
Price of futures contract when sold = 113
Target price per bond for FNMA bonds = 84.453
Effective minimum sale price = 83.908
Par value hedged = $10,000,000
Strike price for put = 110
Number of puts on futures = 109
Price per contract = $500.00
Cost of put position = $54,500

| (1) | (2) | (3) | (4) | (5) | (6) | (7) | (8) |
|---|---|---|---|---|---|---|---|
| Actual Sale Price of FNMA Bonds | Yield at Sale | Yield of 11.25% Treasury Bond | Price of 11.25% Treasury Bond[1] | Futures Price | Value of Put Options[2] | Cost of Put Position | Effective Sale Price[3] |
| 8,000,000 | 8.027 | 7.327 | 135.813 | 105.85581 | 451,717 | 54,500 | 8,397,217 |
| 8,100,000 | 7.922 | 7.222 | 137.031 | 106.80514 | 348,239 | 54,500 | 8,393,739 |
| 8,200,000 | 7.818 | 7.118 | 138.234 | 107.74279 | 246,036 | 54,500 | 8,391,536 |
| 8,300,000 | 7.717 | 7.017 | 139.422 | 108.66875 | 145,107 | 54,500 | 8,390,607 |
| 8,400,000 | 7.617 | 6.917 | 140.609 | 109.59392 | 44,263 | 54,500 | 8,389,763 |
| 8,500,000 | 7.520 | 6.820 | 141.781 | 110.50740 | 0 | 54,500 | 8,445,500 |
| 8,600,000 | 7.424 | 6.724 | 142.938 | 111.40920 | 0 | 54,500 | 8,545,500 |
| 8,700,000 | 7.330 | 6.630 | 144.094 | 112.31021 | 0 | 54,500 | 8,645,500 |
| 8,800,000 | 7.238 | 6.538 | 145.250 | 113.21122 | 0 | 54,500 | 8,745,500 |
| 8,900,000 | 7.148 | 6.448 | 145.391 | 114.10055 | 0 | 54,500 | 8,845,500 |
| 9,000,000 | 7.059 | 6.359 | 147.531 | 114.98909 | 0 | 54,500 | 8,945,500 |
| 9,100,000 | 6.972 | 6.272 | 148.656 | 115.86594 | 0 | 54,500 | 9,045,500 |
| 9,200,000 | 6.886 | 6.186 | 149.766 | 116.73110 | 0 | 54,500 | 9,145,500 |
| 9,300,000 | 6.802 | 6.102 | 150.875 | 117.59548 | 0 | 54,500 | 9,245,500 |
| 9,400,000 | 6.719 | 6.019 | 151.984 | 118.45986 | 0 | 54,500 | 9,345,500 |
| 9,500,000 | 6.637 | 5.937 | 153.078 | 119.31255 | 0 | 54,500 | 9,445,500 |

[1] These numbers are approximate because futures trade in 32nds.
[2] From Maximum of [(110/100 − Futures price/100) × $100,000 × 109, 0]
[3] Does not include transaction costs or the financing of the options position.

(141.136 divided by 1.283). This means that a strike price of 110 for a put option on a Treasury bond futures contract is roughly equivalent to a put option on our FNMA bond with a strike price of 84.453.

The foregoing steps are always necessary to obtain the appropriate strike price on a put futures option. The process is not complicated. It simply involves (1) the relationship between price and yield, (2) the assumed relationship between the yield spread between the bonds to be hedged and the cheapest-to-deliver issue, and (3) the conversion factor for the cheapest-to-deliver issue. As with hedging employing futures illustrated in the previous chapter, the success of the hedging strategy will depend on (1) whether the cheapest-to-deliver issue changes and (2) the yield spread between the bonds to be hedged and the cheapest-to-deliver issue.

### Calculating the Number of Options Contracts

The hedge ratio is determined using the following equation similar to Eq. (56–7) since we will assume a constant yield spread between the bond to be hedged and the cheapest-to-deliver issue:

$$\text{number of options contracts} = \frac{\text{current dollar duration without options}}{\text{dollar duration of the CTD issue} \times \text{conversion factor for CTD issue}}$$

The dollar durations are as follows per 50 basis point change in rates:

$$\text{current dollar duration without options} = \$512{,}320$$
$$\text{dollar duration of the CTD issue} = \$6{,}021$$

Notice that the dollar durations are different from those used in calculating the number of futures contracts for the futures hedge. This is because the dollar durations are calculated at prices corresponding to the strike price of the futures option (110), rather than the futures price (113). The number of futures options contracts is then:

$$\text{number of options contracts} = \frac{\$512{,}320}{\$6{,}021} \times 1.283 = 109 \text{ put options}$$

Thus, to hedge the FNMA bond position with put options on Treasury bond futures, 109 put options must be purchased.

### Outcome of the Hedge

To create a table for the protective put hedge, we can use some of the numbers from Exhibit 56–2. Exhibit 56–8 shows the scenario analysis for the protective put buying strategy. The first five columns are the same as in Exhibit 56–2. For the put option hedge, Column (6) shows the value of the put option position at the expiration date. The value of the put option position at the expiration date will be equal to zero if the futures price is greater than or equal to the strike price of 110. If the futures price is below 110, then the options expire in the money and the value of the put option position is:

value of put option position
= (110/100 − futures price/100) × \$100,000 × number of put options

For example, for the first scenario in Exhibit 56–8 of \$8 million for the actual sale price of the FNMA bond, the corresponding futures price is 105.85581. The number of put options purchased is 109. Therefore,

$$(110/100 - 105.85581/100) \times \$100,000 \times 109 = \$45,717$$

The effective sale price for the FNMA bonds is then equal to

effective sale price = actual sale price + value of put option position
− option cost

Let's look at the option cost. Suppose that the price of the put option with a strike price of 110 is \$500 per contract. With a total of 109 options, the cost of the protection is \$54,500 (109 × \$500, not including financing costs and commissions). This cost is shown in Column (7) and is equivalent to 0.545 per \$100 par value hedged.

The effective sale price for the FNMA bonds for each scenario is shown in the last column of Exhibit 56–8. This effective sale price is never less than 83.908. This equals the price of the FNMA bonds equivalent to the futures strike price of 110 (i.e., 84.453), minus the cost of the puts (that is, 0.545 per \$100 par value hedged). This minimum effective price is something that can be calculated before the hedge is ever initiated. (As prices decline, the effective sale price actually exceeds the target minimum sale price of 83.908 by a small amount. This is due only to rounding and the fact that the hedge ratio is left unaltered although the relative dollar durations that go into the hedge ratio calculation change as yields change.) As prices increase, however, the effective sale price of the hedged bonds increases as well; unlike the futures hedge shown in Exhibit 56–2, the options hedge protects the investor if rates rise, but allows the investor to profit if rates fall.

## Covered Call Writing Strategy with Futures Options

Unlike the protective put buying strategy, covered call writing is not entered into with the sole purpose of protecting a portfolio against rising rates. The covered call writer, believing that the market will not trade much higher or much lower than its present level, sells out-of-the-money calls against an existing bond portfolio. The sale of the calls brings in premium income that provides partial protection in case rates increase. The premium received does not, of course, provide the kind of protection that a long put position provides, but it does provide some additional income that can be used to offset declining prices. If, instead, rates fall, portfolio appreciation is limited because the short call position constitutes a liability for the seller, and this liability increases as rates decline. Consequently, there is limited upside price potential for the covered call writer. Of course, this is not so bad if prices are essentially going nowhere; the added income from the sale of call options is obtained without sacrificing any gains.

To see how covered call writing with futures options works for the bond used in the protective put example, we construct a table much as we did before. With futures selling around 113 on the hedge initiation date, a sale of a 117 call option on futures might be appropriate. As before, it is assumed that the hedged bond will remain at a 70 basis point spread over the CTD issue. We also assume for simplicity that the price of the 117 calls is $500 per contract. The number of options contracts sold will be the same, namely 109 contracts for $10 million face value of underlying bonds. So, the proceeds received from the sale of the 109 call options is $54,500 (109 contracts × $500) or 0.545 per $100 par value hedged.

Exhibit 56–9 shows the outcomes of the covered call writing strategy given these assumptions. The first five columns of the exhibit are the same as for Exhibit 56–8. In Column (6), the liability resulting from the call option position is shown. The liability is zero if the futures price for the scenario is less than the strike price of 117. If the futures price for the scenario is greater than 117, the liability is calculated as follows:

$$(\text{futures price}/100 - 117/100) \times \$100,000 \times \text{number of put options}$$

For example, consider the scenario in Exhibit 56–9 where the actual sale price of the FNMA bond is $9.5 million. The corresponding futures price is 119.31255. The number of call options sold is 109. Therefore,

$$(119.31255/100 - 117/100) \times \$100,000 \times 109 = \$252,068$$

That is,

$$\begin{aligned} \text{effective sale price} = {} & \text{actual sale price} \\ & + \text{proceeds from sale of the call options} \\ & - \text{liability of call position} \end{aligned}$$

Since the proceeds from sale of the call options is $54,500, then

$$\text{effective sale price} = \text{actual sale price} + \$54,000 - \text{liability of call position}$$

The last column of Exhibit 56–9 shows the effective sale price for each scenario.

Just as the minimum effective sale price could be calculated beforehand for the protective put buying strategy, the maximum effective sale price can be calculated beforehand for the covered call writing strategy. The maximum effective sale price will be the price of the hedged bond corresponding to the strike price of the option sold, plus the premium received. In this case, the strike price on the futures call option is 117. A futures price of 117 corresponds to a price of 150.111 (from 117 times the conversion factor of 1.283), and a corre-

**EXHIBIT 56–9**

Writing Calls on Futures against a Nondeliverable Bond

Instrument to be hedged: $10 million FNMA 6.25% of 05/15/29
Price of FNMA as of hedge date (6/24/99) = 88.39
Conversion factor for September 1999 = 1.283
Price of futures contract when sold = 113
Target maximum price for FNMA bonds per bond = 92.858
Par value hedged = $10,000,000
Strike price for call = 117
Number of calls on futures = 109
Price per contract = 500.00
Value of call position = 54,500
Target maximum value for FNMA bonds = $9,285,800

| (1) | (2) | (3) | (4) | (5) | (6) | (7) | (8) |
|---|---|---|---|---|---|---|---|
| Actual Sale Price of FNMA Bonds | Yield at Sale | Yield of 11.25% Treasury Bond | Price of 11.25% Treasury Bond | Futures Price[1] | Liability of Call Options[2] | Proceeds from Call Position | Effective Sale Price[3] |
| 8,000,000 | 8.027 | 7.327 | 135.813 | 105.85581 | 0 | 54,500.00 | 8,054,500 |
| 8,100,000 | 7.922 | 7.222 | 137.031 | 106.80514 | 0 | 54,500.00 | 8,154,500 |
| 8,200,000 | 7.818 | 7.118 | 138.234 | 107.74279 | 0 | 54,500.00 | 8,254,500 |
| 8,300,000 | 7.717 | 7.017 | 139.422 | 108.66875 | 0 | 54,500.00 | 8,354,500 |
| 8,400,000 | 7.617 | 6.917 | 140.609 | 109.59392 | 0 | 54,500.00 | 8,454,500 |
| 8,500,000 | 7.520 | 6.820 | 141.781 | 110.50740 | 0 | 54,500.00 | 8,554,500 |
| 8,600,000 | 7.424 | 6.724 | 142.938 | 111.40920 | 0 | 54,500.00 | 8,654,500 |
| 8,700,000 | 7.330 | 6.630 | 144,094 | 112.31021 | 0 | 54,500.00 | 8,754,500 |
| 8,800,000 | 7.238 | 6.538 | 145.250 | 113.21122 | 0 | 54,500.00 | 8,854,500 |
| 8,900,000 | 7.148 | 6.448 | 146.391 | 114.10055 | 0 | 54,500.00 | 8,954,500 |
| 9,000,000 | 7.059 | 6.359 | 147.531 | 114.98909 | 0 | 54,500.00 | 9,054,500 |
| 9,100,000 | 6.972 | 6.272 | 148.656 | 115.86594 | 0 | 54,500.00 | 9,154,500 |
| 9,200,000 | 6.886 | 6.186 | 149.766 | 116.73110 | 0 | 54,500.00 | 9,254,500 |
| 9,300,000 | 6.802 | 6.102 | 150.875 | 117.59548 | 64,907 | 54,500.00 | 9,289,593 |
| 9,400,000 | 6.719 | 6.019 | 151.984 | 118.45986 | 159,125 | 54,500.00 | 9,295,375 |
| 9,500,000 | 6.637 | 5.937 | 153.078 | 119.31255 | 252,068 | 54,500.00 | 9,302,432 |

[1] These numbers are approximate because futures trade in 32nds.
[2] From Maximum of [(Futures price/100 − 117/100) × $100,000 × 109, 0]
[3] Does not include transaction costs or interest on the option premium received.

sponding yield of 6.159% for the cheapest-to-deliver issue. The equivalent yield for the hedged bond is 70 basis points higher, or 6.859%, for a corresponding price of 92.313. Adding on the premium received of 0.545 per $100 par value hedged, the final maximum effective sale price will be about 92.858. As Exhibit 56–10 shows, if the hedged bond does trade at 70 basis points over the CTD issue as assumed, the maximum effective sale price for the hedged bond is, in fact, slightly over 92.858. The discrepancies shown in the exhibit are due to rounding and the fact that the position is not adjusted even though the relative dollar durations change as yields change.

## Comparing Alternative Strategies

In this chapter we reviewed three basic strategies for hedging a bond position: (1) hedging with futures, (2) hedging with out-of-the-money puts, and (3) covered call writing with out-of-the-money calls. Similar, but opposite, strategies

**E X H I B I T   56–10**

Comparison of Alternative Strategies

| (1) | (2) | (3) | (4) |
|---|---|---|---|
| Actual Sale Price of FNMA Bonds | Effective Sale Price with Futures Hedge | Effective Sale Price with Protective Puts | Effective Sale Price with Covered Calls |
| 8,000,000 | 8,800,150 | 8,397,217 | 8,054,500 |
| 8,100,000 | 8.793,824 | 8,393,739 | 8,154,500 |
| 8,200,000 | 8.788,807 | 8,391,536 | 8,254,500 |
| 8,300,000 | 8.785,101 | 8,390,607 | 8,354,500 |
| 8,400,000 | 8,781,481 | 8,389,763 | 8,454,500 |
| 8,500,000 | 8,779,171 | 8,445,500 | 8,554,500 |
| 8,600,000 | 8,778,170 | 8,545,500 | 8,654,500 |
| 8,700,000 | 8,777,256 | 8,645,500 | 8,754,500 |
| 8,800,000 | 8,776,343 | 8,745,500 | 8,854,500 |
| 8,900,000 | 8.776,739 | 8,845,500 | 9,954,500 |
| 9,000,000 | 8,777,222 | 8,945,500 | 9,054,500 |
| 9,100,000 | 8,779,015 | 9,045,500 | 9,154,500 |
| 9,200,000 | 8,782,117 | 9,145,500 | 9,254,500 |
| 9,300,000 | 8,785,306 | 9,245,500 | 9,289,593 |
| 9,400,000 | 8,788,496 | 9,345,500 | 9,295,375 |
| 9,500,000 | 8,792,995 | 9,445,500 | 9,302,432 |

exist for managers who are concerned that rates will decrease. As might be expected, there is no "best" strategy. Each strategy has its advantages and its disadvantages, and we never get something for nothing. To get anything of value, something else of value must be forfeited.

To make a choice among strategies, it helps to lay the alternatives side by side. Using the futures example and the futures options examples, Exhibit 56–10 shows the final values of the portfolio for the various hedging alternatives. It is easy to see from Exhibit 56–10 that if one alternative is superior to another alternative at one level of rates, it will be inferior at some other level of rates.

Consequently, we cannot conclude that one strategy is the best strategy. The manager who makes the strategy decision makes a choice among probability distributions, not usually among specific outcomes. Except for the perfect hedge, there is always some range of possible final values of the portfolio. Of course, exactly what that range is, and the probabilities associated with each possible outcome, is a matter of opinion.

## Hedging with Options on Cash Instruments

Hedging a position with options on cash bonds is relatively straightforward. Most strategies, including the purchase of protective puts, covered call writing, and buying collars, are essentially the same whether futures options or options on physicals are used. There are some mechanical differences in the way the two types of option contracts are traded, and there may be substantial differences in their liquidity. Nonetheless, the basic economics of the strategies are virtually identical.

Using options on physicals frequently relieves the manager of much of the basis risk associated with a futures options hedge. For example, a manager of Treasury bonds or notes can usually buy or sell options on the exact security held in the portfolio. Using options on futures, rather than options on Treasury bonds, is sure to introduce additional elements of uncertainty.

Given the illustration presented above, and given that the economics of options on physicals and options on futures are essentially identical, additional illustrations for options on physicals are unnecessary. The only important difference is the hedge ratio calculation and the calculation of the equivalent strike price. To derive the hedge ratio, we always resort to an expression of relative dollar durations. Thus, for options on physicals assuming a constant spread the hedge ratio is:

$$\frac{\text{current dollar duration without options}}{\text{dollar duration of underlying for option}}$$

If a relationship is estimated between the yield on the bonds to be hedged and the instrument underlying the option, the appropriate hedge ratio is:

$$\frac{\text{current dollar duration without options}}{\text{dollar duration of underlying for option}} \times \text{yield beta}$$

Unlike futures options, there is only one deliverable, so there is no conversion factor. When cross hedging with options on physicals, the procedure for finding the equivalent strike price on the bonds to be hedged is very similar. Given the strike price of the option, the strike yield is easily determined using the price/yield relationship for the instrument underlying the option. Then given the projected relationship between the yield on the instrument underlying the option and the yield on the bonds to be hedged, an equivalent strike yield is derived for the bonds to be hedged. Finally, using the yield-to-price formula for the bonds to be hedged, the equivalent strike price for the bonds to be hedged can be found.

## SUMMARY

Buying an interest rate futures contract increases a portfolio's duration, selling an interest rate futures contract decreases a portfolio's duration. The advantages of adjusting a portfolio's duration using futures rather than cash market instruments are that transaction costs are lower, margin requirements are lower, and selling short in the futures market is easier.

The general principle in controlling interest rate risk with futures is to combine the dollar exposure of the current portfolio and that of a futures position so that it is equal to the target dollar exposure. The number of futures contracts needed to achieve the target dollar duration depends on the current dollar duration of the portfolio without futures and the dollar duration per futures contract.

Hedging with futures calls for taking a futures position as a temporary substitute for transactions to be made in the cash market at a later date, with the expectation that any loss realized by the manager from one position (whether cash or futures) will be offset by a profit on the other position. Hedging is a special case of controlling interest rate risk in which the target duration or target dollar duration is zero. Cross hedging occurs when the bond to be hedged is not identical to the bond underlying the futures contract. A short or sell hedge is used to protect against a decline in the cash price of a bond; a long or buy hedge is employed to protect against an increase in the cash price of a bond.

The steps in hedging include: (1) determining the appropriate hedging instrument; (2) determining the target for the hedge; (3) determining the position to be taken in the hedging instrument; and, (4) monitoring and evaluating the hedge. The key factor to determine which futures contract will provide the best hedge is the degree of correlation between the rate on the futures contract and the interest rate that creates the underlying risk that the manager seeks to eliminate. The manager should determine the target rate or target price, which is what is expected from the hedge. The hedge ratio is the number of futures contracts needed for the hedge.

The basis is the difference between the spot price (or rate) and the futures price (or rate). In general, when hedging to the delivery date of the futures contract, a manager locks in the futures rate or price. Hedging with Treasury bond futures and Treasury note futures is complicated by the delivery options embedded in these contracts. When a hedge is lifted prior to the delivery date, the effective rate (or price) that is obtained is much more likely to approximate the current spot rate than the futures rate the shorter the term of the hedge.

The proper target for a hedge that is to be lifted prior to the delivery date depends on the basis. Basis risk refers only to the uncertainty associated with the target rate basis or target price basis. Hedging substitutes basis risk for price risk. Hedging non-Treasury securities with Treasury bond futures requires that the hedge ratio consider two relationships: (1) the cash price of the non-Treasury security and the cheapest-to-deliver issue and (2) the price of the cheapest-to-deliver issue and the futures price.

In computing the hedge ratio for nondeliverable securities, the yield beta should be considered; regression analysis is used to estimate the yield beta and captures the relationship between yield levels and yield spreads. After a target is determined and a hedge is set, the hedge must be monitored during its life and evaluated after it is over. It is important to ascertain the sources of error in a hedge in order to gain insights that can be used to advantage in subsequent hedges.

Three popular hedge strategies using options are the protective put buying strategy, the covered call writing strategy, and the collar strategy. A manager can use a protective put buying strategy to hedge against rising interest rates. A protective put buying strategy is a simple combination of a long put option with a long position in a cash bond. A covered call writing strategy involves selling call options against the bond portfolio. A covered call writing strategy entails much more downside risk than buying a put to protect the value of the portfolio and many managers do not consider covered call writing a hedge. It is not possible to say that the protective put buying strategy or the covered call writing strategy is necessarily the better or more correct options hedge. The best strategy (and the best strike prices) depends upon the manager's view of the market. A collar strategy is a combination of a protective put buying strategy and a covered call writing strategy. A manager who implements a collar strategy eliminates part of the portfolio's downside risk by giving up part of its upside potential.

The steps in options hedging include determining the option contract that is the best hedging vehicle, finding the appropriate strike price, and determining the number of options contracts. At the outset of options hedging, a minimum effective sale price can be calculated for a protective put buying strategy and a maximum effective sale price can be computed for a covered call writing strategy. The best options contract to use depends upon the option price, liquidity, and correlation with the bond(s) to be hedged. For a cross hedge, the manager will want to convert the strike price for the options that are actually bought or sold into an equivalent strike price for the actual bonds being hedged. When using Treasury bond futures options, the hedge ratio is based on the relative dollar duration of the current portfolio, the cheapest-to-deliver issue, and the futures contract at the option expiration date, as well as the conversion factor for the cheapest-to-deliver issue.

While there are some mechanical differences in the way options on physicals and options on futures are traded and there may be substantial differences in their liquidity, the basic economics of the hedging strategies are virtually identical for both contracts. Using options on physicals frequently relieves the manager of much of the basis risk associated with an options hedge.

## CHAPTER 57

# INTEREST-RATE SWAPS*

**Anand K. Bhattacharya, Ph.D.**
Executive Vice President
Countrywide Capital Markets Inc.

**Frank J. Fabozzi, Ph.D., CFA, CPA**
Adjunct Professor of Finance
School of Management
Yale University

In recent years, significant increases in interest rates and their volatility have resulted in a substantially higher exposure to interest-rate risk for market participants. This risk is especially severe for financial institutions that show a mismatch between the average duration of their assets and liabilities. In such cases, because the interest-rate sensitivity of assets and liabilities is not synchronized, any changes in market interest rates will have a disproportionate effect on the net worth of the institution. Given that direct restructuring of the asset and liability mix, which essentially involves changes in the contractual characteristics of such instruments, may not always be possible, institutions increasingly have to rely on synthetically managing the interest-rate exposure of the firm. This chapter and Chapter 58 examine the role of capital market innovations such as interest-rate swaps, interest-rate caps and floors (and derivatives such as interest-rate collars and corridors), and compound options in asset/liability management. The focus in this chapter is on interest-rate swaps.

There has already been widespread use of swaps, caps, and floors in the management of taxable institutions, and increased use by pension funds, endowment funds, and other tax-exempt investors is expected as a result of an important Internal Revenue Service regulation in July 1992. Specifically, under section 512 of the Internal Revenue Code, income from contracts such as swaps, caps, and floors (called *notional principal contracts*) is excluded from the Unrelated Business Income Tax. Prior to this ruling, there was concern that the income realized by tax-exempt investors using these contracts would be treated as Unrelated Business Income Tax and therefore taxed.

---

* The authors thank Dr. John Breit for his contribution to earlier versions of this chapter.

# INTEREST-RATE SWAPS

An interest-rate swap is an agreement whereby two parties (called *counterparties*) agree to exchange periodic interest payments. The dollar amount of the interest payments exchanged is based on some predetermined dollar principal, which is called the *notional principal amount*. The dollar amount each counterparty pays to the other is the agreed-upon periodic interest rate multiplied by the notional principal amount. The only dollars that are exchanged between the parties are the interest payments, based on the notional principal amount (or simply *notional amount*). The notional amount also provides important documentation for corporate financial statements and helps determine the contingent liability of swap market makers in the event that the market maker is a regulated financial institution, such as a bank. The notional amount of swaps is also relevant for determining capital requirements.

# FEATURES OF A GENERIC SWAP

In the most common type of swap, one party agrees to pay the other party fixed interest payments at designated dates for the life of the contract. This party is referred to as the *fixed-rate payer.* The other party agrees to make interest-rate payments that float with some index and is referred to as *the floating-rate payer.* The fixed-rate payment is determined as a spread over the relevant Treasury rate. Additionally, depending upon the credit risk of the counterparty, the spread may increase.

For example, suppose that for the next five years party X agrees to pay party Y 10% per year, while party Y agrees to pay party X six-month LIBOR. Party X is a fixed-rate payer/floating-rate receiver, while party Y is a floating-rate payer/fixed-rate receiver. Assume that the notional amount is $50 million, and that payments are exchanged every six months for the next five years. This means that every six months, party X (the fixed-rate payer/floating- rate receiver) will pay party Y $2.5 million (10% times $50 million divided by 2). The amount that party Y (the floating-rate payer/fixed-rate receiver) will pay party X will be six-month LIBOR times $50 million divided by 2. For example, if six-month LIBOR is 7%, party Y will pay party X $1.75 million (7% times $50 million divided by 2). Note that we divide by two because a half-year's interest is being paid.

The interest-rate benchmarks that are commonly used for the floating rate in an interest-rate swap are those on various money market rates such as London Interbank Offered Rate (LIBOR), Treasury bills, commercial paper composite, prime rate, certificate of deposit composite, and federal funds rate. Although the fixed rate at which the cash flows are determined is fixed over the life of the swap, the floating-rate cash flows vary based on the periodic valuation of the index at the swap reset date. Swaps may be structured so that the floating rate resets on a daily, weekly, monthly, quarterly, or semiannual basis for either monthly, quarterly, semiannual, or annual settlement.

## INTERPRETING A SWAP POSITION

There are two ways that a swap position can be interpreted: (1) as a package of forward/futures contracts and (2) as a package of cash flows from buying and selling cash market instruments.

### Package of Forward Contracts

Interest-rate swaps can be viewed as a package of more basic interest-rate control tools, such as forward rate contracts. The pricing of an interest-rate swap will then depend on the price of a package of forward contracts with the same settlement dates and similar indices. Although an interest-rate swap may be nothing more than a package of forward contracts, it is not a redundant contract for several reasons. First, for forward or futures contracts, the longest maturity does not extend out as far as that of an interest-rate swap; an interest-rate swap with a term of 15 years or longer can be obtained. In view of this observation, the analogy with respect to forward/futures contracts applies mainly for short dated swaps since liquidity for futures/forwards is the highest for shorter maturities. Second, an interest-rate swap is a more transactionally efficient instrument; in one transaction an entity can effectively establish a payoff equivalent to a package of forward contracts. The forward contracts would each have to be negotiated separately. In recent years, due to the increased usage of swaps as hedging alternatives to Treasurys, the liquidity of the generic swap market has increased exponentially.

### Package of Cash Market Instruments

In order to understand the equivalence of a swap as a package of cash market instruments, consider the following. Suppose that an investor enters into the following transaction:

- Buys $50 million par of a five-year floating-rate bond that pays six-month LIBOR every six months.
- Finances the purchase of the five-year floating-rate bond by borrowing $50 million for five years with the following terms: 10% annual interest rate paid every six months.

The cash flow of the above transaction is presented in Exhibit 57–1. The second column of the exhibit sets out the cash flow from purchasing the five-year floating-rate bond. There is a $50 million cash outlay and then cash inflows. The amount of the cash inflows is uncertain because they depend on future

**E X H I B I T    57–1**

Cash Flow for the Purchase of a Five-Year Floating-Rate Bond Financed by Borrowing on a Fixed-Rate Basis

Transaction: Purchase for $50 million a five-year floating-rate bond: floating rate = LIBOR, semiannual payments

Borrow $50 million for five years: fixed rate = 10% semiannual payments

| Six-Month Period | Cash Flow (*in Millions of Dollars*) from: | | |
| | Floating-Rate Bond[a] | Borrowing Cost | Net[a] |
|---|---|---|---|
| 0 | −$50 | +$50.0 | $0 |
| 1 | +(LIBOR$_1$/2) × 50 | −2.5 | +(LIBOR$_1$/2) × 50 − 2.5 |
| 2 | +(LIBOR$_2$/2) × 50 | −2.5 | +(LIBOR$_2$/2) × 50 − 2.5 |
| 3 | +(LIBOR$_3$/2) × 50 | −2.5 | +(LIBOR$_3$/2) × 50 − 2.5 |
| 4 | +(LIBOR$_4$/2) × 50 | −2.5 | +(LIBOR$_4$/2) × 50 − 2.5 |
| 5 | +(LIBOR$_5$/2) × 50 | −2.5 | +(LIBOR$_5$/2) × 50 − 2.5 |
| 6 | +(LIBOR$_6$/2) × 50 | −2.5 | +(LIBOR$_6$/2) × 50 − 2.5 |
| 7 | +(LIBOR$_7$/2) × 50 | −2.5 | +(LIBOR$_7$/2) × 50 − 2.5 |
| 8 | +(LIBOR$_8$/2) × 50 | −2.5 | +(LIBOR$_8$/2) × 50 − 2.5 |
| 9 | +(LIBOR$_9$/2) × 50 | −2.5 | +(LIBOR$_9$/2) × 50 − 2.5 |
| 10 | +(LIBOR$_{10}$/2) × 50 + 50 | −52.5 | +(LIBOR$_{10}$/2) × 50 − 2.5 |

[a] The subscript for LIBOR indicates six-month LIBOR as per the terms of the floating-rate bond at time *t*.

LIBOR. The third column shows the cash flow from borrowing $50 million on a fixed-rate basis. The last column shows the net cash flow from the entire transaction. As can be seen in the last column, there is no initial cash flow (no cash inflow or cash outlay). In all 10 six-month periods the net position results in a cash inflow of LIBOR and a cash outlay of $2.5 million. This net position, however, is identical to the position of a fixed-rate payer/floating-rate receiver.

It can be seen from the net cash flow in Exhibit 57–1 that a fixed-rate payer has a cash market position that is equivalent to a long position in a floating-rate bond and borrowing the funds to purchase the floating-rate bond on a fixed-rate basis. But the borrowing can be viewed as issuing a fixed-rate bond, or equivalently, being short a fixed-rate bond. Consequently, the position of a fixed-rate payer can be viewed as being long a floating-rate bond and short a fixed-rate bond.

What about the position of a floating-rate payer? It can be easily demonstrated that the position of a floating-rate payer is equivalent to purchasing a fixed-rate bond and financing that purchase at a floating rate, with the floating rate being the reference interest rate for the swap. That is, the position of a floating- rate payer is equivalent to a long position in a fixed-rate bond and a short position in a floating-rate bond.

## TERMINOLOGY, CONVENTIONS, AND MARKET QUOTES

Here we review some of the terminology used in this market and explain how swaps are quoted.

The date that the counterparties commit to the swap is called the *trade date.* The date that the swap begins accruing interest is called the *effective date,* and the date that the swap stops accruing interest is called the *maturity date.* The *settlement date* refers to the actual date on which cash flows are exchanged.

Although our illustrations assume that the timing of the cash flows for both the fixed-rate payer and floating-rate payer will be the same, this is rarely the case in a swap. In fact, an agreement may call for the fixed-rate payer to make payments annually but the floating-rate payer to make payments more frequently (semiannually or quarterly). Also, the way interest accrues on each leg of the transaction differs, because there are several day-count conventions in the fixed income markets.

The terminology used to describe the position of a party in the swap markets is a blend of cash market jargon and futures jargon. The obvious reason as we just explained is that a swap position can be interpreted as a position in a package of cash market instruments or a package of futures/forward positions. The counterparty to an interest-rate swap is either a fixed-rate payer or floating-rate payer. There are a number of ways to describe these positions:

*Fixed-Rate Payer*
• Is short the bond market
• Has bought a swap
• Is long a swap
• Has established the price sensitivities of a longer-term liability and a floating-rate asset

*Floating-Rate Payer*
• Is long the bond market
• Has sold a swap
• Is short a swap
• Has established the price sensitivities of a longer-term asset and a floating-rate liability

To understand why the fixed-rate payer is viewed as short the bond market and the floating-rate payer is viewed as long the bond market, consider what happens when interest rates change. Those who borrow on a fixed-rate basis will benefit if interest rates rise because they have locked in a lower interest rate. But those who have a short bond position will also benefit if interest rates rise. Thus, a fixed-rate payer can be said to be short the bond market. A floating-rate payer benefits if interest rates fall. Because a long position in a bond benefits if interest rates fall, terminology describing a floating-rate payer as long the bond market has been adopted. From the discussion of both the interpretation of a swap as a package of cash market instruments above and the duration of a swap discussed later in this chapter, the description of a swap in terms of the sensitivities of long and short cash positions follows accordingly.

The convention that has evolved for quoting swaps levels is for a swap dealer to set the floating rate equal to the index and then quote the fixed rate that will apply. To illustrate this convention, consider the following 10-year swap offered by a dealer to market participants.

> *Floating-rate payer:*
> Pay floating rate of 6-month LIBOR
> Received fixed rate of 8.75%

> *Fixed-rate payer:*
> Pay fixed rate = 8.85%.
> Receive floating rate = 6-month LIBOR

The offer price that the dealer would quote the fixed-rate payer would be to pay 8.85% and receive LIBOR flat. (The term *flat* means with no spread.) The bid price that the dealer would quote the floating-rate payer would be to pay LIBOR flat and receive 8.75%. The bid-offer spread is 10 basis points.

The fixed rate is some spread above the Treasury yield curve with the same term-to-maturity as the swap. In our illustration, suppose that the 10-year Treasury yield is 8.35%. Then the offer price that the dealer would quote to the fixed-rate payer is the 10-year Treasury rate plus 50 basis points versus receiving LIBOR flat. For the floating-rate payer, the bid price quoted would be LIBOR flat versus the 10-year Treasury rate plus 40 basis points. The dealer would quote the swap above as 40–50, meaning that it is willing to enter into a swap to receive LIBOR and pay a fixed rate equal to the 10-year Treasury rate plus 40 basis points; it would be willing to enter into a swap to pay LIBOR and receive a fixed rate equal to the 10-year Treasury rate plus 50 basis points. The difference between the Treasury rate paid and received is the bid-offer spread.

## APPLICATIONS

Here we describe how interest-rate swaps can be used in asset/liability management.

### Converting Floating-Rate Debt to Fixed-Rate Debt Using Swaps

Fixed-rate payer/floating-rate receiver swaps can be used to convert floating-rate liabilities synthetically to fixed-rate liabilities, because the floating cost of liabilities is "counterbalanced" by floating-rate receipts associated with the swap. Any increase or decrease in liability costs is matched by a similar change in the floating-rate inflows, as long as the notional amount of the swap is equal to the principal amount of the liability. The net effect of this strategy is to lock in the liability cost at a fixed rate as long as the swap is not terminated prior to maturity.

As an example, consider the case of a financial institution issuing floating-rate liabilities that are priced at a spread of 10 basis points over three-month LIBOR at a rate of 9.10%. The preponderance of the institution's assets, however, are fixed-rate instruments. As long as interest rates either remain stable or fall, the institution will be able to earn a spread over its floating-rate funding costs. However, if interest rates increase, the institution's spread will decrease. In order to synthetically convert the floating liability cost to fixed debt expense, the institution enters into an interest-rate swap for five years with another entity paying fixed and receiving floating cash flows. Suppose that the fixed-rate side of the swap is priced at a spread of 80 basis points over the five-year Treasury rate at a rate of 9.40% and that the floating side of the swap is three-month LIBOR at 9.00%. The funding cost to the institution in various interest-rate scenarios is illustrated in Exhibit 57–2.

In this example, if the institution had not swapped the floating-rate debt cost for fixed-rate cash flows, the liability rate would have repriced in every interest-rate scenario at a spread of 10 basis points over three-month LIBOR, assuming parallel shifts in the yield curve. By entering into the interest-rate swap, the floating outflow of the liability is partially canceled by the floating inflow from the swap in all interest-rate scenarios. The net funding cost is determined as follows:

Floating-rate liability cost + Fixed rate of swap − Floating rate of swap

The effectiveness of this strategy will depend on the extent of basis risk

**E X H I B I T    57–2**

Converting Floating-Rate Debt to Fixed-Rate Debt Using Interest-Rate Swaps

| | Swap Cash Flows | | | |
|---|---|---|---|---|
| Interest-Rate Scenario | Liability Cost | Fixed Outflow | Floating Inflow (LIBOR) | Net Funding Cost |
| +300 bp | 12.10% | 9.40% | 12.00% | 9.50% |
| +200 | 11.10 | 9.40 | 11.00 | 9.50 |
| +100 | 10.10 | 9.40 | 10.00 | 9.50 |
| Stable | 9.10 | 9.40 | 9.00 | 9.50 |
| −100 | 8.10 | 9.40 | 8.00 | 9.50 |
| −200 | 7.10 | 9.40 | 7.00 | 9.50 |
| −300 | 6.10 | 9.40 | 6.00 | 9.50 |

between the liability rate and the swap floating-rate index (usually LIBOR). In the previous example, because the liability rate and the floating side of the swap are both based on three-month LIBOR, there is no basis risk. However in other instances, where the liability rate is keyed off another indicator, such as the Treasury bill index or the prime rate, the existence of basis risk may mitigate the swap's effectiveness. For instance, if the liability rate increases by 1% and LIBOR increases by only 0.85%, the synthetic fixed rate will be 0.15% higher than it would have been in the absence of such imperfect correlation. Conversely, if the liability rate increases by 0.85% and LIBOR by 1%, the synthetic liability rate will be 0.15% lower than the swap fixed rate. The synthetic funding rate will also be affected by any discrepancies in the repricing frequency of the liability and the reset period of the swap. Ideally, close synchronization between these dates will minimize the deviation of the synthetic liability cost from the swap fixed rate that occurs because of reset date mismatch.

## Converting Fixed-Rate Debt to Floating-Rate Debt Using Reverse Swaps

A similar strategy using reverse swaps, where the financial institution receives fixed-rate cash flows and pays floating-rate cash flows, is used to convert the fixed cost of liabilities to a synthetic floating rate. In this case, the fixed-rate interest cost of the liability is offset by the fixed-rate inflow of the swap. If the liability rate is higher (lower) than the swap fixed rate, then the synthetic floating rate will be higher (lower) than the swap floating rate. A financial institution that has fixed-rate debt and a preponderance of floating-rate assets, such as adjustable-rate mortgages, collateralized mortgage obligation (CMO) floater bonds, or floating-rate notes, may adopt this strategy to better match the average duration of their assets and liabilities.

As an example, consider the case of an institution that has three-year fixed-rate debt at a coupon rate of 8.85%. In order to convert this fixed-rate debt into floating-rate liabilities, the institution enters into a reverse swap (floating-rate payer/fixed-rate receiver) for three years. The terms of the swap involve paying three-month LIBOR and receiving fixed-rate cash flows at a spread of 65 basis points over the three-year Treasury yield at a rate of 8.70%. An illustration of this example is presented in Exhibit 57–3. An analysis of this illustration reveals that the effective funding cost is determined as follows:

Fixed-rate liability cost − Fixed-rate of swap + Floating-rate of swap

The institution has converted fixed-rate debt to LIBOR-based debt at a spread of 15 basis points over LIBOR. A schematic of the cash flows involved in synthetically converting floating-rate liability costs to fixed-rate funding and vice versa is presented in Exhibit 57–4. Although the dynamics of the cash flow are essentially reversed, most dealers will charge a higher spread (offer side) for

**EXHIBIT 57–3**

Converting Fixed-Rate Debt to Floating-Rate Debt Using Interest-Rate Swaps

| | Swap Cash Flows | | | |
|---|---|---|---|---|
| Interest-Rate Scenario | Liability Cost | Fixed Outflow | Floating Inflow (LIBOR) | Net Funding Cost |
| +300 bp | 8.85% | 8.70% | 12.00% | 12.15% |
| +200 | 8.85 | 8.70 | 11.00 | 11.15 |
| +100 | 8.85 | 8.70 | 10.00 | 10.15 |
| Stable | 8.85 | 8.70 | 9.00 | 9.15 |
| −100 | 8.85 | 8.70 | 8.00 | 8.15 |
| −200 | 8.85 | 8.70 | 7.00 | 7.15 |
| −300 | 8.85 | 8.70 | 6.00 | 6.15 |

**EXHIBIT 57–4**

Synthetic Conversion of Interest-Rate Liability

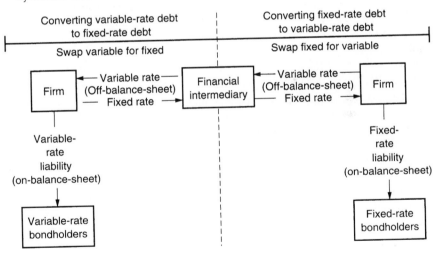

fixed- rate-paying swaps than fixed-rate-receiving swaps (bid side). This bid-ask differential, which is a function of variables such as hedging costs, dealer inventory, relative supply of fixed- and floating-rate payers in the market, conditions in the Treasury market, and quality spreads in the domestic and international bond markets, is used to compensate the dealers for the market-making function.

In the foregoing discussion, it has been tacitly assumed that the payment frequencies and the payment basis of the fixed and floating legs of the swap and the liability being swapped are identical. Any differences in the frequencies or basis will change the net spread calculations. This observation also applies to asset swaps (discussed later). For example, in swapping a fixed liability to a floating-rate obligation, the net spread over LIBOR usually will be slightly different from the spread between the liability coupon and the coupon of the swap. This difference arises because swaps usually pay fixed on an actual/365 or 30 /360 basis and floating on an actual/360 basis. Hence, the net spread over LIBOR will be 360/365 of the nominal spread between coupons.

## DOLLAR DURATION OF A SWAP

As with any fixed income contract, the value of a swap will change as interest rates change. As explained in Chapter 5, dollar duration is a measure of the change in the dollar value of an asset due to a change in interest rates. From our earlier discussion of how to interpret an interest-rate swap, it was explained that from the perspective of the party who pays floating and receives fixed, the position can be viewed as follows:

> Long a fixed-rate bond + Short a floating-rate bond

This means that the dollar duration of an interest-rate swap from the perspective of a floating-rate payer is just the difference between the dollar duration of the two bond positions that constitute the swap. That is,

> Dollar duration of a swap = Dollar duration of a fixed-rate bond
> − Dollar duration of a floating-rate bond

Most of the interest-rate sensitivity of a swap will result from the dollar duration of the fixed-rate bond because the dollar duration of the floating-rate bond will be small. It will always be less than the length of time to the next reset date. Therefore, the dollar duration of a floating-rate bond for which the coupon rate resets every six months will be less than six months. The dollar duration of a floating-rate bond becomes smaller as the swap gets closer to its reset date.

## INNOVATIONS IN SWAP MARKETS

In addition to allowing a firm to issue debt for which it has a comparative relative advantage and then swapping the cash flows to fine-tune the asset/liability gap, interest-rate swaps also serve other useful purposes, especially because of the off-balance-sheet treatment accorded them. It often has been argued that swaps are preferable to refunding because the latter often is constrained by restrictive covenants. Periodically, firms may want to make adjustments in the capital structure with respect to the composition of debt by refinancing longer-term debt with short-term debt at lower interest costs. In certain instances, this may not be easy to accomplish, especially if the debt is noncallable. Swaps provide an effective means to alter the covenants of a debt issue to accomplish asset/liability objectives without incurring the administrative, legal, and underwriting costs of issuing additional debt. In this case, the firm may swap the higher-coupon debt to a cheaper floating-rate liability based on a variety of indexes, such as the Treasury bill index, prime rate, and LIBOR. In recent years, swaptions have been increasingly used to contractually create callable liabilities at issuing entities.

In order to address such specific investor needs, several innovations, such as basis swaps, yield-curve swaps, amortizing swaps, asset swaps, forward swaps, equity swaps, and swaptions have been developed over the last several years to further expand the degree of flexibility provided by generic swaps. A discussion of the salient features of these capital market innovations is presented in this section.

## Basis Swaps

Basis swaps are designed to manage the basis risk inherent in a balance sheet where the asset returns and liability costs are based on different indexes. For instance, a financial institution that invests in a CMO floater with a return of 60 basis points over one-month LIBOR funded by six-month certificates of deposit at an interest cost of prime less 200 basis points is subject to basis risk, despite the minimal duration mismatch. This risk arises because the asset resets monthly off LIBOR, whereas the liability resets every six months based on movements in the prime rate. To alleviate this risk, the institution could enter into a floating-to- floating basis swap, where the institution receives cash flows that are reset every six months at a rate of prime less 150 basis points and pays swap cash flows on a monthly basis indexed off one-month LIBOR. The basis risk will be controlled for the *tenor,* or time period, of the swap.

As an illustration, assume one-month LIBOR is 9% and the prime rate is 10%. Without the basis swap, the spread earned by the institution is defined as the difference between the asset return and the liability cost, 1.60% (9.60% − 8.00%) in our illustration. (For the sake of simplicity, it is assumed that the asset returns are not constrained by caps inherent in CMO floaters.[1]) Assuming that the correlation between the prime rate and one-month LIBOR is imperfect, in that a 1% change in the prime results in less or more than a 1% change in one-month LIBOR, the spread will not be maintained in all interest-rate scenarios. As previously indicated, the institution enters into a basis swap to lock

---

1. A discussion of synthetically "stripping" these caps in Chapter 58.

in the spread over funding costs without incurring the basis risk between the prime rate and LIBOR. Although basis swaps are used most often to refine the interest-rate sensitivity of assets and liabilities, these swaps can also be used to arbitrage spreads between various funding sources. The dynamics of the basis swap are illustrated in Exhibit 57–5.

## Yield-Curve Swaps

In a yield-curve swap, the counterparties agree to exchange payments based on the difference between interest rates at two points on a given yield curve. These swaps are therefore an example of a floating-rate for floating-rate swap, or basis swap.

To illustrate a yield-curve swap, suppose party A agrees to receive six-month Treasury bill rate and to pay party B the yield on a 10-year Treasury minus 200 basis points, with the rate on both reset every six months. If at a reset date the six-month T-bill rate is 3.5% and 10-year Treasury yield is 6%, party A receives 3.5% and pays party B 4%. If the yield curve flattens such that the six-month Treasury bill rate is 5% and the 10-year Treasury is 6.5%, then party A receives 5% and pays 4.5%.

## Amortizing and Accreting Swaps

In the preceding discussion, it was implicitly assumed that the notional amount does not change over the life of the swap. However, with respect to amortizing assets such as mortgage loans and other mortgage-backed instruments such as CMO bonds and automobile receivables, the spread over funding costs will not

**EXHIBIT 57–5**

Locking in a Floating Spread over Funding Costs Using Basis Swaps

| | | | Swap Cash Flows | | | |
|---|---|---|---|---|---|---|
| LIBOR | Asset Return[a] | Prime | Liability Costs[b] | Floating Inflows[c] | Floating Outflows[d] | Net Spread[e] |
| 7.0% | 7.60% | 9.5% | 7.5% | 8.00% | 7.00% | 1.10% |
| 9.0 | 9.60 | 10.0 | 8.0 | 8.50 | 9.00 | 1.10 |
| 11.0 | 11.60 | 12.0 | 10.0 | 10.50 | 11.00 | 1.10 |

[a] Asset return = LIBOR + 60 basis points.
[b] Liability costs = Prime − 200 basis points.
[c] Swap floating inflows = Prime − 150 basis points.
[d] Swap floating outflows = LIBOR.
[e] New spread = Asset return + Swap inflows − Liability costs − Swap outflows.

be maintained because of the asset principal balance declining over time. This declining spread is especially critical for assets whose average life and duration may exhibit dramatic changes due to the possibility of prepayments. In such instances, if bullet swaps with the same notional amount are used, there is the risk of being either underhedged or overhedged with respect to liability costs. If interest rates decrease and prepayments increase substantially, the average life of the asset will shorten. In such instances, the asset may not generate funds sufficient to earn a positive spread. On the other hand, if interest rates rise and prepayments slow down, resulting in an extension of the average life of the asset, the swap may have to be extended or additional swap coverage obtained (at higher cost, owing to bearish interest-rate conditions[2]) to maintain a positive spread.

In such instances, the institution may enter into an amortizing swap, which permits the notional amount of the swap, and hence the exchange of the cash flows, to change in accordance with the amortization rate of the asset. Note that the amortization rate of the notional amount cannot usually be changed over the life of the swap. Because the amortizing swap can be replicated by using a strip of swaps, the swap rate is determined as a blended rate of individual bullet swap rates. This feature of amortizing swaps also provides a market participant with the choice of entering into a series of swaps to match the amortization rate of assets or entering into an amortizing swap at an annual blended rate.

Although amortizing swaps improve the match between the asset and hedged liability cash flows, such swaps do not completely alleviate the risk of being overhedged with respect to liability costs. A major portion of this risk is mitigated for assets such as Planned Amortization Class (PAC) CMO bonds, which provide for a specified amortization rate within a wide band of prepayment scenarios. For assets that exhibit a higher degree of prepayment volatility, if falling interest rates lead to an increase in prepayments and an attendant shortening of average life, the firm may have to continue exchanging swap cash flows for a period longer than the average life of the asset, unless the swap can be terminated. An alternative version of amortizing swaps, labeled "balance guaranteed swaps," has been used to guarantee floating-rate returns to investors. In such instances, instead of the investor managing the prepayment risk, the financial intermediary (typically, the swap dealer) manages the cash flows of the asset and the swap to guarantee the investor a floating rate lower than the contractual rate of the asset. Any changes in cash flows resulting from prepayment related amortization are the responsibility of the dealer.

In instances where the liability schedule is expected to increase, an interest- rate swap with an accreting balance may be used to fix the interest cost

---

2. A bearish interest-rate scenario refers to one in which rates are rising and market prices are falling (a bearish market). In a bullish interest-rate scenario, rates are falling and market prices are rising.

of the liabilities. Perhaps the most common example of this type of swap application is found in the construction industry, where accreting swaps may be used to fix the rate on a project funded with a floating-rate drawdown facility.

## Forward Swaps

A forward swap allows a market participant to initiate a swap with a specified delayed start. Such swaps can be used to hedge debt refinancings or anticipated debt issuance in conjunction with expenditures expected in the future. For instance, suppose a firm has $200 million of noncallable fixed-rate debt maturing in three years. In order to lock in anticipated funding requirements three years hence for a period of five years at current rates, the firm could enter into a forward swap to pay fixed and receive floating cash flows starting three years from now. If rates have increased at the time of issuance, the firm would issue floating-rate debt and effectively convert the floating-rate funding to a fixed-rate liability, because the firm would be a floating-rate receiver.

## Equity Swaps

In recent years, the concept of swapping cash flows has been applied to the equity area. In an *equity swap,* the cash flows that are swapped are based on the total return on some stock market index and an interest rate (either a fixed rate or a floating rate). Moreover, the stock market index can be a non-U.S. stock market index and the payments could be non-dollar denominated. For example, a money manager can enter into a two-year quarterly reset equity swap based on the German DAX market index versus LIBOR in which the money manager receives the market index in deutsche marks and pays the floating rate in deutsche marks.

## Swaptions

Swaptions are representative of the new class of second-generation derivative products that have developed around the swaps, caps, and floor markets. Swaptions can take many forms, but typically they are options to pay or receive a predetermined fixed rate in exchange for LIBOR at some time in the future. As the market develops, it is likely that additional variable-rate indexes will be used to determine floating-rate cash flows. Alternatively, swaptions can contain an option to cancel an existing swap. The second structure is essentially the same as the first, because a swap can be canceled by entering into a new swap in the opposite direction.

In view of this overlap between options to enter swaps and options to cancel swaps, the usual shorthand terminology of puts and calls is rarely used for swaptions. Rather, the option characteristic is spelled out in more detail, for instance, an option to receive fixed at 9% for three years, starting two years hence. Swaption exercise can be European (exercisable on only one date in the future) or American (exercisable on any date up to and including the expiration date), with the bulk of the interbank market for European exercise. A typical American swaption structure would be to enter into, say, a seven-year swap paying fixed at 9% at any time before maturity. As an example, if the option is exercised after one year, the option holder will pay 9% and receive LIBOR for six years.

In terms of flexibility and costs, swaptions lie between swaps and customized interest-rate protection instruments, such as caps and floors. If LIBOR increases, the fixed payer of a swap, the holder of an option to pay fixed, and the cap buyer all benefit equally. If LIBOR decreases, the fixed payer of a swap incurs an opportunity loss and the holder of the swaption or cap loses only the up- front premium. The premium for a cap is greater than that for a swaption because the buyer of the cap essentially has purchased a strip of options, whereas the holder of a swaption owns only one option. If rates increase and the swaption is exercised, the owner of the swaption is exposed to the risk of a fall in interest rates. However, the holder of the cap can still take advantage of the beneficial movement in rates. In view of this observation, swaptions can be viewed as instruments that provide some of the protection and flexibility afforded by caps and floors.

The pricing of swaptions is still somewhat of an art. The development of models for pricing and hedging swaptions is on the cutting edge of options theory. Dealers differ greatly in the models they use to price such options, and the analytical tools range from modified Black-Scholes models to binomial lattice versions to systems based upon Monte Carlo simulations. As a result, bid-ask spreads are wide, and it pays to shop around, particularly for more complicated structures that cannot be backed off in the interbank markets.

Swaptions provide the sophisticated firm with an additional, flexible tool for asset/liability management. On the liability side, the primary uses of swaptions have been in hedging uncertain funding requirements and issuing synthetically callable debt. With respect to fixing liability costs, a corporation can lock in coupon rates for future funding by paying fixed in a forward swap. However, the firm may desire to preserve the opportunity to save on these funding costs in the event that rates decline in the future by purchasing a swaption, despite the attractiveness of the current interest-rate structure. In the event that funding requirements are uncertain, the flexibility of these instruments really comes into play as swaptions can lock in current rates without committing the firm to future borrowing.

Much of the current activity in swaptions has been fueled by an arbitrage between the swaption and callable bond markets. Historically, investors have not demanded full compensation for call options embedded in corporate bonds. Hence, corporations can issue callable debt and then effectively strip off the embedded call option by writing a swaption, thereby lowering the all-in cost of the debt. On the asset side, the primary use of swaptions has been in hedging prepayable swapped assets, such as mortgage-backed instruments. An investor may purchase fixed-rate mortgage-backed securities, swap the fixed rate to floating, and earn an attractive spread over LIBOR. However, this spread is subject to erosion if the asset balance declines because of high prepayments. By giving up some of this spread and purchasing swaptions, the investor can reduce prepayment risk exposure. In addition to these types of specific uses, swaption volatility has also become a widely used indicator of future volatility embedded in current expectations.

# ASSET SWAP

Our earlier applications focused exclusively on the use of interest-rate swaps and associated issues in swap-based liability hedging. Such swaps are referred to as *liability-based swaps. Asset-based swaps,* which use principles involved in liability hedging, are becoming increasingly popular to customize asset coupons and maturities, thereby expanding the asset universe available to portfolio managers. Asset swaps serve several useful functions, such as facilitating yield enhancement, creating assets that are not available in the marketplace, and changing the interest-rate sensitivity of the portfolio, without actually trading the securities.

Similar to the use of swaps in converting fixed-rate debt to floating-rate debt and vice versa, interest-rate swaps also can be used to accomplish the same objective with fixed- and floating-rate assets. For instance, floating-rate notes (FRNs) can be converted synthetically to fixed-rate assets using a receive fixed-rate and pay floating-rate swap. Similarly, fixed-rate assets such as mortgage-backed securities (especially certain types of CMO bonds such as PAC classes) and receivable-backed securities (such as manufactured housing, credit card, and automobile loan collateralized bonds) can be converted to floating-rate instruments by using a receive floating-rate and pay fixed-interest-rate swap. Asset-based swaps can also be used to alter the duration characteristics and, hence, the interest-rate sensitivity of an asset portfolio. For instance, a financial institution that has a predominance of long-term fixed-rate assets can reduce the duration of its portfolio, thereby increasing the interest-rate sensitivity of the assets by creating synthetic floating-rate assets. Characteristics of interest-rate swaps, such as amortizing features and option covenants, can be used to customize and reasonably ensure a particular yield level.

The flexibility afforded by swaps in the design of such synthetic assets becomes apparent when it is realized that investors seeking a particular type of asset, say, a floating-rate asset, can evaluate traditional floating-rate instruments, such as FRNs and CMO floaters as well as fixed-rate assets, by using interest-rate swaps to synthetically convert them to floating-rate assets. Asset-based swaps can also tailor the maturity (tenor) of the swap without having to depend on conditions in the debt markets. The latter feature is especially important for institutions that have "underwater" assets. With recent developments in the asset securitization market, which portend increased securitization of a gamut of assets, firms can always use a collateralized financing structure to raise funds and then reinvest the proceeds in assets of desired maturity and coupon. However, this option, besides being time-consuming, involves administrative, legal, and investment banking costs. Also, assets of particular maturity and coupon may not always be traded in the markets. Asset-based swaps fulfill this particular need in the market mainly because of ease of execution, customization features, and flexibility of swap termination.

## TERMINATION OF INTEREST-RATE SWAPS

There are two ways to terminate a swap: (1) a reverse swap and (2) a swap sale.

### Reverse Swap

The simplest way to terminate an interest-rate swap is to enter into an offsetting position. For illustrative purposes, assume that a firm entered into a five-year swap, paying fixed at a rate of 9.40% and receiving three-month LIBOR. After two years, the firm decides to terminate the swap by entering into a reverse swap, paying floating rate and receiving fixed rate. By matching the reset and settlement periods of the *reverse swap* to those of the original swap, the floating-rate payment of the reverse swap is counterbalanced by the floating-rate inflow from the original swap.

Two cases are illustrated in Exhibit 57–6—a bearish scenario and a bullish scenario. In a bearish interest-rate scenario, the new fixed rate on the reverse swap is likely to be higher than the fixed rate on the original swap. The new fixed rate in Exhibit 57–6 is assumed to be 10.40%. In this bearish scenario, there will be a profit associated with the reverse swap. The firm has effectively created an annuity of 1% of the notional amount for the remaining period of the swap.

In a bullish interest-rate scenario, rates are falling and market prices are rising. In the illustration in Exhibit 57–6, the new fixed rate is assumed to be 8.40%, resulting in a loss on the reverse swap. In this illustration, the firm has created a reverse annuity of 1% per annum for three years.

In either case, because the closing transaction involves receiving the fixed side of a swap, the spread over Treasury is based on the bid side of the market, whereas the original swap involves payment of the swap at the offer spread.

### Swap Sale

Instead of managing the cash flows of two swaps and the credit risk of two counterparties, the firm may sell the swap for either a profit or loss in the

**EXHIBIT 57–6**

Termination of Interest-Rate Swaps

|  | Termination Interest-Rate Scenario | |
| --- | :---: | :---: |
|  | **Bearish** | **Bullish** |
| Swap | | |
| Pay fixed (5-year original maturity / 3-year remaining maturity) | 9.40% | 9.40% |
| Receive 3-month LIBOR | LIBOR | LIBOR |
| Reverse Swap | | |
| Receive fixed (3-year remaining maturity) | 10.40% | 8.40% |
| Pay 3-month LIBOR | LIBOR | LIBOR |
| Profit (Loss) | 1.00% | (1.00%) |

secondary market. In the event that current market swaps with a maturity equal to the remaining maturity of the swap to be terminated are being offered at a higher fixed rate, the swap could be sold for a fee. On the other hand, if current market swaps with a maturity similar to the swap to be liquidated are being originated at lower rates, then an exit fee may have to be paid for terminating the swap. Formally, the termination value of a swap is determined as the present value of an annuity discounted for the remaining term-to-maturity at the current swap rate. The periodic value of the annuity payments is approximated as the difference between the old fixed swap rate and the new fixed swap rate multiplied by the remaining notional amount of the original swap.[3] Formally, this is stated as

$$\text{Termination value of swap} = \text{PV of Annuity at } r_s t$$

where

$$\text{Annuity payments} = (r_s - r_m) \times \text{Notional amount}$$
$$r_s = \text{Original swap fixed rate}$$
$$r_m = \text{Current swap fixed rate}$$
$$t = \text{Time remaining to maturity of swap}$$

---

3. For a more detailed discussion of the calculation of the termination of the value of a swap that takes into days in payment periods, see Chapter 14 in Frank J. Fabozzi, *Valuation of Fixed Income Securities and Derivatives* (New Hope, PA: Frank J. Fabozzi Associates, 1998).

# SUMMARY

In the management of interest-rate volatility and associated asset/liability structural decisions, customized risk-management instruments such as swaps, caps and floors, and split-fee options provide a high degree of coverage flexibility and customization. Interest-rate swaps can be used either to synthetically extend or to shorten the duration characteristics of any asset or liability. The benefit of swaps is that direct changes in the contractual characteristics of either assets or liabilities are associated with administrative, legal, and investment banking costs. Additional swaps covenants, such as amortizing and accreting features and option riders, can be included in the contractual agreement either to better match the funding of an asset or to lock in the return of a synthetic asset.

## CHAPTER 58

# INTEREST-RATE CAPS AND FLOORS AND COMPOUND OPTIONS*

Anand K. Bhattacharya, Ph.D.
Executive Vice President
Countrywide Capital Markets Inc.

Interest-rate caps and floors provide asymmetric interest-rate risk management capabilities similar to those provided by options, except that protection can be customized to a much greater degree. As indicated by the nomenclature, *interest-rate caps,* also referred to as *interest-rate ceilings,* allow the purchaser to "cap" the contractual rate associated with a liability. Alternatively, interest-rate floors allow the purchaser to protect the total rate of return of an asset. The seller of the cap pays the purchaser any amount above the periodic capped rate on the settlement date. Conversely, the purchaser of the floor receives from the seller any amount below the periodic protected rate on the relevant date. The protection provided by caps and floors is asymmetric, in that the purchaser is protected from adverse moves in the market but maintains the advantage of beneficial moves in market rates. In this respect, caps and floors differ from interest-rate swaps. Recall that interest-rate swaps seek to insulate the user from the economic effects of interest-rate volatility, regardless of the direction of interest rates.

Interest-rate protection obtained by purchasing caps and floors can be customized by selecting various contractual features. The following decision variables are commonly used in determining the parameters of either interest-rate caps or floors.

## FEATURES OF INTEREST-RATE CAPS AND FLOORS

The *underlying index* from which the contractual payments will be determined can be chosen from a set of indexes based on LIBOR, commercial paper, prime rate, Treasury bills, or certificates of deposit. Because these instruments are

---

* The version of this chapter that appeared in the third edition was coauthored with Dr. John Breit.

originated along several maturities, an additional variable associated with the index concerns the maturity of the index.

The *strike rate* is the rate at which the cash flows will be exchanged between the purchaser and seller of the customized interest-rate protection instrument. Caps with a higher strike rate have lower up-front premiums, although the trade-off between the premium and the strike rate is not directly proportional. Similarly, floors with a lower strike rate have a lower up-front premium. Increasing (decreasing) the strike rate does not result in a proportionate decrease in the up-front fee for interest-rate caps (floors).

The term of the protection may range from several months to about 30 years, although the liquidity of longer dated caps is not sufficiently high.

The *settlement frequency* refers to the frequency with which the strike rate will be compared to the underlying index to determine the periodic contractual rate for the interest-rate protection agreement. The most common frequencies are monthly, quarterly, and semiannually. At settlement, the cash flows exchanged could be determined on either the average daily rate prevalent during the repricing interval or the spot rate on the settlement date.

The *notional amount* of the agreement on which the cash flows are exchanged is usually fixed, unless the terms of the agreement call for the amortization of the notional amount. For instance, in "spread enhancement" strategies, which involve the purchase of an amortizing asset, such as a fixed-rate mortgage-backed security funded by floating-rate capped liabilities, amortization of the cap notional amount may be necessary in order to maintain the spread. Unless the amortization feature is included in the design of the cap, the spread between the asset cash flows and the liability costs will be eroded.

## PRICING OF CAPS AND FLOORS

The *up front premium* is the fee paid by the purchaser to the seller of the interest-rate agreement at the inception of the contract. This fee is similar to the premium paid to purchase options and is determined by factors such as the strike rate, volatility of the underlying index, the length of the agreement, the notional amount, and any special features, such as amortization of the notional principal.

The pricing of both caps and floors draws heavily on option pricing theory; for instance, an increase in market volatility results in a higher premium for both the cap and the floor. The strike rate for a cap is inversely related to the premium paid for the cap because rates have to advance before the cap is in the money or the payoff is positive. On the other hand, the strike rate for interest-rate floors is directly related to the up-front premium. A higher strike indicates that the likelihood of the index falling below this rate is greater, which indicates a higher likelihood of positive payoff from the floor. The longer the term-to-maturity, the greater the premium because optional protection is available for a longer period of time. Hence, there is a higher probability that the payoff associated with these instruments will be positive. With respect to the payment frequency, the agreement with a shorter payment frequency will command a higher premium because there is a greater likelihood of payoff and the payments are determined only on the settlement date. This may be an important determinant of cash flows, especially in highly volatile markets. Any advantageous changes in market volatility for interest-rate agreements with longer settlement frequencies may not result in a payoff for the purchaser of the agreement because the option-like characteristics of caps and floors are European rather than American in design.

There also may be additional contractual features, such as variable premiums, cost of termination options prior to stated maturity, conversion privileges from one program to another, and purchase of a combination of programs, such as *interest-rate collars* and *corridors.*

## INTEREST-RATE CAPS

As noted above, an interest-rate cap can be used to create an upper limit on the cost of floating-rate liabilities. The purchaser of the cap pays an up-front fee to establish a ceiling on a particular funding rate. If the market rate exceeds the strike rate of the cap on the settlement date, the seller of the cap pays the difference. As an illustration, consider the following example, where an institution purchases an interest-rate cap to hedge the coupon rate of LIBOR-indexed liabilities, which reprice every three months.

| | |
|---|---|
| Notional amount: | $10,000,000 |
| Underlying index: | 3-month LIBOR |
| Maturity: | 3 years |
| Cap strike level: | 10% |
| Premium: | 145 basis points or 1.45% of $10,000,000 = $145,000 |
| Settlement frequency: | Quarterly |
| Day count: | Actual/360 |

The up-front premium can be converted to an annual basis-point equivalent by treating $145,000 as the present value of a stream of equal quarterly payments with a future value of zero at the maturity of the cap. Ideally, this should be computed at the rate at which the up-front premium can be funded for three years. Assuming that this premium can be funded at a rate of 9% and the cap has 12 reset periods, the annual basis-point equivalent of the up-front premium is 56 basis points.[1]

---

1. This represents the annuity over three years, which when discounted quarterly at an annual rate of 9% equals the up-front premium of 145 basis points.

In this example, the payments to the purchaser of the cap by the seller can be determined as the quarterly difference between the three-month LIBOR index and the cap strike rate of 10% times the notional amount of the agreement. Specifically, the cap payments are computed as follows:

$$\text{(Index rate} - \text{Strike rate)} \times \text{(Days in settlement period}/360)}$$
$$\times \text{Notional amount}$$

For instance, where three-month LIBOR is 11%, the payments made by the cap seller, assuming 90 days in the settlement period, would be determined as follows:

$$(11\% - 10\%) \times (90/360) \times 10,000,000 = \$25,000$$

The purchaser does not receive any payments when the reference rate, as indicated by the value of three-month LIBOR, is below the strike rate of 10%. The payoff profile of this capped liability is illustrated in Exhibit 58–1. Because the annual amortized premium of the cap is 56 basis points, the maximum rate associated with the capped liability at a strike of 10% is 10.56%. In interest-rate scenarios where the value of three-month LIBOR is below 10%, the interest expense of the capped liability is higher than the unhedged interest expense by the amount of the amortization of the up-front premium. Given that the maximum risk exposure associated with the purchase of the cap is limited to the up-front premium, the dynamics of caps are similar to those of debt

**EXHIBIT 58–1**

Effective Interest Expense of a Capped Liability

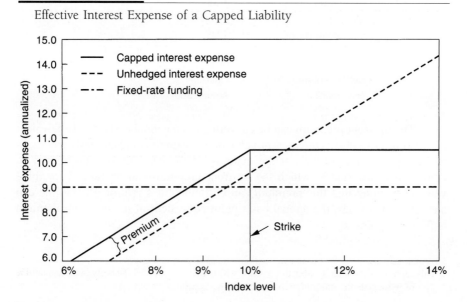

options. On a more specific basis, because the purchaser of the cap benefits in rising rate scenarios, the conceptual options analog is a strip of put options. However, caps can be purchased for maturities longer than those associated with a strip of puts. By increasing the strike rate of the cap, say, from 10% to 10.5%, the up-front premium (and hence the annual amortized premium) can be reduced. However, as illustrated in Exhibit 58–2, the maximum interest expense of the capped liability increases with a higher cap strike rate.

There are several advantages associated with the use of the cap in protecting the interest expense of a floating-rate liability. The purchaser of the cap can obtain protection against higher rates and also fund the liabilities at a floating rate to take advantage of lower interest rates. In this respect, the capped liability strategy can result in a lower cost of funds than certain fixed-rate alternatives.

In addition to capping the cost of liabilities, interest-rate caps can also be used to synthetically strip embedded caps in floating-rate instruments such as CMO floaters and adjustable-rate mortgages. For instance, consider the case of an institution owning a CMO floater bond that reprices monthly at a spread of 60 basis points over LIBOR, with a cap of 600 basis points over the initial coupon rate. If the initial coupon rate is 9.60%, the coupon is capped at 15.60%. Because the only sources of cash flow available to CMO bonds are the principal, interest, and prepayment streams of the underlying mortgages, CMO floaters are by definition capped. In this respect, CMO floaters are different from other LIBOR-indexed bonds, such as floating-rate notes. The institution could strip off the embedded cap in the CMO floater by buying a cap at a strike rate of

**E X H I B I T   58–2**

Effective Interest Cost under Two Cap Levels

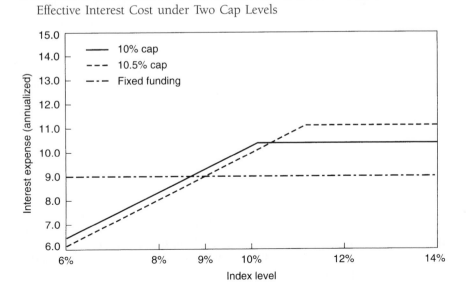

15% or 16%. With a strike rate about 600 to 700 basis points out of the money, the cap could be purchased quite inexpensively. As interest rates increase, the loss in coupon by the embedded cap feature of the CMO bonds would be compensated by the cash inflows from the cap. The same strategy could be applied to strip caps inherent in adjustable-rate mortgages. However, the exercise of stripping caps associated with adjustable-rate mortgages is somewhat more difficult because of the existence of periodic and lifetime caps. While there is theoretical appeal in this strategy, the efficacy of the process may be hampered by unexpected prepayments associated with the assets.

## PARTICIPATING CAPS

It is difficult to pinpoint the exact nature of financial instruments labeled as participating caps. A common theme in the definition of such instruments is the absence of an up-front fee used to purchase the cap. The confusion in definition arises from the variations of the term *participating*. One type of participating cap involves the purchase of cap protection where the buyer obtains full protection in the event that interest rates rise. However, in order to compensate the seller of the cap for this bearish protection, the buyer shares a percentage (the participation) of the difference between the capped rate and the level of the floating-rate index in the event that interest rates fall.

For illustrative purposes, assume that a firm purchases a LIBOR participating cap at a strike rate of 10% with a participation rate of 60%. If LIBOR increases to levels greater than 10%, the firm will receive cash flows analogous to a nonparticipating cap. However, if LIBOR is below the capped rate, say 8%, then the firm gives up 60% of the difference between LIBOR and the capped rate, that is, $(10\% - 8\%) \times 0.6 = 1.2\%$. In this case the effective interest expense would be 9.20% (8.00% + 1.20%) instead of LIBOR plus the annual amortized premium, as in a nonparticipating cap. In bullish interest-rate scenarios, the effective interest expense using a participating cap would be higher than a nonparticipating cap owing to the participation feature. However, in bearish interest-rate scenarios, the effective interest cost of the floating-rate liability would be higher for a nonparticipating cap owing to the annualized cost of the up-front premium. An illustration of the effective interest costs using both hedging alternatives is presented in Exhibit 58-3.

Other participating instruments, also known as *participating swaps,* combine the analytical elements of interest-rate swaps and caps to create a hedge for floating-rate liability costs. In a participating cap structure, the firm uses interest-rate swaps to convert the floating liability rate to a fixed rate and uses caps to create a maximum upper limit on the remainder of the interest expense of the floating-rate liability. However, what distinguishes this structure is that the caps are purchased without paying an up-front fee. The purchase is funded by executing the swap (fixed-rate payer/floating-rate receiver) at an off-market rate involving a higher spread than the current market rate for equivalent maturity swaps. Such participations can be structured in one of the following ways.

**EXHIBIT   58–3**

Effective Interest Expense for Participating Cap

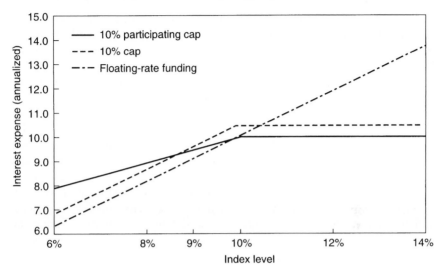

- The buyer decides the maximum rate on the floating-rate liability, which leads to the problem of determining the mixture of notional amounts of caps and swaps.
- The buyer decides on the relative mix of swaps and caps, which leads to the problem of determining the maximum rate level that can be attained with this combination.

Regardless of the choice by the buyer, the following relationship should hold in this type of participating structure:

$$\text{(Present value of annuity at } r_o - r_m, t) \times (\% \text{ of swap})$$
$$= \text{Cap premium} \times (\% \text{ of cap})$$

or

$$\text{(Present value of annuity at } r_o - r_m, t \times (\% \text{ of swap})$$
$$= \text{Cap premium} \times (1 - \% \text{ of swap})$$

or

$$\% \text{ of cap} = \frac{\text{Present value of annuity at } r_o - r_m, t}{\text{Cap premium} + \text{Present value of annuity at } r_o - r_m, t}$$

where

$r_m$ = Current market swap fixed rate for $t$ periods
$r_o$ = Off-market swap fixed rate for $t$ periods

As an example, consider the case of an institution desiring to cap a floating-rate liability expense that floats at a spread of 10 basis points over three-month LIBOR at a maximum rate of around 10% for a period of five years using this type of participating cap structure. The current market rate on a five-year pay-fixed and receive-floating (three-month LIBOR) swap is 80 basis points over the five-year Treasury yield at a rate of 9.40%. The current level of LIBOR is 9% and off-market five-year swaps are priced at a fixed rate of 10%. The cap premium for a five-year cap indexed off three-month LIBOR at a strike rate of 10% is 200 basis points, or 2% of notional amount.

The value of the annuity for five years is the difference between the off-market and the current market swap rate (that is, $10\% - 9.40\% = 0.60\%$). The present value of this annuity for five years at a discount rate of 9.4% (current swap rate) is 2.37185%. Therefore, using the above equation for participating structures, the amount of the caps is defined as $[2.37185/(2.37185 + 2.0000)] = 54\%$. Hence, the amount of swaps is $(1 - 0.54) = 0.46$, or 46%. Using this structure, the effective liability expense in various interest-rate scenarios is presented in Exhibit 58–4. In this example, the synthetic fixed rate using swaps is based on the higher off-market rate, whereas the blended rate is determined as a weighted average of the cap and the swap fixed rate.

In bullish interest-rate scenarios, the blended rate is higher than the un-hedged expense owing to the existence of the swap. The full benefit of the fall in rates is attained only partially by the portion of the liability mix that is capped. As interest rates increase, the blended rate is also higher than current market swaps owing to the existence of the higher-priced off-market swap that is used to fund the cap premium.

## INTEREST-RATE FLOORS

Interest-rate floors are used to protect the overall rate of return associated with a floating-rate asset. As an example, consider the case of a financial institution that owns adjustable-rate mortgages in its portfolio. In the event that interest

### E X H I B I T   58–4

Effective Interest Expenses Using Participating Cap Structure

| LIBOR | Unhedged | Capped Rate 54% Caps | Synthetic Fixed Rate 46% Swaps | Blended Rate |
|-------|----------|----------------------|-------------------------------|--------------|
| 11.0% | 11.10%   | 10.10%               | 10.00%                        | 10.046%      |
| 9.0   | 9.10     | 10.10                | 9.00                          | 9.506        |
| 7.0   | 7.10     | 10.10                | 7.00                          | 8.426        |

rates decrease, the coupon payments on floating-rate assets will be lower, because the repricing of variable-coupon assets is based on a floating-rate index. In order to protect the asset rate of return in bullish interest-rate scenarios, the firm could purchase an interest-rate floor. Analogous to caps, the protective features of a floor can be customized by choosing various attributes of interest-rate protection.

As an illustration, consider the following interest-rate floor purchased by an institution to protect the return on Treasury bill–indexed floating-rate assets:

| | |
|---|---|
| Notional amount: | $10,000,000 |
| Underlying index: | 3-month Treasury bill |
| Maturity: | 3 years |
| Floor strike level: | 8% |
| Premium: | 85 basis points or 0.85% of $10,000,000 = $85,000 |
| Settlement frequency: | Quarterly |
| Day count: | Actual/360 |

The cash flow dynamics of interest-rate floors are opposite to those of interest-rate caps, as illustrated in Exhibit 58–5. As can be seen in this illustration, a floor is beneficial in bullish interest-rate scenarios. Hence, purchasing a floor is analogous to buying a strip of call options. In bearish interest-rate scenarios, the floating-rate asset earns returns constrained only by the contractual

**E X H I B I T   58–5**

Effective Return of a Floored Asset

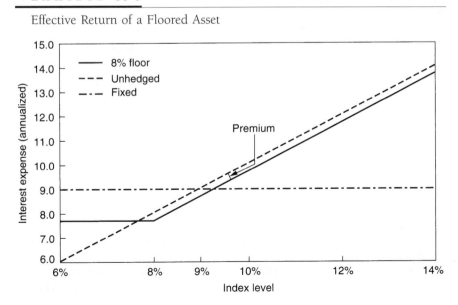

features of such instruments (if any), such as embedded caps. However, the asset return is reduced marginally by the amortization of the floor premium. In bullish interest-rate scenarios, where the asset returns are subject to erosion, the seller of the floor pays the buyer the difference between the strike rate of the floor and the value of the underlying index, adjusted for the days in the settlement period to compensate for the loss in asset coupon.

## INTEREST-RATE COLLARS

Interest-rate collars involve the purchase of a cap to hedge a floating-rate liability at a higher strike rate and the sale of a floor at a lower strike rate to offset the cost of purchasing the cap. If the underlying index rate exceeds the capped rate on the reference date, the seller of the cap pays the firm the amount above the capped rate; if the market rate is less than the floor strike rate, the firm pays the buyer the difference between the floor rate and the index level. If the market rate is between the strike rate of the cap and the strike rate of the floor, the effective interest costs of the firm are normal floating-rate funding costs plus the amortized cap premium (outflow) less the amortized floor premium (inflow). The net effect of this strategy is to limit the coupon rate of the floating-rate liability between the floor strike rate and the cap strike rate. The coupon liability rate is adjusted by the net amount of the amortized cap premium paid and the amortized floor premium received to determine the effective interest cost.

For example, assume that a firm has floating-rate liabilities that are indexed at three-month LIBOR. In order to cap this floating-rate liability for one year, the firm purchases an interest-rate floor at a strike rate of 11% for a premium of 85 basis points. In order to offset this cost, the firm sells a floor at a strike rate of 8% for a premium of 60 basis points. The profit and loss profile of this strategy is presented in Exhibit 58–6. As interest rates rise above the cap strike rate, the firm receives cash flows from the seller of the cap offsetting the higher outflow on the floating-rate liability. As interest rates fall below the floor strike rate, the falling interest expenses associated with the floating-rate liability are offset by the cash outflows to the buyer of the floor. In interest-rate scenarios between the floor and cap strike rate, there are no cash outflows or inflows associated with the hedges. This results in interest expenses associated with the floating-rate liability equal to normal borrowing costs. However, effective interest costs will be slightly higher to account for the net cap less floor premium, unless the collar is structured with a zero premium. In zero premium collars, the idea is to equate the premium paid for the premium received. However, this strategy could be potentially risky as a higher notional amount may have to be sold to equate the premia. In view of this consideration, the short side of the zero premium strategy involves notional amounts greater than the notional amount of the long side of the strategy.

The main benefit from an interest-rate collar is that the firm obtains protection from interest-rate increases at a considerably lower cost than with the

## EXHIBIT 58–6

Interest-Rate Collar

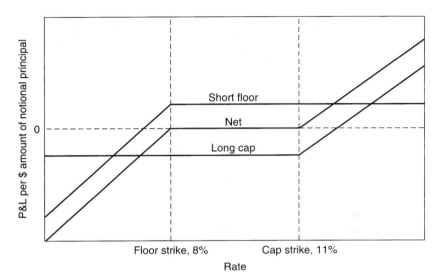

purchase of a cap. However, in return for the benefit of lower-cost interest-rate protection, the firm gives up the benefit from market rallies below the floor strike rate. Because the interest-rate protection is obtained without fixing rates, interest-rate collars are sometimes also described as *swapping into a bond.* However, this is an inefficient form of creating a collar because of the bid-ask volatility spread[2] associated with the structure. Given that the strategy involves buying a cap and selling a floor, the premium paid for the cap is based on a higher offer volatility, whereas the premium received for the floor is based on a lower bid volatility.

## INTEREST-RATE CORRIDORS

An alternative strategy to reduce the cost of the cap premium is to buy a cap at a particular strike rate and sell a cap at a higher strike rate, reducing the cost of the lower strike cap and hedging the interest expense of a floating-rate liability. In contrast to an interest-rate collar, the firm maintains all the benefit of falling interest rates, because there is no sale of a floor. As long as rates are below the strike rate of the lower strike cap, the effective interest expense of the firm is limited to normal borrowing cost plus the amortized net cap premium. As interest rates increase above the lower strike rate, the interest cost to the firm

---

2. See the discussion on termination of caps and floors later in this chapter.

is capped until market rates are above the higher strike cap. As interest rates rise above the strike rate of the second cap, interest costs increase by the amount of the outflow of the cap.

As an illustration, consider the case of a firm that purchases a cap at a strike rate of 11% and sells a cap at a strike rate of 15% to offset the cost of the first cap. The profit and loss profile of this strategy is presented in Exhibit 58–7. At market rates below 11%, the caps are out of the money, and the firm's effective interest cost floats at normal borrowing costs plus the net amortized cap premium. As interest rates increase above 11%, the first cap is in the money and starts paying cash flows to the firm to offset the higher coupon associated with the floating-rate liability. This allows the firm to cap the effective interest expense at a rate of 11% plus the net amortized cap premium. However, at rates higher than 15%, the second cap becomes in the money, and the firm has to start paying cash flows to the cap buyer. The net effect of this development is to increase the liability costs by the amount of cash outflows associated with the second cap.

Although interest-rate collars allow the firm to offset the cost of capping floating-rate liabilities, a word of caution is in order, especially if the caps are struck under the auspices of a zero-premium strategy. Cap premiums are determined by principles of option pricing theory; consequently, the premium received for a 15% cap will be less than the premium paid for the 11% cap because of the higher strike rate and bid-offer volatility spreads. Therefore, in a zero-

**E X H I B I T    58–7**

Interest-Rate Corridor

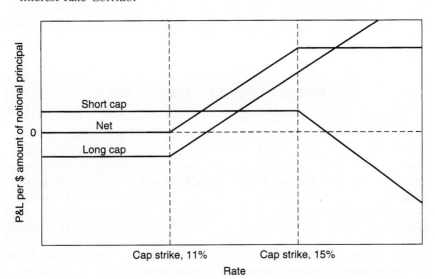

premium strategy, to equate the premium received for the higher strike cap to that paid for the lower strike cap, the notional amount of caps sold must be larger than the notional amount of caps purchased. Although this allows the firm to cap the liability rate at zero cost up to the strike rate of 15%, the firm is exposed to tremendous risk in a high-interest-rate, or "doomsday," scenario. As market interest rates increase to over 15%, the cash outflows paid to the buyer of the higher-strike cap may negate any cash flows received from the lower-strike cap and result in much higher interest costs than the lower-strike cap rate. The extent of this offsetting effect will be an inverse function of the ratio of the notional amount of higher-strike to lower-strike caps—the greater this ratio, the smaller will be the effect of the cash inflows of the lower-strike cap and the higher will be the effective interest cost.

## CAP/FLOOR PARITY

Similar to put/call parity for options, which essentially specifies the relationship between these types of options and the price of the underlying security, caps and floors are related to interest-rate swaps. As an example, consider a strategy that involves buying a cap at 9.50% and selling a floor at 9.50%, both based off the same index, for example, LIBOR. This is equivalent to entering into an interest-rate swap, paying fixed at 9.5%, and receiving floating payments based on LIBOR. If interest rates increase to above the cap level, say 11%, the cap will pay 1.5%. At the same level, the holder of the swap will receive LIBOR at 11%. This translates into a positive cash flow of the difference between LIBOR and the fixed rate of the swap, that is, $11\% - 9.5\% = 1.5\%$. If interest rates decrease to below the floor level, say 7.5%, the holder of the floor pays the difference between the index and the floor strike rate, that is, $9.5\% - 7.5\% = 2\%$. At the same level, the swap holder loses the difference between the swap fixed rate and LIBOR, that is, 2%. Therefore, the cap/floor swap parity may be stated as

Long cap + Short floor = Fixed swap

However, for cap/floor swap parity to hold, the fixed rate of the swap should be paid on the same basis (actual/360 days, 30/360 days, or actual/365 days) as the floating rate, not a varying basis on the two rates. A graphical illustration of cap/floor swap parity is presented in Exhibit 58–8.

The cost of a market swap is zero because no premium cash flows are exchanged at inception. Therefore, using cap/floor swap parity, the cost of a cap should be the same as the cost of a floor struck at the same rate on an identical index. This relationship should hold irrespective of the pricing model used to value the caps and floors. Unless this relationship is true at every point, an arbitrage exists in these markets that could be used to emulate the characteristics of the overpriced instrument. For instance, if caps are overpriced, a

**E X H I B I T   58–8**

Synthetic Swap Cap/Floor Swap Parity

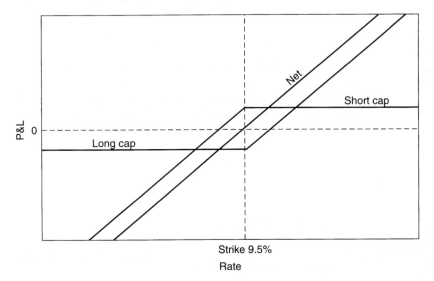

synthetic cap could be created by buying a floor and entering into an interest-rate swap, paying fixed at the floor strike rate and receiving floating using the same underlying index as the floor. Such arbitrage possibilities due to deviation from cap/floor swap parity also ensure efficient pricing in these markets.


## TERMINATION OF CAPS AND FLOORS

As is apparent from the discussion on the characteristics of caps (floors), these instruments are essentially a strip of put (call) options on forward interest rates. Hence, caps and floors are priced using the same theoretical and analytical concepts involved in pricing options. The termination value of caps and floors can be determined using concepts similar to those involved in determining the market value of options (premium) prior to expiration; in interest-rate swaps, where the termination of swaps is based on the bid-ask spread to the Treasury yield, the bid-ask spread for caps and floors is stated in terms of volatility. On a practical basis, this is a much "cleaner" method of determining bid-ask spreads in the cap and floor market than deriving forward curves using bid and ask yield spreads. In order to compensate the financial intermediary for the market-making function, the offer volatility is higher than the bid volatility. Because option premiums are directly related to volatility, the difference between the offer premium and bid premium for either a cap or floor prior to maturity will be directly related to the magnitude of the spread between bid and offer volatility.

## COMPOUND OPTIONS

Interest-rate protection provided by conventional options, such as puts and calls, and derivative optionlike instruments, such as caps and floors, extends over a specified period of time. During this time period, the option may be either "exercised," terminated prior to maturity, or allowed to expire worthless. The exercise (or lack thereof) is triggered by movements either in the price of the underlying security (as in the case of debt options) or in the underlying index (as in the case of caps and floors). However, any termination of the optional contract prior to maturity is incurred at the expense of the bid-offer spread. Given that swaps, caps, and floors are usually longer in maturity than conventional put and call options, termination costs are likely to be higher for such instruments. Additionally, the interest-rate protection provided by swaps, caps, and floors falls more in the category of passive hedging because, with the exception of the exchange of cash flows, there is no ongoing active management of the hedge.

For a shorter time horizon where the holding (outstanding) period of the asset (liability) is subject to change, firms can use interest-rate debt options. Such options can be used to manage asset/liability spreads or offset short-term opportunity losses associated with long-term interest-rate protection instruments. For instance, in rising interest-rate scenarios, where liability costs rise more quickly than the return on assets or the return on assets is fixed, put options can be used to offset the erosion in spread. The benefit of falling rates is still maintained as the loss on puts is limited to the up-front premium. Entities paying fixed in an interest-rate swap would be able to offset the opportunity loss in falling-rate scenarios by purchasing calls on Treasuries. In recent years, an important innovation known as *compound options* or *split-fee options* has allowed investors to limit losses of such short-term option strategies by permitting them to assess market conditions before purchasing additional optional coverage.

Compound options, which are essentially options on options, allow the firm to purchase a window on the market by paying a premium that is less than the premium on a conventional option on the same underlying instrument. The optional coverage can be extended at expiration of the window period by paying another premium. In essence, compound options provide an additional element of risk management by providing the opportunity to further limit downside losses associated with asymmetric coverage without sacrificing the essential ingredients of optional coverage.

Compound options allow the investor to purchase an option to exercise another option by paying a fee known as the *up front premium* for a specified period of time. At the end of this period, known as the *window date,* the investor may exercise the option on the option by paying another fee known as the *back-end fee.* Therefore, the label *split-fee* stems from the dichotomous nature of the fees paid for the combined option. Split-fee options also have been labeled *up and on* options; this terminology refers to the up-front fee and the back-end fee paid on the window date.

## Comparison with Conventional Option Strategies

Compound options offer several advantages over conventional options, such as additional leverage and greater risk-management capabilities. This point is illustrated by contrasting the coverage provided by compound puts and calls with conventional options. The graphical representation of the profit profile of a long put versus a compound put is illustrated in Exhibit 58–9. As indicated in the graph, the net profit profile of a long put is the standard textbook representation. As interest rates decline, causing increases in the value of the underlying security, the losses associated with the purchase of an at-the-money conventional put are limited to the up-front premium (*CE*). As interest rates increase, resulting in a fall in the price of the underlying security, the option can be exercised and the underlying security sold at the higher strike price. The net profit from exercising the option is the difference between the strike price and the value of the underlying security less the cost of the option. The net profit profile of the

**E X H I B I T   58–9**

Long Put vs. Split-Fee Option

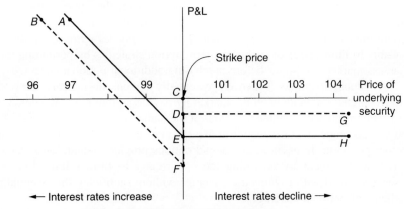

CE = Conventional put option premium
CD = Front-end fee for compound put option
DF = Back-end fee for compound put option

conventional put option in bullish and bearish interest-rate scenarios is denoted by *HEA*.

However, with the compound put option, the same degree of protection afforded by the conventional put is available in bullish interest-rate scenarios at a much lower cost, as indicated by the up-front premium of *CD* in Exhibit 58–9. In the event that interest rates continue to decline, the compound option can be allowed to expire unexercised. On the other hand, if interest rates are expected to increase, the optional coverage can be extended by exercising the second leg of the compound option. The total profit from the exercise of the compound option may be less than that obtained from exercising the conventional put if the sum of the up-front fee and the back-end fee is greater than the up-front put premium. In the event that the compound option is not exercised at the window date, the profit profile of the split-fee option strategy will be discontinuous, as indicated by *GD* in the graph. If the back-end fee is paid and the option exercised on the window date, the profit profile of the compound put is *HEFB*.

Portfolio managers frequently will purchase call options to profit from impending bullish changes in the market. The rationale underlying this strategy is based on the expectation that if interest rates decline, leading to an increase in the price of the underlying security, the portfolio manager will be able to purchase the asset at the lower strike price. The profit profile of this conventional call option is compared to that of a compound call in Exhibit 58–10. As indicated in the illustration, if interest rates remain unchanged or increase, the losses

**EXHIBIT  58–10**

Long Call vs. Split-Fee Option

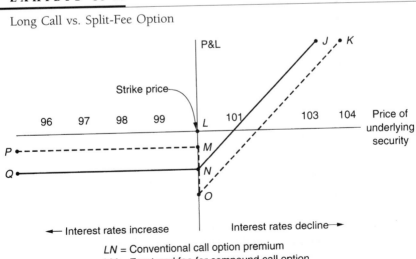

LN = Conventional call option premium
LM = Front-end fee for compound call option
MO = Back-end fee for compound call option

of a conventional call strategy are limited to the up-front call premium. The profit profile of the call is labeled *QNJ* in the graph; the call strategy is profitable in bullish interest-rate scenarios. In bearish interest-rate scenarios, the use of split-fee options results in losses lower than those associated with the conventional call strategy because of the lower up-front premium. However, if at the window date interest rates are lower, resulting in the exercise of the compound option, the profit profile of the compound call is denoted by *PMOK*. If the compound call is not exercised, the profit profile of the split-fee option will be denoted by *PM*.

## Uses of Compound Options

Compound options have been used mainly to hedge mortgage pipeline risk, especially the risk of applicants seeking alternative sources of financing or canceling the loan. This risk, known as *fallout risk,* is usually hedged by purchasing put options. The ramifications of fallout risk are especially severe if the expected mortgage production has already been sold forward. If interest rates fall and mortgage loans fall out of the pipeline, the mortgage lender can let the option expire unexercised. On the other hand, if rates increase, the lender can participate in the upside movement of the market by selling originated loans at the higher put strike price. With a compound put option, the mortgage lender can obtain the same optional protection at a much lower cost and retain the flexibility of extending the protection after assessing market conditions. If at the window date there is no need for put protection, the loss is lower than that of the premium of a conventional put. On the other hand, if additional protection is required, it can be purchased by either extending the compound option or by purchasing a conventional put option. For instance, it is possible that if forward market prices are higher (lower) on the window date, the purchase of a put (call) may be cheaper than exercising the option on the option.

Portfolios using active call-buying programs as yield-enhancement vehicles may purchase compound calls when there is uncertainty regarding an impending fall in interest rates. Instead of purchasing a higher-premium conventional call, the compound call allows the portfolio manager to purchase a window on the market for a lower cost. At the window date, if there is a greater degree of certainty regarding bullish market conditions, the compound options can be extended. However, if the degree of uncertainty increases, the loss is limited to the lower up-front premium.

Compound options, such as calls, can also be used in conjunction with longer-term instruments, such as fixed interest-rate swaps, to offset short-term opportunity losses caused by a fall in interest rates. However, perhaps the largest potential use of compound option technology lies in the application of these concepts to the cap and floor market in designing long-term options on options. Recall that caps (floors) are essentially a package of European puts (calls) on forward interest rates. The market for options on caps and floors, which allow the buyer to either cancel or initiate customized interest-rate protection, is still fairly undeveloped, but the potential uses of such instruments are enormous. As with any optional coverage, the development of such options on a series of options will add another element of flexibility provided by customized risk-management instruments.

# CONCLUDING COMMENTS

Swaps, floors, and compound options are customized risk-management instruments. Whereas interest-rate swaps are intended to insulate the user from changes in interest-rate volatility, caps and floors are designed to provide asymmetric coverage in capping liability costs and protecting the rate of return on assets. In either case, the user retains the right to participate in upside movements of the market. In order to reduce the up-front cost of purchasing caps and floors, the user can either enter into participating agreements that involve giving up a proportional share of beneficial market moves or enter into agreements, such as collars and corridors, that are analogous to option spread strategies.

Because the termination of such agreements involves exit costs, these instruments may prove beneficial for passive hedging where interest-rate protection is desired for longer periods of time. By the same token, these agreements also should not be used if the holding period of either the asset or liability is flexible or subject to change. For shorter periods of time, the user may decide to use split-fee options, which provide greater leverage and risk-management capabilities similar to conventional options, although contemporary use of split-fee options has been mainly in mortgage pipeline hedging. However, compound option technology can be applied readily to develop options on caps and floors, thereby adding an additional element of flexibility for these instruments in designing customized interest-rate protection.

# INDEX

## ABOUT THE EDITOR

**Frank J. Fabozzi** is editor of the *Journal of Portfolio Management*, an Adjunct Professor of Finance at Yale University's School of Management, and a consultant in the fixed-income and derivatives area. Prior to joining Yale's faculty, Dr. Fabozzi was on the faculty of MIT's Sloan School of Management. He is the author and editor of dozens of widely acclaimed books on fixed income securities and portfolio management, including *Fixed Income Mathematics*, *The Handbook of Mortgage-Backed Securities*, The *Handbook of Structured Financial Products*, *Collateralized Mortgage Obligations: Structures and Analysis*, and *Bond Portfolio Management*, and numerous others. Dr. Fabozzi has earned the Chartered Financial Analyst and Certified Public Accountant designations.